AN

ILLUSTRATED FLORA

OF THE

NORTHERN UNITED STATES
AND CANADA

FROM NEWFOUNDLAND TO THE PARALLEL OF THE SOUTHERN BOUNDARY OF
VIRGINIA, AND FROM THE ATLANTIC OCEAN WESTWARD
TO THE 102D MERIDIAN

BY

NATHANIEL LORD BRITTON, Ph.D., Sc.D., LL.D.
DIRECTOR-IN-CHIEF OF THE NEW YORK BOTANICAL GARDEN; PROFESSOR IN COLUMBIA UNIVERSITY

AND

HON. ADDISON BROWN, A.B., LL.D.
PRESIDENT OF THE NEW YORK BOTANICAL GARDEN

THE DESCRIPTIVE TEXT
CHIEFLY PREPARED BY PROFESSOR BRITTON, WITH THE ASSISTANCE OF SPECIALISTS IN
SEVERAL GROUPS; THE FIGURES ALSO DRAWN UNDER HIS SUPERVISION

SECOND EDITION—REVISED AND ENLARGED

IN THREE VOLUMES

VOL. II.

AMARANTHACEAE TO LOGANIACEAE
AMARANTH TO POLYPREMUM

DOVER PUBLICATIONS, INC., NEW YORK

Published in Canada by General Publishing Company, Ltd., 30 Lesmill Road, Don Mills, Toronto, Ontario.
Published in the United Kingdom by Constable and Company, Ltd., 10 Orange Street, London WC 2.

This Dover edition, first published in 1970, is an unabridged and unaltered republication of the second revised and enlarged edition as published by Charles Scribner's Sons in 1913 under the title *An Illustrated Flora of the Northern United States, Canada and the British Possessions.*

International Standard Book Number: 0-486-22643-3
Library of Congress Catalog Card Number: 76-116827

Manufactured in the United States of America
Dover Publications, Inc.
180 Varick Street
New York, N.Y. 10014

Contents of Volume II.

ENGLISH FAMILY NAMES

SYMBOLS USED

° is used after figures to indicate feet.
′ is used after figures to indicate inches.
″ is used after figures to indicate lines, or twelfths of an inch.
´ over syllables indicates the accent, and the *short* English sound of the vowel.
˘ over syllables indicates the accent, and the long, broad, open or close English sound of the vowel.

IN THE METRIC SYSTEM.
    The metre = 39.37 inches, or 3 feet 3.37 inches. ⎫
    The decimetre = 3.94 inches.   ⎪
    The centimetre = $\frac{2}{5}$ of an inch, or 4$\frac{3}{4}$ lines. ⎬ very nearly
    The millimetre = $\frac{1}{25}$ of an inch, or $\frac{1}{2}$ a line.   ⎪
    2$\frac{1}{9}$ millimeters = 1 line.   ⎭

ILLUSTRATED FLORA.

VOL. II.

Family 16. **AMARANTHÁCEAE** J. St. Hil. Expos. Fam. 1: 204. 1805.

AMARANTH FAMILY.

Herbs, some exotic genera low shrubs, with alternate or opposite simple mostly entire thin leaves. Flowers small, green or white, perfect, monoecious, polygamous, or dioecious, bracteolate, variously clustered, usually in terminal spikes or axillary heads. Petals none. Calyx herbaceous or membranous, 2–5-parted, or 5-cleft, the segments distinct or somewhat united, equal, or the inner ones smaller. Stamens 1–5, mostly opposite the calyx-segments, hypogynous; filaments distinct, united at the base, or into a tube; anthers 1-celled or 2-celled. Ovary ovoid or subglobose, 1-celled; ovule solitary in the following genera, amphitropous (several in some tropical genera); style short, elongated or none; stigmas 1–3. Fruit a utricle, circumscissile, bursting irregularly or indehiscent, 1-seeded in our genera. Seed mostly smooth; embryo annular; endosperm mealy, usually copious.

About 40 genera and 475 species, widely distributed, most abundant in warm regions.

Anthers 2-celled; leaves alternate.	
Calyx 2–5-parted or of 2–5 sepals.	
Calyx of the pistillate flowers wanting.	1. *Amaranthus.*
Anthers 1-celled; leaves opposite.	2. *Acnida.*
Flowers in small axillary clusters.	
Flowers variously spicate or paniculate.	3. *Cladothrix.*
Calyx 5-cleft; filaments united into a tube.	4. *Froelichia.*
Calyx 5-parted; filaments united at the base.	5. *Iresine.*

1. AMARÁNTHUS [Tourn.] L. Sp. Pl. 989. 1753.

Annual branched erect or diffusely spreading glabrous or pubescent herbs, most of the species weeds, with alternate, petioled pinnately veined entire, undulate or crisped leaves and small monoecious polygamous or dioecious green or purplish mostly 3-bracteolate flowers in dense terminal spikes or axillary clusters. Calyx of 2–5 distinct sepals. Stamens 2–5; anthers 2-celled, longitudinally dehiscent. Styles or stigmas 2 or 3. Fruit an ovoid or oblong utricle, circumscissile, bursting irregularly or indehiscent, 2–3-beaked by the persistent styles. Embryo annular. [Greek, unfading flower, from the dry, unwithering bracts.]

About 50 species of wide geographic distribution. Besides the following some 22 others occur in the southern and western United States. Type species: *Amaranthus caudàtus* L.

Utricle circumscissile, the top falling away as a lid.	
Flowers, at least the upper, in dense terminal spikes.	
Axils not spine-bearing.	
Sepals oblong to lanceolate.	
Spikes stout, 4″–7″ thick.	1. *A. retroflexus.*
Spikes slender, 2″–3″ thick.	2. *A. hybridus.*
Sepals spatulate.	3. *A. Palmeri.*
A pair of stout spines in each axil.	4. *A. spinosus.*
Flowers all in small axillary clusters, mostly shorter than the leaves.	
Plant prostrate; bracts oblong; utricle smooth.	
Plant erect, bushy-branched; bracts subulate; utricle wrinkled.	5. *A. blitoides.*
Utricle indehiscent, membranous, coriaceous or fleshy.	6. *A. graecizans.*
Upper flowers in terminal, more or less elongated spikes.	
Sepals 5, clawed; flowers dioecious; southwestern species.	7. *A. Torreyi.*
Sepals 2 or 3, oblong or spatulate; flowers monoecious or polygamous; in waste places.	
Utricle smooth, dry, scarious.	8. *A. lividus.*
Utricle fleshy, 3–5-nerved.	9. *A. deflexus.*
Flowers all in small axillary clusters shorter than the leaves.	
Plant not fleshy; stem prostrate; leaves crisped.	10. *A. crispus.*
Sea-coast fleshy plant; stem short, erect; leaves not crisped.	11. *A. pumilus.*

1

1. Amaranthus retrofléxus L.   Green Amaranth, Red Root.   Fig. 1659.

Amaranthus retroflexus L. Sp. Pl. 991. 1753.

Roughish-puberulent, rather light green, stem stout, erect or ascending, commonly branched, 1°–10° tall. Leaves ovate, rhombic-ovate or the upper lanceolate, slender-petioled, acute or acuminate at the apex, narrowed or acuminate at the base, the larger 3′–6′ long, their margins undulate or entire; flowers green, polygamous, densely aggregated in terminal and axillary spikes, which are sessile, stout, obtuse or subacute, ovoid-cylindric, erect or ascending, ½′–2½′ long, 4″–7″ thick; bracts subulate, twice as long as the 5 scarious narrowly oblong or slightly spatulate mucronate-tipped obtuse or often emarginate sepals; stamens 5; utricle slightly wrinkled, thin, circumscissile, rather shorter than the sepals.

A weed, in cultivated and waste soil, throughout North America, north to Nova Scotia, North Dakota and Washington. Also in Europe. Naturalized from tropical America. Rough pigweed. Aug.–Oct.

2. Amaranthus hýbridus L.   Spleen Amaranth.   Pilewort.   Fig. 1660.

Amaranthus hybridus L. Sp. Pl. 990. 1753.
Amaranthus hypochondriacus L. Sp. Pl. 991. 1753.
A. chlorostachys Willd. Amaranth. 34. *pl. 10. t. 19.* 1790.
A. paniculatus L. Sp. Pl. Ed. 2, 1406. 1763.

Similar to the preceding species but darker green, or purple, pubescent or nearly glabrous; stem usually slender, erect, usually branched, 2°–8° tall. Leaves bright green on both sides or paler beneath, usually smaller, slender-petioled; spikes linear-cylindric, axillary and forming dense terminal panicles, ascending, somewhat spreading or drooping; bracts awned or awn-tipped, twice as long as the 5 oblong acute or cuspidate sepals; stamens 5; utricle scarcely wrinkled, circumscissile.

A weed, in waste grounds, range nearly of the preceding species, its races differing in color, pubescence and length of the awns of the bracts. Naturalized from tropical America. Slender pigweed. Red amaranth or cockscomb. Prince's-feather. Flower-gentle. Careless. Floramor. Aug.–Oct.

3. Amaranthus Pàlmeri S. Wats.   Palmer's Amaranth.   Fig. 1661.

A. Palmeri S. Wats. Proc. Am. Acad. **12**: 274. 1876.

Somewhat resembling the two preceding species, stem erect, slender, branched, 2°–3° tall, usually pubescent above. Leaves ovate, rhombic-ovate or the upper lanceolate, blunt at the apex, narrowed at the base, prominently veined, slender-petioled, the lower petioles often longer than the blades; flowers polygamous or dioecious, borne in elongated erect or drooping spikes often 1° long or more, and some of them commonly in small clusters in the upper axils; bracts subulate, spiny-awned, spreading, twice as long as the sepals; sepals 5, spatulate, clawed; utricle dry, circumscissile.

In dry soil, Missouri and Kansas to Texas and in eastern Massachusetts. Adventive. Native from New Mexico to California and Chihuahua. June–Sept.

Amaranthus caudàtus L., with long dense red nodding terminal spikes, has been found in waste grounds in Connecticut.

4. Amaranthus spinòsus L.   Spiny or Thorny Amaranth.   Fig. 1662.

Amaranthus spinosus L. Sp. Pl. 991. 1753.

Rather dark green, glabrous or somewhat pubescent above, stem stout, erect or ascending, ridged, usually much branched, sometimes red, 1°–4° high. Leaves ovate, rhombic-ovate or the upper lanceolate, slender-petioled, acute at both ends, 1′–3′ long, with a pair of rigid stipular spines ¼′–1′ long at each node, the midvein excurrent; flowers monoecious, the pistillate in numerous capitate axillary clusters, mostly shorter than the petioles, the staminate in dense terminal linear-cylindric spreading or drooping spikes 1′–6′ long; bracts lanceolate-subulate about as long as the 5 scarious oblong mucronate-tipped 1-nerved sepals, and the thin imperfectly circumscissile utricle; stamens 5.

In waste and cultivated soil, Maine to Minnesota, Florida and Mexico. Naturalized from tropical America. A troublesome weed southward. Red amaranth. June–Sept.

5. Amaranthus blitoìdes S. Wats.   Prostrate Amaranth.   Fig. 1663.

A. blitoides S. Wats. Proc. Am. Acad. **12** : 273. 1877.

Nearly or quite glabrous, rather pale green, stem diffusely branched, prostrate and spreading on the gorund, ridged, 6′–2° long, often forming mats. Leaves obovate or spatulate, ¼′–1′ long, obtuse or acute at the apex, narrowed into slender petioles, sometimes longer than the blades; flowers polygamous, in small axillary clusters mostly shorter than the petioles; bracts oblong to lanceolate-subulate, little longer than the 3 to 5 oblong-lanceolate acute or cuspidate sepals; stamens 3; utricle nearly smooth, circumscissile, equalling or slightly longer than the sepals.

In waste places, especially along the principal routes of travel, Maine to southern Ontario and North Dakota, south to New Jersey, Missouri and Kansas. Naturalized from west of the Rocky Mountains, where it appears to be indigenous from Washington to Utah, Colorado and Mexico. June–Oct.

6. Amaranthus graecìzans L.   Tumble-weed.   Fig. 1664.

Amaranthus graecizans L. Sp. Pl. 990. 1753.
Amaranthus albus L. Sp. Pl. Ed. 2, 1404. 1763.

Glabrous, pale green, stem erect, bushy-branched, whitish, 6′–2° tall, the branches slender, ascending. Leaves oblong, spatulate or obovate, ½′–1½′ long, slender-petioled, papillose, the midvein excurrent; flowers polygamous, several together in small axillary clusters shorter than the leaves, commonly not longer than the petioles; bracts subulate, pungent-pointed, spreading, much longer than the 3 membranous sepals; stamens 3; utricle wrinkled, circumscissile, longer than the sepals.

In waste and cultivated soil, throughout North America, except the extreme north. The leaves fall away in autumn, and on the western plains the plant, thus denuded, is freely uprooted and blown before the wind, whence the popular name. June–Sept.

$\frac{3}{4}$

7. Amaranthus Tórreyi (A. Gray) Benth. Torrey's Amaranth. Fig. 1665.

Amblogyne Torreyi A. Gray, Proc. Am. Acad. **5**: 167. 1861.
Amaranthus Torreyi Benth.; S. Wats. Bot. Cal. **2**: 2: 42. 1889.

Glabrous or nearly so, stem stout or slender, erect, grooved, usually much branched above, 2°-3° tall. Leaves lanceolate or rhombic-lanceolate, thin, narrowed above to a rather blunt apex, mostly cuneate at the base, 1½'-4' long, ¼'-1' wide, slender-petioled; flowers dioecious, borne in terminal slender some-times panicled spikes and in small axillary clusters; bracts shorter than or about equal-ling the 5 sepals, cuspidate; sepals of the pistillate flowers obovate or broadly spatu-late, clawed, obtuse or emarginate, those of the staminate flowers narrower and subacute; utricle dry, indehiscent.

In dry soil, western Nebraska to Nevada, south to Mexico. Plant with the aspect of *Acnida*. June–Aug.

8. Amaranthus lívidus L. Purplish Ama-ranth. Fig. 1666.

Amaranthus lividus L. Sp. Pl. 990. 1753.
Euxolus lividus Moq. in DC. Prodr. **13²**: 275. 1849.

Glabrous, rather succulent, purplish-green or red; stem erect, slender, branched, 1°-3° tall. Leaves ovate, entire, 1'-3' long, strongly emarginate at the apex, narrowed at the base, slender-petioled; flow-ers monoecious or polygamous, in dense terminal spikes and in capitate axillary clusters usually much shorter than the petioles; bracts shorter than the 2 or 3 oblong or spatulate sepals; utricle dry, sca-rious, smooth, indehiscent, longer than the sepals.

In waste places, eastern Massachusetts to southern New York. Adventive from tropical America. July–Sept.

Amaranthus grácilis Desf., which differs mainly from this species by its warty utricle, has been found in bal-last at the seaports and is reported from Ohio. It is native of tropical America and has been confused with *A. viridis* L.

$\frac{2}{3}$

$\frac{2}{3}$

9. Amaranthus defléxus L. Low Amaranth. Fig. 1667.

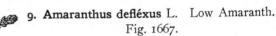

Amaranthus deflexus L. Mant. **2**: 295. 1771.

Euxolus deflexus Raf. Fl. Tell. **3**: 42. 1836.

Glabrous, purplish-green, rather succulent, stem usually much branched, erect, stout or slender, 1°-3° tall. Leaves ovate or oval, obtuse retuse or emarginate at the apex, mostly narrowed at the base, 1'-3' long, ½'-1½' wide, slender-petioled, the petioles often as long as the blades or the lower ones longer; flowers polygamous in dense, mostly short and thick terminal spikes and capitate in the axils; bracts shorter than the 2 or 3 oblong or spatulate sepals usually very short; utricle fleshy, 3-5-nerved, smooth, indehiscent, longer than the sepals when ripe.

In waste places and ballast along the coast, Massa-chusetts to southern New York. Also in California. Probably adventive from Europe. July–Sept.

10. Amaranthus críspus (Lesp. & Thev.) A. Braun. Crisp-leaved Amaranth. Fig. 1668.

Euxolus crispus Lesq. & Thev. Bull. Soc. Bot. France 6 : 656. 1859.

Amarantus crispus A. Braun ; A. Gray, Man. Ed. 6, 428. 1890.

Pubescent, stem copiously branched, slender, spreading on the ground, prostrate, forming mats 8′–2½° in diameter. Leaves oblong or lanceolate, mostly acute at the apex and narrowed at the base, petioled, 4″–1′ long, their margins remarkably crisped ; petioles shorter than or exceeding the blades ; flowers all in small axllary clusters shorter than the petioles ; bracts lanceolate, cuspidate, shorter than the 5 sepals ; utricle wrinkled, indehiscent, about as long as the sepals.

In waste places, New York city, Brooklyn and Albany, N. Y. Also in France. Native region unknown. June–Sept.

11. Amaranthus pùmilus Raf. Coast Amaranth. Fig. 1669.

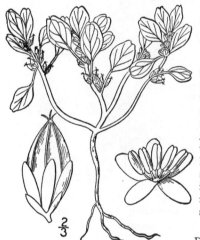

Amarantus pumilus Raf. Med. Rep. (II.) 5 : 360. 1808.

Euxolus pumilus Chapm. Fl. S. States 381. 1860.

Glabrous, fleshy, branched, the branches prostrate or ascending, 3′–8′ long. Leaves ovate, rhombic-ovate, obovate or suborbicular, most of them clustered toward the ends of the branches, obtuse or emarginate at the apex, narrowed or rounded at the base, prominently veined, petioled, 3″–10″ long, the veins often purple ; flowers few together in small axillary clusters ; bracts lanceolate, subacute, shorter than the 5 oblong obtuse sepals ; stamens 5 ; anthers yellow ; utricle fleshy, indehiscent, faintly 5-ribbed, slightly wrinkled, nearly twice as long as the sepals when mature ; seed very large for the genus.

On sea beaches, Rhode Island to North Carolina. Dwarf amaranth. June–Sept.

2. ACNÌDA L. Sp. 1027. 1753.

Annual, erect or decumbent, glabrous branching herbs, similar to the dioecious Amaranths, with alternate petioled thin pinnately veined leaves. Flowers small, green, 1–3-bracted, in terminal and axillary, continuous or interrupted spikes, or clustered in the axils. Staminate flowers consisting of 5 scarious erect 1-nerved mucronate sepals longer than the bracts, and as many stamens ; filaments subulate, distinct ; anthers 2-celled. Pistillate flowers without a calyx ; ovary ovoid or subglobose ; stigmas 2–5, papillose or plumose, short or elongated. Utricle fleshy and indehiscent, or membranous and bursting irregularly or circumscissile ; seed erect, smooth and shining. [Greek, without nettle.]

About 6 species, natives of eastern North America and the West Indies. Type species : *Acnida cannabina* L.

Utricle fleshy, angled, indehiscent ; salt-marsh plant.   1. *A. cannabina.*
Utricle membranous, irregularly dehiscent or circumscissile ; plants of fresh water swamps.
    Utricle circumscissile.   2. *A. tamariscina.*
    Utricle irregularly dehiscent.   3. *A. tuberculata.*

1. Acnida cannábina L. Salt-marsh Water-hemp. Fig. 1670.

Acnida cannabina L. Sp. Pl. 1027. 1753.
A. rusocarpa Michx. Fl. Bor. Am. 2 : 234, *pl. 50.* 1803.

Succulent, stem stout or slender (sometimes 1′ in diameter at the base), usually much branched, 1°–10° tall, the branches ascending. Leaves lanceolate, acuminate but generally blunt-pointed and apiculate at the apex, 2′–6′ long, ¼′–1¼′ wide, narrowed at the base, entire or slightly undulate; petiole usually shorter than the blade; staminate spikes 1′–5′ long, usually dense; sepals oblong-lanceolate or ovate-oblong, acute, acuminate or obtusish, cuspidate or mucronate; fertile spikes dense or loose; stigmas slender, papillose-hispid, ½″ long; utricle fleshy, indehiscent, 3–5-angled, subglobose or obovoid, 1″–2″ long when mature, becoming black, much longer than the bracts.

In salt and brackish marshes, and up the rivers to fresh water, New Hampshire to Florida. Water-leaf. July–Aug.

Acnida floridàna S. Wats. Proc. Am. Acad. 10: 376, a more slender plant, of the southern Atlantic coast, with narrower slender-petioled leaves, the flowers in elongated interrupted spikes, and a smaller utricle, may occur in southern Virginia.

2. Acnida tamaríscina (Nutt.) Wood. Western Water-hemp. Fig. 1671.

Amarantus tamariscinus Nutt. Trans. Am. Phil. Soc. (II.)
5: 165. 1833–37.
Acnida tamariscina Wood, Bot. & Fl. 289. 1873.

Similar to the preceding species, much branched, erect, the branches usually slender, erect-ascending. Leaves lanceolate or ovate-lanceolate, 2′–6′ long, mostly long-acuminate, but sometimes obtuse at the apex and mucronate or cuspidate-tipped, narrowed at the base, the petioles commonly shorter than the blades; spikes mostly loose or interrupted, often 5′ long; sepals lanceolate, subulate-acuminate; stigmas plumose, rather short; utricle membranous, not angled, ½″–1″ long, circumscissile; bractlets lanceolate, cuspidate.

In swamps, Illinois to South Dakota, Texas and New Mexico. July–Sept.

3. Acnida tuberculàta Moq. Rough-fruited Water-hemp. Fig. 1672.

A. tuberculata Moq. in DC. Prodr. 13²: 278. 1849.
A. tamariscina subnuda S. Wats. in A. Gray, Man. Ed. 6,
429. 1890.
A. tamariscina concatenata Uline & Bray, Bot. Gaz. 20 :
158. 1895.
A. tamariscina prostrata Uline & Bray, Bot. Gaz. 20 :
158. 1895.

Erect ascending or prostrate, sometimes 10° high, the branches flexuous. Leaves lanceolate to rhombic-spatulate, acute or obtuse, 6′ long or less; inflorescence spicate, or glomerate in the axils; utricle ovoid, often tubercled, irregularly dehiscent, about ½″ long.

Swamps and river shores, Quebec to North Dakota, south to Kentucky, Louisiana and Missouri. Consists of several races, differing in size and habit. July–Sept.

Celòsia argéntea L., a tall glabrous herb with white or pink flowers subtended by a bract and bractlets in a long dense spike, having 5 sepals, filaments adnate at the base, and the ovary with several ovules, widely distributed in tropical regions, has been found as a waif in Montgomery County, Pennsylvania.

3. CLÁDOTHRIX Nutt.; Moq. in DC. Prodr. 13^2: 359. 1849.

Annual or perennial diffusely branched stellate-pubescent herbs, with opposite entire or slightly undulate petioled leaves, and very small perfect 3-bracted flowers, solitary or clustered in the axils. Calyx of 5 equal pilose erect dry oblong 1-nerved sepals. Stamens 5, hypogynous, their filaments united at the base, their anthers 1-celled. Ovary subglobose; style short; stigma capitate or 2-lobed. Utricle globose, indehiscent. [Greek, branch-hair, from the stellate pubescence.]

About 4 species, natives of southwestern North America and Mexico, the following the generic type.

1. Cladothrix lanuginòsa Nutt. Cladothrix.
Fig. 1673.

Achyranthes lanuginosa Nutt. Trans. Am. Phil. Soc. (II.) 5: 166. 1833–37.
Cladothrix lanuginosa Nutt.; Moq. in DC. Prodr. 13^2: Part 2, 360, as synonym. 1849.

Perennial, somewhat woody at the base, or sometimes annual, stem terete, much branched, sometimes thickened at the nodes, the branches prostrate or ascending, 4'-12' long. Leaves orbicular, broadly ovate or rhombic-ovate, obtuse or acute, usually narrowed at the base, entire, inconspicuously veined, rather firm, 2"-12" wide, the petioles shorter than or equalling the blades; flowers ½" broad or less, mostly clustered in the axils of small upper leaves toward the ends of the branches.

In dry soil, South Dakota to Kansas, Texas, Colorado, Arizona and Mexico. June–Sept.

4. FROELÍCHIA Moench, Meth. 50. 1794.

Annual, erect woolly or silky, branching or simple herbs, with opposite sessile entire or slightly undulate narrow leaves, or the lower and basal ones contracted into petioles. Flowers perfect, 3-bracted, often bracteolate, in panicled dense spikes. Calyx tubular, nearly terete, 5-cleft or 5-toothed, very woolly, its tube longitudinally crested and sometimes tubercled in fruit. Stamens 5, their filaments united into a tube, which is 5-cleft at the summit and bears the 1-celled anthers between its lobes. Ovary ovoid; style slender or wanting; stigma capitate or penicillate. Utricle indehiscent, enclosed by the tube of united filaments. [Name in honor of J. A. Froelich, a German botanist.]

About 12 species, all American. Besides the following, 2 others occur in the Southwestern States. Type species: *Gomphrena interrupta* L.

Stout, 2°-4° tall; crests of fruiting calyx continuous, dentate.   1. *F. campestris.*
Slender, 10'-20' tall; crests of fruiting calyx interrupted.   2. *F. gracilis.*

1. Froelichia campéstris Small. Prairie Froelichia. Fig. 1674.

Froelichia campestris Small, Fl. SE. U. S. 397. 1903.

Stem stout, woolly, 2°-4° tall, the branches slender, erect-ascending, leafless above. Upper leaves linear or linear-oblong, sessile, acute or acuminate at both ends, 1'-3' long, the lower spatulate or oblanceolate, obtuse or acute at the apex, 3'-6' long, ¼'-1' wide, narrowed into margined petioles; spikes mostly opposite, narrowly ovoid or oblong, obtuse or subacute, ½'-1' long; fruiting calyx with prominent longitudinal wing-like toothed crests.

In dry soil, Illinois and Minnesota to Nebraska and Colorado, Tennessee, Kansas and Texas. June–Sept.

Froelichia floridàna (Nutt.) Moq. in which this was included in our first edition, has a hairy, not woolly stem and calyx-crests more deeply cut. It inhabits the Southern States and is recorded from Delaware.

2. Froelichia grácilis Moq.　Slender Froelichia.
Fig. 1675.

Froelichia gracilis Moq. in DC. Prodr. 13^2: 420. 1849.

Similar to the preceding species but the stem slender, branched, especially from the base, or sometimes simple, 10'–20' tall.　Leaves all linear or linear-oblong, acute at both ends, 9''–2' long, sessile or the lower commonly spatulate, obtusish and narrowed into very short petioles; spikes alternate or opposite, oblong, mostly obtuse, ¼'–1' long; fruiting calyx with 5 longitudinal rows of processes or these confluent into interrupted crests.

In dry soil, western Missouri and Nebraska to Colorado and Texas.　June–Sept.

Gomphrena globòsa L., the Globe Amaranth, cultivated for ornament, native of the Old World tropics, with densely capitate red or white flowers, the filaments united into a long tube, has been found in waste grounds in Ohio.

5.　IRESÌNE P. Br. Civ. & Nat. Hist. Jam. 358.　1756.

Annual or perennial tall herbs, with opposite broad petioled thin leaves and very small polygamous perfect or dioecious 3-bracted white flowers, in large terminal panicles or panicled spikes.　Calyx 5-parted, the pistillate usually woolly-pubescent.　Stamens 5, rarely less; filaments united by their bases, filiform; anthers 1-celled.　Utricle very small, subglobose, indehiscent.　[Greek, in allusion to the woolly pubescence.]

About 20 species, natives of warm and temperate regions.　Besides the following typical species another occurs in the southwestern United States.

1. Iresine paniculàta (L.) Kuntze.　Bloodleaf.　Juba's Bush.　Fig. 1676.

Celosia paniculata L. Sp. Pl. 206. 1753.

Iresine celosioides L. Sp. Pl. Ed. 2, 1456. 1763.

Iresine paniculata Kuntze, Rev. Gen. Pl. 542. 1891.

Annual, stem erect, usually branched, slender, 2°–5° tall, glabrous or nearly so.　Leaves ovate, ovate-lanceolate or the upper lanceolate, 2'–6' long, slender-petioled, pinnately veined, nearly or quite glabrous; flowers very numerous, 1'' broad or less, in large terminal much branched panicles; calyx and bracts silvery, dry; pistillate flowers whitevillous at the base, about twice as long as the bracts.

In dry soil, Ohio to Kansas, south to Florida and Texas.　Widely distributed in tropical America.　Aug.–Sept.

Family 17.　CHENOPODIÀCEAE Dumort. Anal. Fam. 15.　1829.
Goosefoot Family.

Annual or perennial herbs, rarely shrubs, with angled striate or terete stems. Leaves alternate or sometimes opposite, exstipulate, simple, entire, toothed or lobed, mostly petioled (in *Salicornia* reduced to mere ridges).　Flowers perfect, pistillate, polygamous, monoecious or dioecious, small, green or greenish, regular, or slightly irregular, variously clustered, commonly in panicled spikes, bractless or bracteolate, occasionally solitary in the axils.　Petals none.　Calyx persistent, 2–5-lobed, 2–5-parted or rarely reduced to a single sepal, wanting in the pistillate flowers of some genera.　Stamens as many as the lobes or divisions of the calyx, or fewer, and opposite them; filaments slender; anthers 2-celled, longitudinally dehiscent.　Disk usually none.　Ovary mostly superior and free from the calyx, 1-celled; ovule solitary, amphitropous; styles 1–3; stigmas capitate, or 2–3-lobed or divided.　Fruit a utricle, with a thin or coriaceous pericarp.　Seed vertical or horizontal; endosperm mealy, fleshy or wanting; embryo partly or completely annular or conduplicate, or spirally coiled.

About 75 genera and 550 species, of wide geographic distribution.

* **Embryo annular or conduplicate, not spirally coiled; endosperm copious**
(except in *Salicornia* and *Kochia*).

Leafy herbs; endosperm copious.
  Fruit enclosed by or not longer than the calyx or bractlets.
    Flowers perfect or some of them pistillate; calyx herbaceous or fleshy.
      Calyx 2–5-lobed or 2–5-parted; stamens 1–5.
        Fruiting calyx wingless, its segments often keeled.
          Calyx herbaceous or but slightly fleshy in fruit; flowers mostly in panicled spikes.

1. *Chenopodium.*

            Fruiting calyx dry, strongly reticulated; leaves pinnatifid.   2. *Roubieva.*
            Calyx very fleshy and bright red in fruit; flowers densely capitate.   3. *Blitum.*
        Fruiting calyx horizontally winged.
          Endosperm mealy; leaves sinuate-dentate.   4. *Cycloloma.*
          Endosperm none; leaves linear, entire.   5. *Kochia.*
      Calyx of 1 sepal; stamen 1.   6. *Monolepis.*
    Flowers monoecious or dioecious.
      Calyx of pistillate flowers none; fruit enclosed by 2 bractlets.
        Bractlets flat or convex, not silky.   7. *Atriplex.*
        Bractlets silky-pubescent, conduplicate.   8. *Eurotia.*
      Calyx of both kinds of flowers 3–5-parted; fruit ebracteolate.   9. *Axyris.*
  Fruit much exserted beyond the 1-sepaled calyx; flowers perfect.   10. *Corispermum.*
Leafless fleshy herbs with opposite branches; endosperm none.   11. *Salicornia.*

** **Embryo spirally coiled; endosperm little or none.**

Shrub; flowers monoecious, not bracteolate.
Herbs; flowers perfect, bracteolate.   12. *Sarcobatus.*
  Fruiting calyx wingless; leaves fleshy, not spiny.   13. *Dondia.*
  Fruiting calyx bordered by a thin horizontal wing; leaves very spiny.   14. *Salsola.*

1. CHENOPÒDIUM [Tourn.] L. Sp. Pl. 218. 1753.

Annual or perennial, green and glabrous, white-mealy or glandular-pubescent herbs, with alternate petioled entire sinuate-dentate or pinnately lobed leaves. Flowers very small, green, perfect, sessile, bractless, clustered in axillary or terminal, often panicled or compound spikes. Calyx 2–5-parted or 2–5-lobed, embracing or enclosing the utricle, its segments or lobes herbaceous or slightly fleshy, often keeled or ridged. Stamens 1–5; filaments filiform or slender. Styles 2 or 3; seed horizontal or vertical, sometimes in both positions in different flowers of the same plant, firmly attached to or readily separable from the pericarp; endosperm mealy, farinaceous; embryo completely or incompletely annular. [Greek, goose-foot, from the shape of the leaves.]

About 60 species, mostly weeds, of wide geographic distribution. Besides the following, some 5 others occur in the western parts of North America. Type species: *Chenopodium rubrum* L.

* **Embryo a complete ring; plants not glandular.**

Leaves white-mealy on the lower surface (except in some races of No. 1).
  Leaves or some of them mostly sinuate-toothed or lobed.
    Sepals strongly keeled in fruit.
      Pericarp firmly attached to the seed; stem erect, tall.   1. *C. album.*
      Pericarp readily detached from the seed; stem low.   2. *C. incanum.*
    Sepals not keeled in fruit; stem decumbent.   3. *C. glaucum.*
  Leaves mostly entire.
    Leaves linear to oblong, short-petioled.   4. *C. leptophyllum.*
    Leaves broadly ovate, long-petioled.   5. *C. Vulvaria.*
Leaves green and glabrous or nearly so on both surfaces when mature.
  Leaves oblong or ovate-oblong, entire.   6. *C. polyspermum.*
  Leaves, at least the lower, sinuate, toothed or incised.
    Stamens 5; calyx not fleshy.
      Pericarp readily separable from the seed.
        Leaves oblong or lanceolate; calyx-lobes scarcely keeled.   7. *C. Boscianum.*
        Leaves triangular-hastate; calyx-lobes keeled.   8. *C. Fremontii.*
      Pericarp firmly attached to the seed.
        Flower-clusters, at least the upper, longer than the leaves.   9. *C. urbicum.*
        Spikes loosely panicled in the axils, the panicles shorter than the leaves.
                                                                            10. *C. murale.*
    Stamens only 1 or 2; calyx slightly fleshy, red.   12. *C. rubrum.*
  Leaves very coarsely 2–6-toothed.   11. *C. hybridum.*
  Leaves broadly triangular-hastate, entire or merely undulate.   13. *C. Bonus-Henricus.*

** **Embryo an incomplete ring; plants glandular aromatic.**

Leaves ovate or oblong, pinnately lobed; flowers in long loose panicles.   14. *C. Botrys.*
Leaves lanceolate; flowers in continuous or interrupted spikes.   15. *C. ambrosioides.*

1. Chenopodum álbum L. Lamb's Quarters. White Goosefoot. Pigweed. Fig. 1677.

Chenopodium album L. Sp. Pl. 219. 1753.
Chenopodium viride L. Sp. Pl. 219. 1753.
C. Berlandieri Moq. Enum. Chenop. 23. 1840.
C. paganum Reichenb. Fl. Germ. 579. 1830.
Chenopodium album viride Moq. in DC. Prodr. 13²: 71. 1849.

Annual, stem striate and grooved at least when dry, erect, commonly branched, 1°–10° tall. Leaves rhombic-ovate or the upper lanceolate or linear-lanceolate, narrowed at the base, acute, cuspidate or sometimes obtuse at the apex, 3-nerved, white-mealy beneath or sometimes green on both sides, dentate, sinuate lobed, or entire, 1'–4' long; petioles often as long as the blades; spikes terminal and axillary, often panicled; calyx about ½" broad in fruit, its segments strongly keeled, usually completely enclosing the utricle; styles short, seed horizontal, black, shining, firmly attached to the pericarp; embryo a complete ring.

In waste places. A common weed throughout North America except the extreme north. Naturalized from Europe. Native also of Asia. Wild spinach. Frost-blite. Baconweed. Muckweed. Fat-hen. June–Sept. Consists of many races.

2. Chenopodium incànum (S. Wats.) Heller. Mealy Goosefoot. Fig. 1678.

C. Fremonti incanum S. Wats. Proc. Am. Acad. 9: 94. 1874.
C. incanum Heller, Plant World 1: 23. 1897.

Annual, densely white-mealy nearly or quite to the base, usually much-branched, 1° high or less, the branches ascending. Leaves ovate to rhombic, ½'–1' long, often nearly as wide as long, few-toothed with rather blunt teeth or some of them entire, paler beneath than above, the slender petioles mostly shorter than the blades; spikes short, borne in the upper axils and in terminal panicles; calyx densely mealy.

In dry soil, Nebraska to Wyoming, Kansas and Arizona. May–July.

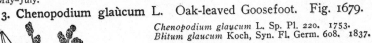

3. Chenopodium glaùcum L. Oak-leaved Goosefoot. Fig. 1679.

Chenopodium glaucum L. Sp. Pl. 220. 1753.
Blitum glaucum Koch, Syn. Fl. Germ. 608. 1837.

Annual, succulent, stem usually much branched, decumbent or prostrate, or with erect branches, 4'–18' high. Leaves oblong, lanceolate or ovate-lanceolate, slender-petioled or the uppermost nearly sessile, obtuse or acute at the apex, mostly narrowed at the base, white-mealy beneath, dark green above, 1'–2' long, the lower or all of them sinuate-dentate or lobed; flowers in small axillary often branched spikes, the clusters usually shorter than the leaves, or the upper panicled; calyx about ½" broad, its segments oblong or obovate, obtuse, neither fleshy nor keeled in fruit; utricle brown, depressed, its summit not completely covered by the calyx; styles short; seed sharp edged, that of lateral flowers vertical, somewhat exserted, that of terminal flowers commonly horizontal; embryo a complete ring.

A weed in waste places throughout North America except the extreme north. Naturalized from Europe; now found in most cultivated areas of the globe. June–Sept.

4. Chenopodium leptophýllum (Moq.) Nutt. Narrow-leaved Goosefoot. Fig. 1680.

Chenopodium album var. *leptophyllum* Moq. in DC. Prodr. 13²: 71. 1849.

Chenopodium leptophyllum Nutt.; Moq. in DC. Prodr. 13²: 71. As synonym. 1849.

Chenopodium leptophyllum var. *oblongifolium* S. Wats. Proc. Am. Acad. 9: 95. 1874.

Chenopodium leptophyllum subglabrum S. Wats. Proc. Am. Acad. 9: 95. 1874.

C. oblongifolium Rydb. Bull. Torr. Club 33: 137. 1906.

Annual, scarcely succulent, stem slender, usually erect, striate or grooved, at least when dry, branched, 6′–2½° tall, mealy above, the branches erect-ascending. Leaves linear to oblong, white-mealy beneath, green above, acute or acuminate, or the lower obtuse, entire or the lower rarely toothed, short-petioled, ½′–1⅓′ long, 1″–3″ wide, 1–3-nerved; flowers in continuous or interrupted axillary and terminal simple or branched spikes; calyx about ½″ broad, its segments strongly keeled and nearly covering the fruit; styles short; seed horizontal, readily detached from the pericarp; embryo a complete ring.

In dry soil, Manitoba to Wisconsin, Missouri, New Mexico and Arizona. Also on the shores of Lake Erie and on sands of the seashore, Maine to New Jersey. July–Sept.

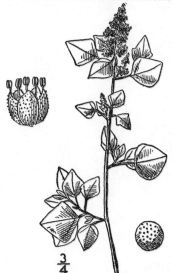

5. Chenopodium Vulvària L.   Stinking Goosefoot. Fig. 1681.

Chenopodium Vulvaria L. Sp. Pl. 220. 1753.

Annual, white-mealy, unpleasantly odorous, much branched, the procumbent branches 1° long or more. Leaves broadly ovate, entire, 1′ long or less, the slender petioles about as long as the blades; flowers in dense short axillary and terminal simple or branched spikes mostly shorter than the leaves; calyx-segments ovate-lanceolate, keeled in fruit, obtusish; seed horizontal, shining, the pericarp coherent; styles short.

Waste grounds, Ontario to Delaware and Florida. Adventive from Europe. July–Sept.

6. Chenopodium polyspérmum L.   Many-seeded Goosefoot. Fig. 1682.

Chenopodium polyspermum L. Sp. Pl. 220. 1753.

Annual, glabrous, not mealy, stem stout or slender, erect or decumbent, commonly much branched, striate, 6′–3° high. Leaves oblong, elliptic or ovate, slender-petioled, entire, thin, green on both sides, obtuse at the apex, narrowed rounded or truncate at the base, 1′–3′ long, 4″–1½′ wide; flowers in loose axillary and terminal panicles; calyx less than 1″ wide, its segments oblong, subacute or obtuse, somewhat scarious, not keeled, not completely covering the top of the fruit; styles short; seed firmly attached to the pericarp, horizontal; embryo a complete ring.

In waste places and ballast, Massachusetts to New Jersey. Adventive from Europe. July–Sept. Allseed.

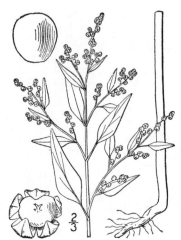

7. Chenopodium Bosciànum Moq. Bosc's Goosefoot. Fig. 1683.

Chenopodium Boscianum Moq. Enum. Chenop. 21. 1840.

Annual, light green, stem slender, erect, striate, usually much branched, 1°–3° tall, the branches very slender, divergent or ascending. Leaves thin, green on both sides, lanceolate or oblong-lanceolate, acute or acuminate at the apex, narrowed at the base, slender-petioled, 1′–2½′ long, the lower sinuate-dentate or nearly all of them entire; flowers in slender terminal and axillary spikes; calyx-segments broadly oblong, obtuse, scarious-margined, not keeled, or scarcely so in fruit, herbaceous, nearly covering the utricle; styles short; seed horizontal, readily separating from the pericarp, black, shining; embryo completely annular.

In woods and thickets, Connecticut to New Jersey, Indiana and Minnesota, south to North Carolina and Texas. July–Sept.

8. Chenopodium Fremóntii S. Wats. Fremont's Goosefoot. Fig. 1684.

Chenopodium Fremontii S. Wats. Bot. King's Exp. 287. 1871.

Annual, glabrous or very nearly so, light green, stem stout or slender, erect, grooved, branched, 1°–3° tall. Leaves thin, green on both sides, broadly triangular-hastate, sinuate-dentate or the upper entire, mostly obtuse at the apex, truncate or abruptly narrowed at the base, slender-petioled, 1′–4′ long and nearly as wide, the uppermost sometimes very small, oblong or lanceolate and acute; spikes slender, axillary to the upper leaves and in terminal panicles; calyx ½″ wide, its segments keeled in fruit, and nearly enclosing the utricle; pericarp easily separable from the seed; seed horizontal, shining; embryo completely annular.

In woods and thickets, South Dakota and Nebraska to Montana and Nevada, south to New Mexico, Arizona and northern Mexico. July–Sept.

9. Chenopodium úrbicum L. Upright or City Goosefoot. Fig. 1685.

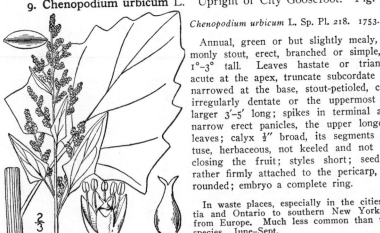

Chenopodium urbicum L. Sp. Pl. 218. 1753.

Annual, green or but slightly mealy, stem commonly stout, erect, branched or simple, channeled, 1°–3° tall. Leaves hastate or triangular-ovate, acute at the apex, truncate subcordate or abruptly narrowed at the base, stout-petioled, coarsely and irregularly dentate or the uppermost entire, the larger 3′–5′ long; spikes in terminal and axillary narrow erect panicles, the upper longer than the leaves; calyx ½″ broad, its segments oblong, obtuse, herbaceous, not keeled and not entirely enclosing the fruit; styles short; seed horizontal, rather firmly attached to the pericarp, its margins rounded; embryo a complete ring.

In waste places, especially in the cities, Nova Scotia and Ontario to southern New York. Adventive from Europe. Much less common than the following species. June–Sept.

10. Chenopodum muràle L.   Nettle-leaved Goosefoot.   Sow-bane.   Fig. 1686.

Chenopodium murale L. Sp. Pl. 219. 1753.

Annual, scarcely or not at all mealy, somewhat scurfy above, stem erect or decumbent, usually branched, 1°–2½° high, leafy to the summit. Leaves rhombic-ovate, thin, bright green on both sides, acute or acuminate at the apex, sharply and coarsely sinuate-dentate, broadly cuneate or subtruncate at the base, slender-petioled, 2′–4′ long; flowers in loose axillary panicles shorter than the leaves, often not longer than the petioles; calyx-segments not entirely enclosing the utricle; styles short; seed sharp-edged, horizontal, firmly attached to the pericarp; embryo completely annular; stamens 5.

In waste places, Maine to Michigan and British Columbia, south to Florida and Mexico. Naturalized from Europe. Widely distributed as a weed in civilized regions. June–Sept.

11. Chenopodium hýbridum L.   Maple-leaved Goosefoot.   Fig. 1687.

Chenopodium hybridum L. Sp. Pl. 219. 1753.

Annual, bright green, not mealy, sometimes more or less scurfy; stem slender, erect, usually branched, 2°–4½° tall. Leaves ovate or rhombic-ovate, long-acuminate at the apex, truncate rounded or subcordate at the base, thin, slender-petioled, sharply dentate with 1–4 large acute teeth on each side, or the upper lanceolate and entire, the lower 4′–7′ long; flowers in large axillary and terminal panicles; calyx about 1″ broad, its segments oblong, rather obtuse, herbaceous, slightly keeled, incompletely covering the fruit; stamens 5; styles short; seed horizontal, sharp-edged, firmly attached to the pericarp; embryo a complete ring.

In woods and thickets, sometimes in waste places, Quebec to British Columbia, south to southeastern New York, Kentucky, Arkansas, Utah and New Mexico. Also in Europe. Sow-bane, Swine's-bane. July–Sept.

12. Chenopodium rùbrum L.   Red Goosefoot.   Pigweed.   Fig. 1688.

Chenopodium rubrum L. Sp. Pl. 218. 1753.
Blitum rubrum Reichb. Fl. Germ. Exc. 582. 1830–32.

Annual, glabrous, somewhat fleshy, not mealy, stem erect, leafy, 1°–2½° tall, often much branched, the branches strict or ascending. Leaves thick, 1½′–4′ long, rhombic-ovate or rhombic-lanceolate, petioled, acute acuminate or obtuse at the apex, narrowed at the base, coarsely sinuate-dentate or the upper entire; flowers in erect compound leafy-bracted axillary and terminal spikes often exceeding the leaves; calyx 3–5-parted, its segments slightly fleshy, red, not keeled, obtuse, about as long as the utricle; stamens 1 or 2; styles short; seed horizontal, ½″ wide, shining, rather sharp-edged, separating from the pericarp; embryo annular.

On the seacoast, Newfoundland to New Jersey, and in saline soil in the interior across the continent, south to central New York, Nebraska and British Columbia. Also in Europe and Asia. Swine's-bane. July–Sept.

Chenopodium hùmile Hook., of similar situations, is lower, has flowers in axillary clusters and a smaller seed, and may be specifically distinct.

13. Chenopodium Bònus-Henrìcus L.   Good King Henry.   Perennial Goosefoot.   Fig. 1689.

Chenopodium Bonus-Henricus L. Sp. Pl. 218. 1753.
Blitum Bonus-Henricus Reichb. Fl. Germ. Exc. 582.
1830–32.

Perennial by a thick rootstock, glabrous, dark green, not mealy; stem erect, usually stout, simple or little branched, channeled, 1°–2½° tall. Leaves broadly triangular-hastate, palmately veined, entire or undulate (rarely with 1 or 2 small teeth), the apex and basal lobes usually acute, the lower long-petioled (petiole often twice as long as the blade), the upper much smaller and short-petioled; flowers in terminal and axillary, simple or panicled, commonly dense spikes sometimes 3′–4′ long; calyx 4-5-parted, the segments not longer than the fruit; styles elongate; seed vertical, or that of terminal flowers horizontal, black, shining, blunt-edged; embryo a complete ring.

In waste places, Nova Scotia and Ontario to Massachusetts and southern New York. Naturalized from Europe. All good. English mercury. Wild spinach. Fat-hen. Roman plant. Blite. Mercury-goosefoot. Smiddy-leaves. Markery. June–Sept.

14. Chenopodium Bòtrys L.   Feather Geranium.   Jerusalem Oak.   Fig. 1690.

Chenopodium Botrys L. Sp Pl. 219. 1753.

Annual, green, glandular-pubescent and viscid, strong-scented; stem slender, erect, simple or branched, 8′–2° tall. Leaves ovate or oblong, deeply and usually irregularly pinnately lobed, acute or obtuse at the apex, petioled, ½′–2′ long, or the uppermost much smaller, the lobes mostly obtuse and dentate; flowers in numerous loose axillary cymose panicles mostly longer than the leaves; calyx 3-5-parted, the segments lanceolate, acute, thin, very pubescent, rather longer than the utricle; seed horizontal or vertical, firmly attached to the pericarp; embryo an incomplete ring.

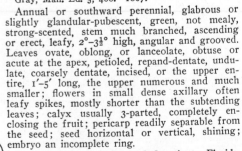

In waste places, Nova Scotia to Minnesota and Washington, southeastern New York, Kentucky and Mexico. Naturalized from Europe. Native also of Asia. The leaves fall in autumn, leaving the panicles as narrow naked wands. Turnpike-geranium. Hindheal. Ambrose. July–Sept.

Chenopodium incìsum Poir., of tropical America, with puberulent flowers and acute leaf-lobes is reported as established in Maine.

15. Chenopodium ambrosioìdes L.   Mexican Tea.   Fig. 1691.

Chenopodium ambrosioides L. Sp. Pl. 219. 1753.
Chenopodium anthelminticum L. Sp. Pl. 220. 1753.
Chenopodium ambrosioides var. *anthelminticum* A. Gray, Man. Ed. 5, 408. 1867.

Annual or southward perennial, glabrous or slightly glandular-pubescent, green, not mealy, strong-scented, stem much branched, ascending or erect, leafy, 2°–3½° high, angular and grooved. Leaves ovate, oblong, or lanceolate, obtuse or acute at the apex, petioled, repand-dentate, undulate, coarsely dentate, incised, or the upper entire, 1′–5′ long, the upper numerous and much smaller; flowers in small dense axillary often leafy spikes, mostly shorter than the subtending leaves; calyx usually 3-parted, completely enclosing the fruit; pericarp readily separable from the seed; seed horizontal or vertical, shining; embryo an incomplete ring.

In waste places, Maine and Ontario to Florida, west across the continent to California. Naturalized from tropical America. Introduced as a weed also into southern Europe and Asia. Consists of numerous races, the spikes leafy to leafless. Aug.–Oct.

2. ROUBIÈVA Moq. Ann. Sci. Nat. (II.) 1: 292. 1834.

A perennial herb, glandular-pubescent, strong-scented, prostrate, and diffusely branched, with narrow small short-petioled deeply pinnatifid leaves. Flowers small, green, perfect, or pistillate, solitary, or in small axillary clusters. Calyx urn-shaped, 3-5-toothed, narrowed at the throat, in fruit becoming obovoid, strongly reticulated and closed. Stamens 5. Styles 3, exserted. Wall of the pericarp thin, glandular. Seed vertical. Embryo a complete ring in the mealy endosperm. [Name in honor of G. J. Roubieu, French botanist.]

A monotypic genus of South America, often included in *Chenopodium.*

1. Roubieva multífida (L.) Moq. Cut-leaved Goosefoot. Fig. 1692.

Chenopodium multifidum L. Sp. Pl. 220. 1753.

Roubieva multifida Moq. Ann. Sci. Nat. (II.) 1: 293. *pl. 10.* 1834.

Usually much branched, very leafy, prostrate, or the branches ascending, 6′-18′ long. Leaves lanceolate or linear-lanceolate or linear-oblong in outline, ½′-1½′ long, 1½″-4″ wide, deeply pinnatifid into linear-oblong acute entire or toothed lobes; flowers 1-5 together in the axils, sessile, less than ½″ broad, some perfect, some pistillate; fruiting calyx obovoid, obtuse, 3-nerved and strongly reticulate-veined, ½″ thick; utricle compressed.

In waste places and ballast, southern New York to Virginia. Naturalized or adventive from tropical America. June–Sept.

3. BLÌTUM L. Sp. Pl. 2. 1753.

Annual glabrous or sparingly pubescent succulent branching herbs, with alternate hastate petioled rather light green leaves. Flowers small, green, or reddish, aggregated in globose axillary sessile heads, or the upper heads forming an interrupted spike. Calyx 2-5-lobed, becoming pulpy and bright red in fruit. Stamens 1-5. Pericarp separating from the seed. Seed vertical, shining. Embryo a complete ring in the mealy endosperm. [The classical name of orache.]

One or perhaps two species, natives of North America and Europe, the following the generic type.

1. Blitum capitàtum L. Strawberry Blite or Spinach. Fig. 1693.

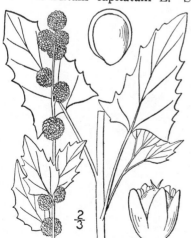

Blitum capitatum L. Sp. Pl. 2. 1753.

Chenopodium capitatum Aschers. Fl. Brand. 572. 1864.

Stem ascending, erect, or prostrate, 6′-2° long, commonly much branched, the branches ascending. Leaves usually longer than wide, 1½′-3′ long, rather thin, sinuate-dentate, or the upper or sometimes all of them entire, cordate or reniform, the apex and basal lobes acute or acuminate; lower petioles often longer than the blades; heads sessile in the axils and on the sides of the upper part of the stem or branches, 2″-3″ in diameter in flower, becoming bright red and 5″-8″ in diameter in fruit, and then somewhat resembling strawberries; seed compressed, ovate, enclosed by the calyx, or when quite mature slightly exserted.

In dry soil, Nova Scotia to Alaska, south to New Jersey, Illinois, Minnesota, in the Rocky Mountains to Colorado and Utah and to Nevada. Also in Europe. Indian paint. Indian strawberry. June–Aug.

4. CYCLOLÒMA Moq. Enum. Chenop. 17. 1840.

An annual diffusely branched glabrous or cobwebby-pubescent herb, with alternate petioled irregularly toothed leaves, and small sessile bractless perfect or pistillate flowers in panicled interrupted spikes. Calyx 5-lobed, the lobes keeled in flower, a thin horizontal irregularly dentate wing developing below them in fruit. Stamens 5. Styles 2–3. Fruit (except its summit) enclosed by the calyx, depressed. Seed horizontal; embryo a complete ring in the mealy endosperm. [Greek, circle-border, alluding to the calyx-wing.]

A monotypic genus of north central North America.

1. Cycloloma atriplicifòlium (Spreng.) Coult. Winged Pigweed. Fig. 1694.

Kochia atriplicifolia Spreng. Nactr. Fl. Hal. **2**: 35. 1801.

Cyclòloma platyphyllum Moq. Enum. Chenop. 18. 1840.

C. atriplicifolium Coult. Mem. Torr. Club **5**: 143. 1894.

Pale green or becoming dark purple, bushy-branched, 6′–20′ high, the stem and branches angular and striate. Leaves lanceolate, mostly acuminate at the apex, narrowed into slender petioles, irregularly sinuate-dentate with acute teeth, 1′–3′ long or the upper much smaller; spikes numerous in terminal panicles, loosely flowered, 1′–3′ long, slender; fruit, including the winged calyx, 2″ broad; calyx-lobes not completely covering the summit of the utricle, which appears as a 5-rayed area.

Along streams and on banks, Manitoba to Indiana and Illinois, Nebraska and Arizona. Tumble-weed. Occasional in waste grounds farther east. Summer.

5. KÓCHIA Roth; Schrad. Journ. Bot. **1**: 307. *pl. 2.* 1799.

Perennial or annual herbs or low shrubs, with alternate sessile narrow entire leaves, and perfect or pistillate flowers, sometimes bracteolate, clustered in the axils. Calyx 5-lobed, herbaceous or membranous, wingless, or sometimes developing a horizontal wing, enclosing the fruit. Stamens 3–5, their filaments linear. Ovary ovoid, narrowed upward into the style; stigmas 2. Utricle pear-shaped or oblong, the pericarp membranous, not adherent to the seed. Seed invertèd; the testa thin; embryo annular; endosperm none. [Name in honor of W. D. J. Koch, 1771–1849, Director of the Botanical Garden at Erlangen.]

About 35 species, mostly natives of the Old World, the following introduced from Europe. An indigenous species, *K. americana,* occurs in the western United States. Type species: *Kochia Scoparia* (L.) Roth.

1. Kochia Scopària (L.) Roth. Kochia. Fig. 1695.

Chenopodium Scoparia L. Sp. Pl. 221. 1753.
Kochia Scoparia Roth; Schrad. Neues Journ. Bot. **3**: 85. 1809.

Annual, pubescent or becoming glabrate, stem erect, slender, rather strict, branched, leafy, 1°–2½° tall. Leaves linear-lanceolate or linear, ciliate, acuminate at the apex, 1′–2′ long, 1″–2″ wide, the upper gradually smaller; flowers sessile, in the axils of the upper leaves, forming short dense bracted spikes; fruiting calyx-segments each with a short triangular horizontal wing.

In waste places, Ontario, Vermont and northern New York. Adventive from Europe. Native also of Asia. Belvedere-, broom- or summer-cypress. July–Sept.

Bassia hirsùta, a related pubescent annual, native of Europe, has been found in Massachusetts and New Jersey. Its fruiting calyx is not winged.

6. MONÓLEPIS Schrad. Ind. Sem. Gott. 4. 1830.

Low annual branching herbs, with small narrow alternate entire toothed or lobed leaves, and polygamous or perfect flowers in small axillary clusters. Calyx of a single persistent herbaceous sepal. Stamen 1. Styles 2, slender. Utricle flat, the pericarp adherent to the smooth vertical seed. Embryo a very nearly complete ring in the mealy endosperm, its radicle turned downward. [Greek, single-scale, from the solitary sepal.]

About 5 species, natives of western North America and northern Asia. Type species: *Monolepis trifida* Schrad.

1. Monolepis Nuttalliàna (R. & S.) Greene. Monolepis. Fig. 1696.

Blitum chenopodioides Nutt. Gen. 1: 4. 1818. Not Lam. 1783.
Blitum Nuttallianum R. & S. Mant. 1: 65. 1822.
Monolepis chenopodioides Moq. in DC. Prodr. 13²: 85. 1849.
Monolepis Nuttalliana Greene, Fl. Fran. 168. 1891.

Slightly mealy when young, pale green, glabrous or nearly so when old; stem 3′–12′ high; branches many, ascending. Leaves lanceolate in outline, short-petioled, or the upper sessile, ½′–2½′ long, narrowed at the base, 3-lobed, the middle lobe linear or linear-oblong, acute or acuminate, 2–4 times as long as the ascending lateral ones; flowers clustered in the axils; sepal oblanceolate or spatulate, acute or subacute; pericarp minutely pitted, about ½″ broad; margins of the seed acute.

In alkaline or dry soil, Manitoba and the Northwest Territory to Minnesota, Missouri, Nebraska, New Mexico and southern California. June–Sept.

7. ÁTRIPLEX [Tourn.] L. Sp. Pl. 1052. 1753.

Annual or perennial herbs or low shrubs, often scurfy-canescent or silvery. Leaves alternate, petioled or sessile, or soime of them opposite. Flowers dioecious or monoecious, small, green, in panicled spikes or capitate-clustered in the axils. Staminate flowers bractless, consisting of a 3–5-parted calyx and an equal number of stamens; filaments separate or united by their bases; a rudimentary ovary sometimes present. Pistillate flowers sübtended by 2 bractlets which enlarge in fruit and are more or less united, sometimes quite to their summits, their margins entire or toothed, their sides smooth, crested, tubercled or winged; perianth none; ovary globose or ovoid; stigmas 2. Utricle completely or partially enclosed by the fruiting bractlets. Seed vertical or rarely horizontal; embryo annular, the radicle pointing upward or downward; endosperm mealy. [From a Greek name of orache.]

About 130 species, of very wide geographic distribution. Besides the following, some 50 others occur in the western parts of North America. Type species: *Atriplex hortensis* L.

Annual herbs; stems or branches erect, diffuse or ascending.
  Leaves hastate, ovate to rhombic-lanceolate or linear-lanceolate.
    Plant green, glabrous or sparingly scurfy, not silvery; leaves slender-petioled.

	1. *A. hastata.*
Plant very scurfy; leaves rhombic-ovate, short-petioled.	2. *A. rosea.*
Plant densely silvery; leaves hastate, entire or little toothed.	3. *A. argentea.*
Leaves oblong, densely silvery, entire; plant of sea beaches.	4. *A. arenaria.*
Perennial herbs or shrubs; leaves oblong or oblanceolate, entire; plants of the western plains.	
Fruiting bractlets suborbicular, wingless, their sides crested or tubercled.	5. *A. Nuttallii.*
Fruiting bractlets appendaged by 4 vertical reticulated wings.	6. *A. canescens.*

1. Atriplex hastàta L.   Halberd-leaved Orache.   Fig. 1697.

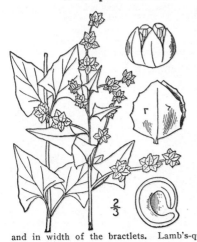

Atriplex hastata L. Sp. Pl. 1053. 1753.
Atriplex patula L. Sp. Pl. 1053. 1753.
Atriplex littoralis L. Sp. Pl. 1054. 1753.
A. patulum var. hastatum A. Gray, Man. Ed. 5, 409. 1867.

Annual, green or purple, somewhat scurfy, at least when young; stems erect, diffuse or ascending, branched, 1°–3° tall. Leaves slender-petioled, acuminate, linear-lanceolate to broadly triangular-hastate, entire or sparingly toothed, 1′–6′ long, truncate or narrowed at the base, the basal lobes divergent, acute or acuminate; flowers in panicled interrupted slender mostly leafless spikes, and usually also capitate in the upper axils; fruiting bractlets united only at the base, fleshy, triangular or rhombic, 3″–4″ wide, their sides often tubercled; radicle of the embryo ascending.

In salt meadows and waste places, most abundant near the coast, Nova Scotia to South Carolina, Ohio and Missouri and in saline soil, Manitoba to British Columbia, Nebraska and Utah and on the Pacific Coast. Also in Europe. Consists of many races, differing in leaf-form and in width of the bractlets. Lamb's-quarters. Fat-hen. Aug.–Oct.

2. Atriplex ròsea L.   Red Orache.   Fig. 1698.

Atriplex rosea L. Sp. Pl. Ed. 2, 1493. 1763.

Annual, pale green and very scurfy, stem erect or decumbent, usually much branched, 1°–2½° high. Leaves ovate or rhombic-ovate, short-petioled or the upper sessile, coarsely sinuate-dentate, obtuse or acute at the apex, narrowed or subtruncate at the base, ½′–3½′ long, ¼′–3½′ wide, often turning red; flowers mostly in axillary capitate clusters, often dense, or some in few terminal spikes; fruiting bractlets broadly ovate or triangular-hastate, strongly veined, mealy-white, dry, about 3″ broad, united only at their bases, their margins toothed or lacerate and sides tubercled.

In waste places and ballast, Nova Scotia to New York and New Jersey. Adventive from Europe. Aug.–Oct.

3. Atriplex argéntea Nutt.   Silvery Orache.   Saltweed.   Fig. 1699.

Atriplex argentea Nutt. Gen. 1: 198. 1818.

Atriplex volutans A. Nelson, Bull. Torr. Club 25: 203. 1898.

Annual, pale, densely silvery-scurfy or becoming smooth, stem erect or ascending, bushy-branched, 6′–20′ high, angular. Leaves firm, triangular-hastate or rhombic-ovate, mostly acute at the apex, narrowed or subtruncate at the base, petioled or the upper sessile, entire or sparingly dentate, ½′–2′ long, the basal lobes short; flowers in capitate axillary clusters, or the staminate in short dense spikes; fruiting bractlets suborbicular, rhombic or broader than high, 2″–4″ wide, united nearly to their summits, the margins sharply toothed, the sides sometimes tubercled or crested; radicle of the embryo pointing downward.

In dry or saline soil, Minnesota to British Columbia, Missouri, Kansas, Colorado and Utah. June–Sept.

Atriplex expánsa S. Wats., admitted into our first edition, is not definitely known within our area.

4. Atriplex arenària Nutt.   Sea-beach Atriplex.   Fig. 1700.

Atriplex arenaria Nutt. Gen. 1: 198.   1818.

Annual, pale, densely silvery-scurfy; stem bushy-branched, 6'–18' high, the branches ascending or decumbent, angular, slender. Leaves oblong, entire, acute or obtuse and mucronulate at the apex, narrowed or rounded at the base, very short-petioled or sessile, ½'–1½' long, 2½"–10" wide, the midvein rather prominent, the lateral veins few and obscure; flowers in axillary clusters much shorter than the leaves; fruiting bractlets triangular wedge-shaped, broadest above, 2"–3" wide, united nearly to the several-toothed summits, their margins entire, their sides reticulated, or sometimes crested or tubercled; radicle of the embryo pointing downward.

On sandy sea beaches, Massachusetts to Florida. July–Sept.

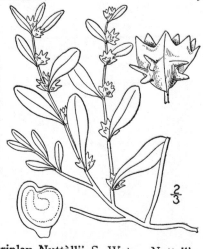

5. Atriplex Nuttàllii S. Wats.   Nuttall's Atriplex.   Fig. 1701.

A. Nuttallii S. Wats. Proc. Am. Acad. 9: 116.   1874.

A finely scurfy pale green shrub, 1°–2½° tall, the branches erect or ascending, rather stiff, striate or terete, leafy, the bark nearly white. Leaves oblong, linear-oblong or oblanceolate, obtuse or subacute at the apex, narrowed at the base, sessile, entire, ½'–2' long, 2"–5" wide; flowers in terminal spikes and capitate clustered in the axils, often strictly dioecious; fruiting bractlets ovate or suborbicular, united to above the middle, 1½"–2½" broad, the margins toothed, the sides crested, tubercled or spiny.

In dry or saline soil, Manitoba to Saskatchewan, south to Nebraska, Colorado and Nevada. Aug.–Oct.

6. Atriplex canéscens (Pursh) James.   Bushy Atriplex.   Fig. 1702.

Calligonum canescens Pursh, Fl. Am. Sept. 370.   1814.

Atriplex canescens James, Trans. Am. Phil. Soc. (II.) 2: 178.   1825.

A pale densely scurfy shrub, 1°–3° high, resembling the preceding species and with similar foliage. Flowers in short terminal spikes and in axillary clusters, commonly dioecious, sometimes monoecious; bractlets ovate in flower, united nearly to their summits; in fruit appendaged by 4 broad thin distinct wings, which are 2"–4" broad at the middle and usually about twice as high, strongly reticulate-veined, not tubercled nor crested, toothed near their summits or entire.

In dry or saline soil, South Dakota to Kansas, Texas, New Mexico and Mexico, west to Oregon and California. Sage-brush. Cenizo. July–Sept.

8. EURÒTIA Adans. Fam. Pl. 2: 260.   1763.

Pubescent perennial herbs or low shrubs, with alternate entire narrow leaves and monoecious or dioecious flowers, capitate or spicate in the axils. Staminate flowers not bracteolate, consisting of a 4-parted calyx and as many exserted stamens. Pistillate flowers 2-bracteolate, the bractlets united nearly or quite to their summits, densely covered with long silky hairs, 2-horned; calyx none; ovary ovoid, sessile, pubescent; styles 2, exserted.   Seed vertical;

embryo nearly annular in the mealy endosperm, its radicle pointing downward. [From the Greek for hoariness or mould.]

Two known species, the following of western North America; the other, of western Asia and eastern Europe is the generic type.

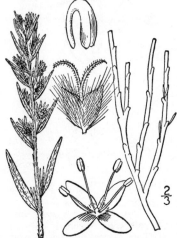

1. Eurotia lanàta (Pursh) Moq. American Eurotia. White Sage. Fig. 1703.

Diotis lanata Pursh, Fl. Am. Sept. 602. 1814.
Eurotia lanata Moq. Enum. Chenop. 81. 1840.

A stellate-pubescent erect much-branched shrub 1°-3° high, the hairs long, white when young, becoming reddish brown, the branches ascending, very leafy. Leaves linear or linear-lanceolate, short-petioled or the upper sessile, obtuse at the apex, narrowed at the base, ½-2′ long, 2″-4½″ wide, their margins revolute, the midvein prominent, the lateral veins few; flowers monoecious, densely capitate in the upper axils, forming terminal leafy spikes; bracts lancolate, 2″-4″ long in fruit, appendaged by 4 tufts of spreading hairs; calyx-lobes acute, pubescent; utricle loose, the pericarp readily separating from the large seed.

$\frac{2}{3}$

In dry soil, Saskatchewan to western Nebraska, Texas, California and Washington. Winter-fat. Romeria. June-Sept.

9. ÁXYRIS L. Sp. Pl. 979. 1753.

Annual herbs with alternate entire petioled leaves and small monoecious flowers, the pistillate ones pilose or villous, the staminate ones uppermost, very small. Staminate calyx 3-5-parted; stamens 2-5. Pistillate calyx 3-4-parted; ovary suborbicular, somewhat flattened; stigmas 2, filiform, connate at the base. Utricle obovate to cuneate, winged or crested at the apex, enclosed in the perianth. Seed erect; embryo horseshoe-shaped; endosperm copious. [Greek, mild to the taste.]

Five or six species, natives of northern Asia, the following typical.

1. Axyris amarantoìdes L. Upright Axyris. Fig. 1704.

Axyris amarantoides L. Sp. Pl. 979. 1753.

Erect, often much branched, 1°-2° high, pubescent, the slender branches ascending. Leaves ovate, elliptic or lanceolate, entire, acute or obtusish, narrowed at the base, thin, 1½′-3′ long, the slender petioles 3″-7″ long; staminate flowers minute, glomerate-spicate; fruit oval or obovate, more or less winged at the top, flattened.

Waste and cultivated grounds, Manitoba and North Dakota. Naturalized from Russia or Siberia.

10. CORISPÉRMUM [A. Juss.] L. Sp. Pl. 4. 1753.

Annual herbs, with alternate narrow entire 1-nerved leaves, and perfect bractless small green flowers, solitary in the upper axils, forming terminal narrow leafy spikes, the upper leaves shorter and broader than the lower. Calyx of a solitary thin broad sepal, or rarely 2. Stamens 1-3, rarely more, and one of them longer. Ovary ovoid, styles 2. Utricle ellipsoid, mostly plano-convex, the pericarp firmly adherent to the vertical seed, its margins acute or winged. Embryo annular in the somewhat fleshy endosperm, its radicle pointing downward. [Greek, bug-seed.]

About 10 species, natives of the north temperate and subarctic zones the following typical.

1. Corispermum hyssopifòlium L.   Bug-seed.   Fig. 1705.

Corispermum hyssopifolium L. Sp. Pl. 4. 1753.

Glabrous or pubescent, rather pale green, somewhat fleshy, stem striate, erect, sometimes zigzag, usually much branched, 6'–2° tall, the branches slender, ascending or divergent, sparingly leafy. Leaves narrowly linear, sessile, ½'–2' long, 1"–2" wide, cuspidate at the apex; upper leaves ovate or lanceolate, appressed-ascending, or at length spreading, acute or acuminate at the apex, ¼'–½' long, scarious-margined; utricle 1½"–2" long, ½"–1" thick, narrowly winged, obtuse, subacute or mucronate by the persistent styles.

In sandy soil, shores of the Great Lakes to the Northwest Territory, Arctic America and British Columbia, south to Missouri, Texas and Arizona. Also in Europe and Asia. Bugweed. Tumble-weed.

Corispermum nítidum Kit. (*C. hyssopifolium microcarpum* S. Wats.) with smaller fruit and upper leaves usually not imbricated, is a race of this, or a closely related species, ranging from Nebraska to Texas and Arizona and also occurring in Europe.

11. SALICÓRNIA [Tourn.] L. Sp. Pl. 3.   1753.

Fleshy glabrous annual or perennial herbs, with opposite terete branches, the leaves reduced to mere opposite scales at the nodes, the flowers sunken 3–7 together in the axils of the upper ones, forming narrow terminal spikes, perfect or the lateral ones staminate. Calyx obpyramidal or rhomboid, fleshy, 3–4-toothed or truncate, becoming spongy in fruit, deciduous. Stamens 2, or sometimes solitary, exserted; filaments cylindric, short; anthers oblong, large; ovary ovoid; styles or stigmas 2. Utricles enclosed by the spongy fruiting calyx, the pericarp membranous. Seed erect, compressed; embryo conduplicate; endosperm none. [Name Greek, salt-horn; from the saline habitat, and horn-like branches.]

About 10 species, natives of saline soil, widely distributed in both the Old World and the New. Only the following are known to inhabit North America. Type species: *Salicornia europaea* L.

Annuals; stems mostly erect.
Scales very short, acute or blunt; spikes 1"–1½" in diameter.   1. *S. europaea.*
Scales mucronate-tipped; spikes 2"–3" in diameter.   2. *S. Bigelovii.*
Perennial by a woody rootstock; stems trailing or decumbent.   3. *S. ambigua.*

1. Salicornia europaèa L.   Slender or Jointed Glasswort.   Fig. 1706.

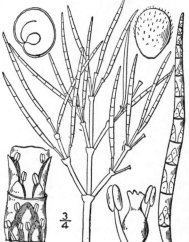

Salicornia europaea and var. *herbacea* L. Sp. Pl. 3. 1753.
Salicornia herbacea L. Sp. Pl. Ed. 2, 5. 1762.
Salicornia rubra A. Nelson, Bull. Torr. Club **26**: 122. 1899.
S. europaea prostrata Fernald, Rhodora **9**: 206. 1907.

Annual, 6'–2° tall, stem usually erect, much branched, the branches slender, ascending, spreading or nearly upright, their joints 2–4 times as long as thick. Scales acute or rather obtuse, 1" long or less, broadly ovate or wider than long; fruiting spikes 1'–3' long, about 1½" in diameter; middle flower of the 3 at each joint twice as high as the lateral ones, reaching nearly or quite to the top of the joint; utricle pubescent.

In salt marshes, Anticosti to Georgia; about salt springs in central New York; in saline soil from Manitoba to British Columbia, south to Kansas and Utah. Also in Europe and Asia. The plant often turns bright red in autumn, forming vividly colored areas, hence called Marsh-samphire. Frog-, crab- or sea-grass. Pickle-plant. Saltwort. English sea-grass. Chickens'-toes. July–Sept.

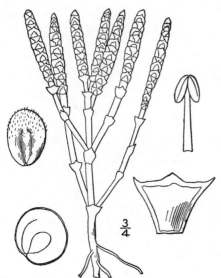

2. Salicornia Bigelòvii Torr. Bigelow's Glasswort. Fig. 1707.

Salicornia mucronata Bigel. Fl. Bost. Ed. 2, 2.
  1824. Not Lag. 1817.
Salicornia virginica Moq. in DC. Prodr. 13^2: 145.
  1849. Not L. 1753.
Salicornia Bigelovii Torr. Bot. Mex. Bound. Surv.
  184. 1859.

Annual, stem and branches stout, erect or nearly so, 2'–12' tall. Scales ovate or triangular-ovate, sharply mucronate, 1"–1½" long, at length spreading; fruiting spikes ½'–2½' long, 2"–3" in diameter, their joints not longer than thick; middle flower slightly higher than the lateral ones, reaching very nearly to the end of the joint; utricle pubescent.

In salt marshes, Nova Scotia to Florida and Texas. Also in the Bahamas, Cuba, Porto Rico and on the Pacific Coast. Plant bright red in autumn. July–Sept.

3. Salicornia ambígua Michx. Woody Glasswort. Fig. 1708.

Salicornia ambigua Michx. Fl. Bor. Am. 1: 2.
  1803.

Perennial by a woody rootstock, stem trailing or decumbent, 6'–2° long, the branches ascending or erect, slender, nearly or quite simple, rather long-jointed, 3'–8' long. Scales broadly ovate or wider than high, acute or obtuse, appressed or slightly divergent; fruiting spikes ½'–1½' long, about 2" in diameter, their joints not longer than thick; flowers all about equally high and about equalling the joints.

On sea beaches and salt meadows, New Hampshire to Florida and Texas, and on the Pacific Coast from British Columbia to California. Bermuda; Bahamas; Cuba to Santa Cruz. Aug.–Sept.

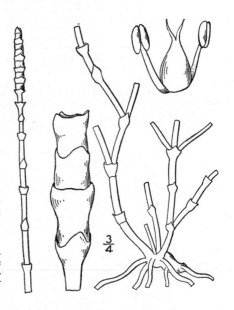

12. SARCÓBATUS Nees in Max. Reise N. A. 1: 510. 1839.

An erect much branched shrub, with spiny branches, alternate linear fleshy entire sessile leaves. Flowers monoecious or dioecious, the staminate in terminal ament-like spikes, the pistillate solitary in the axils, or rarely several together. Staminate flowers without a calyx; stamens 2–5 together under peltate rhombic-ovate acute spirally arranged scales; filaments short. Pistillate flowers sessile or very nearly so; calyx compressed, ovoid or oblong, slightly 2-lipped, adnate to the bases of the 2 subulate exserted papillose stigmas, appendaged by a narrow border which expands into a membranous horizontal wing in fruit. Seed vertical, the testa translucent, double; embryo coiled into a flat spiral, green; endosperm none. [Name Greek, flesh-thorn, from the fleshy leaves and thorny stems.]

A monotypic genus of western North America.

1. Sarcobatus vermiculàtus (Hook.) Torr. Grease-wood. Fig. 1709.

Batis (?) *vermiculata* Hook. Fl. Bor. Am. **2**: 128. 1838.

Sarcobatus vermicularis Torr. Emory's Rep. 150. 1848.

Glabrous or the young foliage somewhat pubescent, much branched, 2°–10° high, the branches slightly angled, leafy, nearly white, some of them leafless and spine-like. Stem 1′–3′ in diameter; wood yellow, very hard; leaves obtuse or subacute, ½′–1½′ long, 1″–1½″ wide, narrowed at the base; spikes of staminate flowers ¼′–1′ long, 1½″–2″ in diameter, cylindric, short-peduncled or sessile; wing of the calyx 4″–6″ broad when mature, conspicuously veined.

In dry alkaline and saline soil, western Nebraska, Wyoming to Nevada and New Mexico. Wood used for fuel, for want of better, in the regions where it occurs. June–July. Fruit mature Sept.–Oct.

13. DÓNDIA Adans. Fam. Pl. **2**: 261. 1763.

[SUAÈDA Forsk. Fl. AEg. Arab. 69. *pl. 18b.* 1775.]

Fleshy annual or perennial herbs, or low shrubs, with alternate narrowly linear thick or nearly terete entire sessile leaves, and perfect or polygamous bracteolate flowers, solitary or clustered in the upper axils. Calyx 5-parted or 5-cleft, the segments sometimes keeled or even slightly winged in fruit, enclosing the utricle. Stamens 5. Styles usually 2, short. Pericarp separating from the vertical or horizontal seed. Embryo coiled into a flat spiral. Endosperm wanting or very little. [In honor of Jacopodi Dondi, Italian naturalist of the fourteenth century.]

About 50 species, of wide geographic distribution. Besides the following, some 6 others occur in the western and southern parts of North America. Type species: *Chenopodium altissimum* L.

Annuals of the Atlantic sea coast; leaves not broadened at the base.
　　Dark green, not glaucous; sepals acutely keeled; seed black.　　　　　　1. *D. linearis.*
　　Light green, glaucous; sepals scarcely keeled; seed dark red.　　　　　　2. *D. maritima.*
Perennial of the western plains; leaves broadened at the base.　　　　　　3. *D. depressa.*

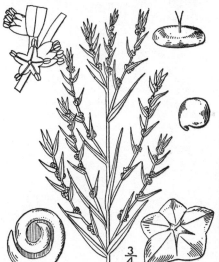

1. Dondia linearis (Ell.) Heller. Tall Sea-Blite. Fig. 1710.

Salsola salsa var. *americana* Pers. Syn. **1**: 296. 1805.
Salsola linearis Ell. Bot. S. C. & G. **1**: 332. 1821.
Dondia linearis Heller, Cat. N. Am. Pl. 69. 1900.
D. americana Britton, in Britt. & Brown, Ill. Fl. **1**: 584. 1896.
Suaeda americana Fernald, Rhodora **9**: 146. 1907.

Annual, dark green or purplish green, not glaucous, stem erect or procumbent, 1°–3° tall, pale green or nearly white, branched, the branches slender, very leafy, erect-ascending or sometimes recurved, more or less secund. Leaves of the stem linear-subulate, ½′–1½′ long, those of the branches much shorter, somewhat 3-angled, lanceolate-subulate, widest just above the base, the upper surface flat; sepals purple-green, glaucous, all or some of them acutely keeled or almost winged; seed orbicular, black, shining, ½″ broad.

On salt marshes, beaches, and along salt water ditches, Nova Scotia to New Jersey and Texas. Bahamas; Cuba. Sea-goosefoot. Aug.–Sept.

2. **Dondia marítima** (L.) Druce. Low or Annual Sea-Blite. Fig. 1711.

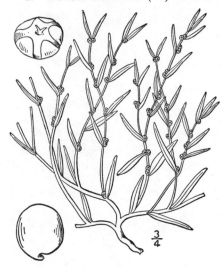

Chenopodium maritimum L. Sp. Pl. 221. 1753.
Suaeda maritima Dumort. Prodr. Fl. Belg. 22.
1827.
Dondia maritima Druce, Ann. Scot. Nat. Hist.
1896: 42. 1896.

Annual, pale green and somewhat glaucous, stem mostly decumbent, bushy-branched, 5'-15' high, becoming brownish, the branches ascending. Leaves 5"-12" long, those of the branches not conspicuously shorter than the upper ones of the stem, 3-angled, broadest at the base; sepals pale green, rounded or very obtusely keeled, somewhat roughened; seed orbicular, dark brownish red, shining, about 1" in diameter.

On sea beaches, stony and muddy shores, and in salt marshes, Quebec to southern New York, New Jersey and southward. Also on the coasts of Europe and of northwestern North America. July–Sept.

Suaeda Ríchii Fernald, of the coasts of Maine and Nova Scotia, has smaller seeds, the leaves not glaucous.

3. **Dondia depréssa** (Pursh) Britton.
Western Sea-Blite. Fig. 1712.

Salsola depressa Pursh, Fl. Am. Sept. 197. 1814.

Suaeda depressa S. Wats. Bot. King's Exp. 294.
1871.

Dondia depressa Britton; Britt. & Brown, Ill. Fl.
1: 585. 1896.

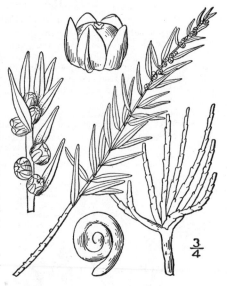

Perennial by a deep slender woody root or sometimes annual, branched from the base and usually also above, 6'-2° tall, the branches decumbent or ascending, usually very leafy. Leaves narrowly linear, ½'-1' long, broadest at or just above the base, or the upper lanceolate or ovate-lanceolate and commonly much shorter; sepals acute, one or more of them strongly keeled in fruit; seed about ½" in diameter, rather dull, minutely reticulated.

In saline soil, Minnesota to Saskatchewan Territory, Nebraska, Kansas, Colorado and Nevada. June–Aug.

14. SÁLSOLA L. Sp. Pl. 222. 1753.

Annual or perennial bushy-branched herbs, with rigid subulate prickle-pointed leaves, and sessile perfect 2-bracteolate flowers, solitary in the axils, or sometimes several together. Calyx 5-parted, its segments appendaged by a broad membranous horizontal wing in fruit and enclosing the utricle. Stamens 5. Ovary depressed; styles 2. Utricle flattened. Seed horizontal; embryo coiled into a conic spiral; endosperm none. [Name Latin, a diminutive of salsus, salty.]

About 50 species, of wide geographic distribution on seashores and in saline districts, occasionally pernicious weeds in cultivated grounds. Type species: *Salsola Soda* L.

Calyx coriaceous, not conspicuously veined; plant maritime.   1. *S. Kali.*
Calyx membranous. very strongly veined; plant an inland weed.   2. *S. pestifer.*

1. Salsola Kàli L. Saltwort. Prickly Glasswort. Fig. 1713.

Salsola Kali L. Sp. Pl. 222. 1753.
Salsola Tragus L. Sp. Pl. Ed. 2, 322. 1762.
Salsola caroliniana Walt. Fl. Car. 111. 1788.

Annual, glabrous or often pubescent, loosely much branched, 1°–2° high, the branches ascending or spreading, mostly stout, somewhat ridged. Leaves dull green or grayish, 3″–10″ long, succulent, lanceolate-subulate, swollen at the base, the midvein excurrent into a stout yellowish green prickle; flowers solitary in the axils; wing of the persistent calyx nearly orbicular, lobed, becoming lacerate, not conspicuously veined, 2″– 4″ in diameter; calyx coriaceous, veined, its wing about as long as the ascending lobe.

On sea beaches, Cape Breton Island to Florida. Also in Europe and Asia. Sea- or Salt-grape. Sea-thrift. Russian thistle. Kelpwort. July–Sept.

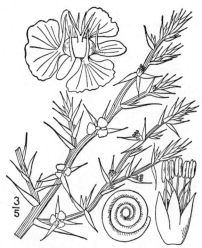

2. Salsola péstifer A. Nelson. Russian Thistle or Cactus. Fig. 1714.

S. Kali rosacea Pall. Ill. Pl. 36, pl. 28, f. 1. 1803.
Not S. rosacea L.
S. Kali tenuifolia F. W. Meyer, Chlor. Han. 470. 1836.
S. pestifer A. Nelson, Rocky Mt. Bot. 169. 1909.

Similar to the preceding species, but bushy branched, the branches usually slender. Leaves and outer branches usually bright red at maturity; leaves not noticeably swollen at the base, linear, prickle-tipped, less fleshy; calyx membranous, veiny, its wing as long as the ascending lobe or longer.

In cultivated fields and waste places, New Jersey to Ontario, the Northwest Territory, Kansas and Washington. A very troublesome weed in many parts of the Central and Western States. Naturalized from northern Europe or Asia. July–Sept.

Family 18. PHYTOLACCÀCEAE Lindl. Nat. Syst. Ed. 2, 213. 1836.

POKEWEED FAMILY.

Herbs (some tropical species shrubs or trees) with alternate entire mostly exstipulate leaves, and perfect regular polygamous or monoecious usually racemose flowers. Calyx 4–5-parted or of 4 or 5 distinct sepals, its segments or sepals imbricated in the bud. Petals wanting. Stamens as many as the calyx-segments or sepals and alternate with them, or more numerous, hypogynous; filaments subulate or filiform, distinct or united at the base; anthers 2-celled, the sacs longitudinally dehiscent, often nearly separated. Ovary superior, several-celled in most of the genera; ovules solitary in the cavities, amphitropous. Styles as many as the carpels, short or none; stigmas linear or filiform. Fruit a berry in the following genus, capsular or samaroid in some others. Endosperm mealy or fleshy.

About 22 genera and 110 species, mostly in the tropics.

1. PHYTOLÁCCA L. Sp. Pl. 41. 1753.

Tall perennial herbs (some tropical species woody), with ample petioled exstipulate leaves, and small flowers in terminal racemes, which by the further growth of the stem become opposite the leaves. Pedicels bracted at the base and often 1–3 bracted above Calyx of 4 or 5 persistent rounded sepals. Stamens 5–30, inserted at the base of the calyx; anthers mostly oblong. Ovary subglobose, composed of 5–15 distinct or somewhat united carpels. Fruit a depressed-globose 5–15-celled juicy, fleshy berry. Seeds 1 in each cavity, erect, compressed; embryo annular in the mealy endosperm. [Name Greek and French, referring to the crimson juice of the berries.]

About 24 species, the following typical one of eastern North America, the others tropical.

1. Phytolacca americàna L. Poke. Scoke. Pigeon-berry. Garget. Fig. 1715.

Phytolacca americana L. Sp. Pl. 41. 1753.
Phytolacca decandra L. Sp. Pl. Ed. 2, 631. 1762.

.A glabrous strong-smelling succulent erect branching herb, 4°–12° tall, the root perennial, large, poisonous, the stem stout, its pith divided into disks separated by lens-shaped cavities. Leaves oblong-lanceolate or ovate-lanceolate, pinnately veined, acute or acuminate at both ends, 8′–12′ long; petioles ½′–4′ long; racemes peduncled, 2′–8′ long; pedicels divergent, 2″–6″ long, each with a subulate-lanceolate bractlet at its base and usually 2 similar ones above; flowers perfect; calyx white, 2″–3″ broad, its sepals suborbicular, or oval; stamens 10, slightly shorter than the sepals; ovary green, 10-celled; styles recurved; berry dark purple, 5″–6″ in diameter, 3″–4″ high, its 10 carpels conspicuous when dry.

In various situations, Maine and Ontario to Minnesota, Arkansas, Florida and Mexico. Bermuda. Sometimes a troublesome weed. Naturalized in Europe. Young shoots eaten like asparagus. June–Sept. Berries ripe Aug.–Oct. Inkberry. Redweed. Red-ink plant. Pocan-bush. Coakum. Cancer-jalap. American nightshade. Pokeweed.

Family 19. CORRIGIOLÀCEAE Reichenb.; Moessl. Handb. 1¹: 51. 1827.

WHITLOW-WORT FAMILY.

Low herbs, erect or prostrate, with opposite mostly stipulate entire leaves, and small, perfect flowers in cymes. Sepals 4 or 5, distinct, or partly united, white or greenish, persistent. Petals none. Stamens 1–10, usually 4 or 5, borne at the base of the ovary, or rarely on the calyx-tube (hypanthium); filaments slender; anthers 2-celled, short. Ovary sessile, 1-celled; styles mostly 2, more or less united, often short; ovule solitary, amphitropous. Fruit an achene or utricle, 1-seeded. Endosperm nearly enclosing the embryo.

About 18 genera and 100 species of wide geographic distribution.

Leaves stipulate.
  Sepals awn-tipped; calyx sessile.   1. *Paronychia.*
  Sepals not awned; calyx pedicelled.
    Styles long; sepals cuspidate; radicle ascending.   2. *Anychiastrum.*
    Styles very short or wanting; sepals mucronate; radicle descending.   3. *Anychia.*
                                                   4. *Scleranthus.*
Leaves not stipulate.

1. PARONÝCHIA [Tourn.] Adans. Fam. Pl. 2: 272. 1763.

Tufted herbs, our species perennials, often woody at the base, with opposite leaves, scarious stipules, and small clustered scarious-bracted apetalous flowers. Calyx 5-parted, the segments awn-tipped. Stamens 5, inserted at the base of the calyx, sometimes alternate with as many staminodia. Ovary ovoid or subglobose, narrowed upward into the style; styles united nearly to the stigmas; ovule solitary, amphitropous. Utricle membranous, included in the calyx, 1-seeded. [Greek, for a disease of the fingers and a plant supposed to cure it.]

About 50 species, natives of warm and temperate regions. Besides the following about 7 others occur in the southern and western United States. Type species: *Illecebrum Paronychia* L.

Flowers clustered.
  Flowers hidden among the bracts and stipules.   1. *P. argyrocoma.*
  Flowers not hidden among the bracts and stipules.
    Stems erect; inflorescence open.
      Calyx 1″–1¼″ long, the sepals oblong to oblong-lanceolate.
        Branches of the inflorescence ascending.   2. *P. Jamesii.*
        Branches of the inflorescence spreading.   3. *P. Wardii.*
      Calyx 2″ long, the sepals lanceolate.   4. *P. dichotoma.*
    Stems prostrate or diffuse; inflorescence contracted.   5. *P. depressa.*
Flowers solitary.   6. *P. sessiliflora.*

1. Paronychia argyrócoma (Michx.) Nutt. Silver Whitlow-wort. Fig. 1716.

Anychia argyrocoma Michx. Fl. Bor. Am. 1: 113. 1803.

Paronychia argyrocoma Nutt. Gen. 1: 160. 1818.

Stem erect or ascending, much branched, 3'–8' high, clothed with silvery appressed scale-like hairs. Leaves linear, 1-nerved, acute or mucronate at the apex, pubescent or nearly glabrous; stipules silvery-white, scarious, entire, usually shorter than the leaves; flowers in forking cymes, subtended and concealed by the large silvery membranous bracts; calyx-segments 2"–2½" long, their awns erect, nearly as long as the segments, pubescent or glabrous; staminodia minute and much shorter than the filaments or wanting.

In rocky places, mostly on mountains, Maine, New Hampshire and Massachusetts, and from Virginia to Tennessee and Georgia, the northern plant less pubescent than the southern, and more floriferous. Ascends to 4200 ft. in North Carolina. Called also silver chickweed and silverhead. July–Sept.

2. Paronychia Jàmesii T. & G. James' Whitlow-wort. Fig. 1717.

Paronychia Jamesii T. & G. Fl. N. A. 1: 170. 1838.

Scabrous-pubescent, stems 3'–10' high, much branched from the base. Leaves linear-subulate, 10" long or less, the lowest obtuse, the uppermost mucronate or bristle-pointed; stipules entire; flowers in small cymes, the branches of the inflorescence ascending; bracts shorter than the calyx; calyx 1"–1¼" long, the segments lanceolate, gradually acuminate, tipped with divergent awns of about one-fourth their length; staminodia about as long as the filaments.

In dry soil, Nebraska and Colorado to Texas and New Mexico. July–Oct.

3. Paronychia Wàrdi Rydb. Ward's Whitlow-wort. Fig. 1718.

Paronychia Wardi Rydb.; Small, Fl. SE. U. S. 400. 1903.

Branched from a woody base, or simple up to the inflorescence, minutely pubescent, the branches slender. Leaves linear-filiform, 3"–10" long, acute, early deciduous; branches of the inflorescence spreading, very slender; calyx puberulent, only about 1" long; sepals oblong, abruptly acuminate, the short awns at length divergent-ascending.

In dry or stony soil, Kansas and Colorado to Texas and New Mexico. Aug.–Oct.

4. Paronychia dichótoma (L.) Nutt. Forking Whitlow-wort. Nailwort. Fig. 1719.

Achyranthes dichotoma L. Mant. 51. 1767.

Paronychia dichotoma Nutt. Gen. 1: 159. 1818.

Much branched from the thick woody base, glabrous or puberulent, 4'–14' tall. Leaves subulate, smooth, all acute, mucronate or bristle-tipped; stipules - entire, silvery, often 5"–6" long, tapering into a slender awn; cyme loose, its branches ascending; calyx 2" long, glabrous or merely puberulent, the awns of its segments divergent, short; staminodia of minute bristles hardly one-fourth as long as the filaments; styles nearly as long as the perianth-segments, the stamens fully one-half as long.

In dry soil, Maryland to North Carolina, west to Arkansas and Texas. July–Oct.

5. Paronychia depréssa (T. & G.) Nutt. Depressed Whitlow-wort. Fig. 1720.

P. Jamesii depressa T. & G. Fl. N. Am. 1: 171. 1838.
Paronychia depressa (T. & G.) Nutt.; A. Nelson, Bull. Torr. Club 26: 236. 1899.

Root deep, woody, the numerous prostrate or spreading branches 3' long or less, forming dense mats, roughish-puberulent. Leaves linear, 3"–7" long, cuspidate; stipules silvery, as long as the leaves or shorter, long-acuminate; flowers in small cymes, or solitary in the axils; calyx pubescent, about 1¼" long, exceeded by the bracts; awns of the sepals divergent-ascending; filaments shorter than the slender staminodia.

In dry soil, South Dakota to Nebraska and Wyoming. June–Aug.

Paronychia diffùsa A. Nelson, of South Dakota, Nebraska, Wyoming and Colorado, differing in shorter bracts and stipules, does not appear specifically distinct.

6. Paronychia sessiliflòra Nutt. Low Whitlow-wort. Fig. 1721.

Paronychia sessiliflora Nutt. Gen. 1: 160. 1818.

Densely tufted from stout thick roots, low, the internodes very short and hidden by the imbricated leaves and stipules. Leaves linear-subulate, glabrous or puberulent, the lowest erect and obtuse, the uppermost recurved-spreading, mucronate or bristle-pointed; stipules 2-cleft, usually shorter than the leaves; bracts entire, mostly shorter than the flowers; flowers sessile, solitary at ends of branchlets; calyx 1"–1½" long, its segments hooded at the apex, tipped with at length divergent awns of nearly their own length; staminodia about as long as the filaments.

In dry soil, Saskatchewan to Montana, Nebraska and Colorado. Aug.–Sept.

2. ANYCHIÁSTRUM Small, Fl. SE. U. S. 400. 1903.

Annual or perennial, diffusely spreading or prostrate herbs, the foliage finely pubescent or glabrous, the stipules short or elongated, the small flowers in dichotomous cymes, with bracts similar to the leaves. Flowers manifestly pedicelled. Sepals distinct or nearly so, erect, cuspidate or abruptly tipped, not awned. Stamens mostly 5, borne at the base of the ovary. Styles united nearly to the stigmas. Utricle nearly or quite enclosed by the calyx. [Greek, star-*Anychia*.]

Four known species, of the southeastern United States. Type species: *Anychiastrum ripàrium* (Chapm.) Small.

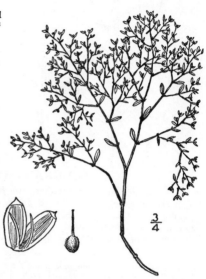

1. Anychiastrum montànum Small. Mountain Anychiastrum. Fig. 1722.

Anychiastrum montanum Small, Torreya 10: 230. 1910.

Annual or biennial, minutely pubescent. Stem branched at the base, the branches spreading, diffuse, 2′–8′ long, slender, purplish; leaves spatulate to elliptic-spatulate, acuminate or acutish, 2″–5½″ long; stipules silvery; calyx ¾″ long in fruit; sepals ovate to oblong-ovate, glabrous, abruptly tipped, but not cuspidate.

$\frac{3}{4}$

In dry soil, mountains of Pennsylvania to Georgia. Aug.–Sept.

3. ANÝCHIA Michx. Fl. Bor. Am. 1: 112. 1803.

Annual herbs, with repeatedly forking stems, elliptic oval or oblanceolate opposite mostly punctate very short-petioled leaves, small scarious stipules, and minute green apetalous flowers. Calyx 5-parted, its segments oblong, concave, not awned. Stamens 2–5, inserted on the base of the calyx; filaments filiform. Staminodia wanting. Ovary subglobose, compressed; styles 2, distinct, or united at the base; ovule solitary, amphitropous. Utricle subglobose, somewhat compressed, longer than the calyx. [Derivation same as *Paronychia*.]

Only the following species, natives of eastern North America. Type species: *Anychia dichotoma* Michx.

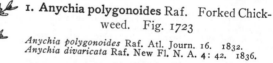

Pubescent; flowers sessile; stems mostly prostrate or ascending.   1. *A. polygonoides*.
Glabrous or nearly so; flowers pedicelled; stems usually erect.   2. *A. canadensis*.

1. Anychia polygonoides Raf. Forked Chickweed. Fig. 1723

Anychia polygonoides Raf. Atl. Journ. 16. 1832.
Anychia divaricata Raf. New Fl. N. A. 4: 42. 1836.

Pubescent, stems mostly prostrate or ascending, much forked, 3′–10′ high, the internodes often shorter than the leaves. Leaves narrowly elliptic, 2″–4″ long, ½″–1″ wide, mucronate or acute at the apex, sessile, or the base tapering into a very short petiole, usually very numerous and crowded; flowers sessile in the forks, more or less clustered, scarcely ½″ high, inconspicuous except when fully expanded; stamens commonly 2 or 3, sometimes 5.

$\frac{3}{5}$

In dry woods, thickets and in open places, Maine to Minnesota, south to Florida, Alabama and Texas. Ascends to 5200 ft. in Georgia. Illustrated in our first edition as *A. dichotoma* Michx., but this proves to be the same as the following species. June–Sept.

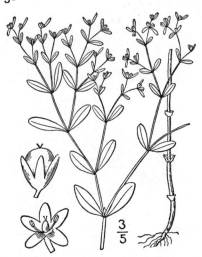

2. Anychia canadénsis (L.) B.S.P. Slender Forked Chickweed. Fig. 1724.

Queria canadensis L. Sp. Pl. 90. 1753.

Anychia dichotoma Michx. Fl. Bor. Am. 1: 113. 1803.

Queria capillacea Nutt. Gen. 1: 159. 1818.

Anychia capillacea DC. Prodr. 3: 369. 1828.

Anychia canadensis B.S.P. Prel. Cat. N. Y. 1888.

Glabrous or very nearly so, stem very slender or filiform, usually erect, repeatedly forked above, 6′–12′ tall, the internodes sometimes 1′ long, much longer than those of the preceding species. Leaves elliptic, oval or sometimes oblanceolate, 3″–8″ long, 1″–4″ wide, obtuse or short-pointed at the apex, narrowed into petioles about 1″ long, not crowded; flowers minute, more or less pedicelled.

In dry woods, Vermont and Ontario to Massachusetts and Georgia, west to Minnesota, Kansas and Arkansas. Ascends to 4200 ft. in North Carolina. June–Sept.

4. SCLERÁNTHUS L. Sp. Pl. 406. 1753.

Low annual herbs, with rather stiff forking stems, opposite subulate leaves connate at the base, no stipules and minute green clustered apetalous flowers. Calyx not bracted, deeply 5-lobed (rarely 4-lobed), the lobes awnless, the cup-like tube (hypanthium) hardened. Stamens 1–10, inserted on the calyx-tube. Ovary ovoid; styles 2, distinct; ovule solitary, pendulous, amphitropous. Utricle 1-seeded, enclosed by the calyx. [Greek, referring to the hard calyx-tube.]

About 10 species, of wide geographic distribution in the Old World, the following naturalized from Europe as a weed. Type species: *Scleranthus annuus* L.

1. Scleranthus ánnuus L. Knawel. German Knotgrass. Fig. 1725.

Scleranthus annuus L. Sp. Pl. 406. 1753.

Much branched from long and rather tough roots, the branches prostrate or spreading, 3′–5′ long, roughish-puberulent or glabrous. Leaves subulate, 2″–12″ long, ciliate, light green, often recurved, their bases membranous at the junction; tube of the calyx 10-angled, rather longer than the lobes, usually glabrous, the lobes somewhat angled on the back and their margins incurved.

In fields and waste places or on dry rocks, Quebec and Ontario to Pennsylvania and Florida, mostly near the coast. Naturalized from Europe. Very common in parts of the Eastern and Middle States. Gravel-chickweed. Parsley-piert. March–Oct.

Family 20. NYCTAGINÀCEAE Lindl. Nat. Syst. Ed. 2, 213. 1836.

FOUR-O'CLOCK FAMILY.

Herbs (some tropical genera trees or shrubs) with simple entire leaves, and regular flowers in terminal or axillary clusters, in the following genera subtended by involucres of distinct or united bracts. Petals none. Calyx inferior, usually corolla-like, its limb campanulate, tubular or salverform, 4–5-lobed or 4–5-toothed. Stamens hypogynous; filaments filiform; anthers 2-celled, dehiscent by lateral slits. Ovary enclosed by the tube of the perianth, sessile or stipitate, 1-celled, 1-ovuled; ovule campylotropous; style short or elongated; stigma capitate. Fruit a ribbed, grooved or winged anthocarp.

About 25 genera and 350 species, of wide geographic distribution, most abundant in America.

Involucre of united bracts; pairs of leaves equal.   1. *Allionia.*

Involucre of separate bracts; pairs of leaves mostly unequal.

     Wings or ridges of the fruit not completely encircling it.   2. *Abronia.*

     Wings of the fruit completely encircling it.   3. *Tripterocalyx.*

1. ALLIÒNIA Loefl.; L. Syst. Ed. 10, 890. 1759.

[Oxybaphus L'Her.; Willd. Sp. Pl. 1: 185. 1797.]

Forking herbs, with opposite equal leaves, and involucres in loose terminal panicles or solitary in the axils of the leaves. Involucre 5-lobed (of 5 partially united bracts), 3-5-flowered, becoming enlarged and reticulate-veined after flowering. Perianth campanulate, its tube constricted above the ovary, its limb corolla-like, deciduous. Stamens 3-5, generally 3, unequal, hypogynous. Fruit obovoid or clavate, strongly ribbed, pubescent in most species. [Name in honor of Chas. Allioni, 1725-1804, a botanist of Turin.]

About 40 species, natives of North and South America, one Asiatic. Type species: *Allionia violacea* L.

Fruit pubescent.
Leaves narrowly linear, sessile or very nearly so, 4″ wide or less.   1. *A. linearis.*
Leaves from linear-lanceolate to ovate-cordate.
  Leaves sessile or nearly so, lanceolate to oblong.
    Pubescence fine and short, often wanting below the inflorescence.   2. *A. albida.*
    Pubescence, or some of it, of long hairs, especially below, and at the nodes.
                                                                              3. *A. hirsuta.*
  Leaves manifestly petioled, ovate, often cordate.   4. *A. nyctaginea.*
Fruit glabrous.   5. *A. Carletoni.*

1. Allionia leneàris Pursh. Narrow-leaved Umbrella-wort. Fig. 1726.

Allionia linearis Pursh, Fl. Am. Sept. 728. 1814.
Calymenia angustifolia Nutt. Fraser's Cat. Name only.
    1813.
Oxybaphus angustifolius Sweet, Hort. Brit. 429. 1830.

Stem slender, terete or somewhat 4-angled below, glabrous, glaucous, 3′-4¼° tall, erect, the branches and peduncles sometimes puberulent. Leaves linear, thick, 1-nerved, ½-2½′ long, 1″-4″ wide, obtuse or acute at the apex, sessile or the lower occasionally short-petioled; involucre about 3-flowered, green before flowering; perianth purple, longer than the involucre; stamens and style exserted; fruit commonly roughened in the furrows between the 5 prominent ribs, pubescent.

In dry soil, Illinois to Minnesota, Wyoming, south to Texas and Mexico. Adventive in Connecticut. June–Aug.

Allionia Búshii Britton and **Allionia Bodini** (Holz.) Morong, admitted as species in our first edition, prove to be conditions of this species with the involucres solitary in the axils.

Allionia glàbra (S. Wats.) Kuntze, of the Southwest, differing in being glabrous throughout, has recently been collected in western Kansas.

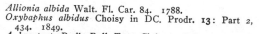

2. Allionia álbida Walt. Pale Umbrella-wort. Fig. 1727.

Allionia albida Walt. Fl. Car. 84. 1788.
Oxybaphus albidus Choisy in DC. Prodr. 13: Part 2,
    434. 1849.
A. bracteata Rydb. Bull. Torr. Club 29: 690. 1902.
A. lanceolata Rydb. Bull. Torr. Club 29: 691. 1902.
A. chersophila Standley, Contr. Nat. Herb. 12: 354.
    1909.

Stem erect, furrowed or striate, 4-sided below, 1°-3° tall, glabrous or short-pubescent above, or pubescent to the base, the peduncles and branches commonly glandular and viscous. Leaves lanceolate or oblong-lanceolate, 3-veined from the base, glabrous, pubescent or ciliate, the upper sessile, sometimes bract-like, the lower short-petioled; involucre much enlarged in fruit, pubescent, ciliate, becoming whitish and purple-veined; perianth pink, white or lilac; fruit with hispid ribs, roughened in the furrows.

South Carolina to Tennessee, South Dakota and Colorado, Florida, Louisiana and Texas. Consists of numerous races, differing in pubescence and width of leaves. May–Aug.

3. Allionia hirsùta Pursh. Hairy Umbrella-wort. Fig. 1728.

Allionia hirsuta Pursh, Fl. Am. Sept. 728. 1814.
Oxybaphus hirsutus Choisy in DC. Prodr. **13**: Part 2, 433. 1849.
Calymenia pilosa Nutt. Gen. **1**: 26. 1818.
Allionia pilosa Rydb. Bull. Torr. Club **29**: 690. 1902.

Stem slender, 1°–3° tall, erect, angled and striate, glandular-pubescent and pilose, especially at the nodes, occasionally glabrate toward the base. Leaves lanceolate or linear-lanceolate, obtuse at the apex, sessile or the lowest sometimes short-petioled, pubescent, 1′–3′ long; branches and petioles very pubescent; inflorescence usually contracted; stamens often 5; fruit narrowly obovoid, the ribs obtuse, pubescent, sometimes with low intermediate ribs in the furrows.

In dry soil, Illinois to Saskatchewan, Wisconsin, Oklahoma and New Mexico. July–Aug.

4. Allionia nyctagínea Michx. Heart-leaved Umbrella-wort. Fig. 1729.

Allionia nyctaginea Michx. Fl. Bor. Am. **1**: 100. 1803.
Oxybaphus nyctagineus Sweet, Hort. Brit. 429. 1830.
Allionia nyctaginea ovata Morong, Mem. Torr. Club **5**: 146. 1894.
Allionia ovata Pursh, Fl. Am. Sept. 97. 1814.

Stem angled, often 4-sided below, rather slender, glabrous or but slightly pubescent, 1°–3° tall. Leaves broadly ovate to oblong, 2′–4′ long, 1′–3′ wide, acute at the apex, cordate, rounded, truncate or narrowed at the base, all petioled except the small bract-like uppermost ones, glabrous or nearly so; peduncles and pedicels commonly pubescent; pedicels 6″ long or less; involucre shorter than the flowers; perianth red; stamens 3–5, exserted; style exserted; fruit oblong or narrowly obovoid, very pubescent.

In dry soil, Illinois to Manitoba, Louisiana, Texas and Colorado. Adventive further east. May–Aug.

Allionia comàta Small, of Texas, Arizona and New Mexico, differs in being viscid-hirsute; it is reported from Nebraska, perhaps erroneously.

5. Allionia Càrletoni Standley. Carleton's Umbrella-wort. Fig. 1730.

Allionia Carletoni Standley, Contr. U. S. Nat. Mus. **12**: 355. 1909.

Stem stout, simple or branched, softly pubescent to the base, about 3° high. Leaves ovate to lanceolate, thick, acutish at the apex, narrowed or rounded at the base, 2′–3′ long, 1¼′ wide or less, puberulent on both sides, short-petioled or almost sessile; inflorescence paniculate; involucres about 8″ broad, softly pubescent, their lobes obtuse, ciliolate, their stalks 4″–5″ long; fruit oblong, narrowed to both ends, glabrous, 2½″ long, prominently ribbed.

Kansas and Oklahoma. June–July.

2. ABRÒNIA Juss.; Gmel. Syst. 1008. 1791.

Annual or perennial herbs, with opposite petioled thick entire leaves, one of each pair somewhat larger than the other. Stems ascending, erect or prostrate, branching, mostly glandular-pubescent, with clustered or solitary numerous-flowered involucres on long axillary peduncles. Flowers sessile, usually conspicuous. Perianth-tube elongated, tubular or funnelform, the limb spreading, 5-lobed, the lobes obcordate or emarginate. Stamens 3-5, unequal, inserted on the tube of the perianth; anthers linear-oblong, included. Style filiform. Fruit dry, 1-5-winged or ridged, the wings broad or narrow, reticulate-veined. Seed cylindric, smooth, shining; one of the cotyledons is abortive, the seedling appearing monocotyledonous. [Name from the Greek, graceful.]

About 45 species, all American, mostly of western North America. Type species: *Abronia califórnica* Gmel.

1. Abronia fràgrans Nutt.   White Abronia.
Fig. 1731.

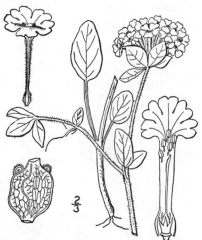

Abronia fragrans Nutt.; Hook. Kew Journ. Bot. **5**: 261. 1853.

Perennial, viscid-pubescent, stem erect or ascending, usually much branched, 1°–2° high. Leaves oval, ovate or oblong-elliptic, petioled, obtuse or acutish at the apex, cuneate, truncate or rounded at the base, 1'–2½' long; bracts of the involucre 5 or 6, ovate or elliptic, white, 5"–8" long; flowers greenish-white, very numerous in the involucres, 8"–12" long, fragrant, opening at night; fruit 4"–6" high, coriaceous with 5 or sometimes fewer, undulate coarsely reticulated ridges about 1" wide, which do not close over its summit.

In dry soil, South Dakota to Nebraska, Colorado, Texas and Mexico. Reported from Iowa. June–Aug.

3. TRIPTERÓCALYX [Torr.] Hook. Kew Journ. Bot. **5**: 261. 1853.

Annual much-branched herbs, more or less pubescent with flattened hairs, with opposite, usually unequal leaves, and axillary or lateral long-peduncled involucres subtending numerous pink or whitish flowers, the involucral bracts separate. Perianth-tube elongated, the limb 5-lobed. Stamens 5, inserted on the perianth-tube; filaments short. Fruit dry, leathery, completely encircled by 2 to 4 broad reticulated membranous wings. [Greek, three-winged calyx.]

About 5 species, natives of western North America, the following the generic type.

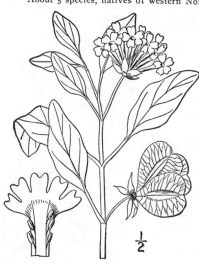

1. Tripterocalyx micránthus (Torr.) Hook.
Pink Abronia.   Fig. 1732.

Tripteridium micranthum Torr. Frem. Rep. 96. 1845.

Abronia micrantha Chois. in DC. Prodr. **13**: Part 2, 436. 1849.

Tripterocalyx micranthus Hook. Kew Journ. Bot. **5**: 261. 1853. [By typographical error *macranthus*.]

Annual, glabrous below, more or less glandular-pubescent above, stem ascending, branched, 1°–2° high. Leaves quite similar to those of *Abronia fragrans* in size and outline; involucral bracts ovate or ovate-lanceolate, acute or acuminate; flowers several or numerous, about 6" long, greenish-white; calyx-limb about 4" broad; fruit nearly 1' high, its 2–4 membranous wings 4"–7" broad, entire-margined, shining, very conspicuous, glabrous, united over the body of the fruit, beautifully reticulate-veined.

In dry soil, South Dakota to Montana, Nevada, Kansas and New Mexico. June–Aug.

Family 21. **AIZOÀCEAE** A. Br.; Aschers. Fl. Brand. 60. 1864.

CARPET-WEED FAMILY.

Herbs, rarely somewhat woody, mostly prostrate and branching, with (in our species) opposite or verticillate leaves and solitary cymose or glomerate perfect, small, regular flowers. Stipules none or scarious, or the petiole-bases dilated. Calyx 4–5-cleft or 4–5-parted. Petals small or none in our species. Stamens perigynous, equal in number to the sepals, fewer, or more numerous. Ovary usually free from the calyx, 3–5-celled, and ovules numerous in each cell in our species. Fruit a capsule with loculicidal or circumscissile dehiscence. Seeds amphitropous; seed-coat crustaceous or membranous; endosperm scanty or copious; embryo slender, curved.

About 22 genera and 500 species, mostly of warm regions, a few in the temperate zones.

Fleshy, sea-coast herbs; leaves opposite; capsule circumscissile.   1. *Sesuvium.*
Not fleshy; leaves verticillate; capsule 3-valved.   2. *Mollugo.*

1. SESÙVIUM L. Syst. Ed. 10, 1058. 1759.

Fleshy decumbent or prostrate herbs, with opposite leaves and solitary or clustered axillary pink or purplish flowers. Stipules none, but the petioles often dilated and connate at the base. Calyx top-shaped, 5-lobed, the lobes oblong, ovate or lanceolate. Petals none. Stamens 5–60, inserted on the tube of the calyx. Filaments filiform, sometimes united at the base. Ovary 3–5-celled. Styles 3–5, papillose along the inner side. Capsule membranous, oblong, 3–5-celled, circumscissile. Seeds round-reniform, smooth; embryo annular.

About 4 species, natives of sea-coasts and saline regions. Besides the following, another, *S. Portulacastrum* L., the generic type, occurs in the Southern States.

Stamens 5; coastal species.   1. *S. maritimum.*
Stamens numerous; inland species.   2. *S. sessile.*

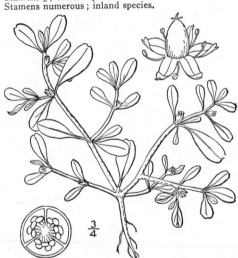

3/4

1. Sesuvium marítimum (Walt.) B.S.P. Sea Purslane. Fig. 1733.

Pharnaceum maritimum Walt. Fl. Car. 117. 1788.
Sesuvium pentandrum Ell. Bot. S. C. & Ga. 1: 556. 1821.
Sesuvium maritimum B.S.P. Prel. Cat. N. Y. 20. 1888.

Annual, glabrous, decumbent or ascending, rarely erect, branches 2′–12′ long. Leaves obovate or spatulate, entire, rounded or slightly emarginate at the apex, narrowed into a petiole or the upper ones sessile, 4″–12″ long; flowers sessile or very nearly so, about 2″ broad, mostly solitary in the axils; stamens 5, alternate with the calyx-lobes; capsule ovoid, about 2″ high, scarcely longer than the calyx.

Sands of the seashore, eastern Long Island to Florida. Bahamas; Cuba. July–Sept.

2. Sesuvium séssile Pers. Western Sea Purslane. Fig. 1734.

Sesuvium sessile Pers. Syn. 2: 39. 1807.

Annual, glabrous, fleshy, usually much branched, the branches erect or ascending, 4′–16′ long. Leaves oblanceolate to obovate, obtuse, 1′ long or less, narrowed into short petioles; flowers sessile or nearly so, 4″–6″ wide; calyx-lobes lanceolate to ovate-oblong, acute or acuminate, short-horned near the apex; stamens numerous; capsule about as long as the calyx.

On beaches, and saline plains, Kansas to Utah, Nevada, California, Texas and northern Mexico; also in southern Brazil. March–Nov.

Tetragonia expánsa Murr., New Zealand spinach, a succulent herb with large deltoid or rhomboid leaves and indehiscent axillary, tubercled fruit, has been found in waste grounds in Connecticut.

1/2

2. MOLLÙGO L. Sp. Pl. 89. 1753.

Herbs, mostly annual, much branched, with verticillate, or in some species basal or alternate leaves, and small cymose or axillary whitish flowers. Stipules scarious, membranous, deciduous. Calyx 5-parted. Sepals persistent, scarious-margined. Petals none. Stamens 3–5, when 3 alternate with the cells of the ovary, when 5 alternate with the sepals. Ovary ovoid or globose, usually 3-celled. Capsule usually 3-celled, 3-valved, loculicidally dehiscent. Seeds small, the testa smooth, granular or sculptured.

About 12 species, most of them of tropical distribution. Besides the following typical one, another occurs in the Southwestern States.

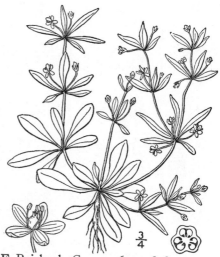

1. Mollugo verticillàta L. Carpet-weed. Fig. 1735.

Mollugo verticillata L. Sp. Pl. 89. 1753.

Prostrate, glabrous, not fleshy, much branched, spreading on the ground and forming patches sometimes 20′ in diameter. Leaves verticillate, in 5's or 6's, spatulate, obovate or linear, entire, obtuse, 6″–12″ long, narrowed into a petiole; flowers axillary, less than 1″ broad; pedicels filiform; sepals oblong, slightly shorter than the ovoid capsule, which appears roughened by the projecting seeds; seeds reniform, usually smooth and shining.

In waste places and cultivated grounds, New Brunswick and Ontario to Minnesota, Washington, Florida, Texas and Mexico. Native of the warmer parts of America, now widely distributed as a weed. Also called Indian chickweed. Devil's-grip. May–Sept.

Family 22. PORTULACÀCEAE Reichenb. Consp. 161. 1828.

PURSLANE FAMILY.

Herbs, generally fleshy or succulent, rarely somewhat woody, with alternate or opposite leaves, and regular perfect but unsymmetrical flowers. Sepals commonly 2 (rarely 5). Petals 4 or 5, rarely more, hypogynous, entire or emarginate, imbricated. Stamens hypogynous, equal in number to the petals or fewer, rarely more; filaments filiform; anthers 2-celled, longitudinally dehiscent. Ovary 1-celled; style 2–3-cleft or 2–3-divided, the divisions stigmatic on the inner side; ovules 2–∞, amphitropous. Capsule membranous or crustaceous, circumscissile, or dehiscent by 3 valves. Seeds 2–∞, reniform-globose or compressed; embryo curved.

About 180 species, mostly natives of America.

Calyx free from the ovary; capsule 3-valved.
  Seeds numerous; stamens 5–∞.
  Seeds not more than 6; stamens 2–5.   1. *Talinum.*
    Perennials; petals distinct.
      Plants with corms or thick rootstocks.   2. *Claytonia.*
      Plants with bulblet-bearing runners.   3. *Crunocallis.*
    Mostly annuals; roots fibrous; petals united at the base or distinct.
      Petals 3, united at base, unequal, the corolla-tube slit down one side; stamens 3.
                                                       4. *Montia.*
      Petals 5, equal, distinct or very nearly so; stamens 5.   5. *Limnia.*
Calyx partly adnate to the ovary; capsule circumscissile.   6. *Portulaca.*

1. TALÌNUM Adans. Fam. Pl. 2: 245. 1763.

Fleshy glabrous erect or ascending, perennial or annual herbs, with scapose or leafy stems, alternate terete or flat exstipulate leaves (terete and clustered at the base in the following species), and mainly cymose racemose or panicled flowers. Sepals 2, ovate. Petals 5, hypogynous, fugacious. Stamens as many as or more numerous than the petals and adherent to their bases. Ovary many-ovuled; style 3-lobed or 3-cleft. Capsule ovoid, oval or globose, 3-valved. Seeds numerous, borne on a central globose placenta. [Aboriginal name of a Senegal species.]

A genus of about 12 species, all but 1 or 2 natives of America. In addition to the following, about 6 others occur in the western United States. Type species: *Portulaca triangularis* Jacq.

Flowers 4″–8″ broad ; sepals deciduous.
 Stamens 10–30 ; capsule globose.
  Stigma-lobes very short.
  Stigma-lobes about one-third as long as the style.
 Stamens only 5 ; capsule oval.
Flowers 10″–15″ broad ; sepals persistent.

1. *T. teretifolium.*
2. *T. rugospermum.*
3. *T. parviflorum.*
4. *T. calycinum.*

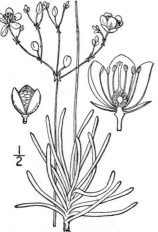

1. Talinum teretifòlium Pursh. Fame-flower.
Fig. 1736.

Talinum teretifolium Pursh, Fl. Am. Sept. 365. 1814.

Perennial, erect, 4′–12′ high, leafy at the base. Leaves linear, terete, ½′–2′ long, about 1″ wide, the base broadened and prolonged posteriorly; scape-like peduncles 1–5, terminal, branched, leafless, slender, bracted at the nodes, 3′–6′ long; cymes terminal, loose, the branches ascending or divaricate; flowers pink, 6″–8″ broad, opening for a day; sepals membranous, deciduous, ovate, obtuse, 2″ long, about half the length of the petals; stamens 10–30; style as long as the stamens; stigma-lobes very short; capsule globose, 2″ in diameter; bracts of the cyme ovate or ovate-lanceolate, 1″ long, prolonged posteriorly.

On dry rocks, Pennsylvania to Minnesota, Kansas, Georgia and Texas. Ascends to 3800 ft. in North Carolina. May–Aug.

2. Talinum rugospérmum Holzinger. Prairie
Talinum. Fig. 1737.

T. rugospermum Holzinger, Asa Gray Bull. 7 : .117. 1899.

Perennial or perhaps biennial, though first described as annual, the root deep, the slender scape-like peduncles 10′ high or less. Leaves basal, linear, terete, 1′–2′ long; cymes and petals like those of *T. teretifolium*, the pink flowers 6″–8″ wide, opening late in the afternoon; sepals deciduous; stamens 12–25, the red filaments very slender, the anthers short, nearly spherical; lobes of the stigma nearly linear, one-fourth to one-third as long as the style; capsule globose, about 2″ in diameter; seeds faintly roughened, but scarcely rougher than those of *T. teretifolium.*

Prairies, Indiana to Minnesota and Wisconsin. Summer.

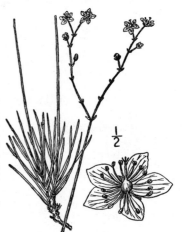

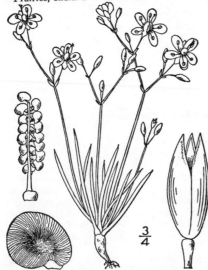

3. Talinum parviflòrum Nutt. Small-
flowered Talinum. Fig. 1738.

Talinum parviflorum Nutt.; T. & G. Fl. N. A. 1 : 197. 1838.

Perennial, similar to the preceding species, leafy below. Leaves terete or nearly so, linear, rather more slender, broadened at the base; scape-like peduncles very slender, 3′–8′ tall; cymes loose, their branches and pedicels ascending; flowers pink, 4″–5″ broad; sepals ovate, deciduous, acute or subacute; stamens 5 (or sometimes fewer?); style somewhat longer than the stamens; capsule oval, 2″ high, about 1″ in diameter; bracts of the cyme narrowly lanceolate, slightly prolonged posteriorly.

In dry soil, Minnesota to Missouri, South Dakota, Colorado, New Mexico and Texas. May–Sept.

4. Talinum calycìnum Engelm. Large-flowered Talinum. Fig. 1739.

Talinum calycinum Engelm. in Wisliz. Rep. 88. 1848.

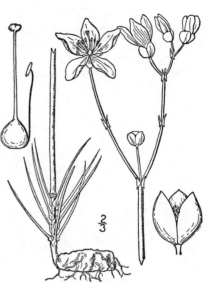

Perennial, erect from a very thick root, slender, 6'–10' high. Leaves nearly terete, clustered at the base, 1½'–2' long, the base triangular-broadened, slightly prolonged posteriorly; cyme terminal, somewhat compound, scarious-bracted, its branches ascending; flowers pink, 10''–15'' broad; sepals broadly ovate, persistent, cuspidate; petals twice as long as the calyx; stamens 12–30; style about twice as long as the stamens; capsule globose-ovoid, about 3'' in diameter.

In dry soil, western Missouri, Nebraska and Kansas to Texas. Rock-pink. June.

2. CLAYTÒNIA [Gronov.] L. Sp. Pl. 204. 1753.

Perennial succulent glabrous herbs, with corms, or thick rootstocks, petioled basal leaves, and opposite or alternate cauline ones. Flowers terminal, racemose. Sepals 2, ovate, persistent. Petals 5, hypogynous, distinct. Stamens 5, inserted on the bases of the petals. Ovary few-ovuled; style 3-lobed or 3-cleft. Capsule ovoid or globose, 3-valved, 3–6-seeded. Seeds compressed, orbicular or reniform. [In honor of John Clayton, 1686?–1773, American botanist.]

About 10 species, natives of northern North America. Type species: *Claytonia virginica* L.

Leaves linear-lanceolate, 3'–7' long.   1. *C. virginica*.
Leaves ovate-lanceolate or ovate, 2'–3' long.   2. *C. caroliniana*.

1. Claytonia virgínica L. Spring Beauty. May- or Grass-flower. Fig. 1740.

Claytonia virginica L. Sp. Pl. 204. 1753.

Ascending or decumbent, perennial from a deep tuberous root, stem 6'–12' long, simple or rarely with a few branches. Leaves elongated, linear or linear-lanceolate, obtuse or acute, narrowed into a petiole, the basal 3'–7' long, 1''–6'' wide, the cauline shorter and opposite; raceme terminal, loose, at length 3'–5' long, somewhat secund; flowers white or pink, with darker pink veins, 6''–10'' broad; pedicels slender, at length 1'–1½' long and recurved; petals emarginate; capsule shorter than the sepals.

In moist woods, Nova Scotia to Saskatchewan, south to Georgia, Montana and Texas. Very variable in the breadth of leaves. Ascends to 2400 ft. in Virginia. Good-morning-spring. Wild potatoes. March-May.

2. Claytonia caroliniàna Michx. Carolina or White-leaved Spring Beauty.
Fig. 1741.

Claytonia caroliniana Michx. Fl. Bor. Am. 1: 160. 1803.

Similar to the preceding species but sometimes more nearly erect. Basal leaves ovate-lanceolate or oblong, 1½'-3' long, 6''-9'' wide, obtuse; stem-leaves on petioles 3''-6'' long; flowers fewer.

In damp woods, Nova Scotia to Saskatchewan, Connecticut, south to North Carolina along the Alleghanies, and to Ohio and Missouri. Rare or absent near the coast in the Middle States. Ascends to 5000 ft. in Virginia. March–May.

Claytonia lanceolàta Pursh, a related species, with sessile shorter stem-leaves, occurs from the Rocky Mountain region to the Pacific Coast, and perhaps in the extreme western portion of our territory.

3. CRUNOCÁLLIS Rydb. Bull. Torr. Club **33**: 139. 1906.

A somewhat succulent low herb, perennial by long stolons, bearing bulblets, the leaves opposite, the inflorescence a few-flowered terminal raceme. Sepals 2, nearly equal. Corolla regular, of 5 similar and equal distinct petals. Stamens 5. Ovary about 3-ovuled. Capsule 1-3-seeded, the seeds roughened. [Greek, beauty of a spring, in allusion to the habitat of the plant.]

A monotypic genus of western North America.

1. Crunocallis Chamissònis (Ledeb.) Rydb. Crunocallis. Fig. 1742.

Claytonia Chamissoi Ledeb.; Spreng. Syst. Veg. 1: 790. 1825.

Montia Chamissonis Greene, Fl. Fran. 180. 1891.

Crunocallis Chamissoi Rydb. Bull. Torr. Club **33**: 139. 1906.

Annual, glabrous, stoloniferous at the base, stems weak, ascending or procumbent, 3'-9' long. Leaves spatulate or oblanceolate, obtuse, narrowed into a petiole or sessile, 1'-2' long, 3''-5'' wide; flowers few, pink, racemose, 3''-4'' broad, the petals much longer than the calyx; pedicels slender, 4''-15'' long, recurved in fruit; capsule very small.

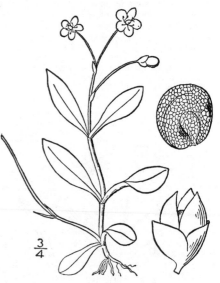

In wet places, Minnesota to British Columbia and Alaska, south in the Rocky Mountains to New Mexico, and to California. May–June.

4. MÓNTIA [Micheli] L. Sp. Pl. 87. 1753.

Small annual glabrous herbs, with opposite fleshy leaves and minute nodding solitary or loosely racemed white flowers. Sepals 2 (rarely 3), broadly ovate, persistent. Petals 3, hypogynous, more or less united. Stamens 3 (very rarely 5), inserted on the corolla. Ovary 3-ovuled; style short, 3-parted. Capsule 3-valved, 3-seeded. Seeds nearly orbicular, compressed, minutely tuberculate. [In honor of Guiseppe Monti, Italian botanist and author of the eighteenth century.]

A genus of few species, widely distributed in the colder parts of both hemispheres, the following typical.

1. Montia fontàna L   Water or Blinking Chickweed. Blinks. Water-blinks. Fig. 1743.

Montia fontana L. Sp. Pl. 87. 1753.

Densely tufted, very green, weak, diffuse or ascending, 1'–6' long, freely branching. Leaves opposite, spatulate or obovate, mainly obtuse, 3"–6" long, 1" broad or less; flowers nodding, solitary and terminal or in a small loose leafy-bracted raceme; sepals obtuse, slightly shorter than the ovate-oblong petals; capsule globose, nearly 1" in diameter.

In springs and wet places, St. Anne des Monts, Quebec; Maine, Nova Scotia, New Brunswick, Labrador, Newfoundland, and across arctic America, extending south in the mountains to California. Also in the Andes of South America, in Australasia and in northern Europe and Asia. Summer.

5. LÍMNIA [L.] Haw. Syn. Pl. Succ. 11. 1812.

Fibrous-rooted succulent herbs, mostly annual in duration, with basal petioled leaves, and a pair of sessile or connate-perfoliate leaves on the stem below the inflorescence. Flowers pink or white, racemose. Calyx of 2 persistent sepals. Petals 5, distinct and equal. Stamens 5. Ovary 2–3-ovuled. Capsule 3-valved, 2–3-seeded   [Greek, referring to the marsh habitat of some species.]

Twelve species, or more, natives of western North America. Type species: *Limnia sibírica* (L.) Haw.

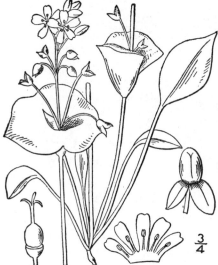

1. Limnia perfoliàta (Donn) Haw. Spanish Lettuce. Fig. 1744.

Claytonia perfoliata Donn; Willd. Sp. Pl. 1: 1186. 1798.
L. perfoliata Haw. Syn. Pl. Succ. 12. 1812.
Montia perfoliata Howell, Erythea 1: 38. 1893.

Annual, roots fibrous, stems several, erect or ascending, simple, 3'–12' high, bearing a pair of connate-perfoliate leaves near the summit, completely or partially united into an orbicular concave disk, 2' broad or less. Basal leaves rhomboid-ovate, long-petioled, the blade 1' long or more, obtuse or acute at apex, narrowed into the petiole; petioles shorter than the stems; raceme usually peduncled, loosely or compactly several-flowered, sometimes compound; bracts broad, deciduous; flowers white or pink, 3"–5" broad; petals and stamens 5; capsule globose, 1"–2" in diameter, 2–5-seeded.

Established near Painesville, Ohio. Native from British Columbia to Mexico. April–May.

6. PORTULÀCA [Tourn.] L. Sp. Pl. 445. 1753.

Diffuse or ascending, glabrous or pubescent fleshy herbs, with terminal flowers. Sepals 2, united at the base and partly adnate to the ovary. Petals 4–6 (mainly 5), inserted on the calyx, fugacious. Stamens 7–∞, also on the calyx. Ovary many-ovuled; style deeply 3–9-cleft or parted   Capsule membranous, dehiscent by a lid, many-seeded. [Latin, in allusion to the purging qualities of some species.]

A genus of about 20 species, all but 2 or 3 natives of America. In addition to the following, some 7 others occur in the southern United States. Type species: *Portulaca oleracea* L.

Glabrous throughout; flowers small, yellow; leaves flat.
   Leaves mainly rounded at the apex; seeds minutely rugose.   1. *P. oleracea,*
   Leaves mainly retuse; seeds prominently tuberculate.   2. *P. retusa.*
Pilose-pubescent especially in the axils; leaves terete
   Flowers red, 4"–6" broad.   3. *P. pilosa.*
   Flowers variously colored, 1'–2' broad.   4. *P. grandiflora.*

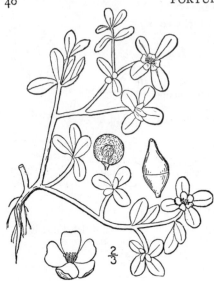

1. Portulaca oleràcea L.   Purslane. Pussley.   Fig. 1745.

Portulaca oleracea L. Sp. Pl. 445. 1753.

Annual, prostrate, freely branching from a deep central root, branches 4′–10′ long. Leaves alternate and clustered at the ends of the branches, obovate or cuneate, 3″–10″ long, rounded at the apex, very fleshy; flower-buds flat; flowers solitary and sessile, 2″–3″ broad, yellow, opening in bright sunshine for a few hours in the morning; sepals broad, keeled, acutish; style 4–6-parted; capsule 3″–5″ long; seeds finely rugose, about ¼″ long.

In fields and waste places, nearly throughout our area, and in warm and tropical America. Native in the southwest, but naturalized northward. Widely naturalized as a weed in the warmer parts of the Old World. Summer.

2. Portulaca retùsa Engelm.   Notched or Western Purslane. Fig. 1746.

Portulaca retusa Engelm. Bost. Journ. Nat. Hist. 6: 154. 1850.

Closely resembles the preceding species. Leaves cuneate, generally broader, mostly retuse or emarginate, but some of them rounded; sepals broad, obtusish, carinate-winged; style larger, 3–4-cleft; capsule 2″–3″ long; seeds distinctly tuberculate, nearly ½″ long; petals smaller than those of *P. oleracea* and the flowers opening earlier in the morning than those of that species, where the two grow together.

Minnesota (?), Missouri to Arkansas and Texas, west to Nevada. Growing in large patches, sometimes several feet in diameter. Pigweed. Summer.

Portulaca neglécta Mackenzie & Bush, of Missouri, is described as having larger flowers.

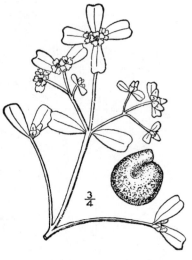

3. Portulaca pilòsa L.   Hairy Portulaca. Fig. 1747.

Portulaca pilosa L. Sp. Pl. 445. 1753.

Annual, spreading or ascending from a deep root, more or less densely pilose-pubescent, with small tufts of light-colored hairs in the axils of the leaves. Branches 2′–6′ long; leaves linear, terete, obtuse, 4″–8″ long, about 1″ wide, alternate, and clustered at the ends of the branches; sepals oblong acute, membranous, not carinate, deciduous with the operculum of the capsule; flowers red, 4″–6″ broad; stamens numerous; style 5–6-parted; seeds minutely tuberculate.

In dry soil, North Carolina to Florida, Missouri, Kansas, Texas and Mexico. Also in tropical America. Summer.

4. Portulaca grandiflòra Hook. Garden Portulaca or Purslane. Sun-plant. Fig. 1748.

Portulaca grandiflora Hook. Bot. Mag. *pl. 2885.* 1829.

Ascending or spreading, sometimes densely pilose, but often with but a few scattered hairs and tufts of others in the axils. Branches 6′-12′ long; leaves alternate, and clustered at the ends of the branches, terete, ¼′-1′ long, about 1″ wide; flowers 1′-2′ broad, pink, yellow, red, or white, very showy, open in sunshine only; sepals broad, obtuse, scarious-margined; petals obovate; capsule ovoid; seeds gray, shining.

In waste places, occasionally escaped from gardens. Introduced from South America. Summer. Cultivated in a large number of forms differing in color and size of flowers. Rose- or Kentucky-moss. Showy portulaca. French pussley. Wax-pinks. Mexican rose.

½

Family 23. **ALSINÀCEAE** Wahl. Fl. Suec. **2** : LXXIV. 1824.
CHICKWEED FAMILY.

Annual or perennial herbs with opposite entire leaves, estipulate or stipulate, and mostly small perfect flowers, solitary or in cymes or umbels. Calyx of 4 or 5 sepals, imbricated, at least in the bud, separate to the base, or nearly so. Petals as many as the sepals, not clawed, rarely wanting. Stamens twice as many as the sepals, or fewer, inserted at the base of the sessile ovary, or on a small disk; filaments distinct, or cohering below; anthers introrse, longitudinally dehiscent. Ovary usually 1-celled; styles 2-5, distinct; ovules several or numerous, amphitropous or campylotropous, borne on a central column. Fruit a capsule, dehiscent by valves or by apical teeth. Embryo mostly curved and with incumbent cotyledons.

About 32 genera and 500 species, of wide distribution, most abundant in temperate regions.
Styles separate to the base.
  Stipules wanting.
    Plants not fleshy; disk of the flower inconspicuous or none.
      Petals deeply 2-cleft or 2-parted (rarely none)
        Capsule ovoid or oblong, dehiscent by valves.   1. *Alsine.*
        Capsule cylindric, commonly curved, dehiscent by teeth.   2. *Cerastium.*
      Petals entire or emarginate (rarely none).
        Capsule cylindric.
        Capsule ovoid or oblong.   3. *Holosteum.*
          Styles as many as the sepals, alternate with them.   4. *Sagina*
          Styles fewer than the sepals.
             Seeds not appendaged by a strophiole.   5. *Arenaria.*
             Seeds strophiolate.   6. *Moehringia*
    Plants fleshy, maritime; disk conspicuous, 8-10-lobed.   7. *Honkenya.*
  Stipules present, scarious.
    Styles and capsule-valves 5.   8. *Spergula.*
    Styles and capsule-valves 3.   9. *Tissa.*
Styles united below; southwestern herb with subulate leaves.   10. *Loeflingia.*

1. **ALSÌNE** [Tourn.] L. Sp. Pl. 274. 1753.
[STELLÀRIA L. Sp. Pl. 421. 1753.]

Mostly annual, generally diffuse herbs, with cymose white flowers. Sepals 5, rarely 4. Petals of the same number, usually deeply 2-cleft, or 2-parted, white in our species, rarely none. Stamens 10 or fewer, hypogynous. Ovary 1-celled, several or many-ovuled; styles commonly 3, rarely 4-5, usually opposite the sepals. Capsule globose, ovoid or oblong, dehiscent by twice as many valves as there are styles. Seeds smooth or roughened, globose or compressed. [Greek, grove, the habitat of some species.]

Species about 75, widely distributed, most abundant in temperate or cold climates. Linnaeus divided the ancient genus *Alsine* into *Alsine* and *Stellaria,* united again by subsequent authors. Type species: *Alsine media* L.

Styles 5; leaves ovate, 1′-2′ long.   1. *A. aquatica.*
Styles 3, rarely 4.
  Leaves broad, ovate, ovate-oblong or oblong-lanceolate.
    Plants glabrous, or with a few scattered hairs.
      Flowers few, terminal; leaves ovate, 2″-3″ long.   2. *A. humifusa.*
      Cymes lateral; leaves oblong, 5″-12″ long.   3. *A. uliginosa.*
    Stems with 1 or 2 pubescent lines; petioles often ciliate.

Petals shorter than the calyx ; lower leaves petioled.   4. *A. media.*
Petals longer than the calyx, or as long ; lower leaves rarely petioled.
    Petals longer than the blunt sepals.   5. *A. pubera.*
    Petals as long as the acute or acuminate sepals.   6. *A. tennesseensis.*
Leaves narrow, linear, oblong, oblanceolate or spatulate.
  Flowers 7″–10″ broad.
    Leaves lanceolate, ciliate.   7. *A. Holostea.*
    Leaves linear, glabrous.   8. *A. glauca.*
  Flowers only 2″–6″ broad.
    Bracts of the cyme small, scarious.
      Pedicels widely spreading ; cyme diffuse.
        Leaves linear, acute at each end ; seeds smooth.   9. *A. longifolia.*
        Leaves lanceolate, broadest below ; seeds rough.   10. *A. graminea.*
      Pedicels erect ; flowers few or solitary.   11. *A. longipes.*
    Bracts of the cyme foliaceous, resembling the upper leaves.
      Capsule 1½–2 times as long as the calyx ; leaves lanceolate or oblong-lanceolate.
        Seeds rough ; petals equalling or longer than the calyx.   12. *A. crassifolia.*
        Seeds smooth ; petals much shorter than the calyx or none.   13. *A. borealis.*
      Capsule not longer than the calyx ; leaves linear or linear-spatulate ; petals none.
                                  14. *A. fontinalis.*

1. **Alsine aquática** (L.) Britton.   Water Mouse-ear Chickweed.   Fig. 1749.

Cerastium aquaticum L. Sp. Pl. 439. 1753.
Stellaria aquatica Scop. Fl. Carn. Ed. 2, 1 : 319. 1772.
Alsine aquatica Britton, Mem. Torr. Club 5 : 356. 1894.

Perennial, stem angled, mostly glandular-pubescent above, nearly glabrous below, ascending or decumbent, branched, 1°–2½° long. Leaves ovate or ovate-lanceolate, acute at the apex, the upper sessile and subcordate, the lower petioled, rounded at the base, 1′–2′ long; flowers about ½′ broad, solitary in the forks of the stem and in terminal cymes; pedicels slender, glandular, deflexed and much longer than the calyx in fruit; calyx campanulate; sepals ovate, acute, about one-half as long as the 2-cleft petals; stamens 10; styles 5, alternate with the sepals, rarely 6; capsule ovoid-oblong, slightly longer than the calyx; seeds rough.

    In wet and waste places, Quebec and Ontario to Pennsylvania. Also in British Columbia. Adventive from Europe. Water-chickweed. May–Aug.

2. **Alsine humifùsa** (Rottb.) Britton.   Low Chickweed.   Fig. 1750.

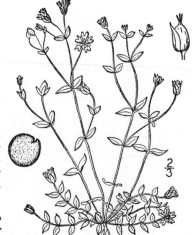

Stellaria humifusa Rottb. Skrift. Vid. Selsk. 10 : 447. 1770.

Arenaria thymifolia Pursh, Fl. Am. Sept. 317. 1814.

Alsine humifusa Britton, Mem. Torr. Club 5 : 150. 1894.

Glabrous, stems branching, spreading and ascending, 1′–3′ long, purplish. Leaves ovate or oblong, fleshy, 2″–3″ long, acutish or obtuse, sessile; bracts foliaceous; flowers few or solitary, terminal or axillary, 3″–5″ broad; sepals ovate-lanceolate, acute or acutish, 2″ long; petals 2-parted, equalling or somewhat exceeding the calyx; capsule ovoid, as long as the sepals; seeds smooth, brown.

    In moist or wet places, Greenland and Labrador to New Brunswick and Maine, west to Alaska and Oregon. Also in northern Europe and Asia. Summer.

3. Alsine uliginòsa (Murr.) Britton. Bog Starwort. Marsh Chickweed. Fig. 1751.

Stellaria uliginosa Murr. Prodr. Goett. 55. 1770.
Alsine uliginosa Britton. Mem. Torr. Club 5: 150. 1894.

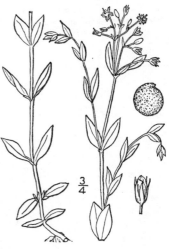

Weak, decumbent or ascending, slender, generally growing in dense masses, stems nearly simple, 6'–16' long. Leaves oblong to oblong-lanceolate, 5''–12'' long, 2''–5'' wide, narrowed at the base, the lower slightly petioled and sometimes ciliate, the upper sessile; flowers 3'' broad, in lateral sessile cymes, rarely terminal; pedicels slender; sepals 1''–1½'' long, lanceolate, acute; petals 2-parted, about the length of the calyx and the ovoid pod; seeds rough.

In cold brooks and springs, Maryland, eastern Pennsylvania and western New Jersey, north to Newfoundland, and in Michigan. Also in British Columbia and the Northwest Territory, Europe and Asia. Bog-, swamp- or marsh stitchwort. Summer.

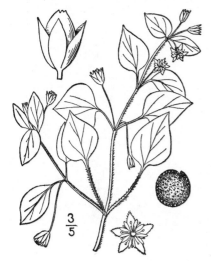

4. Alsine mèdia L. Common Chickweed. Satin-flower. Tongue-grass. Fig. 1752.

Alsine media L. Sp. Pl. 272. 1753.
Stellaria media Vill. Hist. Pl. Dauph. 3: 615. 1789.

Annual, weak, tufted, much branched, decumbent or ascending, 4'–16' long, glabrous except a line of hairs along the stem and branches, the pubescent sepals and the sometimes ciliate petioles. Leaves ovate or oval, 2''–1½' long, acute or rarely obtuse, the lower petioled and often cordate, the upper sessile; flowers 2''–4'' broad, in terminal leafy cymes or also solitary in the axils; pedicels slender; sepals oblong, mostly acute, longer than the 2-parted petals; stamens 2–10; capsule ovoid, longer than the calyx; seeds rough, sometimes crested.

In waste places, meadows and woods, nearly throughout North America. Naturalized from Europe, though possibly native northward. Native also of Asia and now almost universally distributed as a weed. White bird's-eye. Chicken- or winter-weed. Jan.–Dec.

5. Alsine pùbera (Michx.) Britton. Great or Star Chickweed. Fig. 1753.

Stellaria pubera Michx. Fl. Bor. Am. 1: 273. 1803.

Alsine pubera Britton, Mem. Torr. Club 5: 150. 1894.

Perennial, erect or decumbent, 4'–12' high, branching, the stems and branches with two finely hairy lines. Leaves oblong or ovate-oblong, ½'–2½' long, acute or obtuse, their margins more or less ciliate, the upper generally sessile, the lower sometimes narrowed at the base or on broad petioles, those of sterile shoots sometimes all petioled; flowers 4''–6'' broad, in terminal leafy cymes; pedicels rather stout, more or less pubescent; sepals ovate to lanceolate, blunt or acutish, often scarious-margined, shorter than the 2-cleft or 2-parted petals; capsule subglobose or ovoid, its teeth revolute after splitting; seeds rough.

In moist, rocky places, New Jersey and Pennsylvania to Indiana, south to Kentucky, Georgia and Alabama. Ascends to 4500 ft. in North Carolina. May–June.

6. Alsine tennesseénsis (C. Mohr) Small. Tennessee Chickweed. Fig. 1754.

Alsine pubera tennesseensis C. Mohr, Contr. U. S. Nat. Herb. **6**: 499. 1901.

Alsine tennesseensis Small, Fl. SE. U. S. 422. 1903.

Perennial, branched at the base, the branches decumbent, 4′–12′ long, pubescent in lines. Lower leaves oval to suborbicular, petioled, acute or short-acuminate, those of sterile branches often larger; upper leaves sessile or short-petioled, elliptic to elliptic-lanceolate, acute or acuminate, 1′–2′ long, ½′–¾′ wide; flowers slender-pedicelled, about 10″ broad; sepals lanceolate, acuminate, 5″ long, the outer ciliate; petals about as long as the sepals, or shorter, cleft to below the middle; capsule 2″–3″ long.

Rocky woods, West Virginia and Kentucky to Alabama. April–June.

7. Alsine Holóstea (L.) Britton. Greater Stitchwort or Starwort. Adder's Meat. Fig. 1755.

Stellaria Holostea L. Sp. Pl. 422. 1753.
Alsine Holostea Britton, Mem. Torr. Club **5**: 150. 1894.

Erect from a creeping rootstock, glabrous or slightly downy, perennial, 8′–2° high, simple or sparingly branched. Leaves sessile, lanceolate, 1′–3′ long, 2″–3″ wide at the base, tapering to a long slender tip, ciliate on the midvein and margin; flowers showy, 7″–10″ broad, in terminal leafy cymose panicles; pedicels rather slender, downy; sepals 3″–6″ long, lanceolate, acute, scarious-margined, one-half to two-thirds the length of the 2-cleft petals; capsule globose-ovoid. Stem angled, rough on the angles.

Fields and meadows, Maine to Long Island. Fugitive or adventive from Europe. Native also of northern Asia. Also called Allbone, from its brittle nodes. Snake-, star- or thunder-flower. Snappers. Snap-jack. Piskies. Pixie. White bird's-eye. Easter-bell. Snakegrass. Lady's-lint. April–June.

8. Alsine glaùca (With.) Britton. Glaucous Starwort. Fig. 1756.

Stellaria glauca With. Bot. Arr. Br. Plants, Ed. 3, **2**: 420. 1796.

Perennial, glabrous, pale green and glaucous; stem very slender, 1°–2° high, usually branched. Leaves glabrous, linear, 2′ long or less, acute, the upper reduced to small bracts; flowers relatively few, cymose, 6″–8″ wide, on very slender pedicels 1′–2½′ long; sepals linear-lanceolate, 3-ribbed, acute; petals longer than the sepals, deeply cleft.

Grassy places, Quebec. Naturalized from Europe and native also of northern Asia. May–June.

9. Alsine longifòlia (Muhl.) Britton.
Long-leaved Stitchwort. Fig. 1757.

Stellaria longifolia Muhl.; Willd. Enum. Hort. Ber.
479. 1809.
S. graminea Bigel. Fl. Bost. 110. 1814. Not L. 1753.
Stellaria Friesiana Ser. in DC. Prodr. 1: 400. 1824.
A. longifolia Britton, Mem. Torr. Club 5: 150. 1894.

Weak, glabrous, or the stem rough-angled,
freely branching, erect or ascending, 8′–18′ high.
Leaves linear, spreading, acute or acutish at each
end, ½′–2½′ long, 1″–3″ wide, the lower smaller;
bracts lanceolate, 1″–1½″ long, scarious; pedicels slender, divaricate; cymes at length ample,
mostly lateral; flowers numerous, 3″–5″ broad;
sepals lanceolate, acute, about 1½″ long, 3-nerved,
equalling or somewhat shorter than the 2-parted
petals; capsule ovoid-oblong, nearly twice as long
as the calyx; seeds smooth, shining.

In low meadows and swamps, Newfoundland to
Alaska, Maryland, Kentucky and Louisiana, in the
Rocky Mountain region and British Columbia. North-
ern Europe and Asia. May–July.

$\frac{1}{2}$

10. Alsine gramínea (L.) Britton. Lesser
Stitchwort. Lesser Starwort. Fig. 1758.

Stellaria graminea L. Sp. Pl. 422. 1753.
A. gramínea Britton, Mem. Torr. Club 5: 150. 1894.

Weak, glabrous, ascending from creeping rootstocks, branching above, 1°–2° high or long, stem
4-angled. Leaves sessile, lanceolate or oblong-
lanceolate, spreading or ascending, 10″–15″ long,
2″–3″ wide, broadest just above the ciliolate base,
acute, the lower smaller; cymes diffuse, terminal,
or at length lateral; pedicels slender, spreading;
bracts scarious, often ciliate, lanceolate, 2″–3″ long;
flowers 3″–5″ broad; sepals lanceolate, acute, 2″–
2½″ long, 3-nerved; petals 2-cleft, about the length
of the sepals; capsule oblong, exceeding the sepals;
seeds finely roughened.

In fields and along roadsides, Newfoundland to Ontario and Maryland. Considered by Prof. Macoun as
native in Canada; in southern New York and New Jersey
it is certainly introduced and adventive from Europe.
Native of Europe and northern Asia. May–July.

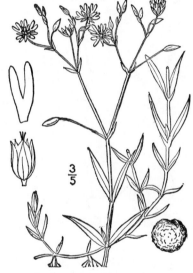

$\frac{3}{5}$

11. Alsine lóngipes (Goldie) Coville.
Long-stalked Stitchwort. Fig. 1759.

Stellaria longipes Goldie, Edinb. Phil. Journ. 6:
327. 1822.
A. longipes Coville, Contr. Nat. Herb. 4: 70. 1893.
Stellaria Edwardsii R. Br. in Parry's Voy. App.
cclxxi. 1824.
A. longipes Edwardsii Britton, Mem. Torr Club 5:
150. 1894.

Erect or ascending, tufted, simple or rarely
sparingly branched, 3′–12′ high, glabrous, shining, glaucous or pubescent. Leaves lanceolate
or linear-lanceolate, 5″–18″ long, 1″–3″ wide
at the base, rigid, ascending or erect; flowers
few, 3″–5″ broad, terminal, on long slender
erect pedicels; bracts scarious, lanceolate;
sepals ovate or lanceolate, acute or acutish;
petals 2-cleft, exceeding the calyx; capsule
ovoid, longer than the sepals; seeds smooth.

In moist places, Labrador and Nova Scotia to
Quebec, west to Alaska and Minnesota, south in
the Rocky Mountains to Colorado, and to Cali-

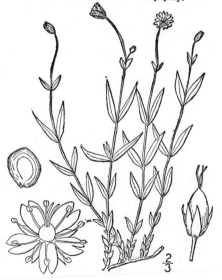

$\frac{2}{3}$

fornia. Also in northern Asia. Summer. Consists of many races, differing mainly in size of plant, size of flowers and pubescence.

12. Alsine crassifòlia Ehrh.   Fleshy Stitchwort.
Fig. 1760.

Stellaria crassifolia Ehrh. Hannov. Mag. 8 : 116. 1784.
Alsine crassifolia Britton, Mem. Torr. Club 5 : 150. 1894.

Diffuse or ascending, weak, slender, simple or branched, glabrous, 2′–10′ long. Leaves somewhat fleshy, oblong-lanceolate to linear-oblong, acute or obtuse, narrowed at the base, 3″–8″ long, 1″–2½″ wide; cymes terminal, few-flowered, or flowers axillary and solitary; bracts foliaceous, small; peduncles slender, ascending; flowers 2″–3″ broad; sepals lanceolate-oblong, acute; petals longer than the calyx; capsule ovoid, longer than the sepals; seeds rough.

In springs and moist places, Labrador to Quebec, Illinois, Manitoba and in arctic America, south in the Rocky Mountains to Colorado. Also in northern Europe and Asia. Summer.

13. Alsine boreàlis (Bigel.) Britton.   Northern Stitchwort.   Fig. 1761.

Stellaria borealis Bigel. Fl. Bost. Ed. 2, 182. 1824.
Stellaria alpestris Fries, Mant. 3 : 194. 1843.
S. borealis var. *alpestris* A. Gray, Man. Ed. 5, 93. 1867.
Alsine borealis Britton, Mem. Torr. Club 5 : 150. 1894.
Alsine borealis alpestris Britton, Mem. Torr. Club 5 : 150. 1894.

Erect or ascending, weak, much branched, glabrous, or pubescent above, 6′–18′ long. Leaves membranous, lanceolate or oblong-lanceolate, ½′–1½′ long, 2″–5″ wide, acute, sessile, their margins ciliate or naked; inflorescence a leafy terminal compound cyme; pedicels slender, ascending or spreading; flowers 2″–4″ broad; sepals ovate-lanceolate, acute; petals 2–5, shorter than the sepals, or none; capsule oblong, much exceeding the sepals; seeds smooth or obscurely roughened.

In wet places, Newfoundland to Rhode Island, New Jersey, Minnesota and Alaska, south in the Rocky Mountains to Colorado. Also in northern Europe and Asia. Ascends to 5000 ft. in New Hampshire. Summer.

14. Alsine fontinàlis (Short & Peter) Britton.   Water Stitchwort.   Fig. 1762.

Sagina fontinalis Short & Peter, Transylv. Journ. Med. 7 : 600. 1834.
Stellaria fontinalis Robinson, Proc. Am. Acad. 29 : 286. 1894.
Alsine fontinalis Britton, Mem. Torr. Club 5 : 356. 1894.

Annual, glabrous, stems weak, very slender, branched, ascending or diffuse, 4′–12′ long. Leaves linear-spatulate, 4″–12″ long, about 1″ wide, the upper sessile, acute or subacute at the apex, the lower obtuse and narrowed into short petioles; pedicels filiform, 3″–15″ long, erect or ascending, solitary or 2–3 together in the forks of the stem and branches and axils; calyx oblong-campanulate, 1″ long; sepals 4 or 5, oblong or linear, obtuse, about equalling the ovoid-oblong obtuse capsule; stamens 4–8; petals wanting; styles very short; seeds densely tuberculate-roughened.

In wet places, Kentucky and Tennessee. April–May.

2. CERÁSTIUM L. Sp. Pl. 437. 1753.

Annual or perennial, generally pubescent or hirsute herbs, with terminal dichotomous cymes of white flowers. Sepals 5, rarely 4. Petals of the same number, emarginate or bifid (rarely wanting). Stamens 10, rarely fewer. Styles equal in number to the sepals and opposite them, or in some species fewer. Capsule cylindric, 1-celled, many-ovuled, often curved, dehiscent by 10, rarely 8, apical teeth. Seeds rough, more or less flattened, attached by their edges. [Greek, horny, referring to the horn-like capsule of many species.]

About 50 species, of wide geographic distribution, most abundant in the temperate zones. Type species: *Cerastium arvense* L.

Petals equalling the sepals, or shorter ; annuals.
  Pedicels not longer than the sepals ; flowers glomerate.   1. *C. viscosum.*
  Pedicels at length longer than the sepals ; flowers cymose.
    Leaves 2″–4″ long ; capsule nearly straight.   2. *C. semidecandrum.*
    Leaves 4″–12″ long ; capsule curved upward.   3. *C. vulgatum.*
Petals manifestly longer than the sepals (rarely wanting).
  Annuals, viscid-pubescent ; flowers 2″–3″ broad.
    Pedicels much longer than the calyx.   4. *C. longipedunculatum.*
    Pedicels shorter than or but little exceeding the calyx.   5. *C. brachypodum.*
  Perennials, glabrous or pubescent ; flowers 6″–10″ broad.
    Styles always 5.
      Leaves linear or lanceolate-oblong, mainly acute.
        Leaves linear to linear-lanceolate ; pod about half as long again as the calyx.
                                              6. *C. arvense.*
        Leaves lanceolate to oblong-lanceolate ; pod twice as long as the calyx.
                                             7. *C. velutinum.*
      Leaves oblong-ovate, obtuse.   8. *C. alpinum.*
    Styles 3 (very rarely 4 or 5) ; leaves linear-oblong.   9. *C. cerastioides.*

1. Cerastium viscòsum L. Mouse-ear Chickweed. Fig. 1763.

Cerastium viscosum L. Sp. Pl. 437. 1753.
Cerastium glomeratum Thuill. Fl. Paris, Ed. 2, 226. 1824.

Annual, tufted, stems ascending or spreading, densely viscid-pubescent, 4′–12′ long. Leaves ovate or obovate, or the lower spatulate, 4″–12″ long, 3″–7″ wide, obtuse ; bracts small, herbaceous ; flowers about 2″–3″ broad, in glomerate cymes, becoming paniculate in fruit ; pedicels shorter than or equalling the acute sepals ; petals shorter than the calyx, 2-cleft.

In waste places and meadows, New Brunswick to Ontario, Florida, Arkansas and Mexico. Naturalized from Europe. Naturalized also in the West Indies, Central America, and on the Pacific Coast. April–July.

2. Cerastium semidecándrum L. Small or Five-stamened Mouse-ear Chickweed. Fig. 1764.

Cerastium semidecandrum L. Sp. Pl. 438. 1753.
Cerastium vulgatum var. *semidecandrum* A. Gray, Man. Ed. 5, 94. 1867.

Low, tufted, erect or decumbent, annual, 2′–6′ high, finely viscid-pubescent. Leaves ovate, or the lower spatulate, 2″–4″ long, obtuse ; bracts scarious, membranous ; inflorescence cymose ; pedicels at length longer than the calyx ; flowers 1″–1½″ broad ; sepals lanceolate, acute, scarious-margined, slightly exceeding the emarginate petals ; capsule narrow, nearly straight ; stamens often 5.

In dry, sterile soil, Massachusetts to Virginia. Naturalized from Europe. Called also spring mouse-ear. April–May.

3. Cerastium vulgàtum L.   Larger Mouse-ear Chickweed.   Fig. 1765.

Cerastium vulgatum L. Sp. Pl. Ed. 2, 627.   1762.

Cerastium triviale Link, Enum. Hort. Ber. 1 : 433.   1821.

Biennial or perennial, viscid-pubescent, tufted, erect or ascending, 6′–18′ long. Lower and basal leaves spatulate-oblong, obtuse; upper leaves oblong, 6″–12″ long, 3″–5″ wide, acute or obtuse; bracts scarious-margined; inflorescence cymose, loose, the pedicels at length much longer than the calyx; sepals obtuse or acute, about equalling the 2-cleft petals, 2″–3″ long; capsule curved upward.

In fields and woods, nearly throughout our area. Naturalized from Europe. Often a troublesome weed. Occcurs also in the Southern and Western States, and is native in northern Asia. Mouse-ear. May–Sept.

4. Cerastium longipedunculàtum Muhl.
Nodding Chickweed.   Powder-horn.
Fig. 1766.

C. longipedunculatum Muhl. Cat. 46.   1813.
Cerastium nutans Raf. Prec. Decouv. 36.   1814.

Annual, bright green, stem weak, reclining or ascending, diffusely branched, 6′–24′ long, striate, finely clammy-pubescent to glabrate. Lower and basal leaves spatulate, obtuse, petioled, ½′–1′ long, those of the middle part of the stem lanceolate or oblong, 1′–2′ long, 3″–4″ wide, the upper similar, acute, sessile, gradually smaller; inflorescence loosely cymose; pedicels slender, in fruit several times the length of the calyx; flowers 2″–3″ broad; sepals lanceolate, obtuse or acutish, about one-half the length of the 2-cleft petals; pods nodding, 5″–9″ long, curved upward, much exceeding the calyx.

In moist, shaded places, Nova Scotia and Hudson Bay to North Carolina, west to British Columbia, Nevada and northern Mexico. The plant sometimes produces capsules from apparently apetalous flowers. Ascends to 2200 ft. in Pennsylvania. Clammy chickweed.   April–June.

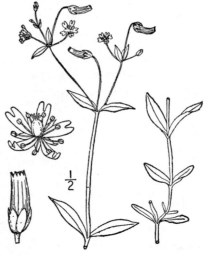

5. Cerastium brachýpodum (Engelm.) Robinson.   Short-stalked Chickweed.
Fig. 1767.

Cerastium nutans var. *brachypodum* Engelm.; A. Gray, Man. Ed. 5, 94.   1867.
Cerastium brachypodium Robinson; Britton, Mem. Torr. Club 5 : 150.   1894.
Cerastium brachypodium compactum Robinson, Proc. Am. Acad. 29 : 278.   1894.

Annual, light green, viscid-pubescent or puberulent all over, stems tufted, erect, 3′–10′ tall. Lower and basal leaves oblanceolate or spatulate, obtuse or subacute at the apex, 3″–12″ long, narrowed into short petioles, the upper linear or linear-oblong, acute, sessile, sometimes erect-appressed; cymes terminal, few–several-flowered; flowers about 2″ broad; fruiting pedicels, or some of them, deflexed, not more than twice as long as the calyx; capsules straight or slightly curved upward, 2–3 times as long as the calyx.

In dry soil, southwestern Illinois and Missouri to Nebraska, South Dakota, Montana, Oregon, Texas, Arizona and Mexico.   March–July.

6. Cerastium arvénse L.   Field or Meadow Chickweed.   Fig. 1768.

Cerastium arvense L. Sp. Pl. 438. 1753.

Perennial, densely tufted, erect or ascending, pubescent or nearly glabrous, flowering stems simple or sparingly branched, 4′–10′ high. Basal leaves and those of the sterile shoots linear-oblong, close, slightly narrowed at the base; stem-leaves distant, linear or narrowly lanceolate, 5″–15″ long, 1″–2″ wide, acute; flowers several, cymose, 6″–8″ broad; pedicels slender, erect; petals obcordate, much exceeding the lanceolate acute sepals which equal or are a little shorter than the slightly oblique pod.

In dry, rocky places, Labrador to Alaska, south to Georgia, Missouri, Nevada and California. Also in Europe and Asia. April–July.

7. Cerastium velùtinum Raf.   Barren Chickweed.   Fig. 1769.

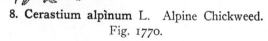

C. velutinum Raf. Med. Rep. II. 5 : 359. 1808.
C. oblongifolium Torr. Fl. U. S. 460. 1824.
C. arvense villosum Holl. & Britt. Bull. Torr. Club 14 : 49. 1887.
C. arvense oblongifolium Holl. & Britt. loc. cit. 47. 1887.

Perennial, tufted, erect or diffuse, pubescent or villous; flowering stems 12′ high or less. Leaves lanceolate to oblong or ovate-lanceolate, mostly obtuse, 1½′ long or less, 2″–5″ wide, those of the flowering stems distant; flowers several, cymose, 7″–10″ wide; petals obcordate, much longer than the sepals; pod 12″–15″ long, about twice as long as the sepals.

On serpentine and limestone rocks, New York to Maryland, southern Ontario, Minnesota and Colorado. May–July.

8. Cerastium alpìnum L.   Alpine Chickweed.   Fig. 1770.

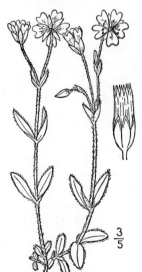

Cerastium alpinum L. Sp. Pl. 438. 1753.

Cerastium Fischerianum Ser. in DC. Prodr. 1 : 419. 1824.

Cerastium alpinum Fischerianum T. & G. Fl. N. A. 1 : 188. 1838.

Perennial, generally silky-hairy, sterile stems prostrate, flowering stems erect, 2′–12′ high. Lower leaves somewhat oblanceolate or spatulate, dense, 2″–4″ long, obtuse; upper leaves distant, ovate-oblong, obtusish, 4″–8″ long; flowers solitary or 2–3, 6″–9″ broad; pedicels slender; petals 2-lobed, twice the length of the lanceolate acute scarious-tipped sepals; pod longer than the calyx, nearly straight.

In moist, rocky places Gaspé, Quebec; Greenland, Labrador and in arctic America to Alaska. Also in arctic and alpine Europe and Asia. Consists of numerous races, differing in size of the plant, size of the flowers, character and amount of pubescence. Summer.

9. Cerastium cerastioìdes (L.) Britton. Starwort Chickweed. Fig. 1771.

Stellaria cerastioides L. Sp. Pl. 422. 1753.

Cerastium trigynum Vill. Hist. Pl. Dauph. 3: 645. 1789.

C. cerastioides Britton, Mem. Torr. Club 5: 150. 1894.

Perennial, glabrous except a line of minute hairs along one side of the stem and branches, rarely pubescent throughout. Flowering branches ascending, 3′–6′ long; leaves linear-oblong, 4″–8″ long, about 1″ wide, obtuse, the lower often smaller and slightly narrowed at the base; flowers solitary or few, 5″–6″ broad, long-pedicelled; petals 2-lobed, mostly twice as long as the obtuse or acutish scarious-margined sepals; capsule nearly straight, twice the length of the calyx; styles 3, rarely 4 or 5; sepals and petals 5 or 4.

Gaspé, Quebec, and in arctic America. Also in arctic and alpine Europe and Asia. Summer.

3. HOLÓSTEUM [Dill.] L. Sp. Pl. 88. 1753.

Annual erect herbs, often viscid-pubescent above, with cymose-umbellate, white flowers on long terminal peduncles. Sepals 5. Petals 5, emarginate or eroded. Stamens 3–5, hypogynous. Styles 3. Ovary 1-celled, many-ovuled. Capsule ovoid-cylindrical, dehiscent by 6 short valves or teeth. Seeds compressed, attached by the inner face, rough. [Greek, signifying all bone, an antiphrase, the herbs being tender.]

About 3 species, natives of Europe and temperate Asia, the following typical.

1. Holosteum umbellàtum L. Jagged Chickweed. Fig. 1772.

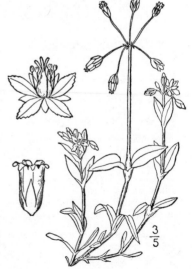

Holosteum umbellatum L. Sp. Pl. 88. 1753.

Glabrous or slightly downy below, viscid and glandular-pubescent above, simple, tufted, 5′–12′ high. Basal leaves spreading, oblanceolate or oblong; stem-leaves oblong, acute or obtuse, sessile, ½′–1′ long; umbel terminal, 3–8-flowered; pedicels very slender, about 1′ long, erect or ascending in flower, subsequently reflexed and again erect when the fruit is mature; flowers white, 2″–3″ broad; sepals obtuse, about 2″ long, scarious-margined, somewhat shorter than the eroded petals; capsule ovoid, nearly twice the length of the sepals, its teeth recurved.

Very abundant in the vicinity of Lancaster, Pa. ; Delaware ; Georgia. Naturalized from Europe. Native also of northern Asia. April–May.

Moenchia erécta (L.) Gaertn., a low annual, native of Europe, with entire petals, an 8-toothed ovoid pod, the styles opposite the sepals, collected many years ago about Philadelphia and Baltimore, has not been found there recently, and is not illustrated in this edition.

4. SAGINA L. Sp. Pl. 128. 1753.

Tufted matted low annual or perennial herbs, with subulate leaves, and small pedicelled whitish flowers. Sepals 4 or 5. Petals of the same number, entire, emarginate or none. Stamens of the same number, or fewer, or twice as many. Ovary 1-celled, many-ovuled. Styles as many as the sepals and alternate with them. Capsule 4–5-valved, at length dehiscent to the base, the valves opposite the sepals. [Ancient name of the spurry.]

About 10 species, natives of the northern hemisphere. Type species: *Sagina procumbens* L.

Parts of the flower in 4's (or some flowers in 5's); seeds not resinous-dotted.   1. *S. procumbens.*
Parts of the flower in 5's, rarely some in 4's.
  Leaves opposite, not fascicled.
    Petals equalling or shorter than the sepals; seeds resinous-dotted.   2. *S. decumbens.*
    Petals and pods longer than the sepals.   3. *S. saginoides.*
  Leaves fascicled in the axils; petals exceeding the sepals.   4. *S. nodosa.*

1. Sagina procúmbens L. Procumbent Pearlwort. Fig. 1773.

Sagina procumbens L. Sp. Pl. 128. 1753.

Annual or perennial, branching, decumbent, depressed or spreading, glabrous or minutely downy, matted, 1'–3' high. Leaves linear, subulate, 1"–3" long, connate at the base; flowers about 1" broad, numerous; peduncles capillary, longer than the leaves, often recurved at the end after flowering; sepals 4, sometimes 5, ovate-oblong, obtusish, generally longer than the petals, which are occasionally wanting; stamens 4, rarely 5; capsule about equalling the calyx; seeds dark brown, not resinous-dotted.

In moist places, Newfoundland and Greenland to Delaware and Michigan. Native of Europe and Asia. Our plant is probably in part naturalized from Europe, as it is in Mexico and in South America. Breakstone. Bird's-eye. Poverty. May–Sept.

Sagina nivális Fries, a very diminutive species, inhabits Greenland and arctic Europe and is recorded from Labrador.

2. Sagina decúmbens (Ell.) T. & G. Decumbent Pearlwort. Fig. 1774.

Spergula decumbens Ell. Bot. S. C. & Ga. 1: 523. 1817.
Sagina decumbens T. & G. Fl. N. A. 1: 177. 1838.
Sagina subulata T. & G. Fl. N. A. 1: 178. 1838. Not Presl, 1826.
Sagina subulata var. *Smithii* A. Gray, Man. Ed. 5, 95. 1867.
Sagina decumbens Smithii S. Wats. Bibl. Index 1: 105. 1878.

Annual, tufted, stems decumbent, erect or ascending, 2'–4' long, glabrous or minutely glandular-pubescent above. Leaves narrowly linear, sometimes bristle-tipped, 3"–5" long; peduncles filiform, 3"–15" long; flowers 1"–1½" broad; sepals, petals and styles 5, or rarely 4; stamens 5 or 10; petals equalling or shorter than the calyx or none; pod ovoid-oblong, nearly twice as long as the calyx; sepals acutish or obtuse; seeds with resinous glands.

In dry soil, eastern Massachusetts to Illinois, south to Florida, Missouri and Louisiana. Slender races with 4-parted flowers, the petals minute or wanting have been mistaken for *S. apetala* Ard. of Europe. March–May.

3. Sagina saginoìdes (L.) Britton. Arctic Pearlwort. Fig. 1775.

Spergula saginoides L. Sp. Pl. 441. 1753.
Sagina Linnaei Presl, Rel. Haenk. 2: 14. 1835.
Sagina saginoides Britton, Mem. Torr. Club 5: 151. 1894.

Perennial, glabrous, tufted, 1'–4' high, few-flowered or the flowers solitary at the ends of the stems. Leaves linear-subulate, or filiform, 2"–5" long, acuminate or mucronate; flowers 1½"–2½" broad; sepals, petals and styles 5; stamens 10; sepals oval, obtuse, half the length of the ovoid-oblong capsule.

On rocks, Labrador, Anticosti, Quebec, and in arctic America. Also in the higher Rocky Mountains south to Colorado and Utah, and in California. Also in alpine and arctic Europe and Asia. Summer.

4. Sagina nodòsa (L.) Fenzl. Knotted Pearlwort or Spurry. Fig. 1776.

Spergula nodosa L. Sp. Pl. 440. 1753.
Sagina nodosa Fenzl, Verbr. Alsin. 18. 1833.

Perennial, tufted, erect or decumbent, 2′–6′ high, stems sparingly branched, slender, glabrous, or slightly glandular-pubescent above. Lower leaves linear, teretish, 4″–8″ long, mucronulate, the upper shorter and with clusters of minute ones in their axils; flowers few, about 3″ broad, terminating the stem and branches; sepals, petals and styles 5; stamens 10; peduncles 3″–8″ long; sepals obtuse, 1″ long; petals obovate, longer than the calyx, as is also the ovoid pod.

In wet places, Massachusetts to Greenland; Lake Superior, Lake Winnipeg and Arctic Sea. Northern Europe and Asia. Summer.

5. ARENÀRIA L. Sp. Pl. 423. 1753.

Annual or perennial, mainly tufted herbs, with sessile leaves, and terminal cymose or capitate, rarely axillary and solitary, white flowers. Sepals 5. Petals 5, entire or scarcely emarginate, rarely none. Stamens 10. Styles generally 3 (rarely 2–5). Ovary 1-celled, many-ovuled. Capsule globose or oblong, dehiscent at the apex by as many valves or teeth as there are styles, or twice as many. Seeds reniform-globose or compressed. [Latin, sand, in allusion to the habitat of many species.]

About 150 species, of wide geographic distribution. Type species: *Arenaria serpyllifolia* L.

Valves of the capsule 2-cleft or 2-toothed, sometimes appearing as if double the number of the styles.
  Leaves ovate or oblong.
    Sepals acuminate; annual herbs of waste places.
      Capsule flask-shaped, firm.   1. *A. serpyllifolia.*
      Capsule nearly cylindric, papery.   2. *A. leptoclados.*
    Sepals obtuse or scarcely acute; perennial; arctic.   3. *A. ciliata.*
  Leaves subulate or setaceous.
    Cymes very dense; stems 1′–4′ tall.   4. *A. Hookeri.*
    Cymes loose; stems 4′–15′ tall.   5. *A. Fendleri.*
Valves of the capsule entire (Genus ALSINE Wahl., ALSINOPSIS Small).
  Leaves rigid, subulate or setaceous.
    Arctic or alpine, densely tufted, 1′–3′ high.
      Flowers 5″–8″ broad.   6. *A. arctica.*
      Flowers 2″–4″ broad.
        Sepals acuminate.   7. *A. verna.*
        Sepals obtuse.   8. *A. sajanensis.*
    Neither arctic nor alpine, tufted but diffuse, 4″–16″ high.
      Leaves densely imbricated; pine barren species.   9. *A. caroliniana.*
      Leaves fascicled in the axils.
        Sepals ovate or ovate-lanceolate, 2″ long; plant bright green.
          Petals longer and capsule shorter than the sepals.   10. *A. stricta.*
          Petals shorter and capsule longer than the sepals.   11. *A. litorea.*
        Sepals narrowly lanceolate, long-acuminate, 2½″ long; plant pale. 12. *A. texana.*
  Leaves soft, herbaceous; narrowly linear or filiform.
    Sepals prominently ribbed; southern.   13. *A. patula.*
    Sepals not ribbed; alpine and northern.   14. *A. groenlandica.*

1. Arenaria serpyllifòlia L. Thyme-leaved Sandwort. Fig. 1777.

Arenaria serpyllifolia L. Sp. Pl. 423. 1753.

Annual, slender, slightly downy-pubescent, widely branched and diffuse, 2′–8′ high. Leaves ovate, 2″–4″ long, 1½″–2″ wide, acute; pedicels slender, 2″–6″ long; bracts ovate, resembling the leaves; flowers 2″ broad or less, very numerous in cymose panicles; sepals ovate, 1½″ long, acute or mucronate, 3–5-nerved, scarious-margined; petals obovate or oblong, usually shorter; capsule ovoid, slightly shorter than or equalling the calyx, dehiscent by 6 short apical valves; seeds rough.

In dry or rocky places, nearly throughout eastern North America, extending across the continent. Naturalized from Europe. Native also of northern Asia, and widely distributed as a weed. May–Aug.

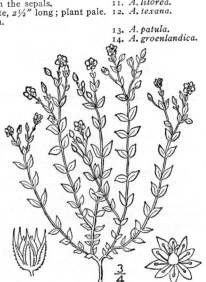

¾

2. Arenaria leptóclados Reichenb. Slender Sandwort. Fig. 1778.

Arenaria leptoclados Reichenb.; Guss. Fl. Sic. Syn. 2 : 284. 1844.

Annual, tufted, much branched, roughish-puberulent, resembling *Arenaria serpyllifolia* L. Leaves lanceolate or ovate-lanceolate, 1½″–2½″ long, about one-half as wide as long, acute or acuminate; bracts similar to the leaves, but usually much smaller; sepals lanceolate, acuminate, narrowly scarious-margined; petals oblong, about half as long as the sepals; capsule oblong or subcylindric, equalling the calyx or a little longer.

Dry soil, Maine to Michigan and westward. Adventive from Europe. May–July.

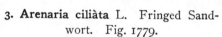

3. Arenaria ciliàta L. Fringed Sandwort. Fig. 1779.

Arenaria ciliata L. Sp. Pl. 425. 1753.

Perennial, tufted, glandular-puberulent, stems very slender, creeping or ascending, pubescent in lines, 1′–5′ long, or the flowering branches erect. Leaves ovate or oblong, obtuse or acute at the apex, sessile or very nearly so, 1″–3″ long, ciliate or glabrous; peduncles filiform, erect, mostly 1-flowered; flowers about 3″ broad; sepals ovate or oblong, obtuse, nerveless or faintly 1-nerved, about as long as the petals; capsule oblong, twice as long as the calyx, its 3 valves deeply 2-cleft; seeds slightly roughened.

Quebec to Greenland. Also in arctic and alpine Europe. The American plant is referred by Dr. B. L. Robinson to the var. *humifusa* Hornem.,—having glabrous leaves and nerveless sepals so far as observed, and may be specifically distinct from the European. In Europe the species has been separated into several varieties. Summer.

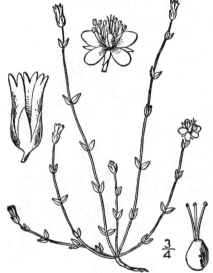

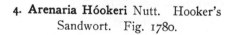

4. Arenaria Hóokeri Nutt. Hooker's Sandwort. Fig. 1780.

Arenaria Hookeri Nutt.; T. & G. Fl. N. A. 1 : 178. 1838.

Arenaria pinetorum A. Nelson, Bull. Torr. Club 26 : 350. 1899.

Tufted from a deep woody root, 2′–3′ high. Leaves linear-subulate, rigid, very sharp-pointed, densely imbricated, glabrous, 6″–12″ long; flowering stems short, finely and densely pubescent; bracts lanceolate-subulate, scarious-margined, the margins ciliolate; cyme dense, 8″–18″ broad, its rays short and pubescent; sepals lanceolate-subulate, pubescent, shorter than the similar bracts and about one-half the length of the petals; capsule not seen.

In dry or rocky soil, South Dakota, Nebraska and Colorado to Wyoming and Montana. June–Aug.

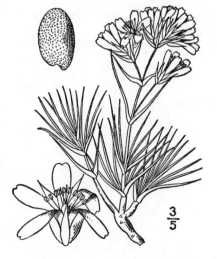

5. Arenaria Féndleri A. Gray.   Fendler's Sandwort.   Fig. 1781.

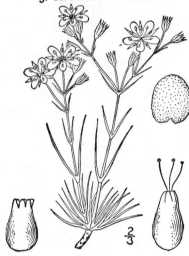

A. *Fendleri* A. Gray, Mem. Am. Acad. (II.) 4: 13.
1849.

Perennial by a woody root, pale green, glandular-pubescent above; stems tufted, erect, very
slender, usually several times forked, 4'-15' tall,
the internodes 1'-2' long. Lower leaves subulate
or setaceous, glabrous or minutely ciliate, 1'-4'
long, about ¼" wide, the upper gradually smaller
and somewhat connate at the base; cyme loose,
its forks filiform, several-flowered; pedicels very
glandular, 3"-12" long; flowers 4"-6" broad;
sepals linear-lanceolate, acuminate, scarious-
margined, nearly as long as the obovate petals;
capsule narrowly oblong, rather shorter than the
sepals, 3-valved, the valves 2-toothed.

In dry, usually rocky soil Nebraska and Wyoming
to Utah, south to New Mexico and Arizona. June–
Aug.

6. Arenaria àrctica Stev.   Arctic Sandwort.   Fig. 1782.

Arenaria arctica Stev.; DC. Prodr. 1: 404. 1824.

Perennial, stem woody below, tufted, glandular-pubescent,
1'-2' high. Leaves linear or linear-lanceolate, sessile and sheathing, densely imbricated, somewhat broadest at the base, 3"-4"
long, semiterete, obtuse, glabrous, ciliate or glandular-pubescent,
generally falcate, strongly keeled by the midvein; peduncles
slender, terminal, 1-2-flowered; flowers 5"-8" broad; sepals
linear-oblong, 3-nerved, obtusish; petals obovate, twice as long
as the calyx; capsule slightly longer than the sepals; seeds smooth.

Greenland and Labrador to Quebec, west through Arctic America
to Alaska, south in the Rocky Mountains to Arizona. Also in Asia.
Summer. Described in our first edition as *Arenaria biflòra* (L.)
S. Wats.

7. Arenaria vérna L.   Vernal Sandwort.   Fig. 1783.

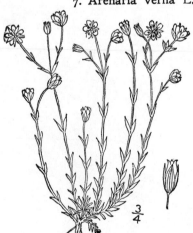

Arenaria verna L. Mant. 72. 1767.

A. *propinqua* Richards. Frankl. Journ. 738. 1823.

A. *verna propinqua* Fernald, Rhodora 8: 32. 1906.

Perennial, densely tufted, flowering stems erect
or ascending, 1'-5' high, branching, glabrous or
sparingly pubescent. Leaves subulate-linear,
rather rigid, imbricated below, more distant
above, 2"-4" long, the upper a little shorter and
broader than the lower; flowers 2"-3" broad,
numerous in loose cymes; pedicels 2"-4" long;
sepals lanceolate, acuminate, 1½"-2" long, 3-ribbed;
petals slightly longer than the sepals; capsule
3-valved, exceeding the sepals; seeds rugose.

In rocky places, Smuggler's Notch, Vt.; Mt. Albert,
Gaspé, Quebec; Labrador and arctic America, south
in the Rocky Mountains to Arizona. Also in northern and alpine Europe and Asia. Summer.

8. Arenaria sajanénsis Willd.   Siberian Sandwort. Fig. 1784.

Stellaria biflora L. Sp. Pl. 422. 1753. Not *A. biflora* L.
Arenaria sajanensis Willd.; Schlecht. Mag. Naturfr. 1816: 200. 1816.
Arenaria biflora S. Wats. Bibl. Index 1: 91. 1878.

Tufted, perennial, stems decumbent, glandular-pubescent, 4' high or less, densely leafy below, the flowering upper parts and the branches with 1–4 distant pairs of smaller leaves, and erect or nearly so; lower leaves linear, stiff, appressed or ascending, 2''–4'' long, glabrous, ciliolate or glandular-pubescent; flowers about 4'' wide; sepals oblong, glandular-pubescent, obtuse; petals equalling or somewhat longer than the sepals; capsule longer than the calyx, 3-valved.

Greenland, Labrador and Quebec to Alaska, south in the Rocky Mountains. Northern Asia. Summer.

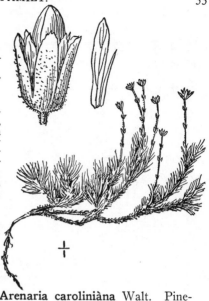

9. Arenaria caroliniàna Walt.   Pine-barren Sandwort. Fig. 1785.

Arenaria caroliniana Walt. Fl. Car. 141. 1788.
Arenaria squarrosa Michx. Fl. Bor. Am. 1: 273. 1803.

Perennial from a deep root, tufted, more or less glandular-pubescent, base woody, flowering stems ascending or erect, 4'–10' high, nearly simple up to the cymose inflorescence. Lower leaves subulate, rigid, 2''–3'' long, channeled on the inner surface, keeled by the prominent midrib, densely imbricated; upper leaves similar, distant; cymes terminal, few-flowered; pedicels ascending or erect; flowers 5''–8'' broad; sepals ovate-oblong, obtuse, nerveless; petals oblanceolate, 3–4 times as long as the calyx; pod short-ovoid, twice as long as the calyx, 3-valved; seeds very nearly smooth.

In dry sand, southeastern New York, pine barrens of New Jersey, south near the coast to Florida and Georgia. May–July.

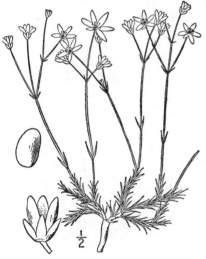

10. Arenaria strícta Michx.   Rock Sandwort. Fig. 1786.

Arenaria stricta Michx. Fl. Bor. Am. 1: 274. 1803.
Alsine Michauxii Fenzl, Verbr. Alsin. table, p. 18. 1833.
Arenaria Michauxii Hook. f. Trans. Linn. Soc. 23: 287. 1867.

Perennial from a short root, tufted, slender, erect or ascending, glabrous, bark green, 6'–16' high, simple or nearly so to the diffuse cymose bracted inflorescence. Leaves slender, rigid, subulate or filiform, broadest at the sessile base, 4''–10'' long, distinctly 1-ribbed, spreading, with numerous others fascicled in the axils; pedicels 3''–18'' long; flowers 4''–5'' broad; calyx ovoid-oblong in fruit; sepals lanceolate or ovate-lanceolate, acute, 3-ribbed, 2'' long, about half the length of the petals and slightly shorter than the ovoid pod; seeds minutely rugose.

In dry rocky places, especially limestone bluffs, Ontario to New Hampshire, Virginia, Minnesota, South Dakota and Missouri. June–July.

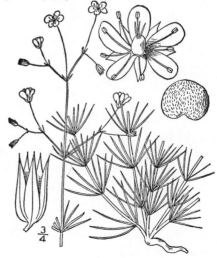

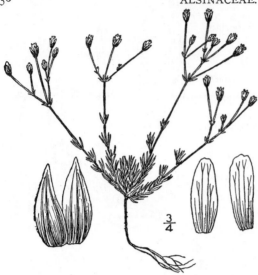

$\frac{3}{4}$

11. Arenaria litòrea Fernald. Beach Sandwort. Fig. 1787.

Arenaria litorea Fernald, Rhodora **8**: 33. 1906.

Perennial, similar to the preceding species, tufted, glabrous, slender, 8' high or less, leafy below. Leaves linear-subulate, somewhat 3-angled, fascicled at the nodes, about 5" long; cymes 1–several-flowered; pedicels slender, 5"–12" long, ascending; sepals $1\frac{1}{2}$"–$2\frac{1}{4}$" long, ovate, acuminate, scarious-margined; petals oblong, shorter than the sepals or nearly equalling them; capsule ovoid, somewhat longer than the calyx.

Sandy and gravelly shores, Quebec, Ontario and Manitoba. June–July.

$\frac{2}{3}$

12. Arenaria texàna (Robinson) Britton. Texas Sandwort. Fig. 1788.

Arenaria stricta texana Robinson; Britton, Mem. Torr. Club **5**: 152. 1894.
Arenaria texana Britton in Britt. & Brown, Ill. Fl. **2**: 34. 1897.

Similar to the preceding species but lower, stiffer, pale green, stems erect, 4'–7' tall, simple up to the inflorescence, conspicuously thickened at the nodes, the internodes mostly very short. Leaves subulate, stiff, 3"–6" long, strongly connate, with numerous minute or similar ones fascicled in their axils; cymes small, rather few-flowered, compact or rather loose; pedicels rarely more than 8" long; flowers 4"–5" broad; calyx narrowly conic in fruit; sepals narrowly lanceolate, strongly 3-ribbed, long-acuminate, 2" long, longer than the capsule.

In dry, rocky soil, Missouri and Kansas to Texas. June–July.

13. Arenaria pátula Michx. Pitcher's Sandwort. Fig. 1789.

Arenaria patula Michx. Fl. Bor. Am. **1**: 273. 1803.

Arenaria Pitcheri Nutt.; T. & G. Fl. N. A. **1**: 180. 1838.

Annual, branched from the base, slender or even filiform, erect or ascending, 4'–10' high, finely pubescent or glabrous. Leaves soft, herbaceous, linear-filiform, 4"–12" long, $\frac{1}{2}$" wide or less, obtuse or acutish; cyme terminal, several-flowered, diffuse; pedicels slender; sepals lanceolate, acuminate, 3–5-nerved, about half the length of the emarginate petals and equalling the pod; seeds rough.

In open, dry places, Kentucky to Illinois, Minnesota, Kansas, Alabama, Tennessee and Texas. April–May.

$\frac{3}{4}$

14. Arenaria groenlándica (Retz) Spreng.
Mountain Sandwort or Starwort. Fig. 1790.

Stellaria groenlandica Retz, Fl. Scand. Ed. *2*, 107. 1795.

Arenaria groenlandica Spreng. Syst. **2**: 402. 1825.

Perennial from a slender rootstock, densely tufted, glabrous, flowering stems slender, 2′–5′ high; leaves linear-filiform, the upper distant, the lower matted, 3″–6″ long; cyme terminal, several-flowered; pedicels 2″–6″ long, filiform; flowers 4″–6″ broad; sepals oblong, obtuse, scarious-margined, nerveless; half the length of the entire or retuse petals and shorter than the oblong pod; seeds compressed, smooth.

On dry rocks, Labrador and Greenland to northern New York, Connecticut, the mountains of southern New York and Pennsylvania, and on the higher Alleghanies of Virginia and North Carolina. Flowers rarely apetalous. June–Sept.

6. MOEHRÍNGIA L. Sp. Pl. 359. 1753.

Low herbs, our species perennial, with oblong ovate ovate-lanceolate or linear soft leaves, sessile or very short-petioled, and small white flowers solitary in the axils or in terminal cymes. Sepals and petals 4 or 5. Stamens 8 or 10. Capsule oblong or ellipsoid, few-seeded. Seeds mostly smooth and shining, appendaged at the hilum by a membranous broad strophiole. [In honor of P. H. G. Moehring, naturalist of Danzig.]

About 20 species, natives of the northern hemisphere. Only the following are known to occur in North America. Type species: *Moehringia muscosa* L.

Leaves oblong or oval, usually obtuse; sepals obtuse or acute, shorter than the petals.   1. *M. lateriflora.*
Leaves lanceolate, usually acute; sepals acuminate, longer than the petals.   2. *M. macrophylla.*

1. Moehringia lateriflòra (L.) Fenzl. Blunt-leaved Moehringia or Sandwort. Fig. 1791.

Arenaria lateriflora L. Sp. Pl. 423. 1753.

Moehringia lateriflora Fenzl, Verbr. Alsin. table, p. 18. 1833.

Stems erect or ascending, simple or at length sparingly branched, finely pubescent throughout, 4′–12′ high. Leaves thin, oval or oblong, ½′–1′ long, obtuse, spreading, the margins and nerves ciliate; cymes lateral and terminal, few-flowered or flowers sometimes solitary; flowers 3″–4″ broad, their parts in 4's or 5's; sepals oblong, obtuse or acute, half as long as the nearly entire petals; ovary at first 3-celled; capsule ovoid, nearly twice as long as the calyx, dehiscent by 3 2-cleft valves.

In moist places and on shores, southern New York and New Jersey to Missouri, north to Newfoundland and Alaska, extending south in the Rocky Mountains to New Mexico. Also in Oregon and British Columbia and in northern Europe and Asia. Showy-sandwort. May–July.

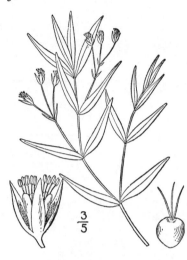

2. Moehringia macrophýlla (Hook.) Torr.
Large-leaved Moehringia or Sandwort.
Fig. 1792.

Arenaria macrophylla Hook. Fl. Bor. Am. 1: 102. *pl. 37.* 1830.

Moehringia macrophylla Torr. Bot. Wilkes' Exp. 246. 1874.

Stems decumbent, puberulent, usually branched, 6'–15' long. Leaves lanceolate, acute or acuminate (rarely obtusish) at the apex, narrowed at the base, 1'–3' long, 2"–5" wide; cymes terminal or becoming axillary by the elongation of the stem, 1–5-flowered; flowers about 3" broad; sepals lanceolate or ovate-lanceolate, long-acuminate, longer than the small petals; capsule rather shorter than the calyx, 3-valved, the valves 2-cleft.

$\frac{3}{5}$

On shores and banks, Labrador to Connecticut, Lake Superior, Idaho and British Columbia, south to California. May–Aug.

7. HONKÉNYA Ehrh. Beitr. 2: 180. 1788.

[AMMODÈNIA J. G. Gmel. Fl. Sib. 4: 160. Hyponym. 1769.]

Perennial fleshy maritime herbs, with ovate obovate oblong or oblanceolate leaves, and rather small flowers, solitary in the axils and in the forks of the stem or branches. Sepals 5 (rarely 4). Petals the same number, entire. Stamens 8 or 10. Disk prominent, 8–10-lobed, glandular. Styles 3–5. Capsule subglobose, fleshy, 3–5-valved when mature, the valve entire. Seeds numerous, obovate, not strophiolate. [In honor of Gerhart August Honckeny, German botanist, 1724–1805.]

Two species, the following of sea beaches throughout the north temperate zone, the other of the coasts of northwestern America and northeastern Asia. Type species: *Honkenya peploides* (L.) Ehrh.

1. Honkenya peploìdes (L.) Ehrh.   Sea-beach Sandwort.   Fig. 1793.

Arenaria peploides L. Sp. Pl. 423. 1753.
Honkenya peploides Ehrh. Beitr. 2: 181. 1788.
Ammodenia peploides Rupr. Beitr. Pfl. Russ. Reich. 2: 25. 1845.

Perennial from long rootstocks, glabrous, fleshy throughout, stems stout, tufted, simple or branched, erect, diffuse or ascending, 3'–10' long. Leaves sessile, clasping, ovate or oval, acute or mucronate, 5"–10" long; flowers axillary and terminal, 3"–4" broad; peduncles stout, 2"–8" long; ovary 3-celled (rarely 4–5-celled); sepals ovate, obtusish, about equalling the petals, shorter than the depressed-globose mostly 3-valved pod; seeds smooth, short-beaked at the hilum, not strophiolate.

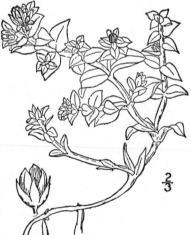

$\frac{2}{3}$

On sands of the seashore, Virginia to New Jersey and arctic America. Also in the shores of northern Europe and Asia. Called also sea-chickweed and sea-purslane or -pimpernel. June–July.

8. SPÉRGULA L. Sp. Pl. 440. 1753.

Annual branched herbs, with subulate stipulate leaves, much fascicled in the axils, and terminal cymes of white flowers. Sepals and petals 5. Stamens 10 or 5. Styles 5, alternate with the sepals. Capsule 5-valved, the valves opposite the sepals. Seeds compressed, acute-margined or winged. [Latin (from *spergo*), to scatter.]

Two or three species, natives of the Old World. The following typical species is widely distributed as a weed.

1. Spergula arvénsis L. Spurry. Poverty-weed. Corn Spurry. Pine-cheat.
Fig. 1794.

Spergula arvensis L. Sp. Pl. 440. 1753.

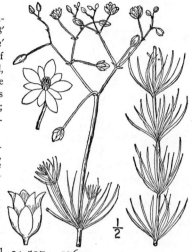

Slender, glabrous or sparingly pubescent, branching at or near the base, erect or ascending, 6'-18' high. Leaves narrowly linear or subulate, 1'-2' long, clustered at the nodes in two opposite sets of 6-8 together, appearing verticillate; stipules small, connate; flowers 2''-3'' broad, numerous in loose terminal cymes; pedicels slender, divaricate; sepals ovate, 1½''-2'' long, slightly longer than the petals; stamens 10 or 5 in flowers on the same plant; capsule ovoid, longer than the calyx; seeds papillose.

In fields and waste places, frequent as a weed throughout eastern Canada and the Eastern and Middle States, south to South Carolina, west to California. Adventive or naturalized from Europe. Sandweed. Pick-purse. Yarr. Cow-quake. Summer.

Spergula satìva Boenn, which differs in being viscid, and with dotted but not papillose seeds, has been collected in New England and in Ontario. Native of Europe.

9. TÍSSA Adans. Fam. Pl. 2: 507. 1763.

[BUDA Adans. Fam. Pl. 2: 507. 1763.]

[SPERGULARIA Pers. Syn. 1: 504. 1805.]

Low annual or perennial herbs, mostly with fleshy linear or setaceous leaves, often with others clustered in the axils, and small pink or whitish flowers in terminal racemose bracted or leafy cymes. Stipules scarious. Sepals 5. Petals the same number, rarely fewer, or none, entire. Stamens 2-10. Ovary 1-celled, many ovuled; styles 3. Pod 3-valved to the base. Seeds reniform-globose or compressed, smooth, winged or tuberculate. [Name unexplained.]

About 20 species, of wide geographic distribution, most of them inhabitants of saline shores or salt marshes. Type species: *Arenaria rubra* L.

Species of salt marshes or sea beaches; leaves very fleshy.
   Pedicels 1½-2 times the length of the sepals; flowers pink.   1. *T. marina.*
   Pedicels 2-4 times the length of the sepals; flowers pale or white.   2. *T. canadensis.*
Species mostly of dry sandy soil; leaves scarcely fleshy.   3. *T. rubra.*

1. Tissa marìna (L.) Britton. Salt-marsh Sand Spurry. Fig. 1795.

Arenaria rubra var. *marina* L. Sp. Pl. 423. 1753.
Spergularia salina Presl, Fl. Cech. 95. 1819.
Buda marina Dumort. Fl. Belg. 110. 1827.
Spergularia media A. Gray, Man. Ed. 5, 95. 1867.
Tissa marina Britton, Bull. Torr. Club 16: 126. 1889.
Buda marina var. *minor* S. Wats. in A. Gray, Man. Ed. 6, 90. 1890.

Annual or biennial, erect, ascending or nearly prostrate, 4'-8' high, freely branching, glabrous or glandular-pubescent. Stipules ovate; leaves linear, terete, very fleshy, ½'-1½' long, ½''-1'' wide, often much fascicled in the axils; pedicels spreading or ascending, 2''-5'' long; flowers numerous, pink; sepals ovate, acute or obtuse, 1''-3'' long; capsule a little longer than the calyx; seeds smooth, or roughened with projecting processes, wingless or winged.

In salt marshes, New Brunswick to Florida and locally in the interior. Also in those of the Pacific Coast, and of Europe and northern Asia. Sea-side or bed-sandwort. Summer.

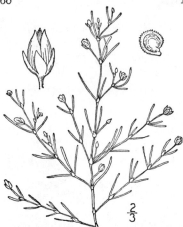

2. Tissa canadénsis (Pers.) Britton. Northern Sand Spurry. Fig. 1796.

Arenaria canadensis Pers. Syn. 1 : 504. 1805.
Tissa salina Britton, Bull. Torr. Club 16 : 127. 1889.
    Not *Spergularia salina* Presl.
Buda borealis S. Wats. in A. Gray, Man. Ed. 6, 90. 1890.
Tissa canadensis Britton, Mem. Torr. Club 5 : 152. 1894.

Annual, slender, diffuse and spreading, entirely glabrous, 2'–5' high. Leaves linear, fleshy, teretish, 5"–8" long, mainly obtuse, generally simply opposite and not fascicled; stipules broadly ovate; pedicels slender, spreading, 3"–6" long, at length much exceeding the calyx; sepals 1" long; flowers pale or white; capsule twice the length of the calyx; seeds smooth or papillose, usually wingless.

On muddy shores, Labrador to Rhode Island. Bed-sandwort. Summer.

3. Tissa rùbra (L.) Britton. Sand Spurry. Purple Sandwort. Fig. 1797.

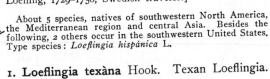

Arenaria rubra L. Sp. Pl. 423. 1753.
Buda rubra Dumort. Fl. Belg. 110. 1827.
Spergularia rubra Presl, Fl. Cech. 93. 1819.
Tissa rubra Britton, Bull. Torr. Club 16 : 127. 1889.

Annual or biennial, depressed or ascending, very leafy up to the inflorescence, glabrous or sparingly glandular-pubescent above, 2'–6' high, often forming dense little mats. Leaves linear, flat, scarcely fleshy, 2"–4" long; flowers bright pink, 1"–1½" broad; stipules ovate-lanceolate, acuminate; sepals ovate-lanceolate, acutish; pedicels slender, spreading, 2"–4" long; pods about equalling the calyx; seeds wingless, rough with projecting points.

In waste places and along roadsides, or sometimes maritime, Nova Scotia to Pennsylvania, western New York, Ohio and Virginia. Apparently adventive from Europe in large part, but perhaps indigenous northward. Also introduced in California and Oregon. Native of Europe and Asia. Bed-sandwort. Summer.

20. LOEFLÍNGIA L. Sp. Pl. 35. 1753.

Low annual glandular-puberulent diffusely branched herbs, with small subulate or setaceous stipulate leaves and very small sessile flowers, solitary or glomerate in the axils. Sepals 5, rigid, keeled, acuminate or awn-tipped, the outer ones commonly with a tooth on each side. Petals 3–5, minute or wanting. Stamens 3–5, perigynous. Ovary triangular-pyramidal, 1-celled, many-ovuled. Capsule 3-valved. Seeds oblong or obovate, attached near their bases; embryo somewhat curved; cotyledons accumbent. [In honor of Peter Loefling, 1729–1756, Swedish traveler.]

About 5 species, natives of southwestern North America, the Mediterranean region and central Asia. Besides the following, 2 others occur in the southwestern United States. Type species : *Loeflingia hispánica* L.

1. Loeflingia texàna Hook. Texan Loeflingia. Fig. 1798.

Loeflingia texana Hook. Ic. Pl. 3 : *pl. 275.* 1840.

Finely and densely glandular-puberulent, stems much branched, bushy, 3'–6' high, the branches slender, terete, ascending or those bearing flowers secund and recurved. Leaves subulate, 2"–3" long, appressed-ascending; flowers less than 1" broad; sepals nearly or quite straight, the 3 outer ones or all with a setaceous tooth on each side; petals much shorter than the sepals; stamens usually 3; capsule shorter than the calyx; seeds obovate.

In dry soil Nebraska to Texas. April–June.

Family 24. **CARYOPHYLLÀCEAE** Reichenb. Consp. 206. 1828.

P<small>INK</small> F<small>AMILY</small>.

Annual or perennial herbs, often swollen at the nodes, with opposite entire exstipulate leaves, and perfect, polygamous, or rarely dioecious regular flowers, the sap watery. Sepals 4 or 5, persistent, united into a tube or cup. Petals equal in number to the sepals, or rarely none, often with a scale at the base of the blade. Stamens twice as many as the sepals, clawed, perigynous; anthers longitudinally dehiscent. Ovary 1, stipitate, mainly 1-celled (rarely 3–5-celled); styles 2–5; ovules and seeds several or many (in all our species), attached to a central column. Fruit generally membranous, a capsule, dehiscent by valves or teeth. Seeds mainly amphitropous; embryo nearly straight, and peripheral to the endosperm; cotyledons mainly incumbent.

About 20 genera and perhaps 600 species, widely distributed, most abundant in the northern hemisphere.

Calyx-ribs at least twice as many as the teeth, running both into the teeth and into the sinuses.
  Styles 5, alternate with the foliaceous calyx-teeth.
  Styles 3–5, when 5, opposite the short calyx-teeth.   1. *Agrostemma.*
    Styles 5, capsule several-celled at the base.
    Styles 3, rarely 4.   2. *Viscaria.*
    Styles 5, capsule 1-celled to the base.   3. *Silene.*
Calyx 5-ribbed, 5-nerved, or nerveless, or striate-nerved.   4. *Lychnis.*
Calyx conspicuously scarious between its green nerves.
  Calyx not bracteolate at the base.
  Calyx bracteolate at the base.   5. *Gypsophila.*
Calyx not at all scarious.   6. *Petrorhagia.*
  Petals appendaged at the base of the blade.
  Petals not appendaged at the base of the blade.   7. *Saponaria.*
    Calyx strongly 5-angled, not bracteolate.
    Calyx terete or nearly so, subtended by bractlets.   8. *Vaccaria.*
                                        9. *Dianthus.*

1. **AGROSTÉMMA** L. Sp. Pl. 435. 1753.

Annual or biennial pubescent often branching herbs, with linear or linear-lanceolate acute or acuminate sessile leaves, and large purple, red or white erect flowers, solitary at the ends of axillary peduncles. Calyx ovoid-oblong, not inflated, narrowed at the throat, 10-ribbed, 5-lobed, the lobes linear, elongated and foliaceous. Petals 5, shorter than the calyx-lobes, their blades obovate or cuneate, emarginate, not appendaged; stamens 10. Styles 5, alternate with the calyx-lobes, opposite the petals. Capsule 1-celled. Seeds numerous, black. [Greek, a field-garland.]

Two known species, natives of Europe and Asia, the following typical.

1. Agrostemma Githàgo L. Corn Cockle. Corn Rose. Corn Campion. Fig. 1799.

Agrostemma Githago L. Sp. Pl. 435. 1753.

Lychnis Githago Scop. Fl. Carn. Ed. 2, 1: 310. 1772.

Erect, 1°–3° high, simple or with few erect branches, densely pubescent throughout with whitish appressed hairs. Leaves linear-lanceolate, acute or long-acuminate, erect, 2′–4′ long, 2″–3″ wide, the lowest narrowed at the base; flowers showy, 1′–3′ broad; peduncles stout, 3′–8′ long, erect; calyx ovoid, its lobes linear, foliaceous, 3 or 4 times the length of the tube and much exceeding the petals, deciduous in fruit; petals usually slightly emarginate, the blade obovate-cuneate.

In grain fields and waste places, frequent or occasional throughout our area. Adventive from Europe, occurring also in northern Asia. Corn-, mullen- or old-maid's pink. Crown-of-the-field. July–Sept.

2. VISCARIA [Rivin.] Roehl. Deutsch. Fl. Ed. 2, 2: 37, 275. 1812.

Perennial or biennial glabrous herbs, with erect, nearly or quite simple stems, and narrow leaves, the basal densely tufted, those of the stem sessile, and small red to rarely white flowers in clustered terminal cymes, the inflorescence in our species almost capitate. Calyx oblong-campanulate, not inflated, 4-5-toothed, 8-10-ribbed. Petals 4 or 5. much exceeding the calyx, each with a 2-cleft appendage at the base of the obovate emarginate blade. Stamens 10, exserted. Styles opposite the calyx-teeth, alternate with the petals. Capsule several-celled at the base, its teeth as many as the styles. [Latin, glutinous.]

About 5 species, the following of arctic and subarctic regions; the others European and Asiatic. Type species: *Viscaria vulgaris* Roehl.

1. Viscaria alpìna (L.) G. Don. Red Alpine Campion. Fig. 1800.

Lychnis alpina L. Sp. Pl. 436. 1753.

Viscaria alpina G. Don, Gen. Syst. 1: 415. 1831.

Tufted, 3'-12' high, rather stout, glabrous, somewhat glaucous, not viscid. Basal leaves narrowly oblanceolate or linear, densely rosulate, ½'-1½' long, 1"-2" wide; stem-leaves distant, linear-lanceolate, erect, acute or obtuse, about 1' long; inflorescence dense, terminal, ½'-1' broad; bracts small, membranous; flowers pink, 3"-4" wide; calyx campanulate, 2" long, its teeth short, rounded; petals about twice the length of the calyx, obovate, 2-lobed; appendages minute.

Mt. Albert, Gaspé, Quebec; Labrador, Newfoundland Hudson Bay, Greenland, and in arctic and alpine Europe and Asia. Summer.

3. SILÈNE L. Sp. Pl. 416. 1753.

Annual or perennial herbs, with cymose or solitary, mainly pink, red or white flowers. Calyx more or less inflated, tubular, ovoid or campanulate, 5-toothed or 5-cleft, 10-many-nerved, not bracted at the base. Petals 5, narrow, clawed, usually with a scale at the base of the blade. Stamens 10. Styles 3 (rarely 4 or 5); ovary 1-celled, or incompletely 2-4-celled. Pod dehiscent by 6 or rarely 3 apical teeth. Seeds mainly spiny or tubercled. [Greek, saliva, in allusion to the viscid secretions of many species.]

About 250 species of wide geographic distribution. In addition to the following, some 35 others occur in the southern and western parts of the continent. Type species: *Silene anglica* L.

Dwarf, arctic-alpine; flowers solitary.   1. *S. acaulis.*
Erect or ascending herbs; flowers clustered (sometimes solitary in nos. 3-7).
     Leaves or some of them verticillate in 4's.   2. *S. stellata.*
     Leaves all opposite.
        Calyx much inflated and bladdery.
           Flowers few, leafy-bracted.   3. *S. alba.*
           Flowers numerous, in leafless cymes.   4. *S. latifolia.*
        Calyx merely expanded by the ripening pod.
           Flowers cymose or paniculate.
              Day-blooming; flowers rarely white, mostly pink or red.
                 Perennials, more or less viscid-pubescent.
                    Petals 2-cleft, 2-lobed, or irregularly incised, scarlet or crimson.
                      Leaves lanceolate or spatulate; flowers numerous.
                        Flowers in slender panicles, nodding.   5. *S. nutans.*
                        Flowers in terminal cymes, erect.   6. *S. virginica.*
                      Leaves broadly oblong to obovate; flowers few or solitary. 7. *S. rotundifolia.*
                   Petals erose, entire, or emarginate.
                      Petals scarlet; plant 3°-4° tall.   8. *S. regia.*
                      Petals pink; plant 4'-10' high.   9. *S. caroliniana.*
                 Annuals, glutinous at or below the nodes.
                   Calyx ovoid.   10. *S. antirrhina.*
                      Flowers small, panicled; calyx-teeth ovate.   11. *S. conica.*
                      Flowers large, cymose; calyx-teeth subulate.   12. *S. Armeria.*
                   Calyx club-shaped; flowers large, cymose.   13. *S. noctiflora.*
              Night-blooming; flowers large, white; annual.
        Flowers spicate or racemose, short-pedicelled.
           Spicate raceme simple; flowers small.   14. *S. anglica.*
           Raceme forked; flowers 6"-8" broad.   15. *S. dichotoma.*
        Flowers axillary and terminal, slender-pedicelled; western.   16. *S. Menziesii.*

1. Silene acàulis L.   Moss Campion.   Fig. 1801.

Silene acaulis L. Sp. Pl. Ed. 2, 603. 1762.

Perennial, puberulent or glabrous, branched, densely tufted, 1'-3' high. Leaves sessile, crowded, linear, 4"-6" long, about ½" wide, obtuse or acutish at the apex, the margins ciliate-serrulate; flowers solitary at the ends of the branches, sessile or slender-peduncled, 4"-6" broad, purple or purplish, rarely white; calyx campanulate, glabrous, 4" high; petals entire or emarginate, with a scale at the base of the blade; pod oblong, equalling or exceeding the calyx.

Summits of the White Mountains, N. H.; Gaspé, Quebec; Cape Breton Island, Labrador and throughout arctic America, south in the higher Rocky Mountains to Arizona. Also in arctic and alpine Europe and Asia. Cushion- or moss-pink. Summer.

2. Silene stellàta (L.) Ait.   Starry Campion.   Thermon Snake-root.   Fig. 1802.

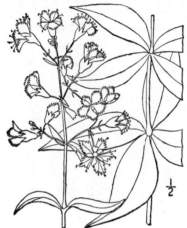

Cucubalus stellatus L. Sp. Pl. 414. 1753.
Silene stellata Ait. f. Hort. Kew. 3: 84. 1811.

Perennial, erect, 2°-3½° high, densely and minutely rough-pubescent throughout. Leaves ovate-lanceolate, acuminate, 2'-4' long, ½'-1' wide, verticillate in 4's or the lowest opposite, their margins finely ciliate; flowers white, 7"-10" broad, in panicled cymes, forming a large showy inflorescence; calyx campanulate, inflated, 7"-8" high, its teeth triangular, acute; petals crownless, fimbriate, about equalling the stamens; pod globose-ovoid, about the length of the calyx.

In woods, Massachusetts to Minnesota, Nebraska, Georgia and Arkansas. June–Aug.

Silene ovàta Pursh, which has the habit of this species but the leaves opposite, is recorded by Pursh from "the western parts of Virginia and Carolina," but is not definitely known from Virginia.

3. Silene álba Muhl.   Western White or Snowy Campion.   Fig. 1803.

Silene alba Muhl. Cat. 45. 1813.

Cucubalus niveus Nutt. Gen. 1: 287. 1818.

Silene nivea Otth in DC. Prodr. 1: 377. 1824.

Perennial, ascending or erect, rather weak, simple, or divergently branched above, minutely puberulent or glabrate. Leaves lanceolate or oblong-lanceolate, 3'-5' long, 5"-8" wide, acuminate, the upper gradually smaller, and subtending the flowers; pedicels about 1' long, divaricate; flowers few, often solitary, about 10" broad; petals white above, yellowish-green beneath; calyx inflated, elongated-campanulate, pubescent, its teeth ovate, obtuse, more or less scarious-margined; petals cuneate, 2-cleft, or 2-lobed, minutely crowned.

In shaded or moist places, Pennsylvania to District of Columbia, Minnesota and Nebraska. June–July.

4. Silene latifòlia (Mill.) Britten & Rendle. Bladder Campion. Fig. 1804.

Cucubalus Behen L. Sp. Pl. 414. 1753. Not Silene
    Behen L.
Cucubalus latifolius Mill. Gard. Dict. Ed. 8, no. 2.
    1768.
Behen vulgaris Moench, Meth. 709. 1794.
S. vulgaris Garcke, Fl. Deutsch. Ed. 9, 64. 1869.
Silene inflata J. E. Smith, Fl. Brit. 2: 292. 1800.
S. latifolia Britten & Rendle, List Brit. Seed-Plants
    5. 1907.

Perennial, branched from the base, glaucous
and glabrous, or rarely pubescent, 6′–18′ high.
Leaves opposite, ovate-lanceolate or oblong,
acute, variable in size, the lower often spatulate;
flowers white, 6″–10″ broad, in loose cymose
panicles, often drooping; calyx at first tubular-
campanulate, at length inflated and globose, 4″–
6″ long, strongly veined; petals 2-cleft, with or
without a small crown.

In meadows and waste places, New Brunswick to
Ontario, Washington, New Jersey and Missouri.
Also on the Pacific Coast. Naturalized from Europe
and native also of Asia. Summer. Called also Behen,
White Ben, Cow-bell, Spattling or Frothy poppy.
Bull-rattle, Rattle-bags, Devil's rattle-box. Snappers.
Knap-bottle. Bird's-eggs. Sea-pink. Maiden's-tears.

5. Silene nùtans L. Nodding Catchfly.
Fig. 1805.

Silene nutans L. Sp. Pl. 417. 1753.

Perennial, glandular-pubescent above or nearly
glabrous, stem slender, erect, 1°–2° tall. Lower and
basal leaves spatulate, subacute at the apex, 2′–5′
long, 3″–8″ wide, tapering into slender petioles;
stem-leaves few and distant, narrowly oblong or
lanceolate, acute or acuminate at the apex, sessile,
the uppermost (bracts) very small; flowers 6″–8″
broad, white or pink, nodding or spreading in a
loose panicle; pedicels slender, 4″–12″ long; calyx
oblong-cylindric in flower, 4″–5″ long, glandular, its
teeth triangular, acute; petals 2-cleft or sometimes
4-cleft, the lobes narrowly oblong; capsule ovoid,
5″–6″ high, distending the calyx.

Mt. Desert Island, Maine, and Staten Island, N. Y.
Fugitive from Europe. English names, Dover catchfly,
Nottingham catchfly. June–Sept.

6. Silene virgínica L. Fire Pink. Fig. 1806.

Silene virginica L. Sp. Pl. 419. 1753.

Perennial, slender, ascending or erect, viscid-
pubescent, branching above, 1°–2° high. Leaves
thin, those of the base and lower part of the stem
spatulate or oblanceolate, 3′–5′ long, obtuse or acute,
tapering into a winged petiole; upper leaves oblong-
lanceolate, acute, sessile; inflorescence loosely
cymose-paniculate; flowers crimson, 1′–1½′ broad;
pedicels slender, ½′–2′ long; calyx tubular-campanulate, 9″–12″ long, enlarged by the ripening pod, its
teeth ovate, acute, scarious-margined; petals 2-cleft,
2-lobed, or irregularly incised, crowned, the limb
oblong or linear-oblong.

In dry woods, southern New Jersey, western New York
and southwestern Ontario to Minnesota, south to Georgia and Missouri. Ascends to 4200 ft. in Virginia. Indian pink. May–Sept.

7. Silene rotundifòlia Nutt. Round-leaved Catchfly. Fig. 1807.

Silene rotundifolia Nutt. Gen. **1**: 288. 1818.

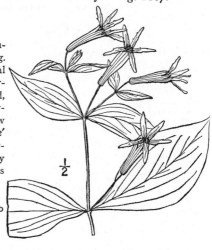

Perennial, stem slender, ascending or reclining, viscid-pubescent, branched, 1½°–2° long. Leaves thin, membranous, the lower and basal ones obovate or broadly spatulate, 2′–4′ long, narrowed into a winged petiole, obtuse but pointed, the cauline obovate, broadly oblong or orbicular-ovate, acute, the uppermost sessile; flowers few and loosely cymose, or solitary, scarlet, 1′–2′ broad; pedicels slender, 1′–2′ long; calyx tubular-campanulate, 10″–15″ long, somewhat enlarged by the ripening pod, its teeth ovate, acute; petals 2-cleft, lobed, or laciniate, crowned.

In shaded places, southern Ohio and Kentucky to Georgia. Summer.

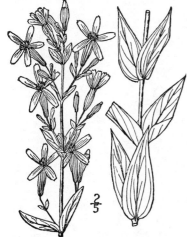

8. Silene règia Sims. Royal Catchfly. Wild Pink. Fig. 1808.

Silene regia Sims, Bot. Mag. *pl. 1724.* 1814.

Perennial, erect, stout, 3°–4° high, simple or sparingly branched, minutely rough-pubescent, slightly viscid. Leaves all but the lowest sessile, thick, ovate-lanceolate, acute or acuminate, 2′–3′ long; inflorescence a narrow strict panicle of few-flowered cymose clusters; pedicels generally less than ½′ long; flowers numerous, deep scarlet, about 1′ broad; calyx oblong-tubular, 10″ long, slightly enlarged by the ripening pod, its teeth ovate, acute; petals emarginate or laciniate, crowned.

Prairies, Ohio to eastern Tennessee, Alabama, west to Missouri. July.

9. Silene caroliniàna Walt. Wild Pink. Fig. 1809.

Silene caroliniana Walt. Fl. Car. 142. 1788.
S. pennsylvanica Michx. Fl. Bor. Am. **1**: 272. 1803.

Perennial, tufted, 4′–10′ high, viscid-pubescent, especially above, generally nearly glabrous below. Basal leaves spatulate, or oblanceolate, acute or obtuse, 2′–4′ long, narrowed into a broad petiole, the margins often ciliate; stem-leaves shorter, sessile, oblong or lanceolate; flowers pink, about 1′ broad, in terminal cymes; pedicels 2″–15″ long; calyx narrow, tubular, much enlarged by the ripening pod, its teeth ovate, acute; petals cuneate, emarginate, eroded, crowned at the base of the claw.

In dry, sandy or rocky soil, Maine to Georgia, west to central New York, Pennsylvania and Kentucky. Ascends to 3300 ft. in West Virginia. April–June.

10. Silene antirrhìna L.   Sleepy Catchfly.   Fig. 1810.

Silene antirrhina L. Sp. Pl. 419. 1753.
Silene antirrhina divaricata Robinson, Proc. Am. Acad.
28: 132. 1893.

Annual, slender, erect or ascending, puberulent
or glabrous, glutinous about the nodes, simple, or
branched above, 8′–2½° high, the branches ascending. Basal and lower leaves spatulate or oblanceolate, 1′–2′ long, narrowed into a petiole, obtuse or
acute, sometimes slightly ciliate; upper leaves linear
and gradually reduced to subulate bracts; inflorescence a loose cymose panicle; pedicels slender,
erect; corolla pink, about 1″–2″ broad, sometimes
wanting; calyx narrowly ovoid, 2″–3″ long, much
expanded by the ripening pod, its teeth ovate, acute;
petals obcordate, minutely crowned.

In waste places and woods, Maine to southern Ontario and British Columbia, south to Florida and Mexico.
Flowers opening for a short time in sunshine. Ascends
to 3200 ft. in Virginia. Summer.

11. Silene cónica L.   Striate, or Corn Catchfly.
Fig. 1811.

Silene conica L. Sp. Pl. 418. 1753.

Annual, canescent or puberulent; stems solitary,
or several together, erect, commonly forked above,
6′–24′ high. Leaves linear-lanceolate, acute, sessile,
1½′ long, or less, about 1½″ wide; inflorescence cymose;
flowers 1–several; pedicels ¼′–1′ long; calyx ovoid,
rounded or truncate at the base, densely about 30-
nerved, about 8″ long, its teeth triangular-subulate;
petals rose or purple, obcordate; capsule oblong-ovoid,
distending the calyx and nearly equalling it.

Dartmouth, Massachusetts, and Clyde, Ohio. Adventive
or naturalized from Europe. June–July.

12. Silene Armèria L.   Sweet William or Lobel's Catchfly.   Fig. 1812.

Silene Armeria L. Sp. Pl. Ed. 2, 601. 1762.

Annual, erect, branching, glabrous and glaucous, or minutely puberulent, about 1° high,
glutinous below each node. Basal leaves oblanceolate, 2′–3′ long, obtuse; stem-leaves ovate
or ovate-lanceolate, 1′–3′ long, acute or obtuse;
inflorescence a terminal compact compound
cyme; flowers purple or pink, 6″–8″ broad; calyx
club-shaped, 5″–8″ long, slightly enlarged by the
ripening pod; pedicels about 1″ long; petals
emarginate, crowned with narrow scales.

In waste places and spontaneous in gardens, New
Brunswick and Ontario to Michigan south to New
Jersey and Pennsylvania. Introduced from Europe.
Pretty-Nancy, Sweet-Susan. None-so-pretty. Old-
maid's- or mice pink. Dwarf French-pinks. Wax-
plant. Mock sweet-william. Limewort- or garden-
catchfly. June–July.

13. Silene noctiflòra L.   Night-flowering Catchfly. Fig. 1813.

Silene noctiflora L. Sp. Pl. 419. 1753.

Annual, stout, viscid-pubescent, simple, or branchin'g, 1°–3° high. Lower and basal leaves obovate or oblanceo-late, 2′–5′ long, obtuse, narrowed into a broad petiole; upper leaves sessile, ovate-lanceolate, acute or acuminate, 1′–3′ long; flowers few, pedicelled, white or pinkish, 8″– 12″ broad, in a loose dichotomous panicle; calyx 10″–15″ long, tubular, 10-nerved and beautifully veined, much enlarged by the ripening pod, its teeth linear, acute; petals 2-cleft.

In waste places, Nova Scotia and New Brunswick to Mani-toba, Montana, Florida, Missouri and Utah. Adventive from Europe. Flowers opening at dusk and remaining so until the morning of the next day, fragrant. July–Sept.

14. Silene ánglica L.   English or Small-flowered Catchfly. Fig. 1814.

Silene anglica L. Sp. Pl. 416. 1753.
Silene gallica L. Sp. Pl. 417. 1753.

Annual, hirsute-pubescent, stem slender, usually erect, simple or branched, 1°–2° high. Leaves spatulate or oblanceolate, 6″–2′ long, obtuse, sometives mucronate, narrowed into a margined petiole, or the upper ones narrower and acute; flowers in a terminal simple 1-sided spicate raceme, nearly sessile or the lower ones distant and longer-pedicelled, sometimes all distinctly pedi-celled; calyx cylindric or oblong-tubular in flower, 10-nerved, villous, 4″–5″ long, much enlarged by the ripening pod and becoming ovoid with a contracted throat, its teeth lanceolate, spreading; petals toothed, entire or somewhat 2-cleft, white, somewhat longer than the calyx.

In waste places, Maine to Ontario, southern New York, Pennsylvania and Missouri. Adventive from Europe. Ex-tensively naturalized as a weed on the Pacific Coast, and widely distributed in nearly all warm-temperate regions. Has been mistaken for *S. nocturna* L. April–July.

15. Silene dichótoma Ehrh.   Forked Catchfly. Fig. 1815.

Silene dichotoma Ehrh. Beitr. 7: 143. 1792.

Silene racemosa Otth in DC. Prodr. 1: 384. 1824.

Annual, erect, branching, pubescent, 1°–2° high. Lower and basal leaves lanceolate or oblanceolate, 2′– 3′ long, acuminate or acute, tapering into a villous petiole; upper leaves sessile, lanceolate or linear; flow-ers white, sessile or very short-pedicelled, distant in forking 1-sided spikes; calyx cylindric, 6″–8″ long, hirsute, much enlarged by the ripening pod, its teeth ovate-lanceolate, acute; petals white, bifid, with a short obtuse crown.

In fields and waste places, Maine to New Jersey, Pennsyl-vania and Texas. Also in California. Adventive from southern Europe. Summer.

16. Silene Menzièsii Hook.　Menzies' Pink.
Fig. 1816.

Silene Menziesii Hook. Fl. Bor. Am. 1 : 90. *pl. 30.*　1830.

Perennial, slender, ascending or decumbent, leafy, widely branching, minutely and densely glandular-pubescent, 6'–18' high. Leaves sessile, or the lowest narrowed into a petiole, oval, ovate-lanceolate or slightly oblanceolate, acute or acuminate at each end, minutely ciliate on the margins, 1'–2½' long; flowers axillary and terminal, numerous, slender-peduncled, white, 4''–5'' long; petals 2-cleft, crownless, longer than the 5-toothed calyx; capsule about the length of the calyx; seeds black, minutely tuberculate.

In damp soil, Assiniboia to western Nebraska, Missouri, British Columbia, California and New Mexico. June–Aug.

4. LÝCHNIS [Tourn.] L. Sp. Pl. 436.　1753.

Herbs, mainly erect, some with the aspect of *Silene.* Calyx ovoid, tubular, or inflated, 5-toothed, 10-nerved. Petals 5, narrowly clawed, the blade entire, 2-cleft, or laciniate, generally crowned. Stamens 10. Ovary 1-celled or incompletely several-celled at the base, many-ovuled; styles 5, opposite the calyx-teeth (occasionally 4 or rarely even 3). Capsule dehiscent by 10 or fewer apical teeth or valves. [From the Greek, for lamp, in allusion to the flame-colored flowers of some species.]

　A genus of about 35 species, natives of the north temperate and arctic zones. In addition to the following about 8 others occur in the northern and western parts of North America. Type species : *Lychnis chalcedonica* L.

Calyx-teeth not twisted; plants pubescent, glandular or glabrate.
　Flowers cymose or panicled ; calyx enlarged by the ripening pod.
　　Fruiting calyx much enlarged, ovoid, obovoid or globose.
　　　Plants viscid-pubescent; flowers usually dioecious.
　　　　Flowers white or pink, opening in the evening.　　　　　　1. *L. alba.*
　　　　Flowers red, opening in the morning.　　　　　　　　　　2. *L. dioica.*
　　　Plant roughish-pubescent ; flowers perfect, scarlet.　　　　3. *L. chalcedonica.*
　　Fruiting calyx campanulate or tubular.
　　　Petals large, deeply laciniate ; introduced species.　　　　4. *L. Flos-cuculi.*
　　　Petals small, entire or emarginate ; native western species.　5. *L. Drummondii.*
　Flowers solitary ; calyx inflated ; plants arctic-alpine.
　　Flower nodding ; pod erect.　　　　　　　　　　　　　　　6. *L. apetala.*
　　Flower and pod erect or nearly so.　　　　　　　　　　　　7. *L. affinis.*
Calyx-teeth twisted ; plant densely white-woolly all over.　　　8. *L. Coronaria.*

1. Lychnis álba Mill.　White Campion.
Evening Lychnis.　Fig. 1817.

Lychnis alba Mill. Gard. Dict. Ed. 8, no. 4.　1768.
Lychnis vespertina Sibth. Fl. Oxon. 146.　1794.

Biennial, viscid-pubescent, loosely and freely branching, 1°–2° high. Leaves ovate-oblong or ovate-lanceolate, acute, 1'–3' long, the lower tapering into a margined petiole, the upper sessile; flowers few, loosely paniculate, 9''–12'' broad, white or pinkish, opening at dusk and remaining open into the morning of the next day, slightly fragrant, often dioecious; calyx at first tubular, 6''–9'' long, about 2'' wide, swelling with the ripening pod so as to become ovoid and 6''–7'' in diameter, its teeth short, lanceolate; petals obovate, 2-cleft, crowned; teeth of the capsule 2-cleft, nearly erect.

In waste places and on ballast, Nova Scotia to Ontario, Michigan, New York and Pennsylvania. Adventive or naturalized from Europe. Snake-, cuckoo- or thunder-flower. Bull- or cow-rattle. White-robin. Summer.

2. Lychnis diòica L.   Red Campion.   Red
bird's-eye.   Fig. 1818.

Lychnis dioica L. Sp. Pl. 437. 1753.
Lychnis diurna Sibth. Fl. Oxon. 145. 1794.

Biennial, very viscid-pubescent, branching above,
1°–2° high. Basal leaves long-petioled, oblong,
obtuse put pointed, the blade 2′–3′ long; stem-
leaves sessile or the lower short-petioled, ovate,
acute, 1′–2′ long, ½–1½′ wide; flowers numerous
in panicled cymes, red or nearly white, scentless,
9″–12″ broad, dioecious, opening in the morning;
calyx at first tubular, about 4″ long and 2½″ wide,
swollen in fruit to nearly globular by the ripening
pod, its teeth ovate-lanceolate, acute; petals obovate, 2-cleft, crowned; teeth of the capsule 2-cleft,
recurved.

In waste places and ballast, Nova Scotia to Ontario,
New York and Virginia. Adventive from Europe. Sum-
mer. Robins. Red- or poor-robin. Bachelor's-buttons.
White soapwort. Soldiers. Adder's- or Devil's-flower.

3. Lychnis chalcedónica L.   Scarlet Lychnis.
Fire-balls.   Fig. 1819.

Lychnis chalcedonica L. Sp. Pl. 436. 1753.

Perennial, stem stout, erect, simple or little
branched, finely pubescent or hirsute, 1°–2½° tall.
Leaves ovate, ovate-lanceolate or the upper lanceolate, acute or acuminate at the apex, rounded or
subcordate at the base, sessile or somewhat clasping,
dark green, 2′–5′ long, 6″–18″ wide; flowers perfect, numerous, about 1′ broad, scarlet, in one or
more usually dense terminal cymes; calyx oblong
in flower, becoming obovoid, its teeth triangular,
acute; petals 2-cleft or laciniate; capsule borne on
a stipe nearly its own length, its teeth entire.

Escaped from gardens to roadsides, Massachusetts to
southern New York. Native of eastern Europe and
western Asia. Flowers, in cultivation, often double.
Sweet-william. None-such. Old English names, Scarlet-
lightning. Cross-of-Jerusalem, Maltese- or Knight's-cross.
June–Sept.

4. Lychnis Flós-cùculi L.   Cuckoo Flower.
Ragged Robin.   Fig. 1820.

Lychnis Flos-cuculi L. Sp. Pl. 436. 1753.

Perennial, slender, erect, 1°–2° high, freely
branching, downy-pubescent below, slightly viscid above. Lower and basal leaves oblanceolate
or spatulate, 2′–3′ long, tapering into a broad
petiole; upper leaves sessile, lanceolate or linear-
lanceolate, distant, the uppermost reduced to
lanceolate bracts; inflorescence paniculate; flowers pink, blue or white, 8″–12″ broad; calyx at
first cylindric, 3″ long, 10-nerved, becoming
campanulate in fruit, its teeth triangular, acute;
petals cleft into 4 linear lobes, the middle pair
of lobes longer; capsule globose.

In moist waste places, New Brunswick to New
Jersey and Pennsylvania. Commonly cultivated.
Fugitive from Europe. Crow-flower. Meadow-pink
or -campion. Cuckoos. Indian-pink. Ragged Jack.
Marsh-gilliflower. June–Sept.

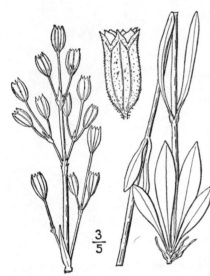

5. Lychnis Drummóndii (Hook.) S. Wats. Drummond's Pink. Fig. 1821.

Silene Drummondii Hook. Fl. Bor. Am. 1 : 89. 1830.

L. Drummondii S. Wats. Bot. King's Exp. 37. 1871.

Erect from a perennial root, simple or sparingly branched, finely glandular-pubescent and viscid, 1°–3° high. Leaves oblanceolate or linear, acute, narrowed into a margined petiole or the upper sessile, 1′–3½′ long; flowers few, slender-pedicelled, white or purplish, 6″–10″ long; petals scarcely longer than the tubular calyx, entire or emarginate at the apex, narrower than the auricled claw; capsule oblong-cylindric, 6″–8″ long; seeds tuberculate.

In dry soil, Nebraska to Minnesota, Manitoba, west to California and Oregon. June–July.

6. Lychnis apétala L. Nodding Lychnis. Fig. 1822.

Lychnis apetala L. Sp. Pl. 437. 1753.

Tufted, arctic or alpine, perennial, 3′–8′ high, glandular-pubescent at least above. Stems 1-flowered; leaves linear or oblanceolate, ½′–2½′ long, 1″–3″ wide, sessile, or the lower narrowed into a petiole; flower nodding, 6″–8″ long; petals narrow, 2-cleft, included in the calyx; calyx inflated, strongly purple-veined, its teeth triangular-ovate, acute; petals narrow, about 1″ wide, minutely appendaged, equalling or shorter than the calyx, deeply 2-cleft; capsule erect, ovoid, 4″ in diameter.

Labrador and throughout arctic America. Also in arctic and alpine Europe and Asia. Summer.

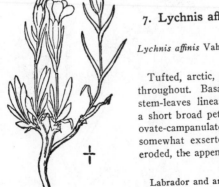

7. Lychnis affìnis Vahl. Arctic Lychnis. Fig. 1823.

Lychnis affinis Vahl, in Fries, Mant. 3: 36. 1843.

Tufted, arctic, perennial, erect, 2′–4′ high, glandular-pubescent throughout. Basal leaves spatulate, obtuse, about ½′ long, ciliate; stem-leaves linear, ½′–1′ long, obtuse, sessile, or narrowed into a short broad petiole; flower erect, 4″–6″ long; calyx oblong or ovate-campanulate, slightly inflated, its teeth short, acute; petals somewhat exserted, the blade narrowed below, emarginate and eroded, the appendages minute.

Labrador and arctic America and Europe. Summer.

8. Lychnis Coronària (L.) Desr. Mullein Pink. Fig. 1824.

Agrostemma Coronaria L. Sp. Pl. 436. 1753.

Lychnis Coronaria Desr. in Lam. Encycl. 3 : 643. 1789.

Perennial, densely white-woolly all over; stem stout, erect or ascending, simple or branched, 1°–3° tall. Lower leaves spatulate, 2′–4′ long, 6″–15″ wide, narrowed into margined petioles; upper leaves oblong or lanceolate, sessile, acute or acuminate at the apex, narrowed or rounded at the base, the uppermost (bracts) usually small; flowers few, 1′ broad or more, long-pedicelled in open terminal panicles; calyx oblong-campanulate, its teeth filiform-subulate, twisted, shorter than the tube; petals crimson.

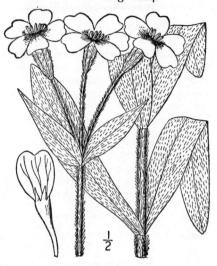

Escaped from gardens to roadsides and waste-places, Maine to southern New York and Michigan and in Washington and Oregon. Native of Europe. Also called Rose-campion. Gardener's-eye. Gardener's-delight. June–Aug.

5. GYPSÓPHILA L. Sp. Pl. 406. 1753.

Annual or perennial, branching or diffuse, mostly glabrous and glaucous herbs, with narrow leaves, and small numerous axillary or paniculate flowers. Calyx turbinate or campanulate, 5-toothed, 5-nerved, bractless. Petals 5, entire or emarginate, their claws narrow. Stamens 10; styles 2. Capsule dehiscent by 4 valves extending to or below the middle Seeds reniform, laterally attached; embryo coiled. [Greek, in allusion to the supposed preference of some species for gypsum soils.]

About 60 species, natives of Europe, Asia and northern Africa. Type species: *Gypsophila repens* L.

Annual, diffuse ; leaves narrowly linear ; flowers axillary on filiform peduncles.   1. *G. muralis.*
Erect perennial ; leaves lanceolate ; flowers paniculate.   2. *G. paniculata.*

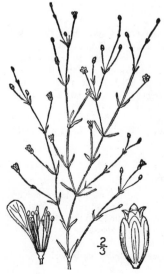

1. Gypsophila muràlis L. Low Gypsophyll. Fig. 1825.

Gypsophila muralis L. Sp. Pl. 408. 1753.

Annual, diffuse, slender, much branched, glabrous or slightly rough at the base, 4′–7′ high. Leaves narrowly linear or subulate, attenuate at each end, 3″–10″ long, ¼″–½″ wide; peduncles slender, spreading or ascending, 3″–10″ long; flowers purplish, 1½″–2″ broad; calyx turbinate, 1½″–2″ long, 5-toothed, the teeth rounded; petals crenate or emarginate, 2″–3″ long, much exceeding the calyx; pod about 2″ long, slightly longer than the calyx.

In waste places, Maine and Ontario to Michigan. Minnesota, Massachusetts, southern New York and New Jersey. Adventive or naturalized from Europe. June–Sept.

2. Gypsophila paniculàta L.   Tall Gypsophyll. Fig. 1826.

Gypsophila paniculata L. Sp. Pl. 407. 1753.

Perennial, glabrous or sometimes pubescent below, stem slender, erect, much branched, 1°–2° tall. Leaves lanceolate, those of the stem 1′ long or more, 2″–4″ wide, acuminate at the apex, narrowed at the base, those of the branches much smaller, the bracts and bractlets minute; flowers 1½″–2″ broad, very numerous in panicled cymes; pedicels 2″–5″ long; calyx campanulate, 1″ high, deeply 5-lobed, the segments with broad scarious margins; petals white or pink, slightly emarginate, one-fourth to one-half longer than the calyx.

Manitoba and Nebraska, escaped from cultivation. Fugitive from northern Europe or Asia. Mist. Baby's-breath. Summer.

6. PETRORHAGIA (Ser.) Link, Handb. 2: 235. 1831.

Rigid and slender mainly perennial herbs, with small glomerate panicled or solitary flowers, bracted at the base. Calyx top-shaped or campanulate, 5-toothed, 5–15-nerved. Petals 5, long-clawed, the limb emarginate or bifid. Stamens 10. Styles 2. Capsule ovoid or oblong, dehiscent by 4 apical teeth or valves. Seeds compressed, laterally attached; embryo straight, eccentric. [Greek, stone-breaking.]

A genus of about 20 species, natives of southern Europe and western Asia, the following typical.

1. Petrorhagia Saxífraga (L.) Ser. Tunica. Saxifrage Pink. Fig. 1827.

Dianthus Saxifraga L. Sp. Pl. 413. 1753.

Tunica Saxifraga Scop. Fl. Carn. Ed. 2, 300. 1772.

Petrorhagia Saxifraga Ser.; Link, Handb. 2: 235. 1831.

Perennial, tufted, sparsely pubescent or glabrous; stems diffuse or ascending, 4′–8′ long, terete, branching. Leaves linear-subulate, erect, very acute, 3″–5″ long, less than ½″ wide, connate at the base, the lower imbricated, the upper distant, their margins scabrous or ciliate; flowers panicled, about 3″ broad, pink or purple; calyx campanulate, 5-ribbed, 3″ long, twice the length of the scarious-margined acute bracts.

Roadsides, Flushing, Long Island, N. Y., and London, Ontario. Adventive from Europe. Summer.

7. SAPONÀRIA L. Sp. Pl. 408. 1753.

Annual or perennial, erect or diffuse herbs, mostly with broad leaves and large flowers. Calyx ovoid, oblong or tubular, 5-toothed, obscurely nerved. Petals 5, entire or emarginate, long-clawed. Stamens 10. Ovary 1-celled or incompletely 2–4-celled; styles 2. Capsule ovoid or oblong, dehiscent by 4 short apical teeth or valves. [Latin, soap; its juices abound in saponin, and have cleansing qualities.]

About 35 species, natives of Europe, Asia and northern Africa the following typical.

1. **Saponaria officinàlis** L.   Soapwort.   Bouncing Bet.
London Pride.   Bruise-wort.   Fig. 1828.

Saponaria officinalis L. Sp. Pl. 408. 1753.

Perennial, glabrous, erect, stout, sparingly branched, leafy,
1°–2° high. The leaves ovate or oval, 2'–3' long, about 1' wide,
strongly 3–5-ribbed, acute, narrowed at the base into a broad
short petiole; flowers pink or whitish, about 1' broad, in
dense terminal corymbs, with numerous small lanceolate
bracts or floral leaves; calyx tubular, 8"–10" long, faintly
nerved, 5-toothed; petals obcordate with a scale at the base
of the blade; pod narrowly oblong, shorter than the calyx.

Roadsides and waste places, common in most districts and escaped from gardens, spreading by underground stolons. Naturalized from Europe. Flowers sometimes double. Summer.
Called also Fuller's-herb. Boston-, chimney-, hedge- or old-
maid's pink. Sheepweed. Soap-root. Soapwort-gentian. World's-
wonder. Sweet-betty. Wild sweet-william. Lady-by-the-gate.
Wood's-phlox. Mock-gilliflower.

8. **VACCÀRIA** Medic. Phil. Bot. 1 : 96.   1789.

Annual glabrous and glaucous erect dichotomously branching herbs, with sessile clasping
ovate or lanceolate acute leaves, and rather small red or pink slender-pedicelled flowers in
terminal cymes. Calyx cylindric in flower, becoming sharply 5-angled and inflated in fruit,
5-toothed, not bracted at the base. Petals much longer than the calyx, not appendaged.
Stamens 10. Styles 2. Capsule 4-toothed. Seeds laterally attached; embryo curved. [Latin,
cow, in allusion to its value for fodder.]

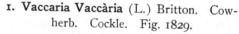

About 3 species, natives of Europe and Asia, the
following typical.

1. **Vaccaria Vaccària** (L.) Britton.   Cow-
herb.   Cockle.   Fig. 1829.

Saponaria Vaccaria L. Sp. Pl. 409. 1753.
Vaccaria vulgaris Host, Fl. Aust. 1 : 518. 1827.
Vaccaria Vaccaria Britton, in Britt. & Br. Ill. Fl. 2 :
1897.

Branching above, 1°–3° high. Leaves lanceolate or ovate-lanceolate, 1'–3' long, ¼'–1' wide,
acute, connate at the base; flowers pale red, 3"–
4" broad, borne in loose corymbose cymes; calyx
oblong or ovate, 5"–7" long, 5-ribbed, much inflated and wing-angled in fruit; petals crenulate,
with no scale at the base of the blade.

In waste places, Ontario to British Columbia,
Florida, Louisiana and California. Locally abundant.
Naturalized or adventive from Europe. Cow-basil.
June–Aug.

9. **DIÁNTHUS** L. Sp. Pl. 409.   1753.

[Tunica Boehm. in Ludw. Def. Gen. 298. 1760.]

Stiff perennial (rarely annual) herbs, mainly with narrow leaves. Flowers terminal,
solitary or cymose-paniculate, generally purple. Calyx 5-toothed, finely and equally many-
striate, tubular, several-bracted at the base. Petals 5, long-clawed, dentate or crenate.
Stamens 10. Styles 2. Ovary 1-celled, stipulate. Capsule cylindric or oblong, stalked,
dehiscent by 4 or 5 short teeth at the summit. Seeds compressed, laterally attached. Embryo
straight, eccentric. [Greek, the flower of Jove.]

Species about 200, natives of the Old World; one of Siberia extending into arctic America.
Type species : *Dianthus caryophyllus* L.

Annuals ; flowers clustered.
　Bracts broad, scarious.   1. *D. prolifer.*
　Bracts narrow, herbaceous, long-pointed.   2. *D. Armeria.*
Perennials.
　Flowers solitary ; leaves linear, short.   3. *D. deltoides.*
　Flowers clustered ; leaves lanceolate or ovate-lanceolate.   4. *D. barbatus.*

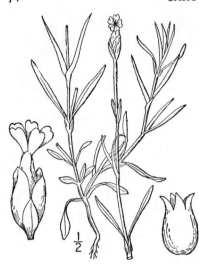

1. Dianthus prólifer L.   Proliferous or Childing Pink.   Fig. 1830.

Dianthus prolifer L. Sp. Pl. 410. 1753.

Annual, erect, slender, glabrous, 6′–15′ high, simple, or with few erect branches. Leaves distant, linear, erect, acute, ½″–1″ wide, 9″–15″ long; flowers small, pink, clustered in terminal oblong or obovoid heads, and appearing successively from behind the bracts, which are broad, ovate, scarious, imbricated, shining, obtuse or mucronate, equalling and concealing the calyx.

In waste places and ballast, Staten Island, N. Y., New Jersey and eastern Pennsylvania to Ohio and South Carolina. Adventive from Europe. Summer. Childing sweet-william.

2. Dianthus Armèria L.   Deptford Pink. Grass Pink.   Fig. 1831.

Dianthus Armeria L. Sp. Pl. 410. 1753.

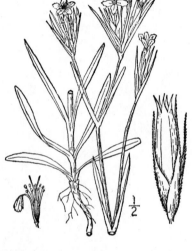

Annual, erect, stiff, finely pubescent, 6′–18′ high; branches few, nearly erect. Leaves linear, erect, acute or the lower obtusish, 1′–3′ long, 1″–1½″ wide; flowers small, pink with whitish dots, borne in terminal often dense clusters; bracts lanceolate-subulate, long-pointed, erect, mostly longer than the sharply-toothed calyx; capsule sometimes 5-toothed.

In fields and along roadsides, Quebec and southern Ontario to Iowa, Michigan, Virginia and Georgia. Naturalized from Europe. Summer.

3. Dianthus deltoìdes L.   Maiden or Meadow Pink.   Fig. 1832.

Dianthus deltoides L. Sp. Pl. 411. 1753.

Perennial, tufted, glabrous or somewhat hoary; stems ascending, 6′–15′ long; branches usually several, nearly erect. Leaves linear-lanceolate, 6″–9″ long, 1″ wide, those of the flowering stems erect, acutish, the lower obtuse and spreading; flowers pink or whitish, solitary at the ends of the stem and branches; petals dentate at the end; bracts ovate, pointed, about half as long as the calyx or less.

In waste places, Vermont, eastern Massachusetts and Connecticut to northern New York and Michigan. Adventive from Europe. Native also of western Asia. Spink. Summer.

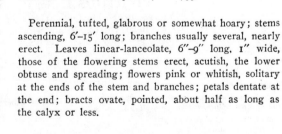

4. Dianthus barbàtus L.   Sweet William.   Bunch or French Pink.   Fig. 1833.

Dianthus barbatus L. Sp. Pl. 409. 1753.

Perennial, tufted, glabrous, stems erect, rather stout, 1°–2° high, branching above or sometimes unbranched. Leaves lanceolate or ovate-lanceolate, 1½–3′ long, 4″–9″ wide, acute or the basal ones oblong or obovate; bracts linear-filiform, about equalling the long-toothed calyx; flowers pink or whitish, in large terminal clusters.

In waste places, escaped from gardens, occasional in the Eastern and Middle States. Introduced from Europe. Snow-flake. London-tuft or -pride. Sweet-johns. Bloomy-down. Summer.

Family 25.   CERATOPHYLLÀCEAE A. Gray,
Ann. Lyc. N. Y. 4: 41. 1837.

HORNWORT FAMILY.

Submerged aquatics, with slender widely branching stems, and verticillate leaves, the monoecious or dioecious flowers solitary and sessile in the axils. Involucre many-parted, the segments entire or toothed. Perianth none. Stamens numerous, crowded on a flat or convex receptacle; anthers sessile or nearly so, linear-oblong, extrorse, the connective prolonged into a thick appendage beyond the sacs. Pistillate flowers with a superior 1-celled ovary; ovule 1, orthotropous, pendulous; style filiform, stigmatic at the summit. Fruit an indehiscent nut or achene. Endosperm none; embryo composed of 4 verticillate oval cotyledons, with a short hypocotyl and a plumule of several nodes and leaves.

The family contains only the following genus.

1. CERATOPHÝLLUM L. Sp. Pl. 992. 1753.

Leaves crowded in verticils, linear or filiform, spinulose-serrulate, forked. Sterile flowers with 10–20 stamens, the anthers about as long as the involucre. Fertile and sterile flowers generally at different nodes, but sometimes in opposite axils at the same node. Ovary and fruit somewhat longer than the involucre, the fruit beaked with the long persistent style.

One or possibly two species, widely distributed in fresh water, the following typical.

1. Ceratophyllum demérsum L.   Hornwort.   Hornweed.   Fig. 1834.

Ceratophyllum demersum L. Sp. Pl. 992. 1753.

Stem 2°–8° long, according to the depth of water. Leaves in verticils of 5′s–12′s, linear, 2–3 times forked, the ends of the segments capillary and rigid, 4″–12″ long; ripe fruit oval, 2″–3″ long with a straight or curved spine-like beak 2″–4″ long, smooth and spurless or with a long basal spur on each side, or tuberculate and with narrowly winged spiny margins or broadly winged without spines.

In ponds and streams, throughout North America except the extreme north. Cuba. Several species and varieties have been proposed, based on the spurs, spines or wings of the fruit, but none of them seem to be more than races. Morass-weed. June–July.

Family 26.   CABOMBÀCEAE A. Gray,
Ann. Lyc. N. Y. 4: 46. 1837.

WATER-SHIELD FAMILY.

Aquatic perennial herbs, with rootstocks, mucilage-coated stems, floating or immersed leaves, and solitary axillary flowers. Sepals 3, rarely 4. Petals 3, rarely 4. Stamens 3–18; anthers extrorse, the connective continuous with the filament. Carpels 2–18, distinct. Stigmas sessile or nearly so; ovules 2 or 3, orthotropous. Fruits indehiscent, coriaceous, separate. Seeds 1–3, borne on the dorsal suture; embryo at the base of fleshy endosperm; cotyledons fleshy; hypocotyl very short.

Two genera and about 5 species, widely distributed in fresh-water lakes and streams.

Leaves dissected, excepting the small floating ones ; stamens 3–6. 1. *Cabomba.*
Leaves peltate, entire, floating ; stamens 12–18. 2. *Brasenia.*

1. CABÓMBA Aubl. Pl. Guian. 1 : 321. 1775.

Stems slender, coated with gelatinous matter, branching. Leaves petioled, peltate, the floating ones small, entire; submerged ones opposite, palmately dissected into numerous

capillary segments. Flowers small, white or yellow. Sepals and petals 3. Stamens 3–6; filaments slender; anthers extrorse. Carpels 2–4. Stigmas small, terminal; ovules commonly 3, pendulous. Fruit coriaceous, indehiscent, about 3-seeded. [Guiana name.]

A genus of 4 species, natives of the warmer parts of America. Type species : *Cabomba aquatica* Aubl.

1. Cabomba caroliniàna A. Gray. Cabomba. Carolina Water-shield. Fig. 1835.

Cabomba caroliniana A. Gray, Ann. Lyc. N. Y. 4 : 47. 1837.

Stem several feet long, branching. Submerged leaves opposite or sometimes verticillate, petioled, 1'–2' broad, centrally peltate, repeatedly divided; floating ones alternate or opposite, linear-oblong, 6"–10" long; flowers long-peduncled from the upper axils, 6"–8" wide, white, or yellow at base within; petals obovate; ripened carpels 3, separate, flask-shaped.

In ponds and slow streams, Missouri and Illinois to North Carolina, south to Florida and Texas. May–Aug.

2. BRASÈNIA Schreb. Gen. Pl. 372. 1789.

Stem slender, several feet long, branching, covered with gelatinous matter as are the petioles, peduncles and lower leaf-surfaces. Leaves alternate, oval, entire, 2'–4' long, long-petioled, centrally peltate, floating, palmately veined. Flowers axillary, purple. Sepals and linear petals 3. Stamens 12–18; filaments filiform. Carpels 4–18, separate. Ovules 2 or 3, pendulous from the dorsal suture. Ripe carpels indehiscent, coriaceous, 1–2-seeded. [Name unexplained.]

A monotypic genus of continental North America, Cuba, eastern and tropical Asia, west tropical Africa, and Australia.

1. Brasenia Schréberi Gmel. Water-shield or Water-target. Fig. 1836.

Menyanthes nymphaeoides Thunb. Fl. Jap. 82. 1784. Not L. 1753.
Brasenia Schreberi Gmel. Syst. Veg. 1 : 853. 1796.
Hydropeltis purpurea Michx. Fl. Bor. Am. 1 : 324. *pl. 29.* 1803.
Brasenia peltata Pursh, Fl. Am. Sept. 389. 1814.
Brasenia purpurea Casp. in Engl. & Prantl, Nat. Pfl. Fam. 3 : Abt. 2, 6. 1890.

Rootstock slender. Leaves 2'–4' long, 1½'–2' wide, thick, rounded at each end; flowers 5"–6" in diameter, on long stout peduncles; fruit oblong, 3"–4" long.

In ponds and slow streams, locally distributed from Nova Scotia to Florida, Manitoba, Nebraska and Texas. Also in Cuba, Mexico, and on the Pacific Coast from California to Washington. Deer-food. Frog-leaf. Little water-lily. Summer.

Family 27. NELUMBONÀCEAE Lindl. Nat. Syst. Ed. 2, 13. 1836.

SACRED BEAN FAMILY.

Comprises only the following genus.

1. NELÚMBO [Tourn.] Adans. Fam. Pl. 2 : 76. 1763.

Large aquatic herbs, with thick rootstocks, long-petioled concave emersed or floating leaves, and small and scale like submerged ones borne sessile on the rootstock. Flowers large, showy, yellow, pink or white. Sepals 4 or 5, imbricate. Petals and stamens ∞, inserted on the calyx, caducous. Filaments more or less petaloid; anthers introrse. Carpels

∞, distinct, contained in pits in the large convex receptacle. Style short; ovules 1 or 2, pendulous or anatropous; endosperm none; cotyledons thick, fleshy. Nuts globose or oblong. [Ceylon name for *N. Nelumbo.*]

A genus of 2 or 3 species, one North American, one Jamaican, the other Asiatic and Australasian, known as Sacred Bean or Water-bean. Type species: *Nymphaea Nelumbo* L.

Flowers pale yellow; plant native.   1. *N. lutea.*
Flowers pink or white; plant introduced.   2. *N. Nelumbo.*

1. Nelumbo lùtea (Willd.) Pers. American Nelumbo or Lotus. Fig. 1837.

Nelumbium luteum Willd. Sp. Pl. 2: 1259. 1799.
Nelumbo lutea Pers. Syn. 1: 92. 1805.

Rootstock nearly horizontal, tuberiferous. Emersed leaves 1°–2° broad, nearly orbicular but often somewhat constricted in the middle, centrally peltate, raised high out of water or floating, prominently ribbed, glabrous above, more or less pubescent and lepidote beneath, the lower surface marked with an oblong, transverse area; petioles and peduncles thick, 3°–7° long, with several large air-canals; flowers pale yellow, 4′–10′ broad; petals concave, obovate, obtuse; anthers appendaged; fruit obconic or somewhat hemispheric, 3′–4′ long; seeds nearly globular, 6″ in diameter.

In rivers and lakes, locally distributed from Massachusetts to Minnesota, Nebraska and Louisiana. Cuba. *N. jamaicensis,* of Jamaica, closely resembles this species, but may be specifically distinct. Tubers and seeds farinaceous, edible. Great yellow water-lily. Water-chinkapin. Wankapin or yankapin. Duck-acorn. Rattle- or water-nut. July–Aug.

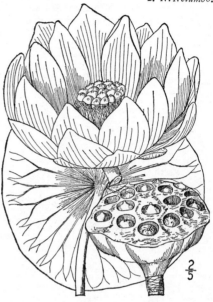

2. Nelumbo Nelúmbo (L.) Karst. Sacred Bean. Indian Lotus. Fig. 1838.

Nymphaea Nelumbo L. Sp. Pl. 511. 1753.
Nelumbo nucifera Gaertn. Fruct. & Sem. 1: 73. *pl. 19.* 1788.
Nelumbium speciosum Willd. Sp. Pl. 2: 1258. 1799.
N. Nelumbo Karst. Deutsch. Fl. 553. 1880–83.

Leaves 2°–3° in diameter, high exserted above the water or some of them floating, thin, concave, glaucous; petioles and peduncles 3°–6° long, glabrous or with scattered minute prickles; flowers 4′–10′ broad, pink or sometimes white; petals oblong or elliptic, obtuse; fruit obconic, 4′–5′ long, 3′–4′ in diameter; seeds oblong or ovoid.

Naturalized in ponds about Bordentown, N. J., where it was introduced by Mr. E. D. Sturtevant. Native of India, Persia, China, Japan and Australia. A superb plant, often cultivated. July–Aug.

Family 28. NYMPHAEÀCEAE DC. Propr. Med. Ed. 2, 119. 1816.

WATER LILY FAMILY.

Perennial acaulescent herbs, with more or less elongated often tuber-bearing rootstocks. Leaves alternate: blades leathery or those of submersed leaves membranous and delicate, all with a sinus at the base, petioled. Flowers perfect, terminating elongated scapes. Sepals 4–6, often green. Petals numerous, usually passing into staminodia or stamens, decaying. Androecium of numerous stamens. Anthers introrse, adnate. Gynoecium of several or many carpels united into a compound ovary. Stigmas united into a disk with radiating stigmatic lines.

Ovules very numerous on the walls of the ovary. Fruit a leathery several-seeded berry. Seeds often shining, with the embryo enclosed in a sac at the base of the fleshy endosperm.

Five genera and about 45 species, widely distributed in fresh water.
Petals small or minute; stamens hypogynous.   1. *Nymphaea.*
Petals large, numerous; stamens epigynous.   2 *Castalia.*

1. NYMPHAÈA [Tourn.] L. Sp. Pl. 510. 1753.

[Nuphar Sibth. & Smith, Fl. Graec. Prodr. 1 : 391   1806.]

Aquatic herbs, with cylindric thick horizontal rootstocks, and large cordate leaves with a deep sinus. Flowers showy, yellow, or sometimes purplish. Sepals 5–6, concave, thick. Petals ∞, small, stamen-like, hypogynous. Stamens ∞, hypogynous. Carpels ∞, many-ovuled, united into a compound pistil. Stigmas disciform, 8–24-radiate. Fruit ovoid, naked. Seeds with endosperm. [Greek, water-nymph.]

A genus of about 8 species, natives of the north temperate zone. Type species: *Nymphaea lutea* L.

Leaves broadly ovate or oval.
    Leaves 5′–12′ long; stigma 12–24-rayed; petals truncate, fleshy.   1. *N. advena.*
    Leaves 2′–4′ long; stigma 7–10-rayed; petals spatulate, thin.   2. *N. microphylla.*
Leaves narrowly ovate or ovate-lanceolate.   3. *N. sagittaefolia.*

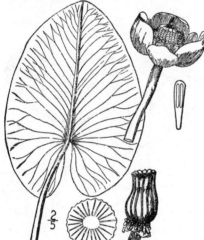

1. Nymphaea ádvena Soland. Large Yellow Pond Lily. Kelp. Fig. 1839.

Nymphaea advena Soland. in Ait. Hort. Kew. **2** : 226. 1789.
Nuphar advena R. Br. in Ait. Hort. Kew. Ed. 2, **3** : 295. 1811.
N. advena minor Morong, Bot. Gaz. **11** : 167. 1886.

Floating and emersed leaves 5′–12′ long, 5′–9′ broad, ovate or orbicular-oval, thick, the sinus 2′–5′ deep, generally open; submerged leaves, when present, thin-membranous, nearly orbicular, otherwise similar; petioles, peduncles and lower surfaces of the leaves often pubescent; flowers 1¾′–3½′ in diameter, depressed-globose, yellow or tinged with purple; sepals 6, oblong, about 1½″ long; petals fleshy, oblong, truncate, 4″–5″ long; stamens in 5–7 rows; anthers about the length of the filaments; stigmatic disc undulate, yellow, or pale red, rays 12–24; fruit ovoid, not deeply constricted into a neck, 1½′–2′ long, about 1′ thick.

In ponds and slow streams, Labrador and Nova Scotia to the Rocky Mountains, south to Florida, Texas and Utah. April–Sept. Beaver-root. Bonnets. Cow-, frog-, dog-, horse- or beaver-lily. Spatter-dock. Apparently consists of several races, or, as here described, includes more than one species.

Nymphaea rubrodísca (Morong) Greene, differing by fewer stigma-rays and spatulate petals, admitted as a species in our first edition, is probably a hybrid between *N. advena* and *N. microphylla.*

Nymphaea fratérna Miller & Standley, recently described from the pine-barrens of New Jersey, has smaller flowers and fruit than *N. advena.*

2. Nymphaea microphýlla Pers. Small Yellow Pond Lily. Fig. 1840.

Nymphaea lutea var. *Kalmiana* Michx. Fl. Bor. Am. **1** : 311. 1803.
Nymphaea microphylla Pers. Syn. **2** : 63. 1807.
Nuphar Kalmianum R. Br. in Ait. Hort. Kew. Ed. 2, **3** : 295. 1811.
N. Kalmiana Sims, Bot. Mag. *pl. 1243.* 1809.

Leaves 2′–4′ long, 1′–3′ broad, the sinus open or closed, commonly more or less pubescent beneath; submerged ones always present, membranous, orbicular, larger; flowers 1′ in diameter or less, yellow; sepals 5; petals thin and delicate, 2″ long; stamens in 3 or 4 rows, narrowly linear, the anther one-fourth the length of the filaments; stigmatic disk crenate or stellate, 2″–3″ broad, 6–7-rayed, dark red; fruit ovoid, 6″–7″ long, with a short neck.

In ponds and slow streams, Newfoundland to southern New York and Pennsylvania. Summer, flowering later than the preceding.

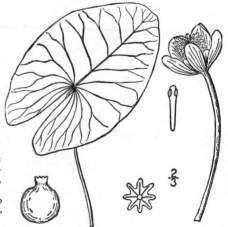

3. Nymphaea sagittaefòlia Walt. Arrow-leaved Pond Lily. Fig. 1841.

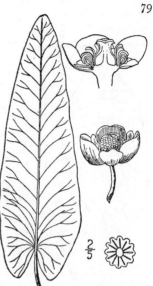

Nymphaea sagittaefolia Walt. Fl. Car. 155. 1788.

Nuphar sagittaefolia Pursh, Fl. Am. Sept. 370. 1814.

Floating leaves narrowly ovate or ovate-lanceolate, glabrous, obtuse, 8'-15' long, 2'-3' wide; submerged ones numerous, similar, but membranous and commonly larger; flowers yellow, about 1' broad; sepals 5; petals broadened above, 3" long; stamens in 4 or 5 rows, the filaments about equalling the anthers; stigmatic disk crenate, 11-15-rayed; fruit ovoid, not constricted into a neck, about 1' long.

In ponds and streams, eastern North Carolina and South Carolina. Recorded as occurring in ponds (now drained) in southern Indiana and Illinois. Plants of the Gulf States formerly referred to this species prove to be distinct. Alligator-bonnets. Summer.

2. CASTÀLIA Salisb. in Konig & Sims, Ann. Bot. 2 : 71. 1805.

Aquatic herbs, with horizontal perennial rootstocks, floating leaves and showy flowers. Sepals 4. Petals ∞, imbricated in few to many series, inserted on the ovary, gradually passing into stamens; stamens ∞, the exterior with large petaloid filaments and short anthers, the interior with linear filaments and elongated anthers. Carpels ∞, united into a compound pistil with radiating linear projecting stigmas. Fruit globose, covered with the bases of the petals, ripening under water. [A spring of Parnassus.]

About 40 species, of wide geographic distribution. Type species: *Castalia pudica* Salisb.

Flowers 3'-5½' broad, fragrant; leaves orbicular to reniform, purplish beneath.	1. *C. odorata.*
Flowers 4'-9' broad, not fragrant; leaves orbicular, green both sides.	2. *C. tuberosa.*
Flowers 1'-1½' broad not fragrant; leaves oval.	3. *C. tetragona.*

1. Castalia odoràta (Dryand.) Woodv. & Wood. Sweet-scented White Water Lily. Pond Lily. Water Nymph. Water Cabbage. Fig. 1842.

Nymphaea odorata Dryand. in Ait. Hort. Kew. 2 : 227. 1789.
Castalia pudica Salisb. in Konig. & Sims, Ann. Bot. 2 : 72. 1805.
Castalia odorata Woodv. & Wood in Rees' Cyclop. 6: no. 1. 1806.
Nymphaea odorata var. *minor* Sims, Bot. Mag. *pl. 1652.* 1814.
Nymphaea odorata var. *rosea* Pursh, Fl. Am. Sept. 369. 1814.

Rootstock thick, simple or with few branches. Leaves floating, orbicular or nearly so, 4'-12' in diameter, glabrous, green and shining above, purple and more or less pubescent beneath, cordate-cleft or reniform, the sinus open but sometimes narrow; petioles and peduncles slender, with 4 main air-channels; flowers white, or sometimes pink, 3'-6' broad, fragrant; petals numerous, in many rows, narrowly oblong, obtuse; fruit globose, or slightly depressed; seeds stipitate, oblong, shorter than the aril.

In ponds and slow streams, Newfoundland to Manitoba, south to Florida, Louisiana and Kansas. Toad-lily. June-Sept.

2. Castalia tuberòsa (Paine) Greene. Tuberous White Water Lily. Fig. 1843.

Nymphaea tuberosa Paine, Cat. Pl. Oneida Co., N. Y. 132. 1865.
Castalia tuberosa Greene, Bull. Torr. Club 15: 84. 1888.

Rootstock thick, with numerous lateral tuberous-thickened branches, which become detached and propagate the plant. Leaves orbicular, 5′–12′ in diameter, floating, sometimes slightly pubescent beneath, green both sides, the veins very prominent on the lower surface; sinus open or closed; petioles stout; flowers pure white, 4′–9′ broad, inodorous or very slightly scented; petals oblong, in many rows, broader than those of *C. odorata*, obtuse; fruit depressed-globose; seeds globose-ovoid, sessile, longer than or about equalling the aril.

Lake Champlain, west through the Great Lakes to Michigan, south to Delaware and eastern Nebraska and Arkansas. Summer.

3. Castalia tetragòna (Georgi) Lawson. Small White Water Lily. Fig. 1844.

Nymphaea tetragona Georgi, Reise in Russ. Reichs, 1: 220. 1775.
Castalia pygmaea Salisb. Parad. Lond. *pl.* 68. 1807.
C. Leibergii Morong. Bot. Gaz. 13: 134. 1888.
Castalia tetragona Lawson, Trans. Roy. Soc. Canada 6: Sec. IV. 112. 1888.

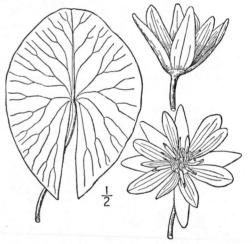

Leaves floating, oval or oblong, 2′–4′ long, 1½′–3′ wide, green above, green or purplish beneath, the basal lobes acute or rounded; sinus open, narrow; petioles and peduncles nearly or quite glabrous; flowers white, inodorous, 1′–2′ broad; petals in about 2 rows, faintly striped with purple, obtuse or acutish, oblong or obovate, thin, about the length of the sepals.

In the Misinaibi River, Ontario (R. Bell); in ponds along the Severn River, Keewatin (J. M. Macoun); near Granite Station, northern Idaho (Leiberg). Also in Siberia, Japan and the Himalayas. Summer.

Family 29. MAGNOLIÀCEAE J. St. Hil. Expos. Fam. 2: 74. 1805.

MAGNOLIA FAMILY.

Trees or shrubs with pinnately veined, alternate, entire or rarely lobed leaves, large solitary flowers, and bitter aromatic bark. Sepals and petals arranged in 3 or more series of 3's, hypogynous, deciduous. Stamens ∞; anthers adnate. Carpels ∞, separate or coherent, borne on the surface of the elongated receptacle, ripening into an aggregate fruit composed of 1–2-seeded dry or fleshy follicles or achenes. Seeds 1 or 2 in each carpel; endosperm fleshy; embryo very small.

About 10 genera and 75 species, of wide geographic distribution.

Anthers introrse; leaves entire, or with 2 basal lobes; carpels follicular.   1. *Magnolia.*
Anthers extrorse; leaves lobed or truncate; carpels samaroid.   2. *Liriodendron.*

1. MAGNÒLIA L. Sp. Pl. 535. 1753.

Trees or shrubs. Leaves large and generally thick, entire. Buds covered with conduplicate sheathing stipules. Flowers large, fragrant. Sepals 3, petaloid. Petals 6–12, imbricated in 2–4 series. Anthers linear, introrse. Carpels spiked or capitate on the elevated or elongated receptacle, 2-ovuled, forming follicles at maturity. Seeds fleshy, anatropous, suspended from the ripe cones by slender filamentous threads. [In honor of Pierre Magnol, 1638–1715, Professor of Botany in Montpellier.]

A genus of about 25 species, natives of eastern North America, the West Indies, Mexico, eastern Asia and the Himalayas. Type species: *Magnolia virginiana* L.

Leaves auriculate, glabrous.   1. *M. Fraseri.*
Leaves cordate, white-pubescent beneath.   2. *M. macrophylla.*
Leaves acute at base.
  Leaves 8′–20′ long, light green and somewhat pubescent beneath.   3. *M. tripetala.*
  Leaves 3′–6′ long, glaucous beneath.   4. *M. virginiana.*
Leaves rounded or truncate at the base, thin.   5. *M. acuminata.*

1. Magnolia Fràseri Walt. Fraser's Magnolia. Long- or Ear-leaved Umbrella-tree. Fig. 1845.

Magnolia Fraseri Walt. Fl. Car. 159. 1788.

Magnolia auriculata Lam. Encycl. 3 : 673. 1789.

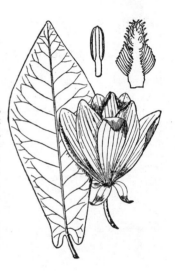

A tree 25°–50° high, the trunk 5′–2° in diameter, straight, the branches widely spreading. Leaf-buds glabrous; leaves clustered at the ends of the branches, auriculate, 6′–20′ long, 3′–8′ broad, elongated-obovate or oblong, contracted below, glabrous, the lower surface light green, the upper surface darker; petioles slender, 1′–3′ long; flowers white, 3′–8′ broad; petals spatulate or obovate, obtuse, much longer than the sepals; cone of fruit 3′–4′ long, rose-colored when mature.

In mountain woods, Virginia and Kentucky to Florida and Mississippi. Heart-wood soft, brown; sap-wood white. Weight per cubic foot 31 lbs. North Carolina-bay. Cucumber-tree. Indian-physic. Water-lily tree. May–June.

2. Magnolia macrophýlla Michx. Great-leaved Magnolia. Large-leaved Umbrella-tree, or Cucumber-tree. Fig. 1846.

Magnolia macrophylla Michx. Fl. Bor. Am. 1 : 327. 1803.

A tree 20°–60° high, the trunk 6′–20′ in diameter, bark gray. Leaf-blades silky-pubescent; leaves oblong or obovate, blunt, cordate, 1°–3½° long, 8′–14′ broad, glabrous and green above, glaucous-white and pubescent beneath; petioles stout, 2′–4′ long; flowers 8″–15′ in diameter, white with a large purple center; petals ovate-oblong, obtuse, thrice the length of the rounded sepals; cone of fruit ovoid-cylindric, 4′–6′ long, bright rose-colored at maturity.

In woods, southeastern Kentucky to North Carolina, Florida, Arkansas and Louisiana. Heart-wood brown, satiny, hard; sap-wood light yellow; weight per cubic foot 33 lbs. Elk-bark. Silver-leaf. Big-bloom. May–June.

3. Magnolia tripétala L.   Umbrella- or Cucumber-tree.   Elk-wood.   Fig. 1847.

Magnolia tripetala L. Sp. Pl. Ed. 2, 756.   1763.
Magnolia virginiana var. *tripetala* L. Sp. Pl. 536.   1753.
Magnolia umbrella Lam. Encycl. 3 : 673.   1789.

A tree 20°-45° high, trunk 4′-18′ in diameter. Leaf-buds glabrous; leaves clustered at the summits of the flowering branches, 1°-1½° long, 4′-8′ wide, obovate to oblanceolate, acute, cuneate at the base, dark green and glabrous above, light green and more or less pubescent beneath, at least when young; petioles stout, 1′-3′ long; flowers 8′-10′ in diameter, white, slightly odorous; sepals broad, reflexed, early deciduous; petals oblong-lanceolate or obovate-lanceolate, acutish; cone of fruit 4′-6′ long, rose-colored when mature.

In woods, southeastern Pennsylvania to Georgia, west to Missouri, Arkansas and Mississippi. Heart-wood brown, soft; sap-wood white; weight per cubic foot 28 lbs. The name *tripetala* is in allusion to the 3 petaloid petals.   May.

4. Magnolia virginiàna L.   Laurel Magnolia.   Sweet Bay.   Fig. 1848.

M. virginiana and var. *glauca* L. Sp. Pl. 535.   1753.
Magnolia glauca L. Sp. Pl. Ed. 2, 755.   1763.

A shrub, or tree 15°-75° high, trunk 5′-3½° in diameter. Leaf-buds pubescent; leaves scattered along the flowering branches, 3′-6′ long, 1′-2′ broad, oval or oblong, obtuse or blunt-acuminate, acute at the base, coriaceous, dark green above, glaucous and more or less pubescent beneath, deciduous in the North, persistent in the South; petioles about 1′ long; flowers white, depressed-globose, deliciously fragrant, 2′-3′ in diameter; sepals spreading, obtuse, nearly as large as the obovate rounded petals; cone of fruit oblong, 1½′-2′ high, pink.

In swamps and swampy woods, eastern Massachusetts, Long Island, Lebanon County, Pa., and southward, mainly east of the Alleghanies to Florida, west through the Gulf States to Arkansas and Texas. Heart-wood soft, reddish-brown; sap-wood nearly white; weight 31 lbs. White-bay, swamp- or white-laurel. Swamp-magnolia or -sassafras. Beaver-tree. Indian-bark. May–June.

5. Magnolia acumináta L.   Cucumber-tree.   Mountain Magnolia.   Fig. 1849.

Magnolia virginiana var. *acuminata* L. Sp. Pl. 536.   1753.

Magnolia acuminata L. Sp. Pl. Ed. 2, 756.   1763.

A tree 60°-90° high, the trunk up to 4½° in diameter. Leaf-buds silky-pubescent; leaves scattered along the branches, 6′-10′ long, 3′-4′ wide, thin, oval, acute or somewhat acuminate, rounded or truncate at the base, light green and more or less pubescent on the lower surface, especially along the veins; petioles 1′-1½′ long; flowers oblong-campanulate, greenish-yellow, 2′ high; petals obovate or oblong, much longer than the spreading deciduous sepals; cone of fruit cylindric, 3′-4′ long, about 1′ in diameter, rose-colored when mature.

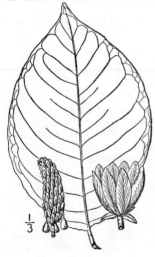

In woods, New York and Ontario to Illinois, Missouri, Georgia, Mississippi and Arkansas. Heart-wood soft, yellowish-brown; sap-wood lighter. Weight per cubic foot 29 lbs. Ascends to 4200 ft. in Virginia. Yellow or black linn. May–June.

2. LIRIODÉNDRON L. Sp. Pl. 535. 1753.

A large forest tree. Leaves alternate, truncate or broadly emarginate, 4–6-lobed or rarely entire, recurved on the petiole in the laterally compressed obtuse buds. Stipules united at the base. Flowers large, slightly fragrant. Sepals 3, petaloid, reflexed. Petals 6, connivent. Anthers linear, extrorse. Carpels spiked on the elongated receptacle, 2-ovuled, samaroid, 1–2-seeded; seeds pendulous by a short slender funiculus at maturity. [Greek, a tree bearing lilies.]

Two species, natives of eastern North America and China, the following one the generic type.

1. Liriodendron Tulipífera L.   Tulip-tree. Lime-tree.   White-wood.   Fig. 1850.

Liriodendron Tulipifera L. Sp. Pl. 535. 1753.

A magnificent tree 60°–190° high with diverging curved branches, the trunk 4°–12° in diameter. Leaves glabrous, very broadly ovate or nearly orbicular in outline, truncate or broadly notched at the apex, truncate, rounded or cordate at the base, 3′–6′ long with 2 apical and 2–4 basal lobes, or occasionally entire; flowers about 2′ high, erect, greenish-yellow, orange-colored within; petals obovate, obtuse, about equalling the reflexed sepals; cone of fruit dry, oblong, acute, 3′ long.

In woods, Vermont to Rhode Island, Florida, Michigan, Arkansas and Mississippi. May–June. Wood soft, yellowish or brownish; sap-wood nearly white. Weight per cubic foot 26 lbs. Cucumber-tree. Blue-, white- or yellow-poplar. Lynn- or saddle-tree. Hickory- or tulip-poplar. Basswood. Saddle-leaf. Canoe-wood.

Family 30. ANNONÀCEAE DC. Syst. 1: 463. 1818.

CUSTARD-APPLE FAMILY.

Trees or shrubs, generally aromatic, with alternate entire pinnately veined leaves. Stipules none. Sepals 3 (rarely 2), valvate or rarely imbricate. Petals about 6, arranged in 2 series. Stamens ∞; anthers adnate, extrorse. Carpels ∞, separate or coherent, mainly fleshy in fruit. Seeds large, anatropous; embryo minute; endosperm copious, wrinkled.

About 46 genera and 550 species, mostly in the tropics, a few in the temperate zones.

1. ASÍMINA Adans. Fam. Pl. 2: 365. 1763.

Small trees, or shrubs, with alternate leaves and lateral or axillary nodding flowers. Buds naked. Sepals 3, ovate, valvate. Petals 6, arranged in 2 series, valvate or imbricated in the bud, those of the outer series the larger when mature. Receptacle subglobose. Stamens and carpels 3–15. Style oblong, stigmatic along the inner side; ovules numerous, in 2 rows. Fruit, large fleshy oblong berries. Seeds large, flat, horizontally placed, enclosed in fleshy arils. [From the aboriginal name *Assimin.*]

About 7 species, natives of eastern and southeastern North America, the following typical.

1. Asimina tríloba (L.) Dunal.   North American Papaw.   False banana.   Fig. 1851.

Annona triloba L. Sp. Pl. 537. 1753.
Asimina triloba Dunal, Mon. Anon. 83. 1817.

A tall shrub or tree 10°–45° high, the trunk 5′–10′ in diameter. Shoots and young leaves dark-pubescent, becoming glabrous at maturity; leaves obovate, acute, 6′–12′ long, cuneate or rounded at the base; petioles 4″–6″ long; flowers axillary, on shoots of the preceding year, appearing with the leaves, 1′–1½′ in diameter, dark purple; sepals ovate, 4″–6″ long, densely dark-pubescent, as are the short peduncles; outer petals spreading, nearly orbicular, slightly exceeding the ovate inner ones; stamens numerous, short; fruit a fleshy berry, 3′–7′ long, 1′–2′ thick, sweet, edible and brown when ripe, pendulous, several on a thick peduncle.

Along streams, southwestern Ontario and western New York, Pennsylvania and western New Jersey to Michigan, Florida, Kansas and Texas. March–April, the fruit mature in October. Wood light, soft, weak, greenish-yellow. Weight per cubic foot 24 lbs. Custard-apple. Fetid shrub.

Family 31. **RANUNCULÀCEAE** Juss. Gen. 231. 1789.

CROWFOOT FAMILY.

Annual or perennial herbs, or rarely climbing shrubs, with acrid sap. Leaves alternate (except in *Clematis*), simple or compound. Stipules none, but the base of the petiole often clasping or sheathing. Pubescence, when present, composed of simple hairs. Sepals 3–15, generally caducous, often petal-like, imbricate, except in *Clematis*. Petals about the same number (occasionally more), or wanting. Flowers regular or irregular. Stamens ∞, hypogynous, their anthers innate. Carpels ∞ or rarely solitary, 1-celled, 1–many-ovuled. Ovules anatropous. Fruit achenes, follicles or berries. Seeds with endosperm.

About 35 genera and 1100 species, distributed throughout the world; not abundant in the tropics.

* Carpels several-ovuled (1-2-ovuled in nos. 1 and 8); fruit a follicle or berry; sepals imbricated in the bud. (HELLEBOREAE.)

Flowers regular; leaves palmately nerved or palmately compound.
  Petals wanting.
    Carpels ripening into a head of red berries.   1. *Hydrastis.*
    Carpels ripening into a head of dry follicles.   2. *Caltha.*
  Petals present, narrow or small, linear, flat.   3. *Trollius.*
  Petals present, narrow or small, tubular, at least at the base.
    Sepals persistent; stem tall, leafy.   4. *Helleborus.*
    Sepals deciduous; stem scape-like, bearing one leaf.   5. *Eranthis.*
Flowers regular; leaves ternately or pinnately compound or decompound.
  Petals not spurred.
    Low herbs with solitary or panicled flowers.
      Carpels and follicles stalked.   6. *Coptis.*
      Carpels and follicles sessile.   7. *Isopyrum.*
    Low shrub with racemose flowers, the fruits follicles.   8. *Xanthorrhiza.*
    Tall erect herbs with racemose flowers.
      Fruit berries.   9. *Actaea.*
      Fruit follicles.   10. *Cimicifuga.*
  Petals prolonged backward into hollow spurs.   11. *Aquilegia.*
Flowers irregular.
  Posterior sepal spurred.   12. *Delphinium.*
  Posterior sepal hooked helmet-like.   13. *Aconitum.*

** Carpels 1-ovuled; fruit an achene.

Sepals imbricated in the bud. (ANEMONEAE.)
  Flowers subtended by involucres remote from the calyx or close under it.
    Styles short, glabrous or pubescent, or none.
      Involucre remote from the calyx; styles short, subulate.   14. *Anemone.*
      Involucre of 3 simple sessile leaves close under the flower.   15. *Hepatica.*
      Involucre of 3 compound sessile leaves; leaflets stalked; stigma sessile.   16. *Syndesmon.*
    Styles elongated, densely plumose.   17. *Pulsatilla.*
  Flowers not subtended by involucres.
    Small annual herbs; leaves basal, linear; sepals spurred.   18. *Myosurus.*
    Low or tall herbs, mostly with both basal and stem leaves; sepals spurless.
      Petals none; leaves palmately lobed.   19. *Trautvettaria.*
      Petals present, bearing a nectariferous pit at the base of the blade.
        Achenes compressed, smooth, papillose or spiny; flowers yellow.   20. *Ranunculus.*
        Achenes transversely wrinkled; flowers white.   21. *Batrachium.*
        Achenes swollen, smooth; sepals 3; petals mostly 8.   22. *Ficaria.*
        Achenes compressed or terete, longitudinally nerved.   23. *Halerpestes.*
      Petals none; leaves ternately decompound.   24. *Thalictrum.*
      Petals present, with no nectar-bearing pit; leaves dissected.   25. *Adonis.*
Sepals valvate in the bud; leaves opposite. (CLEMATIDEAE.)
  Petals none.
    Sepals and stamens spreading; flowers panicled.   26. *Clematis.*
    Sepals and stamens erect or ascending; flowers mostly solitary.   27. *Viorna.*
  Petals present, small, spatulate.   28. *Atragene.*

1. HYDRÁSTIS Ellis; L. Syst. Ed. 10, 1088. 1759.

Erect perennial pubescent herbs, with palmately lobed reniform leaves, and small solitary greenish-white flowers. Sepals 3, petaloid, falling away at anthesis. Petals none. Stamens numerous. Carpels ∞, each bearing two ovules near the middle, and in fruit forming a head of 1-2-seeded crimson berries, somewhat resembling a raspberry; stigma flat. [Greek, water-acting, from its supposed drastic properties.]

Two known species, the typical one of eastern North America, the other Japanese.

1. Hydrastis canadénsis L. Orange-root. Golden Seal. Fig. 1852.

Hydrastis canadensis L. Syst. Ed. 10, 1088. 1759.

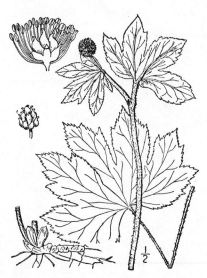

Perennial from a thick yellow rootstock, about 1° high. Basal leaf long-petioled, 5'-8' broad, palmately 5-9-lobed, the lobes broad, acute, sharply and unequally serrate; cauline leaves 2, borne at the summit of the stem, the upper one subtending the greenish-white flower, which is 4"-5" broad when expanded; filaments widened, about 2" long; anthers oblong, obtuse; head of fruit ovoid, blunt, about 8" long, the fleshy carpels tipped with a short curved beak.

In woods, Connecticut to Minnesota, western Ontario, Georgia, Missouri and Kansas. Ascends to 2500 ft. in Virginia. April. Called also yellow puccoon, yellow-root, turmeric-root, yellow Indian paint. Indian-dye, -iceroot or -turmeric. Ohio cucuma. Eye-balm or -root. Yellow eye. Ground-raspberry.

2. CÁLTHA [Rupp.] L. Sp. Pl. 558. 1753.

Succulent herbs, with simple entire or crenate mostly basal cordate or auriculate leaves. Flowers yellow, white or pink. Sepals large, deciduous, petal-like. Petals none. Stamens numerous, obovoid. Carpels numerous or few, sessile, bearing ovules in 2 rows along the ventral suture, in fruit forming follicles; stigmas nearly sessile. [Latin name of the Marigold.]

A genus of beautiful marsh plants, comprising about 15 species, distributed through the temperate and arctic regions of both hemispheres. In addition to those here described, four or five others are found on the western side of the continent. Type species: *Caltha palustris* L.

Stems erect or ascending; flowers yellow.
    Leaves cordate, generally with a narrow sinus; flowers ¾'-1½' wide.   1. *C. palustris.*
    Leaves flabelliform with a broad sinus; flowers 6"-9" wide.   2. *C. flabellifolia.*
Stems floating or creeping; flowers white or pink.   3. *C. natans.*

1. Caltha palústris L. Marsh-marigold. Meadow-gowan. Fig. 1853.

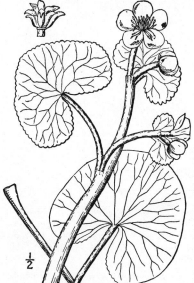

Caltha palustris L. Sp. Pl. 558. 1753.

Stout, glabrous, stem hollow, erect or ascending, 1°-2° high, branching and bearing several flowers. Basal leaves on long and broad petioles, cordate or reniform, 2'-7' wide, with a narrow sinus, entire, crenate or dentate, the upper shorter-petioled or sessile, with nearly truncate bases; flowers bright yellow, 1'-1½' broad; sepals oval, obtuse; follicles 3-12 or even more, compressed, 5"-6" long, slightly curved outward, many-seeded.

In swamps and meadows, Newfoundland to South Carolina, west to Saskatchewan and Nebraska. Ascends to 2500 ft. in Virginia. Locally called cowslip and used as a spring vegetable. April-June. Old English names, water-dragon, water-, mire-, horse- or may-blobs. Meadow-buttercups. American or spring cowslips. Capers. Cow-lily. Crowfoot. Coltsfoot. King-cup. Open or water gowan. Soldiers-buttons. Palsy-wort. Great bitter-flower. Meadow-bouts. Boots. Crazy-bet. Gools. Bull-flower. Drunkards. Water-goggles.

Caltha radicans Forst., which roots at the lower nodes of the stem, and has somewhat smaller flowers, is apparently a race of this species, mostly of high boreal range.

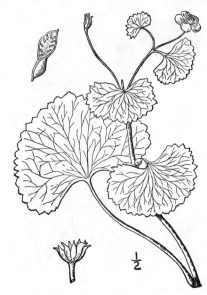

2. Caltha flabellifòlia Pursh. Mountain Marsh-marigold. Fig. 1854.

Caltha flabellifolia Pursh, Fl. Am. Sept. 390. 1814.

Caltha palustris var. *flabellifolia* T. & G. Fl. N. A. 1 : 27. 1838.

Weak, slender, reclining or ascending, $1°-1\frac{1}{2}°$ long, glabrous. Basal leaves $2'-4'$ broad, long-petioled, flabelliform or reniform, with a wide open sinus; the upper sessile or short-petioled, similar or with truncate bases, all crenate or dentate; flowers yellow, $6''-9''$ wide, solitary or 2–3 together; sepals oval; achenes 4–10, about $4''$ long, compressed.

In cold shaded mountain springs, Pocono plateau of Pennsylvania and northern New Jersey to Maryland and recorded from New York. Strikingly different from the preceding in habit and appearance. June–July.

3. Caltha nàtans Pall. Floating Marsh-marigold. Fig. 1855.

Caltha natans Pall. Reise Russ. 3 : 284. 1776.

Stems slender, floating or creeping in wet places, rooting at the nodes, $6'-18'$ long, branching. Lower and basal leaves slender-petioled, cordate-reniform, $1'-2'$ wide, crenate or entire, thin, cordate with a narrow sinus; upper leaves short-petioled, smaller; flowers white or pink, $5''-9''$ broad; sepals oval, obtusish; follicles several or numerous, rather densely capitate, about $2''$ long, the beak short and straight.

In pools and streams, Tower, Mich., Athabasca, arctic America and northern Asia. Summer.

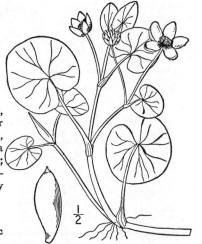

3. TRÓLLIUS L. Sp. Pl. 556. 1753.

Erect or ascending perennial herbs, with palmately divided or lobed leaves, thickened fibrous roots, and large usually solitary yellowish, white, or purplish flowers. Sepals 5–15, petaloid, deciduous. Petals $5-\infty$, small, unguiculate, linear, with a nectariferous pit at the base of the blade. Carpels $5-\infty$, sessile, many-ovuled, forming a head of follicles in fruit. Stamens numerous. [Old German, *trol,* something round.]

About 12 species, mainly inhabiting marshy places, natives of the north temperate zone. Besides the following, another occurs in western North America. Type species : *Trollius europaeus* L.

1. Trollius láxus Salisb. American Globe-flower. Fig. 1856.

Trollius americanus Muhl. Trans. Amer. Phil. Soc. **3** : 172, name only. 1791.
Trollius laxus Salisb. Trans. Linn. Soc. **8** : 303. 1803.

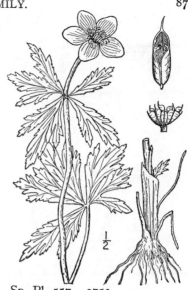

Stems slender, weak, ascending, 1°–2° long. Leaves all but the upper petioled (the lower petioles sometimes a foot long), palmately 5–7-parted, 2'–4' wide, the segments obovate, cuneate, lobed, cleft or toothed; flowers generally solitary, 1½' broad; sepals 5–7, ovate or obovate, obtuse, yellowish-green, spreading; petals 15–25, minute, much shorter than the numerous stamens; filaments filiform; anthers linear, 1" long; head of fruit nearly an inch broad, the follicles 4" long, each tipped with a straight subulate beak of one-fourth its length.

In swamps, New Hampshire (?), Connecticut to Delaware, west to Michigan. May–July.

T. albiflòrus (A. Gray) Rydb., of the Rocky Mountain region, differs in having white sepals.

4. HELLÉBORUS [Tourn.] L. Sp. Pl. 557. 1753.

Erect perennial herbs, with large palmately divided leaves, the basal long-petioled, the upper sessile and sometimes reduced to bracts. Flowers large, white, greenish or yellowish. Sepals 5, broad, petaloid, mainly persistent. Petals 8–10, small, unguiculate, tubular. Stamens ∞. Carpels generally few, sessile, in fruit forming several-seeded capsules, which are dehiscent at the apex at maturity. [The classical name for *H. orientalis;* derivation unknown.]

A genus of coarse herbs, comprising about 15 species, natives of Europe and western Asia. Type species : *Helleborus niger* L.

1. Helleborus víridis L. Green Hellebore. Fig. 1857.

Helleborus viridis L. Sp. Pl. 558. 1753.

Stout, erect, 1°–2° high, glabrous. Basal leaves 8'–12' broad, on petioles 6'–10' long, palmately divided into 7–11 oblong acute sharply serrate segments 3'–4' long; stem hardly exceeding the basal leaves, and bearing several sessile similar leaves near the top subtending the large drooping yellowish-green flowers; sepals broadly oblong, obtuse, spreading, about 1' long; petals tubular, 2-lipped, 2" long; stamens widened; anthers oblong, obtuse; pods 8" long, tipped with a slender beak one-third their length or longer.

In waste places, locally adventive from Europe in New York, New Jersey, Pennsylvania and West Virginia. Christmas-rose [properly *H. niger*]. Chris-root. May.

5. ERÁNTHIS Salisb. Trans. Linn. Soc. **8** : 303. 1803.

[CAMMARUM Hill, Brit. Herb. 47, *pl. 7.* Hyponym. 1756.]

Low herbs, with perennial tuberiferous rootstocks. Cauline leaf one, borne near the summit of the stem, sessile or amplexicaul, immediately subtending the large yellow flower. Sepals 5–8, narrow, petaloid, deciduous Petals, small two-lipped nectaries. Stamens numerous. Carpels commonly few, stipitate, many-ovuled, in fruit forming a head of follicles. [Greek, flower of spring.]

A genus of about 5 species, natives of Europe and the mountains of Asia, the following typical.

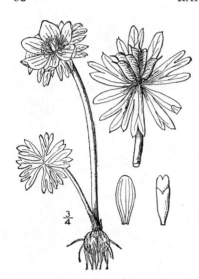

1. Eranthis hyemàlis (L.) Salisb. Winter Aconite or Hellebore. Fig. 1858.

Helleborus hyemalis L. Sp. Pl. 557. 1753.

Eranthis hyemalis Salisb. Trans. Linn. Soc. 8 : 304.   1803.

Cammarum hyemale Greene, Pittonia 3 : 152. 1897.

Erect, simple, 5′–8′ high from a tuberous-thick-ened rootstock; roots fibrous. Basal leaves long-petioled, 1½′ broad, divided and cleft into numerous linear or oblong lobes; cauline leaf similar, invo-lucrate, sessile, clasping; flower solitary, 1½′ wide, sessile; sepals 5–9, membranous, obovate, obtuse, occasionally lobed; petals several, clawed, 2-lipped; stamens numerous; filaments filiform; anthers ob-long, obtuse; carpels several, stipitate; follicles com-pressed, 5″ long, tipped with a sharp beak.

Naturalized from Europe at Bartram's Garden, Phila-delphia, and at Media, Pa. Wolf's-bane. Christmas-flower. February.

6. CÓPTIS Salisb. Trans. Linn. Soc. 8 : 305. 1803.

Low herbs, with slender perennial rootstocks, basal compound or divided leaves, and scapose white flowers. Sepals 5–7, petaloid, deciduous; petals 5–7, small, linear, cucullate. Stamens numerous. Carpels stipitate, few, in fruit forming an umbel of follicles. [Name from the Greek, referring to the cut or divided leaves.]

A genus of about 9 species, inhabiting the cooler portions of the north temperate zone. In addition to the following, three others are found on the Pacific Coast of North America. Type species : *Coptis trifolia* (L.) Salisb.

1. Coptis trifòlia (L.) Salisb. Gold-thread. Fig. 1859.

Helleborus trifolius L. Sp. Pl. Ed. 2, 784. 1762.

Coptis trifolia Salisb. Trans. Linn. Soc. 8 : 305. 1803.

Isopyrum trifolium Britton, Bull. Torr. Club 18 : 265. 1891.

Tufted, glabrous, 3′–6′ high from a slender or filiform yellow bitter rootstock. Leaves all basal, evergreen, long-petioled, the blade reni-form, 1′–2′ broad, 3-divided; petioles very slen-der; segments broadly obovate, cuneate, obtuse, prominently veined, crenate or slightly lobed, dark green and shining above, paler beneath, the teeth mucronate; scape 1-flowered, occasionally 2-flowered, slender; sepals oblong, obtuse; petals small, club-shaped; follicles 3–7, about 3″ long, borne on stipes of about their own length, spread-ing, tipped with a beak 1″–1½″ long.

In damp mossy woods, and bogs, Newfoundland to Maryland and eastern Tennessee, Iowa, Minnesota, British Columbia and Alaska. Ascends to 3500 ft. in the Adirondacks. Called also canker-root, mouth-root, yellow-root. May–Aug.

7. ISOPÝRUM L. Sp. Pl. 557. 1753.

Slender glabrous herbs, with ternately decompound leaves, and solitary or panicled white flowers. Sepals 5 or 6, petaloid, deciduous. Petals 5, nectariform or none. Stamens numerous. Carpels 2–20, sessile (stalked in a western species), several-ovuled, forming a head of follicles in fruit. [Old Greek name for some *Fumaria*.]

A genus of about 15 species, natives of the north temperate zone. Besides the following, there are 3 other North American species, natives of the Pacific Coast. Type species: *Isopyrum rhalictroides* L.

1. Isopyrum biternàtum (Raf.) T. & G.
False Rue Anemone. Fig. 1860.

Enemion biternatum Raf. Journ. Phys. **91**: 70. 1820.
I. biternatum T. & G. Fl. N. A. **1** : 660. 1840.

Slender, erect, paniculately branching above; roots
fibrous and sometimes tuberiferous. Basal leaves
long-petioled, biternate, thin, the ultimate segments
broadly obovate, obtuse, lobed or divided; upper
ones similar but sessile or short-petioled; flowers
several, terminal and axillary, white, 5″–9″ broad;
sepals 5, oblong or somewhat obovate, obtuse; petals
none; stamens many; filaments slender, white, thickened above; carpels few; follicles widely spreading,
ovate, 2″ long, several-seeded, tipped with a beak
nearly one-half their length.

In moist woods and thickets, Ontario to Minnesota,
Kansas, Florida and Texas. May.

8. XANTHORRHÌZA L'Her. Stirp. Nov.
79. 1784.

A low shrubby plant, with pinnate or bipinnate leaves, and small compoundly racemose
flowers. Sepals 5, petaloid, deciduous. Petals 5, smaller than the sepals, unguiculate, concave, 2-lobed. Stamens 5 or 10. Carpels 5–15, sessile, 2-ovuled, forming 1-seeded follicles
at maturity by the suppression of one of the ovules; styles short, at length dorsal. [Greek,
yellow root.]

A monotypic genus of eastern North America.

1. Xanthorrhiza apiifòlia L'Her. Shrub
Yellow-root. Fig. 1861.

X. apiifolia L'Her. Stirp. Nov. 79. 1784.
Xanthorrhiza simplicissima Marsh. Arb. Amer.
168. 1785.

Glabrate, 1°–2° high, the bark and long
roots yellow and bitter. Leaves pinnate or
sometimes bipinnate, clustered at the summit
of the short stem, the blade 5′–6′ long, slender-
petioled; leaflets 5, thin, 1′–3′ long, incisely
toothed, cleft or divided, sessile, ovate or
oblong, acute, cuneate, shining; branches of
the raceme or panicle slender, drooping, 2′–3′
long; flowers about 2″ broad, pedicelled, solitary or 2–3 together, brownish-purple; sepals
ovate, acute; follicles 4–8, inflated, light yellow, 1-seeded, diverging, curved at the apex,
minutely beaked.

In woods, southwestern New York to Kentucky
and Florida. Also called Yellow-wood. The lowest leaves are sometimes 3-foliolate. Parsley-
leaved yellow-root. April–May.

9. ACTAÈA L. Sp. Pl. 504. 1753.

Erect perennial herbs, with large ternately compound leaves, and small white flowers
in terminal racemes. Sepals 3–5, petaloid, fugacious. Petals 4–10, small, spatulate or narrow,
clawed. Stamens numerous; filaments slender. Ovary 1, many-ovuled, forming in fruit a
large somewhat poisonous berry; stigma broad, sessile. Seeds numerous, in 2 rows, horizontal. [An ancient name of the elder.]

About 6 known species, natives of the north temperate zone. Besides the following another
occurs in the western United States. Type species: *Actaea spicata* L.

Pedicels slender ; berries red.   1. *A. rubra.*
Pedicels stout ; berries white.   2. *A. alba.*

1. Actaea rùbra (Ait.) Willd. Red Baneberry. Black Cohosh. Fig. 1862.

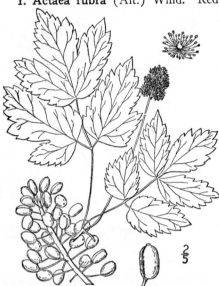

Actaea spicata var. *rubra* Ait. Hort. Kew. **2**: 221. 1789.
Actaea rubra Willd. Enum. 561. 1809.
A. rubra dissecta Britton; Britt. & Brown, Ill. Fl. **2**: 55. 1897.

Erect, bushy, $1°-2°$ high, pubescent or glabrate. Leaves petioled, or the upper sessile, ternate, the divisions pinnate with the lower ultimate leaflets sometimes again compound; leaflets ovate or the terminal one obovate, toothed or somewhat cleft, or all deeply incised, the teeth mainly rounded or mucronate, or acutish; raceme ovoid; petals spatulate, shorter than the stamens; pedicels mainly slender, $5''-7''$ long; berries red, oval or ellipsoid, $5''-6''$ long.

In woods, Nova Scotia to New Jersey and Pennsylvania, west to South Dakota and Nebraska. April–June. *A. spicata* L., of Europe, has purplish-black berries. Coral- and -pearl. Red-berry. Snake-root. Poison-berry. Snakeberry. Toad-root. This and the following species are called also herb-christopher, grapewort and rattlesnake-herb.

Actaea argùta Nutt., of western North America, with smaller globose red berries, enters our western limits in western Nebraska and South Dakota.

2. Actaea álba (L.) Mill. White Baneberry. Fig. 1863.

Actaea spicata var. *alba* L. Sp. Pl. 504. 1753.
Actaea alba Mill. Gard. Dict. Ed. 8, no. 2. 1768.

Closely resembles the preceding species in habit and aspect. Leaflets generally more cut and the teeth and lobes acute or acuminate; raceme oblong; petals truncate at the apex; fruiting pedicels as thick as the peduncle and often red; berries short-oval, white, often purplish at the end.

In woods, Nova Scotia and Anticosti to Georgia, west to Minnesota and Missouri. Ascends to 5000 ft. in Virginia. April–June. Races or hybrids with white berries and slender pedicels (*A. neglecta* Gillman, *A. eburnea* Rydb.), and red berries on thickened pedicels are occasionally met with. White or blue cohosh. White-beads. Necklace-weed. Whiteberry. Snake-root.

10. CIMICIFUGA L. Syst. Ed. 12, 659. 1767.

Tall erect perennial herbs, with large decompound leaves, and white racemose flowers. Sepals 2–5, petaloid, deciduous. Petals 1–8, small, clawed, 2-lobed or none. Stamens numerous, the filaments filiform. Carpels 1–8, many-ovuled, sessile or stipitate, forming follicles at maturity. Stigma broad or minute. [Latin, to drive away bugs.]

A genus of about 10 species, natives of North America, Asia and eastern Europe. Besides the following, there are 3 on the western side of the continent. Type species: *Cimicifuga foetida* L.

Carpels 1 or 2, sessile ; seeds in 2 rows, smooth.
    Leaflets ovate, oblong or obovate, narrowed, truncate or subcordate at the base. 1. *C. racemosa.*
    Leaflets broadly ovate or suborbicular, deeply cordate.   2. *C. cordifolia.*
Carpels 2–8, stalked ; seeds in 1 row, chaffy.   3. *C. americana.*

1. Cimicifuga racemosa (L.) Nutt. Black Snakeroot. Black Cohosh. Fig. 1864.

Actaea racemosa L. Sp. Pl. 504. 1753.
Cimicifuga racemosa Nutt. Gen. 2 : 15. 1818.
Cimicifuga racemosa dissecta A. Gray, Man. Ed. 6, 47. 1890.

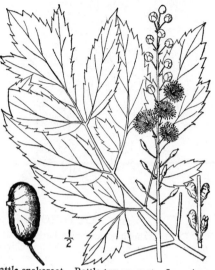

Stem slender, 3°–8° high, leafy above ; rootstock thick. Leaves ternate, the divisions pinnate and the ultimate leaflets often again compound ; leaflets ovate or oblong, or the terminal one obovate, acute or sometimes obtusish at the apex, narrowed, truncate or the lower subcordate at base, incisely-toothed, cleft, divided, or occasionally dissected, thickish, nearly glabrous ; racemes compound, terminal, 6′–3° long, usually finely pubescent ; pedicels bracted ; flowers 6″–7″ broad, foetid ; petals 4–8, 2-cleft ; stamens very numerous ; pistils 1 or 2, sessile ; stigma broad ; follicles oval, 3″–4″ long, minutely beaked ; seeds in 2 rows, smooth, flattened.

In woods, Maine and Ontario to Wisconsin, south to Georgia and Missouri. Ascends to 4000 ft. in North Carolina. Rich-weed. Rattle-weed. Rattle-snakeroot. Rattle-top or -root. June–Aug.

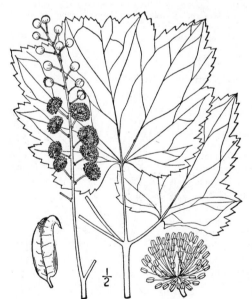

2. Cimicifuga cordifòlia Pursh. Heart-leaved Snakeroot. Fig. 1865.

Cimicifuga cordifolia Pursh, Fl. Am. Sept. 373. 1814.

Cimicifuga racemosa var. *cordifolia* A. Gray, Syn. Fl. 1 : Part 1, 55. 1895.

Tall, similar to the preceding species. Leaflets few, very broadly ovate or orbicular, acute, obtuse or acuminate at the apex, deeply cordate at the base, sometimes 6′ wide ; pistil 1, sessile ; follicles apparently very similar to those of *C. racemosa.* An imperfectly understood species, reported to flower later than *C. racemosa* where the two grow together.

In woods, southwestern Virginia to North Carolina and Tennessee. Tennessee specimens agree exactly with the figure of this plant given in Botanical Magazine. *pl. 2069.* Heart-leaved rattle-top. June–July.

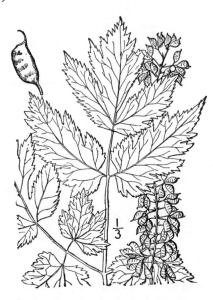

3. Cimicifuga americàna Michx. American Bugbane. Fig. 1866.

C. americana Michx. Fl. Am. 1 : 316. 1803.

Stem slender, 3°–5° high, leafy. Leaves ternate, the divisions pinnate with many of the ultimate leaflets again compound; leaflets ovate or oblong, the terminal one generally cuneate, acute, thin, glabrate, all incisely toothed, cleft or divided, 1′–3′ long; racemes terminal, slender, compound, densely and finely pubescent, 1°–2° long; flowers pedicelled, 4″–6″ broad; pedicels minutely bracted; petals few, 2-lobed; stamens numerous; pistils 3–8, stipitate, stigma minute; follicles inflated, membranous, 5″ long, narrowed below, tipped with a short oblique subulate beak; seeds in 1 row, flattened, chaffy.

Central New York and Pennsylvania, south along the mountains to Georgia and Tennessee. Mountain rattle-top. Aug.–Sept.

11. AQUILÈGIA [Tourn.] L. Sp. Pl. 533. 1753.

Erect branching perennial herbs, with ternately decomposed leaves, and large showy flowers. Sepals 5, regular, petaloid, deciduous. Petals concave, produced backward between the sepals into hollow spurs; stamens numerous, the inner ones reduced to staminodia. Carpels 5, sessile, many-ovuled, forming heads of follicles in fruit. [Latin, eagle, from the fancied resemblance of the spurs to the eagle's claws.]

A genus of beautiful plants, comprising about 50 species, distributed throughout the north temperate zone and extending into the mountains of Mexico. Besides the following, some 20 others occur in the western parts of North America. Type species: *Aquilegia vulgaris* L.

Spur of petals nearly straight; flowers scarlet, white or yellow.   1. *A. canadensis.*
Spur incurved; flowers blue or purple, about 9″ long.   2. *A. brevistyla.*
Spur strongly hooked; flowers white or purple, 1′–2′ long.   3. *A. vulgaris.*

1. Aquilegia canadénsis L. Wild Columbine. Rock-bells. Fig. 1867.

Aquilegia canadensis L. Sp. Pl. 533. 1753.
Aquilegia flaviflora Tenney, Am. Nat. 1 : 389. 1867.
Aquilegia canadensis flaviflora Britton, Bull. Torr. Club 15 : 97. 1888.
Aquilegia coccinea Small, Bull. N. Y. Bot. Gard. 1 : 280. 1899.

Glabrous or somewhat pubescent, 1°–2° high, branching. Lower and basal leaves slender-petioled, biternate, 4′–6′ broad, the ultimate leaflets sessile or on very short stalks, obovate, obtuse, cuneate, obtusely lobed and toothed, pale beneath; leaves of the upper part of the stem lobed or divided; flowers nodding, 1′–2′ long, scarlet or rarely white, or yellow, the spurs nearly straight, 6″ long, thickened at the end; stamens and styles long-exserted; head of fruit erect; follicles slightly spreading, about 8″ long, tipped with a filiform beak of about the same length.

In rocky woods, Nova Scotia to the Northwest Territory, south to Florida and Texas. Ascends to 5000 ft. in Virginia. Consists of several races, differing in size and color of the flowers, and in pubescence. Also at high altitudes in the Rocky Mountains. Honeysuckle. Rock-lily. Bells. Meeting-houses. Jack-in-trousers. Cluckies. April–July.

2. Aquilegia brevístyla Hook. Small-flowered Columbine. Fig. 1868.

Aquilegia brevistyla Hook. Fl. Bor. Am. 1 : 24. 1829.

Slender, erect, sparingly pubescent, branching, 6'-18' high. Basal leaves 2'-5' broad, long-petioled, biternate, the ultimate leaflets nearly sessile, broadly obovate, lobed and crenate; leaves of the stem few, nearly sessile, lobed or divided; flowers small, nodding, about as broad as long (8"), blue or purple; spurs short, incurved, about 2" long; stamens and short styles barely exserted; head of fruit erect; follicles slightly spreading, 8" long, pubescent, tipped with a subulate beak about 2" long.

South Dakota to Alaska and British Columbia. June–July.

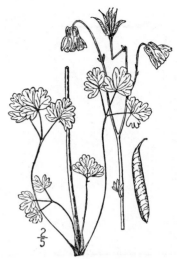

3. Aquilegia vulgàris L. European Columbine. Culverwort. Fig. 1869.

Aquilegia vulgaris L. Sp. Pl. 533. 1753.

Stout, erect, pubescent or nearly glabrous, 1°-2° high, branching above. Basal and lower leaves 4'-6' broad, petioled, 2–3-ternate, the lateral divisions broadly obovate, obtuse, lobed and crenate, glaucous beneath, dark green above; the upper few, lobed or divided; flower 1½'-2' broad and about as long, showy, blue, purple or white; spurs 3"-4" long, stout, strongly hooked; sepals spreading; stamens and styles hardly exserted.

Escaped from gardens into woods and fields, frequent in the Eastern and Middle States, in Nova Scotia and New Brunswick. Adventive or naturalized from Europe. Blue-bells. Lady's-shoes. Capon's-tail. Cock's-foot. Snapdragon. May–July.

12. DELPHÍNIUM L. Sp. Pl. 530. 1753.

Annual or perennial erect branching herbs, with racemose or paniculate showy flowers. Leaves palmately lobed or divided. Sepals 5, the posterior one prolonged into a spur. Petals 2 or 4, small, the two posterior ones spurred, the lateral, when present, small. Carpels few, sessile, many-ovuled, forming follicles at maturity. [Latin, from the supposed resemblance of the flowers to a dolphin.]

A genus of beautiful plants, with large irregular flowers, comprising some 125 species, natives of the north temperate zone. Besides the following, many others grow in western North America and several in the mountains of Mexico. Type species: *Delphinium Consolida* L.

Delphinium Consólida L., a European species which has a glabrous style and capsule, is widely recorded as naturalized in the eastern United States, and was admitted into our first edition; but all specimens examined prove to be *D. Ajacis.*

Annual; pistil 1 ; plant pubescent.   1. *D. Ajacis.*
Perennials; pistils 3.
    Follicles erect or nearly so.
       Leaf-segments broadly cuneate-obovate or cuneate-oblanceolate ; plant glabrous.
                                                  2. *D. exaltatum.*
       Leaf-segments linear.
          Panicle pyramidal ; plant glabrous.
          Panicle narrow ; plants pubescent or puberulent, at least above.
             Raceme open ; roots tuberous.
             Raceme strict ; roots not tuberous.
                Flowers bright blue ; bractlets close to the calyx.
                Flowers bluish-white ; bractlets distant from the calyx.
    Follicles widely divergent.

           3. *D. Treleasei.*

           4. *D. Nelsoni.*

           5. *D. carolinianum.*
           6. *D. virescens.*
           7. *D. tricorne.*

$\frac{1}{2}$

1. Delphinium Ajàcis L. Rocket Larkspur.
Fig. 1870.

Delphinium Ajacis L. Sp. Pl. 531. 1753.

Annual, finely pubescent, somewhat branched, 3°
high or less, usually branched. Leaves finely dissected into narrowly linear, acutish segments, mostly
less than 1″ wide, or those of the lower leaves
somewhat wider; lower leaves petioled, the upper
sessile or nearly so; flowers racemose; racemes
short or elongated, sometimes 10′ long, the pedicels
¼′–1′ long; flowers blue, rarely white; spur slender,
somewhat curved, about 1′ long; pistil 1; style pubescent; follicle erect, pubescent, beaked.

Fields, meadows and waste grounds, Nova Scotia to
South Carolina, Montana and Kansas. June–Aug.

2. Delphinium exaltàtum Ait. Tall
Larkspur. Fig. 1871.

Delphinium exaltatum Ait. Hort. Kew. **2**: 244.
1789.

Slender, 2°–6° high, glabrous or sparingly hairy below, densely pubescent above.
Leaves large, all but the upper petioled,
deeply 3–5-cleft, the divisions lanceolate or
oblanceolate, cuneate, acuminate, cleft and
toothed toward the apex, upper ones reduced to small linear or lanceolate bracts
subtending the flowers; racemes dense,
elongated (sometimes over 1° in length);
flowers purple or blue, 8″–10″ long, downy-
pubescent, the lower pedicels about 1′ long;
spur nearly straight, 4″ long; follicles 3,
erect, 4″–5″ long, pubescent, tipped with a
subulate beak.

In woods, Allegheny and Huntingdon Cos.,
Pa., to Minnesota, south to North Carolina,
Alabama and Nebraska. Has been mistaken
for *D. urceolatum* Jacq. July–Aug.

$\frac{2}{5}$

$\frac{1}{2}$

3. Delphinium Trelèasei Bush. Trelease's
Larkspur. Fig. 1872.

Delphinium Treleasei Bush; Davis, Minn. Bot. Stud.
2: 444. 1900.

Perennial, with fascicled roots, glabrous,
slightly glaucous, 2°–4° high, the stem-leaves
few. Basal leaves long-petioled, deeply palmatifid into linear segments 2″ wide or less;
raceme loose, pyramidal in outline, often a foot
long, the pedicels very slender, ascending, the
lower 2′–4′ long, sometimes branched, the upper
shorter; flowers blue or blue-purple; sepals and
spur about equal in length, puberulent; spur
straight, ¾′ long; sepals narrowly ovate; bractlets
borne somewhat below the calyx; petals yellow-
bearded; follicles 3, erect, slightly puberulent.

In barrens, Missouri. May–June.

4. Delphinium Nélsoni Greene. Nelson's Larkspur. Fig. 1873.

Delphinium Nelsoni Greene, Pittonia 3: 92. 1896.

Finely puberulent, at least above; stem slender, simple, 8'–1½° high from a cluster of tuberous roots near the surface of the ground. Leaves firm, the lower pedately divided into linear lobes or segments, long-petioled, the petioles sheathing the stem, the upper short-petioled, less divided; flowers in the upper axils and forming a loose terminal raceme, blue, slightly villous, slender-pedicelled; lower pedicels 1'–2' long, longer than the flowers; sepals oblong, shorter than the slender spur; lower petal 2-cleft, with a tuft of hairs about the middle; follicles 3, appressed-pubescent; seeds wing-angled above.

Western Nebraska and Colorado to Wyoming, and British Columbia. May–June.

5. Delphinium caroliniànum Walt. Carolina Larkspur. Fig. 1874.

D. carolinianum Walt. Fl. Car. 155. 1788.
D. azureum Michx. Fl. Bor. Am. 1: 314. 1803.
Delphinium Nortonianum Mackenzie & Bush, Trans. Acad. St. Louis 12: 82. 1902.

Stem slender, more or less pubescent, 1°–2° high. Leaves deeply cleft into linear toothed or cleft segments; raceme terminal, 4'–8' long; flowers pedicelled, blue, about 1' long, the spur curved upward, horizontal or nearly erect, 8" long; follicles 3, erect or slightly spreading, downy, 7"–9" long, tipped with a subulate beak; seed coat rugose.

Prairies and open grounds, Virginia to Missouri, Florida and Texas. Prairie, blue or azure larkspur. May–July.

6. Delphinium viréscens Nutt. Prairie Larkspur. Fig. 1875.

D. virescens Nutt. Gen. 2: 14. 1818.
D. albescens Rydberg, Bull. Torr. Club 26: 583. 1899.

Perennial, with branched woody roots, pubescent and often somewhat glandular. Stem stout, 1°–3° high; leaf-segments linear, 1"–3" wide; raceme narrow, rather densely flowered; lower pedicels sometimes 2' long, the upper much shorter; flowers white, or bluish-white, finely pubescent; spur horizontal or ascending, 6"–8" long, straight, or slightly curved upward; follicles 6"–9" long, erect, puberulent.

Prairies, Illinois to Minnesota, Manitoba, Kansas and Texas. *D. Penardi* Huth, of the Rocky Mountains, is closely related to this species. May–July.

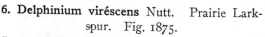

7. **Delphinium tricórne** Michx.   Dwarf
Larkspur.   Fig. 1876.

Delphinium tricorne Michx. Fl. Bor. Am. **1**: 314.
1803.

Stout, glabrous or pubescent, simple, 1°–3°
high. Leaves slender-petioled, deeply 5–7-cleft
or divided, the divisions linear or obovate,
obtuse, entire, or again cleft and toothed;
raceme loose, 4′–5′ long, mostly several-flowered;
flowers 1′–1½′ long, blue or white; spur generally
slightly bent, ascending, 10″–15″ long; follicles
3, widely spreading, 5″–6″ long, tipped with a
short beak; seed-coat smooth, dark.

Pennsylvania to the mountains of Georgia, west to
Minnesota, Nebraska and Arkansas. Roots tuberous.
April–June.

13. **ACONÌTUM** [Tourn.] L. Sp. Pl. 532. 1753.

Tall or long, erect ascending or trailing perennial herbs, with palmately lobed or divided
leaves, and large irregular showy flowers. Sepals 5, the posterior (upper) one larger, hooded
or helmet-shaped. Petals 2–5, small, the two superior ones hooded, clawed, concealed in
the helmet, the three posterior ones, when present, minute. Stamens numerous. Carpels 3–5,
sessile, many-ovuled, forming follicles at maturity. [Ancient Greek name for these plants.]

A genus of beautiful plants including some 70 species, mostly natives of mountainous regions
in the north temperate zone. Besides the following, several others are found in the Rocky Mountains
and on the Pacific Coast. Roots poisonous, as are also the flowers of some species. Type species:
Aconitum lycoctonum L.

Flowers blue; roots tuberous-thickened.
   Helmet arched, tipped with a descending beak.
   Helmet conic, slightly beaked.
Flowers white; stem trailing; helmet elongated-conic.

   1. *A. noveboracense.*
   2. *A. uncinatum.*
   3. *A. reclinatum.*

1. **Aconitum noveboracénse** A. Gray. New
York Monkshood. Fig. 1877.

Aconitum noveboracense A. Gray; Coville, Bull. Torr.
Club **13**: 190. 1886.

Slender, erect, about 2° high, leafy. Lower
leaves all petioled, 3′–4′ broad, nearly orbicular,
deeply 5–7-cleft, the divisions obovate, cuneate,
toothed and cut, acute or acuminate, glabrous,
rather thin; upper leaves nearly sessile, 3–5-cleft,
otherwise similar, subtending branches of the
loose pubescent few-flowered panicle; flowers
blue, 6″ broad, about 1′ high, the arched gibbous
helmet tipped with a prominent descending beak
about 3″ long; follicles erect, 3″ long, subulate-
beaked.

Orange, Ulster and Chenango Counties, N. Y.,
and Summit County, Ohio. Reported from Iowa.
Nearest *A. paniculatum* Lam. of central Europe.
June–Aug.

2. Aconitum uncinàtum L Wild Monkshood or Wolfbane. Fig. 1878.

Aconitum uncinatum L. Sp Pl. Ed. 2, 750. 1762.

Slender, weak, 2°-4° long, ascending or climbing, leafy. Leaves thick, broader than long, 3'-4' wide, deeply 3-5-lobed or cleft; lobes oblong or ovate-lanceolate, cleft or toothed, acute, glabrous or nearly so; panicle few-flowered, pubescent; flowers clustered at the ends of its branches, blue, 1' broad or more; helmet erect, obtusely conic, acute in front but scarcely beaked; follicles 3, 6"-7" long, subulate-beaked

In woods, southern Pennsylvania, south along the mountains to Georgia, west to Wisconsin and Kentucky. Ascends to 3000 ft. in Virginia. June-Sept.

3. Aconitum reclinàtum A Gray. Trailing Wolfsbane. Fig 1879.

A. reclinatum A. Gray, Am. Journ. Sci. 42 : 34. 1842.

Trailing, 2°-8° long. Leaves 3-7-cleft, all but the upper petioled, thin, the lower 6'-8' broad, mainly obovate, acute, toothed and cleft toward the apex; simple panicle or raceme loose, pubescent; flowers white, 8"-10" long; helmet horizontal or nearly so, elongated-conic, with a straight, short beak; follicles 3, 5" long, with slender divergent beaks.

In woods, Cheat Mountain and Stony Man Mountain, Virginia, south along the Alleghanies to Georgia. Ascends to 5500 ft. in North Carolina. Trailing monkshood. July-Aug.

14. ANEMÒNE L. Sp. Pl. 538. 1753.

Erect perennial herbs. Basal leaves lobed, divided or dissected, those of the stem forming an involucre near to or remote from the peduncled flower or flowers. Sepals 4-20, petaloid. Petals none. Stamens ∞, shorter than the sepals. Carpels ∞. Achenes compressed, 1-seeded. [From the Greek, a flower shaken by the wind.]

About 85 species, widely distributed through the temperate and subarctic regions of both hemispheres. About 20 species are natives of North America. Type species: *Anemone coronaria* L.

* Achenes densely woolly.

Stem simple, slender, 1-flowered.
  Root tuberous ; sepals 6-20, narrow.   1. *A. caroliniana.*
  Rootstock slender ; sepals 5-6, oval.   2. *A. parviflora.*
Stem commonly branching above, tall, generally 2-several-flowered.
  Leaves of the involucre sessile or short-petioled ; sepals red ; head of fruit globose or oval.
                                              3. *A. hudsoniana.*
  Leaves of the involucre slender-petioled ; sepals white or green ; head cylindric, oval, or oblong.
    Head of fruit cylindric ; divisions of the leaves wedge-shaped, narrow.   4. *A. cylindrica.*
    Head of fruit oblong or oval ; divisions of the leaves ovate, broad.   5. *A. virginiana.*

** Achenes pubescent, or nearly glabrous.

Leaves of the involucre sessile.
  Stout, 1°-2° high, branching and bearing several flowers ; carpels nearly orbicular ; flowers white.
                                           6. *A. canadensis.*
  Slender, 2'-12' high, 1-flowered ; carpels narrow ; flowers yellow.   7. *A. Richardsonii.*
Leaves of the involucre petioled.
  Involucral leaf-divisions lobed and incised ; plant 4'-9' high.   8. *A. quinquefolia.*
  Involucral leaf-divisions dentate ; plant 10'-16' high.   9. *A. trifolia.*

1. Anemone caroliniàna Walt.   Carolina Anemone.
Fig. 1880.

Anemone caroliniana Walt. Fl. Car. 157. 1788.

Sparsely hairy, 4'–10' high, arising from a tuber 3"–4" in diameter. Basal leaves slender-petioled, 3-divided, the divisions variously toothed, lobed and parted, those of the involucre sessile and 3-cleft; flower erect, 9"–18" broad; sepals 6–20, linear-oblong, purple, varying to white; head of fruit oblong; achenes densely woolly.

Open places, Illinois to Wisconsin and South Dakota, south to Florida and Texas. Mayflower. April–May.

Anemone decapétala Ard., of the southern United States, Mexico and South America, ranging north to Kansas, differs by some or all of its basal leaves having the divisions merely crenate.

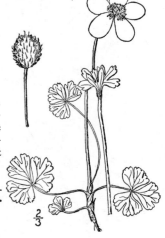

2. Anemone parviflòra Michx.   Northern or Small-flowered Anemone.   Fig. 1881.

Anemone parviflora Michx. Fl. Bor. Am. 1: 319. 1803.

Sparingly hairy, 4'–12' high from slender rootstocks. Basal leaves long-petioled, 3-parted, the broadly wedge-shaped divisions obtusely lobed or crenate, those of the involucre nearly sessile, similarly lobed; flower 1' in diameter or less; sepals oval, very obtuse, white; head of fruit short-oval or globose; achenes densely woolly.

Labrador, Newfoundland and Quebec to Wisconsin, Minnesota and Alaska, south in the Rocky Mountains to Colorado. Also in northern Asia. May–June.

3. Anemone hudsoniàna Richards.   Cut-leaved Anemone.   Red Wind-flower.
Fig. 1882.

Anemone hudsoniana Richards. Franklin's Journey 741. 1823.

Silky-hairy, 6'–18' high, sparingly branched, the lateral peduncles involucrate. Basal leaves long-petioled, reniform, 3–5-parted, the divisions cleft into linear acute lobes, those of the involucres short-petioled and more or less cuneate, otherwise similar; sepals 5–9, greenish or red, oblong, forming a flower ½'–1' broad; head of fruit globose or oblong, ½'–1' long; achenes compressed, densely woolly, tipped with the short subulate styles.

Anticosti and New Brunswick to Maine, New York, Michigan and Minnesota. Summer.

The similar **A. globòsa** Nutt., of the Rocky Mountains, with larger flowers, occurs in the Black Hills of South Dakota and Manitoba, and is reported from Nebraska. Both have been confused with *A. multifida* Poir, of southern South America, which they much resemble.

4. Anemone cylíndrica A. Gray. Long-fruited Anemone. Fig. 1883.

Anemone cylindrica A. Gray, Ann. Lyc. N. Y. **3** : 221. 1836.

Silky-hairy throughout, 1°–2° high, branched at the involucre. Basal leaves tufted, long-petioled, broader than long, 3–5-parted, the divisions cuneate-obovate or cuneate-oblanceolate, narrow; those of the involucre similar, their petioles about 1′ long; sepals 5–6, greenish-white, oblong, generally obtuse; flowers about 9″ broad, on elongated generally naked peduncles; head of fruit cylindric, 1′ in length or more; achenes compressed, woolly, tipped with the minute styles.

Open places, eastern New Brunswick to Massachusetts, New York, New Jersey, Kansas and Saskatchewan. Also in the Rocky Mountains, south to New Mexico, and in British Columbia. June–Aug.

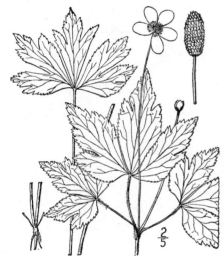

5. Anemone virginiàna L. Tall Anemone. Fig. 1884.

Anemone virginiana L. Sp. Pl. 540. 1753.
A. riparia Fernald, Rhodora **1** : 51. 1899.

Hairy, 2°–3° high, stout, branching at the involucre, the lateral peduncles bearing secondary involucres. Basal leaves long-petioled, broader than long, 3-parted, the divisions broadly cuneate-oblong, variously cleft and divided into acute serrate lobes; those of both primary and secondary involucres similar, on petioles 1′–2′ long; sepals generally 5, white or greenish, acute or obtuse; flowers 9″–18″ broad; head of fruit oblong to subcylindric, 9″–12″ long; achenes compressed, woolly, tipped by the spreading or ascending subulate styles.

In woods, Nova Scotia to South Carolina, Kansas, Alberta and Arkansas. Consists of several races, differing in size and color of flower, shape of fruit and in the styles. Tumble-weed. Thimble-weed. June–Aug.

6. Anemone canadénsis L. Canada or Round-leaved Anemone. Fig. 1885.

Anemone canadensis L. Syst. Ed. 12, **3** : App. 231. 1768.

Anemone pennsylvanica L. Mant. **2** : 247. 1771.

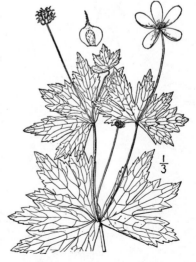

Rather stout, 1°–2° high, somewhat hairy, especially on the lower surfaces of the leaves, branching at the involucre. Basal leaves long-petioled, broader than long, 3–5-parted, the divisions broad, oblong, acute, variously cleft and toothed, those of both primary and secondary involucres similar, sessile; sepals white, oblong, obtuse; flower 1′–1½′ broad; head of fruit globose; achenes flat, nearly orbicular, pubescent, tipped with the stout persistent style, which is about their own length.

Low grounds, Labrador to Assiniboia, Massachusetts, Maryland, Illinois, Kansas and Colorado. *A. dichotoma* L., to which this has been referred, is a Siberian species with glabrous ovate achenes. Crowfoot. Round-headed anemone. May–Aug.

7. Anemone Richardsònii Hook. Richardson's Anemone. Fig. 1886.

Anemone Richardsonii Hook. Fl. Bor. Am. **1**: 6. 1829.

Low, slender, pubescent, 2'–12' high from slender rootstocks. Basal leaves reniform, slender-petioled, 3–5-parted, the lobes acute, broadly oblong, dentate or crenate; those of the involucre similar, sessile; flower solitary, 9" broad, yellow; sepals about 6, oblong; head of fruit depressed-spherical; achenes nearly glabrous, compressed, ovate-oblong, reflexed, tipped with a hooked persistent style of about their own length.

Labrador to Hudson Bay and in arctic America generally. Also widely distributed in Siberia. Summer.

8. Anemone quinquefòlia L. Wind-flower. Snowdrops. Fig. 1887.

$\frac{1}{2}$

Anemone quinquefolia L. Sp. Pl. 541. 1753.
Anemone nemorosa var. *quinquefolia* A. Gray, Man. Ed. 5, 38. 1867.

Low, simple, nearly glabrous, 4'–9' high, from horizontal rootstocks. Basal leaves long-petioled, appearing later than the flowering stem, 5-parted, the divisions oblong, cuneate, dentate; those of the involucre on slender petioles about 9" long, 3–5-parted, the divisions 1½' long, acute, variously cut and lobed; flower solitary, 1' broad; sepals 4–9, obovate or oval, white, or purplish without; head of fruit globose, inclined; achenes pubescent, oblong, tipped with the hooked styles.

In low woods, Nova Scotia to Georgia, western Ontario, Minnesota and Tennessee. Ascends to 3500 ft. in Virginia. Readily distinguishable from the European *A. nemorosa* L., which is sometimes cultivated in our area and reported as escaped in Massachusetts, by its slender habit, slender petioles, less lobed divisions of the involucral leaves, paler green foliage, more slender rootstocks, and smaller flowers. Wood-flower. May-flower. Nimble-weed. Wood-anemone. Wild cucumber. April–June.

$\frac{2}{5}$

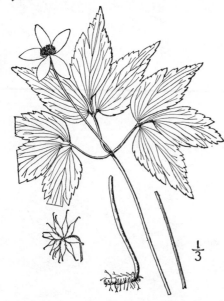

9. Anemone trifòlia L. Mountain Anemone. Fig. 1888.

Anemone trifolia L. Sp. Pl. 540. 1753.

A. lancifolia Pursh, Fl. Am. Sept. 387. 1814.

Stout, 6'–16' tall, nearly glabrous throughout. Basal leaves mostly 3-divided (sometimes 4–5-divided), long-petioled, dentate, often somewhat lobed; involucral leaves stout-petioled, 3-parted, the divisions oblong-lanceolate, acute or acuminate at the apex, dentate, often slightly lobed, 1'–3' long; flower solitary, white, 1'–1½' broad when expanded; peduncles 1'–4' long; sepals oblong to oval; head of fruit globose, 5"–6" in diameter; achenes 10–20, oblong, finely pubescent, tipped with the hooked style.

$\frac{1}{3}$

Southern Pennsylvania, southwestern Virginia, North Carolina and Georgia, chiefly in the mountains; in Virginia usually in company with the lily-of-the-valley. Also in the south Austrian Alps and the mountains of northern Italy. May.

15. HEPÁTICA [Rupp.] Mill. Gard. Dict. Abr. Ed. 4. 1754.

Perennial scapose herbs, with long-petioled thick 3-lobed evergreen basal leaves, and large white or purple flowers, solitary on slender scapes. Involucre of 3 small sessile leaves close under the flowers, simulating a calyx. Sepals membranous, petal-like. Stamens all anther-bearing. Achenes short-beaked, pubescent. [Name ancient, from the supposed resemblance of the leaves to the liver.]

A genus of about 4 species, natives of the north temperate zone. Only the following are known from North America. Type species: *Anemone Hepatica* L.

Lobes of the leaves rounded or obtuse.   1. *H. Hepatica.*
Lobes of the leaves acute.   2. *H. acutiloba.*

1. Hepatica Hepática (L.) Karst. Round-lobed or Kidney Liver-leaf. Noble Liverwort. Fig. 1889.

Anemone Hepatica L. Sp. Pl. 538. 1753.

Hepatica triloba Chaix in Vill. Hist. Pl. Dauph.
1 : 336. 1786.

Hepatica Hepatica Karst. Deutsch. Fl. 559.
1880–83.

Scapes 4'–6' high, villous; roots fibrous. Leaves long-petioled, reniform, 2'–2½' broad when mature, spreading on the ground, 3-lobed, and the lobes sometimes toothed or again lobed, obtuse; involucre of 3 sessile obtuse oblong leaves immediately under the flowers; flowers blue, purple or white, 6"–10" broad; sepals oval or oblong, obtuse, longer than the stamens; achenes several, 2" long, oblong, acute, hairy.

In woods, often in large tufts, Nova Scotia to northern Florida, west to Manitoba, Iowa and Missouri. Alaska. Ascends to 2600 ft. in Virginia. Also in Europe and Asia. Dec.–May. Heart- or three-leaf liverwort. Liver-moss. Mouse-ears. Spring-beauty. Crystal-wort. Golden trefoil. Ivy-flower. Herb Trinity. Squirrel-cup.

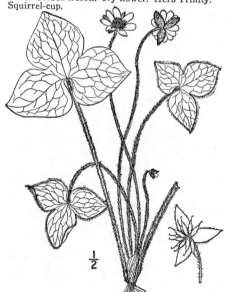

2. Hepatica acutíloba DC. Sharp-lobed or Heart Liver-leaf or Liverwort. Fig. 1890.

Hepatica triloba var. *acuta* Pursh, Fl. Am.
Sept. 391. 1814.

Hepatica acutiloba DC. Prodr. 1 : 22. 1824.

Hepatica acuta Britton, Ann. N. Y. Acad. Sci.
6 : 234. 1891.

Scapes 4'–9' high, villous. Plant closely resembling the preceding, differing in that the leaf-lobes and those of the involucre are acute or acutish.

In woods, Maine, Quebec and throughout Ontario, south in the Alleghanies to Georgia, but rare or absent near the Atlantic Coast, west to Missouri and Minnesota. Puzzling forms occur which are referable with about equal certainty to the preceding species of which it may be regarded as a geographical race. The leaf-form of the German plant is quite intermediate between our *Hepatica* and *acutiloba.* A dioecious tendency of this species has been observed. March–April. Spring-beauty. May-flower.

16. SYNDÉSMON Hoffmg. Flora, 15: Part 2, Intell. Bl. 4, 34. 1832.

[ANEMONELLA Spach, Hist. Veg. 7: 239. 1839.]

A glabrous perennial herb from a cluster of tuberous-thickened roots, with basal 2-3-ternately compound leaves, those of the involucre similar but sessile, and large terminal umbellate slender-pedicelled white flowers. Sepals thin, petaloid. Petals none. Stamens all anther-bearing. Achenes terete, deeply grooved; stigma sessile, truncate. [Greek, bound together, the plant uniting many of the characters of *Anemone* and *Thalictrum*.]

A monotypic genus of eastern North America.

1. Syndesmon thalictroìdes (L.) Hoffmg. Rue-Anemone. Fig. 1891.

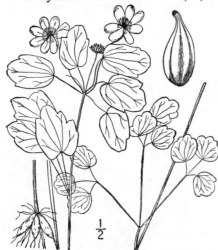

Anemone thalictroides L. Sp. Pl. 542. 1753.
Thalictrum anemonoides Michx. Fl. Bor. Am. 1:
    322. 1803.
Syndesmon thalictroides Hoffmg. Flora 15:
    Part 2, Intell. Bl. 4, 34. 1832.
Anemonella thalictroides Spach, Hist. Veg. 7:
    240. 1839.

Low, glabrous, 4'-9' high, the flowering stem arising in early spring from the cluster of tuberous roots, the ternately-compound basal leaves appearing later and resembling those of *Thalictrum*. Leaves of the involucre similar, sessile, the leaflets long-petioled; sepals 5-10, white or pinkish, longer than the stamens; flower ½'-1' broad; flowers perfect, umbellate immediately above the involucre; achenes sessile, pointed, 4"-6" long.

In woods, New Hampshire and Massachusetts to Florida, Ontario, Minnesota and Kansas. Leaflets are occasionally borne on the stem below those of the involucre. March–June. Wind-flower. May-flower.

17. PULSATÍLLA [Tourn.] Mill. Gard. Dict. Abr. Ed. 4. 1754.

Perennial scapose herbs, with thick rootstocks, basal long-petioled digitately divided leaves, and large purple or white solitary flowers. Involucre remote from the flower, 3-leaved. Sepals petaloid. Petals none. Inner stamens anther-bearing, the outer ones often sterile. Achenes with long persistent plumose styles. [Latin name, unexplained.]

About 18 species, natives of the north temperate and subarctic zones. Besides the following, another occurs in northwestern North America. Type species: *Anemone Pulsatilla* L.

1. Pulsatilla patens (L.) Mill. Pasque Flower. Fig. 1892.

Anemone patens L. Sp. Pl. 538. 1753.
P. patens Mill. Gard. Dict. Ed. 8, No. 4. 1768.
?*Clematis hirsutissima* Pursh. Fl. Am. Sept. 385. 1814.
Anemone Nuttalliana DC. Syst. 1: 193. 1818.
Anemone patens var. *Nuttalliana* A. Gray, Man. Ed. 5,
    36. 1867.
P. hirsutissima Britton, Ann. N. Y. Acad. Sci. 6: 217.
    1891.

Villous, 6'-16' high. Leaves much divided into narrow linear acute lobes, the basal on slender petioles, those of the involucre sessile and erect or ascending; sepals ovate-oblong, light bluish-purple; fruit a head of silky achenes with long plumose styles, like those of some *Clematis*.

In dry soil, prairies of Illinois to British Columbia, Nebraska and Texas. Europe and northern Asia. After flowering the peduncle elongates, sometimes to a foot or more. Consists of several races, the American ones mostly with wider leaf-lobes than the European. March–April. American pulsatilla. Hartshorn- or head-ache-plant. Wild crocus. Mayflower. Easter-flower. Gosling. Badger. April-fools. Prairie-smoke or -anemone. Wind-flower. Rock-lily.

18. MYOSURUS L. Sp. Pl. 284. 1753.

Diminutive annual herbs, with fibrous roots, tufted, basal linear or linear-spatulate, entire leaves and 1-flowered scapes. Sepals 5 (rarely 6–7), long-spurred at the base. Petals the same number or none, when present greenish-yellow, narrow, the claw bearing a nectariferous pit at the summit, the limb spreading. Stamens 5–25, about equalling the sepals. Pistils numerous, borne on a central axis, which becomes greatly elongated in fruit. Ovule 1, suspended. Achenes apiculate or aristate. [Greek, mouse-tail.]

A genus of insignificant plants of local but wide geographic distribution, consisting of the species here figured and about 4 others found in west America and Australia. Type species: *Myosurus minimus* L.

1. Myosurus mínimus L. Mouse-tail. Fig. 1893.

Myosurus minimus L. Sp. Pl. 284. 1753.

Myosurus Shortii Raf. Am. Journ. Sci. 1 : 379. 1819.

Myosurus minimus var. *Shortii* Huth, Engler's Bot. Jahrb. 16 : 284. 1893.

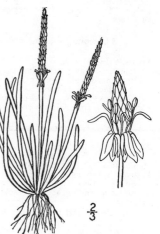

Low, glabrous, 1'–6' high, the scape at length surpassing the leaves and the elongated receptacle attaining the length of 1'–2'. Leaves all basal, 2'–4' long, narrowly spatulate to linear, blunt; petals present, small; achenes glabrous, apiculate.

In moist places, southern Ontario to British Columbia, Indiana, Virginia, Florida, Texas and New Mexico. Reported from the Pacific Coast. Also in central Europe. At Norfolk, Va., the plant seems to have been introduced. Little mouse-tail. Blood-strange. April–July.

19. TRAUTVETTÈRIA F. & M. Ind. Sem. Petr. 1 : 22. 1834.

Tall erect perennial herbs, with large palmately-lobed leaves, those of the stem distant. Sepals 3–5, concave, caducous. Petals none. Carpels ∞, 1-ovuled. Achenes capitate, sharply angular, inflated, tipped with the minute styles. Embryo large. Flowers small, white, corymbosely paniculate. [In honor of Prof. Trautvetter, a Russian botanist.]

A monotypic genus of North America and eastern Asia.

1. Trautvetteria carolinénsis (Walt.) Vail. False Bugbane. Fig. 1894.

Hydrastis carolinensis Walt. Fl. Car. 156. 1788.

Cimicifuga palmata Michx. Fl. Bor. Am. 1 : 316. 1803.

Trautvetteria palmata F. & M. Ind. Sem. Petr. 1 : 22. 1834.

Trautvetteria carolinensis Vail, Mem. Torr. Club 2 : 42. 1890.

T. applanata Greene, Leaflets 2 : 191. 1912.

Stout, 2°–3° high, branching, nearly glabrous, except the lower surfaces of the leaves. Basal leaves long-petioled, 6'–8' broad, 4'–5' long, deeply 5–11-lobed, the lobes acute and sharply dentate; panicle ample, the flowers 3''–6'' broad, borne in cymose clusters at the ends of its branches; filaments slender, slightly widened; anthers oblong.

Southwestern Pennsylvania to the mountains of Virginia and Kentucky, south to Florida, west to Indiana and Missouri. Ascends to 6000 ft. in North Carolina. June–July.

20. RANÚNCULUS [Tourn.] L. Sp. Pl. 548. 1753.

Annual or perennial herbs, with alternate simple entire lobed or divided or dissected leaves, and yellow white or red flowers. Sepals mostly 5, deciduous. Petals equal in number or more, conspicuous or minute, provided with a nectariferous pit and a scale at the base of the blade. Carpels ∞, 1-ovuled. Achenes capitate or spicate, generally flattened, smooth, papillose or echinate, tipped with a minute or an elongated style. [Latin for a small frog, in allusion to the marsh habitat of many species.]

Some 275 species, widely distributed in the temperate and cool regions of both hemispheres and on mountain tops in the tropics. In addition to those here described, many others inhabit the western and northwestern parts of the continent. The names *Crowfoot* or *Buttercup* are popularly applied to most of the species with large flowers and divided leaves. Type species: *Ranunculus auricomus* L.

† **Creeping, floating or decumbent perennials, with palmately lobed, dissected or divided leaves.**

Plants leafy-stemmed.
  Aquatics; leaves orbicular, palmately divided.
    Achenes callous-margined.   1. *R. delphinifolius.*
    Achenes marginless.   2. *R. Purshii.*
  Glabrous; leaves 3-lobed or 3-cleft, cuneate at the base; arctic.   3. *R. hyperboreus.*
Plant scapose from filiform rootstocks.   4. *R. lapponicus.*

†† **Plants of swamps or muddy shores; leaves entire or denticulate.**

Annuals; achenes beakless.
  Petals 1″–2″ long; stamens few.   5. *R. pusillus.*
  Petals 2″–3″ long; stamens numerous.   6. *R. oblongifolius.*
Perennials, rooting from the nodes; achenes beaked.
  Stems trailing; achenes minutely beaked.   7. *R. reptans.*
  Stems ascending or erect; achenes subulate-beaked.   8. *R. obtusiusculus.*

††† **Terrestrial or marsh species with some or all the leaves toothed, lobed or divided.**

Calyx conspicuously black-pubescent; arctic; flowers white or light yellow.   9. *R. nivalis.*
Calyx glabrous or pubescent; flowers yellow.
  1. Achenes smooth, neither papillose, muricate nor spiny.
    Plant low, arctic-alpine; leaves small, palmately lobed.   10. *R. pygmaeus.*
    Plants neither arctic nor alpine.
      Basal leaves, some or all of them, merely crenate (deeply cleft in no. 11).
        Head of fruit oblong, 2–3 times as long as thick.
          Flowers 6″ broad or less; sepals slightly hairy.   11. *R. pedatifidus.*
          Flowers 8″–10″ broad, sepals densely tomentose.   12. *R. cardiophyllus.*
        Head of fruit globose or subglobose.
          Petals longer than the sepals.
            Petals not twice as long as the loosely villous sepals.   13. *R. Alleni.*
            Petals several times longer than the glabrous calyx.
              Basal leaves oval or ovate, not cordate.   14. *R. ovalis.*
              Basal leaves reniform or orbicular, cordate.   15. *R. Harveyi.*
          Petals small, shorter than or equalling the sepals.
            Styles very short.
              Basal leaves cordate; plant glabrous or nearly so.   16. *R. abortivus.*
              Basal leaves not cordate; plant villous at least below. 17. *R. micranthus.*
          Styles subulate, hooked, nearly one-half as long as the achene.
                                            18. *R. alleghaniensis.*
    Leaves all lobed or divided.
      Plant glabrous; stem hollow; flowers very small.   19. *R. sceleratus.*
      Plants more or less pubescent.
        Beak of the achene strongly hooked; flowers 4″–5″ wide.   20. *R. recurvatus.*
        Beak of the achene short.
          Erect plants, naturalized in fields; flowers 1′ broad.
            Calyx spreading; roots fibrous.   21. *R. acris.*
             Calyx reflexed; stem bulbous-thickened at base.   22. *R. bulbosus.*
          Erect or ascending plants of moist soil; flowers 3″–6″ broad.
            Petals not longer than the reflexed sepals.   23. *R. pennsylvanicus.*
            Petals longer than the sepals.   24. *R. Macounii.*
          Ascending and creeping by stolons; flowers 1′ broad.   25. *R. repens.*
          Beak of the achene long, stout or slender; flowers 6″–18″ broad.
            Roots slender; beak stout; leaflets cuneate at base.   26. *R. septentrionalis.*
            Roots thickened; beak of achene slender, subulate.
              Leaf-segments broad, oblong or obovate.   27. *R. hispidus.*
              Leaf-segments narrow, linear-oblong.   28. *R. fascicularis.*
  2. Achenes with scattered papillae, at least near the margins; perennial. 29. *R. parvulus.*
  3. Achenes rough-papillose all over; annual.   30. *R. parviflorus.*
  4. Achenes muricate or spiny.
    Leaf-lobes broad, obtuse.   31. *R. muricatus.*
    Leaf-lobes narrow, subacute.   32. *R. arvensis.*

1. **Ranunculus delphinifòlius** Torr.   Yellow Water-Crowfoot.   Fig. 1895.

Ranunculus multifidus Pursh, Fl. Am. Sept. 736. 1814.
  Not Forsk. 1775.
R. delphinifolius Torr.; Eaton, Man. Ed. 2, 395. 1818.
Ranunculus lacustris Beck & Tracy, N. Y. Med. and
  Phys. Journ. 2: 112. 1823.
R. missouriensis Greene, Erythea 3: 20. 1895.

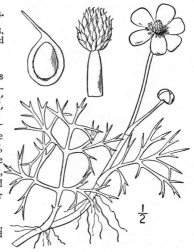

Aquatic or partly emersed, branching, sometimes
several feet long. Immersed leaves repeatedly divided into capillary segments, short-petioled, 1′–3′
long; emersed leaves glabrous or pubescent, ½′–2′
broad, petioled or the upper nearly sessile, 3–5-di-
vided, the divisions cleft into linear or cuneate
segments; flowers yellow, 3″–18″ broad; petals 5–8,
much longer than the sepals; head of fruit globose
or oblong, 3″–5″ long; achenes less than 1″ long,
callous-margined, at least toward the base, tipped
with a straight persistent beak of one-half their
length or more.

In ponds, Maine and Ontario to Michigan, Oregon,
North Carolina, Missouri and Arkansas. The so-called
var. *terrestris* is an emersed form. June–Aug.

2. **Ranunculus Púrshii** Richards.   Pursh's Buttercup.   Fig. 1896.

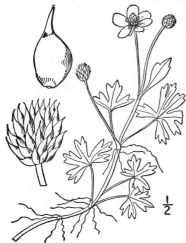

Ranunculus Purshii Richards. Frank. Journ. 741. 1823.
Ranunculus limosus Nutt.; T. & G. Fl. N. A. 1: 20. 1838.
Ranunculus multifidus var. *repens* S. Wats. Bot. King's
  Exp. 8. 1871.

Perennial, floating or creeping, usually pubescent
at least on the younger parts, sometimes densely so;
stems slender, often rooting from the lower nodes,
2′–8′ long. Leaves slender-petioled, orbicular or
reniform in outline, ¼′–1′ wide, palmately divided
nearly to the base into obtuse lobes or segments;
flowers yellow, long-peduncled, 2″–7″ broad; sepals
spreading, ovate, obtusish, early deciduous; petals
about 5; head of fruit subglobose or ovoid-oblong,
obtuse, 2″–3″ long; achenes little compressed,
smooth, not margined, ½″ long, acutish on the back,
abruptly tipped with a slender style of about one-
third their length.

In moist soil, Nova Scotia to Alaska, Michigan, North
Dakota, south in the Rocky Mountains to New Mexico
and Utah. July–Aug.

3. **Ranunculus hyperbòreus** Rottb.   Arctic Buttercup.   Fig. 1897.

Ranunculus hyperboreus Rottb. Skrift. Kjoeb. Selsk. 10: 458. 1770.

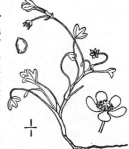

Stem slender, glabrous, filiform, creeping, 2′–6′ long. Leaves
petioled, 3-lobed or cleft, broadly ovate, 2″–5″ broad, 2″–4″
long, obtuse, the base cuneate or rounded, the lobes oblong, obtuse, the lateral ones sometimes toothed; petioles sheathing and
biauriculate; flowers few, 2″–3″ broad, yellow; petals slightly
shorter than the reflexed sepals; peduncles 4″–6″ long; head of
fruit globose, 2″ broad; achenes slightly compressed, with a
minute blunt point.

Labrador, Greenland, arctic America, Iceland, northern Europe and
Siberia. Summer.

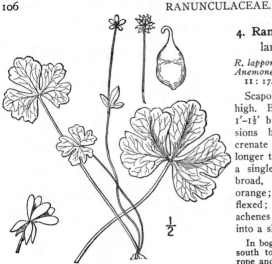

½

4. Ranunculus lappónicus L. Lapland Buttercup. Fig. 1898.

R. lapponicus L. Sp. Pl. 553. 1753.
Anemone nudicaulis A. Gray, Coult. Bot. Gaz.
11 : 17. 1886.

Scapose from running rootstocks, 3′–6′ high. Basal leaves long-petioled, the blade 1′–1½′ broad, reniform, 3-parted, the divisions broadly obovate, cuneate, obtuse, crenate or lobed; scape 1-flowered, slender, longer than the leaves, occasionally bearing a single deeply lobed leaf; flower 3″–5″ broad, yellow; petals 5–6, veined with orange; sepals generally fewer and reflexed; head of fruit globose, 6″ broad; achenes flattened, ovate, gradually narrowed into a slender hooked beak.

In bogs, Greenland and Labrador to Alaska, south to northern Minnesota. Northern Europe and Siberia. Summer.

5. Ranunculus pusíllus Poir. Low Spearwort. Fig. 1899.

R. pusillus Poir. in Lam. Encycl. 6 : 99. 1804.

Annual, slender, weak, glabrous, branching, 6′–18′ long. Leaves entire or denticulate, the lower oblong or ovate, sometimes cordate, on long petioles, the upper narrower, lanceolate or linear, short-petioled or sessile; flowers yellow, 2″–3″ broad, the petals few, often barely exceeding the sepals; stamens 1–10; head of fruit globose, 2″ broad; achenes beakless, merely tipped by the very short persistent style-base.

Marshes, southern New York and New Jersey near the coast, southeastern Pennsylvania, south to Florida and west through the Gulf States to Texas, north to Tennessee and Missouri. Dwarf crowfoot. April–July.

⅗

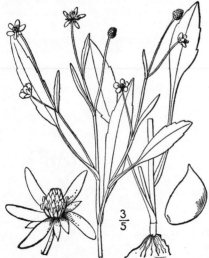

⅗

6. Ranunculus oblongifòlius Ell. Oblong-leaved Spearwort. Fig. 1900.

Ranunculus oblongifolius Ell. Bot. S. C. & Ga. 2 : 58.
1821–24.
Ranunculus pusillus var. *oblongifolius* T. & G. Fl.
N.-A. 1 : 16. 1838.

Annual, branched above, erect or ascending, 1°–2° high, glabrous or pubescent. Leaves entire or denticulate, oblong, or oblong-lanceolate, the lower on long petioles, the blade sometimes 3′ long, the upper narrower, lanceolate or linear; flowers yellow, 3″–6″ broad, the 5 petals much exceeding the sepals; stamens numerous; head of fruit 2″ broad; achenes merely tipped by the very short style-base.

In swamps, near the coast, Delaware to Florida and Texas, north to southern Illinois and Missouri. April–Sept.

7. Ranunculus réptans L.   Creeping Spearwort.   Fig. 1901.

Ranunculus reptans L. Sp. Pl. 549. 1753.
Ranunculus filiformis Michx. Fl. Bor. Am. 1 : 320. 1803.
Ranunculus Flammula var. *reptans* E. Meyer. Pl. Lab. 96. 1830.
R. Flammula intermedius Hook. Fl. Bor. Am. 1 : 11. 1829.

Trailing or reclining, glabrous or pubescent, rooting from the nodes, the flowering stems and peduncles ascending. Leaves linear, lanceolate or spatulate, 1'–2' long, mainly entire, gradually narrowed into the petiole; flowers bright yellow, 4"–5" broad, solitary on peduncles 1'–3' long, petals 4–7, much exceeding the calyx; achenes flattish, with a minute sharp beak; stamens numerous.

On shores, Newfoundland and arctic America, south to New Jersey, Pennsylvania and Michigan, and in the Rocky Mountains to Colorado. Also in Europe. Summer.

Ranunculus Flámmula L., which has larger mostly broader leaves, the stout stem rooting only at the lower nodes, is recorded from Newfoundland, and is widely distributed in Europe and Asia.

8. Ranunculus obtusiúsculus Raf.   Water Plantain Spearwort.   Fig. 1902.

Ranunculus obtusiusculus Raf. Med. Rep. (II.) 5 : 359. 1808.
Ranunculus alismaefolius A. Gray, Man. Ed. 5, 41. 1867. Not Geyer, 1848.
Ranunculus ambigens S. Wats. Bibliog. Index 1 : 16. 1878.

Mostly stout and 1°–3° high, ascending, glabrous, rooting from the lower nodes; stem hollow, sometimes nearly 1' thick at the base. Leaves lanceolate or oblong-lanceolate, 3'–6' long, 5"–12" wide, denticulate or entire, all but the uppermost on broad petioles, which clasp the stem by a broad base; flowers yellow, panicled, 6"–8" broad; petals 5–7, much exceeding the sepals; head of fruit globose or slightly elongated, 5"–6" in diameter; achenes compressed, ½" long, subulate-beaked, but the beak early deciduous.

Marshes, Maine and Ontario to Georgia, Tennessee, Minnesota and Arkansas. June–Aug.

9. Ranunculus nivàlis L.   Snow Buttercup.   Fig. 1903.

Ranunculus nivalis L. Sp. Pl. 553. 1753.

Stem simple, 4'–12' high. Basal leaves long-petioled, 3–7-lobed, or crenate, thick, glabrous, the blade about 1' broad, those of the stem short-petioled or sessile, deeply lobed; flowers solitary, 6"–9" broad, white or light yellow; calyx nearly half the length of the petals, densely black or brown hairy all over, as is the upper part of the peduncle; head of fruit oblong, 6" long; achenes tipped with the subulate style.

Labrador and arctic America generally; also in northern Europe and Asia. Summer.

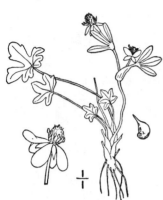

10. Ranunculus pygmaèus Wahl.   Pigmy Butter-cup. Fig. 1904.

Ranunculus pygmaeus Wahl. Fl. Lapp. 157. 1812.

Small, 1′-2′ high, glabrous or sparsely pubescent. Basal leaves slender-petioled, deeply 3–5-lobed or divided, the blade 3″–6″ wide; those of the stem similar and nearly sessile; flowers yellow, 2″–3″ wide, the petals slightly exceeding the glabrous or slightly pubescent sepals; head of fruit short-oblong, 2″ long; achenes ½″ long, lenticular, tipped with a slender beak.

Quebec, Labrador, arctic America, and in the Rocky Mountains. Also in Europe and Asia.

Ranunculus Sàbini R. Br. is another arctic and Rocky Mountain species, differing from this by larger flowers and densely pubescent sepals.

11. Ranunculus pedatífidus J. E. Smith. Northern Buttercup. Fig. 1905.

Ranunculus pedatifidus J. E. Smith in Rees' Cyclop. no. 72. 1813–16.

R. affinis R. Br. in Parry's Voy. App. 265. 1823.

Erect, 4′-12′ high, branching. Basal leaves petioled, broadly ovate or nearly orbicular, about 1′ broad, obtuse, irregularly deeply cleft, those of the stem deeply lobed, nearly sessile, the lobes narrow; flowers yellow, 4″–6″ broad, the petals exceeding the spreading pubescent calyx; head of fruit oblong, 3″–6″ long; achenes oval, tipped with a short beak, often hairy.

Labrador to Alaska, south in the Rocky Mountains to Arizona. Also in northern Asia. Rough-fruited crowfoot. Summer.

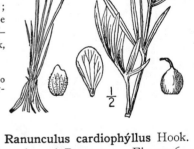

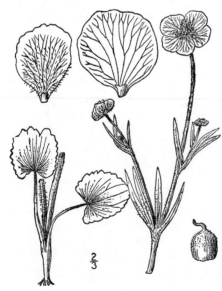

12. Ranunculus cardiophýllus Hook. Heart-leaved Buttercup. Fig. 1906.

R. cardiophyllus Hook. Fl. Bor. Am. 1: 14. 1829.

Ranunculus pedatifidus cardiophyllus Britton, Bull. Torr. Club 18: 265. 1891.

Erect, 4′-15′ high, simple or usually sparingly branched. Basal leaves long-petioled, orbicular to ovate or oblong-ovate, mostly 1′–1½′ broad, coarsely crenate, incised or shallowly lobed, those of the stem short-petioled or nearly sessile, deeply lobed or parted, the lobes narrow, mostly acute or acutish; flowers yellow, larger than in *R. pedatifidus*, 8″–10″ broad, the petals much exceeding the densely tomentose calyx; head of fruit cylindric or ovoid-cylindric, 6″–8″ long; achenes suborbicular, slender-beaked, finely hairy.

In wet meadows and low grounds, Alberta and Saskatchewan to Nebraska and Colorado. May-Aug.

13. Ranunculus Álleni Robinson. Allen's Buttercup. Fig. 1907.

Ranunculus Alleni Robinson, Rhodora **7**: 220. 1905.

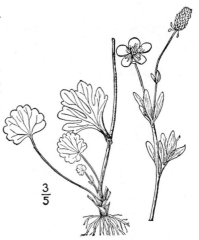

Sparingly pubescent, 4'–8' high, usually branched. Basal leaves long-petioled, orbicular to reniform, 7"–11' wide, coarsely crenate or incised, broadly cuneate to subcordate at the base; cauline leaves sessile or nearly so, deeply cleft or parted into 3–5 mostly oblong or elliptic segments; flowers bright yellow, 5½"–6½" broad, the petals broad, not twice exceeding the loosely villous calyx; head of fruit ovoid to oval; achenes obliquely obovoid, glabrous, minutely beaked.

In moist grounds, Quebec. Aug. Confused with *R. pedatifidus* in our first edition.

$\frac{3}{5}$

$\frac{1}{2}$

14. Ranunculus ovàlis Raf. Prairie Crowfoot. Fig. 1908.

Ranunculus ovalis Raf. Proc. Dec. 36. 1814.
Ranunculus rhomboideus Goldie, Edinb. Phil. Journ. **6**: 329. 1822.

Pubescent, branching, 6'–18' high. Lower and basal leaves oval, oblong, or ovate-oblong, long-petioled, the blade 1' in length or more, crenate or slightly lobed, obtuse, the base more or less cuneate, rarely subcordate; upper cauline leaves sessile or short-petioled, deeply divided into 3–7 linear or oblong obtuse lobes; flowers yellow, 9"–12" broad, the petals narrow and much exceeding the calyx; head of fruit spherical; carpels and achenes oval or orbicular, minutely beaked.

In fields and on prairies, Labrador (?), Quebec and Ontario to Saskatchewan, Alberta, Illinois, Wisconsin and Nebraska. March–May.

15. Ranunculus Hàrveyi (A. Gray) Britton. Harvey's Buttercup. Fig. 1909.

Ranunculus abortivus var. *Harveyi* A. Gray, Proc. Am. Acad. **21**: 372. 1886.
R. Harveyi Britton, Mem. Torr. Club **5**: 159. 1894.

Glabrous, stem erect, slender, branched, 8'–18' tall, from a cluster of narrowly fusiform roots. Leaves thin, the basal and lower ones long-petioled, reniform or suborbicular, obtusely crenate or somewhat lobed, 5"–18" wide, cordate, or some of them truncate at the base, the upper sessile or nearly so, deeply 3-cleft or 3-parted into linear or narrowly oblong entire or few-toothed obtuse segments; flowers bright yellow, 6"–9" broad; petals 4–8, oblong, 4 or 5 times as long as the reflexed sepals; head of fruit globose, 2" in diameter; achenes oblique, compressed, tipped with a minute straight beak.

On dry hillsides, Missouri and Arkansas. April–May.

$\frac{1}{2}$

16. Ranunculus abortìvus L. Kidney- or Smooth-leaved Crowfoot. Fig. 1910.

Ranunculus abortivus L. Sp. Pl. 551. 1753.

R. abortivus encyclus Fernald, Rhodora I : 52. 1899.

Glabrous, or but sparingly pubescent, 6'-2° high, branched. Basal leaves long-petioled, bright green, thick, crenate or sometimes lobed, broadly ovate, obtuse, and generally cordate or reniform, the cauline sessile or nearly so, divided into oblong or linear somewhat cuneate lobes; head of fruit globose, the receptacle short, pubescent; flowers yellow, 2″-3″ broad, the petals oblong, shorter than the reflexed calyx; achenes tipped with a minute curved beak.

In woods and moist grounds, Labrador and Nova Scotia to Manitoba, south to Florida, Arkansas and Colorado. Recorded as biennial in duration. April–June.

17. Ranunculus micránthus Nutt. Rock Crowfoot. Fig. 1911.

R. micranthus Nutt.; T. & G. Fl. N. A. I : 18. 1838.
Ranunculus abortivus var. *micranthus* A. Gray, Man. Ed. 5, 42. 1867.

Similar to the preceding species but usually smaller, villous with spreading hairs, flowering when very young, 6'-18' tall. Leaves thin, dull green, the basal ones ovate, obovate, or suborbicular, 3-lobed or crenate, narrowed, rounded or subcordate at the base; segments of the upper leaves narrow, entire or sharply toothed; flowers yellow, about 3″ broad; sepals narrowed into a short claw; petals oblong or oval, 2–3 times as long as wide; head of fruit rather longer than thick, the receptacle linear, glabrous or very nearly so.

In rich woods, often on rocks, Maine to Minnesota, Saskatchewan, Georgia, Arkansas and Colorado. In New York it blooms somewhat earlier than the preceding species. Roots tuberous. April–May.

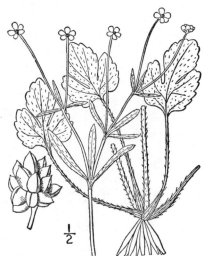

18. Ranunculus alleghaniénsis Britton. Mountain Crowfoot. Fig. 1912.

Ranunculus alleghaniensis Britton, Bull. Torr. Club 22 : 224. 1895.

Similar in aspect to *R. abortivus* and *R. micranthus*, glabrous, stem widely branched, 1°-2° tall. Basal leaves reniform or suborbicular, 6″-2′ wide, long-petioled, crenate or some of them lobed, the teeth and lobes subacute; stem leaves sessile or the lower petioled, divided nearly or quite to the base into linear acute entire toothed or cleft segments; flowers 2″-3″ broad; petals oblong, not exceeding the calyx, yellow, glandular; head of fruit globose or globose-oblong, 2″ in diameter; achenes slightly compressed and margined, tipped with subulate hooked or recurved styles of about one-half their length.

In rich woods, Vermont, Massachusetts and New York to the mountains of North Carolina. Plant slightly glaucous. April–May.

19. Ranunculus sceleràtus L. Celery-leaved Crowfoot. Fig. 1913.

Ranunculus sceleratus L. Sp. Pl. 551. 1753.
R. eremogenes Greene, Erythea 4: 121. 1896.

Stout, glabrous, or nearly so, 6'-2° high, freely branching, stem hollow, sometimes 1¾' thick. Basal leaves thick, 3-5-lobed, on long and broad petioles, the blade 1'-2' broad, reniform or cordate, those of the stem petioled or the upper sessile, deeply lobed or divided, the lobes obtuse, cuneate-oblong or linear, several-toothed or entire; flowers yellow, numerous, 3"-4" broad, the petals about equalling the calyx; head of fruit oblong or cylindric, 4"-6" long; achenes ½" long, very numerous, merely apiculate.

In swamps and wet ditches, New Brunswick to Florida, abundant along the coast, and locally westward to North Dakota, Kansas and Nebraska, extending to Alberta, New Mexico and California, preferring saline or alkaline situations. Also in Europe and Asia. Ditch- or marsh-crowfoot. Biting- or cursed-crowfoot. Water-celery. Blister-wort. Consists of several races. April-Aug.

20. Ranunculus recurvàtus Poir. Hooked or Rough Crowfoot. Fig. 1914.

R. recurvatus Poir. in Lam. Encycl. 6: 125. 1804.

Erect, 6'-2° high, usually hirsute, branching. Leaves all petioled, broadly reniform, 2'-3' wide, deeply 3-cleft, the divisions broadly cuneate, acute, toothed and lobed; flowers light yellow, 4"-5" broad, the petals shorter than or equalling the reflexed calyx; head of fruit globose, 6" wide; achenes compressed, margined, tipped with a recurved hooked beak of one-half their length.

In woods, Nova Scotia to Manitoba, south to Florida, Alabama, Missouri and Kansas. Ascends to 4200 ft. in North Carolina. April-June.

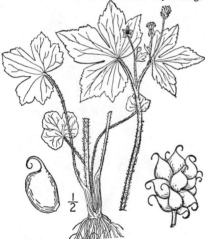

21. Ranunculus àcris L. Tall or Meadow Buttercup. Fig. 1915.

Ranunculus acris L. Sp. Pl. 554. 1753.

Erect, hairy, branched above, 2°-3° high; roots fibrous. Basal leaves tufted, petioled, 3-7-divided, the divisions sessile and cleft into numerous linear to obovate mainly acute lobes; upper leaves short-petioled and merely 3-parted, distant; flowers numerous, bright yellow, about 1' broad; petals twice or thrice the length of the spreading calyx, obovate; head of fruit globose, 6"-7" broad; achenes compressed, short-beaked.

In fields and meadows, Newfoundland to Virginia, British Columbia and Missouri. Bermuda. Naturalized from Europe. Stem sometimes nearly glabrous. Yellow gowan. Gold-knops. Butter-rose, -cresses or -daisy. Horse-gold. Bachelor's-buttons. Blister-plant. May-Sept.

22. Ranunculus bulbòsus L. Bulbous Buttercup. Yellow weed or Gowan. Fig. 1916.

Ranunculus bulbosus L. Sp. Pl. 554. 1753.

Erect from a bulbous-thickened base, hairy, 6'–18' high. Leaves petioled, 3-divided, the terminal division stalked, the lateral ones sessile or nearly so, all variously lobed and cleft, flowers bright yellow, about 1' broad; petals 5–7, much longer than the reflexed sepals, obovate, rounded; head of fruit globose, 5''–6'' broad; achenes compressed, very short-beaked.

In fields and along roadsides, New England to North Carolina, Tennessee and Louisiana. Naturalized from Europe. May–June. In England the name Buttercups is chiefly applied to this species and to *R. repens* and *R. acris*; called also in middle English Kingcups, Goldcups, Butter-flowers and Blister-flowers. Frogwort. Pilewort. Golden knops. Cuckoo-buds. Pissabed. Horse-gold. St. Anthony's-turnip. May–July.

23. Ranunculus pennsylvánicus L. f. Bristly Buttercup or Crowfoot Fig. 1917.

Ranunculus pennsylvanicus L. f. Suppl. 272 1781.

Erect, branching, pilose-hispid, 1°–2° high, leafy. Leaves thin, 3-divided; divisions stalked, deeply 3-cleft, the lobes lanceolate, cuneate, acute, incised; flowers yellow, 3''–4'' wide; petals equalling the reflexed sepals or shorter; head of fruit oblong or cylindric, 3'' thick, sometimes 6'' long; achenes smooth, pointed with a sharp beak one-third their length; receptacle conic, hairy.

In wet, open places, Nova Scotia to Georgia, British Columbia, Kansas and Colorado. June–Aug.

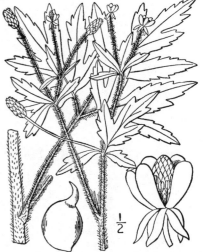

24. Ranunculus Macòunii Britton. Macoun's Buttercup. Fig. 1918.

Ranunculus hispidus Hook. Fl. Bor. Am. 1 : 19. 1829. Not Michx. 1803.
Ranunculus Macounii Britton, Trans. N. Y. Acad. Sci. 12 : 3. 1892.

Erect or diffuse, hairy, branching, 1°–2° high. Leaves 3-divided, the blade 2'–3' long, the divisions broadly oblong to ovate, acute, cuneate, variously cleft and lobed; flowers 5''–6'' broad, yellow, the petals exceeding the spreading or slightly reflexed calyx; head of fruit globose to oblong, 4'' thick; achenes smooth, pointed with a sharp beak about one-fourth their length; receptacle obovoid.

Quebec and Ontario to Illinois, Minnesota and west to British Columbia and Washington, extending south in the Rocky Mountains to Arizona. Summer.

25. Ranunculus rèpens L. Creeping Buttercup. Gold-balls. Fig. 1919.

Ranunculus repens L. Sp. Pl. 554. 1753.

R. Clintoni Beck, Bot. N. & Mid. States 9. 1833.

Generally hairy, sometimes only slightly so, spreading by runners and forming large patches. Leaves petioled, 3-divided, the terminal division, or all three stalked, all ovate, cuneate or truncate, acute, cleft and lobed, often blotched; flowers nearly 1' broad; petals obovate, much exceeding the spreading sepals; head of fruit globose, 4″ in diameter; achenes margined, tipped with a stout short slightly bent beak.

Fields, roadsides, and in wet grounds, Newfoundland to Virginia, Ontario and British Columbia. Bermuda; Jamaica. Mainly introduced from Europe, but regarded as indigenous in its western range. Ram's-claws. Gold-knops. Butterdaisy. Horse-gold. Sitfast. Yellow gowan. Spotted-leaf buttercup. May–July.

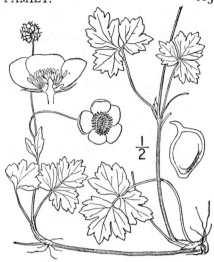

26. Ranunculus septentrionàlis Poir. Swamp or Marsh Buttercup. Fig. 1920.

Ranunculus septentrionalis Poir. in Lam. Encycl. 6: 125. 1804.

Roots simply fibrous; plant branching, 1°–3° high, glabrous, or pubescent, the later branches procumbent and sometimes rooting at the nodes. Leaves large, petioled, 3-divided; divisions mostly stalked, usually cuneate at the base, cleft into broad lobes; lower petioles occasionally a foot long; flowers 1' in diameter or more, bright yellow; petals obovate, twice the length of the spreading sepals; head of fruit globose or oval, 4″ in diameter; achenes flat, strongly margined, subulate-beaked by the stout sword-shaped style which is of nearly their length and often early deciduous.

Mainly in swamps and low grounds, New Brunswick to Manitoba, Georgia and Kansas. April–July.

Ranunculus sicaefórmis Mack. & Bush, of Missouri and Minnesota, seems to be a hispid-pubescent race of this species.

27. Ranunculus híspidus Michx. Hispid Buttercup. Fig. 1921.

R. hispidus Michx. Fl. Bor. Am. 1: 321. 1803.

Usually densely villous when young, sometimes merely appressed-pubescent or glabrate when old; stems ascending or spreading, 8'–2° long; plant not stoloniferous; roots a cluster of thickened fibers. Leaves pinnately 3–5-divided, the divisions ovate, oblong or obovate, narrowed or cuneate at the base, sharply cleft or lobed, usually thin; flowers 6″–18″ broad; petals oblong, about twice as long as the spreading sepals, entire or emarginate; head of fruit globose-oval or globose; achenes broadly oval, lenticular, narrowly margined, abruptly tipped by a subulate style of about onehalf their length.

In dry woods and thickets, Vermont and Ontario to North Dakota, south to Georgia and Arkansas. The earliest flowering buttercup of the vicinity of New York. Ascends to 6000 ft. in North Carolina. March–May.

3/5

28. Ranunculus fasciculàris Muhl. Early or Tufted Buttercup. Fig. 1922.

Ranunculus fascicularis Muhl. Cat. 54. 1813.

Appressed-pubescent; fibrous roots thickened; plant generally low, 6'–12' high, tufted. Leaves petioled, 3–5-divided; divisions stalked (especially the terminal one), deeply lobed and cleft, the lobes oblong or linear; flowers about 1' broad; petals yellow, obovate-spatulate, much longer than the spreading sepals, rounded, truncate or even emarginate; head of fruit globose, about 4" in diameter; achenes flat, slightly margined, beaked with the subulate persistent style which is nearly or quite their length.

Woods, Ontario to Massachusetts, North Carolina, Wisconsin, Kansas and Texas. Reported from Manitoba. Not common near the Atlantic coast. Bundle-rooted buttercup. Cowslip. April–May.

29. Ranunculus pàrvulus L. Hairy Buttercup. Fig. 1923.

Ranunculus parvulus L. Mant. 1: 79. 1767.
Ranunculus Philonotis Retz, Obs. 6: 31. 1791.

Erect, hairy, 6'–15' high, branching. Basal and lower leaves broad-petioled, the blade 1'–2' broad and long, 3-divided or cleft, the divisions broadly ovate, cuneate, stalked, cleft and lobed, the terminal sessile or nearly so, deeply cleft into linear-oblong obtuse segments; flowers yellow, 12" broad or less; petals much exceeding the reflexed calyx; head of fruit oblong, 2"–3" thick; achenes flat, strongly margined, short-beaked, provided with a series of small tubercles or papillae which become more prominent in drying, or nearly smooth.

In ballast grounds and waste places, New Brunswick; Pennsylvania to Florida. Adventive from Europe. Summer.

1/2

30. Ranunculus parviflòrus L. Small-flowered Crowfoot. Fig. 1924.

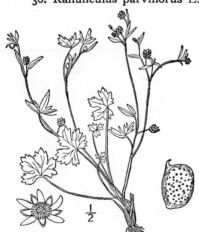

1/2

Ranunculus parviflorus L. Sp. Pl. Ed. 2, 780. 1763.

Hairy, slender, diffuse, annual, branching from the base, 6'–10' high. Basal leaves long-petioled, the blade reniform or cordate-orbicular, 1' broad or less, 3-cleft, the lobes broadly oval, obtuse, cut and toothed; upper leaves short-petioled or nearly sessile, 3–5-parted into linear-oblong lobes; flowers yellow, 1"–2" wide; petals not much longer than the calyx; head of fruit globose, 2" broad; achenes flat, margined, densely papillose, 1½" long, tipped with a sharp beak of about one-fourth their length.

In waste places, Maryland and eastern Virginia to Florida, Arkansas and Texas, and in ballast grounds about the northern seaports. Naturalized or fugitive from Europe. Also naturalized in Bermuda and in Jamaica. Summer.

31. Ranunculus muricàtus L. Spiny-fruited Crowfoot. Fig. 1925.

Ranunculus muricatus L. Sp. Pl. 555. 1753.

Annual, glabrous or sparingly pubescent, branched from the base, 1°–2° high. Lower and basal leaves on long broad petioles, the blade reniform or cordate-orbicular, 1′–2′ wide, 3-lobed, cleft, or crenate; the upper 3-divided, cuneate, short-petioled or sessile; flowers light yellow, 3″–5″ wide, the petals exceeding the calyx; head of fruit globular, 5″–6″ wide; achenes flat, with a broad smooth margin, densely muricate and spiny on the sides, 2″ long, tipped with a stout slightly curved beak of one-half their length, the stout margin unarmed.

Waste places and fields, eastern Virginia to Arkansas, Florida and Texas. Bermuda. Naturalized or adventive from Europe. Also on the Pacific Coast. Native also in Asia. Summer.

32. Ranunculus arvénsis L. Corn Crowfoot. Hunger-weed. Fig. 1926.

Ranunculus arvensis L. Sp. Pl. 555. 1753.

Erect, glabrous or sparingly pubescent, branched above, 1° or more high. Lower leaves petioled, the upper sessile, all deeply cleft or divided into linear-oblong, obtuse cuneate, lobed or toothed segments or the lowest entire; flowers 6″–8″ broad, pale yellow, the petals exceeding the sepals; achenes 4–8, flattened, margined, spiny-tuberculate on the sides and margin, 2″ long, tipped with a subulate beak more than one-half their length.

In waste grounds, southern New York and New Jersey to Ohio, and in ballast. Fugitive from Europe, where it is abundant in grain-fields. Called Hunger-weed because supposed to indicate, when prevalent, a poor crop and consequent want. Starve-acre. Devil's-claws. Hell-weed. Horsegold. Gold-weed. Summer.

21. BATRÀCHIUM S. F. Gray, Nat. Arr. Brit. Pl. 2: 720. 1821.

Perennial aquatic or ditch herbs, with alternate dissected or palmately lobed leaves, the segments of the submerged ones often filiform, and solitary rather small white flowers, borne on peduncles opposite the leaves. Sepals and petals usually 5. Petals oblong or oval, the base sometimes yellowish, the claw bearing a small pit. Stamens several or numerous. Achenes oblique, compressed, not margined, beakless or short-beaked, transversely wrinkled. [Greek, referring to the aquatic habitat.]

About 20 species of very wide geographic distribution. Besides the following, several others occur in western North America. Type species: *Batrachium hederaceum* (L.) S. F. Gray.

Leaves all dissected into filiform segments and lobes.
 Leaves 1′–2′ long, flaccid, collapsing when taken from the water. 1. *B. trichophyllum.*
 Leaves 1′ long or less, rigid when taken from the water. 2. *B. circinatum.*
Leaves all reniform or broadly ovate, 3–5-lobed, 5″–10″ wide. 3. *B. hederaceum.*

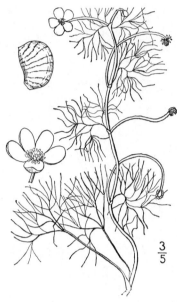

1. Batrachium trichophýllum (Chaix) F. Schultz. White Water-Crowfoot. Fig. 1927.

Ranunculus trichophyllus Chaix in Vill. Hist. Pl. Dauph.
1 : 335. 1786.
Batrachium trichophyllum F. Schultz, Arch. Fl. France
et All. 1 : 107. 1848.
Ranunculus aquatilis var. *trichophyllus* A. Gray, Man.
Ed. 5, 40. 1867.
R. aquatilis var. *caespitosus* DC. Prodr. 1 : 26. 1824.
R. aquatilis capillaceus DC. Prodr. 1 : 26. 1824.

Submerged; stems branching, usually 1° long or more. Leaves petioled, 1'–2' long, flaccid and collapsing when withdrawn from the water, repeatedly forked into capillary divisions; flowers white, 6''–9'' broad, on stout peduncles 1'–2' long, blooming at the surface of the water; head of fruit globose, 2'' broad; receptacle hairy; achenes apiculate.

In ponds and streams, Nova Scotia to British Columbia, south to North Carolina and California. Also in Europe and Asia. Consists, apparently, of numerous races, differing in habit, in size of flowers, number of stamens and shape of petals; several of these have been recognized as species. Water-milfoil. Green eel-grass. Pickerel-weed. June–Sept.

2. Batrachium circinàtum (Sibth.) Rchb. Stiff White Water-Crowfoot. Fig. 1928.

Ranunculus circinatus Sibth.; J. E. Smith, Fl. Brit. 2 : 596. 1800.
Batrachium circinatum Rchb.; Spach, Hist. Veg. 7 : 201. 1839.
R. aquatilis var. *divaricatus* A. Gray, Man. Ed. 2, 7. 1856.

Similar to the preceding species, but the leaves are shorter, less than 1' long, spreading nearly at right angles from the stem, rigid when withdrawn from the water and sessile or nearly so; there appear to be no constant differences in flower or fruit.

In ponds and slow streams, Ontario, New England, northern New Jersey and Pennsylvania, and west to the Pacific Coast, extending south in the Rocky Mountains to Arizona. Also in Europe. Summer. Referred in our first edition to *Batrachium divaricatum* (Schrank) Wimmer.

Batrachium longiróstre (Godr.) F. Schultz, if distinct from this species, differs in having a longer beak to the achene.

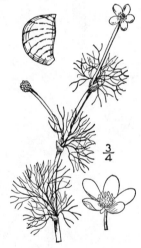

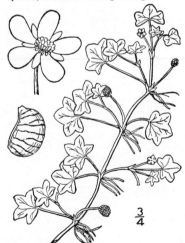

3. Batrachium hederàceum (L.) S. F. Gray. Ivy-leaved Crowfoot. Fig. 1929.

Ranunculus hederaceus L. Sp. Pl. 556. 1753.

Batrachium hederaceum S. F. Gray, Nat. Arr. Brit. Pl. 2 : 721. 1821.

Semi-aquatic, rooting extensively at the joints, branching, entirely glabrous. Leaves floating, or spreading on the mud, semi-circular, reniform or broadly ovate in outline, 3–5-lobed, 3''–6'' long, 5''–10'' broad, the lobes obtuse; flowers 2''–3'' broad; head of fruit globose, 2'' wide; receptacle glabrous; achenes minutely beaked.

In ponds and pools, Newfoundland; southeastern Virginia and Maryland. Naturalized from Europe. June–

22. FICÀRIA [Rupp.] Huds. Fl. Angl. 213. 1762.

Glabrous slightly fleshy perennial herbs, with thickened tuberous roots, branched or simple spreading or erect stems, petioled entire or toothed cordate leaves, and large solitary yellow terminal or axillary flowers. Sepals 3 or sometimes 5, deciduous. Petals 7–12 (commonly 8), yellow, or red at the base, bearing a small pit and scale at the base of the blade. Stamens and pistils numerous. Achenes slightly compressed, blunt, not wrinkled nor ribbed. Cotyledon only one. [Latin, fig, from the fig-like thickened roots.]

About 4 species, natives of the Old World. Type species: *Ficaria verna* Huds.

1. Ficaria Ficària (L.) Karst.   Lesser Celandine.   Fig. 1930.

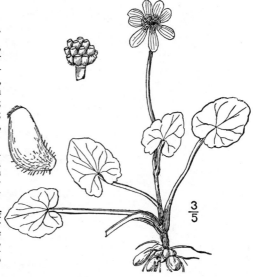

Ranunculus Ficaria L. Sp. Pl. 550. 1753.
F. verna Huds. Fl. Angl. 214. 1762.
F. ranunculoides Moench, Meth. 215. 1794.

Glabrous, flowering stems scapose, 4′–5′ high, bearing 1 or 2 leaves or naked, erect from large fleshy thickened roots. Leaves ovate, cordate, obtuse, crenate, somewhat fleshy, on broad petioles, the blade 1′–2′ long; flowers yellow, 1′ broad; sepals 3; petals 8 or 9; head of fruit globose, ½′ broad; carpels beakless, truncate.

Massachusetts to the District of Columbia. Fugitive from Europe, where it is a common pasture weed, occurring also in western Asia. Pilewort. Crain. Figwort-buttercup. Golden guineas. Golden cup. April–May.

Cyrtorhyncha ranunculìna Nutt., of Wyoming and Colorado, admitted into our first edition as also of Nebraska, is here omitted, as the specimens so determined, and recorded in the "Catalogue of Nebraska Plants," prove, on examination, to be *Ranunculus delphinifolius* Torr.

23. HALERPÉSTES Greene, Pittonia 4: 207. 1900.

Perennial herbs, with crenate dentate or lobed long-petioled leaves, and small yellow flowers, solitary or 2–7 together on scapes or scape-like peduncles. Sepals usually 5, spreading, tardily deciduous. Petals 5–12, yellow, each bearing a small nectar-pit and scale near the base. Stamens and pistils numerous. Head of fruit oblong, oval or subglobose. Achenes compressed, sometimes swollen, longitudinally striate, without a hard coat. [Greek, coastal creeper.]

Two species, the following typical one of North America, Asia and southern South America, the other Asiatic.

1. Halerpestes Cymbalària (Pursh) Greene.   Seaside Crowfoot.   Fig. 1931.

Ranunculus Cymbalaria Pursh, Fl. Am. Sept. 392. 1814.
Oxygraphis Cymbalaria Prantl, in Engl. & Prantl, Nat. Pfl. Fam. 3: Abt. 2, 63. 1891.
Cyrtorhyncha Cymbalaria Britton, Mem. Torr. Club 5: 161. 1894.
H. Cymbalaria Greene, Pittonia 4: 208. 1900.

Low, glabrous, somewhat succulent, spreading by runners. Leaves mostly basal, slender-petioled, the blade cordate-oval or reniform, crenate, 2″–9″ long; flowers 1–7, about 3″–4″ broad, borne on scapes 1′–9′ long, these sometimes bearing one or more leaves toward the base; head of fruit oblong, 3″–8″ long; achenes compressed, somewhat swollen, distinctly striate, minutely sharp-pointed.

On sandy shores, Labrador to New Jersey, west along the St. Lawrence River and the Great Lakes to Minnesota, Kansas and the Northwest Territory, and in saline soil throughout the western half of the continent, extending into Mexico. Also in Asia and South America. The so-called var. *alpina* Hook. is a small northern race. Summer.

24. THALÍCTRUM [Tourn.] L. Sp. Pl. 545. 1753.

Erect perennial herbs. Leaves ternately decompound, basal and cauline, the latter alternate. Flowers perfect, polygamous or dioecious, generally small, greenish-white or purplish, panicled or racemed. Sepals 4 or 5, caducous or early deciduous. Petals none. Achenes commonly few, one-seeded, ribbed or nerved, inflated in some species, stipitate or sessile. Stamens ∞, exserted. [Derivation doubtful, name used for same plant by Dioscorides.]

A genus of about 85 species, most abundant in the north temperate zone, a few in the Andes of South America, India and South Africa. In addition to the species described below, about 12 others are North American, natives of the Southern States, the Rocky Mountains and the Pacific Coast. Type species: *Thalictrum foetidum* L.

Flowers perfect.
  Stem simple, scape-like; achenes sessile; filaments slender.   1. *T. alpinum.*
  Stem branched, leafy; achenes long-stipitate; filaments petal-like.   2. *T. clavatum.*
Flowers dioecious or polygamous.
  Achenes distinctly stipitate.
    Roots bright yellow; terminal leaflets not wider than long.   3. *T. coriaceum.*
    Roots not yellow; terminal leaflets wider than long.   4. *T. caulophylloides.*
  Achenes sessile or nearly so.
    Leaflets waxy-glandular beneath.   5. *T. revolutum.*
    Leaflets not waxy-glandular.
      Filaments capillary or slightly thickened upward.
        Leaflets oblong, longer than wide, mostly puberulent beneath.   6. *T. dasycarpum.*
        Leaflets suborbicular, pale and glabrous beneath.
          Achenes thick-walled, indistinctly ridged.   7. *T. venulosum.*
          Achenes thin-walled, distinctly ribbed.   8. *T. dioicum.*
      Filaments club-shaped, often as wide as the anthers.   9. *T. polygamum.*

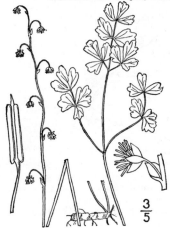

3/5

1. Thalictrum alpìnum L. Arctic or Dwarf Meadow-Rue. Fig. 1932.

Thalictrum alpinum L. Sp. Pl. 545. 1753.

Smooth or slightly glandular, 1′–12′ high. Leaves small, tufted at the summits of scaly rootstocks, biternate; the scapiform stem leafless or 1-leaved near the base; leaflets cuneate-obovate or orbicular, firm, 3–5-lobed at the apex, margins revolute; panicle very simple, often racemose; flowers perfect; stamens about 10; filaments filiform, about equalling the sepals; anthers oblong-linear, mucronate; stigma linear; achenes 1½″ long, obliquely obovoid, sessile.

Anticosti, Newfoundland and arctic America generally. Also in the Rocky Mountains, and in Europe and Asia. Summer.

2. Thalictrum clavàtum DC. Mountain Meadow-Rue. Fig. 1933.

Thalictrum clavatum DC. Syst. 1: 171. 1818.

Glabrous, branching, 6′–24′ high. Leaves basal and cauline, biternate; leaflets oval, ovate, or the terminal obovate-cuneate, thin, pale beneath, stalked, with 3 main lobes and a few secondary ones, their margins not revolute; inflorescence cymose; flowers perfect; filaments clavate and petal-like; anthers oblong, blunt; achenes spreading, equalling their stipes or longer, obliquely oblong, narrowed at each end, flattened; stigma minute.

Mountains of Virginia and West Virginia to Georgia and Alabama. Slender meadow-rue. May–June.

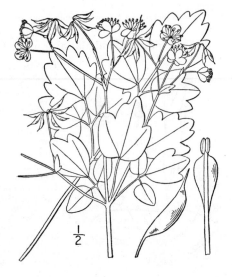

1/2

3. Thalictrum coriàceum (Britton) Small.　Thick-leaved Meadow-Rue. Fig. 1934.

Thalictrum dioicum var. *coriaceum* Britton, Bull. Torr. Club **18**: 363. 1891.

Thalictrum coriaceum Small, Mem. Torr. Club **4**: 98. 1893.

Tall, 3°–5° high, the large rootstocks and roots bright yellow. Stem striate, paniculately branched above; leaves 3–4-ternate, short-petioled, the lower petioles expanded at the base into stipule-like appendages; leaflets obovate or reniform-orbicular, coriaceous, nearly white beneath, usually deeply and sharply incised, the veins prominent on the lower surface; flowers dioecious, the staminate nearly white, the anthers linear, subulate-tipped, longer than the filiform filaments; pistillate flowers purple; achenes oblong-ovoid, subacute, stalked, sharply ribbed, somewhat longer than the persistent style.

In open places, Pennsylvania to Virginia, North Carolina and Tennessee. May–June.

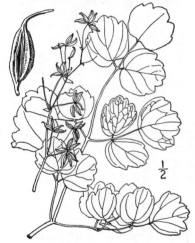

4. Thalictrum caulophylloìdes Small.　Cohosh Meadow-Rue. Fig. 1935.

Thalictrum caulophylloides Small, Bull. Torr. Club **25**: 136. 1898.

Tall, 2½°–5½° high, the creeping rootstocks and the roots, pale. Stem finely striate, rather widely branched above; leaves 3–4-ternate, very short-petioled, with the stipular appendages smaller than in *T. coriaceum;* leaflets thinnish, but firm, broadly oval, suborbicular or somewhat reniform in outline, larger than in *T. coriaceum,* the terminal ones wider than long, all 3–5-lobed, pale or glaucous beneath; flowers dioecious, the staminate greenish, the anthers narrowly linear, larger, longer- and more slender-tipped than in *T. coriaceum;* pistillate flowers greenish-purple; achenes elliptic, acute, decidedly stalked, sharply ridged, much longer than the persistent style.

On mountain sides and river banks, Maryland and Virginia near the District of Columbia and in eastern Tennessee. May–July.

5. Thalictrum revolùtum DC.　Waxy Meadow-Rue. Fig. 1936.

Thalictrum revolutum DC. Syst. **1**: 173. 1818.
T. purpurascens var. *ceriferum* Austin; A. Gray, Man. Ed. 5, 39. 1867.

Stem mostly stout, often purplish, 3°–7° high, glabrous or nearly so. Leaves 3–4-ternate, the lower petioled, the upper sessile or short petioled; leaflets firm in texture, ovate to obovate, 1–3-lobed above the middle or entire, dark green above, paler and waxy-resinous or glandular-pubescent beneath, their margins somewhat revolute; flowers dioecious or polygamous; filaments capillary or slightly thickened above, twice as long as the linear anthers, early drooping; achenes very short-stipitate or sessile, ridged.

Woodlands, thickets and river-banks, Massachusetts to South Carolina, Ontario, Tennessee and Missouri. May–June. Plant strongly odorous.

6. Thalictrum dasycàrpum Fisch. & Lall. Purplish or Tall Meadow-Rue. Fig. 1937.

Thalictrum dasycarpum Fisch. & Lall. Ind. Sem. Hort. Petrop. **8** : *72*. 1842.

Stout, erect, purplish, 4°–7° high, leafy, branching above, pubescent or glabrous; leaves 3–4-ternate, those of the stem sessile or short-petioled; leaflets oblong or obovate, dark green above, commonly somewhat pubescent, but neither waxy nor glandular beneath, and with 3 main apical pointed lobes; panicle compound, leafy, 1° long or more; flowers dioecious or perhaps sometimes polygamous; filaments narrow, slightly widened above; anthers linear or linear-oblong, cuspidate; achenes ovoid, glabrous or pubescent, short-stipitate, with 6–8 longitudinal wings.

In copses and woodlands, New Jersey to North Dakota, Saskatchewan, Nebraska and Arizona. Illustrated in our first edition as *T. purpurascens* L. June–Aug.

7. Thalictrum venulòsum Trelease. Veiny Meadow-Rue. Fig. 1938.

Thalictrum venulosum Trelease, Proc. Bost. Soc. Nat. Hist. **23** : *302*. 1886.
T. campestre Greene, Erythea **4** : *123*. 1896.
T. confine Fernald, Rhodora **2** : *232*. 1900.

Glabrous, pale green and glaucous, stem erect, or assurgent at the base, 6'–2° tall. Leaves 3–4-ternate, long-petioled; leaflets firm, obovate or suborbicular, rounded at the apex, cuneate, obtuse or subcordate at the base, 4''–8'' long, 3–5-lobed, the lower surface rather prominently rugose-veined; panicle narrow, its branches nearly erect; flowers dioecious; stamens 8–20; filaments slender; anthers linear, slender-pointed; achenes ovoid, nearly sessile, tapering into a short beak, thick-walled, slightly 2-edged.

In gravelly and rocky soil, Nova Scotia to Maine, New York, Manitoba, Washington, South Dakota and Colorado. Has been confused with *T. occidentale* A. Gray. May–July.

8. Thalictrum diòicum L. Early Meadow-Rue. Fig. 1939.

Thalictrum dioicum L. Sp. Pl. 545. 1753.

Glabrous, erect, 1°–2° high, slender, leafy. Roots not yellow; leaves 3–4-ternate; leaflets thin, pale beneath, orbicular or broader, often cordate and the terminal one somewhat cuneate, 5–9-lobed; flowers dioecious, greenish, drooping or spreading; panicle elongated, of numerous lateral corymbs or umbels; filaments longer than the sepals; anthers linear, blunt, longer than the filaments; stigma elongated; achenes ovoid, sessile or minutely stipitate, strongly ribbed, much longer than the style.

In woods, Maine to Alabama, Saskatchewan and Missouri. Ascends to 4500 ft. in North Carolina. Poor-man's rhubarb. Shining grass. Quicksilverweed. Feathered columbine. April–May. Recorded from Labrador.

9. Thalictrum polýgamum Muhl.   Fall Meadow-Rue.   Fig. 1940.

Thalictrum polygamum Muhl. Cat. 54. 1813.
Thalictrum Cornuti T. & G. Fl. N. A. 1: 38. 1838.
    Not L. 1753.

Stout, 3°–11° high, branching, leafy, smooth or pubescent but not glandular nor waxy. Leaves 3–4-ternate; leaflets moderately thick, light green above and paler beneath, oblong, obovate or orbicular, with 3 main apical pointed or obtuse lobes; panicle compound, leafy, a foot long or more; flowers polygamous, white or purplish; filaments broadened, narrowly clavate; anthers oblong, short; achenes ovoid, short-stipitate, 6–8-winged, glabrous or pubescent.

Newfoundland to Florida, Ontario and Ohio. Its favorite habitat is in open sunny swamps. Ascends to 2500 ft. in Virginia. Silver-weed. Rattlesnake-bite. Musket- or musquash-weed. Celandine. Several additional species of *Thalictrum* from within our range have been described by Professor Greene, at least some of which are referable to *T. polygamum* as races.

25. ADÒNIS [Dill.] L. Sp. Pl. 547. 1753.

Erect, annual or perennial herbs. Leaves alternate, pinnately dissected into numerous linear segments. Flowers yellow or red, solitary, terminal. Petals 5–16, conspicuous. Carpels ∞, 1-ovuled. Achenes capitate or spicate, rugose-reticulated, tipped with the persistent styles. [Mythological name for a favorite of Venus, changed into a flower.]

A genus of showy-flowered plants, natives of the north temperate regions of Europe and Asia, consisting of the following and about five other species. Type species: *Adonis annua* L.

1. Adonis ánnua L.   Pheasant's or Bird's Eye.   Fig. 1941.

Adonis annua L. Sp. Pl. 547. 1753.

Adonis autumnalis L. Sp. Pl. Ed. 2, 771. 1763.

Annual, erect, 1°–2° high, branched, glabrous. Leaves finally dissected, the lower petioled, the upper sessile, the segments acute; sepals smooth, deciduous; flowers 9″–18″ broad, nearly globular, orange or red, the petals obovate, and darker colored at the base; achenes spicate.

Commonly cultivated for ornament; spontaneous in gardens and occasionally escaped into waste places, especially southward. Fugitive from Europe. Summer. Adonis'-flower. Red-morocco. Camomile.

26. CLÉMATIS L. Sp. Pl. 543. 1753.

Climbing vines, more or less woody. Leaves opposite, slender-petioled, pinnately compound. Flowers cymose-paniculate, our species dioecious, or nearly so. Sepals 4 or 5, valvate in the bud, spreading, petaloid. Petals none. Stamens numerous, spreading; filaments mostly glabrous; anthers short, blunt. Pistils numerous. Achenes 1-seeded. Style long, persistent, plumose. [Greek name for some climbing plant.]

About 25 species of very wide geographic distribution. Besides the following, several others occur in the southern and western parts of North America. Type species: *Clematis vitalba* L.

Leaves 3-foliolate; eastern.   1. *C. virginiana*.
Leaves pinnately 5–7-foliolate; western.   2. *C. ligusticifolia*.

1. Clematis virginiàna L. Virginia Virgin's Bower. Fig. 1942.

Clematis virginiana L. Amoen. Acad. 4 : 275. 1759.

A long vine, climbing over bushes in low woodlands and along fences and water-courses. Leaves glabrous or nearly so, trifoliolate; leaflets mostly broadly ovate, acute at the apex, toothed or lobed, sometimes slightly cordate; flowers white, in leafy panicles, polygamo-dioecious, 8''–15'' broad when expanded; filaments glabrous; persistent styles plumose, 1' long or more.

Georgia to Tennessee, northward to Nova Scotia and Manitoba. Leaves rarely 5-foliolate. Ascends to 2600 ft. in Virginia. Woodbine. Traveler's-joy. Love-vine. Devil's-hair or -darning-needle. Wild hops. July–Sept.

Clematis missouriénsis Rydb., of Missouri, Kansas and Nebraska, differs in having marginless achenes and in being more pubescent; it has been confused with *C. Catesbyana* Pursh, of the southern states and may be specifically distinct.

2. Clematis ligusticifòlia Nutt. Western Virgin's Bower. Fig. 1943.

C. ligusticifolia Nutt.; T. & G. Fl. N. A. 1 : 9. 1838.

A trailing and climbing vine, nearly glabrous. Leaves pinnately 5-foliolate, the lower pair of leaflets generally remote from the upper; leaflets oblong or ovate-lanceolate, acute and sometimes acuminate at the apex, rounded or cuneate at the base, toothed, lobed or divided; flowers white, in leafy panicles, 6''–9'' broad when expanded, the stamens about equalling the sepals; filaments glabrous; persistent styles plumose throughout, nearly white, 1'–2' long.

Western Nebraska, Missouri, and throughout the Rocky Mountain region, west to the Pacific Coast. Windflower. June–Aug.

27. VIÓRNA Reichb.; Spach, Hist. Veg. 7 : 268. 1839.

Vines or erect perennial herbs, with opposite pinnately compound or simple leaves. Flowers mostly solitary. Sepals 4 or 5, petal-like, valvate in the bud, erect or converging. Petals none. Stamens numerous, parallel with the sepals; anthers narrow, linear. Pistils numerous; styles plumose or silky. Achenes flattish, the long styles persistent. [Name unexplained.]

About 20 species, natives of Europe and North America, extending into Mexico. In addition to the following, some 10 species inhabit the southern and western parts of North America. Type species: *Clematis Viorna* L. (*Viorna urnigera* Spach.). Called Leather-flower or Clematis.

* Climbing vines (no. 2 suberect).

Sepals thin, conspicuously dilated.   1. *V. crispa.*
Sepals thick, not dilated, their tips recurved.
   Leaves, or most of them, simple, entire or little lobed; filaments twice as long as the anthers.
                                                                          2. *V. Addisonii.*
   Leaves, or some of them, pinnate or trifoliolate.
     Fruiting styles silky, not plumose.   3. *V. Pitcheri.*
     Fruiting styles plumose.
       Leaves strongly reticulated.   4. *V. versicolor.*
       Leaves not strongly reticulated.
         Calyx pubescent; anthers long-tipped.   5. *V. Viorna.*
         Calyx glabrous; anthers short-tipped.   6. *V. glaucophylla.*

** Erect perennial herbs.

Leaves simple, entire or rarely lobed.
   Fruiting styles long, plumose; eastern species.
     Flowers yellowish-green; achenes straight.   7. *V. ochroleuca.*
     Flowers purple; achenes distinctly oblique.   8. *V. ovata.*
   Fruiting styles short, silky; western species.   9. *V. Fremontii.*
Leaves pinnate, or the lowest entire.   10. *V. Scottii.*

1. Viorna críspa (L.) Small. Marsh Leather-flower. Fig. 1944.

Clematis crispa L. Sp. Pl. 543. 1753.

Clematis cylindrica Sims, Bot. Mag. *pl. 1160.* 1809.

Viorna cylindrica Spach, Hist. Veg. **7** : 269. 1839.

Viorna crispa Small, Fl. SE. U. S. 437. 1903.

A climbing vine. Leaves pinnate; leaflets mostly trifoliolate, the ultimate divisions entire or occasionally lobed, glabrous and thin; flowers solitary, nodding, bluish-purple, 9″–18″ long; calyx cylindric below, but the sepals thin and widely spreading above, their margins undulate; filaments hairy; persistent styles silky, not plumose.

In marshes, Pennsylvania to Missouri, Arkansas, Florida and Texas. Blue-jessamine. Blue-bell. Curl-flowered clematis. May–June.

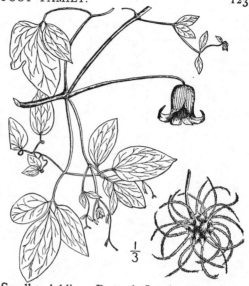

$\frac{1}{3}$

2. Viorna Addisònii (Britton) Small. Addison Brown's Leather-flower. Fig. 1945.

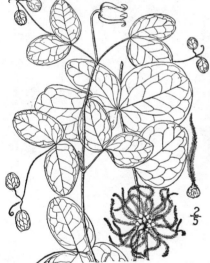

$\frac{2}{5}$

C. Addisonii Britton, Mem. Torr. Club **2** : 28. 1890.
Viorna Addisonii Small, Fl. SE. U. S. 439. 1903.

Ascending or suberect, 1°–3° long, simple or branched, tufted, glaucous and glabrous. Lower leaves simple, entire or 1–4-lobed, obtuse, deep bluish-green above, glaucous beneath, sessile, clasping, 2′–4′ long; upper leaves pinnate, or sometimes simple, tendril-bearing; leaflets 2–4, ovate, sessile; flowers solitary, terminal and axillary, purplish, nodding; calyx ovoid, 9″–15″ long, 5″–7″ broad, contracted near the summit; sepals thick, lanceolate, acute, their tips recurved; stamens numerous, pubescent above, filaments twice as long as the anthers; achenes flat, nearly orbicular, silky-pubescent; persistent styles 1′–1¼′ long, brownish-plumose throughout.

Banks, southwestern Virginia and North Carolina; recorded from Tennessee. May–June.
Clematis viorniòides Britton is a hybrid between this and *V. Viorna*. Roanoke, Va.

3. Viorna Pitcheri (T. & G.) Britton. Pitcher's Leather-flower. Fig. 1946.

Clematis Pitcheri T. & G. Fl. N. A. **1** : 10. 1838.
V. Simsii Small, Fl. SE. U. S. 438. 1903. Not *Clematis Simsii* Sweet.

A high climbing vine, the branches more or less pubescent. Leaves pinnate; leaflets entire, lobed or trifoliolate, thick, reticulated, generally mucronate; flowers solitary; calyx campanulate, less than 1′ long, purplish, pubescent; sepals with recurved margined tips; filaments hairy; persistent styles more or less pubescent, about 1′ long.

Southern Indiana to Missouri, Nebraska and Texas. May–Aug.

$\frac{1}{2}$

4. Viorna versícolor Small. Pale Leather-flower. Fig. 1947.

Clematis versicolor Small; Britton, Man. 421. 1901.

Viorna versicolor Small, Fl. SE. U. S. 438. 1903.

A branching vine, up to 12° long, glabrous or slightly pubescent below the nodes. Leaves pinnate, slender-petioled; leaflets firm, apiculate, oblong to ovate-lanceolate, ¾-3′ long, conspicuously reticulate, very glaucous beneath; sepals thin, purplish, lanceolate, about 10″ long, glabrous, slightly recurved at the tip, achenes pubescent; persistent styles plumose, white or nearly so.

Rocky ledges, Missouri and Arkansas. July.

5. Viorna Viórna (L.) Small. Leather-flower. Fig. 1948.

Clematis Viorna L. Sp. Pl. 543. 1753.
Viorna Viorna Small, Fl. SE. U. S. 439. 1903.

A vine, climbing to the height of 10° or more over bushes in rich soil. Leaves mostly pinnate; leaflets glabrous, entire, lobed or trifoliolate; uppermost and lowest leaves often entire; calyx ovoid-campanulate, purple, the sepals remarkably thick; filaments about as long as the anthers; persistent styles plumose throughout, 1′ long or more, brownish.

Banks and thickets, southern Pennsylvania to West Virginia, Georgia and Indiana. Ascends to 4000 ft. in Virginia. May–July.

Viorna flàccida Small, differing by entire, more pubescent leaflets, the calyx lavender with green tips, occurs in Kentucky and Tennessee.

Viorna Rìdgwayi Standley, of Illinois, has long-tipped leaf-lobes or leaf-segments.

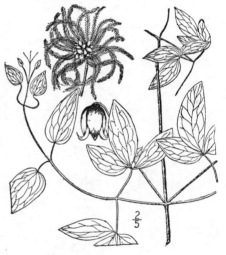

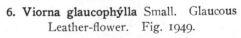

6. Viorna glaucophýlla Small. Glaucous Leather-flower. Fig. 1949.

Clematis glaucophylla Small, Bull. Torr. Club 24 : 337. 1897.

Viorna glaucophylla Small, Fl. SE. U. S. 439. 1903.

A red-stemmed vine up to 15° long. Leaves either simple and entire or lobed, or trifoliolate, ovate, 4′ long or less, acute, acuminate or apiculate at the apex, mostly cordate or subcordate at the base, rather strongly nerved, pale and glaucous beneath when mature; calyx red-purple, glabrous, glossy, conic-ovoid, about 1′ long, the sepals thick, lanceolate, their tips a little spreading; anthers short-tipped, about as long as the filaments; achenes nearly orbicular; persistent styles plumose.

Thickets and river-banks, Kentucky and North Carolina to Alabama and northern Florida. May–July.

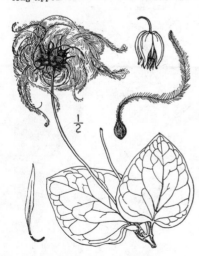

7. Viorna ochroleùca (Ait.) Small. Erect Silky Leather-flower. Fig. 1950.

Clematis ochroleuca Ait. Hort. Kew. **2**: 260. 1789.
Clematis sericea Michx. Fl. Bor. Am. **1**: 319. 1803.
Viorna ochroleuca Small, Fl. SE. U. S. 439. 1903.

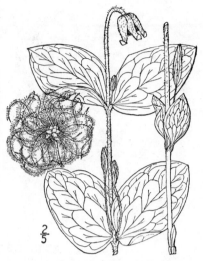

An erect silky-hairy plant, 1°–2° high, somewhat woody at the base. Leaves simple, sessile, ovate, obtuse, glabrous and reticulated above, silky beneath, entire or occasionally lobed, mucronate; flower terminal, nodding, 10″ long; calyx cylindraceous, green; sepals thick, very silky without, their tips recurved; head of fruit erect; achenes scarcely oblique; persistent styles yellowish-brown, plumose throughout, 1′–2′ long.

Staten Island, Pennsylvania, and southward to Georgia. Local. Dwarf clematis. Curly-heads. May–June.

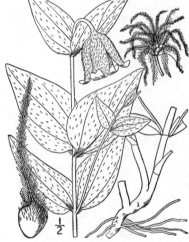

8. Viorna ovàta (Pursh) Small. Erect Mountain Leather-flower. Fig. 1951.

Clematis ovata Pursh, Fl. Am. Sept. 736. 1814.
V. ovata Small, Fl. SE. U. S. 439. 1903.

Similar to the preceding species, stems stiff, 1°–2° tall, pubescent when young, becoming nearly glabrous when old. Leaves ovate, entire, 1½′–2′ long, strongly reticulate-veined and nearly glabrous when mature; flowers solitary at the ends of the stem or branches, purple, nodding, nearly 1′ long; achenes distinctly oblique; persistent styles plumose throughout, the plumes white, turning brown, 1′–1½′ long.

Rocky soil, mountains of Virginia and West Virginia to South Carolina. May–June.

9. Viorna Fremóntii (S. Wats.) Heller. Fremont's Leather-flower. Fig. 1952.

Clematis Fremontii S. Wats. Proc. Am. Acad. **10**: 339. 1875.
Clematis ochroleuca var. *Fremontii* J. F. James, Journ. Cinc. Soc. Nat. Hist. 6: 120. 1883.
V. Fremontii Heller, Muhlenbergia **6**: 96. 1910.

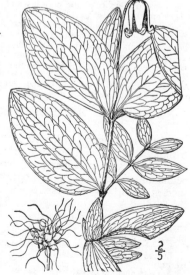

Stout, erect, 6′–15′ high, the stem villous-pubescent, especially at the nodes, woody at the base, simple or branched. Leaves simple, sessile, coriaceous, conspicuously reticulated, glabrous except on the veins beneath, broadly ovate, obtuse or acutish, entire or sparingly toothed; flowers terminal, nodding; calyx purple, 1′ long; sepals thick, tomentose on the margins, their tips recurved; head of fruit 1′ in diameter or more, erect; persistent styles about ½′ long, silky below, naked above.

Prairies and limestone hills, Kansas, Nebraska, and Missouri. April–May.

½

10. Viorna Scóttii (Porter) Rydb. Scott's Leather-flower. Fig. 1953.

Clematis Scottii Porter, in Porter & Coulter, Fl. Colo. 1. 1874.
Clematis Dóuglasii var. *Scottii* Coulter, Man. Bot. Rocky Mts. 3. 1885.
V. Scottii Rydb. Fl. Colo. 141. 1906.

Somewhat villous when young, nearly glabrous when old, stems erect, simple, or nearly so, or branched from the base, 10′–2° tall. Leaves petioled, the upper pinnate or bipinnate, 3′–6′ long, their segments lanceolate, oblong or ovate, entire or few-toothed, stalked, acuminate or acute at the apex, narrowed at the base, 6″–18″ long; lower leaves sometimes entire, or pinnately cleft, smaller than the upper; flowers solitary, terminal or also axillary, long-peduncled, nodding, nearly 1′ long, purple; sepals ovate-lanceolate, thick; persistent styles plumose throughout, 1′ long or more, the plumes brown.

In dry soil, South Dakota to Nebraska, Colorado and Idaho. May–July.

28. ATRÁGENE L. Sp. Pl. 543. 1753.

Perennial climbing vines, with opposite petioled compound leaves, and large showy peduncled flowers, solitary in the axils, or at the ends of the branches. Sepals very large, spreading, petaloid, mostly membranous and prominently veined. Petals small, spatulate.

Stamens very numerous, the outer ones usually with broadened filaments. Styles long, persistent, plumose. [Ancient Greek name for some vine.]

About 5 species, natives of the north temperate zone. In addition to the following, another occurs in the Rocky Mountains and one in northwestern North America. Type species: *Atragene alpina* L.

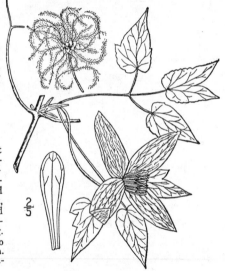

1. Atragene americàna Sims. Purple Virgin's Bower. Fig. 1954.

A. americana Sims, Bot. Mag. *pl. 887.* 1806.
Clematis verticillaris DC. Syst. 1: 166. 1818.

A trailing or partly climbing, somewhat woody, nearly glabrous vine. Leaves trifoliolate; leaflets thin, ovate, acute, toothed or entire, more or less cordate; petioles and petiolules slender; flowers purplish blue, 2′–4′ broad when expanded; sepals 4, thin and translucent, strongly veined, silky along the margins and the veins; petals spatulate, 6″–9″ long; persistent styles plumose throughout, about 2′ long.

Rocky woodlands and thickets, Hudson Bay to Manitoba, Connecticut, Virginia and Minnesota. Ascends to 3000 ft. in the Catskills. Mountain-or Whorl-leaved-clematis. May–June.

⅖

Family 32. BERBERIDÀCEAE T. & G. Fl. N. A. 1: 49. 1838.

BARBERRY FAMILY.

Shrubs or herbs, with alternate or basal, simple or compound leaves, with or without stipules, and solitary or racemed mostly terminal flowers. Sepals and petals generally imbricated in two to several series. Stamens as many as the petals and opposite them, hypogynous. Flowers perfect and pistil one in all our species. Anthers extrorse, opening by valves (except in *Podophyllum*). Style short; ovules 2–∞, anatropous. Fruit a berry or capsule.

About 10 genera and 130 species, widely distributed in the north temperate zone, the Andes and temperate South America, a few in tropical regions.

Shrubs; fruit baccate.
  Leaves unifoliolate, on short branches, in the axils of spines.   1. *Berberis.*
  Leaves pinnate; no spines.   2. *Odostemon.*
Herbs.
  Anthers opening by valves.

Pericarp early bursting, leaving two large naked stalked seeds, resembling berries.

Fruit baccate; stamens 6.   3. *Caulophyllum.*
Fruit capsular, half circumscissile.   4. *Diphylleia.*
Anthers longitudinally dehiscent; fruit baccate; stamens 6–18.   5. *Jeffersonia.*
                                                     6. *Podophyllum.*

1. BÉRBERIS [Tourn.] L. Sp. Pl. 330. 1753.

Shrubs with yellow wood, often unifoliolate leaves, those of the primary shoots reduced to spines, and yellow racemose flowers. Sepals 6–9, petaloid, bracted. Petals 6, imbricated in 2 series, each with 2 basal glands. Stamens 6, irritable, closing around the stigma when shocked; anthers dehiscent by valves opening from the apex. Pistil 1; stigma peltate. Berry 1–few-seeded, mostly red. [Said to be from the Arabic name of the fruit.]

A genus of about 80 species, natives of North America, Europe, northern Asia and South America. Besides the following, another is found in western North America. Type species: *Berberis vulgaris* L.

Twigs ash-colored; racemes many-flowered; petals entire.   1. *B. vulgaris.*
Twigs dark brown; racemes few-flowered; petals notched.   2. *B. canadensis.*

1. Berberis vulgàris L. European Barberry. Fig. 1955.

Berberis vulgaris L. Sp. Pl. 330. 1753.

A glabrous shrub, 6°–8° high, the branches arched and drooping at the ends, the twigs gray. Leaves alternate or fascicled, obovate or spatulate, unifoliolate, obtuse, thick, 1′–2′ long, bristly serrate, many of those on the young shoots reduced to 3-pronged spines, the fascicles of the succeeding year appearing in their axils; racemes terminating lateral branches, many-flowered, 1′–2′ long (3′–4′ in fruit); flowers yellow, 3″–4″ broad with a disagreeable smell; petals entire; berries oblong or ellipsoid, scarlet when ripe, acid.

In thickets, naturalized from Europe in the Eastern and Middle States, adventive in Canada and the West. Native of Europe and Asia. Consists of numerous races. Pep-

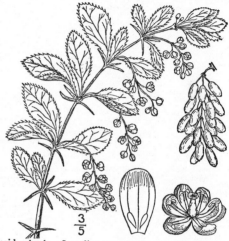

peridge-bush. Jaundice-tree or -berry. Wood-sour. May–June.

2. Berberis canadénsis Mill. American Barberry. Fig. 1956.

B. canadensis Mill. Gard. Dict. Ed. 8, no. 2. 1768.
Berberis vulgaris var. *canadensis* Ait. Hort. Kew. 1: 479. 1789.

A shrub, 1°–6° high, with slender, reddish-brown branchlets. Leaves similar to those of *B. vulgaris,* but with more divergent and distant teeth, or sometimes nearly entire; axillary spines 3-pronged; racemes few-flowered; petals conspicuously notched or emarginate at the apex; flowers about 3″ broad, berries scarlet, oval or subglobose.

In woods, mountains of Virginia to Georgia along the Alleghanies, and in Missouri. June. Referred by Regel to *B. sinensis* Desf., as a variety. Readily distinguished from all races of *B. vulgaris* by its dark-colored twigs.

2. ODOSTÈMON Raf. Am. Month. Mag. 2: 265. Feb. 1818.

[MAHONIA Nutt. Gen. 1: 211. 1818.]

Shrubs, with pinnate leaves of several or many coriaceous leaflets, and yellow racemose flowers, the branches not spiny, but the leaflets often with bristle-tipped teeth. Sepals mostly 6. Petals and stamens of the same number as the sepals. Filaments often dilated; anthers dehiscent by valves. Berries mostly blue or white. [Greek, swollen stamen.]

About 20 species, natives of North America and Asia. Type species: *Berberis Aquifolium* Pursh.

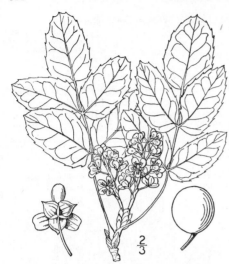

1. Odostemon Aquifòlium (Pursh) Rydb. Trailing Mahonia. Fig. 1957.

Berberis Aquifolium Pursh, Fl. Am. Sept. 219. 1814.
Berberis repens Lindl. Bot. Reg. *pl. 1176.* 1828.
Mahonia repens Don, Gard. Dict. 1: 118. 1831.
Odostemon Aquifolium Rydb. Bull. Torr. Club 33: 141. 1906.

A low trailing glabrous shrub. Leaves petioled, pinnate; leaflets 3–7, ovate, oval, or nearly orbicular, obtuse or acute at the apex, oblique and obtuse, truncate or slightly cordate at the base, sessile, thick, persistent, finely reticulated, dentate with spine-bearing teeth, 1′–2′ long; racemes several, erect, dense, terminal, many-flowered; flowers yellow, 3″–4″ broad, short-pedicelled; bracts ovate, persistent; berry globose, blue or purple, about 3″ in diameter.

Western Nebraska and throughout the Rocky Mountain region, extending to Arizona and British Columbia. Holly-leaf barberry. Grape-root. Rocky mountain or Oregon grape. April–May.

3. CAULOPHÝLLUM Michx. Fl. Bor. Am. 1: 205. 1803.

An erect perennial herb, with thickened rootstocks, and ternately compound leaves. Sepals 6, oblong, the calyx 3–4-bracted. Petals 6, smaller, cucullate, opposite the sepals. Stamens 6; anthers oblong, dehiscent by valves. Pistil 1; style short; stigma lateral; ovules 2, ripening into large globose stipitate blue seeds, resembling berries, which in growth soon rupture the membranous caducous pericarp. [Greek, stem-leaf.]

Two known species; the following typical one of eastern and central North America, the other of eastern Asia.

1. Caulophyllum thalictroìdes (L.) Michx. Blue Cohosh. Fig. 1958.

Leontice thalictroides L. Sp. Pl. 312. 1753.

C. thalictroides Michx. Fl. Bor. Am. 1: 205. 1803.

Glabrous, glaucous when young, 1°–3° high, with 2 or 3 large sheathing bracts at the base, a large triternate nearly sessile leaf near the summit, and generally a smaller similar one near the base of the inflorescence. Divisions of the leaves long-petioled, ternately or pinnately compound, the ultimate segments thin, 1′–3′ long, oval, oblong or obovate, 3–5-lobed near the apex; panicle terminal, 2′–3′ long; flowers greenish purple, 4″–6″ broad; seeds globular, 4″ in diameter, glaucous, borne on stout stalks about 3″ long.

In woods, New Brunswick to South Carolina, west to Manitoba, Tennessee, Nebraska and Missouri. Ascends to 5000 ft. in North Carolina. April–May. Blueberry. Blue-ginsing. Blueberry-, squaw- or papoose-root.

4. DIPHYLLEÌA Michx. Fl. Bor. Am. 1: 203. 1803.

Perennial herbs with horizontal rootstocks, large peltate leaves, and cymose white flowers. Sepals 6, petaloid, falling away early. Petals 6, flat. Stamens 6; anthers dehiscent by valves. Pistil 1; ovules few, arranged in 2 rows on one side of the ovary. Fruit a berry. Seeds oblong, curved. [Greek, double-leaf.]

A genus of 2 species, the typical one native of eastern North America, the other of Japan.

1. Diphylleia cymòsa Michx. Umbrella-leaf. Fig. 1959.

D. cymosa Michx. Fl. Bor. Am. **1**: 203. 1803.

Erect, stout, 1°–2° high, glabrous or nearly so Basal leaves solitary, long-petioled, 1°–2° in diameter, peltate near the center, deeply 2-cleft, many-lobed, the lobes acute or acuminate, sharply dentate; cauline leaves 2, similar, smaller, petioled, constricted in the middle and generally peltate near the margin; cyme many-flowered, 2′–3′ broad; flowers white; petals flat, oblong, obtuse; fruiting pedicels slender, 1′ long or more; berries blue, globose to oblong, 6″ long.

In woods, Virginia to Georgia and Tennessee, along the mountains, mainly at higher altitudes. May–June.

5. JEFFERSÒNIA B. S. Barton, Trans. Am. Phil. Soc. **3**: 342. 1793.

Glabrous perennial herbs, with basal palmately-veined or palmately-lobed leaves, and solitary white flowers borne on slender scapes. Sepals 4, occasionally 3 or 5, petaloid, caducous. Petals 8, flat, longer than the sepals. Stamens 8; filaments slender; anthers dehiscent by valves. Pistil 1; ovary ovoid, many-ovuled; stigmas 2-lobed. Capsule leathery, pyriform, half-circumscissile near the summit. Seeds oblong, arillate. [In honor of Thomas Jefferson.]

A genus of 2 species, the typical one native of eastern North America, the other of Manchuria.

1. Jeffersonia diphýlla (L.) Pers. Twin-leaf. Fig. 1960.

Podophyllum diphyllum L. Sp. Pl. 505. 1753.

Jeffersonia binata B. S. Barton, Trans. Am. Phil. Soc. **3**: 342. 1793.

Jeffersonia Bartonis Michx. Fl. Bor. Am. **1**: 237. 1803.

Jeffersonia diphylla Pers. Syn. **1**: 418. 1805.

Erect, 6′–8′ high when in flower, attaining 16′–18′ in fruit. Leaves glaucous beneath, long-petioled, cordate or reniform, 3′–6′ long, 2′–4′ wide, parted longitudinally into 2 obliquely ovate obtuse lobed or entire divisions; lobes rounded, the sinuses sometimes 9″ deep; scape naked, 1-flowered; flowers white, about 1′ broad; petals oblong, stigma peltate; capsule about 1′ long, short-stipitate.

In woods, eastern Pennsylvania, New York and Ontario to Wisconsin, Iowa, Virginia and Tennessee. Ascends to 2500 ft. in Virginia. May. Ground-squirrel pea. Helmet-pod. Rheumatism-root.

6. PODOPHÝLLUM L. Sp. Pl. 505. 1753.

Erect perennial herbs, with horizontal poisonous rootstocks, large peltate palmately lobed leaves, and solitary white flowers. Sepals 6, petaloid, fugacious, the bud with 3 fugacious bractlets. Petals 6–9, flat, obovate, longer than the sepals. Stamens as many or twice as many as the petals; anthers linear, longitudinally dehiscent. Pistil 1 (rarely several); ovary ovoid, many-ovuled, forming a large fleshy berry in fruit. Seeds numerous, obovate, enclosed in fleshy arils. [Greek, Anapodophyllum, duck-foot-leaf.]

A genus of about 4 species, the following typical one native of eastern North America and Japan, the others Asiatic.

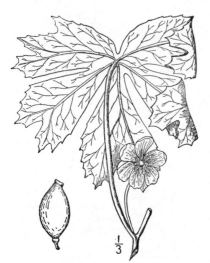

$\frac{1}{3}$

1. Podophyllum peltàtum L.   May Apple. Wild Mandrake.   Fig. 1961.

Podophyllum peltatum L. Sp. Pl. 505. 1753.

Erect, 1°–1½° high. Basal leaves centrally peltate, nearly 1° in diameter, long-petioled, deeply 5–9-lobed, glabrous, or pubescent and light green on the lower surface, darker above; lobes 2-cleft and dentate at the apex; flowering stems appearing from different rootstocks, bearing 1–3 similar leaves, or occasionally leafless; flower white, stout-peduncled, nodding, 2' broad, appearing from the base of the upper leaf and generally from immediately between the two leaves; stamens twice as many as the petals; fruit ovoid, yellowish, 2' long, edible.

In low woods, western Quebec and throughout southern Ontario to Minnesota, Kansas, Florida, Louisiana and Texas. Ascends to 2500 ft. in Virginia. Indian- or hog-apple. Devil's-apples. Wild- or ground-lemon. Puck's-foot. Raccoon-berry. May.

Family 33. MENISPERMÀCEAE DC. Prodr. 1: 95. 1824.

MOONSEED FAMILY.

Climbing or twining woody or herbaceous vines, with alternate entire or lobed leaves, no stipules, and small dioecious panicled racemose or cymose flowers. Sepals 4–12.   Petals 6, imbricated in 2 rows, sometimes fewer, or none.   Stamens about the same number as the petals.   Carpels 3–∞ (generally 6), 1-ovuled, separate; styles commonly incurved.   Fruit drupaceous, often oblique.   Endosperm little.   Embryo long, curved.

About 55 genera and 150 species, mainly of tropical distribution, a few extending into the temperate zones.

Petals none; anthers 2-celled.   1. *Calycocarpum.*
Petals present; anthers 4-celled or 4-lobed.
    Stamens 6; drupe red.   2. *Epibaterium.*
    Stamens 12–many; drupe black.   3. *Menispermum.*

1. CALYCOCÀRPUM Nutt.; T. & G. Fl. N. A. 1: 48. 1838.

A high climbing vine, with large petioled palmately lobed leaves, and greenish flowers in long narrow drooping panicles. Sepals 6, oblong, obtuse. Petals none. Stamens about 12, nearly equalling the sepals; anthers 2-celled. Pistils 3, narrow; stigma laciniate. Drupe oval or globose, the stone flattened and hollowed out on one side, the embryo cordate. [Greek, cup-fruit, in allusion to the cup-like stone.]

A monotypic genus of eastern North America.

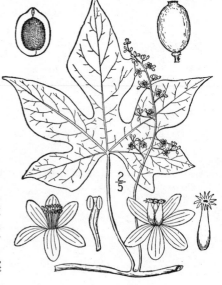

$\frac{2}{5}$

1. Calycocarpum Lỳoni (Pursh) Nutt Cup-seed. Fig. 1962.

Menispermum Lyoni Pursh, Fl. Am. Sept. 371. 1814.
C. Lyoni Nutt.; A. Gray, Gen. Ill. 1: 76. 1848.

Climbing to the tops of trees, glabrous or slightly pubescent. Leaves long-petioled, thin, very broadly ovate or nearly orbicular in outline, 5'–8' long, cordate with a broad round sinus, palmately 3–7-lobed, glabrous above, more or less pubescent on the veins beneath; lobes ovate or oblong, acute or acuminate, repand, dentate or entire; panicles axillary, 5'–10' long, loose; flowers 2" broad; drupe nearly 1' long, black, the stone toothed or erose along the margin of its lateral cavity; pistillate flowers sometimes containing abortive stamens.

In rich woods, Illinois to Missouri and Kansas, south to Florida and Texas. May–June, the fruit ripe in August.

2. EPIBATÈRIUM Forst. Char. Gen. 107. 1776.

[CÉBATHA Forsk. Fl. AEgypt. 171 Hyponym. 1775.]

[COCCULUS DC. Syst. Veg. 1: 515. 1818.]

Climbing vines with small dioecious panicled flowers. Sepals 6, arranged in 2 series. Petals 6, shorter than the sepals, concave. Stamens 6; anthers 4-celled or 4-lobed. Pistils 3–6, sometimes accompanied by sterile filaments; styles erect; stigma entire. Drupe globose or ovoid, the stone flattened, curved. [Greek, referring to the climbing habit.]

A genus of about 11 species, mainly of tropical regions, two or three in the temperate zones. Type species: *Epibaterium pendulum* Forst.

1. Epibaterium carolìnum (L.) Britton.
Carolina Moonseed. Fig. 1963.

Menispermum carolinum L. Sp. Pl. 340. 1753.

Cocculus carolinus DC. Syst. Veg. 1: 524. 1818.

Cebatha carolina Britton, Mem. Torr. Club 5: 162. 1894.

A slender vine, trailing, or climbing to the height of several feet, the stem glabrous or pubescent. Leaves broadly ovate, 2′–4′ long, cordate or rounded at the base, entire or lobed, acute or obtuse, sometimes densely pubescent beneath, mainly glabrous above; petioles slender, 1′–4′ long; panicles axillary and terminal, loose, 1′–5′ long; flowers about 1″ broad; drupe red, laterally flattened, 2″–3″ in diameter, the stone curved into a closed spiral, crested on the sides and back.

Along streams, Virginia to Illinois and Kansas, south to Florida and Texas. Red-berry moonseed. June–Aug.

3. MENISPÉRMUM [Tourn.] L. Sp. Pl. 340. 1753.

High climbing vines, with small whitish panicled flowers. Sepals 4–8, arranged in 2 series, longer than the 6–8 petals. Stamens 12–24. Anthers 4-celled. Pistils 2–4, inserted on a slightly elevated receptacle and generally accompanied by 6 sterile filaments. Drupe nearly globular, or ovoid, laterally flattened, the stone curved into a spiral and crested on the sides and back. [Greek, moonseed.]

A genus of 2 species, the typical one native of eastern. North America, the other of eastern Asia.

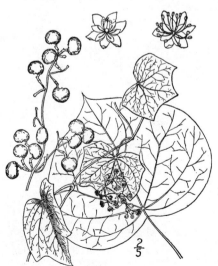

1. Menispermum canadénse L. Canada
Moonseed. Fig. 1964.

Menispermum canadense L. Sp. Pl. 340. 1753.

Stem climbing over bushes or walls, 6°–12° in length, slender, slightly pubescent, or glabrous. Leaves slender-petioled, very broadly ovate, 4′–8′ wide, cordate or sometimes nearly truncate at base, acuminate, acute or obtuse, entire or with 3–7 lobes, pale beneath, peltate near the base, although the petiole is sometimes inserted so near the margin that this character is not apparent; flowers white, 2″ wide; panicles loose, bracteolate; drupe globose-oblong, 3″–4″ in diameter, the stone spirally curved.

In woods along streams, western Quebec to Manitoba, south to Georgia, Nebraska and Arkansas. Ascends to 2600 ft. in Virginia. Bunches of fruit bluish black, with the aspect of small grapes. Texas or yellow sarsaparilla. Yellow parilla. June–July.

Family 34. **CALYCANTHÀCEAE** Lindl. Nat. Syst. Ed. 2, 159.   1836.
STRAWBERRY-SHRUB FAMILY.

Shrubs, with aromatic bark, opposite entire short-petioled leaves, no stipules, and solitary large flowers on lateral leafy branches. Sepals and petals similar, imbricated in many series. Stamens ∞, inserted on the receptacle, the inner sterile, short; anthers extrorse innate. Pistils ∞, nearly enclosed in the hollow receptacle; ovary 1-celled; ovules 1 or 2, anatropous, style filiform. Fruit accessory, consisting of the enlarged ovoid oblong or pyriform receptacle, to which the bases of petals, sepals and bracts are adnate, enclosing few to many smooth shining achenes. Seed erect; endosperm none; cotyledons foliaceous, convolute.

A family of 2 genera and about 6 species, natives of North America and eastern Asia, perhaps of closer affinity with the Rosaceae than where here inserted.

1. **CALYCÁNTHUS** L. Syst. Ed. 10, 1066.   1759.

[BUTNÈRIA Duham. Trait. Arb. 1: 113. *pl. 45.* Hyponym. 1755.]
Stamens inserted in several rows. Flowers purple or red. Otherwise as in the family.
[Greek, cup-flower.]

The genus comprises 4 species, one additional to those here described occurring on the Pacific Coast, and one in Alabama. *Chimonanthus* Lindl. of Japan and China comprises 2 species with yellow flowers smaller than those of *Calycanthus.* The species are called sweet-scented shrub and Carolina allspice. Type species: *Calycanthus floridus* L.

Leaves pubescent beneath; flowers fragrant.   1. *C. floridus.*
Leaves green, often glaucous beneath, smooth or rough above; flowers not fragrant.   2. *C. fertilis.*

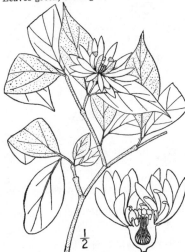

1. **Calycanthus flóridus** L.   Hairy Strawberry-shrub.   Fig. 1965.

Calycanthus floridus L. Syst. Ed. 10, 1066. 1759.
Buettneria florida Kearney, Bull. Torr. Club 21: 175. 1894.

A branching shrub, 2°–9° high, the branchlets and petioles pubescent. Leaves ovate or oval, acute or obtuse, narrowed at the base, soft-downy or pubescent beneath, rough above; flowers dark purple, about 1′ broad, with a strong odor of strawberries when crushed; sepals and petals linear or oblong, pubescent, acutish or blunt, 6″–10″ long; fruit obovoid or oblong; seeds about 5″ long.

In rich soil, Virginia and North Carolina to Florida, Alabama and Mississippi. Freely planted for ornament. Spice-bush. Sweet shrub. Sweet bubby or betties. Strawberry-bush. April–Aug.

2. **Calycanthus fértilis** Walt.   Smooth Strawberry-shrub.   Fig. 1966.

Calycanthus fertilis Walt. Fl. Car. 151. 1788.
Calycanthus laevigatus Willd. Enum. 559. 1809.
Calycanthus glaucus Willd. Enum. 559. 1809.
Buettneria fertilis Kearney, Bull. Torr. Club 21: 175. 1894.

A branching shrub, 4°–9° high, the branchlets and petioles glabrous or nearly so. Leaves ovate, ovate-lanceolate or oblong-lanceolate, acute or acuminate, rough and dark green above, glaucous and sometimes slightly pubescent beneath or bright green and smooth on both sides; sepals and petals linear or linear-lanceolate, acute, 15″ long or less; flowers greenish-purple, inodorous or nearly so.

In rich woods, Pennsylvania to North Carolina, east Tennessee, Georgia and Alabama, along the mountains. March–Aug. Occasional in cultivation. Fruit reputed to be poisonous to sheep. Bubby-bush. Sweet shrub.

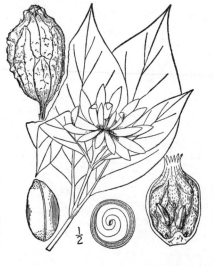

Family 35. **LAURÀCEAE** Lindl. Nat. Syst. Ed. 2, 200. 1836.

Laurel Family.

Aromatic trees and shrubs, with simple, alternate (very rarely opposite) mostly thick evergreen or deciduous, punctate exstipulate leaves. Flowers small, perfect, polygamous, dioecious, or sometimes monoecious, usually fragrant, yellow or greenish in panicles, corymbs, racemes or umbels. Calyx 4–6-parted, the segments imbricated in 2 series in the bud. Corolla none. Stamens inserted in 3 or 4 series of 3 on the calyx, distinct, some of them commonly imperfect or reduced to staminodia; anthers 2-celled or 4-celled, opening by valves. Ovary superior, free from the calyx, 1-celled; ovule solitary, anatropous, pendulous; style filiform or short, rarely almost wanting; stigma discoid or capitate. Fruit a 1-seeded drupe or berry. Endosperm of the seed none. Cotyledons plano-convex, accumbent.

About 40 genera and probably 1000 species, widely distributed in tropical regions; a few in the temperate zones.

Flowers perfect, panicled; leaves evergreen.   1. *Persea.*
Flowers mostly dioecious, racemose or umbellate; leaves deciduous.
  Anthers 4-celled, 4-valved.
    Flowers in umbelled racemes; leaves, or some of them, lobed.   2. *Sassafras.*
    Flowers in capitate umbels; leaves all entire.   3. *Glabraria.*
  Anthers 2-celled, 2-valved; leaves entire.   4. *Benzoin.*

1. PÉRSEA [Plum.] Gaertn. f. Fr. & Sem. 3: 222. 1805.

Trees or shrubs, with alternate coriaceous persistent entire leaves, and perfect panicled flowers. Calyx 6-parted, persistent, its segments equal or unequal. Stamens 12, in 4 series of 3, the inner series reduced to gland-like staminodia, the 3 other series anther-bearing, their anthers 4-celled, 4-valved, those of the third series extrorse and the others introrse in our species. Staminodia large, cordate, stalked. Fruit a globose or oblong berry. [Ancient name of some oriental tree.]

About 50 species, natives of America. Besides the following another occurs in Florida. Type species: *Persea gratissima* Gaertn. f. (*Persea Persea* (L.) Cockerell, the alligator-pear.)

Twigs and petioles puberulent or nearly glabrous.   1. *P. Borbonia.*
Twigs and petioles densely tomentose.   2. *P. pubescens.*

1. **Persea Borbònia** (L.) Spreng.   Red or Sweet Bay.   Isabella-wood.
Fig. 1967.

Laurus Borbonia L. Sp. Pl. 370. 1753.
Persea Borbonia Spreng. Syst. **2**: 268. 1825.
Persea carolinensis Nees, Syst. 150. 1836.
Notaphoebe Borbonia Pax in Engler & Prantl, Nat. Pflf.
  3· Abt. 2, 116. 1889.

A tree, with dark red bark, reaching a maximum height of about 65° and a trunk diameter of 3°. Twigs puberulent or nearly glabrous. Leaves lanceolate, oblong or oblong-lanceolate, bright green above, paler beneath, glabrous when mature, 2′–7′ long, 1′–2′ wide, obscurely pinnately veined, acute, acuminate or some of them obtuse at the apex, narrowed at the base; petioles ½′–1′ long; peduncles short, axillary, often little longer than the petioles, bearing few-flowered panicles; calyx puberulent, spreading in fruit, its inner segments longer than the outer; berries dark blue, ½′ in diameter or more, their pedicels thick, red.

Along streams and borders of swamps, Delaware to Florida and Texas, near the coast, north to Arkansas. Wood hard, strong; color bright red; weight per cubic foot, 40 lbs. April–June. Fruit ripe Aug.– Sept. False mahogany. Bay-galls. White bay. Tisswood.

2. Persea pubéscens (Pursh) Sarg. Swamp Bay. Fig. 1968.

Laurus carolinensis var. *pubescens* Pursh, Fl. Am. Sept. 1814.
Persea carolinensis var. *palustris* Chapm. Fl. S. States, 393. 1860.
Persea pubescens Sarg. Silva 7: 7 *pl. 302.* 1895.

A tree, seldom over 35° high, the trunk sometimes 15′ in diameter. Bark brown; twigs densely brown-tomentose; leaves oval, oblong or lanceolate, glabrous and shining above when mature, pubescent beneath or also tomentose on the veins, acute, acuminate or obtuse at the apex, usually narrowed at the base, strongly pinnately veined, 3′–7′ long, ½′–1½′ wide; petioles 4″–8″ long; peduncles tomentose, mostly longer than the petioles, sometimes 2′–3′ long; calyx tomentose, its inner segments longer than the outer; berry dark blue, 6″–9″ in diameter.

In swamps and along streams, southern Virginia to Florida and Mississippi, near the coast. Great Bahama Island. Wood hard, orange-brown; weight per cubic foot, 40 lbs. May–July. Fruit ripe Sept.

2. SÁSSAFRAS Nees & Eberm. Handb. Med. Pharm. Bot. 2: 418. 1831.

A rough-barked tree, with broad entire or 1–3-lobed deciduous leaves, and yellow dioecious flowers in involucrate umbelled racemes at the ends of twigs of the preceding season, unfolding with or before the leaves, the involucre composed of the persistent bud-scales. Calyx 6-parted, that of the pistillate flowers persistent, its segments equal. Staminate flowers with 3 series of 3 stamens, the 2 outer series with glandless filaments, those of the inner series with a pair of stalked glands at the base. Anthers all 4-celled and introrse, 4-valved. Pistillate flowers with about 6 staminodia and an ovoid ovary. Fruit an oblong-globose blue drupe. [The popular Spanish name.]

Two species, the following typical one of eastern North America, the other Asiatic.

1. Sassafras Sássafras (L.) Karst. Sassafras or Ague Tree. Fig. 1969.

Laurus Sassafras L. Sp. Pl. 371. 1753.
Sassafras officinale Nees & Eberm. Handb. Med. Pharm. Bot. 2: 418. 1831.
Sassafras Sassafras Karst. Deutsch. Fl. 505. 1880–83.
S. variifolium Kuntze, Rev. Gen. Pl. 574. 1891.

A tree sometimes 125° high, the trunk 7° in maximum diameter; the bark rough in irregular ridges, aromatic, the young shoots yellowish-green, the twigs and leaves mucilaginous, pubescent when young but becoming glabrous. Leaves oval and entire or mitten-shaped, or 3-lobed to about the middle and often as wide as long, pinnately veined, petioled; petioles 1′ long or less; racemes several or numerous in the umbels, peduncled; flowers about 3″ broad; stamens about equalling the calyx-segments; fruiting pedicels red, much thickened below the calyx; drupe nearly ½′ high.

In dry or sandy soil, Maine to Ontario, Michigan, Iowa, Florida and Texas. Root largely used for the aromatic oil. Wood soft, weak, durable, brittle; color dull orange; weight 31 lbs. per cubic foot. April–May. Fruit ripe July–Aug. Cinnamon-wood. Smelling-stick. Saloop.

3. GLABRÀRIA L. Mant. 2: 156, 276. 1771.

[MALAPOÈNNA Adans. Fam. Pl. 2: 447. Hyponym. 1763.]

[TETRANTHERA Jacq. Hort. Schoen. 1: 59. *pl. 113.* 1797.]

Trees or shrubs, with entire leaves, deciduous in our species, and small greenish or yellow dioecious flowers in small umbels or almost capitate, involucrate by the bud-scales, axillary, or in the following species unfolding before the leaves at the nodes of twigs of the previous season. Calyx 6-parted, deciduous. Staminate flowers much as in *Sassafras*, bearing 3 series of 3 stamens, their anthers all 4-celled, 4-valved and introrse. Pistillate flowers with 9 or 12 staminodia and a globose or oval ovary. Fruit a small globose or oblong drupe. [Latin, smooth.]

About 100 species, natives of tropical and warm regions of both the Old World and the New, only the following known in North America. Type species: *Glabraria tersa* L.

1. Glabraria geniculàta (Walt.) Britton.
Pond Spice. Fig. 1970.

Laurus geniculata Walt. Fl. Car. 133. 1788.
Tetranthera geniculata Nees, Syst. 567. 1836.
Litsea geniculata Nicholson, Dict. Gard. 2: 287. 1885.
Malapoenna geniculata Coulter, Mem. Torr. Club 5: 164. 1894.

A much-branched shrub, with terete smooth zigzag spreading twigs. Leaves oblong, firm, $\frac{1}{2}'$–$2'$ long, $\frac{1}{4}'$–$\frac{1}{2}'$ wide, acute or rounded at the apex, narrowed at the base, glabrous and rather dark green above, paler and puberulent, at least on the veins, beneath, or quite glabrous when mature; umbels 2–4-flowered, sessile; involucres of 2–4 scales; flowers yellow, less than $2''$ broad; drupe globose, red, about $3''$ in diameter.

In swamps and wet soil, southern Virginia to Florida. Pond-bush. March–April.

4. BÉNZOIN Fabric. Enum. Pl. Hort. Helmst. 1763.

Shrubs (some Asiatic species trees), with alternate entire pinnately veined and in our species deciduous leaves, and dioecious or polygamous yellow flowers, in lateral sessile involucrate clusters unfolding before the leaves, the involucre of 4 deciduous scales. Calyx-segments 6, equal, deciduous. Staminate flowers with 3 series of 3 stamens, the filaments of the inner series lobed and gland-bearing at the base, those of the 2 outer series glandless; anthers all introrse, 2-celled, 2-valved. Pistillate flowers with 12–18 staminodia and a globose ovary. Fruit an obovoid or oblong red drupe. [Named from the Benzoin gum, from its similar fragrance.]

About 7 species, of eastern North America and Asia. Only the following are North American. Type species: *Laurus Benzoin* L.

Shrub glabrous or nearly so throughout; leaves narrowed at the base.   1. *B. aestivale.*
Twigs and lower surfaces of the leaves pubescent; leaves rounded or subcordate at the base.
                                                                    2. *B. melissaefolium.*

1. Benzoin aestivàle (L.) Nees. Spice-bush or -wood. Benjamin-bush. Fig. 1971

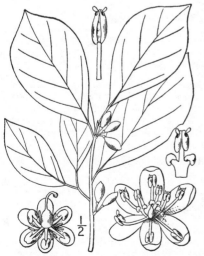

Laurus aestivalis L. Sp. Pl. 370. 1753.
Laurus Benzoin L. Sp. Pl. 370. 1753.
Benzoin aestivale Nees, Syst. Laur. 495. 1836.
Lindera Benzoin Blume, Mus. Bot. Lugd. 1: 324. 1857.
B. Benzoin Coulter, Mem. Torr. Club 5: 164. 1894.

A glabrous or nearly glabrous shrub, $4°$–$20°$ high, with smooth bark and slender twigs. Leaves obovate oval or elliptic, $2'$–$5'$ long, $1'$–$2\frac{1}{2}'$ wide, acute, short-acuminate or some of them rounded at the apex, narrowed at the base, pale beneath; petioles $3''$–$6''$ long; flowers about $1\frac{1}{2}''$ broad, bright yellow, fragrant; pedicels about equalling the calyx-segments; anthers oval, minutely emarginate at the summit; ovary about as long as the style; drupe $4''$–$5''$ long, about $3''$ in diameter.

In moist woods, thickets and along streams, Maine and New Hampshire to Ontario, Michigan, North Carolina, Tennessee and Kansas. March–May. Fruit ripe Aug.–Sept. Ascends to 2500 ft. in Virginia. Snap-wood or -weed. Feverbush. Wild allspice. Leaves of young shoots much larger.

½

2. Benzoin melissaefòlium (Walt.) Nees.
Hairy Spice-bush. Fig. 1972.

Laurus melissaefolia Walt. Fl. Car. 134. 1788.

Lindera melissaefolia Blume, Mus. Bot. Lugd. 1 : 324. 1857.

Benzoin melissaefolium Nees, Syst. 494. 1836.

A shrub similar to the preceding species but the young twigs, buds and lower surfaces of the leaves densely pubescent. Leaves ovate-lanceolate or oblong, acute or acuminate at the apex, rounded or subcordate at the base, 2'–4' long, 9"–18" wide; petioles 1"–3" long; pedicels equalling or slightly longer than the calyx-segments; anthers truncate at the summit; drupe 3"–5" high.

In swamps and wet soil, Illinois and Missouri to North Carolina, south to Alabama and Florida. Jove's-fruit. Feb.–March.

Family 36. PAPAVERÀCEAE B. Juss. Hort. Trian. 1759.

POPPY FAMILY.

Herbs, with milky or colored sap, and alternate leaves or the upper rarely opposite. Stipules none. Flowers solitary or in clusters, perfect, regular. Sepals 2 (rarely 3 or 4), caducous. Petals 4–6 or rarely more, imbricated, often wrinkled, deciduous. Stamens mostly numerous, hypogynous, distinct; filaments filiform; anthers innate, longitudinally dehiscent. Ovary 1, many-ovuled, mainly 1-celled, with parietal placentae; style short; stigma simple or divided; ovules anatropous. Fruit a capsule, dehiscent by a pore, or by valves. Seeds mostly numerous; embryo small at the base of fleshy or oily endosperm.

About 23 genera and 115 species, widely distributed, most abundant in the north temperate zone.
Pod dehiscent at the top, or only to the middle.
    Leaves not spiny-toothed.   1. *Papaver.*
    Leaves spiny-toothed.   2. *Argemone.*
Pod dehiscent to the base.
    Flowers white; petals 8–16 ; juice red.   3. *Sanguinaria.*
    Flowers and juice yellow ; petals 4.
        Capsule oblong or short-linear, bristly.   4. *Stylophorum.*
        Capsule long-linear, rough, tipped with a dilated stigma.   5. *Glaucium.*
        Capsule linear, smooth, tipped with a short subulate style and minute stigma.
                                                                6. *Chelidonium.*

1. PAPÀVER [Tourn.] L. Sp. Pl. 506. 1753.

Hispid or glaucous herbs, with white milky sap, lobed or dissected alternate leaves, nodding flower-buds and showy regular flowers. Sepals 2 or occasionally 3. Petals 4–6. Stamens ∞. Anthers extrorse. Ovules ∞, borne on numerous internally-projecting placentae. Stigmas united into a radiate persistent disc. Capsule globose, obovoid, or oblong, dehiscent near the summit by slits or pores. Seeds marked with minute depressions. [Classic Latin name of the poppy.]

About 45 species, mostly natives of the Old World, but 4 or 5 indigenous in western America. Type species : *Papaver somniferum* L.

Glabrate and glaucous ; leaves lobed, clasping ; capsule subglobose.   1. *P. somniferum.*
Green, hirsute ; leaves pinnately divided.
    Stems branching, leafy ; weeds of waste or cultivated ground.
        Capsule glabrous.
            Capsule subglobose or top-shaped.   2. *P. Rhoeas.*
            Capsule oblong-clavate, narrowed below.   3. *P. dubium.*
        Capsule oblong, hispid with a few erect hairs.   4. *P. Argemone.*
    Leaves all basal ; capsule obovoid, densely hispid with erect hairs ; arctic.   5. *P. nudicaule.*

1. Papaver somníferum L.   Opium or Garden Poppy.   Marble-flower.   Fig. 1973.

Papaver somniferum L. Sp. Pl. 508.   1753.

Erect, sparingly branched, glaucous, 1°–3° high. Leaves clasping by a cordate base, 4'–8' long, 2'–3' wide, oblong, wavy, lobed or toothed; flowers 3'–4' broad, bluish-white with a purple center; filaments somewhat dilated upward; capsule globose, glabrous.

Occasional in waste grounds and on ballast. Also in Bermuda. Fugitive from Europe. Often cultivated for ornament. Widely cultivated in Europe and Asia for its capsules, from which the drug opium, and poppy-oil are derived. Native of the Mediterranean region. Summer. Mawseed. Joan silver-pin. Cheesebowl. Balewort.

2. Papaver Rhoèas L.   Field, Red or Corn Poppy. African Rose.   Fig. 1974.

Papaver Rhoeas L. Sp. Pl. 507.   1753.

Erect, branching, 1°–3° high, hispid with spreading bristly hairs. Lower leaves petioled, 4'–6' long, the upper smaller, sessile, all pinnatifid; lobes lanceolate, acute, serrate; flowers 2'–4' broad, scarlet with a darker center; filaments not dilated; capsule subglobose or top-shaped, glabrous, the disk with 10 or more stigmatic rays.

In waste places and on ballast, Maine to Connecticut and Virginia. Vancouver Island. Bermuda. Occasionally cultivated. Fugitive from Europe. Summer. Old English names. Corn-rose, Red-weed, Headache, Canker-rose and Cheesebowl. Thunder-flower. Blue-eyes.

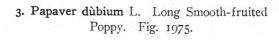

3. Papaver dùbium L.   Long Smooth-fruited Poppy.   Fig. 1975.

Papaver dubium L. Sp. Pl. 1196.   1753.

Slender, branching, 1°–2° high, hirsute with spreading hairs. Lower leaves petioled, 4'–6' long, the upper smaller, nearly sessile, all deeply pinnately divided; lobes oblong, pinnatifid, cleft or sometimes entire; flowers 2' broad, scarlet, sometimes darker in the center; filaments not dilated; capsule oblong-clavate, glabrous, 8"–10" long, narrowed below; stigmatic rays 6–10.

In waste and cultivated grounds, Massachusetts and Rhode Island to Pennsylvania, Virginia, West Virginia and southward. Also in ballast about the seaports and in Bermuda. Adventive from Europe. Summer. Blind-eyes. Headache. Blaver.

4. Papaver Argemòne L.   Pale or Long Rough-fruited Poppy.   Fig. 1976.

Papaver Argemone L. Sp. Pl. 506. 1753.

Slender, hirsute, or nearly glabrous, 1°–2° high, branching. Leaves all but the upper petioled, lanceolate in outline, pinnately divided, the divisions pinnatifid and toothed; flowers 1′–2′ broad, pale red, often with a darker center; filaments not dilated; capsule oblong, 8″–10″ long, narrowed at the base, bristly-hairy.

Waste grounds, Philadelphia, and in ballast about the seaports. Fugitive from Europe. Summer. Old name, wind-rose. Headache.

5. Papaver nudicàule L.   Arctic or Iceland Poppy.   Fig. 1977.

Papaver nudicaule L. Sp. Pl. 507. 1753.

Papaver radicatum Rottb.; DC. Prodr. 1: 118. 1824.

Perennial, more or less hirsute. Leaves all basal, pinnately lobed or cleft, the lobes linear-oblong, acute or obtuse; scape erect, slender, 2′–12′ tall, much exceeding the leaves; flower solitary, 1′–3′ broad, yellow or red; filaments filiform; capsule narrowly obovoid, 5″–8″ high, about 4″ in greatest diameter, densely beset with erect bristly hairs.

Greenland and Labrador to Alaska and British Columbia. Also in northern Europe and Asia. Included in our first edition, in *P. alpinum* L. Summer.

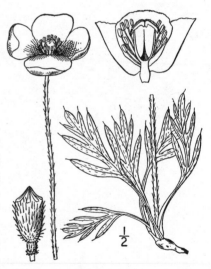

2. ARGEMÒNE L. Sp. Pl. 508. 1753.

Glaucous herbs, with yellow sap, spiny-toothed leaves and large showy flowers. Sepals 2 or 3. Petals 4–6. Stamens ∞. Placentae 4–6, many-ovuled. Style very short or none. Stigma dilated, 3–6-radiate. Capsule prickly, oblong, dehiscent at the apex by valves. Seeds numerous, cancellate. [Greek, an eye disease, supposed to be relieved by the plant so called.]

A genus of about 10 species, natives of America. Type species: *Argemone mexicana* L.

Petals yellow, or rarely cream-colored; flowers nearly or quite sessile.	1. *A. mexicana.*
Petals white, or pinkish.	
Flowers distinctly peduncled; spines of the sepal-tips nearly erect.	2. *A. alba.*
Flowers sessile or nearly so; spines of the sepal-tips spreading.	3. *A. intermedia.*

1. Argemone mexicàna L. Mexican Prickly or Thorn Poppy. Fig. 1978.

Argemone mexicana L. Sp. Pl. 508. 1753.

Stem stout, 1°–2° high, simple or sparingly branched, spiny or sometimes nearly unarmed. Leaves sessile, clasping by a narrowed base, 4′–10′ long, 2′–4′ wide, glaucous, white-spotted, runcinate-pinnatifid, spiny-toothed and more or less spiny on the veins; flowers yellow or cream-colored, sessile or subsessile, 1′–2′ broad; sepals acuminate, bristly-pointed; stamens 4″–5″ long; filaments slender, much longer than their anthers; stigma sessile or nearly so; capsule 1′ long or more.

In waste places, Massachusetts to New Jersey, Pennsylvania, Florida and Texas. Also in ballast about the northern seaports. Adventive from tropical America. A common weed in the American tropics, and introduced into the Old World. The seed yields a valuable painter's oil. June–Sept. Bird-in-the-bush. Devil's-fig. Yellow, Flowering or Jamaica thistle.

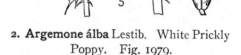

3/5

2. Argemone álba Lestib. White Prickly Poppy. Fig. 1979.

Argemone alba Lestib. Bot. Belg. Ed. 2 : 3 : Part 2, 132. 1799.

A. albiflora Hornem. Hort. Havn. 469. 1815.

Commonly stouter and taller than the preceding species. Leaves pinnatifid or pinnately lobed, glaucous or green, not blotched, but sometimes whitish along the veins; flowers white, usually much larger, 3′–4′ broad, distinctly peduncled; petals rounded; spines of the sepal-tips stouter; capsules 1′–1½′ long.

Georgia and Florida to Missouri and Texas. Spontaneous after cultivation in northern gardens. May–Aug.

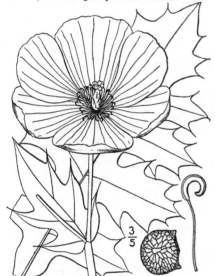

3/5

3. Argemone intermedia Sweet. Leafy White Prickly Poppy. Fig. 1980.

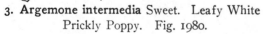

Argemone intermedia Sweet, Hort. Brit. Ed. 2, 585. 1830.

Stem stout, prickly, glabrous and glaucous, often 2° high or more. Leaves lobed or pinnatifid, very prickly, usually whitish-blotched; flowers large, white, sessile or nearly so, 3′–4′ wide; petals rounded; spines of the sepal-tips spreading; capsule oblong, prickly, about 1′ long.

Prairies and plains, Illinois to South Dakota, Wyoming, Nebraska, Texas and Mexico. Has been confused with the preceding species, and with *A. platyceras* Link & Otto. May–Aug.

Argemone híspida A. Gray, ranging from Wyoming to Utah and New Mexico, differs in the stem and branches being hispid-pubescent. It has been recorded from Kansas, perhaps erroneously.

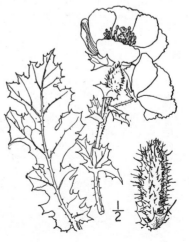

½

3. SANGUINÀRIA [Dill.] L. Sp. Pl. 505. 1753.

Rootstock horizontal, thick; juice red. Leaves basal, palmately veined and lobed, cordate or reniform. Scape 1-flowered (rarely 2). Flower white. Sepals 2, fugacious. Petals 8–16, oblong-spatulate, arranged in 2 or 3 rows. Stamens ∞. Stigma grooved. Placentae 2. Capsule oblong or fusiform, dehiscent to the base, the valves persistent. Seeds smooth, crested. [Name from the red color of the juice.]

A monotypic genus of eastern North America.

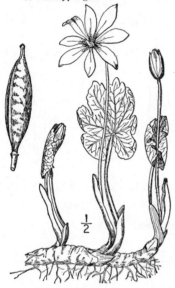

1. Sanguinaria canadénsis L. Bloodroot. Puccoon-root. Tetterwort. Fig. 1981.

Sanguinaria canadensis L. Sp. Pl. 505. 1753.

Glabrous, glaucous, especially when young. Rootstock ½–1′ thick, several inches long, densely clothed with thick fibrous roots; petioles 6′–14′ long; leaves 6′–12′ broad, 4′–7′ long, palmately 5–9-lobed, the lobes repand, or cleft at the apex; flowering scape at length overtopped by the leaves; flower 1′–1½′ broad; petals early deciduous; capsule narrow, 1-celled, 2-valved, 1′ long.

In rich woods, Nova Scotia to Manitoba and Nebraska, south to Florida, Alabama and Arkansas. Ascends to 2500 ft. in Virginia. Also called red puccoon and red Indian-paint. Turmeric. Redroot. Corn-root. Pauson. Sweet-slumber. White puccoon. Snake-bite. Flower sometimes pinkish. The scape rarely bears 2 or 3 flowers and bracts. April–May. The species consists of several races, differing in the leaf-lobing and in size and form of the capsule.

4. STYLÓPHORUM Nutt. Gen. 2: 7. 1818.

Herbs, with stout rootstocks, yellow sap, pinnatifid leaves and clustered or solitary flowers, the buds nodding. Sepals 2. Petals 4. Stamens ∞. Placentae 2–4; style distinct; stigma 2–4-lobed, radiate. Capsule linear or ovoid, bristly, dehiscent to the base by 2–4 valves. Seeds cancellate, crested. [Name Greek, style-bearing.]

A genus of about 4 species, natives of eastern North America, the Himalayas, Japan and Manchuria, the following typical.

1. Stylophorum diphýllum (Michx.) Nutt. Yellow or Celandine Poppy. Fig. 1982.

Chelidonium diphyllum Michx. Fl. Bor. Am. 1: 309. 1803.
Stylophorium diphyllum Nutt: Gen. 2: 7. 1818.
Meconopsis diphylla DC. Syst. Veg. 2: 88. 1821.

Glaucous, especially the lower surfaces of the leaves, sparingly pubescent, 12′–18′ high. Leaves basal and cauline, 4′–10′ long, slender-petioled, 1-2-pinnatifid, the divisions obovate, obtuse, lobed or irregularly crenate, those of the stem 2–4, the upper opposite; flowers 2–4, terminal, about 1′ broad, deep yellow; sepals hirsute, caducous; petals obovate, rounded; capsule 1′ long, ovoid, acute at each end, tipped with the persistent style.

In low woods, western Pennsylvania and Ohio to Tennessee, west to Wisconsin and Missouri. March–May.

Macleya cordàta (Willd.) R. Br. (*Bocconia cordata* Willd.), the Plume-poppy, a tall glaucous perennial, with palmately lobed leaves and large panicles of small greenish-white apetalous flowers, native of eastern Asia, is much planted for ornament, and is spontaneous after cultivation in Pennsylvania and Ohio.

5. GLAUCIUM Mill. Gard. Dict. Abr. Ed. 4. 1754.

Glaucous annual or biennial herbs, with alternate lobed or dissected leaves, large yellow flowers, and saffron-colored sap. Sepals 2. Petals 4. Stamens ∞. Placentae 2, rarely 3; stigma sessile, dilated, 2-lobed, the lobes convex. Capsule long-linear, 2-celled, dehiscent to the base. Seeds cancellate, crestless. [Name Greek, from the glaucous foliage.]

About 6 species, of the Old World, mainly of the Mediterranean region, the following typical.

1. Glaucium Glaucium (L.) Karst. Yellow Horned or Sea Poppy. Fig. 1983.

Chelidonium Glaucium L. Sp. Pl. 506. 1753.
Glaucium flavum Crantz, Stirp. Aust. **2**: 131. 1763.
Glaucium luteum Scop. Fl. Carn. Ed. 2, **1**: 369. 1772.
Glaucium Glaucium Karst. Deutsch. Fl. 649. 1880–83.

Stout, 2°–3° high, rigid, branching. Leaves thick, ovate or oblong, 3'–8' long, 1'–2' wide, scurfy, the basal and lowest cauline petioled, the upper sessile, clasping, pinnatifid, the divisions toothed, or the upper merely lobed; flowers axillary and terminal, 1'–2' broad; sepals scurfy; capsule narrowly-linear, 6'–12' long, tipped with the persistent stigma

In waste places, Rhode Island, southward near the coast to Virginia, and in central New York. Widely diffused as a weed in maritime regions of the Old World. Adventive from Europe. Summer. Bruisewort. Squatmore.

6. CHELIDONIUM [Tourn.] L. Sp. Pl. 505. 1753.

An erect biennial, brittle, branching herb, with alternate deeply pinnatifid leaves, yellow sap and yellow flowers in umbels. Sepals 2. Petals 4. Stamens ∞. Placentae 2. Style short, distinct; stigma not dilated, 2-lobed. Capsule linear, upwardly dehiscent from the base. Seeds smooth, shining, crested. [Name Greek for the swallow, which appears at about its flowering time.]

A monotypic genus of temperate Europe and Asia.

1. Chelidonium majus L. Celandine. Fig. 1984.

Chelidonium majus L. Sp. Pl. 505. 1753.

Weak, 1°–2° high, sparingly pubescent. Leaves thin, 4'–8' long, glaucous beneath, 1–2-pinnatifid, the segments ovate or obovate, crenate or lobed; petioles often dilated at the base; flowers 6"–8" broad, in axillary pedunculate umbels; petals rounded; pedicels slender, 2"–6" long, elongating in fruit; capsule glabrous, 1'–2' long, tipped with the persistent style and stigma.

Waste places, roadsides and even in woods, Maine to Ontario, Pennsylvania, and North Carolina. Naturalized or adventive from Europe. Summer. Called also greater celandine, to distinguish it from *Ficaria*, the small or lesser celandine. Swallow-wort. Tetterwort. Killwort. Wartwort. April–Sept.

Family 37. FUMARIACEAE DC. Syst. 2: 104. 1821.

Fumewort Family.

Annual, biennial or perennial herbs, with watery sap, dissected alternate or basal leaves without stipules, and perfect, irregular flowers variously clustered. Sepals 2, small, scale-like. Petals 4, somewhat united, the 2 outer ones spreading above, one or both saccate or spurred at the base, the 2 inner smaller, narrower, thickened at the tips and united over the stigma. Stamens 6, diadelphous, hypogynous, in 2 sets of 3; anther of the middle ones 2-celled, of the lateral ones 1-celled. Carpels 2, united into a single pistil, the ovary 1-celled; stigma 2-lobed or 2-horned; ovules anatropous or amphitropous. Fruit a 2-valved several-seeded capsule, or 1-seeded and indehiscent.   Seeds with a minute embryo in fleshy endosperm.

Five genera and about 170 species, natives of the north temperate zone and southern Africa.
Each of the 2 outer petals spurred at the base.
   Corolla deeply cordate at base ; petals slightly coherent.   1. *Bicuculla.*
   Corolla rounded or slightly cordate ; petals permanently coherent, persistent.   2. *Adlumia.*
One of the outer petals spurred at base.
   Capsule 2-valved, few–several-seeded.   3. *Capnoides.*
   Fruit globose, indehiscent, 1-seeded.   4. *Fumaria.*

1. BICUCÚLLA Adans. Fam. Pl 2 : App. 23. 1763.

[DICLYTRA Borck. Roem. Arch. 1 : Part 2, 46. 1797. DICENTRA Bernh. Linnaea 8 : 468. 1833.]

Herbs, with dissected leaves, basal in our species, and racemose flowers. Pedicels 2-bracted. Corolla cordate at base; petals 4, in 2 pairs, connivent. slightly coherent, the exterior pair oblong, concave, spurred at the base, spreading at the apex, the inner narrow, clawed, coherent above, crested or winged on the back. Placentae 2; style slender. Capsule oblong or linear, dehiscent to the base by 2 valves. Seeds crested. [Latin, double-hooded.]

A genus of about 16 species, natives of North America and Asia. Type species : *Fumaria Cucullaria* L. The original spelling is *Bikukulla.*
Raceme simple ; flowers white or whitish.
   Spurs divergent ; inner petals minutely crested.   1. *B. Cucullaria.*
   Spurs short, rounded ; inner petals conspicuously crested.   2. *B. canadensis.*
Racemes paniculate ; flowers pink.   3. *B. eximia.*

1. Bicuculla Cucullària (L.) Millsp.   Dutchman's Breeches.   Soldier's Cap.   Monks-hood.   Breeches-flower.   Fig. 1985.

Fumaria Cucullaria L. Sp. Pl. 699. 1753.
Diclytra Cucullaria DC. Syst. Veg. 2 : 108. 1821.
Dielytra Cucullaria T. & G. Fl. N. A. 1 : 66. 1838.
Dicentra Cucullaria Torr. Fl. N. Y. 1 : 45. 1843.
Bicuculla Cucullaria Millsp. Bull. West Va. Agric. Exp. Sta. 2 : 327. 1892.

Delicate, glabrous, arising from a granulate bulbous base. Leaves all basal, pale beneath, slender-petioled, ternately compound, the divisions stalked and finely dissected into linear or oblanceolate segments ; scape slender, 5′–10′ high; raceme secund, 4–10-flowered ; flowers nodding, pedicelled, 6″–8″ long, 8″–10″ broad at the base, white, or faintly pink, yellow at the summit; spurs widely divergent; inner petals minutely crested.

In woods, Nova Scotia to Minnesota, North Carolina, Missouri and Kansas. Ascends to 4500 ft. in Virginia. Colic-weed. Bachelor's- or little-boy's-breeches. Kitten-breeches. Boys-and-girls. Indian boys-and-girls. White-hearts. Butterfly-banners. April–May.

2. Bicuculla canadénsis (Goldie) Millsp.   Squirrel or Turkey Corn.   Fig. 1986.

Corydalis canadensis Goldie, Edinb. Phil. Journ. 6 : 329. 1822.
Diclytra canadensis DC. Prodr. 1 : 126. 1824.
Dicentra canadensis Walp. Rep. 1 : 118. 1842.
B. canadensis Millsp. Bull. West Va. Agric. Exp. Sta. 2 : 327. 1892.

Glabrous, the rootstock bearing numerous small tubers. Leaves all basal and nearly similar to those of the preceding species, decidedly glaucous beneath; scape slender, 6′–12′ high; raceme 4–8-flowered; flowers nodding, short-pedicelled, 7″–9″ long, 5″ broad at the base, greenish-white, purplish tinged, slightly fragrant; spurs short, rounded; inner petals prominently crested.

In rich woods, Nova Scotia to Ontario, Minnesota. Virginia, Tennessee, Missouri and Nebraska. Turkey-pea. Colic-weed. Wild hyacinth. April–June.

3. Bicuculla exímia (Ker) Millsp. Wild Bleeding-heart. Fig. 1987.

Fumaria eximia Ker, Bot. Reg. 1: pl. 50. 1815.
Diclytra eximia DC. Syst. 2: 109. 1821.
Dicentra eximia Torr. Fl. N. Y. 1: 46. 1843.
Bicuculla eximia Millsp. Bull. West Va. Agric. Exp. Sta. 2: 327. 1892.

Glabrous, somewhat glaucous, weak, 10'-2° high; rootstock scaly. Leaves all basal, larger than those of the other eastern species, ternately parted, the divisions stalked, finely pinnatifid into oblong or ovate segments; scape slender, about equalling the leaves; raceme compound; flowers clustered in cymes, slender-pedicelled, pink, nodding, 8"–10" long, 3"–4" broad at the base; spurs short, rounded, incurved; inner petals with projecting crests.

In rocky places, western New York, south to Georgia and Tennessee along the Alleghanies. Turkey-corn. Stagger-weed. May–Sept.

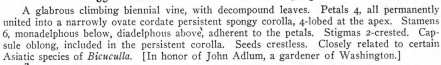

2. ADLÙMIA Raf. Med. Rep. (II.) 5: 352. 1808.

A glabrous climbing biennial vine, with decompound leaves. Petals 4, all permanently united into a narrowly ovate cordate persistent spongy corolla, 4-lobed at the apex. Stamens 6, monadelphous below, diadelphous above, adherent to the petals. Stigmas 2-crested. Capsule oblong, included in the persistent corolla. Seeds crestless. Closely related to certain Asiatic species of Bicuculla. [In honor of John Adlum, a gardener of Washington.]

A monotypic genus of eastern North America.

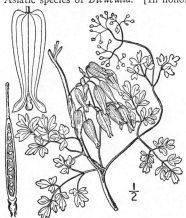

1. Adlumia fungòsa (Ait.) Greene. Climbing Fumitory. Fig. 1988.

Fumaria fungosa Ait. Hort. Kew. 3: 1. 1789.
Adlumia cirrhosa Raf. Med. Rep. (II.) 5: 352. 1808.
A. fungosa Greene; B.S.P. Prel. Cat. N. Y. 3. 1888.

Weak, slender, climbing over other plants by its slender petioles. Leaves 2–3-pinnate, the primary divisions distant, the second more approximate, all slender-stalked; ultimate segments lobed or entire, very thin, ovate or cuneate, pale beneath; flowers numerous in axillary drooping cymes, 5"–7" long, 3" broad at the base, narrowly ovate, greenish purple; capsule 2-valved, few-seeded.

In moist woods and thickets, New Brunswick to Ontario and Michigan, south to North Carolina and Tennessee. Recorded from Kansas. Mountain-fringe. Alleghany-, canary- or cypress-vine. Fairy-creeper. Alleghany- or wood-fringe. June–Oct.

3. CAPNOÌDES [Tourn.] Adans. Fam. Pl. 2: 431. 1763.

[NECKERIA Scop. Introd. 313. 1777.]
[CORYDALIS Medic. Phil. Bot. 96. 1789.]

Erect or climbing herbs, with basal and cauline decompound leaves, and racemose flowers, terminal, or opposite the petioles. Sepals 2, small. Corolla irregular, deciduous; petals 4, erect-connivent, one of the outer pairs spurred at the base, the interior ones narrow, keeled on the back. Stamens 6, in 2 sets, opposite the outer petals. Placentae 2; style entire, dilated or lobed, persistent. Capsule linear or oblong, 2-valved. [Greek, smoke-like, in allusion to the smoke-like odor of some species, as in Fumaria.]

About 110 species, natives of the north temperate zone and South Africa. Type species: Fumaria sempervirens L.

Stems tall; flowers pink with yellow tips.   1. C. sempervirens.
Stems low, diffuse or ascending; flowers yellow.
   Flowers 3"–4" long; spur short.
      Seeds sharp-margined, wrinkled; pods drooping or spreading.   2. C. flavulum.
      Seeds blunt-margined, smooth, shining; pods ascending.   3. C. micranthum.
   Flowers 6"–8" long; spur conspicuous.
      Pods smooth.
         Seeds smooth or obscurely reticulated; pods spreading, ascending or pendulous.

Capsules spreading or drooping, distinctly torulose ; eastern.　　　4. *C. aureum.*
Capsules ascending, terete or slightly torulose ; western.　　　5. *C. montanum.*
Seeds finely reticulated ; pods ascending.　　　6. *C. campestre.*
Pods densely covered with transparent vesicles.　　　7. *C. crystallinum.*

1. **Capnoides sempérvirens** (L.) Borck. Pink or Pale Corydalis. Fig. 1989.

Fumaria sempervirens L. Sp. Pl. 700.　1753.
Capnoides sempervirens Borck. in Roem. Arch. 1 : Part 2, 44.　1797.
Corydalis sempervirens Pers. Syn. 2 : 269.　1807.
Corydalis. glauca Pursh, Fl. Am. Sept. 463.　1814.

Glabrous, glaucous, erect or ascending, 5'–2° high, freely branching. Lower leaves 1'–4' long, short-petioled, the upper nearly sessile, pinnately decompound, the primary divisions distant, the ultimate segments obovate or cuneate, toothed or entire, obtuse, often mucronulate; flowers numerous, panicled, borne in cymose clusters at the ends of the branches, 5"–8" long, pink or rarely white, with a yellow tip; spur rounded, about 1" long; capsules narrowly linear, erect, 1'–2' long, nodose when mature; seeds shining, minutely reticulated.

In rocky places, Nova Scotia to Alaska, Georgia, Minnesota, Montana and British Columbia. Ascends to 4500 ft. in North Carolina. Roman wormwood. April–Sept.

2. **Capnoides flávulum** (Raf.) Kuntze. Pale or Yellow Corydalis. Fig. 1990.

Corydalis flavula Raf.; DC. Prodr. 1 : 129.　1824.
Capnoides flavulum Kuntze, Rev. Gen. Pl. 14.　1891.

Slender, glabrous, diffuse or ascending, 6'–14' high, freely branching. Lower leaves slender-petioled, the upper nearly sessile, all finely dissected into linear or oblong, sometimes cuneate, acute or obtuse segments; pedicels very slender; bracts conspicuous, broadly oblong, acute or acuminate, 3"–4" long; spur ½" long, rounded; outer petals slightly longer than the inner, yellow, sharp-pointed; crest dentate; pods torulose, drooping or spreading; seeds sharp-margined, finely reticulated.

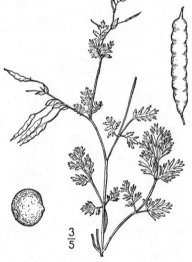

In rocky woods, New York to southwestern Ontario, Minnesota, Virginia and Louisiana. Ascends to 4000 ft. in Virginia. Colic-weed. May–June.

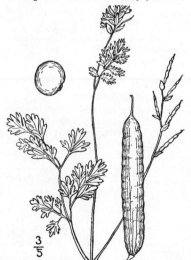

3. **Capnoides micránthum** (Engelm.) Britton. Small-flowered Corydalis. Fig. 1991.

Corydalis aurea var. *micrantha* Engelm.; A. Gray, Man. Ed. 5, 62.　1867.
Corydalis micrantha A. Gray, Coult. Bot. Gaz. 11 : 189. 1886.
Capnoides micranthum Britton, Mem. Torr. Club 5 : 166. 1894.

Habit and foliage nearly as in the preceding species, the ultimate leaf segments generally slightly broader. Flowers similar, the crest entire; or sometimes cleistogamous and minute, spurless and slightly or not at all crested; pods ascending, short-pedicelled, torulose; seeds obtuse-margined, smooth, shining.

In woods, Minnesota to Missouri, Kansas, Texas, Virginia and Florida. Feb.–April.

4. Capnoides àureum (Willd.) Kuntze.
Golden Corydalis. Fig. 1992.

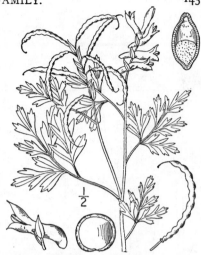

Corydalis aurea Willd. Enum. 740. 1809.

Capnoides aureum Kuntze, Rev. Gen. Pl. 14. 1891.

Glabrous, 6'–14' high, diffuse, branching. Leaves all but the uppermost petioled, finely dissected into oblong obovate or cuneate segments, mainly broader than those of related species; flowers 6" long, bright yellow; spur one-half the length of the body of the corolla, or more, rounded; outer petals keeled, not crested; pedicels short, slender; pods spreading or pendulous, torulose, especially when dry; seeds obtuse-margined, shining, obscurely reticulated.

In woods, Nova Scotia to Minnesota, Alaska, Pennsylvania and Missouri, south in the Rocky Mountains to Arizona and California. March–May.

5. Capnoides montànum (Engelm.) Britton. Mountain Corydalis. Fig. 1993.

Corydalis montana Engelm.; A. Gray, Mem. Am. Acad. 4: 6. 1849.
Corydalis aurea var. *occidentalis* Engelm.; A. Gray, Man. Ed. 5, 62. 1867.
Capnoides aureum var. *occidentale* A. S. Hitchcock, Spring Fl. Manhattan, 17. 1894.
Capnoides montanum Britton, Mem. Torr. Club 5: 166. 1894.

Closely resembles *C. aureum*, but is lighter green and the leaves are rather more finely divided. Flower-clusters spicate-racemose, the pedicels usually very short; flowers bright yellow, 6"–8" long; spur of the corolla as long as its body, or less; capsules spreading or somewhat ascending; seeds sharp-margined, shining or obscurely reticulated.

In dry soil, South Dakota to Kansas, Texas, Utah and Mexico. Perhaps a race of the preceding species. April–Aug.

6. Capnoides campéstre Britton. Plains Corydalis. Fig. 1994.

Capnoides campestre Britton, Man. Ed. 2, 1065. 1905.

Similar to the two preceding species, Flowers spicate-racemose, about 8" long, conspicuous, bright yellow; spur of the corolla blunt, nearly straight, 2"–2½" long; pods curved upward, very short-pedicelled, stout, somewhat 4-sided; seeds sharp-margined, finely and distinctly reticulated.

In fields and woods, Illinois to Nebraska, Arkansas and Texas. April–June. Mistaken in our first edition for the Texan *Capnoides curvisiliquum*. Golden corydalis.

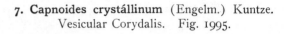

7. Capnoides crystállinum (Engelm.) Kuntze.
Vesicular Corydalis. Fig. 1995.

Corydalis crystallina Engelm.; A. Gray, Man. Ed. 5, 62. 1867.

Capnoides crystallinum Kuntze, Rev. Gen. Pl. 14. 1891.

Erect or ascending, glabrous, 8′–20′ high, branching. Lower leaves slender-petioled, the upper sessile, all finely dissected into oblong or cuneate segments; pedicels stout, short, diverging; flowers spicate, 6″–8″ long, bright yellow; spur 3″–4″ long; crest large, dentate; capsules 9″ long, ascending or erect, densely covered with transparent vesicles; seeds acute-margined, tuberculate-reticulated.

Prairies, Missouri, Kansas and Arkansas. April–June.

4. FUMÀRIA [Tourn.] L. Sp. Pl. 699. 1753.

Diffuse or erect (sometimes climbing) herbs, with finely dissected leaves, and small racemose flowers. Petals 4, erect-connivent, the outer pair larger, 1 of them spurred, the inner narrow, coherent at the apex, keeled or crested on the back. Stamens 6, diadelphous, opposite the outer petals. Ovule 1; style slender, deciduous; stigma entire or lobed. Fruit 1-seeded, nearly globose, indehiscent. Seeds not crested. [Name from the Latin, smoke, from the smoke-like smell of some species.]

About 40 species, all natives of the Old World, the following typical.

1. Fumaria officinàlis L. Fumitory. Hedge Fumitory. Fig. 1996.

Fumaria officinalis L. Sp. Pl. 700. 1753.

Glabrous, stems diffuse or ascending, freely branching, 6′–3° long. Leaves petioled, finely dissected into entire or lobed linear oblong or cuneate segments; racemes axillary and terminal, 1′–3′ long, narrow; pedicels 1″–2″ long, axillary to small bracts; flowers purplish, 2″–3″ long, crimson at the summit; sepals acute, toothed; spur rounded, ½″ long; nut 1″ in diameter, depressed-globose.

In waste places and on ballast, occasionally about towns and villages, Newfoundland to Florida and the Gulf States, and locally in the interior. Bermuda. Fugitive or adventive from Europe. Summer. Waxdolls. Earth-smoke.

Fumaria parviflòra Lam., found on ballast about the seaports, may be distinguished by its still smaller paler flowers (2″), very narrow sharp and channeled leaf-segments, and its apiculate nut.

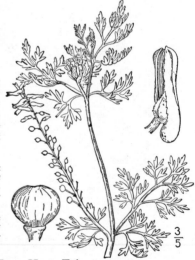

Family 38. CRUCÍFERAE B. Juss. Hort. Trian. 1759.

MUSTARD FAMILY.

Herbs, rarely somewhat woody, with watery acrid sap, alternate leaves, and racemose or corymbose flowers. Sepals 4, deciduous, or rarely persistent, the 2 outer narrow, the inner similar, or concave, or saccate at the base. Petals 4, hypogynous, cruciate, nearly equal, generally clawed. Stamens 6, hypogynous, tetradynamous, rarely fewer. Pistil 1, compound, consisting of 2 united carpels, the parietal placentae united by a dissepiment; style generally persistent, sometimes none; stigma discoid or usually more or less 2-lobed. Fruit a silique or silicle, generally 2-celled, rarely 1-celled, in a few genera indehiscent or lomentaceous. Seeds campylotropous, attached to both sides of the septum; endosperm none; cotyledons incumbent, accumbent or conduplicate, or the embryo rarely straight.

About 200 genera and 1800 species, of wide geographic distribution. Also known as BRAS-SICACEAE.

1. Pod continuous, not transversely 2-jointed.

A. Cotyledons accumbent or incumbent ; pods dehiscent (except in *Neslia, Myagrum*).

a. Pods globose to linear, not greatly elongated nor very broad and flat.

* Pubescence stellate, or of forked hairs.
  Pubescence stellate, or the hairs 2-lobed.
    Pods orbicular to linear, more or less flattened parallel to the broad partition (Alysseae).
      Seeds many in each cell of the oval to linear flat pod.   1. *Draba.*
      Seeds few in each cell of the short pod.
        Pods little flattened ; petals 2-cleft.   2. *Berteroa.*
        Pods much flattened ; petals entire.
          Flowers white ; pubescence of 2-lobed hairs.   3. *Koniga.*
          Flowers yellow ; pubescence stellate.   4. *Alyssum.*
    Pods globose or didymous, swollen (Physarieae).
      Pods globose.   5. *Lesquerella.*
      Pods didymous.   6. *Physaria.*
  Pubescence of forked hairs ; pods little longer than wide (Camelineae).
    Pods dehiscent, several–many-seeded.
      Pods obovoid, swollen ; flowers yellow.   7. *Camelina.*
      Pods not swollen, flattened at right angles to the partition ; flowers white.
        Pods cuneate to triangular-obcordate.   8. *Bursa.*
        Pods elliptic, the valves with a strong midvein.   9. *Hutchinsia.*
    Pods indehiscent, reticulated, mostly 1-seeded.   10. *Neslia.*
** Pubescence of simple hairs, or wanting.
  Pods globose to oblong, scarcely or not at all flattened.
    Aquatic with subulate leaves and minute white flowers ; cotyledons incumbent (Subularieae).
                           11. *Subularia.*
    Aquatic or terrestrial ; leaves not subulate ; cotyledons accumbent (Cochlearieae).
      Flowers yellow, small.   12. *Radicula.*
      Flowers white, large.
        Leaves pinnately divided ; pods linear.   13. *Sisymbrium.*
        Leaves crenate, lobed or pinnatifid ; pods globose or oblong.
          Terrestrial ; leaves undivided or the lower pinnatifid ; style very short.
            Tall herbs ; perennials.   14. *Armoracia.*
            Low arctic and alpine herbs ; annual or biennial.   15. *Cochlearia.*
          Aquatic : submersed leaves finely dissected. style slender ; pod 1-celled.
                           16. *Neobeckia.*
  Pods short, strongly flattened at right angles to the narrow partition ; flowers white or purplish.
    Pods dehiscent (Lepidieae).
      Seeds solitary in each cell of the pod.
        Pods smooth, orbicular or ovate.   17. *Lepidium.*
        Pods rugose-reticulate or tuberculate.   18. *Carara.*
      Seeds 2–several in each cell of the winged pod.   19. *Thlaspi.*
    Pods indehiscent (Isatideae).   20. *Myagrum.*

b. Pods elongated-linear, or large, broad and very flat in Lunaria and Selenia.

Pods stipitate (Stanleyae).
  Pods long-stipitate ; sepals reflexed.   21. *Stanleya.*
  Pods short-stipitate ; sepals not reflexed.   22. *Thelypodium.*
Pods sessile or very nearly so.
  Cotyledons incumbent (Sisymbrieae).
    Stigma simple, not 2-lobed.
      Leaves broad, cordate ; flowers white.   23. *Alliaria.*
      Leaves finely dissected ; flowers yellow.   24. *Sophia.*
    Stigma 2-lobed, the lobes over the placentae.
      Flowers yellow or orange.
        Leaves various, not cordate-clasping.
          Pods 4-angled ; hairs of the stem 2-forked with appressed branches.
                           25. *Cheirinia.*
          Pods terete ; pubescence, if present, of simple hairs.
            Pods narrowly conic, ribbed.   26. *Erysimum.*
            Pods linear-cylindric.   27. *Norta.*
          Leaves cordate-clasping, sessile, entire.   28. *Conringia.*
      Flowers white, purple or pink.
        Flowers very large, deep purple.   29. *Hesperis.*
        Flowers small, white or pale purple.   30. *Arabidopsis.*
  Cotyledons accumbent (Arabideae).
    Pods narrowly linear, rarely oblong.
      Stems leafy, at least above.
        Flowers pure yellow ; pods terete or nearly so.   31. *Barbarea.*
        Flowers white, pink, violet or purple.
          Pods terete, not flattened parallel with the partition.   32. *Iodanthus.*
          Pods more or less flattened parallel with the partition.
            Seeds winged or wing-margined ; pods not elastically dehiscent ; pubescence,
              or some of it, when present, of branched hairs.   33. *Arabis.*
            Seeds wingless ; pods mostly elastically dehiscent the base ; pubescence, if
              present, of simple hairs.
              Stem leafy below or throughout.   34. *Cardamine.*
              Stem leafless below, 2–4-leaved above.   35. *Dentaria.*
      Stem scapose, 1–few-flowered.   36. *Leavenworthia.*

Pods very broad and flat.
  Flowers yellow ; pods finely veined.   37. *Selenia.*
  Flowers purple ; pods reticulate-veined.   38. *Lunaria.*

    B. Cotyledons conduplicate; pod (silique) elongated, beaked; weeds of cultiva-
tion (Brassiceae).

Silique dehiscent.
  Beak of the silique stout, flat or angled.
    Valves 3-nerved.   39. *Sinapis.*
    Valves with 1 strong nerve.   40. *Eruca.*
  Beak of the silique conic, often short.
    Silique terete ; seeds in 1 row in each cell.   41. *Brassica.*
    Silique flattened ; seeds in 2 rows in each cell.   42. *Diplotaxis.*
Silique indehiscent.   43. *Raphanus.*

        2. Pod transversely 2-jointed; fleshy, seaside herbs (Cakileae). 44. *Cakile.*

1. DRÀBA [Dill.] L. Sp. Pl. 642. 1753.

    Low tufted mostly stellate-pubescent herbs, with scapose or leafy stems, simple leaves, and mainly racemose flowers. Silicles elliptic, oblong or linear, flat, few to many-seeded, glabrous or pubescent. Stigma nearly entire. Seeds wingless, arranged in 2 rows in each cell of the pod, numerous; valves dehiscent, nerveless; cotyledons accumbent. [Greek name for some plant of this family.]

    Species about 175, mainly natives of the north temperate and arctic regions, a few in southern South America. Besides the following, some 30 others are natives of western North America. Type species : *Draba verna* L.

Flowers white.
  Petals deeply 2-cleft.   1. *D. verna.*
  Petals entire, toothed, or emarginate.
    Flowering stems scapose, leafy only below.
      Plants annual, not arctic.
        Leaves entire, obovate or oblong.   2. *D. caroliniana.*
        Leaves dentate, cuneate.   3. *D. cuneifolia.*
      Low arctic perennials.
        Leaves stellate-canescent.   4. *D. fladnizensis.*
        Leaves pilose-ciliate or glabrous.   5. *D. nivalis.*
    Flowering stems leafy throughout up to the inflorescence.
      Leaves remotely low-dentate or entire.
        Basal leaves loosely pubescent, ciliate.   6. *D. incana.*
        Basal leaves densely stellate-canescent.
          Fruiting pedicels divergent.   7. *D. arabisans.*
          Fruiting pedicels nearly erect.   8. *D. stylaris.*
      Leaves sharply dentate.   9. *D. ramosissima.*
Flowers yellow.
  Stems leafy.
    Pods oblong, 1″–2″ long.   10. *D. brachycarpa.*
    Pods linear or lanceolate, 3″–6″ long.
      Annual ; pods 3″–4″ long ; pedicels divaricately spreading. 11. *D. nemorosa.*
      Perennial ; pods 4″–7″ long ; pedicels erect. 12. *D. aurea.*
  Stems scapose.   13. *D. alpina.*

1. Draba vérna L. Vernal Whitlow-grass. Shad-flower. Nailwort. Fig. 1997.

    Draba verna L. Sp. Pl. 642. 1753.

    Erophila vulgaris DC. Syst. Veg. **2** : 356. 1821.

    Annual or biennial, the leafless scapes numerous, 1′–5′ high, erect or ascending, arising from a tuft of basal leaves, which are oblong or spatulate-oblanceolate, ½′–1′ long, dentate or nearly entire, acutish and pubescent with stiff stellate hairs; scapes nearly glabrous; flowers white, cleistogamous, 1½″–2″ broad; petals deeply bifid; pedicels ascending, ½′–1′ long in fruit; racemes elongating; pods oblong to oval, glabrous, 3″–4″ long, 1″ broad, obtuse, shorter than their pedicels; style minute; seeds numerous.

    In fields, Massachusetts to New York, Minnesota, Georgia and Tennessee. Recorded from Quebec. Naturalized from Europe. Occurs also in Washington and British Columbia. Native of Europe and western Asia. Consists of a great many slightly differing races. White-blow. Feb.–May.

2. Draba caroliniàna Walt. Carolina Whitlow-grass. Fig. 1998.

Draba caroliniana Walt. Fl. Car. 174. 1788.
Draba hispidula Michx. Fl. Bor. Am. 2 : 28. 1803.
Draba caroliniana micrantha A. Gray, Man. Ed. 5, 72. 1867.
Draba micrantha Nutt.; T. & G. Fl. N. A. 1 : 109. 1838.

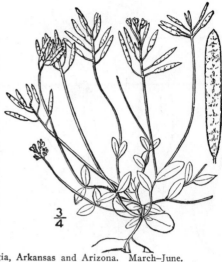

Winter-annual, the flowering scapes 1′–5′ high from a short leafy stem. Leaves tufted, obovate, 4″–10″ long, obtuse, entire or rarely with 3 or 4 teeth, pubescent with stiff stellate hairs; scapes nearly glabrous; flowers white, 1½″–2″ broad; petals entire, sometimes wanting in the later flowers; pedicels 1″–2″ long in fruit, clustered near the summit of the scape; pods linear, 4″–6″ long, nearly 1″ broad, glabrous or appressed-pubescent; style none.

$\frac{3}{4}$

In sandy fields, eastern Massachusetts to southern Ontario, Nebraska, Minnesota, Idaho, Georgia, Arkansas and Arizona. March–June.

$\frac{3}{5}$

3. Draba cuneifòlia Nutt. Wedge-leaved Whitlow-grass. Fig. 1999.

Draba cuneifolia Nutt.; T. & G. Fl. N. A. 1 : 108. 1838.

Winter-annual, stellate-pubescent all over, 4′–8′ high, branching and leafy below. Leaves obovate, cuneate, or the lowest spatulate, ½′–1½′ long, obtuse, dentate toward the summit; flowering branches erect or ascending; flowers white, 2″ broad; petals emarginate, twice or thrice the length of the calyx; pedicels ascending or spreading, 2″–4″ long in fruit; raceme elongating; petals emarginate; pods linear-oblong, obtuse, 4″–5″ long, 1″ wide, minutely hairy; style none.

In fields, Kentucky to Kansas, south to Florida, Texas and northern Mexico, west to southern California. Feb.–April.

4. Draba fladnizénsis Wulf. White Arctic Whitlow-grass. Fig. 2000.

Draba fladnizensis Wulf. in Jacq. Misc. 1 : 147. 1778.

Draba androsacea Wahl. Fl. Lapp. 174. 1812.

Draba cormybosa R. Br. in Ross, Voy. App. 143. 1819.

A low tufted arctic or alpine perennial. Leaves oblanceolate basal, rosulate, acutish, entire, stellate-pubescent or with some simple hairs, ciliate or rarely nearly glabrous, 4″–8″ long; flowers whitish; scapes glabrous; pedicels ascending, 1″–2″ long in fruit; raceme at length somewhat elongated; pods oblong, glabrous, 2″–3″ long, nearly 1″ wide. style almost wanting.

Labrador; Mt. Albert, Gaspé, Quebec; and through arctic America, south in the higher Rocky Mountains to Colorado. Also in arctic and alpine Europe and Asia. Summer.

$\frac{3}{5}$

5. Draba nivàlis Lilj. Yellow Arctic Whitlow-grass. Fig. 2001.

Draba nivalis Lilj. Vet. Akad. Handl. **1793** : 208. 1793.

Perennial by a short branched caudex; scapes tufted, somewhat pubescent, slender, leafless or sometimes bearing a small sessile leaf, 1'–4' high. Basal leaves usually numerous, tufted, oblanceolate or spatulate, 2"–7" long, entire, acutish or acute at the apex, narrowed into a short petiole, stellate-canescent, not ciliate, or slightly so near the base; flowers yellow, about 2" broad; calyx pubescent; style short; pods oblong or linear-oblong, narrowed at both ends, glabrous or but little pubescent, on ascending pedicels 1"–3" long.

Labrador and Greenland, through arctic America to Alaska, south in the Rocky Mountains to Colorado, and in the Sierra Nevada to Nevada. Also in northern Europe and Asia. Summer.

6. Draba incàna L. Hoary or Twisted Whitlow-grass. Fig. 2002.

Draba incana L. Sp. Pl. 643. 1753.
Draba confusa Ehrh. Beitr. **7** : 155. 1792.

Perennial or biennial; flowering stems erect, simple or somewhat branched, leafy, loosely pilose-pubescent, 16' high or less. Leaves 4"–12" long, acutish or obtuse, dentate or nearly entire, the basal ones oblanceolate, those of the flowering stems lanceolate to ovate; flowers white, 1"–1½" broad; petals notched, twice as long as the calyx; pods oblong or lanceolate, acute, twisted when ripe, on short nearly erect pedicels, densely pubescent or glabrous; style minute.

In rocky places, Newfoundland and Labrador to Quebec. Also in arctic and alpine Europe. Hunger-flower. Nailwort. Summer.

Draba hìrta L. of high boreal regions has fewer stem-leaves and longer fruiting pedicels.

$\frac{1}{2}$

7. Draba aràbisans Michx. Rock-cress Whitlow-grass. Fig. 2003.

D. arabisans Michx. Fl. Bor. Am. **2** : 28. 1803.
D. incana arabisans S. Wats. Proc. Am. Acad. **23** : 260. 1888.
D. arabisans orthocarpa Fernald, Rhodora **7** : 66. 1905.

Perennial by a slender branched caudex, the flowering stems 6'–20' high, sparingly stellate-pubescent, often numerous. Leaves thin, green, loosely and mostly sparingly stellate-pubescent, the tufted basal ones spatulate to oblanceolate, ½'–2½' long, 2"–4" wide, usually remotely dentate, sometimes entire, those of the flowering stems similar, oblong to spatulate; flowers white; fruiting pedicels slender, divergent-ascending, 5" long or less; pods narrowly oblong, glabrous, 3"–7" long, 1"–2" wide, twisted or straight.

On cliffs and in rocky and sandy soil, Newfoundland and Labrador to Maine, Vermont, northern New York and western Ontario. June–Aug.

$\frac{3}{4}$

8. Draba stylàris J. Gay.   Canescent Whitlow-grass.
Fig. 2004.

Draba stylaris J. Gay, in Thomas, Cat. 1818.
D. confusa Reichenb. Ic. Crit. **8**: 1033. 1830. Not Ehrh.

Perennial or biennial; flowering stems simple or little branched, 15' high or less, loosely pilose. Basal leaves oblanceolate, few-toothed, $\frac{1}{2}$'–$1\frac{1}{2}$' long, densely stellate-canescent; stem-leaves oblong-lanceolate to ovate, somewhat toothed or entire, more or less stellate-canescent; flowers white; fruiting pedicels nearly erect, 1''–2$\frac{1}{2}$'' long; pods oblong to lanceolate, $3\frac{1}{2}$''–6'' long, mostly twisted when mature, stellate-canescent.

Cliffs and rocks, Newfoundland and Labrador to the mountains of Vermont; Alberta and British Columbia; Colorado. Europe. Previously confused with *D. incana* L.

Draba megaspérma Fernald & Knowlton, found on a gravelly beach in Bonaventure County, Quebec, differs in having broader pods, larger seeds and the flowering stems stellate-canescent.

Draba pycnospérma Fernald & Knowlton, of limestone cliffs and ledges in Quebec, has shorter pods with crowded angled seeds.

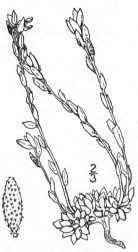

9. Draba ramosíssima Desv.   Branching Whitlow-grass. Fig. 2005.

Draba ramosissima Desv. Journ. Bot. **3**: 186. 1814.

Erect, much branched below, 6'–18' high, stellate-pubescent throughout, the branches bearing tufts of leaves, the inflorescence corymbosely paniculate. Lower leaves spatulate or oblanceolate, 1'–2' long, acute, dentate with spreading teeth; upper leaves oblong or ovate, similarly dentate; branches of the panicle erect or ascending; flowers white, 2''–3'' broad; petals entire or erose, twice or thrice the length of the sepals; pedicels spreading or ascending, 3''–4'' long in fruit; pods oblong or lanceolate, hairy, 3''–4'' long, twisted; style slender, 1''–2'' long.

Mountains of Virginia and Kentucky, south to North Carolina and Tennessee. April–May.

10. Draba brachycàrpa Nutt.   Short-fruited Whitlow-grass. Fig. 2006.

Draba brachycarpa Nutt.; T. & G. Fl. N. A. **1**: 108. 1838.

Annual, tufted, 2'–5' high, loosely stellate-pubescent, leafy to the inflorescence. Basal leaves ovate or obovate, 4''–6'' long, obtuse, sparingly dentate or entire; stem-leaves smaller, sessile, oblong, entire; pedicels ascending, 1''–2'' long in fruit; raceme elongating; flowers yellow, 1'' broad; petals somewhat longer than the calyx, sometimes wanting; pods oblong, acute, $1\frac{1}{2}$''–2'' long, $\frac{1}{2}$'' broad; style minute.

Dry hills and fields, Virginia to Illinois, Missouri, Kansas, Georgia, Louisiana and Arkansas. Montana to Oregon. March–May.

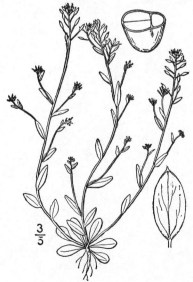

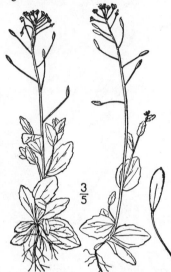

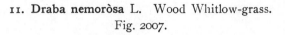

11. **Draba nemoròsa** L.   Wood Whitlow-grass.
Fig. 2007.

Draba nemorosa L. Sp. Pl. 643.   1753.

Winter-annual, loosely stellate-pubescent, 6′–12′ high, branching below, leafy to the inflorescence.   Leaves oblong-ovate, or lanceolate, obtuse, sessile, dentate, the lower 10″–12″ long, 5″–7″ wide, the upper smaller; flowers yellow, fading to whitish, 1″ broad; petals notched, slightly exceeding•the calyx; pedicels divaricately spreading in fruit, glabrous, 3″–10″ long; racemes open, much elongating; pods pubescent, or glabrous, oblong, obtuse, 3″–4″ long; style none.

Western Ontario, Michigan, Minnesota, South Dakota and western Nebraska to Oregon, arctic America and south in the Rocky Mountains to Colorado and Utah.   Also in northern Europe and Asia.   Summer.

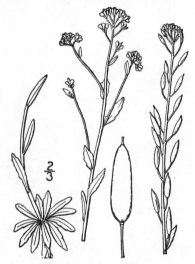

12. **Draba àurea** Vahl.   Golden Whitlow-grass. Fig. 2008.

D. aurea Vahl in Hornem. Fl. OEcon. Ed. 2, 599.   1806.

Perennial, pubescent throughout with stellate and simple hairs; stem branching or nearly simple, 6′–10′ high, leafy to the inflorescence.   Basal leaves oblanceolate or spatulate, 6″–12″ long, obtuse or acutish, slightly dentate or entire, often ciliate at the base; stem-leaves oblong or lanceolate, acute; pods lanceolate or oblong-lanceolate, 4″–6″ long; flowers yellow, 2″ broad; petals twice the length of the calyx, emarginate or entire; pods acute, pubescent or rarely glabrous, at length slightly twisted, 4″–7″ long, on erect pedicels one-half their length; style stout, ½″ long.

Mignon Island, Gulf of St. Lawrence to Labrador, Greenland; arctic America and in the Rocky Mountains south to Arizona.   Summer.

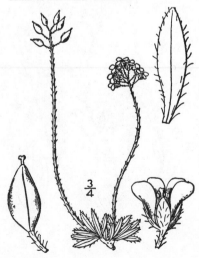

13. **Draba alpìna** L.   Alpine Whitlow-grass. Fig. 2009.

Draba alpina L. Sp. Pl. 642.   1753.

Perennial by a branched caudex, densely tufted, scapes pubescent, ½′–6′ high.   Leaves all basal, entire or few-toothed, oblong, or oblong-lanceolate, obtuse or acute at the apex, mostly narrowed at the base, ciliate, or villous-pubescent, sometimes with some stellate hairs, 2″–6″ long, sessile or short-petioled; flowers yellow, about 3″ broad; calyx pubescent or villous; style ½″ long or less; pod oval or ovate, narrowed at both ends, glabrous, or somewhat pubescent, 2½″–4″ long, 1″–1¼″ wide; pedicels ascending, 1″–5″ long

Greenland to Hudson Bay, the mountains of British Columbia and Alaska.   Also in northern Europe and Asia.   Summer.

Draba crassifòlia Graham, a low annual or biennial species, with tufted basal ciliate leaves, small yellowish scapose flowers, of arctic and alpine distribution, ranges south to Labrador.

2. BERTEROA DC. Mem. Mus. Paris, 7: 232. 1821.

Annual or perennial herbs, stellate-pubescent or canescent, the leaves mostly narrow and entire, and the flowers white in terminal racemes. Petals 2-cleft. Filaments 2-toothed at the base. Silicles oblong or subglobose, somewhat compressed. Seeds several in each cell, winged. Cotyledons accumbent. [In honor of C. G. Bertero, a botanist of Piedmont, 1739–1831.]

About 5 species, natives of Europe and Asia, the following typical.

1. Berteroa incàna (L.) DC. Hoary Alyssum.
Fig. 2010.

Alyssum incanum L. Sp. Pl. 650. 1753.
Berteroa incana DC. Syst. 2: 291. 1821.

Erect or ascending, 1°–2° high, hoary-pubescent, branching above. Leaves lanceolate or oblong, ½′–1½′ long, obtuse, entire or slightly undulate, the lower narrowed into a petiole; flowers white, 1″–1½″ broad; pedicels ascending, 2″–3″ long in fruit; pod canescent, swollen, oblong, 3″–4″ long and about half as broad; style 1″–1½″ long; stigma minute.

In waste places, Maine to Ontario, Minnesota, Massachusetts, New Jersey and Missouri. Adventive or naturalized from Europe. Racemes elongating, the flowers and pods very numerous. June–Sept.

Berteroa mutábilis (Vent.) DC., also native of Europe, has a more compressed, sparingly pubescent and slightly larger pod; it is recorded as adventive in Massachusetts.

3. KÒNIGA* Adans. Fam. Pl. 2: 420. 1763.
[Lobularia Desv. Journ. Bot. 3: 172. 1813.]

Perennial herbs or shrubs, pubescent or canescent with forked hairs, with entire leaves, and small white flowers in terminal racemes. Petals obovate, entire. Filaments slender, not toothed, but with two small glands at the base. Silicle compressed, oval or orbicular. Seeds 1 in each cell. Cotyledons accumbent. [Name in honor of Charles Konig, a curator of the British Museum.]

About 4 species, natives of the Mediterranean region, the following typical.

1. Koniga marítima (L.) R. Br. Sweet Alyssum. Seaside Koniga. Madwort. Snow-drift. Fig. 2011.

Clypeola maritima L. Sp. Pl. 652. 1753.
Alyssum maritimum Lam. Encycl. 1: 98. 1783.
Koniga maritima R. Br. in Denh. & Clapp, Narr. Exp. Afric. 214. 1826.

Procumbent or ascending, freely branching, 4′–12′ high, minutely pubescent with appressed hairs Stem-leaves nearly sessile, lanceolate or linear, ½′–2′ long, 1″–2½″ wide; basal leaves oblanceolate, narrowed into a petiole. flowers white, fragrant, about 2″ broad; pedicels ascending, 3″–4″ long in fruit; pods glabrous, pointed, oval or nearly orbicular, 1″–1½″ long; calyx deciduous; stamens not appendaged.

In waste places, occasional. Vermont to Pennsylvania and on the Pacific Coast. Bermuda. Cuba. Escaped from gardens. Adventive from Europe. Sweet allison. Summer.

4. ALÝSSUM [Tourn.] L. Sp. Pl. 650. 1753.

Low branching stellate-pubescent annual or perennial herbs, with small racemose yellow or yellowish flowers. Petals entire. Filaments often dilated and toothed or appendaged. Silicle ovate, oblong or orbicular, compressed, its valves nerveless, the septum thin. Stigma

---

* Originally spelled *Konig*. Latinized by R. Brown in 1826.

nearly entire. Seeds 1 or 2 in each cell of the pod, wingless; cotyledons accumbent. [Greek, curing madness.]

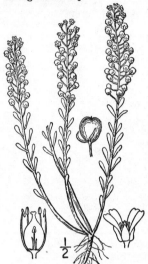

A genus of 100 species or more, natives of the Old World, some of them known as Madwort. Type species: *Alyssum montanum* L.

1. Alyssum alyssoìdes L.   Yellow or Small Alyssum. Fig. 2012.

Clypeola alyssoides L. Sp. Pl. 652. 1753.
Alyssum alyssoides L. Syst. Ed. 10, 1130. 1759.
Alyssum calycinum L. Sp. Pl. Ed. 2, 908. 1763.

Annual, densely erect, simple, or branching from the base, tufted, 3′–10′ high. Leaves linear-oblong or spatulate, narrowed at the base, obtuse, entire, 3″–15″ long, the lower somewhat petioled; flowers yellowish-white, 1″ broad; pedicels spreading or ascending, 2″ long in fruit; pods orbicular, 1½″ in diameter, margined, minutely pubescent, notched at the apex, tipped with the minute style; sepals persistent around the base of the pod; seeds 2 in each cell; style minute; filaments of the shorter stamens minutely toothed at the base.

In fields, Ontario to Massachusetts, southeastern New York, New Jersey and Iowa, and in ballast about the seaports. Also in the Far West. Naturalized or adventive from Europe. Heal-bite. Heal-dog. Summer.

5. LESQUERÉLLA S. Wats. Proc. Am. Acad. 23: 249.   1888.

Low annual or perennial herbs, with stellate pubescence, simple leaves, and racemose mainly yellow flowers. Petals entire. Anthers sagittate. Pod generally inflated, globose or oblong; valves nerveless; septum translucent, nerved from the apex to the middle. Seeds several or many in each cell of the pod, flattened, marginless or narrow-margined; cotyledons accumbent. [Dedicated to Leo Lesquereux, 1805–1889, Swiss and American botanist.]

A genus of about 35 species, natives of America, and mainly of the western parts of the United States. Type species: *Lesquerella Lescurii* (A. Gray) S. Wats.

Pods stellate-pubescent.
  Pods ob'ong, acute, 2″ long; low perennial.   1. *L. spathulata.*
  Pods globose, 1″ in diameter; tall annual or biennial.   2. *L. globosa.*
  Pods oval or subglobose, 2″ long; tall biennial or perennial.   3. *L. argentea.*
Pods glabrous or very nearly so.
  Annual, sparingly pubescent; stem slender, 1°–2° tall, much branched; southwestern.
                                                             4. *L. gracilis.*
  Perennial, densely stellate; stem rather stout, 6′–12′ tall, simple; western.   5. *L. ovalifolia.*
  Perennial, 1′–6′ tall; stem simple; arctic.   6. *L. arctica.*

1. Lesquerella spathulàta Rydberg.   Low Bladder-pod. Fig. 2013.

Lesquerella spathulata Rydberg, Contr. U. S. Nat. Herb. 3: 486.   1896.

Perennial, tufted from a deep root, very finely canescent and stellate, 4′–5′ high; stems slender, generally numerous, simple. Lower leaves oblanceolate or spatulate, 6″–12″ long, acutish, narrowed into a petiole; the upper linear, mainly less than 1″ wide; flowers yellow, about 2″ broad; racemes rather few-flowered; pedicels 3″–6″ long, ascending, or recurved in fruit; pods oblong or nearly globose, slightly compressed, acute, subacute or rarely obtuse at each end, finely canescent, about 2″ long, few-seeded, tipped with a style of about their own length; septum commonly unperforated.

Dry hills, Nebraska and South Dakota to Montana and the Northwest Territory. June.

2. Lesquerella globòsa (Desv.) S. Wats.
Short's Bladder-pod. Fig. 2014.

Vesicaria globosa Desv. Journ. Bot. **3**: 184. 1814.
Vesicaria Shortii T. & G. Fl. N. A. **1**: 102. 1838.
L. globosa S. Wats. Proc. Am. Acad. **23**: 252. 1888.

Slender, erect or ascending, sparingly branch-ing, 6′–20′ high, finely stellate-pubescent all over. Basal leaves obovate, 1′–1½′ long, obtuse; stem-leaves narrower, linear or oblong, smaller, sessile, entire or with slightly undulate margins, the lowest sometimes narrowed into a petiole; flow-ers yellow; petals 2″–3″ long; pedicels slender, spreading, 4″–5″ long in fruit; raceme elongat-ing; pod nearly globular, 1″ in diameter, glabrous when mature; seeds 1 or 2 in each cell; style very slender, 2″ long.

In open places, Kentucky and Tennessee to eastern Missouri. April.

3. Lesquerella argéntea (Pursh) MacM.
Silvery Bladder-pod. Fig. 2015.

Myagrum argenteum Pursh, Fl. Am. Sept. 434. 1814.
Vesicaria argentea DC. Syst. **2**: 297. 1821.
Lesquerella Ludoviciana S. Wats. Proc. Am. Acad. **23**: 252. 1888.
L. argentea MacM. Met. Minn. 263. 1892.

Biennial or perennial, tufted, nearly simple, 6′–18′ high, densely stellate-pubescent through-out. Leaves linear, oblong or oblanceolate, the lower 2′–3′ long, blunt, entire or sparingly repand-toothed; flowers yellow; petals 3″ long; pedicels slender, 8″–12″ long in fruit, spreading or recurved; pod slightly stipitate, stellate-pubescent, globose to oval, 2″–2½″ long; style about equalling the pod.

Prairies, Minnesota, Nebraska and Kansas to North Dakota, Wyoming and Arizona. May–June.

4. Lesquerella grácilis (Hook.) S. Wats.
Slender Bladder-pod. Fig. 2016.

Vesicaria gracilis Hook. Bot. Mag. *pl. 3533.* 1836.

L. gracilis S. Wats. Proc. Am. Acad. **23**: 253. 1888.

Annual, weak, green, stem slender, 10′–20′ high, freely branching, sparsely stellate-pubescent. Leaves linear or oblanceolate, the lower slightly petioled, the upper sessile, 9″–2′ long, their margins often undulate; flowers yellow; petals about 3″ long; pedicels spreading, sometimes 1′ long in fruit, ascending or upwardly curved; pod globose, glabrous, 2″ in diameter, stipitate at the end of the pedicel; style 2″ long; seeds several in each cell.

Prairies, Missouri and Nebraska to Texas. March–May.

$\frac{3}{5}$

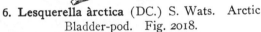

5. Lesquerella ovalifòlia Rydb. Oval-leaved Bladder-pod. Fig. 2017.

Lesquerella ovalifolia Rydb.; Britt. & Brown, Ill. Fl. 2 : 137. 1897.

Perennial from a tufted caudex, pale, densely stellate-canescent. Basal leaves tufted, broadly oval to obovate, sometimes nearly orbicular, entire, obtuse or subacute, 1′–2′ long, narrowed into rather long petioles; stem-leaves distant, sessile, or the lowest short-petioled, linear-oblanceolate or narrowly spatulate; fruiting pedicels comparatively stout, ascending, 6″–10″ long; pods very short-stipitate, subglobose, obtuse, 2½″–3″ in diameter, glabrous; style about 3″ long; seeds about 6 in each cell.

In dry soil, Nebraska, Kansas and Colorado.

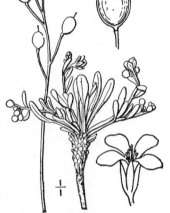

6. Lesquerella àrctica (DC.) S. Wats. Arctic Bladder-pod. Fig. 2018.

Alyssum? *arcticum* DC. Syst. 2 : 324. 1821.
Vesicaria arctica Richards. Frank. Journ. 743. 1823.
Lesquerella arctica S. Wats. Proc. Am. Acad. 23 : 254. 1888.

Perennial, tufted, densely stellate-pubescent, stem nearly or quite simple, erect, 1′–5′ tall. Leaves oblanceolate, or spatulate, or the upper oblong, 1′ long or less, obtuse, entire, the basal ones narrowed into broad petioles, the upper sessile; petals about 2″ long; pods oval or subglobose, obtuse, 2″–3″ high, glabrous or somewhat stellate-pubescent, few-seeded; septum perforated; style 1″ or less long.

Greenland and arctic America. Summer.

The plant described as **Lesquerella àrctica Pùrshii** S. Watts., is taller, sometimes 6′ high ; the septum of the sparsely stellate-pubescent pod unperforated. Anticosti.

6. PHYSÀRIA A. Gray, Gen. Ill. 1 : 162. 1848.

Low perennial stellate-canescent herbs, with erect or ascending usually quite simple stems, spatulate mostly entire leaves, the basal ones tufted, and medium-sized yellow flowers in terminal racemes. Petals longer than the sepals. Style filiform. Silicles membranous, stellate-pubescent, their cells inflated, the septum narrow. Seeds not margined; cotyledons accumbent. [Greek, bellows, from the resemblance of the inflated fruit.]

About 6 species, natives of western North America, the following typical.

$\frac{1}{2}$

1. Physaria didymocàrpa (Hook.) A. Gray. Double Bladder-pod. Fig. 2019.

Vesicaria didymocarpa Hook. Fl. Bor. Am. 1 : 49. *pl. 16.* 1830.
Physaria didymocarpa A. Gray, Gen. Ill. 1 : 162. 1848.
Physaria brassicoides Rydb. Bull. Torr. Club 29 : 237. 1902.

Densely stellate-canescent, pale green; root long and deep. Stems decumbent or ascending, slender, simple, 3′–12′ long; leaves spatulate, the basal ones obtuse, entire, or few-lobed, narrowed into margined petioles, 1′–5′ long; stem-leaves nearly sessile, acute or subacute, much smaller; racemes 2′–5′ long in fruit; flowers 5″–6″ broad; pods didymous, variable, often 6″ thick through the strongly inflated cavities, emarginate at base and summit or narrowed at base, commonly broader than high; seeds numerous.

In dry soil, North Dakota to Saskatchewan, British Columbia, Nebraska, Colorado and Nevada. May–Aug.

7. CAMÉLINA Crantz, Stirp. Austr. 1 : 18. 1762.

Erect annual herbs, with entire toothed or pinnatifid leaves, and small yellowish flowers. Silicles obovoid or pear-shaped, slightly flattened; valves very convex, 1-nerved. Seeds several or numerous in each cell, oblong, marginless, arranged in 2 rows. Stigma entire; style slender. Cotyledons incumbent. [Greek, low flax.]

A genus of about 5 species, natives of Europe and eastern Asia. Type species: *Camelina sativa* (L.) Crantz.

Glabrous, or nearly so ; pod 3″-4″ long.   1. *C. sativa.*
Pubescent, at least below ; pod 2″-3″ long.   2. *C. microcarpa.*

1. Camelina satìva (L.) Crantz. Gold-of-Pleasure. False or Dutch Flax. Fig. 2020.

Myagrum sativum L. Sp. Pl. 641. 1753.

Camelina sativa Crantz, Stirp. Austr. 1 : 18. 1762.

Glabrous, or nearly so, simple, or branching above, 1°-2° high. Lowest leaves petioled, entire or toothed, 2′-3′ long, lanceolate, acutish; upper leaves sessile, smaller, clasping by a sagittate base, mostly entire; pedicels slender, spreading or ascending, 6″-10″ long in fruit; flowers numerous, about 3″ long; pod obovoid or pyriform, margined, slightly flattened, 3″-4″ long, about 2″-3″ wide; style slender, 1½″ long.

In fields (especially where flax has been grown) and waste places, Nova Scotia to British Columbia, Pennsylvania, Kansas and California, naturalized from Europe. Old name, myàgrum. Cultivated in Europe for the fine oil of its seeds; nutritious to cattle. Oil-seed. Siberian oilseed. Cheat. Madwort. June–July.

2. Camelina microcàrpa Andrz. Small-fruited False-flax. Fig. 2021.

Camelina microcarpa Andrz.; DC. Syst. 2 : 517. 1821.

Camelina sylvestris Wallr. Sched. Crit. 347. 1822.

Stem pubescent, at least below, simple or with few elongated branches. Leaves lanceolate, sessile, auricled, or the lower narrowed at the base; fruiting racemes much elongated, often 1° long or more; pedicels relatively somewhat shorter than those of *C. sativa;* pod smaller, rather more flattened, 2″-3″ long, strongly margined.

In waste places, Ontario to Rhode Island, Virginia, British Columbia, Kansas and Arizona. Naturalized or adventive from Europe. May–July.

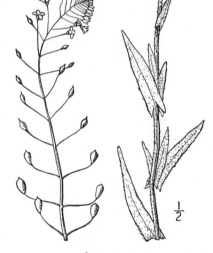

8. BÚRSA [Siegesb.] Weber in Wigg. Prim. Fl. Holst. 47. 1780.

[CAPSELLA Medic. Pfl. Gatt. 1 : 85. 1792.]

Annual or winter-annual erect herbs, pubescent with forked hairs; basal leaves tufted. Flowers racemose, small, white. Silicles cuneate, obcordate or triangular, compressed at right angles with the septum, the valves boat-shaped, keeled. Style short. Seeds numerous, marginless; cotyledons accumbent. [Middle Latin, purse, from the shape of the pod.]

About 4 species, natives of the northern hemisphere, the following typical. In addition to the following, another occurs in the western parts of North America.

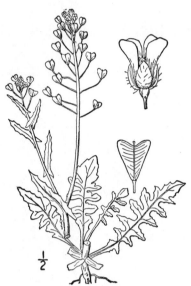

1, **Bursa Bursa-pastòris** (L.) Britton. Shepherd's-purse, -bag or -pouch. Fig. 2022.

Thlapsi Bursa-pastoris L. Sp. Pl. 647. 1753.
B. pastoris Weber in Wigg. Prim. Fl. Holst. 47. 1780.
Capsella Bursa-pastoris Medic. Pfl. Gatt. 1: 85. 1792.
Bursa Bursa-pastoris Britton, Mem. Torr. Club **5**: 172. 1894.

Erect, branching, 6′–20′ high from a long deep root, pubescent below, mainly glabrous above. Basal leaves more or less lobed or pinnatifid, forming a large rosette, rarely entire, 2′–5′ long; stem-leaves few, lanceolate, auricled dentate or entire, flowers white, about 1″ long; pedicels slender, spreading or ascending, 5″–7″ long in fruit; pods triangular, cuneate at the base, truncate or emarginate at the apex, 2″–4″ long; seeds 10 or 12 in each cell.

In fields and waste places, very common. Naturalized from Europe, and widely distributed as a weed over all parts of the globe. Consists of several races. Jan.–Dec. Other names are St. James'-weed, case-weed, mother's heart. Pick-purse. Pick-pocket. Lady's-purse. Witches'-pouches. Shovel-weed. Wind-flower. Pepper-plant. Toothwort. Toywort.

9. **HUTCHÍNSIA** R. Br. in Ait. Hort. Kew. Ed. 2, **4**: 82.   1812.

[Hymenolobus Nutt.; T. & G. Fl. N. A. 1: 117. 1838.]

Low mostly diffuse herbs, more or less pubescent with forked hairs, our species annual, with entire or pinnately lobed leaves, and very small white flowers in terminal racemes, the axis of the racemes much elongating in fruit. Stamens 6. Style wanting or very short. Silicles oval, obcompressed (*i. e.*, at right angles to the partition), the valves with a strong midvein. Seeds numerous in each cell; cotyledons incumbent or accumbent. [Name in honor of Miss Hutchins, of Bantry, Ireland, an eminent botanist.]

About 8 species, natives of the northern hemisphere, only the following known in North America. Type species: *Hutchinsia petraea* (Willd.) R. Br.

1. **Hutchinsia procúmbens** (L.) Desv.   Prostrate Hutchinsia.   Fig. 2023.

Lepidium procumbens L. Spec. Pl. 643. 1753.

Hutchinsia procumbens Desv. Journ. Bot. **3**: 168. 1814.

Hymenolobus divaricatus Nutt.; T. & G. Fl. N. A. 1: 117. 1838.

Capsella elliptica C. A. Meyer; Ledeb. Fl. Alt. 3: 199. 1831.

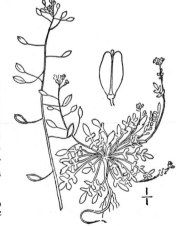

Tufted, somewhat pubescent, or glabrous, branching near the base, the branches ascending or procumbent, slender, 2′–6′ long. Lower leaves short-petioled, pinnatifid, lobed, dentate or sometimes entire, ½′–1′ long; upper leaves sessile or very nearly so, entire or lobed; flowers about ½″ broad; pedicels very slender, ascending or spreading, 3″–6″ long in fruit; pods elliptic or oval, mostly obtuse or emarginate, 1½″–2″ long; seeds several in each cell.

In moist ground, often in saline situations, Labrador to British Columbia, and widely distributed in the Pacific States. Also in Europe, Asia and Australia. June–Aug.

10. **NÉSLIA** Desv. Journ. Bot. **3**: 162.   1814.

[Sphaerocarpus Heist.; Fabr. Enum. Pl. Hort. Helmst. 1763. Not. Adans. 1763.]

An annual or biennial erect branching herb, hispid with branched hairs, with entire leaves, and small yellow racemose flowers. Silicles small, globose, wingless, reticulated, indehiscent, 1-celled, 1-seeded or rarely 2-seeded. Style filiform. Seed horizontal; cotyledons incumbent. [Dedicated to J. A. N. De Nesle, a French botanist.]

A monotypic genus of Europe and eastern Asia.

1. Neslia paniculàta (L.) Desv. Ball Mustard. Fig. 2024.

Myagrum paniculatum L. Sp. Pl. 641. 1753.

Neslia paniculata Desv. Journ. Bot. 3 : 162. 1814.

Slender, branched above, rather densely rough-hispid, 1°–2° high. Leaves lanceolate, or the upper linear-lanceolate, acute or obtusish at the apex, sagittate-clasping at the base, 1′–2½′ long, 2″–8″ wide; racemes elongated; flowers yellow, nearly 1″ broad; pedicels filiform, ascending, 3″–5″ long in fruit; silicles globose, or slightly depressed, about 1″ in diameter, finely reticulated.

In waste places, Quebec to Manitoba, North Dakota, British Columbia and Pennsylvania, and in ballast about the eastern seaports. Adventive or fugitive from Europe. May–Sept.

Rapistrum rugòsum (L.) All., a plant with 2-jointed indehiscent pods, erect on appressed pedicels, in long racemes, has been found as a waif at Easton, Penn., and plentifully in ballast about the seaports. It is related to *Raphanus*.

11. SUBULÀRIA L. Sp. Pl. 642. 1753.

Small annual aquatic submerged herbs, with basal linear subulate leaves, and minute racemose white flowers. Silicles short-stipitate, globose to oblong or elliptic, the valves convex, 1-ribbed on the back, the partition broad. Stigma sessile, entire. Seeds few, in 2 rows in each cell, marginless. Cotyledons narrow, incumbent, curved above their base. [Latin awl, from the awl-shaped leaves.]

A monotypic genus of the northern hemisphere.

1. Subularia aquática L. Water Awlwort. Fig. 2025.

Subularia aquatica L. Sp. Pl. 642. 1753.

Tufted, glabrous, 1′–4′ high, growing on the margins and bottoms of lakes in shallow water. Flowering scape simple, lateral, 1′–3½′ high; leaves nearly cylindric, 6″–15″ long; flowers few, racemose, distant; pedicels slender, 1″–3″ long in fruit; petals white, minute; pods 1″–1½″ long.

In clear, cold lakes, Newfoundland to British Columbia, Maine, New Hampshire and Ontario, south in the Rocky Mountains to Wyoming, and to California. Also in Europe and Siberia. June–Sept.

12. RADÍCULA Hill, Brit. Herb. 265. 1756.

[RORIPA Scop. Fl. Carn. 520. 1760.]

[NASTURTIUM R. Br. in Ait. Hort. Kew. Ed. 2, 4 : 109. 1812.]

Branching herbs, with simple or pinnate lobed dissected or rarely entire leaves, and small yellow flowers. Sepals spreading. Stamens 1–6. Pods short, terete or nearly so. Stipe none. Valves nerveless or 1-nerved. Style short or slender. Stigma 2-lobed or nearly entire. Seeds turgid, minute, in 2 rows in each cell or very rarely in 1 row. Cotyledons accumbent. [Name Latin, diminutive of *radix*, root.]

About 50 species, of wide geographic distribution, most abundant in the north temperate zone. Besides the following, there are about 12 other North American species, natives of the southern and western parts of the continent. Type species: *Sisymbrium amphibium* L.

Flowers and pods distinctly pedicelled ; pods smooth or nearly so.
  Plants perennial by creeping or subterranean branches.
    Leaves pinnately divided ; style very short ; naturalized European species. 1. *R. sylvestris*.
    Leaves pinnatifid ; style slender ; native western species.   2. *R. sinuata*.
  Plants annual, biennial or perennial, with fibrous roots.
    Fruiting pedicels 1″–2″ long ; stem diffuse.
      Pods linear to oblong, 3″–5″ long.   3. *R. obtusa*.
      Pods subglobose, about 1″ in diameter.   4. *R. sphaerocarpa*.
    Fruiting pedicels 2″–4″ long ; stem erect.
      Stem nearly or quite glabrous ; pods linear or linear-oblong. 5. *R. palustris*.
      Stem hispid-pubescent ; pods globose or oval. 6. *R. hispida*.
Flowers and pods very nearly sessile. 7. *R. sessiliflora*.

3/5

2. Radicula sinuàta (Nutt.) Greene. Spreading Yellow-cress. Fig. 2027.

Nasturtium sinuatum Nutt.; T. & G. Fl. N. A. 1: 73. 1838.
Roripa sinuata A. S. Hitchcock, Spring Fl. Manhattan 18. 1894.
Radicula sinuata Greene, Leaflets 1: 113. 1905.

Perennial, diffuse, glabrous, the branches ascending. Leaves oblong, lanceolate, or oblanceolate, 2'–3' long, ½'–1' wide, pinnatifid, the lobes linear or oblong, obtuse, entire, or sparingly dentate; pedicels slender, 3" long; flowers yellow, about 2" broad; pods linear-oblong, sometimes slightly curved, smooth or a little roughened, 4"–6" long; style slender, 1"–1½" long.

In dry or moist sandy soil, Illinois and Minnesota to Assiniboia, Washington, Missouri, Texas and Arizona. St. Thomas, Canada. June–Sept. Has been mistaken for *R. curvisiliqua* (Hook.) Greene.

2/3

1. Radicula sylvéstris (L.) Druce. Creeping Yellow Water-cress. Fig. 2026.

Sisymbrium sylvestre L. Sp. Pl. 657. 1753.
Nasturtium sylvestre R. Br. in Ait. Hort. Kew. Ed. 2, 4: 110. 1812.
Roripa sylvestris Bess. Enum. 27. 1821.
Radicula sylvestris Druce, List Brit. Plants 4. 1908.

Perennial, glabrous; stems creeping, branches ascending. Leaves pinnately divided or deeply pinnatifid, petioled, 3'–5' long, 1'–2' broad, ovate in outline, the divisions obovate, or oblong, toothed or lobed, the terminal one often somewhat larger than the lateral; pedicels slender, 3" long; flowers yellow, 3"–4" broad; pod linear, 4"–6" long; style very short.

In wet grounds and waste places, Newfoundland to Ontario, Virginia and Michigan. Adventive or naturalized from Europe. Native also of northern Asia. Yellow-cress. Summer.

3/5

3. Radicula obtùsa (Nutt.) Greene, Blunt-leaved Yellow-cress. Fig. 2028.

Nasturtium obtusum Nutt.; T. & G. Fl. N. A. 1: 74. 1838.
Roripa obtusa Britton, Mem. Torr. Club 5: 169. 1894.
Radicula obtusa Greene, Leaflets, 1: 113. 1905.

Annual or biennial, diffuse, much-branched, the branches ascending or erect. Leaves oblong or oblanceolate, 2'–4' long, pinnately divided, or pinnatifid, the lobes obtuse, repand-toothed, or sometimes entire; pedicels 1"–2" long; flowers yellow, 1" broad or less; pods narrowly oblong, or linear, 3"–5" long, ascending; style ½" long.

In low grounds, Michigan to Missouri, Texas, Montana and California. April–Aug.

4. Radicula sphaerocàrpa (A. Gray) Greene. Round-fruited Cress. Fig. 2029.

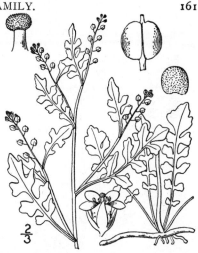

Nasturtium sphaerocarpum A. Gray, Mem. Am. Acad.
  4: 6. 1849.
Roripa sphaerocarpa Britton, Mem. Torr. Club 5:
  170. 1894.
R. obtusa sphaerocarpa Robinson, Rhodora 10: 32.
  1908.
Radicula sphaerocarpa Greene, Leaflets, 1: 113. 1905.

Glabrous, stem erect or decumbent, usually
branched, slender, 4'–12' high. Leaves oblong,
obtuse, the lower lyrate-pinnatifid or incised, the
upper sometimes nearly entire, all petioled or the
upper subsessile; petioles narrowly margined,
somewhat clasping at the base; flowers 1'' broad
or less; petals yellow, about equalling the sepals;
silicle globose, or subglobose, 1''–2'' in diameter,
about as long as its pedicel; style very short.

Illinois to Kansas, Texas and California. Perhaps
a short-podded race of the preceding species. June–
July.

5. Radicula palústris (L.) Moench. Marsh or Yellow Water-cress. Fig. 2030.

Sisymbrium amphibium var. palustre L. Sp.
  Pl. 657. 1753.
Radicula palustris Moench, Meth. 263. 1794.
Nasturtium terrestre R. Br. in Ait. Hort. Kew.
  Ed. 2, 4: 110. 1812.
Nasturtium palustre DC. Syst. 2: 191. 1821.
Roripa palustris Bess. Enum. 27. 1821.

Annual, or biennial, erect, branching,
glabrous or slightly pubescent, 1°–3½° high.
Lower leaves petioled, 3'–7' long, oblong
or oblanceolate, deeply pinnatifid (rarely
only dentate), the lobes acutish or blunt,
repand or toothed; upper leaves nearly sessile, dentate or somewhat lobed; base of
the petiole often dilated and clasping; pedicels slender, 3'' long in fruit; flowers yellow, 2''–3'' broad; pods linear, or linear-
oblong, 2–6 times as long as thick, about
equalling the pedicels, spreading or curved;
style ½'' long or less.

In wet places, nearly throughout North
America except the extreme north. Apparently in part naturalized from Europe on the
eastern side of the continent, but widely
indigenous. Yellow wood-cress. May–Aug.

6. Radicula híspida (Desv.) Britton. Hispid Yellow-cress. Fig. 2031.

Brachylobus hispidus Desv. Journ. Bot. 3: 183. 1814.
Nasturtium hispidum DC. Syst. 2: 201. 1821.
Nasturtium palustre var. hispidum A. Gray, Man. Ed. 2,
  30. 1856.
Roripa hispida Britton, Mem. Torr. Club 5: 169. 1894.
Radicula hispida Britton, Torreya 6: 30. 1906.
R. palustris hispida Robinson, Rhodora 10: 32. 1908.

Resembling the preceding species, but often stouter,
sometimes 4° high and with lower leaves 10' long,
the stem, branches, petioles and veins of the lower
surfaces of the leaves hirsute with spreading hairs.
Leaves lyrate-pinnatifid; pedicels slender, spreading,
about 3'' long, longer than the globose or ovoid pod,
which is 1–2 times as long as thick.

In wet places, New Brunswick to Alaska, British Columbia, Florida and New Mexico. Europe. Summer.

Radicula curvisíliqua (Hook.) Greene, admitted into our first edition as reported from Nebraska is here omitted; it is not definitely known to range east of Wyoming.

7. Radicula sessiliflòra (Nutt.) Greene.
Sessile-flowered Cress.   Fig. 2032.

Nasturtium sessiliflorum Nutt.; T. & G. Fl. N. A. 1: 73. 1838.
Roripa sessiliflora A. S. Hitchcock, Spring Fl. Manhattan 18. 1894.
Radicula sessiliflora Greene, Leaflets 1: 113. 1905.

Annual or biennial, erect, glabrous, 8'–20' high, sparingly branched above, the branches ascending. Leaves petioled, the lower 3'–4' long, obovate or oblong, obtuse, crenate, lobed or pinnatifid, with obtuse lobes; flowers yellow, 1" broad, nearly sessile; pods very slightly pedicelled, spreading or ascending, 3"–6" long, 1" broad, narrowly oblong; style very short; seeds minute, mostly in 2 rows in each cell.

Wet grounds, Virginia to Illinois, Iowa, Nebraska, Arkansas, Florida and Texas. April–June.

13. SISÝMBRIUM [Tourn.] L. Sp. Pl. 657. 1753.

An aquatic or uliginous herb, with pinnately divided leaves, and small white flowers in terminal racemes. Pods linear to linear-oblong, slender-pedicelled, tipped with the rather stout style, the valves nerveless. Seeds in 2 rows in each cell of the pod. Cotyledons accumbent. [Ancient Greek name.]

A monotypic genus of the Old World.

1. Sisymbrium Nastúrtium-aquáticum L.   True Water-cress.   Fig. 2033.

Sisymbrium Nasturtium-aquaticum L. Sp. Pl. 657. 1753.
Nasturtium officinale R. Br. in Ait. Hort. Kew. Ed. 2, 4: 110. 1812.
Roripa Nasturtium Rusby, Mem. Torr. Club 3: Part 3, 5. 1893.
Radicula Nasturtium-aquaticum Britten & Rendle, Brit. Seed Plants 3. 1907.

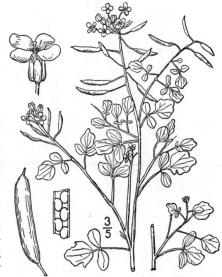

Glabrous, branching, floating or creeping, rooting from the nodes. Leaves of 3–9 segments, the terminal one larger than the lateral, all obtuse, ovate or oval, or the terminal one nearly orbicular; racemes elongating in fruit; flowers 2"–2½" broad; petals twice the length of the calyx; pods 6"–16" long, 1" wide, spreading and slightly curved upward, on pedicels of about their length; seeds distinctly in 2 rows.

In brooks and streams, Nova Scotia to Manitoba, Virginia, Missouri, Arizona and California. Common in most districts. Naturalized from Europe. Native also of northern Asia and introduced into the West Indies and South America. Widely cultivated for salad. Well- or water-grass. Crashes. Brook-lime. Brown-cress. April–Nov.

14. ARMORÀCIA Gaertn. Meyer & Schreb. Fl. Wett. 2: 426. 1800.

Tall perennial glabrous herbs, with large pungent roots, leafy flowering stems and rather large white flowers in terminal racemes, the pedicels slender. Silicles short, little, if any, longer than wide. Style short; stigma subcapitate. Seeds few, in 2 rows in each cell. Cotyledons accumbent. [Name from the Celtic, referring to the favorite (saline) habitat of the plant.]

A genus of a few species, natives of Europe and Asia, the following typical.

1. Armoracia Armoràcia (L.) Britton. Horse-radish. Fig. 2034.

Cochlearia Armoracia L. Sp. Pl. 648. 1753.
Nasturtium Armoracia Fries; A. Gray, Man. Ed. 2, 31. 1856.
Roripa Armoracia A. S. Hitchcock, Spring Fl. Manhattan 18. 1894.
Armoracia rusticana Gaertn. Meyer & Schreb. Fl. Wett. **2**: 426. 1800.

Erect, 2°–3° high, from deep thick roots. Basal leaves on thick petioles 6′–12′ long, the blade oblong, often nearly as long, crenate, sinuate or even pinnatifid, rough but glabrous; upper leaves smaller, sessile, narrowly oblong or lanceolate, crenate or dentate; racemes paniculate, terminal and axillary; pedicels very slender, ascending, 2″–3″ long; flowers white, showy, 2″–4′ broad; pods oblong or nearly globose; style very short

Escaped from gardens into moist grounds, especially along streams. Frequent. Adventive from Europe. The roots furnish the well-known sauce. Summer.

15. COCHLEÀRIA [Tourn.] L. Sp. Pl. 647. 1753.

Annual or biennial maritime herbs, with simple alternate mostly fleshy leaves, and white or rarely purplish or yellowish racemose flowers. Silicle inflated, oblong or globose. Valves very convex, dehiscent. Stigma nearly simple, or capitate. Seeds several in each cell of the pod, usually in 2 rows, marginless. Cotyledons mainly accumbent. [Greek, spoon, from the shape of the leaves.]

A genus of about 25 species, all natives of the colder parts of the north temperate zone. Besides the following, about three others are found on the arctic and northern Pacific coasts of North America. Type species: *Cochlearia officinàlis* L.

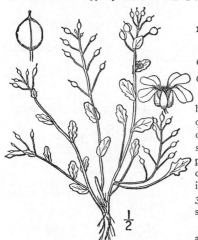

1. Cochlearia officinàlis L. Scurvy-grass or weed. Spoonwort. Fig. 2035.

Cochlearia officinalis L. Sp. Pl. 647. 1753.

Cochlearia oblongifolia DC. Syst. Veg. **2**: 363. 1821.

Diffuse, branching, glabrous, somewhat fleshy, the branches 6′–12′ long. Lower leaves long-petioled, oblong, orbicular or reniform, obtuse, ½′–1′ long, dentate or entire; upper leaves ovate or oblong, sessile or short-petioled; flowers white, 2″–3″ broad; petals emarginate, or entire, thrice as long as the calyx; raceme elongating in fruit; pedicels ascending, 3″–4″ long in fruit; pods globose or ovoid, 2″–3″ long, smooth or reticulated; valves convex, strongly 1-nerved; style ½″ long.

Along seacosts and rivers, Anticosti to Greenland and arctic America generally. Also in arctic Europe and Asia. Summer. A valued antiscorbutic salad.

Cochlearia dànica L., Danish scurvy-grass, of the arctic coasts of America and Europe, differs in having the stem-leaves deltoid to hastate, all but the uppermost slender-petioled, and ranges south to Newfoundland.

16. NEOBÉCKIA Greene, Pittonia **3**: 95. 1896.

An aquatic herb, the immersed leaves finely dissected, with large white racemose flowers. Style slender. Silicles ovoid, 1-celled. Seeds small, few, in 2 rows in each cell. Cotyledons accumbent. [In honor of Lewis Caleb Beck, 1798–1853, American chemist and botanist.]

A monotypic genus of eastern North America.

1. Neobeckia aquática (Eaton) Britton. Lake Water-cress. River-cress. Fig. 2036.

Cochlearia aquatica Eaton, Man. Ed. 5, 181. 1829.
Nasturtium natans var *americanum* A. Gray, Ann. Lyc. N. Y. 3 : 223. 1836.
Nasturtium lacustre A. Gray, Gen. Ill. 1 : 132. 1848.
Roripa americana Britton, Mem. Torr. Club 5 : 169. 1894.
Neobeckia aquatica Greene, Pittonia 3 : 95. 1896.
Radicula aquatica Robinson, Rhodora 10 : 32. 1908.

Branching, 1°–2° long. Immersed leaves 2'–6' long, pinnately dissected into numerous filiform divisions; emersed leaves lanceolate to oblong, obtuse or acute, 1'–3' long, entire, serrate or lobed, readily detached from the stem; pedicels 3"–4" long, slender, spreading or ascending; petals longer than the sepals; style about 1" long; pods 2" long.

In lakes and slow streams, Quebec and Ontario to northern New York, Minnesota, south to Florida and Louisiana. Local. Summer.

17. LEPÍDIUM [Tourn.] L. Sp. Pl. 643. 1753.

Erect, or rarely diffuse, glabrous or pubescent herbs, with pinnatifid lobed or entire leaves and racemose white or whitish flowers. Pubescence, when present, of simple hairs. Stamens often fewer than 6. Petals short, sometimes none. Silicles orbicular to oblong or obovate, flattened contrary to the partition, mostly emarginate, winged or wingless; valves keeled, dehiscent. Seeds solitary in each cell, pendulous, flattened; cotyledons incumbent or rarely accumbent. [Greek, a little scale, from the flat scale-like pods.]

About 65 species, widely distributed. In addition to the following, about 16 others occur in western North America. Called indifferently Cress, Pepperwort or Pepper-grass. Type species: *Lepidium latifolium* L.

Stem-leaves clasping by an auriculate base.
 Pods broadly ovate, winged; annual or biennial.   1. *L. campestre.*
 Pods wingless, broader than long; perennial.   2. *L. Draba.*
Stem-leaves petioled or sessile, not clasping.
 Pods and seeds entirely wingless; petals none; cotyledons incumbent. 3. *L. ruderale.*
 Pods slightly winged above, orbicular or oval, about 1" broad; petals present or none.
  Cotyledons accumbent; petals generally present.   4. *L. virginicum.*
  Cotyledons incumbent; petals minute or wanting.   5. *L. densiflorum.*
 Pods oblong, winged all around, longer than wide, about 2" high. 6. *L. sativum.*

1. Lepidium campéstre (L.) R. Br. Field, Cow or Bastard Cress. Fig. 2037.

Thlaspi campestre L. Sp. Pl. 646. 1753.
L. campestre R. Br. in Ait. f. Hort. Kew. 4 : 88. 1812.

Annual or biennial, erect, 10'–18' high, branching above, hoary-pubescent with scale-like hairs or rarely nearly glabrous. Basal leaves oblong, or spatulate-oblong, entire, or pinnatifid in the lower part, obtuse, petioled, 2'–3' long; stem-leaves oblong or lanceolate, entire or slightly dentate, sessile, clasping the stem by an auricled base; flowers white or yellowish; pedicels rather stout, spreading, 2"–4" long in fruit; pods very numerous, forming dense elongated racemes, broadly ovate, slightly curved upward, about equalling their pedicels, or shorter, broadly winged at the apex, rough, notched, tipped with a minute style.

In fields and waste places, New Brunswick and Ontario to Virginia, Kansas, and on the Pacific Coast, a bad weed in the Middle States. Naturalized from Europe. May–July. Yellow seed. Mithridate mustard. Glen-, or poor-man's-pepper. Glen- or crowdweed. False flax. English pepper-grass.

2. Lepidium Dràba L.　Hoary Cress.
Fig. 2038.

Lepidium Draba L. Sp. Pl. 645. 1753.

Perennial, erect or ascending, 10′–18′ high, hoary-pubescent, branched at the inflorescence. Leaves oblong or lanceolate-oblong, obtuse, slightly dentate or entire, 1½′–2′ long, the lower petioled, the upper sessile and clasping; pedicels slender, ascending or spreading, 3″–6″ long in fruit; flowers white, about 1″–2″ broad; pods very broadly ovate, or cordate, 1½″ long, 2″ broad, arranged in short corymbose racemes; valves distinct, papillose, keeled, wingless, tipped with a slender style ½″–1″ long.

Waste grounds, Astoria and Syracuse, N. Y., Washington, D. C., and on ballast about the seaports. Also from Colorado and Wyoming to California and British Columbia. Fugitive from Europe. Native also of Asia. April–June.

3. Lepidium ruderàle L.　Roadside or Narrow-leaved Pepper-grass.　Fig. 2039.

Lepidium ruderale L. Sp. Pl. 645. 1753.

Annual, erect, 6′–15′ high, glabrous, wiry, freely branching. Basal and lower leaves oblong in outline, 1′–4′ long, 1–2-pinnatifid into linear or oblong obtuse segments; upper leaves smaller, entire or with a few lobes; flowers ½″ broad or less, greenish; petals none; stamens 2; pods flat, not margined, about 1″ in length, short-oval; pedicels spreading or somewhat ascending, very slender, 1½″–2″ long in fruit; valves sharply keeled, barely winged; seeds marginless; cotyledons incumbent.

In waste places, on ballast and along roadsides about the cities, Nova Scotia to Texas, and recorded from Bermuda. Naturalized from Europe. Has the unpleasant odor of wart-cress. Occurs also in Australia. Summer.

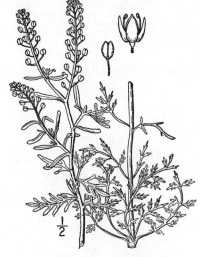

4. Lepidium virgínicum L.　Wild Pepper-grass.　Fig. 2040.

Lepidium virginicum L. Sp. Pl. 645. 1753.

Basal leaves obovate or spatulate in outline, generally with a large terminal lobe and numerous small lateral ones, all dentate, glabrous or slightly pubescent; stem-leaves lanceolate or oblong-linear, sharply dentate or entire, sessile, or the lower stalked; flowers ½″–1″ broad, white, petals generally present, sometimes wanting in the later flowers; stamens 2; pedicels very slender, spreading, 2″–3″ long in fruit; pod flat, short-oval or orbicular, minutely winged above; cotyledons accumbent.

In fields and along roadsides, Quebec to Minnesota, Colorado, Florida, Texas and Mexico. Also in the West Indies, and introduced as a weed into southern Europe. Bird's-pepper. Tongue-grass. May–Nov.

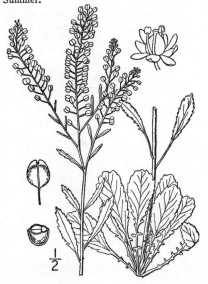

5. **Lepidium densiflòrum** Schrad.   Wild Tongue- or Pepper-grass.   Fig. 2041.

3/5

Lepidium densiflorum Schrad. Ind. Sem. Goett. 4. 1835.

Lepidium intermedium A. Gray, Man. Ed. 2. 1856. Not A. Rich. 1847.

L. ramosissimum A. Nelson, Bull. Torr. Club **26**: 124. 1899.

Much like *L. ruderale* and *L. virginicum.* Basal leaves pinnately lobed or pinnatifid. Pods obovate-orbicular to ovate, sometimes broader than long, slightly wing-margined above, about 1″ in diameter; flowering pedicels ascending, forming narrow racemes, or in fruit spreading; petals small or wanting; seeds nearly wingless; cotyledons incumbent.

In dry soil, Maine and Ontario to British Columbia, Virginia, Texas and Nevada. Naturalized in Europe and native also of Asia. May–Aug. Has been confused with the Asiatic *L. apetalum* Willd. and with *L. mèdium* Greene.

Lepidium neglèctum Thellung, differing by slightly longer capsules with more distinctly winged seeds, is widely distributed within the range of the preceding species and is also naturalized in Europe; but it does not appear to be specifically distinct.

6. **Lepidium satìvum** L.   Garden, Town or Golden Pepper-grass or Cress. Fig. 2042.

Lepidium sativum L. Sp. Pl. 644.   1753.

Annual, glabrous, bright green, stem slender, usually much branched, about 1° high. Lower leaves 2-pinnate, or pinnate with the segments lobed or pinnatifid, 3′–7′ long, the lobes entire or incised; upper leaves sessile or nearly so, entire or incised, much smaller; flowers in loose elongated racemes, about 1″ broad; petals present; stamens 6; silicles ovate-oval, about 2″ high and 1″ wide, equalling or longer than their pedicels, emarginate, winged all around; style short.

3/4

In waste places, Quebec to New York and British Columbia. Escaped from gardens. Native of Europe. Much cultivated for its pungent foliage. Petals often pinkish. Tongue-grass. May–Aug.

18. **CARÀRA** Medic. Pflg. **1**: 34.   1792.

[CORÓNOPUS Gaertn. Fruct. & Sem. **2**: 293.   1791.   Not Mill. 1754.]

Annual or biennial, diffuse, unpleasantly odorous herbs, with mostly pinnatifid leaves, and small whitish flowers. Pubescence of simple hairs. Silicles small, didymous, laterally compressed, sessile. Stamens often only 2 or 4. Valves of the capsule oblong or subglobose, obtuse at each end, rugose or tuberculate, indehiscent, falling away from the septum at maturity. Seeds 1 in each cell, cotyledons narrow, incumbent. [Ancient Italian name.]

About 6 species, of wide geographic distribution in warm and temperate regions.   Type species: *Carara Coronopus* (L.) Medic.

Pod rugose, not crested, emarginate.   1. *C. didymus.*
Pod coarsely wrinkled, crested, tuberculate.   2. *C. Coronopus.*

1. Carara dídyma (L.) Britton. Lesser Wart-cress. Fig. 2043.

Lepidium didymum L. Mant. 92. 1767.

Senebiera didyma Pers. Syn. **2**: 185. 1807.

Coronopus didymus J. E. Smith, Fl. Brit. **3**: 691. 1800.

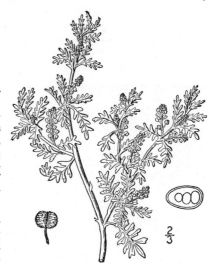

Tufted, spreading on the ground, sparingly pubescent. Stems 2′–15′ long, branching; leaves deeply 1–2-pinnatifid, the lower slender-petioled, the upper sessile; flowers minute, white, racemose; pedicels slender, 1″–1½″ long in fruit; pod didymous, about 1″ broad and slightly more than ½″ high; valves rugose, obtuse at each end and readily separating into 2 ovoid nutlets.

In waste places, Newfoundland to Florida, Missouri and Texas, west to British Columbia, California. Abundant in ballast about the northern seaports. Also throughout tropical America and widely distributed in the Old World where it is native. Summer.

2. Carara Corónopus (L.) Medic. Wart or Swine's Cress. Wartwort. Fig. 2044.

Cochlearia Coronopus L. Sp. Pl. 648. 1753.

Carara Coronopus Medic. Pflg. **1** : 35. 1792.

Senebiera Coronopus Poir. in Lam. Encycl. **7** : 76. 1806.

Coronopus Coronopus Karst. Deutsch. Fl. 673. 1880–83.

Tufted, spreading on the ground, succulent, glabrous and glaucous, or with a few spreading hairs. Stems 2′–15′ long; leaves similar to those of the last species, generally larger, sometimes less divided; flowers similar; pedicels stout, 1″ long or less; pod 2″ broad and about 1½″ high, flattish, rounded, apiculate at the summit, marked with coarse wrinkles which form a crest around the margin; valves not distinctly separate.

In waste places and on ballast, New Brunswick to Florida and the Gulf States. Fugitive or adventive from Europe. Sometimes called buck's-horn and herb-ivy. Sow-grass. Summer.

19. THLÁSPI [Tourn.] L. Sp. Pl. 645. 1753.

Erect glabrous annual or perennial herbs, with entire or dentate leaves, the basal ones forming a rosette, those of the stem, or at least the upper ones, auriculate and clasping. Flowers white or purplish. Siliques obcuneate, obcordate, or oblong-orbicular, mostly emarginate, flattened at right angles to the narrow septum, crested or winged. Valves dehiscent. Seeds 2 or several in each cell, wingless. Cotyledons accumbent. [Greek, to flatten, from the flat pod.]

A genus of about 25 species, natives of temperate, arctic and alpine regions. In addition to the following, 2 others occur in arctic America, the Rocky Mountains and California. Type species: *Thlaspi arvense* L.

Lower stem-leaves not clasping; seeds rugose.   1. *T. arvense.*
All the stem-leaves cordate-clasping; seeds smooth.   2. *T. perfoliatum.*

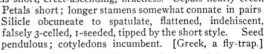

1. Thlaspi arvénse L. Field Penny-cress. Frenchweed. Fig. 2045.

Thlaspi arvense L. Sp. Pl. 646. 1753.

Annual, erect, glabrous, 6′–18′ high, simple or branching above. Basal leaves petioled, oblanceolate, early deciduous; stem-leaves oblong or lanceolate, sparingly dentate, the upper clasping the stem by an auricled base, the lower merely sessile; flowers white, about 1″ long, ½″ broad; pedicels spreading or curved upward, slender, 5″–9″ long in fruit; pods nearly orbicular when ripe, 4″–6″ broad, very flat, broadly winged all around, notched at the apex, in long racemes; style minute, or none; seeds rugose, about 6 in each cell.

In waste places and on ballast, Quebec to New York, Manitoba and Kansas. Naturalized from Europe. Native also of Asia. June–Aug. Bastard cress. Dish-mustard. Treacle-wort.

2. Thlaspi perfoliàtum L. Perfoliate Penny-cress. Fig. 2046.

Thlaspi perfoliatum L. Sp. Pl. 646. 1753.

Annual, glabrous, branched at the base, stems commonly simple, slender, ascending or erect, 3′–7′ tall. Basal leaves ovate or suborbicular, often petioled; stem-leaves oblong or oblong-lanceolate, sessile, auricled at the base and clasping the stem, ½′–1′ long, 3″–6″ wide, obtuse or acute at the apex; pedicels filiform, spreading; silicle obovate-orbicular, 2″–3″ broad, rather narrowly winged, broadly notched at the summit; style short but manifest; seeds usually 4 in each cell.

Hamilton, Ontario, and Geneva, New York. Adventive from Europe. May–Aug.

20. MYÀGRUM L. Sp. Pl. 640. 1753.

An annual glabrous glaucous branching herb, with entire or undulate oblong to lanceolate leaves, the lower petioled, the upper sessile and deeply auricled at the base. Flowers small, yellow, in elongating racemes; pedicels short, erect-ascending, bractless. Sepals nearly erect. Petals short; longer stamens somewhat connate in pairs. Silicle obcuneate to spatulate, flattened, indehiscent, falsely 3-celled, 1-seeded, tipped by the short style. Seed pendulous; cotyledons incumbent. [Greek, a fly-trap.]

A monotypic genus of Europe and western Asia.

1. Myagrum perfoliàtum L. Myagrum. Fig. 2047.

Myagrum perfoliatum L. Sp. Pl. 640. 1753.

Lower leaves oblong, narrowed into petioles; upper leaves 2′–5′ long, ½′–1′ wide, obtuse or acutish at the apex, the basal auricles mostly rounded; racemes, in fruit, elongating to several inches in length; pedicels 1″–2″ long, 2–3 times shorter than the pods, equalling or a little longer than the calyx; longer stamens about equalling the petals.

In waste places about Quebec. Fugitive or adventive from Europe. Summer.

21. STÁNLEYA Nutt. Gen. 2 : 71. 1818.

Glabrous and glaucous, perennial tall mostly erect and branching herbs, with entire toothed lobed or pinnately divided leaves, and large yellow bractless flowers in elongated terminal racemes. Sepals linear, narrow. Petals narrow, long-clawed. Stamens 6, very nearly equal; anthers twisted. Ovary short-stipitate; style short or none. Siliques linear, long-stipitate, spreading or recurving, somewhat compressed, dehiscent, the valves with a strong midnerve. Seeds in 1 row in each cell, numerous, pendulous. Cotyledons straight, incumbent. [Named for Lord Edward Stanley, President of the Linnaean Society.]

About 3 species, of western North America, the following typical.

1. Stanleya pinnàta (Pursh) Britton. Stanleya. Fig. 2048.

Cleome pinnata Pursh, Fl. Am. Sept. 739. 1814.
Stanleya pinnatifida Nutt. Gen. 2 : 71. 1818.
Stanleya pinnata Britton, Trans. N. Y. Acad. Sci. 8 : 62. 1888.

Stems stout, 2°–5° tall, sometimes decumbent. Lower leaves pinnatifid or pinnately divided, or entire, 5′–8′ long, 1′–3′ wide, long-petioled; upper leaves similar, or less divided, or narrowly oblong or lanceolate, entire, short-petioled and narrowed at the base; flowers numerous, showy; petals 8″–12″ long; filaments filiform, exserted; siliques 2′–3′ long, about 1″ thick, 2–3 times as long as their stipes, spreading, downwardly curved, somewhat constricted between the seeds when dry.

In dry soil, South Dakota and Nebraska to California, New Mexico and Arizona. Plant with the aspect of a *Cleome*. May–July.

22. THELYPÒDIUM Endl. Gen. 876. 1839.

[PACHYPODIUM Nutt. 1838. Not Lindl. 1830.]

Erect glabrate biennial or perennial herbs, with simple entire toothed or pinnatifid leaves, and racemose purplish or white flowers. Siliques nearly terete, linear, with a short stipe in some species; valves nerved, dehiscent; style short; stigma nearly entire. Seeds in 1 row in each cell of the pod, oblong, marginless; cotyledons obliquely incumbent. [Greek, female-stalk, from the stiped ovary.]

A genus of about 18 species, natives of North America. All but the following occur only in the western part of the continent. Type species: *Pachypodium laciniàtum* (Hook.) Nutt.

1. Thelypodium integrifòlium (Nutt.) Endl. Entire-leaved Thelypodium. Fig. 2049.

Pachypodium integrifolium Nutt.; T. & G. Fl. N. A. 1 : 96. 1838.
Thelypodium integrifolium Endl.; Walp. Rep. 1 : 172. 1842.
Pleurophragma integrifolium Rydb. Bull. Torr. Club 34 : 433. 1907.

Glabrous, erect, branching above, 3°–6° high. Leaves entire, thickish, the basal and lower ones petioled, narrowly oval or oblong, 2′–4′ long, the upper or sometimes nearly all the cauline ones sessile, linear, lanceolate or oblong-lanceolate, acute or acuminate; flowers pink, in short dense racemes; pedicels slender, spreading, 2″–4″ long; petals obovate or spatulate, long-clawed; pods narrowly linear, about 1′ long and ½″ wide; stipe 1″–2½″ long; style slender, nearly 1″ long.

Nebraska and Wyoming to Oregon, Utah and New Mexico. July–Sept.

23. ALLIÀRIA Adans. Fam. Pl. 2 : 418. 1763.

Biennial or perennial, sparingly pubescent or glabrous, erect branching herbs, with broad dentate cordate or reniform leaves, and rather large racemose white flowers. Sepals short.

Petals oblong, clawed.   Stamens 6   Style very short, conic.   Siliques linear, narrowly cylindric, terete or nearly so, slightly constricted between the seeds when dry, the valves with a strong midnerve, dehiscent from the base.   Seeds oblong, striate, in 1 row in each cell; cotyledons flat, incumbent.   [From *Allium*, garlic, on account of its similar odor.]

About 5 species, natives of Europe and Asia, the following typical.

1. Alliaria Alliària (L.) Britton.   Hedge-garlic.   Garlic Mustard or Root.   Fig. 2050.

Erysimum Alliaria L. Sp. Pl. 660.   1753.
Sisymbrium Alliaria Scop. Fl. Carn. Ed. 2, **2**: 26. 1772.
A. Alliaria Britton, Mem. Torr. Club **5**: 167.   1894.

Erect, branching, 1°–3° high, glabrous or with a few hairs on the petioles and leaf-margins. Leaves reniform, broadly ovate or cordate, rarely nearly orbicular, crenate or undulate, the lower 2′–7′ broad on long petioles, the upper smaller, sessile or nearly so; pedicels 2″–3″ long, spreading and very stout in fruit; flowers white, 3″–4″ broad; pods glabrous, stiff, 1′–2′ long, 1″ thick, pointed, 4-sided when dry.

Waste places, woods and along roadsides, Quebec and Ontario to southern New York, New Jersey and Virginia.   Naturalized from Europe.   Native also of northern Asia.   May–June.   Called also Jack-by-the-hedge and sauce-alone.   Jack-in-the-bush.   Poorman's mustard.   Penny-hedge.

24. SÒPHIA Adans. Fam. Pl. **2**: 417.   1763.

[DESCURAINIA Webb & Barth. Phyt. Can. **1**: 71. 1836.]

Annual or perennial herbs (some exotic species shrubby), canescent or pubescent with short forked hairs, with slender branching stems, 2-pinnatifid or finely dissected leaves, and small yellow flowers in terminal racemes, the racemes much elongating in fruit.   Calyx early deciduous.   Style very short; stigma simple.   Siliques linear or linear-oblong, slender-pedicelled, the valves 1-nerved.   Seeds very small, oblong, wingless, in 1 or 2 rows in each cell; cotyledons incumbent.   [Name in allusion to reputed medicinal properties.]

About 20 species, natives of the north temperate zone, the Canary Islands and the Andes of South America.   Besides the following, several others occur in the western United States.   Type species: *Sisymbrium Sophia* L.

Pods narrowly linear, 8″–12″ long, ½″ wide, curved upward; pedicels ascending.   1. *S. Sophia.*
Pods linear-oblong, 4″–7″ long, nearly or quite 1″ wide, straight or nearly so; pedicels divergent or ascending, mostly longer than the pods.
    Pedicels diverging nearly at right angles.   2. *S. pinnata.*
    Pedicels ascending.   3. *S. incisa.*
Pods linear, 4″–5″ long, about ½″ wide; pedicels erect-appressed or narrowly ascending, equalling or shorter than the pods.
    4. *S. Hartwegiana.*

1. Sophia Sòphia (L.) Britton.   Flixweed.   Herb-Sophia.   Fig. 2051.

Sisymbrium Sophia L. Sp. Pl. 659.   1753.

Descurainia Sophia Webb; Prantl in Engler & Prantl, Nat. Pflf. **3²**: 192.   1892.

Sophia Sophia Britton, in Britt. & Brown, Ill. Fl. **2**: 144.   1897.

Minutely hoary-canescent, stem usually much branched, 1°–2½° tall, quite bushy.   Leaves 2–3-pinnatifid into narrowly linear or linear-oblong segments; flowers very numerous, about 3″ long; pedicels ascending, very slender, 6″–8″ long, glabrous or nearly so; pods narrowly linear, 8″–12″ long, ½″ thick, ascending, curved upwards; seeds in 1 row in each cell of the pod.

In waste places, New Brunswick to Ontario, Washington, Oregon, New York, Illinois, Nebraska and Utah.   Naturalized from Europe.   Native also of Asia.   June–Aug.   Fine-leaved hedge-mustard.   Flaxweed.

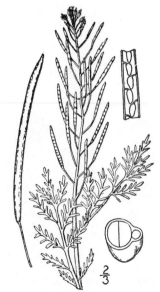

2. Sophia pinnàta (Walt.) Howell. Tansy-Mustard. Fig. 2052.

Erysimum pinnatum Walt. Fl. Car. 174. 1788.
Sisymbrium canescens Nutt. Gen. 2 : 68. 1818.
Descurainia pinnata Britton, Mem. Torr. Club 5 : 173. 1894.
S. pinnata Howell, Fl. N. W. Am. 1 : 56. 1897.
Sophia brachycarpa (Richards.) Rydb.; Britton, Man. 462. 1901.

Densely canescent nearly all over, to glabrate; stem erect, branched, 8′–24′ tall, slender, the branches ascending. Leaves 2′–4′ long, oblong in outline, 2-pinnatifid into very numerous small toothed or entire obtuse segments; pedicels very slender, spreading nearly or quite at right angles to the axis, 5″–7″ long, usually longer than the pods; flowers 1″–1½″ broad; pods horizontal or ascending, oblong or linear-oblong, compressed, 3″–4″ long, 1″ wide, glabrous or somewhat canescent; style minute; seeds plainly in 2 rows in each cell.

In dry soil, Pennsylvania to Florida, Iowa, North Dakota, Colorado, California and Texas. May–July.

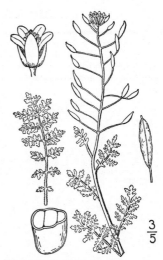

3. Sophia incìsa (Engelm.) Greene. Western Tansy-Mustard. Fig. 2053.

Sisymbrium incisum Engelm.; A. Gray, Mem. Am. Acad. 4 : 8. 1849.
Descurainia incisa Britton, Mem. Torr. Club 5 : 173. 1894.
Sophia incisa Greene, Pittonia 3 : 95. 1896.
Sophia intermedia Rydb. Mem. N. Y. Bot. Gard. 1 : 184. 1900.

Resembles the preceding species, but is greener, nearly glabrous, or the pubescence is mixed with short glandular hairs. Leaves pinnately divided, and the pinnae 1–2-pinnatifid into linear-oblong entire or toothed segments; fruiting pedicels widely ascending, filiform, 5″–10″ long, usually longer than the pods; pods 4″–7″ long, about 1″ thick, somewhat swollen, erect or ascending; seeds in 1 row or indistinctly in 2 rows.

In dry soil, Minnesota to Saskatchewan and British Columbia, south to Tennessee, Kansas, Texas and California. May–Aug.

4. Sophia Hartwegiàna (Fourn.) Greene. Hartweg's Tansy-Mustard. Fig. 2054.

Sisymbrium Hartwegianum Fourn. Sisymb. 66. 1865.
Sisymbrium incisum var. Hartwegianum Brew. & Wats. Bot. Cal. 1 : 41. 1876.
Descurainia Hartwegiana Britton, Mem. Torr. Club 5 : 173. 1894.
Sophia Hartwegiana Greene, Pittonia 3 : 95. 1896.

Similar to the two preceding species, densely minutely canescent or puberulent, stem 1°–2° tall, the branches slender, ascending. Leaves usually less finely dissected, pinnately divided into 5–7 pinnae, which are pinnatifid with obtuse segments and lobes; fruiting pedicels erect-appressed or closely ascending, 1½″–4″ long, shorter than or equalling the pods; pods erect or nearly so, linear, 4″–5″ long, about ½″ thick; seeds in 1 row.

In dry soil, Minnesota to Saskatchewan, British Columbia, Colorado, Utah, Mexico and California. May–July.

25. CHEIRINIA Link, Enum. Hort. Berol. 2: 170. 1820.

Annual, biennial or perennial, mainly erect and branching herbs, more or less pubescent or hoary, with 2-branched hairs, the leaves simple, entire, toothed or lobed. Flowers yellow. Siliques elongated, linear, 4-angled or rarely terete; valves strongly keeled by a prominent midvein. Stigma lobed. Seeds oblong, in 1 row in each cell, marginless or narrowly margined at the top; cotyledons incumbent. [Greek name from similarity of this genus to *Cheiri* Adans.]

A genus of about 90 species, natives of the north temperate zone, most abundant in eastern Europe and central Asia. In addition to the following, several others are found in the Rocky Mountains and on the California coast. Type species: *Cheirinia cheiranthoides* (L.) Link.

Flowers 2″–4″ high.
    Pedicels slender, spreading; pods very narrow, 6″–12″ long.   1. *C. cheiranthoides.*
    Pedicels stout, short.
        Perennial; native; pods ascending.   2. *C. inconspicua.*
        Annual; introduced; pods spreading.   3. *C. repanda.*
Flowers 8″–12″ high, conspicuous.   4. *C. aspera.*

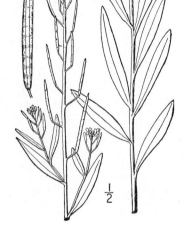

1. Cheirinia cheiranthoìdes (L.) Link. Worm-seed or Treacle Mustard. Fig. 2055.

Erysimum cheiranthoides L. Sp. Pl. 661. 1753.

Cheirinia cheiranthoides Link, Enum. Hort. Berol. 2: 170. 1820.

Cheiranthus cheiranthoides Heller, Cat. N. A. Pl. 4. 1898.

Erect, minutely rough-pubescent, branching, 8′–2° high. Leaves lanceolate or oblong-lanceolate, 1′–4′ long, acutish or obtuse, entire or slightly dentate, tapering at the base into a short petiole or the upper sessile; pedicels slender, spreading or somewhat ascending, 3″–4″ long in fruit; flowers about 2½″ high; pods linear, obtusely 4-angled, glabrous, 6″–12″ long, less than 1″ broad, nearly erect on slender spreading pedicels; valves strongly keeled; styles ½″ long.

Along streams and in fields, Newfoundland to New Jersey, Pennsylvania, Tennessee and Missouri, west to the Pacific Coast. Appears in some places as adventive. Also in northern Europe. Tarrify. June–Aug.

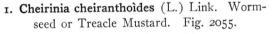
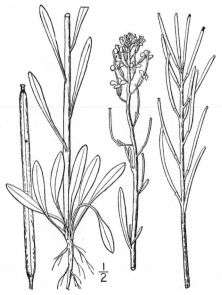

3. Cheirinia inconspícua (S. Wats.) Britton. Small-flowered Prairie-rocket. Fig. 2056.

Erysimum parviflorum Nutt.; T. & G. Fl. N. A. 1: 95. 1838. Not Pers.
Erysimum asperum var. *inconspicuum* S. Wats. Bot. King's Exp. 24. 1871.
E. inconspicuum MacM. Met. Minn. 268. 1892.
Erysimum syrticolum Sheldon, Bull. Torr. Club 20: 285. 1893.

Perennial, roughish-puberulent or canescent, stem erect, 1°–2° tall, simple or sparingly branched. Leaves oblanceolate or linear, 1′–3′ long, obtuse, entire or dentate, the upper sessile, the lower slender-petioled; flowers about 4″ high and broad; pedicels stout, about 2″ long in fruit, ascending; pod narrowly linear, ¾′–2½′ long, about 1″ wide, minutely rough-puberulent, narrowly ascending or erect; style very stout, ½″–1″ long.

In dry soil, Ontario to Manitoba, British Columbia and Alaska, south to Kansas, Colorado and Nevada. Adventive farther east. July–Aug.

3. Cheirinia repánda (L.) Link. Repand Cheirinia. Fig. 2057.

Erysimum repandum L. Amoen. Acad. **3**: 415. 1756.

Cheirinia repanda Link, Enum. Hort. Berol. **2**: 171. 1820.

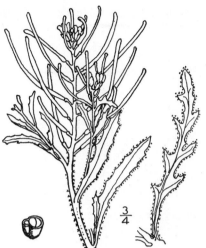

Annual, pubescent, about 1° high, often much branched. Leaves lanceolate to oblong-lanceolate, 1½'–3½' long, repand-denticulate or the lower ones coarsely toothed; flowers 3''–4½'' high; pedicels stout, 2''–3'' long; style short and stout; pods widely spreading, 1½'–3½' long, about 1'' thick.

$\frac{3}{4}$

Waste and cultivated grounds, Ohio to Kansas and Arizona, and in ballast at eastern seaports. Adventive or naturalized from Enrope. May–July.

4. Cheirinia áspera (DC.) Britton. Western Wall-flower. Yellow Phlox. Fig. 2058.

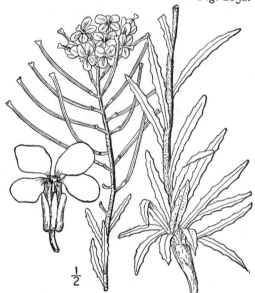

$\frac{1}{2}$

Erysimum lanceolatum Pursh, Fl. Am. Sept. 436. 1814. Not R. Br. 1812.
Erysimum asperum DC. Syst. **2**: 505. 1821.
Erysimum, arkansanum Nutt.; T. & G. Fl. N. A. **1**: 95. 1838.

Rough-pubescent or hoary, 1°–3° high, simple or branching above. Lower leaves lanceolate or linear, tapering into a petiole, dentate or sometimes entire, mainly acute; upper leaves smaller, sessile or nearly so, entire or rarely toothed; flowers orange-yellow, large and showy, 6''– 12'' high and nearly as broad; pedicels stout, spreading, 2''–3'' long in fruit; pods linear, rough, 1½'–4' long, nearly 1'' wide, 4-sided; styles short, thick.

In open places, Newfoundland and Quebec; Ohio and Illinois to Texas, Saskatchewan, Colorado and New Mexico. The eastern plant generally has broader leaves than the western. Prairie-rocket. Orange-mustard. May–July.

26. ERÝSIMUM [Tourn.] L. Sp. Pl. 660. 1753.

Annual or binennial, mostly tall and erect herbs, with simple entire lobed or pinnatifid leaves, and yellow flowers. Siliques linear-conic, terete, many-seeded. Valves mostly 3-nerved, dehiscent. Stigma with 2 short lobes. Seeds in 1 row in each cell of the pod, marginless. Cotyledons incumbent. [Greek name of some garden plant.]

A genus of few species, natives of the Old World, the following typical.

1. Erysimum officinàle L.   Scop.   Hedge Weed or Mustard.   Fig. 2059.

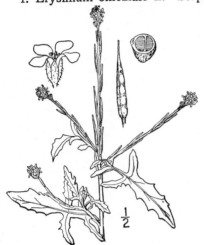

Erysimum officinale L. Sp. Pl. 660. 1753.
Sisymbrium officinale Scop. Fl. Carn. Ed. 2, 2: 26.
1772.
S. leiocarpum Jord. Diag. 1: 139. 1864.

Erect, more or less pubescent, or glabrous, 1°–3° high, with rigid spreading branches. Leaves runcinate-pinnatifid, the lower petioled, the upper nearly sessile; lobes 3–6 pairs and an odd one, oblong, ovate or lanceolate, dentate, crenate or nearly entire, acutish or obtuse, the lower ones often recurved; pedicels 1″ long, erect in fruit; flowers yellow, 1½″ broad, pods 5″–7″ long, linear, acuminate, glabrous or pubescent, closely appressed to the stem; valves with a strong prominent midrib.

In waste places, common throughout our area, except the extreme northwest to the Pacific Coast. Also in Bermuda and in southern South America. Naturalized from Europe. Native also of northern Asia. May–Nov. California mustard. Bank-cress. Scrambling rocket.

27. NÓRTA Adans. Fam. Pl. 2: 417.   1763.

Biennial herbs, with alternate pinnatifid or dentate leaves and medium-sized yellow flowers. Pubescence, when present, of simple hairs. Sepals spreading. Pods narrowly linear, much elongated, terete or nearly so, divergent or ascending. Stigma 2-lobed. Seeds in 1 or 2 rows in each cell of the pod, oblong, not winged. Cotyledons incumbent. [Name unexplained.]

About 10 species, natives of the Old World.   Type species: Sisymbrium strictissimum L.

1. Norta altíssima (L.) Britton.   Tall Sisymbrium.   Fig. 2060.

Sisymbrium altissimum L. Sp. Pl. 659. 1753.
Sisymbrium Sinapistrum Crantz, Stirp. Aust. Ed. 2, 52.
1769.
Sisymbrium pannonicum Jacq. Coll. 1: 70. 1786.

Erect, 2°–4° high, freely branching, glabrous or nearly so. Lowest leaves runcinate-pinnatifid, petioled, the lobes lanceolate, often auriculate; upper leaves smaller, shorter petioled or nearly sessile, very deeply pinnatifid, the lobes linear or lanceolate, dentate or entire, often with a narrow projection on the lower side near the base; uppermost leaves often reduced to linear nearly entire bracts; flowers yellowish, about 3″ broad; pedicels 3″–4″ long, spreading or ascending, thickened in fruit; pods very narrowly linear, stiff, divergent, 2′–4′ long, ½″ wide; valves with a prominent midrib.

In waste places, Nova Scotia to Ontario, British Columbia, Virginia, Missouri, Colorado, Utah and Oregon. Adventive from Europe. A bad weed in the Northwest. Summer.

Norta Irio (L.) Britton [Sisymbrium Irio L.] differs by runcinate-pinnatifid leaves, the terminal segment usually larger than the lateral ones, and soft ascending pods; it occurs occasionally in ballast and waste grounds.

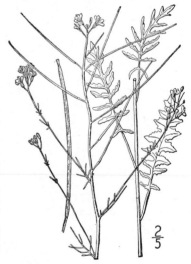

28. CONRÍNGIA [Heist.] Adans. Fam. Pl. 2: 418.   1763.

Erect glabrous annual herbs, with elliptic or ovate entire leaves, sessile and cordate or the lower narrowed at the base, and middle-sized yellowish flowers in terminal racemes. Sepals and petals narrow. Style 2-lobed or entire. Siliques elongated-linear, 4-angled, the valves firm, 1–3-nerved. Seeds in 1 row in each cell, oblong, marginless; cotyledons incumbent. [In honor of Hermann Conring, 1606–1681, Professor at Helmstädt.]

About 7 species, natives of Europe and Asia.   Type species: Brassica orientalis L.

1. Conringia orientàlis (L.) Dumort.
Hare's-ear, Treacle Mustard.
Fig. 2061.

Brassica orientalis L. Sp. Pl. 666. 1753.
E. perfoliatum Crantz, Stirp. Aust. 1: 27. 1762.
Brassica perfoliata Lam. Encycl. 1: 748. 1783.
Erysimum orientale R. Br. Hort. Kew. Ed. 2, 4: 117. 1812.
Conringia perfoliata Link, Enum. 2: 172. 1822.
C. orientalis Dumort. Fl. Belg. 123. 1827.

Stem usually erect, simple, or somewhat branched, 1°–3° high. Leaves light green, obtuse at the apex, 2'–5' long, ¾'–2' wide, the upper smaller; racemes at first short, much elongating in fruit; pedicels slender, ascending, 4"–8" long; petals about ½' long; nearly twice as long as the sepals; pods 3'–5' long, about 1" wide, 4-angled, spreading.

In waste places, New Brunswick to Manitoba, Oregon, Delaware, Missouri and Colorado. A bad weed in the Northwest. May–Aug.

$\frac{3}{5}$

29. HÉSPERIS [Tourn.] L. Sp. Pl. 663. 1753.

Erect perennial or biennial herbs, pubescent with forked hairs, with simple leaves and large racemose purple or white flowers. Stigma with 2 erect lobes. Siliques elongated, nearly cylindric, the valves keeled, dehiscent, 1-nerved. Seeds in 1 row in each cell, globose, wingless; cotyledons incumbent. [Name from *Hesperus*, evening, when the flowers are most fragrant.]

About 25 species, natives of Europe and Asia. Type species: *Hesperis matronalis* L.

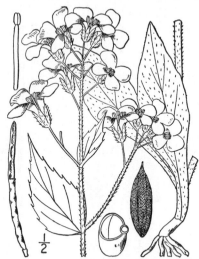

$\frac{1}{2}$

1. Hesperis matronàlis L.　Dame's Rocket or Dame's Violet.　Fig. 2062.

Hesperis matronalis L. Sp. Pl. 663. 1753.

Erect, simple or sparingly branched above, 2°–3° high. Lower leaves 3'–8' long, tapering into a petiole, ovate or ovate-lanceolate, acute, dentate with minute teeth, pubescent on both sides; upper leaves similar but smaller, sessile or short-petioled; flowers 8"–12" broad, pink, purple or white, fragrant; blade of the petals widely spreading, about as long as the claw; pods 2'–4' long, spreading or ascending, contracted between the seeds when ripe.

In fields and along roadsides, escaped from gardens, Nova Scotia to Ontario, Pennsylvania and Iowa. Native of Europe and Asia. May–Aug. Old English names are Queen's- or Dame's-gilliflower; night-scented, rogue's- or winter-gilliflower. Damask-violet. Sweet-rocket. Summer-lilac.

30. ARABIDÒPSIS (DC.) Schur.
Enum. Pl. Trans. 55. 1866.

[PILOSELLA (Thal) Kostel. Enum. Hort. Prag. 104. Hyponym. 1844.]
[STENOPHRÁGMA Celak. Flora 55: 438. 1872.]

Annual or perennial herbs with the aspect of some species of *Arabis*, pubescent with forked hairs, with branched slender erect stems, entire or toothed leaves and small white or pink flowers in terminal racemes. Style very short; stigma 2-lobed. Siliques narrowly linear, the valves rounded, nerveless or finely nerved, dehiscent. Seeds in 1 row in each cell in the following species, in some European species in 2 rows; cotyledons incumbent. [Named from its resemblance to *Arabis*.]

About 12 species, natives of Europe, Asia and North America. Type species: *Arabis Thaliana* L.
Annual; introduced weed.
Perennial; indigenous.

　　　　　　　　1. *A. Thaliana.*
　　　　　　　　2. *A. novae-angliae.*

1. Arabidopsis Thaliàna (L.) Britton. Mouse-ear or Thale-cress. Wall-cress. Fig. 2063.

Arabis Thaliana L. Sp. Pl. 665. 1753.

Sisymbrium Thalianum Gay, Ann. Sci. Nat. 7: 399. 1826.

Stenophragma Thaliana Celak. OEster. Bot. Zeitsch. 27: 177. 1877.

Annual, stem slender, erect, 1′–16′ high, freely branching, more or less pubescent with short stiff hairs, especially below. Basal leaves 1′–2′ long, obtuse, oblanceolate or oblong, narrowed into a petiole, entire or slightly toothed; stem-leaves smaller, sessile, acute or acutish, often entire; pedicels very slender, spreading or ascending, 2″–4″ long in fruit; flowers about 1½″ long; petals about twice the length of the sepals; pods narrowly linear, 4″–10″ long, acute, often curved upward, glabrous.

In sandy fields and rocky places, Massacusetts and southern Ontario to Minnesota, Georgia, Missouri, Arkansas and Utah. Very common eastward. Naturalized from Europe. Native also of northern Asia. Turkey-pod. April–May.

2. Arabidopsis nòvae-ángliae (Rydb.) Britton. Low or Northern Rock-cress. Fig. 2064.

Arabis petraea Hook. Fl. Bor. Am. 1: 42, in part. 1829. Not Lam.

Sisymbrium humile Wats. & Coult. in A. Gray, Man. Ed. 6, 71. 1890. Not Meyer, 1831.

Braya humilis Robinson, in Gray & Wats. Syn. Fl. 1¹: 141, in part. 1895.

Pilosella novae-angliae Rydb. Torreya 7: 158. 1907.

Perennial, erect, 4′–10′ high, branching below, sparingly pubescent. Leaves spatulate, or oblanceolate, the lower obtuse, 1′–2′ long, narrowed into a petiole, sharply dentate or rarely entire, the upper smaller, narrower, often acute; flowers white or pink, 1½″–2″ broad; pedicels ascending or erect, 2″–3″ long in fruit; pods nearly terete, glabrous, narrowly linear, 6″–10″ long, ½″ wide; valves finely nerved; style ½″ long.

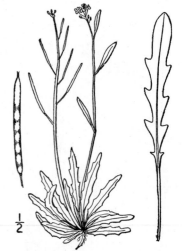

In rocky places, Anticosti, Willoughby Mountain, Vt., near Michipicoten Harbor, Lake Superior. July.

31. BARBARÈA R. Br. in Ait. Hort. Kew. Ed. 2, 4: 109. 1812.

Erect glabrous biennial or perennial branching herbs, with angled stems, pinnatifid leaves, and racemose yellow flowers. Stamens 6. Silique elongated, linear, 4-angled, the valves keeled or ribbed. Style short. Stigma 2-lobed or nearly capitate. Seeds in 1 row in each cell, flat, oblong, marginless; cotyledons accumbent. [Name from St. Barbara, to whom the plant was anciently dedicated.]

A genus of about 7 species, natives of the temperate zones. Besides the following, another occurs in western North America. Type species: *Barbarea vulgaris* R. Br.

Pods obtusely 4-angled, slender-pedicelled; leaf-segments 1–4 pairs.
    Pods divergent or ascending.   1. *B. Barbarea.*
    Pods erect, appressed.   2. *B. stricta.*
Pods sharply 4-angled, stout-pedicelled; leaf-segments 4–8 pairs.   3. *B. verna.*

1. Barbarea Barbarèa (L.) MacM. Yellow Rocket or Cress. Fig. 2065.

Erysimum Barbarea L. Sp. Pl. 660. 1753.
Barbarea vulgaris R. Br. in Ait. Hort. Kew. Ed. 2,
4: 109. 1812.
Barbarea vulgaris var. *arcuata* A. Gray, Man. Ed. 2,
35. 1856.
Barbarea Barbarea MacM. Met. Minn. 259. 1892.

Tufted, stems erect, 1°–2° high. Lower leaves petioled, 2'–5' long, pinnatifid; terminal division much larger than the 1–4 pairs of lateral ones, all oval or obovate, repand-toothed or sometimes entire; upper leaves sessile or nearly so, sometimes clasping; flowers bright yellow, 3''–4'' broad; pods spreading or ascending, about 1' long, obscurely 4-angled; pedicels about 2'' long.

In fields and waste places, Labrador to southern New York and Virginia and locally in the interior. Also on the Pacific Coast. Naturalized from Europe. Leaves thickish, shining above. April–June. Bitter, winter- or rocket-cress. Winter- or wound-rocket. Herb Barbara.

2. Barbarea strícta Andrz. Erect-fruited Winter Cress. Fig. 2066.

Barbarea stricta Andrz. in Bess. Enum. Pl. Volh.
72. 1821.
Barbarea vulgaris var. *stricta* A. Gray, Man. Ed.
2, 35. 1856.

Similar to the preceding species, about equally tall. Lateral segments of the leaves comparatively larger; flowers pale yellow; pods obtusely or obscurely 4-angled, about 1' long, erect and appressed against the rachis of the raceme on erect or ascending slender pedicels.

In fields and waste places, Quebec to Alaska, south to Virginia and Nebraska. Recorded from Florida. The plant is apparently naturalized from Europe in the East, but is reported as indigenous in the North and Northwest. It is abundant in northern Europe and Asia. Leaves shining above. April–June.

3. Barbarea vérna (Mill.) Aschers. Early Winter Belle Isle or Land Cress. Fig. 2067.

Erysimum vernum Mill. Gard. Dict. Ed. 8, No. 3.
1768.
Erysimum praecox J. E. Smith, Fl. Brit. 2: 707.
1800.
Barbarea praecox R. Br. in Ait. Hort. Kew. Ed. 2,
4: 109. 1812.
B. verna Aschers, Fl. Prov. Brandenb. 1: 36.
1864.

Closely resembles the last species. Divisions of the leaves more numerous (4–8 pairs); pods sharply 4-sided, slightly compressed, 1½'–3' long, borne on stout pedicels.

In waste places, Massachusetts to southern New York, Pennsylvania, Tennessee and Florida. Adventive from Europe. Sometimes cultivated for salad. Bank-, American- or Bermuda-cress. In the Southern States called scurvy-grass. April–June.

32. IODÁNTHUS T. & G.; A. Gray, Man. 32. 1848.

A glabrous erect perennial herb, with dentate leaves auricled at the base, or the lower and basal ones lyrate-pinnatifid, and violet or white flowers in panicled racemes. Sepals much shorter than the petals, the inner ones slightly gibbous at the base. Petals long-clawed. Styles stout; stigma subcapitate. Silique linear-cylindric, slightly compressed, somewhat constricted between the seeds. Seeds oblong, rounded, in 1 row in each cell. Cotyledons accumbent. [Greek, violet-colored flower.]

A monotypic genus of southeastern North America.

1. Iodanthus pinnatífidus (Michx.) Steud. Purple or False Rocket.
Fig. 2068.

Hesperis (?) *pinnatifida* Michx. Fl. Bor. Am. **2**: 31. 1803.
Iodanthus hesperidoides T. & G.; A. Gray, Gen. Ill. **1**: 134. 1848.
Thelypodium pinnatifidum S. Wats. Bot. King's Exp. 25. 1871.
Iodanthus pinnatifidus Steud. Nomencl. Ed. 2, 812. 1841.

Glabrous, stem slender, 1°–3° high, branching above. Lower leaves ovate or oblong, occasionally cordate, 2′–8′ long, dentate, tapering into a margined petiole which is clasping and auriculate at the base, the lower part of the blade often pinnatifid into 2–6 pairs of small oblong segments; stem-leaves similar or merely dentate, narrower, sometimes ovate-lanceolate, the upper nearly sessile; flowers numerous, 3″–4″ broad; pedicels spreading, 2″–3″ long in fruit; pods linear, ¾′–1½′ long, ½″ wide, spreading or ascending; style stout, 1″ long.

On river banks, western Pennsylvania to Minnesota, south to Tennessee, Missouri, Louisiana and Texas. May–June.

33. ÁRABIS L. Sp. Pl. 664. 1753.
[Turritis L. Sp. Pl. 666. 1753.]

Annual, biennial or perennial, glabrous or pubescent herbs, with entire lobed or pinnatifid leaves and white or purple flowers. Siliques linear, elongated, flat; valves smooth, mostly 1-nerved, not elastically dehiscent at maturity. Stigma 2-lobed or nearly entire. Seeds in 1 or 2 rows in each cell, flattened, winged, margined or marginless; cotyledons accumbent. [Name from Arabia.]

A genus of about 120 species, mainly natives of the northern hemisphere. In addition to the following, about 35 other species occur in the northern and western parts of the continent. Type species: *Arabis alpina* L. Called also Wall-cress.

Seeds in 1 row or 2 incomplete rows in each cavity of the pod.
  Basal leaves pinnatifid; pods ascending.
    Seeds large, orbicular, wing-margined; stem-leaves pinnatifid.   1. *A. virginica.*
    Seeds minute, oblong, wingless; stem-leaves entire, or dentate.   2. *A. lyrata.*
  Leaves small, mostly entire; pods drooping; seeds oblong, wingless; arctic.   3. *A. arenicola.*
  Basal leaves merely dentate or lyrate.
    Seeds minute, oblong, wingless.   4. *A. dentata.*
    Seeds larger, oblong, winged or margined.
      Pods curved upward, nearly 1″ broad.   5. *A. alpina.*
      Pods nearly erect, ½″ broad.
        Flowers white, 4″ broad; pods not appressed; style ½″ long.   6. *A. patens.*
        Flowers white or greenish-white, 2″–3″ broad; pods appressed; style none.
          Seeds wing-margined; plant not glaucous.   7. *A. hirsuta.*
          Seeds wingless; plant glaucous.   8. *A. glabra.*
      Pods recurved-spreading.
        Plant glabrous throughout.   9. *A. laevigata.*
        Leaves and lower part of stem hairy.   10. *A. canadensis.*
Seeds in 2 distinct rows in each cavity of the pod.
  Pods spreading, erect or ascending; seeds winged.
    Pods erect; basal leaves glabrous or nearly so.   11. *A. Drummondii.*
    Pods spreading; basal leaves stellate-pubescent.   12. *A. brachycarpa.*
  Pods reflexed; seeds winged.
    Basal and lower leaves loosely long-pubescent; pods blunt.   13. *A. Holboellii.*
    Basal and lower leaves finely stellate-pubescent; pods acute.   14. *A. Collinsii.*

1. Arabis virgínica (L.) Trelease. Virginia Rock-cress. Fig. 2069.

Cardamine virginica L. Sp. Pl. 656. 1753.
Cardamine ludoviciana Hook. Journ. Bot. 1: 191. 1834.
A. ludoviciana Meyer, Ind. Sem. Petr. 9: 60. 1842.
Arabis virginica Trelease; Branner & Coville, Rep. Geol. Surv. Ark. 1884: Part 4, 165. 1891.
Planodes virginicum Greene, Leaflets 2: 221. 1912.

Annual or biennial, diffuse, glabrate, the stems ascending, 6'-12' high. Leaves oblong, narrow, deeply pinnatifid, 1'-3' long, the lower petioled, the upper nearly sessile and sometimes reduced to lobed or entire bracts; pedicels spreading or ascending, 2'' long in fruit; flowers very small, white; pods linear, ascending, 8''-12'' long, about 1'' broad; seeds in 1 row in each cell, nearly as broad as the pod, orbicular, wing-margined.

In open places, Virginia and Kentucky to Illinois, Kansas, Arkansas, south to Florida and Texas, west to southern and Lower California. March–May.

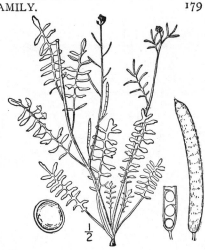

2. Arabis lyràta L. Lyre-leaved Rock-cress. Fig. 2070.

Arabis lyrata L. Sp. Pl. 665. 1753.
Cardamine spathulata Michx. Fl. Bor. Am. 2: 29. 1803.

Arabis lyrata occidentalis S. Wats.; Robinson in Gray & Wats. Syn. Fl. 1: Part 1, 159. 1895.

Tufted, perennial or biennial, erect, 4'-12' high, glabrous above, pubescent below, or sometimes glabrous throughout. Basal leaves lyrate-pinnatifid, 1'-2' long, spatulate or oblanceolate, pubescent or glabrous; stem-leaves entire or dentate, spatulate or linear, ½'-1' long; pedicels slender, ascending, 3''-4'' long in flower, elongating in fruit; flowers pure white, 3''-4'' broad; petals much exceeding the calyx; pods 9''-15'' long, linear, ascending, less than 1'' broad, their valves firm, nerved; style ½'' long or less; seeds in 1 row, oblong, ¼'' long, wingless.

Rocky and sandy places, Ontario to Connecticut, Virginia and Tennessee, west to Manitoba, Alaska, British Columbia and Missouri. Ascends to 2500 ft. in Virginia. Also in Japan. April–Sept.

3. Arabis arenícola (Richards.) Gelert. Arctic Rock-cress. Fig. 2071.

Entrema arenicola Richards.; Hook. Fl. Bor. Am. 1: 67. 1833.
Sisymbrium humifusum J. Vahl, Fl. Dan. *pl.* 2297. 1840.
A. humifusa S. Wats. Proc. Am. Acad. 25: 124. 1890.
A. arenicola Gelert, Bot. Tidskr. 21: 270. 1898.

Perennial from a slender root, somewhat pubescent at least below, or entirely glabrous, the stems diffuse or ascending, slender, mostly simple, 3'-6' long. Leaves spatulate or oblong, nearly entire, 4''-8'' long, 1''-2'' wide, the lower petioled, the upper sessile; flowers purplish or white, about 3'' broad; style very short; pods linear, flat, at length drooping, 8''-12'' long, rather more than ½'' wide, the valves very faintly nerved; seeds oblong, wingless, in 2 incomplete rows in each cell; cotyledons imperfectly accumbent.

Greenland and Labrador to Hudson Bay and the Northwest Territory. Summer.

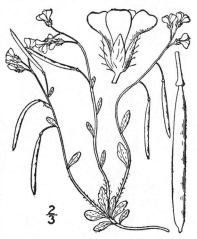

5. Arabis alpìna L.   Alpine Rock-cress. Snow-drift. Fig. 2073.

Arabis alpina L, Sp. Pl. 664. 1753.

Erect or ascending, 4′–12′ high, densely and finely pubescent. Basal leaves 1′–2′ long, obovate or spatulate, obtuse, dentate, on margined petioles; stem-leaves ovate, sessile, clasping by an auricled base, dentate; flowers white, 2″–3″ broad; petals much exceeding the calyx; pedicels slender, spreading or ascending, 4″ long in fruit; pods 1′–1½′ long, curved upward, narrowly linear, 1″ broad; seeds in 1 row in each cell, oblong, narrowly winged; style scarcely any.

Gaspé, Quebec, to Labrador, arctic America and Alaska. Also in northern and central Europe and in northern Asia. White allison. Bishop's-wig. Dusty-husband. Summer.

4. Arabis dentàta T. & G.   Toothed Rock-cress. Fig. 2072.

Sisymbrium dentatum Torr. Transyl. Journ. Med. 10: 338. Hyponym. 1837.

Arabis dentata T. & G. Fl. N. A. 1: 80. 1838.

Slender, erect or ascending, 1°–2° high, sparingly branching, finely rough-pubescent. Basal leaves on margined petioles, obovate, dentate, 2′–4′ long, obtuse; stem-leaves sessile, clasping by an auricled base, dentate, oblong or oblanceolate, obtuse or the upper acute; pedicels 1″–2″ long, spreading; flowers greenish-white, 1″–2″ broad, the petals hardly exceeding the calyx; pods narrowly linear, 10″–15″ long, spreading; style almost none; seeds in 1 row in each cell, oblong, marginless.

Western New York to Minnesota, south to Tennessee, Missouri and Kansas. April–June.

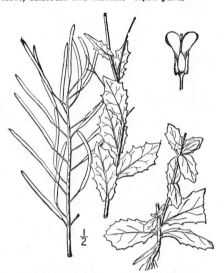

6. Arabis pàtens Sulliv.   Spreading Rock-cress. Fig. 2074.

Arabis patens Sulliv. Am. Journ. Sci. 42: 49. 1842.

Erect, 1°–2° high, mostly pubescent with spreading hairs, at least below. Basal leaves dentate, 1′–3′ long, on marginal petioles; stem-leaves 1′–2′ long, ovate or oblong, acute or acutish, sessile, dentate or nearly entire, partly clasping by a cordate base; pedicels ascending, 6″–8″ long in fruit, slender; flowers white, 4″ broad; pods 1′–1½′ long, ½″ broad, narrowly ascending, not appressed; seeds in 1 row in each cell, oblong, narrowly winged; style 1″ long.

Eastern Pennsylvania to Minnesota, south to Alabama and Missouri. Summer.

7. Arabis hirsùta (L.) Scop. Hairy Rock-cress. Fig. 2075.

Turritis hirsuta L. Sp. Pl. 666. 1753.
Arabis hirsuta Scop. Fl. Carn. Ed. 2, 2 : 30. 1772.
Arabis ovata Poir. in Lam. Encycl. Suppl. 5 : 557. 1817.

Stem strictly erect, nearly simple, 1°–2° high, rough-hairy or nearly glabrous. Basal leaves on margined petioles, obovate or spatulate, obtuse, dentate or repand, 1'–2' long; stem-leaves sessile, clasping by an auricled base, lanceolate or oblong; pedicels nearly erect, or appressed, 3"–6" long in fruit; flowers 2"–3" long, white or greenish-white; petals more or less longer than the calyx; pods narrowly linear, erect or appressed, 1'–2' long, about ½" wide; seeds 1-rowed, or when young obscurely 2-rowed, oblong or nearly orbicular, narrowly margined; style very short.

In rocky places, New Brunswick to Yukon, British Columbia, south to Georgia, Missouri, Kansas, Arizona and California. Also in Europe and Asia. May–Sept.

$\frac{1}{2}$

8. Arabis glàbra (L.) Bernh. Tower Mustard or Cress. Fig. 2076.

Turritis glabra L. Sp. Pl. 666. 1753.
Arabis glabra Bernh. Verz. Syst. Erf. 195. 1800.
Arabis perfoliata Lam. Encycl. 1 : 219. 1783.

Biennial, erect, glabrous and decidedly glaucous above, pubescent at the base, nearly simple, 2°–4° high. Basal leaves petioled, 2'–10' long, oblanceolate or oblong, dentate or sometimes lyrate, hairy with simple pubescence, or with hairs attached by the middle; stem-leaves sessile, with a sagittate base, glabrous, entire or the lower sparingly dentate, 2'–6' long, lanceolate or oblong, acutish; pedicels 2"–6" long, erect; flowers yellowish-white, 2" broad; petals slightly exceeding the calyx; pods narrowly linear, 2'–3' long, ½" wide, strictly erect and appressed; seeds marginless; style none.

In fields and rocky places, New Brunswick to southern New York and Pennsylvania, west to the Pacific Coast. Appears in some places as if not indigenous. Also in Europe and Asia. May–Aug.

$\frac{2}{5}$

9. Arabis laevigàta (Muhl.) Poir. Smooth Rock-cress. Fig. 2077.

Turritis laevigata Muhl. ; Willd. Sp. Pl. 3 : 543. 1801.
A. laevigata Poir. in Lam. Encycl. Suppl. 1 : 411. 1810.
Arabis laevigata Burkii Porter, Bull. Torr. Club 17 : 15. 1890.
A. laevigata laciniata T. & G. Fl. N. A. 1 : 82. 1838.

Glaucous, entirely glabrous, 1°–3° high, nearly simple. Basal leaves petioled, spatulate or obovate, sharply and deeply dentate, or sometimes laciniate, 2'–3' long; stem-leaves sessile, lanceolate, or the upper linear, acute, entire or dentate, usually clasping by an auricled or sagittate base; pedicels ascending or spreading, 4"–5" long in fruit; flowers greenish white, 2"–3" high; petals nearly twice the length of the calyx or less; pods 3'–4' lcng, 1" wide, recurved-spreading; seeds in 1 row, oblong, broadly winged; style almost none.

In rocky woods, Quebec to Ontario, South Dakota, Georgia and Arkansas. April–June.

Arabis serótina Steele, found at Millboro, Virginia, differs in being widely branched, its narrower leaves not clasping, its flowers smaller, appearing in August.

Arabis víridis Harger, a recently proposed New England species, differs in being green, more leafy, the pedicels erect in flower, the petals longer.

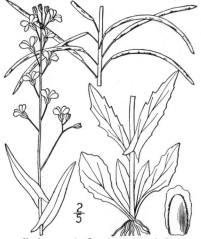

$\frac{2}{5}$

10. Arabis canadénsis L. Sickle-pod.
Fig. 2078.

Arabis canadensis L. Sp. Pl. 665. 1753.

Stem nearly simple, 1°–3° high, pubescent below, glabrous above. Basal leaves narrowed into a petiole, blunt but sometimes acutish, dentate or lyrately lobed, 3′–7′ long; stem-leaves sessile, not clasping, lanceolate or oblong, narrowed at each end, toothed, or the upper entire, pubescent; pedicels hairy, ascending and 2″–4″ long in flower, spreading or recurved and 4″–6″ long in fruit; flowers greenish-white, 2″–3″ long; petals twice as long as the calyx; pods 2′–3½′ long, 1½″–2″ broad, scythe-shaped, pendulous; seeds in 1 row in each cell, oblong, wing-margined; style almost none.

In woods, Maine, Vermont and Ontario to Georgia, west to Minnesota, Kansas, Arkansas and Texas. Ascends to 4200 ft. in North Carolina. June–Aug.

11. Arabis Drummóndii A. Gray. Drummond's Rock-cress. Fig. 2079.

A. Drummondii A. Gray, Proc. Am. Acad. 6: 187. 1866.

Turritis stricta Graham, Edinb. New Phil. Journ. 1829: 350. Not *Arabis stricta* Huds.

Biennial, glabrous throughout, or the basal leaves sometimes sparingly pubescent; stem erect, 8′–3° tall, slightly glaucous. Basal leaves oblanceolate, long-petioled, dentate or entire, those of the stem lanceolate to oblong, erect or nearly so, entire, sessile, sagittate; flowers pink or nearly white, 4″–5″ long, their pedicels erect; fruiting pedicels and pods erect or in age slightly spreading; pods 2′–4′ long, ½″–1½″ wide, rather blunt; seeds in 2 rows in each cell, winged.

Cliffs and rocky soil, Quebec to Connecticut, Ontario, northern Ohio, Illinois, Michigan, British Columbia, Oregon, south in the Rocky Mountains to Colorado and Utah. May–Aug.

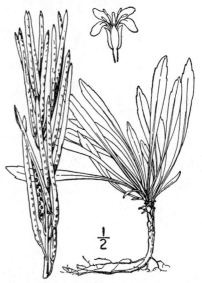

12. Arabis brachycàrpa (T. & G.) Britton. Purple Rock-cress. Fig. 2080.

Turritis brachycarpa T. & G. Fl. N. A. 1: 79. 1838.
A. confinis S. Wats. Proc. Am. Acad. 22: 466. 1887.
A. brachycarpa Britton, Mem. Torr. Club 5: 174. 1894.

Biennial, somewhat glaucous, generally purplish, glabrous except at the base, simple or sparingly branched, 1°–3° high. Basal leaves stellate-pubescent, obovate or spatulate, 1′–3′ long, dentate, narrowed into a petiole; stem-leaves sessile, glabrous, auricled at the base, lanceolate or oblong-linear, about 1′ long, entire or with a few teeth; pedicels spreading, 3″–5″ long in fruit; flowers white or pink, 4″ broad; petals twice the length of the calyx; pods narrowly linear, nearly straight, 1′–4½′ long, 1″ wide or less, spreading or loosely ascending; seeds in 2 rows in each cavity, oblong, wing-margined.

Sandy or rocky soil, Quebec to Manitoba, Assiniboia, Vermont, western New York, Illinois, Minnesota, and in the Rocky Mountains to Colorado. June–July.

13. Arabis Holboèllii Hornem.   Holboell's Rock-cress.   Fig. 2081.

A. Holboellii Hornem. Fl. Dan. 11: *pl 1879*. 1827.
Arabis retrofracta Graham, Edinb. Phil. Journ.
   1829: 344. 1829.

Erect, simple or branching above, 10'–24'
high, stellate-pubescent, hirsute or even nearly
glabrous. Lower leaves spatulate or oblanceolate, tufted, petioled, ½'–2' long, obtuse, entire
or sparingly toothed, more or less long-pubes-
cent and ciliate; stem-leaves sessile, erect,
clasping by a narrow auricled base; pedicels
slender, reflexed or the upper ascending, 3"–5"
long in fruit; flowers purple or whitish, 3"–4"
long, becoming pendent; petals twice the length
of the calyx; pods linear, 1'–2' long, slightly
more than ½" wide, at length reflexed; seeds
margined, in 2 rows in each cell; style very
short or none.

Greenland to Quebec, Lake Superior, Alaska
and British Columbia. Summer.

14. Arabis Collínsii Fernald.   Collin's Rock-cress.   Fig. 2082.

A. Collinsii Fernald, Rhodora **7**: 31. 1905.

Perennial, similar to *Arabis Holboellii*, but the
basal and lower leaves are finely and densely
stellate-pubescent. Stems slender, 1° high or less,
erect, glabrous and glaucescent above, densely
pubescent near the base; basal leaves oblanceolate
to obovate, petioled, tufted, ½'–1' long; stem-leaves
lanceolate, acute at apex, sagittate at base; flowers 2"–2½" long; fruiting pedicels 2½"–4" long,
strongly reflexed; pods linear, 1'–1¾' long, about
¼" wide, acute or acutish; seeds narrowly winged
above, in 2 rows in each cell.

On dry limestone rocks, Rimouski County, Quebec. June–July.

34. CARDÁMINE [Tourn.] L.
Sp. Pl. 654. 1753.

Erect or ascending herbs, with scaly or bulbiferous rootstocks, or fibrous roots, entire
lobed or divided leaves, and racemose or corymbose white or purple flowers. Stamens 6,
rarely 4. Siliques elongated, flat, generally erect; elastically dehiscent at maturity; valves
nerveless or faintly nerved. Stipe none. Seeds in 1 row in each cell, compressed, marginless; cotyledons accumbent, equal or unequal. [Greek, heart-strengthening, a name for some
cress supposed to have that quality.]

A genus of about 125 species, natives of the temperate regions of both hemispheres. Type
species: *Cardamine pratensis* L.

* **Leaves pinnately divided, or some of them of but a single terminal segment.**

Flowers 6"–9" broad, white or purplish; perennial.   1. *C. pratensis.*
Flowers 1"–4" broad, white.
    Leaf-segments numerous, small, the terminal one 2"–10" wide, narrowed, rounded or subcor-
       date at the base; annuals or biennials.
       Leaves nearly all basal, pubescent.   2. *C. hirsuta.*
       Stem leafy; leaves glabrous or very nearly so.
          Flowers 2"–2½" wide; plants of swamps, streams, or wet grounds.
            Segments of basal leaves 2"–12" wide; plant 8'–3° tall.   3. *C. pennsylvanica.*
            Segments of basal leaves ½"–1¼" wide; plant 6'–12' tall.   4. *C. arenicola.*
          Flowers 1"–1½" wide; plant of dry rocky situations.   5. *C. parviflora.*
    Leaf-segments few, large, the terminal one 1'–2' wide, deeply cordate; perennial.
                                                  6. *C. Clematitis.*

** **Leaves entire, toothed, or rarely with 1 or 2 lateral segments; perennials.**
                                             7. *C. bellidifolia.*
Dwarf, alpine; leaves nearly entire, long-petioled.
Erect or decumbent; leaves more or less toothed or lobed.
    Flowers purple; stem erect, from a tuberous base.   8. *C. Douglassii.*
    Flowers white.
       Stem erect from a tuberous base.   9. *C. bulbosa.*
       Stem decumbent, stoloniferous; roots fibrous.   10. *C. rotundifolia.*

$\frac{1}{2}$

1. Cardamine praténsis L. Meadow Bitter-cress. Cuckoo-flower or -spit. Fig. 2083.

Cardamine pratensis L. Sp. Pl. 656. 1753.

Perennial by a short rootstock, glabrous, stem erect or ascending, nearly simple, 8'–20' high. Leaves pinnately divided, lanceolate or oblong in outline, the lower petioled, the upper sessile; divisions 3–7 pairs and an odd one, dentate or entire, those of the basal leaves larger and broader than those of the stem; flowers showy, white or rose, 6"–9" broad; petals three times the length of the calyx; pedicels slender, 4"–6" long in fruit; pods 8"–15" long, 1" wide; style less than 1" long, thick.

In wet meadows and swamps, Labrador to northern New Jersey, west to the Pacific coast of British America and Minnesota. Also in Europe and northern Asia. April–May. Ladies'-smock or smick-smock. Milk-maid. Spink. May-flower.

2. Cardamine hirsùta L. Hairy Bitter-cress. Fig. 2084.

Cardamine hirsuta L. Sp. Pl. 655. 1753.

Annual or biennial, stem erect, usually little branched, slender, 4'–10' tall. Leaves nearly all basal and forming a rosette, more or less pubescent, 1'–4' long, the terminal segment orbicular or broader than long, entire or few-toothed, 3"–10" broad, the lateral ones 2–5 pairs, usually smaller and narrower; stem-leaves few and mostly borne near the base, their segments linear, or linear-oblong; flowers 2" broad, white; pods linear, about 1' long and ½" wide, strictly erect on ascending pedicels 2"–4" long when mature; style almost none.

In moist places and waste grounds, Pennsylvania to Michigan, Nebraska and North Carolina. Doubtfully native of America. Widely distributed in Europe and Asia. Touch-me-not. Land-cress. Lamb's-cress. March–May.

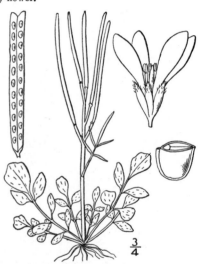

$\frac{3}{4}$

3. Cardamine pennsylvánica Muhl. Pennsylvania Bitter-cress. Fig. 2085.

Cardamine pennsylvanica Muhl.; Willd. Sp. Pl. 3: 486. 1800.
Cardamine pennsylvanica Brittoniana Farwell, Asa Gray Bull. 6: 46. 1894.

Annual, or perhaps sometimes biennial, glabrous or rarely with a few scattered hairs, stem erect, stout or slender, 8'–3° tall, usually much branched, somewhat succulent, leafy up to the racemes. Basal leaves 2'–6' long, the terminal segment obovate, oval or suborbicular, usually narrowed at the base, 3"–10" wide, the lateral 4–8 pairs oblong, oval, or obovate, all toothed, or some of them entire; flowers about 2" broad, white; pods very narrowly linear, 8"–15" long, less than ½" wide, erect ascending or divergent, on ascending or divergent pedicels 2"–3" long; style about ½" long.

In swamps and wet places, Newfoundland to Minnesota, Montana, Florida, Tennessee and Kansas. April–June. The plant described and figured as *Cardamine flexuosa* With., in our first edition, appears to be not specifically distinct from this.

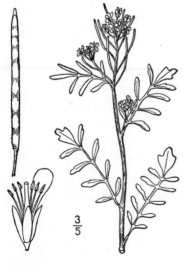

$\frac{3}{5}$

4. Cardamine arenícola Britton. Sand Bitter-cress. Fig. 2086.

Cardamine virginica Michx. Fl. Bor. Am. **2**: 29. 1803. Not L. 1753.

Cardamine arenicola Britton, Bull. Torr. Club **19**: 220. 1892.

Annual, glabrous, usually much branched from the base, leafy nearly or quite up to the racemes, erect, 6′–12′ high. Segments of the leaves numerous, linear or linear-oblong, ½″–1½″ wide, obtusish, entire, or with 1–3 small teeth, those of the basal ones slightly wider than those of the upper; flowers about 2″ broad, white; mature pods strictly erect, less than 1′ long, ¼″–½″ wide, their pedicels ascending; styles almost wanting.

In moist or wet sandy soil, Connecticut to Florida, Kentucky and Tennessee. March–April.

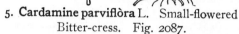

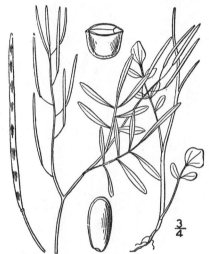

5. Cardamine parviflòra L. Small-flowered Bitter-cress. Fig. 2087.

Cardamine parviflora L. Sp. Pl. Ed. 2, 914. 1763.
Cardamine hirsuta var. *sylvatica* A. Gray, Man. Ed. 5, 67. 1867.

Annual or biennial, glabrous or very sparingly pubescent, stem weak, erect or ascending, very slender or almost filiform, 2′–15′ long, usually leafy up to the racemes, but the leaves scattered. Segments of the leaves numerous, oblong or linear, or the terminal ones sometimes orbicular, entire or sparingly toothed, ½″–2″ wide; mature pods 1′ long or less, rather less than ½″ wide, erect on ascending pedicels, 2″–5″ long, the axis of the racemes commonly zigzag; flowers scarcely more than 1″ broad, white; style almost wanting.

On dry rocks, Quebec to western Ontario and Oregon, south to Massachusetts and Georgia. Also in northern Europe and Asia. April–May.

6. Cardamine Clematìtis Shuttlw. Mountain Bitter-cress. Fig. 2088.

Cardamine Clematitis Shuttlw.; S. Wats. Bibl. Index **1**: 53. 1878.

Perennial, glabrous, dark green, somewhat succulent, stem weak, ascending or erect, slender, 5′–15′ long. Leaves remarkably various, some of them of a single orbicular or reniform, deeply cordate, entire or undulate terminal segment, some of them with two additional ovate oblong or rounded lateral segments, the uppermost occasionally linear-oblong and entire; petioles of the stem-leaves sagittate at base; flowers in short racemes, white, 3″–4″ wide; pedicels ascending, 3″–6″ long; pods ascending or divergent, 1′–1½′ long, less than 1″ wide; style 1″–2″ long, subulate.

In wet woods, high mountains of southwestern Virginia and North Carolina to Alabama. May–July.

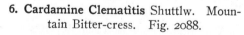

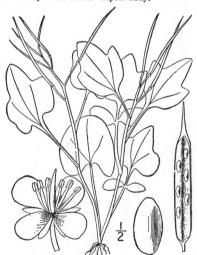

7. **Cardamine bellidifòlia** L.   Alpine Cress.
Fig. 2089.

Cardamine bellidifolia L. Sp. Pl. 654. 1753.

Perennial, tufted, glabrous, 2'–5' high, with fibrous roots. Lower leaves long-petioled, ovate, obtuse, the blades 4''–8'' long, 3''–4'' broad, abruptly contracted into the petiole, entire, or with a few rounded teeth; upper leaves similar, shorter-petioled; flowers 1–5, white; petals about twice the length of the calyx; pods erect, linear, ¾–1¼' long, 1'' wide, narrowed at each end; pedicels 1''–3'' long; style stout, less than 1'' long.

Alpine summits of the White Mountains, N. H.; Mt. Katahdin, Me.; Greenland and arctic America; the Canadian Rocky Mountains; California. Also in Europe and Asia. July.

8. **Cardamine Douglássii** (Torr.) Britton.
Purple Cress.   Fig. 2090.

Arabis rhomboidea var. *purpurea* Torr. Am. Journ. Sci. **4**: 66. 1822.
Arabis Douglassii Torr.; T. & G. Fl. N. A. **1**: 83. As synonym. 1838.
Cardamine Douglassii Britton, Trans. N. Y. Acad. Sci. **9**: 8. 1889.
C. purpurea Britton, in Britt. & Brown, Ill. Fl. **2**: 139. 1897.

Glabrous or somewhat pubescent, generally slender, 6'–15' high, perennial by tuberiferous rootstocks. Basal leaves slender-petioled, about 1' broad, ovate or orbicular, cordate, thickish; lower stem-leaves similar, but short-petioled, the upper sessile, mostly close together, dentate or entire; pedicels 4''–12'' long; flowers purple, showy, 5''–10'' broad; pods nearly erect, 1' long, 1'' broad, pointed at each end; pedicels 4''–12'' long; style 2'' long.

In cold springy places, Quebec and arctic America to the Canadian Rocky Mountains, south to Maryland, Kentucky and Wisconsin. Blooming two or three weeks earlier than the next, and more abundant northward. Mountain water-cress. April–May.

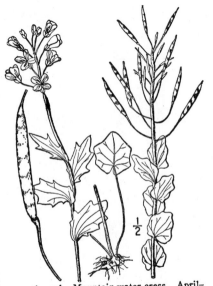

9. **Cardamine bulbòsa** (Schreb.) B.S.P.
Bulbous Cress.   Fig. 2091.

Arabis bulbosa Schreb.; Muhl. Trans. Am. Phil. Soc. **3**: 174. 1793.
Cardamine rhomboidea DC. Syst. Veg. **2**: 246. 1821.
Cardamine bulbosa B.S.P. Prel. Cat. N. Y. **4**. 1888.

Perennial, glabrous, erect from a tuberous base, with tuber-bearing rootstocks, simple or sparingly branched above, 6'–2° high. Basal leaves oval, or nearly orbicular, 1'–1½' long, sometimes cordate, angled or entire, long-petioled; stem-leaves sessile or the lower petioled, mostly distant, oblong or lanceolate, dentate or entire, 1'–2' long; pedicels 4''–12'' long; flowers white, 5''–7'' broad; petals three or four times the length of the calyx; pods 1' long, erect, linear-lanceolate, narrowed at each end; style 1''–2'' long; stigma prominent; seeds short-oval.

In wet meadows and thickets, Nova Scotia(?); Vermont to southern Ontario and Minnesota, south to Florida and Texas. Ascends to 2000 ft. in Virginia. Spring-cress. April–June.

10. Cardamine rotundifòlia Michx.
Round-leaved or American
Water-cress. Fig. 2092.

Cardamine rotundifolia Michx. Fl. Bor. Am. **2**: 30. 1803.

Perennial, weak, ascending or decumbent, forming long stolons; roots fibrous. Basal leaves and stem-leaves similar, the lower petioled, the upper sessile, ovate, oval, or orbicular, obtuse, undulate angled or entire, thin, the base rounded, truncate or cordate; pedicels 4″–12″ long; flowers white, 2″–3″ broad; pods linear, 7″–8″ long, ½″ wide, pointed; style 1″ long; stigma minute; seeds oblong.

In cold springs, New York to Ohio, Missouri, North Carolina and Kentucky. Ascends to 3500 ft. in Virginia. Mountain water-cress. May–June.

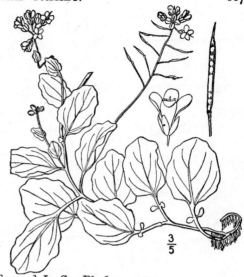

$\frac{3}{5}$

35. DENTÀRIA [Tourn.] L. Sp. Pl. 653. 1753.

Perennial herbs, with fleshy horizontal scaly or toothed rootstocks, erect mostly unbranched stems leafless below, 3-divided or palmately laciniate petioled leaves, and corymbose or short-racemose, white, rose-colored or purple flowers. Petals much longer than the sepals. Stamens 6. Style slender. Silique linear, flat, elastically dehiscent from the base, its valves nerveless or with a faint midnerve; stipe none. Seeds in 1 row in each cell, thick, oval, flattened, wingless; cotyledons thick, nearly or quite equal, accumbent. [Greek, tooth, from the tooth-like divisions of the rootstock.]

About 15 species, natives of the northern hemisphere. Besides the following, some 7 others occur in the western parts of North America. The species are called Pepper-root and Tooth-root, from their pungent and toothed rootstocks. Type species: *Dentaria pentaphyllos* L.

Basal leaves and stem-leaves similar.
  Leaf-divisions lanceolate or oblong, lobed or cleft; joints of the rootstock readily separable.
                                                           1. *D. laciniata.*
  Leaf-divisions ovate or ovate-oblong, crenate or lobed.
    Stem-leaves 2, opposite, or close together; rootstock continuous.   2. *D. diphylla.*
    Stem-leaves 2–5, alternate; rootstock jointed.   3. *D. maxima.*
Divisions of the stem-leaves linear or lanceolate; those of the basal leaves ovate, much broader; joints of the rootstock readily separable.   4. *D. heterophylla.*

$\frac{1}{2}$

1. Dentaria laciniàta Muhl. Cut-leaved Toothwort or Pepper-root. Fig. 2093.

D. laciniata Muhl.; Willd. Sp. Pl. **3**: 479. 1800.
Cardamine laciniata Wood, Bot. & Fl. 38. 1870.
Dentaria furcata Small, Fl. SE. U. S. 480. 1903.

Erect, pubescent or glabrous, 8′–15′ high; rootstock deep, tubercled, jointed, the joints readily separable. Leaves all petioled, 2′–5′ broad, those of the stem generally 3 and approximate or verticillate, rarely distant, 3-parted nearly to the base; divisions lanceolate, linear or oblong, the lateral ones often deeply 2-cleft, all incisely toothed or lobed, or the lateral ones entire; basal leaves similar, rarely developed at flowering time; pedicels stout, 8″–10″ long in fruit; flowers 7″–9″ broad, white or pink; pods linear, ascending, 1′–1½′ long.

In moist or rich woods, Quebec to Florida, west to Minnesota, Kansas and Louisiana. Purple-flowered toothwort. Crow-foot. Crow-toes. April–June.

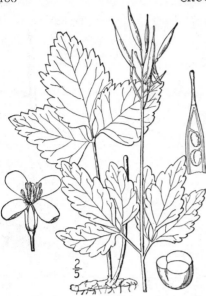

3. Dentaria máxima Nutt. Large Tooth-wort. Fig. 2095.

Dentaria maxima Nutt. Gen. **2** : 66. 1818.
Cardamine maxima Wood, Bot. & Fl. 38. 1870.

Glabrous, similar to the last species but larger; rootstock jointed, prominently tuber-cled. Stem-leaves 2-7 (generally 3), alternate, similar to the basal ones, their divisions short-stalked, ovate to obovate, toothed or cleft; flowers pale purple, 8″–10″ broad.

Maine to Michigan and Pennsylvania. Local. May.

Dentaria incisifòlia Eames, known only from Sherman, Connecticut, differs in having lanceo-late, incised-dentate sessile leaf-segments.

2. Dentaria diphýlla Michx. Two-leaved Toothwort. Fig. 2094.

D. diphylla Michx. Fl. Bor. Am. **2** : 30. 1803.
Cardamine diphylla Wood, Bot. & Fl. 37. 1870.

Stout, erect, simple, glabrous, 8′–14′ high; rootstock continuous, toothed. Basal leaves long-petioled, 4′–5′ broad, ternate, the divisions short-stalked, broadly ovate, dentate, or some-what lobed, about 2′ long; stem-leaves gen-erally 2, opposite or nearly so, similar, shorter petioled and sometimes slightly narrower, ovate or ovate-lanceolate; pedicels 1′–1½′ long; flowers white, 6″–8″ broad; pods 1′ long or more.

In rich woods and meadows, Nova Scotia and New Brunswick to Minnesota, south to South Carolina and Kentucky. Crinkle-root. Trickle. Two-toothed pepper-root. May.

Dentaria anómala Eames, known only from Connecticut, growing with this species and *D. laciniata*, is probably a hybrid between them.

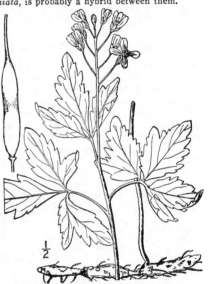

4. Dentaria heterophýlla Nutt. Slender Toothwort. Fig. 2096.

Dentaria heterophylla Nutt. Gen. **2** : 66. 1818.
Cardamine heterophylla Wood, Bot. & Fl. 38. 1870.

Erect, simple, slender, scapose, glabrous or some-what pubescent, 6′–14′ high; rootstock near the sur-face, jointed. Basal leaves long-petioled, ternate, 2′–3′ broad; divisions short-stalked or sessile, ovate, 1′–1½′ long, the terminal one cuneate or rounded at the base, the lateral ones inequilateral, all crenately toothed, lobed or cleft, the lobes or teeth mucronate; stem-leaves generally 2, opposite or nearly so, peti-oled, ternate, the divisions linear or lanceolate, short-stalked, 1′–1½′ long, entire or dentate; pedicels 1′ long in fruit; flowers light purple, 8″–12″ broad; pods ascending, linear, narrowed at each end, 1′ long; style slender, 2″–3″ long.

In low woods, New Jersey and Pennsylvania, south along the mountains to Georgia and Tennessee. The stem-leaves often closely resembling those of *D. laciniata*, which blooms a little earlier. April–May.

36. LEAVENWÓRTHIA Torr. Ann. Lyc. N. Y. 4: 87. 1837.

Low winter-annual glabrous scapose herbs, with lyrate-pinnatifid basal leaves, and few or solitary terminal flowers. Petals wedge-shaped. Siliques flat, broadly linear or oblong, short-stipitate; valves dehiscent, nerveless, finely reticulate-veined. Seeds in 1 row in each cell of the pod, flat, winged or margined; embryo straight, or nearly so, the redicle short, slightly bent toward the cotyledons. [In honor of Dr. M. C. Leavenworth, U. S. A.]

A genus of about 4 species, natives of southeastern North America. Type species: *Leavenworthia aurea* Torr.

Pods not constricted between the seeds   1. *L. uniflora.*
Pods constricted between the seeds.   2. *L. torulosa.*

1. Leavenworthia uniflòra (Michx.) Britton.   Michaux's Leavenworthia.
Fig. 2097.

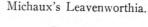

Cardamine uniflora Michx. Fl. Bor. Am. **2**: 29. 1803.
Leavenworthia Michauxii Torr. Ann. Lyc. N. Y. **4**: 89. 1837.
L. uniflora Britton, Mem. Torr. Club **5**: 171. 1894.

Tufted, 2′-6′ high. Basal leaves rosulate, numerous, 1′-4′ long, the segments 5-17, irregularly dentate or angled, 2″-3″ long, the terminal one somewhat larger, all narrowed near the base, but slightly expanded at the junction with the rachis; stem-leaves none, or 1-3, similar, but smaller; flowers about 3″ broad; petals white or purplish with a yellow base, about twice the length of the sepals; pods oblong or linear, 6″-15″ long, 2″ wide when mature; style stout, about ½″ long.

In open dry places, southern Indiana to Missouri and Tennessee, west to Missouri. April.

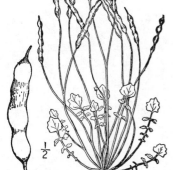

2. Leavenworthia torulòsa A. Gray.   Necklace
Leavenworthia.   Fig. 2098.

Leavenworthia torulosa A. Gray, Bot. Gaz. **5**: 26. 1880.

Closely resembles the preceding species, but the pods are narrower and distinctly constricted between the seeds. Style conspicuous, 1½″-2″ long; seeds sharp-margined, barely winged; terminal segment of the basal leaves decidedly broader and larger than the lateral ones; petals notched.

Barrens of Kentucky and Tennessee. April.

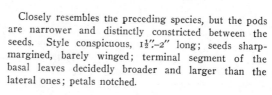

37. SELÈNIA Nutt. Journ. Acad. Phila. 5: 132. 1825.

Annual tufted glabrous herbs, with pinnatisect leaves, and racemose leafy-bracted yellow flowers. Sepals spreading. Petals narrow, erect, with 10 hypogynous glands at their bases. Silique stalked, very flat, oblong, narrowed at each end. Valves nerveless, thin, finely veined, dehiscent. Style long, slender. Seeds few, in 2 rows in each cell of the pod, orbicular, flat, broadly winged, free from the septum. Cotyledons accumbent. [Greek, moon, from the resemblance of this genus to *Lunaria*.]

Two or three species, natives of the south-central United States and northern Mexico, the following typical.

1. **Selenia aùrea** Nutt.   Selenia.
Fig. 2099.

Selenia aurea Nutt. Journ Acad. Phila. **5**: 132.   1825.

Stems simple, numerous, 2'-8' high. Basal leaves 1'-2' long, narrow, 1-2-pinnatifid into numerous oblong dentate or entire segments; stem-leaves similar, smaller; bracts of the raceme pinnatifid, resembling the upper leaves; flowers 3"-4" high, numerous; pedicels 5"-7" long in fruit, spreading or ascending; pod 6"-10" long, 2"-3" broad; style 2" long, very slender.

In open sandy places, Missouri and Kansas to Texas. March–April.

38. LUNÀRIA [Tourn.] L. Sp. Pl. 653. 1753.

Annual, biennial or perennial, more or less pubescent erect branching herbs, with broad simple dentate or denticulate mostly cordate leaves, and large violet or purple flowers in terminal racemes. Lateral sepals saccate at the base. Petals obovate, clawed. Siliques long-stipitate, very flat, oblong or elliptic, the papery valves reticulate-veined, dehiscent. Style filiform; septum hyaline, translucent, shining. Seeds circular or reniform, very large, winged, borne on long funiculi, which are adnate to the septum; cotyledons large, accumbent. [Latin, moon, in allusion to the shining partition of the pod.]

Two known species, natives of Europe and Asia. Type species: *Lunaria annua* L.

Siliques oblong, pointed at both ends; perennial.   1. *L. rediviva.*
Siliques elliptic, rounded at both ends; annual or biennial.   2. *L. annua.*

1. **Lunaria redivìva** L.   Perennial Satin-pod, or Satin-flower.   Fig. 2100.

Lunaria rediviva L. Sp. Pl. 653. 1753.

Perennial, pubescent with short simple hairs, stem rather stout, 2°-4° tall. Leaves broadly ovate, acuminate at the apex, deeply cordate, or the upper rounded at the base, thin, the lower long-petioled, 3'-6' long; flowers 8"-12" broad, slender-pedicelled; pods oblong, 2'-3' long, drooping, about 1' wide at the middle, borne on slender stipes of about one-half their length; seeds reniform, broader than long.

In thickets, Canadian side of Niagara Falls. Escaped from gardens or fugitive from Europe. Determination based on flowering specimens collected by Professor Macoun which may, per-haps, belong to the following species. The plant is commonly cultivated for its ornamental flowers and pods. May–July.

2. Lunaria ánnua L. Honesty. Satin. Satin-flower. Fig. 2101.

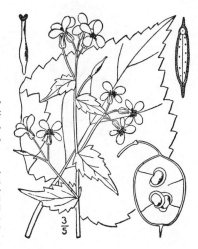

Lunaria annua L. Sp. Pl. 653. 1753.

Lunaria biennis Moench, Meth. 126. 1794.

Resembles the preceding species when in flower, but the root is annual or biennial. Siliques elliptic or broadly oval, 1¾′–2′ long, 1′ wide or rather more, rounded at both ends; seeds suborbicular, cordate, about as long as wide.

Escaped from gardens in southern Ontario, south-western Connecticut and eastern Pennsylvania. Both this species and the preceding are occasionally culti-vated for their remarkable large pods, which are gathered for dry bouquets, the valves falling away at maturity and leaving the septum as a shining membrane. Money-plant. Penny-flower. Matrimony-plant or -vine. May–June.

39. SINÀPIS L. Sp. Pl. 668. 1753.

Annual or biennial, usually erect, branching more or less hispid herbs, with pinnatifid or lobed leaves, and rather large, mostly yellow flowers in terminal racemes. Siliques linear, nearly terete, constricted between the seeds, sessile in the calyx, smooth or densely hispid, tipped with a very long flat sword-like or angled beak which often contains a seed near its base, the valves 3-nerved. Seeds subglobose, in one row in each cell, not winged nor margined. Cotyledons conduplicate. [Name Greek, said to come from the Celtic for turnip.]

About 5 species, natives of southern Europe. Type species: *Sinapis alba* L.

Leaves lyrate pinnatifid; fruiting pedicels 4″–5″ long.　　　　　　　　　　1. *S. alba.*
Leaves dentate or lobed; fruiting pedicels 2″–3″ long.　　　　　　　　　　2. *S. arvensis.*

1. Sinapis álba L. White Mustard. Charlock. Fig. 2102.

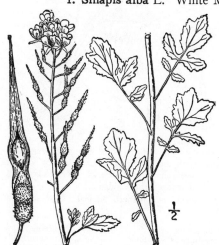

Sinapis alba L. Sp. Pl. 668. 1753.
Brassica alba Boiss. Voy. Espag. 2 : 39. 1839–45.

Erect, annual, 1°–2° high, more or less pu-bescent with stiff spreading hairs. Lower leaves 6′–8′ long, obovate in outline, deeply pinnatifid or pinnate, with a large terminal leaflet or lobe and several pairs of smaller lateral ones, dentate all around; uppermost leaves lanceolate or oblong, often merely dentate, short-petioled; flowers yellow, 7″–9″ broad; pedicels rather stout, spreading, 5″–7″ long in fruit; pods spreading or ascending, terete, constricted between the seeds; beak flat, equalling or sometimes longer than the rest of the pod; seeds light brown.

In waste places and fields, occasional, mostly escaped from cultivation. Adventive from Eu-rope. Native also of western Asia. Senvie. Ked-lock. Summer.

2. Sinapis arvénsis L. Charlock. Wild Mustard. Fig. 2103.

Sinapis arvensis L. Sp. Pl. 668. 1753.

Brassica Sinapistrum Boiss. Voy. Espagne **2**: 39. 1839–45.

Brassica arvensis B.S.P. Prel. Cat. N. Y. 1888.

Erect, annual, 1°–2° high, hispid with scattered stiff hairs, or glabrate, branching above. Leaves variously irregularly toothed or lobed; flowers 6″–8″ broad; pedicels stout, 2″–3″ long in fruit; pods glabrous or slightly bristly, spreading or ascending, somewhat constricted between the seeds, 6″–8″ long, 1″ wide, tipped with a flattened elongated-conic often 1-seeded beak 5″–6″ long, the valves strongly nerved.

In fields and waste places, frequent. Adventive from Europe and widely distributed as a weed. Corn-mustard, chadlock, corn- or field-kale. Kedlock. Kerlock or curlock. Bastard-rocket. Runch-, crowd- or kraut-weed. Yellow-flower. Water-cress. May–Nov.

40. ERÙCA [Tourn.] Mill. Gard. Dict. Abr. ed. 4. 1754.

Annual or biennial branching herbs, with pinnately lobed or dentate leaves, and rather large racemose flowers, the petals yellowish to purplish with brown or violet veins. Style elongated. Siliques linear-oblong, dehiscent, long-beaked, the 3-nerved valves concave. Seeds in 2 rows on each cell. Cotyledons conduplicate. [Latin name for some crucifer.]

Ten species, or fewer, natives of Europe and western Asia, the following typical.

1. Eruca Erùca (L.) Britton. Garden Rocket. Fig. 2104.

Brassica Eruca L. Sp. Pl. 667. 1753.

Eruca sativa Mill. Gard. Dict. Ed. 8, No. 1. 1768.

Annual, somewhat succulent, glabrous, 1°–1¼° high, commonly much branched. Basal and lower leaves pinnately lobed or pinnatifid, 3′–6′ long; upper leaves smaller, lobed, dentate or denticulate; flowers ½′–¾′ wide, variously colored, the petals strongly veined; raceme much elongated in front, the short pedicels and the pods erect-appressed; pods ½′ long or more, tipped by a stout flat beak.

Waste grounds, Ontario to Pennsylvania and Missouri. Adventive from Europe. Also introduced into Mexico. May–Oct.

41. BRÁSSICA [Tourn.] L. Sp. Pl. 666. 1753.

Erect branching annual, biennial or perennial herbs, with pinnatifid basal leaves, those of the stem dentate or often nearly entire, and showy yellow flowers in elongated racemes. Siliques elongated, sessile, terete or 4-sided, tipped with an indehiscent conic beak. Valves convex, 1–3-nerved. Stigma truncate or 2-lobed. Seeds in 1 row in each cell, globose to oblong, marginless; cotyledons conduplicate. [Latin name of the Cabbage.]

A genus of about 80 species, natives of Europe, Asia and northern Africa. Type species: *Brassica oleracea* L.

None of the leaves clasping the stem, the upper sessile.
    Pods slender, ½′–1′ long, appressed; pedicels 2″ long.   1. *B. nigra.*
    Pods rather slender, 1′–2′ long, erect, on slender pedicels 3″–5″ long.   2. *B. juncea.*
Upper leaves clasping by an auricled base.   3. *B. campestris.*

1. Brassica nìgra (L.) Koch. Black Mustard. Fig. 2105.

Sinapis nigra L. Sp. Pl. 668. 1753.
Brassica nigra Koch, in Roehl, Deutsche Fl.
Ed. 3, 4: 713. 1833.

Annual, erect, 2°–7° high, freely and widely branching, pubescent or glabrate. Lower leaves slender-petioled, deeply pinnatifid, with 1 terminal large lobe and 2–4 smaller lateral ones, dentate all around; upper leaves shorter-petioled or sessile, pinnatifid or dentate, the uppermost reduced to lanceolate or oblong entire blades; flowers bright yellow, 3''–5'' broad; pedicels slender, appressed, 2'' long in fruit; pods narrowly linear, 4-sided, 5''–7'' long, ½'' wide, appressed against the stems and forming very narrow racemes; beak slender, 1''–2'' long; seeds dark brown.

In fields and waste places, common throughout our area, except the extreme north, west to the Pacific Coast. Bermuda. Naturalized from Europe. Native also of Asia. Cadlock. Warlock. Kerlock. Scurvy-senvie. June–Nov.

2. Brassica júncea (L.) Cosson. Indian Mustard. Fig. 2106.

Sinapis juncea L. Sp. Pl. 668. 1753.
B. juncea Cosson, Bull. Soc. Bot. Fr. 6: 609. 1859.

Annual, pale, glabrous, or slightly pubescent, somewhat glaucous, stem erect, usually stout, 1°–4° tall. Lower leaves runcinate-pinnatifid and dentate, long-petioled, 4'–6' long, the uppermost sessile or nearly so, lanceolate or linear, commonly entire, much smaller; flowers 6''–9'' wide; fruiting racemes sometimes 1° long; pods erect or nearly so, on slender ascending pedicels 3''–5'' long, not appressed to the axis, 1'–2' long, more than 1'' wide, the conic-subulate beak one-fourth to one-third the length of the body.

In waste places, New Hampshire to Pennsylvania, Michigan, Kansas and Virginia. Adventive or naturalized from Asia. May–July.

3. Brassica campéstris L. Turnip. Wild Navew. Fig. 2107.

Brassica campestris L. Sp. Pl. 666. 1753.
Brassica Rapa L. Sp. Pl. 666. 1753.

Biennial; stem 1°–3° high, branching, glabrous and glaucous, or sometimes slightly pubescent below. Lower leaves petioled, pubescent, more or less lobed or pinnatifid; upper leaves lanceolate or oblong, acute or obtusish, sessile and clasping the stem by an auricled base, entire or dentate, glabrous; flowers bright yellow, 4''–5'' broad; pedicels spreading or ascending, often 1' long in fruit; pods 1½'–2' long, tipped with a beak 4''–5'' long.

In cultivated grounds, sometimes persisting for a year or two, and occasional in waste places eastward. Fugitive from Europe. Summer-rape. Nape. Bergman's-cabbage. Coleseed. April–Oct. Consists of many races.

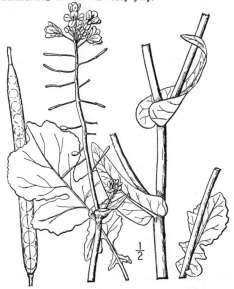

Brassica Nàpus L. (RAPE) is like the preceding species but has all the leaves glabrous; sometimes found in waste places.

Brassica oleràcea L. (CABBAGE) is occasionally spontaneous after cultivation.

Brassica japònica Siebold, occasionally spontaneous after cultivation, has laciniate, often crisped leaves.

42. DIPLOTÁXIS DC. Syst. 2: 628. 1821.

Annual, biennial or perennial herbs, similar to the Mustards, with basal and alternate pinnatifid or lobed leaves, and rather large yellow flowers in terminal racemes. Silique elongated, linear, flat or flattish, short-beaked or beakless, the valves mostly 1-nerved. Style usually slender. Seeds in 2 complete or incomplete rows in each cavity of the silique, marginginless; cotyledons conduplicate. [Greek, referring to the double rows of seeds.]

About 20 species, natives of the Old World, the following fugitive or adventive in our territory. Type species: *Diplotaxis tenuifolia* (L.) DC.

Perennial; stem leafy nearly to the inflorescence.   1. *D. tenuifolia.*
Annual; leaves mostly basal, oblanceolate.   2. *D. muralis.*

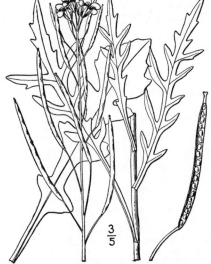

1. Diplotaxis tenuifòlia (L.) DC. Wall Rocket. Fig. 2108.

Sisymbrium tenuifolium L. Cent. Pl. 1: 18. 1755.
Diplotaxis tenuifolia DC. Syst. 2: 632. 1821.

Perennial, glabrous or nearly so, somewhat glaucous, stem branched, bushy, leafy, 1°–4° high. Leaves pinnatifid, often nearly to the midrib, thin, the lower 3'–6' long, the lobes distant or close together, mostly narrow; racemes elongated in fruit, loose; flowers 8"–10" broad; pods 1'–1¼' long, about 1¼" wide, nearly erect; pedicels slender, 10"–20" long in fruit.

In waste places and ballast, Nova Scotia to Ontario, New Jersey and Pennsylvania, chiefly about the cities and in California. Adventive from Europe. Cross-weed. June–Aug.

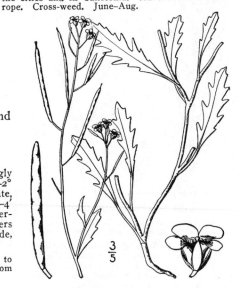

2. Diplotaxis muràlis (L.) DC. Sand Rocket. Fig. 2109.

Sisymbrium murale L. Sp. Pl. 658. 1753.
Diplotaxis muralis DC. Syst. 2: 634. 1821.

Annual, branched from the base, sparingly hispid or glabrous, the slender branches 1°–2° high, leafy only below. Leaves oblanceolate, sinuate-lobed or sometimes pinnatifid, 2'–4' long, narrowed at the base, mostly slender-petioled; fruiting racemes long, loose; flowers 6"–8" broad; pod about 1' long and 1" wide, erect, flattish; fruiting pedicels 4"–8" long.

In waste places and ballast, Nova Scotia to Pennsylvania and in Bermuda. Adventive from Europe. Flix- or cross-weed. June–Aug.

43. RÁPHANUS [Tourn.] L. Sp. Pl. 669. 1753.

Erect branching annual or biennial herbs, with lyrate leaves and showy flowers. Silique linear, coriaceous, fleshy or corky, constricted or continuous and spongy between the seeds, indehiscent. Style slender. Seeds subglobose; cotyledons conduplicate. [Greek, quickappearing, from its rapid germination.]

A genus of about 6 species, natives of Europe and temperate Asia. Type species: *Raphanus sativus* L.

Flowers yellow, fading white; pod longitudinally grooved, 4–10-seeded.   1. *R. Raphanistrum.*
Flowers pink or white; pod not longitudinally grooved, 2–3-seeded.   2. *R. sativus.*

1. Raphanus Raphanístrum L. Wild Radish. Jointed or White Charlock. Wild Rape. Fig. 2110.

Raphanus Raphanistrum L. Sp. Pl. 669. 1753.

Biennial or annual, erect or ascending from a slender root, freely branching, 1°–2½° high, sparsely pubescent with stiff hairs especially below, or rarely glabrous throughout Basal and lower leaves deeply lyrate-pinnatifid, 4′–8′ long, with a large terminal lobe and 4–6 pairs of successively smaller lateral ones, all crenate or dentate; upper leaves few, small, oblong; flowers 6″–9″ broad, yellow (sometimes purplish), fading to white, purplish-veined; pedicels 3″–8″ long in fruit; pods 1′–1½′ long, 6–10-seeded, nearly cylindric when fresh, constricted between the seeds when dry, longitudinally grooved, tipped with a conic beak 5″–10″ long.

In fields and waste places, Pennsylvania to Ontario and Newfoundland. Often a troublesome weed. Introduced also in California and British Columbia and in Bermuda. Naturalized from Europe. Native also of northern Asia. Black or wild mustard. Warlock. Cadlock. Curlock. Skedlock. Kraut-weed. Erroneously called Rape. Summer.

2. Raphanus satìvus L. Garden Radish. Fig. 2111.

Raphanus sativus L. Sp. Pl. 669. 1753.

Similar to the last, but flowers pink or white. Root deep, fusiform or napiform, fleshy. Pods fleshy, 2–3-seeded, not longitudinally grooved, often equalled or exceeded by the long conic beak.

Cultivated and occasionally spontaneous for a year or two in gardens or fields, rarely in waste places. Also in Cuba. Native of Asia. June–Oct.

44. CAKÌLE [Tourn.] Mill. Gard. Dict. Abr. ed. 4. 1754.

Annual, diffuse or ascending, glabrous fleshy branching herbs, with purplish or white flowers. Siliques sessile on the calyx, flattened or ridged, indehiscent, 2-jointed, the joints 1-celled and 1-seeded, or the lower one seedless, separating when ripe. Style none; cotyledons accumbent. [Old Arabic name.]

A genus of several species, natives of sea and lake shores of Europe and North America, one of them extending into tropical regions. Type species: *Bunias Cakile* L.

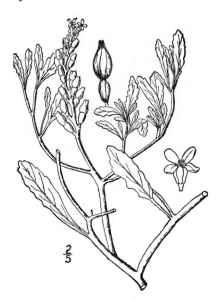

1. Cakile edéntula (Bigel.) Hook. American Sea Rocket. Fig. 2112.

Bunias edentula Bigel. Fl. Bost. 157. 1814.

Cakile americana Nutt. Gen. 2 : 62. 1818.

Cakile edentula Hook. Fl. Bor. Am. 1 : 59. 1830.

Very fleshy throughout, bushy-branched from a deep root, the lower branches spreading or ascending, the central ones erect, 1° in height or less. Leaves oblanceolate, or obovate, obtuse, sinuate-dentate or lobed, narrowed at the base, the lower 3′–5′ long; flowers light purple, 2″–3″ broad; petals long-clawed, more than twice the length of the sepals; pod 6″–10″ long, upper joint slightly longer than the lower, ovoid, angled, flattened, narrowed into a beak above; lower joint obovoid, not flattened.

In sands of the seashore, Newfoundland to New Jersey and Florida, and along the Great Lakes, New York to Minnesota. Also on the California coast. Summer.

Family 39.   **CAPPARIDÀCEAE** Lindl. Nat. Syst. Ed. 2, 61. 1836.

CAPER FAMILY.

Herbs or shrubs (rarely trees), with a watery sap, alternate or very rarely opposite, simple or palmately compound leaves and axillary or terminal, solitary or racemose, regular or irregular, mostly perfect flowers. Sepals 4–8. Petals 4 (rarely none), sessile or clawed. Receptacle elongated or short. Stamens 6–∞, not tetradynamous, inserted on the receptacle; anthers oblong. Ovary sessile or stipitate; style generally short; ovules ∞, borne on parietal placentae. Fruit a capsule or berry. Seeds mainly reniform in our species; endosperm none; embryo generally coiled.

A family of about 35 genera and 450 species, mostly of warm regions.

Pod long-stipitate on its pedicel; stamens 4–6.
     Pod linear-elongated; petals generally clawed.
         Petals entire.   1. *Cleome.*
         Petals laciniate.   2. *Cristatella.*
     Pod short, rhomboid; petals sessile.   3. *Cleomella.*
Pod nearly or quite sessile on its pedicel; stamens more than 6.   4. *Polanisia.*

1.   **CLEÒME** L. Sp. Pl. 671. 1753.

Herbs or low shrubs, generally branching. Leaves digitately 3–5-foliolate, or simple. Leaflets entire or serrulate. Calyx 4-divided or of 4 sepals, often persistent. Petals 4, cruciate, nearly equal, entire, more or less clawed. Receptacle short, slightly prolonged above the petal-bases. Stamens 6 (rarely 4), inserted on the receptacle above the petals. Ovary stalked, with a gland at its base. Capsule elongated, long-stipitate, many-seeded. [Derivation uncertain; perhaps from the Greek, to shut.]

About 75 species, mainly natives of tropical regions, especially American and African. In addition to the following, 4 others occur in the western part of the United States. Type species: *Cleome gynandra* L., of tropical regions, which has been found as a waif in waste grounds on Staten Island, N. Y.

Leaves 3-foliolate; flowers pink, or white.   1. *C. serrulata.*
Leaves, at least the lower, 5–7-foliolate.
     Flowers pink, or white.   2. *C. spinosa.*
     Flowers yellow.   3. *C. lutea.*

1　Cleome serrulàta Pursh.　Pink Cleome.
Fig 2113.

Cleome serrulata Pursh, Fl. Am. Sept. 441　1814.
Peritoma serrulatum DC. Prodr 1: 237　1824.
Cleome integrifolia T. & G. Fl. N. A. 1: 122.　1838.

Annual, erect, glabrous, 2°–3° high, branching above. Leaves 3-foliolate, the lower long and slender-petioled, the upper sessile or nearly so; leaflets lanceolate or oblong, acute, entire or distantly serrulate, 1′–3′ long; fruiting racemes greatly elongated; bracts lanceolate or linear, often mucronate; pedicels slender, spreading or recurved and 6″–10″ long in fruit; stipe of the pod about equalling the pedicel; flowers pink or white, very showy; petals oblong, slightly clawed, 5″–6″ long, obtuse; pods linear, acute, 1′–2′ long.

Prairies, northern Illinois to Minnesota, Saskatchewan, Assiniboia, Missouri, New Mexico and Arizona. Occasional in waste grounds farther east. Rocky Mountain bee-plant. July–Sept.

$\frac{1}{2}$

2.　Cleome spinòsa L.　Spider-flower.
Fig. 2114.

Cleome spinosa L. Sp. Pl. Ed. 2, 939.　1763.
Cleome pungens Willd. Enum. Pl. 689.　1809.

Annual, erect, 2°–4° high, branching above, clammy-pubescent. Leaves 5–7-foliolate, the lower long-petioled, 5′–8′ in diameter, the upper shorter-petioled or nearly sessile, passing into the simple lanceolate or cordate-ovate bracts of the raceme; petioles spiny at the base; leaflets lanceolate or oblong-lanceolate, acute, minutely serrulate; flowers numerous, long-pedicelled, showy, purple or whitish, 1′ broad or more; petals obovate, long-clawed; stipe of the linear glabrous pod at length 2′–6′ long; stamens variable in length, often long-exserted.

In waste places, southern New York to Florida, west to Illinois, Arkansas and Louisiana. Sometimes cultivated for ornament. Fugitive or adventive from tropical America. Prickly cleome. Summer.

$\frac{2}{5}$

3.　Cleome lùtea Hook.　Yellow Cleome.　Fig. 2115.

Cleome lutea Hook. Fl. Bor. Am. 1: 70. pl. 25.　1830.

Annual, erect, glabrous, branching, 1½°–3½° high. Leaves 5-foliolate, slender-petioled, or the upper 3-foliolate and nearly sessile; leaflets oblong or oblong-lanceolate, entire, short-stalked or sessile, narrowed at the base, obtuse or acute and mucronulate at the apex, ½′–2′ long; racemes elongating in fruit; bracts linear-oblong, mucronate; pedicels slender, 5″–6″ long; flowers densely racemose, yellow; petals obovate or oblonceolate, about 1″ long; pod linear, 1½′–3′ long, acute, borne on a stipe becoming longer than the pedicel.

In dry soil, Nebraska to Washington and Arizona. June–Sept.

$\frac{2}{3}$

2. CRISTATÉLLA Nutt. Journ. Acad. Phil. 7 : 85. *pl. 9.* 1834.

Annual viscid glandular-pubescent herbs, with digitately 3-foliolate leaves, and small white or yellowish flowers in terminal bracted racemes. Sepals spreading, slightly united at the base. Petals 4, laciniate or fimbriate at the summit, borne on long slender claws, the 2 lower smaller than the 2 upper. Receptacle short, with a short petaloid nectary between the ovary and the upper sepal. Stamens 6–14; filaments slender, declined. Ovary stalked, also declined. Capsule linear, nearly terete, many-seeded. [Diminutive of *cristatus,* crested, referring to the lacinitale petals.]

A genus of 2 species natives of the south-central United States. Type species : *Cristatella erosa* Nutt.

1. Cristatella Jàmesii T. & G.   James' Cristatella.   Fig. 2116.

Cristatella Jamesii T. & G. Fl. N. A. **1** : 124. 1838.

Erect, slender, branching, 6′–15′ high. Leaves slender-petioled ; leaflets nearly sessile, linear or linear-oblong, longer than the petiole, entire, obtuse, 4″–12″ long ; flowers slender-pedicelled, whitish or yellowish, the pedicels diverging ; bracts mostly 3-foliolate ; claws of the larger petals 1½″–2½″ long ; sepals acute or obtusish ; pod ascending, much longer than its stipe and somewhat longer than the pedicel.

In dry soil, Iowa to Nebraska, Colorado, Louisiana and Texas Reported from Illinois. June–Dec.

3. CLEOMÉLLA DC. Prodr. 1: 237. 1824.

Annual glabrous branching erect or diffuse herbs, with small yellow flowers and 3-foliolate leaves. Calyx of 4 sepals. Petals 4, sessile, not clawed. Receptacle short, glandless. Stamens 6, inserted on the receptacle. Ovary short, long-stalked. Capsule short, rhomboid or trapezoid, often broader than long, 4–10-seeded. [Diminutive of *Cleome.*]

A genus of about 8 species, natives of southwestern North America, extending into Mexico. Type species : *Cleomella mexicana* DC.

1. Cleomella angustifòlia Torr.   Northern Cleomella.   Fig. 2117.

Cleomella angustifolia Torr.; A. Gray, Pl. Wright. **1** : 12. 1852.

Generally erect, 1°–1½° high, branching above. Leaflets linear-lanceolate or linear-oblong, longer than the petiole ; bracts linear, simple ; flowers yellow, 2″–3″ broad ; pedicels very slender, ½′ long in fruit ; pod flattened, rhomboid, 2″–3″ broad, about 2″ high, pointed, raised on a very slender stipe 2″–4″ long, its valves almost conic ; placentae persistent after the valves fall away, each bearing about 3 seeds.

Plains, Nebraska and Colorado to Texas and New Mexico. Summer.

4. POLANÍSIA Raf. Journ. Phys. **89**: 98. 1819.

Annual branching herbs, mainly glandular-pubescent and exhaling a strong disagreeable odor, with whitish or yellowish flowers, and palmately compound or rarely simple leaves. Sepals 4, lanceolate, deciduous. Petals slender or clawed. Receptacle depressed, bearing a gland at the base of the ovary. Stamens 8-∞, somewhat unequal. Pod nearly or quite sessile on its pedicel, elongated, cylindric or compressed, its valves dehiscent from the summit. Seeds rugose or reticulated. [Greek, very unequal, referring to the stamens.]

A genus of about 30 species, natives of temperate and tropical regions. In addition to the following, 2 other species are found in the southern and western parts of North America. Type species: *Polanisia graveolens* Raf.

Stamens equalling or slightly exceeding the petals; flowers 2″-3″ long.   1. *P. graveolens.*
Stamens much exceeding the petals; flowers 4″-6″ long.   2. *P. trachysperma.*

1. Polanisia gravèolens Raf. Clammy-weed. Fig. 2118.

Cleome dodecandra Michx. Fl. Bor. Am. **2**: 32. 1803. Not. L. 1753.
Polanisia graveolens Raf. Am. Journ. Sci. **1**: 378. 1819.

Viscid and glandular-pubescent, branching, 6′-18′ high. Leaves 3-foliolate, slender-petioled; leaflets oblong, obtuse, entire, 6″-12″ long; sepals purplish, slightly unequal; petals cuneate, clawed, deeply emarginate or obcordate, yellowish-white; stamens 9-12, purplish, equalling or slightly exceeding the petals; style about 1″ long; pod lanceolate-oblong, slightly compressed, 1′-1½′ long, 3″-4″ wide, slightly stipitate, rough, reticulated; seeds rough.

Sandy and gravelly shores, western Quebec to Manitoba, Maryland, Tennessee, Kansas and Colorado. Wormweed. False-mustard. Summer.

2. Polanisia trachyspérma T. & G.. Large-flowered Clammy-weed. Fig. 2119.

Pòlanisia trachysperma T. & G. Fl. N. A. **1**: 669. 1840.

Jacksonia trachysperma Greene, Pittonia **2**: 175. 1891.

Similar to the last, but flowers twice the size (4″-6″ long); style slender, 2″-3″ long; stamens much exserted, often twice the length of the petals; filaments purple, conspicuous; pod slightly larger, nearly or quite sessile.

Prairies and plains, Iowa to Missouri, Texas, west to British Columbia and California. Summer.

Family 40. RESEDÀCEAE S. F. Gray, Nat. Arr. Brit. Pl. **2**: 665. 1821.

MIGNONETTE FAMILY.

Annual or perennial herbs, rarely somewhat woody, with alternate or fascicled leaves, gland-like stipules and racemose or spicate, bracted flowers. Flowers unsymmetrical. Calyx 4-7-parted, more or less inequilateral. Petals generally 4-7, cleft or entire, hypogynous. Disk fleshy, hypogynous, 1-sided. Stamens 3-40, inserted on the disk; filaments generally unequal. Ovary 1, compound, of

3-6 carpels; styles or sessile stigmas 3-6; ovules ∞. Fruit capsular in all but one genus, 3-6-lobed. Seeds reniform, without endosperm; cotyledons incumbent.

Six genera and about 65 species, mainly natives of the Mediterranean region.

1. RESÈDA [Tourn.] L. Sp. Pl. 448. 1753.

Erect or decumbent herbs, with entire lobed or pinnatifid leaves, and small spicate or narrowly racemose fiowers. Petals 4-7, toothed or cleft. Disk cup-shaped, glandular. Stamens 8-40, inserted on one side of the flower and on the inner surface of the disk. Capsule 3-6-lobed, horned, opening at the top before the seeds mature. [Ancient Latin name, referring to the supposed sedative effects of some of the species.]

About 55 species, all natives of the Old World. Type species: *Reseda lutea* L.

Leaves entire; upper petals lobed, the lower entire.   1. *R. Luteola.*
Leaves lobed or pinnatifid.
  Petals greenish-yellow, 3 or 4 of them divided.   2. *R. lutea.*
  Petals white, all of them cleft or divided.   3. *R. alba.*

$\frac{2}{3}$

1. Reseda Lutèola L. Dyer's Rocket. Yellow-weed. Fig. 2120.

Reseda Luteola L. Sp. Pl. 448. 1753.

Glabrous, erect, simple, or sparingly branched above, 1°-2½° high. Leaves lanceolate or linear, entire, obtuse, sessile or the lowest narrowed into a petiole; flowers greenish-yellow, 1″-2″ broad, in long narrow spikes; sepals 4; petals 4 or 5, very unequal, the upper ones lobed, the lower one linear, entire; capsule globose, 2″-3″ in diameter, with 3 or 4 apical teeth and 6-8 lateral ridges.

In waste places and in ballast, Massachusetts to New York and Pennsylvania. Mexico. Adventive from Europe. Cultivated for its yellow dye. Summer. Dyer's-weed. Dyer's-mignonette. Weld. Yellow or Italian rocket. Dutch pink. Wild woad.

2. Reseda lùtea L. Yellow Cut-leaved Mignonette. Fig. 2121.

Reseda lutea L. Sp. Pl. 449. 1753.

Ascending or decumbent, pubescent with short scattered stiff hairs, or nearly glabrous. Leaves 2′-4′ long, broadly ovate or oblong in outline, deeply lobed or divided, sometimes pinnatifid, their segments linear or oblong, obtuse, the margins undulate; flowers greenish-yellow, 2″-3″ broad, in narrow racemes; pedicels ascending, about 2″ long in fruit; petals 6 or 5, all but the lowest irregularly cleft; sepals of the same number; stamens 15-20; capsule oblong, about 4″ long, 1½″-2″ wide, with three or rarely 4 short teeth.

$\frac{2}{3}$

In waste places, Massachusetts to New Jersey, Pennsylvania and Michigan, and in ballast about the seaports. Adventive from Europe. Summer. Called also crambling rocket.

Reseda odoràta L., the mignonette of the gardens, has wedge-shaped entire or 3-lobed leaves, and very fragrant flowers with deeply cleft petals.

3. Reseda álba L.   White Cut-leaved
Mignonette.   Fig. 2122.

Reseda alba L. Sp. Pl. 449. 1753.

Erect, glabrous, somewhat glaucous, 1°–3°
high. Leaves often crowded, pinnate or deeply
pinnatifid, the segments 9–12, linear, linear-
oblong or lanceolate, obtusish, entire or undulate, 4″–12″ long; flowers nearly white, 2″–3″
broad, in dense spike-like racemes; pedicels
short; petals 6 or 5, all 3-cleft at the summit;
sepals of the same number; stamens 12–15;
capsule ovoid-oblong, usually 4-toothed, 5″–6″
long.

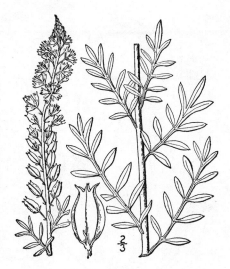

In waste places, Connecticut to Pennsylvania
and Ohio, in ballast about the eastern seaports
and in British Columbia. Adventive from southern Europe. July–Aug.

Family 41. **SARRACENIÀCEAE** La Pyl. Mem. Soc. Linn. Paris **6**: 379.   1827.

PITCHER-PLANT FAMILY.

Marsh herbs, with basal tubular or pitcher-shaped leaves, and large scapose
nodding solitary flowers. Sepals 4 or 5, hypogynous, imbricated, persistent.
Petals 5, imbricated, hypogynous, deciduous or none. Stamens ∞, hypogynous;
anthers versatile. Ovary 1, 3–5-celled; ovules ∞, in many rows. Capsule
3–5-celled, loculicidally dehiscent; style terminal, peltate, lobed, or in one genus
simple. Seeds small, the testa reticulated; embryo small; endosperm fleshy.

Three genera and about 10 species, all natives of America. Besides the following genus, *Chrys-
amphora* of California and *Heliamphora* of Venezuela are the only known members of the family.

1. SARRACÈNIA [Tourn.] L. Sp. Pl. 510.   1753.

Leaves hollow, pitcher-form or trumpet-shaped, with a lateral wing and a terminal lid
or lamina. Sepals 5, with 3 or 4 bracts at the base. Petals 5, ovate or oblong. Ovary
5-celled. Style dilated at the apex into a peltate umbrella-like structure with 5 rays which
terminate under its angles in hooked stigmas. Capsule 5-celled, granular, rugose. Seeds
numerous, anatropous. [Named in honor of Dr. Jean Antoine Sarracin, a botanist of
Quebec.]

About 8 species natives of eastern and southeastern North America. Type species: *Sarracenia
purpurea* L.

Leaves pitcher-shaped, curved; flower purple or greenish (rarely yellow).   1. *S. purpurea.*
Leaves tubular-trumpet-shaped; flower yellow.   2. *S. flava.*

$\frac{2}{5}$

1. Sarracenia purpùrea L. Pitcher-plant. Side-saddle Flower. Fig. 2123.

Sarrecenia purpurea L. Sp. Pl. 510. 1753.

Sarracenia purpurea heterophylla (Eaton) Torr. Fl. N. Y. 1 : 41. 1843.

Sarracenia heterophylla Eaton, Man. Ed. 3, 447. 1822.

Glabrous, except the inner side of the lamina and inner surface of the pitchers, which are densely clothed with stiff reflexed hairs. Leaves tufted, ascending, curved, 4′–12′ long, purple-veined, or sometimes green or yellowish all over, much inflated, narrowed into a petiole below, broadly winged, persistent; scapes 1°–2° high, slender, bearing a single nodding, deep purple or occasionally yellow, nearly globose flower 2′ in diameter or more; petals obovate, narrowed in the middle, incurved over the yellowish style.

In peat bogs, Labrador to the Canadian Rocky-Mountains, Florida, Kentucky and Iowa. May–June. The hollow leaves are commonly more or less completely filled with water containing drowned insects. Young plants often bear several smaller flat obliquely ovate leaves. Huntsman's-cup. Indian cup or pitcher. Adam's- or forefathers'-cup or -pitcher. Whippoorwill's-boots or -shoes. Skunk-cabbage. Watches. Foxglove. Small-pox plant. Fly-trap. Meadow- or fever-cup.

2. Sarracenia flàva L. Trumpets. Trumpet-leaf. Water-cup. Fig. 2124.

Sarracenia flava L. Sp. Pl. 510. 1753.

Glabrous throughout, or the leaves minutely pubescent. Leaves trumpet-shaped, 1°–3° long, 1′–2′ wide at the orifice, narrowly winged prominently ribbed, green, the lid 1′–4′ wide, obtuse or acuminate, erect, contracted at the base; scape 1°–2° high, slender; flower 2′–3′ broad, yellow; petals narrow, oblanceolate or obovate, sometimes 3′ long, drooping, slightly contracted at the middle.

In bogs, Virginia and North Carolina to Florida, west to Louisiana. Yellow trumpets. Watches. Biscuits. April.

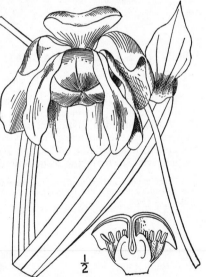

$\frac{1}{2}$

Family 42. DROSERÀCEAE S. F. Gray, Nat. Arr. Brit. Pl. 2 : 664. 1821.

SUNDEW FAMILY.

Perennial or biennial glandular-pubescent herbs, exuding a copious viscid secretion, mostly with basal leaves circinate in the bud, and fugacious perfect flowers, racemose in our species. Calyx persistent, 4–5-parted or the sepals distinct and imbricated. Petals 5, hypogynous, convolute, marcescent, distinct or slightly united at the base. Stamens 4–20, hypogynous or perigynous; filaments subulate or filiform; anthers usually versatile. Disk none. Ovary free, or its base adnate to the calyx, globose or ovoid, 1–3-celled; styles 1–5, simple, 2-cleft or multifid; ovules numerous. Capsule 1–5-celled, loculicidally dehiscent. Seeds several or numerous; anatropous; endosperm fleshy; embryo straight, cylindric.

Four genera and about 90 species, of wide geographic distribution.

1. DRÓSERA L. Sp. Pl. 281. 1753.

Bog herbs, with tufted basal leaves clothed with glandular hairs which secrete a fluid that entraps insects, and scapose racemose flowers. Calyx-tube short, free from the ovary, very deeply 4–8-parted (commonly 5-parted). Petals usually 5, spatulate. Stamens as many as the petals; anthers short, extrorse. Ovary 1-celled; styles 2–5, usually 3, distinct or united at the base, often deeply 2-parted so as to appear twice as many, or fimbriate. Capsule 3-valved (rarely 5-valved), many-seeded, generally stipitate in the calyx. [Name from the Greek, dew, in allusion to the dew-like drops exuded by the glands of the leaves.]

About 85 species, most abundant in Australia. Besides the following, 2 others occur in the southeastern States. Our species are known as Sundew, or Dew-plant. Type species: *Drosera rotundifolia* L.

Blade of the leaf orbicular, or wider than long; petals white. 1. *D. rotundifolia.*
Blade of the leaf linear, or longer than wide
  Leaves linear or spatulate with a distinct petiole; petals white.
    Blade of the leaf spatulate.
      Blade 2–3 times as long as wide. 2. *D. intermedia.*
      Blade 6–8 times as long as wide. 3. *D. longifolia.*
      Blade linear, 10–15 times as long as wide. 4. *D. linearis.*
  Leaves filiform, much elongated, with no distinct petiole; petals purple. 5. *D. filiformis.*

1. Drosera rotundifòlia L. Round-leaved Sundew or Dew-plant. Eyebright. Fig. 2125.

Drosera rotundifolia L. Sp. Pl. 281. 1753.

Drosera rotundifolia comosa Fernald, Rhodora 7: 9. 1905.

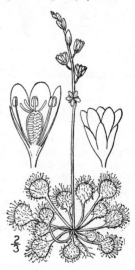

Scape slender, erect, glabrous, 4'–10' high. Leaves orbicular or broader, spreading on the ground, the blade 3"–6" long, abruptly narrowed into a flat pubescent petiole ½'–2' long, the upper surface covered with slender glandular hairs; raceme 1-sided, simple or sometimes once forked, 1–25-flowered; pedicels 1"–2" long; flowers about 2" broad, opening in sunshine; petals white to red, oblong, somewhat exceeding the sepals; seeds fusiform, pointed at both ends, the testa loose.

In bogs or wet sand, Newfoundland and Labrador to Alaska, south to Florida and Alabama, in the Rocky Mountains to Montana and Idaho, and in the Sierra Nevada to California. Ascends to 2500 ft. in the Catskills. Also in Europe and Asia. Rootstock usually short. Parts of the flower are sometimes transformed into small green leaves. Rosa-solis. Youth-wort. Moor-grass. Red-rot. Lustwort. July–Aug.

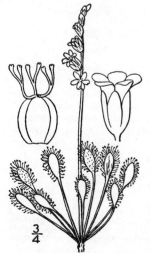

2. Drosera intermèdia Hayne. Spatulate-leaved Sundew. Fig. 2126.

Drosera intermedia Hayne in Schrad. Journ. Bot. **1800**: Part 1, 37.

Drosera longifolia Michx. Fl. Bor. Am. 1: 186. 1803. Not L. 1753.

Drosera americana Willd. Enum. 340. 1809.

Drosera intermedia var. *Americana* DC. Prodr. 1: 318. 1824.

Rootstock elongated (2'–4' long when growing in water). Scape erect, glabrous, 2'–8' high. Blades of the leaves ascending, spatulate, obtuse at the apex, 3"–7" long, 1½"–2" wide, their upper surfaces clothed with glandular hairs, gradually narrowed into a glabrous petiole ½'–1½' long; raceme 1-sided; flowers several; pedicels about 1½" long; petals white, slightly exceeding the sepals; seeds oblong, the testa close, roughened.

In bogs, Newfoundland to Saskatchewan, south to Florida and Louisiana. Also in Cuba, and in northern Europe. June–Aug.

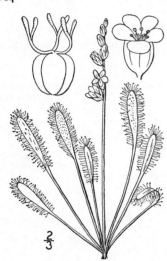

3. Drosera longifòlia L.   Oblong-leaved Sundew.   Fig. 2127.

Drosera longifolia L. Sp. Pl. 282. 1753.

Drosera anglica Huds. Fl. Angl. Ed. 2, 135. 1778.

Similar to the preceding species, but the leaf-blade is erect, longer (8″–15″ long, 1½″–2″ wide), elongated-spatulate and narrowed into a glabrous or sparingly hairy petiole 1′–4′ long; pedicels ½″–3″ long; flowers usually several, racemose, white, 2″–2½″ broad, rarely only one; seeds oblong, obtuse at both ends, the testa loose.

In bogs, Newfoundland and arctic America to Manitoba and British Columbia, Ontario, Michigan, Idaho and California. Also in northern Europe and Asia. Summer.

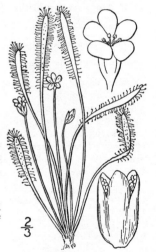

4. Drosera lineàris Goldie.   Slender-leaved Sundew.   Fig. 2128.

Drosera linearis Goldie, Edinb. Phil. Journ. 6: 325. 1822.

Scape low but sometimes exceeding the leaves, glabrous. Petioles erect, glabrous, 2′–4′ long; blade linear, ½′–3′ long, about 1″ wide, densely clothed with glandular hairs, obtuse at the apex; flowers few, or solitary, white; petals somewhat exceeding the sepals; seeds oblong, black, the testa close, smooth and somewhat shining.

In bogs, Quebec to Ontario, Alberta, Maine, Wisconsin and Minnesota. Blooms a little later than *D. rotundifolia* when the two grow together.

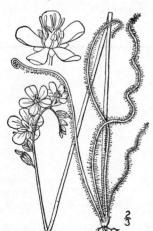

5. Drosera filifórmis Raf.   Thread-leaved Sundew.   Fig. 2129.

Drosera filiformis Raf. Med. Rep. (II.) 5: 360. 1808.

Drosera tenuifolia Willd. Enum. 340. 1809.

Scape erect, glabrous, 8′–20′ high. Leaves narrowly linear or filiform, glandular-pubescent throughout, 6′–15′ long, about 1″ wide, usually acutish at the apex, with no distinction between blade and petiole, woolly with brown hairs at the very base; racemes 1-sided, 10–30-flowered; pedicels 2″–4″ long; flowers purple, 4″–12″ broad; petals obovate, much exceeding the sepals; seeds fusiform, acute at each end, the testa minutely punctate.

In wet sand, near the coast, eastern Massachusetts to Florida and Mississippi. July–Sept. Earliest leaves short, lanceolate, acute, the apex glandular. A hybrid with *D. intermedia* is described.

Drosera brevifòlia Pursh, a species of the southeastern United States, with cuneate-obovate leaves and glandular-pubescent scapes, enters our territory in extreme southeastern Virginia.

Family 43. **PODOSTEMÀCEAE** Lindl. Nat. Syst. Ed. 2, 190. 1836.

River-weed Family.

Small aquatic fresh-water mostly annual fleshy herbs, the leaves usually poorly differentiated from the stem, the whole structure commonly resembling the thallus of an alga or hepatic, the small usually perfect flowers devoid of any perianth and subtended by a spathe-like involucre, or in some genera with a 3–5-cleft membranous calyx. Stamens hypogynous, only 2 in the following genus, numerous in some others; filaments united or distinct; anthers 2-celled, the sacs longitudinally dehiscent. Ovary stalked or sessile, 2–3-celled; ovules usually numerous in each cell, anatropous; styles 2 or 3, short. Capsules 2–3-celled, ribbed. Seeds numerous, minute, without endosperm; embryo straight.

About 21 genera and 175 species, mostly in the tropics, only the following North American.

1. **PODOSTÈMUM** Michx. Fl. Bor. Am. **2**: 164. *pl. 44.* 1803.

Habit of the several species various. Flowers sessile or very nearly so in the spathe-like involucre. Perianth none. Stamens 2, their filaments united to near the summit; anthers 2, oblong or oval. Staminodia 2, filiform. Ovary ovoid, 2-celled; stigmas 2, nearly erect, short, subulate. Capsule ovoid, 6–10-ribbed, 2-valved. [Greek, stalked-stamens.]

About 12 species of rather wide geographic distribution, the following typical. Besides the following, another occurs in the southern United States.

1. **Podostemum ceratophýllum** Michx. River-weed. Thread-foot. Fig. 2130.

Podostemum ceratophyllum Michx. Fl. Bor. Am. **2**: 165. 1803.

Plant dark green, rather stiff, firmly attached to stones in running water, densely tufted, 1'–10' long, the leaves narrowly linear, sheathing at the base, commonly split above into almost filiform segments or lobes. Flowers less than 1" broad, at length bursting from the spathes; capsule oblong-oval, rather more than 1" long, obtuse, borne on a stipe of about its own length, 8-ribbed; stigmas at length recurved.

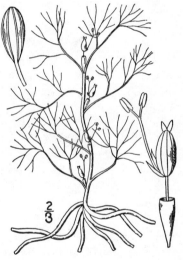

Firmly attached to stones in shallow streams, New Brunswick to Ontario and Minnesota, south to Georgia, Alabama and Kentucky. July–Sept.

Family 44. **CRASSULÀCEAE** DC. Fl. Franc. **4**: 382. 1805.

Orpine Family.

Herbs, or somewhat shrubby plants, mostly fleshy or succulent, with cymose or rarely solitary regular or symmetrical flowers. Stipules none. Calyx persistent, free from the ovary or ovaries, mostly 4–5-cleft or 4–5-parted. Petals equal in number to the calyx-lobes, distinct, or more or less united, usually persistent, rarely wanting. Stamens of the same number or twice as many as the petals; filaments filiform or subulate; anthers longitudinally dehiscent. Receptacle with a scale at the base of each carpel. Carpels equal in number to the sepals, distinct, or united below; styles subulate or filiform; ovules numerous, arranged in 2 rows along the ventral suture. Follicles membranous or coriaceous, 1-celled, dehiscent along the ventral suture. Seeds minute; endosperm fleshy; embryo terete; cotyledons short, obtuse.

About 30 genera and 600 species, of wide geographic distribution.

Stamens of the same number as the sepals ; minute herbs.   **1.** *Tillaeastrum.*
Stamens twice as many as the sepals ; succulent herbs.
    Flowers 4–5-parted.
       Carpels erect ; flowers often polygamous.   **2.** *Rhodiola.*
       Carpels spreading ; flowers perfect.   **3.** *Sedum.*
    Flowers 6–12-parted.   **4.** *Sempervivum.*

1. TILLAEÁSTRUM Britton, Bull. N. Y. Bot. Gard. **3**: 1. 1903.

    Minute, mostly glabrous, aquatic or mud-loving succulent herbs, with opposite entire leaves and very small solitary axillary flowers. Calyx 3–5-parted. Petals 3–5, distinct, or united at the base. Stamens 3–5. Carpels 3–5, distinct. Styles short. Ovules usually few. Follicles few-seeded or several-seeded. [Latin, from the affinity of these plants with the genus *Tillaea*.]

    About 20 species, of wide geographic distribution. Besides the following, another occurs in the western and southern States.

Flowers sessile or short-peduncled.   **1.** *T. aquaticum.*
Fruiting peduncles as long as the leaves or longer.   **2.** *T. Vaillantii.*

1. Tillaeastrum aquáticum (L.) Britton. Pigmy-weed. Fig. 2131.

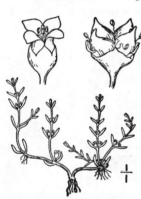

Tillaea aquatica L. Sp. Pl. 128. 1753.
Tillaea simplex Nutt. Journ. Acad. Phil. **1**: 114. 1817.
Bulliarda aquatica DC. Prodr. **3**: 382. 1828.
Tillaeastrum aquaticum Britton, Bull. N. Y. Bot. Gard. **3**: 1. 1903.

    Stems ascending or erect, ½′–3′ high, glabrous. Leaves linear-oblong, entire, acutish or obtuse at the apex, connate at the base, 2″–3″ long, at length shorter than the internodes; flowers sessile or short-peduncled, ½″ broad ; calyx-lobes, petals, stamens and carpels 4, rarely 3, petals greenish, about twice the length of the calyx-lobes; follicles ovoid, longer than the calyx-lobes, 8–10-seeded.

    Muddy banks of streams, Nova Scotia to Massachusetts and Maryland, Louisiana and Texas, near the coast, Washington to Lower California and Colorado. Stem often rooting at the nodes. Also in Europe and northern Africa. July–Sept.

2. Tillaeastrum Vaillántii (Willd.) Britton. Vaillant's Pigmy-weed. Fig. 2132.

Tillaea Vaillantii Willd. Sp. Pl. **1**: 720. 1798.
Tillaeastrum Vaillantii Britton, Bull. N. Y. Bot. Gard. **3**: 2. 1903.

    Similar to the preceding species, 4′ long or less, the oblong to linear-oblong leaves about 2″ long. Fruiting peduncles elongated, becoming as long as the leaves or longer.

    Prince Edward Island ; Nantucket. Europe and northern Africa. Perhaps a race of the preceding species.

2. RHODÌOLA L. Sp. Pl. 1035. 1753.

    Fleshy perennial herbs, with erect, mostly simple stems, broad, rather thin dentate or entire leaves and dioecious or polygamous, yellow, greenish or purplish flowers in terminal cymes. Flowers 4-parted or 5-parted. Calyx shorter than the petals. Carpels distinct, erect. Style very short or none. [Greek, rose, referring to the rose-scented roots.]

    About 8 species, natives of the north temperate zone. Besides the following, 4 others occur in western North America and 1 on Roan Mountain, North Carolina. Type species : *Rhodiola rosea* L.

1. **Rhodiola ròsea** L. Roseroot. Rosewort.
Fig 2133.

$\frac{2}{3}$

Rhodiola rosea L. Sp. Pl. 1035. 1753.
Sedum roseum Scop. Fl. Carn. Ed. 2, 326. 1772.
Sedum Rhodiola DC. Plantes Gras. *pl. 143.* 1805.

Perennial, branched at the base, or simple, erect or ascending, glabrous and somewhat glaucous, 4′–12′ high. Leaves sessile, oval or slightly obovate, acute or obtuse at the apex, narrowed or rounded at the base, dentate or entire, 6″–12″ long, 3″–5″ wide, the lower ones smaller; cyme terminal, dense, ½′–2′ broad; flowers dioecious, yellowish-green or purplish, 2½″–4″ broad; sepals oblong, narrower and shorter than the petals; staminate flowers with 8 (rarely 10) stamens, the pistillate ones with 4 (rarely 5) carpels; follicles purple, about 2″ long, only their tips spreading.

In rocky places, Labrador and arctic America to Maine and Vermont; Chittenango Falls, New York; cliffs on the Delaware River in eastern Pennsylvania. Northern and alpine Europe and Asia. Root rose-scented. Snowdon rose. May–July.

3. **SÈDUM** [Tourn.] L. Sp. Pl. 430. 1753.

Fleshy mostly glabrous herbs, erect or decumbent, mainly with alternate, often imbricated, entire or dentate leaves, and perfect flowers in terminal often 1-sided cymes. Calyx 4-5-lobed. Petals 4-5, distinct. Stamens 8-10, perigynous, the alternate ones usually attached to the petals. Filaments filiform or subulate. Scales of the receptacle entire or emarginate. Carpels 4-5, distinct, or united at the base, spreading; styles usually short; ovules ∞. Follicles many-seeeded or few-seeded. [Latin, to sit, from the lowly habit of these plants.]

About 200 species, mostly natives of temperate and cold regions of the northern hemisphere, but many in the mountains of Mexico and a few in the Andes of South America. Besides the following, about 15 others occur in the western parts of North America. Type species: *Sedum Telephium* L.

Cyme regular, compound, the flowers not secund; leaves broad, flat.
Petals purple; plant somewhat glaucous; petals twice as long as sepals.   1. *S. triphyllum.*
Petals pink; plant very glaucous; petals 3-4 times as long as the sepals.   2. *S. telephioides.*
Flowers secund along the branches of the cyme.
Petals yellow.
Leaves short, thick, ovate, densely imbricated.   3. *S. acre.*
Leaves linear or terete, scattered on the stems.
Annual; petals little longer than the sepals.   4. *S. Nuttallianum.*
Perennial; petals twice as long as the sepals.
Plant 3′–6′ high; native, western.   5. *S. stenopetalum.*
Plant 8′–12′ high; introduced in a few places.   6. *S. reflexum.*
Petals purple or white.
Leaves terete; petals purple, pink, or white.   7. *S. pulchellum.*
Leaves flat, spatulate or obovate; petals white.
Lower leaves verticillate in 3's.   8. *S. ternatum.*
Leaves all alternate.   9. *S. Nevii.*

$\frac{2}{3}$

1. **Sedum triphýllum** (Haw.) S. F. Gray. Orpine.
Live-forever. Fig. 2134.

Anacampseros triphylla Haw. Syn. Pl. Succ. 111. 1812.
Sedum triphyllum S. F. Gray, Nat. Arr. Brit. Pl. **2:** 510. 1821.
Sedum Fabaria Koch, Syn. Pl. Germ. 258. 1837.
S. purpureum Link, Enum. Hort. Berol. 1: 437. 1821.

Perennial, stems erect, stout, simple, tufted, glabrous and slightly glaucous, 1°–1½° high. Leaves alternate, ovate, broadly oval or obovate, obtuse, 1′–2′ long, coarsely dentate, the upper sessile and rounded at the base, the lower larger, narrowed at the base or sometimes petioled; cyme dense, regular, compound, 2′–3′ broad; flowers perfect, 2½″–4″ broad, 5-parted; petals purple, twice as long as the ovate acute sepals; stamens 10; follicles about 2″ long, tipped with a short style.

In fields and along roadsides, Quebec to Ontario, south to Maryland and Michigan. Naturalized from Europe and native of western Asia. Blooms sparingly, but spreads freely by its joints. Garden-orpine. Evergreen. Everlasting. Bog-leaves. Life-of-man. Frog's-mouth or -bladder. Leeks. Frog-plant. Witches'-money-bags. Live-long. Aaron's rod. Midsummer-men. Illustrated in our first edition as *S. Telephium* L. June–Sept.

2. **Sedum telephioìdes** Michx. American Orpine. Wild Live-forever. Fig. 2135.

Sedium telephioides Michx. Fl. Bor. Am. 1 : 277. 1803.

Similar to the preceding species, but more slender, seldom over 10′ high, very glaucous and purplish throughout. Leaves oval or obovate, obtuse, coarsely dentate or entire, 1′–2′ long, all narrowed at the base and petioled or the uppermost sessile; cyme dense, regular, 2′–4′ broad; flowers perfect, 3″–4″ broad, 5-parted; petals pale pink, much longer than the lanceolate sepals; follicles about 2″ long, tipped with a slender style.

On dry rocks, southern Pennsylvania and Maryland to western New York and southern Indiana, south to North Carolina and Georgia. Reported from farther north. Ascends to 4200 ft. in North Carolina. Sweet-heart. Aug.–Sept.

Sedum Siebóldi Sweet, an Asiatic species commonly cultivated, is occasionally found as an escape; its leaves are nearly orbicular and mostly whorled in 3's.

3. **Sedum àcre** L Wall-pepper. Biting or Mossy Stonecrop. Fig. 2136.

Sedum acre L. Sp. Pl. 432. 1753.

Perennial, densely tufted, spreading and matted, glabrous; sterile branches prostrate, the flowering ones erect or ascending, 1′–3′ high. Leaves sessile, alternate, ovate, very thick, densely imbricated, light yellowish green, entire, about 1½″ long, those of the sterile branches usually arranged in 6 rows; cyme 2–3-forked, its branches ½′–1′ long; flowers sessile, about 4″ broad; petals bright yellow, linear-lanceolate, acute, 3 or 4 times as long as the ovate sepals; central flower of the cyme commonly 5-parted, the others usually 4-parted; follicles spreading, 1½″–2″ long, tipped with a slender style.

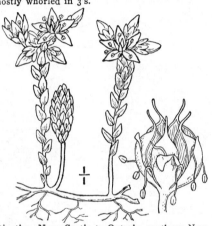

On rocks and along roadsides, escaped from cultivation, Nova Scotia to Ontario, southern New York and Virginia. Adventive from Europe. Native also in northern Asia. Also called bird's-bread. Creeping Jack or Charlie. Pricket. Golden-moss. Little houseleek. Gold-chain. Wall-moss. Tangle-tail. Rock-plant. Pepper-crop. Mountain-moss. Ginger. Poor-man's pepper. Prick-madam. Treasure-of-love. Love-entangled. June–Aug.

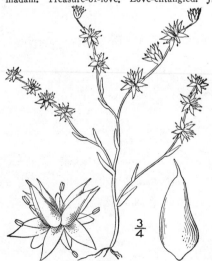

4. **Sedum Nuttalliànum** Raf. Nuttall's Stonecrop. Fig. 2137.

Sedum Nuttallianum Raf. Atl. Journ. 1 : 146. 1832.

Sedum Torreyi Don, Gard. Dict. 3 : 121. 1834.

Sedum sparsiflorum Nutt.; T. & G. Fl. N. A. 1 : 559. 1840.

Annual, low, tufted, glabrous, 2′–3′ high. Leaves alternate, scattered, linear-oblong, teretish, sessile, entire, 2″–6″ long; cyme 2–5-forked, its branches ½″–2′ long; flowers sessile or very short-pedicelled, about 3½″ broad; petals yellow, lanceolate, acute, somewhat longer than the ovate sepals; follicles widely divergent, tipped with the short subulate style.

In dry, open places, Missouri and Arkansas to Texas. May.

5. Sedum stenopétalum Pursh.　Narrow-petaled Stonecrop.　Fig. 2138.

Sedum stenopetalum Pursh, Fl. Am. Sept. 324. 1814.

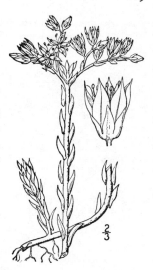

Perennial, tufted, glabrous; flowering branches erect, 3'–7' high. Leaves alternate, crowded but scarcely imbricated, except on the sterile shoots, sessile, terete or linear, 3"–8" long, entire; cyme 3–7-forked, compact, the branches ½'–1' long; flowers mostly short-pedicelled, 4"–5" broad; petals narrowly lanceolate, very acute, yellow, much exceeding the calyx-lobes; follicles about 2" long, their subulate style-tips at length somewhat divergent.

In dry rocky places, South Dakota to Alberta, Nebraska, Oregon and California. May–June.

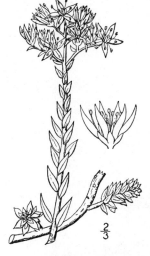

6. Sedum refléxum L.　Crooked Yellow or Reflexed Stonecrop.　Dwarf House-leek.　Fig. 2139.

Sedum reflexum L. Sp. Pl. Ed. 2, 618. 1762.

Perennial by a creeping stem producing numerous short barren shoots, the flowering branches erect, 8'–14' high. Leaves alternate, sessile, densely imbricated on the sterile shoots, terete, somewhat spurred at the base, 3"–9" long; cyme 4–8-forked, its branches recurved in flower; flowers 4"– 6" broad; petals linear, yellow, two to three times as long as the short ovate sepals; follicles about 1½" long, tipped with a very slender somewhat divergent style.

Eastern Massachusetts and western New York, locally escaped from gardens. Native of Europe. Summer. Indian-fog. Love-in-a-chain. Prick-, trip- or trick-madam. Creeping Jennie. Ginger.

7. Sedum pulchéllum Michx.　Widow's Cross. Rock- or Mountain-moss.　Fig. 2140.

Sedum pulchellum Michx. Fl. Bor. Am. 1: 277. 1803.

Perennial (?), glabrous, ascending or trailing, branched at the base, 4'–12' long. Leaves densely crowded, terete or linear, sessile, obtuse at the apex, slightly auriculate at the base, 3"–12" long, about 1" wide; cyme 4–7-forked, its branches spreading or recurved in flower; flowers sessile, close together, 4"–6" broad; petals rose-purple, pink, or white, linear-lanceolate, acute, about twice the length of the lanceolate obtusish sepals; follicles 2"–3" long, tipped with a slender style.

On rocks, Virginia to Georgia, west to Indiana, Kentucky, Missouri, Kansas and Texas. May–July. Cultivated in the South under the above name. Flowering-moss.

8. Sedum ternàtum Michx. Wild Stonecrop. Fig. 2141.

S. *ternatum* Michx. Fl. Bor. Am. 1 : 277. 1803.

Perennial by rootstocks, tufted, stem creeping, flowering branches ascending, 3′–8′ high.
Lower leaves and those of the sterile shoots
flat, obovate, entire, 6″–12″ long, sometimes
9″ wide, rounded at the apex, cuneate at the
base or narrowed into a petiole, verticillate
in 3's; upper leaves oblanceolate or oblong,
alternate, sessile; cyme 2–4-forked, its branches
spreading or recurved in flower; flowers rather
distant, often leafy-bracted, about 5″ broad;
petals linear-lanceolate, acute, white, nearly
twice the length of the oblong obtuse sepals;
follicles 2½″ long, tipped with the slender style.

On rocks, Connecticut to New Jersey, Georgia,
west to Indiana, Missouri, Tennessee and Michigan. Also escaped from gardens to roadsides in
the Middle and Eastern States. Ascends to 3000
ft. in Virginia. Iceland-moss. Three-leaved
stonecrop. April–June.

9. Sedum Nèvii A. Gray. Nevius' Stonecrop. Fig. 2142.

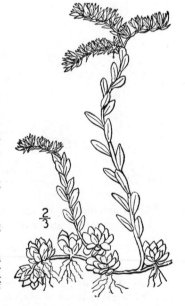

Sedum Nevii A. Gray, Man. Ed. 5, 172. 1867.

Densely tufted, glabrous, stems spreading or decumbent, flowering branches ascending, 3′–5′ high. Leaves
of the sterile shoots very densely imbricated, spatulate
or obovate, narrowed or cuneate at the base, mostly
sessile, rounded at the apex, entire, 3″–6″ long, 1″–2″
wide, the lower ones smaller; leaves of the flowering
branches spatulate or linear-oblong, alternate; cyme
about 3-forked, its branches usually recurved in flower;
flowers close together, 3″–4″ broad; petals linear,
acuminate, longer than the sepals; follicles about 2″
long, widely divergent, tipped with the short style.

On rocks, mountains of Virginia to Alabama, Illinois and
Missouri. May–June.

Sedum stolonìferum Gmel., a perennial species, with
opposite obovate-cuneate crenate leaves and pale rose-
colored petals twice as long as the calyx, occurs on roadsides and in fields in Maine and Nova Scotia. Native of
the Orient.

4. SEMPERVÌVUM [Rupp.] L. Sp. Pl. 464. 1753.

Fleshy perennial herbs, the thick succulent leaves densely imbricated on the short sterile
shoots and scattered on the erect flowering stems, with compound terminal usually dense
cymes of showy flowers. Flowers 6–20-parted. Petals distinct, oblong or lanceolate, acute
or acuminate. Stamens twice as many as the petals. Styles filiform; ovules ∞. Follicles
many-seeded. [Latin, always living.]

About 40 species, natives of the Old World, chiefly distinguished from *Sedum* by the more
numerous parts of the flower, the following typical.

1. Sempervivum tectòrum L. Houseleek. Fig. 2143.

Sempervivum tectorum L. Sp. Pl. 464. 1753.

Flowering stems about 1° high, the barren shoots forming lateral nearly globular tufts. Leaves oval or ovate, the lower 1′–1½′ long, very thick, short-pointed, bordered by a line of stiff short hairs; cyme large, dense; flowers sometimes 1′ broad, pink, sessile along its spreading or recurved branches; petals lanceolate, acute, 2 to 3 times as long as the obtuse ciliate sepals.

Essex Co., Mass., escaped from gardens and reported as well established; Somerset Co., N. J. Native of continental Europe. Summer. Healing-blade. Aye-green. Bullock's-eye. Poor Jan's-leaf. Jupiter's-beard. Hen-and-chickens. Old English names, homewort, sengreen and thunder-plant; a fancied protection against lightning, as well as fire.

Family 45. PENTHORÀCEAE Rydb. N. A. Fl. 22: 75. 1905.

VIRGINIA STONECROP FAMILY.

Erect perennial scarcely succulent herbs, with alternate sessile serrate thin leaves, and greenish perfect flowers in forked secund cymes. Calyx 5-parted or 6-parted. Petals usually wanting, if present 5 or 6. Stamens twice as many as the sepals, hypogynous; filaments filiform. Carpels 5 or 6, united to the middle, ovules ∞. Fruit depressed, 5–6-lobed, 5–6-beaked, the lobes dehiscent, tipped with divergent styles, many-seeded.

The family consists of the following genus.

1. PÉNTHORUM L. Sp. Pl. 432. 1753.

Characters of the family, as given above. [Greek, five, from the symmetrical flower.]

Three known species, natives of eastern North America, Japan and China, the following typical. The following is the only one known in North America. The genus is referred to the Saxifrage Family by some authors and to the Orpine Family by others.

1. Penthorum sedoìdes L. Ditch or Virginia Stonecrop. Fig. 2144.

Penthorum sedoides L. Sp. Pl. 432. 1753.

Glabrous, erect, stem usually branched and angled above, terete below, 6′–2° high. Leaves lanceolate or narrowly elliptic, acuminate at each end, finely serrate, 2′–4′ long, 6″–12″ wide; cymes 2–3-forked, the branches 1′–3′ long; flowers short-pedicelled, about 2″ broad; sepals triangular-ovate, acute, shorter than the flattish capsule; petals linear or linear-spatulate, often or generally wanting.

In ditches and swamps, New Brunswick to Florida, west to Minnesota, Nebraska, Kansas and Texas. July–Sept.

Family 46. PARNASSIÀCEAE Dumort. Anal. Fam. 37, 42. 1829.

GRASS-OF-PARNASSUS FAMILY.

Glabrous perennial scapose herbs, with short rootstocks, basal petioled entire leaves, usually with a single sessile leaf on the scape, and solitary terminal white or pale yellow flowers. Calyx 5-lobed nearly to the base, its short tube free from or adnate to the ovary. Petals 5, spreading, marcescent, each with a cluster of gland-tipped staminodia at the base, united into a scale below, or distinct. Fertile stamens 5, alternate with the petals. Ovary superior or half inferior, 1-celled; style very short or none; stigmas usually 4; ovules ∞. Capsule 1-celled, with 3 or 4 placentae projecting within, loculidically 3–4-valved. Seeds numerous. Seed-coat winged.

1. PARNÁSSIA [Tourn.] L. Sp. Pl. 273. 1753.

Characters of the family as given above. [From the Greek, mount; the plant called Grass of Parnassus by Dioscorides.]

About 15 species, natives of the north temperate and arctic zones. Besides the following, 6 or 7 others occur in northwestern America and one in Florida. Type species: *Parnassia palustris* L.

Petals sessile; leaves ovate, oval, orbicular or cordate.
  Staminodia 3–5 at the base of each petal.
    Flower 9″–18″ broad; petals much exceeding the calyx-lobes.
      Staminodia not longer than the stamens, stout.   1. *P. caroliniana.*
      Staminodia longer than the stamens, slender.   2. *P. grandifolia.*
    Flower 4″–5″ broad; petals equalling the calyx-lobes.   3. *P. Kotzebuei.*
  Staminodia 5–15 at the base of each petal, slender, united into a scale below.
    Flower 1′ broad; leaves cordate at base.   4. *P. palustris.*
    Flower 4″–5″ broad; leaves narrowed at base.   5. *P. parviflora.*
Petals clawed; leaves reniform; staminodia 3 at each petal, distinct.   6. *P. asarifolia.*

$\frac{1}{2}$

1. Parnassia caroliniàna Michx. Carolina Grass-of-Parnassus. Fig. 2145.

Parnassia caroliniana Michx. Fl. Bor. Am. **1**: 184. 1803.

Scape 6′–24′ high, with a nearly sessile ovate clasping leaf below the middle. Basal leaves long-petioled, ovate, broadly oval or orbicular, obtuse at the apex, rounded or sometimes cordate at the base, or decurrent into the petiole, 1′–2′ long; flower 9″–18″ broad; calyx-lobes ovate-oblong, obtuse, much shorter than the sessile broadly oval white greenish-veined petals; staminodia generally 3 in each set, stout, distinct to the base, not longer than the stamens; capsule 4″–5″ long.

In swamps and low meadows, New Brunswick to Manitoba, south to Virginia, Illinois and Iowa; Carolina? June–Sept.

2. Parnassia grandifòlia DC. Large-leaved Grass-of-Parnassus. Fig. 2146.

Parnassia grandifolia DC. Prodr. **1**: 320. 1824.

Similar to the preceding species, the scape bearing an ovate clasping leaf at the middle or much below it. Basal leaves as in *P. caroliniana,* but often larger and narrowed at the base; flower 1′–2′ broad; calyx-lobes shorter than the sessile white petals; staminodia 3–5 in each set, slender or almost filiform, united only at the base, exceeding the anther-bearing stamens.

In moist soil, southwestern Virginia to Florida, Missouri and Louisiana. Ascends to 2200 ft. in Virginia. July–Sept.

3. Parnassia Kotzebùei C. & S. Kotzebue's Grass-of-Parnassus. Fig. 2147.

Parnassia Kotzebuei C. & S. Linnaea 1: 549. 1826.

Scape slender, 3'-7' high, leafless, or sometimes with a single sessile oval leaf near the base. Basal leaves short-petioled, membranous, ovate or oval, narrowed or sometimes cordate at the base, 3"-12" long; flower 4"-5" broad, calyx-lobes oblong, equalling or slightly shorter than the elliptic white 3-5-veined sessile petals; staminodia 3-5 at the base of each petal, rather slender, united below.

Quebec to Labrador, Alaska, Alberta and Wyoming. Summer.

4. Parnassia palústris L. Marsh or Northern Grass-of-Parnassus. Fig. 2148.

Parnassia palustris L. Sp. Pl. 273. 1753.

Scape slender, 3'-12' high, bearing a clasping ovate leaf below the middle, or rarely leafless. Basal leaves slender-petioled, ovate, obtuse at the apex, usually cordate at the base, 9"-18" long; flower 6"-12" broad; calyx ¼-⅓ shorter than the elliptic few-veined sessile petals; staminodia 9-15 at the base of each petal, slender, united below.

In wet places, Newfoundland, Quebec and Labrador to the Canadian Rocky Mountains and Alaska, south to Minnesota, Michigan, North Dakota, and in the Rocky Mountains to Wyoming. Also in Europe and Asia. July-Sept.

5. Parnassia parviflòra DC. Small-flowered Grass-of-Parnassus. Fig. 2149.

Parnassia parviflora DC. Prodr. 1: 320. 1824.

Scape 4'-12' high, very slender, usually bearing a clasping oval leaf at about the middle. Basal leaves petioled, oval or ovate, narrowed at the base, not cordate, 6"-12" long; flower 4"-8" broad; sepals equalling or somewhat shorter than the elliptic sessile petals; staminodia 5-7 at the base of each petal, slender, united below.

In wet places, Newfoundland and Labrador to Alaska, Quebec, Michigan, Wisconsin, and in the Rocky Mountains to Colorado and Utah. July-Sept.

6. Parnassia asarifòlia Vent. Kidney-leaved Grass-of-Parnassus.
Fig. 2150.

Parnassia asarifolia Vent. Jard. Malm. *pl. 39.*
1803.

Scape 10'–20' high, bearing a clasping nearly orbicular leaf at about the middle. Basal leaves long-petioled, orbicular or much broader than long, rounded, broadly kidney-shaped at the base, often 2'–3' wide; flower about 1' broad; calyx-lobes oval, much shorter than the strongly veined elliptic petals, which are rather abruptly narrowed into a claw; staminodia 3 in each set, slender, about the length of the stamens, or somewhat shorter, distinct to the base.

3⁄5

In wet places, mountains of Virginia, West Virginia, North Carolina and South Carolina. July–Sept.

Family 47. **SAXIFRAGÀCEAE** Dumort. Anal. Fam. 36. 1829.*

SAXIFRAGE FAMILY.

Herbs with basal or alternate or opposite leaves. Flowers perfect or polygamo-dioecious, solitary, racemose, cymose or paniculate. Calyx 5-lobed or 5-parted (rarely 4–12-lobed or parted), free, or adnate to the ovary, usually persistent. Petals usually 4 or 5, rarely none. Stamens equal in number or twice as many as the petals, in apetalous species as many or twice as many as the calyx-lobes, perigynous or epigynous; filaments distinct. Disk generally present. Carpels 1–several, often 2, distinct or united, mostly fewer than the stamens; styles as many as the carpels or cavities of the ovary. Fruit a capsule or follicle. Seeds commonly numerous; endosperm generally copious, fleshy; embryo small, terete.

About 90 genera and 650 species, of wide geographic distribution, mainly natives of the temperate zones, rare in the tropics.

Large herbs; leaves 3-ternate; flowers polygamous.   **1.** *Astilbe.*
Small herbs; leaves simple, entire, toothed or cleft, or 3-foliolate.
  Placentae axial; carpels equal or nearly so.
    Stamens 10.
      Calyx-tube only slightly developed, unchanged at maturity; or if slightly accrescent, then flat or flattish and plants acaulescent.
        Leaves opposite, except sometimes on flower-stalks.   **2.** *Antiphylla.*
        Leaves alternate, sometimes all basal.
          Plants caulescent.   **3.** *Leptasea.*
          Plants acaulescent.
            Corolla essentially regular, the petals about equal in length and shape.
                 4. *Micranthes.*
            Corolla irregular, except sometimes that of the terminal flower, three of the petals with blades of an ovate-lanceolate or sagittate type, and two of them narrower and longer.   **5.** *Hydatica.*
      Calyx-tube well-developed, and accrescent, at maturity longer than the lobes.
        Plants without caudices, only producing annual flowering stems. **6.** *Saxifraga.*
        Plants with perennial leafy caudices, often with offsets, the flowering stem very different from the caudex.
          Leaves of the caudex with lobed blades, the margins poreless. **7.** *Muscaria.*
          Leaves of the caudex with serrate blades, each tooth with an encrusted pore.
                 8. *Chondrosea.*
    Stamens 5.
      Calyx-lobes valvate; petals deciduous; seeds wingless.   **9.** *Therofon.*
      Calyx-lobes imbricated; petals persistent; seeds winged.   **10.** *Sullivantia.*

*Revised for this edition by DR. JOHN KUNKEL SMALL.

Placentae almost basal; carpels very unequal.

Placentae parietal; carpels equal or nearly so.

    Flowers in elongated racemes or panicles.

        Petals entire or erose.

        Petals pinnately cleft or parted.

    Flowers solitary and axillary to leaf-like bracts or 2–4 together and each subtended by a leaf-like bract.

        11. *Tiarella.*

        12. *Heuchera.*
        13. *Mitella.*

        14. *Chrysosplenium.*

1. ASTÍLBE Hamilt.; D. Don. Prodr. Fl. Nepal. 210. 1825.

Erect perennial herbs, with large 2–3-ternate leaves, and small spicate polygamous flowers in terminal panicles. Calyx campanulate, 4–5-lobed. Petals 4–5 (in our species), linear-spatulate, inserted at the base of the calyx. Stamens 8–10, all perfect, inserted with the petals; filaments elongated. Ovary superior or nearly so, 2–3-celled, deeply 2–3-lobed; styles 2–3; stigmas obtuse; ovules · ∞. Capsule 2–3-lobed, separating into 2–3 follicle-like carpels, each usually few-seeded. Seeds small, the testa loose, tapering at each end. [Greek, without brightness.]

About 7 species, natives of eastern North America, eastern Asia and the Himalayas. Besides the following another species occurs in the southern Alleghanies. Type species: *Astilbe rivulàris* D. Don.

1. Astilbe biternàta (Vent.) Britton. False Goat's Beard. Astilbe. Fig. 2151.

Tiarella biternata Vent. Jard. Malm.
   pl. 54. 1803.
Spiraea Aruncus var. *hermaphrodita*
   Michx. Fl. Bor. Am. 1: 294. 1803.
Astilbe decandra D. Don, Prodr. Fl.
   Nepal. 211. 1825.
Astilbe biternata Britton, Bull. Torr.
   Club 20: 475. 1893.

Erect, 3°–6° high, more or less pubescent. Leaves petioled, 2–3-ternately compound, often 2° broad; leaflets thin, stalked, ovate, cordate, truncate or rounded at the base, the lateral ones usually oblique, acuminate at the apex, sharply serrate or incised, 2′–5′ long; panicles often 1° long; flowers sessile or nearly so, about 2″ broad, yellowish white; petals of the staminate flowers spatulate, those of the perfect ones much smaller or none; stamens 10; follicles 2, acute, glabrous, about 1½″ long.

In woods, mountains of Virginia to North Carolina, Georgia and Tennessee. Plant with the aspect of *Aruncus*. June.

2. ANTIPHÝLLA Haw. Saxifr. Enum. 43. 1821.

Perennial densely matted herbs, with copiously leafy stems and sterile branches, naked or sparingly leafy flower-stalks and opposite (except sometimes on the flower-stalks) often 4-ranked imbricated broad keeled ciliate leaves each with an almost apical pore, the flowers solitary, erect. Calyx-lobes 5, strongly ciliate. Corolla mostly blue or purple, sometimes white, regular, the petals much longer than the calyx, narrowed into claw-like bases. Stamens 10; filaments subulate to triangular. Ovary less than one-half inferior, the carpels united to above the middle. Follicles erect, except the more or less spreading tips. [Greek, opposite leaved.]

About 4 species, natives of northern regions. Type species: *Saxifraga oppositifolia* L.

1. Antiphylla oppositifòlia (L.) Fourr.   Purple or Mountain Saxifrage. Fig. 2152.

Saxifraga oppositifolia L. Sp. Pl. 402. 1753.

Antiphylla oppositifolia Fourr. Ann. Soc. Linn. Lyons II. 16: 386. 1868.

Tufted, stems prostrate, densely leafy, 2'-10' long. Leaves sessile, ovate, obovate or nearly orbicular, purplish, persistent, keeled, fleshy, opposite, or imbricated in 4 rows on the sterile shoots, obtuse, punctate with 1-3 pores, 1"-2½" long, the margins ciliate; flowers solitary, peduncled or nearly sessile, 4"-6" broad; calyx-lobes obtuse, much shorter than the obovate purple petals; calyx free from the ovary and capsule; follicles abruptly short-pointed; seeds rugose.

On wet rocks, Mt. Mansfield and Willoughby Mountain, Vt.; Anticosti, Newfoundland and throughout arctic America to Alaska, south in the Rocky Mountains to Wyoming and to Oregon. Also in Europe and Asia. Summer.

3. LEPTÀSEA Haw. Saxifr. Enum. 39. 1821.

Perennial, gregarious or matted herbs, with copiously leafy caudices and offsets and less leafy flower-stalks, and alternate fleshy or parchment-like entire or 3-pronged leaves, the flowers solitary or in terminal simple or compound cymes. Calyx-lobes 5, often spreading or reflexed. Corolla white or yellow, regular, the petals with claw-like bases or claws. Stamens 10; filaments subulate or clavate. Ovary almost superior, the carpels united to above the middle. Follicles erect, except for the more or less spreading tips. [Greek, referring to the small size of the plant.]

About 18 species, natives of boreal regions and the higher mountains of North America, Europe and Asia. Type species: *Saxifraga aizoides* L.

Leaves entire.
  Flowers typically solitary or 2 together ; calyx-lobes ciliate.   1. *L. Hirculus.*
  Flowers typically several ; calyx-lobes eciliate.   2. *L. aizoides.*
Leaves 3-pronged at the apex.   3. *L. tricuspidata.*

1. Leptasea Hírculus (L.) Small. Yellow Marsh Saxifrage. Fig. 2153.

Saxifraga Hirculus L. Sp. Pl. 402. 1753.

Leptasea Hirculus Small, N. A. Flora 22²: 152. 1905.

Erect from a slender caudex, glabrous or somewhat pubescent, simple, leafy, 4'-10' high. Leaves alternate, oblong or linear-oblong, entire, ½'-1½' long, the lower petioled, the upper sessile; flower terminal, solitary (rarely 2-4), bright yellow with scarlet spots, ½'-1' broad; calyx-lobes oval or oblong, obtuse, reflexed; petals erect or ascending, obovate or oblong, about 3 times as long as the calyx-lobes; capsule free from the calyx or nearly so, about 4" long, its beaks at length diverging.

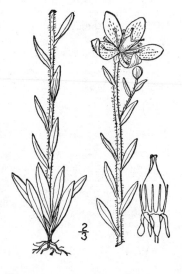

In bogs, Labrador and arctic America. Also in northern and alpine Europe and Asia. Summer.

2. Leptasea aizoìdes (L.) Haw. Yellow Mountain Saxifrage. Fig. 2154.

?Saxifraga autumnalis L. Sp. Pl. 402. 1753.

Saxifraga aizoides L. Sp. Pl. 403. 1753.

Leptasea aizoides Haw. Saxifr. Enum. 40. 1821.

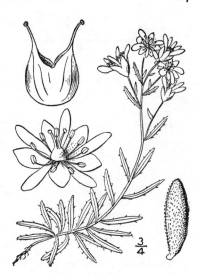

Tufted, glabrous, stems leafy, 2'-6' high. Leaves alternate, linear, thick, fleshy, mucronate-tipped, narrowed at the base, sessile, 4"-9" long, 1"-1½" wide, the margins often sparingly ciliate; flowers several, corymbose, 4"-7" broad; pedicels rather slender; petals oblong, yellow and sometimes spotted with orange, exceeding the ovate-oblong calyx-lobes; carpels abruptly acuminate; base of the capsule adnate to the calyx; seeds minutely rugose.

On wet rocks, Newfoundland and Labrador to Vermont and western New York, west through arctic America to the Rocky Mountains, south to Michigan. Also in alpine and arctic Europe and Asia. Summer. Also called sengreen saxifrage.

3. Leptasea tricuspidàta (Retz.) Haw. Three-toothed Saxifrage. Fig. 2155.

Saxifraga tricuspidata Retz, Prodr. Fl. Scand. Ed. 2, 104. 1795.

Leptasea tricuspidata Haw. Saxifr. Enum. 39. 1821.

Tufted, flowering stems strict, erect, 2'-8' high, the leaves densely clustered at the base, oblong or oblong-spatulate, parchment-like, 4"-7" long, sharply 2-3-dentate at the apex, narrowed at the base, sessile, the margins ciliate with short hairs; scapes bracted; flowers several, corymbose, yellow, 4"-5" broad; sepals ovate, coriaceous, obtusish, much shorter than the oblong-obovate or narrowly oblong petals; capsule tipped with the diverging styles, its lower part adnate to the calyx.

In rocky places, Newfoundland and Labrador to Hudson Bay, west through arctic America to Alaska, south to Lake Superior and in the Canadian Rocky Mountains. Also in arctic Europe. Summer.

4. MICRÁNTHES Haw. Syn. Pl. Succ. 320. 1812.

Perennial herbs, with short leafy caudices and solitary or clustered scapes, and basal entire or toothed leaves, the flowers in terminal compact or open compound cymes. Calyx-lobes 5, erect or reflexed. Corolla white or mainly so, essentially regular, the petals clawless or rarely clawed. Stamens 10; filaments subulate or clavate. Ovary slightly inferior, the carpels slightly united. Follicles spreading or with spreading tips. [Greek, small-flower.]

About 65 species, natives of the north temperate and boreal parts of both hemispheres. Type species: *Micranthes semipubescens* Haw.

Filaments subulate or filiform-subulate; petals not yellow-blotched.
Cymules wholly or mainly aggregated into a head; follicles red.   1. *M. nivalis.*
Cymules in pyramidal or corymb-like panicles; follicles green.
    Corolla white; petals broad; calyx-lobes not reflexed at maturity.
      Cymules permanently compact; petals not twice exceeding the calyx.
           2. *M. texana.*
      Cymules ultimately lax; petals more than twice exceeding the calyx.
           3. *M. virginiensis.*
    Corolla greenish; petals narrow; calyx-lobes reflexed at maturity.   4. *M. pennsylvanica.*
Filaments clavate; petals yellow-blotched.
    Leaves with elongated blades.
           5. *M. micranthidifolia.*
    Leaves with short or suborbicular blades.
      Leaf-blades narrowed at the base; neither cordate nor of an orbicular type.
           6. *M. caroliniana.*
      Leaf-blades cordate at the base, orbicular or nearly so.   7. *M. Geum.*

3/4

1. Micranthes nivàlis (L.) Small. Clustered Alpine Saxifrage. Fig. 2156.

Saxifraga nivalis L. Sp. Pl. 401. 1753.
Micranthes nivalis Small, N. A. Flora 22²: 136. 1905.

Seldom over 6' high. Scape viscid, naked, or bracted at the base of the capitate sometimes branched inflorescence; leaves ovate or oval, narrowed into a margined petiole, thick; flowers white, 3''-5'' broad, in a compact cluster; calyx-lobes ovate or oblong, spreading, obtuse, about one-half the length of the oblong or oblong-ovate petals; ovary half-inferior; follicles deep purple, divergent.

Labrador and arctic America, south in the Rocky Mountains to Arizona. Also in northern and alpine Europe and Siberia. Summer. Said to flower beneath the snow.

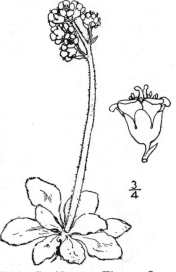

3/4

2. Micranthes texàna (Buckl.) Small. Texan Saxifrage. Fig. 2157.

Saxifraga texana Buckl. Proc. Acad. Phila. 1861: 455. 1862.
Micranthes texana Small, Fl. SE. U. S. 501. 1903.

Scape sparingly pubescent up to the inflorescence, 2'-7' high. Leaves ovate to obovate, narrowed into broad petioles, entire or shallowly toothed, ½-2½' long; inflorescence with the branches ending in congested cymules; flowers white, regular, 2''-3'' broad; calyx-lobes erect, broadly oblong to ovate, somewhat shorter than the suborbicular or obovate petals; follicles erect or nearly so.

On hillsides or in sandy barrens, Missouri and Texas. March–April.

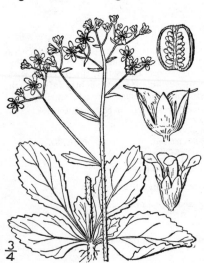

3/4

3. Micranthes virginiénsis (Michx.) Small. Early Saxifrage. Fig. 2158.

Saxifraga virginiensis Michx. Fl. Bor. Am. 1: 260. 1803.
Micranthes virginiensis Small, Fl. SE. U. S. 501. 1903.

Scape viscid-pubescent, 4'-12' high, naked, or with a few bracts at the base of the pedicels. Leaves obovate, or oval with a spatulate base, narrowed into a margined petiole, dentate or crenate, obtuse or acutish at the apex, 1'-3' long or longer; inflorescence cymose, at length loose and paniculate with the lower peduncles elongated; flowers white, regular, 2''-3'' broad; calyx-lobes erect, triangular or triangular-ovate, much shorter than the oblong-spatulate, obtuse petals; ovary nearly free from the calyx; carpels nearly separate, the follicles at length widely divergent.

In dry or rocky woodlands, New Brunswick to Minnesota, south to Georgia and Tennessee. Ascends to 3500 ft. in Virginia. March–May. Forms with 15 stamens occur on New York Island, and with green petals in Essex Co., Mass. Spring-saxifrage. May-flower. Sweet wilson. Everlasting.

4. Micranthes pennsylvánica (L.) Haw. Pennsylvania or Swamp Saxifrage. Fig. 2159.

S. pennsylvanica L. Sp. Pl. 399. 1753.
Saxifraga Forbesii Vasey, Am. Entom. & Bot.
2 : 288. 1870.
M. pennsylvanica Haw. Saxifr. Enum. 45. 1821.

Scape stout, terete, viscid-pubescent, 1°–3½° high, bracted at the inflorescence. Leaves large, oval, ovate, obovate or ob-lanceolate, pubescent or glabrate, 4′–10′ long, 1½′–3′ wide, obtuse at the apex, nar-rowed at the base into a broad petiole, the margins denticulate or repand; cymes in an elongated open panicle; flowers greenish, regular, 1½″–2½″ broad; calyx-tube nearly free from the ovary, its lobes ovate, ob-tusish, reflexed, one-half shorter than the lanceolate or linear-lanceolate petals; fila-ments subulate or filiform; follicles ovoid, their tips divergent when mature.

Swamps and wet banks, Maine to Ontario, Minnesota, Virginia, Iowa and Missouri. May.

5. Micranthes micranthidifòlia (Haw.) Small. Lettuce Saxifrage. Fig. 2160.

Robertsonia micranthidifolia Haw. Syn. Pl. Succ.
322. 1812.
Saxifraga erosa Pursh, Fl. Am. Sept. 311. 1814.
S. micranthidifolia B.S.P. Prel. Cat. N. Y. 17. 1888.
M. micranthidifolia Small, Fl. SE. U. S. 501. 1903.

Scape rather slender, more or less viscid, 1°–3° high, bracted above. Leaves oblanceo-late or oval, sometimes 1° long, obtuse at the apex, tapering downward into a long margined petiole, coarsely and sharply den-tate; panicle loose, elongated; flowers white, regular, 2″–3″ broad; calyx-lobes reflexed, slightly shorter than the oval or oblong ob-tuse petals; calyx-tube free from the ovary; filaments club-shaped; follicles lanceolate, sharp-pointed, 2″–3″ long, their tips at length divergent.

In cold brooks, Bethlehem, Pa., south along the mountains to North Carolina. May–June.

6. Micranthes caroliniàna (A. Gray) Small. Gray's Saxifrage. Fig. 2161.

Saxifraga caroliniana A. Gray, Mem. Am.
Acad. 3 : 39. 1846.
Saxifraga Grayana Britton, Mem. Torr. Club
5 : 178. 1894.
M. caroliniana Small, N. A. Flora 22²: 146. 1905.

Glandular-pilose all over, scapose from a corm-like rootstock, scape 6′–18′ tall. Basal leaves clustered, oblong, oval or nearly orbicular, 1′–5′ long, crenate-den-tate, narrowed into margined petioles, mostly shorter than the blade and dilated at the base; inflorescence cymose-panicu-late, ample; bracts spatulate or lanceolate; flowers white, 4″–5″ broad; calyx-tube adnate to the ovary, its segments ovate-oblong, reflexed, obtuse; petals ovate or oblong-ovate, obtuse, 2-spotted, narrowed into a slender claw; filaments club-shaped; follicles oblong, 2″–3″ long, united only at the base, diverging; styles subulate.

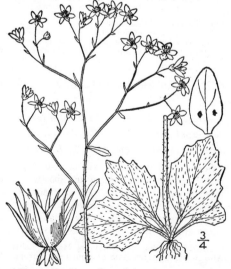

In rocky situations, mountains of Virginia and North Carolina. June–July.

7. Micranthes Gèum (L.) Small. Kidney-leaved Saxifrage. Fig. 2162.

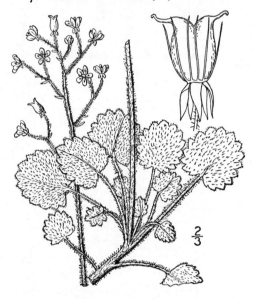

Saxifraga Geum L. Sp. Pl. 401. 1753.

M. Geum Small, N. A. Flora 22²: 148. 1905.

Densely glandular-pubescent, scapose, scape erect, 3′-10′ high. Leaves all clustered at the base, cordate, kidney-shaped or orbicular, ½′-1′ wide, coarsely crenate all around, borne on stout densely pubescent petioles 1′-2½′ long; inflorescence terminal, paniculate; bracts small, linear, obtuse; branches of the panicle ascending, 2-6-flowered; flowers 2″-3″ broad; petals white, oblong or ovate-oblong, with a yellow spot at the base and several smaller purplish spots at the middle; calyx-lobes lanceolate or ovate-lanceolate, reflexed; capsule oblong, its beaks slightly divergent.

Newfoundland and in the mountainous parts of Europe. June–July.

5. HYDÁTICA Neck.; S. F. Gray, Nat. Arr. Brit. Pl. 2: 530. 1821.

SPATULARIA Haw. Saxifr. Enum. 47. 1821. Not Pers. 1791.

Perennial herbs, with leafy caudices and solitary or tufted scapes and basal usually spatulate toothed leaves, the flowers in open panicled cymes, their parts sometimes changed into bulblets. Calyx-lobes 5, reflexed. Corolla white or mainly so, irregular, the petals all clawed, the 3 upper with ovate, lanceolate or sagittate blades, the 2 lower ones with elliptic or spatulate blades, or in plants that bear terminal flowers, the lower petals somewhat simulate the upper ones. Stamens 10; filaments subulate. Ovary chiefly superior, the carpels united at the base or to below the middle. Follicles erect, except the ascending or diverging tips. [Greek, referring to the turgid follicles.]

About 12 species, natives of the north temperate and boreal parts of both hemispheres. Type species: Saxifraga leucanthemifolia Michx.

Inflorescence with bulblets.   1. H. foliolosa.
Inflorescence without bulblets.
   Primary bracts of the inflorescence not leaf-like; petals stout-clawed.   2. H. stellaris.
   Primary bracts of the inflorescence leaf-like; petals slender-clawed.   3. H. petiolaris.

1. Hydatica foliolòsa (R. Br.) Small. Foliose Saxifrage. Fig. 2163.

Saxifraga stellaris var. comosa Poir. in Lam. Encycl. 6: 680. 1804.

Saxifraga foliolosa R. Br. in Parry's Voy. 275. 1824.

Saxifraga comosa Britton, Mem. Torr. Club 5: 178. 1894.

Scape slender, slightly viscid, 2′-6′ high. Leaves oblanceolate, cuneate at the base, dentate and mostly obtuse at the apex, 4″-9″ long; flowers few, white, regular, many or sometimes all of them replaced by little tuftes of leaves; calyx nearly free from the ovary, its lobes reflexed, much shorter than the sagittate obtusish petals which are narrowed into a claw, or sometimes cordate at the base.

In rocky places, Mt. Katahdin, Maine; Labrador and arctic America. Also in northeastern Asia and northern Europe. Summer.

2. Hydatica stellàris (L.) S. F. Gray. Star or Starry Saxifrage. Fig. 2164.

Saxifraga stellaris L. Sp. Pl. 400. 1753.

Hydatica stellaris S. F. Gray, Nat. Am. Brit. Pl. **2** : 530. 1821.

Scape naked below, bracted at the inflorescence, glabrous or slightly viscid, 4′–12′ high. Leaves oblong, oblanceolate or obovate, sharply and coarsely dentate, tapering into a broad petiole, ½′–2′ long; flowers loosely cymose-paniculate, regular, about 5″ broad; petals white, yellow-spotted at the base; calyx nearly free from the ovary, its lobes reflexed, lanceolate, obtusish, about one-half the length of the oblong acutish petals, which are narrowed into a short claw; capsule 2″–3″ long, its tips acuminate, at length somewhat divergent.

In rocky places, reported from Labrador and Greenland. Also in arctic and alpine Europe and Asia. Kidneywort. Summer.

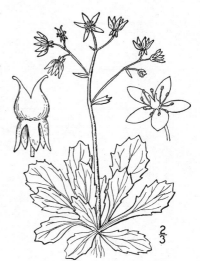

3. Hydatica petiolàris (Raf.) Small. Michaux's Saxifrage. Fig. 2165.

Saxifraga leucanthemifolia Michx. Fl. Bor. Am. **1** : 268. 1803. Not LePeyr. 1803.
Hexaphoma petiolaris Raf. Fl. Tell. **2** : 67. 1836.
Saxifraga Michauxii Britton, Mem. Torr. Club **4** : 118. 1894.
Spatularia petiolaris Small, N. A. Flora **22²** : 150. 1905.
H. petiolaris Small, Fl. SE. U. S. Ed. 2, 760. 1911.

Erect, viscid-pubescent, 6′–20′ high. Basal leaves clustered, oblanceolate or oblong, acute or obtuse at the apex, 3′–7′ long, narrowed into a margined petiole, coarsely and deeply dentate; flowering stem naked below, leafy-bracted above; inflorescence widely paniculate; flowers 2″–3″ broad, irregular; petals clawed, white, the 3 larger ones sagittate or truncate and usually with a pair of yellowish spots at the base, the outer 2 spatulate and unspotted, narrowed at the base; calyx-tube free from the ovary, its lobes reflexed; follicles lanceolate, sharppointed, little divaricate, about 2½″ long.

In dry rocky places, mountain summits of Virginia to Georgia. May–Sept.

6. SAXÍFRAGA [Tourn.] L. Sp. Pl. 398. 1753.

Perennial herbs, with flowering stems arising from the small rootstocks and alternate, entire or 3–7-lobed leaves. The flowers solitary or in terminal cymes, rarely represented by bulblets. Calyx-lobes 5, erect, usually with a terminal gland. Corolla white, regular, the petals somewhat narrowed at the base, but usually clawless. Stamens 10; filaments subulate. Ovary about one-half inferior, the carpels united to about the middle. Follicles well united, erect, except the more or less spreading tips, partly included in the calyx-tube. [Greek, stone-breaking, from reputed medicinal qualities.]

About 20 species, most abundant in the cooler parts of the northern hemisphere. Type species: *Saxifraga granulata* L.

Flowers below the terminal nodding flower replaced by bulblets; petals 4″–5″ long.   1. *S. cernua.*
Flowers not replaced by bulblets; petals about 2″ long.   2. *S. rivularis.*

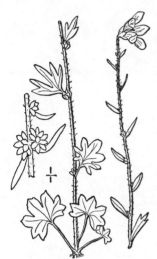

1. Saxifraga cérnua L. Nodding or Drooping Bulbous Saxifrage. Fig. 2166.

Saxifraga cernua L. Sp. Pl. 403. 1753.

Stem weak, slender, ascending, pubescent but scarcely glutinous, 4'-12' long. Leaves alternate, the basal and lower ones petioled, broadly reniform, palmately 5-7-lobed, usually less than 1' wide; upper leaves smaller, sessile, 3-lobed or entire and bract-like, often bearing small bulblets in their axils; flowers 1-3, terminal, nodding, white, 8"-10" broad; petals obovate, sometimes retuse, 3-4 times as long as the ovate calyx-lobes.

Newfoundland, Labrador, and through arctic America to Alaska. Also in arctic and alpine Europe and Asia. Summer.

2. Saxifraga rivulàris L. Alpine Brook Saxifrage. Fig. 2167.

Saxifraga rivularis L. Sp. Pl. 404. 1753.

Densely tufted, glabrous or sparingly pubescent, matted, 1'-3' high. Leaves alternate, the basal and lower ones slender-petioled, reniform, 3-5-lobed, seldom more than 3" wide; petioles dilated at the base; upper leaves lanceolate or ovate, entire or slightly lobed, mainly sessile; flowers 1-5, terminal, erect, white, about 3"-5" broad; calyx-lobes ovate, obtuse, slightly shorter than the ovate-oblong petals; tips of the capsule widely divergent, its base adnate to the calyx.

Alpine summits of the White Mountains, Labrador, arctic America and south in the Rocky Mountains to Colorado. Also in arctic and alpine Europe and Asia. Summer.

7. MUSCÀRIA Haw. Saxifr. Enum. 36. 1821.

Perennial low herbs, with densely tufted or matted copiously leafy caudices, sparingly leafy flower-stems, and alternate, 3-lobed or rarely 5-7-lobed leaves, the flowers solitary or few together in terminal cymes. Sepals 5, erect. Corolla white, regular, the petals relatively broad, clawless. Stamens 10; filaments subulate. Ovary about one-half inferior, the carpels united to above the middle. Follicles erect, except the sometimes slightly spreading tips, mostly included in the calyx-tube. [Latin, referring to the moss-like growth of the plants.]

About 35 species, most abundant on high mountains and in boreal regions. Type species: *Saxifraga muscoides* Wulf.

1. Muscaria caespitòsa (L.) Haw. Tufted Saxifrage. Fig. 2168.

Saxifraga caespitosa L. Sp. Pl. 404. 1753.

Muscaria caespitosa Haw. Saxifr. Enum. 37. 1821.

Densely tufted, leaves clustered at the base, spatulate or fan-shaped, 3"-9" long, deeply 3-5-cleft or lobed into linear obtuse segments, glabrous; flowering stem erect, 2'-8' high, viscid-pubescent, at least above, linear-bracted or with several 3-lobed leaves; flowers 1-8, corymbose, 4"-7" broad, white; calyx-lobes ovate-oblong, obtuse or obtusish, much shorter than the obovate petals; capsule-tips divergent; base of the capsule adnate to the calyx.

On rocks, Quebec, Labrador and Newfoundland, west through arctic America to Alaska, south to Oregon and in the Rocky Mountains to Colorado. Also in arctic and alpine Europe and Siberia. Summer.

8. CHONDRÒSEA Haw. Saxifr. Enum. 10. 1821.

Perennial herbs, with densely leafy short caudices and offsets and sparingly leafy flower-stems, and alternate serrate leaves with each tooth white-encrusted, the flowers in terminal compound cymes. Calyx-lobes 5, erect. Corolla white or sometimes colored, regular, the petals broad, clawless. Stamens 10; filaments lanceolate to lanceolate-subulate. Ovary about one-half inferior, the carpels united to above the middle. Follicles united up to the more or less spreading tips. [Greek, referring to the texture of the leaves.]

About 9 species, most abundant in the mountains of middle Europe. Type species: *Chondrosea pyramidalis* Haw.

1. Chondrosea Aizòon (Jacq.) Haw. Livelong Saxifrage. Fig. 2169.

Saxifraga Aizoon Jacq. Fl. Austr. 5: 18. *pl. 438.* 1778.
Chondrosea Aizoon Haw. Saxifr. Enum. 11. 1821.

Leaves clustered in a dense rosette at the base of the bracted flowering stem; plant spreading by offsets, so that several are often joined together. Leaves 4″-12″ long, spatulate, thick, obtuse and rounded at the apex, the margins serrulate with sharp hard white teeth; scape erect, viscid-pubescent, 4′-10′ high; flowers several or numerous, corymbose, yellowish, about 3″ broad; calyx-lobes ovate-oblong, obtuse, viscid, shorter than the obovate, often spotted petals; capsule tipped by the divergent styles, its base adnate to the calyx.

On dry rocks, Mt. Mansfield, Vermont; Quebec to Labrador, west to Lake Superior and Manitoba. Also in alpine and arctic Europe. Summer.

9. THÉROFON Raf. New Fl. N. A. 4: 66. 1836.

[Boykinia Nutt. Journ. Acad. Phila. 7: 113. 1834. Not Raf.]

Glandular-pubescent perennial herbs, with alternate petioled orbicular or reniform leaves, and small white perfect flowers in branching panicles. Calyx-tube top-shaped or subglobose, adnate to the ovary, its limb 5-lobed. Petals 5, deciduous, inserted on the calyx-tube. Filaments short. Ovary 2-celled (rarely 3-celled); styles 2, rarely 3. Capsule 2-celled, the beaks of the carpels divergent. Seeds numerous, the testa shining, minutely punctate. [Greek, beast-killing; an old name of aconite.]

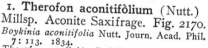

About 10 species, natives of the southern Alleghanies and the mountains of western North America. Type species: *Boykinia aconitifolia* Nutt.

1. Therofon aconitifòlium (Nutt.) Millsp. Aconite Saxifrage. Fig. 2170.

Boykinia aconitifolia Nutt. Journ. Acad. Phil. 7: 113. 1834.
Therofon napelloides Raf. New Fl. 4: 66. 1836.
Saxifraga aconitifolia Field. Sert. Pl. *pl. 57.* 1844.
Therofon aconitifolium Millsp. Bull. West Va. Agric. Exp. Sta. 2: 561. 1892.

Stem rather stout, erect, 1°-2° high. Lower and basal leaves long-petioled, reniform-orbicular, cordate or truncate at the base, slightly scabrous above, glabrous or with a few scale-like hairs along the veins beneath, palmately 5-7-lobed, the lobes obovate or oval, sharply incised-serrate; upper leaves short-petioled; bracts of the inflorescence foliaceous, incised; cymes panicled; pedicels and calyx viscid; flowers white, about 2″ broad; calyx-lobes lanceolate, erect; petals oblanceolate, spatulate at base; capsule adnate to the calyx-tube, only its divergent beaks free.

In woods, mountains of southwestern Virginia to North Carolina, Tennessee and Georgia. July.

10. SULLIVÁNTIA T. & G. Am. Journ. Sci. 42: 22. 1842.

Slender perennial herbs, with mainly basal long-petioled reniform-orbicular crenate or slightly lobed leaves, and small white cymose-paniculate flowers. Calyx-tube campanulate, adnate to the base of the ovary, its limb 5-lobed, the lobes erect. Petals 5, spatulate, marcescent. Stamens 5, inserted at the base of the calyx-lobes. Filaments short. Ovary 2-celled, 2-beaked, ripening into a 2-beaked capsule. Styles 2. Ovules ∞. Seeds winged on both sides. [Named in honor of William Starling Sullivant, 1803–1873, American botanist.]

Four known species, the following of eastern North America, the others of the western States. Type species: *Saxifraga Sullivantii* T. & G.

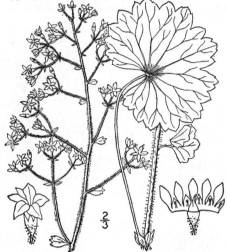

$\frac{2}{3}$

1. Sullivantia Sullivántii (T. & G.) Britton. Sullivantia. Fig. 2171.

Saxifraga (?) *Sullivantii* T. & G. Fl. N. A. 1: 575. 1840.
S. ohionis T. & G. Am. Journ. Sci. 42: 22. 1842.
Sullivantia Sullivantii Britton, Mem. Torr. Club 5: 178. 1894.

Stem scapose, nearly leafless, weak, re-clined, slightly glandular-pubescent, 6′–15′ long. Leaves long-petioled, 1′–3′ wide, and wider than long, reniform-cordate at the base, crenate-dentate or somewhat lobed, sparingly pubescent or glabrous; panicle ample, sometimes leafy-bracted, loose, glandular; pedicels slender, recurved in fruit; flowers white, about 2″ broad; calyx-lobes ovate, not nerved, acutish; petals spatulate, entire, exceeding the stamens.

On cliffs, Ohio and Indiana. June.

Sullivantia Hapemanii (Coult. & Fisher) Coulter, with 3-nerved calyx-lobes and obo-vate or oval-rhombic petal-blades, has been found in Wisconsin and Minnesota and ranges to Wyoming and Colorado.

11. TIARÉLLA L. Sp. Pl. 405. 1753.

Perennial slender erect herbs, with the leaves mainly basal, long-petioled, lobed or 3-foliolate, small stipules adnate to the petiole, and white pedicelled racemose or paniculate flowers. Calyx-tube campanulate, nearly or quite free from the base of the ovary, its limb 5-lobed. Petals 5, clawed. Stamens 10; filaments elongated. Ovary 1-celled; styles 2; ovules ∞. Capsule membranous, 1-celled, 2-valved, the valves usually unequal. Seeds usually few, ovoid or globose, smooth, not winged. [Diminutive of *tiara*, from the form of capsule.]

About 6 species, natives of North America, Japan and the Himalayas. Besides the following, and one in the southern Alleghanies, 5 others occur in the western parts of North America. Type species: *Tiarella cordifolia* L.

1. Tiarella cordifòlia L. Coolwort. False Mitrewort. Fig. 2172.

Tiarella cordifolia L. Sp. Pl. 405. 1753.

Scape 6′–12′ high, slender, pubescent. Leaves long-petioled, broadly ovate, or nearly orbicular, cordate at the base, 3–7-lobed, obtuse or acutish at the apex, 2′–4′ long, crenate or dentate all around, pubescent with scattered hairs above, glabrate or downy along the veins beneath; inflorescence simply racemose or the lowest pedicels sometimes branched, glandular-puberulent; flowers white, about 3″ broad; petals oblong, entire or slightly dentate, clawed, somewhat exceeding the white calyx-lobes; capsule reflexed, about 3″ long, its valves very unequal.

$\frac{3}{5}$

In rich moist woods, Nova Scotia to Ontario and Minnesota, south, especially along the mountains, to Georgia, Indiana and Michigan. Ascends to 5600 ft. in Virginia. White coolwort. Foam-flower. Gem-fruit. April–May.

12. HEÙCHERA L. Sp. Pl. 226. 1753.

Erect or ascending perennial herbs, with mainly basal long-petioled ovate or orbicular leaves, and small paniculate or racemose, white green or purple flowers, on naked or leafy-bracted scapes. Calyx-tube campanulate, often oblique, adnate to the base of the ovary, 5-lobed. Petals small, spatulate, often shorter than the calyx-lobes, entire, inserted on the throat of the calyx. Stamens 5, inserted with the petals. Ovary 1-celled; styles 2, slender. Ovules ∞. Capsule 2-valved, 2-beaked. Seeds minutely hispid or muricate. [Named for Johann Heinrich von Heucher, 1677–1747, a German botanist.]

About 70 species, natives of North America and Mexico. Type species : *Heuchera americana* L. Flowers regular or nearly so.
  Petals with long very slender claws and narrow blades, much exceeding the calyx.
    Leaves, at least the larger ones, low rounded lobes.
      Petioles villous ; calyx-lobes ovate, much shorter than the hypanthium during anthesis.
                                          1. *H. parviflora.*
      Petioles puberulent ; calyx-lobes broadly ovate, as long as the hypathium during anthesis
        or nearly so.   2. *H. puberula.*
    Leaves, at least the larger ones, with prominent angular lobes.
      Leaves deeply lobed, the terminal lobe longer than wide.   3. *H. villosa.*
      Leaves not deeply lobed, the terminal lobe broad and short.   4. *H. macrorhiza.*
  Petals with short claws and broad blades, shorter than the calyx or slightly longer.
    Petals as long as the calyx or shorter.   5. *H. americana.*
    Petals decidedly longer than the calyx.   6. *H. Curtisii.*
Flowers very irregular.
  Stamens long-exserted.   7. *H. hirsuticaulis.*
  Stamens slightly exserted or included.
    Flowering stem leafless ; flowers gibbous below near the base.
      Panicle narrow, strict ; stamens exserted.   8. *H. hispida.*
      Panicle wide, lax ; stamens included.   9. *H. longiflora.*
    Flowering stem leafy ; flowers not gibbous.   10. *H. pubescens.*

1. Heuchera parviflòra Bartl. Rugel's Heuchera. Fig. 2173.

Heuchera parviflora Bartl. Ind. Sem. Hort. Götting. 1838.—Linnaea 13: Litt. 96. 1839. *H. Rugelii* Shuttlw.; Kunze, Linnaea 20: 43. 1847.

Stems slender, 6'–24' long, weak, glandular-hirsute or villous, leafless or bearing a few leaves below. Basal leaves with long slender glandular-villous petioles, broadly reniform, 2'–5' wide, cordate at the base, with 7–9 broad rounded or rarely pointed lobes, crenately toothed, the teeth mucronate; inflorescence very loosely paniculate; flowering calyx regular, campanulate, about 1" long; petals linear-spatulate, 2–3 times as long as the calyx-lobes; stamens somewhat exserted.

Shaded cliffs, Missouri and Illinois to western Virginia and northern Georgia. July–Sept.

$\frac{3}{5}$

2. Heuchera pubérula Mackenzie & Bush. Puberulent Heuchera. Fig. 2174.

H. puberula Mackenzie & Bush, Rep. Mo. Bot. Gard. 16: 103. 1905.

Stems very slender, 4'–12' long, puberulent, leafless. Basal leaves with very slender puberulent petioles, suborbicular to reniform, 1'–2¾' wide, shallowly or deeply cordate at the base, with 5–9 rounded lobes and broad mucronate teeth, finely pubescent on both sides; inflorescence lax, few- or many-flowered; flowering calyx regular, campanulate or turbinate, about 1" long, the lobes broader and the tube relatively shorter than in *H. parviflora;* petals spatulate or linear-spatulate, about twice as long as the calyx-lobes; stamens exserted.

On bluffs, Kentucky and Missouri. July–Oct.

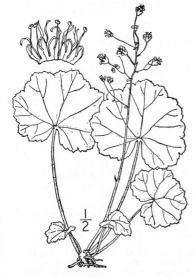

$\frac{1}{2}$

3. Heuchera villòsa Michx. Hairy Heuchera. Fig. 2175.

H. villosa Michx. Fl. Bor. Am. 1 : 172. 1803.

Stem erect, leafless, or rarely bearing a few small leaves below, generally villous-pubescent with brownish hairs, as are also the long petioles and the veins on the lower surfaces of the leaves. Basal leaves 3′–5′ wide, ovate to orbicular, sharply or obtusely and deeply 7–9-lobed, the lobes dentate or serrate, the terminal lobe usually longer than wide; flowering calyx 1″–1½″ long, campanulate, regular; petals linear-spatulate, white or nearly so, twice as long as the calyx-lobes or more; stamens much exserted.

In rocky places, Virginia, West Virginia and Kentucky to Georgia and Tennessee. June–Sept. Called also American sanicle.

4. Heuchera macrorhìza Small. Big-rooted Heuchera. Fig. 2176.

H. macrorhiza Small, Bull. Torr. Club 25 : 466. 1898.

Stem erect, usually leafless, stout, from a very thick scaly rootstock, densely villous or hirsute-villous with usually sordid hairs. Basal leaves, 3′–8′ wide, suborbicular in outline, shallowly lobed, with the terminal lobe usually wider than long, the teeth broad, mucronate; flowering calyx short-hairy, often larger than in *H. villosa*, regular; petals linear or nearly so, about twice as long as the calyx-lobes or less; stamens much-exserted.

On bluffs and river banks, West Virginia, Kentucky and Tennessee. July–Oct.

Heuchera crinìta Rydb., from Kentucky and adjacent states, seems to be a robust form of *H. macrorhiza.*

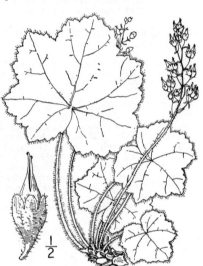

5. Heuchera americàna L. Alum-root. Fig. 2177.

Heuchera americana L. Sp. Pl. 226. 1753.

Stem rather stout, 2°–3° high, leafless, more or less glandular-hirsute. Basal leaves long-petioled, 3′–4′ wide, with 7–9 rounded crenate-dentate lobes, the older ones glabrous, or with scattered hairs on the upper surface; flowering calyx broadly campanulate, nearly regular, 1½″–3″ long; petals very small, greenish, usually not exceeding the calyx-lobes; stamens much exserted; anthers orange.

In dry or rocky woods, Ontario to Connecticut, west to Minnesota, south to Alabama and Louisiana. Ascends to 3000 ft. in Virginia. American sanicle. Common alum-root. May–Aug.

Heuchera lancipétala Rydb., from Kentucky, has a leafless flower-stem as in *H. americana;* but the petals are much longer than the calyx-lobes.

6. Heuchera Curtísii T. & G. Curtis' Heuchera. Fig. 2178.

H. Curtisii T. & G.; A. Gray, Am. Journ. Sci. **42**: 15. 1841.

H. roseola Rydb.; Britton, Man. 481. 1901.

Stem rather stout, 1°-3° high, leafy, glabrous below, puberulent above. Basal leaves ovate to suborbicular, 1¾'-9' wide, with rounded lobes and broad mucronate teeth, glabrous or sparingly pubescent and ciliate; flowering-calyx nearly regular, larger than in *H. americana;* petals purple or pink, usually much exceeding the calyx-lobes; stamens exserted.

In woods and on river bluffs, New York to Tennessee and South Carolina. May–July.

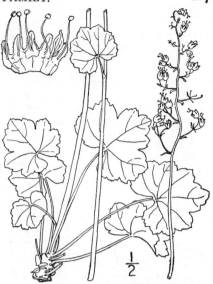

7. Heuchera hirsuticaùlis (Wheelock) Rydb. Rough-stemmed Heuchera. Fig. 2179.

H. hispida hirsuticaulis Wheelock, Bull. Torr. Club 17: 199. 1890.
Heuchera hirsuticaulis Rydb.; Britton, Man. 482. 1901.

Stem 1°-2½° tall, villous-hirsute, leafless. Leaves 1½'-3½' wide, on slender petioles which are pubescent like the stem, reniform to orbicular-ovate, with 7-11 rounded crenate-mucronate lobes; panicle lax, rather wide; flowering calyx campanulate, oblique, 2"-2½" long, its lobes unequal; petals broadly spatulate, equalling the calyx-lobes or shorter; stamens long-exserted.

In dry woods and on bluffs, Michigan to Missouri, Indiana and Arkansas. May–June.

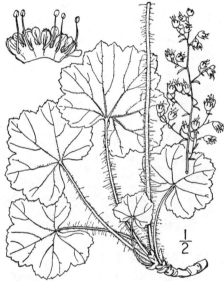

8. Heuchera híspida Pursh. Rough Heuchera. Fig. 2180.

H. hispida Pursh, Fl. Am. Sept. 188. 1814.

Heuchera Richardsonii R. Br. Frankl. Journ. 766. *pl. 29.* 1823.

Stem 2°-4° tall, hirsutely-pubescent or rarely nearly glabrous, usually leafless. Leaves 2'-3' wide, on long and slender petioles, broadly ovate-orbicular, with 5-9 shallow rounded dentate lobes; panicle strict, narrow; flowering calyx campanulate, very oblique, 3"-5" long, its lobes unequal; petals spatulate, slightly exceeding the calyx-lobes; stamens exserted.

In woods, Virginia to western Ontario, west to Kansas, Manitoba and Saskatchewan, south in the Rocky Mountains to Idaho. May–June.

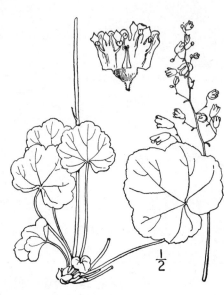

9. Heuchera longiflòra Rydb. Long-flowered Heuchera. Fig. 2181.

Heuchera longiflora Rydb.; Britton, Man. 482. 1901.

Stems $1\frac{1}{2}°-3°$ high, glabrous or hirsutulous above, leafless. Leaves long-petioled, orbicular-reniform to orbicular-ovate, $2'-4'$ wide, shallowly lobed and with very broad teeth; panicle lax, wide, with slender branches; flowering calyx $4''-5''$ long, oblique, the lobes unequal; petals rhombic-spatulate, equalling the calyx-lobes; stamens included.

On hillsides, Kentucky to Alabama. May–June.

10. Heuchera pubéscens Pursh. Downy Heuchera. Fig. 2182.

H. pubescens Pursh, Fl. Am. Sept. 187. 1814.

Stems rather stout, $1°-3°$ high, densely glandular-pubescent, at least above, usually bearing 1 or 2 small leaves. Basal leaves slender-petioled, broadly ovate or orbicular, cordate, $2'-4'$ wide, 5–7-lobed, the lobes rounded or acute, crenate or dentate; panicle loose; flowering calyx oblong-campanulate, somewhat oblique, $3''-4''$ long, minutely glandular, its lobes usually unequal; petals broadly spatulate, purplish, slightly exceeding the calyx-lobes; stamens scarcely or slightly exserted.

In rich woods, mountains of Pennsylvania to Kentucky, Missouri and North Carolina. Ascends to 4000 ft. in North Carolina. May–June.

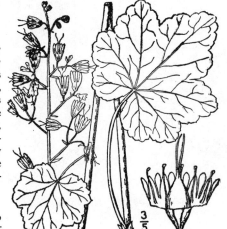

13. MITÉLLA [Tourn.] L. Sp. Pl. 406. 1753.

Erect perennial herbs, with long-petioled ovate or orbicular basal leaves, naked or 2-leaved scapes, and small white or greenish flowers in elongated spiciform racemes. Calyx-tube campanulate or hemispheric, adnate to the base of the ovary, its limb 5-lobed. Petals 5, 3-cleft or pinnatifid. Stamens 10 (sometimes 5); filaments short. Ovary globose, 1-celled; styles 2, short; ovules ∞. Capsule 1-celled, 2-valved at the apex, many-seeded. Seeds smooth, shining. [Diminutive of *mitra*, a cap, from the form of the young pod.]

About 4 species, natives of North America and eastern Asia. Type species: *Mitella diphylla* L.

Basal leaves ovate; scape with 2 opposite leaves.   1. *M. diphylla.*
Basal leaves reniform; scape naked or 1-leaved near the base.   2. *M. nuda.*

1. Mitella diphýlla L.   Two-leaved Bishop's Cap or Mitre-wort.   Fig. 2183.

Mitella diphylla L. Sp. Pl. 406.   1753.

Scape 10'–18' high, pubescent, bearing a pair of opposite nearly or quite sessile leaves near its middle. Basal leaves broadly ovate, cordate at the base, acute or acuminate at the apex, 3–5-lobed, dentate, scabrous and with scattered hairs on both sides, 1'–2' long; leaves of the scape similar, usually smaller; spiciform raceme erect, 3'–8' long, the flowers distant; calyx-lobes and petals white; capsule flattish, broad, dehiscent above, the valves spreading.

In rich woods, Quebec to Minnesota, North Carolina and Missouri. Ascends to 2600 ft. in Virginia. A third leaf is rarely borne on the scape at the base of the inflorescence. Currant-leaf. False sanicle. Fringe- or fairy-cup. April–May.

Mitella oppositifòlia Rydb., native in central New York, and cultivated at South Hadley, Massachusetts, differs from *M. diphylla* in the long-petioled stem-leaves, the lanceolate calyx-lobes and the filiform divisions of the petals.

2. Mitella nùda L.   Stoloniferous or Naked Bishop's Cap or Mitrewort.   Fig. 2184.

Mitella nuda L. Sp. Pl. 408.   1753.

Stem usually stoloniferous, scape erect, very slender, pubescent, 3'–7' high. Basal leaves reniform-orbicular, obtuse, cordate at the base, crenate or doubly crenate, 1'–1½' wide, pubescent with scattered hairs on both sides; stem-leaves usually none; flowers pedicelled, greenish, about 2'' broad; capsule similar to that of the preceding species.

In cold woods and peat-bogs, Newfoundland and Labrador to the Pacific Coast, south to New England, Pennsylvania, Michigan, and in the Canadian Rocky Mountains. Ascends to 3000 ft. in the Adirondacks. Also in northeastern Asia. April–June, or blooming again in the autumn.

Mitella intermèdia Bruhin, from the vicinity of Centerville, Wisconsin, differs from *M. nuda* in the acute-lobed leaves and the subulate divisions of the petals.

14. CHRYSOSPLÈNIUM [Tourn.] L. Sp. Pl. 398. 1753.

Low decumbent or erect somewhat succulent mainly semi-aquatic herbs, with petioled opposite or alternate crenate leaves, with no stipules. Flowers minute, greenish, axillary or terminal, solitary or clustered, perfect. Calyx-tube urn-shaped or obconic, adnate to the ovary, its limb 4–5-lobed. Petals none. Stamens 8–10 (rarely 4–5), inserted on the margin of a disk; filaments short. Ovary 1-celled, flattish, 2-lobed; styles 2, short, recurved; ovules ∞. Capsule membranous, short, inversely cordate or 2-lobed, 2-valved above, few- or many-seeded. Seed-coat muricate or pilose. [Greek, golden spleen, from some reputed medicinal qualities.]

About 15 species, natives of the north temperate zone and southern South America. Besides the following, 2 others occur in northwestern America. Type species: *Chrysosplenium oppositifolium* L.

Lower leaves opposite; flowers mostly solitary.   1. *C. americanum.*
Leaves all alternate; flowers corymbose.   2. *C. alternifolium.*

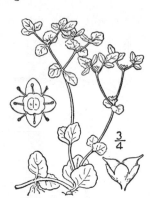

1. Chrysosplenium americànum Schwein.   Golden Saxifrage.   Water Carpet.   Fig. 2185.

Chrysosplenium oppositifolium Walt. Fl. Car. 140.   1788.   Not L.
C. americanum Schwein.; Hook. Fl. Bor. Am. 1 : 242.   1832.

Stems slender, decumbent, forked above, glabrous or very nearly so, 3′–8′ long. Lower leaves opposite, the upper often alternate, broadly ovate, orbicular or somewhat reniform, obtuse or truncate at the base, rounded at the apex, crenate or obscurely lobed, 2″–10″ wide; flowers sessile, axillary, usually solitary, about 1″ broad; calyx-lobes commonly 4, yellowish, or purplish within; stamens commonly 8; anthers orange-red.

In wet, shaded places, Nova Scotia to the Saskatchewan region, south, along the mountains to Georgia, and to Ohio, Michigan and Minnesota.   March–June.

2. Chrysosplenium iowense Rydb.   Iowa Golden Saxifrage.   Fig. 2186.

Chrysosplenium iowense Rydb.; Britton, Man. 483.   1901.

Flowering stems erect, glabrous or pubescent, 2′–6′ high, branched above. Leaves all alternate, the basal ones long-petioled, reniform, or cordate, often pubescent on the upper surface, 3″–18″ wide, or crenate with 5–11 rather broad lobes; flowers mainly terminal, corymbose; calyx-lobes commonly 4, orange-yellow within; stamens usually 8.

On wet mossy slope, Decorah, Iowa.   May–June.   Confused with *Chrysosplenium alternifolium* of Europe, in our first edition.

Family 48.   HYDRANGEÀCEAE Dumort. Anal. Fam. 36, 38.   1829.

HYDRANGEA FAMILY.

Shrubs or trees or vines with simple opposite leaves and no stipules.   Flowers perfect or the exterior ones of the clusters sterile and conspicuous.   Petals and sepals generally 5.   Stamens twice as many as the sepals, or numerous, epigynous. Carpels 2–10, wholly united or the apex free, the lower half at least enclosed by and adnate to the calyx.   Seeds numerous; endosperm generally copious; embryo small.

About 16 genera and 80 species, of temperate and tropical regions.

Sepals and petals 5 or fewer; shrubs.
    Petals valvate; stamens 8 or 10; corolla small.   1. *Hydrangea.*
    Petals convolute; stamens 15–60; corolla large.   2. *Philadelphus.*
Sepals and petals 7 or more; woody vine.   3. *Decumaria.*

1.   HYDRÁNGEA [Gronov.] L. Sp. Pl. 397.   1753.

Shrubs, or some Asiatic species small trees, with opposite simple petioled leaves and terminal corymbose flowers.   Stipules none.   Exterior flowers of the corymb often apetalous, slender-pedicelled, sterile, but with enlarged and very conspicuous calyx-lobes, or sometimes the whole corymb changed to these sterile flowers; fertile flowers small.   Calyx-tube (hypanthium) hemispheric or obconic, adnate to the ovary, 4–5-lobed.   Petals 4 or 5, valvate. Stamens 8 or 10, inserted on the disk.   Filaments filiform.   Ovary 2–4-celled; styles 2–4, distinct, or united at the base; ovules ∞.   Capsule membranous, usually 2-celled, ribbed, many-seeded, dehiscent at the bases of the styles.   [Greek, water-vessel, from the shape of the capsule.]

About 35 species, natives of eastern North America, eastern Asia and the Himalayas, and South America.   Besides the following, 2 or 3 others occur in the southeastern States.   Type species: *Hydrangea arborescens* L.

Leaves glabrous or somewhat pubescent beneath.   1. *H. arborescens.*
Leaves tomentose beneath.   2. *H. cinerea.*

1. Hydrangea arboréscens L.   Wild Hydrangea.   Fig. 2187.

H. arborescens L. Sp. Pl. 397. 1753.
Hydrangea vulgaris Michx. Fl. Bor. Am.
  1 : 268. 1803.
Hydrangea arborescens kanawhana
  Millsp. Bull. W. Va. Agric. Exp. Sta.
  2 : 363. 1891.

A shrub, 4°–10° high, the young
twigs pubescent or glabrate. Petioles slender, 1′–4′ long; leaves ovate,
thin, 3′–6′ long, acute or often acuminate at the apex, rounded, cordate
or rarely broadly cuneate at the base,
sharply dentate, green both sides, or
pale beneath, glabrous above, sometimes pubescent beneath; cymes 2′–5′
broad; marginal sterile flowers usually few or none, but sometimes
numerous, or forming the entire inflorescence, capsule wider than long.

On rocky stream or river banks,
southern New York and New Jersey,
very abundant in the valley of the Delaware, to Iowa, south to Florida, Louisiana and Missouri. Ascends to 4200 ft.
in North Carolina. June–July, sometimes blooming again in Sept. Seven-
barks. Hills-of-snow.

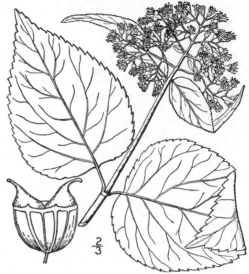

2. Hydrangea cinèrea Small.   Ashy Hy-drangea.   Fig. 2188.

Hydrangea cinerea Small, Bull. Torr. Club **25** : 148.
  1898.

A shrub 6°–8° high, the twigs finely pubescent
or glabrate. Leaves slender-petioled, ovate,
rounded or cordate at the base, acute or acuminate at the apex, 3′–6′ long, slightly thicker than
those of the preceding species, green and nearly
glabrous above, tomentose beneath; marginal
flowers, or at least some of them, sterile and conspicuous; capsule longer than wide.

Missouri to Tennessee and North Carolina, south
to Georgia. Snowy-hydrangea. June–July. Confused in our first edition with *Hydrangea radiata*
Walt., of the southeastern states which has leaves
silvery-white beneath.

2. PHILADÉLPHUS L. Sp. Pl. 470. 1753.

Shrubs, with opposite petioled simple deciduous leaves, and no stipules. Flowers large,
terminal or axillary, corymbose, racemose or solitary, white or cream-colored. Calyx-tube
top-shaped, adnate to the ovary, 4–5-lobed. Petals 4–5, convolute, rounded or obovate.
Stamens 20–40, inserted on the disk; filaments linear. Ovary 3–5-celled; styles 3–5, filiform,
distinct, or united at the base; ovules ∞. Capsule top-shaped, 3–5-celled, at length loculicidally dehiscent by 3–5 valves, many-seeded. Seeds oblong, the testa membranous, produced at each end. [Named after King Ptolemy Philadelphus.]

About 50 species, natives of North America, Mexico, Asia and central Europe. Besides the
following, about 25 others occur in the southern and western parts of North America. Called Mock
Orange from the orange-like blossoms of the various species. The common name Syringa is
unfortunate, being the generic name of the Lilac.

Flowers inodorous, solitary or few.
  Calyx-lobes about equalling the tube.   1. *P. inodorus.*
  Calyx-lobes about twice as long as the tube.   2. *P. grandiflorus.*
Flowers racemose, numerous, fragrant.   3. *P. coronarius.*

2. Philadelphus grandiflòrus Willd. Large-flowered Syringa. Fig. 2190.

Philadelphus grandiflorus Willd. Enum. Hort. Berol. 511. 1809.

A shrub, 6°–10° high, resembling the preceding species and perhaps not specifically different. Leaves broadly ovate or oval, more or less pubescent, especially beneath, 3′–5′ long, acuminate at the apex, rounded or narrowed at the base, sharply dentate, 3-nerved; flowers 1–3 together at the ends of the branches, and sometimes also axillary to the upper leaves, white, inodorous, 1½′–2′ broad; calyx-lobes lanceolate, acuminate, twice as long as the tube; capsule about 3″ high.

In low grounds, Pennsylvania to Virginia, Tennessee and Florida. April–May.

1. Philadelphus inodòrus L. Scentless Syringa. Fig. 2189.

Philadelphus inodorus L. Sp. Pl. 470. 1803.

A shrub, 6°–8° high, glabrous or very nearly so throughout. Leaves ovate or oval, acute or acuminate at the apex, rounded or sometimes narrowed at the base, 2′–5′ long, strongly 3-nerved, serrate with small distant teeth, or entire; flowers white, inodorous, about 1′ broad, solitary or 2 or 3 together at the ends of short branches; calyx-lobes triangular-ovate, acute, about as long as the tube; capsule about 3″ high.

In thickets, Virginia to Georgia, Kentucky and Mississippi, principally in the mountains. Escaped from cultivation in Pennsylvania. May.

3. Philadelphus coronàrius L. Garden Syringa. Mock Orange. Fig. 2191.

Philadelphus coronarius L. Sp. Pl. 470. 1753.

A shrub 8°–10° high. Leaves short-petioled, oval, elliptic or ovate-elliptic, 2′–4′ long, glabrous above, pubescent beneath, acute or acuminate at the apex, rounded or narrowed at the base, denticulate with distant teeth, 3-nerved; flowers numerous, racemose at the ends of the branches, 1′–1½′ broad, creamy white, very fragrant; calyx-lobes ovate, acute, longer than the tube.

Escaped from gardens in Virginia and Ohio, and sparingly in the Middle and Eastern States. Native of central Europe. Orange-flower tree, May–June.

3. DECUMÀRIA L. Sp. Pl, Ed. 2, 1663. 1763.

Woody climbing vines, with opposite petioled leaves, and terminal corymbose perfect flowers. Stipules none. Calyx-tube top-shaped, adnate to the ovary, its limb 7–10-toothed.

Petals 7–10, narrow. Stamens 20–30, inserted on the disk; filaments subulate. Ovary 5–10-celled, 10–15-ribbed, its apex conic; style thick; stigma capitate, 5–10-lobed; ovules ∞. Capsule fragile, ribbed, opening between the ribs. Seeds numerous, the testa membranous, reticulated, produced into a club-shaped appendage. [Latin, *decem,* ten; the parts being often in 10's.]

A monotypic genus of southeastern North America.

1. Decumaria bàrbara L. Decumaria. Fig. 2192.

D. barbara L. Sp. Pl. Ed. 2, 1663. 1763.

Glabrous, or the shoots pubescent, climbing by aerial rootlets to a height of several feet. Petioles ½–1′ long; leaves ovate, acute or obtuse at the apex, rounded or narrowed at the base 2′–4′ long, entire or repand-denticulate, sometimes pubescent on the veins of the lower surface, glabrous and shining above; corymbs terminal, compound, 2′–3′ broad; flowers white, fragrant, 3″–4″ broad; calyx-teeth deciduous; capsule top-shaped, 2″–3″ high, tipped with the conic persistent style, opening between the ribs and remaining on the plant after the seeds fall away.

In swamps, southeastern Virginia to Florida, west to Louisiana. May–June.

Family 49. ITEÀCEAE Agardh, Theor. Syst. Pl. 151. 1858.
VIRGINIA WILLOW FAMILY.

Consists of the following genus:

1. ÌTEA L. Sp. Pl. 199. 1753.

Shrubs or small trees, with simple alternate petioled deciduous leaves, no stipules, and small white flowers in terminal narrow racemes. Calyx-tube obconic or campanulate, 5-lobed, its base adnate to the ovary. Petals 5, linear, their apices inflexed. Stamens 5, inserted on the disk. Ovary 2-celled; style slender; stigma 2-grooved in our species; ovules few or numerous. Capsule oblong or narrowly conic, 2-valved, several–many-seeded. Seeds narrow, flattish, the testa produced at each end. [Greek for willow, which its leaves somewhat resemble.]

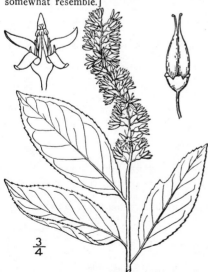

About 5 species, natives of the eastern United States and Asia. The following typical species is the only one known to occur in North America.

1. Itea virgínica L. Itea. Virginia Willow. Fig. 2193.

Itea virginica L. Sp. Pl. 199. 1753.

A shrub 4°–10° high, the twigs and inflorescence finely pubescent. Leaves short-petioled, narrowly oval, oblanceolate or rarely obovate, 1′–3′ long, acute or acuminate at the apex, narrowed at the base, sharply serrulate, glabrous, or with a few hairs along the veins beneath; racemes terminal, dense, 2′–6′ long; flowers short-pedicelled; petals linear, erect or slightly spreading, about 2½″ long; capsule 2-grooved, 2″–3″ long, pubescent, narrow, tipped with the persistent at length 2-parted style.

In wet places, pine barrens of New Jersey, and eastern Pennsylvania to Florida, west to western North Carolina, Missouri and Louisiana. May–June.

Family 50. **HAMAMELIDÀCEAE** Lindl. Veg. Kingd. 784. 1847.

Trees or shrubs, with alternate petioled simple leaves, and perfect, polygamous monoecious flowers, variously clustered. Perianth often imperfect. Calyx-tube, when present, more or less adnate to the ovary, its limb truncate or 4- or 5-lobed. Petals, when present, 4 or 5, perigynous. Stamens 4–∞, perigynous; filaments distinct. Disk circular or none. Overy compound, of 2 carpels united below, 2-celled; styles 2, subulate, erect or recurved; ovules 1, suspended. Fruit a 2-celled 2-beaked woody or coriaceous capsule, dehiscent at the summit. Seeds 1 in each cavity, anatropous; embryo large; endosperm scanty.

About 13 genera and 40 species, natives of North America, Asia and South Africa.

Flowers white, in catkin-like spikes; petals none.   1. *Fothergilla.*
Flowers yellow, in axillary clusters; petals long.   2. *Hamamelis.*

1. **FOTHERGÍLLA** Murr. Syst. Veg. 418. 1774.

Shrubs, the foliage somewhat stellate-pubescent. Leaves alternate, obovate. Flowers perfect, or often polygamous (sometimes monoecious) in catkin-like bracted terminal spikes, appearing a little before the leaves. Calyx campanulate, slightly 5–7-lobed. Petals none. Stamens about 24, inserted on the edge of the calyx; anthers subglobose. Ovary 2-celled; styles slender; ovules 1 in each cell. Capsule cartilaginous, 2-celled, 2-seeded. Seeds bony, pendulous. [Named for Dr. John Fothergill, 1712–1780, an English naturalist.]

A monotypic genus of eastern North America.

1. Fothergilla Gàrdeni Murr.   Fothergilla.
Fig. 2194.

Hamamelis virginiana carolina L. Mant. 333. 1771.
Fothergilla Gardeni Murr. Syst. Veg. 418. 1774.
Fothergilla alnifolia L. f. Suppl. 267. 1781.
F. *carolina* Britton, Mem. Torr. Club **5**: 180. 1894.

A shrub, 2°–5° high, the young twigs densely stellate-pubescent. Leaves short-petioled, 2′–3′ long, obovate or broadly oval, obtuse or short-pointed at the apex, rounded or narrowed at the base, usually inequilateral, coarsely dentate-crenate above the middle, or entire, more or less stellate-pubescent; spikes dense, erect, 1′–2′ long; bracts densely pubescent, the lower ones sometimes lobed; stamens white or pinkish, 2″–4″ long; capsule very pubescent.

In wet grounds, Virginia to Georgia.   Witch- or dwarf-alder.   April.

2. **HAMAMÈLIS** L. Sp. Pl. 124. 1753.

Shrubs, with alternate leaves, and clustered lateral yellow bracted flowers, appearing in late summer or autumn. Calyx 4-parted, persistent, adnate to the lower part of the ovary. Petals 4, elongated, linear, persistent, or in the staminate flowers sometimes wanting. Stamens 4, alternating with 4 scale-like staminodia; filaments very short; anthers dehiscent by a valve. Ovary 2-celled; styles 2, short; ovules 1 in each cell, pendulous. Capsule woody, at length 2-valved at the summit. Seed oblong, its testa shining. [Greek, with the apple, flower and fruit being borne together.]

A genus of 3 known species, one native of eastern North America, the others of Japan.

1. Hamamelis virginiàna L. Witch-Hazel. Fig. 2195.

Hamamelis virginiàna L Sp. Pl. 124. 1753.

A shrub, or rarely a small tree with maximum height of about 25°, the twigs slightly scurfy, or glabrous. Leaves short-petioled, obovate or broadly oval, obtuse or pointed at the apex, somewhat cordate and inequilateral at the base, stellate-pubescent, at least when young, 2'–5' long, thick, repand-dentate; flowers in axillary clusters, nearly sessile, bright yellow, appearing late in the season, when the leaves are falling and while the previous fruit remains; petals narrow, about ½" wide, 6"–9" long; calyx-lobes spreading or recurved, oval, ciliate, pubescent on the outer surface; capsule maturing the next season, beaked with the 2 persistent styles, densely pubescent, 3"–4" high, at length bursting elastically; seeds bony.

In low woods, Nova Scotia to Ontario, Minnesota, Florida, Texas. Wood hard; weight per cubic foot 43 lbs. Spotted-alder. Tobacco-wood. Snapping-hazel. Pistachio. Winter-bloom. Aug.–Dec. Jan.–March in the southwest.

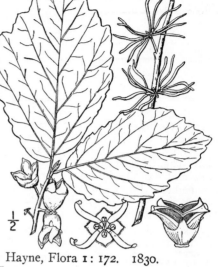

Family 51. ALTINGIÀCEAE Hayne, Flora 1 : 172. 1830.

ALTINGIA FAMILY.

Forest trees producing a balsamic resin, with furrowed bark, and terete or sometimes corky-winged branchlets. Leaves alternate, glandular-serrate, palmately lobed or unlobed; stipules mostly deciduous. Flowers usually monoecious, sometimes perfect, in heads surrounded by three or four deciduous bracts. Perianth wanting. Heads of staminate flowers in terminal racemes or panicles; androecium of numerous stamens, interspersed with minute scales. Pistillate flowers in solitary, long-peduncled axillary heads; gynoecium of two united carpels; ovary partly inferior; stigmas stout; ovules several or numerous in each carpel, horizontal. Fruit a hard, dry, multicapsular head, sometimes armed with the stout persistent stigmas. Capsules opening at the apex, between the bases of the stigmas. Fertile seeds few, winged; testa crustaceous; embryo straight, imbedded in fleshy endosperm; cotyledons flat. Sterile seeds numerous, wingless, angled.

Five genera and about 10 species, natives of southern Europe, Asia, and eastern North America.

1. LIQUIDÁMBAR L. Sp. Pl. 999. 1753.

Large trees with resinous sap, simple alternate lobed petioled leaves, and small monoecious flowers in heads, the staminate clusters racemose, the pistillate ones usually solitary. Calyx and corolla of the staminate flowers none; stamens numerous; filaments short;

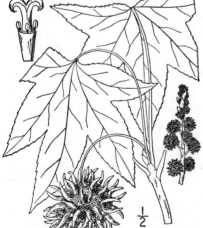

anthers longitudinally dehiscent. Calices of the pistillate flowers confluent; petals none; anthers rudimentary, borne on the edge of the calyx; ovary partly inferior, 2-celled; ovules several or numerous, styles 2. Capsules 2-beaked, 2-valved at the summit, dry, hard, forming a dense spinose globular head. [Name Latin-Arabic referring to the fragrant sap.]

1. Liquidambar Styracíflua L. Sweet Gum. Star-leaved or Red Gum. Fig. 2196.

Liquidambar Styraciflua L. Sp. Pl. 999. 1753.

A forest tree, maximum height about 150°; bark very rough, branches usually winged with corky ridges. Twigs glabrous or slightly pubescent; leaves broader than long, 3'–9' wide, subcordate at base, deeply 3-7-lobed, glabrous above, often pubescent in the axils of the veins beneath, the lobes triangular-ovate, acute, sharply and finely serrate; sterile flower-clusters erect or spreading, conic, consisting of numerous small heads, greenish; fertile heads long-peduncled, at length drooping, borne near the base of the sterile; head of fruit about $1'-1\frac{1}{2}'$ in diameter, the fertile seeds few, with numerous minute sterile ones.

In low woods, Connecticut and southern New York to Florida, Illinois, Missouri and Mexico. Wood hard, not strong, reddish brown; weight per cubic foot 37 lbs. Leaves fragrant when bruised, brilliant in autumn. Its gum, *copal-balsam* or *copalm*, used as a substitute for storax. Satin-walnut. Opossum-tree. Bilsted. Alligator-tree. White-gum. Liquidamber. April–May.

Family 52. GROSSULARIACEAE Dumort. Anal. Fam. 37. 1829.

GOOSEBERRY FAMILY.

Shrubs, with alternate often fascicled usually lobed petioled leaves, and racemose or subsolitary regular flowers, the pedicels mostly bracteolate. Calyx-tube (hypanthium) ovoid, cylindric or hemispheric, adnate to the ovary, the limb 4–5-lobed, often colored. Petals 4 or 5, inserted on the throat of the calyx, small, scale-like, often included. Stamens 4 or 5, inserted with the petals, included or exserted. Ovary inferior, 1-celled; styles 2, distinct or united; ovules few or numerous. Berry globose or ovoid, pulpy, the calyx persistent on its summit. Seeds horizontal, obscurely angled, their outer coat gelatinous, the inner crustaceous. Embryo small, terete, in fleshy endosperm.

Two genera and about 120 species, widely distributed. Currantworts.

Pedicels jointed beneath the ovary; fruit disarticulating from the pedicels; plants without nodal spines.   1. *Ribes*.
Pedicels not jointed; fruit not disarticulating from the pedicels; plants with nodal spines.   2. *Grossularia*.

1. RIBES L. Sp. Pl. 201. 1753.

Shrubs, mostly unarmed, a few species bristly. Leaves palmately veined, usually lobed. Racemes several–many-flowered; pedicels jointed beneath the ovary, usually with a pair of bractlets just below the joint. Ovary not spiny. Fruit disarticulating from its pedicel. [The

About 65 species, natives of the north temperate zone, Mexico and the Andes of South America. Besides the following, some 25 others occur in western North America. Type: *Ribes rubrum* L.

Stems bristly and spiny.	1. *R. lacustre*.
Stems unarmed.	
Ovary with sessile glands.	2. *R. hudsonianum*.
Ovary without glands, or with stalked glands.	
Calyx-tube (hypanthium) obsolete.	
Ovary glabrous.	
Petals yellowish-green.	3. *R. vulgare*.
Petals red.	4. *R. triste.*
Ovary with stalked glands.	5. *R. glandulosum*
Calyx-tube (hypanthium) evident.	
Calyx-tube greenish to yellowish-white.	
Racemes very short; leaf-lobes rounded; fruit red.	6. *R. inebrians.*
Racemes long, drooping; leaf-lobes acutish; fruit black.	7. *R. americanum.*
Calyx-tube bright yellow.	8. *R. odoratum.*

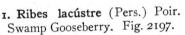

1. Ribes lacústre (Pers.) Poir.
Swamp Gooseberry. Fig. 2197.

Ribes oxyacanthoides var. *lacustre* Pers. Syn. 1 : 252. 1805.
Ribes lacustre Poir. in Lam. Encycl. Suppl. 2 : 856. 1811.

Spines slender, weak, generally clustered. Branches usually densely bristly; petioles slender, more or less pubescent; leaves nearly orbicular, thin, glabrous or nearly so, deeply 5–7-lobed, $1'-7'$ wide, the lobes obtuse or acutish, incised-dentate; flowers racemose, green or purplish, about $2''$ long; pedicels slender, bracted at the base, about $2''$ long; calyx-tube short, its lobes short, broad, spreading; stamens very short, not exserted; berry $2''-5''$ in diameter, reddish, covered with weak gland-tipped bristles.

In swamps and wet woods, Newfoundland to Massachusetts, New York, Pennsylvania, Michigan, Alaska and California. May–June.

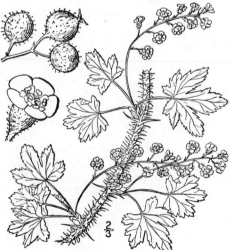

2. Ribes hudsoniànum Richards. Northern Black Currant. Fig. 2198.

Ribes hudsonianum Richards. Bott. App. Frank. Journ. Ed. 2, 6. 1823.

Branches erect, unarmed. Petioles slender, 1'-4' long; leaves broader than long, 1'-4' wide, more or less pubescent and resinous-dotted beneath, 3–5-lobed, the lobes obtuse or acutish, coarsely dentate; racemes 2½' long or less; pedicels 2" long or less; flowers white, 2"-3" broad; calyx broadly campanulate, its lobes oval, obtuse, spreading; stamens short, not exserted; ovary dotted with sessile glands; bracts setaceous, usually nearly equalling the pedicels, deciduous; fruit black, glabrous, 3"-5" in diameter.

Hudson Bay and western Ontario to Alaska, Minnesota and British Columbia. Quinsy-berry. May–June.

Ribes nìgrum L., the black currant of the gardens, with similar leaves, loosely flowered drooping racemes, the calyx-lobes ascending and recurved, has escaped from cultivation in the Middle States.

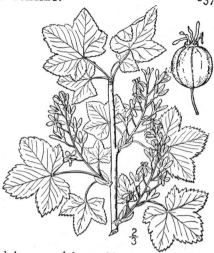

3. Ribes vulgàre Lam. Red Garden Currant. Fig. 2199.

Ribes vulgare Lam. Encycl. 3 : 47. 1789.

Unarmed; stems nearly erect. Petioles slender, glabrous or sparingly pubescent, 1'-3' long; leaves pubescent beneath, at least when young, orbicular or broader, cordate at the base, 3–5-lobed, the lobes acutish, sharply dentate; racemes pendulous, loosely flowered; pedicels 2"-3" long, curved and sometimes ascending, longer than the ovate bractlets; flowers greenish, about 2" broad; calyx flat-campanulate; stamens short; anther-sacs divergent; fruit red, glabrous, 2"-5" in diameter.

Raisin-tree.   Garnet-berry.   Wine-berry. May–June. Escaped from cultivation, Massachusetts to Ontario, Virginia and Wisconsin, and in Oregon and British Columbia. Native of Europe. Included in our first edition in *R. rubrum* L.

4. Ribes trìste Pall. American Red Currant. Fig. 2200.

Ribes triste Pall. Nova Acta Acad. Petrop. 10 : 378. 1797.

Ribes rubrum subglandulosum Maxim. Bull. Acad. St. Petersb. 19 : 261. 1874.

Similar to the preceding species, unarmed, the stems creeping or ascending. Leaves glabrous above, more or less pubescent beneath; racemes several-flowered, as long as the leaves or shorter, drooping; pedicels 4" long or less, longer than the ovate bractlets; flowers purplish; calyx saucer-shaped; anther-sacs contiguous, parallel or nearly so; ovary glabrous; fruit red, glabrous, 3"-4" in diameter.

Wet woods and bogs, Newfoundland to Alaska, New Jersey, Michigan, South Dakota and Oregon. Northern Asia. June–July.

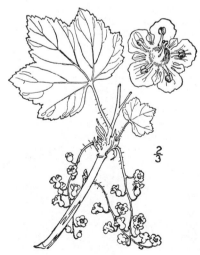

$\frac{3}{5}$

6. Ribes inèbrians Lindl. White-flowered Currant. Fig. 2202.

Ribes inebrians Lindl. Bot. Reg. *pl. 1471.* 1832.

Unarmed. Petioles slender, more or less glandular-pubescent, 3″–10″ long; leaves reniform-orbicular, cordate at the base, ½′–1½′ wide, sparingly glandular-pubescent, or glabrate on both sides, 3–5-lobed, the lobes very obtuse, crenate or crenulate; racemes short, pubescent, pendulous, bractlets rhombic, much longer than the pedicels, persistent, usually entire-margined and glandular-ciliate; flowers sessile or short-pedicelled, white or greenish-white; calyx tubular, glandular; petals minute, nearly orbicular; stamens short; fruit red, insipid, glandular or rarely smooth, about 3″ in diameter.

South Dakota to Idaho, Nebraska, New Mexico and California. May–June. Confused in our first edition with the similar *R. cereum* Dougl.

5. Ribes glandulòsum Grauer. Fetid Currant. Fig. 2201.

Ribes glandulosum Grauer, Pl. Min. Cog. 2. 1784.
R. prostratum L'Her. Stirp. Nov. 3. *pl. 2.* 1785.

Branches decumbent or spreading, thornless and without prickles. Petioles slender, 1′–3′ long, pubescent or glabrous, the dilated base sometimes ciliate; leaves nearly orbicular, sharply and deeply 5–7-lobed, 1′–3′ wide, usually somewhat pubescent along the veins beneath, the lobes acute or acutish, dentate-serrate; flowers racemose, about 2½″ broad; pedicels 2″–2½″ long, glandular, calyx broadly campanulate, its lobes short and broad; stamens short, not exserted; fruit red, glandular-bristly, about 3″ in diameter.

In cold wet places, Newfoundland to Athabasca, British Columbia, south, especially along the mountains, to North Carolina, Michigan and Wisconsin. Plant with a disagreeable odor. Ascends to 6000 ft. in North Carolina. Skunk-currant. May–June.

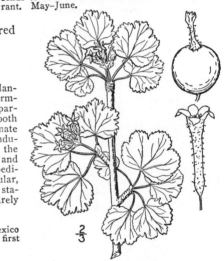

$\frac{2}{3}$

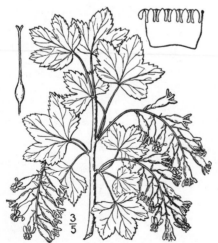

$\frac{3}{5}$

7. Ribes americànum Mill. Wild Black Currant. Fig. 2203.

Ribes americanum Mill. Gard. Dict. Ed. 8, No. 4. 1768.
Ribes floridum L'Her. Stirp. Nov. 1: 4. 1784.
Ribes nigrum var. *pennsylvanicum* Marsh. Arb. Amer. 132. 1785.
Ribes pennsylvanicum Lam. Encycl. 3: 49. 1789.

Branches erect, unarmed. Petioles slender, loosely pubescent, or glabrous; leaves nearly orbicular, glabrous above, somewhat pubescent and resinous-dotted beneath, 1′–3′ wide, sharply 3–5-lobed, the lobes dentate-serrate, acutish; racemes pendulous, rather loosely flowered, pubescent; bractlets linear, much exceeding the pedicels, or shorter; flowers greenish-white, or yellowish, 4″–5″ long; calyx tubular, its lobes short, broad, obtuse; stamens not exserted; fruit globose-ovoid, black, glabrous, 3″–5″ in diameter.

In woods, Nova Scotia to Virginia, Manitoba, Assiniboia, Kentucky, Iowa and Nebraska. Also in New Mexico. Quinsy-berry. April–May.

8. Ribes odorátum Wendl. Golden, Buffalo or Missouri Currant. Fig. 2204.

R. odoratum Wendl. in Bartl. & Wendl. Beitr. **2**: 15. 1825.

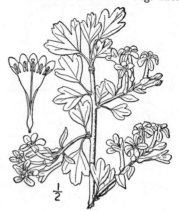

Unarmed. Petioles rather slender, pubescent; leaves convolute in the bud, at length glabrous, often broader than long, thick, 3-lobed or sometimes 5-lobed, broadly cuneate or truncate at the base, the lobes obtuse, few-toothed or entire; racemes leafy-bracted, few-flowered, the rachis and pedicels villous; flowers bright yellow, spicy-scented, 6″–12″ long; calyx-tube cylindric, glabrous, 2–3 times as long as the oval spreading lobes; petals 1″–1½″ long; stamens slightly exserted; fruit black, glabrous, 3″–5″ in diameter.

Along streams, Minnesota and South Dakota to Missouri and Texas. Common in cultivation. Clove- or flowering-current. April–May.

2. GROSSULÀRIA [Tourn.] Mill. Gard. Dict Abr. Ed. 4. 1754.

Shrubs, with erect ascending or trailing branches, the nodes armed with simple or 3-forked spines, rarely spineless. Racemes 1–few-flowered. Pedicels not jointed. Hypanthium evident. Fruit not disarticulating from the pedicel. [Ancient name of the gooseberry.]

About 55 species, natives of the north temperate zone. Besides the following, some 30 others occur in the western states. Type species: *Ribes Grossularia* L.

Ovary bristly; fruit prickly.	1. *G. Cynosbati.*
Ovary glabrous, pubescent, or with stalked glands.	
Flowers white; filaments long.	2. *G. missouriensis.*
Flowers green or purplish; filaments shorter.	
Stamens equalling the petals.	
Calyx-tube (hypanthium) tubular.	3. *G. setosa.*
Calyx-tube (hypanthium) campanulate.	4. *G. oxyacanthoides.*
Stamens twice as long as the petals or longer.	
Ovary villous.	5. *G. reclinata.*
Ovary glabrous or with some stalked glands.	
Calyx-lobes twice as long as the tube.	6. *G. rotundifolia.*
Calyx-lobes about as long as the tube.	7. *G. hirtella.*

1. Grossularia Cynósbati (L.) Mill. Wild Gooseberry. Dogberry. Fig. 2205.

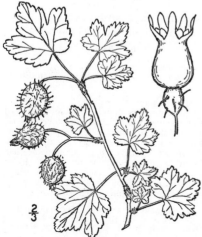

Ribes Cynosbati L. Sp. Pl. 202. 1753.
Grossularia Cynosbati Mill. Gard. Dict. Ed. 8, No. 5. 1768.
Ribes Cynosbati glabratum Fernald, Rhodora **7**: 156. 1905.

Nodal spines slender, solitary or sometimes 2–3 together, erect or spreading, 3″–6″ long, or often wanting. Prickles of the branches few and weak or none; petioles 6″–18″ long, slender, generally pubescent; leaflets nearly orbicular, 1′–2′ broad, pubescent, at least when young, truncate or cordate at the base, deeply 3–5-lobed, the lobes crenate-dentate or incised; peduncles and pedicels slender; flowers 1–3, green, 3″–4″ long; calyx-lobes oblong, shorter than the ovoid tube; stamens not exserted; berry 4″–6″ in diameter, with few or many subulate prickles.

In rocky woods, New Brunswick, south, especially along the Alleghanies to North Carolina, west to Manitoba, Alabama and Missouri. Prickly wild-gooseberry. Dog-bramble. April–June.

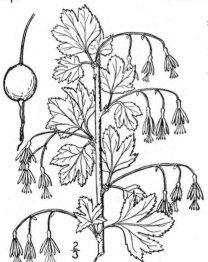

2. Grossularia missouriénsis (Nutt.) Cov. & Britt. Missouri Gooseberry. Fig. 2206.

Ribes gracile Pursh, Fl. Am. Sept. 165. 1814. Not Michx.
Ribes missouriensis Nutt.; T. & G. Fl. N. A. 1 : 548. 1840.
Grossularia missouriensis Cov. & Britt. N. A. Fl. 22 : 221. 1908.

Nodal spines slender, solitary, or 2–3 together, reddish, 3″–8″ long or more. Prickles generally few or none; leaves slender-petioled, somewhat pubescent when young, orbicular or broader, 9″–18″ wide, truncate, slightly cordate, or sometimes obtuse at the base, 3–5-lobed, the lobes rather blunt, dentate; pedicels very slender, 4″–6″ long; flowers white or greenish tinged, drooping, 6″–9″ long; calyx-tube narrow, shorter than the linear lobes; stamens connivent or parallel, much exserted; berry brown to purple, 5″–7″ in diameter.

In dry or rocky soil, Illinois to Minnesota, South Dakota, Kansas and Tennessee. Slender or Illinois gooseberry. May.

3. Grossularia setòsa (Lindl.) Cov. & Britt. Bristly Gooseberry. Fig. 2207.

Ribes setosum Lindl. Trans. Hort. Soc. 7 : 243. 1830.

Grossularia setosa Cov. & Britt. N. A. Fl. 22 : 222. 1908.

Nodal spines 10″ long or less, spreading, sometimes none. Bristles usually numerous, scattered; leaves slender-petioled, more or less pubescent, at least when young, 1½′ in width or less, broadly ovate or orbicular, 3–5-lobed, the lobes incised-dentate; flowers 1–4, white, 3″–5″ long; calyx-tube cylindric, longer than the oblong lobes; stamens not exserted; fruit red to black, sparingly bristly, or often glabrous.

On lake shores, and in thickets, western Ontario and Manitoba to Assiniboia, Nebraska and Wyoming. May.

4. Grossularia oxyacanthòides (L.) Mill. Hawthorn or Northern Gooseberry. Fig. 2208.

Ribes oxyacanthoides L. Sp. Pl. 201. 1753.
Grossularia oxyacanthoides Mill. Gard. Dict. Ed. 8, No. 4. 1768.

Nodal spines generally solitary, light colored, 3″–6″ long, sometimes none. Prickles scattered or wanting; leaves suborbicular, the lobes obtuse or acute; petioles and lower leaf-surfaces commonly pubescent; peduncles short, commonly less than 6″ long; flowers 1–3, short-pedicelled, greenish-purple or white, about 3″–4″ long; calyx-lobes oblong; stamens short, not exserted; berry globose or globose-ovoid, glabrous, 4″–6″ in diameter, reddish-purple when ripe.

In wet woods and low grounds, Newfoundland to Hudson Bay, Yukon, British Columbia, Michigan, North Dakota and Montana. Smooth gooseberry. May–July.

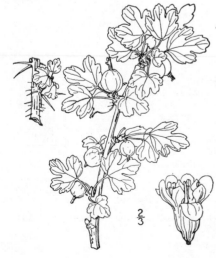

5. Grossularia reclinata (L.) Mill.
Garden Gooseberry. Fig. 2209.

Ribes reclinatum L. Sp. Pl. 201. 1753.
Ribes Uva-crispa L. Sp. Pl. 201. 1753.
Ribes Grossularia L. Sp. Pl. 201. 1753.
G. reclinata Mill. Gard. Dict. Ed. 8, No. 4. 1768.

Nodal spines stout, spreading or reflexed, usually 3 together but sometimes solitary or 2. Prickles scattered or none; leaves rather short-petioled, orbicular or broader, pubescent, at least when young, $\frac{3}{4}'-2\frac{1}{2}'$ wide, 3-5-lobed, the lobes obtuse and crenate-dentate; peduncles very short, 1-flowered or sometimes 2-flowered, glandular-pubescent; flowers green, about $3''$ long; calyx-tube campanulate, pubescent, its lobes oval; stamens somewhat exserted or included; fruit globose-ovoid, or often with weak bristles, often 1' long in cultivation.

Along roadsides in eastern New Jersey and southeastern New York, escaped from gardens. Native of Europe and Asia. Teaberry. Fea- or fay-berry. Berry-tree. Carberry. Dayberry. Wine-berry. Fabes. Honey-blobs. Goggles. Gaskins. May.

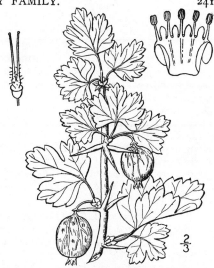

$\frac{2}{3}$

6. Grossularia rotundifòlia (Michx.)
Cov. & Britt. Eastern Wild Goose-
berry. Fig. 2210.

Ribes rotundifolium Michx. Fl. Bor. Am. 1: 110. 1803.
Grossularia rotundifolia Cov. & Britt. N. A. Fl. 22: 223. 1908.

Nodal spines commonly short, or often altogether wanting, and the prickles few or none. Leaves suborbicular, broadly cuneate to subcordate at the base, pubescent, at least beneath, when young; peduncles rather short, nodding; flowers 1–3, greenish-purple, $3''-4''$ long, pedicelled; calyx-lobes linear-oblong, at least twice as long as the tube; stamens exserted for about $\frac{1}{4}$ their length; berry globose, glabrous, purplish, usually not more than $4''$ in diameter.

In rocky woods, western Massachusetts and southeastern New York to North Carolina, especially along the mountains. Smooth gooseberry. May–July.

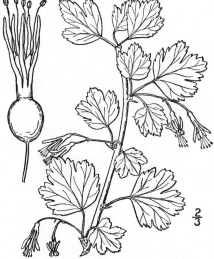

$\frac{2}{3}$

7. Grossularia hirtélla (Michx.) Spach. Low
Wild Gooseberry. Fig. 2211.

Ribes hirtellum Michx. Fl. Bor. Am. 1: 111. 1803.
R. huronense Rydb.; Britton, Man. 487. 1901.
R. oxyacanthoides calcicola Fernald, Rhodora 7: 155. 1905.
R. saxosum Hook. Fl. Bor. Am. 1: 231. 1834.

A shrub, 4° high or less, the branches usually without spines, sometimes bristly, the older ones dark brown. Nodal spines rarely present and $6''$ long or less; leaves suborbicular or ovate-orbicular in outline, incisely 3-5-lobed and dentate, mostly cuneate at the base, $\frac{3}{4}'-2\frac{1}{2}'$ wide, glabrous or sparingly pubescent; peduncles short, 1-3-flowered; bracts much shorter than the pedicels; ovary glabrous or rarely pubescent or with stalked glands; calyx-tube narrowly campanulate; sepals green or purplish; petals obovate; berry black or purple, $4''-5''$ in diameter.

Swamps and moist woods, Newfoundland to Manitoba, West Virginia and South Dakota. Confused in our first edition with *Ribes oxyacanthoides* L.

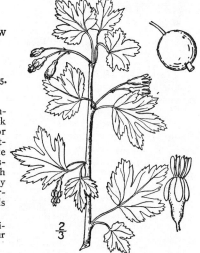

$\frac{2}{3}$

Family 53. **PLATANÀCEAE** Lindl. Nat. Syst. Ed. *2*, 187. 1836.

PLANE-TREE FAMILY.

Large trees, with thin exfoliating bark, alternate petioled palmately lobed and veined leaves, the hollowed petiole bases enclosing the buds for the following season, and very small green monoecious flowers in dense globular heads. Receptacle somewhat fleshy. Flowers very small, bracted; calyx and corolla apparently none. Staminate flowers with 3–8 stamens; filaments short; connective broad, dilated; anthers oblong or linear, longitudinally dehiscent. Pistillate flowers with 2–9 distinct pistils and several staminodes; ovary linear, 1-celled; style elongated; stigma lateral. Ripened head of fruit composed of very numerous narrowly obpyramidal nutlets which are densely pubescent below with long nearly erect hairs. Seed pendulous; endosperm thin; cotyledons linear.

The family contains only the following genus, comprising some 8 species, natives of the north temperate zone. Its relationship to other families is doubtful.

1. **PLÁTANUS** [Tourn.] L. Sp. Pl. 999. 1753.

Characters of the family. [Name ancient.]

Besides the following species, 2 others occur in the western United States and 3 in Mexico. Type species: *Platanus orientàlis* L.

1. **Platanus occidentàlis** L. Button-wood. Button-ball. Plane-tree. Fig. 2212.

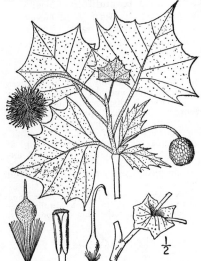

Platanus occidentalis L. Sp. Pl. 999. 1753.

A large tree; maximum height about 130°; and trunk diameter 14°; outer bark freely peeling off in thin plates, uncovering the bright white inner layers. Leaves orbicular, or wider than long, 4′–9′ wide when mature, cordate or truncate at the base, 3–5-lobed, densely floccose-pubescent with whitish branched hairs when young, less so above and becoming nearly glabrous when old, the lobes mostly large, sharply serrate, or rarely entire; petiole mostly shorter than the blade; stipules with broad spreading toothed borders, conspicuous on young shoots; fruiting heads 1′ in diameter, usually solitary, hanging on a long peduncle, persistent through the winter, the nutlets at length scattered by the wind.

Along streams and in wet woods, Maine to Ontario and Minnesota, Florida, Kansas and Texas. Wood hard, weak, difficult to split, reddish brown; weight per cubic foot 35 lbs. The largest tree of east America; often called sycamore. The outer bark of the lower part of old trunks does not freely exfoliate. False sycamore. Water-beech. May.

Family 54. **ROSÀCEAE** B. Juss. Hort. Trian. 1759.

ROSE FAMILY.

Herbs, shrubs, or trees, with alternate (in some exotic genera opposite), simple or compound leaves, and regular perfect or rarely polygamo-dioecious flowers. Stipules commonly present, sometimes large. Calyx free from or adnate to the ovary, 5-lobed (rarely 4–9-lobed), often bracteolate. Disk adnate to the base of the calyx. Petals equal in number to the calyx-lobes, distinct, or none. Stamens usually numerous, distinct; anthers small, 2-celled. Carpels 1–∞, distinct, or adnate to the calyx. Ovary 1-celled or rarely imperfectly 2-celled; style terminal or lateral. Ovules 1, 2, or several, anatropous. Fruit various, mostly follicles or achenes; endosperm none, or rarely copious.

A family comprising about 75 genera and more than 1200 species, of wide geographic distribution.

A. Fruit of 1–5 dehiscent follicles.

* Carpels alternate with the sepals; stipules deciduous or none.

Carpels, if more than 1, united below; seeds with endosperm (NEILLIEAE). 1. *Opulaster.*

Carpels normally 5, distinct; seeds without endosperm (SPIRAEEAE).

Flowers perfect; shrubs with simple leaves. 2. *Spiraea.*

Flowers dioecious; tall herbs with pinnately 2–3-compound leaves. 3. *Aruncus.*

** Carpels opposite the sepals ; stipules persistent (Sorbarieae).

Petals obovate or spatulate, imbricated ; leaves pinnate.   4. *Schizonotus.*
Petals strap-shaped, convolute in the bud ; leaves trifoliolate.   5. *Porteranthus.*

B. Fruit indehiscent, of achenes or drupelets.

* Carpels not enclosed in the fleshy calyx-tube (hypanthium).

  1. *Fruit of dry achenes.*

Ovaries 2-ovuled (Ulmarieae).   6. *Filipendula.*
Ovaries 1-ovuled.
    Seed pendulous or ascending, borne in the ovary opposite to the base of the style.
        Style articulated with the ovary ; calyx-tube from campanulate to nearly flat (Potentilleae).
            Style terminal or nearly so ; ovule and seed pendulous.   7. *Potentilla.*
            Style lateral ; ovule and seed ascending.
                Herbs ; achenes glabrous.
                    Achenes numerous ; stamens about 20.
                        Leaves odd-pinnate.
                            Receptacle not enlarged in fruit ; petals yellow, obtuse or retuse.
                                                                             8. *Argentina.*
                            Receptacle somewhat enlarged in fruit, spongy ; petals red, acute or acuminate.
                                                                             9. *Comarum.*
                        Leaves 3-foliolate ; receptacle much enlarged in fruit.
                            Receptacle not pulpy ; petals yellow.   10. *Duchesnea.*
                            Receptacle very pulpy ; petals white or pinkish. 11. *Fragaria.*
                    Achenes 10–15 ; stamens 5 ; leaves 3-foliolate.   12. *Sibbaldia.*
                Shrubs ; achenes hairy.
                    Style filiform ; leaves 3-foliolate.   13. *Sibbaldiopsis.*
                    Style club-shaped ; leaves pinnate.   14. *Dasiphora.*
            Style nearly basal ; ovule and seed ascending.
                Stamens numerous ; flowers bracteolate ; leaves pinnate.   15. *Drymocallis.*
                Stamens 5 ; flowers ebracteolate ; leaves 2–3-ternately compound.   16. *Chamaerhodos.*
        Style not articulated with the ovary ; calyx-tube urn-shaped or cup-shaped, contracted at the
            throat or mouth.
            Style nearly basal ; inflorescence cymose ; petals none (Alchemilleae).
                Perennial herbs ; stamens 4, alternate with the sepals.   17. *Alchemilla.*
                Small annual herbs ; stamen 1, opposite a sepal, rarely 2–5. 18. *Aphanes.*
            Style terminal ; inflorescence spicate, racemose or capitate (Sanguisorbeae).
                Calyx-tube not prickly ; petals none.
                    Stamens 2–4, not declined ; pistil 1.
                        Perennial herbs ; stigma papillose ; leaflets toothed.   19. *Sanguisorba.*
                        Annual or biennial herbs ; stigma brush-like ; leaflets pectinate-pinnatifid.
                                                                             20. *Poteridium.*
                    Stamens of staminate flowers numerous, declined ; pistils 2.   21. *Poterium.*
                Calyx-tube and fruit prickly ; petals present, yellow.   22. *Agrimonia.*
    Seed erect, basal.
        Style wholly deciduous (Colurieae).   23. *Waldsteinia.*
        Style persistent in whole or in part.
            Calyx-tube hemispheric to turbinate, persistent ; herbs (Dryadeae).
                Calyx-lobes and petals 5 ; leaves pinnate.
                    Styles jointed, the upper part deciduous.   24. *Geum.*
                    Styles not jointed, wholly persistent, mostly plumose.   25. *Sieversia.*
                Calyx-lobes and petals 8 or 9 ; leaves simple ; styles plumose.   26. *Dryas.*
            Calyx-tube salver-shaped, the limb deciduous ; the tube persistent, investing the achene ;
                shrubs or trees (Cercocarpeae).   27. *Cercocarpus.*

  2. *Fruit of fleshy or nearly dry drupelets ; ovary 2-ovuled* (Rubeae).

Drupelets very pulpy.   28. *Rubus.*
Drupelets nearly dry, enclosed by the calyx.   29. *Dalibarda.*

** Carpels enclosed in the fleshy calyx-tube (Roseae).   30. *Rosa.*

1. OPULÁSTER Medic. Pfl. Anat. 2: 109. 1799.

[Physocarpa Raf. New Fl. N. A. 3: 73. 1836.]

[Physocarpus Maxim. Acta Hort. Petrop. 6: 219. 1879.]

Branching shrubs, with petioled simple palmately lobed leaves, and white flowers in terminal corymbs. Calyx campanulate, 5-lobed. Petals 5, rounded, inserted in the throat of
the calyx. Stamens 20–40, inserted with the petals. Pistils 1–5, short-stipitate, when 5 alternate with the calyx-lobes. Stigma terminal, capitate. Pods 1–5, inflated, in our species at
length dehiscent along both sutures, 2–4-seeded. Seeds ovoid or globose, crustaceous, shining ; endosperm copious. [Greek, resembling Opulus, the cranberry-tree.]

Species about 12, of North America, and 1 in Mantchuria. Type species : *Spiraea opulifolia* L.
Follicles glabrous, shining.   1. *O. opulifolius.*
Follicles stellate-pubescent.   2. *O. intermedius.*

1. Opulaster opulifòlius (L.) Kuntze.   Ninebark.   Fig. 2213.

Spiraea opulifolia L. Sp. Pl. 489. 1753.
Neillia opulifolia Brew. & Wats. Bot. Cal. 1 : 171. 1876.
Opulaster opulifolius Kuntze, Rev. Gen. Pl. 949. 1891.

A shrub 3°–10° high, with recurved branches, glabrous twigs and foliage, the bark peeling off in thin strips.   Stipules caducous; leaves petioled, ovate-orbicular, obtusely or acutely 3-lobed, cordate, truncate or broadly cuneate at the base, 1′–2′ long, or larger on the young shoots, the lobes irregularly crenate-dentate; corymbs terminal, peduncled, nearly spherical, many-flowered, 1′–2′ broad; pedicels slender, glabrous or slightly pubescent, 5″–8″ long; flowers white or purplish; calyx glabrous or somewhat pubescent; follicles 3–5, glabrous, shining, 3″–5″ long, obliquely subulate-tipped, twice as long as the calyx.

River-banks and in rocky places, Quebec to Georgia, Tennessee and Michigan.   June.

Opulaster austràlis Rydb., growing in the mountains from Virginia to South Carolina, appears to be a race of this species with smaller follicles.

2. Opulaster intermèdius Rydb.   Prairie Nine-bark.   Fig. 2214.

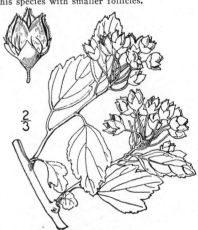

O. intermedius Rydb. in Britton, Man. 492. 1901.

Physocarpus intermedius C. K. Schneider, Handb. Laubh. 1 : 807. 1906.

P. missouriensis Daniels, Univ. Mo. Stud. Sci. 1 : 291. 1907.

A shrub similar to O. opulifolius in aspect, foliage and inflorescence, the leaves mostly narrower, and narrowed at the base.   Calyx densely stellate-pubescent; follicles 3 or 4, abruptly acuminate, 3½″–4″ long, permanently stellate-pubescent.

River-banks and rocky woodlands, southern Ontario and western New York to South Dakota, Illinois, Missouri, Arkansas and Colorado.

2.   SPIRAÈA [Tourn.] L. Sp. Pl. 489.   1753.

Shrubs, with alternate simple pinnate or pinnatifid mainly stipulate leaves.   Flowers terminal or axillary, racemose, cymose, corymbose or paniculate, white or pink, perfect. Calyx persistent, its tube mainly campanulate, 4–5-lobed.   Petals 4–5, inserted on the calyx, short-clawed.   Stamens 20–60, distinct, inserted on the calyx; filaments filiform; anthers didymous.   Disk adnate to the calyx-tube.   Pistils commonly 5 (rarely 1–8), superior, sessile or short-stipitate, alternate with the calxy-lobes.   Stigmas capitate or discoid; ovules 2–∞. Follicles usually 5, not inflated, dehiscent along 1 suture.   Seeds linear, pendulous, the testa dull; endosperm none.   [Greek, twisting, the pods twisted in some species.]

About 70 species, natives of the north temperate zone.   Besides the following, about 12 others occur in the southern and western parts of North America.   Type species: Spiraea salicifolia L.

Flowers in dense terminal panicles.
  Glabrous or puberulent.
    Leaves broadly obovate ; inflorescence glabrous or nearly so.   1. S. latifolia.
    Leaves narrowly oblanceolate or oblong ; inflorescence densely puberulent or tomentulose.
                                                                    2. S. alba.
  Twigs and lower surfaces of the leaves woolly-pubescent.   3. S. tomentosa.
Flowers in terminal corymbs.
  Calyx glabrous ; native.
    Leaves broadly oval or ovate, thick, serrate.   4. S. corymbosa.
    Leaves oblong, thin, nearly entire.   5. S. virginiana.
  Calyx pubescent ; introduced.   6. S. japonica.

1. Spiraea latifòlia (Ait.) Borkh. American Meadow-sweet. Quaker Lady. Fig. 2215.

S. salicifolia latifolia Ait. Hort. Kew. **2** : 198. 1789.
S. latifolia Borkh. Handb. Forstbot. 1871. 1803.

An erect shrub, 2°–6° high, simple, or branched above, nearly glabrous, the stems reddish or purplish. Leaves petioled, broadly oblanceolate or obovate, glabrous or very nearly so, sharply and rather coarsely serrate, especially above the middle, 1′–2′ long, 4″–18″ wide, or on young shoots much larger, obtuse or acutish at the apex, cuneate to rounded at the base, pale beneath; stipules deciduous or none; flowers white or pinkish-tinged, 2″–3″ broad, in dense terminal panicles; follicles glabrous.

In moist or rocky ground, Newfoundland to Saskatchewan, Virginia and western Pennsylvania. Called also queen-of-the-meadow. Spice hardhack. June–Aug.

Included in our first edition in the description of the Asiatic *S. salicifolia* L., which has pubescent inflorescence, pink flowers and narrower oblong leaves; it is sometimes cultivated and has escaped to roadsides in northern New York.

2. Spiraea álba DuRoi. Narrow-leaved Meadow-sweet. Fig. 2216.

S. alba DuRoi, Harbk. Baumz. **2** : 430. 1772.

S. salicifolia lanceolata T. & G. Fl. N. A. **1** : 415. 1840.

A shrub up to 6° high, the twigs yellowish-brown, puberulent when young. Leaves petioled, narrowly oblanceolate to oblong, puberulent on the veins beneath, sharply and mostly finely serrate, acute at each end, 1′–2½′ long, 5″–8″ wide; inflorescence narrowly paniculate, densely puberulent or tomentulose; petals white, suborbicular about 1″ long; follicles glabrous.

In wet soil, Ontario to New York, North Carolina, Saskatchewan, Indiana and Missouri. June–Aug.

3. Spiraea tomentòsa L. Hardhack. Steeple-bush. Fig. 2217.

Spiraea tomentosa L. Sp. Pl. 489. 1753.

Erect, shrubby, usually simple, the stems floccose-pubescent. Leaves short-petioled, ovate or oval, 1′–2′ long, 6″–12″ wide, unequally serrate, obtuse or acutish at the apex, narrowed or rounded at the base, glabrous and dark-green above, woolly-pubescent with whitish hairs beneath; stipules deciduous or none; flowers pink or purple, rarely white, about 2″ broad, in dense terminal panicles; follicles pubescent.

In swamps and low ground, Nova Scotia to Manitoba, south to Georgia and Kansas. Silver-leaf or -weed. White cap. Meadow-sweet. Poor man's-soap. Spice-hardhack. Rosy-bush. July–Sept.

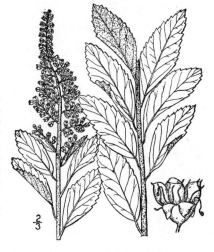

4. Spiraea corymbòsa Raf. Corymbed Spiraea. Fig. 2218.

Spiraea corymbosa Raf. Prec. Decouv. 36. 1814.
Spiraea betulifolia var. *corymbosa* S. Wats. in A. Gray, Man. Ed. 6, 153. 1890.

A shrub, 1°–3° high, simple or little branched, nearly glabrous throughout. Leaves petioled, rather thick, oval, ovate or orbicular, narrowed, rounded or slightly cordate at the base, obtuse at the apex, unequally serrate with pointed teeth, especially above the middle, green above, paler and sometimes minutely pubescent beneath, 1½'–3' long, 1'–2' wide; stipules deciduous or none; flowers white, about 2" broad in dense compound terminal often leafy corymbs; follicles glabrous.

On banks or in rocky places, New York and New Jersey to the mountains of Georgia and Kentucky. Birch-leaved meadow-sweet. May–June.

5. Spiraea virginiàna Britton. Virginia Spiraea. Fig. 2219.

S. virginiana Britton, Bull. Torr. Club **17**: 314. 1890.

A much-branched shrub, the branches forming wands 1°–4° long, more or less pubescent when young, becoming glabrous. Stipules deciduous or none; leaves petioled, oblong or oblanceolate, thin, obtuse or acutish at the apex, cuneate or rounded at the base, 1½'–2' long, 5"–8" wide, green above, pale or slightly glaucous beneath, entire, or with a few low teeth above the middle; petioles 1"–2½" long; flowers white, about 3" wide, in terminal compound corymbs; petals ovate-orbicular; pedicels and calyx glaucous; follicles glabrous.

On damp rocks, West Virginia to the mountains of North Carolina and Tennessee. June.

6. Spiraea japónica L. f. Japanese Spiraea. Fig. 2220.

S. japonica L. f. Suppl. 262. 1781.
S. callosa Thunb. Fl. Jap. 209. 1784.

A shrub 2½°–4½° high, the twigs purplish-brown, finely villous when young. Leaves petioled, ovate to lanceolate, 4' long or less, ¾'–1½' wide, glabrous above, somewhat pubescent beneath, acute or acuminate at the apex, sharply serrate; inflorescence compound, corymbose, 2'–6' broad, finely villous; calyx turbinate, pubescent, its lobes triangular; petals pink or rose, obovate, 1½" long; follicles glabrous.

Escaped from gardens, Connecticut to Pennsylvania. Native of eastern Asia.

Spiraea prunifòlia Sieb. & Zucc., a low shrub with lateral umbels of white, commonly double flowers 5"–6" broad, is much planted for ornament, and has escaped to roadsides in Connecticut and Massachusetts. It is native of Japan and China.

Spiraea chamaedrifòlia L., also Asiatic, and much planted, has simple terminal corymbs of white flowers and small obovate leaves dentate above the middle. It has escaped to roadsides in New York.

3. ARÚNCUS [L.] Adans. Fam. Pl. 2: 295. 1763.

Tall perennial herbs, with large 2–3-pinnate leaves, stipules minute or wanting, and very numerous white dioecious flowers in panicled spikes. Calyx mostly 5-lobed. Petals as many as the calyx-lobes. Stamens numerous, inserted on the calyx; filaments filiform. Pistils usually 3, alternate with the calyx-lobes. Follicles glabrous, at length reflexed, usually 2-seeded. Seeds minute, not shining. [Greek, goat's-beard.]

About 3 species, the following typical one widely distributed in the north temperate zone, one in northwestern America, the other Japanese.

1. Aruncus Arúncus (L.) Karst. Goat's-beard. Fig. 2221.

Spiraea Aruncus L. Sp. Pl. 490. 1753.
Aruncus sylvester Kostel. Ind. Hort. Prag. 15. Name only. 1844.
Aruncus Aruncus Karst. Deutsch. Fl. 779. 1880–83.

Glabrous or pubescent; stem erect, somewhat branched, 3°–7° high. Leaves long-petioled, the lower 1° long or more, pinnate, 3–7-foliolate; leaflets ovate, lanceolate or oval, thin, stalked or sessile, acuminate or acute at the apex, rounded, slightly cordate or sometimes narrowed at the base, sharply doubly serrate or incised, 1′–3′ long; spikes slender, elongated, erect or spreading; flowers 1″–2″ wide; follicles short.

In rich woods, mountains of Pennsylvania to Iowa, south to Georgia and Missouri, and in northern Europe and Asia. Consists of several races, differing in pubescence and slightly in the size and shape of the fruit. Ascends to 4200 ft. in North Carolina. May–July.

4. SCHIZONÒTUS Lindl. Introd. Nat. Syst. 81. 1830.

Shrubs, with odd-pinnate leaves, the large stipules conspicuous. Flowers perfect, in terminal panicles. Calyx-tube hemispheric, its 5 lobes imbricated, early reflexed. Petals 5, imbricated. Stamens numerous, borne on the margin of the disk. Pistils mostly 5, opposite the calyx-lobes, connate below; styles terminal or nearly so; ovules several, pendulous. Follicles thin, dehiscent along both sutures. Seeds few, with endosperm. [Greek, referring to the pinnately compound leaves.]

About 3 species, natives of Asia, the following typical.

1. Schizonotus sorbifòlius (L.) Lindl. Sorb-leaved Schizonotus. Fig. 2222.

Spiraea sorbifolia L. Sp. Pl. 490. 1753.

Schizonotus sorbifolius Lindl.; Steud. Nomencl. Ed. 2, 2: 531. 1841.

Sorbaria sorbifolia A. Braun; Aschers. Fl. Brand. 177. 1864.

Stems 6° high, or less, little branched. Leaflets 13–21, lanceolate, acuminate, finely double-serrate, glabrous or more or less stellate-puberulent; panicle often 1° long, densely very many-flowered; calyx-lobes ovate; petals white, obovate, about 1½″ long; filaments about twice as long as the petals; follicles oblong, pilose; styles recurved.

Locally spontaneous after cultivation, Ontario to New York and Maryland. Native of northern Asia. Summer.

5. PORTERÁNTHUS Britton, Mem. Torr. Club 4: 115. 1894.

[GILLENIA Moench, Meth. Suppl. 286. 1802. Not GILLENA Adans. 1763.]

Erect perennial herbs, with nearly sessile stipulate 3-foliolate or 3-parted leaves, and white or pinkish perfect long-pedicelled flowers in loose terminal panicles. Calyx cylindric, persistent, narrowed at the throat, 10-nerved, 5-toothed, the teeth imbricated, slightly glandular. Petals 5, linear-lanceolate, spreading, convolute in the bud, somewhat unequal, inserted on the calyx. Stamens 10–20, included; filaments short; anthers large. Carpels 5, villous-pubescent, opposite the calyx-lobes. Ovules ascending; style filiform. Follicles 5, 2–4-seeded. Seeds with endosperm. [In honor of Thomas Conrad Porter, Professor in Lafayette College.]

A genus of 2 species, of North America. Type species: *Porteranthus trifoliatus* (L.) Britton.

Leaflets serrate; stipules subulate, mainly entire.   1. *P. trifoliatus.*
Leaflets incised; stipules broad, foliaceous, incised.   2. *P. stipulatus.*

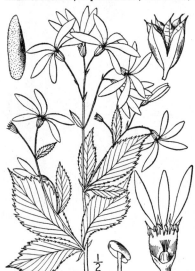

1. Porteranthus trifoliàtus (L.) Britton.

Indian Physic. Bowman's-root. False Ipecac. Fig. 2223.

Spiraea trifoliata L. Sp. Pl. 490. 1753.
Gillenia trifoliata Moench, Meth. Suppl. 286. 1802.
P. trifoliatus Britton, Mem. Torr. Club 5: 115. 1894.

Herbaceous from a perennial root, erect, branching, 2°–4° high, glabrous or somewhat pubescent. Stipules subulate, 2″–4″ long, entire or serrate; leaflets short-stalked, oval, ovate, lanceolate or slightly obovate, acuminate at the apex, narrowed at the base, 2′–3′ long, irregularly serrate; upper leaves often 3-lobed, or sometimes merely serrate; panicles few-flowered; pedicels slender; petals white or pinkish, 5″–6″ long; calyx reddish; pods pubescent, subulate-tipped, little exceeding the calyx.

Woodlands, Ontario and New York to Michigan, Georgia and Missouri. Ascends to 4500 ft. in North Carolina. Stipules rarely larger, lanceolate. Meadowsweet. Indian hippo. Western dropwort. May–July.

2. Porteranthus stipulàtus (Muhl.) Britton. American Ipecac. Fig. 2224.

Spiraea stipulata Muhl.; Willd. Enum. 542. 1809.
Gillenia stipulacea Nutt. Gen. 1: 307. 1818.
P. stipulatus Britton, Mem. Torr. Club 5: 115. 1894.

Resembling the preceding species, but generally more pubescent. Stipules foliaceous, broad, ovate, acuminate or acute, 4″–12″ long, sharply incised-serrate; leaflets commonly narrower than those of the preceding, incised-serrate, or those of the lower leaves deeply pinnatifid; flowers commonly fewer and slightly smaller; pods less pubescent or sometimes quite glabrous.

In woods, western New York to Indiana and Kansas, south to Georgia, Louisiana and Oklahoma. Indian physic. June–July.

6. FILIPÉNDULA [Tourn.] Mill. Gard. Dict. Abr. Ed. 4. 1754.

[ULMÀRIA Hill, Hort. Kew. 213. 1768.]

Tall perennial herbs, with alternate petioled pinnately divided stipulate leaves, and small white, pink or purple perfect flowers in large cymose panicles. Calyx 5-lobed. Petals 5, clawed. Stamens numerous, inserted on the flat or slightly concave receptacle; filaments narrowed at the base. Pistils about 10 (5–15), distinct; ovary 2-ovuled. Ripe carpels capsular, indehiscent, 1-seeded. Seed pendulous. [Latin, a hanging thread.]

About 10 species, natives of the north temperate zone. Besides the following, 2 others occur in northwestern America. Type species: *Spiraea Filipendula* L.

Lateral leaflets palmately 3–5-lobed ; flowers pink or purple.   1. *F. rubra.*
Lateral leaflets merely serrate, or slightly lobed ; flowers white.   2. *F. Ulmaria.*

1. Filipendula rùbra (Hill) Robinson. Queen-of-the-Prairie. Fig. 2225.

Ulmaria rubra Hill. Hort. Kew. 214. *pl. 7.* 1769.

Spiraea lobata Gronov. ; Jacq. Hort. Vind. 1 : 38. *pl. 88.* 1770.

Spiraea rubra Britton, Bull. Torr. Club 18 : 270. 1891.

F. rubra Robinson, Rhodora 8 : 204. 1906.

Glabrous, stem branched, grooved, 2°–8° tall. Leaves large, green on both sides, the lower sometimes 3° long, pinnately 3–7-foliolate, commonly with smaller leaf-segments interposed or borne on the petiole; lateral leaflets sessile, opposite, palmately 3–5-lobed or 3–5-parted, the lobes acute, unequally serrate or incised; terminal leaflet larger, 7–9-parted; stipules serrate, persistent, 4″–8″ long; flowers pink or purple, fragrant, about 4″ broad; capsules glabrous.

In moist grounds and on prairies, western Pennsylvania to Illinois and Michigan, south to Georgia, Kentucky and Iowa. Escaped from gardens farther east. June–July.

2. Filipendula Ulmària (L.) Maxim. Meadow-sweet or Meadow-Queen. Honey-sweet. Sweet-hay. Fig. 2226.

Spiraea Ulmaria L. Sp. Pl. 490. 1753.
Ulmaria palustris Moench, Meth. 663. 1794.
Ulmaria Ulmaria Barnhart, Bull. Torr. Club 21 : 491. 1894.
F. Ulmaria Maxim. Acta Hort. Petrop. 6 : 251. 1879.

Stem branched, angular or grooved, 2°–4° tall. Leaves pinnately 3–9-foliolate, densely and finely white-downy beneath, green above, sometimes with several or numerous much smaller leaf-segments interposed between the leaflets or borne on the petiole; lateral leaflets sessile, opposite, ovate or ovate-lanceolate, acute or acuminate, serrate or sometimes slightly lobed, the terminal one larger and deeply 3–5-lobed, the lobes acute and serrate; stipules about ½′ long; flowers white or greenish-white, fragrant.

Escaped from gardens, Quebec to Massachusetts. Native of Europe and Asia. June–Aug. Meadow-wort. Herb Christopher. My lady's-belt. Bride-wort.

Filipendula denudàta (Presl) Rydb., differs in having the leaves green on both sides, and is established near Dover, Maine. It is also native of Europe and Asia.

7. POTENTÍLLA L. Sp. Pl. 495. 1753.

Herbs, with alternate stipulate digitately or pinnately compound leaves, and cymose or solitary yellow, white or purple perfect flowers. Calyx-persistent, its tube concave or hemispheric, 5-bracteolate (rarely 4-bracteolate), 5-lobed (rarely 4-lobed). Petals 5 or rarely 4, mostly obovate or orbicular, usually emarginate. Stamens ∞, seldom 5 or 10; filaments slender; anthers small. Carpels numerous, inserted on a dry, usually pubescent receptacle; style terminal or nearly so, deciduous. Seed pendulous, anatropous. [Diminutive of *potens*, powerful, from the medicinal properties of some species.]

Over 300 species, nearly all of them natives of the north temperate zone. Besides the following at least 100 others occur in the western and northwestern parts of North America and several in Arctic America. Type species: *Potentilla reptans* L.

A. Flowers solitary, axillary, long-peduncled.

    Flowers 4-parted; upper leaves 3-foliolate.   1. *P. procumbens.*

    Flowers 5-parted; leaves usually all 5-foliolate (genus *Callionia* Greene).

        Pubescence of the stem, petioles and peduncles appressed.

            Leaflets sparingly silky beneath, dentate nearly to the base.   2. *P. simplex.*

            Leaflets densely silky beneath, dentate only above the middle.   3. *P. pumila.*

        Pubescence of the stem, petioles and peduncles spreading.   4. *P. canadensis.*

B. Flowers cymose.

    a. Cymes very leafy, several–many-flowered, the flowers or some of them apparently axillary.

        Mainly annuals or biennials; style fusiform, glandular at the base.

            Achenes corky-gibbous.

                Leaves all pinnate; inflorescence evidently cymose.   5. *P. paradoxa.*

                Upper leaves ternate; inflorescence falsely racemose.   6. *P. Nicolletii.*

            Achenes not gibbous.

                Leaves all ternate; stamens 10–20.

                    Petals about half as long as the calyx-lobes; calyx-tube 2″–2½″ broad in fruit.

                                          7. *P. millegrana.*

                  Petals more than half as long as the calyx-lobes; calyx-tube 3½″ broad in fruit.

                                        8. *P. monspeliensis.*

                Basal leaves apparently 5-foliolate; stamens 5.   9. *P. pentandra.*

        Perennials; style filiform, not glandular.

            Leaves white-tomentose beneath.   10. *P. argentea.*

            Leaves grayish silky beneath.   11. *P. intermedia.*

    b. Cymes not very leafy, usually few-flowered.

        Leaves digitately divided.

            Basal leaves 5–9-foliolate.

                Plant tall, 1° high or more; introduced.   12. *P. recta.*

                Plants low, less than 8′ high; native boreal species.   13. *P. maculata.*

            Basal leaves 3-foliolate; boreal and alpine species.

                Leaves densely white-pubescent beneath.   14. *P. nivea.*

                Leaves green beneath, not densely pubescent.

                    Petals much exceeding the calyx-lobes.   15. *P. emarginata.*

                    Petals scarcely exceeding the calyx-lobes.   16. *P. Robbinsiana.*

        Leaves pinnately divided.

            Style longer than the ripe achene, filiform; leaflets toothed.

                Bractlets much shorter than the acuminate calyx-lobes.   17. *P. effusa.*

                Bractlets at least three-fourths as long as the acute calyx-lobes. 18. *P. Hippiana.*

            Style not longer than the ripe achene; leaflets incised.

                Style not thickened at the base; boreal species.   19. *P. multifida.*

                Style thickened and glandular at the base.

                  Leaves white-tomentose beneath.   20. *P. bipinnatifida.*

                  Leaves grayish pubescent beneath.

                    Leaflets approximate, the leaves suborbicular or pentagonal in outline.

                                          21. *P. pectinata.*

                  Leaflets distant, the leaves obovate in outline.   22. *P. pennsylvanica.*

1. **Potentilla procúmbens** Sibth. Wood Cinquefoil. Fig. 2227.

Tormentilla reptans L. Sp. Pl. 500. 1753. Not *P. reptans* L.

Potentilla procumbens Sibth. Fl. Oxon. 162. 1794.

Potentilla nemoralis Nestl. Mon. Pot. 65. 1816.

Diffusely branched, trailing or ascending, very slender, somewhat strigose-pubescent, 6′–2° long. Stipules foliaceous, entire or dentate; leaves petioled, 3-foliolate (rarely 5-foliolate); leaflets oblanceolate or obovate, obtuse at the apex, cuneate at the base, sharply dentate above; peduncles axillary, filiform, usually much exceeding the leaves, 1-flowered; bractlets narrowly lanceolate; flowers 3″–4″ broad, yellow, generally 4-parted; petals obovate, emarginate, or rounded, exceeding the acute calyx-lobes and narrowly lanceolate bractlets; achenes glabrous; receptacle pubescent.

Labrador and Nova Scotia. Naturalized from Europe. Called also trailing tormentil. Summer.

Potentilla réptans L., another European species found occasionally in grassy and waste places from Massachusetts to New Jersey, and recorded from Ohio, has 5-parted flowers with ovate or elliptic bractlets longer than the calyx-lobes.

2. Potentilla símplex Michx. Decumbent Five-finger. Fig. 2228.

Potentilla simplex Michx. Fl. Bor. Am. 1 : 303. 1803.

Potentilla canadensis simplex T. & G. Fl. N. Am. 1 : 443. 1840.

Rootstock short; stems slender, decumbent, appressed-pubescent, 3° long or less. Leaves glabrous or nearly so above, silky appressed-pubescent beneath, the basal and lower ones 5-foliolate; stipules lanceolate; petioles appressed-pubescent; leaflets oblong to oblanceolate or obovate, coarsely toothed except near the base, ¾'-2½' long; peduncles solitary in the axils of upper leaves, 1'-2' long, appressed-pubescent; bractlets linear-lanceolate, 2"-2½" long, about equalling the slightly broader calyx-lobes; petals yellow, obcordate, 2½"-3" long; stamens 20-25; styles filiform.

Shaded grassy situations, Nova Scotia to North Carolina, Alabama, Minnesota and Missouri. May–July.

3. Potentilla pùmila Poir. Dwarf Five-finger. Fig. 2229.

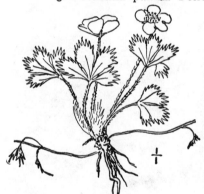

P. pumila Poir. in Lam. Enc. Meth. 5 : 594. 1804.

Potentilla canadensis pumila T. & G. Fl. N. A. 1 : 443. 1840.

Low, seldom more than a few inches high; flowering stems at first very short and upright; later producing slender prostrate runners; whole plant densely silky-strigose, with appressed pubescence; basal leaves digitately 5-foliolate, on slender petioles; stem-leaves few and often only 3-foliolate; leaflets obovate, sharply serrate, usually less than 1' long; stipules small, lanceolate; flowers few, yellow, 3"-5" broad, the first from the axil of the first stem-leaf; petals broadly obovate, slightly exceeding the narrowly lanceolate sepals and bractlets; stamens about 20.

In poor soil, Maine to Ontario, Georgia and Ohio. April–June.

4. Potentilla canadénsis L. Five-finger. Common Cinquefoil. Fig. 2230.

Potentilla canadensis L. Sp. Pl. 498. 1753.

Spreading by slender runners 3'-2° long, the pubescence of the stem, petioles and peduncles spreading. Stipules lanceolate, acute, entire or few-toothed; leaves petioled, digitately 5-foliolate (rarely 3-4-foliolate); leaflets oblanceolate, obovate or oblong, obtuse at the apex, narrowed at the base, 6"-1' long, serrate; peduncles slender, axillary, 1-flowered, the first from the axil of the second stem-leaf; flower yellow, 3"-7" broad; petals 5, broadly oval, slightly longer than the acute calyx-lobes and linear-lanceolate bractlets; stamens about 20; style filiform; achenes glabrous; receptacle villous.

In dry soil, New Brunswick to Georgia, Minnesota and Texas. Ascends to 6300 ft. in North Carolina. April–Aug. Wild or barren strawberry. Sinkfield. Running buttercups. Star-flower.

Potentilla caroliniàna Poir., a plant of the Southern States, with longer spreading pubescence, and broadly obovate leaflets which are cuneate at the base, enters our area in southern Virginia and Missouri. It is probably a race of *P. canadensis* L.

5. Potentilla paradóxa Nutt. Bushy Cinquefoil. Fig. 2231.

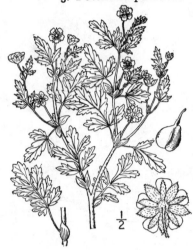

P. paradoxa Nutt.; T. & G. Fl. N. A. **1** : 437. 1840.
Potentilla supina Michx. Fl. Bor. Am. **1** : 304. 1803.
Not L. 1753.

Softly pubescent, annual or biennial, decumbent, ascending or nearly erect, rather stout, bushy, 1°–2° high. Stipules ovate-lanceolate, acute, mainly entire; leaves all but the uppermost petioled, pinnately 7–11-foliolate; leaflets obovate or oval, obtuse, 6″–12″ long, sparingly pubescent, narrowed or rounded at the base, crenate, the upper ones commonly confluent or decurrent on the rachis; flowers terminal, loosely cymose, leafy-bracted, yellow, 3″–5″ broad; petals obovate, cuneate, about equalling the ovate calyx-lobes and lanceolate bractlets; stamens about 20; style thickened below; achenes glabrous, strongly gibbous.

Shores of the Great Lakes from New York, Ontario and Pennsylvania to Minnesota, south in the Mississippi Valley to Missouri, west to Washington, Oregon and New Mexico. Also in Mexico and Mantchuria. June–Sept.

6. Potentilla Nicollétii (S. Wats.) Sheldon. Nicollet's Cinquefoil. Fig. 2232.

Potentilla supina var. *Nicolletii* S. Wats. Proc. Am. Acad.
8 : 553. 1873.
Potentilla Nicolletii Sheldon, Bull. Geol. Nat. Hist. Surv. Minn. 9 : 16. 1894.

Similar to *P. paradoxa,* but more spreading and more branched; lower leaves only pinnate, with several leaflets; upper leaves 3-foliolate; teeth of the leaflets acute; inflorescence elongated, falsely racemose; flowers about 2½″ broad; calyx-tube sparingly hirsute, short and broad; bractlets and calyx-lobes ovate-oblong, mucronate, 1½″ long, petals obovate-cuneate, about as long as the calyx-lobes; stamens 10–15; style fusiform; achenes corky-gibbous.

In sandy soil, North Dakota to Missouri and Kansas. June–Sept.

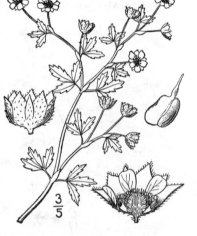

7. Potentilla millegràna Engelm. Diffuse Cinquefoil. Fig. 2233.

Potentilla millegrana Engelm.; Lehm. Ind. Sem. Hamb. 1849 : Add. 12. 1849.
Potentilla rivalis var. *millegrana* S. Wats. Proc. Am. Acad. 8 : 553. 1873.
Potentilla leucocarpa Rydb. in Britt. & Brown, Ill. Fl. 2 : 212. 1897.

Decumbent or ascending, annual, usually weak and diffusely branched, 6′–3° high, softly villous-pubescent, or glabrate. Stipules ovate or ovate-lanceolate, entire or sparingly dentate; leaves all but the uppermost petioled, 3-foliolate; leaflets oblong, cuneate, thin, flaccid, more or less pubescent, incisely serrate, ½′–1½′ long; flowers several, terminal, loosely cymose, yellow, about 2″ broad; calyx-lobes ovate, acute, about equalling the lanceolate bractlets, exceeding the obovate petals; stamens about 10; style slightly thickened below, terminal; achenes small, glabrous.

In damp soil, Illinois to Minnesota, Manitoba, New Mexico, California and Washington. May–Sept.

Potentilla rivàlis Nutt., a western species which may reach our limits in western Nebraska, is distinguished from this by its usually pinnately 5-foliolate leaves, viscid pubescence, stricter erect habit, and more numerous stamens. It has been collected at the stockyards of Chicago.

8. Potentilla monspeliénsis L. Rough Cinque-foil. Barren Strawberry. Fig. 2234.

Potentilla monspeliensis L. Sp. Pl. 499. 1753.
Potentilla norvegica L. Sp. Pl. 499. 1753.
Potentilla hirsuta Michx. Fl. Bor. Am. 1: 302. 1803.
P. labradorica Lehm. Del. Sem. Hort. Hamb. 1849: 12. 1849.

Erect, stout, annual or biennial, branched above, hirsutely rough-pubescent, 6'–2½° high. Stipules foliaceous, incised-dentate or sometimes entire; leaves 3-foliolate, the lower and basal ones petioled, the upper sessile or nearly so; leaflets obovate, green both sides, obtuse at the apex, mostly narrowed at the base, pubescent with spreading hairs, 1'–2' long; flowers yellow, terminal, usually rather densely cymose and leafy-bracted, 3''–6'' broad; calyx-lobes ovate, acute, pubescent, a little longer than the obo-vate retuse petals and somewhat broader than the bractlets; stamens 15–20; style glandular-thickened below; achenes glabrous, rugose or smooth.

In dry soil, Newfoundland and Labrador to South Carolina, Tennessee, Alaska, Kansas, Arizona and Cali-fornia. Also in Mexico, Europe and Asia. Often oc-curs as a weed in cultivated ground; consists of several races. June–Sept.

$\frac{1}{2}$

9. Potentilla pentándra Engelm. Five-stamened Cinquefoil. Fig. 2235.

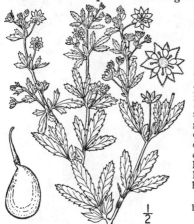

$\frac{1}{2}$

P. pentandra Engelm.; T. & G. Fl. N. A. 1: 447. 1840.
Potentilla rivalis var. *pentandra* S. Wats. Proc. Am. Acad. 8: 553. 1873.

Similar to the preceding species, erect, hirsute, 1°–4° high, simple at the base, much branched above. Stipules lanceolate, somewhat foliaceous, dentate or entire; basal and lower leaves slender-petioled, 3-foliolate, with the lower pair of leaflets parted nearly to the base, so as to appear 4- or 5-foliolate; leaflets oblanceolate or oblong, obtuse at the apex, narrowed or cuneate at the base, incised-dentate, glabrous or sparingly pubescent above, quite pubes-cent beneath, 1'–2' long; flowers terminal, in a more or less flat-topped cyme, pale yellow, 2''–4'' broad; calyx-lobes ovate, acute, exceeding the small spatu-late petals, and equalling or slightly shorter than the lanceolate bractlets; stamens 5–8; style thickened below; achenes glabrous.

In sandy soil, Manitoba to Alberta, Missouri, Ne-braska and Arkansas. June–Sept.

10. Potentilla argéntea L. Silvery or Hoary. Cinquefoil. Fig. 2236.

Potentilla argentea L. Sp. Pl. 497. 1753.

Stems ascending, tufted, branched, slightly woody at the base, 4'–12' long, white woolly-pubescent. Stipules lanceolate, acuminate; leaves all but the uppermost petioled, digitately 5-foliolate; leaflets oblanceolate or obovate, obtuse at the apex, cuneate at the base, green and glabrous above, white-tomentose beneath, laciniate or incised and with revolute margins, 6''–12'' long; flowers cymose, terminal, pedicelled, yellow, 2''–4'' broad; calyx-lobes ovate, acutish, a little shorter than the obovate retuse petals; stamens about 20; style fili-form; achenes glabrous.

In dry soil, Nova Scotia and Ontario to North Dakota, south to Washington, D. C., Indiana and Kansas. Also in Europe and Asia. May–Sept.

Potentilla collina Wibel, of Europe, collected at Winona, Minn., and Cambridge, Mass., differs in its more prostrate habit, broader and not revolute leaflets, and larger calyx.

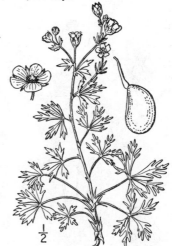

$\frac{1}{2}$

11. Potentilla intermèdia L. Downy Cinque-foil. Fig. 2237.

Potentilla intermedia L. Mant. 1 : 76. 1767.

Perennial, stem 1°–2½° high, usually ascending, leafy and much branched, finely pubescent with long hairs. Leaves green and finely hirsute on both sides, somewhat tomentose beneath, all but the uppermost 5-foliolate, the lower long-petioled; stipules narrow, acute, mostly entire; leaflets obovate or oblong, the teeth rather obtuse; flowers numerous, cymose, yel-low, leafy-bracted; petals obcordate, equalling the triangular-ovate acute sepals and oblong bractlets; stamens about 20; style short, not thickened at the base.

Waste grounds and roadsides, Massachusetts, New York and New Jersey to Michigan. Adventive from Europe. Resembles *P. monspeliensis,* differing in its 5-foliolate leaves, and perennial root.

Potentilla inclinàta Vill., introduced from Europe and established at Kingston, Ontario, and at Buffalo, New York, differs in having leaves grayish-silky beneath with oblanceolate leaflets (*P. canescens* Bess.).

12. Potentilla récta L. Rough-fruited Cinquefoil. Fig. 2238.

Potentilla recta L. Sp. Pl. 497. 1753.
Potentilla sulphurea Lam. Fl. Franc. 3 : 114. 1778.
Potentilla pilosa Willd. Sp. Pl. 2 : 1109. 1799.

Erect, rather stout, branched above, villous-pu-bescent, 1°–2° high. Stipules ovate-lanceolate, the lower foliaceous and laciniate; leaves digitately 5–7-foliolate, all but the uppermost petioled; leaf-lets oblanceolate or oblong-lanceolate, obtuse at the apex, narrowed or cuneate at the base, green both sides, sparingly pubescent with scattered hairs above, more pubescent beneath, incised-dentate, 1′–3′ long, with divergent teeth; flowers terminal, cymose, yel-low, numerous, 6″–9″ broad; stamens about 20; style slender, terminal; carpels rugose.

In waste places, Maine to Ontario, New York, Vir-ginia and Michigan. Adventive from Europe. Native also of Asia. June–Sept.

13. Potentilla maculàta Pourret. Northern Cinque-foil. Fig. 2239.

Potentilla maculata Pourr. Act. Toloss. 3 : 326. 1788.
Potentilla salisbrugensis Haenke in Jacq. Coll. 2 : 68. 1788.

Rootstock prostrate, stems ascending, simple, pubescent, 3′–8′ high. Stipules membranous; basal leaves slender-petioled, digitately 5-foliolate (rarely 3-foliolate); leaflets obovate, obtuse at the apex, narrowed or cuneate at the base, glabrous above, pubescent along the margins and on the veins beneath, green both sides, incisely dentate, with rounded or blunt teeth, 6″–9″ long; flowers few, terminal, loosely cymose, yellow, 6″–9″ broad; pedicels slender; petals obovate, obcordate, cuneate, yellow, orange-spotted at the base, longer than the ovate acutish calyx-lobes; stamens about 20; style filiform, terminal; achenes glabrous.

Labrador and Greenland to James Bay. Also in northern and alpine Europe and Asia. Summer. Confused with *P. rubens* (Crantz) Vill., in our first edition.

Potentilla Ranúnculus Lange, of Greenland and Labrador, differs in having the teeth of the leaflets lanceolate and acute.

14. Potentilla nívea L.   Snowy Cinquefoil.   Fig. 2240.

Potentilla nivea L. Sp. Pl. 499. 1753.

Stems 2'-6' high, woody at the base, ascending or erect, silky-villous, the flowering ones mostly simple. Stipules membranous, silky; leaves 3-foliolate (very rarely 5-foliolate), the lower petioled; leaflets obovate, oblong or oval, obtuse, incised-dentate or crenate, densely white-pubescent beneath, green and loosely villous above, 4"-8" long, the terminal one generally cuneate, the others narrowed or rounded at the base; flowers 1-5, terminal, pedicelled, yellow, 5"-9" broad; bractlets lanceolate to linear; sepals silky, lanceolate, acute, shorter than the broadly obovate emarginate petals, longer than the bractlets; stamens about 20; style filiform, terminal; achenes glabrous.

Quebec, Labrador, Greenland and throughout arctic America to Alaska and British Columbia, south in the Rocky Mountains to Utah and Colorado. Also in arctic and alpine Europe and Asia. Summer.

Potentilla Vahliàna Lehm., another high boreal species, differs in having oval or ovate bractlets and leaflets yellowish-villous beneath.

15. Potentilla emarginàta Pursh.   Arctic Cinquefoil.   Fig. 2241.

Potentilla emarginata Pursh, Fl. Am. Sept. 353. 1814.

Pòtentilla nana Willd.; Schlecht. Berl. Mag. 7: 296. 1815.

Stems villous-pubescent, tufted, ascending or erect, 1'-4' high. Stipules ovate or oblong, membranous, mostly obtuse, entire; leaves 3-foliolate, the basal slender-petioled; leaflets obovate, 2"-6" long, incised-dentate with acute teeth, of which the terminal one is generally the largest, generally villous on both sides, the terminal one narrowed or cuneate, the others sometimes broad at the base; flower solitary, rarely 2, yellow, 5"-7" broad; calyx-lobes ovate, obtuse, pilose, equalling the oblong bractlets, shorter than the obovate obcordate petals; stamens about 20; style filiform; achenes glabrous.

Labrador, Greenland and arctic America to Alaska. Also in eastern Siberia and Spitzbergen. Summer.

16. Potentilla Robbinsiàna Oakes.   Robbins' Cinquefoil.   Fig. 2242.

Potentilla Robbinsiana Oakes; T. & G. Fl. N. A. 1: 441. 1840.
Potentilla minima A. Gray, Man. 122. 1848.
P. frigida A. Gray, Man. Ed. 5, 154. 1867. Not Vill. 1789.

Depressed, ½'-2' high, tufted from a thick woody base, villous-pubescent. Stipules ovate, obtusish, loosely villous; basal leaves petioled, 3-foliolate, those of the flowering stem sessile, small and 3-lobed; leaflets obovate, villous on both sides, and especially so beneath, 2"-4" long, deeply 3-7-dentate above, cuneate or narrowed at the base, obtuse at the apex; flowers solitary, terminal, slender-petioled, yellow, about 3" broad; sepals and bractlets nearly equal, obtuse, slightly shorter than the obcordate petals; stamens about 20; style filiform; achenes glabrous.

White Mountains of New Hampshire. Summer.

17. Potentilla effùsa Dougl. Branched Cinquefoil. Fig. 2243.

P. effusa Dougl.; Lehm. Nov. Stirp. Pug. 2 : 8. 1830.

Plant perennial, 6'-18' high, diffusely branched above. Leaves pinnate, tomentose-canescent, but not silky; leaflets 5-11, or those of the upper leaves only 1-3, oblong, obtuse at the apex, commonly cuneate at the base, incised-dentate, $\frac{1}{2}'-1\frac{1}{2}'$ long; flowers yellow, 3"-5" broad, loosely cymose, yellow; bractlets much shorter than the lanceolate acuminate calyx-lobes; petals obovate, emarginate, exceeding the calyx-lobes; stamens about 20; achenes glabrous.

Prairies, western Minnesota to Saskatchewan, Alberta, Nebraska and New Mexico. Summer.

18. Potentilla Hippiàna Lehm. Woolly Cinquefoil. Fig. 2244.

P. Hippiana Lehm. Nov. Stirp. Pug. 2 : 7. 1830.
Potentilla leucophylla Torr. Ann. N. Y. Lyc. 2 : 197. 1825. Not Pall. 1773.

Erect or ascending, perennial, branched above, rather stout, 1°-2½° high, densely floccose as well as silky. Stipules lanceolate, acuminate, entire; lower and basal leaves petioled, pinnately 5-11-foliolate; leaflets oblanceolate or oblong, obtuse, narrowed or cuneate at the base, 6"-18" long, incisely dentate, very white beneath, the lower ones smaller than the upper, and no smaller ones interspersed; flowers terminal, yellow, loosely cymose, 3"-6" broad; petals obovate, retuse, a little exceeding the lanceolate acute calyx-lobes and slightly narrower bractlets; stamens about 20; style filiform; achenes glabrous.

Dry soil, northwestern Minnesota and Assiniboia to British Columbia, south to New Mexico and Arizona. June-Aug.

19. Potentilla multífida L. Cut-leaved Cinquefoil. Fig. 2245.

Potentilla multifida L. Sp. Pl. 496. 1753.

Perennial, stems several or many from the caudex, low, asceding or spreading, appressed-silky. Stipules large, lanceolate, acuminate, scarious, brown; leaves pinnately 5-9-foliolate, grayish-tomentose beneath, glabrate above; leaflets finely divided to near the midrib into linear acute segments, with more or less revolute margins; petals yellow, a little exceeding the ovate-lanceolate acute sepals; stamens about 20; style terminal, short, not thickened at the base; achenes smooth, or slightly rugose.

Hudson Bay to Great Slave Lake. Also in arctic and alpine Europe and Asia. Summer.

20. Potentilla bipinnatífida Dougl. Plains Cinquefoil. Fig. 2246.

P. bipinnatifida Dougl.; Hook. Fl. Bor. Am. 1: 188. 1833.

P. pennsylvanica bipinnatifida T. & G. Fl. N. Am. 1: 438. 1840.

Perennial; stems several, erect or ascending, usually simple, leafy, finely white-villous, 1°-1½° high. Leaves pinnate, with ovate or lanceolate stipules often 1½' long; leaflets 7-9, obovate in outline, pectinately deeply divided into linear or linear-oblong obtuse segments, finely silky above, white-tomentose beneath; calyx white-silky, 4" broad in fruit, its lobes ovate, 2"-2½" long; bractlets oblong-lanceolate, shorter than the calyx-lobes; stamens about 20; style glandular-thickened at the base.

Plains and hills, Minnesota to Manitoba, Alberta and Colorado. Summer.

21. Potentilla pectinàta Raf. Coast Cinquefoil. Fig. 2247.

Potentilla pectinata Raf. Aut. Bot. 164. 1840.

P. littoralis Rydberg, Bull. Torr. Club 23: 264. 1896.

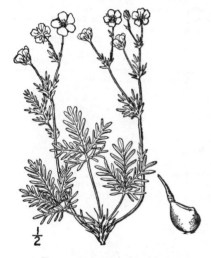

Perennial, tufted, stems ascending or decumbent, branched above, 6'-2° high, appressed-silky, or glabrate. Stipules ovate-lanceolate, cleft or entire, acute; basal and lower leaves petioled, pinnately 5-7-foliolate, the leaflets approximate or apparently digitate; leaflets oblanceolate or obovate, incised-pinnatifid into oblong obtuse segments, grayish-pubescent beneath, green and glabrate above, ½'-2½' long; flowers yellow, cymose, 4"-5" broad; petals obovate, equalling or slightly exceeding the ovate acute veined sepals and the lanceolate bractlets; stamens 20-25; style thickened below; achenes glabrous.

Coast of Newfoundland and Labrador to Hudson Bay, Quebec and New Hampshire. June-July.

22. Potentilla pennsylvánica L. Prairie Cinquefoil. Fig. 2248.

Potentilla pennsylvanica L. Mant. 76. 1767.

P. pennsylvanica strigosa Pursh, Fl. Am. Sept. 356. 1814.

P. strigosa Pall.; Tratt. Ros. Monog. 4: 31. 1824.

Stem generally erect, 15'-30' high, tomentose and more or less villous. Stipules ovate, often much divided; leaves pinnately 5-15-foliolate, grayish tomentose beneath, glabrous above; leaflets oblong or oblanceolate, cleft halfway to the midrib into oblong lobes, margins scarcely revolute; cymes dense, the branches erect; petals yellow, obovate, truncate or slightly emarginate, about equalling the ovate triangular acute sepals and the lanceolate bractlets; stamens 20-25; style thickened below; achenes glabrous.

On plains, Hudson Bay to the Yukon, British Columbia, Kansas and New Mexico. Summer.

8. ARGENTÌNA Lam. Fl. Franc. 3: 118.   1778.

Perennial herbs, with slender stolons, interruptedly pinnate leaves, the flowers solitary, axillary, peduncled. Calyx-tube short and broad. Bractlets, sepals and petals 5, or often more. Petals yellow, not clawed. Stamens 20-25, borne around the base of the hemispheric receptacle; filaments filiform. Pistils numerous on the receptacle; style lateral, filiform. Achenes with thick pericarp. Seeds ascending, amphitropous. [Latin, referring to the silvery white pubescence of the under side of the leaves.]

About 8 species, natives of the north temperate and subarctic zones. Besides the following, 4 others occur in western North America. Type species: *Argentina vulgaris* Lam.

1. Argentina Anserìna (L.) Rydb.   Silver-weed.   Wild or Goose-tansy.   Fig. 2249.

Potentilla Anserina L. Sp. Pl. 495. 1753.
Argentina vulgaris Lam. Fl. Franc. 3: 119. 1778.
A. Anserina Rydb. Mem. Dept. Bot. Col. Univ. 2: 159. 1898.
A. Babcockiana Rydb. N. Am. Fl. 22: 354. 1908.
A. litoralis Rydb. loc. cit. 1908.

Herbaceous, tufted, spreading by slender runners 1°-3° long. Stipules membranous; leaves petioled, pinnate, 3'-18' long; leaflets 7-25, oblong, oblanceolate or obovate, obtuse, the lower generally smaller, often with still smaller ones interspersed, all sharply serrate, nearly glabrous above, white or silky-pubescent beneath; peduncles axillary, solitary, slender, erect, 1-flowered, about equalling the leaves; flower yellow, 8''-12'' broad; petals broadly oval or obovate, entire or emarginate, exceeding the ovate acute calyx-lobes and oval bractlets; stamens about 20; style filiform, lateral; receptacle villous; achenes grooved or grooveless.

On shores and salt meadows, New Jersey to Greenland, west to Nebraska, British Columbia and Alaska, south in the Rocky Mountains to New Mexico and to California. Also in Europe and Asia. Argentina. Silver-feather. Dog's-tansy. Goose-grass. May–Sept. Consists of several or numerous races, differing in size, in shape of the leaflets, and slightly in the achenes; small northern plants have been referred to *A. Egedii* of Greenland.

9. CÓMARUM L. Sp. Pl. 502.   1753.

A stout dark green nearly glabrous herb, with alternate pinnate large-stipuled leaves, the large red or purple flowers cymose or solitary, terminal or also axillary. Calyx deeply 5-lobed, 5-bracteolate, the bractlets narrow. Petals shorter than the calyx-lobes, acute, purple. Stamens numerous, inserted on the large pubescent disk. Pistils numerous, inserted on the somewhat enlarged, pubescent receptacle which becomes spongy in fruit. Style lateral. Achenes glabrous. Seed pendulous. [Greek name of the Arbutus, from the similar fruits.]

A monotypic genus of the north temperate zone.

1. Comarum palústre L.   Purple or Marsh Cinquefoil.   Purple Marshlocks.   Cowberry.   Purplewort.   Fig. 2250.

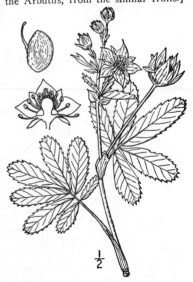

Comarum palustre L. Sp. Pl. 502. 1753.
Potentilla palustris Scop. Fl. Carn. Ed. 2, 1: 359. 1772.

Decumbent and somewhat woody at the base, the upper part of the stems pubescent. Leaves pinnate, the lower long-petioled, 5-7-foliolate; leaflets oblong or oval, sharply or incisely serrate, obtuse or acutish at the apex, narrowed at the base, 1'-3' long; stipules membranous, sometimes adnate to the petiole for half its length; upper leaves nearly sessile, 3-5-foliolate; flowers showy, 9''-15'' broad; calyx-lobes red or purple within, ovate, acuminate, much exceeding the ovate-lanceolate petals; bractlets much shorter than the calyx-lobes; disk lobed.

In swamps and peat-bogs, Greenland and Labrador to New Jersey, Iowa, British Columbia, Wyoming, Alaska and California. Northern Europe and Asia. Marsh five-finger. Meadow-nuts. Bog-strawberry. June–Aug.

10. DUCHÉSNEA J. E. Smith, Trans. Linn. Soc. 10: 372. 1811.

Perennial herbs, with trailing branches often rooting at the nodes (leafy runners), 3-foliolate long-petioled leaves and axillary slender-peduncled yellow perfect flowers. Calyx 5-parted, 5-bracteolate, the bractlets larger than the calyx-segments and alternating with them, dentate or incised, often regarded like those in *Fragaria* and *Potentilla* as an exterior calyx. Petals 5, obovate. Stamens numerous. Pistils numerous, borne on a hemispheric receptacle which greatly enlarges but does not become pulpy in fruit. Achenes superficial on the receptacle. [In honor of A. N. Duchesne, French botanist.]

Two species, natives of southern Asia, the following typical.

1. Duchesnea índica (Andr.) Focke. Mock or Indian Strawberry. Fig. 2251.

Fragaria indica Andr. Bot. Rep. *pl. 479.* 1807.
D. indica Focke, in Engl. & Prantl, Nat. Pfl. Fam. 3³: 33. 1888.

Silky-pubescent, tufted and forming leafy runners, dark green. Leaflets obovate or broadly oval, rather thin, crenate or dentate, obtuse at the apex, rounded or narrowed at the base, the terminal one generally cuneate; peduncles equalling or longer than the leaves; flowers 6″–12″ broad; bractlets of the calyx dentate or incised, exceeding the ovate or lanceolate acuminate spreading calyx-lobes; fruit red, ovoid or globose, insipid.

In waste places, southern New York and Pennsylvania to Florida and Missouri. Also in California, Bermuda and Jamaica. Naturalized or adventive from India. April–July.

11. FRAGÀRIA [Tourn.] L. Sp. Pl. 494. 1753.

Perennial acaulescent herbs propagating by runners, with alternate basal tufted petioled 3-foliolate leaves, and sheathing membranous stipules. Flowers white, corymbose or racemose on erect naked scapes, polygamo-dioecious, the pedicels often recurved. Calyx persistent, its tube obconic or turbinate, 5-bracteolate, deeply 5-lobed. Petals 5, obovate, short-clawed. Stamens ∞; filaments slender. Carpels ∞, inserted on a glabrous convex or elongated receptacle, which becomes fleshy or pulpy in fruit; style lateral. Achenes ∞, minute, dry, crustaceous. Seed ascending. [Latin, *fragum*, strawberry, fragrance.]

About 35 species, natives of the north temperate zone and the Andes of South America. Besides the following, some 15 others occur in western North America. Type species: *Fragaria vesca* L.

Achenes imbedded in pits on the fruit; fruiting scape shorter than the leaves.
　Leaflets oblong or narrowly obovate; fruit oblong-conic. 　　　　1. *F. canadensis.*
　Leaflets broadly oval or obovate; fruit globose or ovoid.
　　Pedicels with long spreading hairs. 　　　　　　　　　　　　　2. *F. Grayana.*
　　Pedicels appressed-pubescent. 　　　　　　　　　　　　　　　3. *F. virginiana.*
Achenes borne on the surface of the fruit; fruiting scape as long as or exceeding the leaves.
　Stout; leaflets thickish; fruit ovoid or ovoid-conic. 　　　　　　4. *F. vesca.*
　Slender; leaflets thin; fruit elongated-conic. 　　　　　　　　　5. *F. americana.*

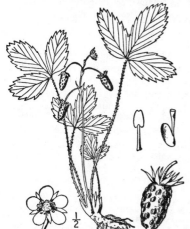

1. Fragaria canadénsis Michx. Northern Wild Strawberry. Fig. 2254.

Fragaria canadensis Michx. Fl. Bor. Am. 1: 299. 1803.

Petioles slender, loosely villous, 4′–7′ high. Leaflets oblong or the middle one narrowly cuneate-obovate, obtuse, rather few-toothed, 9″–2′ long, 5″–10″ wide, glabrous or nearly so above even when young, more or less appressed-pubescent beneath; scapes pubescent with appressed hairs; scape somewhat shorter than the leaves; flowers few, slender-pedicelled, 7″–9″ broad; calyx-lobes lanceolate, acuminate; fruit oblong, or oblong-conic, 5″–6″ long; achenes sunken in pits.

In fields and meadows, Newfoundland to Mackenzie, New York and Michigan. Mountain-strawberry. May–July.

Fragaria multicípita Fernald, from gravelly beaches in Gaspé County, Quebec, differs in being appressed-pubescent and having subglobose fruit.

2. Fragaria Grayàna Vilmorin. Gray's Strawberry. Fig. 2253.

F. *Grayana* Vilmorin; Gay, Ann. Sci. Nat. IV. **8**: 202. 1857.

F. *virginiana illinoensis* Prince; A. Gray, Man. Ed. 5, 155. 1867.

Similar to *F. virginiana,* and perhaps a race of that species, but stouter. Leaves firmer in texture; petioles densely clothed with spreading or reflexed hairs; leaflets acute or obtuse, coarsely serrate; scape stout, 4'–6' high, hirsute like the petioles; pedicels with spreading hairs; calyx-lobes and bractlets linear-lanceolate; petals nearly orbicular; fruit subglobose, 7''–8'' in diameter, the achenes imbedded in pits.

Dry soil, Indiana to Missouri, Alabama and Louisiana. April–May.

3. Fragaria virginiàna Duchesne. Virginia or Scarlet Strawberry. Fig. 2252.

F. *virginiana* Duchesne, Hist. Nat. Fras. 204. 1766.

F. *australis* Rydb. N. Am. Fl. **22**: 361. 1908.

Fragaria terrae-novae Rydb. Mem. Dep. Bot. Col. Univ. **2**: 182. 1898.

Rather stout, tufted, dark green, more or less villous-pubescent with spreading or sometimes appressed hairs. Petioles 2'–6' long; leaflets thick, or even coriaceous, short-stalked or sessile, broadly oval or obovate, obtuse, dentate-serrate, the terminal one generally cuneate, the lateral inequilateral at the base; scape equalling or shorter than the leaves, the fruit being generally borne below them; hairs of the scape more or less spreading; pedicels appressed-pubescent; calyx-lobes, at least of the sterile flowers, erect at maturity, lanceolate; petals obovate; fruit red, ovoid, the achenes imbedded in pits.

In dry soil, Newfoundland to South Dakota, Florida and Oklahoma. Consists of several races. April–June.

4. Fragaria vésca L. European Wood or Hedge Strawberry. Fig. 2255.

Fragaria vesca L. Sp. Pl. 494. 1753.

Stout, tufted, dark-green, generally less villous than the two preceding species. Leaflets ovate or broadly oval, obtuse, dentate, broader but nearly or quite as thick, the terminal one cuneate, the others inequilateral at the base; scape commonly exceeding the leaves, so that the fruit is borne above them, sometimes 12' high, its hairs mostly spreading; calyx-lobes remaining spreading or sometimes reflexed; fruit red, or sometimes white, ovoid-conic, the achenes borne on its smooth and nearly even surface.

In woods, fields and along roadsides. Naturalized from Europe in the Eastern and Middle States; apparently native northward, the white-fruited race native from Connecticut and New York to Ohio and Kentucky. Sow-tit. Sheep-noses. April–June.

5. Fragaria americàna (Porter) Britton. American Wood Strawberry. Fig. 2256.

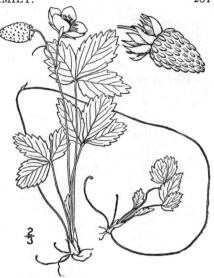

Fragaria vesca var. *americana* Porter, Bull. Torr. Club 17 : 15. 1890.
Fragaria americana Britton, Bull. Torr. Club 19 : 222. 1892.

Slender, light green, loosely villous-pubescent or glabrate, usually producing runners more freely than any of the preceding species. Leaflets thin, ovate or oval, obtuse or acute at the apex, sharply incised-dentate, the terminal one commonly cuneate, the others inequilateral at the base, pubescent with silvery appressed hairs beneath; flowers smaller than in *F. vesca;* calyx-lobes spreading or reflexed in fruit; fruit ovoid or elongated-conic, light red or pink, the achenes borne on its glabrous shining even surface and but slightly attached to it.

In rocky woods, Newfoundland to Manitoba, Virginia and New Mexico. May–June.

12. SIBBÀLDIA L. Sp. Pl. 284. 1753.

Depressed alpine or arctic shrubby plants, with alternate mainly 3-foliolate stipulate leaves, and cymose flowers on scape-like nearly leafless peduncles. Calyx slightly concave, 5-lobed, 5-bracteolate, persistent. Petals 5, oblong or oval, much smaller than the calyx-lobes, yellow. Stamens 5, opposite the calyx-lobes, inserted on the margin of the villous-pubescent disk. Carpels 5–10, on short pubescent stipes; style lateral. Achenes 5–10, glabrous. [Named in honor of Robt. Sibbald, a Scotch naturalist.]

About 5 species, natives of the colder parts of the north temperate zone. The following typical one is the only known American species.

1. Sibbaldia procúmbens L. Sibbaldia. Fig. 2257.

Sibbaldia procumbens L. Sp. Pl. 284. 1753.
Potentilla procumbens Clairv. Man. Herb. Suisse 166. 1811.

Densely tufted, stem woody, decumbent or creeping, a few inches long. Stipules membranous, lanceolate or ovate-lanceolate, adnate; leaves 3-foliolate; petioles slender, 2'–4' long; leaflets obovate or oblanceolate, cuneate at the base, 3–5-toothed at the apex, pubescent with scattered hairs on both sides, resembling in outline those of *Sibbaldiopsis tridentata;* peduncles axillary, nearly naked, about equalling the leaves; flowers yellow, about 2½" broad, numerous; petals oblong or oval, very small; calyx-lobes oblong-ovate, acute, longer and broader than the bractlets.

Summits of the White Mountains; Mt. Albert, Quebec; Labrador, Greenland, arctic America to Alaska, south in the Rocky Mountains to Colorado and Utah and to California. Also in arctic and alpine Europe and Asia. Summer.

13. SIBBALDIÓPSIS Rydb. Mem. Dep. Bot. Col. Univ. 2: 187. 1898.

A depressed tufted shrub with thick trifoliolate leaves and small white flowers in terminal cymes. Calyx-tube nearly flat. Bractlets, calyx-lobes and petals 5. Petals obovate, rounded, not clawed. Stamens about 20, borne in 3 series near the base of the receptacle; filaments filiform; anthers cordate. Receptacle hemispheric, bearing numerous pistils. Style filiform, lateral. Achenes swollen, villous. Seed amphitropous, ascending. [Greek, from the similarity of this plant to *Sibbaldia procumbens.*]

A monotypic genus of eastern North America.

1. Sibbaldiopsis tridentàta (Soland.) Rydb. Three-toothed Cinquefoil. Fig. 2258.

Potentilla tridentata Soland. in Ait. Hort. Kew. **2**: 216. 1789.

Sibbaldiopsis tridentata Rydb. Mem. Dep. Bot. Col. Univ. **2**: 187. 1898.

Tufted, woody at the base, much branched, branches erect, 1'–12' high, pubescent with appressed hairs. Stipules lanceolate, entire; leaves mostly petioled, 3-foliolate; leaflets of the lower one oblanceolate, 3-toothed or sometimes 2–5-toothed at the obtuse apex, cuneate at the base, coriaceous, dark green and shining above, pale and minutely pubescent beneath, ½'–1' long; upper leaflets linear or oblong, often acute and entire; flowers 1–6, in a terminal cyme, white, 3"–5" broad; bractlets shorter and narrower than the ovate acute calyx-lobes, which are shorter than the obovate-oval petals.

In rocky places, especially on mountains, Greenland to New Jersey, on the higher southern Alleghanies, shores of Lake Superior, and west to Manitoba. Mountain five-finger. June–Aug. Recorded from Scotland, apparently erroneously.

14. DASÍPHORA Raf. Aut. Bot. 167. 1838.

Shrubs with firm unequally pinnate leaves, scarious sheathing stipules, and large mostly yellow flowers. Calyx-tube saucer-shaped. Bractlets, calyx-lobes and petals 5. Petals rounded, not clawed. Stamens about 25, in 5 clusters around the hemispheric receptacle; filaments filiform; anthers flat. Pistils numerous on the receptacle; style club-shaped, glandular above, lateral; stigmas lobed. Achenes densely covered with long straight hairs. Seeds amphitropous, ascending. [Greek, bearing hairs, referring to the hairy achenes and receptacle.]

About five species, natives of the north temperate and arctic zones. Only the following typical one occurs in North America.

1. Dasiphora fruticòsa (L.) Rydb. Shrubby Cinquefoil. Fig. 2259.

Potentilla fruticosa L. Sp. Pl. 495. 1753.
Dasiphora riparia Raf. Aut. Bot. 167. 1838.
Dasiphora fruticosa Rydb. Mem. Dep. Bot. Col. Univ. **2**: 188. 1898.

Shrubby, much branched, stems erect or ascending, very leafy, 6'–4° high, the bark shreddy. Stipules ovate-lanceolate, membranous, acute or acuminate, entire; leaflets 5–7, oblong, linear-oblong, or somewhat oblanceolate, entire, acute or acutish at each end, 6"–12" long, silky-pubescent, the margins revolute; flowers terminal, densely cymose, or solitary, bright yellow, 8"–15" broad; petals nearly orbicular, exceeding the ovate calyx-lobes and bractlets; stamens 15–20; style lateral, filiform; achenes, disk and receptacle long-hairy.

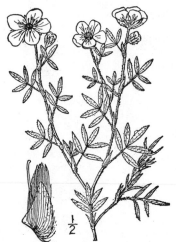

In swamps or moist rocky places, Labrador and Greenland to Alaska, south to New Jersey, Illinois, Minnesota, in the Rocky Mountains to Arizona, and in the Sierra Nevada to California. Also in northern Europe and Asia. Called also hardhack and prairie weed. A troublesome bushy weed in northern New England. June–Sept.

15. DRYMOCÁLLIS Fourr. Ann. Soc. Linn. Lyon II. **16**: 371. 1868.

[Boottia Bigel. Fl. Bost. Ed. 2, 206. 1826. Not Adans. 1763.]

Perennial glandular herbs, with unequally pinnate leaves and cymose flowers. Calyx-tube short and broad. Bractlets, calyx-lobes and petals 5. Petals neither clawed nor emarginate. Stamens 20–30, in 5 clusters on the thickened margin of the 5-angled disc; filaments filiform; anthers flat. Receptacle hemispheric or somewhat elongated, bearing numerous pistils. Style nearly basal; stigma minute. Seed orthotropous, ascending. [Greek, woodland beauty.]

About 30 species, natives of the north temperate and subarctic zone. Besides the following, some 25 others occur in western North America. Type species: *Drymocallis rubricaulis* Fourr.

1. Drymocallis agrimonioides (Pursh) Rydb.   Tall or Glandular Cinquefoil.
Fig. 2260.

Geum agrimonioides Pursh. Fl. Am. Sept. 351. 1814.
Potentilla arguta Pursh, Fl. Am. Sept. 736. 1814.
Drymocallis agrimonioides Rydb. N. A. Fl. **22**: 368. 1908.

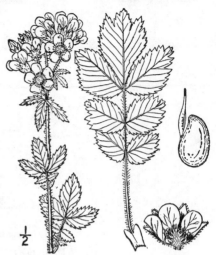

Erect, stout, simple or little-branched above, glandular and villous-pubescent, 1°–4° high. Stipules membranous; basal leaves slender-petioled, pinnately 7–11-foliolate; leaflets ovate, oval or rhomboid, obtuse at the apex, the terminal one cuneate, the others rounded at the base and commonly oblique, all sharply incised-dentate; stem-leaves short-petioled or sessile, with fewer leaflets; flowers white, densely cymose, terminal, numerous, short-pedicelled, 5″–7″ broad; calyx-lobes ovate, acute, shorter than the obovate petals; stamens 25–30, borne on the glandular disk; style nearly basal and fusiform-thickened; achenes glabrous.

On dry or rocky hills, New Brunswick to Mackenzie, south to Virginia, Illinois, Kansas and Colorado. June–July.

16. CHAMAERHODOS Bunge, in Ledeb. Fl. Alt. **1**: 429. 1829.

Perennial or biennial herbs, with ternately divided leaves, and small perfect cymose flowers. Calyx ebracteolate, small, 5-cleft. Petals obovate or cuneate, somewhat clawed. Stamens 5, opposite the calyx-segments; filaments short, subulate, persistent. Pistils 5–20; style filiform, basal. Seed ascending, attached near the base of the style. [Greek, a low rose.]

About 3 species, natives of North America and Asia. Type species: *Chamaerhodos altàica* (L.) Bunge.

1. Chamaerhodos Nuttàllii (T. & G.) Pickering. American Chamaerhodos. Fig. 2261.

C. erecta Nuttallii T. & G. Fl. N. A. **1**: 433. 1840.

C. Nuttallii Pickering; Rydb. N. Am. Fl. **22**: 377. 1908.

Hirsute, glandular, leafy, erect, branched, 1° high or less. Basal leaves 2–4-ternately divided into linear or oblong segments, those of the stem similar, but smaller and less divided; cymes numerous, panicled, the panicle-branches ascending; pedicels nearly erect, not longer than the flowers; calyx-tube 1″–1½″ broad, hispid, the segments narrowly lanceolate, equalling or somewhat shorter than the white petals.

Plains and prairies, Minnesota to Saskatchewan, Alaska and Wyoming. June–Aug.

17. ALCHEMÍLLA L. Sp. Pl. 123. 1753.

Perennial herbs, with basal and alternate lobed or digitately compound leaves, adnate stipules, and small perfect greenish cymose or capitate flowers. Calyx persistent, cup-shaped, contracted at the throat, 4–5-lobed, 4–5-bracteolate. Petals none. Stamens 4, alternate with the sepals; filaments short. Carpel usually solitary; style basal, slender. Achene enclosed in the calyx-tube. Seed ascending, its testa membranous. [Name from its fancied value in alchemy.]

About 10 species, natives of the Old World and of boreal America. Type species: *Alchemilla vulgaris* L.

1. Alchemilla praténsis F. W. Schmidt. Lady's Mantle. Dew-cup. Fig. 2262.

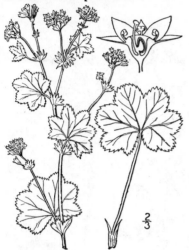

Alchemilla pratensis F. W. Schmidt, Fl. Boem. 3 : 88. 1794.

Perennial from a thick woody rootstock, branched, ascending or erect, pubescent or glabrate. Stipules mostly toothed; leaves orbicular-reniform, 5–9-lobed, more or less pubescent, the lower slender-petioled, the upper sessile or nearly so, lobes broad, not deep, serrate; flowers about 2″ broad, very numerous in terminal and axillary peduncled often leafy corymbs; pedicels filiform; calyx glabrous, its lobes usually 4, ovate, acutish.

In grassy places near the coast, Nova Scotia, Cape Breton and eastern Massachusetts. Naturalized from Europe. Duck's-foot. Padelion or lion's-foot. Syndow. Great sanicle. Bear's-foot. Included in our first edition in *A. vulgaris* L.; *A. glomerulans* Buser, and *A. filicaulis* Buser, are related species of arctic and sub-arctic America and Europe. May–Sept.

Alchemilla alpina L., found on Miquelon Island, and reported by Pursh (probably erroneously) from the White and the Green Mountains, a native of alpine and northern Europe and Asia, is distinguished from the preceding by its 5 oblong silky entire leaflets.

18. ÁPHANES L. Sp. Pl. 123. 1753.

Small annual herbs, with digitately parted, lobed and toothed leaves, and very small apetalous flowers in axillary cymose clusters. Calyx-tube ellipsoid, contracted at the throat, the lobes 4 or 5; bractlets as many as the calyx-lobes, or none. Petals none. Stamens usually only one, borne opposite one of the calyx-lobes; filament short; anthers introrse. Pistils 1–4, usually 2; style basal, slender. Achenes 1 or 2. [Greek, referring to the insignificant aspect of these plants.]

A genus of about twenty species, of the north temperate zone. Besides the following, 2 or 3 others occur in the western United States. Type species: *Aphanes arvensis* L.

1. Aphanes arvénsis L. Parsley-Piert, or Field Lady's Mantle. Argentill. Fig. 2263.

Aphanes arvensis L. Sp. Pl. 123. 1753.
Alchemilla arvensis Scop. Fl. Carn. Ed. 2, 1 : 115. 1770.

Annual, softly pubescent, branching at the base, the branches usually slender, ascending, 1′–6′ high. Stipules toothed or rarely entire; leaves very short-petioled, pubescent, fan-shaped, 2″–5″ long, deeply 3-parted, the lobes cuneate, 2–4-cleft, the segments obtuse or acutish; flowers 1″–1½″ broad, in sessile axillary clusters partly enclosed by the stipules; calyx-lobes usually 4, ovate, obtusish or acute.

In dry fields, District of Columbia to Georgia and Tennessee and in Nova Scotia. Naturalized or adventive from Europe. Breakstone. Parsley-vlix. Parsley-breakstone. Firegrass. Bowel-hivegrass. Colicwort. April–Sept.

The plant of the southeastern states (*A. australis* Rydb.) has smaller leaves and flowers than European specimens examined, but does not appear to be specifically distinct from them.

19. SANGUISÓRBA [Rupp.] L. Sp. Pl. 116. 1753.

Erect, perennial herbs, sometimes decumbent at the base, with alternate odd-pinnate stipulate leaves and small perfect or polygamo-dioecious flowers in dense terminal peduncled spikes. Calyx-tube turbinate, constricted at the throat, angled or winged, persistent, 4-lobed, the lobes petaloid, concave, deciduous. Petals none. Stamens 4, inserted on the throat of the calyx; filaments filiform, elongated, exserted; anthers short; carpel enclosed in the calyx-tube opposite the sepals. Style filiform, terminal; stigmas papillose; ovule suspended. Achene enclosed in the dry angled calyx. Seed pendulous. [Latin, blood-staunching, from its supposed properties.]

About 10 species, natives of the north temperate zone. In addition to the following, 2 or 3 others occur in the western parts of North America. Type species: *Sanguisorba officinalis* L.

1. Sanguisorba canadénsis L. American Great Burnet. Fig. 2264.

Sanguisorba canadensis L. Sp. Pl. 117. 1753.
Poterium canadense A. Gray, Man. Ed. 5, 150. 1867.

Glabrous or slightly pubescent toward the base, erect, simple, or branched above, 1°–6° high, the branches erect. Stipules often foliaceous and dentate; basal leaves long-petioled, sometimes 2° long; leaflets 7–15, ovate, oblong, or oval, obtuse or acutish, cordate or obtuse at the base, serrate with acute teeth, stalked, 1′–3′ long; flowers white, perfect, bracteolate at the base, in dense terminal showy spikes 1′–6′ long; stamens 4; filaments long-exserted, white; achene enclosed in the 4-winged calyx.

In swamps and low meadows, Newfoundland to Michigan, south to Georgia. July–Oct.

Sanguisorba officinalis L., native of Europe and Asia, found in fields in Maine and recorded from Minnesota, differs in having purplish flowers with short stamens not longer than the sepals.

20. POTERÍDIUM Spach, Ann. Sci. Nat. III. 5: 43. 1846.

Annual or perennial herbs, with branched stems, stipulate, odd-pinnate leaves, the leaflets pinnatifid, and greenish perfect bracted flowers in dense oblong spikes. Calyx-tube urn-shaped, constricted at the mouth, 4-winged, its 4 lobes with scarious margins. Stamens 2 or 4; filaments short. Pistil 1; style terminal; stigma brush-like; ovule 1, suspended. Achene enclosed in the dry calyx-tube. [Greek, diminutive of *Poterium*.]

Two species, one of northwestern America and the following typical one.

1. Poteridium ánnuum (Nutt.) Spach. Plains Poteridium. Fig. 2265.

Poterium annuum Nutt.; Hook. Fl. Bor. Am. 1: 198. 1832.

Sanguisorba annua Nutt.; T. & G. Fl. N. A. 1: 429. 1840.

Poteridium annuum Spach, Ann. Sci. Nat. III. 5: 43. 1846.

Glabrous, 4′–15′ high. Leaflets 7–15, broadly obovate, 6″ long or less, pectinate-pinnatifid, with linear-oblong segments; spikes 1¼′ long or less, about 3½″ thick; bracts ovate, shorter than the flowers; calyx-lobes oval, apiculate, 1″ long; stamens usually 4; fruiting calyx-tube strongly 4-winged.

Plains, Kansas to Arkansas and Texas. Summer.

21. POTÈRIUM L. Sp. Pl. 994. 1753.

Perennial herbs, with odd-pinnate, stipulate leaves, and small, perfect and imperfect flowers in dense heads. Calyx-tube 4-angled, constricted at the throat, 4-lobed. Petals 4. Perfect flowers with several or numerous declined stamens, the filaments capillary. Pistils 2; style terminal; stigmas brush-like. Achene enclosed in the thickened, 4-angled calyx-tube. Seed suspended. [Greek, goblet or beaker.]

About four species, natives of the Old World, the following typical.

1. Poterium Sanguisórba L.   Salad Burnet. Fig. 2266.

Poterium Sanguisorba L. Sp. Pl. 994. 1753.
Sanguisorba minor Scop. Fl. Carn. Ed. 2, 1 : 110. 1772.
Sanguisorba Sanguisorba Britton, Mem. Torr. Club 5 : 189. 1894.

Glabrous or pubescent, erect, slender, perennial, branched, 10′–20′ high. Stipules usually small, laciniate; leaflets 7–19, ovate or broadly oval, deeply incised, short-stalked or sessile, 6″–10″ long; flowers greenish, in dense peduncled globose-ovoid heads, 3″–6″ long, the lower ones perfect or staminate, the upper pistillate; stamens 12 or more, drooping; stigmas purple; calyx-lobes ovate, acute or acutish; fruit 1″–2″ long.

In dry or rocky soil and in ballast, southern Ontario, Maine, New York and Pennsylvania to Maryland. Naturalized or adventive from Europe and native also of Asia. Summer. Garden-burnet. Bloodwort. Bibernel. Pimpernelle. Toper's-plant.

22. AGRIMÒNIA [Tourn.] L. Sp. Pl. 448. 1753.

Perennial erect herbs, often glandular. Leaves alternate, petioled, odd-pinnate, with smaller leaf-segments interposed between the larger ones, and conspicuous stipules. Flowers small, regular, perfect, yellow, in narrow spicate racemes. Calyx-tube in fruit obconic, hemispheric or turbinate, often grooved, uncinate-bristly above, somewhat constricted at the throat, the 5 lobes connivent. Petals 5, small. Stamens 5–15, slender. Carpels 2, included; style terminal; stigma 2-lobed; ovules pendulous. Fruit dry, mostly reflexed; achenes 1–2, oblong. Seed suspended, its testa membranous. [Ancient Latin name.]

About 15 species, natives of the north temperate zone, Mexico, and the Andes of South America. Besides the following, another occurs in the Southern States. Type species: *Agrimonia Eupatoria* L.

Racemes and leaves beneath with loose spreading hairs or glabrous.
  Roots not tuberous; fruit large, turbinate, with numerous radiating bristles.   1. *A. gryposepala.*
  Roots tuberous; fruit very small, hemispheric, with few ascending or erect bristles.
                                                                                   2. *A. rostellata.*

Racemes and leaves beneath closely or softly pubescent.
  Roots tuberous; stems pubescent; leaves not glandular-dotted beneath.
    Small, often simple, with elongated terminal raceme; leaflets 3–5.   3. *A. pumila.*
    Larger, paniculate-branched; leaflets 5–11.   4. *A. mollis.*
  Roots not tuberous; stems hirsute; leaves glandular-dotted beneath.
    Leaflets mostly 7–9; fruit large, the bristles connivent.   5. *A. striata.*
    Leaflets mostly 11–17; fruit small, the bristles radiate.   6. *A. parviflora.*

1. Agrimonia gryposépala Wallr.   Tall Hairy Agrimony.   Fig. 2267.

A. Eupatoria hirsuta Muhl. Cat. 47. 1813.
Agrimonia hirsuta Bicknell, Bull. Torr. Club 23 : 509. 1896.
Agrimonia gryposepala Wallr. Beitr. Bot. 1 : 49. 1842.

Mostly 3°–4° tall (2°–6°), minutely glandular, villous. Leaves large; leaflets thin, bright green, mostly 7, spreading, elliptic to broadly oblong, or the odd one obovate, apex acute, base often subcordate, coarsely serrate, the margins and nerves beneath ciliate, the lower surface rarely pubescent; interposed leaf-segments ovate, mostly 3 pairs; stipules broad, coarsely cut-toothed; flowers 4″–6″ broad, the buds ovoid, acute; fruit reflexed, 3″ long, short-turbinate, abruptly contracted at the pedicel, the disk convex, the dilated marginal rim bearing numerous reflexed spreading and erect bristles.

Woods and thickets, Nova Scotia to Minnesota, North Carolina and California. Roots fibrous. Feverfew. Beggar's-ticks. Cockle-bur. Stickweed. Stickseed. June–Aug.

2. Agrimonia rostellàta Wallr. Woodland Agrimony. Fig. 2268.

Agrimonia parviflora DC. Prodr. **2** : 587. 1821. Not
  Soland. 1789.
Agrimonia rostellata Wallr. Beitr. Bot. **1** : 42. 1842.

Mostly about 2° high (1°–5°), minutely glandular, simple or delicately paniculately branched;
racemes filiform, short, loosely flowered. Roots
tuberous. Stem glabrous, or with scattered hairs
above; leaflets thin, commonly 5, mostly oblong
or obovate-oblong and obtuse, crenate or dentate,
often cuneate, scarcely ciliate; interposed leaf-
segments usually a small entire pair; stipules
small, entire and lanceolate, or ovate and laciniate;
flowers 2″–2½″ broad, the buds subglobose, truncate or nearly so; fruit 2″ high or less, spreading
or nodding, hemispheric, the furrows shallow or
obsolete; disk very tumid, its rim unmargined, its
bristles short and weak, erect or ascending.

In dry woods, Connecticut to Virginia, eastern Tennessee, Missouri and Nebraska. Previously mistaken
for *A. striata* Michx. July–Sept.

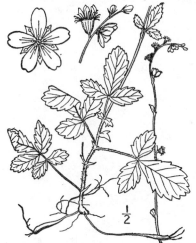

3. Agrimonia pùmila Muhl. Small-fruited Agrimony. Fig. 2269.

Agrimonia pumila Muhl. Cat. 47. 1813.
A. microcarpa Wallr. Beitr. Bot. **1** : 39. *pl. 1. f. 3.* 1842.

Small and slender, 1°–2° high, erect or assurgent, simple, or with a few branches above. Roots
tuberous; stem villous with spreading hairs below,
appressed-pubescent above; leaves often crowded
toward the base of the stem, frequently 3-foliolate;
leaflets 3–5, small, elliptic to obovate or cuneate,
obtuse or acute at the apex, often pilose above,
soft-pubescent and pale beneath; interposed leaf-
segments, if any, a small pair; stipules small, the
lower ones lanceolate and entire, the upper
rounded on the outer side and laciniate; racemes
very loosely flowered, flowers small; fruit 2″ long
or less, minutely glandular, hemispheric to turbinate; disk flat; bristles few, ascending or erect.

In dry soil, Pennsylvania and Maryland to Florida,
Kentucky and Texas. Aug.

4. Agrimonia móllis (T. & G.) Britton. Soft Agrimony. Fig. 2270.

Agrimonia Eupatoria var. *mollis* T. & G. Fl. N. A. **1** :
  431. 1840.
?*A. pubescens* Wallr. Beitr. Bot. **1** : 45. 1842.
A. mollis Britton, Bull. Torr. Club **19** : 221. 1892.
A. mollis Bicknellii Kearney, Bull. Torr. Club **24** : 565.
  1897.

Virgately branched, 1½°–6° tall. Roots tuberous.
Stem pubescent, or villous below, finely pubescent
or canescent above, as also the racemes. Leaves
thickish, dull green, veiny, pale and velvety-pubescent
beneath; leaflets mostly 7 (5–11), spreading, narrowly oblong to obovate, obtuse or acutish at the
apex, crenate to dentate; interposed leaf-segments
oblong, mostly a single pair; stipules lanceolate to
ovate-oblong, cut-toothed or lobed; flowers 3″–4″
broad, the buds subglobose, obtuse; fruit 2″ long or
more, ascending, spreading or loosely reflexed,
oblong, to broadly turbinate; disk flat, or convex,
the ascending slender bristles nearly in a single row.

Dry woods and thickets, Massachusetts to Michigan,
North Carolina and Kansas. July–Oct.

5. Agrimonia striàta Michx.   Britton's Agrimony.   Fig. 2271.

A. striata Michx. Fl. Bor. Am. 1: 287. 1803.
Agrimonia Brittoniana Bicknell, Bull. Torr. Club
23: 517. 1896.

Robust, 2°–6° tall, virgately branched. Roots
fibrous. Stem hirsute-pubescent with short
spreading brownish hairs, sub-appressed above;
leaves numerous; leaflets 7–9, rarely 11, oblique
to the rachis, tetragonal-elliptic to rhomboid-
lanceolate, acute or acuminate, deeply and closely
serrate, dull green, thickish, rugose, softly pubescent beneath, glabrate above, their margins finely
scabrous-ciliolate; interposed leaf-segments narrow, usually several pairs; stipules lanceolate,
acuminate, laciniate; racemes long, erect or ascending; flowers crowded, 3″–5″ wide; fruit 3″–
4″ long, reflexed, long-turbinate, deeply grooved,
unmarginal; disk flat or concave; bristles often
purplish, short, crowded, inflexed and connivent
over the sepals.

Along thickets and roadsides, Newfoundland to
Saskatchewan, West Virginia, Nebraska and New
Mexico. June–Sept.

6. Agrimonia parviflòra Soland.   Many-flowered Agrimony.   Fig. 2272.

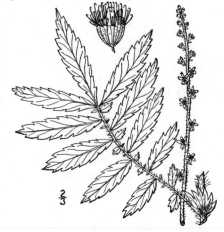

Agrimonia parviflora Soland. in Ait. Hort. Kew.
2: 130. 1789.

Virgately branched, 2°–6° high, with long
racemes. Stem densely hirsute with coarse
brownish hairs, villous abouve; leaves crowded,
the lower often deflexed; leaflets 9–17, close
together, spreading, lanceolate or linear-
lanceolate, acuminate, sharply serrate, rather
thin, glabrous above, pubescent beneath, especially on the veins, very glandular; interposed
leaf-segments mostly 4 or 5 crowded pairs;
stipules laciniate, acuminate; flowers very
numerous, 3″–5″ broad; the buds rounded-
truncate; fruit loosely reflexed, small, glandular, dilated-turbinate with a prominent elevated
disk; bristles reflexed, spreading and erect.

In moist or dry soil, Connecticut, to Michigan,
Kansas, Georgia and Mississippi. Roots fibrous.
July–Oct.

23.   WALDSTEÌNIA Willd. Neue Schr. Gesell. Nat. Fr. 2: 105. pl. 4.   1799.

Perennial herbs, with the aspect of Strawberries, with alternate mainly basal long-petioled
3–5-foliolate or lobed leaves, membranous stipules, and yellow corymbose flowers on bracted
scapes. Calyx persistent, the tube top-shaped, minutely 5-bracteolate or bractless at the
summit, 5-lobed. Petals 5, obovate, longer than the calyx-lobes. Stamens 8, inserted on the
throat of the calyx; filaments rigid, persistent. Carpels 2–6, inserted on a short villous receptacle; style nearly terminal, deciduous, filiform. Achenes 2–6, obliquely obovoid, pubescent.
Seed erect. [Named in honor of Franz Adam von Waldstein-Wartenburg, 1759–1823, a
German botanist.]

Five known species, natives of the north temperate zone. Besides the following, another occurs
in Georgia. Type species: Waldsteinia geoides Willd.

Petals twice as long as the calyx-lobes or longer.	1. W. fragarioides.
Petals as long as the calyx-lobes or shorter.	2. W. Doniana.

1. Waldsteinia fragarioìdes
(Michx.) Tratt.   Barren or Dry Strawberry.   Fig. 2273.

Dalibarda fragarioides Michx. Fl. Bor.
Am. **1**: 300. *pl. 28.* 1803.
Waldsteinia fragarioides Tratt. Ros.
Mon. **3**: 107. 1823.

Pubescent or nearly glabrous, rootstock creeping, rather stout. Stipules ovate-lanceolate, acutish; leaves tufted, long-petioled, 3-foliolate (rarely 5-foliolate); leaflets obovate, obtuse at the apex, broadly cuneate at the base, dentate or crenate and sometimes incised, 1'–2' long; scapes slender, erect, bracted, corymbosely 3–8-flowered; pedicels slender, often drooping; flowers yellow, 3"–5" broad; achenes 4–6, finely pubescent; calyx-lobes ovate-lanceolate, acute.

Woods and shaded hillsides. New Brunswick to Ontario, Minnesota, Michigan, Indiana and Georgia. May–June.

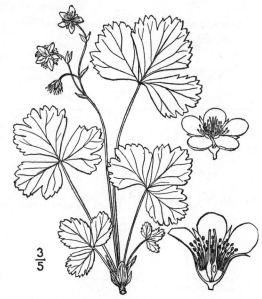

$\frac{3}{5}$

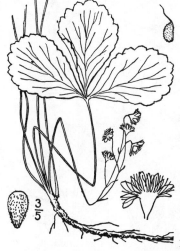

$\frac{3}{5}$

2. Waldsteinia Doniàna Tratt.   Southern Dry Strawberry.   Fig. 2274.

W. Doniana Tratt. Ros. Mon. **3**: 109. 1823.
W. parviflora Small, Bull. Torr. Club **25**: 137. 1898.

Perennial by horizontal rootstocks, villous-hirsute, or glabrous in age. Leaves basal, 5'–12' high; petioles much longer than the blades, usually less densely pubescent than the scapes; leaflets cuneate-obovate or broadly rhomboidal, 1½'–3' long, coarsely and irregularly crenate or lobed; scapes erect, solitary or several together, commonly shorter than the leaves, corymbose at top; calyx usually hairy, the tube broadly turbinate, 1¼"–1½" long, the segments triangular-lanceolate, or lanceolate-acuminate, often shorter than the tube; petals linear-oblong or narrowly elliptic, shorter than the calyx-segments or barely longer; achenes obovoid, 1½" long.

In woods and shaded soil, southwestern Virginia to North Carolina, Tennessee and Georgia. March–May.

24. GÈUM L. Sp. Pl. 500. 1753.

Perennial herbs, with odd-pinnate or deeply pinnatifid, stipulate leaves, those of the base clustered, those of the stem commonly smaller. Flowers cymose-corymbose or solitary, yellow, white or purple. Calyx persistent, its tube obconic or hemispheric, usually 5-bracteolate, 5-lobed. Petals 5, orbicular, oblong or obovate, obtuse or emarginate, exceeding the calyx. Stamens ∞, inserted on a disk at the base of the calyx; filaments filiform. Carpels ∞, aggregated on a short receptacle. Style filiform, jointed, the lower part persistent. Seed erect, its testa membranous. [The ancient Latin name.]

About 40 species, most abundant in the north temperate zone, a few in southern South America, 1 in South Africa. Besides the following, several others occur in western North America. Type species: *Geum urbànum* L.

Calyx-lobes reflexed.
  Head of fruit sessile in the bracteolate calyx.
    Petals small and inconspicuous; stipules small.
      Petals white.
        Hirsute; receptacle glabrous or downy.
        Finely pubescent or glabrate; receptacle densely hairy.
      Petals yellow; stem hirsute.
    Petals large, obovate, golden yellow; stipules large.
      Hirsute; terminal leaf-segment very large, usually cordate.
      Pubescent; terminal leaf-segment ovate, cuneate or oblanceolate.
  Head of fruit stalked in the bractless calyx.
Calyx-lobes erect or spreading; flowers purple, nodding.

1. *G. virginianum.*
2. *G. canadense.*
3. *G. flavum.*

4. *G. macrophyllum.*
5. *G. strictum.*
6. *G. vernum.*
7. *G. rivale.*

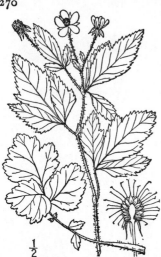

$\frac{1}{2}$

1. Geum virginiànum L. Rough Avens. Bennet. Herb-bennet. Fig. 2275.

Geum virginianum L. Sp. Pl. 500. 1753.

Branched above, rather stout, 2½° high or less. Stem and petioles bristly-pubescent, the stout short peduncles pubescent with reflexed hairs; basal and lower leaves odd-pinnate, the terminal leaflet usually larger than the lateral ones, the lower leaflets mostly very small; upper leaves 3-parted, 3-cleft, or the uppermost merely incised; stipules small; calyx-lobes reflexed, exceeding or about equalling the creamy-white petals; head of fruit globose, very dense, 6″–8″ in diameter; receptacle merely downy or glabrous; style slender, jointed, pubescent below, 4″–5″ long.

Low ground, Nova Scotia to Pennsylvania and southward in the Alleghanies, west through Ontario to Minnesota and to Missouri. Blooms somewhat earlier than *G. canadense.* Basal leaves becoming very large, the terminal leaflet sometimes 6′ wide. White avens. Throat-root. Chocolate-root. May–July.

2. Geum canadénse Jacq. White Avens. Fig. 2276.

Geum carolinianum Walt. Fl. Car. 150. 1788.
Geum album Gmel. Syst. 2: 861. 1791.

Softly and finely pubescent or glabrate, erect, branched above, 1½°–2½° high. Stipules small, dentate; basal leaves petioled, lobed, 3-foliolate or pinnately divided, their segments 3–5, the terminal one broadly ovate or obovate, the lateral ones narrower, all dentate and more or less lobed, sometimes with smaller ones borne on the petiole; stem-leaves short-petioled or sessile, 3–5-lobed or divided; peduncles slender; flowers white, 4″–8″ broad; calyx-lobes lanceolate, reflexed; petals obovate, equalling or shorter than the sepals; head of fruit globose-obovoid, sessile, 4″–6″ long; receptacle densely short-bristly; style glabrous, or pubescent below, jointed, 3″–4″ long.

In shaded places, Nova Scotia to Ontario, Georgia, Minnesota, South Dakota, Louisiana and Kansas. Red-root. Herb-bennet. June–Aug.

$\frac{1}{2}$

3. Geum flàvum (Porter) Bicknell. Cream-colored Avens. Fig. 2277.

Geum album var. *flavum* Porter, Bull. Torr. Club 16: 21. 1889.
Geum canadense var. *flavum* Britton, Bull. Torr. Club 18: 270. 1891.
G. flavum Bicknell, Bull. Torr. Club 23: 523. 1896.

Stem bristly-hairy below, erect, 1½°–3° tall. Stipules large, often 1′ long, foliaceous, dentate or lobed. Basal leaves mostly pinnately divided, sometimes only lobed; lower stem-leaves usually also pinnately divided, the terminal segment often elongated; upper stem-leaves oval or lanceolate, sometimes entire; peduncles slender; flowers cream-yellow, about 3″ broad; petals narrowly oblong, shorter than or little exceeding the reflexed calyx-lobes; head of fruit sessile, about 5″ in diameter; receptacle bristly-villous; style nearly glabrous to the base, jointed, 3″–4″ long.

In woods, Connecticut to North Carolina, Ohio, western Kentucky and Tennessee. June–Aug.

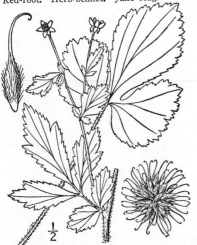

$\frac{1}{2}$

Geum urbànum L., from Europe, distinguished by its bright yellow, broader and longer petals, is escaped from cultivation at Cambridge, Mass.

4. Geum macrophýllum Willd. Large-leaved Avens. Fig. 2278.

Geum macrophyllum Willd. Enum. 557. 1809.

Stout, erect, bristly-pubescent, simple or branched above, 1°–3° high. Stipules broad, foliaceous; basal leaves petioled, lyrate-pinnate, the terminal segment much the largest, reniform, orbicular or cordate, crenulate-dentate, 3–7-lobed; lateral leaflets 3–6, oval or obovate, with smaller ones interspersed or borne on the petiole; stem-leaves short-petioled or sessile, the leaflets or lobes 2–4, cuneate; flowers several, terminal, short-peduncled, yellow, 5″–10″ broad; petals obovate, exceeding the acute reflexed calyx-lobes; receptacle nearly glabrous; style slender, jointed, pubescent, at least below, 3″–5″ long.

In low grounds, Newfoundland to Alaska and British Columbia, south to New York, Missouri, Colorado and California. Also in northern Europe. May–July.

5. Geum stríctum Ait. Yellow Avens. Fig. 2279.

Geum strictum Ait. Hort. Kew. 2 : 217. 1789.
Geum canadense Murr. Comm. Goett. 5 : 34. *pl. 4. f. B.* 1783. Not Jacq. 1772.

Erect or ascending, pubescent, branched above, 2°–5° high. Stipules broad, foliaceous; basal leaves lyrate-pinnate; leaflets 5–7, obovate, cuneate, dentate or lobed, with a few smaller ones interspersed, the terminal one largest, broadly ovate or cuneate; stem-leaves sessile or short-petioled, with 3–5 ovate or oblong acute segments; flowers yellow, similar to those of the preceding species; receptacle downy-pubescent; style slender, 3″–4″ long, jointed, pubescent below.

In swamps or low grounds, Newfoundland to British Columbia, south to New Jersey, Pennsylvania, Missouri and New Mexico. Also in northern Asia. June–Aug. A hybrid with *G. canadense* has been found in eastern Pennsylvania. Herb-bennet. Black-bur. Camp-root.

6. Geum vérnum (Raf.) T. & G. Spring Avens. Early Water Avens. Fig. 2280.

Stylipus vernus Raf. Neog. 3. 1825.
Geum vernum T. & G. Fl. N. A. 1 : 422. 1840.

Erect or ascending, slender, pubescent with spreading hairs, or glabrate, simple or nearly so, 6′–2° high. Basal leaves tufted, petioled, with a single orbicular-reniform dentate 3–5-lobed leaflet, or pinnate with 3–7 obovate or oval more or less dentate and lobed ones; stem-leaves few, sessile or short-petioled, pinnate or pinnatifid; flowers few, terminal, corymbose or racemose, erect, about 2″ broad; calyx-lobes ovate, acute, reflexed; bractlets none; petals yellow, spreading; head of fruit stalked; style glabrous, jointed, about 2″ long; receptacle glabrous.

Shaded places, Ontario to West Virginia and Tennessee, west to Illinois, Kansas and Texas. Naturalized from the West in New Jersey, Pennsylvania and southern New York. April–June.

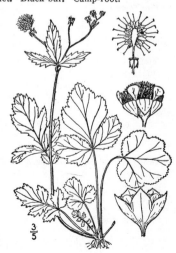

7. Geum rivàle L.   Purple or Water Avens.   Fig. 2281.

Geum rivale L. Sp. Pl. 501. 1753.

Erect, simple or nearly so, pubescent, 1°-3° high. Basal leaves lyrately and interruptedly pinnate, petioled, the lateral segments generally few and small, the terminal 1-3, much larger, all sharply and irregularly lobed and dentate; stem-leaves distant, short-petioled or sessile, simple, or 3-foliolate; flowers few, terminal, purple or purplish, nodding, 9″-12″ broad; petals obovate, emarginate, abruptly narrowed into a claw; calyx-lobes spreading, purple; head of fruit stalked in the calyx; achenes pubescent; style jointed, plumose below, 3″-4″ long.

In swamps and low grounds, Newfoundland to British Columbia, New Jersey, Pennsylvania, Michigan and Colorado. Also in northern Europe and Asia. Indian-chocolate. Evan's- or chocolate-root. Drooping avens. Maiden-hair. Throatwort. Throat-root. Cure-all. May–July.

Geum púlchrum Fernald, similar, but with smaller clear yellow flowers, found in Quebec, Vermont and Alberta, is presumably a hybrid of this species with *G. macrophyllum* Willd.

25. SIEVÉRSIA Willd. Mag. Gesell. Naturfr. Berlin 5: 397.   1811.

Mostly low perennial herbs, with odd-pinnate leaves. Flowers in cymes, or solitary, yellow or purplish. Calyx obconic or hemispheric, 5-lobed and generally 5-bracteolate. Petals 5. Stamens numerous; filaments filiform. Carpels many, on a short hemispheric receptacle. Style terminal, persistent, filiform, pubescent or plumose, not jointed, generally elongating in fruit. Seeds erect, basal. [Named in honor of Sievers.]

About 15 species of temperate alpine or arctic regions; besides the following five or six others occur in western and arctic North America. Type species: *Dryas anemonoides* Pall.

Leaflets 1-9, terminal one of the basal leaves orbicular-reniform; style plumose below; flowers
yellow.   1. *S. Peckii.*
Leaflets numerous, cuneate; style plumose throughout; flowers light purple.   2. *S. ciliata.*

1. Sieversia Peckii (Pursh) Rydb.   Yellow Mountain Avens.   Fig. 2283.

Geum Peckii Pursh, Fl. Am. Sept. 352. 1814.

Geum radiatum var. *Peckii* A. Gray, Man. Ed. 2, 117. 1856.

Sieversia Peckii Rydb. in Britton, Man. 508. 1901.

Sparingly pubescent or glabrate, stem 6′-2° high, erect, simple, 1-8-flowered at the summit. Basal leaves tufted, petioled, lyrately pinnate, the terminal segment very large, reniform-orbicular, sharply and irregularly dentate and slightly 3-5-lobed, 3′-6′ broad; lateral leaflets few or none; flowers yellow, 6″-12″ broad; bractlets of the calyx much shorter than the erect lanceolate calyx-lobes; petals obovate, often emarginate, spreading; style filiform, plumose below, naked above, 6″-8″ long, not jointed.

White Mountains of New Hampshire; Mt. Kineo, Maine. July–Aug.

Sieversia radiàta (Michx.) Greene, of the high mountains of North Carolina, to which this was referred in our first edition, differs in being hirsute-pubescent with spreading hairs, and in its broader ovate calyx-lobes.

2. Sieversia ciliàta (Pursh) Rydb. Longplumed Purple Avens. Prairie-smoke.
Fig. 2282.

Geum ciliatum Pursh, Fl. Am. Sept. 352. 1814.
Geum triflorum Pursh, loc. cit. 736. 1814.
Sieversia ciliata Rydb. in Britton, Man. 509. 1891.

Softly pubescent with short or spreading hairs, scapose; scape 6'–18' high, simple, 3–8-flowered at the summit. Basal leaves tufted, petioled, interruptedly pinnate with many small leaflets interspersed among the obovate or oval laciniate numerous larger ones; leaves of the scape 2 opposite small sessile pairs, the elongated peduncles commonly bearing another similar pair; flowers several, showy, 6''–9'' broad; bractlets linear, slightly exceeding the purple lanceolate acute erect calyx-lobes; petals purplish, erect, about equalling the bractlets; head of fruit sessile; style filiform, 1'–2' long and strongly plumose throughout in fruit, not jointed.

In dry or rocky soil, Newfoundland and Labrador to New York, British Columbia, Illinois, Iowa, North Dakota, and in the Rocky Mountains to Arizona. Races differ in pubescence, and in the shape and toothing of the leaflets. Johnny smokers. May–July.

26. DRYAS L. Sp. Pl. 501. 1753.

Low tufted herbaceous shrubs, with simple petioled stipulate leaves white-canescent beneath, and white or yellow, rather large perfect solitary flowers on slender scapes. Calyx persistent, not bracted, its tube concave, glandular-hirsute, 8–9-lobed. Petals 8 or 9, obovate, larger than the calyx-lobes. Stamens ∞, inserted on the throat of the calyx; filaments subulate. Carpels ∞, sessile, inserted on the dry receptacle; style terminal, persistent, elongated and plumose in fruit. Seed ascending, its testa membranous. [Name Latin, a wood-nymph.]

Three species, natives of the cold-temperate and arctic parts of the north temperate zone. Type species: *Dryas octopetala* L.

Flowers white ; sepals linear.
  Leaves oval or ovate, coarsely crenate.   1. *D. octopetala.*
  Leaves ovate, or ovate-lanceolate, subcordate, entire or nearly so.   2. *D. integrifolia.*
Flowers yellow ; sepals ovate ; leaves crenate.   3. *D. Drummondii.*

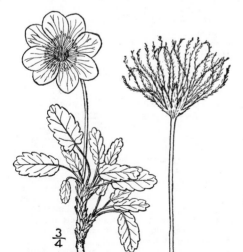

1. Dryas octopétala L. White Mountain Avens. Fig. 2284.

Dryas octopetala L. Sp. Pl. 501. 1753.
Dryas chamaedrifolia Pers. Syn. 2 : 57. 1807.

Stems prostrate, woody at the base, branched, 3'–6' long. Stipules linear, adnate to the petiole; leaves oval or ovate, coarsely crenate all around, green and glabrous above, densely white-canescent beneath, generally obtuse at each end, ½'–1' long; scape terminal, erect, 1'–5' long, pubescent; flower white, about 1' broad; sepals linear, acute or acutish, glandular-pubescent, persistent; style about 1' long, plumose and conspicuous in fruit.

Labrador and Greenland and throughout arctic America, south in the Rocky Mountains to Utah, Colorado, and to British Columbia. Also in arctic and alpine Europe and Asia. Wild betony. June–Aug.

2. Dryas integrifòlia Vahl. Entire-leaved Mountain Avens. Fig. 2285.

Dryas integrifolia Vahl, Act. Havn. 4: Part 2, 171. 1798.
Dryas tenella Pursh, Fl. Am. Sept. 350. 1814.

Similar to the preceding species, but the leaves are ovate or ovate-lanceolate, obtuse and often subcordate at the base, obtusish at the apex, entire or with 1 or 2 teeth near the base, the margins strongly revolute; flowers white, generally slightly smaller; sepals linear.

"White Hills of New Hampshire," collected by Prof. Peck, according to Pursh, Anticosti, Greenland; Labrador, west through arctic America to Alaska. June–Aug.

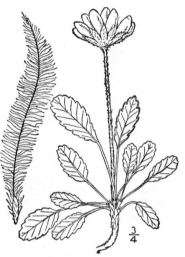

3. Dryas Drummóndii Richards. Drummond's Mountain Avens. Fig. 2286.

Dryas Drummondii Richards.; Hook. Bot. Mag. *pl. 2972.* 1830.
Dryas octopetala var. *Drummondii* S. Wats. Bibliog. Index 1: 281. 1878.

Similar to *D. octopetala*, the leaves crenate-dentate, but generally narrowed at the base. Scape floccose-pubescent, often taller; flower yellow, about 9" broad; sepals ovate, acutish, black glandular-pubescent.

On gravel, Gaspé, Quebec; Anticosti and Labrador, throughout arctic America, south. in the Rocky Mountains to Montana and to Oregon. June–Aug.

27. CERCOCÀRPUS H.B.K. Nov. Gen. et Sp. 6: 232. 1823.

Shrubs or small trees, with alternate simple petioled coriaceous dentate or entire, stipulate, prominently straight-veined leaves, and short-pedicelled or sessile, solitary or clustered, axillary or terminal, perfect flowers. Calyx narrowly tubular, persistent, contracted at the throat, 5-lobed. Petals none. Stamens 15–25, inserted in 2 or 3 rows on the limb of the calyx; filaments very short; anthers oval, often pubescent. Ovary 1, terete, slender, included in the calyx-tube, ripening into a villous achene; style filiform, villous, persistent, plumose and elongated in fruit; stigma obtuse; ovule solitary, nearly erect. Seed linear, its testa membranous. [Greek, tailed-fruit.]

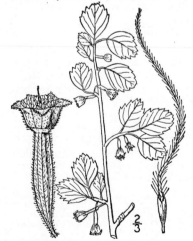

About 10 species, natives of western North America and Mexico. Type species: *Cercocarpus fothergilloides* H.B.K.

1. Cercocarpus montànus Raf. Small-leaved Cercocarpus. Fig. 2287.

Cercocarpus montanus Raf. Atl. Journ. 146.. 1832–33.
Cercocarpus parvifolius Nutt.; H. & A. Bot. Beechey Voy. 337. 1841.

A low branching shrub. Leaves obovate or oval, coriaceous, obtuse at the apex, cuneate or sometimes rounded at the base, short-petioled, dentate, silky-pubescent or canescent below, sparingly so or glabrous above, 6"–12" long, 3"–8" broad; flowers axillary, solitary or in pairs, short-peduncled, recurved, about 3" broad; calyx-tube pubescent, 4"–6" long, its limb deciduous; style becoming 2'–4' long and very plumose in fruit.

In dry or rocky soil, South Dakota to western Kansas, Montana, Wyoming, Utah and New Mexico. April–June.

28. RÚBUS [Tourn.] L. Sp. Pl. 492. 1753.

Perennial herbs, shrubs or trailing vines, often prickly, with alternate simple lobed or 3–7-foliolate leaves, the stipules adnate to the petiole. Flowers terminal or axillary, solitary, racemose or panicled, white, pink or purple, perfect or sometimes dioecious. Calyx persistent, not bracted, deeply 5-parted, its tube short and broad. Petals 5, deciduous. Stamens ∞, usually numerous, inserted on the calyx, distinct. Carpels ∞, rarely few, inserted on a convex or elongated receptacle, ripening into drupelets and forming an aggregate fruit, which in many species is edible, sweet and delicious, in others sour, or nearly tasteless. Ovules 2, one abortive. Style nearly terminal, slender. Seed pendulous. [The ancient name of the bramble, from *ruber*, red.]

Perhaps 200 species, of wide geographic distribution, most abundant in the north temperate zone. Besides the following, several others occur in North America beyond our area. A great many species, based mainly on trivial characters of pubescence, habit and leaf-form have been described since the publication of our first edition; many of these are hybrids between the different blackberries and others are races. There is great difference of opinion, both in Europe and America, regarding the number of valid species. All the British brambles were reduced to a single species, *R. fruticosus* L., by Bentham, but other authors have recognized and described a large number. The stems of many species are biennial. Several species are widely cultivated for their edible fruits, which have been improvd by selection. Type species: *Rubus fruticosus* L.

Leaves simple, crenate or palmately lobed. [Genus RUBACER Rydb.]
  Shrubby, 2°–5° high, branched; flowers corymbose.
    Flowers numerous, red-purple.   1. *R. odoratus.*
    Flowers few, white; western.   2. *R. parviflorus.*
  Herbaceous, 3′–9′ high, simple; flowers solitary, white.   3. *R. Chamaemorus.*
Leaves 3–7-foliolate (rarely simple in a race of No. 4).
  Fruit falling away from the dry receptacle. RASPBERRIES.
    Stems bristly, not glaucous; fruit light red.   4. *R. strigosus.*
    Stems prickly, slightly glaucous; fruit dark red.   5. *R. neglectus.*
    Stems prickly, very glaucous; fruit normally purple-black.   6. *R. occidentalis.*
  Fruit persistent on the fleshy receptacle. BLACKBERRIES.
    Herbaceous, unarmed; fruit red to purple.
      Erect, 10′ high or less; petals obovate, usually pink.   7. *R. arcticus.*
      Trailing or ascending; petals spatulate-oblong, white.   8. *R. triflorus.*
    Shrubby, usually bristly or prickly; fruit black when ripe.
      Leaves white-woolly beneath; stems erect or nearly so.   9. *R. cuneifolius.*
      Leaves not white-woolly beneath.
        Stems erect, ascending, or arching.
          Unarmed, or with very few distant prickles; leaves glabrous on both sides.
                                         10. *R. canadensis.*
         More or less densely prickly, or bristly.
           Leaves glabrous on both sides.   11. *R. nigricans.*
           Leaves velvety-pubescent beneath.
             Inflorescence with few or several unifoliolate leaves; fruit subglobose.
                                         12. *R. frondosus.*
             Inflorescence not leafy; fruit oblong to cylindric.
               Pedicels without prickles.   13. *R. alleghanensis.*
               Pedicels prickly.   14. *R. argutus.*
        Stems trailing or procumbent.
         Leaves dull above; fruit black.
          Leaves deciduous.
            Leaflets pubescent beneath, mostly rounded or cordate at base.
                                    15. *R. Baileyanus.*
            Leaflets glabrous or nearly so, mostly narrowed at base. 16. *R. procumbens.*
         Leaves coriaceous, persistent.   17. *R. trivialis.*
       Leaves shining above; fruit reddish.   18. *R. hispidus.*

½

1. Rubus odoràtus L. Purple-flowering Raspberry. Thimble-berry. Fig. 2288.

Rubus odoratus L. Sp. Pl. 494. 1753.

Erect, branched, shrubby, glandular-pubescent and somewhat bristly, not prickly, 3°–5° high. Stipules small, lanceolate, acuminate; leaves simple, petioled, large (sometimes nearly 1° broad), 3–5-lobed, cordate at the base, pubescent, especially on the veins of the lower surfaces, the lobes acuminate, finely serrate, the middle one longer than the others; flowers terminal, rather numerous, corymbose or paniculate, purple (rarely white), showy, 1′–2′ broad; bracts membranous; calyx-lobes tipped with a long slender appendage; fruit red when ripe, depressed-hemispheric, scarcely edible.

In rocky woods, Nova Scotia to Ontario and Michigan, south to Georgia and Tennessee. June–Aug. Scotch caps. Mulberry. Rose-flowering or Canadian raspberry. In England called Virginia raspberry.

Rubus columbiànus (Millsp.) Rydb., from West Virginia, appears to be a race of this species with narrower leaf-lobes.

2. Rubus parviflòrus Nutt. Salmon-berry. White-flowering Raspberry. Fig. 2289.

Rubus parviflorus Nutt. Gen. 1: 308. 1818.

Rubus nutkanus Mocino; DC. Prodr. 2: 566. 1825.

Similar to the preceding species but usually less glandular and scarcely bristly. Leaves petioled, simple, cordate at the base, 3–5-lobed, the lobes acute or obtusish, rarely acuminate, the middle one equalling or but slightly longer than the others, all coarsely and unequally serrate; flowers few, corymbose, white, terminal, 1′–2′ broad; calyx-lobes tipped with a long, slender appendage; fruit depressed-hemispheric, scarcely edible, red when ripe.

In woods, Michigan, Minnesota and western Ontario to Alaska and California, south in the Rocky Mountains to Utah and Colorado. Thimble-berry. May–July.

½

½

3. Rubus Chamaemòrus L. Cloudberry. Knotberry. Mountain Bramble. Mountain Raspberry. Knoutberry. Fig. 2290.

Rubus Chamaemorus L. Sp. Pl. 494. 1753.

Herbaceous, rootstock creeping, branches erect, 2–3-leaved, 3′–10′ high, unarmed, finely pubescent or nearly glabrous, scaly below; stipules ovate, obtuse; leaves petioled, simple, orbicular or broader, 5–9-lobed, cordate or reniform at the base, pubescent or glabrous, 1′–3′ broad, the lobes usually short, broad, dentate; flowers monoecious or dioecious, solitary, terminal, white, 6″–12″ broad; sepals ovate, shorter than the petals, sometimes toothed toward the apex; fruit reddish to yellow, composed of few drupelets, edible and pleasant, at length separating from the receptacle.

In peat-bogs and on mountains, Maine and New Hampshire to arctic America, extending to Alaska and British Columbia. Also in northern Europe and Asia. An interesting southern colony of this plant has been recently found at Montauk Point, Long Island. Baked-apple berry. June–July.

4. Rubus strigòsus Michx.   Wild Red Raspberry.   Fig. 2291.

Rubus strigosus Michx. Fl. Bor. Am. 1: 297. 1803.
Rubus idaeus var. *strigosus* Maxim. Bull. Acad. St.
Petersb. 17: 161. 1872.

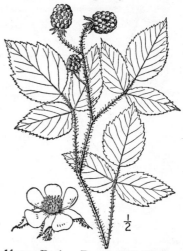

Stems shrubby, biennial, branched, 3°–6° high,
usually densely clothed with weak glandular bristles, or the older stems with small hooked prickles.
Stipules narrow, deciduous; leaves petioled, pinnately 3–5-foliolate, rarely simple and 3-lobed; leaflets ovate or ovate-oblong, acuminate, sharply and
irregularly serrate or slightly lobed, rounded at the
base, 1′–3′ long, whitish-pubescent beneath; inflorescence terminal and axillary, racemose or paniculate,
loose; pedicels slender, curving in fruit; flowers
4″–6″ broad; petals white, ascending, about equalling the spreading acuminate, mostly hispid, velvety
sepals; fruit elongated-hemispheric, light red, rarely
white.

In dry or rocky situations, Newfoundland and Labrador to British Columbia, south in the Alleghanies to
North Carolina, and in the Rocky Mountains to New
Mexico. Ascends to 5500 ft. in North Carolina. The
original of the Cuthbert and Hansall raspberries. Mulberry. May–July. Fruit ripe July–Sept.

Northern races closely resemble the Old World *Rubus
idaeus* L.

5. Rubus negléctus Peck.   Purple Wild Rasp-berry.   Fig. 2292.

Rubus neglectus Peck, Rep. Reg. Univ. N. Y. 22: 53.
1869.
Rubus strigosus × *occidentalis* Aust. Bull. Torr. Club 1:
31. 1870.

Intermediate between the preceding species and the
next, probably originating as a hybrid between
them. Stems usually elongated, recurved and rooting at the tip, glaucous, sparingly bristly and prickly;
leaflets ovate, sharply and irregularly incised-serrate,
very white-pubescent beneath, 1′–3′ long; inflorescence
corymbose, rather compact, terminal and often axillary; pedicels erect or ascending even in fruit; flowers 4″–5″ broad; petals white, erect; fruit nearly
hemispherical, dark-red or purple (yellowish in a
cultivated form).

In dry or rocky soil, Vermont to Ontario, Pennsylvania and Ohio. The original of the Carolina, Gladstone
and other raspberries. June–July. Fruit ripe July–Aug.

6. Rubus occidentàlis L.   Black Raspberry.   Thimble-berry.   Fig. 2293.

Rubus occidentalis L. Sp. Pl. 493. 1753.
Rubus idaeus var. *americanus* Torr. Ann. Lyc. N. Y. 2:
196. 1825.

Very glaucous, stems cane-like, recurved, often
rooting at the tip, sometimes 10°–12° long, sparingly armed with small hooked prickles, rarely
slightly glandular-bristly above. Stipules setaceous,
deciduous; leaves pinnately 3-foliolate (rarely 5-folio-
late); leaflets ovate, acuminate, coarsely incised-
serrate, very white-pubescent beneath; flowers as in
the preceding species; inflorescence corymbose, compact, usually only terminal; pedicels short, ascending
or erect in fruit; fruit purple-black (rarely yellow),
depressed-hemispheric.

New Brunswick to Quebec, Ontario, Georgia and Missouri. Ascends to 3000 ft. in Virginia. The original of
the Gregg, Hilborn and other raspberries. May–June.
Fruit ripe July. Called also scotch-cap and black-cap.
Purple raspberry. Black-berry.

Rubus phoenicolàsius Maxim., the wine-berry, of
Japan, a densely glandular species, has locally escaped from cultivation.

7. Rubus árcticus L.   Arctic Bramble.   Fig. 2294.

Rubus arcticus L. Sp. Pl. 494. 1753.
R. acaulis Michx. Fl. Bor. Am. 1 : 298. 1803.

Stems erect, simple or branched from the base, herbaceous, 3'–10' high, unarmed, finely pubescent, sometimes leafless below. Stipules oval or ovate, obtuse, 2"–4" long; leaves slender-petioled, 3-foliolate (rarely 5-foliolate); leaflets sessile or short-stalked, rhombic-ovate or obovate, coarsely and unequally serrate or slightly lobed, 9"–18" long; flowers solitary, or occasionally 2, terminal, slender-peduncled, pink, or rarely white, 6"–12" broad, sometimes dioecious; sepals acute, equalling or shorter than the obovate, entire or emarginate clawed petals; fruit light red, of several or numerous persistent or tardily deciduous drupelets, edible, fragrant.

In peat-bogs and damp woods, Quebec to Manitoba and British Columbia, and throughout arctic America. Also in northern Europe and Asia. Strawberry-leaved bramble. The petals of the American plant are mostly longer-clawed than those of the European. Summer.

8. Rubus triflòrus Richards.   Dwarf Red Blackberry.   Fig. 2295.

Rubus saxatilis var. *canadensis* Michx. Fl. Bor. Am. 1 : 298. 1803. Not *R. canadensis* L. 1753.
R. saxatilis var. *americanus* Pers. Syn. 2 : 52. 1807.
Rubus triflorus Richards. Franklin Journ. Ed. 2, App. 19. 1823.
R. americanus Britton, Mem. Torr. Club 5 : 185. 1894.

Stem trailing or ascending, unarmed, annual, herbaceous, or slightly woody and sometimes branched below, 6'–18' long, somewhat pubescent. Stipules oval, entire or few-toothed, 3"–5" long; leaves petioled, pedately or pinnately 3-foliolate, rarely 5-foliolate; leaflets rhombic-ovate, glabrous or nearly so, acute, the lateral ones mostly rounded, the terminal ones cuneate at the base, all sharply and often doubly serrate; peduncles slender, 1–3-flowered, glandular-pubescent; flowers 4"–6" broad; petals 5–7, white, spatulate-oblong, erect, rather longer than the acuminate reflexed sepals; fruit red-purple, about 6" long.

In swamps, Newfoundland to Alaska, south to New Jersey, Iowa and Nebraska. Intermediate between blackberries and raspberries. May–July. Running raspberry. Mulberry. Plum-bog-. swamp- or pigeon-berry. Dewberry. Fruit ripe July–Aug.

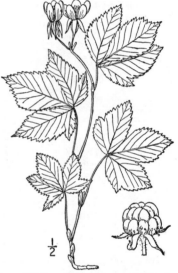

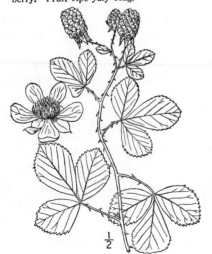

9. Rubus cuneifòlius Pursh.   Sand Blackberry.   Low or Knee-high Blackberry.   Fig. 2296.

Rubus parvifolius Walt. Fl. Car. 149. 1788. Not L. 1753.
Rubus cuneifolius Pursh, Fl. Am. Sept. 347. 1814.

Shrubby, erect or nearly so, 1°–3° high, much branched, armed with stout straight or recurved prickles, the young shoots and lower surfaces of the leaves densely whitish-pubescent. Stipules linear; leaves petioled, 3–5-foliolate; leaflets thick, rugose above, 1'–2' long, obovate or rarely oval, obtuse, dentate, especially above the middle, the terminal one cuneate; peduncles mainly terminal, 2–5-flowered; flowers white or pinkish, nearly 1' broad; petals exceeding the sepals; fruit brownish-black, often 1' long, delicious.

In sandy soil, southern Connecticut to Florida, west to Missouri and Louisiana. Brier-berry. May–July. Fruit ripe July–Aug.

10. Rubus canadénsis L. Millspaugh's Black-berry. Fig. 2297.

Rubus canadensis L. Sp. Pl. 494. 1753.
Rubus Millspaughii Britton, Bull. Torr. Club **18**: 366. 1891.

Ascending, wand-like, entirely unarmed, or with a few weak prickles, glabrous or the younger shoots scurfy-pubescent, the stems 5°–12° long. Leaves long-petioled, pedately 5-foliolate, or some 3-folio-late; leaflets oval, thin, glabrous on both sides, long-acuminate or acute, rounded or narrowed at the base, often 6′ long and 2′ wide, sharply but not very deeply dentate; stalk of the terminal leaflet 1½′–4′ long; inflorescence loosely racemose; bracts linear-lanceo-late; pedicels slender, ascending; sepals lanceolate, acuminate; fruit black, very pulpy, 8″–12″ long.

In thickets and woods, Newfoundland to Michigan, and the higher Alleghanies of North Carolina. June–Aug.

½

11. Rubus nìgricans Rydb. Bristly Black-berry. Fig. 2298.

Rubus hispidus var. *suberecta* Peck, Rep. N. Y. State Mus. **44**: 31. 1891. Not *R. suberectus* Anders. 1815.
Rubus nigricans Rydb. in Britton, Man. 498. 1901.

Stems erect or ascending, 2°–4° high, the older parts densely clothed with slender stiff slightly reflexed bristles. Leaflets generally 5 in leaves of the sterile shoots, 3 in those of the flowering branches, obovate, mostly acute or short-acumi-nate, sometimes 4′ long, short-stalked or sessile, green and glabrous on both sides; flowers 6″–9″ broad, racemose; fruit small, sour.

In dry or marshy soil, Quebec and northern New York to Michigan and eastern Pennsylvania. In-cluded in our first edition under *Rubus setòsus* Bigel., which appears to be a hybrid between this species and *R. hispidus* L. July–Aug.

½

12. Rubus frondòsus Bigel. Leafy-flow-ered Blackberry. Fig. 2299.

Rubus frondosus Bigel. Fl. Bost. Ed. *2*, 199. 1824.

Rubus villosus frondosus Bigel.; Torr. Fl. U. S. **1**: 487. 1824.

Stems erect or arching, 2½°–4° high, angled, bearing rather stout straight prickles, villous, especially when young. Leaves velvety-pubescent beneath, sparingly pubescent or glabrous above; leaflets elliptic to obovate, sharply serrate, acute or acuminate; racemes more or less elongated, the pedicels subtended by petioled, mostly uni-foliolate leaves (bracts); flowers about 1′ broad; petals broadly obovate; fruit subglobose, black, falling away before the subtending leaves.

Mostly in dry soil, Massachusetts to New York, Ohio(?) and Virginia. May–June.

⅗

2/3

14. Rubus argùtus Link. Tall Blackberry. Thimble-berry. Cloud-berry. Fig. 2301.

Rubus argutus Link, Enum. Hort. Berol. **2** : 60. 1822.

Shrubby, branched, perennial, pubescent; stems erect or recurved, 3°–10° long, armed with stout prickles. Stipules linear or lanceolate; leaves 3–5-foliolate; leaflets ovate or ovate-oblong, acute or acuminate, coarsely and unequally serrate, densely pubescent beneath, the terminal one stalked; inflorescence racemose, villous, often glandular and prickly; bracts small; flowers 9″–12″ broad; petals white, obovate, much exceeding the sepals; fruit black, pulpy, 6″–12″ long.

In dry soil, mostly at low altitudes, Massachusetts to Virginia. Finger-berry. Sow-tit. May–June. Fruit ripe July–Aug. Included in our first edition in the description of *Rubus villosus* Ait., which name has been erroneously applied by most authors.

Rubus laciniàtus Willd., found escaped from culti-vation in southern New York, Pennsylvania and Delaware, has laciniate or pinnatifid leaflets. It is a native of Europe.

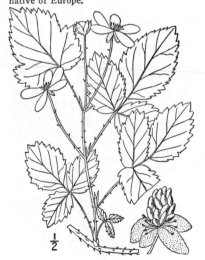

1/2

13. Rubus alleghaniénsis Porter. Mountain Blackberry. Fig. 2300.

Rubus villosus var. *montanus* Porter, Bull. Torr. Club **17** : 15. 1890.
Rubus montanus Porter, Bull. Torr. Club **21** : 120. 1894. Not Ort. 1852.
Rubus alleghaniensis Porter, Bull. Torr. Club **23** : 153. 1896.
R. nigrobaccus Bailey, Sk. Ev. Nat. Fr. 379, *f. 59*, *60.* 1898.

Stems reddish or purple, very prickly, erect, arching or ascending, 2°–8° high. Leaflets ovate to ovate-lanceolate, acute or acuminate, pubescent, at least beneath, the inflorescence more or less glandular-hispid; flowers several in rather loose racemes; fruit oblong, oblong-conic or thimble-shaped, 8″–14″ long, 3″–4″ in diameter; racemes sometimes very long; drupelets oblong when dry, rarely yellowish.

In dry soil, Nova Scotia to Ontario, New York, Virginia and North Carolina. May–July. Fruit ripe Aug.–Sept. High-bush blackberry.

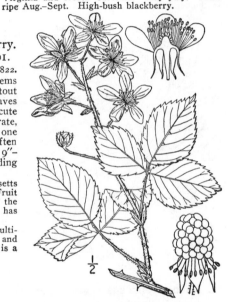

1/2

15. Rubus Baileyànus Britton. Bailey's Blackberry. Fig. 2302.

Rubus villosus var. *humifusus* T. & G. Fl. N. A. **1** : 455. 1840. Not *R. humifusus* Weihe, 1825.
R. Baileyanus Britton, Mem. Torr. Club **5** : 185. 1894.

Stem trailing or ascending, sparingly prickly, 3°–6° long. Leaflets broadly ovate or oval, pubes-cent, at least on the lower surface, mostly rounded or cordate at the base, acute or obtuse, the upper-most leaves almost invariably unifoliolate; flow-ers few, rather large; fruit small, not as succulent as that of the related species.

In dry woods and thickets, Massachusetts to south-ern New York and Virginia. May–June.

Rubus Rándii (Bailey) Rydb., referred to this species in our first edition, appears to be a hybrid, with *R. canadensis* L. as one of its parents.

16. Rubus procumbens Muhl. Low Running Blackberry. Dewberry. Fig. 2303.

?*R. villosus* Ait. Hort. Kew. **2** : 210. 1789. Not Thunb.
Rubus procumbens Muhl, Muhl. Cat. 50. 1813.
R. *canadensis invisus* Bailey, Am. Gard. **12** : 83. 1891.
R. *canadensis roribaccus* Bailey, Am. Gard. **11** : 642. 1890.

Trailing, shrubby, stem often several feet long, armed with scattered prickles or nearly naked. Branches erect or ascending, 4'-12' long, more or less pubescent, sometimes prickly, sometimes slightly glandular; leaves petioled, 3-7-foliolate; leaflets ovate, oval or ovate-lanceolate, thin, deciduous, acute or sometimes obtusish at the apex, rounded or narrowed at the base, sharply dentate-serrate, usually sparingly pubescent; flowers terminal, few and racemose, or sometimes solitary, white, about 1' broad; peduncles leafy; sepals shorter than or exceeding the petals; fruit black, delicious, often 1' long.

In dry soil, Newfoundland(?), Ontario to Lake Superior, south to Virginia, Louisiana and Oklahoma. Creeping blackberry. April–May. Fruit ripe June–July. Referred in our first edition, following previous authors, to *Rubus canadensis* L., long misunderstood

Rubus Ensleni Tratt., of the Southern States, differing by crenate leaflets, is doubtfully recorded as far north as Kansas.

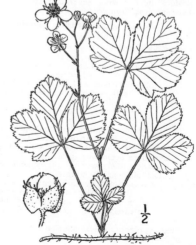

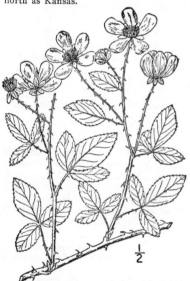

17. Rubus triviàlis Michx. Low Bush Blackberry. Fig. 2304.

Rubus trivalis Michx. Fl. Bor. Am. **1** : 296. 1803.

Stem trailing or procumbent, several feet long, beset with stout hooked prickles, and sometimes bristly. Branches erect, 3'-9' high, prickly and usually pubescent or setose; leaves petioled, 3-foliolate (rarely 5-foliolate); leaflets oval, or sometimes ovate-lanceolate, coriaceous, evergreen, glabrous or very nearly so, acute or obtusish at the apex, narrowed or rounded at the base, sharply serrate; peduncles terminal, prickly, 1-5-flowered; flowers often 1' broad, white; petals much exceeding the reflexed sepals; fruit black, often 1' long, sweet.

In dry sandy soil, Virginia to Florida, west to Texas. Called also southern dewberry. March–May.

Rubus rubrisètus Rydb., ranging from Louisiana northward into Missouri, differs in being copiously glandular-pubescent, with somewhat smaller flowers.

18. Rubus híspidus L. Hispid or Running Swamp Blackberry. Fig. 2305.

Rubus hispidus L. Sp. Pl. 493. 1753.
Rubus obovalis Michx. Fl. Bor. Am. **1** : 298. 1803.

Stems slender, slightly woody, creeping, more or less densely beset with weak, retrorse bristles. Branches erect or ascending, 4'-12' long, naked, or with a few scattered prickles; leaves petioled, 3-foliolate or rarely 5-foliolate; leaflets obovate, obtuse, thick, persistent, somewhat shining above, narrowed at the base, ½'-1½' long, sharply serrate above the middle; peduncles terminal or axillary, nearly or quite leafless; flowers racemose, white, 6"-8" broad; petals exceeding the sepals; fruit reddish, or nearly black when ripe, sour, usually less than ½' long, composed of few drupelets.

In swamps or low grounds, rarely in dry soil, Nova Scotia to Ontario and Minnesota, south to Georgia and Kansas. Ascends to 3500 ft. in North Carolina. Leaves sometimes persistent into the winter. Leaflets of sterile shoots sometimes 2'-3' long. June–July.

29. DALIBÀRDA L. Sp. Pl. 491. 1753.

A low tufted perennial downy-pubescent herb, with simple long-petioled ovate-orbicular cordate and crenate leaves, scape-like peduncles bearing 1 or 2 large perfect white flowers, and short recurved peduncles bearing several or numerous small cleistogamous flowers. Calyx deeply 5–6-parted, its divisions somewhat unequal, the 3 larger ones commonly toothed. Petals 5, sessile, soon deciduous. Stamens numerous. Pistils 5–10; style terminal. Drupelets 5–10, nearly dry, enclosed at length in the connivent calyx-segments. [Named in honor of Thos. Fran. Dalibard, a French botanist of the 18th century.]

A monotypic genus of northeastern North America.

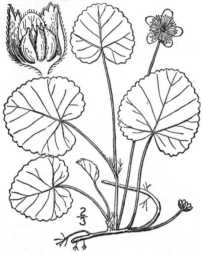

1. Dalibarda rèpens L. Dalibarda. Dewdrop. Fig. 2306.

Dalibarda repens L. Sp. Pl. 491. 1753.

Rubus Dalibarda L. Sp. Pl. Ed. 2, 708. 1762.

Dalibarda violaeoides Michx. Fl. Bor. Am. 1: 299. 1803.

Stems slender, unarmed, much tufted, several inches long. Leaves pubescent on both sides, 9″–2′ in diameter, the crenations low, obtuse or sometimes mucronulate; stipules setaceous; flowers 4″–5″ broad; peduncles slender, 1½′–5′ long; achenes oblong, pointed, slightly curved, minutely roughened, 2″ long, rather more than ½″ in thickness.

In woods, Nova Scotia to Minnesota, south, to Pennsylvania, southern New Jersey, North Carolina, Ohio and Michigan. Plant resembling a low violet. Robin-runaway. June–Sept.

30. RÒSA [Tourn.] L. Sp. Pl. 491. 1753.

Erect or climbing shrubs, generally with subterranean rootstocks. Stems commonly prickly. Leaves alternate, odd-pinnate. Stipules adnate to the petiole. Flowers corymbose or solitary, red, pink or white (in our species). Calyx-tube cup-shaped or urn-shaped, constricted at the throat, becoming fleshy in fruit, 5- (rarely 4-) lobed, the lobes imbricated, spreading, deciduous or persistent. Petals 5 (rarely 4), spreading. Stamens ∞, inserted on the hollow annular disk. Carpels ∞, sessile at the bottom of the calyx; ovaries commonly pubescent; styles distinct or united. Achenes numerous, enclosed in the berry-like fruiting calyx-tube. Seed pendulous. [The ancient Latin name of the rose.]

A large genus, the number of species variously regarded, natives of the northern hemisphere. Besides the following, several others occur in the southern and western parts of North America. Type species: *Rosa centifolia* L.

* Styles cohering in a column; leaflets mostly 3.   1. *R. setigera.*
** Styles all distinct; leaflets 5–11.

Leaves deciduous.
    Calyx-lobes persistent, erect on the fruit, or spreading.
        Infrastipular spines generally none.
            Stems unarmed or nearly so; calyx-lobes erect on the fruit.   2. *R. blanda.*
            Stems armed with numerous prickles.
                Leaflets 3–9, often resinous, obtuse at base; flowers solitary; calyx-lobes erect on the fruit.   3. *R. acicularis.*
                Leaflets 7–11, not resinous, narrowed at base; flowers corymbed; calyx-lobes spreading.   4. *R. pratincola.*
        Infrastipular spines commonly present; stems prickly.
            Calyx-lobes entire; native western species.   5. *R. Woodsii.*
            Calyx-lobes, at least the outer ones, deeply incised; introduced specie   6. *R. canina.*
    Calyx-lobes deciduous, spreading.
        Leaflets finely serrate; spines stout, recurved.   7. *R. carolina.*
        Leaflets coarsely serrate.
            Infrastipular spines slender, nearly straight; native bushy species.
                Stems with scattered prickles or naked; flowers often solitary.   8. *R. virginiana.*
                Stems very densely prickly; flowers usually solitary.   9. *R. nitida.*
            Infrastipular spines stout, hooked; introduced wand-like or climbing species.   10. *R. rubiginosa.*
Leaves evergreen; calyx-lobes persistent.   11. *R. bracteata.*

1. Rosa setígera Michx. Prairie Rose. Climbing Rose. Fig. 2307.

Rosa setigera Michx. Fl. Bor. Am. 1 : 295. 1803.

Stems climbing, several feet long, armed with scattered curved prickles but not bristly, or unarmed. Petioles, twigs and peduncles often glandular-pubescent; stipules very narrow; leaflets 3, or sometimes 5, mostly ovate, acute or obtusish at the apex, rounded at the base, 1'–3' long, sharply serrate; flowers corymbose, about 2½' broad; calyx-lobes ovate, acute, at length reflexed and deciduous, glandular; petals obcordate, varying from rose-color to white; styles cohering in a glabrous column; fruit globose, 4"–5" in diameter, more or less glandular.

In thickets and on prairies, southern Ontario to Wisconsin, West Virginia, Florida and Texas. Escaped from cultivation in Connecticut, New Jersey and Virginia. June–July. Michigan rose. Rose-blush.

2. Rosa blánda Ait. Smooth or Meadow Rose. Fig. 2308.

Rosa blanda Ait. Hort. Kew. 2 : 202. 1789.

Erect, low, 2°–4° high; entirely unarmed or with a few straight slender prickles on the stem. Stipules rather broad; leaflets 5–7, short-stalked, usually pale beneath, oval or obovate, obtuse at the apex, commonly narrowed or cuneate at the base, 1'–1½' long, simply and sharply serrate; flowers pink, sometimes 3' broad, corymbose or solitary; calyx-lobes lanceolate, acuminate, entire, hispid-pubescent, persistent and erect on the fruit; petals obovate, erose or sometimes obcordate; styles separate; fruit globose or pyriform, glabrous or nearly so, about 5" in diameter.

In moist rocky places, Newfoundland to Vermont and northern New Jersey, west to Ontario, Assiniboia and Missouri. Pale or early wild-rose. June–July.

3. Rosa aiculàris Lindl. Prickly Rose. Fig. 2309.

Rosa acicularis Lindl. Ros. Monog. 44. pl. 8. 1820.
Rosa Sayi Schwein. in Keating, Narr. Long's Exp. 2 : 388. 1824.
R. Engelmanni S. Wats. Gard. & For. 2 : 376. 1889.

Bushy, low, 1°–4° high, the stems and often the branches, densely armed with straight prickles; infrastipular spines none. Stipules mostly broad; leaflets 5–9 (rarely 3), oval or oval-lanceolate, obtuse at the apex, rounded at the base, simply or doubly serrate, often more or less resinous-pubescent, 1'–2' long; flowers usually solitary, 2½'–3' broad; calyx-lobes lanceolate, acuminate or sometimes dilated above, entire or few-toothed, persistent and erect upon the fruit; styles distinct; fruit globose or ovoid, sometimes 1' long, generally glabrous.

Anticosti to Ontario, Alaska, northern Michigan, Minnesota, south in the Rocky Mountains to Colorado. Northern Europe and Asia. Consists of several races, differing in the form of the fruit and in the amount of pubescence. June–July.

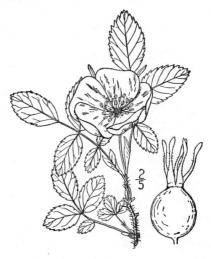

4. Rosa pratíncola Greene.   Arkansas Rose.
Fig. 2310.

Rosa pratincola Greene, Pittonia 4: 13. 1899.

Erect, low, 1°–2° high. Stems densely prickly with very slender bristles; infrastipular spines none; stipules rather narrow, sometimes toothed above; leaflets 7–11, oval or obovate, sessile or nearly so, obtuse at the apex, narrowed or often cuneate at the base, seldom over 1' long, simply and sharply serrate, glabrous on both sides; flowers corymbose or rarely solitary, about 2' broad; sepals lanceolate, acuminate, sparingly glandular-hispid or glabrous, or sometimes lobed, persistent and spreading or reflexed; styles distinct; fruit globose or nearly so, 4"–6" in diameter, glabrous or bristly.

Prairies, Manitoba to Minnesota, Iowa, Missouri, Nebraska, Colorado, Texas and New Mexico. June–July. Confused in our first edition with *Rosa arkansana* Porter.

Rosa spinosíssima L., scotch rose, with densely prickly stems, small roundish leaflets glabrous or nearly so, small pinkish or white flowers and globose black fruit, is locally escaped from cultivation. It is native of Europe and Asia.

5. Rosa Woódsii Lindl.   Woods' Rose.
Fig. 2311.

Rosa Woodsii Lindl. Mon. Ros. 21. 1820.
Rosa Fendleri Crepin, Bull. Soc. Bot. Belg. 15: 91. 1876.

Low, bushy, 1°–3° high, armed with slender mostly straight spines, or naked above. Infrastipular spines commonly present; stipules rather broad, entire; leaflets 5–9, oval or obovate, short-stalked or sessile, obtusish at the apex, narrowed or cuneate at the base, 5"–18" long, simply and sharply serrate, somewhat glaucous beneath; flowers 1'–2' broad, corymbose or solitary, short-pedicelled; sepals lanceolate, acuminate, laterally lobed or entire, erect and persistent on the fruit; styles distinct; fruit globose or globose-ovoid, 4"–5" in diameter, glabrous, sometimes glaucous.

Prairies, Minnesota to Missouri, the Northwest Territory, New Mexico and Colorado. June–July.

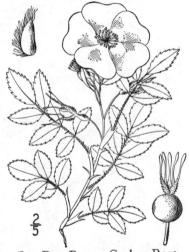

6. Rosa canìna L.   Dog Rose.   Canker Rose.
Wild Brier.   Hip-tree or -rose.   Fig. 2312.

Rosa canina L. Sp. Pl. 491. 1753.

Branches erect or straggling, sometimes 10° long, armed with stout short hooked spines, not bristly but sometimes glandular. Stipules broad, glandular; leaflets 5–7, ovate or oval, rather thick, generally obtuse at each end, usually simply and sharply serrate, sometimes pubescent beneath, glabrous or nearly so above, 1'–1½' long; flowers solitary or few, pink varying to white; calyx-lobes much lobed, lanceolate, reflexed; styles distinct; fruit long-ovoid, 6"–9" long, usually glabrous.

In waste places, especially along roadsides, Nova Scotia to western New Jersey and eastern Pennsylvania, Virginia and Tennessee. Naturalized or adventive from Europe; native also in northern Asia. Cat-whin. Canker-blooms (Shakspere). Bramble-brier or brere-rose. Lawyers (i. e. an old thorny stem). Soldiers. Hedge-peak. Dog-thorn. Horse-bramble. Bird-brier. Bedeguar. June–July.

7. Rosa carolìna L. Swamp or Wild Rose. Hip-tree. Fig. 2313.

Rosa carolina L. Sp. Pl. 492. 1753.

Bushy, 1°–8° high, armed with rather distant stout commonly recurved spines. Prickles not very abundant, sometimes none; stipules very narrow; leaflets 5–9 (usually 7), varying considerably in outline, oval, oblong, ovate-lanceolate or even obovate, 1′–3′ long, finely and simply serrate, generally short-stalked, acute or acutish at each end, pale or pubescent beneath; flowers corymbose or rarely solitary, 2′–3′ broad; calyx-lobes lanceolate, acuminate or dilated above, rarely lobed, hispid-pubescent, spreading or reflexed, deciduous; styles distinct; fruit globose or depressed-globose, about 4″ high, glandular-hispid.

In swamps and low grounds, Nova Scotia to Ontario, Minnesota, Missouri, Florida and Mississippi. June–Aug.

$\frac{2}{5}$

8. Rosa virginiàna Mill. Low or Pasture Rose. Fig. 2314.

Rosa virginiana Mill. Gard. Dict. Ed. 8, no. 10. 1768.
Rosa humilis Marsh. Arb. Am. 136. 1785.
Rosa parviflora Ehrh. Beitr. 4: 21. 1789.
Rosa lucida Ehrh. Beitr. 4: 22. 1789.
Rosa humilis lucida Best, Bull. Torr. Club 14: 256. 1887.

Bushy, 6′–6° high, usually armed with slender or stout, straight or curved infrastipular spines, and more or less prickly. Stipules entire; leaflets usually 5, sometimes 7, rather thin, ovate-oval or obovate, dull or somewhat shining, coarsely and simply serrate, 6″–2′ long, mostly acute or acutish at each end, short-stalked or sessile, glabrous or pubescent beneath; flowers usually few or solitary, 2′–3′ broad; pedicels and calyx usually glandular; calyx-lobes lanceolate, acuminate, or dilated above, commonly lobed, spreading and deciduous; petals obovate, obcordate or sometimes lobed; styles distinct; fruit globose or depressed-globose, glandular-hispid, about 4″ high.

In dry or rocky soil, Newfoundland to Ontario, Wisconsin, Missouri, Georgia and Louisiana. Our commonest wild rose, consisting of many slightly differing races, northern ones with stouter spines than southern. A double-flowered form occurs in Pennsylvania and New Jersey. Dwarf wild rose. May–July.

$\frac{1}{2}$

9. Rosa nítida Willd. Northeastern Rose. Wild or Shining Rose. Fig. 2315.

Rosa nitida Willd. Enum. 544. 1809.

Low, bushy, seldom over 2° high, the stems and branches very densely covered with slender straight prickles nearly as long as the slender infrastipular spines. Stipules usually broad, often glandular; leaflets 5–9, oblong or oval, generally acute at each end, short-stalked, the terminal one sometimes slightly obovate and obtuse at the apex, all finely and sharply serrate, shining above, glabrous or very nearly so, 6″–15″ long; flowers solitary or few, 1′–2½′ broad; calyx-lobes lanceolate, acuminate, entire, hispid or glandular, at length spreading, deciduous; petals often obcordate; styles distinct; fruit glandular-hispid, globose, about 4″ high.

In low grounds, Connecticut and Massachusetts to Newfoundland. June–July.

$\frac{2}{5}$

10. **Rosa rubinòsa** L.   Sweetbrier.   Fig. 2316.

Rosa rubiginosa L. Mant. 2 : 564. 1771.
Rosa micrantha J. E. Smith, Eng. Bot. *pl. 2490*.
Rosa eglanteria Mill. Dict. Ed. 8, no. 4. 1768. Not L. 1753.

Slender, 4°–6° high, or often forming longer wands, armed with stout recurved prickles. Stipules rather broad; rachis of the leaves glandular; leaflets 5–7, generally doubly serrate and densely glandular-pubescent and resinous beneath, very aromatic; flowers pink varying to white; calyx-lobes lanceolate, usually much lobed, spreading, deciduous, glandular-hispid; fruit oval or ovoid, 6″–10″ long.

In thickets, pastures and waste places, Nova Scotia to Ontario, Tennessee, Virginia and Kansas. Adventive or naturalized from Europe; native also in central Asia. June–July. The Eglantine of Chaucer, Spenser and Shakspere. Hip-rose. Hip-brier. Bedeguar. Primrose. Kitchen-rose.

Rosa gállica L., occasionally escaped from cultivation, differs in having weak slender prickles and much larger leaflets; it is native of Europe.

Rosa cinnamòmea L., the cinnamon rose, of Europe and Asia, with small double reddish flowers, and leaves downy-pubescent beneath, is occasionally found along roadsides in the Eastern and Middle States.

11. **Rosa bracteàta** Wendl.   Evergreen Rose.   Fig. 2317.

Rosa bracteata Wendl. Bot. Beob. 50. 1798.

A shrub with dark green, evergreen leaves, the stems and branches diffuse or spreading, sometimes 18°–20° long, armed with recurved prickles. Leaflets 5–11, obovate or oval, ½–1′ long, often wedge-shaped at the base, notched, truncate or apiculate at the apex, serrate, shining above; flowers solitary or few together; calyx-lobes acuminate, reflexed when old, persistent; petals white to yellow, retuse or notched; styles separate; fruit about ¾′ in diameter.

Woods and waste places, Virginia to Florida, Tennessee and Mississippi. Naturalized from China. April–June.

Family 55.   **MALÀCEAE** Small, Fl. SE. U. S. 529.   1903.

APPLE FAMILY.

Trees or shrubs, with alternate pinnately veined or pinnate petioled leaves, the small deciduous stipules free from the petiole. Flowers regular, perfect, racemed, cymose or solitary. Calyx mostly 5-toothed or 5-lobed, its tube (hypanthium) adnate to the ovary. Petals mostly 5, usually clawed. Stamens numerous or rarely few, distinct; anthers small, 2-celled, the sacs longitudinally dehiscent. Ovary 1–5-celled, usually 5-celled, composed of 1–5 wholly or partly united carpels, borne within the hypanthium and adnate to it; ovules 1–2 (rarely several) in each carpel, anatropous, ascending; styles 1–5; stigma small. Fruit a more or less fleshy pome, consisting of the thickened calyx-tube enclosing the bony papery or leathery carpels. Endosperm none; cotyledons fleshy.

About 20 genera and probably not fewer than 500 species, of wide geographic distribution.

Ripe carpels papery or leathery.	
Leaves pinnate.	1. *Sorbus.*
Leaves simple, entire, toothed, or lobed.	
Cavities of the ovary (carpels) as many as the styles.	
Flesh of the pome with grit-cells.	2. *Pyrus.*
Flesh of the pome without grit-cells.	
Cymes simple ; trees.	3. *Malus.*
Cymes compound ; low shrubs.	4. *Aronia.*
Cavities of the ovary becoming twice as many as the styles.	5. *Amelanchier.*
Ripe carpels bony.	
Ovule 1 in each carpel, or if 2, dissimilar.	6. *Crataegus.*
Ovules 2 in each carpel, alike.	7. *Cotoneaster.*

1. SÓRBUS [Tourn.] L. Sp. Pl. 477. 1753.

Trees or shrubs, with alternate pinnate leaves, serrate leaflets, deciduous stipules, and perfect regular white flowers, in terminal compound cymes. Calyx-tube urn-shaped, 5-lobed, not bracteolate. Petals 5, spreading, short-clawed. Stamens ∞. Ovary inferior; styles usually 3, distinct; stigma truncate; ovules 2 in each cavity. Fruit a small red berry-like pome, its carpels not cartilaginous. [The ancient Latin name of the pear or service-tree.]

A genus of about 10 species, natives of the north temperate zone. Besides the following, 2 others occur in western North America. Type species: *Sorbus domestica* L.

Leaflets long-acuminate; fruit 2″–3″ in diameter.   1. *S. americana.*
Leaflets obtuse or short-pointed; fruit about 4″ in diameter.   2. *S. scopulina.*

1. Sorbus americàna Marsh. American Mountain Ash. Dogberry. Fig. 2318.

Sorbus americana Marsh. Arb. Am. 145. 1785.
Sorbus microcarpa Pursh, Fl. Am. Sept. 341. 1814.
Pyrus americana DC. Prodr. 2: 637. 1825.

A small tree, with smooth bark, reaching a maximum height of 30° and a trunk diameter of 18′. Leaf-buds acute; leaves petioled; leaflets 11–17, lanceolate, long-acuminate, glabrous on both sides or slightly pubescent when young, bright green above, generally paler beneath, 1½′–4′ long, sharply serrate with mucronate teeth; cymes densely compound, 3′–6′ broad; flowers 2″–3″ broad; fruit globose, bright red, 2″–3″ in diameter.

In low woods or moist ground, Newfoundland to Manitoba, south, especially along the mountains, to North Carolina and to Michigan. Wood soft, light brown; weight per cubic foot 34 lbs. American rowan- or service-tree. Witch- or round-wood. Round- or wine-tree. Elder-leaved mountain-ash or -sumach. Moose-missy. Missey-moosey. Indian-mozamize. Life-of-man. A closely related form occurs in Japan. May–June.

$\frac{2}{5}$

2. Sorbus scopulìna Greene. Western Mountain Ash. Fig. 2319.

S. scopulina Greene, Pittonia 4: 130. 1900.
S. subvestita Greene, loc. cit. 1900.

A small tree or often a shrub, closely resembling the preceding species. Leaf-buds acute; leaflets 7–15, proportionately broader and shorter, oval or ovate-lanceolate, obtuse or short-pointed at the apex, sharply serrate, glabrous and dark green above, pale and usually more or less pubescent beneath, especially along the veins, seldom over 3′ long; flowers 3″–5″ broad; calyx and pedicels generally pubescent; cymes 2′–4′ broad; fruit globose, red, about 4″ in diameter.

In moist ground, Labrador to Alaska, south to Maine, Pennsylvania, Michigan, and in the Rocky Mountains to Colorado and Utah. Wood similar to that of the preceding; weight per cubic foot 37 lbs. United, in our first edition, as by other authors, with *S. sambucifolia* (C. & S.) Roem., of eastern Asia, which proves to be distinct; it has also been referred to the northwestern *Sorbus sitchensis* Roem. American rowan-tree. June–July.

$\frac{2}{5}$

Sorbus Aucupària L., the European mountain ash, rowan tree or quick-beam, has the leaves pubescent on both sides, especially when young, the calyx and pedicels usually woolly. Often planted; locally escaped from cultivation.

2. PỲRUS [Tourn.] L. Sp. Pl. 479. 1753.

Trees, or some species shrubs, with simple leaves. Flowers large, showy, white or pink, in simple terminal cymes. Calyx urn-shaped, 5-lobed, the lobes acute. Hypanthium nearly closed by a disc-like cushion. Petals 5, rounded, short-clawed. Stamens usually numerous; styles mostly 5, distinct, or united only at the very base; ovules 2 in each cavity; carpels cartilaginous or leathery. Fruit a pome, usually pear-shaped, its flesh abounding in grit-cells. [Latin name of the pear.]

About 12 species, natives of the Old World, the following typical.

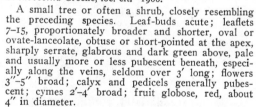

1. Pyrus commùnis L. Pear. Choke Pear. Fig. 2320.

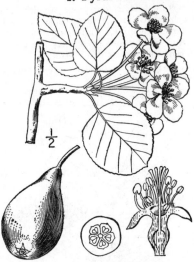

Pyrus communis L. Sp. Pl. 479. 1753.

A tree, sometimes 60° high and with a trunk 2°–3° in diameter, commonly much smaller, the branches usually thorny. Leaves ovate, elliptic or obovate, finely serrulate or entire, slender-petioled, 1½′–3′ long, downy and ciliate when young, becoming glabrous or nearly so when old, the apex acute or acuminate, the base usually rounded; petioles sometimes as long as the blades or longer; cymes few–several-flowered, borne at the ends of short twigs of the preceding year; pedicels 9″–2′ long, at first downy; flowers white, 1′–2′ broad; calyx-lobes about as long as the tube; styles distinct to the base; pome, in the wild form, seldom over 2′ long, in the numerous cultivated forms often much larger.

In thickets and woods, Maine to New York, New Jersey and Pennsylvania, escaped from cultivation. Native of Europe and Asia. Wood hard, fine-grained, reddish-brown; weight per cubic foot 51 lbs. April–May.

3. MÀLUS Mill. Gard. Dict. Abr. Ed. 4. 1754.

Trees or shrubs, with alternate toothed or lobed leaves, and showy pink or white flowers in simple terminal cymes. Calyx-tube urn-shaped or campanulate, 5-lobed. Hypanthium open, not closed by a cushion. Petals 5, rounded, clawed. Styles 2–5 (usually 5), united at the base; ovules 2 in each cavity, carpels papery or leathery. Fruit a pome, usually depressed-globose, mostly hollowed at the base, but sometimes rounded, its flesh not containing grit-cells. [Greek, apple.]

About 15 species, natives of the north temperate zone. Besides the following, another occurs in northwestern America. Type species: *Pyrus Malus* L.

Leaves glabrous, at least when mature.
  Leaves ovate-lanceolate to oblong, narrowed at the base.
    Leaves obtusish or acute.
    Leaves acuminate.
  Leaves ovate, cordate or rounded at the base.
Leaves persistently pubescent or tomentose beneath.
  Leaves mostly narrowed at the base; pome 1′–1½′ in diameter.
  Leaves rounded or subcordate at the base; pome 2′–4′ in diameter.

1. *M. coronaria.*
2. *M. baccata.*
3. *M. glaucescens.*

4. *M. ioensis.*
5. *M. Malus.*

1. Malus coronària (L.) Mill. Narrow-leaved Crab Apple. Fig. 2321.

Pyrus coronaria L. Sp. Pl. 480. 1753.
Malus coronaria Mill. Gard. Dict. Ed. 8, no. 2. 1768.
Pyrus angustifolia Ait. Hort. Kew. 2: 176. 1789.
Malus angustifolia Michx. Fl. Bor. Am. 1: 292. 1803.
Malus lancifolia Rehder, Trees & Shrubs 2: 141. 1911.

A small tree, sometimes 20° high and the trunk 10′ in diameter. Leaves oblong, oblong-lanceolate or oval, thick, shining and dark green above, glabrous when mature, sometimes pubescent beneath when young, dentate or often entire, or those of sterile shoots often lobed, obtusish or acute at the apex, narrowed at the base, 1′–2′ long; cymes few-flowered; pedicels 1′–1½′ long, slender; flowers pink, fragrant, mostly less than 1′ broad; styles nearly separate; calyx-lobes early deciduous; pome about 1′ in diameter, yellowish, hard.

In thickets, New Jersey to Illinois and Missouri, south to Florida and Louisiana. Recorded from Kansas. Wood hard, reddish brown; weight per cubic foot 43 lbs. Crab-apple or -tree. Wild crab. Southern wild crab. March–May.

2. Malus baccàta (L.) Borck. Siberian Crab Apple. Fig. 2322.

Pyrus baccata L. Mant. **1** : 75. 1767.

Malus baccata Borck. Handb. Forstbot. **2** : 1280. 1800–1803.

A small tree, up to 30° high. Leaves glabrous, ovate to ovate-oblong, 2′–4′ long, acuminate at the apex, rounded or narrowed at the base, serrate, rather firm in texture; flowers clustered, on slender pedicels, about 1½′ broad; petals oblong to obovate, narrowed at the base; fruit globose, about 1′ in diameter, yellow or reddish; calyx-lobes glabrous or nearly so, deciduous.

Escaped from cultivation and spontaneous, Maine to Connecticut. Native of Europe and Asia. May.

$\frac{2}{3}$

2. Malus glaucescéns Rehder. American Crab Apple. Fig. 2323.

Malus glaucescens Rehder, Trees and Shrubs **2** : 139. 1911.

A small tree, sometimes reaching a height of 25° and trunk diameter of 12′. Leaves petioled, ovate to triangular-ovate, sparingly pubescent beneath along the veins when young, glabrous when old, sharply serrate and on sterile shoots, often somewhat lobed, obtuse, acute or acutish at the apex, rounded or cordate at the base, 1′–3′ long; flowers rose-colored, very fragrant, 1′–2′ broad; pedicels 6″–18″ long; calyx glabrous or pubescent, its lobes somewhat persistent on the pome; pome fleshy, globose or depressed, 1′–1½′ in diameter, greenish-yellow, fragrant, very acid.

In thickets, Ontario to Michigan, south to New Jersey, South Carolina, Iowa and Missouri. Wood soft, reddish brown; weight per cubic foot 44 lbs. Wild or fragrant crab. Sweet-scented crab. April–May. Fruit ripe Sept. Long mistaken for *M. coronaria*. Consists of several races, or may include more than one species.

$\frac{1}{2}$

3. Malus ioénsis (Wood) Britton. Western Crab Apple. Fig. 2324.

Pyrus coronaria var. *ioensis* Wood, Class-book, 333. 1860.

Pyrus ioensis Carruth, Trans. Kans. Acad. Sci. **5** : 48. 1877.

Malus ioensis Britton, in Britt. & Brown, Ill. Fl. **2** : 235. 1897.

A small tree, resembling *Malus glaucescens.* Leaves simple, firm, white-pubescent beneath, at length glabrous above, obtuse at the apex, mostly narrowed at the base, ovate, oval or oblong, dentate, crenate or with a few rounded lobes, 1′–2′ long, or on young shoots much larger; petioles and calyx pubescent, ½′–1½′ long; flowers much like those of *M. glaucescens;* pedicels villous-pubescent, slender, 1′–1½′ long; calyx-lobes persistent on the pome.

Minnesota, Wisconsin and Illinois to Kentucky, Louisiana, Nebraska and Oklahoma. Iowa crab. April–May.

Malus Soulàrdi (Bailey) Britton, admitted as a species in our first edition, has been shown to be a hybrid between this and *Malus Malus.*

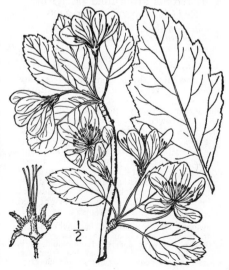

$\frac{1}{2}$

$\frac{1}{2}$

4. Malus Màlus (L.) Britton. Apple.
Scarb- or Wilding-tree. Fig. 2325.

Pyrus Malus L. Sp. Pl. 479. 1753.
Malus sylvestris Mill. Gard. Dict. Ed. 8, no. 1. 1768.

A large tree with spreading branches, the trunk sometimes reaching a diameter of 3° in cultivation. Leaves petioled, broadly ovate or oval, obtuse or abruptly pointed at the apex, rounded or slightly cordate at the base 1'–3' long, dentate or nearly entire, glabrous or nearly so above, pubescent and often woolly beneath, especially when young; pedicels generally tomentose, 1'–2' long; flowers pink, or white, 1½'–3' broad; calyx tomentose; fruit depressed-globose or elongated, hollowed at the base, 1½'–3' in diameter.

In woods and thickets, frequent in southern New England, New York, New Jersey and Pennsylvania. Our common apple, introduced from Europe and escaped from cultivation. Native also of western Asia. Wood hard, reddish brown; weight per cubic foot 50 lbs. Crab-tree or -stock. Nurse-garden. April–May.
The cultivated crab apples are mainly hybrids of this with *M. baccata* and are occasionally spontaneous.

4. ARÒNIA Medic. Phil. Bot. 140. 1789.

Low shrubs, with alternate simple petioled finely serrate leaves, the upper side of the midrib glandular, the narrow stipules early deciduous. Flowers small, white or pink, in terminal compound cymes. Calyx urn-shaped, 5-lobed. Petals 5, concave, spreading. Stamens numerous. Styles 3–5, united at the base. Ovary woolly. Pome small, globose or somewhat top-shaped, not hollowed at the base, its carpels rather leathery. [Name modified from *Aria*, the beam-tree of Europe.]

The genus consists of the following species, the first typical.

Cyme and lower surfaces of the leaves woolly.
    Fruit short-pyriform, bright red; calyx-lobes very glandular.   1. *A. arbutifolia.*
    Fruit oval to globose, purple-black; calyx-lobes glandless, or with very few glands.
                                                      2. *A. atropurpurea.*
Cyme and leaves glabrous or nearly so; fruit black or purplish.   3. *A. melanocarpa.*

1. Aronia arbutifòlia (L.) Ell.
Red Choke-berry. Fig. 2326.

Mespilus arbutifolia L. Sp. Pl. 478. 1753.
Pyrus arbutifolia L. f. Suppl. 256. 1781.
Mespilus arbutifolia var. *erythrocarpa* Michx. Fl. Bor. Am. 1: 292. 1803.
A. arbutifolia Ell. Bot. S. C. & Ga. 1: 556. 1821.

A branching shrub, sometimes reaching a height of 12°, but usually much lower. Leaves petioled, oval, oblong or obovate, obtuse or abruptly short-pointed at the apex, narrowed or somewhat cuneate at the base, 1'–3' long, serrulate-crenulate, glabrous above, generally densely tomentose beneath; cymes terminal, but at length overtopped by the young sterile shoots, compound; flowers white or purplish-tinged, 4''–6'' broad; calyx and pedicels tomentose; calyx-lobes very glandular; pome 2''–3'' in diameter, and bright red when mature, long-persistent.

Swamps and wet woods, Massachusetts to Florida, Ohio and Louisiana, often confused with the following species, from which it is quite distinct in fruit. Recorded from Arkansas. Choke-pear. Dog-berry. March–May.

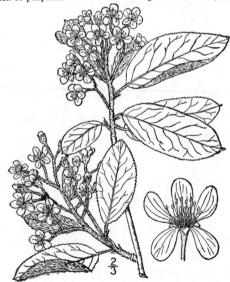

$\frac{2}{3}$

2. Aronia atropurpùrea Britton.
Purple-fruited Choke-berry.
Fig. 2327.

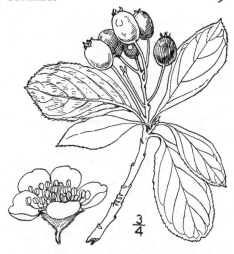

Aronia atropurpurea Britton, Man. 517. 1901.

Pyrus arbutifolia var. *atropurpurea* Robinson, Rhodora **10** : 33. 1908.

A shrub, sometimes 12° high, usually taller than the other species. Calyx, pedicels and lower leaf-surfaces tomentose; leaves oval to obovate; calyx-lobes glandless, or with very few glands; fruit oval to globose, purple-black, 3″–5″ long, persistent into late autumn.

Wet grounds, especially shaded swamps, Newfoundland to Ontario, Michigan and Virginia, perhaps extending south to Florida. April–June.

3. Aronia melanocarpa (Michx.) Britton.
Black Chokeberry. Chokepear.
Fig. 2328.

Mespilus arbutifolia var. *nigra* Willd. Sp. Pl. **2** : 1013. 1800.

Mespilus arbutifolia var. *melanocarpa* Michx. Fl. Bor. Am. **1** : 292. 1803.

Pyrus melanocarpa Willd. Enum. 525. 1809.

Pyrus nigra Sargent, Gard. & For. **3** : 416. 1890.

Aronia nigra Britton, Mem. Torr. Club **5** : 182. 1894.

A shrub resembling the preceding species. Leaves obovate or oval, obtuse, acute or abruptly acuminate at the apex, narrowed or cuneate at the base, short-petioled, crenulate, dark green above, paler beneath, glabrous or nearly so on both surfaces; flowers similar to the preceding; calyx and pedicels nearly glabrous; calyx-lobes glandular; fruit globose or oval, nearly black, or purplish black, 3″–4″ in diameter, early deciduous.

In swamps or low woods, or sometimes in drier soil, Nova Scotia to western Ontario, south to Florida and Michigan. Ascends to 6000 ft. in North Carolina. March–June.

5. AMELÁNCHIER Medic. Phil. Bot. 1 : 155. 1789.

Shrubs or trees, with alternate simple petioled serrate or entire leaves, unarmed branches, and racemose or rarely solitary white flowers. Calyx-tube campanulate, more or less adnate to the ovary, 5-lobed, the lobes narrow, reflexed, persistent. Petals 5. Stamens ∞, inserted on the throat of the calyx; filaments subulate; styles 2–5, connate, pubescent at the base. Ovary wholly or partly inferior, its cavities becoming twice as many as the styles; ovule 1 in each cavity, erect. Pome small, berry-like, 4–10-celled. Testa of the seed cartilaginous. [The Savoy name of the Medlar.]

A genus of about 25 species, natives of the north temperate zone. Besides the following, some 12 others occur in western North America and 1 in Mexico. Type species: *Mespilus amelanchier* L.

The species apparently consist of many races, differing in size, in pubescence, and in size of flowers and fruit. Hybrids are also supposed to exist.

Flowers several or numerous in the racemes; pome globose.
　Glabrous or pubescent trees and shrubs; leaves usually serrate nearly all around.
　　Leaves acute or acuminate at the apex; top of the ovary glabrous or nearly so.
　　　Leaves ovate or ovate-lanceolate, usually glabrous when mature; base cordate or rounded;
　　　　petals narrowly oblong.	1. *A. canadensis*.
　　　Leaves oblong, oval, ovate or obovate, rarely subcordate at base, densely white-woolly
　　　　beneath, at least when young, petals oblong to obovate.	2. *A. intermedia*.
　　Leaves rounded, obtuse or subacute at the apex; top of the ovary woolly.
　　　Low shrub of rocky places, 1°–3° high; petals 2″–4″ long.	3. *A. spicata*.
　　　Tree or small shrub; petals 5″–8″ long; leaves coarsely toothed.	4. *A. sanguinea*.
　Glabrous western shrub; leaves dentate above the middle only.	5. *A. alnifolia*.
Flowers only 1–4 in the clusters; pome oblong or obovoid.	6. *A. Bartramiana*.

1. **Amelanchier canadénsis** (L.) Medic. June-berry. Service-berry. May-or Sand-cherry. Fig. 2329.

Mespilus canadensis L. Sp. Pl. 478. 1753.
Pyrus Botryapium L. f. Suppl. 255. 1781.
A. Botryapium DC. Prodr. 2 : 632. 1825.
A. canadensis Medic. Geschichte 79. 1793.

A tree sometimes reaching the height of 60°, with trunk diameter of 2°, but usually lower, seldom over 25° high. Leaves ovate or oval, acute or acuminate at the apex, rounded or cordate at the base, sharply and finely serrate, sometimes sparingly pubescent when young, soon entirely glabrous, or the under surface sometimes persistently pubescent, 1′–3′ long, or larger on young shoots; racemes spreading or drooping, pedicels long, slender; bracts silky, purplish, deciduous; petals linear, linear-spatulate, or linear-oblong, 6″–9″ long, 3–4 times the length of the nearly or quite glabrous calyx; pome globose, red or purple, sweet.

In dry woodlands, Nova Scotia to western Ontario, Arkansas, Florida and Louisiana. Wood very hard, brown; weight per cubic foot 49 lbs. Service-tree. May-, juice-, or wild Indian-pear. Indian-cherry. Sugarpear, -plum, or -berry. Shad-bush. Boxwood. Bill-berry. June-plum. March–May. Fruit ripe June–July.

Amelanchier laèvis Wiegand, of similar range, extending north to Newfoundland, with leaves glabrous or nearly so from the first, may be distinct.

2. **Amelanchier intermèdia** Spach. Shad-bush. Swamp Sugar-Pear. Fig. 2330.

A. intermedia Spach, Hist. Veg. 2 : 85. 1834.
Amelanchier canadensis var. *oblongifolia* T. & G. Fl. N. A. 1 : 473. 1840.

A shrub or small tree, sometimes 30° high, the foliage and inflorescence densely whitewoolly when young, often nearly or quite glabrous when old. Leaves oval, oblong, elliptic or obovate, acute or obtuse, rounded, or sometimes narrowed or subcordate at the base, finely and sharply serrate nearly all around; racemes short, rather dense; pedicels short, seldom over 1′ long; petals spatulate or linear-spatulate, 5″–7″ long, 2–3 times as long as the calyx-lobes; calyx usually densely whitewoolly; pome globose, 3″–4″ in diameter.

In swamps and moist soil, New England to Ontario, Florida and Louisiana. Wild pear. Currant-tree. Flowering dogwood. May-bush. April–May. Consists of many races.

A. nantuketénsis Bicknell differs in having shorter petals and thicker leaves, and ranges from Massachusetts to New Jersey.

3. **Amelanchier spicàta** (Lam.) C. Koch. Low June-berry. Fig. 2331.

Crataegus spicata Lam. Encycl. 1 : 84. 1783.
Amelanchier spicata C. Koch, Dendr. 1 : 182. 1869.
A. stolonifera Wiegand, Rhodora 14 : 144. 1912.
?*A. humilis* Wiegand, loc. cit. 141. 1912.

Stems 1°–3° high from a long root creeping among rocks. Leaves elliptic or oval, 9″–1¼′ long, rounded at both ends, or sometimes subacute at the apex, sometimes subcordate at the base, serrulate or dentate-serrate nearly all around or sometimes entire below the middle, dark green and quite glabrous when mature, woolly when young; racemes numerous, 4–10-flowered; pedicels slender, ¼′–1′ long in fruit; petals 2″–4″ long; calyx-lobes nearly triangular; top of the ovary woolly; pome globose, about 3″ in diameter.

In dry rocky places, Ontario to Michigan, Iowa, Pennsylvania and North Carolina. May–June.

4. Amelanchier sanguínea (Pursh) DC.
Round-leaved June-berry. Fig. 2332.

Mespilus canadensis var. *rotundifolia* Michx.
Fl. Bor. Am. 1 : 291. 1803.
Pyrus sanguinea Pursh. Fl. Am. Sept. 340. 1814.
A. sanguinea DC. Prodr. 2 : 633. 1825.
A. rotundifolia Roem. Syn. Mon. 3 : 146. 1847.

A tall shrub or small tree, sometimes 25°
high. Leaves broadly oval, ovate or nearly
orbicular, 1'–3' long, obtuse or rounded at
both ends, or rarely subacute, often cordate
at the base, serrate nearly all around with
large teeth, or entire near the base, glabrous
from the time of unfolding or more or less
woolly when very young; racemes several-
flowered; pedicels slender, 1'–1½' long in
fruit; calyx-lobes lanceolate; petals spatulate or oblanceolate, 5''–8'' long; pome globose, 3''–4'' in diameter.

In woods and thickets, New Brunswick to
Minnesota, North Carolina and Michigan. May.

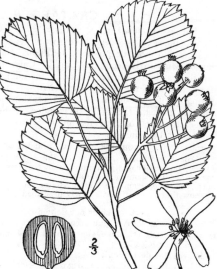

5. Amelanchier alnifòlia Nutt. North-western June or Service-berry.
Fig. 2333.

Aronia alnifolia Nutt. Gen. 1 : 306. 1818.
A. alnifolia Nutt.; Roemer, Syn. Man. 3 : 147.
1847.

A shrub, 6°–8° high, more or less tomentose-pubescent when young, at length
glabrate throughout and somewhat glaucous. Leaves thick, broadly elliptic or
almost orbicular, very obtuse and often
truncate (rarely acutish) at the apex,
rounded or subcordate at the base, coarsely
dentate above the middle, ½'–2' long; racemes short, rather dense; pedicels short;
petals oblanceolate, cuneate, 3''–9'' long,
2–4 times the length of the calyx; pome
purple with a bloom, 3''–4'' high, sweet.

Dry soil, western Ontario to British Columbia, South Dakota, Nebraska, New Mexico and
California. Pigeon-berry. April–May.

6. Amelanchier Bartramiàna (Tausch) Roem. Oblong-fruited June-berry.
Fig. 2334.

Mespilus canadensis var. *oligocarpa*
Michx. Fl. Bor. Am. 1 : 291. 1803.
Pyrus Bartramiana Tausch, Flora
21² : 715. 1838.
Amelanchier oligocarpa Roem. Syn.
Mon. 3 : 145. 1847.
A. Bartramiana Roem. loc. cit. 1847.

A shrub, 2°–9° high, glabrous,
or very nearly so throughout, except the early deciduous bracts,
which are sometimes loosely tomentose. Leaves thin, narrowly
oval or oblong, generally about
3 times as long as broad, narrowed and acute or acutish at
each end, finely and sharply serrate, 1'–3' long; racemes 1–4-flow-
ered; pedicels slender; petals
obovate or oblanceolate, 3''–4''
long, about twice as long as the
calyx; pome oval to pear-shaped,
purple, with a bloom, 3''–4'' long.

Swamps, Labrador to Ontario,
Pennsylvania and Michigan. May.

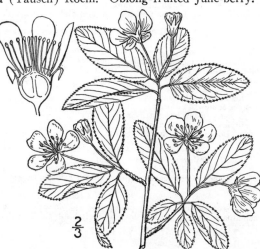

6. CRATAÈGUS L. Sp. Pl. 475. 1753.*

Shrubs or small trees, usually spiny, with alternate, simple, petioled, usually lobed leaves (those on the vegetative shoots generally of different shape than those of flowering branches and more deeply cut), deciduous stipules, and white (rarely pink) terminal corymbose flowers with early-deciduous bracts. Calyx-tube cup-shaped or campanulate, adnate to the carpels, its limb 5-lobed. Petals 5, spreading, rounded, inserted on the margin of the disk in the throat of the calyx. Stamens 5-25, inserted in 1-3 series; filaments filiform; anthers oblong, white, yellow, or red. Ovary inferior, or its summit free, 1-5-celled; styles 1-5, separate, persistent, usually surrounded at the base by tomentum; stigmas terminal; ovules 1 in each carpel, or if 2, dissimilar. Pome small, yellow, red, or rarely blue or black, containing 1-5 bony nutlets, each usually 1-seeded. Seed erect, flattish, the testa membranaceous. [Greek, strong, from the hardness and the toughness of the wood.]

About 300 species, natives of the north temperate zone, the tablelands of Mexico and the Andes; the center of distribution is in the eastern United States. Type species: *Crataegus Oxyacantha* L. The genus has been of great taxonomic interest for ten years, about 1000 species having been described, from the United States, during that period. Data are fast accumulating tending to show that many of these newly described species are hybrids.

    A. Leaves not deltoid-cordate, pubescent or glabrous.

      a. Leaves pubescent or glabrous, if pubescent on one side only, always so beneath; thorns 1'-7' long (*C. monogyna* 3" long); fruit not black.

        * Petioles ½ inch or longer.

1. **Leaves not deeply cut.**

    † LEAVES CUNEATE, BROADEST AT THE MIDDLE OR THE APEX.

      Leaves broadest towards the apex.

Leaves not impressed-veined above, shining.	I. CRUS-GALLI.
Leaves impressed-veined above, dull.	II. PUNCTATAE.

      Leaves broadest at the middle.

        Leaves impressed-veined.

Calyx-lobes usually deeply cut; nutlets deeply pitted on the ventral faces.	
	III. MACRACANTHAE.
Calyx-lobes less deeply cut; nutlets with shallow pits on the ventral faces.	
	IV. BRAINERDIANAE.

      Leaves not impressed-veined.

        Petioles usually glandless.

Calyx-lobes glandular-margined; fruit more than 4" thick; leaves not trilobate.	
	V. ROTUNDIFOLIAE.
Calyx-lobes not glandular-margined; fruit 2"-4" thick; leaves often trilobate towards the apex.	VI. VIRIDES.

        Petioles always glandular.

Petioles with small stalked glands.	VII. INTRICATAE.
Petioles with large, sessile glands.	VIII. FLAVAE.

    †† LEAVES BROADEST AT THE BASE.

      Leaves ½'-2½' long and wide, membranaceous; calyx-lobes usually entire.

Leaves yellow-green, often slightly pubescent; fruit soft at maturity.	IX. TENUIFOLIAE.
Leaves blue-green, glabrous (except *aspera*); fruit hard at maturity.	X. PRUINOSAE.
Leaves 1'-4' long and wide; calyx-lobes usually serrate.	XI. COCCINEAE.

2. **Leaves deeply cut (only those of the vegetative shoots in C. spathulata).**

Leaf-lobes sometimes 15; thorns 3"-9" long.	XII. OXYACANTHAE.
Leaf-lobes 3-7; thorns 1'-1¾'.	XIII. MICROCARPAE.
** Petioles about 1" long.	XIV. PARVIFOLIAE.

      b. Leaves pubescent above, glabrous beneath; thorns ¼'-1' long; fruit black.

                                                        XV. DOUGLASIANAE.

    B. Leaves conspicuously deltoid-cordate, glabrous.   XVI. CORDATAE.

Group I. CRUS-GALLI.

Leaves coriaceous, glandless; petioles ¼'-¾' long; corymbs many-flowered; calyx-lobes lanceolate-acuminate, usually entire; fruit red; calyx-tube flattened; flesh hard thin, greenish.

Leaves entire.

Leaves ¾'-4' long.	1. *C. Crus-galli.*
Leaves ¾'-2½' long.	2. *C. berberifolia.*

Leaves somewhat lobed.

Styles and nutlets usually 2.	3. *C. schizophylla.*
Styles and nutlets usually 3-5.	

    Lobes of the leaves irregular, obtuse.

      Fruit globose.

Vegetative leaves oblong.	4. *C. denaria.*
Vegetative leaves round.	5. *C. Reverchoni.*
Fruit ellipsoidal.	6. *C. Canbyi.*
Lobes of the leaves regular, acute; calyx-lobes serrate.	7. *C. fecunda.*

Group II. PUNCTATAE.

Leaves subcoriaceous; petioles ¼'-½' long; corymbs many-flowered; calyx-lobes lanceolate-acuminate, usually entire; flesh of fruit hard, thick; calyx-tube usually flattened.

* Written by Mr. W. W. EGGLESTON.

Fruit glabrous ; calyx-lobes entire.
Fruit ellipsoidal ; nutlets usually 3 or 4.
Leaves bright yellow-green, slightly impressed-veined above ; fruit ellipsoidal.
8. *C. cuneiformis.*
Leaves dull gray-green, strongly impressed-veined above ; fruit short-ellipsoidal.
Leaves obovate, narrow. 9. *C. punctata.*
Leaves oblong, broad. 10. *C. Jonesae.*
Fruit globose.
Nutlets 2 or 3. 11. *C. Margaretta.*
Nutlets 4 or 5. 12. *C. suborbiculata.*
Fruit villous ; calyx-lobes glandular-serrate. 13. *C. collina.*

Group III. MACRACANTHAE.

Leaves rhombic-elliptic ; petioles ¼'–¾' long ; corymbs many-flowered, pubescent ; calyx-lobes lanceolate, acuminate, glandular-laciniate, villous ; fruit red, its flesh glutinous ; calyx-lobes reflexed.
Leaves dark green, glabrous and shining above, coriaceous.
Fruit sometimes 8″ thick ; stamens usually 10 ; leaves and anthers large. 14. *C. succulenta.*
Fruit sometimes 6″ thick ; leaves and anthers small ; stamens 15–20. 15. *C. neofluvialis.*
Leaves gray-green, pubescent and dull above, subcoriaceous.
Leaves rhombic-ovate, lobed. 16. *C. Calpodendron.*
Leaves oval, more entire. 17. *C. globosa.*

Group IV. BRAINERDIANAE (ANOMALAE).

Leaves elliptic to ovate, subcoriaceous to membranous ; petioles ½'–1½' long ; corymbs many-flowered ; calyx-lobes lanceolate-acuminate, glandular-serrate ; fruit red ; calyx-lobes reflexed ; flesh thin, succulent or glutinous.
Fruit and corymbs pubescent ; calyx-lobes sharply glandular-serrate.
Leaves serrate ; styles and nutlets 2 or 3. 18. *C. pertomentosa.*
Leaves dentate ; styles and nutlets 4 or 5. 19. *C. Vailiae.*
Fruit and corymbs glabrous ; calyx-lobes remotely glandular-serrate. 20. *C. Brainerdi.*

Group V. ROTUNDIFOLIAE.

Leaves elliptic-ovate to orbicular ; subcoriaceous ; petioles ¼'–2' long ; young foliage usually yellow-green ; corymbs many-flowered ; calyx-lobes usually lanceolate-acuminate ; fruit red, the flesh soft ; calyx-lobes reflexed.
Leaves longer than wide.
Leaf-lobes acuminate. 21. *C. laurentiana.*
Leaf-lobes acute. 22. *C. lucorum.*
Leaves of about the same length and breadth.
Leaf-lobes acuminate. 23. *C. irrasa.*
Leaf-lobes acute or obtuse.
Calyx-tube prominent ; fruit subglobose. 24. *C. Macauleyae.*
Calyx-tube obscure.
Leaves acutely lobed toward the apex ; calyx-lobes glandular-laciniate.
25. *C. Bicknellii.*
Leaves not acutely lobed ; calyx-lobes glandular-margined only.
Fruit pyriform, yellow-red ; flowers and fruit maturing early. 26. *C. Oakesiana.*
Fruit globose, red ; flowers 3 or 4 days later.
Fruit round in cross-section, 3″–5″ thick. 27. *C. chrysocarpa.*
Fruit angular in cross-section, 5″–8″ thick. 28. *C. Jackii.*

Group VI. VIRIDES.

Leaves oblong-ovate to oval ; membranous, dark green, shining and glabrous above ; petioles ¼'–1¼' long ; corymbs many-flowered ; calyx-lobes entire ; fruit red, glabrous ; flesh hard, edible.
Leaves ovate ; lobes shallow ; fruit yellow-red. 29. *C. ovata.*
Leaves oblong-ovate ; lobes deep.
Fruit bright red, glaucous, 2″ or 3″ thick ; leaves serrate. 30. *C. viridis.*
Fruit dull dark red, 3″ or 4″ thick ; leaves coarsely serrate. 31. *C. nitida.*

Group VII. INTRICATAE.

Leaves elliptic to ovate, subcoriaceous, the teeth gland-tipped ; petioles ¼'–1¼' long ; young foliage usually yellow-green ; corymbs 3–7-flowered ; bracts glandular, very deciduous ; calyx-lobes lanceolate-acuminate, generally strongly toothed toward the apex ; fruit greenish-yellow to reddish-brown, bluntly angular ; calyx-tube prominent, the lobes reflexed ; flesh hard, thick.
Foliage and fruit pubescent ; corymbs villous.
Fruit globose, greenish- to reddish-brown. 32. *C. intricata.*
Fruit ellipsoid or pyriform, yellow. 33. *C. Stonei.*
Foliage, corymbs and fruit glabrous.
Leaves entire or the lobes crenate. 34. *C. padifolia.*
Leaves lobed, the lobes acute.
Leaves cordate. 35. *C. populifolia.*
Leaves cuneate.
Leaves elliptic-ovate ; fruit pyriform-ellipsoidal ; anthers small. 36. *C. straminea.*
Leaves ovate to oval ; fruit globose or subglobose ; anthers large.
Fruit lemon-yellow. 37. *C. pallens.*
Fruit red-green to red-brown. 38. *C. Boyntoni.*

Group VIII. FLAVAE.

Leaves short-obovate to spatulate, membranous; petioles ¼′–¾′ long; corymbs few-flowered; calyx-lobes glandular-serrate; fruit green to orange or red; calyx-tube prominent, the lobes reflexed; flesh usually soft at maturity. Shrubs and trees of the sandy pinelands of the southern coastal plain; only one, of the several species, reaching southern Virginia.

Easily recognized by the zigzag branches and very glandular foliage.   39. *C. flava.*

Group IX. TENUIFOLIAE.

Leaves ovate, membranous, often slightly pubescent; petioles slender, ½′–1¼′ long; young foliage usually bronze-green; corymbs many-flowered; fruit red, glabrous; calyx-lobes erect or spreading, persistent; flesh succulent.

Fruit ellipsoid, ovoid or pyriform.
   Calyx-lobes serrate.   40. *C. flabellata.*
   Calyx-lobes entire.
     Fruit small, 3″ or 4″ thick, with rather firm flesh; leaves much lobed.   41. *C. roanensis.*
     Fruit large, 5″–9″ thick, with soft flesh; leaves not conspicuously lobed. 42. *C. macrosperma.*
Fruit compressed-globose or subglobose.
   Lobes of the leaves reflexed.   43. *C. Grayana.*
   Lobes of the leaves spreading or ascending.
     Terminal leaves cuneate.   44. *C. alnorum.*
     Terminal leaves cordate.   45. *C. populnea.*

Group X. PRUINOSAE.

Leaves ovate, membranous to subcoriaceous, blue-green, glabrous (except *C. aspera*); petioles ¼′–1¼′ long; young foliage usually bronze-green; corymbs many-flowered; calyx-lobes deltoid-acuminate; fruit pruinose; calyx-tube prominent, the lobes spreading, persistent.

Leaves pubescent.   46. *C. aspera.*
Leaves glabrous.
   Leaves elliptic-ovate.   47. *C. Jesupi.*
   Leaves ovate.
     Leaves usually cordate.
       Fruit conspicuously angled, strongly pruinose.   48. *C. rugosa.*
       Fruit without conspicuous angles, slightly pruinose.   49. *C. filipes.*
     Leaves usually cuneate.
       Lobes of the leaves deep, acuminate.   50. *C. leiophylla.*
       Lobes of the leaves shallow, acute.
         Fruit without conspicuous angles.   51. *C. beata.*
         Fruit conspicuously angled.
           Leaves 1½′–3½′ long, 1¼′–2¾′ wide.   52. *C. disjuncta.*
           Leaves not more than 2½′ long, 2½′ wide.
             Leaves deltoid.   53. *C. Gattingeri.*
             Leaves ovate.   54. *C. pruinosa.*

Group XI. COCCINEAE (MOLLES).

Leaves ovate, membranous to subcoriaceous; petioles ¾′–1½′ long; corymbs many-flowered; calyx-lobes glandular-serrate; fruit usually red and pubescent; calyx-lobes swollen, erect or spreading; flesh thick, soft, edible.

Mature leaves usually glabrous above; young foliage bronze green; anthers pink.
   Fruit yellow.   55. *C. Kelloggii.*
   Fruit red.
     Leaves oblong-ovate.
       Leaves sharply lobed; eastern.
         Corymbs nearly glabrous; lobes reflexed.   56. *C. villipes.*
         Corymbs very pubescent; lobes ascending.   57. *C. anomala.*
       Leaves subentire; southwestern.
         Corymbs and fruit nearly glabrous.   58. *C. dispessa.*
         Corymbs and fruit very tomentose.   59. *C. lanuginosa.*
     Leaves broadly ovate.
       Corymbs and fruit glabrous; stamens about 20.   60. *C. coccinioides.*
       Corymbs and fruit pubescent or tomentose.
         Leaves on vegetative shoots cuneate.
           Leaves concave, 1¼′–3′ long, 1¼′–2¾′ wide.   61. *C. Pringlei.*
           Leaves plane, 1¼′–4′ long, 1¼′–3½′ wide.   62. *C. coccinea.*
         Leaves on vegetative shoots cordate.   63. *C. albicans.*
Mature leaves tomentose above; young foliage yellow-green; anthers yellow.
   Leaves on vegetative shoots cuneate at base.
     Lobes of the leaves broad, shallow, acuminate.   64. *C. Arnoldiana.*
     Lobes narrow, deep, acute.
       Fruit globose; calyx-tube rather prominent; leaves subcoriaceous. 65. *C. canadensis.*
       Fruit ellipsoidal-pyriform; calyx-tube obscure; leaves membranous. 66. *C. submollis.*
   Leaves on vegetative shoots cordate.   67. *C. mollis.*

Group XII. OXYACANTHAE.

Leaves ovate, 3–15-lobed or cleft; corymbs many-flowered; fruit red, styles and nutlets 1; introduced species.   68. *C. monogyna.*

Group XIII. MICROCARPAE.

Leaves membranous, lobed; flowers small; stamens about 20; fruit small, red. Shrubs or trees of the South, with grayish-brown scaly and warty bark.
Leaves deeply lobed or cut; styles and nutlets 2.   69. *C. Marshallii.*
Leaves of the vegetative shoots only, lobed, the other leaves spatulate; styles and nutlets 5.
     70. *C. spathulata.*

Group XIV. PARVIFOLIAE.

Leaves small, subcoriaceous; corymbs 1–3-flowered. Shrubs.   71. *C. uniflora.*

Group XV. DOUGLASIANAE.

Leaves subcoriaceous; petioles ¼'–¾' long; corymbs many-flowered; nutlets roughly pitted on the ventral faces.   72. *C. Douglasii.*

Group XVI. CORDATAE.

Leaves often conspicuously 3–5-lobed; petioles ½'–2' long; corymbs many-flowered; fruit small, scarlet; nutlets bare at the apex.   73. *C. Phaenopyrum.*

1. **Crataegus Crús-Gálli** L.   Cock-spur Thorn.   Newcastle Thorn.   Fig. 2335.

Crataegus Crus-galli L. Sp. Pl. 476. 1753.
Crataegus lucida Mill. Dict. Ed. 8, no. 6. 1768.

A small tree, sometimes 30° high, with spreading branches; spines very numerous, straight, 1'–7' long. Leaves obovate to elliptic, ¾'–4' long, ¼'–1½' wide (sometimes 2¾' wide), sharply serrate, except toward the base, acute or rounded at the apex, cuneate, dark green and shining above, coriaceous, glabrous, or occasionally slightly pubescent, glandless; corymbs glabrous, or occasionally pubescent; flowers about 8″ broad; stamens 10–20; anthers usually pink; calyx-lobes lanceolate; acuminate, entire; styles and nutlets usually 2; fruit ellipsoid-ovoid to subglobose, about 5″ thick, greenish to red; flesh hard and dry.

Sandy soil; northern New York to Ontario, eastern Kansas, south through western Connecticut to Georgia. Introduced near Montreal, about Lake Champlain and on Nantucket Island. An extremely variable species for which many names have been proposed. May–June; fruit ripe October. Red haw. Thorn-apple, -bush or -plum. Pin-thorn. Hawthorn.

2. **Crataegus berberifòlia** T. & G.   Barberry-leaved Haw.   Fig. 2336.

Crataegus berberifolia T. & G. Fl. N. Am. **1**: 469. 1840.
Crataegus Engelmannii Sarg. Bot. Gaz. **31**: 2. 1901.

A small tree, sometimes 30° high, with spreading branches and a broad crown, the spines occasional; twigs pubescent, becoming glabrous. Leaves oblong-cuneiform, spatulate or obovate, rounded or acute at the apex, cuneate, serrate towards the apex, ¾'–2½' long, ½'–1½' wide, rough-pubescent above, white-pubescent or tomentose beneath (in northern forms less pubescent than in southern); corymbs depsely villous; flowers about 8″ broad; stamens 10–20; anthers yellow or pink; styles and nutlets 2 or 3; calyx-lobes entire, slightly pubescent, fruit subglobose to short-ellipsoid, about 5″ thick; yellow, orange or red, slightly pubescent.

Western Kentucky to Missouri and the Gulf states. May; fruit ripe October.

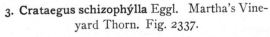

3. Crataegus schizophýlla Eggl. Martha's Vineyard Thorn. Fig. 2337.

Crataegus schizophylla Eggl. Bull. Torr. Club 38 : 243. 1911.

A small tree, sometimes 12° high, with ascending irregular branches. Spines numerous, 1′–3′ long; leaves oblong-obovate to ovate, ¾′–2½′ long, ¼′–1¾′ wide, acute or obtuse at the apex, cuneate at the base, coarsely serrate with short acute lobes towards the apex, glabrous, slightly impressed-veined; petioles ¼′–¾′ long; corymbs glabrous; flowers about 6″ broad; calyx-lobes lanceolate, acute; stamens about 10, anthers pale purple; styles and nutlets usually 2; fruit pyriform-ellipsoid, dark red, about 5″ thick; calyx persistent, its lobes reflexed; flesh hard at maturity; nutlets ridged on the back.

Common on Martha's Vineyard, Massachusetts. June; fruit ripe October.

4. Crataegus denària Beadle. Palmer's Thorn. Fig. 2338.

Crataegus denaria Beadle, Bilt. Bot. Stud. 1 : 2. 131. 1902.
Crataegus Palmeri Sarg. Trees & Shrubs 1 : 57. 1903.

A small tree, sometimes 25° high, with spreading branches and a round-topped crown. Spines ¾′–2½′ long; leaves oval, ovate, to oblong-obovate, 1′–3′ long, ½′–2′ wide, acute or obtuse at the apex, cuneate at the base, serrate, crenate-serrate or doubly so, often slightly lobed towards the apex, dark green and shining above, slightly impressed-veined; corymbs glabrous or slightly pilose; flowers about 6″ broad, stamens usually ten, anthers yellow; styles and nutlets 2–5; fruit globose or subglobose, reddish-green or light red, about 4″ thick.

Low rich soil, western Kentucky and Missouri, south to central Mississippi. Intermediate between *C. Crus-galli* and *C. viridis.* April–May; fruit ripe October.

5. Crataegus Reverchòni Sargent. Reverchon's Thorn. Fig. 2339.

Crataegus Reverchoni Sarg. Trees & Shrubs 1 : 55. 1903.
C. Jasperensis Sarg. Rep. Mo. Bot. Gard. 19 : 61. July 1904.
C. rubrifolia Sarg. Rep. Mo. Bot. Gard. 19 : 66. July 1908.
C. rubrisepala Sarg. Mo. Bot. Gard. 19 : 70. July 1908.

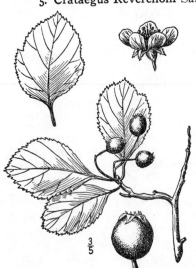

A shrub or tree, sometimes 20° high, with numerous zigzag branches and an irregular round-topped crown. Spines 1′–2′ long; leaves ovate, oval or obovate, 1¾′–1¾′ long, ¾′–1′ wide, acute or obtuse at the apex, broadly cuneate or rounded at the base, serrate or serrate-dentate, often with 1 or 2 pairs of shallow lobes toward the apex, coriaceous, dark green and shining above, glabrous; corymbs glabrous; flowers 6″ or 7″ broad; stamens 10–20; anthers yellow or pink; styles and nutlets 3–5; calyx-lobes lanceolate, entire; fruit subglobose to compressed, globose, light scarlet to orange-red, 4″ or 5″ thick; calyx-lobes reflexed.

Southern Missouri and Dallas County, Texas. April; fruit ripe October.

6. Crataegus Cánbyi Sargent. Canby's Thorn. Fig. 2340.

?*Crataegus elliptica* Ait. Hort. Kew. **2**: 168. 1789.
Mespilus elliptica Hayne, Dendr. Fl. 78. 1822. (Guimpel, Otto and Hayne Abbild. Deutsch. Holz. *pl. 144.* 1819–1830.)
Crataegus Canbyi Sarg. Bot. Gaz. **31**: 3. 1901.
C. Pennypackeri Sarg. Bot. Gaz. **35**: 100. 1903.

A small tree, 20° high, with somewhat ascending branches. Spines straight, 1′–2′ long; leaves oblong-ovate, 1′–3′ long, ¾′–2½′ wide, acute at the apex, cuneate at the base, doubly serrate, often lobed toward the apex, glabrous, dark green and shining above; petioles ¼′–¾′ long; corymbs glabrous; flowers about 8″ broad, sepals lanceolate acuminate, entire; stamens 10–20; anthers pink; styles and nutlets 3–5; fruit short-ellipsoid to globose, 5″–8″ thick, dark crimson.

Occasional, eastern Pennsylvania and Maryland. May; fruit ripe October.

7. Crataegus fecúnda Sargent. Fruitful Thorn. Fig. 2341.

Crataegus fecunda Sarg. Bot. Gaz. **33**: 111. 1902.

A small tree, sometimes 25° high, with spreading branches. Thorns numerous, 1½′–2½′ long; leaves oblong-obovate to oval, 1¾′–3½′ long, ¾′–2¾′ broad, doubly serrate, acute at the apex, cuneate at the base, dark green and shining with veins strongly marked above, paler and glabrous beneath; corymbs slightly villous; flowers about 10″ wide; calyx-lobes coarsely glandular-serrate; stamens about 10; anthers purple; styles and nutlets 2–4; fruit short-ellipsiod to subglobose, 10″–12″ long, orange-red, slightly pubescent; calyx-lobes erect, flesh thick.

Rich bottom lands, Illinois and Missouri in the vicinity of St. Louis. May; fruit ripe October.

8. Crataegus cuneifórmis (Marsh.) Eggleston. Marshall's Thorn. Fig. 2342.

Mespilus cuneiformis Marsh. Arb. Am. 88. 1785.
C. disperma Ashe, Journ. E. Mitch. Soc. **17**[1]: 14. 1900.
C. peoriensis Sarg. Bot. Gaz. **31**: 5. 1901.
C. grandis Ashe, Journ. E. Mitch. Soc. **17**[2]: 9. 1901.
C. pausiaca Ashe, Ann. Carn. Mus. **1**: 390. 1902.
C. porrecta Ashe, Ann. Carn. Mus. **1**: 391. 1902.

A small tree, sometimes 25° high, with widely spreading branches, the bark dark brown, scaly. Spines numerous, often branched, ¾′–7′; leaves oblanceolate-obovate, acute at the apex, cuneate at the base, serrate or doubly serrate, 1′–2½′ long, ½′–1½′ wide, dark vivid yellow-green, glabrous and impressed-veined above when mature; corymbs usually slightly pubescent; flowers 6″–8″ wide; stamens 10–15, anthers dark pink; styles and nutlets 2–4; fruit ellipsoid-pyriform, scarlet or dark red, about 5″ thick.

Western New York and Pennsylvania to southwest Virginia, west to central Illinois. Intermediate between *C. Crusgalli* and *C. punctata*. May; fruit ripe October.

9. Crataegus punctàta Jacq. Large-fruited or White Thorn. Dotted Haw. Fig. 2343.

C. *punctata* Jacq. Hort. Vind. 1 : 10, *pl. 28*. 1770.
C. *flava* Hook. Fl. Bor. Am. 1 : 202. 1832. Not Ait.
C. *tomentosa* var. *punctata* A. Gray, Man. Ed. 2, 124. 1856.

A flat-topped tree, usually with horizontal branches, but branches sometimes ascending, becoming up to 30° high. Spines light gray, ¾′–2′ long; leaves obovate to oblong, ¾′–3′ long, ¼′–2′ broad, impressed-veined and dull gray-green above, pubescent, acute or obtuse at the apex, sharply cuneate at the base, serrate, doubly serrate or lobed at the apex; corymbs tomentose or canescent; flowers about 10″ broad; stamens about 20, anthers white or pink; styles and nutlets usually 3 or 4; fruit yellow or red, short-ellipsoid, 6″–12″ thick.

Quebec to Pennsylvania, Minnesota, Iowa and Kentucky. June; fruit ripe October–November.

10. Crataegus Jònesae Sargent. Miss Jones' Thorn. Fig. 2344.

Crataegus Jonesae Sarg. Bot. Gaz. 31 : 14. 1901.

A shrub, or a tree, occasionally 20° high. Spines 2′ or 3′ long; leaves elliptic-ovate, acute or obtuse at the apex, cuneate, serrate with acute lobes, the tips of the lobes often reflexed, 1½′–4′ long, 1¼′–3′ wide, glabrous, except along the veins beneath; petioles 1′–2′ long, glandless, slightly pubescent; flowers about 12″ broad; calyx-lobes linear, acuminate; calyx villous, the lobes glabrous outside; stamens about 10; anthers large, pink; styles and nutlets 2 or 3; fruit short-ellipsoid to pyriform, about 8″ thick, slightly pubescent, bright carmine-red; flesh thick, yellow, calyx-lobes persistent.

Islands and coast of Maine from Portland to Pembroke, and inland at Skowhegan. June; fruit ripe September.

11. Crataegus Margarétta Ashe. Brown's Thorn. Mrs. Ashe's Thorn. Fig. 2345.

Crataegus Margaretta Ashe, Journ. E. Mitch. Soc. 16: 72. Feb. 1900.
Crataegus Brownii Britton, Bull. N. Y. Bot. Gard. 1 : 5 : 447. March 1900.

A shrub or small tree, sometimes 25° high, with ascending branches forming a round crown. Spines ¾′–1½′ long; leaves oblong-obovate or ovate, sometimes broadly so, ¾′–2½′ long, ¾′–1½′ wide, obtuse or acute at the apex, cuneate or rounded at the base, serrate or doubly serrate with 2 or 3 pairs of acute or obtuse lobes toward the apex, glabrous when mature, dark green above, membranous; corymbs slightly pubescent, becoming glabrous; flowers 7″–10″ broad, calyx-lobes lanceolate, acuminate, slightly pubescent inside; stamens about 20; styles and nutlets 2 or 3; fruit dull rusty green, yellow or red, compressed-globose to short-ellipsoid, angular, 4″–8″ thick, its flesh yellow, mealy, hard; calyx-lobes reflexed, deciduous.

Southern Ontario to central Iowa, western Virginia, Tennessee and Missouri. May; fruit ripe October.

12. Crataegus suborbiculàta Sargent.　Caughua-waga Thorn.　Fig. 2346.

Crataegus suborbiculata Sarg. Rhodora 3 : 72.　1901.
C. nitidula Sarg. Geol. Surv. Mich. 521.　1907.
C. Saundersiana Sarg. Ont. Nat. Sci. Bull. 4 : 66.　1908.
C. Dewingii Sarg. Rep. N. Y. State Bot. 1907 : 34.　1908.

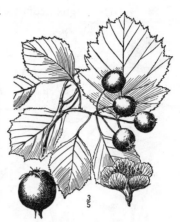

A small tree, sometimes 20° high, with spreading branches and a broad crown. Spines 1¼'–2' long; leaves ovate-orbicular, impressed-veined and dull dark green above, glabrous, serrate or twice serrate, acute at the apex, broadly cuneate at the base, ¾'–2¾' long, ¾'–2¼' wide; corymbs glabrous; flowers about 10" broad; stamens about 20, the anthers rose; styles and nutlets 4 or 5; sepals slightly glandular-margined; fruit globose or compressed-globose, 5"–8" thick; dull green to scarlet; calyx-tube somewhat prominent.

Limestone areas, valley of the St. Lawrence and Great Lakes from Montreal to southeastern Michigan.　May–June; fruit ripe October.

13. Crataegus collìna Chapman.　Chapman's Hill Thorn.　Fig. 2347.

Crataegus collina Chapm. Fl. So. U. S. Ed. 2, suppl. 2. 684. 1892.
C. Lettermani Sarg. Bot. Gaz. 31 : 220. April 1901.
C. sordida Sarg. Bot. Gaz. 33 : 114. Feb. 1902.

A tree, sometimes 25° high, with spreading branches and a flat-topped crown. Spines numerous, 1'–2½' long; leaves obovate or oblanceolate to oval, acute or obtuse at the apex, strongly cuneate, serrate or doubly serrate with obtuse lobes toward the apex, nearly entire below, ¾'–2¼' long, ½'–2' wide; subcoriaceous, yellow-green, somewhat pubescent when young; corymbs and calyx pubescent; flowers 7"–12" broad; stamens 10–20 (commonly 20), the anthers usually yellow; styles and nutlets 4 or 5; calyx-lobes glandular-ciliate or glandular-serrate; fruit globose or compressed-globose, 5"–7" thick, red or orange-red; calyx-tube somewhat prominent, the lobes reflexed.

Virginia to Georgia, Missouri and Mississippi. April–May; fruit ripe October.

14. Crataegus succulénta Schrader.　Long-spined Thorn.　Fig. 2348.

C. succulenta Schrad.; Link, Handb. 3 : 78.　1831.
Crataegus glandulosa var. *macracantha* Lindl. Bot. Reg. 22 : *pl. 1912.* 1836.
Crataegus macracantha var. *minor* Lodd.; Loud. Arb. Brit. 2 : 819.　1838.
Crataegus occidentalis Britton, Bull. N. Y. Bot. Gard. 1 : 5 : 448.　1900.
Crataegus coloradensis A. Nelson, Proc. Biol. Soc. Wash. 17 : 175.　1904.

A small tree, sometimes 25° high, with ascending branches and a broad irregular crown. Spines numerous, 1½'–4' long; leaves rhombic-ovate to obovate, 1¼'–3¼' long, 1'–2½' wide, acute at the apex, broadly cuneate at the base, serrate or doubly serrate with fine teeth, often lobed towards the apex, coriaceous, dark shining green above, pubescent along the veins beneath; corymbs slightly villous; flowers about 10" broad; calyx-lobes lanceolate, acuminate, glandular-laciniate, villous; stamens 10–20, usually 10, the anthers large, pink or occasionally yellow; styles and nutlets usually 2 or 3; fruit subglobose, 3"–8" thick, dark red, shining, villous; calyx-lobes reflexed; flesh thin, glutinous.

Nova Scotia to Minnesota, North Carolina and Nebraska, and in the Rocky Mountains to southern Colorado.　May; fruit ripe September.

15. Crataegus neofluviàlis Ashe. New River Thorn. Fig. 2349.

Crataegus neofluvialis Ashe, Journ. E. Mitch. Soc. **16**:
     71. Feb. 1900.
Crataegus michiganensis Ashe, Bull. N. Car. Agric. Coll.
     175: 111. Aug. 1900.
C. gemmosa Sarg. Bot. Gaz. **33**: 119. 1902.
C. pisifera Sarg. Rhodora **7**: 163. 1905.

A tree, sometimes 30° high, with ascending and spreading branches, and numerous spines 1'-3' long. Leaves elliptic-ovate to obovate, 1'-3' long, ¾'-2½' wide, acute or obtuse at the apex, cuneate at base, sharply and doubly serrate with obtuse or acute lobes towards the apex, coriaceous, dark green and shining above, pubescent along the veins beneath; corymbs and calyx-tube glabrous or slightly villous; flowers 6"-8" broad, calyx-lobes more villous inside, glandular-laciniate; stamens 15-20; anthers usually pink, small; styles and nutlets usually 2 or 3; fruit globose or short-ellipsoid, dark red, 3"-6" thick, glabrous or slightly hairy; calyx-lobes reflexed; flesh thin, glutinous.

Western Vermont to eastern Wisconsin, North Carolina and Iowa. May; fruit ripe September.

16. Crataegus Calpodéndron (Ehrh.) Medic. Pear-thorn. Pear or Red Haw. Fig. 2350.

Crataegus Crus-galli Mill. Dict. Ed. 8, n. 5. 1768.
     Not L.
Crataegus tomentosa Du Roi, Harbk. Baumz. Ed. 1,
     183. 1771. Not L.
Mespilus Calpodendron Ehrh. Beitr. **2**: 67. 1788.
C. Calpodendron Medic. Gesch. Bot. 83. 1793.
C. Chapmani Ashe, Bot. Gaz. **28**: 270. 1899.

A shrub or small tree, sometimes 20° high, with ascending and spreading branches forming a broad crown. Spines occasional, 1'-2' long; leaves rhombic-ovate, acute or acuminate at the apex, 1½'-4½' long, 1¼'-3' wide, finely and doubly serrate, those on the vegetative shoots obtuse and more entire than the others, pubescent on both sides, becoming scabrate above, subcoriaceous, dull green; corymbs white-tomentose; flowers about 7" broad; stamens about 20 (occasionally 10); anthers small, pink; styles and nutlets usually 2 or 3; fruit pyriform or ellipsoid (in var. *microcarpa*, globose), orange-red or red, 4" or 5" thick; calyx-lobes reflexed, laciniate; flesh glutinous; nutlets with deep pits in their ventral faces.

Central New York, northeastern New Jersey and Pennsylvania to Minnesota and Missouri, south in the mountains to northern Georgia. May–June; fruit ripe September. Long mistaken for *C. tomentosa* L. White or common (Pa.) thorn. Thorn-apple or -plum. Black thorn.

17. Crataegus globòsa Sargent. Globose-fruited Thorn. Fig. 2351.

Crataegus globosa Sarg. Rep. Mo. Bot. Gard. **19**: 118. 1908.

A slender shrub, or tree, sometimes 25° high, with numerous spines 1'-2½' long. Leaves oval, obovate or elliptic, 1½'-4' long, 1¼'-3¼' wide, coarsely serrate or doubly serrate with shallow, obtuse lobes towards the apex, acute or bluntish, broadly cuneate at the base, membranous, dark yellow-green and pubescent, becoming scabrate above, pubescent beneath; corymbs villous; flowers 7"-8" broad; calyx-lobes lanceolate, acuminate, glandular-laciniate; stamens about 20; anthers large, pink; styles and nutlets usually 2; fruit globose or short-ellipsoid, about 4" thick, light orange-red, shining; calyx-lobes closely appressed, often deciduous; nutlets with large shallow cavities on the ventral faces.

Southern Missouri to southeastern Kansas. May; fruit ripe October.

18. Crataegus pertomentòsa Ashe.
Prairie Thorn. Fig. 2352.

Crataegus pertomentosa Ashe, Journ. E. Mitch.
Soc. **16**: 70. Feb. 1900.
Crataegus campestris Britton, Bull. N. Y. Bot.
Gard. **1** : 5 : 449. March 1900.

A small tree, sometimes 20° high, with
nearly horizontal branches and a flattened
crown. Spines numerous, curved, 1'–3½'
long; leaves oblong to obovate, 1¾'–2¾' long,
¾'–2¼' wide, acute at the apex, abruptly
cuneate to rounded at the base, finely and
doubly serrate or lobed, slightly villous or
glabrate above, villous beneath, particularly
along the veins, vivid dark green, subcoriaceous; corymbs and calyx densely villous;
flowers about 10″ broad; stamens 10–15;
styles and nutlets 2 or 3; calyx-lobes deeply
serrate; fruit globular or nearly so, 4″–6″
thick, cherry-red, villous when young.

Rocky barrens, Iowa, Kansas and Missouri.
May; fruit ripe September.

19. Crataegus Váiliae Britton.
Miss Vail's Thorn. Fig. 2353.

C. Vailiae Britton, Bull. Torr. Club **24** : 53.
1897.
Crataegus missouriensis Ashe, Bull. N. Car.
Agric. Coll. **175** : 110. 1900.

A shrub, sometimes 10° high, with
ascending branches and a round symmetrical crown. Spines numerous, slender, 1'–2' long; leaves elliptic-ovate to
obovate, ¾'–2¼' long, ½'–1¾' wide, acute
at the apex, cuneate, coarsely serrate
or doubly so, subcoriaceous, rough-
pubescent and shining above, pale-
tomentose beneath; petioles 2″–4″ long;
corymbs pubescent; flowers 6″ or 7″
broad; stamens about 20; anthers pink;
styles and nutlets 3–5; calyx-lobes
laciniate; fruit subglobose to pyriform,
orange-red, about 5″ thick, slightly villous, calyx-tube rather prominent, the
lobes persistent, reflexed.

Rocky bluffs and river banks, southwestern Virginia to North Carolina and
Missouri. May; fruit ripe October.

20. Crataegus Bràinerdi Sargent. Brainerd's
Thorn. Fig. 2354.

C. Brainerdi Sarg. Rhodora **3** : 27. Feb. 1901.
C. scabrida Sarg. Rhodora **3** : 29. 1901.
C. Egglestoni Sarg. Rhodora **3** : 30. 1901.
C. asperifolia Sarg. Rhodora **3** : 31. 1901.
C. Schuettei Ashe, Journ. E. Mitch. Soc. **2** : 7. July 1901.

A shrub or tree, sometimes 20° high, with ascending branches. Spines 1'–2½' long; leaves elliptic to
ovate (in the *Egglestoni* type often oval to orbicular), acute or acuminate at the apex, abruptly
cuneate or rounded at the base; finely serrate or
doubly serrate and lobed, 1¼'–3½' long, ¾'–2½' wide,
subcoriaceous or membranous; bright green and glabrate or occasionally scabrate above, pubescent along
the veins beneath; corymbs glabrous; flowers about
10″ broad; stamens 5–20; anthers pink; styles and
nutlets 2–4; fruit short-ellipsoid to globose, cherry-
red to scarlet, about 5″ thick; nutlets usually with
shallow pits on the ventral faces.

New England to northeastern Iowa, south to Pennsylvania. May; fruit ripe September.

21. **Crataegus laurentiàna** Sargent. Fernald's Thorn. Fig. 2355.

C. *laurentiana* Sarg. Rhodora 3 : 77. April 1901.
C. *Fernaldi* Sarg. Rhodora 5 : 166. June 1903.

A large much branched shrub, sometimes 15° high, with spines 2′ or 3′ long. Leaves oblong to oblong-ovate, 1¼′–3′ long, 1′–2′ wide, acute or acuminate at the apex, cuneate at base, sharply serrate or doubly serrate with 3–5 pairs of acute lobes towards the apex, subcoriaceous, bright yellow-green above, pubescent beneath, becoming glabrous; corymbs white-tomentose; flowers 7″ or 8″ broad; stamens about ten, anthers small, pale pink; calyx-lobes glandular-margined, lanceolate; styles and nutlets 4 or 5; fruit ellipsoid, dark crimson, 5″ or 6″ thick, slightly villose; calyx-lobes reflexed, persistent.

Newfoundland, Nova Scotia, Quebec, Maine, and shores of Lake Superior. June; fruit ripe September.

22. **Crataegus lucòrum** Sargent. Grove Thorn. Fig. 2356.

C. *lucorum* Sarg. Bot. Gaz. 31 : 227. 1901.

A shrub or tree, with ascending branches, the spines 1′–1½′ long. Leaves oblong-ovate to broadly ovate, 1¼′–2½′ long, ¾′–2′ wide, acute or acuminate at the apex, broadly cuneate or rounded at base, serrate or doubly serrate or lobed towards the apex, membranous, dark dull green above, glabrous and pale beneath; corymbs slightly villous; flowers about 10″ broad; stamens about 20; anthers small, purple; styles and nutlets 4 or 5; calyx-lobes nearly glabrous on the inner surface, slightly glandular-serrate; fruit pyriform-ellipsoid, crimson, 5″ or 6″ thick, glabrous; calyx-lobes reflexed; flesh soft, succulent.

Northen Illinois and Wisconsin. May; fruit ripe September.

23. **Crataegus irràsa** Sargent. Blanchard's Thorn. Fig. 2357.

C. *irrasa* Sarg. Rhodora 5 : 116. April 1903.
Crataegus irrasa var. *divergens* Peck, Bull. N. Y. State
    Mus. 75 : 51. 1904.
C. *Blanchardi* Sarg. Rhodora 7 : 218. 1905.

A shrub, sometimes 12° high, with numerous spines 1′–3½′ long. Leaves ovate to elliptic, acute at the apex, broadly cuneate or truncate at the base, serrate, with 4–6 pairs of acute lobes, 1¼′–2½′ long, 1¼′–2½′ wide, membranous, slightly pubescent above, becoming glabrous but remaining pubescent along the veins beneath; corymbs villous; flowers about 8″ broad; stamens about 20; anthers yellow or pink; styles and nutlets 3–5; fruit subglobose to short-ellipsoid, about 5″ thick, slightly angled, red or scarlet, somewhat pubescent; calyx-lobes persistent; flesh soft, reddish.

Montmorency Falls, Quebec, south to southern Vermont and eastern New York. May; fruit ripe September.

24. Crataegus Macaùleyae Sargent.
Miss Macauley's Thorn.   Fig. 2358.

Crataegus Macauleyae Sarg. Proc. Roch. Acad.
Sci. 4 : 130. 1903.

A round-topped tree, sometimes 20°
high, with somewhat pendulous branches.
Leaves ovate to oval, 1½'–2½' long, 1¼'–2'
wide, acute, broadly cuneate or rounded at
the base, doubly serrate or lobed, dark
yellow-green and shining above, membranous, glabrous; corymbs many-flowered,
glabrous; flowers 8''–9'' broad; calyx-lobes
glabrous or pubescent on the inside, lanceolate, acuminate; stamens about 20; anthers
yellow, small; styles and nutlets 4 or 5;
fruit subglobose to short-ellipsoid, dark
crimson, 5'' or 6'' thick, the calyx-tube
prominent; flesh thin, yellow, dry.

Central and western New York. May; fruit
ripe October.

25. Crataegus Bicknélli Eggleston.   Bicknell's Thorn.   Fig. 2359.

Crataegus rotundifolia var. *Bicknellii* Eggl. Rhodora 10 :
79. 1908.
Crataegus Bicknellii Eggl. Bull. Torr. Club 38 : 244. 1911.

A round-topped shrubby tree, not more than 10°
high with numerous stout spines 1'–2½' long. Leaves
ovate or oblong-ovate, 1½'–3' long, 1¼'–2¾' wide, acute
at the apex, broadly cuneate or rounded at the base,
sharply doubly serrate with acute lobes towards the
apex, dark green and shining above, paler and glabrous
beneath; corymbs glabrous; flowers 8'' or 9'' broad;
stamens about 10; anthers light purple; styles and nutlets 4 or 5; calyx-lobes long-acuminate laciniate; fruit
globose, red, about 5'' thick; calyx-lobes reflexed, persistent, conspicuously lobed; flesh soft at maturity.

Nantucket Island, Massachusetts. June; fruit ripe September.

26. Crataegus Oakesiàna Eggleston.   Oakes'
Thorn.   Fig. 2360.

C. Oakesiana Eggl. Torreya 7 : 35. Feb. 1907.

A round-topped shrub or tree, sometimes 20° high.
Spines numerous, ¾'–1½' long. Leaves ovate to broadly
ovate, acute or acuminate at the apex, gradually or
abruptly cuneate at the base, doubly serrate towards the
apex, 1'–2¾' long, 1'–2¼' wide, slightly pubescent above,
becoming glabrate, paler and glabrous beneath; corymbs
slightly villous; flowers about 10'' broad; calyx villous,
its lobes glabrous outside; stamens about 20, anthers
yellow; styles and nutlets 3–5; fruit pyriform-ellipsoid,
slightly angular, yellowish-red, about 10'' thick, calyx-
lobes deciduous; flesh soft, mealy, light yellow.

Locally common along the Connecticut River in Essex
Co., Vermont. May; fruit ripe August.

27. Crataegus chrysocàrpa Ashe. Round-leaved Thorn. Fig. 2361.

Mespilus rotundifolia Ehrh. Beitr. **3**: 30. 1788.
Crataegus rotundifolia Borckh. in Roem. Arch. 1^3: 87. 1798. Not Lam. Ency. **1**: 84. 1783.
Crataegus chrysocarpa Ashe, Bull. N. Car. Agri. Coll. **175**: 110. 1900.
C. sheridana A. Nelson, Bot. Gaz. **34**: 370. 1902.
C. Doddsii Ramaley, Bot. Gaz. **46**: 5: 381. 1908.

A beautiful round-topped shrub, or a tree occasionally 25° high, with numerous spines, $1'-3'$ long. Leaves ovate-orbicular or obovate, $1\frac{1}{4}'-2'$ long, $\frac{3}{4}'-2\frac{1}{4}'$ wide, acute at the apex, broadly cuneate at base, doubly serrate with rather coarse teeth and with 3 or 4 pairs of acute lobes, subcoriaceous, dark yellow-green and shining above, slightly pubescent or glabrous; corymbs pubescent or glabrous; flowers $7''$ or $9''$ broad; stamens 5-10; styles and nutlets usually 3 or 4; calyx-lobes lanceolate, acuminate, usually entire but glandular-margined; fruit depressed-globose to short-ovoid, about $5''$ thick, red; flesh soft; calyx-lobes reflexed.

Nova Scotia and New Brunswick to Saskatchewan, south to North Carolina, Nebraska, and in the Rocky Mts. to New Mexico. May; fruit ripe August–September.

28. Crataegus Jáckii Sargent. Jack's Thorn. Fig. 2362.

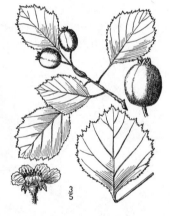

C. Jackii Sarg. Rhodora **5**: 162. 1903.
C. rotundata Sarg. Ont. Nat. Sci. Bull. **4**: 61. 1908.

A round-topped shrub, sometimes 15° high. Spines numerous, $1\frac{1}{2}'-2\frac{1}{2}'$ long; leaves ovate-orbicular to obovate, acute at the apex, cuneate or rounded at the base, $1\frac{1}{4}'-2\frac{1}{2}'$ long, $1'-2'$ wide, doubly serrate, lobes very shallow, dull dark green above, slightly pubescent becoming glabrate above, paler and glabrous beneath; corymbs slightly villous; flowers $10''-12''$ broad; calyx glabrous, its lobes sharply glandular-serrate; stamens 5-10; anthers yellow; styles and nutlets 2 or 3; fruit ovoid-ellipsoid, $5''-8''$ thick, dull dark red, prominently angled; flesh thick, reddish, edible.

Isle of Montreal to southern Ontario. May; fruit ripe September.

29. Crataegus ovàta Sargent. Ovate-leaved Thorn. Fig. 2363.

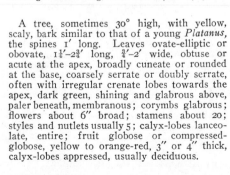

Crataegus ovata Sarg. Man. Trees 402. 1905.

A tree, sometimes 30° high, with yellow, scaly, bark similar to that of a young *Platanus,* the spines $1'$ long. Leaves ovate-elliptic or obovate, $1\frac{1}{4}'-2\frac{3}{4}'$ long, $\frac{3}{4}'-2'$ wide, obtuse or acute at the apex, broadly cuneate or rounded at the base, coarsely serrate or doubly serrate, often with irregular crenate lobes towards the apex, dark green, shining and glabrous above, paler beneath, membranous; corymbs glabrous; flowers about $6''$ broad; stamens about 20; styles and nutlets usually 5; calyx-lobes lanceolate, entire; fruit globose or compressed-globose, yellow to orange-red, $3''$ or $4''$ thick, calyx-lobes appressed, usually deciduous.

River bottoms, western Kentucky and eastern Missouri. April–May; fruit ripe October.

30. Crataegus víridis L. Southern Thorn. Fig. 2364.

Crataegus viridis L. Sp. Pl. 476. 1753.
C. arborescens Ell. Bot. S. C. & Ga. 1 : 550. 1821.

A tree, often 35° high, with ascending branches and a broad crown, the bark gray or light orange. Spines rather uncommon, ¾′–2′ long; leaves oblong-ovate, acute, acuminate or even obtuse at the apex, serrate or doubly serrate, often with acute or obtuse lobes towards the apex, ¾′–3¼′ long, ½′–2′ wide, dark green, shining and slightly impressed-veined above, sometimes pubescent along the veins beneath; corymbs glabrous; flowers 5″–8″ broad; stamens about 20; anthers usually yellow, sometimes pink; styles and nutlets 4 or 5; fruit globose or compressed-globose, bright red or orange, glaucous, 2″ or 3″ thick.

Alluvial soil along streams and lakes, southern Virginia to northern Florida, Indiana, Illinois, Kansas and Texas. Wood hard, reddish-brown, weight per cubic foot 40 lbs. Red haw. Tree-haw or -thorn. March–April; fruit ripe October.

31. Crataegus nítida (Engelm.) Sargent. Shining Thorn. Fig. 2365.

Crataegus viridis nitida Engelm.; Britton & Brown, Ill. Fl. 2 : 242. 1897.
Crataegus nitida Sarg. Bot. Gaz. 31 : 231. 1901.

A tree, sometimes 30° high, with ascending and spreading branches forming a broad irregular crown. Spines occasional, 1′–2′ long; leaves oblong-ovate to oval, 1¼′–3′ long, ¾′–2¼′ wide, acute at the apex, cuneate at the base, coarsely serrate or twice serrate with acute lobes towards the apex, dark green, shining above, paler beneath, glabrous; corymbs many-flowered; flowers 6″–10″ broad; stamens about 20; anthers light yellow; calyx-lobes lanceolate, acuminate; styles and nutlets 3–5; fruit globose to short-ellipsoid, dark dull red, 3″–5″ thick; nutlets small, ridged on the back.

Bottom-lands, southern Indiana and Illinois. May; fruit ripe October.

32. Crataegus intricàta Lange. Lange's Thorn. Biltmore Haw. Fig. 2366.

C. intricata Lange, Bot. Tidssk. 19 : 264. 1894–95.
C. biltmoreana Beadle, Bot. Gaz. 28 : 406. 1899.
Crataegus modesta Sarg. Rhodora 3 : 28. 1901.
Crataegus premora Ashe, Ann. Carn. Mus. 1 : 391. 1902.

An irregularly branched small shrub, occasionally 15° high. Spines infrequent; leaves elliptic-ovate to broadly ovate, ¾′–3½′ long, ¾′–2¾′ wide, acute, broadly cuneate to truncate, doubly serrate or lobed, rough-pubescent, sometimes becoming scabrous; corymbs and calyx villous, few-flowered; flowers about 12″ broad; stamens usually 10, sometimes 20; anthers yellow or pink; styles and nutlets usually 3 or 4; fruit short-ellipsoid to globose, 4″–7″ thick, greenish-yellow or becoming dark reddish-brown, slightly pubescent.

Open rocky woods, western New England and New York south to South Carolina and Missouri. Has been mistaken for *C. coccinea* L. May–June; fruit ripe October–November.

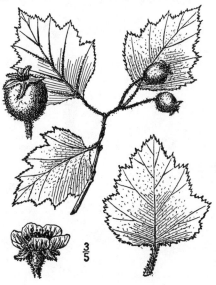

33. Crataegus Stònei Sargent.   Stone's Thorn. Peck's Thorn. Fig. 2367.

Crataegus Stonei Sarg. Rhodora **5** : 62. 1903.
Crataegus Peckii Sarg. Rhodora **5** : 63. 1903.

An intricately branched shrub, sometimes 7° high, armed with spines 1′–2′ long. Leaves oblong to oblong-ovate, 1′–3′ long, 1½′–2½′ wide, serrate or doubly serrate with acute or acuminate lobes toward the apex, acute at the apex, cuneate, yellow-green and scabrate above, slightly pubescent along the veins beneath; corymbs few-flowered, villous; flowers 7″–10″ broad; stamens about 10; anthers pink; styles and nutlets 3 or 4; fruit pyriform to short-ellipsoid, 6″ or 7″ thick, light yellow or yellow-green tinged with red, slightly villous; flesh hard at maturity.

Rocky places, central Massachusetts, Connecticut and eastern New York. May; fruit ripe October.

34. Crataegus padifòlia Sargent.   Padus-leaved Thorn. Fig. 2368.

C. padifolia Sarg. Trees & Shrubs **2** : 75. *pl. 135.* 1908.

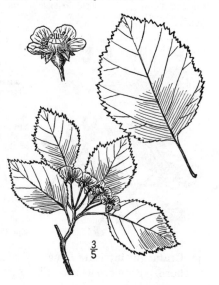

A shrubby tree, sometimes 20° high, with erect and spreading branches forming an open crown. Leaves elliptic-ovate to ovate, ¾′–2¾′ long, ½′–2′ wide, acute at the apex, cuneate or rounded at the base, coarsely serrate or doubly serrate, glabrous, membranous, light yellow-green above; corymbs glabrous; flowers 7″–9″ broad; stamens about 10, the anthers pink; calyx-lobes ovate, acute, slightly glandular; styles and nutlets 2 or 3; fruit short-ellipsoid to depressed-globose, slightly angled, orange-red, 6″ or 7″ thick; calyx-tube but slightly enlarged, the lobes small, spreading, deciduous; flesh thin, hard, dry.

Upland woods, southern Missouri. April; fruit ripe September–October.

35. Crataegus populifòlia Walter.   Poplar-leaved Haw. Fig. 2369.

Crataegus populifolia Walt. Fl. Car. 147. 1788.

A shrub or small tree, about 15° high, with ascending and spreading branches forming a round crown. Spines slender, ¼′–2′ long; leaves deltoid-ovate or oblong-ovate, ¾′–2½′ long, ½′–2′ wide, serrate or doubly serrate with acute lobes, acute at the apex, truncate or cordate at the base, membranous, yellow-green above, paler beneath, usually glabrous, sometimes slightly appressed-pubescent above; petioles slender, ¼′–¾′, glandular; corymbs few-flowered, glabrous (flowers not known); fruit globose, 4″–6″ thick, light red, without angles; styles and nutlets 4 or 5; stamens about 10; calyx-lobes ovate-lanceolate, slightly toothed, appressed, usually deciduous; flesh hard at maturity.

Virginia to South Carolina. Fruit ripe in September.

36. Crataegus stramínea Beadle. Alleghany Thorn. Fig. 2370.

C. straminea Beadle, Bot. Gaz. **30**: 345. 1900.
Crataegus intricata Sarg. Rhodora **2**: 28. 1901. Not J.
Lange.
C. apposita Sarg. Bot. Gaz. **35**: 103. 1903.
C. Bissellii Sarg. Rhodora **5**: 65. 1903.

An irregularly branched shrub, sometimes 10° high, with occasional spines 1′–2′ long. Leaves elliptic-ovate, ¾′–2¾′ long, ½′–2′ wide, subcoriaceous, bright yellow-green above, glabrous, acute at the apex, cuneate at the base, serrate or doubly serrate with 3 or 4 pairs of acute lobes towards the apex, the lower pair often more deeply cut; corymbs 3–7-flowered, glabrous; flowers 7″–10″ broad; stamens about 10; anthers yellow or sometimes pink; styles and nutlets 3 or 4; fruit pyriform to ellipsoid, angular, about 5″ thick, yellow-green; calyx-tube prominent, the lobes reflexed, strongly serrate towards the apex.

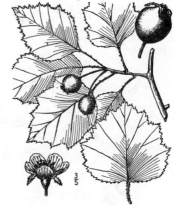

Rocky hills, western Vermont to southern Michigan, south through Connecticut to Delaware, to northern Alabama and southern Missouri. May; fruit ripe October.

37. Crataegus pállens Beadle. Beadle's Yellow-fruited Thorn. Fig. 2371.

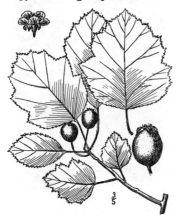

C. pallens Beadle, Bilt. Bot. Stud. **1**: 27. 1901.
C. amara Ashe, Journ. E Mitch. Soc. **18**: 22. 1902.
Crataegus fortunata Sarg. Proc. Acad. Nat. Sci. Phil. **62**[1]: 239. 1910.

A shrub or small tree up to 25° high, with ascending branches and numerous slender thorns 1′–2′ long. Leaves ovate or ovate-oblong, subcoriaceous, glabrous, ¾′–2½′ long, ½′–2½′ wide, acute at the apex, broadly cuneate to slightly cordate at the base, serrate or twice serrate with 2 or 3 pairs of acute lobes, the lower pair more deeply cut; corymbs glabrous, few-flowered, flowers 8″ or 9″ broad; calyx-lobes glabrous outside; stamens 10–20, the anthers usually pink, small; styles and nutlets 2 or 3; fruit globose to short-ellipsoid, greenish-yellow or yellow, 4″–7″ thick; sepals reflexed, usually deciduous; flesh hard at maturity.

Lower altitudes of the Alleghany Mountains, southern Pennsylvania, Virginia, West Virginia and North Carolina. May; fruit ripe October.

38. Crataegus Boÿntoni Beadle. Boynton's Thorn. Fig. 2372.

C. Boyntoni Beadle, Bot. Gaz. **28**: 409. Dec. 1899.
Crataegus polybracteata Ashe, Journ. E. Mitch. Soc. **16**[2]: 79. Feb. 1900.
C. Buckleyi Beadle, Bilt. Bot. Stud. **1**: 25. 1901.
C. foetida Ashe, Ann. Carn. Mus. **1**: 389. 1902.

A round-topped, irregularly branched shrub or tree, sometimes 25° high. Spines occasional; leaves ovate to oval, acute at the apex, broadly cuneate or truncate, serrate or doubly serrate with acute or obtuse lobes towards the apex, 1¾′–2½′ long, 1½′–2¼′ wide, yellow-green above, paler beneath, glabrous; corymbs often slightly pubescent, becoming glabrous; flowers about 10″ wide; calyx-lobes but slightly toothed, sometimes entire, stamens 10–15; styles and nutlets 3–5; fruit subglobose, 5″–8″ thick, orange-red or red-brown; flesh hard at maturity.

Shaly soils, eastern Massachusetts to central Michigan, South Carolina and central Tennessee. May–June; fruit ripe October.

39. Crataegus flàva Aiton. Summer or Yellow Haw. Fig. 2373.

Crataegus flava Ait. Hort. Kew. 2: 169. 1789.
Mespilus caroliniana Poir. in Lam. Encycl. 4: 442. 1797.
Crataegus flexispina Lauche, Deutsch. Dend. 569. 1883.
Not *Mespilus flexispina* Moench.

A slender tree, with rough bark and ascending branches, sometimes 20° high, the thorns slender, ½'–2' long. Leaves obovate or ovate, acute or obtuse at the apex, cuneate at the base, ¾'–2¼' long, ½'–2' broad, dentate-serrate or doubly so, slightly pubescent above when young, glabrous when mature; petioles 3''–12'' long, slightly winged above; corymbs few-flowered; pedicels and calyx slightly pubescent; flowers about 9'' broad; calyx-lobes entire, glandular-margined; stamens about 10; anthers pink; styles usually 3 or 4; fruit ellipsoid-pyriform, yellowish-green, sometimes checked with red, about 8'' thick; flesh hard at maturity.

Summits of sandy ridges, southeastern Virginia to Florida. Red haw. April; fruit ripe October.

40. Crataegus flabellàta (Bosc) K. Koch. Bosc's Thorn. Fig. 2374.

Mespilus flabellata Bosc; Desf. Tab. de L'Ecole 2: 271. 1815.
M. flabellata Bosc; Spach, Hist. Veg. 2: 63. 1834.
C. flabellata K. Koch, Weissd. 240. 1853.
C. crudelis Sarg. Rhodora 5: 143. 1903.
C. blandita Sarg. Rhodora 5: 147. 1903.

A large shrub or small tree, with ascending branches, sometimes 20° high. Spines numerous, 1'–4' long; leaves ovate to broadly ovate, 1¾'–2¾' long, 1'–2¾' wide, acute at the apex, broadly cuneate or truncate at the base, serrate or doubly serrate, sharply lobed, with the tips of the teeth often recurved, slightly villous above, becoming scabrate or glabrate; corymbs many-flowered, slightly villous; flowers 7''–10'' broad; stamens about 10; styles and nutlets 3–5; fruit ellipsoid, 4''–6'' thick, scarlet or crimson; flesh succulent.

Along the St. Lawrence River, Quebec. May; fruit ripe September.

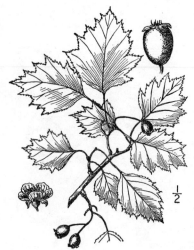

41. Crataegus roanénsis Ashe. Roan Mountain Thorn. Fig. 2375.

C. roanensis Ashe, Bull. N. Car. Agric. Coll. 175: 114. 1900.
C. fluviatilis Sarg. Rhodora 5: 117. April 1903.
C. ascendens Sarg. Rhodora 5: 141. May 1903.

A shrub or small tree, sometimes 20° high, with ascending branches and numerous curved spines ¾'–2½' long. Leaves ovate or oblong-ovate, acute at the apex, broadly cuneate to cordate at the base, serrate with 3-6 pairs of acute straight lobes, 1'–2¾' long, ¾'–2¼' wide, membranous, slightly villous, becoming glabrate, dark yellow-green above; corymbs glabrous or slightly villous; flowers about 8'' broad; stamens 5–20, usually 5–10; styles and nutlets usually 3 or 4; fruit ellipsoid, ovoid or pyriform, crimson, 3'' or 4'' thick; flesh rather firm.

Quebec to Wisconsin, North Carolina and Tennessee. May; fruit ripe September.

42. Crataegus macrospérma Ashe.   Variable Thorn.   Fig. 2376.

C. macrosperma Ashe, Journ. E. Mitch. Soc. **16**: 73. 1900.
? *Mespilus cordata* Mill. Dict. Ed. 8, n. 4. 1768: Fig. Pl. 119.
pl. 179. 1760. Not *Crataegus cordata* Ait.

A shrub or small tree, sometimes 25° high, with ascending branches and numerous curved spines ¾-2¾'
long. Leaves elliptic-ovate to broadly ovate, acute at
the apex, rounded, truncate or rarely cordate at the
base, serrate or doubly serrate, ¾-2¾' long, ¾-2¾' wide,
membranous, slightly villous, becoming glabrate, dark
yellow-green above; petioles slender, ½-1' long; corymbs
glabrous or slightly villous; flowers 7"-10" broad; stamens 5-20, usually 5-10; styles and nutlets usually 3 or
4; fruit ellipsoid or pyriform, scarlet to crimson, often
glaucous, 5"-9" thick, its flesh soft at maturity; calyx-
lobes erect or spreading.

Nova Scotia and Maine to southeastern Minnesota, North
Carolina and Tennessee. May; fruit ripe August–September. More than fifty different names have been given to
what is essentially this species. Figured in our first edition as *C. coccinea* L.

43. Crataegus Grayàna Eggl.   Asa Gray's Thorn.   Fig. 2377.

Crataegus Grayana Eggl. Rhodora **10**: 80.   May 1908.

A large shrub, sometimes 20° high, with ascending
branches, the thorns ¾-2½' long. Leaves ovate, 1'-3¼'
long, ¾-3' wide, acuminate at the apex, broadly cuneate
to truncate at the base, slightly pubescent above, becoming glabrate, serrate or doubly serrate with 4-6 pairs of
acuminate lobes, their tips recurved; corymbs slightly
villous; flowers 7"-8" broad; calyx-tube villous below,
the lobes slightly villous within, glandular-margined;
stamens about 20; styles and nutlets usually 4 or 5;
fruit subglobose to short-ellipsoid, angular, dark cherry-
red, 6"-8" thick; calyx-lobes reflexed.

Montmorency Falls west to Ottawa, Ontario, western
New England and northeastern New York. May; fruit
ripe August–September.

44. Crataegus alnòrum Sargent.   Edson's Thorn.   Fig. 2378.

Crataegus alnorum Sarg. Rhodora **5**: 153.   1903.

Crataegus Edsoni Sarg. Rhodora **7**: 205.   1905.

A broad shrub, sometimes 15° high, with ascending
branches, the spines 1'-1½' long. Leaves ovate, 1¼'-2¾'
long, 1'-2½' wide, acute at the apex, broadly cuneate or
truncate at the base, serrate or doubly serrate with
acute lobes, dull dark yellow-green above, paler beneath; corymbs glabrous, many-flowered; flowers 7"-
10" broad; stamens about 20; styles and nutlets 3-5;
fruit subglobose, slightly angular, dark cherry-red, 6"
or 7" thick; calyx-lobes erect or spreading; flesh succulent.

New England to southern Michigan, south to Pennsylvania. May; fruit ripe September.

45. Crataegus popùlnea Ashe. Gruber's Thorn.
Fig. 2379.

C. populnea Ashe, Ann. Carn. Mus. **1**: 395. 1902.
C. stolonifera Sarg. Bot. Gaz. **35**: 109. 1903.

A shrub or small tree, sometimes 20° high, with a flattened round crown. Spines 1′–2′ long; leaves membranous, slightly villous above, becoming glabrate, broadly ovate to elliptic-ovate, 1′–2¾′ long and wide, acute to acuminate at the apex, broadly cuneate to truncate at the base, those of the vegetative shoots usually cordate, serrate or twice serrate, the lobes broad, acute or none; corymbs glabrous; flowers 8″–10″ broad; stamens 5–10; anthers pink; styles and nutlets usually 3 or 4; fruit glabrous to short-ellipsoid, scarlet, 5″–7″ thick, calyx-lobes appressed or spreading; flesh yellow.

Low grounds, southern Ontario to Pennsylvania and Delaware. May; fruit ripe September.

46. Crataegus áspera Sargent. Rough-leaved Thorn. Fig. 2380.

Crataegus aspera Sarg. Trees & Shrubs **2**: 67. *pl. 131.* 1908.
C. bracteata Sarg. Rep. Mo. Bot. Gard. **19**: 91. July 1908.

A shrub, sometimes 7° high, with slender zigzag branchlets. Spines numerous, curved, 1½′–2½′ long; leaves ovate, 1¼′–2½′ long, ¾′–2′ wide, acute or acuminate at the apex, rounded or truncate at the base, finely serrate or doubly serrate, with 3 or 4 pairs of acute lobes, yellow-green, membranous, appressed-pubescent, becoming scabrate above, tomentose beneath; petioles tomentose, 1′–1½′ long; corymbs few-flowered; pedicels slightly pubescent, becoming glabrous; flowers 8″ or 9″ broad; calyx-lobes triangular; stamens about 10; styles and nutlets usually 4 or 5; fruit short-ellipsoidal to subglobose, scarlet, very pruinose, 5″ or 6″ thick; calyx-tube little enlarged, the lobes obtuse, spreading, often deciduous; flesh thin.

Thickets, southern Missouri. April–May; fruit ripe November.

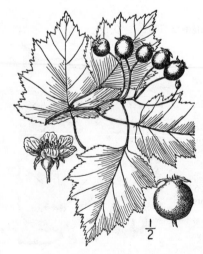

47. Crataegus Jésupi Sargent. Jesup's Thorn. Fig. 2381.

Crataegus Jesupi Sarg. Rhodora **5**: 61. 1903.

A large shrub, sometimes 20° high, with ascending branches. Leaves elliptic-ovate, 1½′–3′ long, 1′–2′ wide, acute or acuminate at the apex, broadly cuneate to truncate-cordate, serrate or doubly serrate with 4 or 5 pairs of acute lobes, yellow-green above, paler beneath, glabrous; corymbs glabrous; flowers about 10″ broad, calyx-lobes entire; stamens about 10; anthers dark red; styles and nutlets usually 3 or 4; fruit short-ellipsoid to pyriform, about 5″ thick, dark red, slightly angled, devoid of bloom when mature; calyx-lobes mostly deciduous; flesh firm at maturity.

Western Vermont to southwestern Wisconsin, south to Pennsylvania. May; fruit ripe October.

48. Crataegus rugòsa Ashe.   Fretz's Thorn.
Fig. 2382.

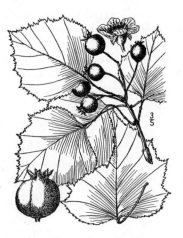

C. rugosa Ashe, Journ. E. Mitch. Soc. **17**[1] : 5.   1900.
C. deltoides Ashe, Journ. E. Mitch. Soc. **17**[2] : 19.   1901.
C. rustica Beadle, Bilt. Bot. Stud. **1**[2] : 122.   1902.

A shrub or tree, sometimes 20° high, with ascending branches. Leaves broadly ovate, 1′–2¾′ long, 1′–2¾′ wide, acute or acuminate at the apex, cordate or truncate at the base, serrate or twice serrate with 4–6 pairs of broad acuminate lobes, membranous, glabrous; corymbs glabrous; flowers about 10″ broad; stamens 10–20; anthers pink; styles and nutlets usually 4 or 5; fruit depressed-globose, bright red, 5″–8″ thick; flesh rather succulent when mature.

Southwestern New England to Pennsylvania, Indiana and the mountains of North Carolina. May; fruit ripe October.

49. Crataegus fílipes Ashe.   Miss Beckwith's Thorn.   Fig. 2383.

C. filipes Ashe, Journ. E. Mitch. Soc. **19**[1] : 18.   April 1903.
C. opulens Sarg. Proc. Roch. Acad. Sci. **4** : 104.   June 1903.
C. Beckwithae Sarg. Proc. Roch. Acad. Sci. **4** : 124.   June 1903.
C. sequax Ashe, Journ. E. Mitch. Soc. **20**[2] : 50.   1904.
C. Robbinsiana Sarg. Rhodora **7** : 197.   1905.   Not *Crataegus silvicola* Beadle, Bot. Gaz. **28** : 414.   1899.

A shrub or tree, sometimes 30° high, with ascending branches. Spines numerous, 1′–2½′ long; leaves ovate, ¾′–2¾′ long, ¾′–2½′ wide, acute or acuminate at the apex, rounded, truncate and in vegetative shoots strongly cordate at the base, serrate or twice serrate and lobed, the lower pair of acuminate lobes often deeply cut, membranous, glabrous; corymbs glabrous; flowers about 10″ broad; stamens about 10; anthers pink; styles and nutlets 3–5; fruit globose or compressed-globose, cherry-red, 6″–8″ thick.

Western New England to central Michigan and south to Pennsylvania. May; fruit ripe October.

50. Crataegus leiophýlla Sargent.   Maine's Thorn.   Fig. 2384.

C. leiophylla Sarg. Proc. Roch. Acad. Sci. **4** : 99.   1903.
C. Maineana Sarg. Proc. Roch. Acad. Sci. **4** : 106.   1903.
C. duracina Sarg. Proc. Acad. Nat. Sci. Phil. **62** : 186.   1910.

A large shrub, sometimes 15° high, with erect branches, and numerous thorns 1′–2½′ long. Leaves broadly ovate, 1¼′–2¾′ long and wide, acute or ·acuminate at the apex, broadly cuneate to truncate at the base, doubly serrate, with 3–5 pairs of acuminate spreading lobes, blue-green above, paler beneath, subcoriaceous, dull; corymbs glabrous; flowers about 10″ broad; stamens 10–20; anthers pink or yellow; styles and nutlets 4 or 5; fruit pyriform to globose, slightly angular, 6″ or 7″ thick, dark green becoming bright or dark scarlet, slightly pruinose; flesh hard at maturity.

Central and western New York to Pennsylvania. May; fruit ripe October.

51. Crataegus beàta Sargent. Dunbar's Thorn. Fig. 2385.

C. beata Sarg. Proc. Roch. Acad. Sci. **4**: 97. 1903.
C. compta Sarg. Proc. Roch. Acad. Sci. **4**: 102. 1903.
C. medioxima Sarg. Proc. Acad. Nat. Sci. Phil. **62**: 190. 1910.
C. effera Sarg. Proc. Acad. Nat. Sci. Phil. **62**: 206. 1910.

A shrub sometimes 20° high, with ascending or erect branches, the thorns 1'–1½' long. Leaves ovate, 1¾'–3' long, 1'–2¾' wide, acute or acuminate at the apex, broadly cuneate to truncate at the base, doubly serrate with acute lobes, blue-green above, paler beneath, membranous to subcoriaceous, dull, those of shoots sometimes cordate; corymbs many-flowered, glabrous; flowers 7''–10'' broad; stamens 5–20; anthers pink; styles and nutlets 3–5; fruit short-ellipsoid, slightly angular, crimson, slightly pruinose, 5''–8'' thick; flesh firm at maturity.

Southern Ontario to western Pennsylvania. May; fruit ripe October.

52. Crataegus disjúncta Sargent. Missouri Thorn. Fig. 2386.

C. disjuncta Sarg. Trees & Shrubs **1**: 109. 1903.

A tree, sometimes 20° high, with ascending and spreading branches forming a broad crown. Thorns 1'–2½' long; leaves broadly ovate, 1½'–3½' long, 1¼'–2¾' wide, acute or acuminate at the apex, broadly cuneate, rounded or truncate at the base, coarsely serrate or twice serrate with 3–5 pairs of short acuminate lobes, membranous, blue-green above, glabrous; corymbs glabrous, 3–6-flowered; flowers 7'' or 8'' broad; stamens about 10; anthers large, pink; calyx-lobes lanceolate, entire; styles and nutlets 4 or 5; fruit short-ellipsoid, angular, 6'' or 7'' thick, green, becoming scarlet, pruinose; calyx-tube conspicuous, its lobes deciduous.

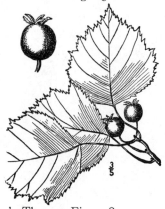

Western Kentucky to southern Missouri. May; fruit ripe October.

53. Crataegus Gattíngeri Ashe. Gattinger's Thorn. Fig. 2387.

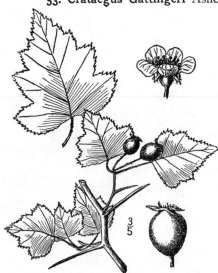

C. coccinea var. *oligandra* T. & G. Fl. N. Am. **1**: 465. 1840.
C. Gattingeri Ashe, Journ. E. Mitch. Soc. **17¹**: 12. 1900.
C. bedfordensis Sarg. Proc. Acad. Nat. Sci. Phil. **62**: 185. 1910.

A shrub, sometimes 15° high, with ascending branches and irregular crown. Spines numerous, 1'–2' long; leaves narrowly ovate to deltoid, 1'–2½' long, ¾'–2' wide, acuminate at the apex, broadly cuneate or rounded at the base, serrate or broadly serrate, lobed toward the apex, membranous, glabrous, dark green above, paler beneath; corymbs glabrous, many-flowered; flowers 7'' or 8'' broad; stamens 10–20; anthers small, pink; calyx-lobes triangular, persistent; styles and nutlets usually 3 or 4; fruit globose, angular, red, slightly pruinose, 4''–6'' thick; flesh hard at maturity.

Southern Pennsylvania to southern Indiana and south to West Virginia and central Tennessee. May; fruit ripe October.

54. Crataegus pruinòsa (Wendl.) K.Koch. Waxy-fruited Thorn. Fig. 2388.

C. populifolia Ell. Bot. S. C. & Ga. 1: 553.
1821. Not Walt.
Mespilus pruinosa Wendl. Flora 6: 700. 1823.
C. pruinosa K. Koch. Hort. Dend. 168 1853.
C. Porteri Britton, Bull. N. Y. Bot. Gar. 1:
5: 448. 1900.

A shrub or tree, sometimes 20° high,
with ascending branches, an irregular crown,
and numerous slender spines, 1'–2½' long.
Leaves elliptic-ovate to broadly ovate, 1'–
2½' long, 1'–2½' wide, acute or acuminate at
the apex, abruptly cuneate, rounded or occasionally cordate at the base, serrate or
doubly serrate with 3 or 4 pairs of broad
acute lobes towards the apex, membranous,
glabrous, blue-green; corymbs glabrous;
flowers about 10" broad; stamens 10–20;
anthers pink or sometimes yellow; styles
and nutlets usually 4 or 5; fruit depressed-
globose to short-ellipsoid, strongly angled,
pruinose, apple-green becoming scarlet or
purple, 6"–8" thick; calyx-tube prominent,
the lobes spreading, entire, persistent.

Rocky open woods, western New England to
Michigan, North Carolina and Misouri. May;
fruit ripe October.

55. Crataegus Kellóggii Sargent. Kellogg's Thorn. Fig. 2389.

C. Kelloggii Sarg. Trees & Shrubs 1: 117. 1903.

A small tree, sometimes 25° high, with erect branches,
rough bark and occasional straight spines, 1' long.
Leaves broadly ovate to suborbicular, rounded at the
apex, broadly cuneate or truncate at the base, 1¼'–2¾'
long, 1'–2¾' wide, serrate or doubly serrate with broad
lobes above the middle, dark yellow-green, slightly pubescent, becoming glabrate above, pubescent along the
veins beneath; petioles slender, villous when young;
corymbs pubescent; flowers about 7" broad; calyx
slightly villous, the lobes glabrous outside, nearly entire;
stamens about 20; anthers red; styles and nutlets usually 5; fruit subglobose to short-ovoid, bright yellow,
10"–12" thick; calyx-lobes spreading.

Occasional in bottom-lands of the River Des Peres,
Carondelet, Mo. April; fruit ripe September.

56. Crataegus víllipes Ashe. Thin-leaved Thorn. Fig. 2390.

Crataegus Holmesiana Ashe, Journ. E. Mitch. Soc. 16: 78.
Feb. 1900. Not *C. Holmesii* Lesq.
Crataegus tenuifolia Britton, Bull. N. Y. Bot. Gard. 1: 448.
March 1900. Not Guild.
Crataegus Holmesiana var. *villipes* Ashe, Journ. E. Mitch.
Soc. 17²: 11. 1901.
C. villipes Ashe, Ann. Carn. Mus. 1: 388. 1902.

A tree, sometimes 30° high, with strongly ascending
branches, the thorns 1½'–2½' long. Leaves elliptic-ovate,
acute or acuminate at the apex, cuneate at the base,
1'–3½' long, ¾'–2½' wide, serrate or doubly serrate with
4–6 pairs of acute or acuminate lobes with tips usually
reflexed, pubescent, or at length scabrous above, pubescent along the veins beneath; corymbs glabrous or
slightly pubescent; flowers about 8" broad; stamens
5–10; styles and nutlets usually 3 or 4; fruit pyriform
or ellipsoid, crimson, about 6" thick, the calyx-lobes
enlarged, erect, persistent.

Maine and Quebec to central Michigan, south in the
mountains to North Carolina. May; fruit ripe August–
September.

57. Crataegus anómala Sargent. Oblong-leaved Thorn. Fig. 2391.

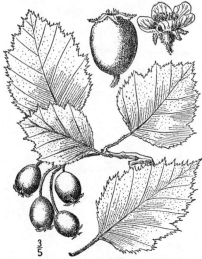

C. anomala Sarg. Rhodora **3**: 74. 1901.
C. oblongifolia Sarg. Bull. N. Y. State Mus. 105: 60. 1906.

A shrubby tree, sometimes 20° high, with numerous spines $1\frac{1}{4}'-2'$ long. Leaves oblong to ovate, $1\frac{1}{4}'-3\frac{1}{2}'$ long, $\frac{3}{4}'-3'$ wide, acute at the apex, broadly cuneate to truncate at the base, serrate or doubly serrate with acute lobes, slightly pubescent, becoming scabrous above, densely villous along the veins beneath, yellow-green; petioles pubescent, $\frac{1}{4}'-\frac{3}{4}'$ long, many-flowered; corymbs and calyx villous; flowers 7″ or 8″ broad; stamens about 10; styles and nutlets 4 or 5; fruit pyriform-ellipsoid, 7″–10″ thick, crimson, the calyx-tube prominent, the lobes slightly spreading, persistent, pubescent; flesh thick, edible.

Quebec to Massachusetts and New York. May; fruit ripe October.

58. Crataegus dispéssa Ashe. Bush's Thorn. Fig. 2392.

Crataegus pyriformis Britton, Journ. N. Y. Bot. Gard. **1**: 5: 449. March 1900. Not Jacques.
C. dispessa Ashe, Journ. E. Mitch. Soc. **17**[1]: 14. Dec. 1900.

A tree, sometimes 30° high, with spreading branches and occasional thorns $\frac{3}{4}'-1\frac{1}{2}'$ long. Leaves broadly oval to obovate-oval, obtuse at the apex, cuneate at base, $1\frac{1}{4}'-2\frac{3}{4}'$ long, $\frac{3}{4}'-2\frac{1}{2}'$ wide, sharply and sometimes doubly serrate, slightly pubescent, becoming glabrate above, pubescent especially along the veins beneath, membranous, yellow-green; corymbs many-flowered, villous; flowers about 12″ broad; calyx villous, its lobes slightly villous, stamens about 20; anthers pink; styles and nutlets 4 or 5; fruit ellipsoid-pyriform, about 6″ thick, bright cherry-red; calyx-lobes reflexed; nutlets ear-shaped; flesh thick, edible.

Rich bottom-lands, southern Missouri. May; fruit ripe September.

59. Crataegus lanuginòsa Sargent. Woolly Thorn. Fig. 2393.

C. lanuginosa Sarg. Trees & Shrubs **1**: 113. 1903.

A tree, sometimes 25° high, with both spreading and erect branches, and numerous thorns $1\frac{1}{4}'-3\frac{1}{2}'$ long, the young thorns often bearing undeveloped leaves. Leaves ovate to suborbicular, acute at the apex, broadly cuneate to truncate at the base, coarsely and doubly serrate, $1'-2\frac{3}{4}'$ long, $\frac{3}{4}'-2\frac{1}{2}'$ wide, appressed-pubescent, becoming scabrous above, densely white-tomentose beneath; corymbs many-flowered, white-tomentose; flowers about 10″ broad; calyx-lobes ovate-lanceolate, acute; stamens about 20; anthers pink; styles and nutlets usually 5; fruit subglobose to short-ellipsoid, about 8″ thick, tomentose, bright cherry-red, the calyx-tube prominent.

Common about Webb City, Missouri. May; fruit ripe September.

60. Crataegus coccinioìdes Ashe. Eggert's Thorn. Fig. 2394.

Crataegus coccinioìdes Ashe, Journ. E. Mitch. Soc. **16**: 74.
Feb. 1900.
Crataegus Eggertii Britton, Bull. N. Y. Bot. Gard. **1**: 447.
March 1900.
C. dilatata Sarg. Bot. Gaz. **31**: 9. 1901.
C. speciosa Sarg. Trees & Shrubs **1**: 65. 1903.

A shrub or tree, sometimes 20° high, with spreading
branches, the spines ¾–2½′ long. Leaves broadly
ovate, acute at the apex, rounded or truncate at the
base, doubly serrate with several pairs of broad acute
lobes, 1¾–3½′ long, 1¾–3′ wide, membranous, dark
green above, paler and slightly tomentose along the
veins beneath; corymbs 5–12-flowered, glabrous; flowers 10″–12″ broad; calyx-lobes ovate, acute, glandular-
serrate; stamens about 20; styles and nutlets usually
4 or 5; fruit subglobose, obtusely angled, 7″–10″
thick with prominent calyx-tube and spreading calyx-
lobes.

Montreal Island south to Rhode Island, west to Missouri and Kansas. May; fruit ripe September.

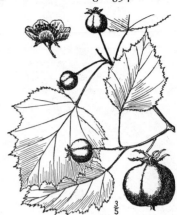

61. Crataegus Prínglei Sargent. Pringle's Thorn. Fig. 2395.

C. Prínglei Sarg. Rhodora **3**: 21. Feb. 1901.
C. exclusa Sarg. Rhodora **5**: 108. April 1903.

A tree, sometimes 25° high, with ascending branches,
and spines 1′–2′ long. Leaves ovate to oval, concave,
1¾–3′ long, 1′–2¾′ wide, obtuse at the apex, rounded or
abruptly cuneate at the base, twice serrate, very shallowly lobed, pubescent, becoming glabrate above, pubescent along the veins beneath, bright yellow-green;
corymbs many-flowered, pubescent; flowers about 10″
broad; stamens about 10; anthers pink; styles and nutlets 3–5; fruit short-ellipsoid to pyriform, pubescent,
red, about 8″ thick; calyx-lobes spreading, persistent;
flesh thick, acid, edible.

Western New England, west to northern Illinois and
south to Pennsylvania. May; fruit ripe September.

62. Crataegus coccínea L. Scarlet Thorn or Haw. Red Haw. Fig. 2396.

Crataegus coccinea L. Sp. Pl. 476. 1753.
C. pedicillata Sarg. Bot. Gaz. **31**: 226. 1901.
C. Ellwangeriana Sarg. Bot. Gaz. **33**: 118. 1902.

A tree, sometimes 25° high, with ascending and spreading branches, armed with
spines 1′–2′ long. Leaves broadly ovate,
acute or acuminate at the apex, broadly
cuneate to truncate at the base, 1¾–4′ long,
1¼–3½′ wide, serrate, doubly serrate or
lobed, slightly pubescent becoming scabrous above, nearly glabrous beneath, membranous; corymbs glabrous or villous;
flowers 8″–10″ broad; stamens 10–20; styles
and nutlets 3–5; fruit pyriform to short-
ellipsoid, red, glabrous or slightly pubescent, 7″–10″ thick; calyx-lobes rather persistent, erect or spreading.

Connecticut to Ontario, Illinois, Delaware
and Pennsylvania. May; fruit ripe September. Hawthorn. White-thorn. Red thorn-bush.
Thorn-apple, -bush or -plum. Red thorn.

63. Crataegus álbicans Ashe.   Tatnall's Thorn.   Fig. 2397.

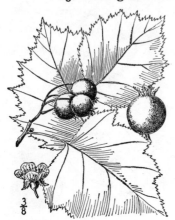

C. *albicans* Ashe, Journ. E. Mitch. Soc. 17²: 20.   July 1901.

C. *Tatnalliana* Sarg. Bot. Gaz. 35: 106.   Feb. 1903.

C. *polita* Sarg. Rhodora 5: 111.   April 1903.

A shrub or small tree, sometimes 20° high, with spreading branches.   Leaves broadly ovate to oblong-ovate, acute or acuminate at the apex, cordate, truncate or broadly cuneate at the base, 1¼′–3½′ long, 1¼′–3½′ wide, serrate, doubly serrate or lobed, membranous, glabrous or slightly pubescent when mature; corymbs many-flowered, glabrous to villous; flowers 8″–10″ broad; stamens 5–10; styles and nutlets 3–5; fruit subglobose to short-ellipsoid-pyriform, glabrous or villous, dark red, 5″–8″ thick; calyx-lobes deciduous; flesh thick, edible.

Western New England to southern Michigan, south to Delaware and in the mountains to northeastern Tennessee. May; fruit ripe September.

64. Crataegus Arnoldiàna Sargent.   Arnold's Thorn.   Fig. 2398.

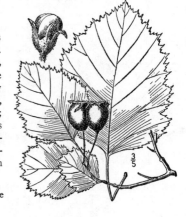

C. *Arnoldiana* Sarg. Bot. Gaz. 31: 221.   1901.

A tree, sometimes 20° high, with ascending branches forming a broad crown; spines numerous, 2′–3′ long. Leaves broadly ovate to oval, 1¼′–4′ long, 1′–3½′ wide, acute at the apex, broadly cuneate to truncate at the base, serrate or doubly serrate with broad shallow acuminate lobes, tomentose, becoming scabrous above, subcoriaceous; corymbs many-flowered, tomentose; flowers about 10″ broad; stamens about 10; anthers yellow; styles and nutlets 4 or 5; fruit globose or sub-globose, 8″–10″ thick, bright crimson, slightly pubescent; calyx-lobes but slightly swollen, spreading; flesh thick, juicy and edible.

Eastern Massachusetts and Connecticut.   May; fruit ripe August.

65. Crataegus canadénsis Sargent.   Canadian Thorn.   Fig. 2399.

Crataegus canadensis Sarg. Rhodora 3: 73.   1901.

A round-topped tree, sometimes 30° high, with spreading branches, and numerous thorns 1′–2½′ long. Leaves ovate, 1¼′–3′ long, 1′–2¾′ wide, acute at the apex, broadly cuneate to truncate at the base, serrate or doubly serrate with acute lobes toward the apex, tomentose, becoming scabrate above, subcoriaceous; corymbs many-flowered, tomentose; flowers about 10″ broad; stamens about 20; anthers yellow; styles and nutlets 4 or 5; fruit short-ellipsoid to subglobose, crimson, 5″–8″ thick, slightly tomentose, calyx-tube rather prominent, the lobes spreading; flesh thick, edible.

About Montreal, Quebec.   May; fruit ripe September.

66. Crataegus submóllis Sargent. Emerson's Thorn. Fig. 2400.

C. tomentosa Emerson, Trees & Shrubs Mass. 430. 1846.
Not L.
C. submollis Sarg. Bot. Gaz. **31**: 7. 1901.

A tree, sometimes 25° high, with spreading branches forming a broad symmetrical crown, the spines numerous, 1′–3′ long. Leaves ovate, 1½′–4¾′ long, 1¾′–3½′ wide, acute at the apex, broadly cuneate at base, serrate or doubly serrate and acutely lobed, membranous, yellow-green, tomentose, becoming scabrate; corymbs many-flowered, tomentose; flowers about 12″ broad; stamens about 10; anthers light yellow; styles and nutlets 4 or 5; fruit short-ellipsoid to pyriform, orange-red, 8″–10″ thick, slightly tomentose, calyx-lobes persistent; flesh thick, edible.

Quebec to southern Ontario, Massachusetts and New York. May; fruit ripe September.

67. Crataegus móllis (T. & G.) Scheele. Red-fruited or Downy Thorn. Fig. 2401.

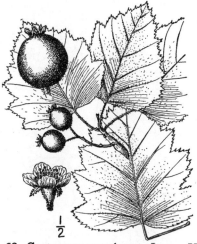

?*C. acerifolia* Lodd.; Moench, Hort. Weiss. 28. 1785.
C. coccinea var. (?) *mollis* T. & G. Fl. N. Am. **1**: 465. 1840.
C. mollis Scheele, Linnaea **21**: 569. 1848.
C. tiliaefolia K. Koch, Weissd. 247. 1853.

A tree, sometimes 40° high, with spreading branches forming a broad-topped crown. Spines 1′–2′ long; leaves broadly ovate, acute at the apex, cordate to truncate at the base, 1½′–5′ long, 1½′–4′ wide, serrate or twice serrate with narrow acute lobes, slightly rugose, membranous, densely tomentose beneath, tomentose above, becoming scabrate; corymbs tomentose; flowers about 12″ broad; stamens about 20; anthers light yellow; styles and nutlets 4 or 5; fruit short-ellipsoid to subglobose, scarlet, 7″–12″ thick, calyx-lobes deciduous; flesh thick, edible.

Southern Ontario to South Dakota, Central Tennessee and Arkansas. May; fruit ripe September. Downy haw.

68. Crataegus monógyna Jacq. Hawthorn. White or May Thorn. Fig. 2402.

C. monogyna Jacq. Fl. Aust. **3**: 50. *pl. 292. f. 1.* 1775.

A shrub or tree, with ascending branches, sometimes 40° high and a trunk diameter of 1½°. Thorns numerous; leaves ovate, sharply 3–15-lobed or cleft, acute at the apex, cuneate to truncate at the base; serrate, ½′–1¾′ long, ½′–2′ wide, dark green and glabrous above when mature, paler and slightly pubescent beneath; corymbs many-flowered, glabrous; flowers white or pink, about 7″ broad; calyx-lobes deltoid, entire, obtuse; stamens about 20; anthers pink; style and nutlet usually one; fruit globose or subglobose, red, about 3″ thick.

Along roadsides and in thickets, sparingly escaped from cultivation. Wood hard, yellowish white; weight per cubic foot 50 lbs. Native of Europe and Asia. May–June; fruit ripe September. Has been confused with *C. Oxyacantha* L. Called also English hawthorn. Hathorn. Hedge-thorn. May-bush. May. Quickset. Quick. Wick. Wicken. Haw-tree. Quickthorn.

69. Crataegus Marshállii Eggl. Parsley Haw, Parsley-leaved Thorn. Fig. 2403.

C. Marshallii Eggl. in Britton & Shafer, N. A. Trees 473. 1908.
Mespilus apiifolia Marsh. Arb. Am. 89. 1785.
C. apiifolia Michx. Fl. Bor. Am. 1: 287. 1803. Not Medic. 1793.

A shrub or small tree, 7°–20° high, the stems usually crooked; branches spreading; bark smooth; twigs tomentose; spines few, 1'–1½' long. Leaves broadly ovate to orbicular, acute, slightly cordate to cuneate at the base, pinnately 3–7-lobed, serrate, ½'–1½' long and wide, pilose above when young, pilose beneath, membranous; petioles 1'–2' long, tomentose; corymbs 3–12-flowered, usually villous; flowers 6"–8" broad; calyx-lobes lanceolate, acuminate, serrate, glabrous outside; stamens about 20; anthers dark red; styles and nutlets usually 2; fruit ellipsoid or ovoid, 2"–4" long, scarlet, slightly pubescent; calyx-lobes reflexed; nutlets smooth on back, bare at apex.

Along streams and swamps, Virginia to Florida, Missouri and Texas. Wood hard, bright reddish-brown; weight per cubic foot 46 lbs. March–April; fruit ripe October.

70. Crataegus spathulàta Michx. Small-fruited Thorn or Haw. Fig. 2404.

C. spathulata Michx. Fl. Bor. Am. 1: 288. 1803.
C. microcarpa Lindl. Bot. Reg. 22: *pl. 1846*. 1836.

A shrub or small tree, 15°–25° high, the bark light brown, smooth, flaky. Twigs glabrous; spines sparse, 1'–1½'; leaves spatulate or oblanceolate, ½'–1½' long, ¼'–¾' wide, acute or rounded and sometimes 3–5-lobed, sharply cuneate into a winged petiole, crenate-serrate, dark green and slightly villous above when young, membranous; flowers about 5" broad, several or numerous in glabrous corymbs; calyx-lobes deltoid, entire; stamens about 20; anthers pink; styles and nutlets usually 5; fruit globose or subglobose, red, 2" or 3" thick, calyx-lobes reflexed; nutlets slightly ridged on back, the apex bare.

Thickets at lower altitudes, Virginia to Florida, Missouri and Texas. Wood hard, reddish-brown. Weight per cubic foot 45 lbs. Narrow-leaved thorn. May–June.

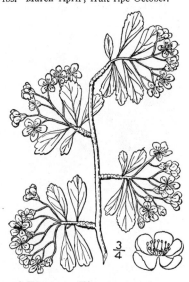

$\frac{3}{4}$

71. Crataegus uniflòra Muench. Dwarf Thorn. Fig. 2405.

C. uniflora Muench. Hausv. 5: 147. 1770.

C. parvifolia Ait. Hort. Kew. 2: 169. 1789.

C. Smithii Sarg. Trees & Shrubs 2: 67. 1903.

A small irregular shrub, 3°–8° high. Spines numerous, slender, straight, often leaf-bearing, ½'–2½' long; leaves obovate to spatulate, ½'–1½' long, ¼'–1¼' wide, obtuse or rounded at the apex, cuneate at base, crenate or crenate-serrate, subcoriaceous, shining above, very pubescent, becoming scabrate; petioles about 1' long, pubescent, winged; corymbs tomentose, 1–3-flowered, flowers 6"–8" wide; calyx-lobes foliaceous, slightly pubescent, laciniate; stamens about 20; anthers white; styles and nutlets 5–7; fruit ellipsoid, pyriform or globose, greenish-yellow or red, 5"–8" thick, pubescent; calyx-tube prominent, its lobes reflexed; flesh firm.

In sandy soil, Long Island, N. Y., to Florida, west to West Virginia, southern Missouri and central Texas. Has been confused with *C. tomentosa* L. April, May; fruit ripe October.

$\frac{3}{5}$

72. Crataegus Douglásii Lindl. Douglas' Thorn. Fig. 2406

Crataegus punctata Jacq. var. *? brevispina* Dougl. ;
Hook. Fl. Bor. Am. **1** : 201. 1832.
C. Douglasii Lindl. Bot. Reg. *pl. 1810.* 1835.
C. brevispina Dougl. ; Steud. Nom. Bot. Ed. 2 :
431. 1841.

A tree or shrub, sometimes 40° high; bark
dark brown and scaly. Spines $\frac{1}{4}'-1'$ long; twigs
reddish; leaves ovate to obovate, $\frac{3}{4}-2\frac{3}{4}'$ long,
$\frac{3}{4}-2\frac{1}{4}'$ wide, acute or obtuse at the apex, cuneate
at the base, doubly serrate and lobed except
near the base, dark green and appressed-pubescent above, glabrous beneath, subcoriaceous;
petioles slightly winged, $1\frac{1}{4}'-1'$ long; corymbs
many-flowered, glabrous or nearly so; flowers
about 8″ broad, calyx-lobes acute or acuminate,
entire, villous above, tinged with red; stamens
10–20; anthers light yellow; styles and nutlets
3–5; fruit short-ellipsoid, 4″ or 5″ thick, dark
purple, becoming black in drying; flesh soft,
sweet; nutlets ear-shaped, roughly pitted on
the inner face.

Thunder Bay Island, Lake Huron and Ke-
weenaw Peninsula, Mich.; Michipicoten Island,
Lake Superior; and far northwestward. May, June; fruit ripe August–September.

73. Crataegus Phaenópyrum (L. f.) Medic. Washington Thorn. Fig. 2407.

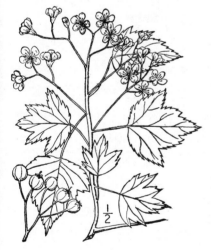

Mespilus Phaenopyrum L. f. Suppl. 254. 1781
Crataegus cordata Ait. Hort. Kew. **2** : 168. 1789.
Not *Mespilus cordata* Mill.
C. Phaenopyrum Medic. Gesch. Bot. 83. 1793.

A shrub or small tree, 15°–30° high, with trunk
diameter up to 1°. Branches strongly ascending;
thorns numerous, $\frac{3}{4}'-2'$ long; leaves ovate-triangular, simply or doubly serrate, often 3–5-lobed,
acute at the apex, rounded to cordate at the base,
$\frac{3}{4}'-3'$ long and wide, bright green above, glabrous;
petioles $\frac{1}{2}'-2'$ long, slender; corymbs many-flowered, glabrous; flowers 4″–6″ wide; calyx-lobes
deltoid, entire; stamens about 20; anthers pink;
styles and nutlets usually 5; fruit depressed-
globose, 2″ or 3″ thick, scarlet; calyx-lobes deciduous; nutlets with bare apex and smooth back.

Moist, rich ground, Virginia to Georgia, Illinois
and Arkansas. Naturalized northward to Pennsylvania and New Jersey. Virginia, -hedge or -heart-
leaved thorn. Red-haw. April–June; fruit ripe October–November.

7. COTONEÁSTER Medic. Phil. Bot. **1**: 155. 1789.

Shrubs, with alternate stipulate coriaceous often evergreen leaves, and small white cymose
or rarely solitary flowers. Calyx-tube adnate to the ovary, the limb 5-lobed, persistent.
Petals 5, scarcely clawed. Stamens numerous; filaments mostly subulate. Ovary 2–5-celled
or of 2–5 carpels, separate at the summit; styles 2–5; ovules 2 in each cavity or carpel, alike,
erect. Pome ovoid, globose or top-shaped, the carpels bony when mature. [Name neo-Latin,
Quince-star or Star-quince.]

About 20 species, natives of the Old World. Type species: *Mespilus Cotoneaster* L.

$\frac{3}{4}$

1. Cotoneaster Pyracántha (L.) Spach.
Evergreen or Fire Thorn.   Pyracanth.
Fig. 2408.

Mespilus Pyracantha L. Sp. Pl. 478.   1753.
Crataegus Pyracantha Medic. Gesch. 84.   1798.
Cotoneaster Pyracantha Spach, Hist. Veg. 2 : 73.
1834.

A shrub, 3°–8° high. Spines slender, $\frac{1}{2}'$–1′ long; leaves evergreen, glabrous on both sides, oval or slightly oblanceolate, crenulate, obtuse at the apex, usually narrowed at the base, somewhat shining above, 1′–2′ long, short-petioled; cymes terminal, compound, many-flowered; pedicels and calyx pubescent; calyx-lobes ovate; flowers about 3″ broad; styles 5; fruit scarlet, depressed-globose, about 2″ high, bitter.

In thickets, escaped from cultivation about Philadelphia and Washington. Native of southern Europe and western Asia. Christ's- or Egyptian-thorn. May.

Family 56.   AMYGDALÀCEAE Reichb. Consp. 177.   1828.
PEACH FAMILY.

Trees or shrubs, the bark exuding gum, the foliage, bark and seeds containing prussic acid, bitter. Leaves alternate, petioled, serrate, the small stipules early deciduous, the teeth and petiole often glandular. Flowers corymbose, umbelled, racemed or solitary, regular, mostly perfect. Calyx inferior, deciduous, free from the ovary, its tube obconic, campanulate or tubular, 5-lobed. Disk annular. Calyx-lobes imbricated in the bud. Petals 5, inserted on the calyx. Stamens numerous, inserted with the petals. Pistil 1 in our genera; ovary 1-celled, 2-ovuled; style simple; stigma mostly small and capitate. Fruit a drupe. Seed 1, suspended; endosperm none; cotyledons fleshy.

About 10 genera and 120 species, widely distributed, most abundant in the north temperate zone.

Drupe glabrous.
    Flowers umbellate or corymbose, appearing before or with the leaves mostly on branches of the
    previous year.   1. *Prunus.*
    Flowers racemose, appearing after the leaves on branches of the year.   2. *Padus.*
Drupe velvety.   3. *Amygdalus.*

1. PRÙNUS [Tourn.] L. Sp. Pl. 473.   1753.

Shrubs or trees, mostly with edible fruits, the white or pink flowers umbellate or corymbose, the leaves conduplicate or convolute in vernation. Petals spreading. Stamens 15–20, distinct; filaments filiform. Style terminal; stigma peltate or truncate. Exocarp of the drupe fleshy, glabrous, the endocarp bony, smooth or a little roughened, globose or oval, or oblong and compressed. [Ancient Latin name of the Plum-tree.]

About 95 species, natives of the north temperate zone, tropical America and Asia. Besides the following, some 15 others occur in the southern and western parts of North America. The genus is often divided into *Prunus* proper, the plums, and *Cerasus*, the cherries; but other than flavor, there appears to be no salient feature separating the two groups. Type species : *Prunus domestica* L.

* Flowers in lateral scaly umbels or fascicles, expanding with or before the leaves.

† Inflorescence umbellate, the clusters sessile or nearly so.

Leaves convolute in vernation ; fruit mostly large ; pit more or less flattened.   (PLUMS.)
    Umbels several-flowered.
        Leaves abruptly acuminate ; drupe red or yellow.
            Calyx-lobes entire, pubescent within ; fruit globose.   1. *P. americana.*
            Calyx-lobes glandular-serrate ; fruit subglobose or oval.
                Calyx-lobes glabrous within ; leaves oval or obovate.   2. *P. nigra.*
                Calyx-lobes pubescent on both sides ; leaves ovate-lanceolate.   3. *P. hortulana.*
        Leaves acute or obtusish ; drupe red or purple.
            Leaves glabrous when mature.
                Fruit red, with little bloom or none.   4. *P. angustifolia.*
                Fruit dark purple, with a bloom ; leaves ovate.   5. *P. alleghaniensis.*

Leaves pubescent, at least on the lower surface, when mature.
  Drupe 8″–12″ in diameter ; coast plants.
    Leaves ovate or oval, acute ; stone pointed at both ends.   6. *P. maritima.*
    Leaves orbicular, very obtuse ; stone pointed at base.   7. *P. Gravesii.*
  Drupe 3″–5″ in diameter ; prairie plant.   8. *P. gracilis.*
Umbels only 1–2-flowered.   9. *P. insititia.*
Leaves conduplicate in vernation ; fruit mostly small ; pit mostly globose. (Cherries.)
  Flowers 3″–6″ broad ; low shrubs.
    Leaves oblanceolate or spatulate ; northern.   10. *P. pumila.*
    Leaves oval, oblong, or slightly obovate.
      Petioles 4″–10″ long ; drupe 4″–5″ in diameter ; eastern.   11. *P. cuneata.*
      Petioles 2″–3″ long ; fruit 6″–8″ in diameter ; western.   12. *P. Besseyi.*
  Flowers 9″–15″ broad ; trees ; leaves ovate.
    Leaves glabrous ; pedicels short ; fruit sour.   13. *P. Cerasus.*
    Leaves pubescent beneath, at least on veins ; pedicels long ; fruit sweet. 14. *P. Avium.*
      †† Inflorescence more or less corymbose ; leaves shining. 15. *P. pennsylvanica.*
  ** **Flowers corymbose, terminating twigs of the season.** 16. *P. Mahaleb.*

1. **Prunus americàna** Marsh. Wild Yellow or Red Plum. Fig. 2409.

Prunus americana Marsh. Arb. Am. 111. 1785.

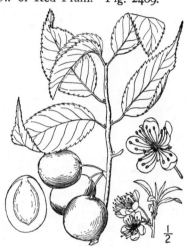

A shrub or small tree, maximum height about 35°, and trunk diameter about 12′; branches more or less thorny; bark thick. Leaves ovate or obovate, acuminate, nearly or quite glabrous when mature, usually pubescent when young, sharply and often doubly serrate, with gland-tipped teeth, rounded at the base, slender-petioled; petioles usually glandless; flowers white, 8″–12″ broad, appearing in lateral sessile umbels before the leaves; pedicels 5″–9″ long; calyx-lobes pubescent within, entire; drupe globose, red or yellow, 9″–12″ in greatest diameter, the skin tough, bloom little or none, the stone somewhat flattened, its ventral edge acute or margined, the dorsal faintly grooved.

Connecticut to Montana, Florida, Texas and Colorado. A southwestern race has very pubescent leaves. April–May. Fruit ripe Aug.–Oct. Horse-, hog's- or goose-plum. Native plum. Plum-granite.

2. **Prunus nìgra** Ait. Canada Plum. Horse Plum. Fig. 2410.

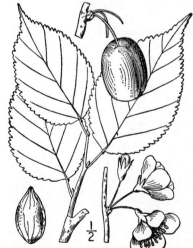

Prunus nigra Ait. Hort. Kew. 2 : 165. 1789.

Prunus mollis Torr. Fl. U. S. 1 : 470. 1824.

A tree, 20°–30° high, the trunk sometimes 10′ in diameter, the bark thin. Leaves oval, ovate or obovate, long-acuminate, pubescent when young, crenulate-serrate, narrowed, obtuse or subcordate at the base, 3′–5′ long; petioles stout, ½′–1′ long, bearing 1 or 2 red glands near the blade; flowers in lateral umbels, expanding before the leaves, 1′–1¼′ broad; pedicels 6″–10″ long, slender, glabrous; calyx-lobes glandular-serrate, glabrous within, sometimes pubescent without; petals white, turning pink; drupe oval, 1′–1⅓′ long, yellow to orange-red, thick-skinned, bloom little or none, the flesh adherent to the oval compressed stone, which is sharply ridged on the ventral edge, somewhat grooved on the dorsal.

Newfoundland to Alberta, Massachusetts, Georgia and Wisconsin. Wood hard, reddish-brown; weight per cubic foot 43 lbs. Red or wild plum. Pomegranate. May. Fruit Aug.

3. Prunus hortulàna Bailey. Wild Goose Plum. Fig. 2411.

P. hortulana Bailey, Gard. & For. **5**: 90. 1892.
Prunus hortulana Mineri Bailey, Bull. Cornell Agric. Exp. Sta. **38**: 23. 1892.

A small tree, similar to the two preceding; branches spreading, bark thin. Leaves ovate-lanceolate to ovate or oblanceolate, long-acuminate, somewhat peach-like, closely glandular-serrate, glabrous, 4′–6′ long; petioles not 1′ long, usually bearing two glands near the blade; flowers few in the lateral umbels, expanding before the leaves; pedicels 5″–10″ long; calyx-lobes glandular-serrate, pubescent without and within; drupe subglobose or short-oval, bright red, thin-skinned; stone swollen, not margined; bloom little or none.

Indiana to Iowa, Missouri, Kansas and Texas. Hog-plum. Apparently erroneously recorded from farther east, unless as an escape from cultivation. Garden wild plum. April–May.

4. Prunus angustifòlia Marsh. Chickasaw Plum. Hog Plum. Fig. 2412.

Prunus angustifolia Marsh. Arb. Am. 111. 1785.
Prunus Chicasa Michx. Fl. Bor. Am. **1**: 284. 1803.
P. Watsoni Sargent, Gard. & For. **7**: 134. *f. 25.* 1894.

A small tree, sometimes 25° high, the trunk 7′ in diameter, the branches somewhat thorny. Leaves lanceolate or oblong-lanceolate, acute at the apex, serrulate, often rounded at the base, glabrous when mature, 3′–5′ long; flowers smaller than those of the preceding species, in lateral umbels, expanding before the leaves; drupe red, globose, 6″–9″ in diameter, nearly destitute of bloom, thin-skinned, its stone ovoid, hardly flattened, both edges rounded, one of them slightly grooved.

In dry soil, southern New Jersey to Florida, west to Arkansas and Texas. Wood soft, reddish-brown; weight per cubic foot 43 lbs. April. Fruit ripe May–July.

5. Prunus alleghaniénsis Porter. Porter's Plum. Fig. 2413.

P. alleghaniensis Porter, Bot. Gaz. **2**: 85. 1877.

A low, straggling shrub or small tree, with maximum height of about 15° and trunk diameter of 5′, seldom thorny. Leaves ovate-oblong or obovate, acute or acuminate, finely and sharply serrate, rounded at the base, pubescent when young, glabrous or very nearly so when old; flowers similar to those of *P. americana,* about 7″ broad; drupe globose-ovoid, about 5″ in greatest diameter, very dark purple with a conspicuous bloom; pulp pleasantly acid; stone slightly flattened, a shallow groove on one margin, a slight expansion on the other.

Barrens of Huntingdon Co., across the Alleghany Mountains to Clearfield Co., Pa.; southern Connecticut. Alleghany sloe. April. Fruit ripe in August.

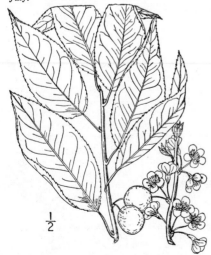

6. Prunus marítima Wang. Beach or Sand Plum. Fig. 2414.

Prunus maritima Wang. Am. 103. 1781.

Prunus cerasifera Ehrh. Beitr. 4: 17. 1789.

Prunus sphaerocarpa Michx. Fl. Bor. Am. 1: 284. 1803.

A low much-branched shrub, 1°–7° high, not thorny. Leaves oval, ovate or obovate, finely and sharply serrate, acutish or acute at the apex, rounded at the base, pubescent beneath even when old; flowers white, numerous, showy, in sessile lateral umbels, expanding before the leaves, 5″–8″ broad; petals obovate; drupe globose, purple, ½′–1′ in diameter, sweet when ripe, covered with a bloom; stone little flattened, acute on one margin, slightly grooved on the other, usually pointed at both ends.

On seabeaches and in sandy soil near the coast, Virginia to New Brunswick. April–May. Fruit ripe in Sept. or Oct.

7. Prunus Gràvesii Small. Graves' Beach Plum. Fig. 2415.

Prunus Gravesii Small, Bull. Torr. Club 24: 45. 1897.

A low shrub, reaching a maximum height of about 4°, not thorny, the twigs of the season mostly puberulent. Leaves orbicular, oval-orbicular, or slightly obovate, 9″–18″ long, rounded, retuse or apiculate at the apex, obtuse or truncate at the base, pubescent, at least on the nerves beneath; flowers white, about 6″ broad, solitary or 2–3 together in lateral umbels, expanding with the leaves; petals suborbicular; drupe globose, 5″–8″ in diameter, nearly black, with a light blue bloom; stone nearly as thick as wide, pointed only at the base.

On a gravelly ridge, Groton, Connecticut. May–June. Fruit ripe in Sept.

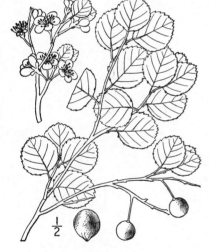

8. Prunus grácilis Engelm. & Gray. Low Plum. Fig. 2416.

Prunus gracilis Engelm. & Gray, Bost. Journ. Nat. Hist. 5: 243. 1847.

A branching shrub, 1°–4° high, the foliage and young twigs densely soft-pubescent. Leaves short-petioled, ovate-lanceolate or oval, acute or acutish at both ends, sharply serrate, glabrate on the upper surface at maturity; flowers white, 3″–4″ broad, in sessile, lateral umbels, appearing before the leaves; pedicels slender, pubescent; drupe oval-globose, 4″–5″ in diameter; stone little flattened, nearly orbicular.

In sandy or dry soil, Tennessee to Kansas and Texas.

9. Prunus insitítia L. Bullace. Fig. 2417.

Prunus insititia L. Sp. Pl. 475. 1753.

A much-branched shrub with thorny branches, 5°–15° high. Leaves mostly obovate, obtuse at the apex, narrowed or rounded at the base, serrate, nearly glabrous above when mature, pubescent beneath; flowers white, about 4″–6″ broad, appearing before the leaves, the lateral clusters usually only 1–2-flowered; pedicels ½′–1′ long; drupe globose, nearly black with a bloom 6″–10″ in diameter; stone little flattened, acute on one edge, ridged and grooved on the other.

Along roadsides and waste grounds, New York to Massachusetts. Naturalized or adventive from Europe. April–May. Has been mistaken for *P. spinosa* L.

Prunus doméstica L., the Garden Plum, a small tree, with larger fruit, flowers and leaves, has locally escaped from cultivation.

10. Prunus pùmila L. Sand or Dwarf Cherry. Fig. 2418.

Prunus pumila L. Mant. Pl. 1: 75. 1767.

Prostrate and spreading or ascending, much branched from the base, sometimes bushy, 6′–6° high. Leaves mostly oblanceolate or spatulate, acute or acutish at the apex, narrowed at the base, serrate, especially toward the apex, usually pale beneath and deep green above, glabrous or very nearly so on both sides when mature; flowers white, 4″–5″ broad, appearing with the leaves in sessile lateral umbels; clusters few-flowered; drupe 4″–6″ in diameter, dark red or nearly black when mature without bloom; flesh thin, acid.

On sandy or gravelly shores, New Brunswick to Manitoba, Maine, New Jersey, Indiana and Wisconsin. April–May. Fruit ripe in August. Beach-plum.

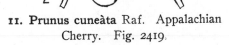

11. Prunus cuneàta Raf. Appalachian Cherry. Fig. 2419.

Prunus cuneata Raf. Ann. Nat. 11. 1820.

An erect shrub, 1°–4° high, the branches often strict, light colored, glabrous or puberulent. Leaves oval, oblong or obovate, obtuse or sometimes acute at the apex, narrowed or wedge-shaped at the base, more or less serrate with rather appressed teeth, rather thin, 1′–3′ long, sometimes nearly 1′ wide; petioles 4″–10″ long; flowers in umbels, appearing with the leaves, about 5″ broad; drupe globose, nearly black and 4″–5″ in diameter when mature; pedicels 1′ long or less.

In wet soil, or among rocks, Maine and New Hampshire to Minnesota, North Carolina and Wisconsin.

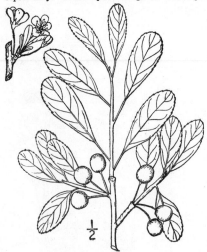

12. **Prunus Bésseyi** Bailey. Western Sand Cherry. Bessey's Cherry. Fig. 2420.

Prunus Besseyi Bailey, Bull. Cornell Agric. Exp. Sta. 70: 261. 1894.
Cerasus Besseyi Smyth, Trans. Kans. Acad. Sci. **15**: 62. 1898.

A shrub, 1°–4° high, the branches diffuse, spreading or prostrate, not strict. Leaves elliptic, oblong or oval, the teeth appressed, the apex and base mostly acute; petioles 2″–3″ long; stipules of young shoots often longer than the petiole; flowers in sessile umbels, expanding with the leaves, 4″–5″ broad; fruit 6″–8″ in diameter, on stout pedicels usually not more than 6″ long, bitterish and astringent, black, mottled or yellowish.

Plains, Manitoba and Minnesota to Kansas and Utah. April–May.

13. **Prunus Cérasus** L. Sour Cherry. Egriot. Fig. 2421.

Prunus Cerasus L. Sp. Pl. 474. 1753.

A tree, reaching in cultivation the height of 50°, with trunk diameter of 3½°, but usually smaller. Leaves ovate or ovate-lanceolate, variously dentate, abruptly acute or acuminate at the apex, rounded at the base, glabrous on both sides, very resinous when young; flowers white, 8″–12″ broad, in sessile, lateral, very scaly umbels, expanding with the leaves or before them, the scales large, spreading; pedicels little over 1½′ long in flower; drupe globose, 4″–6″ in diameter (larger in cultivation), black or red, sour, without bloom; stone globose.

In woods and thickets, New Hampshire to Georgia and Colorado, escaped from cultivation. Native of Europe. Wood strong, reddish-brown; weight per cubic foot 54 lbs. April–May. Fruit June–July. Its leaves unfold several days later than those of *P. Avium* when growing with it. This, and the following species, in the wild state, are the originals of most of the cultivated cherries.

14. **Prunus Àvium** L. Wild or Crab Cherry. Mazard. Gean. Sweet Cherry. Fig. 2422.

Prunus Avium L. Fl. Suec. Ed. 2, 165. 1755.

A large tree, often 70° high, the trunk reaching 4° in diameter. Leaves ovate, oval, or slightly obovate, abruptly short-acuminate at the apex, obtuse or sometimes narrowed at the base, irregularly serrate or doubly serrate, pubescent on the veins beneath, or over the entire lower surface when young; flowers white, about 1′ broad, in scaly lateral umbels, expanding with the leaves, the scales small; pedicels slender, 1′–2½′ long in flower; drupe globose, black or dark red, sweet.

In thickets and woodlands, escaped from cultivation, Ontario to Connecticut, Pennsylvania and Virginia. Native of Europe. April–May. Merry. Blackmerry. Hawkberry. Gaskins.

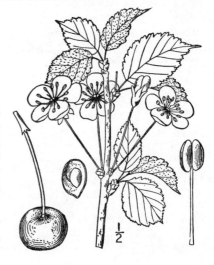

15. Prunus pennsylvánica L. f. Wild Red or Pigeon Cherry. Fig. 2423.

Prunus pennsylvanica L. f. Suppl. 252. 1781.
Cerasus pennsylvanica Lois. Nouv. Duham. 5: 9. 1812.

A small tree, with maximum height of about 35°, and trunk diameter of 1½°, sometimes shrubby. Leaves oval or lanceolate, acute or acuminate at the apex, mainly rounded at the base, glabrous and shining on both sides, serrulate, rather slender-petioled; flowers white, in lateral, corymbose, peduncled or sessile leafless clusters, unfolding with the leaves; pedicels slender, glabrous, 6″–12″ long; drupe globose, red, 2″–3″ in diameter, without bloom, its flesh thin and sour, its stone globular.

In rocky woods, and clearings, Newfoundland to Georgia, British Columbia and Colorado. Woods soft, light brown; weight per cubic foot 31 lbs. Dogwood. Bird-, red-, fire- or pin-cherry. April–June. Fruit ripe in August.

16. Prunus Mahàleb L. Mahaleb. Perfumed Cherry. Fig. 2424.

Prunus Mahaleb L. Sp. Pl. 474. 1753.

Cerasus Mahaleb Mill. Gard. Dict. Ed. 8, no. 4. 1768.

A small tree or shrub, with maximum height of about 25° and trunk diameter of 1° generally flowering when but a few years old. Bark pale, smooth; leaves petioled, ovate, abruptly acute at the apex, rounded or slightly cordate at the base, glabrous on both sides, denticulate, fragrant; flowers white, about 5″ broad, in corymbs borne on short leafy branches of the season, unfolding with the leaves; drupe reddish-black, globose or globose-ovoid, about 4″ long, the flesh thin, the stone slightly flattened.

Roadsides and waste places, Ontario to New York, Pennsylvania and Delaware. Adventive from Europe. Wood hard, brown. Used in Europe for cabinet making. April–May. Fruit ripe July.

2. PÀDUS Mill. Gard. Dict. Abr. Ed. 4. 1754.

Trees or shrubs, with alternate deciduous leaves and small white flowers in narrow racemes terminating leafy branches of the season. Petals spreading. Stamens 15–20. Calyx-tube bell-shaped, with 5 short sepals. Style terminal, simple, the stigma flattish. Drupe small, globose, red to purple or black, the exocarp fleshy, the endocarp hard, smooth. [Greek name for the European species.]

About 15 species, natives of the northern hemisphere. Besides the following, 4 occur in the Southern States and 1 in northwestern America. Type species: *Prunus Padus* L.

Sepals deciduous; teeth of the leaves slender; shrubs or small trees.
    Fruit very astringent; leaves thin.   1. *P. nana.*
    Fruit sweet, little astringent; leaves thick.   2. *P. melanocarpa.*
Sepals persistent; leaves coarsely toothed; large tree.   3. *P. virginiana.*

1. Padus nana (Du Roi) Roemer. Choke Cherry. Fig. 2425.

Prunus nana Du Roi, Harbk. Baumz. 1²: 194. f. 4. 1772.
Padus nana Roem. Arch. 1²: 38. 1797.

A shrub, 2°–10° high, rarely a small tree, with gray bark. Leaves thin, obovate to ovate or oval, abruptly acute or acuminate at the apex, rounded at the base, glabrous or somewhat pubescent on the lower surface, sharply or doubly serrulate with slender teeth; petioles with several glands; flowers white, 4″–5″ broad, in erect or spreading mainly loosely-flowered racemes; petals suborbicular; pedicels 2″–3″ long, drupe red to nearly black, rarely yellow, globose, 4″–5″ in diameter, very astringent; stone globular.

Along river-banks and in rocky situations, Newfoundland to Manitoba, Georgia and Texas. April–May. Fruit ripe in July or August.

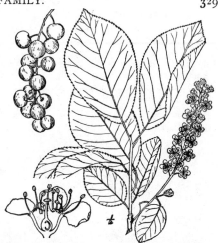

2. Padus melanocàrpa (A. Nelson) Shafer. Rocky Mountain Wild Cherry. Fig. 2426.

Cerasus demissa melanocarpa A. Nelson, Bot. Gaz. 34: 25. 1902.
P. melanocarpa Shafer; Britton & Shafer, N. A. Trees 504. 1908.

A shrub or small tree, with greatest height of about 30° and trunk diameter of 1½°, but usually much smaller. Leaves glabrous, similar to those of the preceding species, but thicker, acute or often obtusish at the apex, and with shorter teeth; flowers white, 4″–5″ broad; racemes generally dense, short or elongated, densely-flowered, terminating leafy branches; drupe dark purple or black (rarely yellow), sweet or but slightly astringent, globose, 3″–4″ in diameter.

Prairies and dry soil, North Dakota to Nebraska and New Mexico, west to British Columbia and California. Wood hard, not strong, light brown; weight per cubic foot 43 lbs. Western choke-cherry. May–July. Fruit ripe in August. Padus demissa (Nutt.) Roemer, of northwestern America, with leaves pubescent beneath, and red or purplish fruit, may not be distinct from P. nana.

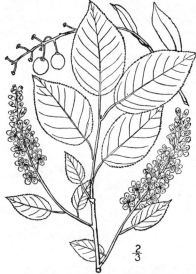

3. Padus virginiàna (L.) Mill. Wild Black Cherry. Cabinet or Rum Cherry. Fig. 2427.

Prunus virginiana L. Sp. Pl. 473. 1753.
Padus virginiana Mill. Gard. Dict. Ed. 8, no. 3. 1768.
Prunus serotina Ehrh. Beitr. 3: 20. 1788.
Prunus serotina Smallii Britton, in Britt. & Brown, Ill. Fl. 2: 253. 1897.

A large tree, with maximum height of about 90° and trunk diameter of 4°, the bark rough and black. Leaves thick, oval, oval-lanceolate or ovate, acuminate or acute at the apex, narrowed or rounded at the base, glabrous, or pubescent along the veins beneath, serrate with appressed callous teeth; flowers similar to those of the two preceding species, the racemes elongated, spreading or drooping, terminating leafy branches, petals obovate; drupe globose, 4″–5″ in diameter; dark purple or black, sweet but slightly astringent.

In woods or open places, Nova Scotia to Florida, South Dakota, Kansas and Texas. Wood hard, strong, reddish-brown; weight per cubic foot 36 lbs.; used in cabinet making. Wild or whiskey cherry. May. Fruit ripe Aug.–Sept.

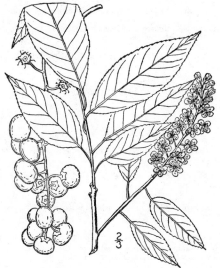

3. AMÝGDALUS L. Sp. Pl. 472. 1753.

Trees or shrubs, with mostly lanceolate serrulate short-petioled leaves, and pink or white flowers solitary or clustered at the nodes of the twigs of the preceding season. Petals spreading. Stamens 20–30, distinct, the filaments filiform. Style and stigma as in *Prunus*. Exocarp of the fruit mostly fleshy, velvety in the following species; endocarp (stone) bony, deeply pitted or nearly smooth, oval or oblong, pointed, more or less compressed. [Name said to be Syrian for the almond.]

About 5 species, natives of Asia, the following the type of the genus.

1. Amygdalus pérsica L. Peach. Fig. 2428.

Amygdalus persica L. Sp. Pl. 472. 1753.

A small tree, the purplish-brown twigs glabrous. Leaves mostly lanceolate or oblong-lanceolate, 3′–5′ long, 8″–18″ wide, glabrous on both sides, long-acuminate at the apex, usually narrowed at the base, finely serrulate nearly all around, thickish; petioles 1″–3″ long; flowers pink, ½′–2′ broad, scaly-bracted; drupe subglobose, grooved, softly velvety, 1½′–3′ in diameter.

Escaped from cultivation, New York to North Carolina and Florida. April–May.

Family 57. MIMOSÀCEAE Reichenb. Fl. Exc. 437. 1832.

MIMOSA FAMILY.

Herbs, shrubs or trees, with alternate mostly compound, commonly 2–3-pinnate leaves, the stipules various, and small regular mostly perfect flowers in heads, spikes or racemes. Calyx 3–6-toothed, or 3–6-lobed, the teeth or lobes mostly valvate in the bud. Corolla of as many distinct or more or less united petals, also valvate. Stamens as many as the petals, or twice as many, or ∞, distinct, or monadelphous. Ovary 1-celled; ovules several or numerous; style simple. Fruit a legume. Seeds without endosperm; cotyledons fleshy.

About 40 genera and 1500 species, mostly of tropical distribution, a few in the temperate zones. This, and the three following families, are often united under the name LEGUMINOSAE.

Stamens numerous, at least more than 10.
    Filaments separate.   1. *Acacia.*
    Filaments united below.   2. *Albizzia.*
Stamens only as many as the petals, or twice as many.
    Petals separate ; pod smooth.
        Pod separating into valves.   3. *Acuan.*
        Pod leathery, indehiscent.   4. *Prosopis.*
    Petals united to about the middle ; pod spiny.   5. *Morongia.*

1. ACÀCIA [Tourn.] Mill. Gard. Dict. Abr. Ed. 4. 1754.

Shrubs or trees, some species nearly herbaceous, with bipinnate leaves, the ultimate leaflets usually small and numerous, or the leaves in many exotic species modified into flat simple phyllodes. Flowers small, in heads or spikes. Calyx campanulate, usually 4–5-toothed, or of 4 or 5 distinct sepals. Petals mostly 4 or 5, separate, united, or wanting. Stamens ∞, exserted; filaments filiform, separate; pollen-grains cohering in 2's–6's. Ovary sessile or stipitate. Pod linear, oblong or oval, flat or swollen, often constricted between the seeds. [Greek, point, or thorn, many species being thorny.]

Perhaps 300 species, chiefly in subtropical regions, most abundant in Africa and Australia, a few in the temperate zones. Besides the following, several others occur in the southern United States. Type species: *Mimosa scorpioides* L.

1. Acacia angustíssima (Mill.) Kuntze.　Prairie Acacia.　Fig. 2429.

Mimosa angustissima Mill. Gard. Dict. Ed. 8, no. 19. 1768.
Mimosa filiculoides Cav. Ic. 1: 55. pl. 78. 1791.
Acacia filicina Willd. Sp. Pl. 4: 1072. 1806.
Acacia filiculoides Trelease; Branner & Coville, Rep. Geol. Surv. Ark. 1888: Part 4, 178. 1891.
A. angustissima Kuntze, Rev. Gen. Pl. 3²: 47. 1898.

A low thornless shrub, varying from glabrous to hirsute-pubescent. Pinnae of the leaves 2–15 pairs, oblong in outline, 1′–2′ long; leaflets 10–50 pairs, oblong or linear-oblong, about 2″ long, less than 1″ wide, obtuse or acute, slightly inequilateral, 1-veined; heads globose, many-flowered, axillary, slender-peduncled, 6″–10″ in diameter; sepals distinct or nearly so; filaments yellow, 3–4 times as long as the sepals; pod linear, acute, often narrowed at the base, stipitate, mostly straight, 1′–2′ long, about 3″ wide, flat, its valves thin, reticulated, glabrous or pubescent, impressed between the seeds.

Prairies, plains and bluffs, Missouri and Kansas to Texas, Arizona and Mexico.　May–July.

2. ALBÍZZIA Durazz. Mag. Tosc. 3⁴: 11.　1772.

Unarmed trees, with large bipinnate leaves, widely spreading branches, and perfect or polygamous capitate pink or white flowers, the heads sometimes panicled. Calyx tubular to campanulate, 5-lobed. Corolla funnelform. Stamens numerous, longer than the corolla; filaments united near the base of the corolla. Pods linear, flat, 2-valved, the margins of the valves not separating from them. [In honor of Albizzi, an Italian naturalist.]

About 50 species, natives of warm and tropical regions of the Old World, the following typical.

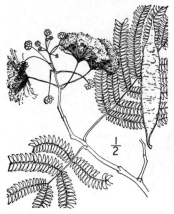

1. Albizzia julibríssin Durazz.　Pink Siris.　Silk-tree.　Fig. 2430.

A. julibrissin Durazz. Mag. Tosc. 3⁴: 11.　1772.

A tree, up to 35° high, and trunk diameter of 1½°, the bark thin and scaly, the slender twigs smooth, reddish-brown. Leaves 8′–16′ long, with 8–16 pairs of pinnae; the rachis tipped by a spine; leaflets 25 to 35 pairs, oblong, inequilateral, acute, 5″–8″ long, revolute-margined, dark green above, pale green and pubescent beneath; heads panicled, about 2′ in diameter; flowers pink; stamens more than 1′ long; ovary short-stalked; pod 4′–6′ long, narrowed at both ends, papery; seeds oval, flat, 4″–5″ long.

Virginia to Florida and Louisiana.　Naturalized from southern Asia.　April–July.

3. ÁCUAN Medic. Theod. Sp. 62.　1786.

[Desmanthus Willd. Sp. Pl. 4: 1044.　1806.]

[Darlingtonia DC. Ann. Sci. Nat. 4: 97.　1825.]

Perennial herbs or shrubs, with bipinnate leaves, small stipules, and greenish or whitish small regular flowers in axillary peduncled heads or spikes. Flowers perfect, sessile, or the lowest sometimes staminate, neutral or apetalous. Calyx campanulate, its teeth short. Petals valvate, distinct, or slightly united or coherent below. Stamens 10 or 5, distinct, mainly exserted; anthers all alike. Ovary nearly sessile; ovules ∞. Pod linear, straight or curved, acute, glabrous, flat, several-seeded, 2-valved, the valves coriaceous or membranous.

About 10 species, natives of warm and tropical America, one of them widely distributed in tropical regions of the Old World.　Type species: Mimosa virgata L.

Pods few, linear, erect, straight.　　　　　　　　　　　　　　　1. A. leptoloba.
Pods numerous in globose heads, oblong, curved.　　　　　　　　　2. A. illinoensis.

1. Acuan leptóloba (T. & G.) Kuntze.
Prairie Mimosa. Fig. 2431.

Desmanthus leptolobus T. & G. Fl. N. A. 1: 402. 1840.

Acuan leptoloba Kuntze, Rev. Gen. Pl. 158. 1891.

Herbaceous, ascending, branched, stems rough-angled, 2°–3° long. Leaves short-petioled, bipinnate; pinnae 5–10 pairs, sessile; leaflets 10–24 pairs, sessile, linear-lanceolate, acute, inequilateral, rounded at the base, usually glabrous, $1\frac{1}{2}''$–$2''$ long, $\frac{1}{4}''$ wide or less; peduncles $6''$–$12''$ long, few-flowered; stamens (always?) 5; pods 3–8, narrowly linear, acuminate, nearly straight, glabrous, about 3 times the length of the peduncle, 6–8-seeded.

Prairies, Kansas to Texas. Summer.

2. Acuan illinoénsis (Michx.) Kuntze.
Illinois Mimosa. Fig. 2432.

Mimosa illinoensis Michx. Fl. Bor. Am. 2: 254. 1803.
Acacia brachyloba Willd. Sp. Pl. 4: 1071. 1806.
Desmanthus brachylobus Benth. in Hook. Journ. Bot. 4: 358. 1842.
A. illinoensis Kuntze, Rev. Gen. Pl. 158. 1891.

Ascending or erect, glabrous or nearly so, stems angled, 1°–3° high. Foliage resembling that of the preceding species, but the pinnae and obtusish leaflets are sometimes more numerous; peduncles $1'$–$2'$ long; pods numerous, densely capitate, oblong or lanceolate, strongly curved, $8''$–$12''$ long, acute, slightly impressed between the 2–5 seeds.

Prairies and river-banks, Ohio to Kentucky, Florida, South Dakota, Colorado, Texas and New Mexico. Illinois acacia. May–Sept.

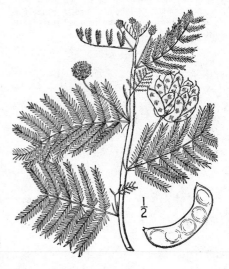

4. PROSÒPIS L. Mant. 1: 10. 1767.

Trees or shrubs often with spines in the axils, with 2-pinnate leaves, the leaflets few or numerous, and small spicate or capitate perfect flowers. Calyx campanulate, with 5 short teeth. Petals 5, valvate, distinct, or connate below. Stamens 10, distinct; filaments long. Ovary often stalked, many-ovuled; styles slender or filiform; stigma very small. Pod linear, straight or curved, compressed, leathery, indehiscent, the mesocarp spongy or dry. Seeds flattened. [Ancient name for some very different plant.]

About 15 species, natives of warm and tropical regions. Besides the following, 2 or 3 others occur in the southwestern United States. Type species: *Prosopis spicígera* L.

1. Prosopis glandulòsa Torr.   Prairie Mesquite.   Fig. 2433.

P. glandulosa Torr. Ann. Lyc. N. Y. **2** : 192. *pl. 2.* 1828.

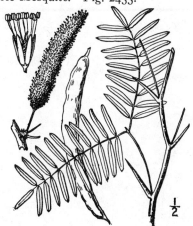

A glabrous or minutely pubescent shrub, the axils usually with a pair of sharp spines. Leaves petioled, with 2 spreading short-stalked pinnae, each of numerous sessile leaflets which are linear or linear-oblong, entire, acute or obtuse, mostly mucronulate, firm, veiny, $\frac{1}{2}$–2′ long, 1″–2″ wide; spikes or spike-like racemes axillary, often numerous, peduncled, very densely many-flowered, 2′–5′ long, nearly $\frac{1}{2}$′ thick; pedicels $\frac{1}{2}$″–1″ long; calyx campanulate; petals 2–4 times as long as the calyx; ovary villous; pods linear, stipitate, 4′–8′ long, 4″–6″ wide, constricted between the seeds.

Kansas to Texas, Arizona, California and Mexico. Apparently distinct from the tropical *P. juliflora* (Sw.) DC. April–June.

5. MORÓNGIA Britton, Mem. Torr. Club **5** : 191.   1894.

[SCHRANKIA Willd. Sp. Pl. **4** : 1041.   1806.   Not Medic. 1792.]

[LEPTOGLOTTIS DC. Mem. Leg. 451.   1823?]

Perennial herbs, or shrubs, mainly prostrate or procumbent, armed with recurved prickles. Leaves bipinnate, usually sensitive; leaflets numerous, small; stipules setaceous. Flowers regular, small, 4–5-parted, pink or purple, perfect or polygamous, in axillary peduncled heads or spikes. Petals united to the middle. Stamens usually 8–12, distinct or united at the base; anthers all alike. Ovary nearly sessile; ovules ∞. Pod linear, acute or acuminate, spiny all over, at length 4-valved, several seeded. [Named in honor of the late Rev. Thos. Morong, a contributor to the first edition of this work.]

About 10 species, natives of temperate and tropical America, 1 in tropical Africa. Type species: *Schrankia aculeata* Willd.

Leaflets elliptic, strongly veined.   1. *M. uncinata.*
Leaflets linear-oblong, scarcely veined.   2. *M. microphylla.*

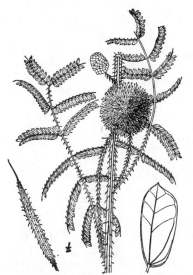

1. Morongia uncinàta (Willd.) Britton.   Sensitive-brier.   Fig. 2434.

Schrankia uncinata Willd. Sp. Pl. **4** : 1043.   1806.

M. uncinata Britton, Mem. Torr. Club **5** : 191.   1894.

Herbaceous, perennial, branched, decumbent, 2°–4° long. Stem, branches, petioles and peduncles thickly armed with hooked prickles $\frac{1}{2}$″–1″ long; stem grooved and angled; leaves petioled; pinnae 4–8 pairs, distant; leaflets 8–15 pairs, obliquely elliptic, thick, obtusish and mucronate at the apex, inequillateral and rounded at the base, slightly ciliate on the margins, strongly marked with few elevated veins beneath, 2″–4″ long; heads globose, very dense, 8″–12″ in diameter; flowers pink; pods terete, very densely spiny, about 2′ long.

In dry soil, Virginia to Illinois and South Dakota, Nebraska, Florida and Texas. May–July. Shame-vine. Sensitive-rose.

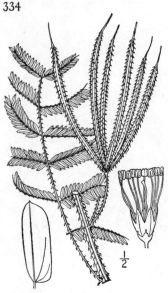

$\frac{1}{2}$

2. Morongia microphylla (Dryand) Britton.
Narrow-leaved Sensitive-brier. Fig. 2435.

Mimosa Intsia Walt. Fl. Car. 252. 1788. Not L. 1753.

Mimosa microphylla Dryand. ; J. E. Smith, Georgia Insects, 2 : 123. *pl. 62.* 1797.

Schrankia angustata T. & G. Fl. N. A. 1 : 400. 1840.

Morongia angustata Britton, Mem. Torr. Club 5 : 191. 1894.

Similar to the preceding species Pinnae 3–6 pairs; leaflets numerous, linear-oblong, thin, acutish or obtuse, not mucronate or but very slightly so, very obscurely veined, not at all reticulated, $1\frac{1}{2}''-3''$ long; peduncles shorter than the leaves; heads densely flowered, $5''-8''$ in diameter; flowers pink; pods linear, sparingly or densely spiny, $2'-5'$ long.

In dry soil, Virginia to Florida, west to Tennessee and Texas. Sensitive plant. June–Aug.

Family 58. **CAESALPINIÀCEAE** Kl. & Garcke, Bot. Erg. Wald. 157. 1862.

SENNA FAMILY.

Trees, herbs or shrubs, with alternate simple or compound mostly stipulate leaves. Flowers mostly clustered and perfect, sometimes monoecious, dioecious or polygamous, nearly regular, or irregular. Calyx mostly of 5 sepals or 5-toothed. Petals usually 5, imbricated, and the upper (unpaired) one enclosed by the lateral ones in the bud. Stamens 10 or fewer in our genera, the filaments distinct, or more or less united. Ovary 1-celled, 1–many-ovuled. Fruit a legume, mostly dehiscent into 2 valves. Seeds with or without endosperm.

About 90 genera and 1000 species, mostly of tropical distribution.

Trees or shrubs ; leaves simple ; corolla irregular, apparently papilionaceous, but the lateral petals enclosing the upper one in the bud.　　　　　　　　　　　　　　　　　　　1. *Cercis.*
Herbs (all our species) ; flowers perfect ; leaves pinnate or bipinnate ; corolla nearly regular.
　　Leaves pinnate, not punctate.
　　　　Pods not elastically dehiscent ; leaves not sensitive to touch.　　　　2. *Cassia.*
　　　　Pods elastically dehiscent , leaves sensitive to touch.　　　　　　　3. *Chamaecrista.*
　　Leaves bipinnate, glandular-punctate.　　　　　　　　　　　　　　　4. *Hoffmanseggia.*
Trees ; leaves pinnate or bipinnate ; flowers dioecious or polygamous.
　　Receptacle short ; stamens 3–5 ; pod flat, short or elongated.　　　　5 *Gleditsia.*
　　Receptacle elongated ; stamens 10 ; pod oblong, woody.　　　　　　　6. *Gymnocladus.*

1. CÉRCIS L. Sp. Pl. 374. 1753.

Small trees or shrubs, with simple broad leaves, and pink flowers in short lateral fascicles borne on the twigs of preceding seasons. Calyx somewhat oblique, broadly campanulate, 5-toothed. Corolla irregular; petals 5; standard enclosed by the wings in the bud; keel larger than the wings. Stamens 10, distinct, declined; anthers all alike, short, versatile, longitudinally dehiscent. Ovary short-stipitate; ovules ∞. Pod linear-oblong or oblong, flat, margined along the upper suture, 2-valved at maturity, the valves thin, reticulate-veined. [Ancient name of the Old World Judas-tree.]

About 7 species, natives of North America, Europe and temperate Asia. Besides the following, two others occur in the south central and western United States. Type species: *Cercis Siliquastrum* L.

1. Cercis canadénsis L. Red-bud. American Judas-tree. Fig. 2436.

Cercis canadensis L. Sp. Pl. 374. 1753.

A tree, with greatest height of about 50° and trunk diameter of 1°, or often shrubby. Stipules membranous, small, caducous; leaves simple, petioled, cordate-orbicular, blunt-pointed, rather thick, glabrous, or pubescent along the veins beneath, 2′-6′ broad; flowers several together in sessile umbellate clusters, appearing before the leaves; pedicels slender, 4″-12″ long; corolla pink-purple, about 4″ long; pod short-stalked in the calyx, linear-oblong, acute at each end, glabrous, 2′-3′ long, 6″ wide, several-seeded.

In rich soil, southern Ontario and New York to Iowa, Nebraska, Arkansas, Florida and Texas. Wood hard, weak, dark reddish-brown; weight per cubic foot 40 lbs. Red Judas-tree. Salad-tree. April.

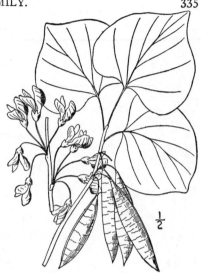

2. CÁSSIA [Tourn.] L. Sp. Pl 376. 1753.

Herbs, shrubs, or in tropical regions trees, with evenly pinnate leaves, not sensitive to the touch, and mainly (in all our species) yellow flowers. Calyx-teeth nearly equal, mostly obtuse, generally longer than the tube. Corolla nearly regular; petals 5, spreading, nearly equal, imbricated, clawed. Stamens usually 10, sometimes 5, often unequal and some of them imperfect; anthers all alike, or those of the lower stamens larger, opening by 2 pores at the summit. Ovary sessile or stalked; ovules ∞. Pod flat or terete, often curved, septate or continuous between the seeds, the valves not elastically dehiscent. Seeds numerous. [Ancient name.]

About 200 species, of wide distribution in warm and temperate regions, very abundant in tropical America. Besides the following, about 15 others occur in the southern and southwestern States. Type species: *Cassia fistula* L.

Leaflets 6 or 4, broadly obovate.   1. *C. Tora.*
Leaflets 8–20, oblong or ovate-lanceolate.
 Perennial; leaflets oblong, obtuse.
  Segments of the pod at least as long as broad; petiolar gland club-shaped.   2. *C. marilandica.*
  Segments of the pod much shorter than broad; petiolar gland cylindric to conic.
                                                                               3. *C. Medsgeri.*
 Annual; leaflets ovate-lanceolate, acute or acuminate.   4. *C. occidentalis.*

1. Cassia Tòra L. Low Senna. Fig. 2437.

Cassia Tora L. Sp. Pl. 376. 1753.

Cassia obtusifolia L. Sp. Pl. 377. 1753.

Annual, glabrous, 1½°-2° high, branched or simple. Stipules linear-subulate, at length deciduous; leaves petioled, the gland borne between or above the lowest pair of leaflets; leaflets 2–4 pairs, thin, obovate, obtuse and mucronulate at the apex, narrowed or rounded at the base, 1′-1½′ long, often 1′ wide; flowers 6″-12″ broad, few, in short axillary racemes; calyx-lobes oblong, obtuse; stamens 10, the anthers of the upper 3 imperfect; pod linear, very slender, strongly curved, 4′-6′ long, about 1½″ wide.

Along rivers, southern Pennsylvania to Indiana and Missouri, south to Florida and Mexico, and throughout tropical America and the warmer parts of the Old World. Sickle-senna. Coffee-weed. July–Oct.

2. Cassia marilándica L.   Wild or American Senna.   Fig. 2438.

Cassia marilandica L. Sp. Pl. 378. 1753.

Perennial, glabrous or pubescent with a few scattered hairs, 3°–8° high, little branched. Stipules subulate-linear, caducous; leaves petioled, the club-shaped gland borne near the base of the petiole; leaflets 12–20, oblong or lanceolate-oblong, obtuse or obtusish, mucronate, rounded at the base, ciliate, 1′–2′ long, 3″–6″ wide; flowers 7″–9″ broad, numerous in pubescent axillary racemes on the upper part of the plant; calyx-lobes ovate or oblong, obtuse; stamens 10, the upper 3 imperfect; pod linear, flat, pubescent or becoming glabrous, 3′–4′ long, 3″ wide, curved, its segments as long as broad or slightly longer; seeds flat, suborbicular.

In swamps and wet soil, Massachusetts to North Carolina, Ohio and Tennessee. July–Aug.

3. Cassia Médsgeri Shafer.   Medsger's Wild Senna.   Fig. 2439.

Cassia Medsgeri Shafer, Torreya 4: 179. 1904.

Biennial (?) or perennial, similar to *C. marilandica*, glabrous or very nearly so throughout. Stipules linear-lanceolate; petiolar gland cylindric to conic; leaflets 8–16, oblong to elliptic, mucronate, glabrous, slightly glaucous beneath, 2′ long or less; inflorescence glabrous or nearly so; pod curved, linear, little compressed, 4′ long or less, tardily dehiscent, its segments much shorter than broad; seeds obovoid, 2″ long, 1″ thick.

In dry gravelly soil, Pennsylvania to Georgia, Iowa, Kansas and Texas. July–Sept.

4. Cassia occidentàlis L.   Coffee Senna.   Styptic-weed.   Fig. 2440.

Cassia occidentalis L. Sp. Pl. 377. 1753.

Annual, glabrous, much branched, erect, 4°–6° high. Stipules caducous; gland short, borne near the base of the petiole; leaflets 8–12, ovate or ovate-lanceolate, acute or acuminate at the apex, rounded at the base, 1′–2′ long, 4″–9″ wide; flowers 7″–9″ broad, in short axillary racemes; stamens 10, the upper 3 imperfect; calyx-lobes oblong, obtuse; pod linear, glabrous, 4′–6′ long, about 3″ wide, somewhat curved, its margins thickened.

In waste places, Virginia to Indiana, Kansas, Florida and Mexico, and throughout tropical America, extending to Chili and Uruguay. Also in the warmer parts of the Old World. In our area adventive from the South. Coffee-weed. The seeds are known as negro or magdad coffee. July–Aug.

3. CHAMAECRÍSTA Moench, Meth. 272. 1794.

Herbs or low shrubs, with evenly pinnate leaves, often sensitive to the touch, mostly persistent strongly nerved stipules, and yellow flowers in small axillary clusters or solitary in the axils. Calyx-lobes acuminate. Corolla somewhat irregular, three of the five petals smaller than the others. Stamens 10, all usually with perfect anthers opening by terminal pores. Pods linear, flat, more or less elastically dehiscent, the valves twisting. [Greek, low crest.]

About 100 species, widely distributed in temperate and tropical regions. Besides the following, some 15 others occur in the southern United States. Type species: *Chamaecrista nictitans* (L.) Moench.

Flowers 2″-4″ wide, short-pedicelled.   1. *C. nictitans.*
Flowers 1′-1½′ wide, slender-pedicelled.   2. *C. fasciculata.*

1. Chamaecrista níctitans (L.) Moench. Sensitive Pea. Wild Sensitive-plant. Fig. 2441.

Cassia nictitans L. Sp. Pl. 380. 1753.
Chamaecrista nictitans Moench, Meth. 272. 1794.

Annual, erect or decumbent, branching, more or less pubescent, 6′-15′ high. Stipules subulate-linear, persistent; leaves petioled, sensitive, bearing a small gland near the base of the petiole; leaflets 12-44, linear-oblong, obtuse and mucronate at the apex, rounded and oblique at the base, inequilateral, 3″-8″ long, 1″-1½″ wide; flowers 2-3 together in the axils, short-pedicelled, 2″-4″ broad; calyx-lobes acute or acuminate; stamens 5, all perfect; pod linear, nearly glabrous, or pubescent, 1′-1½′ long, 2′-2½′ wide.

In dry soil, Maine to Georgia, west to Indiana, Kansas and Texas. Also in the West Indies. July–Oct.

2. Chamaecrista fasciculàta (Michx.) Greene. Partridge Pea. Large-flowered Sensitive Pea. Prairie Senna. Fig. 2442.

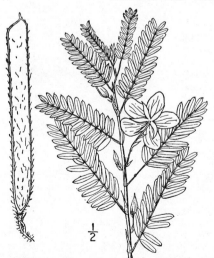

Cassia fasciculata Michx. Fl. Bor. Am. 1: 262. 1803.
Cassia Chamaecrista robusta Pollard, Mem. Torr. Club 21: 218. 1894.
Chamaecrista fascicularis Greene, Pittonia 3: 242. 1897.
C. fasciculata Greene; Pollard in Small, Fl. SE. U. S. 587. 1903.

Annual, erect or spreading, widely branched, pubescent, with spreading hairs, or nearly glabrous, 1°-2½° high. Stipules subulate-linear, persistent; leaves petioled, with a sessile gland on the petiole, sensitive; flowers 2-4 together in the axils, 1′-1½′ broad, slender-pedicelled, showy, some of the petals often purple spotted; leaflets 20-30, linear-oblong or the upper lanceolate, obtuse, mucronate, inequilateral, oblique at the base, 4″-10″ long, 1½″-2″ wide; calyx-lobes long-acuminate; stamens 10, all perfect, 4 of the anthers yellow, 6 purple; pod linear, pubescent or glabrate, 1½′-2½′ long, 2″-3″ wide.

In dry soil, Massachusetts to Florida, Minnesota, Texas and Mexico. Referred to *Cassia* in our first edition. Dwarf-cassia. Magoty-boy-bean. July–Sept.

Chamaecrista L., in our first edition. Dwarf-cassia. Magoty-boy-bean. July–Sept.

Chamaecrista depréssa (Pollard) Greene, of the Gulf States, which is apparently perennial, with fewer leaflets, is recorded from Missouri. It is probably identical with *C. chamaecristoides* (Collad.) Greene, of the same region.

4. HOFFMANSÉGGIA Cav. Icones 4 : 63. *pl. 392, 393.* 1797.

Herbs, or low shrubs, with glandular-punctate bipinnate leaves, small stipules, and yellow flowers in terminal or lateral racemes. Calyx deeply 5-parted, the lobes nearly equal. Petals 5, oval or oblong, imbricated, nearly equal. Stamens 10, distinct, slightly declined; filaments often glandular at the base; anthers all alike, longitudinally dehiscent. Ovary nearly sessile; ovules ∞. Pod flat, linear, oblong or ovate, curved or straight, 2-valved, several-seeded. [In honor of Joh. Centurius, Graf Hoffmansegge, a writer on Portuguese botany.]

About 20 species, natives of western America and South Africa. Besides the following, some 9 others occur in the southwestern United States. Type species: *Hoffmanseggia falcaria* Cav.

Leaflets black-punctate ; pod obliquely oblong.   1. *H. Jamesii.*
Leaflets not punctate ; pod linear-oblong.   2. *H. falcaria.*

1. Hoffmanseggia Jàmesii T. & G.   James' Hoffmanseggia. Fig. 2443

Pomaria glandulosa Torr. Ann. Lyc. N. Y. **2** : 193. 1826.
    Not Cav. 1799.
Hoffmanseggia Jamesii T. & G. Fl. N. A. **1** : 393. 1840.
Caesalpinia Jamesii Fisher, Coult. Bot. Gaz. **18** : 123. 1893.

Herbaceous, glandular, black-punctate and finely pubescent, branching at the base from a deep woody root; stems 6'–12' high. Stipules subulate; leaves petioled, bipinnate; pinnae 5–7; leaflets 9–19, oval or oblong, obtuse at each end, inequilateral, 1½''–3'' long; racemes terminal, or lateral (opposite the leaves), elongated; flowers yellow, distant, deflexed, 3''–4'' long, the upper petal spotted with red; pod flat, obliquely oblong, black-punctate, about 1' long and 5'' wide, 2–3-seeded, tipped with the base of the style.

Plains, Kansas to Texas, Arizona and New Mexico. June–July.

2. Hoffmanseggia falcària Cav.   Sickle-fruited Hoffmanseggia. Fig. 2444.

Hoffmanseggia falcaria Cav. Icones, **4** : 63. *pl. 392.* 1797.
H. stricta Benth. ; A. Gray, Pl. Wright. **1** : 56. 1852.
Caesalpinia Falcaria Fisher, Coult. Bot. Gaz. **18** : 122. 1893.

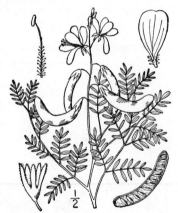

Herbaceous, puberulent, not black-punctate, the glands of the peduncles and petioles stalked; stems ascending or decumbent, 1° high or less. Stipules ovate; leaves slender-petioled, bipinnate; pinnae 7–11; leaflets 12–21, oblong, obtuse, 1½''–3'' long; racemes few–several-flowered, elongating in fruit; pod flat, linear-oblong, curved or nearly straight, 1'–1½' long, about 3'' wide, blunt, 8–12-seeded, the fruiting pedicels recurved.

Kansas (according to Fisher) ; Texas, west to California. Also in Central and South America. April–June.

5. GLEDÍTSIA L. Sp. Pl. 1056. 1753.

Large thorny trees, with evenly once or twice pinnate leaves, small stipules, and small greenish polygamous flowers in slender axillary spicate racemes. Calyx campanulate, 3–5-cleft. Petals 3–5, equal, sessile, inserted at the summit of the calyx-tube. Stamens 3–10, distinct; anthers all alike, longitudinally dehiscent. Ovary rudimentary or none in the staminate flowers, in the fertile ones nearly sessile, elongated or ovoid. Ovules 2–∞. Pod linear or oval, flat, nearly straight, or twisted at maturity, coriaceous, tardily dehiscent, 1-seeded or many-seeded, sometimes pulpy between the flat seeds. [In honor of J. T. Gleditsch, 1714–1786, German botanist, the name often spelled *Gleditschia.*]

About 6 species, natives of eastern North America and Asia. Besides the following, one occurs in Texas. Type species: *Gleditsia triacanthos* L.

Pod linear-oblong, elongated, many-seeded.   1. *G. triacanthos.*
Pod obliquely oval, short, 1-seeded.   2. *G. aquatica.*

1. Gleditsia triacánthos L.   Honey or Sweet Locust.   Three-thorned Acacia.   Black or Thorn Locust.   Fig. 2445.

Gleditsia triacanthos L. Sp. Pl. 1056. 1753.

A large tree, with rough bark, maximum height about 140° and trunk diameter 5½°, usually armed with numerous stout branching or simple thorns. Leaves petioled, 1–2-pinnate; leaflets short-stalked, oblong-lanceolate or oval, obtuse at each end, inequilateral at the base, glabrous above, often pubescent on the veins beneath, crenulate, 8″–15″ long; racemes solitary or clustered, slender, drooping, dense, 3′–5′ long; flowers greenish, about 2″ broad; pod linear-oblong, 1°–1½° long, 1′–1½′ wide, stalked, glabrous and shining, twisted, many-seeded, pulpy within, sometimes eaten.

In woods, western New York and Ontario to Michigan, Georgia, Kansas and Texas. Naturalized and extensively planted further east. Wood durable, bright brownish-red; weight per cubic foot 42 lbs. Pulp of the pod-sweet. May–July. Honey. Honey-shucks. Sweet-bean.

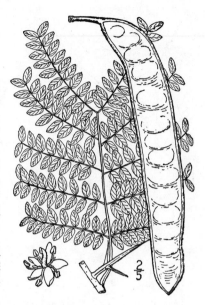

2. Gleditsia aquática Marsh.   Water or Swamp Locust.   Fig. 2446.

Gleditsia aquatica Marsh. Arb. Am. 54. 1785.

Gleditsia monosperma Walt. Fl. Car. 254. 1788.

A tree, with maximum height of about 60°, and trunk diameter of 2½°, the thorns usually simple. Foliage similar to that of the preceding species, but the leaflets thicker, darker green, usually larger, ovate-lanceolate or lanceolate in outline, the margins more conspicuously crenulate; racemes drooping, elongated; pod obliquely oval, flat, glabrous, narrowed at each end, slender-stalked, 1′–1½′ long, 9″–12″ wide, 1-seeded, not pulpy within.

In swamps, Indiana to Missouri, South Carolina, Florida and Texas. Wood very hard, bright reddish-brown; weight per cubic foot 46 lbs. July.

6. GYMNÓCLADUS Lam. Encycl. 1 : 733. 1783.

Trees, with bipinnate leaves, and showy white dioecious or polygamous flowers in terminal racemes. Calyx tubular, 5-lobed, the lobes narrow, nearly equal. Petals 5 (rarely 4), oblong or oval, nearly equal, imbricated, inserted at the top of the calyx-tube. Stamens 10, distinct, shorter than the petals and inserted with them; filaments pubescent; anthers all alike, longitudinally dehiscent. Ovary rudimentary, or none in the staminate flowers, sessile and many-ovuled in the pistillate and polygamous ones; style straight. Pod oblong, thick, large, coriaceous, flat, pulpy between the seeds, 2-valved. [Greek, naked-branch.]

A monotypic genus of eastern North America.

1. Gymnocladus dioìca (L.) Koch. Kentucky Coffee-tree. Fig. 2447.

Guilandina dioica L. Sp. Pl. 381. 1753.
Gymnocladus canadensis Lam. Encycl. 1: 733. 1783.
Gymnocladus dioicus Koch, Dendrol. 1: 5. 1869.

A large forest tree, with rough bark, maximum height about 100°, and trunk diameter of 3°. Leaves large, bipinnate, petioled; pinnae 5–9, odd or evenly pinnate; leaflets 7–15 (or the lowest pair of pinnae of but a single leaflet), ovate, acute or acuminate at the apex, rounded at the base, glabrous, or pubescent on the veins beneath, ciliate on the margins, 1'–3' long; racemes many-flowered, elongated; flowers nearly white, slender-pedicelled, 8''–9'' long; pod 5'–10' long, about 1¼'–1¾' wide, the valves thick and coriaceous.

Rich woods, southern Ontario and New York to Pennsylvania, Tennessee, South Dakota, Nebraska and Oklahoma. Wood soft, strong, light reddish-brown; weight per cubic foot 43 lbs. The fruit called Coffee-nut. May–June. Kentucky mahogany. Chicot. American coffee-bean. Nickar-tree.

Family 59. KRAMERIACEAE Dumort. Anal. Fam. 20. 1829.

KRAMERIA FAMILY.

Pubescent herbs, or low shrubs, with alternate simple or digitately 3-foliolate leaves, and purple or purplish, solitary or racemed, irregular perfect flowers. Peduncles 2-bracted at or above the middle. Stipules wanting. Sepals 4 or 5, usually large, the outer one commonly wider than the others. Petals usually 5, smaller than the sepals, the 3 upper ones long-clawed, often united by their claws, or the middle one of the 3 wanting, the 2 lower ones reduced to suborbicular fleshy glands. Stamens 3 or 4, monadelphous, at least at the base; anther-sacs opening by a terminal pore. Ovary 1-celled, or partly 2-celled; ovules 2, collateral, anatropous, pendulous; style slender, acute or truncate. Fruit globose, or compressed, spiny, indehiscent, 1-seeded. Seed without endosperm; cotyledons fleshy.

The family consists of only the following genus, with about 20 species, distributed from the southern United States to Chile. It has often been included in the POLYGALACEAE, but its affinity to *Cassia* and related genera indicates that it should be placed next to the CAESALPINIACEAE.

1. KRAMÈRIA Loefl.; L. Syst. Ed. 10, 899. 1759.

[In honor of Johann Georg Heinrich Kramer, an Austrian physician of the eighteenth century.]

Type species: *Krameria Ixìne* L.

1. Krameria lanceolàta Torr. Linear-leaved Krameria. Fig. 2448.

K. lanceolata Torr. Ann. Lyc. N. Y. 2: 166. 1828.

A perennial appressed-pubescent herb from a thick woody root, the stems prostrate or ascending, branched, often 1° long or more. Leaves numerous, linear, linear-lanceolate or linear-oblong, sessile, simple, entire, about 1' long, ½''–2'' wide, acute, tipped with a minute prickle; peduncles solitary, axillary, 1-flowered, sometimes secund, as long as the leaves, or shorter, bearing 2 leaf-like bracts just below the flower; flowers about 1' broad, the sepals purple within, pubescent without; claws of the 3 upper petals united; stamens 4, monadelphous; fruit globose, pubescent, very spiny, about ½' in diameter.

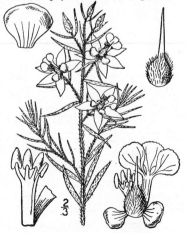

Florida to Kansas, New Mexico and Mexico. April–June. Referred in our first edition to the Mexican *K. secundiflora* DC., which it resembles.

Family 60. FABÀCEAE Reichenb. Consp. 149. 1828.

PEA FAMILY.

Herbs, shrubs, vines or trees, with alternate mostly compound stipulate leaves, and irregular (papilionaceous) perfect or sometimes polygamo-dioecious flowers, mainly in spikes, heads, racemes or panicles. Calyx 4–5-toothed, or 4–5-cleft, the teeth or lobes unequal or equal; sometimes 2-lipped. Petals more or less united, or separate, perigynous or hypogynous, usually consisting of a broad upper one (standard, banner), two lateral ones (wings), and two front ones more or less united (forming the keel); the standard encloses the wings in the bud. Stamens monadelphous, diadelphous, or sometimes separate, 10 in most of the genera, sometimes 9, rarely 5. Pistil 1, simple, superior; ovary mainly 1-celled, sometimes 2-celled by the intrusion of the sutures, or several-celled by cross-partitions; style simple; ovules 1–many, anatropous or amphitropous. Fruit a legume, 1–many-seeded, dehiscent into 2 valves, or indehiscent, in one tribe a loment. Seeds mostly without endosperm; cotyledons thick.

Genera about 325, species over 5000, most abundant in temperate and warm regions; known also as PAPILIONACEAE and PHASEOLACEAE, and included by some authors in the LEGUMINOSAE.

* The 10 stamens distinct.

Leaves pinnate. Tribe 1. SOPHOREAE.
Leaves digitate (in ours 3-foliolate), or simple. Tribe 2. PODALYRIEAE.

** The stamens monadelphous or diadelphous.

Herbs, shrubs, woody vines or trees, the leaves not tendril-bearing.
  Pod not a loment, 2-valved or indehiscent.
    Foliage not glandular-dotted (except in *Glycyrrhiza*, which has many-seeded pods).
      Stamens monadelphous; anthers of 2 kinds. Tribe 3. GENISTEAE.
      Stamens diadelphous (except in *Ononis*); anthers all alike.
        Leaves, in our species, 3-foliolate, rarely 1-foliolate.
          Leaflets denticulate. Tribe 4. TRIFOLIEAE.
          Leaflets entire. Tribe 5. LOTEAE.
        Leaves pinnately several–many-foliolate (except in *Orophaca*). Tribe 7. GALEGEAE.
    Foliage glandular-dotted; pod indehiscent, 1–2-seeded; herbs. Tribe 6. PSORALEAE.
  Pod a loment; herbs. Tribe 8. HEDYSAREAE.
Herbaceous vines, or herbs; leaves evenly pinnate, with tendrils. Tribe 9. VICIEAE.
Vines, ours herbaceous, or herbs; leaves without tendrils. Tribe 10. PHASEOLEAE.

Tribe 1. SOPHOREAE.

Our species herbs; flowers racemed. 1. *Sophora.*
Trees; flowers panicled. 2. *Cladrastis.*

Tribe 2. PODALYRIEAE.

Ovary sessile, or nearly so; pod flat in our species. 3. *Thermopsis.*
Ovary distinctly stipitate; pod inflated. 4. *Baptisia.*

Tribe 3. GENISTEAE.

Herbs, with simple or 5–11-foliolate leaves.
  Leaves simple; pod inflated. 5. *Crotalaria.*
  Leaves 5–11-foliolate; pod flattened. 6. *Lupinus.*
Shrubs with 1–3-foliolate leaves.
  Calyx divided into 2 lips; leaves very prickly. 7. *Ulex.*
  Calyx cleft into 2 lips to about the middle.
    Calyx-teeth long. 8. *Genista.*
    Calyx-teeth short. 9. *Cytisus.*

Tribe 4. TRIFOLIEAE.

Flowers spiked, or capitate; pods curved, or coiled. 10. *Medicago.*
Flowers in long racemes; pods coriaceous. 11. *Melilotus.*
Flowers capitate or umbelled; pods straight, membranous. 12. *Trifolium.*

Tribe 5. LOTEAE.

Filaments diadelphous; pods dehiscent.
  Leaves 5-foliolate. 13. *Lotus.*
  Leaves pinnate; leaflets sometimes only 1 or 3. 14. *Hosackia.*
Filaments monadelphous; pods indehiscent or nearly so. 15. *Anthyllis.*

Tribe 6. PSORALEAE.

Leaves digitately 3–5-foliolate, or pinnately 3-foliolate. 16. *Psoralea.*
Leaves pinnately 5–many-foliolate.
  Stamens 10 or 9, monadelphous, at least at the base.
    Corolla of only 1 petal (the standard). 17. *Amorpha.*
    Corolla of 5 petals, the wings and keel united to the filament-tube. 18. *Parosela.*
  Stamens only 5, monadelphous. 19. *Petalostemum.*

Tribe 7. GALEGEAE.

Standard very broad, ovate or orbicular.
  Herbs; leaves odd-pinnate.
    Pod 4-angled in our species. 20. *Indigofera.*
    Pod flat. 21. *Cracca.*

High-climbing woody vines.   22. *Kraunhia.*
Trees or shrubs.   23. *Robinia.*
Herbs ; leaves evenly pinnate.   24. *Sesban.*
Standard narrow ; our species all herbs.
   Pod not prickly ; foliage not glandular-punctate.
     Keel of the corolla blunt.
      Leaves pinnate, or simple.
       Pods not flattened, swollen, or one or both sutures intruded.
        Pods fleshy, becoming spongy, 2-celled, indehiscent.   25. *Geoprumnon.*
        Pods not fleshy, dehiscent (epicarp slightly fleshy in *Astragalus pectinatus*).
         Pods not much swollen, leathery or papery.   26. *Astragalus.*
         Pods much inflated, membranous, 1-celled.   27. *Phaca.*
       Pods flat, both sutures prominent externally.
        Leaves not bristle-tipped ; pods several-seeded.   28. *Homalobus.*
        Leaves bristle-tipped ; pods only 1–2-seeded.   29. *Kentrophyta.*
      Leaves 3-foliolate.   30. *Orophaca.*
     Keel of the corolla acute.   31. *Oxytropis.*
   Pod prickly ; foliage glandular-punctate.   32. *Glycyrrhiza.*

Tribe 8.   HEDYSAREAE.

Leaves odd-pinnate.
  Flowers purplish, umbellate.   33. *Coronilla.*
  Flowers purple or white, racemose.   34. *Hedysarum.*
  Flowers yellow, small.   35. *AEschynomene.*
Leaves 4-foliolate or 2-foliolate.   36. *Zornia.*
Leaves 3-foliolate, the terminal leaflets stalked.
  Flowers yellow.   37. *Stylosanthes.*
  Flowers purple, blue or white.
   Pod of several joints ; leaflets stipellate.   38. *Meibomia.*
   Pod of 1 or 2 joints ; leaflets not stipellate.   39. *Lespedeza.*

Tribe 9.   VICIEAE.

Style slender, with a tuft of hairs at the summit.   40. *Vicia.*
Style flattened. bearded along the inner side.   41. *Lathyrus.*

Tribe 10.   PHASEOLEAE.

Style bearded along the inner side ; rachis not thickened at the insertion of the flowers ; keel of
  corolla not curved nor coiled.   42. *Clitoria.*
Style glabrous, or pubescent below ; keel of corolla not curved nor coiled.   43. *Bradburya.*
  Standard spurred at the base.
  Standard not spurred.
   Flowers blue, purple, purplish, or white.
    Leaves odd-pinnate ; leaflets 5–7.   44. *Glycine.*
    Leaves 3-foliolate, rarely 1-foliolate.
     Calyx tubular, not bracteolate.   45. *Falcata.*
     Calyx short, bracteolate.   46. *Galactia.*
   Flowers yellow.   47. *Dolicholus.*
Style bearded along the inner side ; rachis thickened at the insertion of the flowers.
  Keel of the corolla spirally coiled ; flowers racemed.   48. *Phaseolus.*
  Keel of the corolla strongly incurved ; flowers purple, capitate.   49. *Strophostyles.*
  Keel of the corolla short, slightly incurved ; flowers capitate.   50. *Vigna.*

1. **SOPHÒRA** L. Sp. Pl. 373. 1753.

Shrubs, perennial herbs, or in tropical regions trees, with odd-pinnate leaves and white
yellow or violet flowers in terminal racemes or panicles. Calyx generally campanulate, its
teeth short. Standard obovate or orbicular, erect or spreading ; wings obliquely oblong ; keel
oblong, nearly straight. Stamens all distinct or very nearly so ; anthers versatile, all alike ;

style incurved. Ovary short-stalked ; ovules ∞. Pod
stalked in the calyx, coriaceous or fleshy, terete, constricted between the subglobose seeds, mainly indehiscent. [Arabic, yellow.]

About 25 species, natives of warm and tropical regions.
Besides the following, about 5 others occur in the southern States. Type species : *Sophora alopecuroides* L.

1. Sophora serícea Nutt. Silky Sophora.
Fig. 2449.

Sophora sericea Nutt. Gen. 1 : 280. 1818.

Herbaceous, woody at the base, erect or ascending,
branched, silky or silvery pubescent with appressed
hairs, 6′–12′ high. Stipules subulate, deciduous ; leaves
short-petioled ; leaflets 7–25, short-stalked, obovate
or elliptic, obtuse or emarginate at the apex, narrowed
or cuneate at the base, 3″–6″ long ; raceme peduncled,
rather loosely flowered, 2′–4′ long ; flowers white,
about 8″ long, nearly sessile ; pod dry, coriaceous,
1′–2′ long, about 2″ thick, pubescent, few-seeded.

Plains and prairies, South Dakota, Nebraska and
Wyoming to Texas, Arizona and Mexico. April–June.

$\frac{3}{5}$

2. CLADRÁSTIS Raf. Neogenyton 1. 1825.

Trees, with odd-pinnate leaves, no stipules nor stipels, the petiole-base hollow. Flowers showy, white, in terminal panicles. Calyx-teeth 5, short, broad. Standard orbicular-obovate, reflexed; wing oblong; keel incurved, obtuse, its petals distinct. Stamens 10, all distinct; filaments slender; anthers all alike, versatile. Ovary sessile or nearly so; ovules few; style incurved. Pod linear or lanceolate, short-stalked, flat, at length 2-valved, few-seeded. [Greek, brittle-branch.]

A monotypic genus of the southeastern United States, related to the Manchurian *Maackia*.

1. Cladrastis lùtea (Michx. f.) Koch.
American or Kentucky Yellow-wood.
Fig. 2450.

Virgilia lutea Michx. f. Arb. Am. **3**: 266. *pl. 3.* 1813.
Cladrastis fragrans Raf. Cat. Bot. Gard. Trans. 12.
Name only. 1824.
Cladrastis tinctoria Raf. Neogenyton 1. 1825.
Cladrastis lutea Koch, Dendrol. **1** : 6. 1869.

A smooth-barked tree, with maximum height of about 50° and trunk diameter of about $3\frac{1}{2}$°. Foliage nearly glabrous; leaves petioled; leaflets 5-11, ovate, oval or obovate, stalked, 2'-4' long, pointed or blunt-acuminate at the apex, obtuse or the terminal one cuneate at the base; panicles many-flowered, drooping, 10'-20' long; pedicels slender, 5"-9" long; calyx tubular-campanulate; corolla white, about 1' long; pod short-stalked, glabrous, 2'-4' long, 4"-5" wide, 2-6-seeded.

In rich soil, Missouri, Kentucky, Tennessee and western North Carolina. Wood yellow, hard, strong, yielding a yellow dye; weight per cubic foot 39 lbs. Flowers fragrant. June. Yellow-ash or -locust. Gopherwood. Fustic-tree.

3. THERMÓPSIS R. Br. in Ait. Hort. Kew. Ed. 2, 3 : 3. 1811.

Perennial branching herbs, with sheathing scales at the base, alternate 3-foliolate leaves, and large yellow or purple flowers in terminal or axillary racemes. Stipules usually large and foliaceous. Calyx campanulate or short-turbinate, its lobes equal and separate, or the two upper ones united. Standard nearly orbicular, equalling the oblong wings and about equalling the keel. Stamens 10, incurved, separate. Ovary sessile or short-stipitate; ovules ∞; style slightly incurved; stigma terminal, small. Pod sessile or short-stalked, flat (in our species), linear or oblong, straight or curved. [Greek, Lupine-like.]

About 20 species, natives of North America and northern and eastern Asia. Besides the following, some 10 others occur in the southern Alleghanies and in the western part of the continent. Type species : *Thermopsis lanceolata* (Willd.) R. Br.

Leaflets 1'-3' long; panicle elongated, usually long-peduncled; eastern.   1. *T. mollis.*
Leaflets ½'-1½' long; panicle short, short-peduncled; western.   2. *T. rhombifolia.*

1. Thermopsis móllis (Michx.) M. A. Curtis.
Alleghany Thermopsis. Fig. 2451.

Podalyria mollis Michx. Fl. Bor. Am. **1** : 264. 1803.

Baptisia mollis DC. Prodr. **2** : 100. 1825.

Thermopsis mollis M. A. Curtis; A. Gray, Chlor. Bor. Am. 47. *pl. 9.* 1846.

Erect, somewhat divaricately branched, 2°-3° high, finely appressed-pubescent. Leaves petioled, 3-foliolate; leaflets oval, rhombic-elliptic or obovate, entire, 1'-3' long, 9"-15" wide, obtuse or acute, nearly sessile; stipules ovate or lanceolate, shorter than the petiole; racemes 6'-10' long, mainly terminal; pedicels 2"-6" long, bracted at the base; flowers yellow, about 9" long; pod short-stalked in the calyx, linear, slightly curved, 2'-4' long.

Southwestern Virginia, eastern Tennessee, North Carolina and Georgia, in the mountains. Bush-pea. July-Aug.

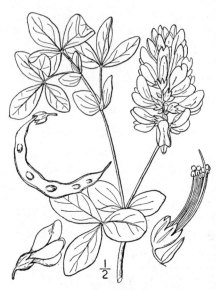

2. Thermopsis rhombifòlia (Nutt.) Richards. Prairie Thermopsis or False Lupine. Fig. 2452.

Cytisus rhombifolius Nutt. Fraser's Cat. 1813.

Thermia rhombifolia Nutt. Gen. 1: 282. 1818.

Thermopsis rhombifolia Richards, Frank. Journ. App. 13. 1823.

Erect, 8'-20' high, branched, appressed silky-pubescent. Leaves petioled; leaflets oval or obovate or rhombic-elliptic, obtuse, entire, $\frac{1}{2}$-$1\frac{1}{2}$' long, 3"-6" wide, sessile; stipules broad; racemes terminal or lateral, rather dense, few-flowered, 2'-5' long; pedicels 2"-4" long, bracted; flowers yellow, about 10" long; pod linear, generally strongly recurved-spreading, several-seeded, stalked in the calyx, 3'-4' long.

In sandy soil, on plains and hills, North Dakota to Nebraska, Kansas, Saskatchewan, Montana and Colorado. Yellow or bush-pea. June–July.

4. BAPTÍSIA Vent. Dec. Gen. Nov. 9. 1808.

Perennial erect branching herbs, with sheathing basal scales, alternate 3-foliolate or sometimes simple perfoliate leaves and showy yellow white or blue flowers in terminal or lateral racemes. Stipules foliaceous, or small, or none. Calyx campanulate, obtuse at base, or sometimes slightly turbinate, the teeth equal and separate, or the two upper ones united. Corolla and stamens as in *Thermopsis*. Ovary stipitate. Pod stalked, ovoid, oblong or nearly globose, pointed, inflated, the valves often coriaceous. [Greek, dyeing.]

About 24 species, natives of eastern and southern North America. Type species: *Sophora alba* L.

Flowers blue ; plant glabrous.
Flowers yellow.
  Racemes numerous, terminal ; plant glabrous.
  Racemes few, lateral ; plant more or less pubescent.
Flowers white or cream color.
  Very pubescent.
  Glabrous or nearly so.
    Leaflets oblong or lanceolate, green in drying.
    Leaflets obovate-cuneate, black in drying.

1. *B. australis.*
2. *B. tinctoria.*
3. *B. villosa.*
4. *B. bracteata.*
5. *B. alba.*
6. *B. leucantha.*

1. Baptisia austràlis (L.) R. Br. Blue Wild or Blue False Indigo. Fig. 2453.

Sophora australis L. Syst. Nat. Ed. 12, 2: 287. 1767.
B. australis R. Br. in Ait. Hort. Kew. Ed. 2, 3: 6. 1811.

Glabrous, stout, 4°-6° high. Leaves short-petioled, 3-foliolate; leaflets oblanceolate or sometimes oval, obtuse at the apex, cuneate at the base, entire, 1'-2$\frac{1}{2}$' long, sessile or nearly so; stipules lanceolate, equalling the petioles, or longer, persistent; racemes terminal, erect, loosely flowered, elongated (sometimes 10' long); bracts narrow, caducous; pedicels 2"-3" long; flowers indigo-blue, 9"-12" long; pod oblong, stout-stalked in the calyx, 1'-1$\frac{1}{2}$' long, 5"-6" thick, tipped with the subulate style.

In rich soil, District of Columbia to western Pennsylvania, Missouri, Kansas, Georgia and Texas. Naturalized in the Connecticut River Valley, in Vermont, escaped from cultivation. June–Aug. Rattle-bush.

A hybrid of this species with *B. bracteata* has been observed by Prof. A. S. Hitchcock in Kansas.

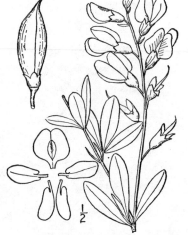

2. Baptisia tinctòria (L.) R. Br. Wild Indigo. Yellow, Indigo or Clover Broom. Horsefly-weed. Fig. 2454.

Sophora tinctoria L. Sp. Pl. 373. 1753.
B. tinctoria R. Br. in Ait. Hort. Kew. Ed. 2, 3: 6. 1811.

Glabrous, erect, succulent, much branched, 2°–4° high. Leaves petioled, 3-foliolate; leaflets obovate or oblanceolate, ½–1½′ long, sessile or nearly so, obtuse, cuneate at the base, entire, turning black in drying; stipules minute, caducous; racemes numerous, few-flowered, terminal; bracts minute, deciduous; pedicels 1″–2″ long; flowers bright yellow, about ½′ long; pods ovoid or nearly globose, 3″–5″ long, tipped with the subulate style.

In dry soil, Maine to Vermont, Ontario, Minnesota, Florida and Louisiana. June–Sept. Indigoweed. Shoofly. Rattle-bush. Horse-fleaweed.

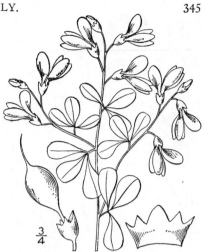

3/4

3. Baptisia villòsa (Walt.) Nutt. Hairy Wild Indigo. Fig. 2455.

Sophora villosa Walt. Fl. Car. 134. 1788.

Baptisia villosa Nutt. Gen. 1: 281. 1818.

Erect, branched, 2°–4° high, more or less pubescent throughout, especially when young. Leaves very short-petioled or sessile, 3-foliolate, turning dark in drying; leaflets oblong, oval, or obovate, obtusish at the apex, narrowed or cuneate at the base, 2′–4′ long, entire; stipules lanceolate or subulate, much longer than the petioles, persistent or the upper deciduous; racemes lateral, sometimes 10′ long, loosely many-flowered; pedicels 3″–4″ long; flowers yellow, about 1′ long; bracts caducous or deciduous; pods oblong-ovoid, about 1½′ long, finely appressed-pubescent, long-stalked in the calyx, tipped with the subulate style.

In dry soil, Virginia and North Carolina to Florida, west to Arkansas. June–July.

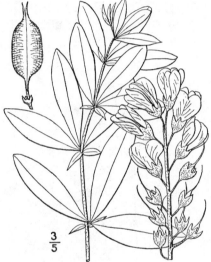

3/5

4. Baptisia bracteàta Ell. Large-bracted Wild Indigo. Fig. 2456.

Podalyria bracteata Muhl. Cat. 42. Without description. 1813.
B. bracteata Ell. Bot. S. C. & Ga. 1: 469. 1817.
Baptisia leucophaea Nutt. Gen. 1: 382. 1818.

Erect or ascending, low, bushy-branched, villous-pubescent throughout. Leaves sessile or short-petioled, 3-foliolate, dark green or brownish in drying; leaflets oblanceolate or spatulate, narrowed or cuneate at the base, obtuse or acutish at the apex, 1½′–3′ long, 4″–8″ wide, thick, reticulate-veined; stipules lanceolate, or ovate, persistent; racemes usually few, mainly lateral, sometimes 1° long, reclining, many-flowered; flowers white or cream-color, about 1′ long, very showy; pedicels slender, 6″–15″ long, spreading, somewhat secund; bracts large and persistent; pods ovoid, mostly narrowed at the base, 1′–2′ long, pubescent, tipped with a long at length deciduous style.

Prairies, Illinois, Michigan and Minnesota to South Carolina, Georgia, Louisiana and Texas. April–May. Yellowish false-indigo.

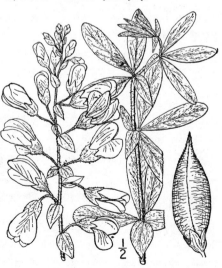

1/2

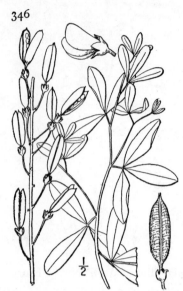

½

5. Baptisia álba (L.) R. Br. White Wild Indigo. Fig. 2457.

Crotalaria alba L. Sp. Pl. 716. 1753.

Baptisia alba R. Br. in Ait. Hort. Kew. Ed. 2, 3 : 6. 1811.

Glabrous throughout, divergently branching, 1°–3° high. Leaves petioled, 3-foliolate; petioles slender, 3″–9″ long; leaflets oblong or oblanceolate, narrowed at the base, obtuse at the apex, 1′–1½′ long, 4″–6″ wide, rather thin, green in drying; stipules and bracts minute, subulate, early deciduous; racemes elongated, erect, 6′–10′ long, lateral, long-peduncled; pedicels 3″–8″ long; flowers white, 6″–7″ long; pod linear-oblong, about 1½′ long, 4″ thick, short-stalked in the calyx, abruptly tipped with an almost filiform deciduous style.

In dry soil, North Carolina to Florida. Recorded from Missouri and southern Indiana, but we have seen no specimens collected west or north of the South Atlantic States. Erroneously recorded from Minnesota and Ontario. May–June. Prairie-indigo.

6. Baptisia leucántha T. & G. Large White Wild Indigo. Fig. 2458.

Baptisia leucantha T. & G. Fl. N. A. 1 : 385. 1840.

Glabrous throughout, succulent, branching, 2°–4° high, the branches stout, ascending. Leaves petioled, 3-foliolate, blackening in drying; leaflets obovate or oblanceolate, 1′–2′ long, 6″–12″ wide, very obtuse, rounded and sometimes slightly emarginate at the apex, narrowed or cuneate at the base; stipules lanceolate or linear, equalling or shorter than the petioles, deciduous; racemes lateral, sometimes 1° long, loosely flowered; flowers white, 9″–10″ long; pedicels 2″–3″ long; pod ellipsoid, long-stalked in the calyx, about 9″ long, tipped with the subulate style.

In rich soil, Ontario to Minnesota, south to Kentucky, North Carolina, Florida, Kansas, Arkansas and Texas. June–July. White false-indigo.

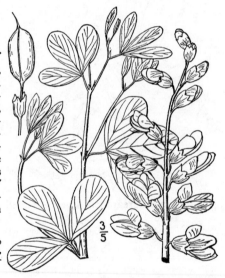

⅗

5. CROTALÀRIA L. Sp. Pl. 714. 1753.

Herbs, sometimes slightly woody, with simple (or in some tropical species 3–7-foliolate) leaves, and racemose flowers. Calyx 5-toothed, slightly 2-lipped. Standard orbicular or ovate, often cordate; wings oblong or obovate; keel curved. Stamens monadelphous, their sheath deeply cleft; anthers of 2 forms, alternating with each other, the one small, versatile, the other larger. Ovary sessile or short-stalked; style more or less curved. Pod oblong or globose, inflated, coriaceous or membranous, many-seeded, the seeds loose at maturity. [Greek, a rattle.]

About 250 species, mainly natives of tropical regions. Besides the following, some 7 others occur in the southern and southwestern United States. Type species: *Crotalaria lotifolia* L.

Stem and branches erect or ascending; leaves, at least the upper, lanceolate or oblong.
            1. *C. sagittalis.*
Stems prostrate, from a deep root; leaves broadly oblong or oval.
            2. *C. rotundifolia.*

$\frac{2}{3}$

1. Crotalaria sagittàlis L.   Rattle-box.
Fig. 2459.

Crotalaria sagittalis L. Sp. Pl. 714. 1753.

Annual, erect or decumbent, villous-pubescent, branching, rarely over 1° high. Leaves simple, oval, lanceolate or oblong, acute or obtusish at the apex, rounded at the base, entire, nearly sessile, 1'–2½' long, 2''–8'' wide; stipules persistent and united, decurrent on the stem, sagittate above, or the lower wanting; peduncles 1'–4' long, 2–4-flowered; pedicels 1''–3'' long; flowers yellow, 4''–6'' long, the corolla about equalling the calyx; pod oblong, glabrous, nearly sessile in the calyx, 1' long, 4''–5'' in thickness, much inflated, nearly black at maturity; seeds shining.

In dry open places, Vermont to Florida, Minnesota, South Dakota, Arkansas and Mexico. Also in Jamaica. June–Sept. Wild pea. Loco-weed.

2. Crotalaria rotundifòlia (Walt.) Poir.

Anonymos rotundifolia Walt. Fl. Car. 181. 1788.
Crotalaria sagittalis var. *ovalis* Michx. Fl. Bor.
Am. 2: 55. 1803.
Crotalaria rotundifolia Poir. in Lam. Encycl.
Suppl. 2: 402. 1811.
Crotalaria ovalis Pursh, Fl. Am. Sept. 469. 1814.

Perennial by a deep somewhat woody root, the slender branches usually prostrate. Pubescence mostly dense, brownish, spreading or ascending; leaves broadly oblong or oval, obtuse at both ends, or narrowed at the base, paler beneath than above, ½'–1½' long; petioles 1''–2'' long; upper stipules usually distinctly sagittate, the lower much smaller, or often wanting; peduncles lateral, 2'–6' long, slender, 2–6-flowered; flowers usually distant, yellow, 6''–8'' long; corolla little longer than the calyx; pod nearly as in the preceding species.

Mostly in dry soil, southern Virginia to Florida, Missouri and Louisiana. May–Aug.

Crotalaria Púrshii DC., of the southern United States, another perennial deep-rooted species, but with leaves linear to oblong, stems erect or ascending, and merely puberulent, is recorded as entering our area in southern Virginia.

Prostrate Rattle-box.   Fig. 2460.

$\frac{2}{3}$

6. LUPÌNUS [Tourn.] L. Sp. Pl. 721. 1753.

Herbs, rarely shrubs, with alternate digitately-compound 7–15-foliolate (rarely simple or 3–5-foliolate) leaves, and showy flowers in terminal spikes or racemes. Calyx deeply toothed and 2-lipped. Standard orbicular or ovate, its margins reflexed; wings oblong or obovate; keel incurved, sometimes beaked. Stamens monadelphous, their sheath not cleft; anthers of two forms as in *Crotalaria*. Ovary sessile; style incurved. Pod flattened, generally constricted between the seeds, the valves coriaceous.   [Latin name of some pulse, from *lupus*, wolf.]

Over 100 species, mainly natives of temperate and warm regions. About 70 occur in North America, mainly on the western side of the continent. Type species: *Lupinus albus* L.

Perennial; flowers 7''–9'' long; leaflets oblanceolate.
  Corolla blue, pink or white, the standard not spotted.   1. *L. perennis.*
  Corolla blue, with a conspicuous dark spot on the standard.   2. *L. plattensis.*
Perennial; flowers 4''–6'' long; leaflets oblong-linear.   3. *L. decumbens.*
Annual; leaflets mainly oblong; pod 2-seeded.   4. *L. pusillus.*

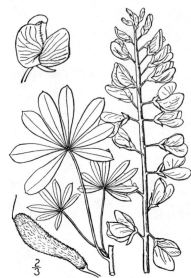

$\frac{2}{3}$

1. Lupinus perénnis L. Wild or Perennial Lupine. Wild Pea. Fig. 2461.

Lupinus perennis L. Sp. Pl. 721. 1753.
Lupinus perennis occidentalis S. Wats. Proc. Am. Acad. 8 : 530. 1873.

Perennial, erect, more or less pubescent, sometimes villous, branched, 1°–2° high. Leaves slender-petioled, 2′–3′ broad, leaflets 7–11 (commonly about 8), oblanceolate, sessile or nearly so, obtuse and mucronate at the apex, 1′–1½′ long, 3″–6″ wide, appressed-pubescent or glabrate; raceme terminal, peduncled, 6′–10′ long, rather loosely flowered; pedicels 3″–6″ long; flowers blue, sometimes pink, or white, 6″–8″ long; pod linear-oblong, very pubescent, 1½′ long, 4″ wide, usually 4-6-seeded, the valves coiling at dehiscence; style subulate.

In dry, sandy soil, Maine and Ontario to Minnesota, Florida, Missouri and Louisiana. Old maid's- or Quaker-bonnets. Sun-dial. May–June.

2. Lupinus platténsis S. Wats. Nebraska Lupine. Fig. 2462.

Lupinus ornatus var. *glabratus* S. Wats. Proc. Am. Acad. 8 : 528. 1873. Not *L. glabratus* Agardh. 1835.
Lupinus plattensis S. Wats. Proc. Am. Acad. 17 : 369. 1882.

Resembling the preceding species, perennial, 1°–1½° high, branching, villous or appressed-pubescent, the living plant with a glaucous appearance; leaflets 7–10, oblanceolate, spatulate or narrowly oval, 1′–1½′ long, 3″–5″ wide; raceme terminal, 4′–8′ long, loosely flowered; pedicels 3″–5″ long; corolla blue, 6″–8″ long, the standard with a conspicuous dark spot.

Plains, Nebraska, Wyoming, Colorado. Recorded from Dakota. June–July.

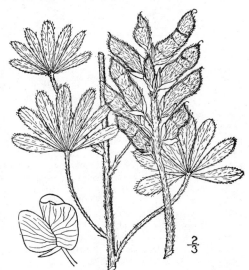

$\frac{2}{3}$

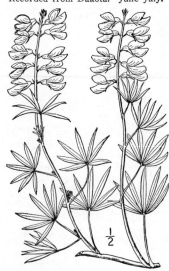

$\frac{1}{2}$

3. Lupinus decúmbens Torr. Silvery Lupine. Fig. 2463.

Lupinus decumbens Torr. Ann. Lyc. N. Y. 2 : 191. 1826.

Perennial, rather shrubby, bushy-branched, 1°–2° high, finely and densely silky-pubescent with appressed hairs, the leaves becoming glabrous on the upper side. Petioles slender, equalling or the lower exceeding the leaves; stipules minute, subulate; leaflets sessile, linear-oblong, acute or obtusish at the apex, narrowed at the base, 9″–18″ long, 2″–4″ wide; racemes terminal, rather dense, 2′–8′ long; pedicels 2″–3″ long; flowers purple, 4″–6″ long; pod silky-pubescent, about 1′ long, mostly 3-5-seeded.

Prairies, western Nebraska and South Dakota to Montana, Oregon and California. In our first edition included in *L. argenteus* Pursh, which ranges from Montana to Colorado. July–Aug.

Lupinus argophyllus (A. Gray) Cockerell, of Colorado and New Mexico, differing in having leaves permanently pubescent above, is recorded from Nebraska.

4. Lupinus pusíllus Pursh. Low Lupine.
Fig. 2464.

Lupinus pusillus Pursh, Fl. Am. Sept. 468. 1814.

Annual (always?), villous-pubescent, 4'–8' high, from a deep root, much branched near the base. Leaves petioled, 1'–2' wide; leaflets 5–7 (commonly 5), oblong or oblanceolate, narrowed at the base, obtuse or acute at the apex, glabrous or nearly so on the upper surface, pubescent with long scattered hairs beneath, 3"–4" wide; racemes numerous, short-peduncled or sessile, 1'–3' long, densely few-flowered; pedicels 1"–2" long; flowers blue, 3"–4" long; pod oblong, very pubescent, 6"–8" long, 2"–3" broad, about 2-seeded; style subulate.

Dry plains, South Dakota to Nebraska, Kansas, Montana, Oregon, Washington, Nevada and New Mexico. March–July.

7. ÙLEX L. Sp. Pl. 741. 1753.

Shrubs, with stiff spine-like branches, simple, linear stiff very prickly leaves, and large yellow solitary or racemed flowers. Calyx membranous, mostly yellow, divided nearly to its base into 2 concave lips; upper lip mostly 2-toothed, and lower 3-toothed; teeth short. Standard ovate; wings and keel oblong, obtuse. Stamens monadelphous; anthers alternately longer and shorter, the shorter versatile. Ovary sessile, several–many-ovuled; style somewhat incurved, smooth. Pod ovoid, oblong or linear. Seeds strophiolate. [The ancient Latin name.]

About 20 species, natives of eastern Europe, the following typical.

1. Ulex europaèus L. Furze. Gorse. Whin. Prickly or Thorn Broom. Fig. 2465.

Ulex europaeus L. Sp. Pl. 741. 1753.

Much branched, bushy, 2°–6° high, more or less pubescent. Branchlets very leafy, tipped with spines; leaves prickly, 2"–7" long, or the lowest sometimes lanceolate and foliaceous; flowers borne on twigs of the preceding season, solitary in the axils, 6"–8" long, the twigs appearing like racemes; pedicels very short, bracted at the base; calyx a little shorter than the petals, minutely 2-bracteolate; pod few-seeded, compressed, scarcely longer than the calyx.

In waste places, eastern Massachusetts to southern New York and eastern Virginia, escaped from cultivation. Also on Vancouver Island. Fugitive from Europe. Ulim. May–July.

8. GENÍSTA [Tourn.] L. Sp. Pl. 709. 1753.

Low branching sometimes thorny shrubs, mainly with 1-foliolate leaves, and showy clustered yellow flowers. Calyx 2-lipped; teeth long. Standard oval or ovate; wings oblong; keel oblong, deflexed, the claws of its petals adnate to the uncleft sheath of the monadelphous stamens; anthers alternately long and short. Ovary sessile, several-ovuled; style incurved at the apex. Pod various, flat in our species, several-seeded. Seeds not strophiolate. [Celtic, gen, a small bush.]

About 80 species, natives of Europe, northern Africa and western Asia, the following typical.

1. Genista tinctòria L.   Dyeweed or Greenweed.
Woad-waxen.   Base Broom.   Fig. 2466.

Genista tinctoria L. Sp. Pl. 710. 1753.

Branching from the base, not thorny, the sterile shoots decumbent, the flowering ones erect, stiff, 1°–2° high, branched
above, slightly pubescent. Leaves 1-foliolate, sessile, lanceolate or elliptic-lanceolate, ½'–1½' long, glabrous or with scattered hairs, acute at the apex, narrowed at the base, entire,
shining; stipules none; racemes numerous, terminal, 1'–2' long,
few-flowered; bracts ovate-lanceolate, acute; flowers yellow,
nearly sessile, about 6" long; calyx bracteolate at the base, its
3 lower teeth narrower than the 2 upper; pod about 1' long,
flat, glabrous.

On dry hills, Maine and Massachusetts to eastern New York.
Naturalized from Europe. Native also of northern Asia. Summer. Known also as wood-wax, green-wood, dyer's-broom, dyer's
green-weed, dyer's-whin and alleluia.

9. CÝTISUS [Tourn.] L. Sp. Pl. 739. 1753.

Shrubs, often stiff or spiny, with 3-foliolate or 1-foliolate leaves, and showy clustered
flowers, mainly in terminal racemes. Calyx 2-lipped, campanulate, the teeth short; standard
ovate or orbicular; wings oblong or obovate; keel straight or curved. Stamens monadelphous;
anthers alternately larger and smaller. Ovary sessile, many-ovuled; style incurved. Pod flat,
oblong or linear, pubescent or glabrous, several-seeded; seeds strophiolate. [From Cythrus,
one of the Cyclades, where the first species was found.]

About 45 species, natives of Europe, western Asia and northern Africa, the flowers very slightly
different from those of *Genista*. Type species: *Cytisus hirsùtus* L.

1. Cytisus scopàrius (L.) Link.   Broom.   Green or
Scotch Broom.   Hagweed.   Fig. 2467.

Spartium scoparium L. Sp. Pl. 709. 1753.

Cytisus scoparius Link, Enum. Hort. Berol. **2**: 241. 1822.

Sarothamnus scoparius Wimm.; Koch, Syn. Fl. Germ. 152. 1837.

Stiff, wiry, 3°–5° high, much branched, nearly glabrous.
Branches elongated, straight, nearly erect, angled; lower leaves
petioled, 3-foliolate, the leaflets obovate, acute, or mucronate-
tipped, 3"–5" long, entire, narrowed at the base; upper leaves
sessile, often 1-foliolate; stipules none; flowers bright yellow,
nearly 1' long, in elongated terminal leafy racemes; pedicels
solitary or 2–3 together, 3"–5" long; pod flat, glabrous on the
sides, but ciliate on the margins, 1'–2' long; style slender, at
length spirally curved.

In waste places, Nova Scotia to Massachusetts, Delaware and
Virginia. Also in California and on Vancouver Island. Adventive or naturalized from Europe. Bannal. Besom. Summer.

10. MEDICÀGO [Tourn.] L. Sp. Pl. 778. 1753.

Herbs (a single shrubby species in southern Europe), with small 3-foliolate leaves, and
small yellow or violet flowers in axillary heads or racemes. Leaflets commonly dentate, pinnately veined, the veins terminating in the teeth. Calyx-teeth short, nearly equal; standard
obovate or oblong; wings oblong; keel obtuse. Stamens diadelphous, the 1 opposite the
standard separate from the other 9; anthers all alike. Ovary sessile or nearly so, 1–several-
ovuled; style subulate. Pod curved or spirally twisted, reticulated or spiny, indehiscent, 1–few-
seeded. [Greek, Medike, from Medea, whence the Medic, or Lucerne, was derived.]

About 50 species, natives of Europe, Asia and Africa. Type species: *Medicago sativa* L.

Perennial; flowers violet, conspicuous.   1. *M. sativa.*
Annual; flowers bright yellow, small.
   Pod 1-seeded, curved, not spiny.   2. *M. lupulina.*
   Pod several-seeded, spiny on the edges, spirally twisted.
      Pod loosely coiled, not furrowed on the edge.   3. *M. hispida.*
      Pod densely coiled, its edge furrowed.   4. *M. arabica.*

1. Medicago satìva L. Purple Medic. Alfalfa. Lucerne. Burgundy, Chilian or Brazilian Clover. Snail Clover. Fig. 2468.

Medicago sativa L. Sp. Pl. 778. 1753.

Perennial, much branched, decumbent or ascending, $1°-1\frac{1}{2}°$ high, the young shoots and leaves with some scattered hairs, glabrous when mature. Leaves petioled; leaflets oblanceolate or obovate, $2''-12''$ long, dentate, especially toward the apex, obtuse, truncate or emarginate and often mucronate, narrowed or cuneate at the base; stipules entire; peduncles $\frac{1}{2}'-2'$ long, bearing a dense short raceme of violet or blue flowers; petals about $3''$ long; pod pubescent, twisted into 2 or 3 spires.

In fields and waste places, New England and Ontario to Minnesota, south to Virginia and Kansas. Much cultivated for fodder in the southern and western States. Introduced from Europe. Great or spanish trefoil. Holy-hay. Sainfoin. Summer.

Medicago falcàta L., similar to this, but with yellow flowers and nearly flat, scarcely coiled pods, is occasionally found in waste places. Native of Europe.

2. Medicago lupulìna L. Black or Hop Medic. Blackseed. Hop Clover. Nonesuch. Fig. 2469.

Medicago lupulina L. Sp. Pl. 779. 1753.

Annual, pubescent, branched at the base, the branches decumbent and spreading, often $1°-2°$ long; leaves petioled; leaflets obovate, oval or nearly orbicular, variable in size, sometimes $6''-8''$ long, denticulate or crenulate, obtuse, mucronate or emarginate, narrowed or rounded at the base; stipules ovate or lanceolate, dentate; peduncles $1'-3'$ long; head oblong or cylindric, dense, $2''-10''$ long; flowers bright yellow, about $1''$ long; pods nearly glabrous, black when ripe, curved into a partial spire, strongly veined, 1-seeded.

In fields and waste places, common throughout our area, except the extreme north, and widely distributed as a weed in all temperate regions. Native of Europe and Asia. Black or melilot-trefoil. Black-grass. Black-nonesuch, natural grass, horned clover, shamrock, sainfoin. March–Dec.

3. Medicago híspida Gaertn. Toothed Medic. Bur Clover. Fig. 2470.

Medicago hispida Gaertn. Fr. & Sem. **2**: 349. 1791.
Medicago denticulata Willd. Sp. Pl. **3**: 1414. 1803.

Annual, branched at the base, the branches spreading or ascending, glabrous or with a few appressed hairs. Leaves petioled; leaflets obovate, rounded, emarginate or obcordate, cuneate, crenulate, $5''-8''$ long; stipules dentate; flowers few, yellow, $1''$ long, in small, peduncled heads; pod several seeded, spirally twisted, the 2 or 3 coils flat and rather loose, elegantly reticulated with elevated veins, the thin edge armed with 1 or 2 rows of curved prickles and not furrowed.

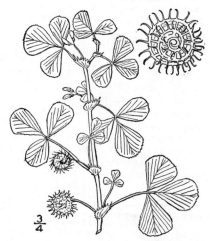

In waste places and in ballast about the seaports, Nova Scotia to Pennsylvania, Florida, Nebraska, Texas and also on the Pacific Coast. Bermuda. Fugitive or adventive from Europe. Native also of Asia and widely distributed as a weed. Summer.

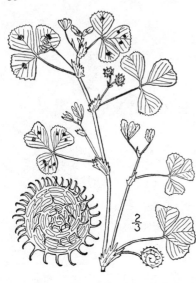

4. Medicago arábica (L.) Huds. Spotted Medic. Fig. 2471.

M. polymorpha arabica L. Sp. Pl. 780. 1753.

Medicago arabica Huds. Fl. Angl. 288. 1762.

Medicago maculata Sibth. Fl. Oxon. 232. 1794.

Annual, usually pubescent, with spreading hairs, closely resembling the preceding species, but generally stouter. Leaflets often nearly 1' long, and with a conspicuous dark spot or spots near the centre; pod nearly globose, of 3 or 4 compactly wound coils, reticulate-veined on the sides, the edge thicker and furrowed between the marginal rows of curved prickles.

In waste places and ballast, New Brunswick · to Pennsylvania and Georgia. Also on the Pacific Coast. Fugitive or adventive from Europe. Summer. Bur-, heart-, California or spotted-clover. Heart-trefoil. Heart-leaf. Purple grass.

11. MELILÒTUS [Tourn.] Mill. Gard. Dict. Abr. Ed. 4. 1754.

Annual or biennial herbs, with 3-foliolate petioled leaves, dentate leaflets, their veins commonly ending in the teeth, and small white or yellow flowers in slender racemes. Calyx-teeth short, nearly equal; standard obovate or oblong; wings oblong; keel obtuse. Stamens diadelphous; anthers all alike. Ovary sessile or stipitate, few-ovuled; style filiform. Pod ovoid or globose, straight, indehiscent or finally 2-valved. Seeds solitary or few. [Greek, Honey-lotus.]

About 20 species, natives of Europe, Africa and Asia. Type species: *Trifolium Melilotus officinalis* L.

Flowers white; standard a little longer than the wings.   1. *M. alba.*
Flowers yellow; standard about equalling the wings.   2. *M. officinalis.*

1. Melilotus álba Desv. White Melilot. White Sweet-clover. Honey. Fig. 2472.

Melilotus alba Desv. in Lam. Encycl. 4: 63. 1797.

M. vulgaris Willd. Enum. Hort. Berol. 790. 1809.

Erect or ascending, 3°–10° high, branching, glabrous, or the young twigs and leaves finely pubescent. Leaves petioled, rather distant; leaflets oblong or slightly ob-lanceolate, serrate, narrowed at the base, truncate, emarginate or rounded at the apex, 6''–10'' long, 2''–5'' wide; stipules subulate; racemes numerous, slender, 2'–4' long, often 1-sided; pedicels 1'' long or less; flowers white; standard 2''–2½'' long, slightly longer than the wings; pod ovoid, slightly reticulated, glabrous, 1½'' long.

In waste places, frequent throughout our area and in the Southern States. Adventive or naturalized from Europe, and native also of Asia. White millet. Honey-lotus. Cabul-, tree-, honey- or bokhara-clover. Leaves fragrant in drying, as in other species of the genus. June–Nov.

Melilotus altíssima Thuill, a European species with narrow, nearly entire leaflets, and pubescent pods, has been found on ballast at Atlantic ports.

2. Melilotus officinàlis (L.) Lam. Yellow Melilot. Yellow Sweet-clover. Yellow Millet. Fig. 2473.

Trifolium Melilotus officinalis L. Sp. Pl. 765. 1753.
Melilotus vulgaris Hill, Brit. Herb. 308. 1756.
Melilotus officinalis Lam. Fl. Fr. 2 : 594. 1778.

Resembling the preceding species, but the flowers are yellow. Standard about equalling the wings and keel; leaflets oblong, oblanceolate, or oval, serrate, the apex rounded, not truncate; pod about 2″ long, with irregularly reticulated veins, often slightly pubescent with appressed hairs.

In waste places, frequent throughout our area and in the southern States. Adventive or naturalized from Europe. Native also of Asia. Summer, blooming later than *M. alba*, where the two grow together in southern New York. Old English names, balsamflowers, hart's-clover, king's-clover, king's-crown, heartwort. Plaster-clover.

Melilotus índica (L.) All., introduced on ballast about the seaports, and an abundant weed in the Far West, may be readily distinguished from this by its much smaller yellow flowers and smaller pods.

Onònis rèpens L., an herb of the tribe TRIFOLIEAE, with axillary flowers, forming terminal leafy racemes, has been found as a waif in central New York. The genus is distinguished from others of the tribe by its monadelphous stamens.

12. TRIFÒLIUM [Tourn.] L. Sp. Pl. 764. 1753.

Herbs, with (in our species) mostly 3-foliolate, denticulate leaves, and purple pink red white or yellow flowers in dense heads or spikes. Stipules adnate to the petiole. Calyx-teeth nearly equal. Petals commonly persistent, their claws more or less completely adnate to the stamen-tube. Stamens diadelphous, or the tenth one separate for only a portion of its length. Ovary sessile or stipitate, few-ovuled. Pod oblong or terete, often included in the calyx, membranous, indehiscent or tardily dehiscent by 1 suture, or by a lid, 1-6-seeded. [Latin, referring to the 3 leaflets.]

About 275 species, most abundant in the north temperate zone, a few in South America and South Africa. Besides the following, about 60 others occur in the western part of the continent. Type species: *Trifolium pratense* L.

Flowers yellow. [Genus CHRYSASPIS Desv.]
  Head 6″-9″ long; leaflets all sessile.
  Head 4″-6″ long, nearly globose; stipules ovate; terminal leaflet stalked.   1. *T. agrarium.*
    Head 20–40-flowered; standard conspicuously striate.
    Head 10–12-flowered; standard scarcely striate.   2. *T. procumbens.*
      3. *T. dubium.*
Flowers red, purple, or white.
  Head or spike much longer than thick; calyx silky, its teeth plumose.
    Corolla crimson, equalling or exceeding the calyx-lobes.   4. *T. incarnatum.*
    Corolla whitish, shorter than the calyx-lobes.   5. *T. arvense.*
  Head globose, oval or ovoid.
    Flowers sessile, or very nearly so ; heads dense, ovoid, oval or globose.
      Heads mostly sessile, or nearly so ; calyx pubescent.   6. *T. pratense.*
      Heads always distinctly peduncled.
        Calyx-teeth pubescent.   7. *T. medium.*
        Plant glabrous throughout.   8. *T. Beckwithii.*
    Flowers pedicelled ; heads umbel-like, globose.
      Heads 1′ in diameter or more ; peduncles 1′–3′ long.
        Prostrate ; pubescent ; perennial.   9. *T. virginicum.*
        Ascending ; pubescent ; annual or biennial.   10. *T. reflexum.*
        Stoloniferous ; glabrous ; perennial.   11. *T. stoloniferum.*
      Heads 6″–9″ in diameter ; lower peduncles 2′–8′ long.
        Ascending or procumbent ; flowers pink, pinkish, or purple.
          Ascending ; calyx much shorter than the pink or nearly white corolla.
              12. *T. hybridum.*
        Procumbent ; tufted ; calyx nearly equalling the purple corolla. 13. *T. carolinianum.*
        Creeping ; flowers white or pinkish.   14. *T. repens.*

23

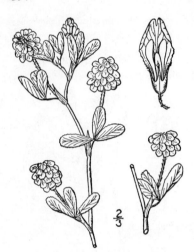

1. Trifolium agràrium L. Yellow or Hop-clover. Fig. 2474.

Trifolium agrarium L. Sp. Pl. 772. 1753.
?*T. aureum* Poll. Hist. Pl. Palat. **2**: 344. 1777.

Glabrous or slightly pubescent, annual, ascending, branched, 6'–18' high. Leaves petioled; stipules linear-lanceolate, acuminate, 4"–7" long, adnate to the petiole for about one-half its length; leaflets all from the same point, sessile, obovate or oblong, finely denticulate, narrowed at the base, rounded, truncate or emarginate at the apex, 6"–9" long; peduncles axillary, ½'–2' long; head oblong, or oval, 6"–9" long, densely many-flowered; flowers yellow, 2"–3" long, at length reflexed; pedicels shorter than the calyx; standard slightly emarginate, exceeding the pod, conspicuously striate, and brown, especially when dry.

Along roadsides and in waste places, Nova Scotia to South Carolina, west to Ontario, western New York and Iowa. Naturalized from Europe. May–Sept.

2. Trifolium procúmbens L. Low, or Smaller Hop-clover or Hop-trefoil. Fig. 2475.

Trifolium procumbens L. Sp. Pl. 772. 1753.

Similar to the preceding species, but lower, more spreading and more pubescent. Leaflets obovate, cuneate at the base, rounded, truncate or emarginate at the apex, finely denticulate, 4"–7" long, the lateral ones nearly sessile, the terminal distinctly stalked; stipules ovate, adnate to the lower part of the petiole, about 2" long; peduncles 3"–12" long; heads 20–40-flowered, globose or short-oval, 4"–6" in greatest diameter; flowers yellow, at length reflexed, about 2" long; standard dilated, not folded, exceeding the pod, striate and brown when dry.

In fields and along roadsides, Nova Scotia to Ontario, Washington, Georgia and Mississippi. Naturalized from Europe. May–Sept.

3. Trifolium dùbium Sibth. Least Hop-clover or Hop-trefoil. Fig. 2476.

Trifolium dubium Sibth. Fl. Oxon. 231. 1794.
Trifolium minus Smith, Engl. Bot. *pl. 1256.* 1799.
Trifolium procumbens var. *minus* Koch, Fl. Germ. & Helv. Ed. 2, 195. 1843.

Straggling or ascending, nearly glabrous, stems 2'–20' long, branching. Leaflets obovate, truncate or emarginate at the apex, or even obcordate, denticulate, cuneate at the base, the lateral ones nearly sessile, the terminal stalked; stipules ovate or lanceolate, adnate to the lower part of the petiole; peduncles 3"–12" long; heads nearly globose, 2"–3" in diameter, 3–20-flowered; flowers about 1½" long, turning brown, at length reflexed; standard exceeding and folded over the pod, scarcely striate.

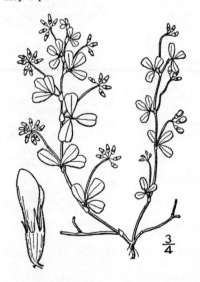

In fields and waste places, Massachusetts to New Jersey, Arkansas, Georgia and Mississippi. Also in Washington, Oregon and British Columbia. Jamaica. Naturalized from Europe. Summer. Said to be the true Shamrock. Called also yellow-suckling. Wild or yellow-trefoil.

4. Trifolium incarnàtum L.   Crimson, Carnation, French or Italian Clover. Fig. 2477.

Trifolium incarnatum L. Sp. Pl. 769. 1753·

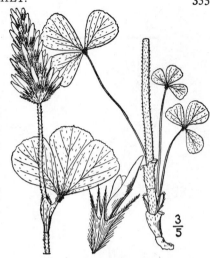

Annual, erect, softly pubescent, little branched, 6'–3° high. Leaves long-petioled; stipules broad, membranous, dentate, 4"–12" wide; leaflets all from the same point, very nearly sessile, obovate or obcordate, narrowed or cuneate at the base, denticulate, 6"–12" long; heads terminal, oblong or ovoid, 1'–2½' long; flowers sessile, 4"–6" long; calyx hairy; corolla crimson, equalling or exceeding the subulate plumose calyx-lobes.

In fields, waste places and ballast, Maine to New York, New Jersey and Virginia. Cultivated for fodder and for nitrogenizing the soil. Introduced from Europe. Called also Napoleons. Summer.

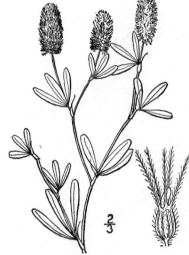

5. Trifolium arvénse L.   Rabbit-foot, Old-field or Stone Clover. Fig. 2478.

Trifolium arvense L. Sp. Pl. 769. 1753·

Annual, erect, freely branching, silky-pubescent, 6'–18' high. Leaves short-petioled; stipules narrow, 3"–5" long, subulate-tipped, entire or nearly so; leaflets all from the same point, linear or oblanceolate, denticulate above, obtuse and often emarginate, narrowed or cuneate at the base, 6"–12" long; heads terminal, peduncled, oblong or cylindric, 6"–12" long, very dense; flowers sessile; calyx very silky; corolla whitish, shorter than the subulate plumose calyx-lobes.

In fields and waste places, Quebec and Ontario to South Carolina, Florida, Tennessee and Missouri. Naturalized from Europe. Native also of northern Asia. Hare's-foot or pussy-clover. Calf-clover. Poverty-grass. Bottle-grass. Dogs and cats. Pussies. Pussy-cats. May–Sept.

6. Trifolium praténse L.   Red, Purple or Meadow Clover. Fig. 2479.

Trifolium pratense L. Sp. Pl. 768. 1753·

Perennial, more or less pubescent, branching, decumbent or erect, 6'–2° high. Leaves long-petioled; stipules ovate, strongly veined, subulate-tipped, 6"–10" long; leaflets short-stalked, all from the same point, oval, oblong, or obovate, narrowed at base, hardly cuneate, obtuse and sometimes emarginate at the apex, often dark-spotted near the middle, finely denticulate, ½'–2' long; heads globose or somewhat ovoid, sessile (rarely peduncled), about 1' long; flowers red (rarely white), sessile, about 6" long, remaining erect in fruit; calyx hairy, its subulate teeth shorter than the corolla.

In fields and meadows, common throughout our area and in the southern States. Bermuda. Naturalized from Europe and widely cultivated for fodder. Native also of northern Asia. Leaflets commonly 3, sometimes 4–11. Marl- or cow-grass. Broad-leaved clover. Sugar-plums. Honeysuckle-clover, knap, suckles. April–Nov.

$\frac{2}{3}$

7. Trifolium mèdium L. Zig-zag or Mammoth Clover. Cow- or Marl-grass. Fig. 2480.

T. medium L. Amoen. Acad. 4: 105. 1759.

Closely resembling the preceding species. Stem sometimes conspicuously zigzag, but often straight, finely pubescent or glabrate. Stipules lanceolate; leaflets lanceolate or oblong, not spotted, frequently entire except for the projecting tips of the veins; heads always more or less peduncled; flowers very nearly sessile; corolla 6″–7″ long, bright purple; calyx-tube nearly glabrous, the teeth slightly pubescent.

In fields and waste places, Nova Scotia, Ontario and Massachusetts. Erroneously recorded from Missouri and elsewhere. Adventive or naturalized from Europe. Native also of Siberia. Cow- or giant-clover. Pea-vine clover. Summer.

8. Trifolium Beckwíthii Brewer. Beckwith's Clover. Fig. 2481.

Trifolium Beckwithii Brewer; S. Wats. Proc. Am. Acad. 11 : 128. 1876.

Perennial, glabrous throughout; stems rather stout, erect or nearly so, straight, 6′–18′ high. Basal leaves on long petioles; stipules narrow, acute, 1′ long or less; leaflets oblong, or somewhat oblanceolate, obtuse, denticulate, 9″–2′ long; heads long-peduncled, globose, 1′–1½′ thick; flowers purple or purplish, 6″–9″ long, very short-pedicelled, the lower at length reflexed; calyx-teeth glabrous, linear-subulate, the longer nearly equalling the tube; pod 2–6-seeded.

Eastern South Dakota, probably introduced from farther west. Native from Montana to California. May–June.

$\frac{3}{5}$

9. Trifolium virgínicum Small. Prostrate Mountain Clover. Fig. 2482.

Trifolium virginicum Small, Mem. Torr. Club 4: 112. 1894.

Perennial from a long large root, diffusely branched at the base, the branches prostrate, pubescent. Leaflets linear, narrowly lanceolate or oblanceolate, 5″–20″ long, obtuse or cuspidate, serrate-dentate, glabrous above, more or less silky beneath, conspicuously veined; flowers in globose heads about 1′ in diameter, whitish, crowded, the slender pedicels 1″–2″ long; standard emarginate-mucronate, striate; calyx silky, the teeth long, subulate.

Slopes of Cate's Mountain, Greenbrier Co., W. Va. June.

$\frac{3}{5}$

10. Trifolium refléxum L. Buffalo Clover.
Fig. 2483.

Trifolium reflexum L. Sp. Pl. 766. 1753.

Annual or biennual, pubescent, ascending, branching, 10'-20' high. Leaves long-petioled; stipules ovate-lanceolate, acuminate, foliaceous, few-toothed or entire, 8"-12" long; leaflets all from the same point, short-stalked, oval or obovate, cuneate at the base, obtuse or emarginate at the apex, denticulate, 5"-12" long; heads peduncled, dense, globose, 1' in diameter or more; flowers 5"-6" long, all on slender pedicels, at length 3"-4" long and reflexed; standard red, wings and keel nearly white; calyx-teeth linear-subulate, shorter than the corolla, finely pubescent; pods 3-6-seeded.

In meadows, southern Ontario, western New York and Pennsylvania to Iowa, South Dakota, Arkansas, Kansas, Florida and Texas. April–Aug.

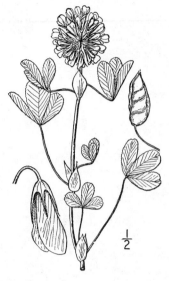

$\frac{1}{2}$

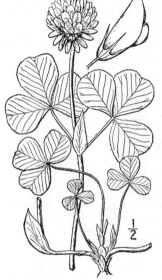

$\frac{1}{2}$

11. Trifolium stoloníferum Muhl. Running Buffalo Clover. Fig. 2484.

Trifolium stoloniferum Muhl. Cat. 70. 1813.

Perennial, glabrous, branching, 6'-12' long, forming runners at the base. Leaves, especially the lower, long-petioled; stipules ovate-lanceolate, acute, membranous, often 1' long; leaflets all from the same point, short-stalked, obovate or obcordate, broadly cuneate at the base, denticulate, 9"-15" long; heads terminal, peduncled, nearly 1' in diameter; flowers white, purplish-tinged, 4"-6" long; pedicels slender, 3"-4" long, at length reflexed; calyx-teeth subulate, longer than the tube; pod commonly 2-seeded.

Prairies and dry woods, Ohio to Iowa, Tennessee, Missouri and Kansas. Introduced into South Dakota. Recorded from Nebraska. May–Aug.

12. Trifolium hýbridum L. Alsike or Alsatian Clover. Fig. 2485.

Trifolium hybridum L. Sp. Pl. 766. 1753.

Perennial, erect or ascending, sometimes rather stout and succulent, 1°-2° high, branching, glabrous or very nearly so, not uniting at the nodes. Leaves long-petioled; stipules ovate-lanceolate, acuminate, membranous, 6"-12" long; leaflets all from the same point, short-stalked, obovate, sometimes emarginate but not obcordate, narrowed or cuneate at the base, serrulate with sharp-pointed teeth, 6"-12" long; heads globose, long-peduncled; flowers pink, or pinkish, 3"-4" long; pedicels slender, 1"-2" long, reflexed when old; corolla 3-4-times as long as the calyx; calyx-teeth subulate, about equalling the tube; pod 2-4-seeded.

In meadows and waste places, Nova Scotia to Ontario, Idaho, British Columbia, New Jersey, Georgia and New Mexico. Bermuda. Cuba. Swedish clover. Sometimes cultivated for fodder. May–Oct.

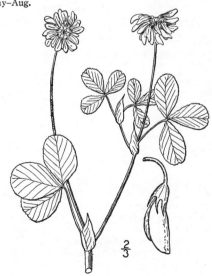

$\frac{2}{3}$

13. Trifolium carolinìànum Michx. Carolina Clover. Fig. 2486.

Trifolium carolinianum Michx. Fl. Bor. Am. **2**: 58. 1803.

Perennial, pubescent, tufted, ascending or procumbent, much branched from the base, 3'–8' high. Leaves slender-petioled; stipules ovate or ovate-lanceolate, foliaceous, 2"–4" long, acute, few-toothed toward the apex, or entire; leaflets all from the same point, short-stalked, obovate, emarginate or obcordate, cuneate at the base, denticulate, 2"–6" long; heads globose; peduncles slender, elongated; flowers purplish, 2"–3" long; standard apiculate; pedicels 1"–2" long, strongly reflexed in fruit; corolla scarcely longer than the calyx; calyx-teeth lanceolate, herbaceous, villous, longer than the tube; pod about 4-seeded.

Naturalized in waste places about Philadelphia; native in fields and open places, Virginia to Florida, west to Kansas, Arkansas and Texas. March–Oct.

14. Trifolium rèpens L. White, Dutch or Honeysuckle Clover. White Trefoil. Purple-grass. Purplewort. Fig. 2487.

Trifolium repens L. Sp. Pl. 767. 1753.

Perennial, glabrous, or with a few scattered hairs, branching at the base, the branches creeping, often rooting at the nodes, 4'–12' long. Leaves long-petioled; stipules ovate-lanceolate membranous, acute, 2"–5" long; leaflets all from the same point, short-stalked, obovate, emarginate or obcordate, broadly cuneate at the base, denticulate, 4"–9" long; heads globose, long-peduncled; flowers white, 3"–5" long; pedicels 1"–2" long, finally reflexed; corolla 2–3-times as long as the calyx; calyx-teeth acuminate, somewhat shorter than the tube; pod about 4-seeded.

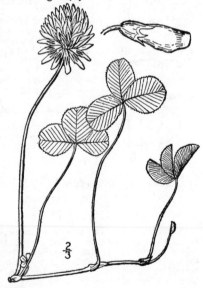

In fields, waste ground and open places, very common throughout our area and in the southern States. Also in the Northwest. Naturalized from Europe, or perhaps native in the extreme north. Naturalized in the mountains of Jamaica and in Bermuda. Native also of Siberia. Widely distributed in all temperate regions. Leaflets sometimes 4–9. Heads occasionally proliferous. Flowers sometimes pinkish. English names, sheep's gowan, honeystalks, lamb-sucklings, and sometimes shamrock. May–Dec.

13. LÒTUS [Tourn.] L. Sp. Pl. 773. 1753.

Herbs with 3–5-foliolate leaves, and umbelled reddish yellow or white flowers. Calyx-teeth nearly equal. Petals free from the stamen-tube; standard ovate or orbicular; wings oblong or obovate; keel incurved, obtuse or beaked. Stamens diadelphous (1 and 9); anthers all alike. Ovary sessile, 1–several-ovuled. Pod linear or oblong, flattish or terete, 2-valved, 1–several-seeded, septate or continuous between the seeds. [The Greek name of several different plants.]

About 90 species, of wide geographic distribution in the Old World, the following typical.

1. Lotus corniculàtus L. Bird's-foot Trefoil. Ground Honeysuckle. Bloom-fell. Fig. 2488.

Lotus corniculatus L. Sp. Pl. 775. 1753.

Perennial from a long root, appressed-pubescent or glabrate. Stems slender, decumbent, or ascending, 3′-2° long; leaves 3-foliolate, short-petioled; leaflets obovate, oblanceolate or oblong, 3″-8″ long, obtuse or acute; stipules similar to the leaflets, and often as large; peduncles elongated, sometimes 4′-6′ long, umbellately 3-12-flowered; calyx-lobes acute, as long as the tube, or shorter; corolla bright yellow, 6″-9″ long, or the standard reddish; pods linear, about 1′ long, spreading, several-seeded.

In waste places and on ballast, Nova Scotia, New Brunswick, and about the seaports of the Eastern and Middle States to Washington, D. C. Adventive from Europe. Native also of Asia, and widely distributed as a weed. Crowtoes (Milton). Cross-toes. Cat's-clover. Sheepfoot. Bird's-eye. Ladies'-fingers. Devil's-fingers. Shoes and stockings. Claver. June-Sept.

14. HOSÁCKIA Dougl.; Benth. Bot. Reg. 15: *pl. 1257.* 1829.

Herbs, mostly with pinnate leaves, but these sometimes with only 1 leaflet or 3, as in the following species, the umbellate or solitary, yellow, red or rose-colored flowers on bracted axillary peduncles. Calyx-teeth nearly equal. Petals free from the stamen-tube, the stamens diadelphous; standard ovate or suborbicular, wings oblong or obovate; keel incurved, mostly pointed or beaked. Pod linear, flattened or nearly terete, not stipitate. [In honor of David Hosack, 1769–1835 professor of botany and materia medica in Columbia College.]

About 50 species, natives of North America, all except *L. Helleri* Britton of North Carolina, and the following species, confined to the western part of the continent. Type species: *Hosackia bicolor* Dougl.

1. Hosackia americàna (Nutt.) Piper. Prairie Bird's-foot Trefoil. Fig. 2489.

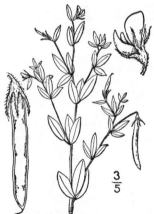

Trigonella americana Nutt. Gen. **2**: 120. 1818.
Lotus sericeus Pursh, Fl. Am. Sept. 489. 1814. Not DC. 1813.
Hosackia Purshiana Benth. Bot. Reg. under *pl. 1257.* 1829.
Lotus americanus Bisch. Litt. Ber. Linnaea 14: 132. 1840.
Hosackia americana Piper, Contr. U. S. Nat. Herb. **11**: 366. 1906.

Annual, erect, branched, villous-pubescent, or glabrate, 10′-20′ high. Leaves 3-foliolate, or the upper sometimes 1-foliolate, sessile or the lower on petioles about 1″ long; stipules minute or none; middle leaflet slightly longer-stalked than the lateral ones, oblong, the lateral lanceolate, rounded at the base, 5″-8″ long, 2″-3″ wide; peduncles axillary, 1-flowered, 9″-12″ long in fruit, leafy-bracted at the summit; flowers rose-color, about 2″ long, the standard darker-veined; calyx-lobes linear, about twice the length of the tube; pods straight, about 1′ long, acute, glabrous, 4-7-seeded, deflexed.

In dry soil, Minnesota to North Dakota, Idaho, Missouri, Arkansas, Texas, New Mexico and Sonora. Recorded as introduced in Illinois. Wild vetch. Summer.

15. ANTHÝLLIS [Tourn.] L. Sp. Pl. 719. 1753.

Herbs, or some species shrubby, with pinnate leaves, the stipules small or none, and bracted capitate flowers. Calyx somewhat swollen, persistent, 5-toothed. Petals long-clawed; standard and wings ovate; keel incurved, shorter than the wings, obtuse or short-pointed;

stamens monadelphous, or the vexillar one distinct; pod ovoid, stalked or sessile, few-seeded, indehiscent, enclosed by the calyx. [Ancient name for some quite different plant.]

Twenty species or more, natives of Europe, Asia and northern Africa, the following typical.

1. Anthyllis Vulneària L. Kidney Vetch. Lady's-fingers. Fig. 2490.

Anthyllis Vulneraria L. Sp. Pl. 719. 1753.

Perennial, pubescent; stems often tufted, 8'–15' long. Leaflets 3–17, oblong, or those of basal leaves reduced to a solitary terminal broad one; peduncles as long as the leaves or longer; heads subtended by a deeply lobed bract; calyx very hairy, much inflated, narrowed at the mouth; corolla yellow to dark red, 6"–10" long.

$\frac{3}{4}$

In fields, Pennsylvania and Ontario, and in waste and ballast grounds at the Atlantic seaports. Adventive from Europe. June–Aug.

16. PSORÀLEA [B. Juss.] L. Sp. Pl. 762. 1753.

Herbs or shrubs, with dark glands or pellucid dots, 1–5-foliolate leaves, and purple blue pink or white flowers, mainly in spikes or racemes. Stipules broad. Calyx-lobes equal or the lower longest, or the two upper ones sometimes united. Standard ovate or orbicular, clawed; wings oblong or falcate; keel incurved, obtuse. Stamens monadelphous or diadelphous; anthers uniform. Ovary sessile or short-stalked, 1-ovuled. Pod ovoid, short, indehiscent, 1-seeded. [Greek, scurfy, from the glandular dots, whence the name scurfy-pea.]

About 120 species, of wide geographic distribution. In addition to the following, about 25 others occur in the western United States. Type species: *Psoralea bituminosa* L.

Leaves digitately 3–5-foliolate (leaflets all from the same point).
  Plants leafy-stemmed.
    Flowers small, 2"–4" long.
      Pods subglobose.   1. *P. lanceolata.*
      Pods ovoid, or ovate.
        Pods with a short, mostly abrupt beak.
          Flowers few, scattered in slender elongated racemes.   2. *P. tenuiflora.*
          Flowers numerous, clustered, or crowded in racemes.   3. *P. floribunda.*
        Pods with a slender sharp or elongated beak.
          Leaflets linear ; flowers in loose elongated racemes.   4. *P. linearifolia.*
          Leaflets linear-lanceolate, oblong, oblanceolate or obovate ; flowers spiked.
            Leaflets oblanceolate or obovate ; pubescence gray.   5. *P. collina.*
            Leaflets linear-lanceolate or oblong ; pubescence silvery.
              Leaflets linear-lanceolate ; calyx inflated in fruit. 6. *P. digitata.*
              Leaflets oblong ; calyx not inflated in fruit.   7. *P. argophylla.*
          Flowers large, 6"–8" long, densely spicate.   8. *P. cuspidata.*
  Plants acaulescent, or nearly so, low, spreading ; roots tuberous.
    Leaflets oblong-cuneate.   9. *P. esculenta.*
    Leaflets linear-oblong.   10. *P. hypogaea.*
Leaves pinnately 3-foliolate (the terminal leaflet stalked).
  Racemes short, on peduncles about equalling the leaves.   11. *P. stipulata.*
  Racemes spicate, the peduncles elongated, much exceeding the leaves.
    Leaflets oblong-lanceolate, obtuse ; pods 2" long, nearly orbicular. 12. *P. pedunculata.*
    Leaflets ovate-lanceolate, acuminate ; pods 4"–5" long, obliquely ovate. 13. *P. Onobrychis.*

1. **Psoralea lanceolàta** Pursh.   Lance-leaved
Psoralea.   Tumble-weed.   Fig. 2491.

Psoralea lanceolata Pursh, Fl. Am. Sept. 475. 1814.
P. micrantha A. Gray; Torr. Pac. R. R. Rep. 4: 77. 1856.

Erect, or assurgent, nearly glabrous, much branched, densely dark-glandular, light green, 1°–2° high. Root not tuberous; petioles equalling or shorter than the leaves; stipules linear, 3″–4″ long, early deciduous; leaflets 3, digitate, sessile, sometimes with a few scattered hairs, linear to oblanceolate, entire, varying from acute to obtuse or even emarginate at the apex, narrowed or cuneate at the base, 8″–15″ long, 2″–4″ wide; peduncles slender; spikes dense, short, 4″–6″ thick, 6–10-flowered; bracts membranous, caducous; flowers bluish-white, 3″ long; corolla 2–3 times as long as the calyx; pod subglobose, about 2″ long, sparingly pubescent, or glabrous, punctate; seed globose, brown.

In dry soil, Iowa to North Dakota, Saskatchewan, Kansas, Arizona and British Columbia. June–July.

2. **Psoralea tenuiflòra** Pursh.   Few-flowered
Psoralea.   Fig. 2492.

Psoralea tenuiflora Pursh, Fl. Am. Sept. 475. 1814.

Erect, finely appressed-canescent, especially when young, punctate, much branched, slender, 2°–4° high. Root not tuberous; leaves short-petioled, digitately 3–5-foliolate; stipules subulate, 1″–2″ long; leaflets very short-stalked, entire, oval, oblong or elliptic, 6″–10″ long, 1½″–3″ wide, obtuse and mucronulate at the apex, narrowed or cuneate at the base; peduncles slender, longer than the leaves; racemes loosely 6–14-flowered, 1′–3′ long; bracts scale-like, persistent; flowers purplish, 2″ long; corolla about twice the length of the calyx; pod ovate, glabrous, punctate, 2″–3″ long; seed ovoid, brown.

Prairies, Illinois to South Dakota, Texas and Sonora, west to Colorado and Montana. Scurvy-pea. May–Oct.

Psoralea obtusíloba T. & G., doubtfully recorded from Kansas in our first edition, is not definitely known within our area.

3. **Psoralea floribúnda** Nutt.   Many-flowered Psoralea.   Fig. 2493.

P. floribunda Nutt.; T. & G. Fl. N. A. 1: 300. 1838.
P. tenuiflora floribunda Rydb. Fl. Neb. 21: 55. 1895.

Stem 1°–4° high, profusely branching, canescent, not glandular. Petioles 2½″–15″ long, mostly shorter than the leaflets; stipules 1½″–3½″ long, subulate, sometimes reflexed; leaves 3–5- sometimes 7-foliolate; leaflets 5″–18″ long, 1½″–4″ wide, oblong, oblong, glandular on both surfaces, rugose, glabrous or with a few scattered hairs above, canescent with closely appressed white hairs beneath; peduncles 2′–7′ long; spikes oblong or cylindric, usually many-flowered, the flowers about 4″ long, at length interrupted and appearing almost as if whorled; bracts 1″–1½″ long, lanceolate, hirsute; calyx canescent, the lobes triangular, acute, the lower one the longest; pod ovoid, glabrous, light brown, covered with darker glands, beak short, stout, straight; seed 2½″ long, compressed.

Prairies, Illinois to Montana, Texas, Arizona and Mexico. Perhaps a large-flowered race of the preceding species. May–Oct. Scurvy-pea.

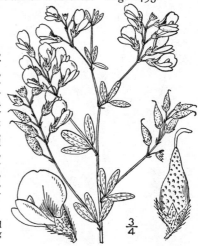

4. Psoralea linearifòlia T. & G. Narrow-leaved Psoralea. Fig. 2494.

Psoralea linearifolia T. & G. Fl. N. A. **1**: 300. 1838.

Erect, 1°–2° high, widely branching; stems not always glandular, glabrous, or sparingly pubescent with appressed hairs. Stipules 1½″–3½″ long, lanceolate or setaceous; leaves sessile or short-petioled, 1–3-foliolate; leaflets 5″–15″ long, 1 '–2″ wide, linear, rugose, glandular, glabrous or with a few appressed hairs; peduncles 1'–9' long; flowers blue, loosely scattered, 1–4 together on slender pedicels 2″–4″ long; bracts 1″ long, ovate, acuminate; mature calyx campanulate, 2″ long, glandular, slightly pubescent; pod 4″ long, narrowly ovoid or oblong, glandular, with a short stout straightish beak; seed flat, oblique, dark brown.

Prairies and hillsides, Nebraska and Colorado to Texas. May–Aug.

5. Psoralea collìna Rydberg. Nebraska Psoralea. Fig. 2495.

Psoralea collina Rydberg, Fl. Neb. **21**: 54. *f. 6, 7.* 1895.

Ascending or diffuse, somewhat grayish-pubescent, 1°–2° high. Stipules narrow, 1″–4″ long; leaves 3-foliolate, or sometimes 5-foliolate; leaflets obovate or oblanceolate, mucronate, mostly glabrous above; bracts pointed, 1½″–2″ long; peduncles slender, 1'–4' long; flowers about 3″ long; calyx-segments linear-lanceolate, much shorter than the ovate pod, the lower one a little longer than the others; pod 2½″–3″ long, tipped with a flat straight beak about 1½″ long.

Hillsides, western Nebraska. July–Aug.

6. Psoralea digitàta Nutt. Digitate Psoralea. Fig. 2496.

Psoralea digitata Nutt.; T. & G. Fl. N. A. **1**: 300. 1838.

Canescent with appressed hairs, slender, erect, widely branching, 1°–2° high. Petioles shorter than or sometimes a very little exceeding the leaves; stipules linear, 1½″–2″ long; peduncles much elongated, often 3–5 times as long as the leaves; leaflets 5, or of the upper leaves 3, digitate, short-stalked, oblong-linear or oblanceolate, 9″–18″ long, 2″–3″ wide, mostly obtuse or mucronulate at the apex, narrowed or cuneate at the base; inflorescence spicate, interrupted, the blue flowers short-pedicelled or sessile in clusters of 3–5; corolla 4″–5″ long, exceeding the broad mucronate bracts; calyx-lobes acute; pod ovoid, flattish, pubescent.

Prairies and hills, South Dakota to Colorado, Kansas and Texas. June–July.

7. Psoralea argophýlla Pursh. Silver-leaf Psoralea. Fig. 2497.

Psoralea incana Nutt. Fraser Cat. Name only. 1813.

Psoralea argophylla Pursh, Fl. Am. Sept. 475. 1814.

Erect, widely branched, densely silvery pubescent with white appressed hairs throughout. Stem often zigzag, 1°–3° high; petioles shorter than or equalling the leaves; stipules narrowly linear, 3"–4" long; leaflets 3–5, digitate, very short-stalked, oval, oblong or obovate, obtuse and mucronate or acutish at the apex, narrowed or rounded at the base, 8"–15" long, 3"–6" wide; peduncles exceeding the leaves; inflorescence spicate, interrupted, the blue flowers sessile, about 4" long, in clusters of 2–4; bracts lanceolate, slightly longer than the corolla, persistent; calyx-lobes lanceolate; pod ovate, straight-beaked.

Prairies and plains, Wisconsin and Minnesota to North Dakota, Saskatchewan, Alberta, Missouri, Colorado and New Mexico. June–Aug.

$\frac{1}{2}$

$\frac{1}{2}$

8. Psoralea cuspidàta Pursh. Large-bracted Psoralea. Fig. 2498.

Psoralea macrorhiza Nutt. Fraser's Cat. Name only. 1813.
Psoralea cuspidata Pursh, Fl. Am. Sept. 741. 1814.
Psoralea cryptocarpa T. & G. Fl. N. A. 1: 301. 1838.

Erect or ascending, stout, branched, finely appressed-pubescent, at least above, 1°–2° high, from a long deep tuberous-thickened root. Petioles equalling or shorter than the leaves, 1½'–2' long; stipules linear, acuminate, 6"–8" long; leaflets 5, digitate, short-stalked, entire, broadly oblanceolate or oval, obtuse and commonly mucronate at the apex, narrowed or cuneate at the base, 1'–2' long, 4"–7" wide; spikes oblong, dense, 1½'–3' long, 1'–1½' thick; peduncles longer than the petioles; bracts lanceolate, long-cuspidate, equalling or exceeding the bluish corolla; pod oval, membranous, enclosed in the calyx.

Prairies and plains, South Dakota to Kansas, Arkansas and Texas. May–June.

9. Psoralea esculénta Pursh. Pomme Blanche. Prairie Apple or Turnip. Indian Bread-root. Fig. 2499.

Psoralea esculenta Pursh, Fl. Am. Sept. 475. 1814.

Rather stout, erect from a large farinaceous root or cluster or roots, little branched, 4'–18' high, densely villous-pubescent with whitish hairs. Lower petioles 2–4 times longer than the leaves; stipules lanceolate, 8"–12" long; leaflets 5, digitate, short-stalked, oval or obovate, entire, obtuse, narrowed at base, 1'–2' long, 4"–10" wide; peduncles equalling or longer than the petioles; spikes oblong, dense, 1½'–3' long, 1'–1½' thick; bracts lanceolate or ovate, acute, 5"–8" long, nearly equalling the bluish corolla; pod oblong, glabrous, about 2½" long, slightly wrinkled, enclosed in the calyx-tube.

Prairies and plains, Manitoba and North Dakota to Wisconsin, Montana, Missouri, Nebraska and Texas. Missouri bread-root. Cree- or prairie-potato. Tipsin. Tipsinna. June.

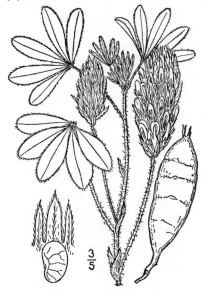
$\frac{3}{5}$

10. Psoralea hypogaèa Nutt. Small Indian Bread-root. Fig. 2500.

Psoralea hypogeae Nutt.; T. & G. Fl. N. A. **1**: 302. 1838.

Similar to the preceding species, but smaller, nearly acaulescent, the stem hardly rising above the ground, densely pubescent with appressed whitish hairs. Petioles 2–4 times as long as the leaves; stipules oblong, acutish, about 6″ long; leaflets 5, digitate, sessile or nearly so, linear-oblong or oblanceolate, 1′–1½′ long, 2″–3″ wide, entire, often mucronate-tipped, narrowed at the base; peduncles ½′–3′ long; spikes short, dense, ½′–1′ long; bracts ovate, acute, shorter than or nearly equalling the dull blue corolla; pod 5″ long or more, somewhat hirsute, slender-beaked.

Plains, Nebraska and Colorado to Texas, Montana and New Mexico. May–June.

11. Psoralea stipulàta T. & G. Large-stipuled Psoralea. Fig. 2501.

Psoralea stipulata T. & G. Fl. N. A. **1**: 688. 1840.

Sparingly pubescent or glabrous, nearly glandless, branched, diffuse or ascending, stems 1°–2° long. Petioles shorter than the leaves; stipules foliaceous, ovate or lanceolate, about 6″ long; leaves pinnately 3-folio-late; leaflets oval or elliptic, 1′–2′ long, entire, narrowed at the base, obtusish at the apex, the terminal one on a stalk 3″–6″ long; peduncles mainly axillary, longer than the petioles; racemes short, dense, 1′ long or less; flowers purple, 4″–5″ long; bracts ovate, acute or acuminate, membranous, deciduous; pod not seen.

In rocky places, Ohio, Indiana and Kentucky. Local. June–July.

12. Psoralea pedunculàta (Mill.) Vail. Samson's Snakeroot. Fig. 2502.

Hedysarum pedunculatum Mill. Gard. Dict. Ed. 8, no. 17. 1768.
Psoralea melilotoides Michx. Fl. Bor. Am. **2**: 58. 1803.
P. pedunculata Vail, Bull. Torr. Club **21**: 114. 1891.

Erect, slender, sparingly branched, 1°–2½° high, more or less pubescent and rough. Glands of the foliage small and inconspicuous; leaves petioled, pinnately 3-foliolate; petioles shorter than or equalling the leaflets; stipules subulate; leaflets oblong-lanceolate, 1½′–3′ long, 4″–7″ wide, entire, obtuse at each end, the apex mucronulate, the terminal one on a stalk 2″–6″ long; racemes axillary and terminal, on peduncles much exceeding the leaves, rather loosely flowered, 2′–5′ long; bracts ovate-lanceolate, acuminate, early deciduous, glandular; flowers purplish, about 2″ long; pod nearly orbicular, strongly wrinkled transversely.

In dry soil, Virginia to Ohio, Illinois, Kansas, south to Florida and Texas. March–July. Congo-root. Bob's-root.

13. Psoralea Onóbrychis Nutt.   Sainfoin Psoralea.   French-grass.   Fig. 2503.

Stylosanthes racemosa Nutt. Fraser Cat. Name only.
1813.

Psoralea Onobrychis Nutt. Gen. **2**: 104. 1818.

Glabrous or slightly pubescent, branched, 3°–6°
high. Glands of the foliage few and small; stipules
subulate; petioles about equalling the 3-foliolate
leaves; leaflets ovate-lanceolate, 2′–4′ long, 1′–2′
wide, entire, rounded or truncate at the base, acuminate at the apex, the terminal one on a stalk about
1′ long; racemes numerous, axillary and terminal,
very slender and loosely flowered, 3′–6′ long; peduncles equalling or shorter than the leaves; flowers
purplish, 1½′–2′ long; pod obliquely ovoid, 4″–6″ long,
transversely wrinkled and roughened with points.

Along rivers, southern Ontario to Tennessee, South
Carolina and Missouri. June–July.

17. AMÓRPHA L. Sp. Pl. 713. 1753.

Glandular-punctate shrubs, with odd-pinnate leaves, and small violet blue or white flowers,
in dense terminal spicate racemes. Calyx-teeth nearly equal, or the lower ones longer;
standard obovate, erect, clawed, folded around the stamens and style; wings and keel none.
Stamens monadelphous below; anthers all alike. Ovary sessile, 2-celled; style curved; stigma
terminal. Pod short, oblong, curved, nearly indehiscent, 1–2-seeded. [Greek, deformed, four
petals being absent.]

About 15 species, natives of North America and Mexico.   Type species: *Amorpha fruticosa* L.

Tall shrub; leaflets 1′–2′ long; pod usually 2-seeded.	1. *A. fruticosa.*
Low shrubs; leaflets 3″–6″ long; pod 1-seeded.	
Glabrous or nearly so; spikes commonly solitary.	2. *A. nana.*
Densely canescent; spikes commonly clustered.	3. *A. canescens.*

1. Amorpha fruticòsa L.   False or Bastard Indigo.   River-locust.   Fig. 2504.

Amorpha fruticòsa L. Sp. Pl. 713. 1753.

A shrub 5°–20° high, with pubescent or glabrous foliage. Leaves thin, petioled, 6′–16′ long;
leaflets 11–21, distant, short-stalked, oval or elliptic, obtuse and mucronulate, or sometimes slightly
emarginate at the apex, rounded or slightly narrowed at the base, 1′–2′ long, 5″–10″ wide, entire;
spike-like racemes dense, clustered or solitary,
3′–6′ long; flowers short-pedicelled, 3″–4″ long;
standard violet-purple, 2–3 times as long as the
calyx, emarginate; stamens exserted; pod glabrous, glandular, thick-stalked, 3″–4″ long, acute,
usually 2-seeded.

Along streams, Pennsylvania and Ohio to Minnesota, Saskatchewan, Florida, Colorado and Chihuahua. Also escaped from cultivation in the Eastern
and Middle States. May–July.

Amorpha angustifòlia (Pursh) Boynton, of
Texas and Oklahoma, with thick leaflets, acute at
both ends, is recorded from Iowa.

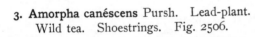

2. Amorpha nàna Nutt. Fragrant or Dwarf False Indigo. Fig. 2505.

Amorpha nana Nutt. Fras. Cat. 1813.

Amorpha microphylla Pursh, Fl. Am. Sept. 466. 1814.

A low bushy shrub, seldom more than 1° high, glabrous or nearly so throughout. Leaves short-petioled, numerous, 1'–3' long; leaflets 13–19, rigid, short-stalked, oval or oblong, rounded or emarginate and mucronate at the apex, obtuse or acute at the base, 3″–6″ long, 1½″–2½″ wide; spike-like racemes commonly solitary; flowers fragrant; standard purplish, about 2″ long; calyx-teeth acuminate; pod short, 1-seeded.

$\frac{3}{4}$

Prairies and plains, Iowa to Minnesota, Manitoba, Kansas and Colorado. May.

3. Amorpha canéscens Pursh. Lead-plant. Wild tea. Shoestrings. Fig. 2506.

Amorpha canescens Pursh, Fl. Am. Sept. 467. 1814.

A bushy shrub, 1°–3° high, densely white-canescent all over. Leaves sessile or very nearly so, numerous, 2'–4' long; leaflets 21–51, approximate, almost sessile, oval or short-lanceolate, obtuse or acutish and mucronulate at the apex, rounded or truncate at the base, 4″–7″ long, 2″–3″ wide, less pubescent above than beneath; spikes usually densely clustered, 2'–7' long; calyx-teeth lanceolate; standard bright blue, nearly orbicular or obcordate, about 2″ long; pod slightly exceeding the calyx, 1-seeded.

Prairies, Indiana to Minnesota, North Dakota and Manitoba, south to Kansas, Colorado, Louisiana and New Mexico. Named from its leaden-hue, not as indicative of lead. July-Aug.

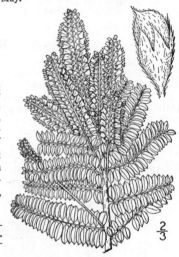

$\frac{2}{3}$

18. PAROSÈLA Cav. Desc. 185. 1802.

[DALEA Willd. Sp. Pl. 3: 1336. 1803.]

Herbs, or sometimes shrubs, with usually glandular-punctate foliage, odd-pinnate leaves, minute stipules, and small purple white or yellow flowers in terminal or lateral spikes. Calyx-teeth nearly equal; standard cordate or auriculate, clawed; wings and keel mainly exceeding the standard; adnate by their claws to the lower part of the stamen-tube. Stamens 10 or 9, monadelphous; anthers uniform. Ovary sessile or short-stalked; ovules 2 or 3; style subulate. Pod included in the calyx, membranous, mostly indehiscent and 1-seeded. [Anagram of *Psoralea*.]

Perhaps 150 species, natives of western North America, Mexico and the Andean region of South America. In addition to the following some 50 others occur in the western United States. Type species: *Dalea obovatifolia* Ort.

Spikes elongated, narrow, loosely flowered.
    Foliage glabrous; corolla white; leaflets linear.   1. *P. enneandra.*
    Foliage pubescent; corolla purple; leaflets obovate.   2. *P. lanata.*
Spikes oblong, thick, densely flowered.
    Foliage glabrous; corolla pink or white; leaflets 15–41.   3. *P. Dalea.*
    Foliage pubescent; corolla yellow to red; leaflets 3–9.
        Plant 1°–2° high; calyx-teeth acuminate.   4. *P. aurea.*
        Plants not over 10″ high; calyx-teeth aristate.   5. *P. nana.*

1. Parosela enneándra (Nutt.) Britton. Slender Parosela. Fig. 2507.

Dalea enneandra Nutt. Fraser's Cat. 1813.

Dalea laxiflora Pursh, Fl. Am. Sept. 741. 1814.

P. enneandra Britton, Mem. Torr. Club 5: 196. 1894.

Erect, glabrous, 1°–4° high, with numerous slender ascending branches. Leaflets 5–11, linear or linear-oblong, obtusish, 2″–5″ long, ½″–1″ wide, narrowed at the base, nearly sessile; spikes numerous, 2′–5′ long, loosely flowered; bracts obtuse, nearly orbicular, punctate, membranous-margined, 1½″ long, often mucronate; flowers 4″–6″ long; calyx-teeth subulate, beautifully plumose, shorter than the white corolla; standard small, cordate; keel exceeding the wings; stamens 9.

Prairies, Iowa to South Dakota and Colorado, south to Mississippi and Texas. June–Aug.

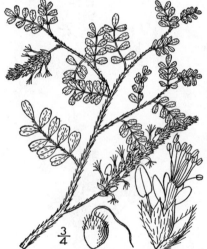

2. Parosela lanàta (Spreng.) Britton. Woolly Parosela. Fig. 2508.

Dalea lanata Spreng. Syst. Veg. 3: 327. 1826.
D. lanuginosa Nutt.; T. & G. Fl. N. A. 1: 307. 1838.
P. lanata Britton, Mem. Torr. Club 5: 196. 1894.

Decumbent, branching, softly and densely pubescent throughout, 1°–2° long. Leaflets 9–13, obovate, obtuse, truncate or emarginate at the apex, narrowed or cuneate at the base, nearly sessile, 4″–6″ long, about 2″ wide above; spikes numerous, short-peduncled, 1′–4′ long, rather loosely flowered; bracts oval or obovate, long-acuminate or mucronate, about 1½″ long; flowers 3″ long; corolla deep purple or red; calyx-teeth subulate, plumose; standard cordate, slightly exceeding the wings and keel; stamens 10.

Prairies, Kansas to Texas, Utah and New Mexico. Summer.

3. Parosela Dàlea (L.) Britton. Pink Parosela. Fig. 2509.

Psoralea Dalea L. Sp. Pl. 764. 1753.

Dalea alopecuroides Willd. Sp. Pl. 3: 1336. 1803.

Parosela Dalea Britton, Mem. Torr. Club. 5: 196. 1894.

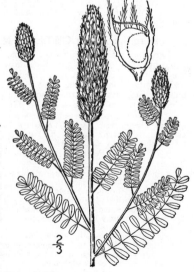

Erect, branched, 1°–2° high, foliage glabrous. Leaflets 15–41, oblanceolate or linear-oblong, obtuse at the apex, narrowed at the base, sessile or nearly so, 2″–3″ long, ½″–1″ wide; spikes terminal, oblong, very dense, 1′–2′ long, about 5″ thick, peduncled; bracts ovate or lanceolate, acuminate, deciduous, about equalling the calyx, hyaline-margined; calyx very silky-pubescent, its teeth linear-lanceolate, acuminate, plumose; corolla pink, or whitish, about 2″ long; keel about equalling the wings.

Prairies, Illinois to Minnesota, Nebraska, South Dakota, Alabama, Texas, Arizona and Mexico. Aug.–Sept.

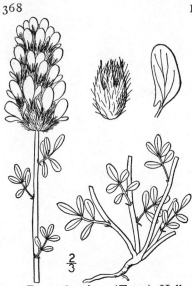

4. Parosela aùrea (Nutt.) Britton. Golden Parosela. Fig. 2510.

Dalea aurea Nutt. Fraser's Cat. 1813.

Psoralea aurea Poir. in Lam. Encycl. Suppl. 4: 590. 1816.

P. aurea Britton, Mem. Torr. Club 5: 196. 1894.

Erect, pubescent, simple, 1°–2° high. Leaflets 5–9, sessile, rather distant, obovate, oblong or oblanceolate, obtuse at the apex, narrowed at the base, 4″–6″ long, 1½″–2½″ wide; spikes solitary, short-peduncled, ovoid or globose, very dense, 1′–3′ long, 6″–8″ thick; bracts ovate, mucronate, shorter than the densely plumose and pubescent calyx-teeth; corolla yellow, 4″–5″ long; standard much shorter than the wings and keel.

Prairies, South Dakota to Missouri (?), Nebraska, Colorado and Texas. Summer.

5. Parosela nàna (Torr.) Heller. Low Parosela. Fig. 2511.

Dalea nana Torr.; A. Gray, Mem. Am. Acad. 4: 31. 1849.
P. nana Heller, Cont. Frank. & Marsh. Coll. 1: 49. 1894.

Suffrutescent, erect, silky-villous throughout. Stems several from the same root, branched, 3′–10′ high; leaflets 3–5, rarely 4″–5″ long, obovate to linear-oblong, obtuse or mucronulate, narrowed at the base, rarely glabrate above, and usually minutely glandular beneath; petioles as long as the leaflets; spikes oblong-ovoid, 5″–10″ long, short-peduncled; bracts ovate, mucronate or aristate, shorter than the calyx, caducous; corolla yellow, longer than the setaceous and plumose calyx-teeth; standard shorter than the wings and keel.

Sand hills and prairies, Comanche Co., Kansas, to Texas and California. Summer.

Parosela Jàmesii (Torr.) Vail, with large thick spikes up to 3½′ long, the bracts as long as the calyx or longer, the leaves 3-foliolate, ranges from Colorado to Texas and New Mexico, and is recorded from Kansas.

19. PETALOSTÈMUM Michx. Fl. Bor. Am. 2: 48. 1803.

Perennial glandular-punctate herbs, with long or deep roots, odd-pinnate leaves, and pink purple or white spicate or capitate flowers. Calyx-teeth nearly equal, rather broad, shorter than the tube. Petals on long slender claws; standard oblong or cordate; wings and keel-petals similar to each other, their claws adnate to the sheath of the stamen-tube almost to its summit. Stamens 5, alternate with the petals. Ovary sessile, 2-ovuled; style subulate. Pod included in the calyx, 1–2-seeded. [Greek, referring to the united petals and stamens.]

About 50 species, natives of North America and Mexico. Type species: *Petalostèmum cándidum* Michx. The generic name *Kuhnistera* Lam., used for these plants in our first edition, is better restricted to its type species, *K. pinnata* (Walt.) Kuntze, of the Southern States, which has the spikes subtended by an imbricated involucre, and long bristle-like calyx-teeth.

    * Foliage glabrous or very slightly pubescent.

Flowers white; leaflets 3–9.
  Leaflets oblong, linear-oblong or oblanceolate; spikes cylindric or oblong.　　　　　　　1. *P. compactum.*
    Calyx villous-pubescent.
    Calyx glabrous or nearly so.
      Stem little branched; spikes cylindric; leaflets ½′–1′ long, thin.　　　2. *P. candidum.*
      Stem much branched; spikes oblong; leaflets smaller, firm.　　　　3. *P. oligophyllum.*
  Leaflets narrowly linear; heads globose or short.　　　　　　　　　　　4. *P. multiflorum.*
Flowers pink or purple.
  Leaflets 3–5; calyx silky-pubescent.
    Bracts glabrous; leaflets mucronulate.　　　　　　　　　　　　　　　5. *P. purpureum.*
    Bracts silky-pubescent; leaflets obtuse.　　　　　　　　　　　　　　6. *P. tenuifolium.*
  Leaflets 13–31; calyx glabrous.　　　　　　　　　　　　　　　　　　　7. *P. foliosum.*
    ** Foliage silky-pubescent; leaflets 9–17.　　　　　　　　　　　　　8. *P. villosum.*

1. Petalostemum compáctum (Spreng.) Swezey. Dense-flowered Prairie-clover. Fig. 2512.

Dalea compacta Spreng. Syst. Veg. **3** : 327. 1826.
Petalostemon macrostachyus Torr. Ann. Lyc. **2** : 176. 1828.
P. compactus Swezey, Nebraska Flow. Pl. 6. 1891.
Kuhnistera compacta Kuntze, Rev. Gen. Pl. 192. 1891.

Erect, dotted with sessile glands, branched, 1°–2½° high. Leaflets 5–7, glabrous, short-stalked, oblong-lanceolate or linear-oblong, acute or obtusish, dotted beneath, 6″–12″ long, about 2″ wide; peduncles terminal, elongated, not bracted; spikes cylindric, 2′–6′ long, about 6″ thick, the rachis pubescent; flowers white or nearly so, about 2″ long; bracts awn-pointed, longer than the densely villous-pubescent calyx; wings and keel-petals oblong; standard cordate; pod pubescent, enclosed by the calyx.

In dry soil, South Dakota to Nebraska, Kansas, Colorado and Wyoming. July–Aug.

$\frac{3}{4}$

$\frac{2}{3}$

2. Petalostemum cándidum (Willd.) Michx. White Prairie-clover. Fig. 2513.

Dalea candida Willd. Sp. Pl. **3** : 1337. 1803.
P. candidum Michx. Fl. Bor. Am. **2** : 49. 1803.
Kuhnistera candida Kuntze, Rev. Gen. Pl. 192. 1891.

Glabrous, stems erect, assurgent, or rarely prostrate, simple, or sparingly branched, 1°–2° high. Leaves petioled; leaflets 5–9, oblong, or oblanceolate, 8″–12″ long, 1½″–3″ wide, obtusish or acute and often mucronulate at the apex, narrowed at the base, very short-stalked; peduncles terminal, elongated, bracted; spikes cylindric, 1′–4′ long, 5″–6″ thick; bracts awn-pointed, longer than the calyx; corolla white, 2″–3″ long; wings and keel-petals oval; standard cordate; calyx-teeth and pod slightly pubescent.

Prairies and plains, Indiana to Minnesota, Manitoba, Tennessee, Louisiana, Texas and Colorado. June–Aug. White tassel-flower.

3. Petalostemum oligophýllum Torr. Slender White Prairie-clover. Fig. 2514.

Petalostemon gracile var. *oligophyllum* Torr. Emory's Mil. Rec. 139. 1848.
Kuhnistera candida var. *occidentalis* Rydberg, Contr. Nat. Herb. **3** : 154. 1895.
Kuhnistera oligophylla Heller, Bull. Torr. Club **23** : 122. 1896.
Petalostemon oligophyllum Torr.; Smyth, Trans. Kans. Acad. **15** : 61. 1898.

Glabrous, stem slender, erect or ascending, usually much branched, 1°–2½° tall, the branches straight, ascending. Leaves short-petioled; leaflets about 7 (5–9), linear, linear-oblong or somewhat oblanceolate, firm, varying from less than 1″ wide to 2″ wide, mostly less than 10″ long, or those of the lower leaves larger; spikes oblong or short-cylindric, blunt; bracts lanceolate, acuminate, equalling the calyx, or longer, deciduous; calyx-teeth usually pubescent; corolla white.

Plains, South Dakota to Nebraska, Wyoming, Texas, Arizona and Mexico. Root sometimes over 1° long. June–Sept.

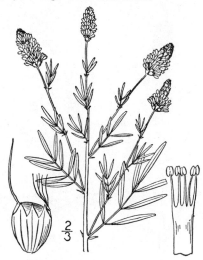

$\frac{2}{3}$

4. Petalostemum multiflòrum Nutt. Round-headed Prairie-clover. Fig. 2515.

P. multiflorus Nutt. Journ. Phil. Acad. **7** : 92. 1834.

Kuhnistera multiflora Heller, Mem. Torr. Club **5** : 197. 1894.

Glabrous, erect, corymbosely much branched, 1°–2° high. Leaves short-petioled, often clustered; leaflets 3–9, linear or somewhat oblanceolate, obtuse or obtusish at the apex, cuneate or narrowed at the base, short-stalked, 4″–6″ long, ¼″–1″ wide; peduncles elongated; heads globose, 4″–6″ in diameter; bracts subulate, shorter than the calyx; calyx-teeth slightly pubescent; corolla white, about 2″ long; wings and keel-petals ovate, oval, or slightly cordate.

Plains, western Iowa to Missouri, Kansas, Arkansas and Texas. Summer.

5. Petalostemum purpùreum (Vent.) Rydb. Violet or Purple Prairie-clover. Fig. 2516.

Dalea purpurea Vent. Hort. Cels, *pl. 40.* 1800.
Petalostemon violaceum Michx. Fl. Bor. Am. **2** : 50. 1803.
Dalea violacea Willd. Sp. Pl. **3** : 1337. 1803.
Kuhnistera purpurea MacM. Met. Minn. 329. 1892.
P. purpureum Rydb. Mem. N. Y. Bot. Gard. **1** : 238. 1900.

Glabrous or slightly pubescent, erect, 1½°–3° high, branching above. Leaves short-petioled, more or less clustered; leaflets 3–5, narrowly linear, 3″–9″ long, ½″–1″ wide, acutish and often mucronate at the apex, narrowed at the base, very short-stalked; spikes peduncled, oblong, or finally cylindric, ½′–2′ long, about 5″ thick; bracts obovate, mucronate, nearly glabrous, equalling the silky-pubescent calyx or shorter; corolla violet or purple, about 2″ long; standard cordate; wings and keel-petals oblong.

Prairies and plains, Indiana to Manitoba, Saskatchewan, Texas and Colorado. Often grows with *P. candidum*. July–Aug. Thimbleweed. Red tassel-flower.

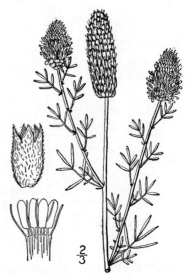

6. Petalostemum tenuifòlium A. Gray. Silky Prairie-clover. Fig. 2517.

P. tenuifolius A. Gray, Proc. Am. Acad. **11** : 73. 1876.

Kuhnistera tenuifolia Kuntze, Rev. Gen. Pl. 192. 1891.

More or less pubescent, erect, branching, 1°–2° high. Leaves short-petioled; leaflets 3–5, linear, obtuse, somewhat involute, dotted with sessile glands, 3″–5″ long, ½″–1″ wide, very short-stalked or sessile; peduncles terminal, elongated, bracted; spikes oblong or cylindric, ½′–1½′ long, about 5″ thick, the rachis pubescent; flowers rose-purple, about 2½″ long; bracts ovate, aristate, silky-pubescent, slightly exceeding the very silky-pubescent calyx; standard nearly orbicular, cordate, cucullate.

In dry soil, Kansas and Arkansas to New Mexico. July–Aug.

7. Petalostemum foliòsum A. Gray. Leafy Prairie-clover. Fig. 2518.

Petalostemon foliosus A. Gray, Proc. Am. Acad. **7**: 336. 1868.

Kuhnistera foliosa Kuntze, Rev. Gen. Pl. 192. 1891.

Erect, branching, or sometimes simple, glabrous throughout, 1°–3° high. Leaves numerous, petioled; leaflets 13–31, close together, short-stalked, linear-oblong or slightly oblanceolate, 4″–7″ long, 1″–1½″ wide, acute or obtuse, mucronate at the apex, narrowed at the base; spikes terminal, long-ovoid or cylindric, 1′–2′ long, 5″–6″ thick, densely-flowered; peduncles short, bracted; bracts lanceolate, awn-pointed, longer than the glabrous calyx; flowers rose-purple, about 2″ long; standard broad, nearly orbicular; wings and keel-petals oval; calyx-teeth finely ciliate.

Along rivers, Illinois, Kentucky (?) and Tennessee. July–Aug.

8. Petalostemum villòsum Nutt. Hairy or Silky Prairie-clover. Fig. 2519.

Petalostemon villosus Nutt. Gen. **2**: 85. 1818.
Dalea villosa Spreng. Syst. Veg. **3**: 326. 1826.
Kuhnistera villosa Kuntze, Rev. Gen. Pl. 192. 1891.

Ascending or decumbent from a deep root, branching at the base, densely villous or silky-pubescent all over, 1°–2° high. Leaves short-petioled or nearly sessile; leaflets 9–17, approximate, linear-oblong or slightly oblanceolate, acute or obtuse and often aristate at the apex, narrowed at the base, 3″–5″ long, 1″–2″ wide; spikes terminal, clustered or solitary, short-peduncled, cylindric, 1′–4½′ long, 5″–6″ thick, very dense; bracts lanceolate, acuminate, exceeding the densely villous calyx; corolla rose-purple or rarely white, standard oblong; wings and keel-petals oblong-obovate.

Prairies and sandy plains, Wisconsin to Saskatchewan, Missouri, Texas and Colorado. Aug.

20. INDIGÓFERA L. Sp. Pl. 751. 1753.

Herbs, or rarely shrubs, often canescent with hairs affixed by the middle, with odd-pinnate leaves, small stipules, and pink or purple spicate or racemose flowers. Calyx-teeth oblique, nearly equal, or the lower longer. Standard ovate or orbicular, sessile or clawed; wings oblong; keel erect, somewhat gibbous, or spurred. Stamens mainly monadelphous; anthers all alike. Ovary sessile or nearly so, 1–∞-ovuled; style slender. Pod linear, 4-angled (in our species), septate between the seeds. [Name from the yield of indigo by some species.]

About 275 species, natives of warm and temperate regions. In addition to the following, some 7 others occur in the southern and southwestern United States. Type species: *Indigofera tinctoria* L.

1. Indigofera leptosépala Nutt. Wild or Western Indigo-plant. Fig. 2520.

Indigofera leptosepala Nutt.; T. & G. Fl. N. A. 1: 298. 1838.

Perennial decumbent, cinereous-pubescent, slender, branching, 6'-24' long. Leaves short-petioled; leaflets 5-9, oblanceolate or oblong-linear, 3"-12" long, 1"-3" wide, obtuse and often mucronulate at the apex, narrowed or cuneate at the base, short-stalked; spikes peduncled, loosely few-flowered; flowers pink or purplish, about 3" long; calyx-teeth subulate, equal; pods linear, acute, obtusely 4-angled, sessile in the calyx, 8"-12" long, 1" thick, reflexed at maturity.

Prairies, Kansas and Arkansas to Texas and Mexico, east to Florida. May-Nov.

21. CRÁCCA L. Sp. Pl. 752. 1753.

[TEPHROSIA Pers. Syn. 2: 328. 1807.]

Herbs, sometimes slightly shrubby, with odd-pinnate not punctate leaves, and purple red or white flowers in terminal or lateral racemes or short clusters. Stipules small. Leaflets entire. Calyx-teeth usually nearly equal. Petals all clawed. Standard orbicular or broadly ovate; wings obliquely obovate or oblong; keel curved. Stamens monadelphous or diadelphous; anthers all alike. Ovary sessile; ovules several or many. Pod linear, flat, 2-valved, several-seeded, continuous, or with membranous septa between the seeds. [Latin, vetch.]

About 120 species, mainly natives of warm and tropical regions. Besides the following, eleven species occur in the southern and southwestern United States. Type species: *Cracca villosa* L.

Raceme terminal, dense, nearly sessile, many-flowered.	1. *C. virginiana.*
Peduncles lateral and terminal, elongated, few-flowered.	
Villous; flowers in an interrupted spike or raceme.	2. *C. spicata.*
Pubescent; peduncles few-flowered near the summit.	3. *C. hispidula.*

1. Cracca virginiàna L. Cat-gut. Wild Sweet-pea. Goat's Rue. Fig. 2521.

Cracca virginiana L. Sp. Pl. 752. 1753.
Galega virginiana L. Sp. Pl. Ed. 2, 1062. 1763.
Tephrosia virginiana Pers. Syn. 2: 329. 1807.

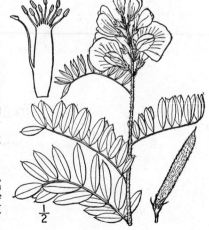

Erect or ascending, more or less villous or silky-pubescent with whitish hairs, 1°-2° high. Roots long, fibrous, tough; leaves short-petioled; leaflets 7-25, oblong, linear-oblong or the terminal one oblanceolate, narrowed or cuneate at the base, rounded, mucronate acutish or emarginate at the apex, 9"-12" long, 2"-4" wide; flowers yellowish-purple, 6"-9" long, crowded in a terminal often compound nearly sessile raceme; pedicels 2"-4" long; pod linear, densely pubescent, 1'-2' long.

In dry sandy soil, Maine to Minnesota, Arkansas, Florida, Louisiana and northern Mexico; western races more copiously pubescent than eastern, have been regarded as specifically distinct as *Cracca holosericea* (Nutt.) Britten & Baker. Turkey-, rabbit- or hoary pea. Devil's shoestrings. June-July.

2. **Cracca spicàta** (Walt.) Kuntze. Loose-flowered Goat's Rue. Fig. 2522.

Galega spicata Walt. Fl. Car. 188. 1788.

Tephrosia spicata T. & G. Fl. N. A. 1 : 296. 1838.

Cracca spicata Kuntze, Rev. Gen. Pl. 175. 1891.

Villous-pubescent with long brown hairs, decumbent or straggling, much branched, 1°–2° long. Leaves few and distant, short-petioled; leaflets 9–15, short-stalked, oval, oblanceolate or narrowly obovate, narrowed, cuneate or rounded at the base, obtuse, mucronate or emarginate at the apex, 9″–15″ long, 3″–6″ wide; peduncles lateral and terminal, slender, 4′–10′ long; inflorescence interrupted, very loose, 2′–5′ long; flowers purplish, 6″–8″ long; pod linear, finely pubescent, about 2′ long, 2½″ wide.

In dry soil, Delaware to Florida, Tennessee, Alabama and Louisiana. This was included by Linnaeus in the preceding species. June–Aug.

$\frac{3}{5}$

3. **Cracca hispídula** (Michx.) Kuntze. Few-flowered Goat's Rue. Fig. 2523.

Galega hispidula Michx. Fl. Bor. Am. 2 : 68. 1803.

Tephrosa hispidula Pers. Syn. 2 : 329. 1807.

Cracca hispidula Kuntze, Rev. Gen. Pl 175. 1891.

More or less pubescent, procumbent or straggling, much branched, slender, 1°–2° long. Leaves petioled; leaflets 5–19, short-stalked, oval, oblong, oblanceolate or obovate, narrowed, rounded or cuneate at the base, obtuse, emarginate or acute at the apex; peduncles lateral or terminal, slender, 2′–4′ long; flowers red-purple, few, terminal, about 6″ long; pod linear, 1′–1½′ long, 2″ wide, minutely pubescent.

Dry sandy soil, Virginia to Florida, Alabama and Louisiana. May–Aug.

$\frac{2}{3}$

22. **KRAÙNHIA** Raf. Med. Rep. (II.) 5: 352. 1808.

[Wisteria Nutt. Gen. 2 : 125. 1818.]

High-climbing woody vines, with odd-pinnate leaves, and showy blue, lilac or purplish flowers in large terminal racemes. Calyx somewhat 2-lipped, the 2 upper teeth slightly shorter than the 3 lower. Standard large, reflexed, clawed, with 2 small appendages at the base of the blade; wings oblong, falcate, auriculate at the base; keel incurved, obtuse. Stamens diadelphous; anthers all alike. Ovary stalked; ovules ∞. Pod elongated, torulose, 2-valved, coriaceous, not septate between the seeds. [Named for Kraunh.]

Five known species, the following of southeastern North America, the others Asiatic, the first of ours typical.

Racemes 2′–4′ long; calyx-teeth shorter than the tube.   1. *K. frutescens.*
Racemes 8′–12′ long; calyx-teeth nearly or about as long as the tube, or the lower one longer.
                                                                              2. *K. macrostachys.*

1. Kraunhia frutéscens (L.) Greene.
American or Woody Wisteria.
Fig. 2524.

Glycine frutescens L. Sp. Pl. 753. 1753.
Wisteria speciosa Nutt. Gen. 2: 116. 1818.
Wisteria frutescens Poir. in Lam. Ill. 3: 674. 1823.
Krauhnia frutescens Greene, Pittonia 2: 175. 1891.
Bradleia frutescens Britton, Man. 549. 1901.

Climbing over trees and bushes to a length of
30°-40° or more, forming a stem several inches
in diameter. Leaves petioled; rachis and short
stalks of the leaflets often pubescent; leaflets 9-15,
ovate or ovate-lanceolate, somewhat acuminate
but blunt at the apex, rounded at the base, entire,
1'-2' long, glabrous and dark-green above, pale
and sometimes slightly pubescent beneath; racemes dense, 2'-7' long; pedicels 2''-3'' long;
calyx finely pubescent, sometimes with club-
shaped glands; corolla lilac-purple, 6''-9'' long;
auricles of the wings one short and one slender;
pod linear, 2'-3' long.

In low grounds, Virginia to Florida, Arkansas and
Texas. Kidney-bean tree. Virgin's-bower. April–
June.

2. Kraunhia macróstachys (T. & G.) Small.   Long-clustered Wisteria.   Fig. 2525.

Wistaria frutescens var. *macrostachys* T. & G. Fl. N. A. 1:
283. 1838.
Wistaria macrostachys Nutt.; T. & G. Fl. N. A. 1: 283.
As synonym. 1838.
K. macrostachys Small, Bull. Torr. Club 25: 134. 1898.

A vine, sometimes 20°-25° long. Stem becoming 1¼'
thick, branching; leaves 4'-8' long; leaflets usually 9,
ovate to elliptic-lanceolate, 1'-2¾' long, acuminate, or
acute, rounded or cordate at the base; racemes 8'-12'
long, loosely-flowered, drooping; rachis and pedicels
densely hirsute and glandular, with club-shaped glands;
calyx pubescent like the pedicels, the tube campanulate,
the segments lanceolate, lateral ones about as long as
the tube, lower one longer; corolla lilac-purple or light
blue; standard with blade 7'' broad, decurrent on the
claw; pods 2'-4' long, constricted between the black lustrous seeds.

In swamps, Indiana (?), Illinois to Missouri, Louisiana
and Arkansas. Spring.

23. ROBINIA L. Sp. Pl. 722. 1753.

Trees or shrubs, spreading freely from undergound parts, with odd-pinnate leaves, and
axillary or terminal racemes of showy flowers. Stipules small, often spiny. Petioles slightly
dilated at the base, enclosing the buds of the next year. Calyx-teeth short, broad, the 2 upper
somewhat united. Standard large, reflexed, not appendaged; wings oblong, curved; keel
curved, obtuse. Stamens diadelphous; anthers uniform, or the alternate ones smaller. Ovary
stalked; ovules ∞. Pod flat, linear, not septate between the seeds, margined along the upper
suture, tardily 2-valved. [Name in honor of John and Vespasian Robin, who first cultivated
the Locust-tree in Europe, 1550–1629.]

About 8 species, natives of North America and Mexico.   Type species: *Robinia Pseudo-Acàcia* L.

Twigs, petioles and pods glabrous; flowers white; a tree.   1. *R. Pseudo-Acacia.*
Twigs and petioles glandular ; pods hispid; flowers pinkish ; a tree.   2. *R. viscosa.*
Twigs and petioles bristly ; pods hispid; flowers pink or purple ; a shrub. 3. *R. hispida.*

1. Robinia Pseudo-Acàcia L. Locust-tree.
False or Bastard Acacia. Fig. 2526.

Robinia Pseudo-Acacia L. Sp. Pl. 722. 1753.
Pseudo-Acacia odorata Moench, Meth. 145. 1789.

A large tree with very rough bark, maximum
height of about 80° and trunk diameter of 3½°, rarely
shrubby. Twigs and foliage nearly glabrous; stipules often spiny; leaflets 9–19, stalked, ovate or oval,
mainly rounded at the base, obtuse or emarginate
and mucronulate at the apex, entire, 1'–2' long;
stipels small, setaceous; racemes loose, drooping;
pedicels slender, 3"–6" long; flowers white, fragrant, 7"–10" long, the standard yellowish at base;
pod glabrous, 2'–4' long, about 6" wide, 4–7-seeded.

. Monroe Co., Pa., south, especially along the western
slopes of the mountains, to Georgia, west to Iowa, Missouri and Oklahoma. Extensively naturalized elsewhere in the United States and eastern Canada and in
Europe. Wood strong, very durable, greenish brown,
the sap-wood yellow; weight per cubic foot 46 lbs.
Much used for posts, in ship-building, and especially
for tree-nails. Called also white, yellow, black, red-
flowering or green locust. Honey-, pea-flower or post-
locust. Silver-chain. May–June.

2. Robinia viscòsa Vent. Clammy or
Honey Locust. Rose Acacia. Fig. 2527.

Robinia viscosa Vent. Hort. Cels, *pl. 4.* 1800.

A small tree, with rough bark, maximum
height about 40° and trunk diameter 10'. Twigs
and petioles glandular-pubescent, viscid; stipules short, sometimes spiny; leaflets 11–25,
stalked, obtuse and mucronate at the apex,
mostly rounded at the base, ovate or oval,
1'–2' long, thicker than those of the preceding
species; stipels small, subulate; racemes rather
dense, often erect; pedicels 2"–4" long; flowers pinkish, 9"–12" long, not fragrant; pod
2'–4' long, about 6" wide, glandular-hispid.

Mountains of Virginia to Georgia. Escaped
in the Middle States and north to Nova Scotia.
Wood brown, the sap-wood yellow; weight per
cubic foot 50 lbs. Rose-flowering or red-locust.
June.

3. Robinia híspida L. Rose Acacia.
Bristly or Moss Locust. Fig. 2528.

Robinia hispida L. Mant. 101. 1767.

A much-branched shrub, 3°–9° high. Twigs,
petioles, pedicels and rachises of the leaves
bristly; stipules very small, or none; leaflets
9–13, stalked, broadly ovate or oblong, entire,
mainly obtuse or rounded at each end, mucronate, 1'–2' long; stipels none or subulate;
racemes loose; pedicels 3"–6" long; flowers
pink or purple, 8"–15" long, not fragrant; pods
linear, bristly-hispid.

Mountains of Virginia to eastern Tennessee and
Georgia. Often cultivated for ornament. Honey
locust. May–June.

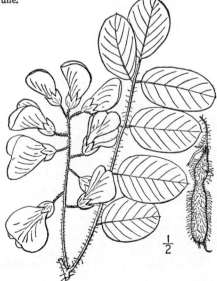

24. SÉSBAN Adans. Fam. Pl. 2: 327. 1763.

[SESBANIA Scop. Introd. 308. 1777.]

Herbs or shrubs, with evenly pinnate leaves, the leaflets numerous, entire, not stipellate, or the stipels minute. Flowers yellow, reddish, purplish or white, in axillary or lateral racemes, the slender pedicels with 2 deciduous bractlets under the calyx. Calyx campanulate, nearly equally 5-toothed. Standard broad, ovate or orbicular; wings oblong, falcate; keel blunt. Stamens diadelphous (9 and 1). Ovary mostly stipitate, many-ovuled; style glabrous; stigma small. Pod elongated-linear, wingless, compressed, partitioned between the oblong seeds. [Name Arabic.]

About 15 species, natives of warm and tropical regions, only the following one known in North America. Type species: *Aeschynomene Sesban* L.

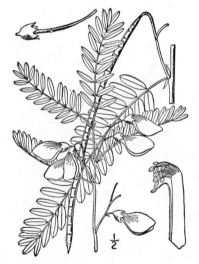

1. Sesban macrocàrpa Muhl. Pea-tree. Long-podded Sesban. Fig. 2529.

Sesbania macrocarpa Muhl.; Ell. Bot. S. C. & Ga. 2: 221. 1821.

Annual, glabrous, widely branching, 4°–12° tall. Leaflets 10–35 pairs, oblong, obtuse, mucronate, thin, 1′ long or less, 2″–3″ wide, pale beneath; racemes shorter than the leaves, 1–5-flowered; calyx-teeth subulate, shorter than the tube; corolla yellowish, purple-spotted, the standard 8″–10″ long; pod 6′–12′ long, about 2″ wide, somewhat curved, drooping, tipped with the subulate style.

In wet or moist soil, Missouri to Texas, Arizona, east to South Carolina and Florida, south to Central America. Collected also in southern Pennsylvania and in ballast deposits on Staten Island, New York. June–Sept.

Colùtea arboréscens L., a European shrub, with odd-pinnate leaves, yellow flowers in short racemes, and much inflated membranous pods, is reported as escaped from cultivation in eastern Massachusetts.

25. GEOPRÙMNON Rydb. in Small, Fl. SE. U. S. 615, 1332. 1903.

Perennial herbs with tufted decumbent or ascending leafy stems, odd-pinnate leaves with numerous entire leaflets, the stipules distinct and nearly free from the petiole, and rather large white, yellowish, violet or purplish flowers in peduncled axillary racemes. Calyx campanulate or nearly cylindric, its teeth nearly equal. Standard rather narrow, erect, notched, longer than the wings; keel shorter than the wings; stamens diadelphous, the anthers all alike. Ovary sessile; ovules numerous. Pod globose to conic-fusiform, fleshy, becoming spongy, indehiscent, completely 2-celled. [Greek, earth-plum.]

Five species, natives of Central North America. Type species: *Geoprumnon crassicarpum* (Nutt.) Rydb.

Pod glabrous, globose, or oval.
　Corolla purple; pod pointed.　　　　　　　　　　　　　　　　　　　　1. G. crassicarpum.
　Corolla yellowish-white; pod obtuse.　　　　　　　　　　　　　　　　2. G. mexicanum.
Pod pubescent, ovoid or oblong.
　Pod ovoid, about 6″ long, not wrinkled.　　　　　　　　　　　　　　3. G. plattense.
　Pod oblong, curved, 1′ long or more, wrinkled.　　　　　　　　　　4. G. tennesseense.

1. Geoprumnon crassicàrpum (Nutt.) Rydb. Ground Plum. Fig. 2530.

Astragalus crassicarpus Nutt. Fraser's Cat. 1813.
Astragalus carnosus Pursh, Fl. Am. Sept. 740. In part. 1814.
A. caryocarpus Ker, Bot. Reg. **2**: *pl. 176.* 1816.
G. crassicarpum Rydb. in Small, Fl. SE. U. S. 616. 1903.

Appressed-pubescent, branching at the base, branches decumbent or ascending, 6'–15' long, mostly simple. Stipules ovate, acute, 2"–3" long; leaflets 15–25, oblong, elliptic or sometimes obovate, obtuse, narrowed at the base, 3"–6" long, 1½"–2½" wide; peduncles equalling or shorter than the leaves; flowers violet-purple, 8"–9" long, in short racemes; pods thick, glabrous, globose or oval, short-pointed, 8"–12" in diameter.

Prairies, Minnesota to Manitoba, Saskatchewan, Iowa, Missouri, Colorado and Texas. Fruit edible, collected by prairie-dogs for their winter store. April–June. Buffalo-pea, -bean or -apple.

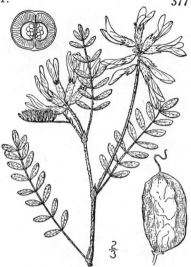

2. Geoprumnon mexicànum (A. DC.) Rydb. Larger Ground Plum. Fig. 2531.

Astragalus mexicanus A. DC. Pl. Rar. Jard. Gen. **4**: 16. 1826.
Astragalus trichocalyx Nutt.; T. & G. Fl. N. A. **1**: 332. 1838.
G. mexicanum Rydb. in Small, Fl. SE. U. S. 616. 1903.

Similar to the preceding species, but less pubescent and with the hairs somewhat spreading. Leaflets 17–33, oblong to obovate, obtuse or emarginate at the apex, narrowed at the base; flowers yellowish-white, or purplish at the tip, 9"–12" long, in short racemes; pod thick, glabrous, globose, not pointed, 1'–1¼' in diameter.

Prairies, Illinois to Nebraska, Kansas, Louisiana and Texas. Fruit edible. May.

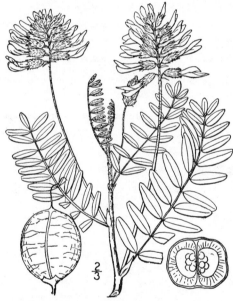

3. Geoprumnon platténse (Nutt.) Rydb. Platte Milk Vetch. Fig. 2532.

Astragalus plattensis Nutt.; T. & G. Fl. N. A. **1**: 332. 1838.
G. plattense Rydb. in Small, Fl. SE. U. S. 616. 1903.

Villous-pubescent with spreading hairs, prostrate or ascending, 6'–12' high or long. Leaflets 13–29, oblong to obovate, obtuse at the apex, narrowed at the base, 4"–9" long, about 2" wide; stipules broad, ovate, pointed, 3"–4" long; flowers yellowish-white or tipped with purple, about 9" long, in short heads; pod ovoid, pointed, smooth, loosely pubescent, nearly straight.

Prairies, Indiana to Minnesota and Nebraska, south to Alabama and Texas. May.

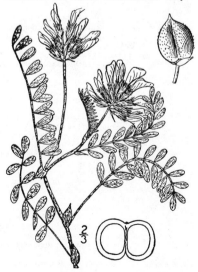

4. **Geoprumnon tennesseénse** (A. Gray) Rydb. Tennessee Milk Vetch.
Fig. 2533.

Astragalus tennesseensis A. Gray; Chapm. Fl. S. States, 98. 1860.
Astragalus plattensis var. *tennesseensis* A. Gray, Proc. Am. Acad. 6 : 193. 1864.
G. tennesseense Rydb. in Small, Fl. SE. U. S. 615. 1903.

Stems erect or ascending from a deep root; plant villous with long whitish hairs. Leaflets 15–31, oblong, or linear-oblong, obtuse, or emarginate, nearly glabrous above, 6″–10″ long, 2″–4″ wide; stipules lanceolate, oval, or ovate-lanceolate; peduncles about equalling the leaves; racemes short, several–many-flowered; flowers about 10″ long; pod oblong, conic, fleshy, 1′ long or rather more, strongly wrinkled, at least when dry, its summit strongly curved.

On hillsides, Illinois to Tennessee, Alabama and Missouri. March–May.

26. **ASTRÁGALUS** [Tourn.] L. Sp. Pl. 755. 1753.

Herbs, sometimes woody, mostly with odd-pinnate leaves of several or many leaflets, and purple violet white or yellow flowers in spikes or racemes, or rarely umbellate or solitary. Stipules present. Calyx tubular, its teeth nearly equal. Petals clawed; standard erect, ovate or oblong; wings oblong; keel obtuse, about equalling the wings. Stamens diadelphous; anthers all alike. Ovary sessile or stipitate; ovules ∞. Pod sessile or stalked, dehiscent, 1–2-celled, very different in different species and affording the best characters in classification, accepted as generic by some authors. [Greek name of some leguminous plant.]

At least 1000 species, of wide geographic distribution, most abundant in northern Asia. In addition to the following, at least 175 others occur in the western and southern United States. Type species: *Astragalus Onóbrychis* L.

* Pod 2-celled.

Plant densely villous-pubescent all over.	1. *A. mollissimus.*
Plants glabrous, or grayish-pubescent.	
Flowers yellowish ; pod terete, glabrous.	2. *A. carolinianus.*
Flowers purple ; pod with a deep furrow, pubescent.	
Pod finely appressed-pubescent.	3. *A. adsurgens.*
Pod densely villous with white hairs.	4. *A. Hypoglottis.*

** Pod 1-celled, but one or both sutures sometimes intruded.

Pod 2-grooved on the upper side (genus *Diholcus* Rydb.).	5. *A. bisulcatus.*
Pod not 2-grooved.	
Pod slightly fleshy ; leaflets persistent (genus *Ctenophyllum* Rydb.).	6. *A. pectinatus.*
Pod papery or leathery ; leaflets deciduous.	
Pod cordate or triangular in section, the dorsal suture intruded (only slightly intruded in *A. Robbinsii*).	
Pod straight or nearly so (genus *Tium* Medic.).	
Flowers white or yellowish-white.	
Pod triangular in cross-section ; plant appressed-pubescent ; western.	
	7. *A. racemosus.*
Pod cordate in cross-section ; plant villous-pubescent ; western	8. *A. Drummondii.*
Pod somewhat compressed, the dorsal suture scarcely intruded.	9. *A. Robbinsii.*
Flowers purple.	
Pod densely blackish or brownish-pubescent ; stems diffuse.	10. *A. alpinus.*
Pod finely pubescent ; stem erect.	11. *A. Blakei.*
Pod crescent-shaped (genus *Holcóphacos* Rydb.).	12. *A. distortus.*
Pod neither cordate nor triangular in cross-section, the dorsal suture not intruded.	
Plants scapose, or very short-stemmed (genus *Xylóphacos* Rydb.).	
Plant villous ; flowers yellow.	13. *A. lotiflorus.*
Plants silky or silvery-canescent ; flowers blue, violet or purple.	
Pod straight or nearly so, nearly circular in cross-section.	14. *A. missouriensis.*
Pod curved, 8-shaped in cross-section.	15. *A. Shortianus.*
Plants leafy-stemmed.	
Pod flattened, with a partial partition (genus *Atelophragma* Rydb.).	
Pod sessile, black-pubescent.	16. *A. eucosmos.*
Pod stipitate, glabrous.	17. *A. aboriginorum.*
Pod not flattened, completely 1-celled.	
Pods small, transversely wrinkled, coriaceous (genus *Micróphacos* Rydb.).	
	18. *A. gracilis.*
Pods large, smooth, papery.	19. *A. flexuosus.*

1. Astragalus mollíssimus Torr. Woolly Loco-weed or Crazy-weed. Fig. 2534.

Phaca villosa James, Trans. Am. Phil. Soc. (II.) **2** : 186. 1825. Not Nutt. 1818.

Astragalus mollissimus Torr. Ann. Lyc. **2** : 178. 1826.

Decumbent or ascending, stout, bushy, densely villous-pubescent, 1°–2° high. Stem very short; stipules membranous, ovate, pointed, 3″–5″ long, adnate to the petiole; leaflets 19–27, oval, obtuse, but pointed at the apex, narrowed or rounded at the base, 4″–6″ long, 2″–3″ wide; peduncles equalling or exceeding the leaves; flowers violet-purple, 8″–12″ long, in dense spikes; pod oblong, dry, cartilaginous, glabrous, dehiscent into 2 valves, somewhat compressed, sessile, 2-celled, 5″–10″ long, about 3″ thick, furrowed at both sutures, slightly curved at maturity.

Prairies, plains and hills, Nebraska to Wyoming. Texas and New Mexico. June. The popular name of the plant is from its poisonous effects on cattle. Rattlebag weed.

2. Astragalus caroliniànus L. Carolina or Canadian Milk Vetch. Fig. 2535.

Astragalus carolinianus L. Sp. Pl. 757. 1753.
Astragalus canadensis L. Sp. Pl. 757. 1753.

Glabrous or slightly pubescent, erect or ascending, branched, 1°–4° high. Stipules membranous, broadly lanceolate, acuminate, 2″–4″ long; leaflets 15–31, elliptic or oval, obtuse or slightly emarginate at the apex, rounded at the base, 1′–2′ long, 3″–9″ wide; peduncles longer than the leaves, or shorter; flowers greenish yellow, 6″–8″ long in dense thick spikes; pod oblong, sessile, 2-celled, coriaceous, dehiscent, glabrous, erect, terete, or sometimes slightly furrowed at the dorsal suture, pointed, nearly straight, 5″–8″ long.

Along streams, Quebec and Hudson Bay to Saskatchewan, western New York, Georgia, Louisiana, Nebraska and Utah. Canadian rattle-weed. July–Aug.

3. Astragalus adsúrgens Pall. Ascending Milk Vetch. Fig. 2536.

A. adsurgens Pall. Astrag. 40. *pl. 31.* 1800.
A. striatus Nutt.; T. & G. Fl. N. A. **1** : 330. 1838.

Minutely cinereous-pubescent or glabrate, ascending or decumbent, 4′–18′ long, simple or branched at the base. Stipules membranous, ovate, acuminate, 3″–5″ long; leaflets 15–25, oval to linear-oblong, obtuse and sometimes emarginate at the apex, narrowed at the base, 8″–12″ long; peduncles exceeding the leaves; flowers purplish, 6″–8″ long, in dense short spikes; pod sessile, 2-celled, oblong, pointed, coriaceous, finely pubescent, erect, dehiscent, cordate-triangular in section, deeply furrowed on the back, 4″–6″ long.

Prairies, Minnesota to Manitoba, Keewatin, British Columbia, Kansas, Colorado and Nevada. Also in northern Asia. June–July.

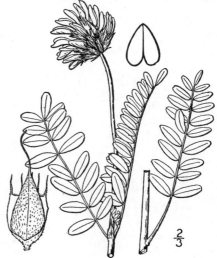

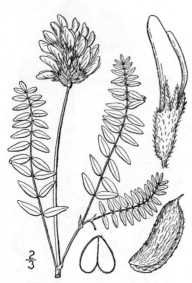

4. Astragalus Hypoglóttis L. Purple Milk Vetch or Cock's-head. Fig. 2537.

Astragalus Hypoglottis L. Mant. **2**: 274. 1771.

Pubescent or glabrate, decumbent or ascending, slender, branched at the base, 6'–24' long. Stipules ovate-lanceolate, acute, 2"–3" long; leaflets 17–25, oblong or elliptic, obtusish and generally emarginate at the apex, rounded at the base, 3"–7" long; flowers violet-purple, 6"–10" long, in dense heads; pods membranous, sessile, 2-celled, dehiscent, densely villous with white hairs, ovoid-oblong, deeply furrowed on the back, 4"–5" long.

Kansas to Minnesota, north to Hudson Bay, west to Alaska. Also in northern Europe and Asia. May–Aug.

5. Astragalus bisulcàtus (Hook.) A. Gray. Two-grooved Milk Vetch. Fig. 2538.

Phaca bisulcata Hook. Fl. Bor. Am. **1**: 145. 1833.

Astragalus bisulcatus A. Gray, Pac. R. R. Rep. **12**: Part 2, 42. *pl. 1.* 1860.

Rather stout, erect, nearly simple, 1°–3° high. Stipules membranous, ovate-lanceolate, acute, 4"–6" long; leaflets 17–27, oval or oblong, obtuse at the apex, narrowed at the base, 8"–12" long; flowers deep purple, 7"–8" long, in elongated narrow racemes; peduncles longer than the leaves; pod 1-celled, linear, stipitate, deflexed, pointed, glabrous at maturity, membranous, with 2 deep furrows on the upper side, 6"–10" long.

Plains and river-valleys, Nebraska and Colorado to Montana and Saskatchewan. June–Aug.

6. Astragalus pectinàtus (Hook.) Dougl. Narrow-leaved Milk Vetch. Fig. 2539.

Phaca pectinata Hook. Fl. Bor. Am. **1**: 141. *pl. 54.* 1830.
Astragalus pectinatus Dougl.; Hook. Fl. Bor. Am. **1**: 142. As synonym. 1830.

Ascending, much branched at the base or also above, 1°–2° high, finely canescent or glabrate. Stipules membranous, ovate-lanceolate, acute or acuminate, 4"–6" long; leaflets 11–21, very narrowly linear, acute, ½'–3' long, persistent; peduncles shorter than or exceeding the leaves; flowers yellow, 8"–12" long, in loose spikes or spike-like racemes; standard much longer than the wings and keel; pod nearly terete, 1-celled, sessile, oblong, pointed, coriaceous, glabrous, dehiscent, not furrowed, keeled along the upper suture, 6"–8" long, the exocarp somewhat fleshy.

Plains, Kansas, Nebraska and Colorado to Saskatchewan and Alberta. June–Aug.

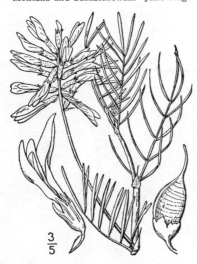

7. Astragalus racemòsus Pursh. Racemose Milk Vetch. Fig. 2540.

A. racemosus Pursh, Fl. Am. Sept. 740. 1814.

Erect or ascending, finely pubescent, branched at the base; stem somewhat zigzag, 1°–2° high. Stipules ovate-lanceolate, membranous, 2″–3″ long; leaflets 17–21, elliptic or linear-oblong, acutish or mucronate, 10″–15″ long; peduncles equalling or exceeding the leaves; flowers yellowish-white, 8″–9″ long, in loose spike-like racemes; pedicels 1″–2″ long; pods linear-oblong, imperfectly 2-celled by the intrusion of the dorsal suture, triangular in section, acute at each end, glabrous, stipitate, broadly sulcate, pendent, about 1′ long.

Plains and hills, North Dakota to Missouri, Kansas, Colorado and New Mexico. June–July.

$\dfrac{3}{5}$

$\dfrac{2}{3}$

8. Astragalus Drummóndii Dougl. Drummond's Milk Vetch. Fig. 2541.

Astragalus Drummondii Dougl.; Hook. Fl. Bor. Am. 1 : 153. 1833.

Loosely woolly-pubescent, erect, 1°–2° high, rather stout, growing in clumps. Stipules ovate, long-acuminate, 3″–5″ long; leaflets 19–33, oblong or sometimes oblanceolate, obtuse at the apex, narrowed at the base, 5″–10″ long; flowers yellowish-white or the keel purplish tinged, 8″–9″ long, in loose spikes; peduncles equalling or exceeding the leaves; pod 1-celled, the dorsal suture somewhat intruded, distinctly stipitate, cartilaginous, linear, pendent, glabrous, grooved, about 2′ long; calyx somewhat enlarged at the base, dark-pubescent above.

Hills, plains and valleys, South Dakota to Nebraska, Saskatchewan, Alberta and Colorado. June–July.

9. Astragalus Robbínsii (Oakes) A. Gray. Robbins' Milk Vetch. Fig. 2542.

Phaca Robbinsii Oakes, Hovey's Mag. Hort. 7 : 179. 1841.
Astragalus Robbinsii A. Gray, Man. Ed. 2, 98. 1856.

Glabrous or nearly so, erect, slender, branched at the base, 9′–18′ high. Stipules ovate-oblong, membranous, 2″–3″ long; leaflets 7–11, oblong, obtuse or slightly emarginate at the apex, narrowed or rounded at the base, 4″–8″ long; flowers white, 3″–5″ long in loose short or elongated racemes; pedicels 1″–2″ long; pod flattened, 1-celled, oblong, short-stipitate, rather abruptly pointed at each end, membranous, finely blackish-pubescent, dehiscent, nearly straight, not furrowed, or obsoletely so, 9″–12″ long.

Known only from rocky ledges of the Winooski River, Vermont; station now obliterated, and the species extinct, unless inhabiting some undiscovered locality. June–July.

$\dfrac{1}{2}$

10. Astragalus alpìnus L.   Alpine Milk Vetch.   Fig. 2543.

Astragalus alpinus L. Sp. Pl. 760. 1753.

Phaca astragalina DC. Astrag. 64. 1803.

A. alpinus Brunetinus Fernald, Rhodora 10: 91. 1908.

Ascending or decumbent, branched from the base 6′–15′ high, slightly pubescent, or glabrous. Stipules ovate, foliaceous, 2″–3″ long; leaflets 13–25, oval or elliptic, obtuse or retuse, narrowed or rounded at the base, 3″–6″ long; flowers violet, the keel commonly darker, in short racemes; peduncles mostly exceeding the leaves; pod 1-celled, somewhat flattened, membranous, stipitate, pendent, dehiscent, rather densely black-pubescent, oblong, acute, somewhat inflated, about 6″ long, deeply furrowed on the under side; calyx dark-pubescent.

On rocks, Maine and Vermont to Newfoundland and Labrador, west to Alaska and British Columbia, south in the Rocky Mountains to Colorado. Also in northern Europe and Asia. June.

11. Astragalus Blàkei Eggleston.   Blake's Milk Vetch.   Fig. 2544.

A. Robbinsii occidentalis S. Wats. Bot. King's Exp. 70. 1871.

A. Robbinsii Jesupi Eggleston & Sheldon, Bull. Geol. Nat. Hist. Surv. Minn. 9: 155. 1894.

A. Blakei Eggleston, Bot. Gaz. 20: 271. 1895.

A. Jesupi Britton, Man. 1048. 1901.

Similar to the two preceding species, but stem rather stouter, erect or nearly so, up to 20′ high, sparingly pubescent. Leaflets 9–15, oblong to elliptic, obtuse or emarginate, glabrous above, pubescent beneath; corolla whitish or bluish purple, 5″–6″ long; pod 1′ long or less, pubescent, swollen, somewhat triangular in section.

Rocky banks and cliffs. Maine and Vermont. May-June. Also in the Rocky Mountains.

12. Astragalus distórtus T. & G.   Bent Milk Vetch.   Fig. 2545.

Astragalus distortus T. & G. Fl. N. A. 1: 333. 1838.

Sparingly pubescent or glabrate, diffuse or ascending, much branched from the base, stems 8′–15′ long. Leaflets 11–25, obovate or oval, emarginate or rounded at the apex, narrowed at the base, 2″–5″ long; flowers purple, 4″–6″ long, in loose short spikes; pod sessile in the calyx, 1-celled, slightly inflated, linear-oblong, coriaceous, strongly curved, glabrous, grooved on the under side, 1′–1½′ long.

In dry soil, Illinois to Iowa, south to West Virginia, Mississippi and Texas. March–July.

13. Astragalus lotiflòrus Hook. Low Milk Vetch. Fig. 2546.

Astragalus lotiflorus Hook. Fl. Bor. Am. **1**: 152. 1833.
Phaca lotiflora T. & G. Fl. N. A. **1**: 349. 1838.
Astragalus elatiocarpus Sheld. Bull. Geol. Nat. Hist. Surv. Minn. **9**: 20. 1894.
Phaca elatiocarpa Rydb. Bull. Torr. Club **32**: 665. 1906.
A. nebraskensis Bates, Torreya **5**: 216. 1906.

Pubescent, with long white hairs, branched from the base, nearly acaulescent, or with stems 1′–3′ long. Stipules ovate, acuminate, 1½″–2″ long; leaflets 7–15, oval or oblong, obtuse and sometimes mucronulate at the apex, narrowed at the base, 5″–8″ long; flowers few, yellow, 4″–6″ long, in rather dense short spikes; calyx campanulate, its teeth subulate; peduncles shorter than or equalling the leaves, sometimes very short; pod 1-celled, sessile, villous-pubescent, ovoid-oblong, coriaceous, somewhat inflated, pointed, dehiscent, keeled along the straight dorsal suture.

Prairies and plains, Manitoba to South Dakota, Missouri, Nebraska, Texas, British Columbia and Colorado. June–July.

14. Astragalus missouriénsis Nutt. Missouri Milk Vetch. Fig. 2547.

Astragalus melanocarpus Nutt. Fraser's Cat. Name only. 1813.

Astragalus missouriensis Nutt. Gen. **2**: 99. 1818.

Densely silky-canescent all over, tufted, branching from the base, 2′–5′ long. Stipules ovate-lanceolate, acute, 2″–4″ long, leaflets 7–21, elliptic or obovate, obtuse but sometimes mucronate at the apex, narrowed or rounded at the base, 3″–5″ long; flowers few, violet-purple, 5″–9″ long in loose heads or short spikes; pod 1-celled, sessile, acute, oblong, pubescent, dehiscent, coriaceous, circular in section, slightly keeled along the ventral suture, transversely wrinkled, about 1′ long.

Plains, Kansas and Nebraska to Saskatchewan and New Mexico. May–July.

15. Astragalus Shortiànus Nutt. Short's Milk Vetch. Fig. 2548.

Astragalus Shortianus Nutt.; T. & G. Fl. N. A. **1**: 331. 1838.

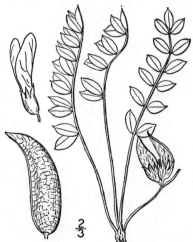

Silvery canescent, nearly acaulescent, somewhat branched from the base. Stipules ovate, acutish, about 2″ long; leaflets 9–15, elliptic or obovate, acutish at the apex, narrowed or rounded at the base, 5″–9″ long; flowers blue or violet, 7″–9″ long; peduncles commonly shorter than the leaves; pod 1-celled, sessile, coriaceous, 8-shaped in section, dehiscent at maturity, lanceolate-ovoid, puberulent, transversely wrinkled, strongly curved and beaked at the summit, 1′–1½′ long.

Plains and hills, North Dakota to Montana, Nebraska, Colorado, New Mexico and Arizona. May–July.

16. Astragalus eucósmos Robinson. Pretty Milk Vetch. Fig. 2549.

Phaca elegans Hook. Fl. Bor. Am. 1 : 144. 1830.
Astragalus oroboides var. *americana* A. Gray, Proc. Am. Acad. 6 : 205. 1864.
Phaca parviflora Nutt.; T. & G. Fl. N. A. 1 : 348. 1838.
A. elegans Britton; Britt. & Brown, Ill. Fl. 2 : 303. 1897. Not Bunge.
A. eucosmos Robinson, Rhodora 10 : 33. 1908.

Glabrous or nearly so, decumbent or nearly erect, slender, somewhat branched, 10′–20′ high. Stipules ovate, acute, about 2″ long; flowers bluish or purple, 3″–4″ long, in elongated spike-like racemes; leaflets 9–17, oblong or linear-oblong, 8″–10″ long; pedicels at length 1″ long; pod sessile, ellipsoid, 1-celled, pendent, slightly inflated, obtuse at each end, apiculate, black-pubescent all over, 2″–3″ long.

Labrador, Quebec and northern Maine; Saskatchewan to Yukon and Colorado. June–Aug.

17. Astragalus aboriginòrum Richards. Indian Milk Vetch. Fig. 2550.

Astragalus aboriginorum Richards. App. Frank. Journ. 28. 1823.
Phaca aborigina Hook. Fl. Bor. Am. 1 : 143. *pl. 56.* 1830.
Homalobus aboriginum Rydb. in Britton, Man. 554. 1901.

Finely canescent or glabrate, erect, somewhat branched, 8′–15′ high. Stipules ovate, acute, membranous or foliaceous, 2″–3″ long; leaflets 9–13, linear or oblong, obtuse or acute, 6″–10″ long; flowers white, tinged with violet, 4″–5″ long, in rather loose racemes; peduncles longer than the leaves; pod slightly inflated, compressed, oval in section, 1-celled, glabrous, half-elliptic, long-stipitate, acute at each end, slightly sulcate, the dorsal suture slightly intruded; calyx blackish-pubescent, its teeth subulate.

South Dakota to Manitoba, Alberta and Colorado. Root long and yellow, "collected by the Cree and Stone Indians in the spring as an article of food" (Richardson). May–June.

18. Astragalus grácilis Nutt. Slender Milk Vetch. Fig. 2551.

Dalea parviflora Pursh, Fl. Am. Sept. 474. 1814. Not *A. parviflorus* Lam. 1783.
Astragalus gracilis Nutt. Gen. 2 : 100. 1818.
Astragalus microlobus A. Gray, Proc. Am. Acad. 6 : 203. 1864.
Astragalus parviflorus MacM. Met. Minn. 325. 1892.

Slender, erect, or ascending, finely pubescent, 1°–2° high, simple or nearly so. Stipules ovate, acute or acuminate, 1½″–3″ long; leaflets 7–21, narrowly linear to linear-oblong, distant, obtuse, truncate or emarginate at the apex, 4″–12″ long, scarcely 1″ wide; flowers purple, 3″–4″ long, in narrow elongated spike-like racemes; pedicels 1″ long or less; pods 1-celled, sessile in the calyx, pendent, straight, coriaceous, ellipsoid, finely appressed-pubescent with white hairs, or at length glabrous or nearly so, transversely veined, 2″–3″ long.

Prairies and plains, Minnesota to Montana, Missouri, Texas, Colorado and Wyoming. May–June.

19. Astragalus flexuòsus (Hook.) Dougl. Flexile Milk Vetch. Fig. 2552.

Phaca elongata Hook. Fl. Bor. Am. **1**: 140. 1830. Not *Astragalus elongatus* Willd. 1803.
Phaca flexuosa Hook. Fl. Bor. Am. **1**: 141. 1830.
Astragalus flexuosus Dougl.; Hook. Fl. Bor. Am. **1**: 140. 1830.

Erect or ascending, finely pubescent, branching from the base, 1°–1½° high. Stipules ovate or ovate-lanceolate, 2″–3″ long; leaflets 9–21, linear, oblong or oblanceolate, obtuse or emarginate at the apex, narrowed or cuneate at the base, 3″–6″ long; peduncles exceeding the leaves; flowers purple or purplish, 4″–5″ long; pod 1-celled, sessile, cylindric, linear or linear-oblong, puberulent, dehiscent, pointed, 8″–12″ long.

Prairies and plains, Minnesota to Kansas, Saskatchewan, Alberta and Colorado. June–Aug.

27. PHÀCA L. Sp. Pl. 755. 1753.

Perennial herbs, similar to *Astragalus,* mostly with pinnate leaves, and racemed or spicate, purplish or purple flowers. Pod much inflated, membranous in texture, strictly 1-celled, neither of the sutures intruded. [Greek, Lentils.]

A large genus, mainly of the north temperate zone. Besides the following, numerous other species occur in the western parts of North America. Type species: *Phaca baetica* L.

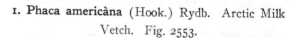

Leaflets 7–21, oblong, elliptic or ovate.
 Pod stalked; flowers slender-pedicelled. 1. P. americana.
 Pod sessile; flowers short-pedicelled. 2. P. neglecta.
Leaflets only 1, or sometimes 3–5, very narrowly linear. 3. P. longifolia.

1. Phaca americàna (Hook.) Rydb. Arctic Milk Vetch. Fig. 2553.

P. frigida var. *americana* Hook. Fl. Bor. Am. **1**: 140. 1830.
Astragalus frigidus var. *americanus* S. Wats. Bibl. Index, **1**: 193. 1878.
Phaca americana Rydb.; Britt. & Brown, Ill. Fl. **2**: 304. 1897.

Erect, nearly simple, glabrous, 1°–2° high. Stipules foliaceous, ovate-oblong, 2″–6″ long; leaflets 7–17, oval or ovate-lanceolate, 9″–18″ long; peduncles generally exceeding the leaves; flowers white, 8″–9″ long, in loose racemes; pedicels filiform, ½′ long in fruit; pod 1-celled, stipitate, inflated, membranous, 10″–12″ long, acute at each end, oblong, dehiscent at maturity, glabrous, shining.

In wet rocky places, Quebec to British Columbia and Alaska, south to South Dakota and in the Rocky Mountains to Wyoming. June–July.

2. Phaca neglécta T. & G. Cooper's Milk Vetch. Fig. 2554.

Phaca neglecta T. & G. Fl. N. A. **1**: 344. 1838.
Astragalus Cooperi A. Gray, Man. Ed. 2, 98. 1856.
Astragalus neglectus Sheldon, Bull. Geol. Surv. Minn. **9**: 59. 1894.

Glabrous or nearly so, erect, 1°–2° high. Stipules ovate, acute, 1″–2″ long; leaflets 9–21, thin, oblong or elliptic, often minutely pubescent beneath, 8″–12″ long, obtuse or emarginate at the apex, narrowed at the base; peduncles shorter than or equalling the leaves; flowers white, 5″–7″ long, in rather loose spikes; calyx pubescent with blackish hairs, its teeth subulate; pod 1-celled, sessile, the ventral suture somewhat intruded, inflated, coriaceous, ovoid, acute, glabrous, slightly furrowed along both sutures, 6″–10″ long, 5″–6″ thick.

On banks and shores, Quebec to Niagara, west to Minnesota and Iowa. June–July.

3. Phaca longifòlia (Pursh) Nutt. Long-leaved Milk Vetch. Fig. 2555.

Psoralea longifolia Pursh, Fl. Am. Sept. 741. 1814.
Phaca longifolia Nutt.; T. & G. Fl. N. A. 1: 346. 1838.
Astragalus pictus var. *filifolius* A. Gray, Proc. Am. Acad. 6: 215. 1864.
A. filifolius Smyth, Trans. Kans. Acad. 15: 61. 1895.

Erect, very slender, branching, finely canescent, 6′–18′ high. Stipules subulate, rigid, those of the lower part of the stem connate; leaflet usually 1, narrowly linear, nearly terete, 1′–4′ long, ½″–1″ wide, sometimes 3 or 5; leaves persistent; flowers few, pink, 3″–5″ long, in short loose racemes; peduncles much shorter than the leaves; pod 1-celled, short-stalked, much-inflated, membranous, spotted, glabrous, ovoid, short-pointed, not furrowed, about 1′ long, ½′ thick.

In sandy soil, South Dakota to Nebraska, Wyoming, Idaho and New Mexico. Bird-egg pea. May–June.

Phaca Bodini (Sheldon) Rydb., a decumbent species with small blackish pubescent pods and purple flowers, common in Wyoming and Colorado, enters our area in western Nebraska.

28. HOMÁLOBUS Nutt.; T. & G. Fl. N. A. 1: 352. 1838.

Perennial herbs, with pinnate simple or pinnately 3–5-foliolate leaves, and racemose mostly small flowers, the peduncles short, or elongated. Keel of the corolla obtuse. Pod flat, glabrous or pubescent, completely 1-celled, few–several-seeded, the sutures both prominent externally. [Greek, regular-lobes.]

Besides the following species, some 30 others occur in western North America. Type species: *Homalobus caespitosus* Nutt.

Plants leafy-stemmed; leaves pinnate; leaflets 9–23, thin.   1. *H. tenellus.*
Plants scapose; leaves simple, or pinnately 3–5-foliolate, the leaflets very narrow. 2. *H. caespitosus.*

1. Homalobus tenéllus (Pursh) Britton. Loose-flowered Milk Vetch. Fig. 2556.

Astragalus tenellus Pursh, Fl. Am. Sept. 473. 1814.
Ervum multiflorum Pursh, Fl. Am. Sept. 739. 1814.
Homalobus multiflorus T. & G. Fl. N. A. 1: 351. 1838.
A. multiflorus A. Gray, Proc. Am. Acad. 6: 226. 1864.
H. stipitatus Rydb. Bull. Torr. Club 34: 419. 1907.

Ascending or diffuse, slender, branched, finely pubescent, or glabrate, 10′–18′ high. Stipules broadly ovate, 1½″–3″ long, acute or obtuse, the upper ones connate; leaflets 9–23, thin, oblong, linear-oblong or oblanceolate, obtuse at the apex, narrowed at the base, 6″–10″ long; flowers yellowish-white, 3″–4″ long, in loose spike-like racemes; pod stalked, straight, oblong, acute at each end, papery, glabrous, 6″–8″ long, 2″ wide.

Dry soil, Minnesota to Nebraska, Colorado, north to Saskatchewan and British Columbia. May–Aug.

2. Homalobus caespitòsus Nutt. Tufted Milk Vetch. Fig. 2557.

Homalobus caespitosus Nutt.; T. & G. Fl. N. A. 1: 352. 1838.

Astragalus caespitosus A. Gray, Proc. Am. Acad. 6: 230. 1864.

Silvery-canescent, much tufted from a deep root, 3′–6′ high. Stipules scarious, much imbricated, lanceolate, acuminate, 4″–6″ long; leaves simple, spatulate-linear, acute, 1′–2′ long, or some of them 3–5-foliolate, with oblong-linear leaflets; peduncles scapiform, exceeding or equalling the leaves; flowers purple, 4″–5″ long, in heads or short spike-like racemes; pod erect, sessile, few-seeded, oblong, acute, coriaceous, slightly curved, pubescent, 4″–5″ long; calyx-teeth subulate.

In dry rocky soil, Nebraska to Colorado, Utah, North Dakota and Assiniboia. May–July.

29. KENTROPHYTA Nutt.; T. & G. Fl. N. A. 1 : 353.   1838.

Low tufted perennial pubescent herbs, with pinnately 3–7-foliolate leaves, the linear persistent leaflets firm in texture, spinulose-tipped. Flowers 2 to 4 together in the axils or solitary, nearly sessile, yellow or yellowish. Calyx campanulate, the teeth nearly equal. Keel obtuse, shorter than the wings. Ovary few-ovuled. Pod short, ovate, 1-celled, somewhat coriaceous, with 1 or 2 seeds. [Greek, referring to the sharp-tipped leaflets.]

About 5 species, natives of central North America, the following typical.

1. Kentrophyta montàna Nutt.   Prickly Milk Vetch.   Fig. 2558.

Kentrophyta montana Nutt.; T. & G. Fl. N. A. 1 : 353. 1838.
Kentrophyta viridis Nutt.; T. & G. Fl. N. A. 1 : 353. 1838.
Astragalus Kentrophyta A. Gray, Proc. Acad. Phil. 1863 : 60. 1863.
Homalobus montanus Britton, in Britt. & Brown, Ill. Fl. 2 : 306. 1897.

Densely tufted, intricately branched, 2′–10′ high, finely canescent. Stipules linear-lanceolate, spiny-tipped, 2″–5″ long; leaflets 3–7, linear, rigid, spiny, widely spreading, 3″–6″ long, ½″ wide; flowers 1–4 together in the axils, nearly sessile, yellowish-white or bluish-tinged, 2″–3″ long; pod sessile or very short-stalked, 1–3-seeded, ovoid-oblong, acute, coriaceous, dehiscent, pubescent, 3″–4″ long.

In dry, rocky places, South Dakota to Nebraska, New Mexico and Saskatchewan. June–Sept.

30. OROPHACA Britton, in Britton & Brown, Ill. Fl. 2 : 306.   1897.

Perennial, silvery or villous-pubescent low tufted herbs, with branched woody caudices, deep roots, membranous scarious stipules, sheathing and united below, and digitately 3-foliolate (rarely 5-foliolate) leaves, resembling those of Lupines. Flowers few, capitate or racemose, the clusters sessile or peduncled. Keel of the corolla blunt. Pod coriaceous, completely 1-celled, ovoid or oval, few-seeded, villous, partly or wholly enclosed by the calyx. [Greek, mountain vetch.]

Three known species, the following, and one in Colorado and Wyoming. Type species: *Orophaca caespitosa* (Nutt.) Britton.

Flowers yellowish, 1–3 together in the axils.
    Corolla glabrous outside.   1. *O. caespitosa.*
    Corolla pubescent outside.   2. *O. argophylla.*
Flowers blue-purple, in peduncled racemes.   3. *O. sericea.*

1. Orophaca caespitòsa (Nutt.) Britton.   Sessile-flowered Milk Vetch.   Fig. 2559.

Astragalus triphyllus Pursh, Fl. Am. Sept. 740. 1814. Not Pall. 1800.
Phaca caespitosa Nutt. Gen. 2 : 98. 1818.
Orophaca caespitosa Britton, in Britt. & Brown, Ill. Fl. 2 : 306. 1897.

Silvery-canescent, densely tufted from a deep root, 2′–4′ high. Stipules scarious, imbricated, glabrous, ovate-lanceolate, 3″–4″ long; leaves digitately 3–5-foliolate, slender-petioled; leaflets oblong or oblanceolate, acute or obtusish at the apex, narrowed or cuneate at the base, 6″–8″ long; flowers yellowish, 6″–8″ long, sessile in the axils of the leaves; calyx-teeth half as long as the tube; corolla glabrous; pod 1-celled, sessile, ovoid, acute or acuminate, coriaceous, dehiscent, villous-pubescent, enclosed by the calyx, 2″–3″ long.

Plains and hills, Kansas, Nebraska and South Dakota to Montana and Saskatchewan. May–July.

2. Orophaca argophýlla (Nutt.) Rydb. Silvery Milk Vetch. Fig. 2560.

Phaca argophylla Nutt.; T. & G. Fl. N. A. 1: 342. 1838.

Astragalus hyalinus M. E. Jones, Proc. Cal. Acad. II. 5: 648. 1895.

Orophaca argophylla Rydb. in Britton, Man. Ed. 2, 1067. 1905.

Similar to the preceding species, but the leaflets relatively shorter and broader. Stipules scarious; corolla about 5″ long, pubescent outside; calyx-teeth a little shorter than the tube.

In dry soil, Nebraska and Wyoming. May–July.

3. Orophaca serícea (Nutt.) Britton. Hoary Milk Vetch. Fig. 2561.

Phaca sericea Nutt.; T. & G. Fl. N. A. 1: 343. 1838.

Astragalus sericoleucus A. Gray, Am. Journ. Sci. (II.) 33: 410. 1862.

Orophaca sericea Britton, in Britt. & Brown, Ill. Fl. 2: 307. 1897.

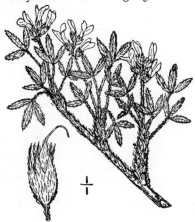

Villous-pubescent, densely tufted, and spreading on the ground from a deep root, the stems 3′–4′ long. Leaves short-petioled, 3-foliolate; leaflets oblong or oblanceolate, acute or obtusish at the apex, narrowed or cuneate at the base, 2″–5″ long; peduncles slender, 2–6-flowered, equalling or exceeding the leaves; flowers bluish-purple, about 3″ long; pod 1-celled, sessile, ovoid-oblong, coriaceous, acute, villous-pubescent, about 3″ long, partly enclosed by the calyx.

In dry, sandy or rocky places, Nebraska to Wyoming and Colorado. May–July.

31. OXÝTROPIS DC. Astrag. 19. 1802.

[ARAGALLUS Neck. Elem. 3: 12. Hyponym. 1790.]
[SPIESIA Neck. Elem. 3: 13. Hyponym. 1790.]

Herbs, sometimes shrubby, and mostly acaulescent, with odd-pinnate leaves, and racemose or spicate flowers. Calyx-teeth nearly equal. Petals clawed; standard erect, ovate or oblong; wings oblong; keel erect, shorter than or equalling the wings, its apex mucronate, acuminate or appendaged; stamens diadelphous; anthers all alike; style filiform. Pod sessile or stipitate, 2-valved, 1-celled, or more or less 2-celled by the intrusion of the ventral suture. [Greek, referring to the sharp-pointed keel of the corolla.]

About 130 species, natives of the north temperate zone. In addition to the following, some 20 others occur in the western and northwestern parts of North America. Type species: *Oxytropis montana* (L.) DC.

Leaves simply pinnate.
  Plants 1′–4′ high; heads few-flowered.
    Pod membranous, pubescent, much inflated, 1-celled.   1. *O. podocarpa.*
    Pod coriaceous, ovoid, little inflated, pubescent, partly 2-celled.
      Calyx gray-pubescent; leaflets 7–9, oblong.   2. *O. multiceps.*
      Calyx dark-pubescent; leaflets 7–21, linear.   3. *O. arctica.*
  Plants 6′–18′ high; heads or spike-like racemes many-flowered.
    Sparingly pubescent; flowers 8″–9″ long; pods papery.   4. *O. campestris.*
    Silky-pubescent; flowers 9″–15″ long; pods coriaceous.   5. *O. Lamberti.*
Leaves pinnate, the leaflets verticillate.
  Pod scarcely longer than the calyx, its tip spreading.   6. *O. splendens.*
  Pod 2–3 times as long as the calyx, its tip erect.   7. *O. Belli.*

1. Oxytropis podocàrpa A. Gray. Inflated Oxytrope. Fig. 2562.

Oxytropis arctica var. *inflata* Hook. Fl. Bor. Am. 1: 146. 1833.
Oxytropis podocarpa A. Gray, Proc. Am. Acad. 6: 234. 1864.
Spiesia inflata Britton, Mem. Torr. Club 5: 201. 1894.
Aragallus inflatus A. Nelson, Erythea 7: 59. 1899.

Acaulescent or nearly so, more or less villous-pubescent, much tufted, 1'–4' high. Stipules membranous, imbricated, adnate to the petiole, lanceolate, about 2'' long; leaves pinnate; leaflets 9–21, linear, 2''–4'' long, about ½'' wide, obtuse or obtusish; peduncles 1–2-flowered, scarcely exceeding the leaves; flowers violet, 7''–8'' long; calyx densely dark-pubescent; pod membranous, much inflated, 1-celled, ovoid, pubescent, short-stalked or sessile in the calyx, about 9'' long, pointed; ventral suture slightly intruded.

Arctic and alpine; Labrador and arctic America, south in the Rocky Mountains to Colorado. Summer.

2. Oxytropis múlticeps Nutt. Tufted Oxytrope. Fig. 2563.

Oxytropis multiceps Nutt.; T. & G. Fl. N. A. 1: 341. 1838.
Spiesia multiceps Kuntze, Rev. Gen. Pl. 207. 1891.
Aragallus multiceps Heller, Cat. N. A. Pl. 4. 1898.

Nearly acaulescent, with a deep root, tufted and matted, silky-canescent, 3' high or less. Stipules membranous, acute, adnate to the petiole; leaves pinnate; leaflets 7–9, oblong, 3''–6'' long, 1''–2'' wide, scape ½'–1½' long, about equalling the leaves, or shorter, 1–3-flowered; flowers purple, nearly 1' long; calyx slightly pubescent, its teeth short; pod short-stalked in the calyx, coriaceous, little inflated, about ½' long, 1-celled, acute, pubescent, enclosed by the swollen calyx.

On dry hills and mountains, western Nebraska, Wyoming and Colorado. Summer.

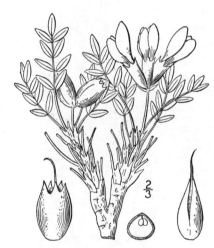

3. Oxytropis àrctica R. Br. Arctic Oxytrope. Fig. 2564.

Oxytropis arctica R. Br. App. Parry's Voy. 278. 1823.
Spiesia arctica Kuntze, Rev. Gen. Pl. 206. 1891.
Aragallus arcticus Greene, Pittonia 3: 211. 1897.

Acaulescent, tufted, villous-pubescent, 1'–4' high. Stipules membranous, lanceolate, imbricated, pubescent; leaves pinnate; leaflets 7–21, linear, or linear-oblong, obtusish, 2''–4'' long, about ½'' wide; peduncles exceeding the leaves, 2–5-flowered at the summit; flowers violet(?), 6''–10'' long; calyx pubescent; pod coriaceous, little or not inflated, oblong or ovoid-oblong, sessile, pubescent, incompletely 2-celled.

Shores of the Gulf of St. Lawrence; Hudson Strait, Hudson Bay, and along the Arctic seacoast. Summer. Several related species occur in high arctic America.

4. Oxytropis campéstris (L.) DC. Yellow or Field Oxytrope. Fig. 2565.

Astragalus campestris L. Sp. Pl. 761. 1753.
Oxytropis campestris DC. Astrag. 74. 1802.
O. campestris coerulea Koch, Syn. 181. 1838.
Spiesia campestris Kuntze, Rev. Gen. Pl. 206. 1891.
O. campestris johannensis Fernald, Rhodora 1 : 88. 1899.
Aragallus johannensis Heller, Cat. N. A. Pl. Ed. 2, 7. 1900.

Acaulescent or nearly so, much tufted, sparingly pubescent, or glabrate, 6'-15' high. Stipules membranous, lanceolate, acuminate, imbricated, 3"-4" long; leaves pinnate,
3'-6' long; leaflets 13-27, lanceolate or oblong, acute or
obtusish at the apex, rounded at the base, sessile, 3"-15"
long, 1"-4" wide; peduncles generally exceeding the leaves;
flowers several or numerous in short spikes or heads, white,
yellow, rose-colored or blue, 6"-8" long; pods sessile, papery
in texture, ovoid or oblong, blackish-pubescent, 6"-12" long,
acuminate with the subulate style, incompletely 2-celled.

In rocky and gravelly places, Quebec, northern Maine and
New Brunswick to Labrador and Hudson Strait. Also in Europe. Summer. Consists of several races, differing in size and
in color and size of the flowers.

5. Oxytropis Lámberti Pursh. Stemless Loco- or Crazy-weed. Colorado Loco Vetch. Fig. 2566.

Oxytropis Lamberti Pursh, Fl. Am. Sept. 740. 1814.
Spiesia Lamberti Kuntze, Rev. Gen. Pl. 207. 1891.
Oxytropis sericea Nutt.; T. & G. Fl. N. A. 1 : 339. 1838.

Silky-pubescent with appressed or slightly spreading hairs,
acaulescent or nearly so, tufted. Stipules imbricated, membranous, pubescent, lanceolate, acute or acuminate, 4"-7"
long; leaves 4'-9' long; leaflets 9-19, linear, oblong or sometimes lanceolate, acute or obtusish at the apex, mainly rounded
at the base, 8"-12" long, 1½"-3" wide; peduncles longer than
the leaves, 6'-12' long; flowers purple, yellow, or purplish,
8"-15" long, in dense heads or spikes; pod incompletely
2-celled, coriaceous, sessile, erect, ovoid-cylindric, densely
pubescent, long-acuminate, 6"-12" long, exceeding the calyx.

Prairies, Minnesota to North Dakota, Saskatchewan and British
Columbia, south to Texas and New Mexico. Consists of several
races, differing in amount of pubescence, shape and size of leaflets, color of flowers, and size of pods. April-Aug.

6. Oxytropis spléndens Dougl. Showy Oxytrope. Fig. 2567.

Oxytropis splendens Dougl.; Hook. Fl. Bor. Am. 1 : 147. 1833.
Spiesia splendens Kuntze, Rev. Gen. Pl. 207. 1891.
Aragallus splendens Greene, Pittonia 3 : 211. 1897.

Densely silvery and silky-villous, acaulescent, tufted.
Stipules imbricated, membranous, villous-pubescent, lanceolate, acute, 4"-6" long; leaves 4'-9½' long, erect; leaflets
very numerous, in verticils of 3-6, oblong or oblong-lanceolate, acute or acutish at the apex, rounded at the base,
6"-10" long, 2"-4" wide; peduncles exceeding the leaves,
sometimes 12' long; flowers deep purple, about 6" long,
in dense spikes; pods ovoid, erect, 2-celled or nearly so,
long-acuminate with a spreading or oblique tip, villous-
pubescent, little exceeding the calyx, 6"-9" long.

Prairies and plains, Minnesota and North Dakota to Saskatchewan, Colorado and New Mexico. June-Aug.

7. Oxytropis Bélli (Britton) Palibine.   Bell's
Oxytrope. Fig. 2568.

Spiesia Belli Britton; J. M. Macoun, Can. Rec. Sci.
1894: 148. 1894.
Aragallus Belli Greene, Pittonia 3: 212. 1897.
O. Belli Palibine, Bull. Soc. Bot. Genève 2: 19. 1910.

Acaulescent, tufted, loosely villous with white
hairs. Stipules membranous, ovate or oblong, acute
or acuminate, imbricated, villous or glabrate, 5″-7″
long; leaves 3′-6′ long; leaflets oblong or oblong-
lanceolate, subacute at the apex, rounded at the base,
3″-4″ long, 1″-2″ wide, in verticils of 3 or 4; peduncles about equalling the leaves; inflorescence capitate; pod oblong, erect-spreading, densely pubescent
with black hairs or some longer whitish ones intermixed, about 9″ long and 3″ thick, 2–3 times as long
as the black-pubescent calyx, very nearly or quite
2-celled by the intrusion of the ventral suture, the tip
erect; corolla not seen.

Hudson Bay. Summer.

32. GLYCYRRHÌZA [Tourn.] L. Sp. Pl. 741. 1753.

Perennial herbs, with thick sweet roots, odd-pinnate leaves, and blue or white flowers in
axillary spikes or heads. Calyx-teeth nearly equal, the two upper sometimes partly united.
Standard narrowly ovate or oblong, short-clawed; wings oblong, acutish; keel acute or obtuse,
shorter than the wings. Stamens mainly diadelphous; anthers alternately smaller and longer.
Pod sessile, covered with prickles or glands, nearly indehiscent, continuous between the seeds.
[Greek, sweet-root.]

About 15 species, natives of the north temperate zone, southern South America and Australia.
Besides the following, another occurs in California. Type species: *Glycyrrhiza echinata* L.

1. Glycyrrhiza lepidòta Pursh.   Wild or
American Licorice. Fig. 2569.

Liquivitia lepidota Nutt. in Fraser's Cat. Hyponym. 1813.

Glycyrrhiza lepidota Pursh, Fl. Am. Sept. 480. 1814.

Erect, branching, 1°-3° high, the foliage with
minute scales or glands. Stipules lanceolate or ovate-
lanceolate, acute, 2″-3″ long, deciduous; leaves petioled; leaflets 11–19, lanceolate, or oblong, acute or
obtuse and mucronate at the apex, rounded or narrowed at the base, entire, very short-stalked, 10″-18″
long, 3″-6″ wide; peduncles much shorter than the
leaves; spikes dense, many-flowered, 1′-2′ long, about
9″ thick; flowers yellowish-white, 6″ long; calyx-
teeth slender, longer than the tube; pod about 6″
long, few-seeded, oblong, densely covered with
hooked prickles.

Hudson Bay to Minnesota, Saskatchewan, Washington,
Iowa, Missouri, Chihuahua and Arizona. Locally in
waste grounds farther east. May–Aug. Licorice-root.

33. CORONÍLLA [Tourn.] L. Sp. Pl. 742. 1753.

Herbs, with odd-pinnate leaves, and purple purplish or yellow flowers, in axillary peduncled heads or umbels. Calyx-teeth nearly equal, the 2 upper more or less united. Petals
clawed; standard nearly orbicular; wings oblong or obliquely obovate; keel incurved, beaked.
Stamens diadelphous (9 and 1); anthers all alike. Pod terete, angled or compressed, curved
or straight, jointed. [Diminutive of *corona*, crown.]

About 25 species, natives of Europe, Asia and northern Africa. Type species: *Coronilla
valentìna* L.

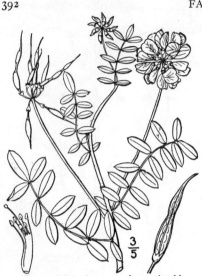

1. Coronilla vària L. Coronilla. Axseed. Axwort. Fig. 2570.

Coronilla varia L. Sp. Pl. 743. 1753.

Perennial, straggling or ascending, glabrous, branching, 1°–2° long. Leaves sessile; leaflets 11–25, oblong or obovate, obtuse and mucronate at the apex, narrowed or rounded at the base, 6″–9″ long, 1½″–3″ wide; peduncles longer than the leaves; flowers 4″–6″ long, pinkish-white (standard pink, wings white or purple-tipped), in dense umbels; pedicels 1″–2″ long; pod coriaceous, linear, 4-angled, the joints 3″–4″ long.

Roadsides and waste places, Massachusetts to southern New York, Maryland and Missouri. Adventive or naturalized from Europe. Hive-vine. June–Aug.

34. HEDÝSARUM L. Sp. Pl. 745. 1753.

Perennial herbs, sometimes shrubby, with odd-pinnate leaves, and showy flowers in axillary peduncled racemes. Calyx bracteolate, its teeth nearly equal. Standard obovate or obcordate, narrowed at the base; wings oblong, shorter than the standard; keel longer than the wings, obtuse, obliquely truncate. Stamens diadelphous (9 and 1). Pod flat, linear, its joints oval, orbicular or quadrate, readily separable. [Greek, sweet-broom.]

About 70 species, natives of the north temperate zone and northern Africa. Besides the following several others occur in western North America. Type species: *Hedysarum coronarium* L.

1. Hedysarum boreale Nutt. Hedysarum. Fig. 2571.

Hedysarum alpinum var. *americanum* Michx. Fl. Bor. Am.
2 : 74. 1803.
Hedysarum boreale Nutt. Gen. 2 : 110. 1818.
Hedysarum americanum Britton, Mem. Torr. Club 5 : 201.
1894.

Stem erect or somewhat decumbent, glabrous or nearly so, 6′–2½° high, generally simple. Leaves short-petioled; stipules lanceolate, long-acuminate, 2″–8″ long; leaflets 11–21, oblong or oblanceolate, obtuse and often mucronulate at the apex, mostly rounded at the base, 6″–10″ long, 2″–5″ wide; racemes longer than the leaves; flowers violet-purple, or sometimes white, numerous, deflexed, 7″–10″ long, in rather loose elongated racemes; calyx-teeth ovate, acute, shorter than the tube; pod ½′–1½′ long, drooping, of 3–5 oval or orbicular, glabrous or somewhat pubescent, strongly reticulated joints, about 2½″ wide.

In rocky places, Labrador and Newfoundland to Alaska, British Columbia, Maine, Vermont, Ontario, South Dakota, south in the Rocky Mountains to Utah. Recorded by Michaux from the Alleghanies. June–July.

Hedysàrum Mackénzii Richards., admitted into our first edition as from Hudson Bay, differs in having longer subulate calyx-teeth; it inhabits northwestern North America.

35. AESCHYNÓMENE L. Sp. Pl. 713. 1753.

Herbs, or in tropical regions shrubs, mainly with odd-pinnate leaves, those of many species sensitive to the touch, and yellow flowers in axillary panicles or racemes. Calyx-teeth nearly equal, more or less united into 2 lips. Standard orbicular, short-clawed; wings oblong or obliquely obovate, about as long as the standard; keel curved. Stamens diadelphous (5 and 5); anthers all alike. Ovary stipitate; ovules 2–∞. Pod stalked in the calyx, flat, jointed. [Greek, to be ashamed, referring to the sensitive leaves.]

About 55 species, widely distributed in warm and tropical regions. Besides the following, another occurs in the southern states. Type species: *Aeschynomene áspera* L.

1. Aeschynomene virgínica (L.) B.S.P.   Sensitive Joint Vetch.   Fig. 2572.

Hedysarum virginicum L. Sp. Pl. 750. 1753.

Aeschynomene hispida Willd. Sp. Pl. 3 : 1163. 1800.

Aeschynomene virginica B.S.P. Prel. Cat. N. Y. 13. 1888.

Annual, herbaceous, branched, erect, rough-pubescent or glabrate, 2°–5° high. Stipules membranous, ovate, acuminate, 3″–4″ long, deciduous; leaves short-petioled; leaflets 25–55, oblong, linear-oblong or oblanceolate, obtuse at the apex, narrowed or rounded at the base, 3″–9″ long; somewhat sensitive; flowers few, racemose, reddish-yellow, about 5″ long; petals veined; pod linear, 1′–2½′ long, 3″ wide, sparingly tuberculate or glabrous, of 5–10 nearly square easily separable joints.

River banks, southeastern Pennsylvania, southwestern New Jersey to Florida, west to Louisiana and Mexico. Jamaica. Called also bastard sensitive plant. Aug.–Sept.

36. STYLOSÁNTHES Sw. Prodr. Fl. Ind. Occ. 108. 1788.

Perennial herbs, mainly with some villous or viscid pubescence, 3-foliolate leaves, and yellow terminal or axillary spicate or capitate flowers. Calyx deciduous, its tube narrow, its teeth membranous, the 4 upper ones more or less united. Petals and stamens inserted at or near the summit of the tube; standard orbicular; wings oblong; keel curved, beaked. Stamens monadelphous; anthers alternately longer and shorter. Ovary nearly sessile; ovules 2–3; style filiform. Pod sessile, flattened, 1–2-jointed, reticulate, dehiscent at the summit. [Greek, column-flower, alluding to the column-like calyx-tube.]

About 30 species, natives of warm and temperate regions. Besides the following, another occurs in the southern States. Type species: *Stylosanthes procumbens* Sw.

Leaflets oblong-linear to oblanceolate; floral bracts entire.	1. *S. biflora.*
Leaflets elliptic to obovate; floral bracts deeply cleft.	2. *S. riparia.*

1. Stylosanthes biflòra (L.) B.S.P.   Pencil-flower.   Fig. 2573.

Trifolium biflorum L. Sp. Pl. 773. 1753.

Stylosanthes elatior Sw. Svensk. Acad. Handl. 1789 : 296. *pl. 2. f. 2.* 1789.

Stylosanthes biflora B.S.P. Prel. Cat. N. Y. 13. 1888.

Wiry, branched from the base and often also above, stems ascending, erect or spreading, villous-pubescent or glabrate, 6′–24′ long. Stipules sheathing the stem, linear-filiform above; leaves short-petioled; leaflets 3, oblong, linear-oblong or oblanceolate, acute or acutish and mucronate at the apex, narrowed or cuneate at the base, 6″–18″ long, 1½″–2″ wide, strongly veined, the terminal one stalked; upper bracts entire; flowers few, mainly terminal, sessile or nearly so, yellow, ciliate-bracted, 3″–4″ long; pod obovate or suborbicular, pubescent, about 2″ long, of 1 perfect and 1 abortive joint.

In dry soil, southeastern New York to Florida, west to Indiana, Kansas, Tennessee, Louisiana and Texas. June–Sept.

A very hairy southern race, ranging north to Virginia and Missouri, is known as *S. biflora hispidissima* (Michx.) Pollard & Ball.

2. Stylosanthes ripària Kearney. Decumbent Pencil-
flower. Fig. 2574.

Stylosanthes riparia Kearney, Bull. Torr. Club **24**: 565. 1897.

Stems decumbent, or ascending, 3'–12' long, usually with a
tomentose line on the elongated internodes. Stipules sheathing, subulate above; petioles pubescent; leaflets elliptic to
obovate-cuneate, the terminal one 5"–9" long, the lateral ones
somewhat smaller; spikes terminal, about 6-flowered, with
only 1 or 2 perfect flowers; calyx-tube conspicuously veined,
about 2" long; vexillum proportionately longer than in *S.
biflora;* floral bracts usually deeply cleft to the middle, or
beyond, 2-nerved; upper (perfect) segment of the pod nearly
twice as broad as in *S. biflora.*

$\frac{3}{5}$

In dry woods, Pennsylvania and Delaware to West Virginia,
Alabama and Tennessee. May–Aug.

37. ZÓRNIA Gmel. Syst. **2**: 1096. 1791.

Herbs, with digitately 4-foliolate or 2-foliolate petioled leaves, the leaflets not stipellate,
the stipules small or foliaceous, sagittate. Flowers yellow in our species, small, interruptedly
spicate, large-bracted, sessile, rarely solitary, the spikes axillary and terminal, peduncled. Bracts
2 together, nearly enclosing the flower. Calyx 2-lipped, 5-lobed, its tube short. Standard
nearly orbicular, clawed; wings oblique; keel incurved. Stamens monadelphous; anthers
alternately longer and shorter. Ovary sessile; ovules several; style very slender. Loment
flat, several-jointed. [In honor of Johann Zorn, a German apothecary.]

About 12 species, all natives of America, 2 of them naturalized in the warmer regions of the
Old World, the following typical. Besides the following, another occurs in the southwestern states.

1. Zornia bracteàta (Walt.) Gmel. Zornia. Fig. 2575.

Anonymos bracteata Walt. Fl. Car. 181. 1788.
Zornia bracteata Gmel. Syst. **2**: 1096. 1791.
Zornia tetraphylla Michx. Fl. Bor. Am. **2**: 76. 1803.

Perennial by a long woody root, glabrous or sparingly finely pubescent; stems wiry, prostrate, 1°–2°
long. Stipules about 3" long; petioles ½'–1' long, slender; leaflets 4, oblong, lanceolate, or oblong-obovate,
acute at both ends, ¼'–1' long, or those of the lower
leaves obtuse at the apex and shorter; peduncles longer
than the petioles; spikes several-flowered, much interrupted in fruit, 2'–4' long; bracts ovate or broadly oval,
3"–5" long, acute or acutish; pod 3–5-jointed, the joints
oval, 1½"–2" long, densely spinulose.

In dry sandy soil, southeastern Virginia to Florida,
Texas and Mexico. May–Aug.

$\frac{3}{5}$

Árachis hypogaèa L., the pea-nut, is occasionally seen
as a waif, not permanently established.

38. MEIBÒMIA Heist. Fabr. Enum. Pl. Hort. Helmst. 168. 1759.

[Desmodium Desv. Journ. Bot. (II.) **1**: 122. *pl. 5, f. 15.* 1813.]

Perennial herbs, sometimes woody at the base, erect, ascending or trailing, with stipellate
3-foliolate or in some species 1- or 5-foliolate leaves, and usually small flowers in terminal
or axillary compound or simple racemes or panicles. Calyx-tube short, its teeth more or less
united into 2 lips, the upper one variously 2-toothed, the 3 lower teeth acute or attenuate.
Standard oblong, ovate or orbicular, narrowed or rarely clawed at the base; wings obliquely
oblong; keel nearly straight, obtuse. Stamens monadelphous or diadelphous (9 and 1);
anthers all alike. Ovary sessile or stalked; ovules 2–∞. Loment flat, sessile or stalked,
several jointed, the joints mainly coriaceous and pubescent or muricate, indehiscent or rarely
partially dehiscent, readily separable. [Named for Dr. Brandus Meibom, died at Helmstadt,
1740.]

A genus of about 160 species, natives of warm and temperate North and South America, South Africa and Australia. Besides the following, about 20 others occur in the southern and southwestern States. Our species are known as Tick-trefoil, or Tick-seed. Type species: *Hedysarum canadense* L.

* **Loment not constricted above, deeply constricted below, long-stalked; leaflets broad.**

Panicle arising from the base of the plant; peduncle usually leafless.

Panicle terminal.   1. *M. nudiflora.*

     Leaves crowded at its base.

     Leaves scattered along the stem.   2. *M. grandiflora.*

                                        3. *M. pauciflora.*

** **Loment constricted on both margins, more deeply below than above.**

† Stems trailing or reclining.

Leaflets orbicular or nearly so.

   Leaflets 1′ long or less, glabrate, coriaceous; stipules subulate.   4. *M. arenicola.*

   Leaflets 1′–2′ long, thinnish, usually quite pubescent; stipules ovate.   5. *M. Michauxii.*

Leaflets ovate or oval.

   Corolla whitish; leaves yellowish green; stipules broadly ovate.   6. *M. ochroleuca.*

   Corolla purple; leaves dull green; stipules subulate.   7. *M. glabella.*

†† Stems erect or ascending.

Leaves sessile or nearly so; leaflets linear or lanceolate.   8. *M. sessilifolia.*

Leaves petioled.

   Leaflets narrowly linear; joints of the loment usually concave on the back.   9. *M. stricta.*

   Leaflets broad (except in races of *M. paniculata*).

     1. Joints of the loment notably longer than broad.

       Leaflets obtuse, rough-pubescent, yellowish green.   10. *M. canescens.*

       Leaflets long-acuminate.   11. *M. bracteosa.*

     2. Joints of the loment little longer than broad.

       (a.) Loment distinctly long-stalked in the calyx.

         Plants glabrous, or nearly so (except in races of *M. paniculata*).

           Leaflets lanceolate or oblong.   12. *M. paniculata.*

           Leaflets broadly ovate or oval, glaucous beneath.   13. *M. laevigata.*

         Plants pubescent or scabrous.

           Leaflets thick, coriaceous.

             Leaves villous and reticulated beneath.   14. *M. rhombifolia.*

             Leaves velvety-pubescent beneath.   15. *M. viridiflora.*

           Leaflets scarcely coriaceous, appressed-pubescent or villous beneath.   16. *M. Dillenii.*

       (b.) Loment sessile in the calyx, or nearly so.

         Loment-joints 4–7; flowers numerous, showy.

           Leaflets coriaceous, strongly reticulated beneath.   17. *M. illinoensis.*

           Leaflets not coriaceous, scarcely reticulated beneath; loments numerous.   18. *M. canadensis.*

         Loment-joints 1–3.

           Leaflets scabrous, 1′–2′ long.   19. *M. rigida.*

           Leaflets not scabrous, 5″–10″ long.

             Plant nearly glabrous throughout.   20. *M. marylandica.*

             Stem pubescent; leaflets and petioles ciliate.   21. *M. obtusa.*

1. Meibomia nudiflòra (L.) Kuntze. Naked-flowered Tick-trefoil. Fig. 2576.

Hedysarum nudiflorum L. Sp. Pl. 749. 1753.

Desmodium nudiflorum DC. Prodr. **2**: 330. 1825.

Meibomia nudiflora Kuntze, Rev. Gen. Pl. 197. 1891.

Slender, erect or ascending, the leaves clustered at the summit of the sterile stems, the peduncle arising from the base of the plant, leafless or rarely with 1 or 2 leaves, 3° high or less. Stipules subulate, deciduous; petioles 1′–4′ long; leaflets oval or ovate, glabrous or slightly pubescent, somewhat acuminate or with a blunt point, pale beneath, 1′–3′ long, the terminal one rhomboidal, the others inequilateral; panicles narrow, few-flowered; flowers rose-purple, 3″–5″ long; bracts deciduous; calyx-teeth obtuse, the lowest one largest; loment 2–3-jointed, the joints longer than wide, straight or concave on the back, obliquely semi-rhomboidal, pubescent with uncinate hairs, the sutures glabrous; stipe nearly as long as the pedicel.

In dry woods, Quebec to Minnesota, Florida, Arkansas and Louisiana. July–Aug.

½

2. Meibomia grandiflòra (Walt.) Kuntze. Pointed-leaved Tick-trefoil. Fig. 2577.

Hedysarum grandiflorum Walt. Fl. Car. 185. 1788.

H. acuminatum Michx. Fl. Bor. Am. **2** : 72. 1803.

Desmodium acuminatum DC. Prodr. **2** : 329. 1825.

Meibomia grandiflora Kuntze, Rev. Gen. Pl. 196. 1891.

Erect, glabrous, or somewhat pubescent, 1°–5° high. Leaves in a cluster at the summit of the stem, from which rises the slender peduncle; petioles 3′–6′ long; stipules subulate, generally persistent; leaflets ovate, acuminate, 2′–6′ long, pubescent with scattered hairs on both surfaces; panicle ample; bracts deciduous; flowers large, purple; loment 2–3-jointed; joints longer than wide, concave above, obliquely rounded below, uncinate-pubescent; stipe as long as the pedicel.

In dry or rocky woods, Quebec to Ontario, South Dakota, Florida, Alabama, Kansas and Oklahoma. June–Sept. Beggar-ticks.

3. Meibomia pauciflòra (Nutt.) Kuntze. Few-flowered Tick-trefoil. Fig. 2578.

Hedysarum pauciflorum Nutt. Gen. **2** : 109. 1818.
Desmodium pauciflorum DC. Prodr. **2** : 330. 1825.
M. pauciflora Kuntze, Rev. Gen. Pl. 198. 1891.

Decumbent or ascending, more or less pubescent with scattered hairs, 1°–3° long. Stipules subulate, deciduous; leaves alternate, distant, petioled; leaflets ovate, obtuse or bluntly acuminate, pubescent, 1′–3′ long, the terminal one rhomboid; racemes terminal or sometimes also axillary, simple, few-flowered; calyx-lobes acute, ciliate; corolla white, about 3″ long; loment 1–4-jointed, the joints concave or straight on the back, obliquely rounded below, larger than those of the preceding species, uncinate-pubescent; stipe slightly shorter than the pedicel.

In woods, Ontario to western New York, southern Pennsylvania, Florida, Ohio, Arkansas and Louisiana. July–Aug.

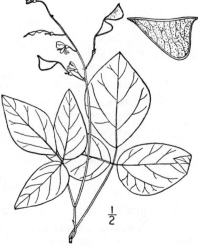

½

4. Meibomia arenícola Vail. Sand Tick-trefoil. Fig. 2579.

Hedysarum lineatum Michx. Fl. Bor. Am. **2** : 72. 1803. Not L. 1759.

Desmodium lineatum DC. Prodr. **2** : 330. 1825.

Meibomia arenicola Vail, Bull. Torr. Club **23** : 140. 1896.

Decumbent or prostrate, pubescent or glabrate, slender, 1°–2° long. Stipules subulate, persistent; petioles about ½′ long; leaflets ovate-orbicular, ½′–1′ long, glabrous or nearly so, coriaceous, reticulate-veined; racemes terminal and axillary, elongated, usually pubescent; flowers purple, about 2″–3″ long; pedicels slender; loment small, 2–4-jointed, the joints uncinate-pubescent, less convex above than below, 1½″–2½″ long; stipe about equalling the calyx-lobes, or shorter.

In dry woods, Maryland to Florida, west to Louisiana. July–Sept.

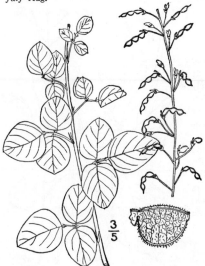

⅗

5. Meibomia Michàuxii Vail. Prostrate Tick-trefoil. Fig. 2580.

Hedysarum rotundifolium Michx. Fl. Bor. Am. **2**:
72. 1803. Not Vahl. 1791.
Desmodium rotundifolium DC. Prodr. **2**: 330.
1825.
Meibomia rotundifolia Kuntze, Rev. Gen. Pl. 197.
1891.
M. Michauxii Vail, Bull. Torr. Club **23**: 140. 1896.

Prostrate, 2°–6° long, softly pubescent, or
densely villous. Stipules ovate or triangular-
ovate, persistent, acuminate, somewhat cordate, striate, ciliate; leaves petioled; leaflets
nearly orbicular, pubescent, 1′–1½′ long; panicles terminal and axillary, loose; bracts deciduous; flowers purple, 3″–5″ long; calyx-lobes
ciliate; loment 1′ long or more, 3–5-jointed;
joints obliquely rhomboid below, slightly convex above, uncinate-pubescent; stipe equalling
or longer than the calyx-lobes.

Dry woods, Maine (?), Ontario to Minnesota,
Massachusetts, Florida, Missouri and Louisiana.
July–Sept. Round-leaved or trailing tick-trefoil.
Hive-vine. Dollar-leaf.

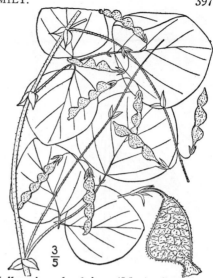

3/5

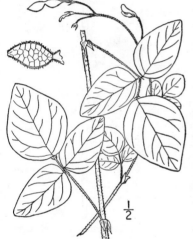

1/2

6. Meibomia ochroleùca (M. A. Curtis) Kuntze. Cream-flowered Tick-trefoil. Fig. 2581.

Desmodium ochroleucum M. A. Curtis; Canby, Proc.
Acad. Phila. 1864: 17. 1864.
Meibomia ochroleuca Kuntze, Rev. Gen. Pl. 198. 1891.

Procumbent or decumbent, hirsute, 1°–3° long.
Stipules ovate, persistent, cordate, striate; petioles
½′–1½′ long; leaflets yellowish green, rugose or nearly
smooth above, reticulate-veined and somewhat scabrous beneath, 8″–2′ long, the terminal one rhomboid,
the lateral obliquely ovate, smaller, or sometimes
wanting; racemes terminal and axillary, simple;
bracts deciduous; flowers whitish; upper calyx-lobe
minutely 2-toothed, the others attenuate; loment 2–3-
jointed, the joints only slightly more convex below
than above, twisted, oval, pale green, glabrous except
the uncinate-pubescent sutures; stipe about as long
as the calyx-lobes.

In woodlands, New Jersey to Georgia, Tennessee and
Missouri. Aug.–Sept.

7. Meibomia glabélla (Michx.) Kuntze. Trailing Tick-trefoil. Fig. 2582.

Hedysarum glabellum Michx. Fl. Bor. Am. **2**: 73. 1803.
Desmodium humifusum Beck. Bot. 86. 1833.
Meibomia glabella Kuntze, Rev. Gen. Pl. 198. 1891.

Procumbent, glabrous or nearly so, stem terete
below, striate above, sometimes 8° long. Stipules
lanceolate or ovate-lanceolate; leaves petioled; leaflets ovate or oval, obtuse, glabrous or sparingly pubescent above, pale beneath, 1′–2½′ long, the terminal
one slightly rhomboid; racemes terminal and axillary,
panicled; bracts deciduous; flowers purple; calyx-
lobes acute, the upper one 2-toothed, the others attenuate; loment 2–5-jointed, the joints obliquely semi-
rhomboidal, less convex above than below, finely
roughened; stipe about 2″ long, equalling or rather
longer than the calyx-lobes.

In dry sandy woods, eastern Massachusetts to New
York, western New Jersey, and eastern Pennsylvania to
South Carolina. Aug.–Sept.

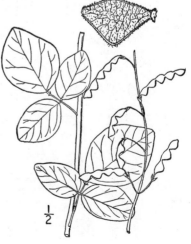

1/2

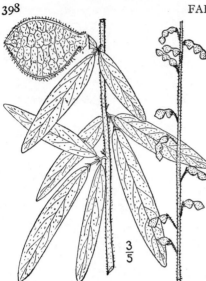

8. Meibomia sessilifòlia (Torr.) Kuntze. Sessile-leaved Tick-trefoil. Fig. 2583.

Hedysarum sessilifolium Torr.; Curtis, Bost. Journ. Nat. Hist. **1** : 123. 1834.
Desmodium sessilifolium T. & G. Fl. N. A. **1** : 363. 1838.
M. sessilifolia Kuntze, Rev. Gen. Pl. 198. 1891.

Erect, 2°–4° high, uncinate-pubescent. Stipules small, deciduous; leaves very nearly sessile; leaflets linear or linear-oblong, obtuse at each end, nearly glabrous above, reticulate-veined and pubescent beneath, 1′–3′ long, 3″–9″ wide; racemes terminal, simple or compound; flowers small, 2″–3″ long, purple; pedicels very short; bracts deciduous; calyx-lobes acute, the upper one obliquely 2-toothed; loment 1–3-jointed, the joints about 2″ long, obliquely obovate, hispid, somewhat twisted, less convex above than below; stipe not exceeding the calyx-lobes.

In dry soil, Massachusetts, Rhode Island and Connecticut to Ontario, Michigan, Kentucky, Louisiana, Kansas, Arkansas and Texas. July–Sept.

9. Meibomia strícta (Pursh) Kuntze. Stiff Tick-trefoil. Fig. 2584.

Hedysarum strictum Pursh, Fl. Am. Sept. 483. 1814.

Desmodium strictum DC. Prodr. **2** : 329. 1825.

Meibomia stricta Kuntze, Rev. Gen. Pl. 198. 1891.

Erect, slender, finely roughish pubescent, 2°–4° high. Stipules subulate, deciduous; leaves petioled; leaflets linear, obtuse or acute, glabrous, thick, reticulate-veined, 1′–2½′ long, about 3″ wide; flowers 1″–2″ long; loment small, 1–3-jointed; joints semi-obovate or semi-rhomboid, often slightly concave on the back, uncinate-pubescent, about 2″ long; pedicels short; stipe about equalling the calyx-lobes.

Pine barrens of New Jersey to Florida, west to Louisiana. July–Sept.

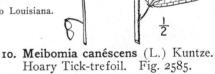

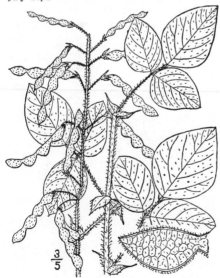

10. Meibomia canéscens (L.) Kuntze. Hoary Tick-trefoil. Fig. 2585.

Hedysarum canescens L. Sp. Pl. 748. 1753.
Desmodium canescens DC. Prodr. **2** : 328. 1825.
M. canescens Kuntze, Rev. Gen. Pl. 195. 1891.
Desmodium canadense var. *hirsuta* Hook. Comp. Bot. Mag. **1** : 23. 1835.
Meibomia canescens hirsuta Vail, Bull. Torr. Club **19** : 111. 1892.

Erect, much branched, densely short- or villous-pubescent, 3°–5° high. Stipules ovate, acuminate, somewhat cordate, persistent; leaves petioled; leaflets ovate, obtuse or acutish, 1′–4′ long, about as long as the petioles, scabrous above, pubescent beneath, ciliate, the terminal one commonly rhomboid and larger than the lateral ones; racemes terminal, compound; bracts deciduous; upper lobe of the calyx 2-toothed, the others attenuate; flowers 2″–2½″ long; loment 4–6-jointed, joints longer than wide, unequally rhomboid, 4″–6″ long; stipe about equalling the upper lobe of the calyx.

In rich soil Ontario to Massachusetts. Florida, Minnesota, Arkansas and Texas. July–Sept.

11. Meibomia bracteòsa (Michx.) Kuntze. Large-bracted Tick-trefoil. Fig. 2586.

Hedysarum bracteosum Michx. Fl. Bor. Am. **2**: 73. 1803.
Desmodium bracteosum DC. Prodr. **2**: 329. 1825.
Desmodium cuspidatum Hook. Comp. Bot. Mag. **1**: 23. 1835.
Desmodium canadense var. *longifolium* T. & G. Fl. N. A. **1**: 365. 1838.
Meibomia bracteosa Kuntze, Rev. Gen. Pl. 195. 1891.
Meibomia longifolia Vail, Bull. Torr. Club **23**: 140. 1896.

Erect, 2°–6° high, glabrous or pubescent below, the panicle finely pubescent. Stipules lanceolate, cuspidate, somewhat cordate, deciduous or persistent; leaves petioled; leaflets 2′–8′ long, longer than the petioles, ovate or ovate-lanceolate, acuminate, glabrous or very nearly so above, often pubescent beneath; flowers large, purple, 4″–5″ long; bracts deciduous, cuspidate, striate; calyx deeply 2-lipped, the upper lip 2-toothed, the others acute; loment 1′–3′ long, 3–7-jointed, the joints obliquely oblong, about twice as long as wide, uncinate-pubescent; stipe about the length of the lower calyx-lobes.

In thickets, Maine to Ontario, Minnesota, Florida, Missouri, Arkansas and Texas. Aug.–Sept.

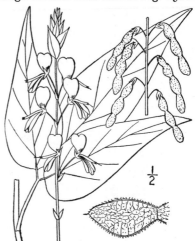

12. Meibomia paniculàta (L.) Kuntze. Panicled Tick-trefoil. Fig. 2587.

Hedysarum paniculatum L. Sp. Pl. 749. 1753.
Desmodium paniculatum DC. Prodr. **2**: 329. 1825.
Desmodium paniculatum var. *angustifolium* T. & G. Fl. N. A. **1**: 364. 1838.
Desmodium paniculatum var. *pubens* T. & G. Fl. N. A. **1**: 364. 1838.
Meibomia paniculata Kuntze, Rev. Gen. Pl. 198. 1891.
Meibomia paniculata Chapmani Britton, Mem. Torr. Club **5**: 204. 1894.
Meibomia paniculata pubens Vail, Bull. Torr. Club **19**: 112. 1892.

Erect, slender, glabrous or more or less pubescent, 2°–4° high. Stipules small, subulate, mainly deciduous; leaves petioled; leaflets oblong-lanceolate to linear-lanceolate, obtuse or acute, 1′–2′ long; racemes terminal, compound; bracts deciduous; upper calyx-lobe deeply 2-toothed, the 3 lower ones attenuate, with the middle one elongated; flowers purple, 3″–4″ long; loment 1′ long or more, 4–6-jointed, the joints obliquely triangular or rhomboid, minutely uncinate-pubescent; stipe nearly equalling the lower lobes of the calyx.

In dry soil, Ontario to Minnesota, Maine, Massachusetts, Florida and Texas. Consists of several races, differing in width of leaflets and in pubescence. July–Sept.

13. Meibomia laevigàta (Nutt.) Kuntze. Smooth Tick-trefoil. Fig. 2588.

Hedysarum laevigatum Nutt. Gen. **2**: 109. 1818.
Desmodium laevigatum DC. Prodr. **2**: 329. 1825.
Meibomia laevigata Kuntze, Rev. Gen. Pl. 198. 1891.

Erect or ascending, 2°–4° high, glabrous or nearly so. Stipules subulate, deciduous; petioles 1′–2′ long; leaflets ovate, blunt or acutish, somewhat glaucous beneath, the terminal one larger than the lateral and more or less rhomboid; racemes terminal, compound, slightly pubescent; bracts deciduous; calyx scabrous, the upper lobe entire or minutely 2-toothed, the 3 lower attenuate; flowers pink, 5″–6″ long; loment 3–4-jointed, the joints triangular, angled on the back, uncinate-pubescent; stipe 2″–3″ long.

In dry woods, southern New York to Florida, Missouri and Texas. Stem terete, glaucous. Aug.–Sept.

14. Meibomia rhombifòlia (Ell.) Vail. Rhomb-leaved Tick-trefoil. Fig. 2589.

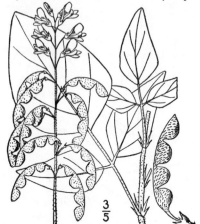

Hedysarum rhombifolium Ell. Bot. S. C. & Ga. **2**: 216. 1824.
Desmodium rhombifolium DC. Prodr. **2**: 330. 1825.
Desmodium floridanum Chapm. Fl. 102. 1860.
Meibomia floridana Kuntze, Rev. Gen. Pl. 198. 1891.
M. rhombifolia Vail, Bull. Torr. Club **19**: 113. 1892.

Erect or ascending, 2°-3° high or more, uncinate-pubescent, simple or branched. Stipules subulate, taper-pointed; leaves ovate, often mucronulate, coriaceous, scabrous above, villous and reticulated beneath, 2′-3½′ long, the terminal rhomboid, the lateral ones often wanting; racemes terminal, simple or panicled, elongated, usually leafless; bracts minute, deciduous; calyx-lobes acute, the upper one 2-toothed; loment 2-5-jointed, the joints obliquely semi-rhomboid, rounded on the back, uncinate-pubescent; stipe often as long as the lowest joint.

In sandy soil and pine lands, Virginia to Florida, west to Alabama and Louisiana. May–Sept.

15. Meibomia viridiflòra (L.) Kuntze. Velvet-leaved Tick-trefoil. Fig. 2590.

Hedysarum viridiflorum L. Sp. Pl. 748. 1753.
Desmodium viridiflorum Beck, Bot. 84. 1833.
Meibomia viridiflora Kuntze, Rev. Gen. Pl. 197. 1891.

Erect, rather stout, downy-pubescent, 2°-4° high. Stipules lanceolate, mainly deciduous; petioles ½′-1½′ long; leaflets broadly ovate, obtuse, rough above, densely velvety-pubescent beneath, 1′-3½′ long, the terminal one somewhat rhomboid; racemes compound, elongated, terminal, uncinate-pubescent; bracts deciduous; upper calyx-lobe minutely 2-toothed, the 3 lower ones attenuate; flowers purple, 3″-4″ long; loment 2-4-jointed, the joints semi-rhomboid, uncinate, about 2″ long; stipe about equalling the lower lobes of the calyx.

Dry woods, eastern Pennsylvania and southern New York to Florida, Michigan, Missouri, Arkansas and Texas. Aug.–Oct.

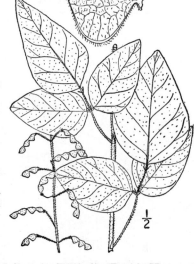

16. Meibomia Dillènii (Darl.) Kuntze. Dillen's Tick-trefoil. Fig. 2591.

Hedysarum marylandicum Willd. Sp. Pl. **3**: 1189. 1803. Not L. 1753.
Desmodium Dillenii Darl. Fl. Cest. 414. 1837.
Meibomia Dillenii Kuntze, Rev. Gen. Pl. 195. 1891.

Erect, 2°-3° high, pubescent with scattered hairs, or nearly glabrous. Stipules subulate, mainly deciduous; petioles 1′-2′ long; leaflets usually thin, oval or oblong-ovate, obtuse, 1½′-4′ long, ½′-1½′ wide, sparingly pubescent or glabrous above, softly pubescent or villous beneath; racemes terminal, compound, loose; bracts small, deciduous; upper calyx-lobe entire or minutely 2-toothed, the lower ones slender; flowers 3″-4″ long; loment 2-4-jointed, the joints nearly triangular, about 3″ long, somewhat convex on the back, uncinate-pubescent; stipe shorter than the calyx-lobes.

Woods, Maine to Ontario, Minnesota, Alabama, Tennessee, Missouri and Texas. June–Sept.

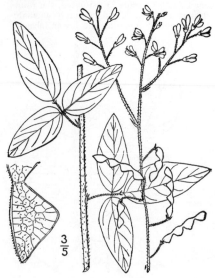

17. Meibomia illinoénsis (A. Gray) Kuntze. Illinois Tick-trefoil. Fig. 2592.

Desmodium illinoense A. Gray, Proc. Am. Acad.
8: 289. 1870.
M. illinoénsis Kuntze, Rev. Gen. Pl 198. 1891.

Erect, stout, 2°–4° high, uncinate-pubescent.
Stipules ovate, acute, cordate, ciliate, pubescent, persistent; petioles 1′–2′ long; leaflets
lanceolate or ovate-lanceolate, obtusish, coriaceous, scabrous above, strongly reticulate-
veined and cinereous beneath, 2′–3½′ long, the
terminal one broader and longer than the lateral; racemes terminal, simple or compound;
bracts deciduous, ovate-lanceolate; calyx-lobes
acute, the upper one minutely 2-toothed; flowers 3″–4″ long; loments ½′–1′ long, often in
pairs, 3–6-jointed, the joints oval or orbicular,
densely uncinate-pubescent; stipe not longer
than the short upper lobe of the calyx.

Prairies and plains, Ontario (according to Macoun); Ohio to Michigan, Iowa, Nebraska, Kansas and Oklahoma. June–Sept.

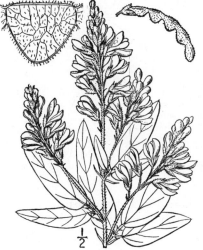

18. Meibomia canadénsis (L.) Kuntze. Canadian or Showy Tick-trefoil. Sain-foin. Fig. 2593.

Hedysarum canadense L. Sp. Pl. 748. 1753.
Desmodium canadense DC. Prodr. 2: 328. 1825.
M. canadensis Kuntze, Rev. Gen. Pl. 195. 1891.

Erect, stout, pubescent, 2°–8° high. Stipules
linear-lanceolate, persistent, or at length deciduous; lower petioles ½′–1′ long, the upper leaves
nearly sessile; leaflets oblong or lanceolate-oblong,
obtuse, glabrous or roughish above, appressed-
pubescent beneath; racemes terminal, densely
panicled; flowers large, 5″–8″ long, conspicuous,
purple or bluish-purple; bracts ovate-lanceolate,
large, acute, ciliate, at length deciduous; calyx-
lobes attenuate, the upper 2-toothed, the lower
ones elongated; loment nearly sessile in the calyx,
about 1′ long, 3–5-jointed; joints triangular,
straight or convex on back, uncinate-pubescent.

Thickets and river-banks, Nova Scotia to Manitoba, North Carolina, Missouri, Nebraska and Oklahoma. Our most showy-flowered species. July–Sept.
Beggars'-lice.

19. Meibomia rígida (Ell.) Kuntze. Rigid Tick-trefoil. Fig. 2594.

Hedysarum rigidum Ell. Bot. S. C. and Ga. 2: 215.
1824.
Desmodium rigidum DC. Prodr. 2: 330. 1825.
Meibomia rigida Kuntze, Rev. Gen. Pl. 198. 1891.

Erect or ascending, rather rigid, finely uncinate-
pubescent, 2°–3° high. Stipules small, lanceolate,
deciduous; leaves petioled; leaflets ovate, oblong
or oval, obtuse, thickish, scabrous above, pubescent, especially along the veins beneath, 1′–2′
long; racemes terminal, compound; flowers very
small, 1″–2″ long, purplish; upper lobe of the
calyx entire or minutely 2-toothed, the 3 lower
ones slender; loment sessile in the calyx, 1–3-
jointed, the joints obliquely ovate, rounded on
the back, uncinate-pubescent, about 1½″ long.

In dry soil, New Hampshire to Florida, Michigan,
Nebraska, Kansas, Arkansas and Louisiana. July–
Oct.

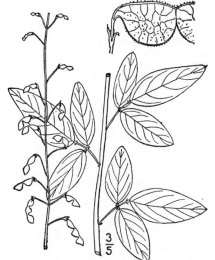

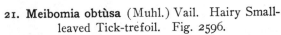

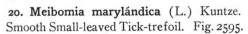

20. Meibomia marylándica (L.) Kuntze.
Smooth Small-leaved Tick-trefoil. Fig. 2595.

Hedysarum marylandicum L. Sp. Pl. 748. 1753.

Desmodium marylandicum Boott.; Darl. Fl. Cestr. 412. 1837.

Meibomia marylandica Kuntze, Rev. Gen. Pl. 198. 1891.

Erect or ascending, glabrous, or rarely with a few scattered hairs, slender, 2°–3° high. Stipules subulate, deciduous or persistent; petioles 3″–6″ long; leaves crowded; leaflets 3″–12″ long, ovate or nearly orbicular, obtuse, glabrous on both sides, the lateral often subcordate; upper lobe of the calyx emarginate or minutely 2-toothed; racemes panicled; corolla purplish, very small, 1″–2″ long; loment sessile in the calyx or nearly so, 1–3-jointed, the joints small, obliquely oval or semi-orbicular.

In dry soil and in copses, Ontario to Massachusetts, Florida, Minnesota, Missouri, Arkansas and Texas. July–Sept.

21. Meibomia obtùsa (Muhl.) Vail. Hairy Small-leaved Tick-trefoil. Fig. 2596.

Hedysarum obtusum Muhl.; Willd. Sp. Pl. 3: 1190. 1803.
Hedysarum ciliare Muhl.; Willd. Sp. Pl. 3: 1196. 1803.
Desmodium ciliare DC. Prodr. 2: 329. 1825.
Meibomia obtusa Vail, Bull. Torr. Club 19: 115. 1892.

Erect or ascending, bushy, 1°–3° high, pubescent. Stipules subulate, deciduous; leaves crowded; petioles ciliate, shorter than the leaflets; leaflets broadly ovate or oval, obtuse, somewhat coriaceous, more or less pubescent on both sides, ciliate, 6″–12″ long; racemes terminal, compound or simple, uncinate-pubescent; upper lobe of the calyx entire or minutely 2-toothed, the lower ones acute; flowers 1″–2″ long; loment 2–3-jointed, the joints obliquely oval; stipe not exceeding the calyx-lobes.

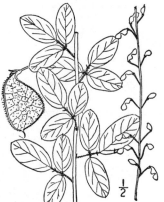

Dry soil, Ontario to Massachusetts and Florida, west to Michigan, Missouri, Arkansas and Texas. Cuba. July–Oct.

39. LESPEDÈZA Michx. Fl. Bor. Am. 2: 70. 1803.

Herbs, often somewhat woody, with pinnately 3-foliolate leaves, small stipules, and small purple or whitish flowers in axillary clusters, heads or panicles. Flowers often of 2 kinds intermixed, the one petaliferous and mainly sterile, the other minute, apetalous, abundantly fertile. Calyx-lobes nearly equal, those of petaliferous flowers often longer than those of apetalous ones. Standard in the petaliferous flowers obovate or oblong, clawed; wings oblong; keel incurved. Stamens more or less diadelphous (9 and 1); anthers all alike. Ovary sessile or stipitate, 1-ovuled. Pods ovate, oblong, oval or suborbicular, flat, indehiscent, reticulated, composed of a single joint, or with a second stalk-like joint at the base, those of petaliferous flowers often sharper-pointed than those of apetalous ones. [Named for Lespedez, governor of Florida, patron of Michaux.]

A genus of about 40 species, natives of eastern North America, Asia and Australia. Type species: *Lespedeza sessiliflora* Michx. The genus is known as bush-clover.

Perennial native species; stipules subulate; calyx-lobes narrow.
Corolla purple or purplish; plants bearing both petaliferous and apetalous flowers.
    Stems prostrate or trailing.
        Glabrous or somewhat appressed-pubescent.   1. *L. repens.*
        Downy-pubescent or tomentose.   2. *L. procumbens.*
    Stems erect or ascending.
        Peduncles manifest, mostly longer than the leaves.
            Bushy-branched; petaliferous flowers paniculate.   3. *L. violacea.*
            Stems simple or little-branched; flowers racemose or subspicate.
                Calyx of petaliferous flowers two-thirds as long as the pod or more.
                          . 4. *L. Manniana.*
            Calyx of petaliferous flowers one-half as long as the pod or less.
                Stem tomentose; leaves tomentose beneath.   5. *L. Brittonii.*
                Stem and leaves glabrate or appressed-pubescent.
                    Leaflets oval to suborbicular.   6. *L. Nuttallii.*
                    Leaflets oblong.   7. *L. acuticarpa.*

Peduncles shorter than the leaves, or flower-clusters sessile.
  Calyx of petaliferous flowers less than one-half as long as the pod.
    Leaflets densely tomentose beneath.   8. *L. Stuvei.*
    Leaflets appressed-pubescent beneath or glabrate.
      Leaflets oval to oblong.   9. *L. frutescens.*
      Leaflets linear to linear-oblong.   10. *L. virginica.*
  Calyx of petaliferous flowers two-thirds as long as the pod or more.
                                     11. *L. simulata.*
Flowers all complete; corolla whitish or yellowish; pod included or scarcely exserted.
  Leaves oblong, ovate-oblong, or nearly orbicular.
    Peduncles mostly exceeding the leaves.   12. *L. hirta.*
    Peduncles shorter than the leaves.   13. *L. capitata.*
  Leaves linear or linear-oblong; peduncles manifest, usually elongated.
    Spikes densely-flowered.   14. *L. angustifolia.*
    Spikes interrupted, loosely-flowered.   15. *L. leptostachya.*
Annual; stipules ovate; calyx-lobes broad; introduced species.   16. *L. striata.*

1. Lespedeza rèpens (L.) Bart.
Creeping Bush-clover. Fig. 2597.

Hedysarum repens L. Sp. Pl. 749. 1753.
L. repens Bart. Prodr. Fl. Phil. **2**: 77. 1818.

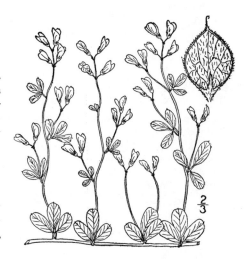

Trailing or diffusely procumbent, glabrate or appressed-pubescent, tufted, stems slender, simple or somewhat branched, 6′–24′ long. Petioles shorter than the leaves; stipules subulate, 1″–2″ long; leaflets oval or obovate, obtuse or retuse at the apex, narrowed or rounded at the base, 3″–8″ long; peduncles of the petaliferous flower-clusters slender, much exceeding the leaves; inflorescence rather loose, few-flowered; corolla violet-purple, 2″–3″ long; pod oval-orbicular, acute, finely pubescent, 1½″ long.

In dry or sandy soil, Connecticut to Florida, Minnesota, Arkansas and Texas. Aug.–Sept.

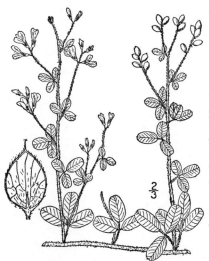

2. Lespedeza procúmbens Michx. Trailing Bush-clover. Fig. 2598.

Lespedeza procumbens Michx. Fl. Bor. Am. **2**: 70. 1803.

Woolly or downy-pubescent, trailing, procumbent or sometimes ascending, stouter than the preceding species, stems 12′–30′ long. Stipules subulate; petioles commonly much shorter than the leaves; leaflets oval or elliptic, rarely slightly obovate, obtuse or retuse at the apex, rounded at the base, 5″–12″ long; peduncles of the petaliferous flower-clusters longer than the leaves, or the flowers sometimes all apetalous and nearly sessile; corolla violet-purple or pinkish purple; pod oval-orbicular, acute, pubescent, 1½″ long.

In dry soil, New Hampshire to Florida, west to Indiana, Missouri, Arkansas and Texas. Aug.–Sept.

3. **Lespedeza violàcea** (L.) Pers. Bush-
clover. Fig. 2599.

Hedysarum violaceum L. Sp. Pl. 749. 1753.

Lespedeza violacea Pers. Syn. **2**: 318. 1807.

Erect or ascending, sparingly pubescent, usually
much branched, 1°–3° high. Stipules subulate,
2″–3″ long; petioles shorter than or equalling the
rather distant leaves; leaflets oval, elliptic or
elliptic-oblong, thin, obtuse or retuse at the apex,
rounded at the base, 6″–2′ long, appressed-pubescent beneath; peduncles, at least the upper ones,
longer than the leaves; inflorescence loose, few-
flowered, paniculate; corolla violet-purple, 3″–5″
long; pod ovate or oval, acute, finely and sparingly pubescent, or glabrate, 2″–3″ long.

In dry soil, New Hampshire to Florida, west to
Minnesota, Kansas, Louisiana and northern Mexico.
Aug.–Sept.

Lespedeza pràirea (Mack. & Bush) Britton, of dry
soil from Illinois and Missouri to Arkansas and
Texas, has smaller leaflets and shorter-pedicelled
flowers.

4. **Lespedeza Manniàna** Mackenzie &
Bush. Mann's Bush-clover. Fig. 2600.

L. Manniana Mackenzie & Bush, Trans. Acad. Sci.
St. Louis **12**: 15. 1902.

Stems erect or ascending, slender, appressed-
pubescent with rather long hairs or somewhat
pilose, 1½°–2½° high. Leaflets oblong or linear-
oblong, 1½′ long or less, obtuse and mucronate
at the apex, sparingly appressed-pubescent above,
densely so beneath; petaliferous flowers short-
racemose on slender peduncles longer than the
leaves; calyx 3″–4″ long, about two-thirds as
long as the corolla and the oval acute somewhat
pubescent pod.

Prairies, Missouri, Kansas and Arkansas. Recorded from Michigan. Aug.–Sept.

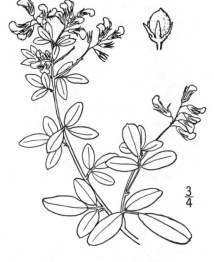

5. **Lespedeza Brittónii** Bicknell. Britton's
Bush-clover. Fig. 2601.

L. Brittonii Bicknell, Torreya **1**: 103. 1901.

Stems ascending, finely pubescent or tomentose at least above, 4° long or less. Leaves
short-petioled; leaflets firm in texture, oblong to
elliptic, obtuse, mucronulate, ¾′–2′ long, finely
pubescent or glabrate above, densely velvety-
pubescent beneath; peduncles longer than the
leaves or some of them shorter, tomentose;
flowers short-racemose; corolla purple and pink,
3″–4″ long, somewhat longer than the calyx;
pods of petaliferous flowers ovate-elliptic, acute,
pubescent, twice as long as the calyx.

Dry woodlands and borders of woods. Massachusetts to New Jersey and Maryland. Aug.–Sept.

6. Lespedeza Nuttàllii Darl.   Nuttall's Bush-clover.   Fig. 2602.

Lespedeza Nuttallii Darl. Fl. Cest. Ed. 2, 420. 1837.

Erect or ascending, simple or branched, more or less pubescent, 2°–3° high.   Stipules subulate; petioles shorter than the leaves; leaflets oval, obovate or suborbicular, thickish, obtuse or emarginate at the apex, narrowed or sometimes rounded at the base, dark green and glabrous or nearly so above, pubescent beneath, 4″–20″ long, 3″–10″ wide; peduncles mostly exceeding the leaves; inflorescence capitate, or spicate, dense; flowers violet-purple, about 3″ long; pod oblong, or oval, acuminate or acute at each end, very pubescent, 2½″–3″ long, longer than the calyx.

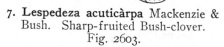

Dry soil, southern New Hampshire and New York to Michigan, Florida and Kansas. Aug.–Sept.

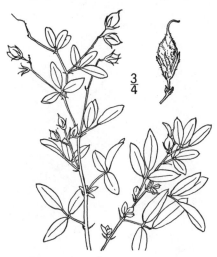

7. Lespedeza acuticàrpa Mackenzie & Bush.   Sharp-fruited Bush-clover.   Fig. 2603.

L. acuticarpa Mackenzie & Bush, Trans. Acad. Sci. St. Louis **12**: 16. 1902.

Stems ascending, slender, 2° long or less, glabrate to quite densely pubescent. Leaflets oblong to oblong-elliptic, ½′–1′ long, 2″–5″ wide, obtuse or acutish and mucronate, glabrate above, appressed-pubescent beneath; petaliferous flowers few, racemose, spicate at the ends of peduncles which are very slender and longer than the leaves; corolla purplish, 3″–4″ long, a little longer than the calyx; pods of petaliferous flowers oval, acute or acuminate, sparingly pubescent, twice as long as the calyx, those of apetalous flowers less acute, much longer than the calyx.

Dry soil, Tennessee to Missouri and Arkansas. Aug.–Sept.

8. Lespedeza Stùvei Nutt.   Stuve's Bush-clover.   Fig. 2604.

Lespedeza Stuvei Nutt. Gen. **2**: 107. 1818.

Erect or ascending, simple and wand-like or sometimes slightly branched, densely velvety or downy pubescent all over, 2°–4° high.   Stipules subulate, 2″–3″ long; petioles commonly much shorter than the leaves; leaflets oval, oblong or suborbicular, obtuse or retuse at the apex, narrowed or rounded at the base, 6″–10″ or rarely 15″ long; flowers of both kinds in nearly sessile axillary clusters; corolla violet-purple, 2″–3″ long; pod ovate-oblong to orbicular, acute, or oblong, 2″–3″ long, downy-pubescent, much longer than the calyx.

Dry soil, Vermont and Massachusetts to Virginia, Alabama, Michigan, Arkansas and Texas. Aug.–Sept.

Lespedeza neglécta (Britton) Mackenzie and Bush, with linear or linear-oblong pubescent leaves, may be a hybrid of this species with *L. virginica.*

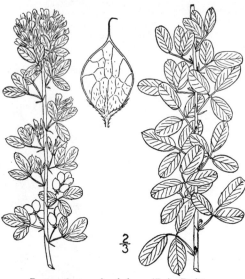

$\frac{2}{3}$

10. Lespedeza virgínica (L.) Britton. Slender Bush-clover. Fig. 2606.

Medicago virginica L. Sp. Pl. 778. 1753.
L. sessiliflora Michx. Fl. Bor. Am. **2**: 70. 1803.
Lespedeza violacea var. *angustifolia* T. & G. Fl. N. A. **1**: 367. 1840.
Lespedeza virginica Britton, Trans. N. Y. Acad. Sci. **12**: 64. 1893.

Erect, slender, simple and wand-like or branch-ed, resembling the preceding species. Leaflets linear or oblong-linear, 6″–18″ long, 1″–2½″ wide, truncate, obtuse or sometimes acute at the apex, finely pubescent beneath, or glabrate on both surfaces; clusters of both kinds of flowers sessile, or nearly so, crowded in the upper axils; flowers violet-purple, 2″–3″ long; pod ovate, or oval-orbicular, acute, or obtuse, 2″ long; pubescent, or nearly glabrous, much longer than the calyx.

Dry soil, New Hampshire to Ontario, Minnesota, Arkansas, Florida and Texas. Aug.–Sept.

$\frac{3}{4}$

9. Lespedeza frutéscens (L.) Britton. Wand-like Bush-clover. Fig. 2605.

Hedysarum frutescens L. Sp. Pl. 748. 1753.
Lespedeza reticulata S. Wats. Bibliog. Index **1**: 233. 1878. Not Pers. 1807.
Lespedeza Stuvei var. *intermedia* S. Wats. in A. Gray, Man. Ed. 6, 147. 1890.
Lespedeza frutescens Britton, Mem. Torr. Club **5**: 205. 1894.

Erect, simple or branched, finely appressed-pubescent or glabrate, 1°–3° high. Stipules subulate, 2″–3″ long; petioles equalling or shorter than the leaves; leaflets oval, oblong or elliptic, obtuse, truncate or retuse at the apex, narrowed or rounded at the base, 6″–18″ long, glabrous and dark green above, paler and pubescent beneath; flowers of both kinds in short-stalked or nearly sessile axillary clusters, generally crowded toward the summit of the stem; corolla violet-purple, 2″–3″ long; pod ovate-oblong, acute, pubescent, about 2″ long, much longer than the calyx.

Dry soil, Maine to Ontario, Minnesota, Florida, Illinois and Texas. Aug.–Sept.

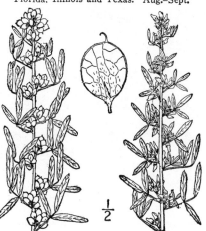

$\frac{1}{2}$

11. Lespedeza simulàta Mackenzie & Bush. Intermediate Bush-clover. Fig. 2607.

L. simulata Mackenzie and Bush, Trans. Acad. Sci. St. Louis **12**: 18. 1902.

Erect, stems glabrate or short-pubescent, 3° high or less. Leaflets oblong-linear to oblong-elliptic, ½″–2′ long, 2″–6″ wide, obtuse and mucronate at the apex, narrowed or rounded at the base, appressed-pubescent and more or less silvery especially beneath; spike sessile or short-peduncled, not longer than the leaves, rather densely several-flowered; petaliferous flowers purplish, 3″–4″ long; calyx densely pubescent, 2½″–3″ long, nearly as long as the corolla, and two-thirds as long to longer than the densely pubescent ovate acute pod.

In dry soil, Connecticut to Ohio, Missouri, Pennsylvania and Oklahoma. Aug.–Oct.

12. Lespedeza hírta (L.) Hornem. Hairy Bush-clover. Fig. 2608.

Hedysarum hirtum L. Sp. Pl. 748. 1753.
Lespedeza hirta Hornem. Hort. Havn. 699. 1807.

Erect or ascending, rather stout, generally branching above, villous or silky-pubescent, 2°–4° high. Stipules subulate, 1″–2½″ long; petioles shorter than the leaves; leaflets oval, or suborbicular, obtuse at each end, sometimes emarginate at the apex, 6″–2′ long; peduncles mostly elongated, often much exceeding the leaves; heads oblong-cylindric, rather dense, ½′–1½′ long; flowers all complete; corolla yellowish-white or the standard purple spotted, about 3″ long; pod oval, acute, very pubescent, about equalling the calyx-lobes.

Dry soil, Maine and Ontario to Florida, Minnesota, Arkansas, Louisiana and Texas. Aug.–Oct.

A plant known as *Lespedeza hírta oblongifòlia* Britton, with leaves oblong, obtuse, 9″–15″ long, 2″–4″ wide, glabrate above, appressed-pubescent below; peduncles slender; spikes looser, 1′–1½′ long; calyx very pubescent; in pine-barrens, Egg Harbor, N. J., and in the Southern States, may be a hybrid with *L. angustifolia* (Pursh) Ell. We do not know its fruit.

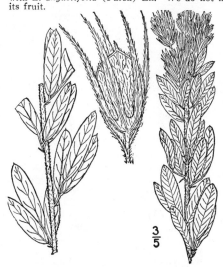

13. Lespedeza capitàta Michx. Round-
     headed Bush-clover. Fig. 2609.

L. capitata Michx. Fl. Bor. Am. **2**: 71. 1803.
Lespedeza capitata var *sericea* H. & A. Comp. Bot. Mag. **1**: 23. 1835.
Lespedeza frutescens Ell. Bot S. C. **2**: 206. 1824.
L. Bicknellii House, Torreya **5**: 167. 1905.
L. velutina Bicknell, Torreya **1**: 102. 1901.

Stiff, erect or ascending, mainly simple and wand-like, silky, silvery pubescent, or somewhat villous, 2°–5½° high. Stipules subulate; leaves nearly sessile; leaflets oblong, linear-oblong or narrowly elliptic, obtuse or acute at each end, 1′–1½′ long, 3″–5″ wide; peduncles much shorter than the leaves, or the dense globose-oblong heads sessile in the upper axils; flowers all complete; corolla yellowish-white, with a purple spot on the standard, 3″ long; pod ovate-oblong, pubescent, about half as long as the calyx-lobes.

Dry fields, Ontario and Maine to Florida, Minnesota, Nebraska, Arkansas and Louisiana. Races differ in pubescence and in width of leaflets. Aug.–Sept. Dusty-clover.

Lespedeza longifòlia DC. (*L. capitata longifolia* T. & G.) of prairies, from Iowa to Missouri, Illinois and Kentucky, has linear to linear-lanceolate acute leaflets, and is a well marked race of *L. capitata* or a distinct species.

14. Lespedeza angustifòlia (Pursh)
Ell. Narrow-leaved Bush-clover.
            Fig. 2610.

Lespedeza capitata var. *angustifolia* Pursh, Fl. Am. Sept. 480. 1814.
L. angustifolia Ell. Bot. S. C. & Ga. **2**: 206. 1824.

Erect, simple, or branched above, slender, appressed-pubescent, or nearly glabrous, 2°–3° high. Stipules subulate; leaves nearly sessile; leaflets linear or oblong-linear, rarely some of the lower ones lance-linear, 1′–1½′ long, 1″–2″ wide, obtuse, truncate or acutish at the apex; peduncles mostly elongated, usually exceeding the leaves; flowers nearly as in the preceding; pod ovate-orbicular, shorter than the calyx-lobes.

Dry sandy soil, eastern Massachusetts, Long Island, south to Florida, west to Louisiana. Records of this species in Iowa and Michigan appear to be erroneous. Aug.–Sept.

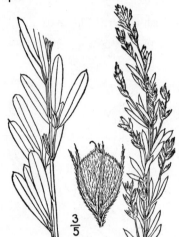

15. Lespedeza leptostàchya Engelm. Prairie Bush-clover. Fig. 2611.

Lespedeza leptostachya Engelm.; A. Gray, Proc. Am. Acad. 12 : 57. 1876.

Erect, simple or branched, 1°–3° high, silvery-pubescent with appressed hairs. Stipules subulate; petioles shorter than the leaves; leaflets linear, 1′–1½′ long, 1″–2″ wide; spikes slender, interrupted and loosely flowered, on peduncles equalling or exceeding the leaves; corolla as in the preceding species; flowers all complete; pod ovate, pubescent, about 1½″ long, nearly equalling the calyx.

Prairies, Illinois to Iowa, Wisconsin and Minnesota. Aug.–Sept.

3/5

16. Lespedeza striàta (Thunb.) H. & A. Japan Clover. Fig. 2612.

Hedysarum striatum Thunb. Fl. Jap. 289. 1784.
Lespedeza striata H. & A. Bot. Beechey 262. 1841.

Annual, diffuse or ascending, branched, tufted, sparingly appressed-pubescent, 6′–12′ long. Stipules ovate, acute or acuminate, 1″–2″ long; petioles much shorter than the leaves; leaflets oblong or oblong-obovate, 4″–9″ long, 1″–4″ wide, obtuse at the apex, narrowed at the base, their margins usually sparingly ciliate; flowers 1–3 together, both petaliferous and apetalous, sessile or nearly so in the axils; corolla pink or purple, about ½″ long; calyx-lobes ovate; pod oval, acute, exceeding the calyx-lobes.

In fields, Pennsylvania to Indiana, Missouri, Kansas, Florida and Texas. Naturalized from eastern Asia. Wild clover. Hoopkoop-plant. July–Aug.

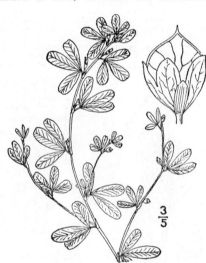

3/5

40. VÍCIA [Tourn.] L. Sp. Pl. 734. 1753.

Climbing or trailing, herbaceous vines, with pinnate tendril-bearing leaves, half-sagittate or entire stipules, and axillary sessile or racemose, blue violet or yellowish flowers. Calyx-tube somewhat oblique, obtuse at the base, its teeth about equal, or the two upper ones slightly shorter or longer. Standard obovate or oblong, emarginate, clawed; wings obliquely oblong, adherent to the shorter oblong curved keel. Stamens diadelphous (9 and 1), or monadelphous below; anthers all alike. Ovary sessile or stipitate; ovules ∞; style very slender, with a tuft or ring of hairs at its summit. Pod flat, dehiscent, 2-valved, continuous between the round seeds. [The classical Latin name of the Vetch.]

About 130 species of wide geographic distribution. In addition to the following, about 15 others occur in the southern and western parts of North America. **Type species:** *Vicia sativa* L.

Flowers racemed or spicate; peduncles elongated.
  Indigenous perennials.
    Spike-like racemes dense, 1-sided, 15–40-flowered.   1. *V. Cracca.*
    Racemes loose, 1–20-flowered.
      Flowers 7″–10″ long.
        Leaflets elliptic, or ovate-oblong.   2. *V. americana.*
        Leaflets narrowly linear; western.   3. *V. sparsifolia.*
      Flowers 2″–5″ long.
        Racemes 8–20-flowered; flowers 4″–5″ long.   4. *V. caroliniana.*
        Racemes 1–6-flowered; flowers 2″–4″ long.
          Leaflets 2–5 pairs, linear, or those of lower leaves oval or obovate. 5. *V. micrantha.*
          Leaflets 4 or 5 pairs, all oval, elliptic or obovate.   6. *V. ludoviciana.*
  Introduced annuals; flowers few, 2″–3″ long.
    Pod glabrous, 3–6-seeded.   7. *V. tetrasperma.*
    Pod pubescent, 2-seeded.   8. *V. hirsuta.*
Flowers sessile or very nearly so, few, axillary.
  Flowers 1 or 2 in the axils; annuals.
    Leaflets oblong, oval or obovate; flowers about 1′ long.   9. *V. sativa.*
    Leaflets, except of lower leaves, linear, or linear-oblong; flowers ¾′ long. 10. *V. angustifolia.*
  Flowers 2–6 in a short nearly sessile raceme; perennial.   11. *V. Sepium.*

1. Vicia Crácca L. Tufted or Cow Vetch. Blue or Bird Vetch. Fig. 2613.

Vicia Cracca L. Sp. Pl. 735. 1753.

Perennial, finely pubescent or sometimes glabrate, stems tufted, slender, weak, climbing or trailing, 2°–4° long. Stipules linear, acute, entire, 1″–4″ long; leaves nearly sessile; leaflets 8–24, thin, linear or linear-oblong, obtuse or acutish, mucronate, 8″–10″ long, 1½″–2″ wide; peduncles axillary, shorter than or equalling the leaves; spike-like racemes dense, secund, 1′–4′ long; flowers bluish-purple, sometimes white, 5″–6″ long, reflexed; pod short-stalked, glabrous, 9″–12″ long, about 3″ wide, 5–8-seeded.

In dry soil, Newfoundland to British Columbia, New York, New Jersey, Kentucky, Iowa and Washington. Also in Europe and Asia. Tinegrass. Cat-peas. Canada-pea. June–Aug.

Vicia villòsa Roth, is a similar Old World species, but villous-pubescent, annual or biennial in duration, and with larger flowers, locally spontaneous after cultivation for fodder.

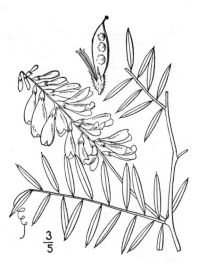

3/5

2. Vicia americàna Muhl. American or Purple Vetch. Pea Vine. Fig. 2614.

Vicia americana Muhl.; Willd. Sp. Pl. 3: 1096. 1803.

Perennial, glabrous or with some appressed pubescence, trailing or climbing, 2°–3° long. Leaves nearly sessile; stipules broad, foliaceous, triangular-ovate, sharply toothed, 2″–5″ long; leaflets 8–14, elliptic, ovate or oblong, obtuse or sometimes emarginate and mucronulate at the apex, rounded at the base, 8″–18″ long, 3″–7″ wide; peduncles usually shorter than the leaves; racemes loose, 2–9-flowered; flowers bluish-purple, 8″–9″ long, spreading; pod short-stalked, glabrous, 1′–1¼′ long, 4–7-seeded.

In moist ground, New Brunswick to Ontario, Manitoba and British Columbia, New York, Virginia, Kentucky and Arizona. Leaflets of lower leaves sometimes narrow. Ascends to 3500 ft. in Virginia. May–Aug. Buffalo-pea.

Vicia oregàna Nutt. (*V. truncata* Nutt.), with obovate or oblong leaflets truncate and dentate at the apex, widely distributed in western North America, enters our area in Kansas and Nebraska.

2/3

3. Vicia sparsifòlia Nutt. Narrow-leaved American Vetch. Fig. 2615.

Vicia sparsifolia Nutt.; T. & G. Fl. N. A. 1: 270. 1838.
Lathyrus linearis Nutt.; T. & G. Fl. N. A. 1: 276. 1838.
Vicia americana var. *linearis* S. Wats. Proc. Am. 11: 134. 1876.
Vicia linearis Greene, Fl. Francis. 3. 1891.

Perennial, glabrous or nearly so, stems weak, often zigzag, 1°–2° long. Leaflets 4–7 pairs, narrowly linear to linear-oblong, 9″–18″ long, ¼″–2″ wide, rather thick, acute or obtusish, the apex not toothed, mucronate; stipules 2″–4″ long, half-sagittate, acuminate, their bases prolonged, sometimes dentate; peduncles shorter than the leaves, or about equalling them; racemes loose, 2–6-flowered; flowers purple or purplish, about 9″ long; pod about 1′ long, 3″ wide or rather more, glabrous, short-stalked.

In dry soil, Manitoba to British Columbia, South Dakota, Kansas, New Mexico and California. Perhaps a narrow-leaved race of *V. americana.* May–Aug.

2/3

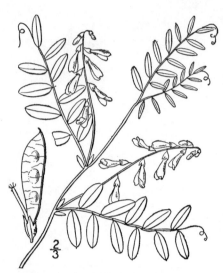

$\frac{2}{3}$

4. Vicia caroliniàna Walt. Carolina or Pale Vetch. Fig. 2616.

Vicia caroliniana Walt. Fl. Car. 182. 1788.

Vicia parviflora Michx. Fl. Bor. Am. 2 : 69. 1803.

Perennial, glabrous or nearly so, trailing or climbing, slender, 2°–3° long. Stipules linear or oblong, entire, 2″–3″ long; leaves short-petioled; leaflets 8–18, oblong or linear-oblong, entire, obtuse or emarginate, or sometimes acutish and mucronate, 6″–10″ long, 1½″–5″ wide; peduncles equalling or shorter than the leaves; racemes loosely 8–20-flowered; flowers nearly white, 4″–5″ long, the keel bluish-tipped; pod glabrous, 8″–14″ long, short-stalked, 5–8-seeded.

River-banks and cliffs, Ontario to Minnesota, south to Georgia, Mississippi and Kansas. Ascends to 3500 feet in Virginia. May–July.

5. Vicia micrántha Nutt. Small-flowered Vetch. Fig. 2617.

Vicia micrantha Nutt.; T. & G. Fl. N. A. 1 : 271. 1838.

Perennial (or sometimes annual?), glabrous, stems very slender, 1°–2° long. Leaflets 2–5 pairs, narrowly linear to linear-oblong, thin, ½′–1½′ long, 1″–2″ wide, obtuse, acutish or emarginate, or those of the lower leaves obovate, oval, or even obcordate, usually shorter; peduncles 4″–15″ long, 1–2-flowered; flowers 2″–3″ long, purplish; pod slightly pubescent or glabrous, about 1′ long, 2½″ wide, 6–12-seeded; seeds compressed.

On prairies and in thickets, Missouri (?), Arkansas to Tennessee, Alabama and Texas. April–May.

$\frac{3}{4}$

6. Vicia ludoviciàna Nutt. Louisiana Vetch. Fig. 2618.

Vicia ludoviciana Nutt.; T. & G. Fl. N A. 1 : 271. 1838.

Perennial, glabrous, or the young parts pubescent; stem rather stout, angled, 1½°–3° long. Leaflets 4 or 5 pairs, elliptic, oval or obovate, thin, 6″–10″ long, 2″–4″ wide, obtuse or emarginate; stipules very narrow, rarely over 3″ long, linear, or half-sagittate; peduncles shorter than the leaves, or about equalling them, or longer, 2–6-flowered (rarely 1-flowered); flowers 3″–4″ long, bluish; pod 1′ long, or rather more, 3″–5″ wide, glabrous, 4–6-seeded, the seeds compressed.

Missouri to Texas, Louisiana and Florida. April–May.

$\frac{3}{4}$

7. Vicia tetraspérma (L.) Moench. Slender Vetch. Smooth or Lentil Tare. Fig. 2619.

Ervum tetraspermum L. Sp. Pl. 738. 1753.

Vicia tetrasperma Moench, Meth. 148. 1794.

Annual, glabrous or nearly so, weak, slender, 6′–24′ long. Stipules linear, long-auriculate at the base; leaves short-petioled; leaflets thin, 6–12, linear or linear-oblong, obtuse or acutish, commonly mucronulate, 6″–8″ long; peduncles filiform. equalling or shorter than the leaves, 1–6-flowered; flowers pale blue or purplish, 2″–3″ long; pod 4″–6′ long, glabrous, 3–6-seeded.

In meadows and waste places, Nova Scotia to Ontario, Florida and Mississippi. Guadeloupe. Naturalized from Europe. Native also of northern Asia. June–Sept.

8. Vicia hirsùta (L.) Koch. Hairy Vetch or Tare. Tineweed. Fig. 2620.

Ervum hirsutum L. Sp. Pl. 738. 1753.
V. Mitchelli Raf. Prec. Decouv. 37. 1814.
V. hirsuta Koch, Syn. Fl. Germ. 191. 1837.

Sparingly pubescent, or glabrous, annual, much resembling the preceding species. Stipules linear, long-auriculate and sometimes toothed; leaves nearly sessile; leaflets 12–14, oblong or linear, obtuse, emarginate or truncate, mucronulate, 4″–8″ long, narrowed at the base; peduncles slender, mainly shorter than the leaves, 2–6-flowered; flowers pale purplish blue, about 1½″ long; pod oblong, pubescent, 4″–6″ long, 2-seeded.

In fields and waste places, Nova Scotia to Virginia, Alberta, Oregon, Florida and Ohio. Naturalized from Europe. Native also of Asia. Called also tine-tare, tare-vetch, strangle-tare. May–Sept.

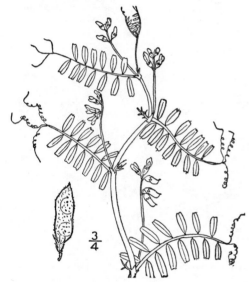

9. Vicia satìva L. Common Vetch or Tare. Pebble-vetch. Spring-vetch. Fig. 2621.

Vicia sativa L. Sp. Pl. 736. 1753.

Annual or winter-annual, pubescent or glabrate, spreading, ascending or climbing, 1°–3° long. Stipules broad, generally sharply toothed; leaves short-petioled; leaflets 8–14, obovate, oblong or oblanceolate, obtuse, truncate or retuse and mucronate at the apex, narrowed at the base, 9″–15″ long, 2″–4″ wide; flowers 1 or 2 in the axils, sessile or short-peduncled, bluish-purple, 9″–15″ long; calyx-teeth about as long as the tube; pod linear-oblong, glabrous, 1½″–3′ long, about 4″ wide, 5–10-seeded.

In fields and waste places, frequent or occasional nearly throughout our area, in the Southern States and on the Pacific Coast. Bermuda; Jamaica. Adventive from Europe. Cultivated for fodder. Native also of Asia. May–Aug.

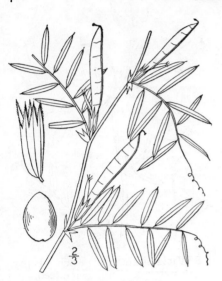

$\frac{2}{3}$

10. Vicia angustifòlia L. Smaller Common Vetch. Fig. 2622.

Vicia angustifolia L. Amoen. Acad. 4: 105. 1759.
Vicia sativa var. *angustifolia* Ser. in DC. Prodr. 2: 361. 1825.

Annual or winter-annual, glabrous or puberulent; stem slender, 1°-2° long. Stipules mostly half-sagittate, toothed, or entire; leaves short-petioled, or nearly sessile; leaflets 4-16, linear, lanceolate, or oblanceolate, 4"-18" long, 1'-2" wide, acute, obtuse, truncate or emarginate at the apex, mucronulate, those of the lower leaves commonly oblong or obovate, broader and shorter; flowers 1 or 2 in the upper axils, purple, 6"-9" long; calyx-teeth as long as the tube or shorter; pod linear, glabrous, 1'-2' long, 2½"-3½" wide.

In fields and waste places, Nova Scotia to Florida, mostly near the coast and in Missouri. Naturalized from Europe. Widely distributed as a weed in temperate regions. April–July.

11. Vicia Sèpium L. Bush Vetch. Wild Tare. Fig. 2623.

Vicia Sepium L Sp. Pl. 737. 1753.

Perennial by slender stolons, minutely pubescent; stem slender, 2°-3° long. Leaves short-petioled, 2'-6' long; leaflets 10-18, ovate or oval, 6"-12" long, 3"-7" wide, emarginate or truncate at the apex, mucronulate, thin; stipules half-sagittate, 5" long or less; racemes in 1 or more of the upper axils, 2-6-flowered, ½'-1' long, nearly sessile; flowers very short-pedicelled, pale purple, 6"-10" long; calyx-teeth unequal, shorter than the tube; pod 10"-15" long, about 3" wide, glabrous.

Waste grounds, Quebec, Maine, Ontario and New Hampshire. Adventive or fugitive from Europe. Native also of Asia. Called also crowpeas. May–July.

Vicia narbonénsis L., an annual European species with large dark purple axillary flowers, and broad ovate toothed leaflets, has escaped from cultivation in Maryland and the District of Columbia.

Ervum Léns L., the lentil, distinguished from all our species of *Vicia* by its elongated calyx-lobes and oval, 1-2-seeded pod, is collected occasionally as a waif, not established.

$\frac{1}{2}$

41. LÁTHYRUS L. Sp. Pl. 729. 1753.

Herbaceous vines, rarely erect herbs, with pinnate mostly tendril-bearing leaves, and racemose or sometimes solitary flowers. Calyx oblique or gibbous at the base, its teeth nearly equal or the upper ones somewhat shorter than the lower. Corolla nearly as in *Vicia*, but commonly larger. Stamens diadelphous (9 and 1), or monadelphous below. Ovary sessile or stalked; ovules generally numerous; style curved, flattened, hairy along its inner side. Pod flat, or sometimes terete, 2-valved, dehiscent, continuous between the seeds. [Ancient Greek name of some leguminous plant.]

About 110 species, natives of the northern hemisphere and of South America. Besides the following, about 25 others occur in the southern and western parts of North America. Type species: *Lathyrus sativus* L.

Leaflets 2-6 pairs.
  Flowers purple.
    Stipules broad, foliaceous; plant of the seashore and the Great Lakes.   1. *L. maritimus.*
    Stipules half-sagittate or small, or wanting; inland plants.
      Plants climbing or trailing; stipules present; pod sessile.
        Leaflets ovate or oval, large; flowers 10-20.   2. *L. venosus.*
        Leaflets linear, oblong or oval, smaller; flowers 2-6.
          Leaflets linear or linear-oblong; stem winged.   3. *L. palustris.*
          Leaflets oblong or oval; stem wingless.   4. *L. myrtifolius.*
      Plants mainly erect; stipules often wanting; pod stipitate.
        Leaflets lanceolate or oblong.   5. *L. decaphyllus.*
        Leaflets linear.   6. *L. ornatus.*
  Flowers yellowish-white; stipules foliaceous.   7. *L. ochroleucus.*
Leaflets 1 pair.
  Perennial introduced species.
    Flowers yellow; stems wingless.   8. *L. pratensis.*
    Flowers purple; stems broadly winged.   9. *L. latifolius.*
  Annual; flowers purple; native species.   10. *L. pusillus.*

1. Lathyrus marítimus (L.) Bigel. Beach Pea. Sea or Seaside Pea. Fig. 2624.

Pisum maritimum L. Sp. Pl. 727. 1753.

Lathyrus maritimus Bigel. Fl. Bost. Ed. 2, 268. 1824.

Perennial, glabrous or nearly so, stout, somewhat fleshy, slightly glaucous; stems angled, decumbent, 1°-2° long. Stipules broad foliaceous, ovate, hastate, acute, 1'-2' long; leaves nearly sessile; leaflets 3-6 pairs, oblong, oval or obovate, obtusish and mucronulate at the apex, mainly narrowed at the base, somewhat larger than the stipules; tendrils branched; peduncles somewhat shorter than the leaves; flowers 6-10, 9"-12" long, purple; calyx-teeth often ciliate; pod sessile, linear-oblong, nearly glabrous, veined, 1½'-3' long, 4"-5" wide

Sea-beaches, New Jersey to arctic America, shores of the Great Lakes, Oneida Lake and on the Pacific Coast. Also in northern Europe and Asia. May-Aug. Sometimes blooming again late in autumn. Also called sea-side everlasting pea.

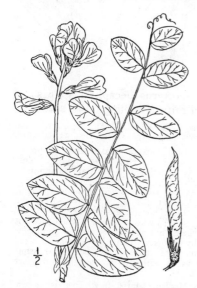

2. Lathyrus venòsus Muhl. Veiny Pea. Fig. 2625.

Lathyrus venosus Muhl.; Willd. Sp. Pl. 3: 1092. 1803.

Finely pubescent or glabrous, perennial, ascending, climbing or decumbent, 2°-3° long. Stems strongly 4-angled; stipules lanceolate, half-sagittate, acute or acuminate, 4"-12" long, much smaller than the leaflets; leaves petioled; leaflets 4-7 pairs, ovate or oval, obtuse or acutish and mucronulate at the apex, mostly rounded at the base, 1'-2' long; tendrils branched; peduncles shorter than the leaves; flowers purple, 6"-8" long; calyx pubescent or glabrous; pod linear, sessile, glabrous, veined, 1½'-3' long, about 3" wide.

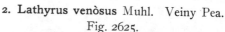

River shores and banks, western New Jersey and Pennsylvania to Ontario, Indiana, Saskatchewan, Georgia, Louisiana and Arkansas. Ascends to 3500 feet in Virginia. Leaflets often strongly reticulated. May-July.

$\frac{1}{2}$

3. Lathyrus palústris L. Marsh Vetchling. Wild Pea. Fig. 2626.

Lathyrus palustris L. Sp. Pl. 733. 1753.
L. palustris linearifolius Ser in DC. Prodr. 2 : 371. 1825.

Perennial, glabrous or somewhat pubescent; stems angled and usually winged, slender, 1°–3° long; stipules half-sagittate, lanceolate, linear or ovate-lanceolate, 5″–10″ long, 1½″–2½″ wide; leaflets 2–4 pairs, lanceolate, oblong, linear or linear-oblong, acute or obtusish and mucronate at the apex, narrowed or rounded at the base, 1′–2½′ long, 2″–5″ wide; tendrils branched; peduncles generally about equalling the leaves, 2–8-flowered; flowers purple, 5″–7″ long; pod linear, sessile, slightly pubescent, or glabrous, 1½′–2½′ long, about 3″ wide.

In moist or wet grounds, Newfoundland to Alaska, Massachusetts, New York, South Dakota and British Columbia. Also in Europe and Asia. May–Aug.

4. Lathyrus myrtifòlius Muhl. Myrtle-leaved Marsh Pea. Fig. 2627.

Lathyrus myrtifolius Muhl.; Willd. Sp. Pl. 3 : 1091. 1803.
L. palustris var. myrtifòlius A. Gray, Man. Ed. 2, 104. 1856.
L. myrtifolius macranthus White, Bull. Torr. Club 21 : 448. 1894.

Perennial, usually quite glabrous sometimes pubescent; stems slender, angled, not winged, 1°–3° long, weak. Stipules obliquely ovate, or half-sagittate, 6″–12″ long, often 4″–6″ wide and toothed; leaflets 2–4 pairs, mostly 3 pairs, oval, oval-oblong or ovate, mucronate and acute or obtuse at the apex, narrowed at the base, 9″–2′ long, 3″–7″ wide, rather thin; tendrils branched, peduncles equalling the leaves, or shorter, 3–9-flowered; flowers purple or purplish, similar to those of the preceding species; pod linear, glabrous, sessile, 1′–2′ long, 3½″ wide or less.

In moist or wet grounds, New Brunswick to Manitoba, south to North Carolina and Tennessee. May–July.

$\frac{3}{5}$

$\frac{3}{5}$

5. Lathyrus decaphýllus Pursh. Prairie Vetchling. Fig. 2628.

L. decaphyllus Pursh, Fl. Am. Sept. 471. 1814.
Lathyrus polymorphus Nutt. Gen. 2 : 96. 1818.

Perennial, erect or ascending, glabrous, or finely pubescent, 6′–18′ high. Stems angled; stipules half-sagittate, acuminate, 4″–12″ long, 1″–3″ wide; leaves petioled; leaflets 3–7 pairs, obtuse or acute and mucronulate at the apex, narrowed at the base, thick, conspicuously reticulated, 1′–2½′ long, 3″–8″ wide; stipules when present branched, but often wanting; peduncles usually shorter than the leaves; flowers purple, 1′–1½′ long, showy; pod linear, stipitate; seeds with a narrow stalk and short hilum.

Kansas (?), Idaho and Colorado to Arizona and New Mexico. March–July. Everlasting-pea.

6. Lathyrus ornàtus Nutt. Showy Vetchling. Fig. 2629.

L ornatus Nutt.; T. & G Fl. N. A. 1 : 277. 1838.

Closely resembling the preceding species, but generally lower, often less than 1° high, glabrous or nearly so. Stipules lanceolate or linear, 2″–10″ long; leaflets narrow, linear or linear-oblong, acute and mucronate, 4″–12″ long, 1″–2″ wide; tendrils commonly wanting; flowers purple, showy, 1′–1½′ long; pod linear, stipitate; seeds with a broad stalk and long hilum.

Prairies and plains, Oklahoma to Kansas and South Dakota, west to Colorado, Wyoming and Utah. May–June.

Lathyrus incànus (Rydb. & Smith) Rydb. differs in being villous-pubescent. It ranges from western Nebraska to Utah and Wyoming.

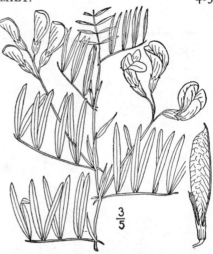

3/5

7. Lathyrus ochroleùcus Hook. Cream-colored or Pale Vetchling. Fig. 26jo.

Lathyrus ochroleucus Hook. Fl. Bor. Am. 1 : 159. 1833.
Lathyrus glaucifolius Beck, Bot. 90. 1833.

Perennial, slender, glabrous and slightly glaucous; stem somewhat angled, climbing or trailing, 1°–2½° long; stipules broad, foliaceous, half-ovate and half-cordate, 8″–12″ long; leaves petioled; leaflets 3–5 pairs, thin, pale beneath, ovate or broadly oval, acute or acutish at the apex, rounded at the base, 1′–2′ long; tendrils branched; peduncles shorter than the leaves; flowers 5–10 yellowish white, 7″–9″ long; pod oblong-linear, sessile, glabrous, 1′–2′ long.

On river-banks and hillsides, Quebec to Mackenzie, British Columbia, New Jersey, Illinois, Iowa, South Dakota and Wyoming. May–July.

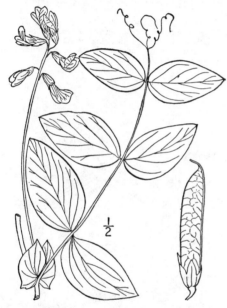

1/2

8. Lathyrus praténsis L. Meadow Pea. Yellow Vetchling. Fig. 2631.

Lathyrus pratensis L. Sp. Pl. 733. 1753.

Perennial, weak, slender, glabrous or sparingly pubescent, climbing or straggling, 1°–3° long. Stems angled, branching; stipules lanolate, foliaceous, half-sagittate, acuminate, 6″–12″ long, nearly as large as the leaflets; leaves sessile; leaflets a single pair, oblong or linear-oblong, acute or acutish, mucronulate, 1′–1½′ long, 2″–4″ wide; tendrils simple or branched; racemes exceeding the leaves; flowers 4–12, yellow, 6″–10″ long; pods linear, glabrous, 1′–1½′ long.

In waste places, New Brunswick, New York, Massachusetts and Ontario. Also throughout Europe and in Russian Asia. Angleberries. Crawpeas. Mouse-pea. Tom Thumb. Yellow tar-fitch [tare vetch]. Lady's-fingers. June–Aug.

2/3

9. Lathyrus latifòlius L. Everlasting Pea. Fig. 2632.

Lathyrus latifolius L. Sp. Pl. 733. 1753.

Perennial, glabrous; stems high-climbing, broadly winged, 3° long or more. Stipules lanceolate, acute, often 1' long; petioles as long as the stipules or longer, winged like the stem; leaflets a single pair, oblong-lanceolate to elliptic, strongly veined, 2'-4' long, acute or mucronate; tendril branched; peduncles stout, curved, mostly longer than the leaves; flowers purple, racemose, purple to white, nearly 1' long.

Escaped from cultivation, Connecticut to District of Columbia. Native of Europe. Summer.

Lathyrus tuberòsus L., another perennial Old World species, with purple flowers, but with smaller thin leaflets and smaller flowers has been found in grassy places in Ontario, Vermont and eastern Massachusetts.

10. Lathyrus pusíllus Ell. Low Vetchling. Fig. 2633.

L. pusillus Ell. Bot. S. C. & Ga. 2 : 223. 1823.

Annual, glabrous; stems usually branched near the base, spreading or climbing, narrowly 2-winged, 2° long or less. Leaflets a single pair, linear to linear-oblong, acute, ½'-2½' long, with a filiform often 3-forked tendril between them; stipules lanceolate, slightly curved, auricled at the base, as long as the petiole or shorter; peduncles 2' long or less, 1-2-flowered; flowers purple, 2½"-3½" long, short-pedicelled; calyx-lobes narrowly lanceolate, acuminate, as long as the tube or somewhat longer; pods linear, 1'-1¾' long.

Sandy soil, North Carolina to Florida, Missouri, Kansas and Texas. April-May.

42. CLITÒRIA L. Sp. Pl. 753. 1753.

Woody vines, or erect or climbing herbs, with pinnately 3-foliolate (sometimes 5-9-foliolate) leaves, persistent stipules, and large showy axillary solitary or racemose flowers. Calyx tubular, 5-toothed, the 2 upper teeth more or less united. Standard large, erect, retuse, narrowed at the base, not spurred; wings oblong, curved; keel acute, shorter than the wings. Stamens more or less monadelphous; anthers all alike. Ovary stipitate; style elongated, incurved, hairy along the inner side. Pod stalked in the calyx, linear or linear-oblong, flattened, 2-valved, partly septate between the seeds.

About 30 species, natives of warm and temperate regions. The following is the only one known to be native in North America. Type species: *Clitoria Ternatea* L., which is naturalized in Florida.

1. Clitoria mariàna L. Butterfly-Pea.
Fig. 2634.

Clitoria mariana L. Sp. Pl. 753. 1753.

Erect or ascending, sometimes twining, glabrous or nearly so, 1°–3° high. Stipules ovate-lanceolate, acute, 1″–2″ long; petioles usually shorter than the leaves; leaflets stipellate, ovate-lanceolate or oblong-lanceolate, obtuse, mucronate, 1′–2′ long, 4″–12″ wide; peduncles short, 1–3-flowered; bracts lanceolate, striate, deciduous; flowers about 2′ long, very showy; calyx tubular, 6″–8″ long, its teeth ovate, acute; corolla pale blue; pods linear-oblong, acute, about 1′ long and 3″ wide.

Dry soil, Snake Hill, N. J., south to Florida, west to Missouri and Texas. Formerly at Brooklyn, N. Y. Clabber-spoon. June–July.

Dólichos Láblab L., the hyacinth bean, native of tropical Asia and widely cultivated in tropical and warm temperate regions for its edible seeds, is a long annual vine with large purple flowers and broad several-seeded pods. It is naturalized in the Southern States, and spontaneous, though scarcely established north to Ohio and the District of Columbia.

½

43. BRADBÙRYA Raf. Fl. Ludov. 104. 1817.

[Centrosema Benth. Ann. Mus. Wien, 2: 117. 1838.]

Slender twining or prostrate vines, with pinnately 3-foliolate leaves (rarely 5–7-foliolate), persistent stipules, and large showy axillary racemose or solitary flowers. Calyx campanulate, its teeth or lobes nearly equal; standard orbicular, nearly flat, spurred on the back near its base, clawed; wings obovate, curved; keel curved. Stamens more or less diadelphous (9 and 1); anthers all alike. Style incurved, bearded at the apex around the stigma. Pod linear, flattened, nearly sessile, partially septate between the seeds, 2-valved, the valves thick-edged, longitudinally nerved along their margins, elastically dehiscent. [In honor of John Bradbury, who travelled in America early in the century.]

About 30 species, natives of America. Besides the following, 2 others occur in the Southern States. Type species: *Bradburya scandens* Raf.

⅗

1. Bradburya virginiàna (L.) Kuntze.
Spurred Butterfly-Pea. Fig. 2635.

Clitoria virginiana L. Sp. Pl. 753. 1753.
Centrosema virginianum Benth. Ann. Mus. Wien 2: 120. 1838.
B. virginiana Kuntze, Rev. Gen. Pl. 164. 1891.

Perennial, climbing or trailing, somewhat branched, finely rough-pubescent, 2°–4° long. Stipules linear, acute, about 2″ long; petioles usually shorter than the leaves; leaflets 3, ovate, or oblong-lanceolate, stipellate, acute and mucronate or blunt, rounded at the base, reticulate-veined, 1′–2′ long, 4″–12″ wide; peduncles about equalling the petioles, 1–4-flowered; bracts ovate, acute, finely striate; flowers short-pedicelled, 1′–1½′ long; corolla violet; calyx-lobes linear; pod linear, 4′–5′ long, about 2″ wide, long-acuminate, its margins much thickened.

Dry sandy soil, New Jersey to Florida, west to Arkansas and Texas. Extends in several races throughout tropical America to Bolivia. July–Aug.

44. GLYCÌNE L. Sp. Pl. 753. 1753.

[BRADLEIA Adans. Fam. Pl. 2: 324. 1763.]

[APIOS Moench, Meth. 165. 1794.]

Twining perennial vines, with pinnately 3-7-foliolate leaves, small stipules and rather large brownish-purple or red flowers, mainly in axillary racemes or panicles. Calyx campanulate, somewhat 2-lipped, the 2 lateral teeth very small, the 2 upper united and short, the lower one long and acute. Standard ovate, or orbicular, reflexed. Wings obliquely obovate, adherent to the elongated incurved at length twisted keel. Stamens diadelphous (9 and 1); anthers all alike; ovary nearly sessile; ovules ∞; style slender. Pod linear, straight or slightly curved, compressed, 2-valved, many-seeded. Rootstocks tuberous. [Greek, from the sweet tubers.]

Five known species, the following of eastern North America, 2 of China and 1 of the Himalayas. Type species: *Glycine Àpios* L.

Standard suborbicular, rounded or retuse at the apex; tubers necklace-like.   1. *G. Apios.*
Standard produced at the apex into a thickened appendage; tubers large, solitary.   2. *G. Priceana.*

$\frac{1}{2}$

1. Glycine Àpios L. Ground-nut. Wild Bean. Fig. 2636.

Glycine Apios L. Sp. Pl. 753. 1753.
Apios tuberosa Moench, Meth. 165. 1794.
Apios Apios MacM. Bull. Torr. Club 19: 15. 1892.

Slender, pubescent or glabrate, climbing over bushes to a height of several feet. Rootstock tuberous, the tubers necklace-shaped; stipules subulate, 1″-2″ long, deciduous; leaves petioled; leaflets 5-7 (rarely 3), ovate or ovate-lanceolate, acute or acuminate at the apex, rounded at the base, 1′-3′ long; racemes axillary, often compound; peduncles shorter than the leaves; flowers numerous, brownish purple, odorous, about 6″ long; standard not appendaged; rachis of the inflorescence knobby; pod linear, straight or slightly curved, pointed, 2′-4½′ long, about 2½″ wide, many-seeded, its valves rather coriaceous.

In moist ground, New Brunswick to Florida, west to western Ontario, Minnesota, Nebraska, Kansas and Texas. Stem with milky juice; tubers edible. July-Sept. Ground-, trailing- or potato-pea. Pig-, Dacotah- or Indian-potato. White apple. Traveler's-delight.

2. Glycine Priceàna (Robinson) Britton. Price's Ground-nut. Fig. 2637.

Apios Priceana Robinson, Bot. Gaz. 25: 451. 1898.

Tuber often 6′-7′ thick, somewhat higher than thick, solitary. Stems pubescent with reflexed hairs, or glabrous, 3°-10° long; leaflets 3-9, ovate or ovate-lanceolate, 4′ long or less, acuminate at the apex, rounded or obtuse at the base, sparingly pubescent on both sides; panicles often 2 or 3 together in the axils, many-flowered, 4′-6′ long; corolla greenish-white, tinged with rose or magenta; blade of the standard about 1′ long, produced at the apex into a spongy or fleshy knob; pods linear, 4′-5′ long.

Rocky woods, Kentucky and Tennessee. Summer.

$\frac{1}{2}$

45. FALCÀTA Gmel in L. Syst. Nat. Ed. 13, 2: 1131. 1796.

[AMPHICÀRPA Ell. Journ. Acad. Phil 1: 372. 1817.]

Twining perennial vines, with pinnately 3-foliolate leaves, small white, violet or purple flowers in axillary racemes, and also solitary apetalous fertile flowers in the lower axils or on the slender creeping branches from the base. Calyx of the petaliferous flowers tubular, 4-5-toothed. Standard obovate, erect, folded around the other petals; wings oblong, curved, adherent to the incurved obtuse keel. Stamens diadelphous (9 and 1); anthers all alike. Style filiform, not bearded. Pods from the upper flowers linear-oblong, several-seeded, 2-valved, those from the lower obovoid, fleshy, mainly 1-seeded. [Latin, referring to the curved keel of the corolla.]

About 7 species, natives of North America, eastern Asia and the Himalayas. Only the following are known in North America. Type species: *Falcata caroliniana* (Walt.) Gmel.

Leaves thin; bracts small; plant pubescent or glabrate.   1. *F. comosa.*
Leaves firm; bracts large; plant villous-brown-pubescent.   2. *F. Pitcheri.*

1. Falcata comòsa (L.) Kuntze. Wild or Hog Pea-nut. Fig. 2638.

Glycine comosa L. Sp. Pl. 754. 1753.
Glycine bracteata L. Sp. Pl. 754. 1753.
Glycine monoica L. Sp. Pl. Ed. 2, 1023. 1763.
Amphicarpa monoica Ell. Journ. Acad. Phil. 1: 373. 1817.
Falcata comosa Kuntze, Rev. Gen. Pl. 182. 1891.

Slender, simple or sparingly branched, climbing, pubescent or glabrate, 1°–8° long. Stipules oblong or ovate, 2″ long, striate; leaflets broadly ovate or rhombic-ovate, acute at the apex, rounded at the base, the lower inequilateral, 1′–3′ long; racemes of petaliferous flowers mainly simple; bracts small, ovate, obtuse; flowers purplish or white, 6″–7″ long; pedicels equalling or exceeding the bracts; pods of the petaliferous flowers about 1′ long, 3″ wide, pubescent.

Moist thickets, New Brunswick to Florida, west to Manitoba, Nebraska and Louisiana. Aug.–Sept. Pea-vine. American licorice.

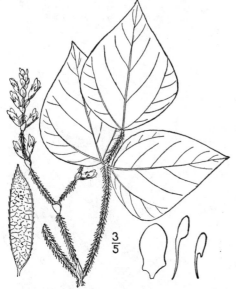

2. Falcata Pítcheri (T. & G.) Kuntze. Pitcher's Hog Pea-nut. Fig. 2639.

Amphicarpaea Pitcheri T. & G. Fl. N. A. 1: 292. 1838.
F. Pitcheri Kuntze, Rev. Gen. Pl. 182. 1891.

Similar to the preceding but generally stouter, villous-pubescent throughout with reflexed brown hairs. Leaflets larger and thicker, sometimes 4′ long; pedicels mostly shorter than the nearly orbicular canescent bracts; ovary and pods of the petaliferous flowers pubescent throughout, subterranean fruit less abundantly produced than in *F. comosa;* calyx larger.

Moist thickets, Massachusetts to Virginia, New York, South Dakota, Tennessee and Texas. Perhaps a race of the preceding species. Aug.–Sept.

46. GALÁCTIA P. Br.; Adans. Fam. Pl. 2: 322. 1763.

Prostrate or climbing perennial vines (sometimes erect and shrubby), mainly with pinnately 3-foliolate leaves, small and deciduous stipules, and purple or violet axillary racemose flowers. Calyx 4-lobed, bracteolate, the lobes acute, often as long as the tube. Standard orbicular or obovate. Wings narrow, obovate, adherent to the narrow, nearly straight keel. Stamens diadelphous or nearly so (9 and 1); anthers all alike. Ovary nearly sessile; ovules ∞; style filiform, not bearded. Pod linear, straight or slightly curved, usually flattened, 2-valved, several-seeded. Fleshy few-seeded pods are sometimes produced from subterranean apetalous flowers. [Greek, milk-yielding, the typical species described as having milky branches.]

About 70 species, natives of warm and temperate regions, most abundant in America. Besides the following, about 25 others occur in the southern and southwestern states. Type species: *Glycine Galactia* L.

Nearly glabrous throughout; pods slightly pubescent.
Finely downy-pubescent; pods very downy.

1. *G. regularis.*
2. *G. volubilis.*

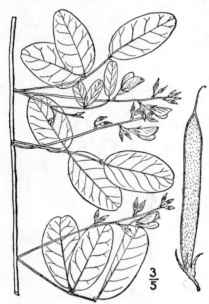

3/5

1. Galactia reguläris (L.) B.S.P. Milk Pea. Fig 2640.

Dolichos regularis L. Sp. Pl. 726. 1753.

Galactia glabella Michx. Fl. Bor. Am. **2**: 62. 1803.

Galactia regularis B.S.P. Prel. Cat. N. Y. 14. 1888.

Prostrate, glabrous or sparingly appressed-pubescent; stems matted, usually branching, 1°–2° long. Stipules minute, deciduous; petioles shorter than the leaves; leaflets elliptic or ovate-oblong, obtuse and often emarginate at the apex, rounded or slightly cordate at the base, ½–1½′ long, 4″–9″ wide; peduncles longer than the petioles and generally exceeding the leaves, erect, 4–10-flowered; racemes loose or dense; pedicels about 1½″ long; flowers reddish-purple, 6″–8″ long; pods linear, straight, or slightly curved, slightly pubescent, 1′–1½′ long, 2″ wide, 4–7-seeded.

In dry sandy soil, southeastern New York, Pennsylvania, pine barrens of New Jersey to Florida, Kansas and Mississippi. July–Aug.

2. Galactia volúbilis (L.) Britton. Downy Milk Pea. Fig. 2641.

Hedysarum volubile L. Sp. Pl. 750. 1753.
Galactia mollis Nutt. Gen. **2**: 117. 1818. Not Michx. 1803.
Galactia pilosa Ell. Bot. S. C. & Ga. **2**: 238. 1824. Not Nutt. 1818.
G. volubilis Britton, Mem. Torr. Club **5**: 208. 1894.
G. volubilis mississippiensis Vail, Bull. Torr. Club **22**: 508. 1895.

Finely downy-pubescent all over, similar to the preceding species. Leaflets ovate, elliptic, or oval, obtuse or acutish, sometimes emarginate at the apex, rounded or slightly cordate at the base, downy beneath, glabrous or with some appressed pubescence above, ¾′–1½′ long, 5″–12″ wide; peduncles sometimes elongated, but variable in length; racemes rather loose; flowers purplish, about 6″ long; pod linear, 1′–1¼′ long, 2″ wide, densely and finely downy-pubescent.

3/4

In dry soil, New York Island; Flushing, Long Island, south to Florida, west to Kentucky, Kansas and Texas. Races differ in pubescence and in form of leaflets. June–July.

Dioclea multiflòra (T. & G.) C. Mohr., a long vine, the purple flowers differing from those of *Galactia* in having the filament opposite the standard adnate to it, has been found along a railroad in western Kentucky. It is native of the southern states.

Pueraria Thunbergiàna (Sieb. & Zucc.) Benth., the kudzu vine, of China, a high-climbing, hairy vine with large 3-foliolate leaves, the leaflets 3-lobed and acuminate, the blue-purple flowers in racemes, is much planted for ornament and has been found in waste grounds on Staten Island.

47. DOLÍCHOLUS Medic. Vorles. Chur. Phys. Gesell. 2 : 354. 1787.

[RHYNCHOSIA Lour. Fl. Cochin. 562. 1793.]

Perennial twining, trailing or erect herbs, with pinnately 1–3-foliolate leaves, and yellow mostly axillary and racemose flowers. Leaflets generally punctate with resinous dots, not stipellate. Calyx 4–5-lobed, somewhat 2-lipped. Standard obovate or orbicular, spreading or reflexed. Wings narrow. Keel incurved at the apex or falcate. Stamens diadelphous (9 and 1). Ovary nearly sessile; ovules 2, rarely 1; style filiform. Pod flat, oblong or obliquely orbicular, 2-valved, 1–2-seeded. [Name diminutive of *Dolichos*.]

About 200 species, natives of warm and temperate regions. In addition to the following, some 12 others occur in the southern States. Type species: *Dolicholus minimus* (L.) Medic.

Leaflets 3.
　Stem twining or trailing.
　　Racemes shorter than the leaves; flowers 3″–4″ long.　　　　　　　　　　1. *D. tomentosus.*
　　Racemes longer than the leaves; flowers about 6″ long.　　　　　　　　　2. *D. latifolius.*
　Stem erect, 1°–2½° high.　　　　　　　　　　　　　　　　　　　　　　　3. *D. erectus.*
Leaflets solitary, very broad; plants low, 3′–9′ high.　　　　　　　　　　　　4. *D. simplicifolius.*

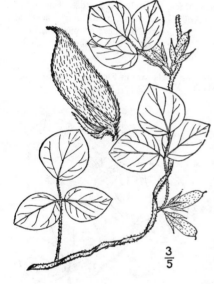

1. Dolicholus tomentòsus (L.) Vail. Twining Dolicholus. Fig. 2642.

Glycine tomentosa L. Sp. Pl. 754. 1753.

Rhynchosia tomentosa var. *volubilis* T. & G. Fl. N. A. 1 : 285. 1838.

Rhynchosia tomentosa H. & A. Comp. Bot. Mag. 1 : 23. 1835.

D. tomentosus Vail, Bull. Torr. Club 26 : 112. 1899.

Trailing or twining, more or less pubescent with spreading hairs, simple or branched, 1°–3° long. Stipules ovate, acute, 2″–4″ long, sometimes wanting; petioles shorter than the leaves; leaflets 3, or the lowest leaves 1-foliolate, ovate, orbicular or broader than long, obtuse but generally pointed, 1′–2′ long; racemes short-peduncled or sessile, 2–8-flowered; flowers 3″–4″ long; calyx deeply 4-parted, the upper lobe 2-cleft; pod oblong, acute, pubescent, 8″–9″ long, about 3″ wide.

In dry sandy soil, Virginia to Florida, west to Texas. May–July.

2. Dolicholus latifòlius (Nutt.) Vail. Prairie Rhynchosia. Fig. 2643.

Rhynchosia latifolia Nutt.; T. & G. Fl. N. A 1 . 285. 1838.

Dolicholus latifolius Vail, Bull. Torr. Club 26 : 114. 1899.

Softly pubescent, stem angled, trailing or climbing, sometimes 5° long, with a few long branches. Stipules lanceolate, small, or wanting; petioles 1′–3′ long; leaflets 3, broadly ovate, or somewhat rhomboid, or the end one orbicular, 1′–3′ long, mostly obtuse; racemes elongated, exceeding the leaves, sometimes 1° long in fruit, many-flowered; pedicels 1″–2″ long; calyx about 6″ long, very deeply parted, the segments narrowly lanceolate, acuminate; corolla little longer than the calyx; pod oblong, acute, very pubescent, about 1′ long.

In dry soil, Missouri to Louisiana and Texas. May–June

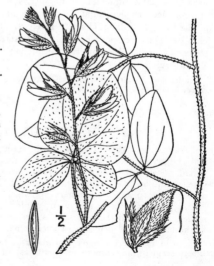

3. Dolicholus eréctus (Walt.) Vail.
Erect Rhynchosia. Fig. 2644.

Trifolium erectum Walt. Fl. Car. 184. 1788.

Rhynchosia erecta DC. Prodr. 2 : 384. 1825.

Rhynchosia tomentosa var. *erecta* T. & G. Fl. N. A.
  1 : 285. 1838.

D. erectus Vail, Bull. Torr. Club 26 : 115. 1899.

Erect, rather stout, simple or slightly branched, velvety-pubescent or tomentose, 1°–2½°
high. Stipules linear-lanceolate, acuminate,
2″–3″ long; petioles shorter than or equalling
the leaves; leaflets 3, oval, ovate or slightly
obovate, thick, densely tomentose, especially
beneath, obtuse or acute, 1′–2′ long; racemes
5–15-flowered, sessile or short-peduncled; flowers 3″–5″ long; pod oblong, pubescent, 6″–8″
long, about 3″ wide.

In dry soil, Delaware to Florida, Tennessee and
Louisiana. May–Sept.

4. Dolicholus simplicifòlius (Walt.) Vail.
Round-leaved Rhynchosia. Fig. 2645.

Trifolium simplicifolium Walt. Fl. Car. 184. 1788.

Rhynchosia reniformis DC. Prodr. 2 : 384. 1825.

Rhynchosia tomentosa var. *monophylla* T. & G. Fl. N. A.
  1 : 284. 1838.

Rhynchosia simplicifolia Wood, Bot. & Fl. 96. 1870.

D. simplicifolius Vail, Bull. Torr. Club 26 : 114. 1899.

Erect, low, simple, pubescent with spreading hairs,
3′–9′ high. Stipules lanceolate, acuminate, 3″–4″ long;
petioles shorter than or exceeding the leaves; leaflet
usually solitary, orbicular or broader, thick, obtuse
and rounded or apiculate at the apex, slightly cordate
at the base, 1′–2′ long (leaflets rarely 3, the lateral
ones ovate) ; racemes rather densely flowered, short-
peduncled or sessile; flowers 3″–5″ long; pod as in
the preceding species.

In dry soil, Virginia to Florida, Tennessee and Louisiana. May–July.

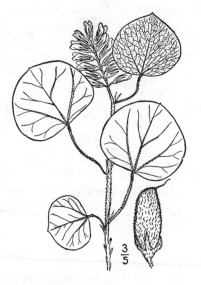

48. PHASÈOLUS [Tourn.] L. Sp. Pl. 723. 1753.

Annual or perennial vines, rarely erect herbs, with pinnately 3-foliolate stipellate leaves,
and axillary racemose flowers. Calyx 5-toothed or 5-lobed, or the 2 upper teeth more or less
united. Standard orbicular, recurved, spreading or somewhat contorted; wings mainly obovate, equalling or exceeding the standard; keel spirally coiled, linear or obovoid. Stamens
diadelphous (9 and 1); anthers all alike. Style longitudinally bearded; stigma oblique or
lateral; ovary sessile or nearly so; ovules ∞. Pod linear, straight or curved, 2-valved, several-
seeded, tipped with the persistent style. Seeds mostly with rounded ends. Rachis thickened
at the bases of the pedicels. [Ancient name of the Kidney Bean.]

About 170 species, natives of warm and temperate regions. Besides the following, about 12
others occur in the southern and southwestern states. Type species: *Phaseolus vulgaris* L.

1. Phaseolus polystàchyus (L.) B.S.P. Wild Bean or Bean Vine. Fig. 2646.

Dolichos polystachyus L. Sp, Pl. 726. 1753.

Phaseolus perennis Walt. Fl. Car. 182. 1788.

Phaseolus polystachyus B.S.P. Prel. Cat. N. Y. 15. 1888.

Climbing over bushes, or trailing, from a perennial root, finely pubescent, branched, 4°–15° long. Stipules lanceolate, deciduous; leaflets broadly ovate or nearly orbicular, acute or acuminate at the apex, rounded at the base, 2′–4′ long, the terminal one often slightly cordate, the lower ones unequal-sided; racemes axillary, usually numerous, peduncled, 4′–12′ long, narrow, loosely-flowered; pedicels 2″–4″ long, minutely bracted at the base; corolla purple, about 4″ long; pods stalked, drooping, somewhat curved, flat, 1¾′–2½′ long, 4″–5″ wide, 4–6-seeded, glabrous or nearly so; seeds chocolate-brown, 3″–4″ long.

In thickets, Canada (Torrey and Gray) ; Connecticut to Florida, Ohio, Nebraska and Texas. Recorded from Minnesota. July–Sept. Called also wild kidney bean.

49. STROPHOSTYLES Ell. Bot. S. C. & Ga. 2: 229. 1822.

Twining or trailing herbaceous vines, rarely erect, mostly pubescent, with pinnately 3-foliolate stipellate leaves, and pink-purple or nearly white flowers capitate at the ends of long axillary peduncles. Calyx as in *Phaseolus*. Standard nearly orbicular; wings mostly obovate; keel strongly curved. Stamens diadelphous (9 and 1). Style longitudinally bearded, bent. Pod linear, nearly terete, or somewhat compressed, usually straight, few–several-seeded, tipped by the persistent style. Seeds truncate at the ends, more or less pubescent or mealy. [Greek, bent style.]

An American genus, of about 6 species. Type species: *Strophostyles angulosa* Ell.

Leaflets mainly lobed, 1′–2′ long ; pod 2′–3′ long ; root annual.   1. *S. helvola.*
Leaflets mainly entire, ½′–1½′ long ; pod 1′–2′ long.
  Flowers several, about 6″ long ; root perennial.   2. *S. umbellata.*
  Flowers few, about 3″ long ; root annual.   3 *S. pauciflora.*

1. Strophostyles hélvola (L.) Britton. Trailing Wild Bean. Fig. 2647.

Phaseolus helvolus L. Sp. Pl. 724. 1753.

Phaseolus angulosus Ort. Nov. Pl. 24. 1797.

Phaseolus diversifolius Pers. Syn. 2: 296. 1807.

Strophostyles angulosa Ell. Bot. S. C. 2: 229. 1822.

S. helvola Britton; Britt. & Brown, Ill. Fl. 2: 338. 1897.

Prostrate or low-twining, rather rough-pubescent, branched at the base, 2°–8° long, rarely erect and 10′–20′ high. Root annual; stipules narrowly lanceolate, 1″–2″ long; leaflets broadly ovate, obtuse or acute at the apex, rounded at the base, thickish, generally more or less obtusely lobed, sometimes entire, 1′–2′ long, the lower ones often inequilateral; peduncles axillary, exceeding the petioles; flowers 3–10, sessile, capitate; corolla greenish-purple, 4″–6″ long; keel slender, curved; pod sessile, linear, nearly terete, slightly pubescent, 2′–3′ long; seeds oblong, pubescent, 2½″–3½″ long.

In sandy soil, Quebec to Massachusetts, Florida, Ontario, South Dakota, Kansas and Texas. July–Oct.

Strophostyles missouriénsis (S. Wats.) Small, regarded as a variety of this species in our first edition, differs by being a longer vine, climbing over trees and bushes, its leaflets nearly entire and its seeds slightly larger. It ranges from Virginia to Illinois and Kansas.

2. **Strophostyles umbellàta** (Muhl.) Britton.   Pink Wild Bean.   Fig. 2648.

Glycine umbellata Muhl.; Willd. Sp. Pl. **3**: 1058.   1803.

Strophostyles peduncularis Ell. Bot. S. C. **2** : 230.   1822.

Phaseolus helvolus T. & G. Fl. N. A. **1** : 280.   1838.   Not L. 1753.

Phaseolus umbellatus Britton, Trans. N. Y. Acad. **9** : 10. 1889.

S. umbellata Britton ; Britt. & Brown, Ill. Fl. **2** : 339.   1907.

Root perennial; stems slender, trailing, branching, more or less pubescent with retrorse hairs, $1°-5°$ long. Stipules ovate-lanceolate, $1''-2''$ long; leaflets ovate, lanceolate or oblong, obtuse or acutish at the apex, rounded at the base, sparingly pubescent, entire, or rarely with 1 or 2 shallow lobes; peduncles generally much longer than the leaves; flowers several, pink, fading yellowish, capitate-umbellate, about $6''$ long, similar to those of the preceding species; pedicels $\frac{1}{2}''-1''$ long; pod linear, straight, little compressed, sessile, $1'-2'$ long, $2''$ wide, sparingly pubescent; seeds mealy-pubescent, $1\frac{1}{2}''-2''$ long.

In sandy soil, Long Island to Florida, Indiana, Arkansas and Texas. July–Sept.

3. **Strophostyles pauciflòra** (Benth.) S. Wats. Small Wild Bean.   Fig. 2649.

Phaseolus pauciflorus Benth. Comm. Leg. Gen. 76.   1837.

Phaseolus leiospermus T. & G. Fl. N. A. **1** : 280.   1838.

Strophostyles pauciflorus S. Wats. in A. Gray, Man. Ed. 6, 145. 1890.

Roots annual; stem slender, finely retrorsely hirsute, low-climbing or trailing, $1°-2\frac{1}{2}°$ long. Stipules ovate-lanceolate, $\frac{1}{2}''-1\frac{1}{2}''$ long; leaflets lanceolate or linear-oblong, obtuse at the apex, rounded at the base, entire, $9''-18''$ long, $3''-5''$ wide; peduncles exceeding the leaves; flowers 2–6, capitate-umbellate, purplish, about $3'$ long; pod flat, linear, about $1'$ long and $2''$ wide, very pubescent; seeds purple, glabrous and shining at maturity, $1\frac{1}{2}''-2''$ long.

Along rivers, Indiana to South Dakota, Colorado, Mississippi, Missouri, Kansas and Texas. July–Sept.

50. **VÍGNA** Savi, Mem. Phas. **3** : 7.   1826.

Climbing or trailing herbaceous vines, or sometimes erect herbs, with pinnately 3-foliolate stipulate leaves, the leaflets broad. Flowers clustered at the ends of long axillary peduncles, yellowish or purplish, the rachis of the head or raceme knotty, the bracts and bractlets early deciduous. Calyx 5-toothed, or the 2 upper teeth united. Standard nearly orbicular, auricled at the base; wings shorter than the standard; keel about equalling the standard, slightly incurved. Stamens diadelphous (9 and 1). Ovary sessile; ovules numerous; style bearded along the inner side. Pod linear, nearly terete, 2-valved. [In honor of Domenic Vigni, a commentator on Theophrastus.]

About 30 species, natives of warm and tropical regions. Besides the following, another occurs in the southern United States. Type species : Dólichos lutèolus Jacq.

1. **Vigna sinénsis** (L.) Endl.   Cow Pea.   China Bean.   Fig. 2650.

Dolichos sinensis L. Cent. Pl. 2 : 28.   1756.
Dolichos Catjang L. Mant. 1 : 269.   1767.
Vigna Catjang Walp. Linnaea 13 : 533.   1839.
Vigna sinensis Endl. ; Hassk. Pl. Jav. Rar. 386.   1848.

Annual, glabrous, or somewhat pubescent; stem twining or trailing, striate. Stipules ovate or ovate-lanceolate, acuminate, prolonged backward, 3″–10″ long; petioles stout, often as long as the leaflets or longer; terminal leaflet rhombic-ovate, acute or blunt, 2′–6′ long, often about as wide, long-stalked; lateral leaflets very obliquely ovate and inequilateral, about as large as the terminal one, short-stalked; flowers few near the knotty ends of the long peduncles, 8″–10″ long; pod fleshy, 4′–7′ long, 3″–4″ thick, nearly straight; seeds with a dark circle around the scar of attachment.

Escaped from cultivation, Missouri to Texas and Georgia. Native of Asia, and called chowley, towcok. Seeds edible. Black-eyed bean. July–Sept.

Vigna repèns (L.) Kuntze, a smaller vine with much shorter pods, widely distributed in tropical America, has been found in ballast about New York.

$\frac{1}{2}$

Family 61.   **GERANIÀCEAE** J. St. Hil. Expos. Fam. 2 : 51.   1805.

GERANIUM FAMILY.

Herbs with alternate or opposite leaves, and axillary solitary or clustered perfect regular flowers. Stipules commonly present. Sepals 5 (rarely fewer), mostly persistent. Petals of the same number, hypogynous. Stamens as many as the sepals, or 2–3 times as many, distinct; anthers 2-celled, versatile. Ovary 1, usually 5-lobed and 5-celled; ovules 1 or 2 in each cavity. Fruit capsular. Embryo straight or curved; cotyledons flat or plicate.

About 12 genera and 470 species, natives of temperate regions, most abundant in South Africa.

Carpel-bodies turgid; carpel-tails (styles) glabrous within, merely recoiling at maturity; anthers usually 10 (or 5 in *Geranium pusillum*).
     Carpel-bodies deciduous from the styles at maturity, each with 2 fibrous appendages near the top; leaves divided.   1. *Robertiella.*
     Carpel-bodies permanently attached to the styles, unappendaged; leaves lobed, cleft or parted.
                                                         2. *Geranium.*
Carpel-bodies spindle-shaped; carpel-tails (styles) pubescent within, spirally coiled at maturity; anthers 5.   3. *Erodium.*

---

1.   **ROBERTIÉLLA** Hanks; Hanks & Small, N. A. Fl. 25^1: 3.   1907.

[ROBERTIUM Picard, Mem. Soc. Agric. Boulogne II. 1 : 99.   1837.   Not *Robertia* Scop. 1777.]

Herbs with 3-divided leaves, the divisions 1–2-pinnatifid, and axillary 2-flowered peduncles. Flowers regular. Sepals 5, awn-tipped. Petals 5, glabrous, each with a slender claw and a broad blade. Stamens 10; filaments glabrous. Ovary 5-lobed, 5-celled, the style-column beaked. Ovules 2 in each cavity. Capsule separating into 5 carpels, the bodies deciduous from the styles at maturity, each bearing 2 fibrous appendages near the top. [Diminutive of *Robertium*.]

Two known species of north temperate regions, the following typical.

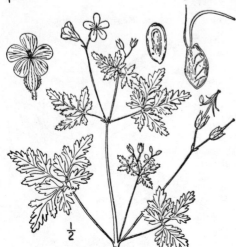

1. Robertiella Robertiàna (L.) Hanks. Herb Robert. Red robin. Fig. 2651.

Geranium Robertianum L. Sp. Pl. 681. 1753.
Robertiella Robertiana Hanks; Hanks & Small, N. A. Fl. **25**: 3. 1907.

Annual or biennial, glandular-villous, weak, extensively branching, erect or decumbent, 6′–18′ high, heavy-scented. Leaves thin, ovate-orbicular in outline, the divisions cleft, finely lobed or toothed, the teeth oblong, mucronate; peduncles slender, 2-flowered, 1′–3′ long; pedicels divaricate, ½′ long; sepals acuminate and awn-pointed; flowers red-purple, about 6″ broad; petals 4″–5″ long, narrow-clawed; beak of the fruit about 1′ long, awn-pointed, nearly glabrous; carpels nearly glabrous, wrinkled.

In rocky woods, rarely in sandy places, Nova Scotia to Manitoba, New Jersey, Pennsylvania and Missouri. Occurs also in Europe, Asia and northern Africa. Odor disagreeable. Fox, mountain or wild geranium. Red robin. Red-shanks. Dragons'-blood. Jenny-wren. Wren's-flower. Red bird's-eye. May–Oct.

2. GERÀNIUM [Tourn.] L. Sp. Pl. 676. 1753.

Herbs with stipulate palmately lobed, cleft or parted leaves, and axillary 1–2-flowered peduncles. Flowers regular, 5-merous. Sepals 5, imbricated. Petals 5, hypogynous, imbricated. Stamens 10 (rarely 5), generally 5 longer and 5 shorter. Ovary 5-lobed, 5-celled, beaked with the compound style. Ovules 2 in each cavity. Capsule elastically dehiscent, the 5 cavities 1-seeded, long-tailed. [Greek, a crane, from the long beak of the fruit.]

About 190 species, widely distributed in temperate regions. Besides the following, some 60 others occur in North America. Type species: *Geranium sylváticum* L.

Perennial; flowers 1′ broad or more.
 Beak of the fruit, and pedicels, glandular-pubescent. 1. *G. pratense.*
 Beak of the fruit, and pedicels, pubescent, but not glandular. 2. *G. maculatum.*
Annuals or biennials; flowers 2″–6″ broad.
 Peduncles 1-flowered. 3. *G. sibiricum.*
 Peduncles 2-flowered.
  Peduncles longer than the leaves; carpels smooth and glabrous. 4. *G. columbinum.*
  Peduncles short; carpels rugose or hairy.
   Seeds reticulated or pitted.
    Glandular-pubescent with long white hairs. 5. *G. rotundifolium.*
    Pubescent with short hairs; leaves deeply lobed.
     Flowers pale purple; seeds minutely reticulated.
      Beak short-pointed; inflorescence compact. 6. *G. carolinianum.*
      Beak long-pointed; inflorescence loose. 7. *G. Bicknellii.*
     Flowers deep purple; seeds deeply pitted. 8. *G. dissectum.*
   Seeds smooth or nearly so.
    Stamens 5; carpels hairy, not rugose. 9. *G. pusillum.*
    Stamens 10; carpels glabrate, rugose. 10. *G. molle.*

1. Geranium praténse L. Meadow Geranium. Fig. 2652.

Geranium pratense L. Sp. Pl. 681. 1753.

Perennial by a stout rootstock, pubescent with spreading or retrorse short hairs, erect, 1°–2½° high. Basal leaves long-petioled, reniform or orbicular-reniform in outline and decidedly pentagonal, mostly 4′–5′ wide, 5–7-parted, the divisions narrower, more attenuate and more finely cut than in *G. maculatum;* stem-leaves usually with narrower divisions and teeth than the basal leaves; peduncles elongated, glandular-pubescent like the pedicels which are very variable in length; flowers deep-purple, 1¼′–1¾′ broad; petals ciliate at the base; beak of the fruit ¾′–1′ long; carpels minutely pubescent; seeds reticulate.

In meadows and fields, New Brunswick and Quebec to Maine and Massachusetts. Adventive from Europe. June–Aug.

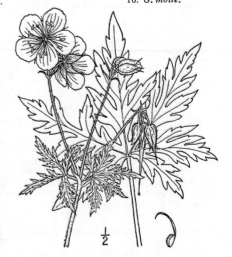

Geranium pyrenàicum L., of Europe, a perennial with much smaller flowers, the sepals obtusish, has been found in waste places in Quebec and Pennsylvania.

2. Geranium maculàtum L.   Wild or Spotted Crane's-bill.   Fig. 2653.

Geranium maculatum L. Sp. Pl. 681. 1753.

Perennial by a thick rootstock, pubescent with spreading or retrorse hairs, erect, simple, or branching above, 1°–2° high. Basal leaves long-petioled, nearly orbicular, broadly cordate or reniform, 3′–6′ wide, deeply 3–5-parted, the divisions obovate, cuneate, variously toothed and cleft; stem-leaves 2, opposite, shorter-petioled, otherwise similar to the basal ones; peduncles 1–5, elongated, generally bearing a pair of leaves at the base of the umbellate inflorescence; ultimate pedicels 1′–2′ long; flowers rose-purple, 1′–1½′ broad; sepals awn-pointed; petals woolly at the base; beak of the fruit 1′–1½′ long; carpels pubescent; seed reticulate.

In woods, Maine and Ontario to Manitoba, Georgia, Alabama and Nebraska. Recorded from Newfoundland. Alum-root or bloom. Crowfoot. American kino-root. Shame-face. Chocolate-flower. Rockweed. Sailor's-knot. April–July.

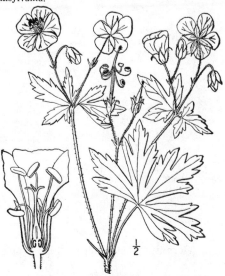

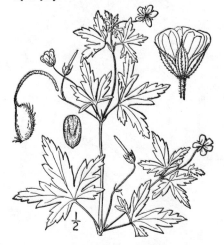

3. Geranium sibíricum L.   Siberian Crane's-bill.   Fig. 2654.

Geranium sibiricum L. Sp. Pl. 683. 1753.

Annual, villous-pubescent, freely branched, decumbent or ascending, 1°–4½° high. Leaves deeply 3–5-parted, 2′–2½′ broad, nearly orbicular, or cordate-reniform, the divisions oval-lanceolate, cleft or toothed; peduncles slender, 1-flowered, 2′–3′ long, 2-bracted near the middle; flowers nearly white, 3″–4″ broad; sepals oval, awned; beak of the fruit canescent, 7″–9″ long, tipped with a short prolongation; lobes of the capsule puberulent or hairy, seed minutely reticulate.

Abundant along roadsides in the northern part of New York City. Adventive from Asia. Some of the pedicels are rarely 2-flowered. June–Sept.

4. Geranium columbìnum L.   Long-stalked Crane's-bill.   Fig. 2655.

Geranium columbinum L. Sp. Pl. 682. 1753.

Annual, slender, decumbent or prostrate, slightly hispid-pubescent with whitish appressed hairs. Leaves 1′–1½′ in diameter, pedately deeply 5–9-divided into narrow, mostly linear variously cleft segments; petioles very slender, those of the lower and basal leaves often 5′–6′ long; peduncles also slender, longer than the upper leaves, 2-flowered; pedicels 1′–3′ long; flowers purple, about 4″ broad; sepals ovate, awn-pointed, enlarging in fruit; petals notched; capsule-lobes nearly glabrous, keeled, not rugose; beak 6″–10″ long, hispid; seeds deeply pitted.

In fields and along roadsides, New Jersey, Pennsylvania, Maryland and Virginia. Also in South Dakota. Naturalized or adventive from Europe. Native also of northern Asia. May–July.

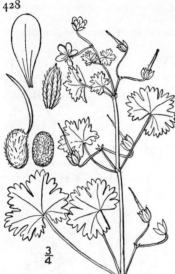

5. Geranium rotundifòlium L.   Round-leaved Crane's-bill.   Fig. 2656.

Geranium rotundifolium L. Sp. Pl. 683. 1753.

Annual, often tufted, 6′–18′ high, much branched, softly pubescent with spreading white purple-tipped glandular hairs. Leaves reniform-orbicular, broader than long, 1½′ wide, cleft about to the middle into 5–9 obtuse broad lobes, which are 3–5-toothed; petioles slender, those of the basal leaves elongated; flowers purple, 2″–3″ broad; sepals ovate, or oval, short-pointed, somewhat shorter than the entire obovate petals; ovary and capsule-lobes hairy, not wrinkled; beak pubescent, about 6″ long, pointed with a short awn; seeds reticulated.

In waste places, Michigan, and in ballast about New York and Philadelphia. Fugitive from Europe. Native also of northern Asia. Summer.

6. Geranium caroliniànum L.   Carolina Crane's-bill.   Fig. 2657.

Geranium carolinianum L. Sp. Pl. 682. 1753.

Annual, erect, generally branched from the base and also above, stout, 6′–15′ high, loosely pubescent with spreading often glandular gray hairs. Leaves petioled, reniform-orbicular in outline, 1′–3′ wide, deeply cleft into 5–9 oblong or obovate cuneate toothed or lobed segments; peduncles rather short and stout, 2-flowered; flowers in compact clusters, pale pink or whitish, 4″–6″ broad; sepals ovate, ciliate, awn-pointed, about equalling the obovate emarginate petals; ovary-lobes hispid-pubescent; persistent filaments not longer than the carpels; beak nearly 1′ long, short-pointed; seeds ovoid-oblong, finely reticulated.

In barren soil, Nova Scotia(?), Ontario to British Columbia, Massachusetts, Florida and Mexico. Also in Bermuda and Jamaica. April–Aug.

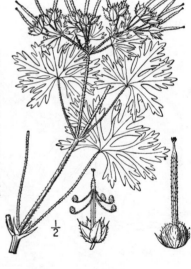

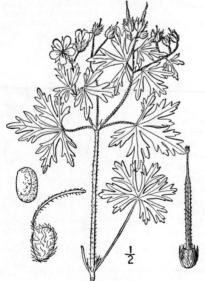

7. Geranium Bicknéllii Britton.   Bicknell's Crane's-bill.   Fig. 2658.

G. Bicknellii Britton, Bull. Torr. Club **24** : 92. 1897.

Similar to the preceding species, but taller, the stems usually more slender, loosely pubescent. Leaves slender-petioled, somewhat angulate in outline, the segments oblong or linear-oblong, mostly narrower; peduncles slender, 2-flowered, the inflorescence loose; sepals lanceolate, awn-pointed; ovary-lobes pubescent; persistent filaments longer than the carpels; beak about 1′ long, long-pointed, its tip 2″–3″ long; seeds reticulated.

Newfoundland to Maine to western Ontario, British Columbia, southern New York, Michigan and Utah. May–Sept.

8. Geranium disséctum L. Cut-leaved Crane's-bill. Fig. 2659.

Geranium dissectum L. Amoen. Acad. 4: 282. 1760.

Closely related to the two preceding species, but smaller in every way, more slender, the branches decumbent or ascending; leaves seldom more than 1½′ wide, deeply cleft into narrower segments; inflorescence loose; peduncles short, 2-flowered; flowers purple, about 3″ broad; sepals ovate, awned, equalling or slightly longer than the notched petals; capsule-lobes and beak pubescent; seeds ovoid or globose, deeply pitted.

In waste places, and in ballast in New York and New Jersey. Also in the far Northwest. Fugitive from Europe. Wood-geranium. June–Sept.

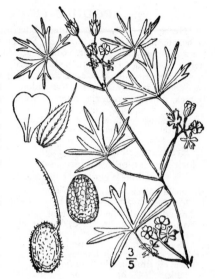

9. Geranium pusíllum L. Small-flowered Crane's-bill. Fig. 2660.

Geranium pusillum L. Sp. Pl. Ed. 2, 957. 1763.

Annual, widely branching, slender, weak, pubescent or villous, 4′–18′ long. Leaves petioled, reniform-orbicular, ½′–1½′ wide, deeply divided into 7–9 oblong, or sometimes linear-oblong, entire or 3-toothed, cuneate lobes; peduncles short, 3″–9″ long, 2-flowered; pedicels 3″–12″ long; sepals acute, awnless; flowers pale-purple, 3″–5″ broad; petals notched; capsule-lobes hairy, keeled, not wrinkled; beak about 5″ long, canescent; seed smooth; anther-bearing stamens commonly only 5, as in *Erodium*.

In waste places, Ontario to British Columbia, Massachusetts, New Jersey, North Carolina, Nebraska and Utah. Also in Bermuda. Adventive from Europe. May–Sept.

10. Geranium mólle L. Dove's-foot Crane's-bill. Fig. 2661.

Geranium molle L. Sp. Pl. 682. 1753.

Resembling the preceding species, but more villous, the leaves nearly orbicular in outline and not as deeply cleft, generally only to just below the middle, into 7–11 obovate or cuneate lobes, which are 3–5-toothed at the apex; flowers dark-purple, 3″–5″ broad; sepals obtusish, not awned; capsule-lobes distinctly marked with transverse wrinkles; beak about 5″ long, sparingly pubescent; seeds smooth or striate, not pitted, nor reticulate; anther-bearing filaments 10.

In lawns and waste places, Maine to Pennsylvania, New York, Ohio and Ontario. Also in Washington and Vancouver. Fugitive from Europe. Other English names are pigeon-foot, starlights, culverfoot. May–Sept.

3. ERÒDIUM L'Her.; Ait. Hort. Kew. 2: 414. 1789.

Herbs, generally with jointed nodes, opposite or alternate stipulate leaves, and axillary umbellate nearly regular flowers. Sepals 5, imbricated. Petals 5, hypogynous, imbricated, the 2 upper slightly smaller. Glands 5. Anther-bearing stamens 5, alternating with as many sterile filaments. Ovary 5-lobed, 5-celled, beaked by the united styles, the beak terminating in 5 stigmas; ovules 2 in each cavity. Capsule-lobes 1-seeded, the styles elastically dehiscent and coiled spirally at maturity, villous-bearded on the inner side. Seeds not reticulate. [Greek, a heron, from the resemblance of the fruit to its beak and bill.]

About 60 species, widely distributed in temperate and warm regions. There are three native species in the southwest and several exotic ones have been collected on ballast at the seaports. Type species: *Erodium crassifolium* Soland.

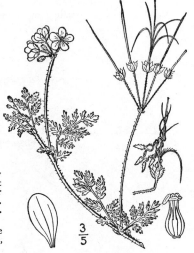

1. Erodium cicutàrium (L.) L'Her. Hemlock Stork's-bill or Heron's-bill. Alfilaria. Pink Needle. Fig. 2662.

Geranium cicutarium L. Sp. Pl. 680. 1753.
E. cicutarium L'Her.; Ait. Hort Kew. 2: 414. 1789.

Annual, tufted, villous-pubescent, somewhat viscid, erect or ascending, branched, 6'–12' high. Basal and lower leaves petioled, 3'–7' long, $\frac{1}{2}'-1'$ wide, pinnate, the divisions finely pinnatifid; upper leaves sessile, otherwise similar; peduncles generally longer than the leaves, umbellately 2–12-flowered; flowers purple or pink, 4"–5" broad; sepals acute, villous, about equalling the entire petals; carpels hairy; beak $\frac{1}{2}'-1\frac{1}{2}'$ long, its divisions spirally coiled when ripe.

Waste places and fields, Nova Scotia to Ontario, New Jersey, Pennsylvania and Michigan and very abundant from Texas to Oregon. Adventive from Europe, in our area. A common weed in the Old World. Pin-clover. Pin-grass. Pinweed. Alfilerilla. Filerie. Wild musk. April–Sept.

Erodium moschàtum Willd., locally naturalized in the eastern states, has much broader less cut leaf-segments, unappendaged sepals and 2-toothed filaments.

Family 62. OXALIDÀCEAE Lindl. Nat. Syst. Ed. 2, 140. 1836.*

WOOD-SORREL FAMILY.

Annual or perennial leafy-stemmed or acaulescent herbs, or rarely shrubs, often with rootstocks or scaly bulbs, the sap sour. Leaves mostly palmately 3-foliolate, in some exotic species pinnate or entire and peltate; stipules commonly present as scarious expansions of the petiole-bases; leaflets mostly obcordate. Flowers perfect, in umbel-like or forking cymes, or sometimes solitary; peduncles mostly long. Sepals 5, often unequal. Petals 5, white, pink, purple or yellow. Stamens 10–15 Ovary 5-celled, 5-lobed; styles united or distinct; ovules 2–many in each cavity; fruit a loculicidal globose or columnar capsule, rarely baccate. Embryo straight, in fleshy endosperm.

About 15 genera and about 300 species, chiefly of tropical distribution.

Plants acaulescent, with bulb-like or scaly rootstocks; corolla white, pink or rose-purple.
    Sepals without apical tubercles; rootstocks elongated.   1. *Oxalis.*
    Sepals with apical tubercles; rootstocks bulb-like.   2. *Ionoxalis.*
Plants caulescent; corolla yellow.   3. *Xanthoxalis.*

1. ÓXALIS L. Sp. Pl. 433. 1753.

Perennial herbs, with slender more or less scaly rootstocks. Leaves basal, solitary or several together, with the petioles dilated at the base, palmately 3-foliolate; leaflets notched at the apex, usually with a membranous fold in the sinus. Scapes solitary or several together, topped by a single pedicel or rarely with an umbel-like cyme. Flowers perfect, homogonous. Sepals 5, the inner longer than the outer. Petals white or pink, delicate, much longer than the sepals, often obliquely notched at the apex. Stamens 10: filaments commonly glabrous. Capsule relatively short. Seeds few or several in each cavity, pitted and grooved or striate. [Greek, sour, from the acid juice.]

About 6 species, natives of the northern hemisphere, the following typical.

*Revised by Dr. J. K. SMALL.

1. Oxalis Acetosélla L.   White or True Wood-sorrel.   Alleluia.   Fig. 2663.

Oxalis Acetosella L. Sp. Pl. 433.   1753.

Perennial by a scaly nearly unbranched root-stock, acaulescent, 2′-6′ high, pubescent with scattered brownish hairs. Leaves 3-6, long-petioled; petioles jointed and dilated at the base; leaflets obcordate, wider than long; scapes 1-3, slightly longer than the leaves, 1-flowered, 2-bracted above the middle; flowers broadly campanulate, about ½′ long; sepals obtusish; petals white or pink, veined with deep pink, emarginate or entire, 3-4 times as long as the calyx; capsule subglobose, 1″-2″ long, glabrous, its cavities 1-2-seeded; seeds ovoid, longitudinally grooved.

In cold damp woods, Nova Scotia to Saskatchewan, the mountains of North Carolina, and the north shore of Lake Superior. Cleistogene flowers are borne on recurved scapes at the base of the plant. Native also in Europe, Asia and northern Africa. Sleeping beauty. Ladies'- or sleeping clover. Sheep-sorrel. Cuckoo-flower. Old names, wood-sower or wood-sour, cuckoo's meat, sour trefoil, stub-wort, shamrock, hearts, sour-trifoly. Yields the druggists' " Salt of Lemons." May–July.

2. IONÓXALIS Small, Fl. SE. U. S. 665.   1903.

Perennial acaulescent herbs, with scaly bulbs. Leaves basal, few or many together, with the petioles dilated at the base, palmately 3-10-foliolate; leaflets notched at the apex, with short or elongated lobes, usually with orange tubercles in each sinus, commonly drooping. Scapes erect, solitary or clustered, usually topped by umbel-like cymes. Flowers perfect, heterogonous. Sepals 5, with tubercles at the apex. Petals 5, rose-purple, rose-violet or white, much longer than the sepals, commonly rounded at the apex. Stamens 10: filaments usually pubescent, united at the base. Capsule sometimes elongated, 5-celled. Seeds wrinkled, grooved or tubercled. [Greek, purple-oxalis.]

About 120 species, natives of North and South America, most abundant in continental tropical America. Type species: *Ionoxalis violacea* (L.) Small.

1. Ionoxalis violàcea (L.) Small.   Violet Wood-sorrel.   Fig. 2664.

Oxalis violacea L. Sp. Pl. 434.   1753.
Ionoxalis violacea Small, Fl. SE. U. S. 665.   1903.

Perennial from a brownish bulb with ciliate scales, acaulescent, 4′-9′ high, nearly or quite glabrous. Leaves generally 4-8, long and slender-petioled, about 1′ wide; leaflets obcordate, minutely reticulated, the midrib sometimes sparingly hairy; scapes several, commonly exceeding the leaves, umbellately 3-12-flowered; pedicels slender; flowers 8″-10″ long, heterogonous; sepals obtuse; petals rose-purple, rarely white, lighter toward the base, obtuse or truncate, 3 times as long as the sepals; capsule ovoid, 2″ in diameter; cavities 2-3-seeded; seeds flattened, rugose-tuberculate.

In woods, Massachusetts to Minnesota and South Dakota, south to Florida and Texas. Purple wood-sorrel. Sheep-sorrel. May–June.

3. XANTHÓXALIS Small, Fl. SE. U. S. 666.   1903.

Annual or perennial caulescent herbs, with descending or horizontal rootstocks. Stems sometimes woody at the base. Leaves alternate, with the stipules obsolete or appearing as narrow dilations at the base of the petiole, palmately 3-foliolate; leaflets broadly obcordate, usually inequilateral, nearly sessile or rarely stalked, sometimes sensitive. Flowers perfect, heterogonous or homogonous. Sepals 5, narrow, imbricated. Corolla yellow, sometimes with a darker eye. Petals 5, surpassing the sepals, rounded or notched at the apex. Stamens 10: filaments glabrous or the longer ciliate. Capsule more or less elongated, columnar or narrowed upward, angled, 5-celled. Seeds several in each cavity, transversely ridged or tuberculate by broken ridges. [Greek, yellow-oxalis.]

About 50 species, of wide geographic distribution. Type species: *Xanthoxylis corniculata* (L.) Small.

Pedicels appressed-pubescent ; cymes typically umbel-like.
  Longer filaments glabrous.
    Stem appressed-pubescent, not creeping ; capsules pubescent.   1. *X. stricta.*
    Stem loosely pubescent ; capsules glabrous except in No. 2, a plant with creeping stems.
      Plants spreading and creeping ; capsules pubescent.   2. *X. corniculata.*
      Plants erect ; capsules glabrous.
        Cymes open at maturity ; capsules gradually pointed.   3. *X. Bushii.*
        Cymes cluster-like at maturity ; capsules abruptly pointed.   4. *X. rufa.*
  Longer filaments pubescent.
    Petals glabrous ; pistil, or styles, short-hairy.
      Stem and branches finely soft-pubescent or nearly glabrous ; primary branches of the
        cyme short or obsolete.
        Leaves numerous ; cymes mostly 1-flowered ; capsules less than thrice as long as the
          calyx.   5. *X. filipes.*
        Leaves few ; cymes mostly several-flowered ; capsules over thrice as long as the calyx.
          6. *X. Brittoniae.*
      Stem and branches hirsute ; primary branches of the cyme long ; leaflets copiously
        strigillose.   7. *X. interior.*
    Petals pubescent ; pistil, or styles, long-hairy.   8. *X. Priceae.*
Pedicels loosely pubescent.
  Capsule-body several times longer than the sepals ; leaflets uniformly green.   9. *X. cymosa.*
  Capsule-body scarcely twice as long as the sepals ; leaflets brown-margined.   10. *X. grandis.*

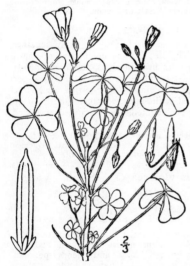

1. **Xanthoxalis stricta** (L.) Small. Upright Yellow Wood-sorrel. Fig. 2665.

Oxalis stricta L. Sp. Pl. 435. 1753.
Oxalis corniculata var. *stricta* Sav. in Lam. Encycl. **4** : 683. 1797.
Xanthoxalis stricta Small, Fl. SE. U. S. 667. 1903.

Plants usually low and erect, pale green. Stem commonly branched at the base, the branches spreading, 5'–6' long, more or less strigose ; leaves 9''–1½' broad ; leaflets coarsely cellular, very sensitive, closing when touched ; petiole-bases narrowly dilated ; flowers yellow, fragrant, in umbel-like cymes, peduncles 1½'–6' long, stout ; pedicels at length deflexed ; sepals linear or lanceolate, about 2½'' long, ciliolate, erect or ascending ; petals 4''–5'' long, commonly reddish at the base ; capsule columnar, 8''–15'' long, abruptly narrowed at the summit.

In woods and fields, Nova Scotia to Wyoming, Colorado, south to Florida and Texas. Introduced into Europe as a weed. Sheep- or poison-sheep-sorrel. Toad-sorrel. Ladies'-sorrel or -sour-grass. April–Oct.

2. **Xanthoxalis corniculàta** (L.) Small. Yellow Procumbent Wood-sorrel. Fig. 2666.

Oxalis corniculata L. Sp. Pl. 435. 1753.
?*O. repens* Thunb. Oxal. 16. 1781.
Xanthoxalis corniculata Small, Fl. SE. U. S. 667. 1903.

Plants depressed, green, sparingly pubescent or nearly glabrous, freely branching from the base and with a few branches above. Stem 1'–6' high, the branches loosely pubescent, diffuse, mainly procumbent and often rooting from the nodes ; leaflets obcordate, wider than long, about ½' wide ; petioles slender, dilated at the base into oblong rounded or truncate stipules ; peduncles 1–3-flowered ; flowers yellow, 2''–6'' long ; pedicels strigillose, more or less reflexed ; capsule oblong, gradually narrowed to the apex, 5''–9'' long, appressed pubescent.

In ballast about the eastern sea-ports, and frequently growing on the ground in greenhouses. Texas and throughout tropical America. Has been found in Ontario. Occurs also in warm and tropical regions of the Old World. Ladies'-sorrel. Feb.–Nov.

3. Xanthoxalis Búshii Small. Bush's Yellow Wood-sorrel. Fig. 2667.

Oxalis Bushii Small, Bull. Torr. Club **25**: 611. 1898.
X. Bushii Small, Fl. SE. U. S. 667. 1903.

Plants bright green. Stems erect, 2'–8' tall, often simple; leaves few; petioles pubescent especially near the base; leaflets with rounded lobes, strigillose; peduncles slender, nearly erect, usually solitary, conspicuously overtopping the leaves, glabrous or nearly so except near the base; cymes umbel-like; sepals oblong, 1¾"–2" long, obtuse; corolla light yellow, 4½"–6" broad; filaments much dilated at the base; styles slightly pubescent; capsules long-columnar, 6"–7½" long.

In dry soil, Nova Scotia to South Dakota, Colorado and Georgia. May–June.

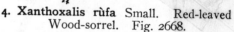

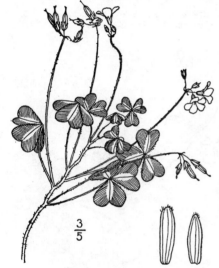

4. Xanthoxalis rùfa Small. Red-leaved Wood-sorrel. Fig. 2668.

Oxalis rufa Small, in Britton, Man. 577. 1901.
X. rufa Small, Fl. SE. U. S. 668. 1903.

Plants reddish-purple. Stems early branched at the base and decumbent, 4'–12' long, sometimes glaucescent; leaves numerous, commonly clustered; leaflets sometimes pale along the midrib; peduncles glabrous or villous, usually surpassing the leaves; cymes dichotomous or the primary branches suppressed, thus umbel-like or clustered; sepals oblong or oblong-lanceolate, 1"–1½" long; corolla light yellow, 3"–5" broad; petals glabrous, sometimes erose at the apex; capsules short-columnar, abruptly pointed, 4"–6" long.

In woods and moist soil, Massachusetts to Minnesota and Georgia. April–Sept.

5. Xanthoxalis fílipes Small. Slender Yellow Wood-sorrel. Fig. 2669.

Oxalis filipes Small, in Britt. & Brown, Ill. Fl. Ed. 1.
2: 349. 1897.
Xanthoxalis filipes Small, Fl. SE. U. S. 667. 1903.

Plants bright green, very slender, sparsely pubescent with appressed hairs. Stem erect or decumbent, nearly simple, usually very leafy, wiry, 10'–2° high; leaves ¼'–½' wide, long-petioled, not stipulate, or the stipules represented by a narrow dilation of the base of the petiole; leaflets obcordate, with unequal sides, peduncles slender, equalling or exceeding the leaves, mostly 1-flowered; flowers yellow; pedicels very slender, strigillose or glabrate, recurved in mature fruit; sepals oblong-lanceolate, 2" long, obtuse, with a tuft of hairs at the apex; petals 4" long, emarginate; capsule 4"–6" long, gradually narrowed to the apex, often curved.

In woods, Virginia to Tennessee, south to Georgia. May–Aug.

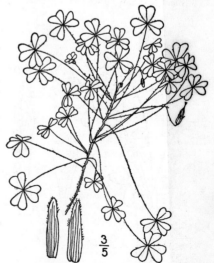

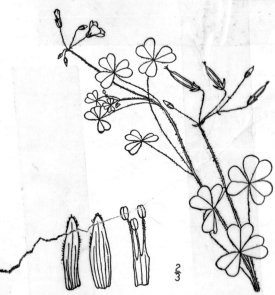

7. Xanthoxalis intèrior Small. Midland Wood-sorrel. Fig. 2671.

X. interior Small, Fl. SE. U. S. 668. 1903.

Stems usually solitary, 1°–2° tall, hirsute; leaflets bright green throughout, 10″–15″ wide, or some of them smaller, copiously strigillose, somewhat ciliate; cymes normally dichotomous, with some of the branches more or less suppressed, commonly raised above the leaves by the elongating peduncles; pedicels strigillose; sepals oblong to oblong-lanceolate, about 2″ long, ciliate at the tip; petals 3″–4½″ long, light yellow; longer filaments sparingly ciliate above; capsules rather slender, 4″–5″ long, on erect or ascending pedicels.

In woods and on partly shaded hillsides, Missouri and Arkansas. July–Oct.

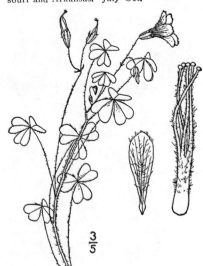

6. Xanthoxalis Brittòniae Small. Britton's Wood-sorrel. Fig. 2670.

Oxalis Brittoniae Small, in Britton, Man. 577. 1901.
X. Brittoniae Small, Fl. SE. U. S. 668. 1903.

Plants often stoutish, loosely pubescent, bright green. Stem sparingly leafy, 4′–16′ tall, often branched; leaves mostly ½′–¾′ broad; petioles filiform, sparingly villous; leaflets broader than long, nearly glabrous; peduncles about twice as long as their subtending petioles; cymes dichotomous or the primary branches suppressed, thus more umbel-like; sepals elliptic to narrowly oblong, 1½″–2″ long; corolla light yellow, 5″–7½″ wide; filaments glabrous; styles glabrous; capsules columnar, abruptly acuminate, 7″–10″ long.

In woods and fields, Massachusetts to Missouri and Florida. May–July.

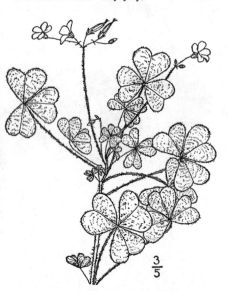

8. Xanthoxalis Prìceae Small. Price's Wood-sorrel. Fig. 2672.

O. Priceae Small, Bull. Torr. Club **25**: 612. 1898.
X. Priceae Small, Fl. SE. U. S. 669. 1903.

Plants mostly villous, deep green. Stems early decumbent, 4′–12′ long; leaves often numerous; leaflets pale or glaucescent beneath, ciliate; peduncles sometimes slightly longer than the petioles; sepals linear or nearly so, 3″–4″ long, pubescent at the base and tip; corolla deep chrome-yellow, 7″–10″ broad; petals pubescent without; styles copiously villous; capsules stout, columnar, 5″–7½″ long.

On rocky hillsides and in open woods, Kentucky to Alabama. June–Nov.

Xanthoxalis recúrva (Ell.) Small, admitted into our first edition, is not definitely known to occur in our range.

9. Xanthoxalis cymòsa Small. Tall Yellow Wood-sorrel. Fig. 2673.

Oxalis cymosa Small, Bull. Torr. Club **23**: 267. 1896.
X. cymosa Small, Fl. SE. U. S. 668. 1903.

Plants normally tall, bright green. Stem usually erect, 6'–4° high, branched above, often villous, reddish or brown; leaves 9''–18'' broad, on petioles 1½'–3' long; leaflets broader than long, sharply notched; petiole-bases scarcely dilated; flowers yellow, in dichotomous cymes; pedicels erect, or ascending, 3''–4'' long, more or less villous; sepals lanceolate or narrowly elliptic, 2''–3'' long, finally spreading; petals obtuse, or emarginate, 4''–5'' long; capsule slender, columnar, 5''–7'' long, gradually narrowed to the summit; seeds obovoid-oblong, ¾'' long, with nearly continuous ridges.

In woods and fields, Ontario to Michigan, Florida, Nebraska and Texas. May–Oct.

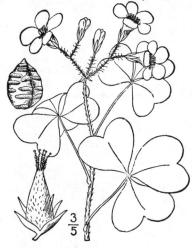

10. Xanthoxalis grándis Small. Great Yellow Wood-sorrel. Fig. 2674.

Oxalis recurva Trel. Mem. Bost. Soc. Nat. Hist. **4**: 89. 1888. Not Ell. 1821.
Oxalis grandis Small, Bull. Torr. Club **21**: 474. 1894.
Xanthoxalis grandis Small, Fl. SE. U. S. 668. 1903.

Plants stout, glabrate below or villous, bright green. Stem erect, 1°–4° tall, simple, or nearly so; leaves 1½'–3' broad; leaflets usually unequal, often with a brown margin, more or less ciliate; petioles villous, hardly dilated at the base, 2'–6' long; flowers yellow, in dichotomous cymes; pedicles 5''–7'' long, erect, or spreading; sepals unequal; ovate, or oblong, 2''–3'' long, often ciliate at the apex; petals rounded at the apex, 6''–8'' long; capsule stout, ovoid, or ovoid-oblong, 3''–5'' long, seeds ovoid or obovoid, 1'' long, with broken transverse ridges.

On river banks, Pennsylvania to Illinois, Georgia and Alabama. May–Aug.

Family 63. LINÀCEAE Dumort. Comm. Bot. 61. 1822.*

FLAX FAMILY.

Herbs, or shrubs, with alternate or opposite leaves, and perfect regular nearly symmetrical flowers. Stipules mostly small or none. Sepals 5, rarely 4, imbricated, persistent. Petals of the same number and alternate with the sepals, imbricated, generally contorted. Stamens of the same number, alternate with the petals; filaments monadelphous at the base; anthers versatile, 2-celled. Ovary 1, 2–5-celled, or by false septa 4–10-celled. Ovules anatropous. Styles 2–5. Fruit mainly capsular. Seeds 1–2 in each cavity, oily; endosperm little or none; embryo straight; cotyledons flat.

About 14 genera and about 160 species of wide geographic distribution.

Stigmas introrse and elongated; sepals glandless; petals mostly blue or red.   1. *Linum.*
Stigmas terminal and capitate; sepals, at least the inner ones, with marginal glands; petals mostly yellow.   2. *Cathartolinum.*

1. LÌNUM [Tourn.] L. Sp. Pl. 277. 1753.

Annual or perennial herbs, sometimes woody at the base, with alternate or opposite, rarely verticillate, sessile leaves, and perfect flowers. Inflorescence axillary or terminal. Stipules or stipular glands wanting. Sepals 5, persistent. Petals 5, blue, red or rarely white, fugacious. Stamens 5, monadelphous, with interspersed staminodia. Ovary 5-celled, or 8–10-celled by false partitions, not cartilaginous at the base, the real cavities 2-ovuled. Capsule

---

* Revised by Dr. JOHN K. SMALL.

5–10-valved, the carpels with incomplete false septa, each one longitudinally ridged and grooved on the back. Seeds flat, lenticular. [The classical Latin name.]

About 8 species, natives of temperate or warm regions. In addition to the following another occurs in the western United States. Type species: *Linum usitatissimum* L.

Annual; introduced; inner sepals ciliate; capsule about as long as the calyx.　1. *L. usitatissimum.*
Perennial; western; sepals eciliate; capsule much exceeding the calyx.　2. *L. Lewisii.*

1. Linum usitatíssimum L. Flax. Lint-bells. Linseed. Fig. 2675

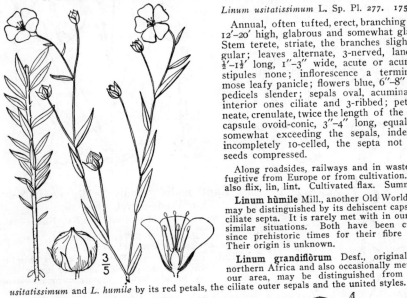

Linum usitatissimum L. Sp. Pl. 277. 1753.

Annual, often tufted, erect, branching above, 12′–20′ high, glabrous and somewhat glaucous. Stem terete, striate, the branches slightly angular; leaves alternate, 3-nerved, lanceolate, $\frac{1}{2}′$–1$\frac{1}{2}′$ long, 1″–3″ wide, acute or acuminate; stipules none; inflorescence a terminal cymose leafy panicle; flowers blue, 6″–8″ broad; pedicels slender; sepals oval, acuminate, the interior ones ciliate and 3-ribbed; petals cuneate, crenulate, twice the length of the sepals; capsule ovoid-conic, 3″–4″ long, equalling or somewhat exceeding the sepals, indehiscent, incompletely 10-celled, the septa not ciliate; seeds compressed.

Along roadsides, railways and in waste places, fugitive from Europe or from cultivation. Called also flix, lin, lint. Cultivated flax. Summer.

Linum húmile Mill., another Old World species, may be distinguished by its dehiscent capsule with ciliate septa. It is rarely met with in our area in similar situations. Both have been cultivated since prehistoric times for their fibre and oil. Their origin is unknown.

Linum grandiflòrum Desf., originally from northern Africa and also occasionally met with in our area, may be distinguished from both *L. usitatissimum* and *L. humile* by its red petals, the ciliate outer sepals and the united styles.

2. Linum Lewísii Pursh. Lewis' Wild Flax. Fig. 2676.

Linum Lewisii Pursh, Fl. Am. Sept. 210. 1814.
Linum perenne var *Lewisii* Eat & Wright, N. A. Bot. 302. 1840.

Perennial by a woody root, 1°–2° high, glabrous, glaucous, densely tufted, simple up to the cymose inflorescence. Leaves crowded, oblong or linear, 3″–20″ long, $\frac{1}{4}″$–2″ wide, acute or acutish, 3–5-nerved; flowers blue, 1′–1$\frac{1}{2}′$ broad; sepals oval, mainly obtuse, one-third or one-fourth the length of the petals; stigmas shorter than the styles; capsule broadly ovoid, 2–3 times as long as the calyx, obtuse, incompletely 10-celled, dehiscent, the septa ciliate.

Prairies, Manitoba to South Dakota, Wisconsin, Texas, Arizona, Utah and Alaska. Prairie-flax. Summer.

The European *L. perenne* L., otherwise nearly identical with this species, differs in having heterogonous flowers.

2. CATHARTOLÌNUM Reichb. Handb. 307. 1837.

Annual or perennial often paniculately or corymbosely branched herbs. Leaves alternate or occasionally opposite, without stipules but sometimes with stipular glands, mostly narrow, entire or serrulate, sometimes ciliate or glandular-margined. Sepals 5, persistent or deciduous, all of them or only the inner ones with gland-tipped teeth. Petals 5, yellow or white, unappendaged but sometimes pubescent within near the entire base. Stamens 5; filaments united at the base, the free portions abruptly or gradually dilated at the base, not accompanied by staminodia, or rarely with a short staminodium in each sinus. Gynoecium 5-carpellary, or rarely 2-carpellary, sometimes cartilaginous at the base; styles filiform, distinct or united; stigmas distinct, terminal, capitate. Capsule ovoid or depressed, 5-celled, or rarely 2-celled and with firm septa, or completely or incompletely 10-celled by false septa, the carpels not ribbed on the back. Seeds flattened, often lunate. [Greek, referring to the medicinal qualities of some of the species.]

About 70 species of wide geographic distribution. Type species: *Linum cathàrticum* L.

Styles distinct.
  Staminodia wanting; plants perennial; corolla yellow.
    Sepals entire at maturity, the inner ones sometimes roughened by the bases of the deciduous glandular hairs.
      Stem paniculately branched; outer sepals short ($1''$–$1\frac{1}{4}''$ long); stem-leaves mostly opposite.   1. *C. striatum.*
      Stem corymbosely branched; outer sepals long ($1\frac{1}{2}''$–$1\frac{3}{4}''$ long); stem-leaves mostly alternate.   2 *C. virginianum.*
    Sepals, either those of both series, or those of the inner or the outer series, glandular-toothed.
      Capsules spheroidal, depressed at the apex.   3. *C. medium.*
      Capsules ovoid; pointed at the apex.   4. *C. floridanum.*
  Staminodia present; plants annual; corolla white.   5. *C. catharticum.*
Styles more or less united.
  Sepals persistent; capsules without thickenings at the base.   6. *C. sulcatum.*
  Sepals deciduous; capsules with cartilaginous thickenings at the base.
    Outer sepals slightly exceeding the capsules; false septa of the capsule slightly thickened.   7. *C. rigidum.*
    Outer sepals greatly exceeding the capsule; false septa of the capsule thickened for about one half their width.   8. *C. Berlanderi.*

1. Cathartolinum striàtum (Walt.) Small. Ridged Yellow Flax. Fig. 2677.

Linum striatum Walt. Fl. Car. 118. 1788.

Linum diffusum Wood, Bot. & Flor. 66. 1870.

C. striatum Small, N. A. Fl. **25**[1]: 71. 1907.

Perennial, paniculately branched, light green and somewhat viscid, so that the plant adheres to paper in which it is dried, the stem and branches sharply angled or even winged by low ridges decurrent from the leaf-bases. Leaves usually opposite nearly up to the inflorescence, oblong, acute or obtuse; branches of the panicle short and divergent; flowers small, yellow, often clustered; capsule subglobose, usually rather longer than the sepals.

In bogs and swamps, rarely in drier ground, Ontario to Massachusetts, Florida, Kentucky, Missouri and Texas. Summer.

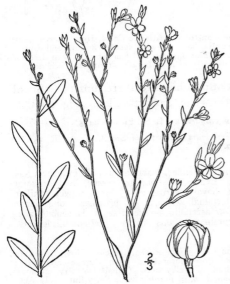

2. Cathartolinum virginiànum (L.) Reichenb. Wild or Slender Yellow Flax. Fig. 2678.

Linum virginianum L. Sp. Pl. 279. 1753.
C. virginianum Reichenb. Handb. 307. 1837.

Perennial by suckers, erect or ascending, glabrous, rather dark green, simple below, corymbosely branched above, $1°$–$2°$ high. Stem and branches terete, slender, not stiff, striate, or slightly angled above; flowering branches ascending, or sometimes weak and recurved; fruiting branches ascending, or somewhat spreading; leaves thin, oblong or oblanceolate, spreading or ascending, 1-nerved, $6''$–$13''$ long, $2''$–$3''$ wide, acute, or the lower opposite and spatulate, obtuse; pedicels filiform, the lower $2''$–$6''$ long, longer than the calyx; flowers yellow, $3''$–$4''$ broad; sepals ovate, about equalling the depressed-globose 10-celled capsule, which is about $1''$ high.

In shaded situations, Maine and Ontario to Georgia and Alabama. June–Aug.

3. Cathartolinum mèdium (Planch.) Small. Stiff Yellow Flax. Fig. 2679.

Linum virginianum var. *medium* Planch. Lond. Bot. **7**: 480. 1848.

Linum medium Britton in Britt. & Brown, Ill. Fl. **2**: 349. 1897.

Cathartolinum medium Small, N. A. Fl. **25¹**: 72. 1907.

Perennial by suckers, glabrous; stems erect, striate, stiff, not angled, corymbosely branched above, the branches erect-ascending both in flower and in fruit; leaves firm, appressed-ascending, the lowest commonly spatulate and opposite, the others lanceolate to linear-lanceolate, acute, 4″–12″ long, ½″–2″ wide; pedicels ½″–3″ long, the lower rarely longer than the calyx; sepals ovate, or ovate-lanceolate, acute, about equalling the depressed-globose capsule, which is about 1″ high.

In dry soil, Vermont to Ontario, Massachusetts, Florida, Missouri and Texas. June–Aug.

4. Cathartolinum floridànum (Planch.) Small. Florida Yellow Flax. Fig. 2680.

Linum virginianum var. *floridanum*(?) Planch. Lond. Journ. Bot. **7**: 480. 1848.
Linum floridanum Trel. Trans. St. Louis Acad. **5**: 13. 1887.
Cathartolinum floridanum Small, N. A. Fl. **25¹**: 72. 1907.

Perennial, glabrous, stem strict, stiff, terete, 1½°–2½° high, corymbosely branched above, the branches erect-ascending, slightly angled. Leaves acute, the lowest mostly opposite, narrowly oblong or oblanceolate, the others linear-lanceolate, appressed-ascending, alternate, 5″–10″ long, ½″–2″ wide; fruiting branches erect-ascending; fruiting pedicels shorter than or little exceeding the calyx, or the lowest ones slightly longer; sepals ovate, acute or acuminate, about equalling the capsule; capsule ovoid, about 1½″ long; petals yellow, twice as long as the calyx.

Eastern Massachusetts and Illinois to Florida and Louisiana. June–Aug.

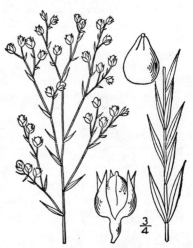

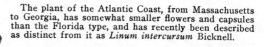

The plant of the Atlantic Coast, from Massachusetts to Georgia, has somewhat smaller flowers and capsules than the Florida type, and has recently been described as distinct from it as *Linum intercursum* Bicknell.

5. Cathartolinum cathàrticum (L.) Small. Dwarf or Cathartic Flax. Fig. 2681.

Linum catharticum L. Sp. Pl. 281. 1753.

Cathartolinum catharticum Small, N. A. Fl. **25¹**: 74. 1907.

Annual, slender, glabrous, usually branched, 3′–8′ high. Leaves all opposite, sessile, oval or somewhat obovate, entire, 2″–4″ long; flowers axillary and terminal, white, 2″–3″ broad, on long slender erect or ascending pedicels; sepals lanceolate, acute or acuminate; petals obovate; pod small, globose.

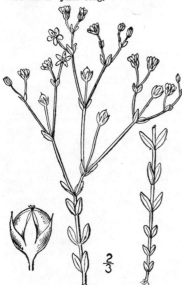

Along low sandy seashore, Pictou, Nova Scotia and in Ontario. Naturalized from Europe where it is abundant on chalky soils. Called also fairy, mountain, mill-mountain, or purging flax. Fairy lint. July–Aug.

6. Cathartolinum sulcàtum (Riddell) Small. Grooved Yellow Flax. Fig. 2682.

Linum sulcatum Riddell, Suppl. Cat. Ohio Pl. 10. 1836.
Linum Boottii Planch. Lond. Journ. Bot. **7** : 475. 1848.
?*Linum simplex* Wood, Bot. & Flor. 66. 1870.
Cathartolinum sulcatum Small, N. A. Fl. **25¹** : 78. 1907.

Annual, simple or branched, 1°–2° high. Stem wing-angled and grooved, at least above; leaves alternate, lanceolate or linear, 8″–12″ long, 1″–1½″ wide, acute or acuminate, 3-nerved, the lower glabrous, the upper smaller and glandular-ciliate, as are the floral bracts and sepals; stipules represented by a pair of small globose dark-colored glands; flowers racemose or corymbose, about 6″ broad, yellow; pedicels 1″–4″ long; sepals lanceolate, acute, slightly longer than the ovoid, acute, incompletely 10-celled pod; styles separate above the middle; septa of the capsule ciliate.

In dry soil, Ontario to Manitoba, Massachusetts, Georgia, west to Texas, rare near the Atlantic coast. Summer.

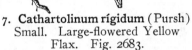

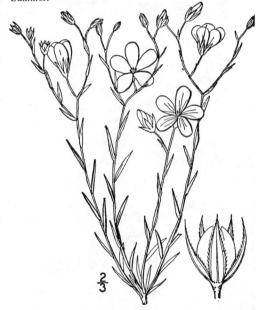

7. Cathartolinum rígidum (Pursh) Small. Large-flowered Yellow Flax. Fig. 2683.

Linum rigidum Pursh, Fl. Am. Sept. 210. 1814.
Cathartolinum rigidum Small, N. A. Fl. **25¹** : 82. 1907.

Perennial(?), 6′–15′ high, branched, glaucous, glabrous or puberulent. Branches stiff, more or less angular; leaves erect, linear or linear-lanceolate, 4″–12″ long, ½″–1″ wide, acute or mucronate, the upper ones glandular-serrulate or ciliate; stipular glands minute, globose, sometimes wanting; flowers yellow, 9″–15″ broad; sepals lanceolate, acute or awn-pointed, glandular-serrulate, the outer ones becoming 3″–4″ long; petals cuneate-obovate, twice the length of the sepals; styles separate only at the summit; capsule ovoid, 5-valved, shorter than the sepals, 2″–2¼″ long.

Prairies, Saskatchewan to Manitoba, Missouri, Texas and Colorado. Summer.

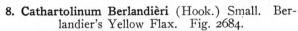

8. Cathartolinum Berlandièri (Hook.) Small. Berlandier's Yellow Flax. Fig. 2684.

Linum Berlandieri Hook. Bot. Mag. *sub pl. 3480.* 1836.
L. arkansanum Osterhout, Bull. Torr. Club **28** : 644. 1901.
C. Berlandieri Small, N. A. Fl. **25¹** : 82. 1907.

Annual (?), 2½′–16′ high, often much-branched, bright green and sometimes glaucescent when young. Branches ascending, striate-winged; leaves spreading or ascending, linear to narrowly linear-lanceolate, mostly 7″–20″ long, acuminate; stipular glands, when present, short; bracts glandular-toothed; flowers bright yellow, 16″–24″ broad; sepals lanceolate, the outer ones becoming 4½″–5½″ long, all evenly glandular-toothed; petals obovate, 8½″–11″ long; capsule ovoid, 2″–2¼″ long.

In dry soil, Kansas and Colorado to Texas. Spring.

Cathartolinum compáctum (A. Nelson) Small, a species related to *C. rigidum*, ranges from the Rocky Mountain region into North Dakota and Kansas. It is a low dull green plant with small flowers, the petals less than 5″ long.

Millegrana Radiola (L.) Druce (*Radiola Linoides* Roth), the All-seed of Europe, has been found on Cape Breton. The genus differs from *Linum* and *Cathartolinum* in its 4-parted flowers.

Family 64. **BALSAMINÀCEAE** Lindl. Nat. Syst. Ed. 2, 138. 1836.

JEWEL-WEED FAMILY.

Succulent herbs, with alternate thin, simple dentate petioled leaves and showy very irregular axillary somewhat clustered flowers. Sepals 3, the 2 lateral ones small, green, nerved, the posterior one large, petaloid, saccate, spurred. Petals 5, or 3 with 2 of them 2-cleft into dissimilar lobes. Stamens 5, short; filaments appendaged by scales on their inner side and more or less united; anthers coherent or connivent. Ovary oblong, 5-celled; style very short, or none; stigma 5-toothed or 5-lobed; ovules several in each cell. Fruit in the following genus an oblong or linear capsule, elastically dehiscent into 5 spirally coiled valves, expelling the oblong ridged seeds. Endosperm none; embryo nearly straight; cotyledons flat. Later flowers small, cleistogamous, apetalous.

About 220 species, mostly natives of tropical Asia. The family consists of the following genus and the monotypic Asiatic *Hydrocera*, differing from *Impatiens* in its indehiscent 4–5-seeded berry. In our first edition it was placed at the end of the order SAPINDALES, but is here grouped in the GERANIALES.

1. **IMPÀTIENS** [Rivin.] L. Sp. Pl. 937. 1753.

Characters of the family, as given above. [Name in allusion to the elastically bursting pods.]

Besides the following species, 3 others occur in Western North America and two in Central America. Type species: *Impatiens Noli-tangere* L., an Old World plant with light yellow flowers, recorded as found in Ontario.

Flowers orange-yellow, mottled; spur incurved.   1. *I. biflora.*
Flowers pale yellow; spur short, spreading.   2. *I. pallida.*

1. **Impatiens biflòra** Walt. Spotted or Wild Touch-me-not. Silver-leaf. Fig. 2685.

Impatiens biflora Walt. Fl. Car. 219. 1788.

Impatiens fulva Nutt. Gen. 1 : 146. 1818.

Annual, glabrous, 2°–5° high, branched, purplish. Leaves thin, ovate or elliptic, pale and glaucous beneath, 1½'–3½' long, generally obtuse, coarsely toothed, the teeth commonly mucronate; petioles slender, ½'–4' long; peduncles axillary, ½'–1½' long, 2–4-flowered; pedicels pendent, slender, bracted above the middle; bracts linear; flowers horizontal, orange-yellow, mottled with reddish-brown (rarely nearly white and not mottled), 9"–12" long; saccate sepal conic, longer than broad, contracted into a slender incurved spur of one-half its length, which is 2-toothed at the apex.

In moist grounds, Newfoundland to Saskatchewan, Florida and Nebraska. Spurs are occasionally developed on the 2 small exterior sepals, and spurless flowers have been observed. This and the next called balsam, jewel-weed. Speckled jewels. Silver-, slipper- or snap-weed. Ear-jewel. Ladies'-slipper, pocket- or ear-drop. Wild or brook-celandine. Solentine. Snap-dragon. Shining-grass. Cowslip. Weather-cock. Kicking-colt or -horses. Wild balsam. July–Oct.

Impatiens Nortónii Rydb., of western Missouri and Kansas, differs from *I. biflora* in the larger and relatively longer and narrower saccate sepal, which tapers gradually into the shorter spur.

Impatiens Balsamina L., with purple or white flowers, much cultivated, has been found in waste grounds in Pennsylvania. It is native of southern Asia.

2. Impatiens pállida Nutt.   Pale Touch-me-not.   Fig. 2686.

Impatiens pallida Nutt. Gen. 1 : 146. 1818.

Impatiens aurea S. Wats. Bibl. Ind. 152, as a synonym. 1878. Not *I. aurea* Muhl. 1813.

Similar to the preceding species, but larger and stouter. Flowers pale yellow, sparingly dotted with reddish-brown, or sometimes dotless, 12″–15″ long; saccate sepal dilated-conic, about as broad as long, abruptly contracted into a short scarcely incurved notched spur, less than one-third its length; bracts of the pedicels lanceolate to ovate, acute.

In similar situations, most abundant northward. Nova Scotia to Saskatchewan, Georgia and Kansas, July–Sept. Snapweed. Balsam. Wild balsam or celandine. Silverweed. Slippers. Quick-in-the-hand. Jewelweed.

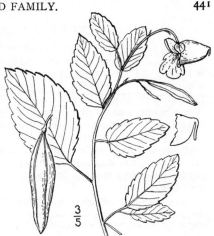

$\frac{3}{5}$

Family 65.   **LIMNANTHÀCEAE** Lindl. Nat. Syst. Ed. 2, 142.   1836.

FALSE MERMAID FAMILY.

Annual herbs, with alternate petioled exstipulate pinnately divided leaves. Flowers perfect, regular, white, pink or red, axillary, long-peduncled. Sepals 2–5, valvate, persistent. Petals the same number as the sepals, alternating with as many small glands, the nearly perigynous stamens twice as many, distinct. Filaments filiform; anthers 2-celled, the sacs longitudinally dehiscent. Carpels as many as the sepals and opposite them, 1-ovuled, nearly distinct, the single slender style arising from the centre as in Geraniaceae, cleft above into as many stigmas as there are carpels; ovule ascending. Fruit very deeply 2–5-lobed, the carpels indehiscent, rough or tubercled. Embryo straight; endosperm none; cotyledons thick.

Two North American genera, the following, and *Limnanthes*, of the Pacific States, with about 9 species. The family was placed in the order SAPINDALES in our first edition, but is here brought into its more natural place in the GERANIALES.

1.   **FLOÉRKEA** Willd. Neue Schrift. Ges. Nat. Fr. 3: 448.   1801.

Annual diffuse glabrous herbs with small white solitary flowers. Sepals 3, valvate. Glands 3. Petals 3, oblong, entire. Stamens 4–6. Ovary 2–3-lobed nearly to the base, 2–3-celled; stigmas 2–3. Mature carpels 1–3, rugose, indehiscent, fleshy. Seed erect. [In honor of H. G. Floerke, 1790–1835, a German botanist.]

Two species, the following typical one, and the closely related *F. occidentalis* Rydb., of the western United States.

1. **Floerkea proserpinacoìdes** Willd.   False Mermaid.
Fig. 2687.

Floerkea prosperpinacoides Willd. Neue Schrift. Ges. Nat. Fr. 3 : 448. 1801.

Slender, weak, 4′–15′ long, branching. Leaves thin, slender-petioled, ½′–3′ long, the segments 5 or 3, distant, lanceolate, oblong or linear-oblong, acute or obtusish, entire or cleft; peduncles slender, elongating in fruit; flowers white, about 1½″ broad; sepals lanceolate to ovate-lanceolate, acute, at length much exceeding the fruit; stamens about equalling the petals; ripe carpels nearly globular, about 1½″ in diameter, tuberculate above.

$\frac{2}{3}$

In marshes and along rivers, Quebec to Ontario, Wisconsin, Delaware, Tennessee and Missouri. April–June.

Family 66.   **ZYGOPHYLLÀCEAE** Lindl. Nat. Syst. 1830.

CALTROP FAMILY.

Herbs, shrubs, or some tropical species trees, the branches often jointed to the nodes. Leaves mostly opposite, stipulate, pinnate, or 2–3-foliolate, the leaflets entire. Stipules persistent. Flowers perfect, axillary, peduncled. Sepals usually 5, distinct, or united by their bases. Petals the same number as the sepals, or none. Stamens as many as the petals, or 2–3 times as many, inserted on the base of the receptacle, the alternate ones sometimes longer; anthers versatile, longitudinally dehiscent; filaments usually with a small scale at the base or near the middle. Ovary 4–12-celled; style terminal; stigma usually simple; ovules 1–numerous in each cavity, pendulous, or ascending. Fruit various, dry in our species. Endosperm of the seed copious or none; embryo straight or curved; cotyledons linear or oblong.

About 20 genera and 160 species, widely distributed in warm and tropical regions.

Fruit spiny, splitting into 5 3–5-seeded segments.   1. *Tribulus.*
Fruit not spiny, often tubercled, splitting into 10–12 1-seeded segments.   2. *Kallstroemia.*

1. TRÍBULUS [Tourn.] L. Sp. Pl. 386. 1753.

Herbs, mostly diffuse or prostrate, with evenly pinnate stipulate leaves and peduncled axillary yellow flowers. Sepals 5, deciduous. Petals 5, deciduous. Stamens 10, hypogynous, the alternate ones somewhat longer. Ovary sessile, 5-lobed, 5-celled, hairy; disk 10-lobed; style short; stigma 5-ridged; ovules 3–10 in each cavity, pendulous. Fruit 5-angled, spiny, splitting into five 3–5-seeded segments. [Greek, three-pronged, Caltrop, from the resemblance of the fruit to that implement.]

About 12 species, natives of warm and tropical regions. Besides the following typical one, another occurs in the Southern States.

1. Tribulus terréstris L. Ground Burnut. Land Caltrop. Fig. 2688.

Tribulus terrestris L. Sp. Pl. 387. 1753.

Annual, pubescent, branched from the base, the stem prostrate or ascending, sometimes 1° long or more. Leaves petioled; stipules small; leaflets 4–8 pairs, oblong, inequilateral, opposite, short-stalked, acutish or obtuse, 3″–8″ long; flowers solitary, about 6″ broad; peduncles shorter than the leaves; petals oblong, about as long as the sepals; segments of the fruit usually with 2 long spines, 2 shorter ones, and a row of very short ones forming a crest on the back, also commonly with some bristle-like hairs.

In ballast and waste places about the eastern seaports, and from Illinois to Nebraska, Arkansas, Arizona and Mexico. Adventive from Europe. June–Sept.

2. KALLSTROÈMIA Scop. Introd. 212. 1777.

Mostly annual branching pubescent herbs, the branches often prostrate, with opposite stipules evenly pinnate leaves, and solitary axillary peduncled yellow flowers. Sepals usually 5, persistent or deciduous. Petals the same number, obovate or oblanceolate, deciduous. Stamens twice as many as the petals. Ovary sessile, 10–12-celled; ovule 1 in each cavity, pendulous; style long, or short, 10–12-grooved, persistent; stigma mostly 10–12-ridged. Fruit 10–12-lobed, not spiny, often tubercled, splitting into 10–12 1-seeded segments. [In honor of Kallstroem.]

About 20 species, of wide distribution in warm and tropical regions. Besides the following, 7 others occur in the southern and western States. Type species: *Tribulus maximus* L.

Persistent style longer than the carpel-bodies; carpel-faces scarcely wrinkled; petals 3½″–5″ long.
                                                1. *K. intermedia.*
Persistent style shorter than the carpel-bodies; carpel-faces prominently wrinkled; petals 2½″–3″ long.
                                                2. *K. hirsutissima.*

1. **Kallstroemia intermèdia** Rydb.   Greater Caltrop.   Fig. 2689.

Kallstroemia intermedia Rydb. N. Am. Fl. **25** : 113. 1910.

Annual, branches slender, hirsute and pilose, prostrate, 6'–18' long. Leaves short-petioled; stipules subulate, shorter than the petioles; leaflets 3–5 pairs, oval,
or oblong, inequilateral, acute or obtuse at the apex,
rounded or subcordate at the base, 4"–10" long; peduncles slender, 6"–2' long in fruit; flowers 1' broad, or
less; sepals linear-lanceolate, very pubescent, persistent,
shorter than the petals; fruit ovoid-conic, strigose-
canescent, about 3" in diameter, shorter than the stout
persistent style, the segments tubercled.

In dry soil, Missouri to Kansas, Texas, New Mexico and
Chihuahua. Included in our first edition in *K. maxima* (L.)
T. & G., which has glabrous fruit. April–Sept.

$\frac{3}{5}$

2. **Kallstroemia hirsutíssima** Vail.   Hirsute Caltrop.   Fig. 2690.

Kallstroemia hirsutissima Vail, in Small, Fl. SE. U. S. 670.
1903.

Annual, branches stout, appressed cinereous-pubescent and hirsute. Leaves short-petioled; stipules lanceolate; leaflets 3–4 pairs, elliptic, 4"–10" long, shaggy-
hirsute, at least beneath; peduncles stoutish, 5"–8" long;
flowers 6"–7" broad, yellow or orange-yellow, fading
whitish; sepals linear-lanceolate, as long as the petals
or nearly so; fruit broadly ovoid-conic, 3"–4" in diameter, longer than the conic style, the segments sharply
tubercled.

In dry soil, Kansas and Colorado to Texas, New Mexico
and Mexico. July–Aug.

$\frac{3}{4}$

Family 67. **RUTACEAE** Juss. Gen. 296. 1789.

RUE FAMILY.

Trees or shrubs, rarely herbs, with heavy-scented and glandular-punctate foliage,
alternate or opposite mainly compound exstipulate leaves, and (in our species)
polygamo-dioecious generally cymose flowers. Sepals 3–5, or none. Petals 3–5,
hypogynous or perigynous. Stamens of the same number, or twice as many, distinct, inserted on the receptacle; anthers 2-celled, mostly versatile. Disk annular.
Pistils 1–5, distinct, or 1 and compound of 2–5 carpels, inserted on the somewhat
elongated receptacle. Fruit (in our species) capsular or a samara. Seeds oblong
or reniform; embryo straight or curved; endosperm generally fleshy, sometimes.
none; cotyledons thick or foliaceous.

About 110 genera and 950 species, most abundant in South Africa and Australia.

Pistils 1–5, distinct; fruit fleshy, capsular.   1. *Zanthoxylum.*
Pistil 1, 2-celled ; fruit a samara.   2. *Ptelea.*

1. **ZANTHÓXYLUM** L. Sp. Pl. 270. 1753.

[XANTHOXYLUM Mill. Gard. Dict. Ed. 8. 1768.]

Trees or shrubs with alternate pinnate leaves, the twigs and petioles commonly prickly.
Flowers axillary or terminal, cymose, whitish or greenish, mostly small. Sepals 3–5, or none.
Petals 3–5, imbricated. Staminate flowers with 3–5 hypogynous stamens. Pistillate flowers
with 1–5 distinct pistils, rarely with some stamens. Carpels 2-ovuled. Pods fleshy, 2-valved,
1–2-seeded. Seeds oblong, black and shining. [Greek, yellow-wood.]

About 150 species, natives of temperate and tropical regions. In addition to the following 2 others occur in the Southern States. Type species: *Zanthoxylum Clava-Herculis* L.

Flowers in small sessile axillary cymes; calyx none.   1. *Z. americanum.*
Flowers in large terminal compound cymes; calyx present.   2. *Z. Clava-Herculis.*

1. Zanthoxylum americànum Mill.
Prickly Ash. Toothache-tree.
Fig. 2691.

Xanthoxylum americanum Mill. Gard. Dict. Ed. 8, no. 2. 1768.

A shrub, or small tree, reaching a maximum height of about 25°, and a trunk diameter of 6'. Leaves alternate, odd-pinnate, pubescent when young, becoming glabrous or nearly so when old; leaflets 3–11, ovate, opposite, dark green above, lighter beneath, nearly sessile, 1½'–2' long, crenulate or entire, acutish; flowers greenish, about 1½'' broad, in sessile axillary cymes, borne on the wood of the previous season and appearing before the leaves; pedicels slender; calyx none; petals 4 or 5; pistils 2–5; follicles black, ellipsoid, about 2'' long, on short stipes, 1–2-seeded.

In woods and thickets, Quebec to Virginia, especially along the mountains, west to western Ontario, South Dakota, Kansas and Nebraska. Wood soft, light brown; weight per cubic foot 35 lbs. Angelica-tree. Suterberry. April–May.

2. Zanthoxylum Clàva-Hérculis L.
Southern Prickly Ash. Sea Ash.
Pepper-wood. Fig. 2692.

Z. Clava-Herculis L. Sp. Pl. 270. 1753.

Z. carolinianum Lam. Encycl. 2: 39. 1786.

A small, very prickly tree, with a maximum height of 45° and trunk diameter of 9', the prickles supported on cushions of cork sometimes 8' broad. Leaves alternate, odd-pinnate, glabrous, shining above, dull beneath; leaflets 5–19, obliquely ovate, nearly sessile, 1½'–3' long, acute, crenulate; flowers greenish-white, in large terminal cymes, appearing before the leaves; sepals 4 or 5; petals 4 or 5; pistils 2 or 3; follicles about 2'' long, sessile.

Along streams, coast of southern Virginia to Florida, west to Texas and Arkansas. Wood light brown; weight per cubic foot 31 lbs. Hercules'-club. Prickly-yellowwood. Yellow prickly ash. Wild orange. June.

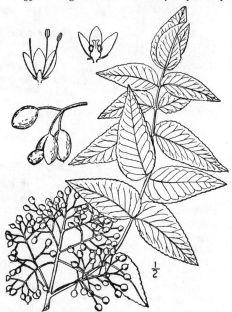

2. PTÈLEA L. Sp. Pl. 118. 1753.

Shrubs or small trees, without prickles, the bark bitter. Leaves 3–5-foliolate, with entire or serrulate leaflets. Flowers greenish white, polygamous, corymbose-paniculate. Calyx 4–5-parted, the lobes imbricated. Petals 4 or 5, much longer than the calyx, also imbricated. Stamens 4 or 5, alternate with the petals; filaments hairy on the inner side, present in the pistillate flowers but the anthers abortive or wanting. Ovary flattened, 2-celled (rarely 3-celled). Fruit a nearly orbicular samara, 2-winged (rarely 3-winged), indehiscent. Cells 1-seeded. Seed oblong-ovoid. [Greek, Elm, from the similarity of the fruits.]

Three species. natives of the United States and Mexico, the following typical.

1. Ptelea trifoliàta L.   Three-leaved Hop-tree.   Shrubby Trefoil.   Fig. 2693.

Ptelea trifoliata L. Sp. Pl. 118. 1753.

A shrub or small tree, with a maximum height of about 20° and trunk diameter of 6′. Leaves long-petioled, 3-foliolate, pubescent when young, glabrate when old, or sometimes persistently pubescent; leaflets ovate or oval, 2′–5′ long, sessile, crenulate, acute or obtuse, the lateral ones somewhat oblique, the terminal one more or less cuneate at the base; flowers about 5″ broad, in terminal compound cymes; odor disagreeable; sepals ½″ long, obtuse; petals about 3″ long, oblong; samara 8″–9″ in diameter, the wing membranous and reticulated, emarginate, tipped with the minute persistent style or this finally deciduous.

In woods, Connecticut to Florida, west to southern Ontario, Minnesota, Kansas and Mexico. Consists of many trivially different races. The fruit is bitter and has been used as a substitute for hops. The foliage has an unpleasant odor. Wood light brown; weight per cubic foot 43 lbs. Ague-bark. Quinine-tree. Pickaway-anise. Prairie-grub. Wafer-ash. Swamp-dogwood. Wingseed. June.

Ptelea tomentosa Raf. (*P. trifoliata mollis* T. & G.) is a very pubescent race, ranging from North Carolina and Georgia to Indiana and Durango.

The common rue, *Ruta gravèolens* L., a native of Europe, has escaped from cultivation in several localities in our range. It is a heavy-scented herb or partially woody plant and differs from our other representatives of the Rue family in the perfect flowers, the 4–5-lobed ovary and the lobed, several-seeded capsule.

Family 68.   SIMAROUBÀCEAE DC. Bull. Soc. Philom. 2: 209. 1811.

AILANTHUS FAMILY.

Trees or shrubs, with bitter bark, and mainly alternate and pinnate not punctate leaves. Stipules minute or none. Inflorescence axillary, paniculate or racemose. Flowers regular, dioecious or polygamous. Calyx 3–5-lobed or divided. Petals 3–5. Disk annular or elongated, entire or lobed. Stamens of the same number as the petals, or twice as many; anthers 2-celled. Ovaries 2–5, or single and 2–5-lobed, 1–5-celled; styles 1–5. Seeds generally solitary in the cells; embryo straight or curved.

About 30 genera and 150 species, natives of warm or tropical regions, distinguished from RUTACEAE mainly by their non-punctate foliage.

1.   AILÁNTHUS Desf. Mem. Acad. Paris, 1786: 265. *pl. 8.* 1789.

Large trees, with odd-pinnate leaves, and terminal panicles of greenish-white polygamo-dioecious flowers. Calyx short, 5-cleft, the lobes imbricated. Petals 5, spreading, valvate. Disk 10-lobed. Staminate flowers with 10 stamens inserted at the base of the disk. Pistillate flowers with a deeply 2–5-cleft ovary, its lobes flat, cuneate, 1-celled, and 2–3 stamens. Ovules solitary in each cavity. Samaras 2–5, linear, or oblong, membranous, veiny, 1-seeded at the middle. Seed compressed; cotyledons flat, nearly orbicular. [From the Chinese name.]

Three species, natives of China and the East Indies. The following typical one has become widely naturalized in eastern North America.

$\frac{2}{5}$

1. Ailanthus glandulòsa Desf. Tree-of-Heaven. Ailanthus. Fig. 2694.

Ailanthus glandulosa Desf. Mem. Acad. Paris 1786: 265. . 1789.

A tree, 40°–90° high. Leaves 1°–3° long, petioled, glabrous, odd-pinnate; leaflets 13–41, opposite or nearly so, stalked, ovate or ovate-lanceolate, cordate or truncate and often oblique at the base, acute or acuminate at the apex, entire, or with 1–4 blunt teeth near the base; flowers greenish, about 3″ broad, pedicelled, the staminate ones ill-scented; samaras twisted, nearly 2′ long, very conspicuous on the pistillate tree in autumn.

Escaped from cultivation, along roadsides and in fields, spreading extensively by suckers, and seeding freely in some localities, southern Ontario to Massachusetts, Virginia and Kansas. Chinese sumac. Heavenward-tree. False varnish-tree. Devil's-walking-stick. Naturalized from China. June–July.

Family 69. **POLYGALÀCEAE**
Reichenb. Consp. 120. 1828.

Milkwort Family.

Herbs, rarely shrubs or small trees in tropical regions, with alternate, or sometimes opposite or verticillate leaves; stipules none. Flowers racemose, spicate, or solitary and axillary. Pedicels generally 2-bracted at the base. Flowers perfect, irregular. Sepals 5, the two lateral ones (wings) large, colored, the others smaller. Petals 3 (or 5), hypogynous, more or less united into a tube, the lower one often crested. Stamens generally 8, united in 1 or 2 sets. Ovary 2-celled; style simple; stigma curved, dilated or lobed; ovules 1 in each cavity, anatropous. Fruit mainly capsular. Seeds generally caruncled, often hairy; embryo straight.

About 10 genera and perhaps 1000 species, widely distributed in temperate and tropical regions.

1. POLÝGALA [Tourn.] L. Sp. Pl. 701. 1753.

Herbs or shrubs, with alternate opposite or verticillate leaves. Flowers racemose, spicate, or capitate, rarely solitary and axillary, sometimes also cleistogamous and subterranean. Sepals very unequal, the two lateral ones large and petaloid. Petals 3, united into a tube which is split on the back, and more or less adnate to the stamens. Stamens 8 or 6, monadelphous below, or diadelphous; capsule membranous, compressed, dehiscent along the margin. Seeds 1 in each cavity, generally hairy. [Greek, much milk.]

A genus of about 450 species, of wide geographic distribution. Besides the following, about 40 others occur in the southern and western parts of North America. Typè species: *Polygala vulgaris* L.

  * **Flowers in corymbed spike-like racemes at the summit of the stem, yellow.**

Basal leaves long, narrow, acuminate.	1. *P. cymosa.*
Basal leaves spatulate, or obovate.	2. *P. ramosa.*

  ** **Flowers in solitary spikes or spike-like racemes, terminating the stem and branches.**

Basal leaves spatulate, or obovate; flowers orange yellow.	3. *P. lutea.*
Basal leaves inconspicuous, or wanting; flowers not yellow.	
Leaves, at least the lower, verticillate; spikes 4″–9″ thick, blunt; flowers purple to greenish white.	
Spikes sessile, or nearly so; wings deltoid.	4. *P. cruciata.*
Spikes peduncled; wings lanceolate-ovate.	5. *P. brevifolia.*
Leaves verticillate and alternate; spikes 2″–3″ thick, acute.	
Verticillate leaves predominating; spikes dense; flowers green to purplish.	6. *P. verticillata.*
Alternate leaves predominating; spikes loose, long; flowers more purple.	7. *P. ambigua.*
Leaves all alternate.	
Petals united into a cleft tube, 3″–4″ long; flowers pink.	8. *P. incarnata.*
Petals not conspicuously united into a tube.	
Spikes ovoid to globose.	
Bracts persistent; flowers rose-purple to white.	
Spikes blunt; wings broadly ovate.	9. *P. viridescens.*
Spikes acutish; wings narrowly ovate or elliptic.	10. *P. Curtissii.*
Bracts deciduous; flowers rose-purple.	11. *P. mariana.*
Spikes cylindric.	
Leaves oblanceolate to linear, 2″–6″ long; flowers greenish to purplish.	
	12. *P. Nuttallii.*

Leaves lanceolate, 1'–2' long; flowers white or greenish.   13. *P. Senega.*
Spikes elongated-conic; flowers white.   14. *P. alba.*
    *** **Flowers distinctly racemose, rose or purple.**   15. *P. polygama.*
**** **Flowers 1–4, large, axillary, but apparently terminal, rose-purple to white.**
    16. *P. paucifolia.*

1. Polygala cymòsa Walt. Tall Pine-barren Milkwort. Fig. 2695.

Polygala cymosa Walt. Fl. Car. 179. 1788.

P. acutifolia T. & G. Fl. N. A. 1 : 128. 1838.

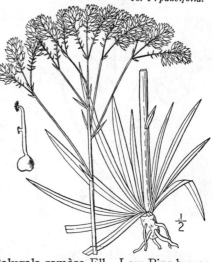

Annual or biennial; stem erect, glabrous, 2°–3° high, simple, slightly angular; roots fibrous. Basal leaves elongated-linear, attenuate at the apex, 2'–3' long, 2''–3'' wide, entire, densely tufted; stem-leaves linear-subulate, bract-like, 5''–8'' long; inflorescence a simple or compound cluster of spike-like racemes; pedicels 1''–2'' long; bracts persistent; flowers yellow, drying greenish black; seed globose, minute, nearly glabrous; caruncle none.

In wet pine barrens, Delaware to Florida, west to Louisiana. May–July.

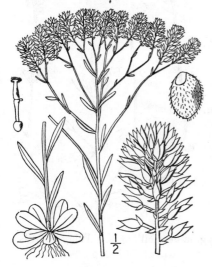

2. Polygala ramòsa Ell. Low Pine-barren Milkwort. Fig. 2696.

P. corymbosa Nutt. Gen. 2 : 89. 1818. Not Michx. 1803.
Polygala ramosa Ell. Bot. S. C. & Ga. 2 : 186. 1822.

Annual or biennial, glabrous; stems tufted or single from fibrous roots, 6'–16' high, simple. Stem-leaves linear-oblong, obtuse, 6''–10'' long, 1''–2'' wide; basal leaves much broader and often larger, spatulate or obovate; inflorescence a terminal compound corymb, 3'–6' broad, of numerous peduncled spike-like racemes; flowers citron-yellow, 1½'' long, drying dark green; pedicels 1'' long or less; wings oblong, acuminate; crest minute; seed ovoid, hairy, twice to thrice the length of the caruncle.

In low pine barrens, Delaware to Florida, west to Louisiana. June–Sept.

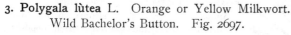

3. Polygala lùtea L. Orange or Yellow Milkwort. Wild Bachelor's Button. Fig. 2697.

Polygala lutea L. Sp. Pl. 705. 1753.

Annual, glabrous; stems tufted from fibrous roots, erect or ascending, or at length divaricately branched, 6'–12' high. Stem-leaves oblong-lanceolate, acute or obtuse, 8''–15'' long, 2''–4'' wide, entire; basal leaves broader and often larger, obovate or spatulate, obtuse; spike-like racemes terminal, solitary, ovoid or oblong, very dense, ½'–1½' long, 6''–9'' thick, obtuse; flowers 2''–3'' long, orange-yellow, preserving their color in drying; pedicels 1''–2'' long; wings oblong-ovate, abruptly acuminate; crest of the corolla-tube minute; caruncle-lobes linear, about equalling the hairy seed, or shorter.

In pine-barren swamps, Long Island to New Jersey, eastern Pennsylvania, Florida, west to Louisiana. June–Oct.

4. Polygala cruciàta L.   Cross-leaved or Marsh Milkwort.   Fig. 2698.

Polygala cruciata L. Sp. Pl. 706. 1753.
P. Torreyi Chodat, Mem. Mus. Gen. 31²: 194. 1893.

Annual, erect, glabrous, 4′–16′ high, at length freely branching above; stem square or slightly wing-angled. Basal leaves none; those of the stem and branches verticillate in 4's, or a few of them scattered, linear or oblanceolate, ½′–1½′ long, 1″–2″ wide, entire, obtuse, mucronulate, the lower smaller; spike-like racemes oval, obtuse, 4″–9″ thick, sessile or short-peduncled; pedicels slender, 1½″–2″ long; bracts persistent; flowers purple, greenish or white; wings triangular-ovate, sessile, somewhat cordate, acute, acuminate or awn-pointed, 1½″–3″ long, much exceeding the pods; crest of the corolla minute; seed oblong, slightly hairy, about equalling the caruncle.

In sandy swamps, Maine to Florida; Michigan to Minnesota, Nebraska and Louisiana. Drumheads. July–Sept.

5. Polygala brevifòlia Nutt.   Short-leaved Milkwort.   Fig. 2699.

Polygala brevifolia Nutt. Gen. 2 : 89.   1818.

Resembling the preceding species, but is lower, more slender and weaker. Leaves shorter, often scattered on the branches and upper part of the stem; spikes smaller (3″–5″ thick), on slender peduncles; wings ovate or ovate-lanceolate, obtuse or mucronulate.

In sandy swamps, coast of Rhode Island to Florida and Mississippi.   Summer.

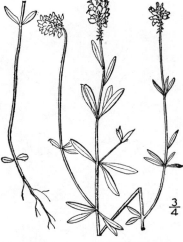

6. Polygala verticillàta L.   Whorled Milkwort.   Fig. 2700.

Polygala verticillata L. Sp. Pl. 706. 1753.

Annual, glabrous, very slender, 6′–12′ high, usually branched, the branches often opposite. Basal leaves none; stem-leaves linear, 3″–15″ long, ½″–2″ wide; acute, entire, punctate, mucronulate, mostly verticillate in 4's or 5's, with some scattered ones on the stem or branches; spikes conic, long-peduncled, acute, 2″ thick at the base, very dense, 4″–10″ long; flowers greenish or purplish; pedicels about ½″ long; wings broadly oval, distinctly clawed, shorter than the pod; crest of the corolla manifest; seed oblong, hairy, twice the length of the caruncle; bracts deciduous.

In dry or moist soil, mostly in fields, southern Quebec and Ontario to Minnesota, Saskatchewan, Nebraska, Florida and Mexico. Ascends to 2,500 ft. in Virginia. June–Nov.

7. Polygala ambígua Nutt. Loose-spiked Milkwort. Fig. 2701.

Polygala ambigua Nutt. Gen. **2**: 89. 1818.
Polygala verticillata var. *ambigua* Wood, Bot. &
Flor. 80. 1870.

Resembling the preceding species, but often taller, 5'–16' high, very slender. Lower stem-leaves commonly verticillate, but the others all alternate; spikes long, loose, the lower flowers often quite distant; peduncles often several inches long; flowers rather larger; wings purple or purplish, nearly circular in outline; mature capsule hardly longer than the wings, which are appressed to it; seed hairy.

In dry soil, Maine to New Jersey, Georgia, Pennsylvania, Michigan, Missouri and Louisiana. Apparently specifically distinct from the preceding species, which it resembles.

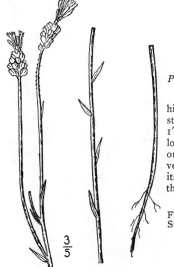

8. Polygala incarnàta L. Pink Milkwort. Fig. 2702.

Polygala incarnata L. Sp. Pl. 701. 1753.

Annual, erect, glabrous, glaucous, very slender, 1'–2° high, simple, or sparingly branched. Basal leaves none; stem-leaves alternate, distant, linear or subulate, sessile, 1"–6" long, rarely wanting; spike terminal, dense, 1'–1½' long, 2"–4" thick; pedicels ½" or less long; bracts minute or none; flowers pink or rose, 5"–6" long; corolla-tube very slender, 3"–4" long, 2–5 times the length of the wings, its keel prominently crested; wings cuspidate; seed hairy, the caruncle-lobes enveloping its beaked extremity.

In dry soil, southern Ontario to Wisconsin, New Jersey, Florida, Arkansas and Mexico. Procession- or rogation-flower. Summer.

9. Polygala viridéscens L. Field or Purple Milkwort. Fig. 2703.

Polygala viridescens L. Sp. Pl. 705. 1753.
Polygala sanguinea L. Sp. Pl. 705. 1753.

Erect, 6'–15' high, annual, glabrous, branching above, leafy. Stem somewhat angled; basal leaves none; stem-leaves oblong, or linear-oblong, 8"–15" long, 1"–2" wide, obtuse or acute, mucronulate; heads globose, becoming oval, 4"–6" thick, obtuse; pedicels about ½" long; flowers rose-purple, greenish, or sometimes white; wings sessile, sometimes slightly cordate, ovate, exceeding the pod; bracts generally persistent on the elongating axis; seed obovoid, hairy, about the length of the caruncle; crest minute.

In fields and meadows, Nova Scotia to southern Ontario, North Carolina, Minnesota, Kansas, Arkansas and Louisiana. June–Sept. The contrast between the green-flowered and purple-flowered forms is striking where the two grow together. Strawberry-tassel.

10. Polygala Curtíssii A. Gray. Curtiss' Milkwort. Fig. 2704.

Polygala Curtissii A. Gray, Man. Ed. 5, 121. 1867.

Erect, slender, 8'–10' high, much resembling the preceding species and the following; heads globose or rarely elongated, at first pointed, blunt when fully developed, loosely flowered, 4"–6" thick; bracts persistent, mainly shorter than the slender pedicels; flowers purple; wings oblong, clawed, nearly erect, twice the length of the pod; seed obovoid, very hairy, apiculate; caruncle minute, much shorter than the seed.

In dry soil, Pennsylvania to Kentucky, Georgia and Alabama. Aug.–Sept.

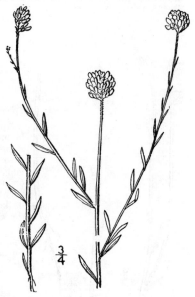

11. Polygala mariàna Mill. Maryland Milkwort. Fig. 2705.

Polygala mariana Mill. Gard. Dict. no. 6. 1768.

Polygala fastigiata Nutt. Gen. 2: 89. 1818.

Annual, slender, glabrous, 6'–16' high, at length much branched above. Basal leaves none; stem-leaves linear, 3"–9" long, about 1" wide, entire, mostly acute, mucronulate; heads globose or slightly longer than thick, obtuse, 3"–4" wide; pediceis slender, 1½"–2" long; flowers rose-purple; wings ovate-oblong or obovate, pointed, narrowed at the base, slightly longer than the pod; bracts deciduous from the elongating axis; caruncle-lobes embracing the smaller extremity of the slightly hairy obovoid seed; corolla minutely crested.

In dry soil, southern New Jersey and Delaware to Florida, west to Kentucky and Texas. July–Sept.

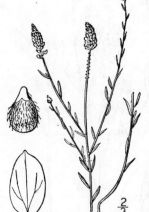

12. Polygala Nuttàllii T. & G. Nuttall's Milkwort. Ground Centaury. Fig. 2706.

Polygala sanguinea Nutt. Gen. 2: 88. 1818. Not L. 1753.

Polygala Nuttallii T. & G. Fl. N. A. 1: 670. 1840.

Annual, glabrous, erect, slender, 4'–7' high, branching above. Basal leaves none; stem-leaves numerous, linear or linear-oblong, 3"–8" long, ½"–1" wide, entire, obtuse or acutish; spikes cylindric or oblong, about 2" thick, 3"–6" long, the floral axis elongating as the fruits fall away from below; pedicels ½" long or less; bracts subulate, persistent; flowers greenish or yellowish-purple, 1" long; seed obovoid, very hairy, longer than the caruncle; wings oblong to oval, about equalling the pod; crest very small.

In dry sandy soil in open places, eastern Massachusetts to North Carolina; apparently erroneously recorded from farther west. Aug.–Sept.

13. Polygala Sénega L. Seneca Snakeroot. Mountain Flax. Fig. 2707.

Polygala Senega L. Sp. Pl. 704. 1753.
Polygala Senega latifolia T. & G. Fl. N. A. 1 : 131. 1838.

Perennial, glabrous or nearly so, stems several, from woody rootstocks, erect or ascending, 6′–18′ high, simple, or branched above. Leaves alternate, lanceolate to ovate or oblong-lanceolate, sessile, 1′–2′ long, 3″–4″ wide, serrulate, the lowest much smaller and scale-like; spike terminal, short-peduncled, dense, acute, 1′–2′ long; flowers 1½″ long, white or tinged with green; pedicels less than ½″ long; wings orbicular-obovate, concave; crest of the corolla short, few-lobed; seed hairy, slightly longer than the lobes of the caruncle.

In rocky woods, New Brunswick to Hudson Bay, Alberta, south to North Carolina along the Alleghanies and to Missouri and Arkansas. Rattlesnake snake-root. Senega-root. May–June.

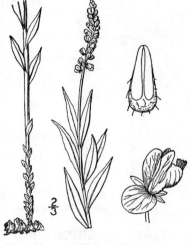

14. Polygala álba Nutt. White Milkwort. Fig. 2708.

Polygala alba Nutt. Gen. 2 : 87. 1818.
Polygala Senega var. *tenuifolia* Pursh. Fl. Am. Sept. 750. 1814. Not *P. tenuifolia* Willd. 1803.

Perennial, glabrous, stems erect from hard woody rootstocks, slender, 6′–15′ high. Leaves alternate, narrowly linear, acute, 3″–12″ long, ½″–1″ wide, their margins entire and revolute, the lower somewhat broader and shorter, clustered; spike terminal, long-peduncled, dense, 1′–2′ long; flowers 1″–1½″ long, white; pedicels less than ½″ long; wings oblong-ovate, slightly concave; crest of the corolla short; seeds silky; about twice the length of the caruncle-lobes.

Prairies, South Dakota to Nebraska, Kansas, Texas and Mexico, Montana, New Mexico and Arizona. May–July.

15. Polygala polýgama Walt. Racemed Milkwort. Fig. 2709.

Polygala polygama Walt. Fl. Car. 179. 1788.
P. polygama abortiva Chodat, Mem. Mus. Gen. 31² : 280. 1893.

Biennial, glabrous; stems numerous, simple, 4′–20′ high, erect from a deep slender root. Stem-leaves crowded, oblong or oblanceolate, obtuse, mucronulate, 8″–12″ long, 1″–2″ wide, entire, the lower gradually smaller; basal leaves spatulate, sometimes smaller; raceme terminal, loose, 1′–4′ long; pedicels spreading or recurved, 1″–2″ long; flowers purple or rose, rarely nearly white, showy, 2″–3″ long, or some of them small and cleistogamous; wings broadly obovate; crest of the corolla large, laciniate; stamens 8; subterranean branches horizontal, bearing numerous, nearly sessile cleistogamous flowers; seeds hairy, longer than the caruncle-lobes.

In dry soil, Nova Scotia to Manitoba, Michigan, Florida and Texas. Local. Bitter or pink milkwort. Centaury. June–July.

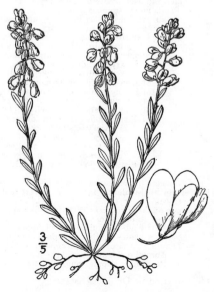

$\frac{2}{3}$

16. Polygala paucifòlia Willd.   Fringed Milkwort.

Flowering Wintergreen.   Gay-wings.   Fig. 2710.

Polygala paucifolia Willd. Sp. Pl. **3** : 880.   1800.

Polygala uniflora Michx. Fl. Bor. Am. **2** : 53.   1803.

Glabrous, perennial from slender prostrate stems and root-stocks 6′–15′ long.   Flowering branches erect or ascending, 4′–7′ high; leaves of the summits of the stems clustered, ovate or oblong, 1′–1½′ long, 7″–10″ wide, acute, rough-margined, on petioles 2″–4″ long; those of the lower part of the shoots successively smaller, distant, the lowest scale-like; flowers 1–4, axillary to the upper leaves, 7″–10″ long, slender-peduncled, rose-purple or rarely white, showy; wings obovate; crest of the corolla beautifully fimbriate; seed slightly shorter than the caruncle; cleistogamous subterranean flowers few, on short lateral branches.

In moist rich woods, New Brunswick and Anticosti to Saskatchewan, south to Georgia, Illinois and Minnesota. Ascends to 2500 ft. in Virginia. Dwarf milkwort. Evergreen snakeroot. May-wings. Little pollom. Baby's-feet, -toes or -slippers. Lady's-slipper. Bird-on-the-wing. Indian pink. May–July.

Family 70.   EUPHORBIÀCEAE J. St. Hil. Expos. Fam. 276.   1805.*

SPURGE FAMILY.

Monoecious or dioecious herbs, shrubs or trees, with acrid often milky sap. Leaves opposite, alternate or verticillate, entire or toothed, sessile or petioled, sometimes with glands at the base; stipules present, obsolete or wanting. Inflorescence various.   Flowers apetalous or petaliferous, sometimes much reduced and subtended by an involucre which resembles a calyx (genera 12–17), the number of parts in the floral whorls often different in the staminate and pistillate flowers. Stamens few, or numerous, in one series or many; filaments separate or united. Ovary usually 3-celled; ovules 1 or 2 in each cavity, pendulous; styles as many as the cavities of the ovary, simple, didvided, or many-cleft.   Fruit a mostly 3-lobed capsule, separating, often elastically, into 3 2-valved carpels from a persistent axis at maturity.   Seeds anatropous; embryo straight, or slightly curved, in fleshy or oily endosperm, the broad cotyledons almost filling the seed-coats.

About 250 genera and over 4000 species, of wide geographic distribution.

Flowers not in an involucre, with a true calyx.
  Ovules 2 in each cavity of the ovary.
    Petals none; stamens usually 3.   1. *Phyllanthus.*
    Petals present at least in the staminate flowers; stamens 5 or 6.   2. *Andrachne.*
  Ovule 1 in each cavity of the ovary.
    Flowers spicate, racemose or axillary; calyx not corolla-like.
      Corolla present in either the staminate or pistillate flowers, or in both.
        Stamens 5 or 6; filaments distinct; pubescence stellate.
          Ovary, and dehiscent capsule, 2–4-celled, mostly 3-celled.   3. *Croton.*
          Ovary, and achene-like capsule, 1-celled.   4. *Crotonopsis.*
        Stamens 10; filaments monodelphous; pubescence not stellate.   5. *Ditaxis.*
      Corolla none; pubescence not stellate.
        Styles many-cleft; pistillate flowers with cleft or laciniate bracts.   6. *Acalypha.*
        Styles not cleft; bracts neither cleft nor laciniate.
          Pistillate flowers with foliaceous or scale-like bracts; stamens 8 or more.
            Flowers in simple spikes or racemes; leaf-blades not peltate.
              Styles 3; ovary 3-celled; capsule 3-lobed.   7. *Tragia.*
              Styles 2; ovary 2-celled; capsule 2-lobed.   8. *Mercurialis.*
            Flowers in panicled racemes; leaf-blades peltate.   9. *Ricinus.*
          Pistillate flowers with glandular saucer-shaped bracts; stamens 2 or 3.
                                      10. *Stillingia.*
    Flowers in cymes; calyx corolla-like, salverform.   11. *Cnidoscolus.*
Flowers in an involucre, the calyx represented by a minute scale at the base of the filament-like pedicel.
  Glands of the involucres with petal-like appendages, these sometimes much reduced.
    Leaves all opposite.
      Leaf-blades inequilateral, oblique at the base.   12. *Chamaesyce.*
      Leaf-blades equilateral, not oblique at the base.   13. *Zygophyllidium.*
    Leaves alternate or scattered at least below the inflorescence.
      Annual or biennial; stipules narrow; bracts petal-like.   14. *Dichrophyllum.*
      Perennial; stipules none; bracts not petal-like.   15. *Tithymalopsis.*

* Revised by Dr. J. K. SMALL.

Glands of the involucres without petal-like appendages, entirely naked, sometimes with crescent-
like horns.
Stem topped by an umbel; stipules none; involucres in open cymes, each with 4 glands and
entire or toothed lobes.   16. *Tithymalus.*
Stem not topped by an umbel; stipules gland-like; involucres in cluster-like cymes, each with
a single gland or rarely 4 glands and fimbriate lobes.   17. *Poinsettia.*

1. PHYLLÁNTHUS L. Sp. Pl. 981. 1753.

Annual, biennial or perennial herbs. Stems wiry. Leaves alternate, entire, often numerous, and so arranged as to appear like the leaflets of a compound leaf. Flowers monoecious,
apetalous, sessile or pedicelled, a staminate and a pistillate one together in the axils. Calyx
mostly 5–6-parted, the lobes imbricated. Stamens usually 3, the filaments more or less united,
rarely separate. Ovary 3-celled; ovules 2 in each cavity; styles 3, each 2-cleft. Capsule
globose, each carpel 2-seeded; endosperm of the seed fleshy. [Greek, leaf-flower.]

More than 125 species, natives of the tropical and temperate zones of both hemispheres. Type
species: *Phyllanthus Nirùri* L.

1. Phyllanthus carolinénsis Walt. Caro-
lina Phyllanthus. Fig. 2711.

Phyllanthus carolinensis Walt. Fl. Car. 228. 1788.
Phyllanthus obovatus Willd. Sp. Pl. 4: 574. 1805.

Annual, dark green, glabrous. Stem slender,
erect, or ascending, 4′–20′ high, simple or branched, the branches 2-ranked; leaves obovate, or
oblong, 3″–10″ long, obtuse, narrowed to a very
short petiole, or subsessile; flowers inconspicuous,
nearly sessile in the axils; calyx 6-parted, its
lobes linear, or oblong; stamens 3; styles 3, each
2-cleft; glands of the pistillate flower more or
less united; capsule about 1″ in diameter; seeds
nearly ½″ long, marked with lines and minute
black papillae.

In sandy or gravelly soil, eastern Pennsylvania to
Illinois, Kansas, Florida, Texas and Central America.
May–Oct.

2. ANDRÁCHNE L. Sp. Pl. 1014. 1753.

Herbs, or shrubby plants, with diffusely branching stems. Leaves alternate, petioled, the blades
often membranous. Flowers monoecious, axillary, pedicelled, the staminate often clustered,
with a 5–6-lobed calyx, 5 or 6 petals, a glandular or lobed disk, 5 or 6 stamens and distinct
filaments; pistillate flowers solitary, with a 5–6-lobed calyx, minute petals or these wanting;
ovary 3-celled; styles stout, 2-cleft or 2-parted; ovules 2 in each cavity. Capsules dry, separating into 3 2-valved carpels. Seed somewhat curved, rugose; endosperm fleshy; embryo
curved. [From the Greek for Portulaca.]

About 12 species, of wide geographic distribution. Type species: *Andrachne Telephioìdes* L.

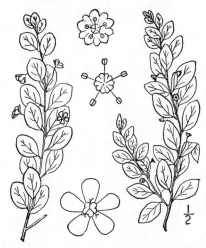

1. Andrachne phyllanthoìdes (Nutt.)
Müll. Arg.   Northern Andrachne.
Fig. 2712.

Lepidanthus phyllanthoides Nutt. Trans. Am. Philos.
Soc. 5: 175. 1837.
Andrachne phyllanthoides Müll. Arg. in DC. Prodr.
15: 435. 1862.

A straggling much branched shrub, 1°–3° tall,
with glabrous lustrous branches and minutely
pubescent twigs. Leaves numerous, the blades
obovate or oval, 4″–9″ long, retuse or obtuse at
the apex, often mucronulate, bright green, paler
beneath than above, short-petioled; pedicels filiform, 3″–10″ long, glabrous; calyx-segments oblong-obovate, ¾″–1½″ long, spreading; petals of
two kinds, those of the staminate flowers narrowly obovate, or oblong-obovate, 3–5-toothed,
greenish-yellow, those of the pistillate flowers
smaller, broadly obovate, entire; capsule subglobose, rather fleshy until mature.

On rocky barrens, Missouri to Arkansas and Texas.
Summer.

3. CRÒTON L. Sp. Pl. 1004. 1753.

Herbs or shrubs, monoecious or rarely dioecious, strong-scented, stellate-pubescent, more or less glandular. Leaves mostly alternate, entire, toothed or lobed, sometimes with 2 glands at the base of the blade. Flowers in axillary or terminal clusters, often spicate or racemose. Staminate flowers uppermost; calyx 4–6-parted (usually 5-parted); petals usually present, but small or rudimentary, alternating with glands; stamens 5 or more, inflexed. Pistillate flowers clustered below the staminate; calyx 5–10-parted; petals usually wanting; ovary mostly 3-celled; ovule 1 in each cavity; styles once, twice or many times 2-cleft. Capsule splitting into 2–4 (usually 3) 2-valved carpels. Seeds 1 in each carpel, smooth, or minutely pitted. Embryo straight in the fleshy endosperm. [The Greek name of the Castor-oil plant.]

About 700 species, mostly of warm and tropical regions, a few in the temperate zones; some of high medicinal value. Type species: *Croton Tiglium* L.

Plants monoecious.
Leaves toothed; staminate calyx 4-lobed, pistillate 5-lobed.   1. *C. glandulosus.*
Leaves entire; staminate calyx 3–5-lobed, pistillate 5–12-lobed.
  Capsules clustered, erect, depressed-globose, 3″–3½″ broad.   2. *C. capitatus.*
  Capsules mostly solitary, nodding, ovoid, or oblong-ovoid.
    Plant silvery; capsules 2″–2½″ long.   3. *C. monanthogynus.*
    Plant whitish; capsules 3″–3½″ long.   4. *C. Lindheimerianus.*
Plant dioecious.   5. *C. texensis.*

1. Croton glandulòsus L. Glandular Croton. Fig. 2713.

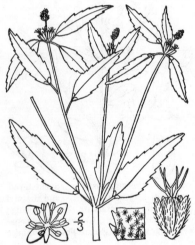

Croton glandulosus L. Amoen. Acad. **5**: 409. 1760.

Annual, monoecious, usually dark green, rough with stellate hairs, and somewhat glandular. Stem erect or assurgent, rather slender, 8′–2½° high, corymbosely branched, or nearly simple; leaves oblong, linear-oblong or ovate, ½′–3′ long, coarsely serrate, bearing 2 glands at the base of the blade; petiole shorter than the blade; flower-clusters terminal or axillary, the staminate in spikes, with a 4-parted calyx, 4 petals, a 4-rayed glandular disk and 8 stamens; pistillate flowers several at the base of the staminate, with 5 sepals, rudimentary petals, and 3 2-cleft styles; capsule subglobose, about 2½″ in length; seeds oblong, minutely wrinkled.

In sandy soil, Virginia to Indiana, Iowa and Kansas, south to Florida and Central America. Also in the West Indies and South America. Consists of many races, differing in shape of leaves, and in amount of pubescence. March–Dec.

2. Croton capitàtus Michx. Capitate Croton. Hogwort. Fig. 2714.

Croton capitatus Michx. Fl. Bor. Am. **2**: 214. 1803.

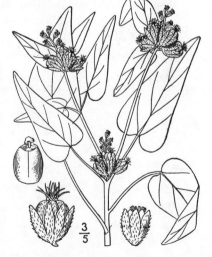

Annual, monoecious, silvery green, densely stellate-pubescent. Stem erect or assurgent, usually corymbosely branched above; leaves lanceolate, oblong, or rarely ovate, entire, often undulate, obtuse or cordate at the base; lower petioles often equalling or exceeding the blades, flowers clustered at the ends of the branches, the staminate racemose, with a 5-parted calyx, 5 petals, and 10–14 stamens; pistillate flowers several, sessile, with 7–12 sepals, no petals, the styles twice or thrice cleft; capsule depressed-globose, 3″–3½″ in diameter; seeds gray, or variegated, turtle-shaped, smooth, or minutely pitted.

In dry soil. New Jersey to Tennessee, Iowa, Kansas, Georgia and Texas. May–Oct.

3. Croton monanthógynus Michx.　Single-fruited Croton.　Fig. 2715.

C. monanthogynus Michx. Fl. Bor. Am. **2**: 215. 1803.

Annual, monoecious, silvery green, rather densely stellate-pubescent and somewhat glandular. Main stem slender, 4′–8′ high, simple, or sparingly branched above, topped by a 3–5-rayed umbel with rays 5′–15′ long, forked or umbellately branched; leaves ovate or oblong, 5″–1½′ long, entire or undulate, obtuse or subcordate at the base; petioles usually about half as long as the blades; staminate flowers clustered at the ends of erect peduncles, with 3–5 unequal calyx-segments, the same number of petals and scale-like glands, and 3–8 stamens; pistillate flowers mostly solitary, on recurved pedicels, with 5 equal calyx-segments, no petals, 5 glands and 2 sessile 2-cleft stigmas; capsule ovoid or oblong-ovoid, 2″–2½″ long, 1–2-celled; seeds oval or orbicular, variegated, minutely pitted, shining.

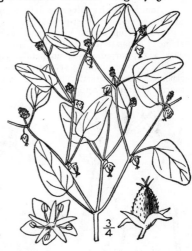

In dry soil, North Carolina to Indiana and Kansas, south to Florida and Mexico. Prairie-tea. June–Oct.

4. Croton Lindheimeriànus Scheele.　Lindheimer's Croton.　Fig. 2716.

Croton Lindheimerianus Scheele, Linnaea **25**: 580. 1852.

Somewhat shrubby, whitish-tomentose. Stems erect, 4′–15′ tall, sometimes diffusely branched; leaves rather numerous, the blades ovate to oblong-ovate, ½′–2′ long, obtuse or acutish, green above, undulate; petioles almost as long as the blades or shorter; pedicels 1″–3″ long, recurving; calyx slightly accrescent, its segments oblong or elliptic-oblong, becoming 2″ long, slightly keeled in age; petals pubescent; capsules oval, 3″–3½″ long, 3-celled, tomentose, truncate-obtuse at both ends, drooping; seeds oblong-elliptic, nearly 2″ long.

In dry soil, Kansas to Texas and New Mexico. Summer.

5. Croton texénsis (Klotzsch) Muell. Arg.　Texas Croton.　Fig. 2717.

Hendecandra texensis Klotzch, Erichs. Arch. **1**: 252. 1841.
Croton texensis Muell. Arg. in DC. Prodr. **15**: Part 2, 692. 1862.

Annual, dioecious, often bronze-green, canescent with stellate pubescence. Stem rather slender, erect or assurgent, 8′–2° high, paniculately or corymbosely branched; leaves ovate to linear-oblong, or almost linear, 10″–3½′ long, entire or undulate; petioles mostly shorter than the blades; staminate flowers racemose; pistillate flowers sessile or nearly so in stalked clusters; calyx equally 5-parted, the segments ovate; petals none; glands 5, minute; stamens mostly 10; styles 3, twice or thrice 2-cleft; capsule subglobose, 2½″–3″ in diameter; somewhat muricate; seeds ovoid or oval, variegated, finely reticulated.

In dry soil, South Dakota to Illinois, Alabama, Wyoming and Arizona. Recorded from Delaware. Skunk-weed. June–Sept.

4. CROTONÓPSIS Michx. Fl. Bor. Am. 2: 185. 1803.

Annual slender silvery-scurfy monoecious herbs with branched stems, narrow alternate or rarely opposite short-petioled leaves, the flowers in terminal and lateral clusters. Staminate flowers uppermost in the clusters, with an equally 5-parted calyx, 5 petals and 5 inflexed stamens opposite the petals, the filaments distinct, enlarged at the summit. Pistillate flowers with a 3-5-parted calyx, no petals, 5 petal-like glands opposite the calyx-segments, and a 1-celled ovary; ovule 1; style twice or thrice cleft. Fruit a small scaly or spiny achene-like capsule. Seed lenticular or terete, longitudinally wrinkled; embryo straight in fleshy endosperm. [Greek, Croton-like.]

Two known species, natives of the southeastern United States. Type species: *Crotonopsis lineàris* Michx.

1. Crotonopsis lineàris Michx. Crotonopsis. Fig. 2718.

C. linearis Michx. Fl. Bor. Am. 2: 186. *pl. 46.* 1803.

Silvery, covered with peltate somewhat fringed scales, except on the green upper surfaces of the leaves. Stem wiry, 4′-1½° high, much branched; leaves oblong-ovate to linear-lanceolate, ½′-1½′ long, entire; staminate flowers with an equally 5-parted calyx, the petals spatulate; calyx of the pistillate flowers unequally 3-5-parted; achene ovoid-elliptic; seed ovoid, 1″-1½″ long.

In dry sandy soil, Connecticut and New Jersey to Tennessee, Illinois, Missouri, Kansas, south to Florida and Texas. July–Sept.

5. DITÁXIS Vahl; Juss. Euphorb. 27, 110. 1824.

Monoecious herbs or shrubs, perennial by rootstocks, silky or pilose, the sap purplish. Leaves alternate, entire, or rarely toothed, often strongly nerved. Flowers in axillary or axillary and terminal clusters, often racemed, usually bracted. Staminate flowers often crowded at the ends of the racemes; calyx 4–5-lobed, the lobes valvate; petals 4 or 5, alternate with the calyx-lobes and with the lobes of the disk; stamens of the same number as the petals or two or three times as many, united into a column. Pistillate flowers with the calyx-lobes imbricated and smaller petals, the ovary 3-celled, each cavity with 1 ovule; styles 3, short, once to thrice cleft. Capsule 3-lobed, depressed, separating into 3 2-valved carpels. Seeds subglobose, wrinkled, or muricate, sometimes crested; embryo straight in the fleshy endosperm. [Greek, double-ranked, in allusion to the stamens.]

About 20 species, natives of temperate and tropical regions. Type species: *Ditaxis fasciculàta* Vahl.

Flowers in terminal and axillary racemes; leaves sessile.   1. *D. mercurialina.*
Flowers in axillary clusters; leaves short-petioled.   2. *D. humilis.*

1. Ditaxis mercuriálina (Nutt.) Coult. Tall Ditaxis. Fig. 2719.

Aphora mercurialina Nutt. Trans. Am. Phil. Soc. (II.) 5: 174. 1833–37.
Argyrothamnia mercurialina Muell. Arg. Linnaea 34: 148. 1865.
Ditaxis mercurialina Coult. Mem. Torr. Club 5: 213. 1894.

Stem slender, strict, usually simple, channeled, silky, 4′-2° high. Leaves alternate, ovate to narrowly lanceolate, 10″-2′ long, undulate, sessile, often strongly 3-nerved, glabrate; flowers in terminal and axillary racemes; staminate flowers with lanceolate or linear-lanceolate acute ciliate calyx-segments, and spatulate-oblong undulate petals; pistillate flowers with a 5-parted calyx, the segments lanceolate, spreading, 3 times as long as those of the staminate, petals none; capsule depressed, 3″-4½″ in diameter, somewhat silky, 3-lobed; seeds globose-ovoid, 2″ long, pointed, wrinkled, indistinctly 3-crested.

In dry soil, Kansas and Arkansas to Texas. Lower leaves sometimes oblanceolate. April–July.

2. Ditaxis hùmilis (Engelm. & Gray) Pax.
Low Ditaxis. Fig. 2720.

Aphora humilis Engelm. & Gray, Bost. Journ. Nat.
  Hist. **5**: 262. 1847.
Argyrothamnia humilis Muell. Arg. Linnaea, **34**:
  147. 1865.
Ditaxis humilis Pax in Engl. & Prantl, Nat Pfl. Fam.
  3: Abt. 5, 45. 1890.

Stem slender, much branched, pubescent, the
branches spreading, 4″–1° long. Leaves alternate,
ovate, oblong, obovate or oblanceolate, 5″–15″
long, entire, narrowed into a short petiole; flowers in axillary clusters; staminate flowers with
petals a little longer than the 5 calyx-segments
and longer than the lobes of the disk; pistillate
flowers with a 5-parted calyx and 3 styles each
usually twice 2-cleft; capsule short-pedicelled,
much depressed, 2″–3″ in diameter, 3–4-lobed;
seeds oval-globose, about 1″ long, muricate.

Prairies, Kansas to Louisiana and Texas. March–
Sept.

6. ACALÝPHA L. Sp. Pl. 1003. 1753.

Herbs or shrubs, our species annual, monoecious. Stems mostly erect and branched.
Leaves alternate, entire or toothed, petioled, stipulate. Flowers in axillary and terminal
spikes or spike-like racemes, the staminate cluster peduncled, each flower in the axil of a
minute bractlet, with a 4-parted calyx and 8–16 stamens united at their bases. Pistillate
flowers subtended by a foliaceous bract which often equals or overtops the staminate, the
calyx 3–5-parted, ovary 3-celled; stigmas fringed; petals wanting in both kinds of flowers;
capsule usually of 3 2-valved carpels, each 1-seeded. [Greek, nettle.]

About 250 species, mostly tropical and subtropical. Type species: *Acalypha virginica* L.

Staminate and pistillate flowers in separate spikes or racemes; capsule spiny.   1. *A. ostryaefolia*.
Staminate and pistillate flowers in the same spike or raceme; capsule smooth.
    Plant not glandular; bract palmately many-lobed, equalling or exceeding the staminate spike.
                                        2. *A. virginica*.
    Plant glandular; bract many-cleft, shorter than the staminate spike.   3. *A. gracilens*.

1. Acalypha ostryaefòlia Ridd. Horn-
beam Three-seeded Mercury. Fig. 2721.

Acalypha caroliniana Ell. Bot. S. C. & Ga. **2**: 645.
  1824. Not Walt. 1788.

Acalypha ostryaefolia Riddell, Syn. Fl. W. States,
  33. 1835.

Dark green, minutely pubescent. Stem
erect, rather stout, simple or branched, 1°–2½°
tall. Leaves thin, or membranous, ovate,
2½′–4′ long, short-acuminate, serrate, obtuse
or cordate at the base, the petioles often as
long as the blades; staminate and pistillate
flowers in separate spikes, the bractlets of the
staminate minute, those of the pistillate conspicuous, lobed; capsule much depressed,
3-lobed, 1½″–2″ in diameter, spiny; seeds
ovoid, 1″ long, wrinkled.

New Jersey to Ohio, Kansas, Florida and
Mexico. Bahamas, Cuba. June–Nov.

2. Acalypha virgínica L.   Virginia Three-seeded Mercury, Mercury-weed.   Fig. 2722.

Acalypha virginica L. Sp. Pl. 1003. 1753.

Dark green or becoming purplish, somewhat pubescent. Stem erect or ascending, 3′–2° tall; leaves ovate or elliptic, 10″–4′ long, thin, coarsely serrate except near the base; staminate and pistillate flowers in the same axillary clusters, the staminate spike peduncled, usually included in the large palmately lobed bract; pistillate flowers 1–3 at the base of the staminate peduncle; capsule 3-lobed, subglobose, about 1½″ in diameter, smooth, sometimes slightly pubescent; seeds ovoid, reddish, striate.

In woods and thickets, Nova Scotia to Minnesota, Florida and Texas. Occurs at 3000 ft. in Georgia. Upper leaves commonly forming a flat-topped cluster. June–Oct.

3. Acalypha grácilens A. Gray.   Slender Three-seeded Mercury.   Fig. 2723.

Acalypha gracilens A. Gray, Man. 408. 1848.

Acalypha virginica var. *gracilens* Muell. Arg. Linnaea **34**: 45. 1865.

Pale green, pubescent, often densely glandular. Stem slender, erect, 4′–2½° tall, usually branched, the branches often nearly filiform, spreading or divergent; leaves lanceolate or linear-oblong, 5″–2′ long, usually firm, acutish, serrate, narrowed to a short petiole; staminate and pistillate flowers in the same axillary clusters; staminate spike very slender, usually exceeding the many-cleft bract; pistillate flowers 1 or several; capsule subglobose, about 1½″ in diameter; seeds globose-ovoid, dark red, or gray mottled with red, striate-pitted.

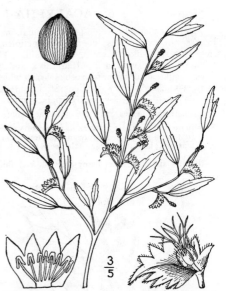

In dry woods and thickets, New Hampshire to Kansas, Florida and Texas. Occurs 2000 ft. in South Carolina. June–Sept.

7. TRÀGIA [Plumier] L. Sp. Pl. 980. 1753.

Monoecious herbs, or shrubs, sometimes climbing, usually armed with stiff stinging hairs. Leaves alternate, toothed or somewhat lobed, mostly cordate, petioled; flowers in racemes, or spicate racemes, bracteolate, apetalous; staminate flowers with a 3–5-parted calyx and 1–3 or rarely numerous stamens; pistillate flowers with a 3–8-lobed calyx, the segments entire or pinnatifid, a 3-celled ovary with 1 ovule in each cavity, and 3 styles, often united to above the middle; capsule 3-lobed, separating into 3 2-valved carpels; seeds subglobose; endosperm fleshy. [From Tragus, the Latin name of Hieronymus Bock, 1498–1553, a German botanist.]

About 50 species, mostly natives of tropical regions. Besides the following, 4 others occur in the southern United States. Type species: *Tragia volubilis* L.

Stems not twining.
    Staminate calyx 4-lobed; stamens 2.   1. *T. urens.*
    Staminate calyx 3-lobed; stamens 3.   2. *T. nepetaefolia.*
    Staminate calyx 4–5-lobed; stamens 4 or 5.   3. *T. ramosa.*
Stems twining.   4. *T. macrocarpa.*

1. Tragia ùrens L.   Eastern Tragia.
Fig. 2724.

Tragia urens L. Sp. Pl. Ed. 2, 1391. 1763.

Tragia innocua Walt. Fl. Car. 220. 1788.

Perennial, dull green, pilose or hirsute. Stem slender, erect, 4′-15′ tall, branched; leaves obovate or ovate to linear, entire, undulate or toothed, mostly obtuse at the apex, narrowed or subcordate at base, short-petioled or sessile, 5″-2′ long; flowers in terminal or lateral spike-like racemes often 4′ long; staminate flowers with a 4-lobed calyx and 2 stamens; pistillate flowers several at the base of the racemes, with a 5-6-lobed calyx; capsule short-pedicelled, much depressed, 4″-5″ in diameter, sparingly pubescent; seeds subglobose, 2″ long, smooth.

In sandy soil, Virginia to Florida and Louisiana. May–Aug.

2. Tragia nepetaefòlia Cav.   Catnep Tragia. Fig. 2725.

T. nepetaefolia Cav. Icones **6**: 37. *pl. 557, f. 1.* 1801.

Tragia urticaefolia Michx. Fl. Bor. Am. **2**: 176. 1803.

Perennial, hispid with stinging hairs. Stem slender, erect or reclining, 6′-15′ long; leaves triangular-ovate or lanceolate, 5″-2′ long, dentate-serrate, cordate, short-petioled, the lower sometimes orbicular; racemes 5″-1½′ long, many-flowered; staminate flowers mostly with a 3-lobed calyx and 3 stamens; pistillate flowers with a 5-lobed calyx; capsule much depressed, 3″ in diameter, hirsute; seeds globose, chestnut brown, smooth, 2″ in diameter.

In sandy soil, Georgia and Florida to Missouri, Kansas, Mexico and New Mexico. Recorded from Virginia. May–Oct.

3. Tragia ramòsa Torr.   Branching Tragia. Fig. 2726.

T. ramosa Torr. Ann. Lyc. N. Y. **2**: 245. 1826.

T. stylaris Muell. Arg. Linnaea **34**: 180. 1860.

Perennial, light green, bristly with stinging hairs. Stem slender, usually much branched, the branches sometimes spreading, 2′-12′ long; leaves lanceolate, ovate-lanceolate or triangular-lanceolate, ½-2′ long, acute at the apex, coarsely and sharply serrate, truncate or cordate at the base, short-petioled; racemes ½′-1½′ long, few-flowered; staminate flowers very short-pedicelled, with a 4-5-lobed calyx and 4-6 stamens; pistillate flowers solitary with a 5-lobed calyx subtended by a 3-lobed bract; capsule much depressed, 3″-4″ in diameter, bristly; seeds globose, 2″ in diameter, orange, more or less variegated.

In dry soil, Missouri to Texas, Colorado and Arizona. July–Aug.

4. Tragia macrocàrpa Willd. Twining or Large-fruited Tragia. Fig. 2727.

Tragia cordata Michx. Fl. Bor. Am. **2**: 176. 1803. Not Vahl. 1790.

Tragia macrocarpa Willd. Sp. Pl. **4**: 323. 1806.

Perennial, twining, slightly hirsute. Stem slender, $10'-4\frac{1}{2}°$ long, branched; leaves ovate, $2'-4\frac{1}{2}'$ long, deeply cordate, coarsely dentate-serrate, long-acuminate; petioles mostly shorter than the blades, staminate flowers with a 3-lobed calyx and 3 stamens; pistillate flowers several at the bases of the spikes, short-pedicelled, the calyx 5-lobed; capsule depressed, $6''-8''$ in diameter; seeds subglobose, $2\frac{1}{4}''$ long, smooth, variegated.

In dry or rocky soil, Kentucky to Missouri, Florida and Texas. June–Sept.

8. MERCURIÀLIS [Tourn.] L. Sp. Pl. 1035. 1752.

Annual or perennial herbs or shrubby plants, with firm or succulent tissues. Leaves opposite, entire or often toothed. Flowers mostly dioecious, apetalous. Staminate flowers in more or less elongated spikes or racemes, the calyx membranous, of 3 valvate sepals; stamens 8–20; filaments distinct; anthers opening lengthwise. Pistillate flowers with a calyx of 3 sepals, the ovary 2-celled; styles 2, distinct or nearly so; stigmas entire; ovules solitary in each cavity. Capsule usually 2-lobed. Seed solitary in each cavity, with a smooth or tuberculate crustaceous testa. [Latin, belonging to the god Mercury.]

About 7 species, mostly natives of the Mediterranean region. Type species: *Mercurialis perennis* L.

1. Mercurialis ánnua L. Herb Mercury. Fig. 2728.

Mercurialis annua L. Sp. Pl. 1035. 1753.

Annual, glabrous. Stems $8'-2°$ tall, more or less widely branched; leaves thinnish, ovate to lanceolate, acute or slightly acuminate, serrate with rounded teeth, or crenate; petioles $2\frac{1}{2}''-7\frac{1}{2}''$ long; staminate flowers in interrupted spikes which surpass the leaves; pistillate flowers clustered in the axils; capsules 2-lobed, $2''-2\frac{1}{2}''$ broad, hispid; seeds subglobose, $\frac{3}{4}''$ in diameter, pitted.

In waste places, Nova Scotia to Florida, Ohio and Texas; Bermuda. Native of Europe and Africa.

9. RÍCINUS [Tourn.] L. Sp. Pl. 1007. 1753.

A tall stout monoecious herb, glabrous and glaucous, with alternate large peltate palmately-lobed petioled leaves, and numerous small apetalous greenish flowers in terminal racemes, the pistillate above the staminate. Staminate flowers with a 3–5-parted calyx, the segments valvate, and numerous crowded stamens; filaments repeatedly branched. Pistillate flowers with a caducous calyx, a 3-celled, 3-ovuled ovary, the 3 red styles united at the base, 2-cleft. Capsule subglobose, or oval, smooth or spiny, separating into 3 2-valved carpels. Seeds ovoid or oblong, usually mottled. Embryo straight. Endosperm fleshy and oily. [The Latin name of the plant.]

A monotypic genus of the warmer parts of Africa and Asia.

1. Ricinus commùnis L.   Castor-oil Plant.   Castor-bean.   Palma Christi.   Fig. 2729.

Ricinus communis L. Sp. Pl. 1007. 1753.

Stem erect, 3°–15° tall, more or less branched, becoming tree-like in warm regions. Leaves nearly orbicular in outline, 4′–2° broad, 6–11-palmately-lobed and peltate, the lobes toothed, acute or acuminate; capsule 6″–8″ in diameter, usually spiny; sometimes smooth; seeds shining, smooth, black, variegated with white, or mottled with gray and brown markings.

In waste places, escaped from cultivation, New Jersey to Florida and Texas. An imposing ornamental plant, and also of medicinal value. Widely naturalized in warm and tropical regions. Oil-plant. Mexico-seed. Stedfast. Man's-motherwort.

10. STILLÍNGIA Garden; L. Mant. 1: 19, 126.   1767.

Monoecious glabrous herbs or shrubs, with simple or branched stems, alternate or rarely opposite, entire or toothed leaves, often with 2 glands at the base, the flowers bracteolate, in terminal spikes, apetalous, the bractlets 2-glandular. Staminate flowers several together in the axils of the bractlets, the calyx slightly 2–3-lobed; stamens 2–3, exserted. Pistillate flowers solitary in the axils of the lower bractlets; calyx 3-lobed, ovary 2-celled or 3-celled with a solitary ovule in each cavity; styles stout, somewhat united at the base. Capsule 2-lobed or 3-lobed, separating into 2 or 3 two-valved carpels. Seeds ovoid or subglobose. Embryo straight in the fleshy endosperm. [In honor of Dr. B. Stellingfleet, an English botanist.]

About 15 species, mostly of tropical America and the islands of the Pacific Ocean, the following typical.

1. Stillingia sylvática L.   Queen's Delight.   Queen-root.   Fig. 2730.

Stillingia sylvatica L. Mant. 1: 126. 1767.

A bright green slightly fleshy perennial herb. Stem rather stout, erect or assurgent, usually branched from the base, 1°–3½° tall. Leaves obovate, oblong or elliptic, 5″–4′ long, obtuse, or subacute, serrate with appressed teeth, often narrowed at the 2-glandular base, sessile; flowers in terminal spikes, lemon-colored, subtended by small bracts furnished with saucer-shaped glands; calyx cup-shaped; petals and glandular disk none; capsule depressed, 5″–7″ in diameter, 3-lobed; seeds ovoid, 3″ long, light gray, minutely pitted and papillose, the base flattened.

In dry soil, Virginia to Florida, Kansas and Texas. Called also Silver-leaf; the root, known as Queen's-root, an alterative. Yaw-root. Nettle-potatoe. March–Oct.

Stillingia salicifòlia (Torr.) Small, with relatively narrower and serrulate leaves, ranges from Kansas to Texas.

11. CNIDÓSCOLUS Pohl, Pl. Bras. 1 : 56. *pl. 49.* 1827.

Monoecious or rarely dioecious perennial stinging bristly herbs, or shrubs, with entire, lobed or divided petioled leaves, the flowers in cymes. Flowers apetalous. Staminate flowers on the upper parts of the cymes, with a corolla-like 5-lobed calyx, the stamens usually numerous (10 or more) and in several series, their filaments mostly united at the base. Pistillate flowers in the lower forks of the cymes; ovary mostly 3-celled and 3-ovuled; styles united at the base; capsule ovoid or subglobose, easily separating into 2-valved carpels; seeds ovoid or obovoid; embryo straight; endosperm fleshy. [Greek, stinging spine.]

About 20 species, widely distributed in warm and tropical America. Besides the following another occurs in the Southern States. Type species: *Cnidoscolus hamosus* Pohl.

1. Cnidoscolus stimulòsus (Michx.) Engelm. & Gray. Spurge Nettle. Tread-softly. Fig. 2731.

Jatropha stimulosa Michx. Fl. Bor. Am. **2** : 216. 1803.

Cnidoscolus stimulosus Engelm. & Gray, Bost. Journ. Nat. Hist. **5** : 234. 1845.

Jatropha urens var. *stimulosa* Muell. Arg. in DC. Prodr. **15** : Part. 2, 1101. 1862.

Perennial by a stout root, herbaceous, bright green, armed with stinging hairs. Stem rather slender, erect, simple or branched, 4′–3½° tall; leaves nearly orbicular in outline, 2½′–12′ broad, truncate or cordate at the base, deeply 3–5-lobed, the lobes entire, toothed or pinnatifid; calyx of the staminate flowers salverform, white or pink, 10″–20″ broad; capsule oblong, 5″–8″ long, papillose, wrinkled; seeds oblong-obovoid, 5″–6″ long, smooth, mottled.

In dry sandy soil, Virginia to Florida and Texas. Sand-nettle. Stinging-bush. March–Aug.

12. CHAMAESÝCE S. F. Gray, Nat. Arr. Brit. Pl. **2** : 260. 1821.

Annual or perennial herbs, or shrubs. Stems often radially branched at the base, the branches ascending or prostrate, sometimes creeping, forking. Leaves opposite, entire or toothed, more or less oblique at the base; stipules delicate, entire or fringed. Involucres solitary in the axils or in axillary cymes; glands 4, sessile or stalked, naked or usually with an appendage, one sinus of each involucre glandless. Capsule smooth, sometimes pubescent, the angles sharp or rounded. Seeds angled, with minute caruncles, white or black, the faces smooth or transversely wrinkled. [Greek, ground-fig.]

About 225 species, widely distributed in temperate and tropical regions. Type species: *Chamaesyce maritima* S. F. Gray.

This genus and the following ones of the family were all included in *Euphorbia* in our first edition, but the true *Euphorbias* are African, nearly or quite leafless tall and stout plants, very different from any of ours.

‡ Leaves entire; seeds smooth.
Plants branched at the base, the branches prostrate.
　Seeds 1½″ long.   1. *C. polygonifolia.*
　Seeds ½″–¾″ long.
　　Leaves usually more than twice as long as broad; seeds nearly terete, ¾″ long.   2. *C. Geyeri.*
　　Leaves usually less than twice as long as broad; seeds obtusely 4-angled, ½″ long.   3. *C. serpens.*
Plants with an erect or ascending stem, branched above, branches ascending.
　Seeds nearly terete, 1″ long; leaves usually flat and straight.   4. *C. petaloidea.*
　Seeds 4-angled, ¾″ long; leaves often involute and curved.   5. *C. zygophylloides.*
‡‡ Leaves entire; seeds variously roughened.
Plants glabrous.   6. *C. Fendleri.*
Plants canescent.   7. *C. lata.*

‡‡‡ Leaves serrate or dentate ; plants prostrate or spreading.
Herbage glabrous.
    Seeds faintly transversely ridged and pitted.
        Seeds brown, about ½″ long ; leaves broad.   8. *C. serpyllifolia.*
        Seeds gray, about ¾″ long ; leaves narrow.   9. *C. albicaulis.*
    Seeds strongly transversely ridged, not pitted.   10. *C. glyptosperma.*
Herbage pubescent, or puberulent.
    Capsules pubescent.
        Seeds narrow, fully ½″ long, fully twice as long as wide, the faces pitted. 11. *C. stictospora.*
        Seeds broad, less than ½″ long, less than twice as long as wide, the faces wrinkled.
            Leaves broad ; involucre deeply split on one side ; seeds blunt-angled. 12. *C. humistrata.*
            Leaves narrow ; involucre not deeply split ; seeds sharp-angled.   13. *C. maculata.*
    Capsules glabrous.   14. *C. Rafinesqui.*
    ‡‡‡‡ Leaves serrate or dentate ; plants erect or ascending.   15. *C. Preslii.*

1. Chamaesyce polygonifòlia (L.) Small. Seaside or Knotweed Spurge. Fig. 2732.

Euphorbia polygonifolia L. Sp. Pl. 455. 1753.

Chamaesyce polygonifolia Small, Fl. SE. U. S. 708.
    1903.

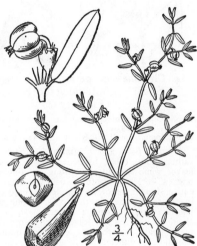

    Annual, pale green, glabrous, stem branched
from the base, the branches radiately spreading,
prostrate, forked, wiry, 3′–8′ long. Leaves opposite, oblong, linear-oblong or linear-lanceolate,
3″–10″ long, fleshy, obtuse, often mucronulate,
entire, obtuse or subcordate and somewhat oblique
at the base, short-petioled ; stipules an inconspicuous fringe of short bristles ; involucres usually
solitary in the axils, turbinate-campanulate, less
than 1″ long, with 4 columnar nearly naked
glands shorter than the lobes ; peduncles twice as
long as the involucres ; capsule globose-ovoid,
1½″–2″ long, nodding, minutely wrinkled ; seeds
ovoid, 1½″ long, somewhat flattened, ash-colored,
very minutely pitted and spotted.

    In sand along the Atlantic coast, Nova Scotia to
Florida, and on the shores of the Great Lakes. Shore-spurge. July–Sept.

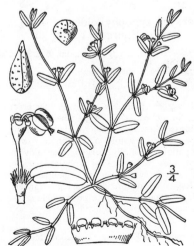

2. Chamaesyce Geỳeri (Engelm. & Gray) Small. Geyer's Spurge. Fig. 2733.

Euphorbia Geyeri Engelm. & Gray, Bost. Journ. Nat.
    Hist. **5**: 260. 1847.
C. Geyeri Small, Fl. SE. U. S. 709. 1903.

    Annual, olive-green, glabrous. Stem branched from
the base, the prostrate branches radiately spreading,
wiry, 2′–15′ long ; leaves oblong or ovate, 2″–6″ long,
obtuse, usually mucronulate, entire or nearly so,
oblique, obtuse or subcordate at the base, short-
petioled ; stipules a fringe of short setae ; involucres
usually solitary in the axils, campanulate, about ¼″
high, with 4 wineglass-shaped glands shorter than
the lobes, each subtended by an inconspicuous white
or red entire or lobed appendage ; peduncles as long
as the involucres, or longer ; capsule globose-reniform, about 1″ long, nodding ; seeds narrowly ovoid,
¾″ long, ash-colored, nearly terete.

    In sandy soil, Illinois to Minnesota, South Dakota and
Kansas. July–Sept.

3. Chamaesyce sérpens (H.B.K.) Small. Round-leaved Spreading Spurge. Fig. 2734.

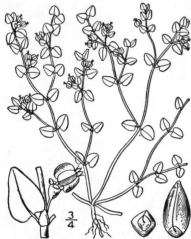

Euphorbia serpens H.B.K. Nov. Gen. **2**: 52. 1817.
Chamaesyce serpens Small, Fl. SE. U. S. 709. 1903.

Annual, pale green, glabrous, sometimes glaucescent. Stem branched from the base. the slender or filiform branches prostrate, 2'–12' long; leaves orbicular, orbicular-ovate or oval, 1"–3" long, obtuse or emarginate, entire, often slightly revolute-margined, short-petioled, the base oblique, rounded or subcordate; stipules triangular, somewhat incised at the apex; peduncles slightly longer than the petioles; involucres solitary in the axils, nearly ½" high, bearing 4 sessile saucer-shaped glands shorter than the lobes, each subtended by a minute irregular crenulate appendage; capsule nodding, depressed-globose, 1" in diameter; seeds oblong-ovoid, ½" long, smooth, obtusely 4-angled, light gray.

Illinois to Iowa, western Ontario, South Dakota and Kansas, south to Mexico. West Indies. In ballast about the eastern seaports. March–Oct.

4. Chamaesyce petaloìdea (Engelm.) Small. White-flowered Spurge. Fig. 2735.

Euphorbia petaloidea Engelm. Bot. Mex. Bound. Surv. 185. 1859.
C. petaloidea Small, Fl. SE. U. S. 711. 1903.

Annual, pale green, glabrous. Stem usually rather stout, erect, branched above, 6'–2° high; leaves opposite, linear, oblong or linear-lanceolate, 5"–1' long, obtuse, usually flat, straight, entire, slender-petioled; stipules a fringe of setae; involucres solitary in the axils, oblong-campanulate, 1" long, bearing 4 wineglass-shaped glands about as long as the lobes, each subtended by a white ovate or orbicular entire or undulate appendage; peduncles as long as the involucres; capsule globose-reniform, 1" long; seeds oblong-ovoid, nearly 1" long, ash-colored, minutely pitted, nearly terete.

Prairies, Iowa to Wyoming, Missouri, Texas and Arizona. July–Sept.

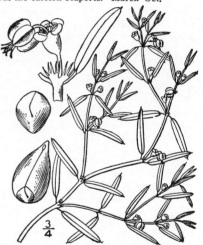

5. Chamaesyce zygophylloìdes (Boiss.) Small. Prairie Spurge. Fig. 2736.

Euphorbia petaloidea var. Nuttallii Engelm. Bot. Mex. Bound. Surv. 185. 1859.
E. zygophylloides Boiss. Cent. Euph. 10. 1860.
Euphorbia arenaria Engelm. & Gray, Bost. Journ. Nat. Hist. **5**: 260. 1847. Not Nutt. 1837.

Annual, bright green, glabrous. Stem slender, erect or ascending, branched, 4'–2° high, the branches wiry, leaves mostly linear and mucronulate or truncate at the apex, often involute, obtuse or narrowed at the base, petioled, usually curved, the midvein prominent; stipules lanceolate or subulate-lanceolate; involucres solitary in the axils, campanulate, less than 1" long, long-peduncled, bearing 4 saucer-shaped glands subtended by white entire oblong or ovate appendages; seeds ovoid, ¾" long, gray, 4-angled.

Prairies, Missouri and Kansas to Texas and Mexico. June–Sept.

6. Chamaescye Féndleri (T. & G.) Small. Fendler's Spurge. Fig. 2737.

Euphorbia Fendleri T. & G. Pac. R. R. Rep. **2**: 175. 1855.
Chamaesyce Fendleri Small, Fl. SE. U. S. 710. 1903.

Annual (or perennial by a woody root), pale green, glabrous. Stem diffusely branched from the base, the spreading wiry branches 4′–8′ long, brittle; leaves suborbicular, oval or elliptic, 1½″–4″ long, obtuse, entire, short-petioled, the base oblique, obtuse or subcordate; stipules usually a fringe of short setae; involucres solitary in the axils, sometimes clustered toward the ends of the branches, campanulate, 1″–2½″ high, with 4 or 5 saucer-shaped oval glands subtended by irregular entire or slightly lobed appendages; peduncles about as long as the involucres; capsule deflexed, 1½″ in diameter, sharply 3-lobed; seeds ovoid, ¾″ long, transversely wrinkled.

Nebraska and Wyoming to Texas. Mexico, Utah and Arizona. April–Oct.

7. Chamaesyce làta (Engelm.) Small. Hoary Spurge. Fig. 2738.

Euphorbia lata Engelm. Bot. Mex. Bound. Surv. 188. 1859.
Chamaesyce lata Small, Fl. SE. U. S. 710. 1903.

Perennial, pale green, canescent all over. Stem branched from the somewhat woody base, the branches spreading or ascending, 2′–4′ long; leaves ovate to lanceolate, 2½″–5″ long, revolute-margined, abruptly narrowed, truncate or cordate at the base, short-petioled; stipules obsolete or of a few short setae; involucres solitary in the axils, ½″ long, short-peduncled, bearing 5 disk-like glands subtended by narrow undulate appendages; capsule subglobose, 1″ in diameter; seeds oblong, ¾″ long, acutish at both ends, 4-angled, the faces inconspicuously transversely wrinkled.

Kansas to Colorado, Texas and New Mexico. April–Aug.

8. Chamaesyce serpyllifòlia (Pers.) Small. Thyme-leaved Spurge. Fig. 2739.

Euphorbia serpyllifolia Pers. Syn. **2**: 14. 1807.
Chamaesyce serpyllifolia Small, Fl. SE. U. S. 712. 1903.

Annual, dark green, or becoming reddish, glabrous. Stem branched from the base, the slender branches prostrate or ascending, 4′–12′ long; leaves oblong to spatulate, 1½″–6″ long, obtuse or retuse, nearly entire, or serrulate to below the middle, short-petioled, the base oblique, mostly truncate or obtuse; stipules at length a fringe of weak setae; involucres solitary in the axils, sometimes clustered toward the ends of the branchlets, less than 1″ long, bearing 4 disk-like glands each subtended by a narrow lobed appendage; capsule 1″ broad, slightly nodding; seeds ovoid, hardly ¾″ long, 4-angled, the faces transversely wrinkled and pitted.

In dry soil, Michigan and Wisconsin to South Dakota, Idaho, Washington, California, south to Missouri, Texas and Mexico. May–Sept.

9. Chamaesyce albicaùlis Rydb. White-stemmed Spurge. Fig. 2740.

Euphorbia albicaulis Rydb. Mem. N. Y. Bot. Gard. 1: 266. 1900.

Chamaesyce albicaulis Rydb. Fl. Colo. 223. 1906.

Annual, pale green or yellowish. Branches procumbent, 4'–12' long, glabrous, shining; leaves linear or slightly broadened upward, 5''–7½'' long, toothed at the apex; involucres turbinate, about ½'' high; appendages minute, rather broad, white, truncate or crenulate; capsule about 1'' long, smooth, acute-angled; seeds light gray, oblong, ¾'' long or less, acutely 4-angled, shallowly transversely wrinkled.

In sandy soil, Nebraska to Montana and New Mexico. June–Sept.

10. Chamaesyce glyptospérma (Engelm.) Small. Ridge-seeded Spurge. Fig. 2741.

Euphorbia glyptosperma Engelm. Bot. Mex. Bound. Surv. 187. 1859.
C. glyptosperma Small, Fl. SE. U. S. 712. 1903.

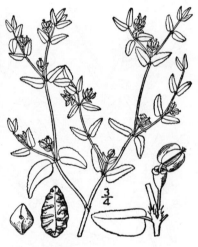

Annual, pale green, glabrous. Stem branched toward the base, the branches ascending, spreading or prostrate, 2'–15' long; leaves oblong, linear-oblong or rarely ovate, 1''–6'' long, more or less falcate, obtuse at the apex, inequilateral, serrulate, very oblique and obtuse or subcordate at the base, short-petioled; stipules becoming a fringe of setae; involucres solitary in the axils, often clustered, campanulate, ½'' long, with 4 dark ribs and 4 saucer-shaped glands, their appendages narrow, crenulate, or slightly lobed; capsule depressed-globose, less than 1'' in diameter, nodding; seeds oblong, ½'' long, ash-colored, strongly transversely wrinkled, not pitted.

In sandy soil, Ontario to British Columbia, Maine, southeastern New York, Wisconsin, Iowa, Texas and Mexico. June–Oct.

11. Chamaesyce stictóspora (Engelm.) Small. Narrow-seeded Spurge. Fig. 2742.

Euphorbia stictospora Engelm. Bot. Mex. Bound. Surv. 187. 1859.

C. stictospora Small, Fl. SE. U. S. 714. 1903.

Annual, yellowish green, pilose throughout. Stem branched from the base, the branches ascending, or radiating, 2'–12' long; leaves oblong to suborbicular, 2''–3'' long, obtuse, dentate-serrate at the apex, short-petioled, the bases truncate or subcordate; stipules fringed; involucres clustered, campanulate, ½'' high, with 4 cup-shaped glands subtended by inconspicuous crenate appendages; peduncles at length longer than the involucres; capsule ovoid, ½''–1'' in diameter; seeds narrowly ovoid, ½'' long, pointed, pitted, gray or ash-colored, sharply 4-angled.

Plains, hills and prairies, South Dakota to Nebraska, Kansas, Colorado and Mexico. June–Oct.

12. Chamaesyce humistràta (Engelm.)
Small. Hairy Spreading Spurge.
Fig. 2743.

Euphorbia humistrata Engelm.; A. Gray, Man. Ed. 2, 386. 1856.
C. humistrata Small, Fl. SE. U. S. 713. 1903.

Annual, light green, puberulent or sparingly pilose. Stem branched from the base, the slender branches radiately spreading, prostrate or ascending, 4′–12′ long; leaves ovate-oblong or obovate-oblong, or sometimes narrower, 2″–7″ long, serrulate, at least above the middle, oblique, obtuse or subcordate at the base, short-petioled; stipules at length fringed; involucres in lateral clusters, split on one side, ½″ long, faintly nerved, with 4 disk-like glands, each subtended by a narrow irregular red or white appendage; capsule depressed-globose, less than 1″ in diameter, its 3 lobes keeled; seeds oblong, ½″ long, papillose, obscurely transversely wrinkled.

Ontario to New York, New Jersey, Minnesota, Kansas and Mississippi. Spotted eyebright. Aug.–Oct.

13. Chamaesyce maculàta (L.) Small.
Milk Purslane. Spotted or Blotched
Spurge. Fig. 2744.

Euphorbia maculata L. Sp. Pl. 455. 1753.
Chamaesyce maculata Small, Fl. SE. U. S. 713. 1903.

Annual, dark green, puberulent or pilose. Stem branched from the base, the branches slender, radiately spreading, prostrate, 2′–15′ long, often dark red; leaves usually blotched, oblong or ovate-oblong, 2″–8″ long, obtuse, more or less serrate, short-petioled, the base oblique, subcordate; stipules a fringe of setae; involucres solitary in the axils, entire, ½″ long, with 4 cup-shaped glands, the appendages narrow, white or red, crenulate; peduncles shorter than the involucres; capsule ovoid-globose, about 1″ in diameter, pubescent; seeds ovoid-oblong, obtusely angled, minutely pitted and transversely wrinkled.

Dry soil, New England to Ontario, Wyoming, Florida and Texas. California. Apparently introduced west of the Rocky Mountains. Spotted or black pusley. Black spurge. Spotted eyebright. Milkweed. June–Nov.

14. Chamaesyce Rafinésqui (Greene) Small.
Hairy Spurge. Fig. 2745.

E. hypericifolia var. *hirsuta* Torr. Fl. N. & Mid. St. 331. 1826. Not *E. hirsuta* Schur, 1853.

Euphorbia hirsuta Wiegand, Bot. Gaz. **24**: 51. 1897.

Euphorbia Rafinesqui Greene, Pittonia 3 : 207. 1897.

Annual, more or less hirsute. Stems branched at the base, the branches prostrate or decumbent, 2′–10′ long, dichotomous, zigzag; leaves ovate-oblong, 4″–8″ long, acutish, serrulate nearly to the oblique base, pale beneath; petioles about ½″ long; stipules lacerate; peduncles surpassing the petioles; involucres funnel-form, ½″ high, glabrous, bearing 4 stalked saucer-shaped dark-brown glands, each subtended by white crenate appendages; capsule about 1″ in diameter, broader than long, glabrous, retuse at the apex, its angles obtuse; seed slightly more than ½″ long, 4-angled, black with a white coating, its faces even or slightly wrinkled.

In sandy or gravelly soil, Quebec and Ontario to Connecticut, New Jersey, Pennsylvania and Illinois. June–Sept.

15. Chamaesyce Préslii (Guss.) Arthur. Large or Upright Spotted Spurge. Fig. 2746.

Euphorbia Preslii Guss. Fl. Sic. Prodr. 1: 539. 1827.
Euphorbia hypericifolia A. Gray, Man. 407. 1848. Not L. 1753.
Chamaesyce Preslii Arthur, Torreya 11: 260. 1912.

Annual, glabrous or sparingly pubescent. Stem branched, at least above, ascending or erect, 7'-2° high, the branches mostly spreading, often recurved at the ends; leaves opposite, oblong, or linear-oblong, varying to ovate or obovate, often falcate, oblique, 3-nerved, unequally serrate, often with a red blotch and red margins, short-petioled; stipules triangular, slightly lacerate; involucres narrowly obovoid, ½" long, one-half or one-third as long as the peduncles, bearing 4 glands subtended by orbicular or reniform entire white or red appendages; capsule glabrous, 1" in diameter; seeds oblong-ovoid, ¾" long, 4-angled, with broken transverse ridges.

In fields and thickets, Ontario to Massachusetts, Florida, Wisconsin, Nebraska and Texas. Has been confused with C. nutans (Lag.) Small, of Mexico. May–Oct.

13. ZYGOPHYLLÍDIUM Small, Fl. SE. U. S. 714. 1903.

Annual herbs, with erect forking stems. Leaves opposite, rarely alternate on the lower part of the stem, narrow, equilateral, not oblique at the base, entire; stipules gland-like, often obsolete. Involucres delicate, short-peduncled in the upper forks. Glands 5, broader than long, subtended by petal-like appendages. Capsules long-pedicelled, 3-lobed. Seeds terete, usually narrowed upward, more or less papillose, the caruncle sometimes wanting. [Greek, resembling Zygophyllum.]

About 5 species, natives of North America. Type species: Zygophyllidium hexagonum (Nutt.) Small.

1. Zygophyllidium hexagònum (Nutt.) Small. Angled Spurge. Fig. 2747.

Euphorbia hexagona Nutt.; Spreng. Syst. 3: 791. 1826.
Zygophyllidium hexagonum Small, Fl. SE. U. S. 714. 1903.

Annual, yellowish green, glabrous or sparingly pubescent. Stem slender, striate-angled, erect, or assurgent, 4'-20' tall, branched, the branches ascending, often almost filiform; leaves opposite, linear, oblong or lanceolate, very short-petioled, obtuse or acute, equilateral; stipules obsolete or very narrow; involucres solitary in the axils, often clustered, 1"-1½" long, ciliate, pubescent, short-peduncled, with 5 glands subtended by triangular-ovate whitish or green appendages; capsule glabrous, 2" in diameter; seeds ovoid or oblong-ovoid, 1½" long, terete, papillose.

Iowa to Montana, Texas and Colorado. Also at Wilmington, Del. June–Oct.

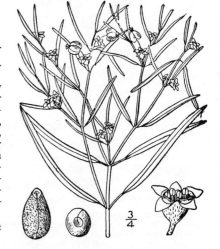

14. DICHROPHÝLLUM Kl. & Garcke, Monatsb. Akad. Ber. 1859: 249.

Annual caulescent herbs, with the erect stems often topped by a several-rayed umbel. Leaves scattered below the umbel, above it opposite or whorled, often petal-like and very showy, entire; stipules at the base of the petioles or leaf-blades, fugacious. Involucres campanulate, in rather dense cymes, pubescent without and within; lobes fimbriate. Glands 5, peltate, somewhat concave, with white or pink petal-like appendages. Capsule exserted, large, pubescent, the lobes rounded. Seeds narrowed upward, reticulated, with caruncles. [Greek, referring to the colored leaves or bracts.]

About 4 species, natives of North America, the following typical.

1. Dichrophyllum marginàtum (Pursh.) Kl. & Garcke. White-margined Spurge. Fig. 2748.

Euphorbia marginata Pursh, Fl. Am. Sept. 607. 1814.
Dichrophyllum marginatum Kl. & Garcke, Monatsb. Akad. Ber. 1859: 249.

Annual, bright green, glabrous or pubescent. Stem rather stout, erect, 10'-3° tall, somewhat channelled, usually pilose, topped by a mostly 3-rayed umbel; leaves except the whorl subtending the umbel, scattered, ovate to obovate, 10''-3½' long, entire, sessile; rays of the umbel forked; bracts large, white-margined; involucres campanulate, often clustered, 2'' long, usually pubescent, bearing 3 glands subtended by white reniform appendages; capsule depressed-globose, 3'' in diameter, usually pubescent, the lobes rounded; seeds ovoid-globose, terete, about 2'' long, dark ash-colored, reticulate-tuberculate.

In dry soil, Minnesota to Colorado, south to Texas. Introduced into waste places in the Central and Atlantic States. Snow-on-the-mountain. Variegated spurge. Mountain snow. May–Oct.

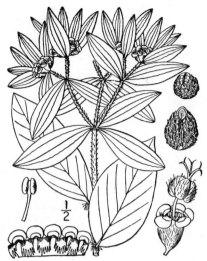

15. TITHYMALÓPSIS Kl. & Garcke, Monatsb. Akad. Ber. 1859: 249.

Perennial herbs, with tough rootstocks and glabrous or pubescent foliage. Stems solitary or tufted, topped by several-rayed umbels. Leaves alternate or scattered below the umbels, thence opposite or whorled, entire, more or less leathery, inclined to be revolute. Involucres sessile or peduncled, few and remote, or in rather close clusters and numerous; lobes toothed or fimbriate Glands sessile or stalked, with white, pink or rose petal-like appendages. Capsule exserted, sometimes conspicuously so, often broader than high; lobes rounded. Seeds narrowed upward, more or less conspicuously punctate, without caruncles. [Greek, resembling *Tithymalus*.]

About 18 species, natives of North America. Type species: *Tithymalopsis corollàta* (L.) Kl. & Garcke.

Involucres with conspicuous petaloid white or pinkish appendages.
   Stems simple below or nearly so, umbellately or paniculately branched above. 1. *T. corollata.*
   Stems tufted or diffusely branched below, dichotomous above.
      Leaves linear-lanceolate to linear; rootstock horizontal.   2. *T. marylandica.*
      Leaves ovate, oval or oblong; rootstock perpendicular.   3. *T. arundelana.*
Involucres with inconspicuous green appendages.   4. *T. Ipecacuanhae.*

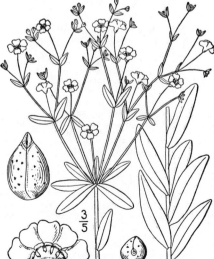

1. Tithymalopsis corollàta (L.) Kl. & Garcke. Blooming or Flowering Spurge. Fig. 2749.

Euphorbia corollata L. Sp. Pl. 459. 1753.
Tithymalopsis corollata Kl. & Garcke, Monatsb. Akad. Ber. 1859: 249.

Perennial by a long stout rootstock, bright green, glabrous or somewhat pubescent. Stem erect, 10'-3° tall, often spotted, usually simple; umbellately or paniculately branched above; leaves linear, oblong or oblong-spatulate, 10''-20'' long, entire, short-petioled or sessile, the lower scattered, those subtending the umbel verticillate; rays of the umbel forked; bracts ovate to linear, green; involucres mostly terminal, less than 1'' long, bearing 4 or 5 yellowish green oblong glands subtended by white petal-like cuneate or orbicular-cuneate appendages; capsule erect, subglobose, 1''-2'' in diameter; seeds ovoid, smooth, sparingly pitted.

In dry soil, Ontario to Massachusetts, Minnesota, Kansas, Florida and Texas. April–Oct. Ascends to 4200 ft. in North Carolina. Apple-, bowman- or purging-root. Picac. Milk- or white purslane. Milk-pusley or -ipecac. Milkweed. Snake-milk. Wild hippo. Naturalized in its northeastern range.

3. Tithymalopsis arundelàna
(Bartlett) Small. Anne Arundel Spurge. Fig. 2751.

Euphorbia arundelana Bartlett, Rhodora 13: 364. 1911.

Perennial, with perpendicular stout rootstocks, glabrous or pubescent, bright green. Stems tufted as in *T. Ipecacuanhae,* stout, 8' tall or less, dichotomous or trichotomous above; leaves scale-like on the lower part of the stems, the upper ones mostly 1' long or less, ovate, oval or oblong, obtuse; involucres hemispheric, about 1" high, those on the lower part of the stem very long-peduncled, the upper ones shorter-peduncled; appendages white or pink, suborbicular.

In sandy places, Anne Arundel County, Maryland. May–June.

2. Tithymalopsis marylándica
(Greene) Small. Maryland Spurge. Fig. 2750.

Euphorbia marylandica Greene, Pittonia 3: 345. 1898.

Perennial, with horizontal rootstocks, glabrous, pale green, glaucescent. Stems trichotomous near the base, thence bushy, 16' tall or less, the branches dichotomous; leaves linear to linear-lanceolate, $\frac{3}{4}'-1\frac{1}{2}'$ long, acute, opposite above the whorl of 3 at the first fork; involucres hemispheric, nearly 1" high, rather short-peduncled; appendages white, suborbicular to reniform.

On sand hills, Anne Arundel County, Maryland. Summer.

4. Tithymalopsis Ipecacuanhae (L.)
Small. Wild Ipecac. Ipecac Spurge. Fig. 2752.

Euphorbia Ipecacuanhae L. Sp. Pl. 455. 1753.
Tithymalopsis Ipecacuanhae Small, Fl. SE. U. S. 716. 1903

Perennial by a deep perpendicular root, glabrous or pubescent. Stems several or many, slender, spreading, ascending or nearly erect, 4'–10' long, branched; leaves green or red, wonderfully variable in outline from linear to orbicular, 5"–3' long, mostly opposite, entire, the upper sometimes whorled, the lower often alternate, short-petioled; involucres axillary, mostly hemispheric, nearly 1" long, slender-peduncled; bearing 5 transversely elliptic or oblong green sessile unappendaged glands; capsule $1\frac{1}{2}''$ in diameter, nodding; seeds light gray, oblong-ovoid or ovoid, $1\frac{1}{2}''$ long, pitted, obscurely 4-sided.

In dry sandy soil, Connecticut to Florida, mostly near the coast. Also in southern Indiana. An emetic. Spurge-ipecac. American white ipecac. May–Oct.

16. TITHYMÀLUS [Tourn.] Adans. Fam. 2: 355. 1763.

Annual or perennial herbs or shrubby plants, with simple or branched stems, which are topped by several-rayed umbel-like cymes. Leaves below the umbel usually scattered or alternate, without stipules, often broadened upward. Bracts of the umbel quite different from the stem-leaves; blades entire or toothed. Involucres sessile or peduncled, axillary, disposed in open or close cymes; lobes often toothed. Glands 4, transversely oblong, reniform or crescent-shaped by the horn-like appendages, the missing one represented by a thin often ciliate lobe. Capsule exserted, smooth or tuberculate; lobes rounded, sharp or keeled. Seeds variously pitted, often with caruncles. [Greek, referring to the milky juice of these plants.]

About 250 species of wide geographic distribution. Besides the following, several others occur in western North America. Type species: *Euphorbia dendroides* L.

Leaves mainly opposite and decussate; capsules 5″ wide or more.   1. *T. Lathyrus.*
Leaves alternate or scattered; capsules less than 5″ wide.
   Leaves serrulate; glands of the involucre oblong, oval or orbicular.
      Seeds smooth or faintly reticulated.
         Glands stalked; warts on the capsules elongated; seeds faintly reticulated.
                                     2. *T. obtusatus.*
         Glands sessile; warts on the capsules depressed; seeds smooth.   3. *T. platyphyllus.*
      Seeds strongly and prominently reticulated.
         Glands nearly sessile; capsules warty.
            Upper stem-leaves with small basal lobes; bracts of the umbel about as broad as long
              or broader.   4. *T. missouriensis.*
            Upper stem-leaves merely sessile; bracts of the umbel manifestly longer than broad.
                                       5. *T. arkansanus.*
         Glands stalked; capsules smooth.   6. *T. Helioscopia.*
   Leaves entire; glands of the involucres crescent-shaped or reniform.
      Plants perennial; seeds smooth.
         Glands crescent-shaped, horned.
            Stem-leaves 2″–6″ broad; capsules smooth.
               Leaves subtending, the umbel lanceolate or oblanceolate.   7. *T. Esula.*
               Leaves subtending, the umbel ovate, oval or obovate.   8. *T. lucidus.*
             Stem-leaves ¼″–1½″ broad; capsules granular on the lobes.   9. *T. Cyparissias.*
         Glands reniform, not horned.   10. *T. Darlingtonii.*
      Plants annual or biennial; seeds pitted or rugose-pitted.
         Leaves thin, petioled.
             Capsules with 2-crested lobes.   11. *T. Peplus.*
             Capsules with rounded lobes.   12. *T. commutatus.*
         Leaves thick, sessile.   13. *T. robustus.*

1. Tithymalus Láthyrus (L.) Hill. Caper or Myrtle Spurge. Fig. 2753.

Euphorbia Lathyrus L. Sp. Pl. 457. 1753.

Tithymalus Lathyrus Hill, Hort. Kew. 172/3. 1768.

Annual or biennial, glabrous, stout, glaucous. Stem usually erect, stout, 8′–3° tall, mostly simple below, umbellately branched above; leaves numerous, the lower scattered, those subtending the umbel verticillate, the lower linear, reflexed, the upper lanceolate or linear-lanceolate, 1½′–5′ long, entire, sessile, subcordate at the base; bracts opposite, ovate or ovate-lanceolate, truncate or subcordate; involucres 2½″ long, bearing 4 crescent-shaped unappendaged glands prolonged into short horns; capsule subglobose, 5″–6″ in diameter, its lobes rounded; seeds oblong-ovoid, 2½″–3″ long, terete, usually wrinkled.

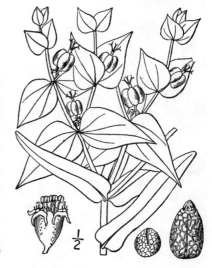

In waste places, Connecticut to North Carolina. Also in California. Native of Europe. Wild caper. Caper-bush. Mole-tree or -plant. Spring-wort; its seeds a cathartic. May–Aug.

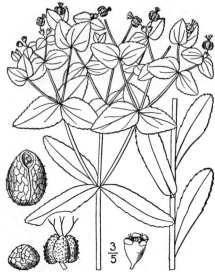

2. Tithymalus obtusàtus (Pursh) Kl. & Garcke. Blunt-leaved Spurge.
Fig. 2754.

Euphorbia obtusata Pursh, Fl. Am. Sept. 606. 1814.

Tithymalus obtusatus Kl. & Garcke, Abh. Akad. Ber. 1859: 69.

Annual, yellowish green, glabrous. Stem slender, erect or assurgent, 1°–2° high, strict, branched above, topped by a 3-rayed umbel; branches simple or forked; leaves, except the whorl, subtending the umbel, scattered, spatulate-oblong, obtuse, serrulate to below the middle, sessile, the base slightly auricled; involucres short-peduncled, ½″ long, bearing 4 stalked unappendaged glands; capsule subglobose, nearly 2″ in diameter, with elongated warts, the lobes rounded; seeds lenticular, oblong, or orbicular-oblong, dark brown, faintly reticulated.

In dry soil, Pennsylvania to Iowa, Kansas, South Carolina and Texas. Warted spurge. March–July.

3. Tithymalus platyphýllus (L.) Hill. Broad-leaved Spurge. Fig. 2755.

Euphorbia platyphylla L. Sp. Pl. 460. 1753.
T. platyphyllus Hill, Hort. Kew. 172/4. 1768.

Annual, glabrous or nearly so. Stems mostly erect, slender, 4′–20′ high, terete, often reddish, topped by a usually 5-rayed umbel; the branches forked or umbellately branched; leaves except the whorl at base of the umbel, scattered, oblong or spatulate-oblong, 10″–15″ long, acute, serrulate, sessile, the base slightly auricled; bracts triangular-ovate or reniform, mucronate, often entire; involucres very thin, campanulate, nearly 1″ long, sessile, bearing 4 sessile glands without appendages; capsule subglobose, about 2″ in diameter, with depressed warts, the lobes rounded; seeds lenticular, oblong or nearly orbicular, smooth, brown.

Along the shores of the St. Lawrence River and the Great Lakes, west to Manitoba. Naturalized from Europe. June–Sept.

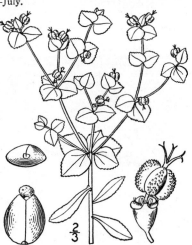

4. Tithymalus missouriénsis (Norton) Small. Reticulate-seeded Spurge.
Fig. 2756.

E. arkansana missouriensis Norton, Rep. Mo. Bot. Gard. 11: 103. 1900.
T. missouriensis Small, Fl. SE. U. S. 721. 1903.

Annual, olive green, glabrous. Stem erect, rather slender, 4′–15′ high, topped by a compound 3-rayed umbel; branches forked; leaves, except those subtending the umbel, scattered, spatulate or oblong, 5″–1½′ long; obtuse, serrate to below the middle, sessile, the upper slightly auricled at the base; bracts roundish or ovate, inequilateral, small, serrate, cordate; involucres solitary in the axils, less than 1″ long, with 4 oblong naked nearly sessile glands; capsule depressed-globose, 1½″ in diameter, with elongated warts; seeds ovoid, lenticular, reddish brown, finely but distinctly reticulated.

Minnesota and Iowa to Montana, Washington, Alabama and New Mexico. Included in our first edition in Euphorbia dictyosperma F. & M., a far western species. May–Aug.

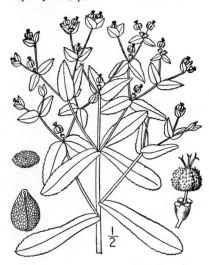

5. Tithymalus arkansànus (Engelm. & Gray) Kl. & Garcke. Arkansas Spurge. Fig. 2757.

Euphorbia dictyosperma Engelm. in Torr. Bot. Mex.
Bound. Surv. 191. 1859. Not F. & M. 1835.
Euphorbia arkansana Engelm. & Gray, Bost. Journ. Nat.
Hist. **5** : 53. 1845.
Tithymalus arkansanus Kl. & Garcke, Abh. Akad. Berlin
1859 : 66.

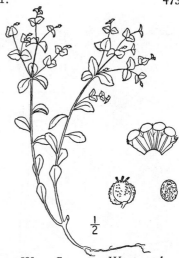

Annual, olive green. Stem slender, 8′–20′ tall, with
few spreading branches above, topped by umbels
with 3 copiously dichotomous rays $\frac{3}{4}′$–$1\frac{1}{4}′$ long; stem-
leaves cuneate or spatulate, $\frac{1}{2}′$–$1\frac{1}{4}′$ long, rather acute,
serrulate above the middle; bracts ovate to triangu-
lar-ovate, $\frac{1}{4}′$–$\frac{3}{4}′$ long, truncate or subcordate at the
base, mucronate at the apex; involucres about $\frac{1}{2}″$
high, with transversely elliptic glands less than $\frac{1}{2}″$
wide, the lobes usually ciliate; capsules $1\frac{1}{4}″$–$1\frac{1}{2}″$ wide,
warty; seeds ovoid, closely reticulated, brown.

Dry soil, Missouri to Colorado, Louisiana and Mexico.
May–Aug.

6. Tithymalus Helioscòpia (L.) Hill. Sun or Wart Spurge. Wartweed. Fig. 2758.

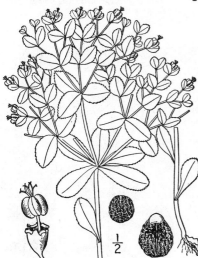

Euphorbia Helioscopia L. Sp. Pl. 459. 1753.
Tithymalus Helioscopia Hill, Hort. Kew. 172/3. 1768.

Annual, glabrous or nearly so. Stem stout,
erect or assurgent, 8′–12′ tall, often branched
from the base, topped like the branches by a more
or less compound 3–5-rayed umbel; leaves, except
the whorl at the base of the umbel, scattered,
spatulate, obovate, oblong, or sometimes nearly
orbicular, $\frac{1}{2}′$–$4\frac{1}{2}′$ long, obtuse or retuse, serrulate,
narrowed to a short petiole; bracts oblong or
ovate, serrulate, inequilateral, sessile; involucres
oblong-campanulate, $1\frac{1}{4}″$ long, nearly sessile,
usually with 4 oblong stalked unappendaged
glands; capsule globose-ovoid, or somewhat depressed, 2″ in diameter, smooth, the lobes rounded; seeds ovoid, nearly $1\frac{1}{2}″$ long, reddish brown,
strongly reticulate.

In waste places, Newfoundland to Quebec, Ontario,
New York and Ohio. Also in Oregon. Naturalized
from Europe. Sun-weed. Turnsole. Little-good. Cat's-
milk. Wolf's-milk. Churnstaff. Wart-grass. Mouse-
milk. Wartwort. Mad-woman's-milk. Devil's-milk.
Seven sisters. June–Oct.

7. Tithymalus Ésula (L.) Hill. Leafy Spurge. Faitour's Grass. Fig. 2759.

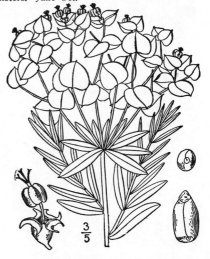

Euphorbia Esula L. Sp. Pl. 461. 1753.
Tithymalus Esula Hill, Hort. Kew. 174/4. 1768.

Perennial by a horizontal rootstock, glabrous.
Stems often clustered, slender, mostly erect, 8′–2°
tall, scaly below, branched above, topped by a
many-rayed umbel; leaves few, all scattered, except the whorl at the base of the umbel, linear or
oblong, 7″–20″ long, 2″–6″ broad, entire, sessile;
those subtending the umbel lanceolate or oblanceolate; bracts subreniform, mucronate; invo-
lucres campanulate, $1\frac{1}{4}″$–$1\frac{1}{2}″$ long, nearly sessile,
bearing 4 unappendaged crescent-shaped glands;
capsule nodding, smooth; seeds oblong, terete,
smooth.

In waste places, Maine to Ontario, New York, New
Jersey and Michigan. Tithymal. Naturalized from
Europe. Summer.

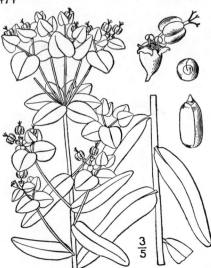

$\frac{3}{5}$

8. Tithymalus lùcidus (Waldst. & Kit.) Kl. & Garcke. Shining Spurge. Fig. 2760.

Euphorbia lucida Waldst. & Kit. Pl. Rar. Hung. 1: 54. *pl. 54*. 1802.
T. lucidus Kl. & Garcke, Abh. Akad. Berlin 1859: 66.

Perennial by a horizontal rootstock, bright green, glabrous. Stems rather stout, usually clustered, erect or assurgent, 8'–20' high, usually very leafy, simple or branched, topped by a 4–7-rayed umbel; branches simple or forked; leaves, except the whorl at the base of the umbel, alternate, linear or linear-oblong, ½'–1½' long, 2''–6'' broad, entire, mostly apiculate, sessile, revolute-margined, those subtending the umbel ovate, oval or obovate; bracts opposite, reniform, obtuse or apiculate; involucres campanulate, 1½'' long, sessile, bearing 4 yellowish oblong crescent-shaped, 2-horned, unappendaged glands; capsule globose-ovoid, 2'' in diameter, nodding, finely wrinkled; seeds 1¼''–1½'' long, nearly terete, whitish, smooth.

In fields along the Susquehanna River, southern New York and Pennsylvania. Formerly mistaken for *Euphorbia nicaeensis* All. Naturalized from Europe. July–Sept.

9. Tithymalus Cyparíssias (L.) Hill. Cypress Spurge. Fig. 2761.

Euphorbia Cyparissias L. Sp. Pl. 461. 1753.
T. Cyparissias Hill, Hort. Kew. 172/4. 1768.

Perennial by horizontal rootstocks, bright green, glabrous. Stems mostly clustered, often growing in large patches, scaly below, leafy above, erect, 1° high, or less, branched, the branches topped by many-rayed umbels; leaves linear, or almost filiform, those subtending the umbels whorled, the others alternate, sessile, 6''–1' long, ¼''–1½'' broad; involucres turbinate-campanulate, 1'' long, short-peduncled, with 4 unappendaged crescent-shaped glands; capsule sub-globose, 1½'' in diameter, spreading, granular on the rounded lobes; seeds oblong, 1'' long, smooth.

Escaped from gardens to roadsides and waste places, Massachusetts to Virginia and Colorado. Naturalized from Europe. Quack salver's spurge. Tree- or Irish-moss. Balsam. Garden-spurge. Graveyard-weed. Welcome-to-our-house. Kiss-me-Dick. Cypress. Bonaparte's crown. Poisonous when eaten in quantities. Bracts yellowish. May–Sept.

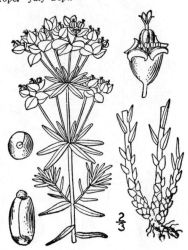

$\frac{2}{3}$

$\frac{3}{5}$

10. Tithymalus Darlingtònii (A. Gray) Small. Darlington's Spurge. Fig. 2762.

Euphorbia Darlingtonii A. Gray, Man. 404. 1848.
T. Darlingtonii Small, Fl. SE. U. S. 719. 1903.

Perennial, dark green, often minutely pubescent. Stem rather stout, erect, 1½°–5° tall, fleshy, topped by a 5–8-rayed umbel, branched above, the branches simple or forked; the leaves oblong or oblanceolate, 1½''–4' long, mostly obtuse at the apex, sessile, often undulate, more or less pubescent beneath, those of the stem scattered, those subtending the umbels verticillate; bracts opposite, ovate or nearly reniform; involucres campanulate, nearly 2'' long, bearing 5 reniform crenulate unappendaged glands; capsule depressed-globose, minutely warty; seeds ovoid-globose.

New York, Pennsylvania and New Jersey to West Virginia and North Carolina. May–Sept.

11. Tithymalus Péplus (L.) Hill. Petty Spurge.
Fig. 2763.

Euphorbia Peplus L. Sp. Pl. 456. 1753.
Tithymalus Peplus Hill, Hort. Kew. 172/3. 1768.

Annual, glabrous. Stem rather slender, erect or nearly so, 4′–12′ high, simple or branched, topped by a 3–5-rayed umbel; stem-leaves scattered, oblong or obovate, ½′–1¼′ long, obtuse or retuse, entire, crisped, narrowed into a slender petiole; those at the base of the umbel whorled; bracts opposite, ovate or triangular-ovate, apiculate, sessile; involucres campanulate, almost sessile, less than 1″ long, bearing 4 crescent-shaped unappendaged glands prolonged into slender horns; capsule globose-ovoid, 1″–1½″ in diameter, slightly nodding, smooth, the lobes 2-keeled; seeds oblong or oblong-ovoid, whitish, nearly terete, marked with 1–4 series of pits.

In waste places, New Brunswick to western New York, Wisconsin, Iowa, New Jersey, Pennsylvania and West Virginia. Bermuda, Jamaica. Adventive from Europe. Devil's-milk. Seven sisters. Wartweed. June–Sept.

12. Tithymalus commutàtus (Engelm.) Kl. & Garcke. Tinted Spurge.
Fig. 2764.

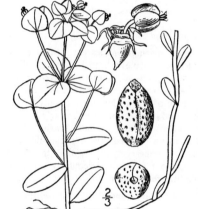

Euphorbia commutata Engelm. in A. Gray, Man. Ed. 2, 389. 1856.
Tithymalus commutatus Kl. & Garcke, Abh. Akad. Ber. 1859: 82.
Euphorbia ohiotica Steud. & Hochst.; Boiss. in DC. Prodr. 15: Part 2, 142. 1862.

Biennial, yellowish green, often tinged with red, glabrous. Stem slender, usually decumbent at the base, 4′–15′ long, branched, topped by a 3-rayed umbel; branches forked or umbellately branched; leaves, except the whorl at the base of the umbel, scattered, spatulate to ovate, ½′–1½′ long, obtuse or mucronulate, entire, flat, narrowed into a slender petiole; bracts opposite, ovate-reniform; involucres campanulate, 1¼″ long, sessile, bearing 3 or 4 crescent-shaped unappendaged glands prolonged into slender horns; capsule globose-ovoid, 1½″ in diameter, glabrous, the lobes rounded; seeds oblong, terete, irregularly pitted.

On hillsides, chiefly along streams, Ontario to Minnesota, Pennsylvania, Florida and Missouri. March–July.

Tithymalus falcàtus (L.) Kl. & Garcke, a native of Europe, with spatulate leaves, subulate-tipped bracts and rugose-pitted seeds, has been found in western Virginia.

13. Tithymalus robústus (Engelm.) Small. Rocky Mountain Spurge. Fig. 2765.

Euphorbia montana β *robusta* Engelm. Bot. Mex. Bound. Surv. 192. 1859.
E. robusta Small, in Britt. & Brown, Ill. Fl. 2: 381. 1897.

Perennial by a perpendicular rootstock, glabrous, glaucous. Stems slender, clustered, erect or assurgent, 4′–14′ tall, slightly angled, scaly below, branched, topped by a 3–5-rayed umbel; leaves, except the whorl subtending the umbel, scattered, ovate or oblong-ovate, 5″–8″ long, thick, obtuse or apiculate, entire, sessile; bracts opposite, triangular-ovate or subreniform, involucres campanulate, 1½″ long, sessile, bearing 4 somewhat crescent-shaped unappendaged buff crenulate glands; capsule globose-ovoid, 2″ long, horizontal, its lobes rounded; seeds oblong or obovoid-oblong, terete, 1¼″ long, gray, minutely pitted.

Hills and plains, South Dakota to Montana, Wyoming, Nebraska, Arkansas and Arizona. May–Oct.

17. POINSÉTTIA Graham, Edinb. N. Phil. Journ. 20: 412. 1836.

Annual or perennial herbs or shrubby plants, with green or partially, often more highly colored, foliage. Stems simple or branched, often irregularly so. Leaves alternate below, opposite above, similar throughout or very variable; stipules gland-like. Involucres in axillary or terminal cymes or solitary; lobes fimbriate. Glands fleshy, solitary, or rarely 3 or 4, sessile or short-stalked, without appendages, the missing ones represented by narrow lobes. Capsule exserted, the lobes rounded. Seed narrowed upward, tuberculate, without a caruncle or with a minute one only. [In honor of Joel Roberts Poinsette, of South Carolina.]

About 12 species, mostly natives of tropical America. Type species: *Poinsettia pulcherrima* (Willd.) Graham.

Glands of the involucre stalked; leaves nearly or quite uniform.
  Leaves linear or linear-lanceolate; seeds narrowly ovoid, not prominently tuberculate.
                                                                          1. *P. cuphosperma.*
  Leaves ovate or ovate-lanceolate; seeds broadly ovoid, prominently tuberculate.
                                                                          2. *P. dentata.*
Glands of the involucre sessile; leaves various.   3. *P. heterophylla.*

1. Poinsettia cuphospérma (Engelm.) Small.   Warty Spurge.   Fig. 2766.

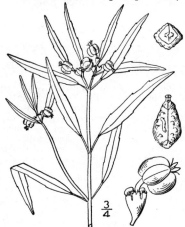

Euphorbia dentata var. *cuphosperma* Engelm. Bot. Mex. Bound. Surv. 190. 1859.

Euphorbia cuphosperma Boiss. in DC. Prodr. 15: Part 2, 73. 1862.

Poinsettia cuphosperma Small, Fl. SE. U. S. 721. 1903.

Annual, usually sparingly pubescent. Stem erect, slender, simple, or sparingly branched, 8′–15′ high. Leaves opposite or alternate, linear, oblong, or linear-lanceolate, 10″–3′ long, entire, undulate, or denticulate, narrowed into a slender petiole; involucres crowded at the ends of the branches, nearly sessile, glabrous, or nearly so, nearly 2″ long, bearing about 4 long-stalked unappendaged glands; capsule glabrous, or sparingly pubescent, 2½″ in diameter, seeds narrowly ovoid, about 1½″ long, irregularly 4-angled, ridged and slightly tuberculate.

South Dakota to Colorado and Mexico   Aug–Sept.

2. Poinsettia dentàta (Michx.) Small.   Toothed Spurge.   Fig. 2767.

Euphorbia dentata Michx Fl. Bor. Am. 2: 211. 1803.
Poinsettia dentata Small, Fl. SE. U. S. 722. 1903.

Annual, dull green, pubescent. Stem erect or ascending, 8′–15′ high, somewhat woody below, branched, the branches mostly ascending; leaves opposite, or the lowest alternate, varying from ovate to nearly linear or orbicular-oblong, 5″–3½′ long, coarsely dentate, narrowed into slender petioles, the nerves prominent beneath; involucres clustered at the ends of the branches, oblong-campanulate, about 1½″ long, 3–5-lobed, bearing 1–4 yellowish short-stalked glands without appendages; capsule glabrous, 2″–2½″ in diameter; seeds ovoid or ovoid-globose, ash-colored, irregularly tuberculate, inconspicuously 4-angled.

In dry or moist soil, Pennsylvania to South Dakota, Wyoming, Tennessee, Louisiana and Mexico. July–Oct.

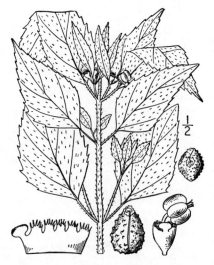

3. Poinsettia heterophýlla (L.) Kl. & Garcke. Various-leaved Spurge. Fig. 2768.

Euphorbia heterophylla L. Sp. Pl. 453. 1753.
P. heterophylla Kl. & Garcke, Monatsb. Akad. Berlin 1859: 253.

Annual or biennial, bright green, pubescent or nearly glabrous. Stem mostly erect, 1°–3° tall, woody below, with the branches ascending, or the lower spreading, leafy at the ends; leaves alternate, very variable, linear to orbicular, entire, undulate, sinuate or dentate, the uppermost often fiddle-shaped and blotched with red; all slender-petioled; involucres clustered at the ends of branches, 1½″ long, about equalling the peduncles; cleft into 5 ovate or oblong laciniate lobes, the sinuses bearing 1 or several sessile glands without appendages; capsule glabrous or minutely pubescent, 3″ in diameter; seeds oblong-ovoid, 1½″ long, transversely wrinkled and tuberculate.

Illinois to South Dakota, Florida, Kansas and Texas. Tropical America. April–Nov.

Family 71. CALLITRICHÀCEAE Lindl. Nat. Syst. Ed. 2, 191. 1836.*

WATER STARWORT FAMILY.

Herbaceous aquatic or rarely terrestrial plants, with slender or capillary stems, opposite exstipulate entire spatulate or linear leaves, and minute perfect or monoecious axillary flowers. Perianth none. Bracts 2, sac-like or none. Stamen 1; filament elongated, filiform; anthers cordate, 2-celled, opening by lateral slits. Pistil 1; ovary 4-celled; ovules 1 in each cavity; styles 2, filiform, papillose nearly the whole length. Fruit compressed, lobed, the lobes more or less winged or keeled on the margins, separating at maturity into 4 flattish 1-seeded carpels. Seed anatropous, pendulous; endosperm fleshy; embryo straight or slightly curved, nearly as long as the endosperm.

Consists of the following genus:

1. CALLÍTRICHE L. Sp. Pl. 969. 1753.

Characters of the family. The affinities are variously regarded by botanical authors, some placing it in HALORAGIDACEAE, some in ONAGRACEAE, others near EUPHORBIACEAE, the position here maintained. [Greek, beautiful hair, from the hair-like stems.]

About 20 species, of very wide geographic distribution. Besides the following, about 7 others occur in the southern and western parts of North America. Type species: *Callitriche palustris* L.

Fruit short-peduncled; bracts wanting; terrestrial.　　1. *C. Austini.*
Fruit sessile; aquatic, or some forms growing in mud.
　Bracts present.
　　Fruit oval, flat on the face, longer than the styles.　　2. *C. palustris.*
　　Fruit obovate, plano-convex, shorter than the styles.　　3. *C. heterophylla.*
　Bracts none; leaves all linear, submersed.　　4. *C. autumnalis.*

1. Callitriche Aùstini Engelm. Terrestrial Water-Starwort. Fig. 2769.

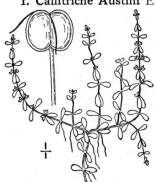

Callitriche terrestre Raf. Med. Rep. (II.) 5: 358. 1808?
Callitriche deflexa var. *Austini* Hegelm. Ver. Bot. Ver. Brand. 9: 15. 1867.
C. Austini Engelm. in A. Gray, Man. Ed. 5, 428. 1867.

Tufted, the branches spreading on the ground or ascending, ½′–2′ long. Leaves spatulate or obovate, 3-nerved, 1½″–2″ long, about 1″ wide, obtuse, tapering at the base into a short margined petiole, destitute of stellate scales; fruit about ¼″ long and nearly ½″ broad, deeply notched at both ends, its lobes with a narrow marginal wing or raised border, with a deep groove between them; peduncle shorter than or slightly exceeding the fruit; styles persistent, not longer than the fruit, spreading or reflexed.

In damp, shaded places, Connecticut to Delaware, Ohio, Missouri, Louisiana, Texas and Mexico. July–Sept. The dried plant exhales a pleasant odor like melilot.

* Text written for the first edition by the late REV. THOMAS MORONG, here slightly revised.

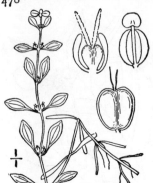

2. Callitriche palústris L.   Vernal Water-Starwort.   Water Fennel.   Fig. 2770.

Callitriche palustris L. Sp. Pl. 969. 1753.
Callitriche verna L. Fl. Suec. Ed. 2, 4. 1755.
Callitriche vernalis Koch, Syn. Fl. Germ. Ed. 2, 245. 1837.

Aquatic or growing in the mud, stems 2′–10′ long. Submerged leaves linear, 1-nerved, retuse or bifid at the apex, 5″–10″ long; emersed or floating leaves obovate, obtuse, truncate or retuse at the apex, narrowed at the base into a margined petiole, dotted with stellate scales; aquatic forms occur with the leaves all linear; fruit 2-bracted, oval, ½″–1″ long, about one-half as broad, nearly flat on the face, slightly notched at the apex, winged only toward the apex, or all around, separated by a deep groove.

Mostly in cold or running water, apparently occurring nearly throughout the United States and Canada. Also in South America, Europe and Asia. Water-chickweed. July–Sept.

3. Callitriche heterophýlla Pursh.   Larger Water-Starwort.   Fig. 2771.

Callitriche heterophylla Pursh, Fl. Am. Sept. 3. 1814.

Similar to the preceding species, either aquatic or growing in the mud. Fruit smaller, mostly obovate, usually slightly less than ½″ long, and about the same breadth, broadly notched at the apex, thick, plano-convex, almost ventricose at the base; lobes obtusely angled with a small intervening groove, wingless, or with a narrow wing or raised border on the margins; styles usually longer than the fruit, erect.

In ponds and slow streams, Newfoundland to Manitoba, Florida, Missouri, Colorado and Louisiana. July–Sept.

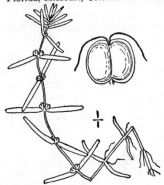

4. Callitriche autumnàlis L.   Autumnal or Northern Water-Starwort.   Fig. 2772.

Callitriche palustris var. *bifida* L. Sp. Pl. 696. 1753.
Callitriche autumnalis L. Fl. Suec. Ed. 2, 4. 1755.
Callitriche bifida Morong, Mem. Torr. Club 5 : 215. 1894.

Entirely submerged. Leaves crowded, linear or linear-lanceolate, clasping at the base, retuse or bifid at the apex, 1-nerved, 5″–8″ long, without stellate scales; fruit sessile, or rarely minutely pedunculate, orbicular or slightly narrower than long, ½″–1″ in diameter, its lobes separated by a deep groove and broadly winged on the margins; styles as long as the fruit, or shorter, soon deciduous; bracts none.

In flowing water, Quebec and Lake Champlain to Michigan, Manitoba and Oregon, south in the Rocky Mountains to Colorado. Also in Europe and Asia. July–Sept.

Family 72. EMPETRÀCEAE Dumort. Fl. Belg. 106. 1827.

CROWBERRY FAMILY.

Low evergreen shrubs, with small narrow nearly sessile exstipulate leaves jointed to short pulvini, channeled on the lower side by the revolute margins, and small dioecious or rerely polygamous flowers, axillary or in terminal heads. Calyx of 3 sepals. Corolla or 2 or 3 petals, or none. Staminate flowers with 2–4 (mostly 3) stamens, the filaments filiform, the anthers 2-celled, longitudinally dehiscent, sometimes with a rudimentary pistil. Pistillate flowers with a 2–several-celled sessile ovary, the single style cleft into as many stigma-bearing segments as there are ovary-cavities; ovules 1 in each cavity, amphitropous. Fruit a berry-like drupe, containing 2–several 1-seeded nutlets. Embryo straight, terete, in copious endosperm.

Three known genera, the following, and the monotypic *Ceratiola* of the southeastern United States.

Flowers axillary ; petals 3.   1. *Empetrum.*
Flowers in terminal heads ; petals none.   2. *Corema.*

1. ÉMPETRUM [Tourn.] L. Sp. Pl. 1022. 1753.

Depressed or spreading herbaceous shrubs, freely branching, dioecious or monoecious, the branches usually densely leafy, the leaves linear-oblong. Flowers inconspicuous, solitary in the upper axils. Sepals and petals mostly 3. Staminate flowers with 3 stamens, the anthers introrse. Pistillate flowers with a globose 6–9-celled ovary, and a short thick style with 6–9-toothed segments. Drupe black to red, containing 6–9 nutlets. [Greek, on rocks, referring to the growth of these plants in rocky places.]

Two known species, the following typical one, and *C. rubrum* of southern South America.

1. Empetrum nìgrum L. Black Crowberry. Heathberry. Fig. 2773.

Empetrum nigrum L. Sp. Pl. 1022. 1753.

Glabrous, or the young shoots and leaves pubescent, usually much branched, the branches diffusely spreading, 2'–10' long. Leaves crowded, dark green, linear-oblong, thick, obtuse, 2"–3½" long, about ½" wide, the strongly revolute margins roughish; flowers very small, purplish; stamens exserted; drupe black, purple or red, 2"–3" in diameter.

In rocky places, Greenland to Alaska, south to the coast of Maine, the higher mountains of New England and northern New York, Michigan and California. Also in Europe and Asia. Crake-berry. Black-berried heath. Wire-ling. Crow-pea. Monox-heather. Heath. Hog-cranberry. Crowberry. Curlew-berry. Grows in dense beds; the fruit much eaten by arctic birds. Summer.

2. CORÈMA Don, Edinb. New Phil. Journ. 15: 63. 1826–27.

[OAKESIA Tuckerm. in Hook. Lond. Journ. Bot. 1: 445. 1842.]

Low, much branched shrubs, with narrowly linear leaves crowded on the branches, and small dioecious or polygamous flowers in terminal heads. Corolla none. Staminate flowers with 3 or sometimes 4 long-exserted stamens, occasionally with a rudimentary or perfect pistil. Pistillate flowers with a 2–5-celled (mostly 3-celled) ovary and a slender 2–5-cleft style, the stigmatic branches very slender, sometimes toothed. Drupe globose, usually with 3 nutlets. [Greek, a broom, in allusion to the bushy habit.]

Two species, the following of the eastern United States, the other, the generic type, of southwestern Europe, the Azores and Canaries.

1. Corema Conràdii Torr. Conrad's Broom Crowberry. Fig. 2774.

Empetrum Conradii Torr. Ann. Lyc. N. Y. 4: 83. 1837.
C. Conradii Torr.; Loudon, Encycl. Trees 1092. 1842.

Much branched, 6'–2° high, the young twigs puberulent and densely leafy, the branches minutely scarred by the persistent pulvini. Leaves 2"–3" long, rather less than ½" wide, obtuse, glabrous when mature, bright green; flowers numerous in the terminal sessile heads, the pistillate ones almost concealed by the upper leaves, the staminate conspicuous by the exserted purple stamens; drupes nearly dry, less than 1" in diameter.

In rocky or sandy soil, Newfoundland to Massachusetts and New Jersey, mostly near the coast; but occurring in one station on the Shawangunk Mountains in Ulster Co., N. Y. Local. Usually growing in large patches. April–May. Brown or Plymouth crowberry. Poverty-grass.

Family 73. **BUXÀCEAE** Dumort. Comm. Bot. 54. 1822.

BOX FAMILY.

Monoecious or dioecious trees, shrubs or perennial herbs, with alternate or opposite simple mostly evergreen leaves, the sap not milky. Flowers clustered or solitary, regular, bracted, with or without a perianth (calyx). Petals none. Staminate flowers with 4–7 distinct stamens, the anthers 2-celled; sometimes with a rudimentary pistil. Pistillate flowers with a 2–4-celled (mostly 3-celled) ovary, with 2 or 1 anatropous ovules in each cavity; styles as many as the ovary-cavities, simple. Fruit a capsule or drupe, its carpels 1–2-seeded. Embryo straight; endosperm fleshy, or almost wanting.

About 6 genera and 35 species, only the following and the Californian *Simmondsia* in continental North America.

I. **PACHYSÁNDRA** Michx. Fl. Bor. Am. **2**: 177. 1803.

Monoecious perennial herbs, with matted rootstocks, the stems procumbent or ascending, leafy above, scaly or naked below. Leaves alternate, exstipulate, petioled, persistent, broad, 3-nerved, coarsely toothed, or entire. Flowers spicate, the pistillate and staminate in the same spike. Staminate flowers with 4 sepals; stamens 4, opposite the sepals; filaments thick, long-exserted; anthers 2-celled, the sacs longitudinally dehiscent. Pistillate flowers with 4 sepals or more; ovary 3-celled, the cavities with a partition at the base; styles 3, spreading; ovules 2 in each cavity. Capsule of 3 2-seeded carpels. [Greek, thick stamen.]

Two species, the following typical one of southeastern North America, the other Japanese.

I. **Pachysandra procúmbens** Michx. Alleghany Mountain Spurge. Fig. 2775.

P. procumbens Michx. Fl. Bor. Am. **2**: 177. *pl. 45.* 1803.

Somewhat pubescent, forming large clumps; stems stout, simple, 1° long or less. Leaves ovate, oval, or obovate, 2′–4′ long, obtuse or acutish at the apex, coarsely dentate or some of them entire, cuneate or abruptly narrowed at the base into a petiole shorter than or equalling the blade; spikes 1 or several in the axils of the lower scales, densely many-flowered, 2′–3′ long, the staminate flowers forming most of the spike, the pistillate few toward its base; sepals green or purplish; filaments white, 4″–5″ long.

In woods, West Virginia to Kentucky, Florida and Louisiana. Flowers fragrant. April–May.

Family 74. **ANACARDIÀCEAE** Lindl. Nat. Syst. 1830.

SUMAC FAMILY.

Trees or shrubs, with acrid resinous or milky sap, alternate or rarely opposite leaves, and polygamo-dioecious or perfect, mainly regular flowers. Calyx 3–7-cleft. Petals of the same number, imbricated in the bud, or rarely none. Disk generally annular. Stamens as many or twice as many as the petals, rarely fewer, or more, inserted at the base of the disk; filaments separate; anthers commonly versatile. Ovary in the staminate flowers 1-celled. Ovary in the pistillate flowers 1- or sometimes 4–5-celled; styles 1–3; ovules 1 in each cavity. Fruit generally a small drupe. Seed-coat bony or crustaceous; endosperm little or none; cotyledons fleshy.

About 60 genera and 500 species, most abundant in warm or tropical regions, a few extending into the temperate zones.

Styles terminal; leaves compound; fruit nearly symmetrical.
  Fruit densely pubescent, its stone smooth.
    Flowers in dense terminal panicles, appearing after the leaves.   1. *Rhus.*
    Flowers in clustered spikes, appearing before the leaves.   2. *Schmaltzia.*
  Fruit glabrous, or sparingly pubescent, its stone striate.   3. *Toxicodendron.*
Styles lateral; leaves simple; fruit gibbous.   4. *Cotinus.*

1. RHÚS [Tourn.] L. Sp. Pl. 265. 1753.

Shrubs or trees, with alternate mostly odd-pinnate leaves, no stipules, and small polygamous flowers in terminal panicles. Calyx 4-6-cleft or parted (commonly 5-cleft), persistent. Petals equal, imbricated, spreading. Disk annular. Stamens (in our species) 5. Pistil 1, sessile; ovary 1-ovuled; styles 3, terminal. Drupe small, 1-seeded, mostly subglobose, pubescent; stone smooth. Seeds inverted on a stalk that rises from the base of the ovary; cotyledons nearly flat. [Ancient Greek and Latin name; Celtic, red.]

About 125 species, natives of warm and temperate regions. Besides the following, about 6 others occur in the southern and western parts of the United States. Type species: *Rhus coriaria* L.

Rachis of the leaf wing-margined.   1. *R. copallina*.
Rachis of the leaf nearly terete.
  Foliage and twigs velvety-pubescent.   2. *R. hirta*.
  Foliage and twigs glabrous. glaucous.   3. *R. glabra*.

1. Rhus copallìna L. Dwarf Black or Mountain Sumac. Upland Sumac. Fig. 2776.

Rhus copallina L. Sp. Pl. 266. 1753.

A shrub, or sometimes a small tree, with maximum height of about 20° and trunk diameter of 6'. Leaves pinnate, 6'-12' long, the petiole and rachis more or less pubescent; leaflets 9–21, ovate-lanceolate or oblong-lanceolate, inequilateral, acute or obtusish at each end, entire, or few-toothed toward the apex, dark green and glabrous above, paler and often pubescent beneath; rachis wing-margined between the leaflets; flowers polygamous, green, 1½″ broad, in dense terminal panicles; pedicels and calyx finely pubescent; drupe compressed, 2″ in diameter, crimson, covered with short fine acid hairs.

In dry soil, Maine and southern Ontario to Florida, west to Minnesota, Nebraska and Texas. Not poisonous. Leaves and bark contain much tannin and are collected in large quantities in the southern States, and ground for tanning leather. Wood soft, light brown; weight per cubic foot 33 lbs. Ascends to 2600 ft. in North Carolina. Smooth or common sumac. June–Aug.

2. Rhus hírta (L.) Sudw. Staghorn Sumac. Fig. 2777.

Datisca hirta L. Sp. Pl. 1037. 1753.
Rhus typhina L. Amoen. Acad. 4: 311. 1760.
Rhus hirta Sudw. Bull. Torr. Club 19: 82. 1892.

A small tree, with maximum height of 40° and trunk diameter of 9', or often shrubby. Leaves pinnate, 8'-15' long; petioles, rachis and twigs more or less densely velvety-pubescent; leaflets 11–31, lanceolate or oblong-lanceolate, 3'-5' long, acuminate at the apex, rounded at the base, sharply serrate, dark green and nearly glabrous above, pale and more or less pubescent beneath; panicles terminal, dense; flowers green, polygamous, 1½″ broad; drupe globose, 1½″-2″ in diameter, very densely covered with bright crimson hairs.

In dry or rocky soil, Nova Scotia to Georgia, especially along the mountains, west to southern Ontario, South Dakota and Iowa. Wood soft, greenish-yellow; weight per cubic foot 27 lbs. Bark rich in tannin. A race with laciniate leaflets has been found in New Hampshire. June. Vinegar-tree. American, Virginia, hairy or velvet-sumac. Staghorn.

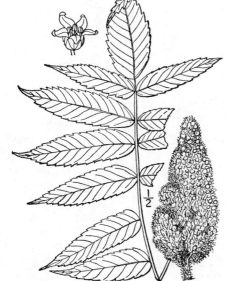

3. Rhus glàbra L.   Smooth Upland or Scarlet Sumac.   White or Sleek Sumac. Fig. 2778.

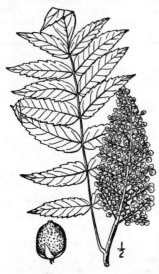

Rhus glabra L. Sp. Pl. 265. 1753.

A shrub or rarely a small tree, 2°–20° high, similar to the preceding species, but glabrous and somewhat glaucous. Leaflets 11–31, lanceolate or oblong-lanceolate, 2′–4′ long, acuminate at the apex, rounded and often oblique at the base, dark green above, whitish beneath, sharply serrate, rachis not winged; pedicels sometimes slightly pubescent; inflorescence and fruit similar to those of the two preceding species; drupe covered with short reddish acid hairs.

In dry soil, Nova Scotia to Minnesota, south to Florida, Mississippi and Louisiana. Several specific names have been proposed for trivially different races of this species. Foliage sometimes used for tanning. This species and the two preceding sometimes have the whole or a part of the flower-clusters changed into small leaves. A race with laciniate leaflets (*R. bipinnata* Greene) occurs in southern Pennsylvania and Delaware. Pennsylvania sumac. Shoe-make. Senhalanac. Vinegartree. June–Aug.

Rhus glàbra boreàlis Britton, with the inflorescence and sometimes also the foliage soft-pubescent, occurring in Michigan and Minnesota, may be a hybrid with *Rhus hirta*.

2. SCHMÀLTZIA Desv. Journ. Bot. 1813: 229. 1813.

Shrubs with polygamo-dioecious small green flowers unfolding before the usually 3-foliolate alternate leaves. Flowers spicate or capitate; calyx 5-cleft; petals 5; stamens 5; ovary 1-ovuled; styles 3, short. Fruit a small pubescent drupe, the stone smooth, the seed inverted. [Named for C. S. Rafinesque-Schmaltz, a copious writer upon natural objects.]

About 8 species, natives of North America and Mexico. Type species: *Rhus aromática* Ait.

Leaflets 1′–3′ long, crenate-dentate, acutish.   1. *S. crenata.*
Leaflets ½′–1½′ long, obtuse or obtusish, with few rounded teeth or lobes.   2. *S. trilobata.*

1. Schmaltzia crenàta (Mill.) Greene.   Fragrant or Sweet-scented Sumac. Fig. 2779.

Toxicodendron crenatum Mill. Gard. Dict. Ed. 8, no. 5. 1768.
Rhus aromatica Ait. Hort. Kew. 1: 367. 1789.
Rhus canadensis Marsh. Arb. Am. 129. 1785. Not Mill. 1768.
S. aromatica Desv.; Steud. Nom. Ed. 2, 2: 531. 1841.
Schmaltzia crenata Greene, Leaflets 1: 128. 1905.

A shrub, 3°–8° high, ascending or diffuse. Leaves petioled, 3-foliolate, 2′–4′ long, aromatic; leaflets ovate or rhomboid, 1′–2′ long, 9″–18″ wide, the lateral ones sessile, the terminal short-stalked, acute or obtusish at the apex, the lateral rounded or truncate, the terminal cuneate at the base, all crenate or crenate-dentate with numerous large teeth, and usually pubescent, especially when young, often permanently so; flowers yellowish green, about 1″ broad, in clustered spikes; drupe globose, red, pubescent.

In rocky woods, Ontario and Vermont to Florida, especially along the mountains, west to Minnesota, Kansas and Louisiana. Consists of numerous races, differing mainly in pubescence. The catkin-like spikes are developed on the branches in late autumn. March–April.

2. Schmaltzia trilobàta (Nutt.) Small. Ill-scented Sumac. Skunk-bush. Fig. 2780.

Rhus trilobata Nutt.; T. & G. Fl. N. A. **1**: 210. 1838.

Rhus aromatica var. *trilobata* A. Gray.; S. Wats. Bot. King's Exp. 53. 1871.

Schmaltzia trilobata Small, Fl. SE. U. S. 728. 1903.

A glabrous or somewhat hairy shrub, 2°–6° high. Leaves petioled, 3-foliolate, unpleasantly odorous, 1′–2′ long; leaf-lets sessile, or nearly so, ½′–1′ long, puberulent when young, usually glabrous when mature, ovate or oval, obtuse or obtusish, the terminal one commonly considerably larger than the lateral and cuneate at the base, all crenately few-lobed or toothed or sometimes entire; flowers as in the preceding species, and fruit similar.

Illinois to South Dakota, Texas, Montana, New Mexico and California. March. Races differ much in pubescence.

3. TOXICODÉNDRON [Tourn.] Mill. Gard. Dict. Abr. Ed. 4. 1754.

Small trees, shrubs, or climbing vines, with 3-foliolate or pinnate leaves, poisonous to the touch, and axillary panicles of small, greenish or white, polygamous flowers unfolding after the leaves. Calyx 5-cleft; petals and stamens 5; ovary 1-ovuled; style terminal. Drupes glabrous or sparingly pubescent when young, the stone striate. [Greek, poison-tree.]

About 20 species, natives of North America and Asia. Type species: *Rhus Toxicodéndron* L.

Leaflets 7–11, glabrous.   1. *T. Vernix.*
Leaflets 3 only.
    Glabrate, or somewhat pubescent; leaflets thin, entire or sinuate; fruit not papillose.
                                              2. *T. radicans.*
    Densely pubescent; leaflets firm in texture, deeply 3–7-lobed; fruit papillose.
                                               3. *T. Toxicodendron.*

1. Toxicodendron Vérnix (L.) Kuntze. Poison or Swamp Sumac. Poison Elder. Fig. 2781.

Rhus Vernix L. Sp. Pl. 265. 1753.

Toxicodendron pinnatum Mill. Gard. Dict. Ed. 8, no. 4. 1768.

Rhus venenata DC. Prodr. **2**: 68. 1825.

Toxicodendron Vernix Kuntze, Rev. Gen. Pl. 153. 1891.

A shrub or small tree, with maximum height of 25° and trunk diameter of 6′. Leaves petioled, pinnate, 6′–15′ long, glabrous or somewhat puberulent; leaflets 7–13, thin, obovate, oval, or the lowest ovate, 2′–4′ long, 1′–1½′ wide, green both sides, entire, short-acuminate at the apex, narrowed or rounded at the base, short-stalked; rachis terete; flowers green, about 1″ broad, in loose axillary panicles 3′–8′ long; drupe globose-oblong, 2″ in diameter, gray, glabrous.

In swamps, Maine to Vermont, southern Ontario, Florida, Minnesota, Missouri and Louisiana. Very poisonous. Wood soft, yellowish brown; weight per cubic foot 27 lbs. June. Poison ash or tree. Swamp or poison dog-wood. Poison-wood.

2. Toxicodendron radìcans (L.) Kuntze. Poison, Climbing or Three-leaved Ivy. Poison Oak. Climath. Fig. 2782.

Rhus radicans L. Sp. Pl. 266. 1753.
Rhus Toxicodendron of American authors, in part, not L.
Toxicodendron vulgare Mill. Gard. Dict. Ed. 8, no. 1. 1768.
Rhus microcarpa Steud. Nomencl. 689. 1821.
T. radicans Kuntze, Rev. Gen. 153. 1891.

A woody vine, climbing by numerous aerial rootlets, or erect and bushy, the stem sometimes 3'-4' in diameter. Leaves petioled, 3-foliolate, glabrate or somewhat pubescent, especially beneath; leaflets ovate or rhombic, 1'-4' long, entire or sparingly dentate or sinuate, acute or short-acuminate at the apex, the lateral sessile or short-stalked, inequilateral, the terminal one stalked, rounded or narrowed at the base; flowers green, 1½" broad, in loose axillary panicles, 1'-3' long; fruit similar to that of the preceding, 1½"-2½" in diameter, glabrous, or sparingly pubescent.

Thickets and along fences, etc., often ascending high trees, Nova Scotia to British Columbia, Florida, Arkansas, Texas and Mexico. Bermuda; Bahamas. Very poisonous. Consists of many races, differing in habit, shape of leaflets and pubescence. Trailing or climbing sumac. Mercury. Black mercury-vine. Markry. Mark-weed. Picry. May–June.

Toxicodendron Rydbergii (Small) Greene, an upright shrub with thicker leaves and larger fruit, enters our western limits in Kansas and North Dakota.

3. Toxicodendron Toxicodéndron (L.) Britton. Poison Oak. Fig. 2783.

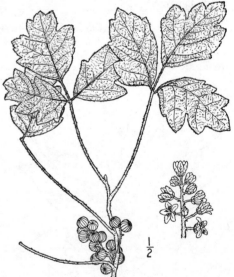

Rhus Toxicodendron L. Sp. Pl. 266. 1753.
T. pubescens Mill. Gard. Dict. Ed. 8, no. 2. 1768.
R. Toxicodendron quercifolium Michx. Fl. Bor. Am. 1: 183. 1803.
R. quercifolia Steud. Nomencl. 689. As synonym. 1821.

A low branching shrub, 3° high or less, spreading by underground branches, the young shoots densely pubescent. Leaves long-petioled, 3-foliolate; leaflets ovate to obovate in outline, firm in texture, dark green and sparingly pubescent above, paler green and densely velvety-pubescent beneath, 4' long or less, irregularly lobed, toothed or sinuate-margined; panicles 1'-3' long; petals oblong, obtuse, veined; fruit pubescent when young, smooth or sometimes papillose when mature, depressed-globose, 3"-4½" in diameter.

Dry woodlands, southern New Jersey and Delaware to Georgia, Alabama and Texas. April–May.

4. CÓTINUS Adans. Fam. Pl. 2: 345. 1763.

Shrubs or small trees, with alternate petioled ovate oval or obovate entire leaves, and small polygamous slender-pedicelled flowers in large terminal panicles. Calyx 5-parted, the segments imbricated, obtuse. Petals longer than the calyx, imbricated. Stamens 5. Ovary obovoid; styles 3, lateral; stigmas very small. Drupe obliquely oblong or oval, compressed, gibbous, 1-seeded. Seed nearly as in Rhus. [Greek name of the oleaster, or wild olive.]

Two known species, the following of southeastern North America, the other, Cotinus Cotinus (L.) Sargent, the generic type, native of Europe and Asia.

1. Cotinus americànus Nutt. Wild or American Smoke-tree. Chittam-wood. Fig. 2784.

Rhus cotinoides Nutt.; T. & G. Fl. N. A. 1: 217. As synonym, 1838.
Cotinus americanus Nutt. Sylva 3: *pl. 81.* 1849.
Cotinus cotinoides Britton, Mem. Torr. Club 5: 216. 1894.

A small widely branched tree, with maximum height of about 40° and trunk diameter of 15'. Leaves oval or slightly obovate, thin, glabrous or sparingly pubescent beneath, 3'–6' long, 1½'–2' wide, obtuse at the apex, narrowed and commonly acute or acutish at the base, the blade slightly decurrent on the petiole; flowers 1"–1½" broad, green, borne in loose large terminal panicles, pedicels elongating to 1'–1½' and becoming very plumose in fruit; drupe reticulate-veined, 2" long.

Rocky hills, Missouri and Oklahoma, east to Tennessee and Alabama. Wood soft, orange-yellow, yielding a rich dye; weight per cubic foot 40 lbs. Very nearly related to the European *C Cotinus,* which differs in its smaller coriaceous leaves, more pubescent, mostly rounded and obtuse at base. Yellow-wood. April–May.

Family 75. CYRILLÀCEAE Lindl. Veg. King. 445. 1847.

CYRILLA FAMILY.

Glabrous shrubs, or small trees, with simple entire thick alternate exstipulate leaves, long-persistent or evergreen, and small regular perfect bracted racemose flowers. Sepals 4–8 (mostly 5), persistent. Petals the same number as the sepals, hypogynous, distinct, or slightly united by their bases, deciduous. Stamens 4–10, in 1 or 2 series, distinct, hypogynous; anthers introrse, 2-celled, the sacs longitudinally dehiscent. Ovary 2–5-celled; ovules 1–4 in each cavity, anatropous, pendulous; style short or none; stigma very small, or 2–3-lobed. Fruit dry, small, 1–5-seeded. Seeds oblong or spindle-shaped; endosperm fleshy; embryo central, cylindric.

Three genera and about 12 species, natives of America.

1. CYRÍLLA Garden; L. Mant. 1: 5, 50. 1767.

Racemes clustered at the ends of twigs of the preceding season. Sepals 5, firm, acute, shorter than the petals. Petals 5, white, acute, spreading. Stamens 5, opposite the sepals, the filaments subulate, the anthers oval. Ovary ovoid, sessile, mostly 2-celled, sometimes 3-celled; ovules 2–4 in each cavity; style short, thick, 2–3 lobed. Fruit ovoid, 2–3-seeded, the pericarp spongy. [In honor of Domenico Cyrillo, professor of medicine at Naples.]

Three or four species, natives of southeastern North America, the West Indies and northern South America, the following the generic type.

1. Cyrilla racemiflòra L. Southern Leatherwood or Ironwood. Fig. 2785.

Cyrilla racemiflora L. Mant. 1: 50. 1867.

A shrub or small tree, sometimes 35° high and the trunk 15' in diameter, the bark at the base spongy. Leaves oblanceolate, obovate or oval, short-petioled, reticulate-veined and the midvein rather prominent beneath, obtuse or acute at the apex, cuneate-narrowed at the base, 2'–4' long, 3"–1' wide; racemes narrow, 2'–6' long, bearing the very numerous small white flowers nearly to the base; pedicels 1"–2" long, somewhat longer than the bracts, or shorter; fruit about 1" long.

Along streams and swamps, southern Virginia to Florida and Texas, mostly near the coast. Also in the West Indies and South America. He-huckleberry. Burn-wood bark. White or red titi. May–July.

Family 76. ILICÀCEAE Lowe, Fl. Mad. 2: 11. 1868.

HOLLY FAMILY.

Shrubs or trees, with watery sap, and alternate petioled simple often coriaceous leaves. Flowers axillary, small, clustered or solitary, white, mainly polygamo-dioecious, regular. Stipules minute and deciduous, or none. Calyx 3–6 parted, generally persistent. Petals 4–6 (rarely more), separate, or slightly united at the base, hypogynous, deciduous, imbricated. Stamens hypogynous, as many as the petals, or sometimes more; anthers oblong, cordate. Disk none. Ovary 1, superior, 3–several-celled; stigma discoid or capitate; style short or none; ovules 1 or 2 in each cavity of the ovary. Fruit a small berry-like drupe, enclosing several nutlets. Seed pendulous; endosperm fleshy; embryo straight.

Three genera and about 300 species, natives of temperate and tropical regions.

Petals oblong or obovate, slightly united.   1. *Ilex.*
Petals linear, distinct.   2. *Nemopanthus.*

1. ÌLEX L. Sp. Pl. 125. 1753.

Shrubs or trees, with entire dentate or spiny-toothed, minutely stipulate leaves, and axillary cymose or solitary, perfect or polygamous flowers. Calyx small, 4–5-cleft or toothed. Petals 4–9, somewhat united at the base, oblong, obtuse. Stamens of the same number, adnate to the base of the corolla. Berry-like drupe globose, with 4–8 bony or crustaceous nutlets. [Ancient name of the Holly oak.]

About 280 species, mostly American, some in Asia, Africa and Australia. Besides the following, some 5 others occur in the southeastern United States. Type species: *Ilex Aquifolium* L.

Leaves thick, evergreen, persistent.
  Nutlets ribbed.
    Leaves spiny-toothed.   1. *I. opaca.*
    Leaves dentate or entire, not spiny.
      Leaves entire or few-toothed; calyx-lobes acute.   2. *I. Cassine.*
      Leaves coarsely crenate; calyx-lobes obtuse.   3. *I. vomitoria.*
  Nutlets not ribbed; leaves dotted beneath.
    Leaves oblanceolate, obtusish; drupe 2″–3″ in diameter.   4. *I. glabra.*
    Leaves obovate, acute; drupe 3″–4″ in diameter.   5. *I. coriacea.*
Leaves thin, deciduous.
  Nutlets ribbed; peduncles 1-flowered.
    Leaves small, obovate or spatulate, crenate.   6. *I. decidua.*
    Leaves large, ovate or lanceolate, sharply serrate.   7. *I. montana.*
  Nutlets not ribbed.
    Flowers all short-pedicelled.
      Twigs brown; leaves oval to oblong.   8. *I. verticillata.*
      Twigs grey; leaves obovate to nearly orbicular.   9. *I. bronxensis.*
    Staminate flowers on long and slender pedicels.   10. *I. laevigata.*

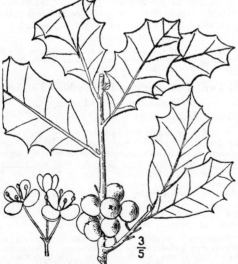

1. Ilex opàca Ait. American or White Holly. Fig. 2786.

Ilex opaca Ait. Hort. Kew. 1: 169. 1789.

A tree of slow growth, sometimes 50° high, and with a trunk diameter of 3½°. Young twigs sparingly pubescent; leaves elliptical or obovate, 2′–4′ long, 1′–1½′ wide, evergreen, glabrous on both sides, obtuse or acutish at the apex, spiny-tipped, spinose-dentate, at least toward the apex, rarely nearly or quite entire; petioles 2″–4″ long, sometimes puberulent; peduncles 2-bracted; staminate cymes 3–10-flowered, ½′–1′ long; fertile flowers mostly scattered and solitary; calyx-lobes acute, ciliate; stigma sessile; drupe globose or globose-oblong, red, rarely yellow, 4″–5″ in diameter; nutlets ribbed.

In moist woods, Massachusetts to Florida, Pennsylvania, Indiana, Missouri and Texas. Most abundant near the coast. Wood hard, nearly white; weight per cubic foot 36 lbs. Ascends to 3000 ft. in North Carolina. April–June.

2. Ilex Cassìne L. Dahoon Holly.
Fig. 2787.

Ilex Cassine L. Sp. Pl. 125. 1753.
Ilex Dahoon Walt. Fl. Car. 241. 1788.

A shrub, or small tree, with maximum
height of about 25° and trunk diameter of 18'.
Twigs pubescent; leaves coriaceous, evergreen,
oblanceolate or oblong-obovate, 2'-4' long,
½'-1' wide, acutish or obtuse at the apex, acute
at the base, entire, or with a few sharp teeth,
glabrous and dark green above, pale and usually pubescent beneath, especially on the strong
midrib; petioles 3''-4'' long; staminate cymes
several- or many-flowered; peduncles and pedicels pubescent; fertile cymes commonly 3-flow-
ered; calyx-lobes acute, ciliate; drupes red,
globose, 2''-3'' in diameter, on pedicels of
about the same length.

In low woods, southern Virginia to Florida,
near the coast, west to Louisiana. Also in the
Bahamas and Cuba. Wood soft, light brown;
weight per cubic foot 30 lbs. Yaupon. May.

Ilex myrtifòlia Walt., with smaller linear to
linear-oblong leaves not over 1½' long, has nearly
the same range, and is probably a race of this
species.

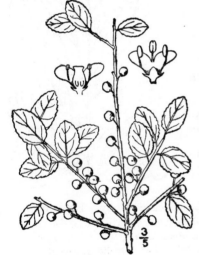

3. Ilex vomitòria Ait. Cassena. Yaupon.
Emetic Holly. Fig. 2788.

Ilex Cassine Walt. Fl. Car. 241. 1788. Not L. 1753.
Ilex vomitoria Ait. Hort. Kew. 1: 170. 1789.

A shrub, or small tree, with maximum height of
about 25° and trunk diameter of 4'-6'. Petioles and
young twigs puberulent; leaves ovate-oblong or
elliptic, ½'-1½' long, 4''-9'' wide, obtuse at both ends,
crenate, glabrous, evergreen, pale beneath, dark
green above; petioles 1''-2'' long; staminate cymes
several-flowered, short-peduncled; fertile cymes sessile, 1-3-flowered; pedicels longer than the petioles;
calyx-lobes obtuse; drupe globose, red, 2''-3'' in
diameter; nutlets ribbed.

In low woods, Virginia to Florida, west to Arkansas
and Texas. Naturalized in Bermuda. Wood hard, nearly
white; weight per cubic foot 45 lbs. Appalachian, Carolina, or South-sea tea. Indian black-drink. Evergreen
cassena. May.

4. Ilex glàbra (L.) A. Gray. Inkberry.
Evergreen Winterberry. Fig. 2789.

Prinos glaber L. Sp. Pl. 330. 1753.
Ilex glabra A. Gray. Man. Ed. 2, 264. 1856.

A shrub, 2°-6° high. Young twigs and petioles
finely puberulent; leaves coriaceous, evergreen, dark
green and shining above, paler and dotted beneath,
oblanceolate or elliptic, 1'-2' long, 5''-9'' wide, generally cuneate at the base, obtusish and few-toothed
at the apex, or sometimes entire; petioles 2''-4''
long; sterile cymes several-flowered, slender-peduncled; fertile flowers generally solitary, sometimes 2
or 3 together; calyx-segments acutish or obtuse;
drupe black, 2''-3'' in diameter; nutlets not ribbed.

In sandy soil, Nova Scotia; eastern Massachusetts to
Florida, west to Louisiana, mainly near the coast. Appalachian tea. Gall-berry. Dye-leaves. June–July.

5. Ilex coriàcea (Pursh) Chapm. Shining Inkberry. Fig. 2790.

Prinos coriaceus Pursh, Fl. Am. Sept. 221. 1814.

Ilex coriacea Chapm. Fl. S. States, 270. 1860.

Ilex lucida T. & G.; S. Wats. Bibl. Index 1. 159. 1878. Not *Prinos lucidus* Ait.

A glabrous shrub, 15° high or less. Leaves thick, evergreen, oval to obovate or oblong, acute at both ends, entire, or with a few small sharp teeth, 1′–3′ long, dark green and shining above, paler and dotted beneath, short-petioled, somewhat viscid when young; flowers clustered in the axils, or the staminate solitary, the cymes sessile; pedicels bractless, short; calyx-segments 6–9; drupe black, 3″–4″ in diameter; nutlets flat, smooth.

Dismal Swamp, Virginia, to Florida and Louisiana. April–May.

6. Ilex decídua Walt. Swamp, Meadow or Deciduous Holly. Fig. 2791.

Ilex decidua Walt. Fl. Car. 241. 1788.

A shrub, or small tree, with a maximum height of 30° and trunk diameter of 8′ or 10′. Twigs light gray, glabrous; leaves obovate or spatulate-oblong, 1½′–3′ long, 4″–8″ wide, crenate, deciduous, dark green, glabrous and with impressed veins on the upper surface, paler and pubescent beneath, especially on the midrib, acute or cuneate at the base, blunt at the apex or sometimes emarginate; pedicels slender, 1-flowered, several often appearing from near the same point, bractless; calyx-lobes ovate, obtuse; drupe red, depressed-globose, 2″–3″ in diameter; nutlets ribbed.

In swamps and low grounds, District of Columbia to Florida, west to Illinois, Kansas and Texas. Wood hard, white; weight per cubic foot 46 lbs. Flowers unfolding with the leaves in May. Bearberry. Possum-haw.

7. Ilex montàna (T. & G.) A. Gray. Large-leaved Holly. Fig. 2792.

I. montana T. & G.; A. Gray, Man. 276. 1848.

Ilex monticola A. Gray, Man. Ed. 2, 264. 1856.

Ilex mollis A. Gray, Man. Ed. 5, 306. 1867.

Ilex monticola mollis Britton, Mem. Torr. Club 5: 217. 1894.

A shrub, or occasionally forming a slender erect tree, with a maximum height of about 40°. Leaves rather thin, deciduous, ovate or ovate-lanceolate, 2′–6′ long, ½′–2½′ wide, sharply serrate or serrulate, acuminate or acute, glabrous on both sides or pubescent beneath, especially along the veins; petioles 4″–8″ long; pedicels 1-flowered, bractless, the sterile clustered, the fertile mostly solitary; calyx-lobes acute or acutish, ciliate or pubescent; drupes red, globose-ovoid, 2″–3″ in diameter; nutlets ribbed.

Mountain woods, New York and Pennsylvania, to Georgia and Alabama. Mountain holly. May.

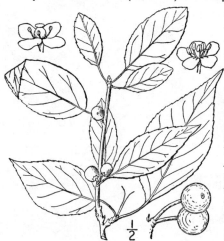

8. Ilex verticillàta (L.) A. Gray. Virginia Winterberry. Black Alder. Fever-bush. Fig. 2793.

Prinos verticillatus L. Sp. Pl. 330. 1753.
Prinos podifolius Willd. Enum. Hort. Berol. 394. 1809.
Ilex verticillata A. Gray, Man. Ed. 2, 264. 1856.

A shrub, 6°–25° high. Twigs brown, glabrous or slightly pubescent; leaves oval, obovate or oblong-lanceolate, 2′–3′ long, about 1′ wide, acute or acuminate at the apex, acute or obtusish at the base, rather thick and coriaceous, dark green and nearly glabrous above, pubescent, at least on the veins beneath, sharply serrate; staminate cymes clustered, 2–10-flowered, the fertile 1–3-flowered; pedicels 2-bracted; calyx-lobes obtuse, ciliate; drupes bright red (rarely yellow or white), clustered so as to appear verticillate, about 3″ in diameter; nutlets smooth.

In swamps, Connecticut to Florida, west to Wisconsin and Missouri, perhaps extending further north. The leaves turn black in autumn. Striped, white or false alder. June–July.

9. Ilex bronxénsis Britton. Northern Winterberry. Fig. 2794.

Ilex verticillata tenuifolia Torr. Fl. North. U. S. 338. 1824. Not *I. tenuifolia* Salisb.

Ilex bronxensis Britton, Man. 604. 1901.

I. verticillata cyclophylla Robinson, Rhodora **2** : 105. 1900.

Similar to the preceding species, but with grey slender twigs. Leaves various, obovate to orbicular, 1′–3′ long, glabrous, or more or less pubescent beneath; fruit often larger than that of *I. verticillata,* orange-red.

In swamps and wet woods, Nova Scotia to Ontario, Michigan, Indiana and New Jersey. June–July.

Ilex fastigiàta Bicknell, of Nantucket, recently described, differs by fastigiate branching and narrower lanceolate to oblong-lanceolate leaves.

10. Ilex laevigàta (Pursh) A. Gray. Smooth Winterberry. Hoop-wood. Fig. 2795.

Prinos laevigatus Pursh, Fl. Am. Sept. 220. 1814.
Ilex laevigata A. Gray, Man. Ed. 2, 264. 1856.

A shrub, somewhat resembling the two preceding. Twigs glabrous; leaves oval or oblong, thin, 1′–2′ long, mainly acute or acutish at each end, glabrous on both sides or sometimes villous on the veins beneath, turning yellow in autumn, finely serrulate; staminate flowers solitary or occasionally 2 together, on very slender pedicels 5″–9″ long; fertile flowers solitary, much shorter-peduncled; calyx-lobes acute, glabrous; drupes larger than in *I. verticillata,* orange-red, rarely yellow, ripening earlier, on stalks about equal to their diameter.

In swamps, Maine and New Hampshire to Pennsylvania and Georgia. Blooms earlier than the preceding. Can-hoop. May–June.

2. NEMOPÁNTHUS Raf. Journ. Phys. **89**: 96. 1819.

[ILICIOÌDES Dumont. Bot. Cult. **4**: 127. *pl. 4.* Hyponym. 1802.]

A glabrous shrub, with slender-petioled oblong deciduous leaves, and polygamo-dioecious axillary small flowers. Calyx of the staminate flowers none, that of the pistillate minute, 4–5-toothed. Petals 4 or 5, distinct, linear. Stamens 4 or 5, free from the corolla; anthers ovoid-globose. Ovary 3–5-lobed, 3–5-celled; ovules 1 in each cavity; stigmas 3–5, sessile. Drupe subglobose. Nutlets 4 or 5. [Greek, referring to the slender pedicels.]

A monotypic genus of eastern North America.

1. Nemopanthus mucronàta (L.) Trelease. Wild or Mountain Holly.
Fig. 2796.

Vaccinium mucronatum L. Sp. Pl. 350. 1753.

Nemopanthus fascicularis Raf. Journ. Phys. **89**: 97. 1819.

N. canadensis DC. Mem. Soc. Gen. **1**: 450. 1821.

Nemopanthes mucronata Trelease, Trans. Acad. St. Louis **5**: 349. 1889.

Ilicioides mucronata Britton, Mem. Torr. Club **5**: 217. 1894.

A shrub, 6°–15° high, with ash-colored bark. Leaves elliptic or obovate, $\frac{1}{2}'-2'$ long, acutish or mucronate at the apex, obtuse or acute at the base, entire or with a few small teeth; petioles 3″–6″ long; flowers of both kinds solitary, or the staminate sometimes 2–4 together; pedicels very slender, often $1\frac{1}{2}'$ long; drupe red, 3″–4″ in diameter; nutlets faintly ribbed.

In swamps, Newfoundland to western Ontario, south to Wisconsin, Indiana and Virginia. Cat-berry. Brick-timber. May.

$\frac{1}{2}$

Family 77. CELASTRÀCEAE Lindl. Nat. Syst. Ed. 2, 119. 1836.

STAFF-TREE FAMILY.

Trees or shrubs, often climbing. Leaves alternate or opposite, simple. Stipules, when present, small and caducous. Flowers regular, generally perfect, small. Pedicels commonly jointed. Calyx 4–5-lobed or parted, persistent, the lobes imbricated. Petals 4–5, spreading. Stamens inserted on the disk, alternate with the petals. Disk conspicuous, flat or lobed. Ovary sessile, its base distinct from or confluent with the disk, mostly 3–5-celled; style short, thick; stigma entire or 3–5-lobed; ovules 2 in each cell, anatropous. Fruit (in our species) a somewhat dehiscent 2–5-celled pod. Seeds arilled; embryo large; cotyledons foliaceous.

About 45 genera and 375 species, widely distributed in warm and temperate regions.

Leaves opposite.
Large erect or decumbent shrubs; fruit 3–5-lobed; aril red. 　　　　　　　　1. *Euonymus.*
Low spreading shrubs; fruit oblong; aril whitish. 　　　　　　　　　　　　2. *Pachystima.*
Leaves alternate; woody vine. 　　　　　　　　　　　　　　　　　　　　3. *Celastrus.*

1. EUÓNYMUS [Tourn.] L. Sp. Pl. 197. 1753.

Shrubs, with opposite petioled entire or serrate leaves, and perfect cymose axillary greenish or purple flowers. Calyx 4–5-cleft, the lobes spreading or recurved. Petals 4 or 5, inserted beneath the 4–5-lobed disk. Stamens 4 or 5, inserted on the disk. Ovary 3–5-celled; style short or none; stigma 3–5-lobed. Capsule 3–5-celled, 3–5-lobed, angular, rounded or winged, the cavities 1–2-seeded, loculicidally dehiscent. Seeds enclosed in the red aril. [Ancient name of the spindle-tree; also spelled *Evonymus.*]

About 65 species, of the north temperate zone. Besides the following, 2 others occur in California. Type species: *Euonymus europaeus* L.

Pods tuberculate; low shrubs; flowers greenish pink; leaves subsessile.
Erect or ascending; leaves ovate-lanceolate, acuminate. 　　　　　　　1. *E. americanus.*
Decumbent, rooting at the nodes; leaves obovate, obtuse. 　　　　　　　2. *E. obovatus.*
Pods smooth; high shrubs; leaves distinctly petioled.
Flowers purple; cymes 6–15-flowered. 　　　　　　　　　　　　　　3. *E. atropurpureus.*
Flowers greenish yellow; cymes 3–7-flowered. 　　　　　　　　　　　4. *E. europaeus.*

1. Euonymus americànus L. Strawberry Bush. Fig. 2797.

Euonymus americanus L. Sp. Pl. 197. 1753.

A shrub, 2°–8° high, with 4-angled and ash-colored twigs, divaricately branching. Leaves ovate-lanceolate or oblong-lanceolate, thick, 1½′–3′ long, ½′–1′ wide, acuminate at the apex, acute or obtuse at the base, nearly sessile, crenulate, glabrous, or sparingly hairy on the veins beneath; peduncles 6″–12″ long, very slender, 1–3-flowered; flowers greenish, 5″–6″ broad; petals separated, the blade nearly orbicular, erose or undulate, the claw short; capsule slightly 3–5-lobed, not angular, depressed, tuberculate.

In low woods, southern New York to Florida, Illinois, Nebraska and Texas. June. Bursting-heart. Fish-wood. Burning bush.

2. Euonymus obovàtus Nutt. Running Strawberry Bush. Fig. 2798.

Euonymus obovatus Nutt. Gen. 1 : 155. 1818.

Euonymus americanus var. *obovatus* T. & G.; A. Gray, Gen. 2 : 188. 1849.

A low decumbent shrub, seldom rising over a foot from the ground, branching, rooting from the prostrate twigs. Branches 4-angled or slightly winged; leaves obovate or elliptic-obovate, rather thin, mostly acute or cuneate at the base, obtuse at the apex, finely crenulate-serrulate, 1′–2′ long, ½′–1½′ wide, glabrous; petioles 1″–2″ long; peduncles 1–4-flowered; flowers greenish, smaller than in the preceding species, about 3″ broad; petals generally 5, nearly orbicular, crenulate or erose, close together or even slightly overlapping, with scarcely any claw; capsule commonly 3-celled, slightly lobed, depressed, tuberculate.

In low woods, southern Ontario to Pennsylvania, northern New Jersey (?), Illinois, Michigan, and Kentucky. Blooms earlier than *E. americànus*. April–May.

3. Euonymus atropurpùreus Jacq. Burning Bush. Wahoo. Fig. 2799.

Euonymus atropurpureus Jacq. Hort. Vind. 2 : 5. *pl. 120.* 1772.

A shrub or small tree, 6°–25° high. Twigs obtusely 4-angled; leaves ovate-oblong or elliptic, 1½′–5′ long, 1′–2½′ wide, acuminate at the apex, acute or obtuse at the base, puberulent, especially beneath, crenulate-serrulate, rather thin; petioles 4″–8″ long; peduncles very slender, 1′–2′ long, bearing a trichotomous 5–15-flowered cyme; pedicels 3″–6″ long; flowers purple, 5″–6″ broad; petals commonly 4, obovate, undulate; capsule smooth, deeply 3–4-lobed, 6″–8″ broad.

Ontario to Florida, Montana, Nebraska and Oklahoma. Wood nearly white; weight per cubic foot 41 lbs. Indian-arrow. Strawberry-tree or -bush. Bitter-ash. Arrow-wood. Spindle-tree. June.

$\frac{2}{3}$

4. Euonymus europaèus L. Spindle-tree. Fig. 2800.

Euonymus europaeus L. Sp. Pl. 197. 1753.

A glabrous shrub, 3°–9° high, resembling the preceding species. Leaves oblong to ovate-lanceolate, acuminate, crenulate; peduncles mostly less than 1' long, stouter; cymes 3–7-flowered; flowers greenish-yellow or yellowish-white, about 5″ broad; petals 4 (rarely 5), oblong or obovate; capsule smooth, deeply 4-lobed.

Escaped from cultivation to copses and roadsides, Virginia, New York and New Jersey. June. Arrow-beam. Prick-timber. Prickwood. Cat-tree. Pegwood. Pincushion-shrub. Skiver- or skewer-wood. Witch-wood. Louseberry. Gatteridge. Butchers' prick-tree. Gaiter- or Gatten-tree. European dogwood.

2. PACHÝSTIMA Raf. Am. Month. Mag. 2 : 176. 1818.

Low branching glabrous shrubs, with corky branches, opposite coriaceous evergreen leaves, and small axillary, solitary or clustered, perfect brownish flowers. Calyx-lobes 4, broad. Petals 4, spreading. Stamens 4, inserted beneath the disk; filaments longer than the anthers. Ovary immersed in the disk, 2-celled; ovules 2 in each cell, erect; style very short; stigma slightly 2-lobed. Capsule oblong, compressed, 2-celled, at length loculicidally dehiscent, 1–2-seeded. Seeds oblong with a white many-lobed aril at the base. [Greek, thick stigma.]

Two species, natives of North America. The typical *P. Myrsinites* (Pursh) Raf. occurs in the Rocky Mountains.

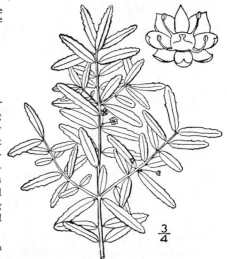

1. Pachystima Cánbyi A. Gray.
Canby's Mountain Lover.
Fig. 2801.

P. Canbyi A. Gray, Proc. Amer. Acad. 8 : 623. 1873.

A shrub 4'–12' high, with decumbent rooting branches. Leaves linear-oblong, or slightly obovate, 3″–12″ long, 1½″–2″ wide, obtuse at each end, very short-petioled, pale green, serrate, the margins revolute; peduncles 1–3-flowered, 2-bracted below the middle; pedicels slender, shorter than the leaves, 2-bracted near the base; calyx-lobes oval, about equalling the petals; capsule oblong, about 4″ long and 2″ in diameter, dehiscent at maturity.

On dry exposed rocks, mountains of Virginia and West Virginia. Rat-stripper. April–May.

$\frac{3}{4}$

3. CELÁSTRUS L. Sp. Pl. 196. 1753.

Shrubs, mainly climbing, with alternate thin deciduous leaves, and terminal or axillary, racemose or paniculate, small dioecious or polygamous flowers. Calyx 5-lobed. Petals 5, inserted under the disk. Stamens in the sterile flowers 5, inserted at the sinuses of the 5-lobed disk. Ovary inserted on the disk, 2–4-lobed, 2–4-celled; style thick; stigma 2–4-lobed; ovules 2 in each cell, erect. Capsule 2–4-celled, loculicidally dehiscent into as many valves. Seeds 1–2 in each cell, enclosed in a scarlet aril; embryo straight; endosperm fleshy; cotyledons flat, coriaceous. [Greek name of some evergreen tree.]

About 30 species, 1 in continental North America, a few in tropical America, numerous in eastern Asia, several in Australia and Madagascar, the following typical.

1. Celastrus scándens L.   Shrubby or Climbing Bittersweet.   Waxwork. Staff-tree.   Fig. 2802.

?*Celastrus bullatus* L. Sp. Pl. 196. 1753.

Celastrus scandens L. Sp. Pl. 196. 1753.

3/5

A twining woody vine, ascending trees to a height of 25° or more, or trailing on the ground where it lacks support. Leaves alternate, somewhat 2-ranked by the twisting of the stem, ovate, oval or obovate, 2′–4′ long, 1′–2′ wide, glabrous on both sides, acuminate or acute at the apex, acute or rounded at the base, crenulate, petioles 6″–9″ long; flowers greenish, about 2″ broad, in terminal compound racemes 2′–4′ in length; petals crenate, much longer than the calyx-lobes; capsule yellow, or orange, 5″–6″ in diameter, opening in autumn and exposing the showy red aril.

In rich soil, Quebec to North Carolina, especially along the mountains, west to Manitoba, Kansas and New Mexico. Foliage sometimes variegated. June. Staff-vine. Fever-twig. False bitter-sweet. Climbing orange-root. Roxbury wax-work. Jacob's-ladder.

Family 78. STAPHYLEÀCEAE DC. Prodr. 2 : 2.   1825.
BLADDER-NUT FAMILY.

Trees or shrubs, with mostly opposite odd-pinnate or 3-foliolate stipulate leaves, and regular perfect flowers in terminal or axillary clusters. Sepals, petals and stamens usually 5. Carpels mostly 3. Disk large, the stamens inserted at its base without. Anthers introrse, 2-celled. Fruit a dehiscent bladdery capsule in the following genus, indehiscent in some others. Seeds solitary or few in each carpel; testa hard; endosperm fleshy; embryo straight.

About 5 genera, and 22 species, widely distributed.

1. STAPHYLÈA L. Sp. Pl. 270. 1753.

Shrubs, with opposite 3-foliolate or pinnate leaves, and axillary drooping racemes or panicles of white flowers. Pedicels jointed. Sepals imbricated. Petals the same number as the sepals and about equalling them. Ovary 2–3-parted, the lobes 1-celled; ovules numerous in each cavity, anatropous. Capsule 2–3-lobed, 2–3-celled. Seeds globose. [Greek, cluster.]

About 6 species, of the north temperate zone. *S. Bolanderi* A. Gray occurs in California. Type species: *Staphylea pinnata* L.

1/2

1. Staphylea trifòlia L.   American Bladder-nut.   Fig. 2803.

Staphylea trifolia L. Sp. Pl. 270. 1753.

A branching shrub, 6°–15° high, or in the south sometimes a tree up to 30° high with a trunk 6′ in diameter, with smooth striped bark. Young leaves and petioles pubescent; mature foliage glabrate; stipules linear, 4″–6″ long, caducous; leaflets ovate or oval, 1½′–2½′ long, acuminate at the apex, obtuse or somewhat cuneate at the base, finely and sharply serrate, the lateral ones sessile or nearly so, the terminal one stalked; stipels subulate; flowers campanulate, racemed, about 4″ long; pedicels bracted at the base, slightly longer than the flowers; capsule about 2′ long, 1′ wide, much inflated, the 3 (rarely 4) carpels separate at the summit and dehiscent along the inner side.

In moist woods and thickets, Quebec and Ontario to Minnesota, South Carolina, Missouri and Kansas. April–May.

Family 79. **ACERÀCEAE** St. Hil. Expos. Fam. **2**: 15. 1805.

MAPLE FAMILY.

Trees or shrubs, with watery often saccharine sap, opposite simple and palmately lobed (rarely entire) or pinnate leaves, and axillary or terminal cymose or racemose regular polygamous or dioecious flowers. Calyx generally 5-parted, the segments imbricated. Petals of the same number, or none: Disk thick, annular, lobed, sometimes obsolete. Stamens 4–12, often 8; filaments filiform. Ovary 2-lobed, 2-celled; styles 2, inserted between the lobes. Fruit of 2 winged samaras, joined at the base and 1-seeded (rarely 2-seeded). Seeds compressed, ascending; cotyledons thin, folded.

The family consists of the following genus and *Dipteronia* Oliver, of central Asia, which differs from *Acer* in the samara being winged all around. There are more than 100 species of Maples.

1. ÀCER [Tourn.] L. Sp. Pl. 1055. 1753.

Besides the following, some 8 others occur in southern and western North America. Type species: *Acer Pseudo-plátanus* L.

Leaves simple, palmately lobed.
  Flowers in dense sessile lateral clusters, unfolding before the leaves.
    Petals none; ovary tomentose; samaras divergent.   1. *A. saccharinum.*
    Petals present; ovary glabrous; samaras incurved.
      Leaves pale and glabrous or but slightly pubescent beneath.
        Leaves bright green above, mostly 5-lobed.
          Wings of the samara broadened above the middle.   2. *A. rubrum.*
          Wings of the samara linear, scarcely broadened above.   3. *A. stenocarpum.*
      Leaves dark green above, mostly 3-lobed.   4. *A. carolinianum.*
    Leaves densely whitish-pubescent beneath; southern.   5. *A. Drummondii.*
  Flowers corymbose, lateral, unfolding with the leaves.
    Flowers long-pedicelled, drooping; large trees.
      Leaves pale and nearly glabrous beneath.   6. *A. Saccharum.*
      Leaves green and pubescent, at least on the veins, beneath.   7. *A. nigrum.*
    Flowers short-pedicelled, erect; shrub or small tree; western.   8. *A. glabrum.*
  Flowers racemed, terminal, unfolding after the leaves.
    Racemes drooping; leaves finely serrate.   9. *A. pennsylvanicum.*
    Racemes erect; leaves coarsely serrate.   10. *A. spicatum.*
Leaves pinnate.   11. *A. Negundo.*

1. Acer sacchárinum L. Silver Maple. Soft or White Maple. Fig. 2804.

Acer saccharinum L. Sp. Pl. 1055. 1753.

Acer dasycarpum Ehrh. Beitr. 4: 24. 1789.

Acer eriocarpum Michx. Fl. Bor. Am. 2: 253. 1803.

A large tree with flaky bark, maximum height of 100°–120° and trunk diameter of 3°–5°. Leaves 4'–6' long, deeply 5-lobed, the lobes rather narrow, acuminate, coarsely and irregularly dentate, truncate or slightly cordate at the base, green above, silvery white and more or less pubescent beneath, especially when young; flowers greenish to red, in nearly sessile lateral corymbs much preceding the leaves; calyx obscurely lobed; petals none; fruiting pedicels elongating; stamens 3–6; samaras pubescent when young, divaricate, at length 2' long, the wing often 6" wide.

Along streams, New Brunswick to Florida, west to southern Ontario, South Dakota, Nebraska and Oklahoma. The samaras are frequently unequally developed. Wood hard, strong, light colored; weight per cubic foot 32 lbs. Used for furniture and floors. Maple sugar is made from the sap in small quantities. River-, silver-leaf-, creek-, water- or swamp-maple. Feb.–April.

Acer Pseùdo-Plátanus L., sycamore-maple, with terminal drooping racemes of yellowish flowers with very woolly ovaries, and deeply 3–5-lobed leaves, and **Acer platanoìdes** L., Norway maple, with terminal corymbs of greenish yellow flowers appearing with or before the 5–7-lobed leaves, commonly planted, have occasionally escaped from cultivation.

2. Acer rùbrum L. Red, Scarlet or Water Maple. Swamp Maple. Fig. 2805.

Acer rubrum L. Sp. Pl. 1055. 1753.

A large tree with flaky or smoothish bark, maximum height about 120° feet and trunk diameter 3°–4½°. Twigs reddish; leaves 3′–4′ long, cordate at the base, sharply 3–5-lobed, the lobes irregularly dentate, acute or acuminate, bright green above, pale and generally whitish beneath, often more or less pubescent; flowers red or yellowish, in sessile lateral clusters much preceding the leaves; petals narrowly oblong; stamens 3–6; fruiting pedicels elongating; samaras glabrous, slightly incurved, 9″–12″ long, the wing 3″–4″ wide, broadest at or above the middle.

In swamps and low grounds, Nova Scotia to Manitoba, Nebraska, Florida and Texas. Wood hard, not strong; color light reddish brown; weight per cubic foot 38 lbs. Used for furniture, gun-stocks, etc. Foliage crimson in autumn. Ascends to 4000 ft. in Virginia. Consists of numerous races; the three following species appear to be distinct. White, soft, shoe-peg, or hard maple. March–April.

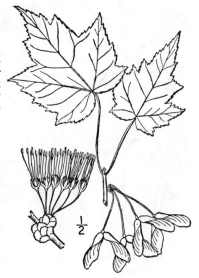

3. Acer stenocàrpum Britton. Narrow-fruited Maple. Fig. 2806.

Acer stenocarpum Britton, N. A. Trees 647. 1908.

A small tree, with leaves similar to those of the Red Maple, thin, light green above, pale beneath, 3-lobed or 5-lobed. Flowers red, appearing before the leaves; samaras on very slender stalks 2′–3′ long, linear, not widened above, about 10″ long, 1½″–2½″ wide, slightly curved, the seed-bearing part very strongly striate.

Flinty soil, Allenton, Missouri. April.

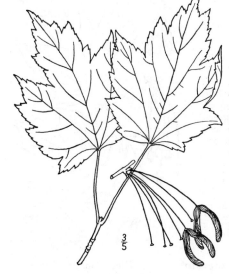

4. Acer caroliniànum Walt. Carolina Maple. Fig. 2807.

Acer carolinianum Walt. Fl. Car. 251. 1788.
Acer rubrum tridens Wood, Classbook 286. 1863.

A tree attaining nearly or quite the dimensions of the Red Maple, with grey, relatively smooth bark. Leaves rather firm in texture, dark green above, white-glaucous and more or less pubescent beneath, mostly 3-lobed and obovate or obovate-orbicular in outline, or 5-lobed and suborbicular, rarely ovate and without lobes, the margin serrate; fruit similar to that of the Red Maple, bright red or sometimes yellow.

Wet or moist soil, Massachusetts to Pennsylvania, Missouri, Florida and Texas. Feb.–April.

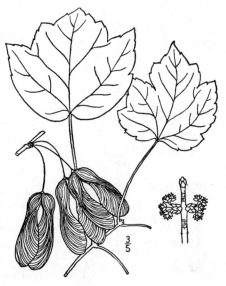

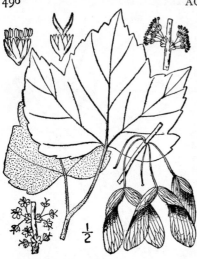

5. Acer Drummóndii H. & A. Drummond's or Hard Maple. Fig. 2808.

Acer Drummondii H. & A.; Hook. Journ. Bot. **1** : 200. 1834.
Acer rubrum var. *Drummondii* Sarg. 10th Census U. S. **9** : 50. 1884.

A large tree, similar to the preceding species. Leaves 3′–6′ long, thicker, 3-lobed, or sometimes 5-lobed, obtuse or cordate at the base, densely whitish tomentose beneath when young, the tomentum persisting, at least along the veins, the lobes short, broad, acute or acuminate; young twigs and petioles more or less tomentose; flowers in lateral sessile fascicles unfolding much before the leaves; petals present; fruiting pedicels 1′–2′ long; samaras glabrous, more or less incurved, 1½′–2½′ long, the wing 5″–10″ broad at middle.

In swamps, southern Missouri to Georgia, Florida and Texas. Fruit brilliant scarlet, ripening in March or April.

6. Acer sáccharum Marsh. Sugar or Rock Maple. Sugar-tree. Fig. 2809.

Acer saccharum Marsh. Arb. Amer. 4. 1785.
Acer saccharinum Wang. Amer. 36. *pl. 2. f. 26.* 1787. Not L. 1753.
Acer barbatum Michx. Fl. Bor. Am. **2** : 252. 1803.

A large and very valuable tree, with maximum height of 100°–120° and trunk diameter of 2½°–3½°. Leaves 3′–6′ long, dark green above, pale beneath, cordate or truncate at the base, 3–7-lobed, the lobes acuminate, irregularly sinuate, the sinuses rounded; flowers in sessile, lateral or terminal corymbs, greenish yellow, drooping on capillary hairy pedicels, appearing with the leaves; petals none; samaras glabrous, slightly diverging, 1′–1½′ long, the wing 3″–5″ wide.

In rich woods, Newfoundland to Manitoba, south, especially along the mountains, to Florida and Texas. Its sap is the main source of maple sugar. Wood hard, strong, light reddish-brown; weight per cubic foot 43 lbs. The bird's-eye and curled maple of cabinet makers are varieties. The tree is widely planted for shade and for ornament. Hard, black or sweet maple. April–May.

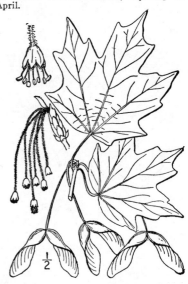

7. Acer nigrum Michx. Black Sugar Maple. Fig. 2810.

Acer nigrum Michx. f. Hist. Arb. Am. **2** : 238. *pl. 16.* 1810.

Acer saccharinum var. *nigrum* T. & G. Fl. N. A. **1** : 248. 1838.

Acer saccharum var. *nigrum* Britton, Trans. N. Y. Acad. Sci. **9** : 10. 1889.

A tree, nearly or quite as large as the Sugar Maple, with rough, blackish bark. Leaves similar, but green both sides, thicker and generally more or less pubescent beneath, especially along the veins; lobes much broader and shorter, with few undulations or frequently entire, the basal sinus often narrow; samaras slightly more divergent.

Quebec, Ontario and Vermont to northern Alabama, west to South Dakota, Louisiana and Arkansas. Wood resembling that of the preceding species, the sap also yielding much sugar. Black or hard maple. April–May.

8. Acer glàbrum Torr.   Dwarf or Rocky Mountain Maple.   Fig. 2811.

Acer glabrum Torr. Ann. Lyc. N. Y. 2 : 172. 1826.
Acer tripartitum Nutt.; T. & G. Fl. N. A. 1 : 247. 1838.

A shrub, or small tree, with maximum height of about 35° and trunk diameter of 12'. Leaves 1'–3' long, often broader, glabrous on both sides, or puberulent when young, 3–5-lobed, the lobes acute or obtusish, sharply serrate, the sinuses acute; flowers yellowish green, in numerous small lateral and terminal sessile corymb-like racemes; pedicels short, glabrous, erect or ascending; samaras glabrous, shining, 9″–15″ long, little diverging; wing 4″–6″ wide.

Borders of streams and hillsides, northwestern Nebraska to Montana and throughout the Rocky Mountain region, south to Arizona, west to the Sierra Nevada. Wood hard, light brown. Weight per cubic foot 37 lbs. Soft, shrubby or bark-maple. May.

9. Acer pennsylvanicum L.   Striped, Goose-foot or Northern Maple.   Moosewood.   Fig. 2812.

Acer pennsylvanicum L. Sp. Pl. 1055. 1753.
Acer striatum Du Roi, Diss. Inaug. 58. 1771.

A small tree, with maximum height of about 35° and trunk diameter of about 8', the smoothish green bark striped with darker bands. Leaves larger, often 6'–8' long, broadest above the middle, thin, glabrous above, sparingly pubescent beneath when young, slightly cordate or truncate at the base, finely serrate or serrulate all around, 3-lobed near the apex, the lobes short and acuminate to a long tip; racemes terminal, narrow, drooping, 3'–4' long; flowers greenish yellow, 3″–4″ broad; unfolding after the leaves; petals obovate; samaras glabrous, 1' long, widely divergent, the wing 4″–5″ wide.

In rocky woods, Nova Scotia to Lake Superior, south, especially along the mountains to Georgia, and Tennessee. False or striped dogwood. Whistle-wood. Wood soft, satiny,

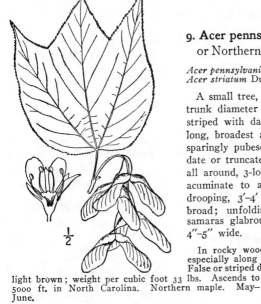

light brown; weight per cubic foot 33 lbs. Ascends to 5000 ft. in North Carolina. Northern maple. May–June.

10. Acer spicàtum Lam.   Mountain Maple.   Fig. 2813.

Acer spicatum Lam. Encycl. 2 : 381. 1786.
Acer montanum Ait. Hort. Kew. 3 : 435. 1789.

A shrub, or rarely a small tree, with maximum height of about 30° and trunk diameter of 8', the bark green, not striped. Leaves 3'–5' long, glabrous above, pubescent beneath, at least when young, 3–5-lobed, coarsely serrate, lobes acute or acuminate; racemes compound, erect, rather dense; flowers 1″–1½″ broad, greenish yellow, unfolding after the leaves; petals linear-spatulate; samaras 9″–10″ long, somewhat divergent, the wing 3″–4″ wide.

Damp rocky woods, Newfoundland and James' Bay to Manitoba, south, especially along the mountains, to North Carolina, Tennessee, Michigan, Iowa and Minnesota. Wood soft, light reddish brown; weight per cubic foot 33 lbs. Ascends to 5000 ft. in North Carolina. Moose-, swamp-, water- or low maple. May–June.

3/5

11. Acer Negúndo L.   Box Elder.   Ash-leaved or Cut-leaved Maple.   Water Ash.   Fig. 2814.

Acer Negundo L. Sp. Pl. 1056. 1753.
Negundo aceroides Moench, Meth. 334. 1794.
Negundo Negundo Karst. Deutsch. Fl. 596. 1880–83.

A tree with maximum height of 60°–70° and trunk diameter of 2°–3½°.   Leaves pinnately 3–5-foliolate; leaflets ovate or oval, thin, pubescent when young, nearly glabrous or pubescent when old, 2′–5′ long, 1′–3′ wide dentate, slightly lobed or sometimes entire, acute or acuminate at the apex, rounded, or the terminal one somewhat cuneate at the base; flowers dioecious, drooping, very small, appearing a little before the leaves; samaras glabrous, 1′–1½′ long, the broad wing finely veined, the united portion constricted at the base.

Along streams, Maine and Ontario to Manitoba, south to Florida, Texas and Mexico.   Rare near the Atlantic Coast.   Wood soft, weak, white; weight per cubic foot 27 lbs.   Used for woodenware and paper pulp.   Sugar maple.   Red river maple.   Black or maple-ash.   April.

Acer intèrior Britton, Western ash-leaved maple, of the Rocky Mountain region, and found in western Kansas and Nebraska, has thicker leaves, the united portions of the samaras not constricted at the base.

Family 80.   **AESCULÀCEAE** Lindley, Orb. Dict. 1: 155. 1841.

BUCKEYE FAMILY.

Trees or shrubs, with opposite petioled digitately 3–9-foliolate leaves, and conspicuous polygamous irregular flowers in terminal panicles, the bark unpleasantly odorous.   Calyx tubular or campanulate, 5-lobed or 5-cleft in the following genus, the lobes unequal.   Petals 4–5, unequal, clawed.   Disk entire, often 1-sided.   Stamens 5–8; filaments elongated.   Ovary sessile, 3-celled; ovules 2 in each cavity; style slender.   Capsule leathery, globose or slightly 3-lobed, smooth or spiny, 3-celled or by abortion 1–2-celled, and often only 1-celled.   Seeds large, shining; cotyledons very thick.

The family consists of the following genus, containing about 15 species, of North America and Asia, and *Billia*, of Mexico, which differs from *Aesculus* in having distinct sepals.

1.   **AÉSCULUS** L. Sp. Pl. 344. 1753.

Characters of the family.   [Ancient name.]   Type species: *Ae. Hippocastanum* L.

Capsules spiny, at least when young; stamens exserted.
  Flowers white, mottled with yellow and purple; introduced.   1. *Ae. Hippocastanum.*
  Flowers yellow or greenish-yellow; native.
    A tree; leaflets 5–7, pubescent.   2. *Ae. glabra.*
    A shrub; leaflets 7–9, glabrate.   3. *Ae. arguta.*
Capsule glabrous; stamens scarcely exceeding the petals.
  Corolla yellow, greenish or purplish; calyx oblong; a large tree.   4. *Ae. octandra.*
  Corolla red; calyx tubular; shrubs or small trees.   5. *Ae. Pavia.*

1. **Aesculus Hippocástanum** L.   Horse-chestnut.   Fig. 2815.

Aesculus Hippocastanum L. Sp. Pl. 344. 1753.

A large tree, reaching a maximum height of about 100° and a trunk diameter of 6°, the buds very resinous.   Leaves long-petioled, pubescent when young, glabrate when mature, or with persistent tufts of hairs in the axils of the veins on the lower surface; leaflets 5–7 (occasionally only 3 on some leaves), obovate, 4′–8′ long, abruptly acuminate at the apex, cuneate-narrowed to the base, irregularly crenulate-dentate; petals 5, spreading, white, blotched with red and yellow, inflorescence rather dense, often 1° long, the pedicels and calyx canescent; stamens declined, exserted; fruit globose, prickly.

Escaped from cultivation, New England, New York and New Jersey.   Native of Asia.   Called also Bongay, and the fruit, in children's games, Conquerors.   Lambs.   June–July.

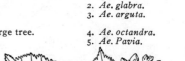

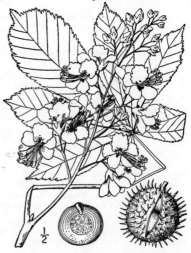

½

2. Aesculus glàbra Willd. Fetid Buckeye Ohio Buckeye. Fig. 2816.

Aesculus glabra Willd. Enum. 405. 1809.

A tree, with maximum height of about 75° and trunk diameter of 2°, the bark rough and fetid. Leaves long-petioled; leaflets 5, rarely 7, 3'–6' long, oval, oblong or lanceolate, acuminate, narrowed at the base, glabrous or slightly pubescent on the veins beneath, finely and sharply serrate, short-stalked or at first sessile; inflorescence loose, pubescent, 4'–6' long; flowers pale yellow; calyx campanulate; petals 4, parallel. 5"–7" long, slightly unequal, their claws about equalling the calyx-lobes; stamens curved, exserted; fruit 1'–1½' in diameter, very prickly when young, becoming smoothish at maturity.

Woods, Pennsylvania to Alabama, west to Michigan, Nebraska and Oklahoma. Wood soft, white, the sapwood slightly darker; weight per cubic foot 28 lbs. Timber used for artificial limbs and a variety of woodenware articles. American horse-chestnut. April–May.

3. Aesculus argùta Buckl. Shrubby or Western Buckeye. Fig. 2817.

Ae. arguta Buckl. Proc. Phil. Acad. 1860: 443. 1860.

A shrub, 3°–10° high, or a small tree, with smooth bark. Twigs, young petioles, leaves and inflorescence somewhat pubescent, becoming glabrate; leaflets 7–9, narrow, 3'–4' long, about 1' wide, long-acuminate, unequally serrate; inflorescence dense, 4'–6' long; flowers yellow, " the centre reddish "; calyx broadly campanulate, its lobes very obtuse; stamens exserted, curved; petals parallel, 5"–6" long; fruit very spiny when young.

Missouri and Kansas to Texas, and recorded from Iowa. Similar to the preceding species, but apparently distinct. March–April.

4. Aesculus octándra Marsh. Yellow Sweet or Big Buckeye. Fig. 2818.

Aesculus octandra Marsh. Arb. Am. 4. 1785.
Ae. lutea Wang. Schrift. Nat. Fr. Berl. 8: 133. *pl. 6.* 1788.
Aesculus flava Ait. Hort. Kew. 1: 494. 1789.
Aesculus hybrida DC. Cat. Hort. Monsp. 75. 1813.
Ae. flava var. *purpurascens* A. Gray, Man. Ed. 3, 118. 1867.

A large tree, with maximum height of 85°–90° and trunk diameter of 2½°–3°, rarely reduced to a shrub; bark dark brown, scaly. Leaves petioled, the petiole commonly slightly pubescent; leaflets 5, rarely 7, 4'–7' long, 2'–3' wide, oval, glabrous or pubescent on the veins above, more or less pubescent beneath, acuminate at the apex, the lower ones oblique, the others cuneate at the base, all finely serrate; inflorescence rather loose, puberulent; flowers yellow; petals 4, long-clawed, connivent, the 2 upper narrower and longer than the lower; stamens included; fruit smooth even when young.

Woods, Alleghany Co., Pa., to Georgia, west to Iowa, Oklahoma and Texas. Wood soft, creamy white; weight per cubic foot 27 lbs. Large buckeye. April–May.

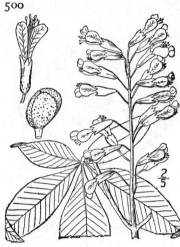

5. Aesculus Pàvia L.　Red or Little Buckeye.　Fig. 2819.

Aesculus Pavia L. Sp. Pl. 344. 1753.

A shrub, 4°–12° high, rarely a small tree up to
18° high.　Leaflets 5–7, stalked, oblong, lanceolate,
or obovate, 3′–5′ long, 1′–1½′ wide, acute or short-
acuminate at the apex, all narrowed at the base,
finely serrate, nearly glabrous on both sides when
mature, shining; inflorescence loose; peduncles 1–3-
flowered; flowers bright red-purple, 1′–1½′ long;
calyx tubular, its lobes short; petals 4, connivent, the
upper longer than the lower; stamens about equalling the longer petals; fruit smooth; seeds dark
brown.

In rich soil, Virginia to Florida, west to Kentucky,
Arkansas and Texas.　Fish-poison.　April–May.

Aesculus austrìna Small, Southern Buckeye, a similar shrub or small tree, has leaves tomentose beneath,
and yellow-brown seeds; it inhabits the South-central
States, ranging north to Missouri.

Family 81.　**SAPINDÀCEAE** R. Br. Exp. Congo, App.　1818.

SOAPBERRY FAMILY.

Trees or shrubs, with watery sap, rarely herbaceous vines.　Leaves alternate
(opposite in one exotic genus), mostly pinnate òr palmate, without stipules.
Flowers polygamo-dioecious, regular or slightly irregular.　Sepals or calyx-
lobes 4–5, mostly imbricated.　Petals 3–5.　Disk fleshy.　Stamens 5–10 (rarely
fewer or more), generally inserted on the disk.　Ovary, 1, 2–4-lobed or entire,
2–4-celled; ovules 1 or more in each cavity.　Fruit various.　Seeds globose or
compressed; embryo mainly convolute; cotyledons often unequal; endosperm
none.

About 125 genera, including over 1000 species, widely distributed in tropical and warm regions.
Trees or shrubs; fruit a berry.　　　　　　　　　　　　　　　　　　1. *Sapindus.*
Herbaceous vines; fruit an inflated pod.　　　　　　　　　　　　　2. *Cardiospermum.*

1. SAPÍNDUS [Tourn.] L. Sp. Pl. 367.　1753.

Trees or shrubs, with alternate mostly odd-pinnate leaves, and regular polygamo-dioecious
flowers in terminal or axillary racemes or panicles.　Sepals 4–5, imbricated in 2 rows.　Petals
of the same number, each with a scale at its base.　Disk annular, hypogynous.　Stamens 8–10,
inserted on the disk; anthers versatile.　Ovary 2–4-lobed (commonly 3-lobed), with the same
number of cavities; ovules 1 in each cavity, ascending; style slender; stigma 2–4-lobed.　Fruit
a globose or lobed berry with 1–3 seeds.　[Name, *Sapo Indicus,* Indian soap, from the soapy
quality of the berries.]

About 10 species, natives of warm and tropical Asia and America. *S. Saponaria* L., the generic
type, occurs in Florida.

1. Sapindus Drummóndii H. & A.　Drummond's Soapberry.　Wild China-tree.
Indian Soap-plant.　Fig. 2820.

S. Drummondii H. & A. Bot. Beechey's Voy. 281.　1841.
Sapindus acuminatus Raf. New Flora N. A. 3: 22.　1836.

A tree, with maximum height of about 50° and trunk
diameter of 2°, the bark fissured when old.　Leaves
pinnate, glabrous above, sparingly pubescent beneath,
5′–18′ long; leaflets 7–19, inequilateral, obliquely lanceolate, often falcate, entire, 1½′–4′ long, acuminate at the
apex and commonly acute at the base; rachis not winged;
panicles terminal, 5′–8′ long, dense; flowers white, about
2″ broad; petals ovate; berry globose or oval, 4″–7″
in diameter, very saponaceous, usually 1-seeded and
with 2 abortive ovules at its base.

River valleys and hillsides, Missouri to Louisiana, Kansas,
Texas, Arizona and northern Mexico.　Wood hard, light
yellowish brown; weight per cubic foot 59 lbs; used in
Texas for cotton baskets.　Berries used as a substitute for
soap.　Included, in our first edition, in the description of
Sapindus marginàtus Willd., of the Southeastern States,
which differs in having lanceolate petals.　May–June.

2. CARDIOSPÉRMUM L. Sp. Pl. 366. 1753.

Climbing and extensively branching herbaceous vines, with alternate bipinnate or decompound leaves, and small axillary tendril-bearing corymbs of slightly irregular polygamodioecious flowers. Tendrils 2 to each corymb, opposite. Pedicels jointed. Sepals 4, the 2 exterior smaller. Petals 4, 2 larger and 2 smaller. Disk 1-sided, undulate. Stamens 8; filaments unequal. Ovary 3-celled; style short, 3-cleft; ovules 1 in each cavity. Capsule inflated, 3-lobed. Seeds arilled at the base; cotyledons conduplicate. [Greek, heart-seed.]

About 15 species, of warm and temperate regions, the following typical.

1. Cardiospermum Halicácabum L. Balloon Vine. Heart-seed. Fig. 2821.

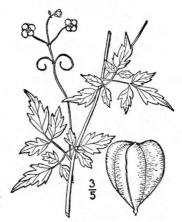

Cardiospermum Halicacabum L. Sp. Pl. 366. 1753.

Slender, glabrous or slightly pubescent, climbing, 2°–6° long. Leaves petioled, biternate or bipinnate, 2'–4' long; segments stalked, ovate or oblong, acute or acuminate, sharply serrate; peduncles commonly longer than the leaves, bearing a few-flowered corymb at the summit; flowers white, 3''–4'' broad; capsule much inflated, about 1' long, globose-pyriform; seeds globose, nearly black.

In waste places, New Brunswick, N. J., Washington, D. C., Kansas, and in ballast about the sea-ports; common in cultivation. Native of tropical America, and widely diffused as a weed in the warmer parts of the Old World. Heart-pea. Winter-cherry. Puff-ball. Summer.

$\frac{3}{5}$

Koelreutèria paniculàta Laxm., a Chinese tree with pinnate leaves and terminal panicles of yellow flowers succeeded by 3-lobed bladery pods, is much planted for shade and ornament and is reported spontaneous from seed in Indiana.

Family 82. RHAMNÀCEAE Dumort. Fl. Belg. 102. 1827.

BUCKTHORN FAMILY.

Erect or climbing shrubs, or small trees, often thorny. Leaves simple stipulate, mainly alternate, often 3–5-nerved. Stipules small, deciduous. Inflorescence commonly of axillary or terminal cymes, corymbs or panicles. Flowers small, regular, perfect or polygamous. Calyx-tube obconic or cylindric, the limb 4–5-toothed. Petals 4–5, inserted on the calyx, or none. Stamens 4–5, inserted with the petals and opposite them; anthers short, versatile. Disk fleshy. Ovary sessile, free from or immersed in the disk, 2–5- (often 3-) celled; ovules 1 in each cavity, anatropous. Fruit a drupe or capsule, often 3-celled. Seeds solitary in the cavities, erect; endosperm fleshy, rarely none; embryo large; coryledons flat.

About 50 genera and 600 species, natives of temperate and warm regions.

Ovary free from the disk; fruit a drupe.
  Petals sessile, entire; stone of the drupe 2-celled.   1. *Berchemia.*
  Petals short-clawed or none; stones of the drupe 2–4.   2. *Rhamnus.*
Ovary adnate to the disk at its base; fruit dry.   3. *Ceanothus.*

1. BERCHÈMIA Neck.; DC. Prodr. 2: 22. 1825.

[?OENOPLEA Hedw. f. Gen. 1: 151. 1806.]

Climbing or erect shrubs, with alternate petioled ovate or oblong coriaceous pinnately-veined leaves, and small greenish-white flowers in axillary or terminal clusters, or rarely solitary. Calyx-tube hemispheric, the limb 5-toothed. Petals 5, sessile, concave or cucullate. Stamens 5; filaments filiform. Disk filling the calyx-tube, covering but not united with the ovary. Drupe oval, obtuse, compressed, its flesh thin and coriaceous, its stone 2-celled. Seeds linear-oblong; cotyledons thin. [Name unexplained.]

About 10 species, the following typical one in southeastern North America, the others in Asia and tropical Africa.

1. Berchemia scándens (Hill.) Trelease.   Supple-Jack.   Rattan-Vine.   Fig. 2822.

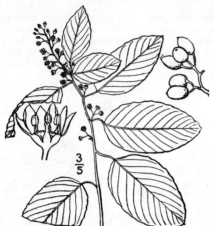

Rhamnus scandens Hill, Hort. Kew. 453. *pl. 20.* 1768.
R. volubilis L. f. Suppl. 152. 1781.
Berchemia volubilis DC. Prodr. **2**: 22. 1825.
Berchemia scandens Trel. Trans. St. Louis Acad. **5**:
  364. 1889.

A glabrous high-climbing shrub, with slender tough terete branches. Leaves ovate or ovate-oblong, 1′–2′ long, ½′–1′ wide, acute, acuminate, or obtuse and cuspidate at the apex, obtuse or somewhat truncate at the base, dark green above, paler beneath, their margins undulate and sometimes slightly revolute; veins 8–12 pairs; petioles slender, 2″–5″ long; flowers about 1½″ broad, mainly in small terminal panicles; petals acute; style short; drupe 3″–4″ long, equalling or shorter than its slender pedicel, its stone crustaceous.

In low woods, Virginia to Florida, Kentucky, Missouri and Texas. Rattan. March–June.

2. RHÁMNUS [Tourn.] L. Sp. Pl. 193. 1753.

Shrubs or small trees, with alternate pinnately veined and (in our species) deciduous leaves, and small axillary cymose, racemose or paniculate, perfect, dioecious, or polygamous flowers. Calyx-tube urceolate, its limb 4–5-toothed. Petals 4–5, short-clawed, mainly emarginate and hooded, or none. Disk free from the 3–4-celled ovary. Style 3–4-cleft. Drupe berry-like, oblong or globose, containing 2–4 separate nutlet-like stones. Seeds mainly obovoid; endosperm fleshy; cotyledons flat or revolute. [The ancient Greek name.]

About 90 species, natives of temperate and warm regions. Besides the following, some 10 others occur in the western United States and British America. Type species: *Rhamnus cathartica* L.

Flowers dioecious or polygamous; nutlets grooved.
  Petals present; flowers mainly 4-merous.
    Leaves broadly ovate; branches thorny; drupe with 3 or 4 nutlets.   1. *R. cathartica.*
    Leaves ovate-lanceolate; drupe with 2 nutlets.   2. *R. lanceolata.*
  Petals none; flowers 5-merous; drupe with 3 nutlets.   3. *R. alnifolia.*
Flowers perfect; nutlets smooth.
  Umbels peduncled; leaves acute; calyx campanulate.   4. *R. caroliniana.*
  Umbels sessile; leaves obtuse; calyx hemispheric.   5. *R. Frangula.*

1. Rhamnus cathàrtica L.   Buckthorn.   Fig. 2823.

Rhamnus cathartica L. Sp. Pl. 193. 1753.

A shrub, 6°–20° high, the twigs often ending in stout thorns. Leaves glabrous, petioled, broadly ovate or elliptic, 1½′–2½′ long, about 1′ wide, regularly crenate or crenulate, acute, obtuse or acuminate at the apex, obtuse or acutish at the base, with 3–4 pairs of veins, the upper running nearly to the apex; flowers dioecious, greenish, about 1″ wide, clustered in the axils, unfolding a little later than the leaves; petals, stamens and calyx-teeth 4; petals very narrow; drupe globose, black, about 4″ in diameter; nutlets 3 or 4, grooved.

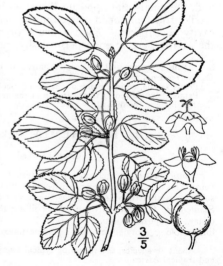

In dry soil, escaped from hedges, New England, the Middle States and Ontario. Introduced from Europe and native also of northern Asia. May–June. Hart's-thorn. Rhineberry. Waythorn. Purging buckthorn. The berries yield a dye, and have powerful medicinal properties.

2. Rhamnus lanceolàta Pursh.
Lance-leaved Buckthorn.
Fig. 2824.

Rhamnus lanceolata Pursh, Fl. Am. Sept. 166.
1814.

A tall erect shrub, with smooth grayish
bark, and unarmed mostly puberulent
branches. Leaves short-petioled, 1′–3½′ long,
½′–1′ wide, ovate-lanceolate to oblong-lanceolate, obtusish or acuminate at the apex,
acute or obtuse at the base, glabrous or
nearly so above, more or less pubescent,
especially on the veins beneath, finely serrulate; veins 6–7 pairs; flowers axillary,
1–3 together, greenish, about 1½″ broad,
appearing with the leaves; pedicels 1″–2″
long; petals, stamens and calyx-teeth 4;
drupe black, about 3″ in diameter, obovoid-
globose; stigmas 2; drupe containing 2
grooved nutlets.

In moist soil, Pennsylvania to Iowa and
Nebraska, south to Alabama and Texas. May.

3. Rhamnus alnifòlia L'Her. Alder-
leaved Buckthorn. Dwarf Alder.
Fig. 2825.

Rhamnus alnifolia L'Her. Sert. Angl. 5. 1788.

A small shrub, with puberulent thornless
branches. Leaves oval to elliptic, 2′–4′ long, 1′–2′
wide, obtuse to acuminate at the apex, mainly
acute at the base, irregularly crenate-serrate; veins
6–7 pairs; petioles 3″–6″ long; flowers 5-merous,
solitary or 2–3 together in the axils, green, about
1½″ broad, mainly dioecious, appearing with the
leaves; petals none; fruiting pedicels 3″–4″ long;
drupe globose, or somewhat obovoid, about 3″ in
diameter; nutlets 3, grooved.

In swamps, Newfoundland to British Columbia,
south to New Jersey, Illinois, Nebraska, Wyoming
and California. Dogwood. May–June.

4. Rhamnus caroliniàna Walt. Carolina
Buckthorn. Bog-birch. Fig. 2826.

Rhamnus caroliniana Walt. Fl. Car. 101. 1788.
Frangula caroliniana A. Gray, Gen. 2: 178. 1849.

A tall thornless shrub, or small tree, with puberulent twigs. Leaves elliptic or broadly oblong,
glabrous, or somewhat hairy on the veins beneath, 2′–6′ long, 1′–2½′ wide, acute or acuminate
at the apex, obtuse or acute at the base, obscurely
serrulate or even entire; veins 6–10 pairs; petioles
6″–9″ long; flowers 5-merous, perfect, greenish,
about 1″ broad, in axillary peduncled umbels, or
some of them solitary, unfolding after the leaves;
calyx finely puberulent, or glabrous, campanulate,
its lobes lanceolate, acuminate; petals present;
drupe globose, sweet, about 4″ in diameter; nutlets 3, not grooved.

In swamps and low grounds, Virginia and Kentucky to Missouri, Kansas, Florida and Texas. Erroneously recorded from New Jersey. Alder-leaved
buckthorn. Indian-cherry. May–June.

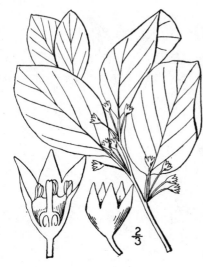

5. Rhamnus Frángula L.　Alder Buckthorn. Black Dogwood.　Fig. 2827.

Rhamnus Frangula L. Sp. Pl. 193. 1753.

A shrub, reaching a maximum height of about 8°, the young twigs finely and sparsely puberulent. Leaves thin, elliptic or obovate, entire or very obscurely crenulate, glabrous on both surfaces, obtuse or cuspidate at the apex, rounded or narrowed at the base, $1\frac{1}{2}'-2\frac{1}{2}'$ long, $1'-1\frac{1}{2}'$ wide; petioles $2''-4''$ long; umbels 1-6-flowered, strictly sessile in the axils; flowers 5-merous, perfect; calyx nearly hemispheric, its lobes ovate, acute; fruiting pedicels $2''-5''$ long; fruit $3''-4''$ in diameter, the 3 nutlets compressed, not grooved.

In bogs, Long Island, northern New Jersey and Ontario. Naturalized from Europe. May–June. Black-alder. Berry-alder. Arrow-wood. Persian-berry.

3. CEANÒTHUS L. Sp. Pl. 195. 1753.

Shrubs, with alternate petioled leaves, and terminal or axillary corymbs or panicles of white blue or yellowish perfect flowers. Calyx-tube hemispheric, or top-shaped, the limb 5-lobed. Petals 5, hooded, clawed, longer than the calyx-lobes, inserted under the disk. Stamens 5; filaments filiform, elongated. Ovary immersed in the disk and adnate to it at the base, 3-lobed. Disk adnate to the calyx. Style short, 3-cleft. Fruit dry, 3-lobed, separating longitudinally at maturity into 3 nutlets. Seed-coat smooth; endosperm fleshy; cotyledons oval or obovate. [Name used by Theophrastus for some different plant.]

About 55 species, natives of North America and northern Mexico.　Type species: *Ceanothus americanus* L.

Leaves ovate or ovate-oblong; peduncles long.　　　　　　　　　　　1. *C. americanus.*
Leaves oblong or oval-lanceolate; peduncles short.　　　　　　　　　2. *C. ovatus.*

1. Ceanothus americànus L.　New Jersey Tea.　Red-root.　Fig. 2828.

Ceanothus americanus L. Sp. Pl. 195. 1753.

Stems erect or ascending, branching, several commonly together from a deep reddish root, puberulent, especially above. Leaves ovate or ovate-oblong, $1'-3'$ long, $\frac{1}{2}'-1'$ wide, acute or acuminate at the apex, obtuse or subcordate at the base, finely pubescent, especially beneath, serrate all around, strongly 3-nerved; petioles $2''-5''$ long; peduncles terminal and axillary, elongated, often leafy, bearing dense oblong clusters of small white flowers; pedicels $3''-6''$ long, white; claws of the petals very narrow; fruit depressed, about $2''$ high, nearly black.

In dry open woods, Maine to Ontario, Manitoba, south to Florida and Texas. May–July. Ascends to 4200 ft. in North Carolina. An infusion of the leaves was used as tea by the American troops during the Revolution. Also called Wild snowball. Spangles. Walpole-tea. Wild pepper. Mountain-sweet.

2. Ceanothus ovàtus Desf. Smaller Red-root. Fig. 2829.

Ceanothus ovatus Desf. Hist. Arb. 2 : 381. 1809.

Ceanothus ovalis Bigel. Fl. Bost. Ed. 2 : 92. 1824.

C. ovatus pubescens T. & G.; S. Wats. Bibl. Index 1 : 166. 1878.

Similar to the preceding species, but generally a smaller shrub and nearly glabrous throughout, or western races densely pubescent. Leaves oblong, or oval-lanceolate, 1'–2' long, 3''–9'' wide, mainly obtuse at each end, but sometimes acute at the apex, glabrous, or with a few hairs on the principal veins, serrate with prominently gland-tipped teeth; peduncles short, nearly always terminal, bearing dense short clusters of white flowers; pedicels slender, 4''–7'' long; fruit nearly as in C. americanus.

In rocky places and on prairies, Vermont and Ontario to Minnesota, Manitoba, the District of Columbia, Illinois and Texas. Rare or absent along the Atlantic coast. May–June.

Family 83. VITÀCEAE Lindl. Nat. Syst. Ed. 2, 30. 1836.

GRAPE FAMILY.

Climbing, woody vines, or erect shrubs, with copious watery sap, nodose joints, alternate simple or compound petioled leaves with deciduous stipules, and small regular greenish perfect or polygamo-dioecious flowers, in panicles, racemes or cymes. Calyx entire or 4–5-toothed. Petals 4 or 5, separate or coherent, valvate, caducous. Stamens 4 or 5, opposite the petals; filaments subulate, inserted at the base of the disk or between its lobes; disk sometimes obsolete or wanting; anthers 2-celled. Ovary 1, generally immersed in the disk, 2–6-celled; ovules 1 or 2 in each cavity, ascending, anatropous. Fruit a 1–6-celled berry (commonly 2-celled). Seeds erect; testa bony; raphe generally distinct; endosperm cartilaginous; embryo short.

About 10 genera and over 500 species, widely distributed.

Hypogynous disk present, annular or cup-shaped, lobed or glandular; leaves not digitately compound in our species.
  Petals united into a cap, falling away without separating.   1. *Vitis.*
  Petals separate, spreading.
    Foliage not fleshy; flowers mostly 5-parted; shrubs or vines.   2. *Ampelopsis.*
    Foliage fleshy; flowers mostly 4-parted; vines.   3. *Cissus.*
Hypogynous disk obsolete or wanting; leaves digitately compound in our species, the leaflets 5–7.
                                          4. *Parthenocissus.*

1. VÌTIS [Tourn.] L. Sp. Pl. 202. 1753.

Climbing or trailing woody vines, rarely shrubby, mostly with tendrils. Leaves simple, usually palmately lobed or dentate. Stipules mainly small, caducous. Flowers mostly dioecious, or polygamo-dioecious, rarely perfect. Petals hypogynous or perigynous, coherent in a cap and deciduous without expanding. Ovary 2-celled, rarely 3-4-celled; style very short, conic; ovules 2 in each cavity. Berry globose or ovoid, few-seeded, pulpy, edible in most species. [The ancient Latin name.]

About 50 species, natives of warm and temperate regions. In addition to the following, some 10 or 15 others occur in the southern and western United States. Type species: *Vitis vinifera* L.
Leaves woolly beneath; twigs woolly or hairy.
  Pubescence rusty-brown; berries large, musky.   1. *V. Labrusca.*
  Pubescence at length whitish; berries small, black, not musky
    Berries with bloom; branches terete.   2. *V. aestivalis.*
    Berries without bloom; branches angular.   3. *V. cinerea.*

Leaves glabrate, sometimes slightly pubescent when young.
  Leaves bluish-white glaucous beneath.   4. *V. bicolor.*
  Leaves not glaucous beneath.
    Leaves 3–7-lobed ; lobes acute or acuminate.
      Lobes and sinuses acute ; berries with bloom.   5. *V. vulpina.*
      Lobes long-acuminate ; sinuses rounded ; berries without bloom.   6. *V. palmata.*
    Leaves sharply dentate, scarcely lobed.
      Bark loose ; pith interrupted by the solid nodes.
        High-climbing ; leaves large ; berries sour.   7. *V. cordifolia.*
        Low ; leaves small ; berries sweet.   8. *V. rupestris.*
      Bark close ; pith continuous through the nodes. Genus Muscadinia Small.
                                                                           9. *V. rotundifolia.*

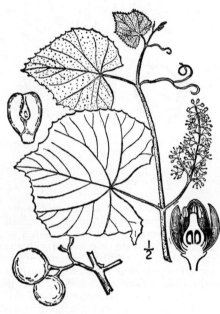

1. Vitis Labrúsca L.   Northern Fox- or Plum-grape.   Wild Vine.   Fig. 2830.

Vitis Labrusca L. Sp. Pl. 203. 1753.

Climbing or trailing, often ascending high trees, sometimes forming a stem a foot in diameter or more, the young twigs, forked tendrils, petioles and lower surfaces of the leaves densely rusty-pubescent, especially when young. Bark loose and separating in strips; nodes solid, interrupting the pith; leaves large, each opposite a forked tendril or a flower cluster, varying from merely dentate to deeply lobed with rounded sinuses; fertile flowers in compact panicles, the sterile looser; berries few, brownish-purple or yellowish, about 9″ in diameter, strongly musky; seeds 3–6, about 4″ long; raphe narrow.

Thickets, Vermont to Indiana, New York, Georgia and Tennessee. Recorded from Minnesota. The cultivated isabella, concord and catawba grapes have been derived from this species. Ascends to 2100 ft. in Virginia. May–June. Fruit ripe Aug.–Sept.

2. Vitis aestivàlis Michx.   Summer Grape.   Small Grape.   Fig. 2831.

Vitis aestivalis Michx. Fl. Bor. Am. 2 : 230. 1803.

High climbing, branches terete, the twigs and petioles pubescent; bark loose and shreddy; pith interrupted at the nodes. Leaves as large as those of *V. Labrusca,* dentate, or 3–5-lobed, floccose-woolly with whitish or rusty pubescence, especially when young, sometimes becoming nearly glabrous when mature; tendrils and flower-clusters intermittent (wanting opposite each third leaf); inflorescence generally long and loose; berries numerous, about 5″ in diameter, black, with a bloom, acid, but edible; seeds 2–3, about 3″ long; raphe narrow.

In thickets, southern New Hampshire to Florida, west to southern Ontario, Wisconsin, Kansas and Texas. Ascends to 3500 ft. in North Carolina. May–June. Fruit ripe Sept.–Oct.

3. Vitis cinèrea Engelm. Fig. 2832.

Vitis aestivalis var. *canescens* Engelm. Am.
　Nat. **2** : 321, name only. 1868.
Vitis aestivalis var. *cinerea* Engelm.; A.
　Gray, Man. Ed. 5, 679. 1867.
V. cinerea Engelm. Bushb. Cat. Ed. 3, 17.
　1883.

Climbing, branches angled, young shoots
and petioles mostly floccose-pubescent;
bark loose; pith interrupted; tendrils
intermittent. Leaves dentate, or somewhat 3-lobed, often longer than wide,
rather densely floccose-pubescent with
whitish, persistent hairs on the lower
surface, especially along the veins, sparingly so on the upper; inflorescence
loose; berries black, without bloom,
3″–4″ in diameter, pleasantly acid, 1–2-
seeded; seeds about 2″ long, the raphe
narrow.

Illinois to Nebraska, Kansas, Louisiana
and Texas. May–June. Downy or ashy
grape.

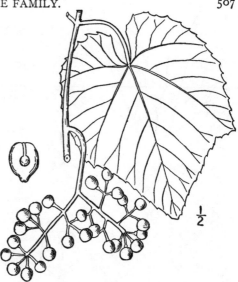

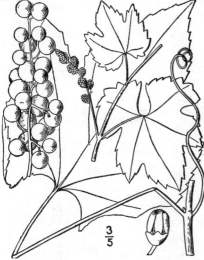

4. Vitis bícolor LeConte. Blue or Winter Grape. Fig. 2833.

Vitis bicolor LeConte, Proc. Phil. Acad. **6** : 272. 1852.
Vitis aestivalis var. *bicolor* LeConte; Wats. & Coult.
　in A. Gray, Man. Ed. 6, 113. 1890.

High-climbing or long-trailing, the tendrils intermittent, the branches terete. Twigs and leaves
glabrous, or somewhat pubescent, bluish-glau-
cous, especially the lower surfaces of the leaves,
the bloom sometimes disappearing by the time
the fruit ripens; internodes long, the pith interrupted at the nodes; leaves usually 3-lobed, cordate at the base, sometimes 12′ long, the sinuses
rounded, the lobes acute or acuminate; inflorescence compact; berries bluish-black with a bloom,
sour, about 4″ in diameter; seeds about 2″ long,
raphe narrow.

New Hampshire to Michigan, North Carolina,
Tennessee and Missouri. May–June.

5. Vitis vulpìna L. Riverside or Sweet Scented Grape. Fig. 2834.

Vitis vulpina L. Sp. Pl. 203. 1753.
Vitis riparia Michx. Fl. Bor. Am. **2** : 231. 1803.
Vitis cordifolia var. *riparia* A. Gray, Man. Ed. 5,
　113. 1867.

Climbing or trailing, glabrous throughout, or
more or less pubescent on the veins of the lower
surfaces of the leaves; branches rounded or
slightly angled, greenish; pith interrupted, the
diaphragm thin; tendrils intermittent. Leaves
thin, shining, almost all sharply 3–7-lobed, the
sinuses angular, the lobes acute or acuminate,
the terminal one commonly long; stipules 2″–3″
long, often persistent until the fruit is formed;
inflorescence compact or becoming loose; berries bluish-black, with a bloom, 4″–5″ in diameter, rather sweet; seeds 2–4, 2″ long, the raphe
narrow and inconspicuous.

Along rocky river-banks, New Brunswick to Manitoba, south to Maryland, West Virginia, Arkansas
and Colorado. May–June. Fruit beginning to ripen
in July or earlier, sometimes continuing until October. Winter-, frost-, bull- or Aroyo-grape.

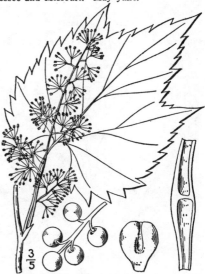

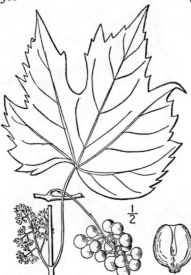

6. Vitis palmàta Vahl. Missouri Grape.
Fig. 2835.

Vitis palmata Vahl, Symbol. Bot. 3 : 42. 1794.

Vitis rubra Michx.; Planch. in DC. Mon. Phan. 5 : 354. 1887.

High-climbing, glabrous or nearly so throughout, or with slight pubescence on the veins of the lower surfaces of the leaves; twigs bright red; bark separating in large flakes; pith interrupted, the diaphragms thick; tendrils intermittent, forked. Leaves dull, darker green than in *V. vulpina*, deeply 3–5-lobed, the sinuses rounded, the lobes long-acuminate; stipules 1½″–2″ long; inflorescence loose; berries black, 4″–5″ in diameter, without bloom; seeds 1 or 2, about 3″ long; raphe indistinct.

River-banks, Illinois, Missouri and Arkansas. Blooming later and ripening its berries after *V. vulpina*. June–July.

7. Vitis cordifòlia Michx. Frost Grape.
Chicken Grape. Fig. 2836.

Vitis cordifolia Michx. Fl. Bor. Am. 2 : 231. 1803.
Vitis virginiana Munson, Gard. & For. 3 : 474. 1890. Not Lam. 1808.
Vitis Baileyana Munson. Vit. Bail. 1893.

High-climbing, the twigs glabrous or slightly pubescent, terete or indistinctly angled; pith interrupted by thick diaphragms; internodes long; bark loose; tendrils intermittent; stem sometimes 1° in diameter or more. Leaves 3′–4′ wide, glabrous, or sparingly pubescent on the veins beneath, thin, sharply and coarsely dentate with very acute teeth, sometimes slightly 3-lobed, mostly long-acuminate at the apex; tendrils forked, intermittent; stipules about 2″ long; inflorescence loose or compact; berries black, shining, about 3″ in diameter, ripening after frost; seeds 1 or 2, about 2″ long; raphe narrow.

Moist thickets and along streams, southern New York and New Jersey to Illinois, Wisconsin, Nebraska, Florida and Texas. Possum-, fox- or winter grape. May–June. Fruit ripe Oct.–Nov.

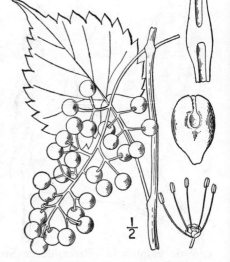

8. Vitis rupéstris Scheele. Sand, Sugar or Mountain Grape.
Fig. 2837.

V. rupestris Scheele, Linnaea 21 : 591. 1848.

Low, bushy or sometimes climbing to a height of several feet, glabrous or somewhat floccose-pubescent on the younger parts; pith interrupted; bark loose; tendrils forked, intermittent or often wanting. Leaves smaller than in any of the preceding species, pale green, shining, sharply dentate with coarse teeth, or sometimes incised, abruptly pointed, rarely slightly 3-lobed, the sides often folded together; stipules 2″–3″ long; inflorescence compact; berries black, with a bloom, 3″–4″ in diameter, sweet, 2–4-seeded; seeds about 2″ long; raphe very slender.

In various situations, Pennsylvania to the District of Columbia, Missouri, Tennessee and Texas. April–June. Fruit ripe in August.

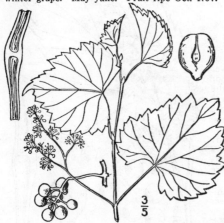

9. Vitis rotundifòlia Michx. Southern Fox-grape. Bullace Grape. Fig. 2838.

Vitis rotundifolia Michx. Fl. Bor. Am. **2**: 231. 1803.
Vitis vulpina T. & G. Fl. N. A. **1**: 245. 1838. Not L. 1753.
Muscadinia rotundifolia Small, Fl. SE. U. S. 757. 1903.

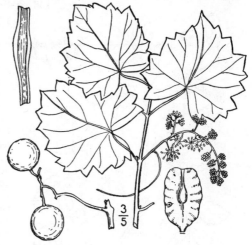

Trailing or high-climbing, glabrous or nearly so throughout; tendrils simple, intermittent, sometimes few; bark close, not shreddy; pith continuous through the nodes.   Leaves nearly orbicular, 2′–3′ wide, dark green, shining, dentate with large triangular teeth; inflorescence dense; berries few, purple, 5″–9″ in diameter, without bloom, tough, musky; seeds several, flat, wrinkled, notched at the apex; raphe indistinct.

In moist, often sandy soil, Delaware to Indiana, Kentucky, Missouri, Kansas, south to Florida, Texas and Mexico. Muscadine grape.   The original of the Scuppernong. The berries fall away singly. May. Fruit ripe Aug.–Sept.

2. AMPELÓPSIS Michx. Fl. Bor. Am. 1: 159. 1803.

[Cissus Pers. Syn. **1**: 143. 1805. Not L. 1753.]

Climbing woody vines, or some species bushy, the coiling tendrils not tipped by adhering expansions. Leaves simple, dentate or lobed, or pinnately or palmately compound. Flowers polygamo-dioecious, or polygamo-monoecious. Petals 5, separate, spreading. Disk cup-shaped, 5-lobed or annular, adnate to the base of the ovary; ovary 2-celled; ovules 2 in each cavity; style subulate. Berry 2–4-seeded, the flesh usually thin and inedible. [Greek, vine-like.]

About 15 species, natives of temperate and warm regions, only the following known to occur in North America. Type species: *Ampelopsis cordata* Michx.

Leaves coarsely serrate, or slightly 3-lobed.   1. *A. cordata.*
Leaves 2–3-pinnately compound.   2. *A. arborea.*

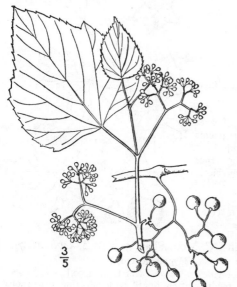

1. Ampelopsis cordàta Michx.
Simple-leaved Ampelopsis.
Fig. 2839.

Ampelopsis cordata Michx. Fl. Bor. Am. **1**: 159. 1803.
Cissus Ampelopsis Pers. Syn. **1**: 142. 1805.
Vitis indivisa Willd. Berl. Baumz. Ed. 2, 538. 1811.

Glabrous or the young twigs sparingly pubescent, climbing, the branches nearly terete; tendrils few or none. Leaves broadly ovate, 2′–4′ long, coarsely serrate, rarely slightly 3-lobed, glabrous on both sides, or pubescent along the veins, truncate or cordate at the base, acuminate at the apex; panicles small, loose, with 2–3 main branches; corolla expanding its petals; disk cup-shaped; berries 2″–3″ in diameter, bluish, 1–2-seeded, the flesh very thin and inedible; seeds about 2″ long; raphe narrow.

Swamps and river-banks, southern Virginia to Florida, west to Illinois, Nebraska and Texas. May–June.

2. Ampelopsis arbòrea (L.) Rusby. Pepper-vine. Pinnate-leaved Ampelopsis. Fig. 2840.

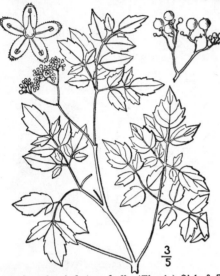

Vitis arborea L. Sp. Pl. 203. 1753.

Cissus stans Pers. Syn. 1: 143. 1805.

Vitis bipinnata T. & G. Fl. N. A. 1: 243. 1838.

Ampelopsis arborea Rusby, Mem. Torr. Club 5: 221. 1894.

Glabrous or nearly so, erect or ascending, bushy, sometimes climbing; tendrils often wanting. Leaves bipinnate, or the lowest tripinnate and sometimes 8′ in length or more; leaflets ovate or rhombic-ovate, ½′–1½′ long, sharply serrate, acute or acuminate at the apex, obtuse or slightly cordate or the terminal one cuneate at the base, glabrous, or somewhat pubescent on the veins beneath; panicles short-cymose; corolla expanding; berries black, depressed-globose, about 3″ in diameter, sometimes pubescent, the flesh thin, inedible; seeds 1–3.

In rich moist soil, Virginia to Missouri, Florida and Mexico. Cuba. June–July.

Ampelopsis heterophylla (Thunb.) Sieb. & Zucc., a climbing eastern Asiatic vine, with deeply palmately 3–5-lobed leaves and short-peduncled compound cymes, was found as a waif from cultivation at Lancaster, Pa., in 1890.

3. CÍSSUS L. Sp. Pl. 117. 1753.

Mostly climbing vines, sometimes prostrate, the foliage usually succulent. Leaves simple or compound, often trifoliolate, the leaflets readily separating in drying. Flowers mostly perfect. Petals usually 4, spreading. Disk cup-shaped, adnate to the base of the ovary. Berries small, inedible; 1–2-seeded. [Greek, ivy.]

Over 225 species, most abundant in tropical regions. Type species: *Cissus vitaginea* L.

1. Cissus incìsa (Nutt.) Des Moulins. Cut-leaved Cissus. Fig. 2841.

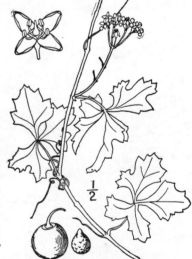

Vitis incisa Nutt. T. & G. N. A. 1: 243. 1838.

Cissus incisa Des Moulins; Durand, Actes Soc. Linn. Bordeaux 24: [reprint 59]. 1862.

A long vine, the stem and leaves succulent. Leaves 3-foliolate or 3-parted; leaflets or leaf-segments ovate or obovate, cuneate at the base, toothed, or the middle one lobed, 2′ long or less; inflorescence umbel-like; berries obovoid, 4″ long, nearly black, 1–2-seeded, borne on recurved pedicels.

Sandy and rocky soil, Missouri and Kansas to Texas, Florida and Arizona. June–Aug.

4. PARTHENOCÍSSUS Planch. in DC. Mon. Phan. 5: Part 2, 447. 1887.

[PSEDERA Neck. Elem. 1: 158. Hyponym. 1790.]

[QUINARIA Raf. Am. Man. Grape-vines, 6. 1830. Not Lour. 1790.]

Climbing or trailing woody vines, the tendrils often tipped with adhering expansions (disks), or sometimes merely coiling, our species with digitately compound leaves, the leaflets

5-7. Flowers perfect, or polygamo-monoecious, in compound cymes or panicles. Petals 5, spreading. Hypogynous disk obsolete or wanting in our species. Stamens 5. Ovary 2-celled; ovules 2 in each cavity; style short, thick. Berry 1-4-seeded, the flesh thin, not edible.

About 10 species, natives of eastern North America and Asia, the following typical. Besides the following, another occurs in Texas.

1. Parthenocissus quinquefòlia (L.) Planch. Virginia Creeper. False Grape. American Ivy. Fig. 2842.

Hedera quinquefolia L. Sp. Pl. 202. 1753.
Vitis quinquefolia Lam. Tabl. Encycl. 2: 135. 1793.
Ampelopsis quinquefolia Michx. Fl. Bor. Am. 1: 160. 1803.
Parthenocissus quinquefolia Planch. in DC. Mon. Phan. 5: Part 2, 448. 1887.
P. vitacea A. S. Hitchc. Spring Fl. Manhattan 26. 1894.

High-climbing or trailing, glabrous or pubescent. Tendrils usually numerous, and often provided with terminal adhering expansions, the vine sometimes supported also by aerial roots; leaves petioled, digitately 5-foliolate (rarely 7-foliolate); leaflets stalked, oval, elliptic, or oblong-lanceolate; 2'-6' long, acute or acuminate, narrowed at the base, coarsely toothed, at least above the middle, pale beneath, dark green above, glabrous or somewhat pubescent; panicles ample, erect or spreading in fruit; berries blue, about 6" in diameter, usually 2-3-seeded; peduncles and pedicels red.

In woods and thickets, Quebec to Assiniboia, Missouri, Florida, Texas and Mexico. Bahamas; Cuba. July. Fruit ripe in October. The foliage turns deep red in autumn. The species consists of numerous races, differing in pubescence, serration of leaflets and in the tendrils. Five-finger-ivy or -creeper. Five-leaf-ivy. Erroneously called woodbine.

Parthenocissus tricuspidàta (Sieb. & Zucc.) Planch., the *Ampelopsis Veitchii* of the gardeners, a Japanese vine, clinging to walls by its very numerous disk-tipped tendrils, has the leaves sharply 3-lobed or sometimes 3-divided; it is freely planted for ornament.

Family 84. TILIÀCEAE Juss. Gen. 289. 1789.

Trees, shrubs or rarely herbs, with fibrous bark, alternate (rarely opposite) simple leaves, mostly small and deciduous stipules, and axillary or terminal generally cymose or paniculate flowers. Sepals 5, rarely 3-4, valvate, deciduous. Petals of the same number, or fewer, or none, alternate with the sepals, mostly imbricated in the bud. Stamens ∞, mostly 5-10-adelphous; anthers 2-celled. Ovary 1, sessile, 2-10-celled; style entire or lobed; ovules anatropous. Fruit 1-10-celled, drupaceous or baccate. Embryo straight, rarely curved; cotyledons ovate or orbicular; endosperm fleshy, rarely wanting.

About 35 genera and 275 species, widely distributed in warm and tropical regions, a few in the temperate zones.

1. TÍLIA [Tourn.] L. Sp. Pl. 514. 1753.

Trees, with serrate cordate mainly inequilateral leaves, and axillary or terminal, cymose white or yellowish perfect flowers, the peduncles subtended by and partly adnate to broad membranous bracts. Sepals 5. Petals 5, spatulate, often with small scales at the base. Stamens ∞; filaments cohering with the petal-scales or with each other in 5 sets. Ovary 5-celled; cells 2-ovuled; style simple; stigma 5-toothed. Fruit dry, drupaceous, globose or ovoid, indehiscent, 1-2-seeded. Seeds ascending; endosperm hard; cotyledons broad, 5-lobed, corrugated. [The ancient Latin name.]

About 20 species, natives of the north temperate zone, 1 in the mountains of Mexico. Type species: *Tilia europaèa* L.

Leaves smooth or very nearly so, sometimes glaucous.
1. *T. americana.*
Leaves mostly densely hairy beneath, not glaucous.
Leaves brown-hairy or rusty-hairy beneath.
2. *T. pubescens.*
Leaves white, grey or silvery beneath.
Bracts mostly abruptly narrowed at the base, sessile or nearly so.
3. *T. heterophylla.*
Bracts mostly attenuate at the base, distinctly stalked.
4. *T. Michauxii.*

1. Tilia americàna L. Bass-wood.   American Linden. White-wood. Fig. 2843.

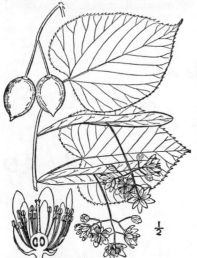

½

Tilia emericana L. Sp. Pl. 514. 1753.
T. glabra Vent. Mem. Acad. Paris 4: 9. *pl. 2.* 1802.
Tilia canadensis Michx. Fl. Bor. Am. **2**: 306. 1803.

A large forest tree, 60°–125° high,. with spreading branches; trunk 2°–5° in diameter. Leaves
obliquely ovate, cordate or sometimes truncate at
the base, 2′–5′ wide, coriaceous, glabrous on both
sides, or with some pubescence on the veins of the
lower surface, sharply serrate with glandular teeth,
abruptly acuminate or acute; petioles 1′–2′ long;
floral bract 2′–4′ long, often narrowed at the base,
strongly veined; cymes drooping, 6–20-flowered;
flowers 5″–7″ broad, fragrant; petals yellowish-
white, crenate, slightly longer than the pubescent
sepals; scales similar to the petals, but smaller; fruit
globose-ovoid, 4″–5″ in diameter.

In rich woods and along river-bottoms, New Brunswick to Georgia, especially along the mountains, west
to Manitoba, Nebraska and Texas. Wood soft, weak,
light brown or reddish; weight per cubic foot 28 lbs.
Used for cabinet work and for paper pulp. Bast-, lin-,
lime-, bee-, black-lime- or monkey-nut-tree. White-lind.
Southern linn. Yellow bass-wood. Wickup. Daddy-
nuts. Spoon-wood. Whistle-wood. May–June.

2. Tilia pubéscens Ait. Southern Bass-wood or
White-wood. Fig. 2844.

Tilia pubescens Ait. Hort. Kew. **2**: 229. 1789.
T. americana var. *pubescens* Loud. Arb. Brit. **1**: 374. 1838.
A small tree, 40°–50° high, with a trunk 1° in diameter. Leaves generally smaller than those of *T. americana*, glabrous above, brown-pubescent, or sometimes
densely woolly beneath; floral bracts commonly broader
and shorter, narrowed or rounded at the base; fruit
globose, 2½″–3″ in diameter.
In moist woods, Virginia to Florida, west to Texas. Erroneously reported from farther north. Wood as in *T.
americana*, but lighter in weight, about 24 lbs. to the cubic
foot. May–June.
Tilia leptophýlla (Vent.) Small, ranging from Missouri
to Texas, differs in its thinner, less hairy leaves, but is probably a race of this species.

½

½

3. Tilia heterophýlla Vent. White Bass-wood.
Bee-tree. Linden. Fig. 2845.

T. heterophylla Vent. Mem. Acad. Paris 4: 16. *pl. 5.* 1802.

A forest tree, 45°–70° high, with a trunk 1½°–3½° in
diameter. Leaves larger than in either of the preceding
species (often 6′–8′ long), inequilateral, cordate or truncate, glabrous and dark green above, white beneath with
a fine downy pubescence, acute or acuminate; floral
bracts 3′–5′ long, narrowed at the base; flowers slightly
larger and often fewer than those of *T. americana*;
fruit globose, about 5″ in diameter.

In woods, New York and Pennsylvania, south along the
Alleghanies and Blue Ridge to Florida and Alabama, west
to central Illinois, Kentucky and Tennessee. White linn.
Teil- or tile-tree. Cottonwood. Silver-leaf poplar. Wahoo.
Wood weak, light brown; weight per cubic foot 26 lbs.
June–July.

The European linden or lime-tree, **Tilia europaèa** L., is planted as an ornamental tree in parks
and on lawns. It may be distinguished from any of our species by the absence of scales at the base
of the petals. Its name, Lin, was the origin of the family name of Linnaeus.

4. Tilia Michaùxii Nutt.   Michaux's Bass-wood.
Fig. 2846.

T. alba Michx. f. Hist. Arb. Am. **3**: 315.   1813.   Not L.

T. Michauxii Nutt. Sylva, Ed. 2, 92.   1842

A forest tree, sometimes 90° tall, the bark broadly furrowed, or that of the branches smooth and silvery gray Leaves firm in texture, 9' long or less, serrate, whitish-pubescent beneath, the apex acuminate, the base usually very oblique; floral bracts spatulate, attenuate toward the base and decurrent on the peduncle to above its base; staminodes spatulate; petals light yellow, 3″–5″ long; fruit ovoid or globose, 4″–7″ long.

In rich soil, Connecticut to Ohio, Georgia, Kentucky and Alabama.   June–July.

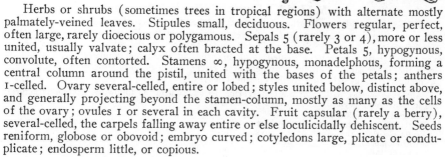

Family 85.   **MALVÀCEAE** Neck. Act. Acad. Theod. **2**: 488.   1770.

Mallow Family.

Herbs or shrubs (sometimes trees in tropical regions) with alternate mostly palmately-veined leaves. Stipules small, deciduous. Flowers regular, perfect, often large, rarely dioecious or polygamous. Sepals 5 (rarely 3 or 4), more or less united, usually valvate; calyx often bracted at the base. Petals 5, hypogynous, convolute, often contorted. Stamens ∞, hypogynous, monadelphous, forming a central column around the pistil, united with the bases of the petals; anthers 1-celled. Ovary several-celled, entire or lobed; styles united below, distinct above, and generally projecting beyond the stamen-column, mostly as many as the cells of the ovary; ovules 1 or several in each cavity. Fruit capsular (rarely a berry), several-celled, the carpels falling away entire or else loculicidally dehiscent. Seeds reniform, globose or obovoid; embryo curved; cotyledons large, plicate or condu-plicate; endosperm little, or copious.

About 45 genera and 900 species, widely distributed in tropical and temperate regions.

Stamen-column anther-bearing at the summit; carpels in a circle around a central axis.
Carpels 1-seeded.
   Flowers perfect.
      Involucels of 6–9 bractlets.   1. *Althaea.*
      Involucels of 1–3 bractlets, or none.
         Stigmas linear, on the inner side of the style-branches.
            Carpels beakless; petals obcordate.   2. *Malva.*
            Carpels beaked; petals truncate.   3. *Callirrhoë.*
         Stigmas capitate, terminal.
            Seed ascending.   5. *Malvastrum.*
            Seed pendulous.   6. *Sida.*
   Flowers dioecious.   4. *Napaea.*
Carpels 2–several-seeded.
   Involucels none.   7. *Abutilon.*
   Involucels of 3 bractlets.
      Carpels continuous.   8. *Phymosia.*
      Carpels septate between the seeds.   9. *Modiola.*
Stamen-column anther-bearing below the entire or 5-toothed summit; fruit a loculicidal capsule.
Carpels 1-seeded.   10. *Kosteletzkya.*
Carpels several-seeded.   11. *Hibiscus.*

1.   **ALTHAEA** L. Sp. Pl. 686.   1753.

Tomentose or pilose herbs, with lobed or divided leaves, and axillary or terminal, solitary or racemose, perfect flowers. Involucels of 6–9 bractlets united at the base. Calyx 5-cleft. Petals 5. Stamen-column anther-bearing at the summit. Cavities of the ovary numerous, 1-ovuled; style-branches the same number as the ovary-cavities, stigmatic along the inner side; carpels numerous, indehiscent, 1-seeded, arranged in a circle around the axis. Seed ascending. [Ancient Greek, signifying to cure.]

About 15 species, natives of the temperate and warm parts of the Old World, the following typical.

1. Althaea officinàlis L.   Marsh-Mallow.
Wymote.   Fig. 2847.

Althaea officinalis L. Sp. Pl. 686. 1753.

Perennial, herbaceous, erect, 2°–4° high, branching, densely velvety pubescent. Leaves broadly
ovate, acute or obtuse, dèntate and generally
3-lobed, the lower ones often cordate; veins elevated on the lower surfaces; petioles ½′–1′ long;
flowers in terminal and axillary narrow racemes,
pink, about 1′–1½′ broad; bractlets of the involucels 6–9, linear, shorter than the 5 ovate-lanceolate
acute calyx-segments; carpels 15–20, tomentose.

In salt marshes, coast of Massachusetts, Connecticut and New York; Pennsylvania, Michigan. Reported from New Jersey and Arkansas. Naturalized
from Europe. Roots thick, very mucilaginous, used
in confectionery, and in medicine as a demulcent.
Summer. Mortification-root. Sweat-weed.

Althaea cannábina L., with digitately 5-parted
leaves, has been found in waste places at Washington, D. C.

Althaea ròsea L., the Hollyhock, is occasionally
seen in waste places, spontaneous after cultivation.

2. MÁLVA [Tourn.] L. Sp. Pl. 687. 1753.

Pubescent or glabrate herbs, with dentate lobed or dissected leaves, and axillary or
terminal solitary or clustered perfect flowers. Calyx 5-cleft. Bractlets of the involucels 3
(rarely none). Petals 5. Stamen-column anther-bearing at the summit. Cavities of the
ovary several or numerous, 1-ovuled; style-branches of the same number, linear, stigmatic
along the inner side. Carpels arranged in a circle, 1-seeded, beakless, indehiscent. Seed
ascending. [Greek, referring to the emollient leaves.]

About 30 species, natives of the Old World. In addition to the following, another is naturalized in California. Type species: *Malva sylvestris* L.

Leaves with 5–9 shallow lobes.
    Petals 2–4 times the length of the calyx.   1. *M. sylvestris.*
    Petals 1–2 times the length of the calyx.
        Procumbent, low.   2. *M. rotundifolia.*
        Erect, tall.   3. *M. verticillata.*
Leaves deeply 5–7-lobed.
    Stem-leaves deeply lobed; carpels glabrous.   4. *M. moschata.*
    Stem-leaves 1–3-pinnatifid; carpels downy.   5. *M. Alcea.*

1. Malva sylvéstris L.   High Mallow.
Fig. 2848.

Malva sylvestris L. Sp. Pl. 689. 1753.

Biennial, erect or ascending, branched, pubescent with
loose spreading hairs, or glabrate. Leaves orbicular, or
reniform, 1½′–4′ wide, with 5–9 shallow angular or
rounded lobes, crenate-denate, truncate or cordate at
the base; petioles 2′–6′ long; flowers reddish-purple,
2–4 times as long as the calyx; carpels about 10, flat
1′–1½′ broad, in axillary clusters; pedicels slender; petals
on the back, rugose-reticulate.

In waste places and along roadsides, sparingly adventive
from Europe in the United States, Canada and Mexico,
escaped from cultivation. Native also in Siberia. Summer.
English names, common mallow, cheese-flower, cheese-cake,
pick-cheese, round dock, maul. Country-mallow.

2. Malva rotundifòlia L. Low, Dwarf or Running Mallow. Cheeses. Fig. 2849.

M. rotundifolia L. Sp. Pl. 688. 1753.

Annual or biennial, procumbent and spreading from a deep root, branched at the base, stems 4'–12' long. Leaves orbicular-reniform, 1'–3' wide, cordate, with 5–9 broad shallow dentate-crenate lobes; petioles slender, 3'–6' long; flowers clustered in the axils, pale blue, 4''–7'' broad; pedicels 6''–15'' long; petals about twice the length of the ovate acute calyx-lobes; carpels about 15, rounded on the back, pubescent.

In waste places, common nearly throughout our territory, and widely distributed as a weed in other temperate regions. Naturalized from Europe. Native also of western Asia. English names, dutch-cheese, doll or fairy cheeses, pellas. Blue, common or country mallow. Malice. May–Nov.

Malva parviflòra L., another European weed, with smaller flowers, the similar carpels reticulated, widely distributed in the Southern and Western States, has been found in Missouri, and in ballast about cities on the Atlantic Coast.

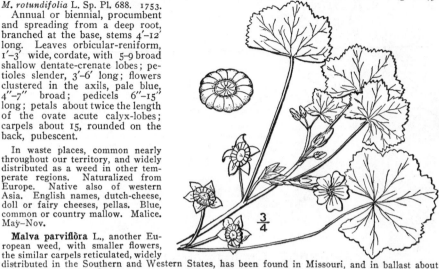

3. Malva verticillàta L. Whorled Mallow. Curled Mallow. Fig. 2850.

Malva verticillata L. Sp. Pl. 689. 1753.
Malva crispa L. Sp. Pl. Ed. 2, 970. 1763.
Malva verticillata crispa L. Sp. Pl. 689. 1753.

Annual, erect, glabrous or nearly so, 4°–6° high. Leaves nearly orbicular with 5–11 shallow, angular dentate lobes, their margins often wrinkled and crisped; petioles elongated; flowers white or whitish, sessile, clustered in the axils, about the size of those of *M. rotundifolia*; petals about twice the length of the calyx-lobes; carpels rugose-reticulated.

In waste places, Nova Scotia to Quebec, South Dakota and Pennsylvania. Adventive from Europe. Summer.

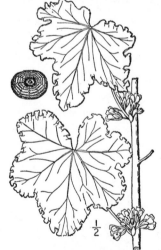

4. Malva moschàta L. Musk Mallow. Muskplant. Musk. Fig. 2851.

Malva moschata L. Sp. Pl. 690. 1753.

Perennial, erect, 1°–2° high, branching, pubescent with long hairs, or glabrate. Basal leaves orbicular, 3'–4' wide, with 5–9 short broad rounded dentate lobes; stem-leaves deeply divided into linear or cuneate, pinnatifid or cleft segments; flowers 1½'–2' broad, pink or white, racemosely clustered at the summits of the stem and branches; petals obcordate or emarginate, 5–8 times as long as the triangular-ovate acute calyx-lobes; carpels 15–20, densely hairy, rounded on the back.

In waste places and along roadsides, Nova Scotia to Ontario, British Columbia, New Jersey, Virginia, Wisconsin and Oregon. Naturalized from Europe. Plant with a faint odor of musk. Summer.

5. Malva Alcea L. European or Vervain Mallow. Fig. 2852.

Malva Alcea L. Sp. Pl. 689. 1753.

Similar to the preceding species, but the stem-leaves are only once 5–7-parted or cleft, the lobes dentate or incised; pubescence shorter and denser, stellate; flowers pink, purplish or white; petals obcordate; carpels glabrous, very finely rugose-reticulated.

In waste places, occasionally escaped from gardens, Vermont to Michigan, New York and Pennsylvania. Introduced from Europe. Summer.

3. CALLÍRHOE Nutt. Journ. Acad. Phil. 2: 181. 1821.

[NUTTALLIA Barton, Fl. N. A. 2: 74. *pl. 62.* 1822.]

Herbs, with lobed or divided leaves, and showy axillary or terminal perfect flowers. Bractlets of the involucel 1–3, separate, or none. Calyx deeply 5-parted. Petals cuneate, truncate, often toothed or fimbriate. Stamen-column anther-bearing at the summit. Cavities of the ovary ∞, 1-ovuled; style-branches of the same number as the cells of the ovary, stigmatic along the inner side. Carpels ∞ (10–20), arranged in a circle, 1-seeded, indehiscent or 2-valved, beaked at the apex, the beak separated from the cavity by a septum. Seed ascending. [A Greek mythological name.]

A genus of about 7 species, natives of the central and southern United States and northern Mexico. Type species: *Callirhoë digitàta* Nutt.

Bractlets of the involucels none.
    Flowers 1′ broad; carpels very pubescent.
    Flowers 1½′–2′ broad; carpels scarcely pubescent.
Bractlets of the involucels 3.
    Leaves triangular, crenate; carpels not rugose.
    Leaves orbicular, palmatifid; carpels rugose.

1. *C. alceoides.*
2. *C. digitata.*

3. *C. triangulata.*
4. *C. involucrata.*

1. Callirhoë alceoïdes (Michx.) A. Gray. Light Poppy-Mallow. Fig. 2853.

Sida alceoides Michx. Fl. Bor. Am. 2: 44. 1803.

Callirhoë alceoides A. Gray, Mem. Am. Acad. (II.) 4: 18. 1848.

Perennial, erect, 8′–20′ high, slender, strigose-pubescent, branched at the base from a thick woody root. Basal leaves triangular, palmately lobed or incised, 2′–3½′ long, slender-petioled; stem-leaves palmatifid, the divisions linear or cuneate, acute or obtuse; flowers corymbose or racemose at the summit, pink or white, about 1′ broad; pedicels 1′–2′ long, slender; involucels none; calyx-lobes triangular, acuminate; petals dentate and somewhat fimbriate; carpels strigose-pubescent and conspicuously rugose-reticulate on the back.

In dry soil, Kentucky to Nebraska, Kansas and Texas. May–Aug.

2. Callirhoë digitàta Nutt. Fringed Poppy-Mallow. Fig. 2854.

Callirhoë digitata Nutt. Journ. Acad. Phila. **2**: 181. 1821.

Nuttallia digitata Bart. Flora N. A. **2**: 74. *pl.* 62. 1822.

Similar to the preceding species, sparsely pubescent or glabrous. Divisions of the stem-leaves longer, narrowly linear, sometimes quite entire and 4′–5′ long, sometimes deeply incised; basal leaves sometimes cordate-triangular, crenate, lobed or divided; involucels none; flowers long-peduncled, 1½′–2′ broad, reddish-purple or lighter; petals beautifully fimbriate; calyx-lobes triangular to lanceolate, acuminate; carpels strongly rugose-reticulate, scarcely pubescent.

In dry soil, Illinois and Missouri to Kansas and Texas. April–July.

3. Callirhoë triangulàta (Leavenw.) A. Gray. Clustered Poppy-Mallow Fig. 2855.

Malva triangulata Leavenw. Am. Journ. Sci. **7**: 62. 1824.

Callirhoë triangulata A. Gray, Mem. Am. Acad. (II.) **4**: 16. 1848.

Perennial, erect or ascending from a deep root, 1½°–2½° high, branched above, stellate-pubescent with short hairs. Leaves triangular-hastate, the lower long-petioled, crenate or slightly lobed, acute or obtusish, 2′–3′ long, the upper short-petioled or nearly sessile, smaller, 3–5-cleft or divided, the lobes narrow, dentate or crenate; flowers in terminal panicled clusters, 1′–2′ broad, short-pedicelled, deep purple; involucel of 3 linear or spatulate bractlets, nearly as long as the 5-lobed calyx; carpels numerous, hairy, not rugose, short-beaked.

Prairies, Indiana to Minnesota, North Carolina, Missouri and Texas. June–Aug.

Callirhoë Bushii Fernald, of the Ozark Mountains, Missouri, has palmatifid leaves similar to those of the following species, but with broader segments; it is described as erect, and its bractlets as ovate, but a specimen examined has an ascending stem and linear bractlets.

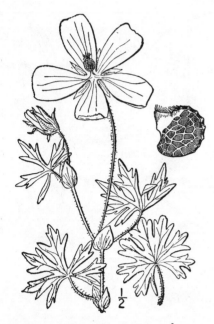

4. Callirhoë involucràta (T. & G.) A. Gray. Purple Poppy-Mallow. Fig. 2856.

Nuttallia involucrata Nutt.; Torr. Ann. Lyc. N. Y. 2: 172. Name only. 1828.

Malva involucrata T. & G. Fl. N. A. 1: 226. 1838.

Callirhoë involucrata A. Gray, Mem. Am. Acad. (II.) 4: 16. 1848.

Perennial, branched from a deep root, procumbent or ascending, $1°-2°$ long, pubescent with long hispid hairs. Leaves cordate-orbicular, palmately lobed or palmatifid, the lobes obtuse or acute, dentate or incised, those of the upper leaves commonly narrower than those of the lower; stipules ovate, conspicuous; peduncles terminal and axillary, slender, 1-flowered; bractlets of the involucel 3, linear, half the length of the lanceolate acute 3–5-nerved calyx-lobes; flowers red-purple, $1'-2\frac{1}{2}'$ broad; carpels rugose-reticulate.

In dry soil, Minnesota and Iowa to Texas, Utah and New Mexico and northern Mexico. April–Aug.

4. NAPAÈA [Clayt.] L. Sp. Pl. 686. 1753.

An erect perennial herb, with palmately-lobed leaves, and small white dioecious flowers in ample terminal corymbose panicles. Involucels none. Calyx 5-toothed. Petals entire. Staminate flowers with 15–20 anthers borne at the summit of the stamen-column. Pistillate flowers with 8–10 styles, stigmatic along their inner surface, the stamen-column present but destitute of anthers. Cavities of the ovary as many as the styles, 1-ovuled. Carpels 8–10, separating at maturity from the axis, beakless, but minutely tipped, imperfectly 2-valved. Seed ascending. [Greek, a dell.]

A monotypic genus of the east-central United States.

1. Napaea dioìca L. Glade Mallow. Fig. 2857.

Napaea dioica L. Sp. Pl. 686. 1753.

Simple, or branching above, $4°-9°$ high, pubescent or glabrate. Basal and lower leaves $6'-12'$ broad, long-petioled, orbicular in outline, 7–11-parted nearly to the base, the divisions acute, dentate and lobed; upper leaves smaller, short-petioled, 5–9-lobed, the lobes incisely cut, acute or acuminate; staminate flowers $6''-9''$ broad, the pistillate somewhat smaller; petals obovate, 2–3 times the length of the calyx; carpels strongly 1-nerved, slightly rugose-reticulate.

In moist grounds, southern Pennsylvania to Virginia, west to Minnesota, Iowa and Tennessee. July.

5. MALVÁSTRUM A. Gray, Mem. Am. Acad. (II.) 4: 21. 1848.

Herbs, with entire cordate or divided leaves, and axillary or terminal, solitary or race-mose, short-pedicelled perfect flowers. Calyx 5-cleft. Bractlets of the involucels small, 1–3 or none. Stamen-column anther-bearing at the apex. Cavities of the ovary 5–∞, 1-ovuled. Style-branches of the same number, stigmatic at the summit only, forming capitate stigmas; carpels indehiscent or imperfectly 2-valved, falling away from the axis at maturity, their apices pointed or beaked. Seed ascending. [Greek, star-mallow.]

About 75 species, natives of America and South Africa, 2 of them widely distributed as weeds in tropical regions. In addition to the following, about 15 other species inhabit the southern and western United States. Type species: *Malvastrum coccíneum* (Pursh) A. Gray.

Leaves lanceolate-oblong, dentate.   1. *M. angustum.*
Leaves pedately 5-parted, the lobes incised.   2. *M. coccineum.*

1. Malvastrum angústum A. Gray. Yellow False Mallow. Fig. 2858.

Sida hispida Pursh, Fl. Am. Sept. 452. 1814?
Malvastrum angustum A. Gray, Mem. Am. Acad. (II.) 4: 22. 1848.
Malveopsis hispida Kuntze, Rev. Gen. Pl. 72. 1891.

Annual, erect with the habit of a *Sida*, slender, branching, pubescent with appressed hairs, 6′–12′ high. Leaves oblong-lanceolate, or linear-oblong, petioled, acute, finely dentate with somewhat distant teeth, 9″–10″ long, 2″–4″ wide; flowers yellow, 4″–6″ broad, mostly solitary in the axils of the upper leaves, short-peduncled; bractlets of the involucels 2–3, linear, shorter than the ovate-triangular pubescent acute calyx-lobes; petals about equalling the calyx; carpels 5, somewhat pubescent, reniform, 2-valved at maturity.

In dry ground, Tennessee and Illinois to Iowa, Missouri and Kansas. Summer.

$\frac{2}{3}$

2. Malvastrum coccíneum (Pursh) A. Gray. Red False Mallow. Fig. 2859.

Malva coccinea Nutt. in Fraser's Cat. Name only. 1813.
Cristaria coccinea Pursh, Fl. Am. Sept. 454. 1814.
M. coccineum A. Gray, Mem. Am. Acad. (II.) 4: 21. 1848.

Perennial, erect or ascending, 4′–10′ high, freely branched, densely and silvery stellate-pubescent. Lower leaves 1′–2′ wide, ovate-orbicular in outline, slender-petioled, the uppermost nearly sessile, all pedately 3–5-parted; lobes cuneate to linear, incised, mainly obtuse; flowers red, 6″–9″ broad, in dense short terminal spicate racemes; bractlets of the involucels commonly none; petals much longer than the lanceolate acutish calyx-lobes; carpels 10–15, rugose-reticulated, indehiscent, 1-seeded (rarely 2-seeded).

Prairies and plains, Iowa to North Dakota, Manitoba, Nebraska, Texas, British Columbia and New Mexico. Prairie-mallow. Moss-rose. May–Aug.

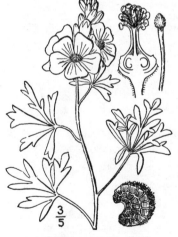

$\frac{3}{5}$

6. SÍDA L. Sp. Pl. 683. 1753.

Herbs, with serrate, crenate or lobed leaves, and solitary or clustered, axillary or terminal, perfect flowers. Bractlets of the involucels none. Calyx 5-toothed or 5-cleft. Stamen-column anther-bearing at the summit. Cells of the ovary 5–∞, 1-ovuled; style-branches of the same number, stigmatic at the summit only. Carpels indehiscent, or at length 2-valved at the apex. Seed pendulous. [Greek, used by Theophrastus.]

About 100 species, natives of the warmer parts of America, Asia, Africa and Australasia. Besides the following, some 20 others occur in the southern and southwestern parts of the United States. Type species: *Sida alnifolia* L.

Leaves linear, ovate or oblong, serrate
    Leaves ovate or oblong-lanceolate; flowers 2"–4" broad   1. *S. spinosa.*
    Leaves linear or linear-oblong; flowers 6"–12" broad.   2. *S. Elliottii.*
Leaves palmately 3–7-lobed.
    Glabrous or nearly so, tall; flowers in terminal panicles.   3. *S. hermaphrodita.*
    Densely stellate-canescent, low; flowers axillary.   4. *S. hederacea.*

1. Sida spinòsa L. Prickly Sida. Indian or False Mallow. Fig. 2860.

Sida spinosa L. Sp. Pl. 683. 1753.

Annual, erect, branching, finely and softly pubescent, 1°–2° high. Leaves ovate to oblong-lanceolate, 1'–2' long, 5"–10" wide, petioled, obtuse or acute, truncate or cordate at the base, crenate-dentate; flowers axillary, short-peduncled, yellow, 2"–4" broad; peduncles shorter than the petioles; calyx-teeth triangular, acute; carpels 5, dehiscent at the apex into 2 beaks; stipules linear; petioles of the larger leaves with a small spine-like tubercle at the base.

In waste places, Maine to New Jersey, Iowa and Michigan, Kansas, Florida and Texas, and widely distributed in tropical America. Supposed by some to be naturalized at the north, but it occurs in New Jersey as if native. Summer.

2. Sida Ellióttii T. & G. Elliott's Sida. Fig. 2861.

Sida Elliottii T. & G. Fl. N. A. 1 : 231. 1838.

Perennial, glabrous or nearly so, branching, 1°–4° high. Leaves short-petioled, linear or linear-oblong, 1'–2' long, 2"–2½" wide, mostly obtuse at each end, serrate-dentate; peduncles 1-flowered, often longer than the petioles; flowers axillary, yellow, 6"–12" broad, calyx-teeth broadly ovate, acute; carpels 8–10, dehiscent at the apex, slightly and abruptly pointed.

In dry soil, southern Virginia to Florida, west to Missouri and Chihuahua. Summer.

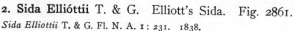

3. Sida hermaphrodìta (L.) Rusby. Virginia Mallow. Fig. 2862.

Napaea hermaphrodita L. Sp. Pl. 686. 1753.
Sida Napaea Cav. Diss. 5 : 277. *pl. 132. f. 1.* 1788.
S. hermaphrodita Rusby, Mem. Torr. Club 5 : 223. 1894.

Perennial, nearly glabrous, branching, 4°–10° high. Leaves petioled, 3'–6' wide, ovate-orbicular, deeply 3-7-lobed or cleft, the lobes lanceolate or ovate, the middle one commonly longest, all incised-dentate, acute or acuminate; flowers white, 9"–12" broad, numerous in terminal corymbose panicles; pedicels, calyx and petioles of the upper leaves finely pubescent; calyx-lobes short and broad, acute; carpels about 10, acute, dehiscent at the top.

Along rivers, in rocky places, southern Pennsylvania to Ohio, Virginia, West Virginia and Tennessee. Summer.

4. Sida hederàcea Torr. Round-leaved Sida. Fig. 2863.

Sida hederacea Torr.; A Gray, Mem. Am. Acad. 4: 23. 1849.
Malva hederacea Dougl.; Hook. Fl. Bor. Am. 1: 107. 1830.

Perennial, decumbent, densely stellate-canescent. Leaves reniform to broadly ovate. inequilateral, 2' wide or less; flowers solitary or few together in the axils, the peduncles recurved in fruit; petals white or yellowish; calyx 5-angled, its lobes ovate-lanceolate, acuminate; fruit short, conic, of 6 to 10 carpels.

In moist, often saline soil, Kansas to Texas, Mexico, Wyoming, Washington and California.

7. ABÙTILON [Tourn.] Mill. Gard. Dict. Abr. Ed. 4. 1754.

Herbs or shrubs, sometimes trees in tropical countries, mostly soft-pubescent, with cordate angular or lobed leaves and axillary flowers. Involucels none. Calyx 5-cleft. Stamen-column anther bearing at the apex. Cavities of the ovary 5–∞, 3-9-ovuled. Style-branches the same number as the ovary-cavities, stigmatic at the apex; carpels 2-valved, often rostrate, falling away from the axis at maturity. Seeds more or less reniform, the upper ascending, the lower pendulous or horizontal. [Name given by the celebrated Arabian physician Avicenna (Ibn Sina), died 1037.]

About 100 species, natives of warm and tropical regions of both hemispheres. In addition to the following typical one, some 15 others inhabit the southern and southwestern parts of the United States.

1. Abutilon Abùtilon (L.) Rusby. Velvet Leaf. Indian Mallow. Fig. 2864.

Sida Abutilon L. Sp. Pl. 685. 1753.
Abutilon Theophrasti Medic. Malv. 28. 1787.
Abutilon Avicennae Gaertn. Fruct. et Sem. 2: 251. *pl. 135.* 1791.
A. Abutilon Rusby, Mem. Torr. Club 5: 222. 1894.

Annual, stout, 3°–6° high, branched, densely and finely velvety-pubescent. Leaves long-petioled, cordate, ovate-orbicular, 4'–12' wide, dentate, or nearly entire, acuminate, the tip blunt; flowers yellow, 6"–9" broad, axillary, solitary; peduncles stout, shorter than the petioles; head of fruit 1' in diameter or more; carpels 12–15, pubescent, dehiscent at the apex, each valve beaked by a slender awn.

In waste places, frequent or common throughout our area, except the extreme north. Naturalized or adventive from southern Asia, and widely distributed as a weed in warm countries. American jute or hemp. Indian hemp. Cotton-, sheep- or mormon-weed. Butter-button- or velvet-weed. Pie-print or -marker. Butter-print. Aug.–Oct.

8. PHYMÒSIA Desv. in Hamilt. Prodr. 49. 1825.

[SPHAERALCEA St. Hil. Plant. Us. Bras. *pl. 52.* 1827.]

Herbs or shrubs. Bractlets of the involucels 3, distinct, or united at the base. Stamen-column anther-bearing at the summit. Cavities of the ovary 5–∞, 2-3-ovuled. Style-branches the same number as the ovary-cavities, stigmatic at the apex; carpels 2-valved, not septate between the seeds, separating from the axis at maturity. Seeds reniform. [Greek, swollen, referring to the somewhat inflated carpels of the typical species.]

About 40 species, natives of America and South Africa. In addition to the following, about 16 others occur in the southwestern United States. Type species: *Phymosia abutiloides* (L.) Desv., of the Bahamas.

Leaves nearly orbicular, 5–7-lobed; flowers pink.   1. *P. remota.*
Leaves lanceolate, crenulate; flowers red.   2. *P. cuspidata.*

3/5

1. Phymosia remóta (Greene) Britton. Maple-leaved Globe-Mallow. Fig. 2865.

Iliamna remota Greene, Leaflets 1: 206. 1906.
Sphaeralcea remota Fernald, Rhodora 10: 52. 1908.

Perennial, erect, branched, 2°–6° high, finely stellate-pubescent and scabrous. Leaves nearly orbicular in outline, palmately 5–7-lobed or cleft, cordate, the lobes ovate or lanceolate, dentate, acute, the middle one generally longest; flowers pink, 1'–1½' broad, short-pedicelled, clustered in the upper axils or in terminal spike-like racemes; bractlets of the involucels linear, shorter than the calyx; calyx densely pubescent, its lobes triangular, acuminate.

In gravelly soil, known only from an island in the Kankakee River, Illinois. Summer. Previously referred to the western *Sphaeralcea acerifolia* Nutt.

2. Phymosia cuspidàta (A. Gray) Britton. Sharp-fruited Globe-Mallow. Fig. 2866.

Sida stellata Torr. Ann. Lyc. N. Y. 2: 171. 1827. Not Cav. 1802.
Sphaeralcea stellata T. & G. Fl. N. A. 1: 228. 1838.
Sphaeralcea angustifolia var. *cuspidata* A. Gray, Proc. Am. Acad. 22: 293. 1887.
Sphaeralcea cuspidata Britton, in Britt. & Brown, Ill. Fl. 3: 519 1898.

Perennial, densely stellate-canescent; stems rather stout, simple, or somewhat branched, leafy, 1°–4° high. Leaves lanceolate, linear-lanceolate, or oblong-lanceolate, obtuse, or acutish, firm, crenulate, the lower with petioles as long as the blade, the others short-petioled, the larger 2'–4' long, ¼'–1' wide, sometimes hastately lobed toward the base; flowers red, 6"–10" broad, clustered in the axils, short-pedicelled; carpels 1–3-seeded, cuspidate, the tip often deciduous, wrinkled on the sides, stellate-canescent, or glabrate.

3/5

Kansas to Texas, Colorado, Arizona and Mexico. April–Aug.

9. MODÌOLA Moench, Meth. 619. 1794.

A prostrate or ascending herb, often rooting from the nodes, with palmately cleft or divided leaves, and small axillary peduncled red to purple flowers. Bracts of the involucre 3, distinct. Calyx 5-cleft. Stamen-column anther-bearing at the apex. Cavities of the ovary ∞, 2–3-ovuled. Style-branches stigmatic at the summit; carpels 15–20, septate between the seeds, dehiscent into 2 valves with awn-pointed tips, and cristate on the back. [Latin, from the likeness of the fruit to the small Roman measure, *modiolus*.]

A monotypic genus of warm and temperate America and South Africa.

1. Modiola caroliniàna (L.) G. Don. Bristly-fruited Mallow. Fig. 2867.

Malva caroliniana L. Sp. Pl. 688. 1753.

Modiola multifida Moench, Meth. 620. 1791.

Modiola caroliniana G. Don, Gen. Hist. Pl. 1 : 466. 1831.

Annual or biennial, more or less pubescent, freely branching; stems slender, 6′–18′ long. Leaves nearly orbicular in outline, ½–2½′ wide, petioled, pedately 3–5-cleft, the lobes dentate or incised; leaves sometimes simply dentate; flowers axillary, solitary, 3″–5″ broad; peduncles at length elongated, slender; petals obovate; fruit depressed-orbicular, the carpels hispid-aristate along the back.

In low grounds, Virginia to Florida, west to Texas, and in Central and South America and the West Indies. The same species apparently occurs in South Africa. Summer.

10. KOSTELÉTZKYA Presl, Rel. Haenk. 2: 130. *pl. 70.* 1836.

Perennial, scabrous or pubescent herbs or shrubs, with hastate or angular leaves, and showy, axillary or paniculate flowers. Bractlets of the involucels several, linear. Calyx 5-toothed or 5-cleft. Stamen-column entire, or 5-toothed at the summit, anther-bearing below for nearly its entire length. Ovary 5-celled, the cells 1-ovuled; style-branches of the same number, stigmatic at the capitate summits. Capsule depressed, 5-angled. Seeds reniform, ascending. [Named in honor of V. F. Kosteletzky, a botanist of Bohemia.]

About 8 species, natives of warm and temperate America. In addition to the following, another occurs in the southwestern United States. Type species: *Kosteletzkya hastàta* Presl.

1. Kosteletzkya virgínica (L.) A. Gray. Virginia Kosteletzkya. Fig. 2868.

Hibiscus virginicus L. Sp. Pl. 697. 1753.

K. virginica A. Gray, Gen. 2 : 80. *t. 132.* 1849.

K. virginica var. *althaeifolia* Chapm. Fl. S. States 57. 1860.

K. althaeifolia A. Gray; S. Wats. Bibl. Index 136. 1878.

Perennial, erect, branching, 2°–4° high, more or less stellate-pubescent and scabrous. Leaves ovate, or hastate, truncate or cordate at the base, 2′–5′ long, unequally dentate and often 3-lobed below, sometimes with an additional lobe or two at the middle, acute, velvety or pubescent; flowers pink, 1½′–2½′ broad, in loose terminal leafy panicles; bractlets of the involucels 8–9, linear, shorter than the lanceolate acute calyx-segments; capsule hispid-pubescent.

In salt or brackish marshes, southeastern New York to Florida and Louisiana. Bermuda; Cuba. Aug.

11. HIBÍSCUS L. Sp. Pl. 693. 1753.

Herbs, shrubs, or in tropical regions even small trees, with dentate or lobed leaves, and showy, axillary or paniculate, mostly campanulate flowers. Bractlets of the involucels numerous, narrow. Calyx 5-cleft or 5-toothed. Column of stamens truncate or 5-toothed at the apex, anther-bearing below along much of its length. Ovary 5-celled, the cells 3–several-ovuled; style-branches 5, stigmatic at the capitate summit. Capsule 5-valved. Seeds reniform. [An ancient name, used by Dioscorides for the Marsh Mallow.]

About 180 species, widely distributed in warm and temperate countries. In addition to the following, about 14 others occur in the southern and western United States. Type species: *Hibiscus Trionum* L.

Tall perennial herbs.
　Leaves white-pubescent beneath ; seeds glabrous, or nearly so.
　Leaves glabrate, or stellate-hairy above ; bractlets not ciliate.
　　Capsule glabrous or nearly so.
　　　Corolla pink ; capsule short-tipped.
　　　Corolla white, with a crimson eye ; capsule beaked.
　　Capsule stellate-pubescent.
　Leaves soft-hairy above ; bractlets ciliate.
　Leaves glabrous on both sides ; seeds hairy.
Low hairy annual of waste places.
Tall woody shrub, escaped from gardens.

1. *H. Moscheutos.*
2. *H. oculiroseus.*
3. *H. incanus.*
4. *H. lasiocarpos.*
5. *H. militaris.*
6. *H. Trionum.*
7. *H. syriacus.*

1. Hibiscus Moscheùtos L.　Swamp Rose-Mallow.　Mallow Rose.　Fig. 2869.

Hibiscus Moscheutos L. Sp. Pl. 693. 1753.
Hibiscus palustris L. Sp. Pl. 693. 1753.
Hibiscus opulifolius Greene, Leaflets **2** : 65.

Erect, 4°–7° high, forming numerous cane-like stems from a perennial root. Leaves ovate or ovate-lanceolate, 3′–7′ long, cordate or obtuse at the base, acute or acuminate at the apex, the lower or sometimes all lobed at the middle, palmately veined, dentate or crenate, densely white stellate-pubescent beneath, green and glabrous or slightly stellate above; petioles 1′–5′ long; flowers 4′–7′ broad, pink, clustered on stout pedicels at the summits of the stems; peduncles often adnate to the petioles; bractlets linear, not ciliate, shorter than the calyx; calyx-lobes ovate; capsule ovoid, 1′ long, glabrous or sparingly pubescent, abruptly short-pointed or blunt; seeds glabrous.

In brackish marshes, eastern Massachusetts to Florida and Louisiana, and on lake shores and in saline situations locally in the interior to western Ontario, Indiana and Missouri. Sea-hollyhock. Water- or swamp-mallow. Aug.–Sept.

2. Hibiscus oculiròseus Britton.　Crimson-eye Rose-Mallow.　Fig. 2870.

Hibiscus oculiroseus Britton, Journ. N. Y. Bot. Gard. **4**: 220. 1903.

Similar to the preceding species in stems, foliage and pubescence, and about as high, the flowers about as large. Calyx-segments triangular-lanceolate, acute, nearly twice as long as wide; corolla white with a dark crimson center; capsule ovoid-conic, long-pointed.

In salt marshes, southeastern New York and New Jersey. A hybrid, with intermediate characters between this and the preceding, occurs on Staten Island, and also appeared in the New York Botanical Garden. Aug.–Sept.

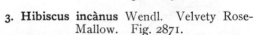

3. Hibiscus incànus Wendl.　Velvety Rose-Mallow.　Fig. 2871.

Hibiscus incanus Wendl. Bot. Beob. 54. 1798.

Perennial, erect, 6° high or less. Leaves ovate *or* broadly lanceolate, 4′–7′ long, acuminate at the apex, obtuse or subcordate at the base, dentate, rarely somewhat lobed, pale and finely velvety beneath, dark green above, long-petioled; bractlets linear, not ciliate, about half as long as the velvety calyx; calyx-segments ovate, acute or acuminate; petals white to pink, blotched at the base, 3′–4′ long; capsule ovoid, stellate-pubescent, rather shorter than the calyx.

Marshes, Maryland to Florida and Louisiana. May–Aug.

4. Hibiscus lasiocàrpus Cav.　Hairy-fruited Rose-Mallow.　Fig. 2872.

Hibiscus lasiocarpus Cav. Diss. 3: 159. *pl. 70. f. 1.* 1787.

Resembles the three preceding species. Leaves broadly ovate, dentate or 3–7-lobed, mostly cordate or truncate at the base; pubescence of the lower surface white and densely stellate, the upper surface darker, with longer soft mostly nearly simple hairs; bractlets of the involucels linear, equalling the calyx or shorter, ciliate; capsule ovoid, densely and finely hairy; seeds nearly glabrous.

In swamps, southern Indiana to Missouri, south to Florida and Texas. Aug.

5. Hibiscus militàris Cav.　Halberd-leaved Rose-Mallow.　Sweating-weed. Fig. 2873.

Hibiscus militaris Cav. Diss. 3: 352. *pl. 198. f. 2.* 1787.

Hibiscus virginicus Walt. Fl. Car. 177. 1788. Not L. 1753.

Erect, 3°–5° high, nearly glabrous throughout. Leaves 4′–5′ long, ovate in outline, acute or acuminate, cordate or truncate at the base, the lower, or sometimes all, hastately lobed, the margins dentate-crenate; petioles 1′–6′ long; flowers pink with a darker eye, 2′–3′ long, axillary or clustered at the ends of the stem or branches; peduncles shorter than the petioles and jointed above the middle; bractlets of the involucels linear, slightly shorter than the calyx, glabrous, or with a few scattered hairs; fruiting calyx inflated; capsule ovoid, enclosed by the calyx, glabrous, or very nearly so; seeds silky.

Along rivers, southern Pennsylvania to Florida, west to Minnesota, Nebraska and Louisiana. Aug.–Sept.

6. Hibiscus Triònum L.　Bladder Ketmia.　Flower-of-an-Hour.　Venice Mallow.　Modesty.　Fig. 2874.

Hibiscus Trionum L. Sp. Pl. 697. 1753.

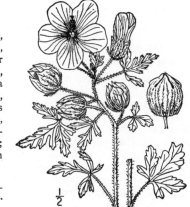

Annual, depressed and branching from the base, pubescent with spreading hairs. Leaves petioled, ovate or orbicular in outline, pedately 3–7-lobed or divided, the lobes obtuse, dentate-crenate or cleft, the middle one longer; flowers pale yellow with a purple eye, 1′–2½′ broad, axillary to the upper leaves, each one remaining open but a few hours; petals tinged with purple on the outer edge; bracts linear, ciliate, much shorter than the membranous beautifully nerved hispid-pubescent 5-angled inflated calyx; capsule globose-ovoid, hairy; seeds roughened with short processes.

In waste places, Nova Scotia to Florida, South Dakota and Kansas. Adventive from southern Europe. Aug.–Sept. Devil's head-in-a-bush. Black-eyed susan.

526 MALVACEAE. VOL. II.

7. Hibiscus Syrìacus L. Shrubby Althaea. Rose-of-Sharon. Fig. 2875.

Hibiscus Syriacus L. Sp. Pl. 695. 1753.

A branching nearly glabrous shrub, 10°–20° high. Leaves short-petioled, ovate, 2'–5' long, obtuse or cuneate at the base, acute but blunt at the apex, 3–5-lobed or the upper merely dentate, sometimes with a few scattered stellate hairs on the upper surface; flowers axillary, short-pedun-cled, pink or white with a crimson centre, 2'–4' broad; bractlets linear, shorter than the calyx, or slightly exceed-ing it; peduncles, bractlets and calyx stellate-pubescent; capsule ovoid, nearly 1' long.

Sparingly escaped from cultivation, Connecticut to Pennsyl-vania, the District of Columbia and Georgia. Introduced from western Asia. Aug.–Sept.

Family 86. THEÀCEAE DC. Prodr. 1: 529. 1824.
TEA FAMILY.

Trees or shrubs, with alternate or rarely opposite pinnately-veined mainly exstipulate leaves, and large axillary or terminal flowers. Flowers regular, mostly perfect. Sepals 5 (rarely 4–7), imbricated, the inner ones generally larger than the outer. Calyx often 2-bracted at the base. Petals 5 (rarely 4–9), hypogynous, imbricated, crenulate. Stamens ∞, numerous, hypogynous, more or less united at their bases. Ovary sessile, 2–several-celled; styles 1 or several; ovules 2 or more in each cavity. Fruit a 3–5-celled generally woody capsule with loculicidal or septicidal dehiscence; endosperm little or none; embryo large, with condupli-cate cotyledons.

About 16 genera and 160 species, natives of tropical and warm regions.

Stamens monadelphous.   1. *Stewartia.*
Stamens 5-adelphous.   2. *Gordonia.*

1. STEWÀRTIA L. Sp. Pl. 698. 1753.

Shrubs, with deciduous membranous serrulate leaves, and large showy axillary solitary flowers on short peduncles. Sepals 5, rarely 6, slightly unequal, ovate or lanceolate. Petals of the same number, obovate. Stamens monadelphous below; anthers versatile. Ovary 5-celled; styles 1 or 5; ovules 2 in each cell, anatropous, ascending; capsule ovoid, woody, 5-celled, loculicidally dehiscent. Embryo straight. Cotyledons oval, longer than the inferior radicle. [Named in honor of John Stuart, Marquis of Bute.]

Six species, natives of North America and Japan. Type species: *Stewartia Malachodendron* L.

Style 1, compound; stigma 5-lobed; seeds marginless; capsule subglobose. 1. *S. Malachodendron.*
Styles 5, distinct; seeds wing-margined; capsule ovoid, 5-angled. 2. *S. pentagyna.*

1. Stewartia Malachodéndron L. Round-fruited Stewartia. Fig. 2876.

Stewartia Malachodendron L. Sp. Pl. 698. 1753.

Stewartia virginica Cav. Diss. 5: *pl. 158. f. 2.* 1787.

A shrub, 6°–12° high, the branches pubescent when young. Leaves oval, acute or acuminate at each end, 2'–3' long, 1½'–2' wide, serrulate with mucronate-tipped teeth, pubescent below, glabrous above; petioles 2''–4'' long; flowers axillary, 3'–4' broad, solitary or occasionally in pairs, very short-peduncled; sepals ovate or orbicular, obtuse, silky-pubescent, united at the base; petals 5, white, sparingly pubescent on the under side, minutely crenulate; filaments purple; anthers blue; style 1, compound; stigma 5-lobed; capsule subglobose, 6''–8'' long, pubescent; seeds marginless.

In woods, Virginia to Florida, west to Louisiana. April–May.

2. Stewartia pentágyna L'Her. Angled-fruited or Mountain Stewartia. Fig. 2877.

Stuartia pentagyna L'Her. Stirp. Nov. 155. *pl. 74.* 1784.

Malachodendron ovatum Cav. Diss. **5**: *pl. 158. f. 2.* 1787.

A shrub resembling the preceding species. Leaves oval, or ovate, larger, 4'-6' long, 2'-3' wide, acuminate at the apex, obtuse or sometimes acute at the base, pubescent beneath, mucronate-serrulate or rarely entire; flowers axillary, solitary, 2'-3' broad; peduncles 3″-7″ long; sepals lanceolate, acutish, hairy; petals 5 or 6, cream-color, crenulate; styles 5, distinct; capsule 5-angled, ovoid, acute, 9″ long, densely pubescent; seeds wing-margined.

In woods, mountains of Kentucky and North Carolina to Georgia and Alabama. June.

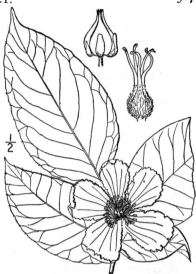

2. GORDÒNIA Ellis, Phil. Trans. 60: 518. *pl. 11.* 1770.

Trees or shrubs, with coriaceous evergreen leaves, and large white solitary axillary flowers, often clustered at the ends of branches. Sepals 5 imbricated, rounded, concave. Petals 5, imbricated, obovate. Stamens ∞, 5-adelphous, each cluster cohering with the base of a petal. Ovary 1, 3-5-celled; style 1; stigma 5-rayed. Capsule woody, ovoid, 5-valved, the axis persistent. Seeds pendulous, compressed, with a short terminal or lateral wing; embryo straight or oblique; cotyledons ovate, longitudinally plaited; radicle short, superior. [Named for James Gordon, a London nurseryman.]

About 16 species, natives of eastern North America, Mexico and eastern Asia. The following is the type of the genus.

1. Gordonia Lasiánthus L. Loblolly Bay. Holly-Bay. Tan-Bay. Swamp or Black Laurel. Fig. 2878.

Hypericum Lasianthus L. Sp. Pl. 783. 1753.

Gordonia Lasianthus L. Mant. **2**: 570. 1771.

A tree 45°-75° high. Leaves lanceolate or oblong, acute, attenuate and involute at the base, very nearly sessile, coriaceous, persistent, 3'-5' long, 1'-2' wide, serrulate, glabrous, shining; peduncles 1'-3' long, ascending, 1-flowered; flowers 1½'-2' broad; sepals orbicular, silky, ciliate; petals slightly pubescent without; capsule ovoid-conic, pointed, 6″-8″ long, sometimes 6-valved; wing of the seed terminal.

In low woods, Virginia to Florida. Wood soft, light red; weight per cubic foot 29 lbs. May-July.

Family 87. HYPERICÀCEAE Lindl. Nat. Syst. Ed. 2, 77. 1836.

ST. JOHN'S-WORT FAMILY.

Herbs or shrubs, sometimes small trees in tropical regions, with opposite or rarely verticillate simple entire or rarely glandular-ciliate or dentate leaves, no stipules, and terminal or axillary, solitary or cymose-paniculate flowers. Foliage pellucid-punctate or black-dotted. Flowers regular and perfect. Sepals 5 or 4, imbricated   Petals of the same number, hypogynous, generally oblique or contorted. Stamens numerous or few, hypogynous, often in sets of 3 or 5; anthers versatile or innate, 2-celled, longitudinally dehiscent. Ovary 1-7-celled, composed of 1–7 carpels; styles as many as the carpels; ovules ∞, in 2 rows in each cavity, anatropous. Fruit mainly capsular; seeds mainly straight; endosperm none.

About 10 genera and over 300 species, mostly of temperate and warm regions.

Sepals 4, in unequal pairs; petals 4.	1. *Ascyrum.*
Sepals and petals 5.	
Petals yellow, convolute in the bud.	
Leaves normal, not reduced to scales.	2. *Hypericum.*
Leaves reduced to minute appressed scales.	3. *Sarothra.*
Petals pink or greenish purple, imbricated in the bud.	4. *Triadenum.*

1. ÁSCYRUM L. Sp. Pl. 787. 1753.

Leafy glabrous low shrubs, with the aspect of *Hypericum.* Flowers bright yellow. Sepals 4, in 2 pairs, the exterior ones broad and round, the interior smaller and narrower. Petals 4, oblique or slightly contorted, deciduous. Stamens ∞, distinct, or united in clusters. Ovary 1-celled, with 2–4 parietal placentae; styles 2–4. Capsule 1-celled, 2–4-valved, dehiscent at the placentae. [Greek, not rough.]

About 5 species, natives of eastern and southeastern North America, the West Indies and Central America. Type species: *Ascyrum hypericoides* L.

Erect, 1°–2° high; leaves clasping; styles 3–4.	1. *A. stans.*
Diffusely branched, 5′–10′ high; leaves sessile; styles 2.	2. *A. hypericoides.*

1. Ascyrum stáns Michx. St. Peter's-wort. Fig. 2879.

Ascyrum stans Michx. Fl. Bor. Am. **2**: 77. 1803.

Erect, simple or with a few upright branches, 1°–2° high. Stems and branches 2-edged or slightly winged; leaves clasping, erect or ascending, oval, or broadly oblong, 9″–18″ long, 5″–7″ wide, obtuse, thick; cymes terminal, few-flowered; pedicels 4″–6″ long, 2-bracted below the middle; flowers 8″–12″ broad; outer sepals nearly orbicular, 4″–6″ long, cordate, the inner lanceolate, 3″–6″ long; petals obovate, longer than the sepals; styles 3 or 4, short; capsule ovoid, about 3″ long.

In dry sandy soil, especially in pine barrens, Long Island to Pennsylvania, Florida, eastern Tennessee and Texas. July–Aug.

2. Ascyrum hypericoìdes L. St. Andrew's Cross. Fig. 2880.

Ascyrum hypericoides L. Sp. Pl. 788. 1753.
Ascyrum Crux-Andreae L. Sp. Pl. Ed. 2, 1107. 1763.

Low, much branched from the base, diffuse or ascending, 5′–10′ high. Stems and branches flattened and 2-edged; leaves oblong or obovate, sessile, narrowed and 2-glandular at the base, ½′–1½′ long, 2″–4″ wide, thin, obtuse; flowers terminal or also axillary; pedicels 1″–3″ long; 2-bracted near the summit; flowers 6″–9″ broad; outer sepals oval or ovate, sometimes cordate, 4″–6″ long, 2″–4″ wide, obtuse, the inner narrower and mainly shorter; petals oblong-linear, about equalling the outer sepals; styles 2; capsule ovoid, about 2″ long.

In dry sandy soil, Nantucket, Mass., to Florida, Illinois, Nebraska and Texas. Ascends to 2800 ft. in Virginia. Cuba; Jamaica. July–Aug.

2. HYPÉRICUM [Tourn.] L. Sp. Pl. 783. 1753.

Herbs or shrubs, with opposite punctate or black-dotted leaves, and mostly cymose yellow flowers. Sepals 5, equal or nearly so. Petals 5, mainly oblique or contorted, convolute in the bud. Stamens ∞, distinct, or more or less united in clusters, sometimes with interposed hypogynous glands. Ovary 1-celled, with 3–5 parietal placentae which sometimes project far into the cavity, or 3–5-celled (rarely 6-celled); ovules ∞, generally numerous; styles 3–6. Capsule 1–5-celled (rarely 6-celled). [The Greek name.]

About 210 species, of wide geographic distribution. In addition to the following, 12 others occur in southern and western North America. Type species: *Hypericum perforatum* L.

* Styles 5; large perennials; pods 5-celled.

Flowers 1'–2' broad; capsules 9"–10" long; plant herbaceous.	1. *H. Ascyron.*
Flowers 6"–12" broad; capsules 3"–6" long; plant shrubby.	2. *H. Kalmianum.*

** Styles 3 (rarely 4).
† Tall leafy shrubs.

Flowers numerous, 4"–8" wide; pods completely 3-celled.	
Flowers 6"–8" broad; pods 4"–6" long.	3. *H. prolificum.*
Flowers 4"–6" broad; pods 2"–3" long.	4. *H. densiflorum.*
Flowers few or solitary, 1'–2' wide; pods incompletely 3-celled.	5. *H. aureum.*

†† Herbaceous, sometimes woody at the base.

‡ Stamens numerous (15–40); flowers 3"–12" broad.

Capsules 1-celled or incompletely 3–4-celled.	
Capsules incompletely 3–4-celled by the projecting placentae.	
Leaves linear, 1"–2" wide.	6. *H. galioides.*
Leaves oblong, 3"–5" wide.	7. *H. adpressum.*
Capsules strictly 1-celled; placentae parietal.	
Styles united into a beak, separate above; stigmas minute.	
Leaves linear or linear-oblong; seeds transversely rugose.	
Nearly simple, erect; pod globose.	8. *H. cistifolium.*
Branched, decumbent; pod 3-sided.	9. *H. dolabriforme.*
Leaves elliptic; seeds minutely pitted and striate.	10. *H. ellipticum.*
Styles separate; stigmas capitate; cyme naked.	11. *H. virgatum.*
Capsules completely 3-celled; styles separate.	
Leaves linear or oblong; sepals lanceolate; introduced.	12. *H. perforatum.*
Leaves broadly oblong, oval or ovate-lanceolate; native species.	
Sepals ovate to ovate-lanceolate.	
Leaves obtuse; sepals acute; petals 2"–3" long.	13. *H. punctatum.*
Leaves acute; sepals acuminate; petals 5"–10" long.	14. *H. pseudomaculatum.*
Sepals lanceolate; petals 5"–7" long; leaves obtuse.	15. *H. graveolens.*

‡‡ Stamens few (5–12); flowers ½"–3" broad.

Leaves spreading or ascending, 3–7-nerved.	
Cyme leafy-bracted.	16. *H. boreale.*
Cymes subulate-bracted.	
Leaves ovate, oval, oblong or lanceolate, 5–7-nerved.	
Leaves ovate, oval or oblong; capsule 1"–2½" long.	
Leaves obtuse; sepals linear-oblong, acutish or obtuse.	17. *H. mutilum.*
Leaves acute, or only the lower obtuse; sepals long-acuminate.	18. *H. gymnanthum.*
Leaves lanceolate or oblong-lanceolate; capsule 4"–5" long.	19. *H. majus..*
Leaves linear, obtuse, 3-nerved.	20. *H. canadense.*
Leaves linear, erect, 1-nerved.	21. *H. Drummondii.*

1. Hypericum Áscyron L. Great or Giant St. John's-wort. Fig. 2881.

Hypericum Ascyron L. Sp. Pl. 783. 1753.
Hypericum pyramidatum Ait. Hort. Kew. 3: 103. 1789.

Perennial, herbaceous, erect, 2°–6° high, branching, the branches often nearly erect, angled. Leaves sessile, clasping, ovate-oblong or ovate-lanceolate, 2'–5' long, ½'–1½' wide, obtuse or acute; cymes terminal, few-flowered; flowers bright yellow, 1'–2' broad; pedicels stout, ½'–2' long; sepals ovate-lanceolate, 4"–6" long, acute; petals obovate or oblanceolate, tardily deciduous; styles usually 5, united below; stigmas capitate; stamens numerous, united in 5 sets; capsule ovoid, 9"–10" long; cells 3.

Banks of streams, western Quebec and Vermont to Manitoba, south to Connecticut, New Jersey, Pennsylvania, Illinois, Iowa, Missouri and Kansas. Also in northern Europe and Asia. July–Aug.

½

3. Hypericum prolíficum L. Shrubby St. John's-wort. Fig. 2883.

Hypericum prolificum L. Mant. 1: 106. 1767.

Shrubby, diffusely branched from near or at the base, 1°–3° high; stems sometimes 1′ in diameter; branches ascending or erect, leafy; branchlets 2-edged. Leaves linear-oblong or oblanceolate, narrowed at the base, or tapering into a short petiole, obtuse, often mucronulate, pale beneath, 1′–3′ long, 3″–9″ wide, with tufts of smaller ones in the axils; cymes several–many-flowered, terminal and sometimes also axillary; pedicels 6″ long or less; flowers 5″–9″ broad; sepals unequal, shorter than petals; stamens numerous, distinct; styles 3; capsules 3-celled, 4″–6″ long.

Sandy or rocky soil, western Ontario and New York to Minnesota, Georgia, Missouri and Arkansas. Rock-rose. Paint-brush. Broom-brush. July–Sept.

2. Hypericum Kalmiànum L. Kalm's St. John's-wort. Fig. 2882.

Hypericum Kalmianum L. Sp. Pl. 783. 1753.

Shrubby, freely branching, 1°–2° high, leafy; branches 4-angled, twigs flattened and 2-edged. Leaves oblong-linear or oblanceolate, sessile, or narrowed into a short petiole, obtuse, 1′–2½′ long, 2″–4″ wide, more or less glaucous beneath, generally with smaller ones clustered in the axils; cymes terminal, few-flowered; pedicels stout, 2″–10″ long; flowers 6″–12″ broad; sepals foliaceous, oblong, acute, 3″–4″ long, usually about half the length of the petals; stamens very numerous, distinct; styles 5 (4-6), united below into a beak; capsule ovoid, 3″ long, completely 5- (4-6-) celled.

Sandy soil, Quebec, Ontario and western New York to Illinois, Wisconsin and Michigan. Shrubby St. johnswort. Aug.

⅗

4. Hypericum densiflòrum Pursh. Bushy or Dense-flowered St. John's-wort. Fig. 2884.

Hypericum densiflorum Pursh, Fl. Am. Sept. 376. 1814.

Hypericum prolificum var. *densiflorum* A. Gray, Man. Ed. 3, 84. 1867.

Erect, 4°–6° high, shrubby, freely branching, densely leafy; branches somewhat angled and branchlets 2-edged. Leaves crowded, 1′–2′ long, 1½″–3″ wide, acutish or obtuse, with smaller ones clustered in the axils; cymes densely many-flowered, mainly terminal; pedicels 1″–4″ long; flowers 5″–8″ broad; sepals narrow, not foliaceous, shorter than the petals; stamens numerous, distinct; styles 3, more or less united; capsule 3-celled, 2″–3″ long.

Pine-barrens of New Jersey to Florida, west to Kentucky, Arkansas and Texas. July–Sept.

½

5. Hypericum aùreum Bartram. Golden St. John's-wort. Fig. 2885.

Hypericum aureum Bartram, Travels 383. 1791.

Perennial, shrubby, 2°-4° high, the twigs 4-sided. Leaves oblong, firm in texture, 1'-3' long, obtuse and mucronulate at the apex, narrowed at the base, pale beneath; petioles very short; flowers solitary or 2 or 3 together, sessile, 1'-2' broad; sepals unequal, shorter than the obovate oblique petals; stamens very numerous; styles 3; capsules conic, incompletely 3-celled, nearly 1' long, long-pointed.

River banks and bluffs, South Carolina to Tennessee, Kentucky and Texas. May–July.

6. Hypericum galioìdes Lam. Bedstraw St. John's-wort. Fig. 2886.

Hypericum galioides Lam. Encycl. 4: 161. 1797.

Perennial, somewhat woody, branching, 1°-2½° high, the stems and branches nearly terete. Leaves linear, linear-oblong or oblanceolate, with smaller ones clustered in their axils, obtusish, thick, spreading, narrowed below, ½'-2½' long, 1"-2" wide, involute in drying; flowers short-pedicelled, 3"-5" broad; sepals narrowly linear, foliaceous, resembling the uppermost leaves, shorter than the pointed oblique petals; stamens numerous, distinct; styles 3; capsule 2"-3" long, incompletely 3-celled by the projecting placentae.

In low grounds, Delaware to Florida, west to eastern Tennessee and Louisiana. July–Sept.

7. Hypericum adpréssum Bart. Creeping St. John's-wort. Fig. 2887.

H. adpressum Bart. Comp. Fl. Phil. 2: 15. 1818.

Stem nearly simple, erect or ascending from a perennial creeping or decumbent sometimes spongy-thickened base, 1°-2° high, angled below, 2-edged above. Leaves oblong or lanceolate, 1'-2' long, 3"-5" wide, obtuse, ascending, often with smaller ones fascicled in the axils; cyme terminal, several-flowered, leafy only at the base; pedicels 1"-3" long; flowers 6"-9" broad; sepals lanceolate, acute, about half the length of the petals; stamens numerous, distinct; styles 3 or 4; capsule about 2" long, incompletely 3-4-celled by the projecting placentae.

In low grounds, Nantucket, Mass., to New Jersey and Pennsylvania, south to Georgia and Louisiana. Recorded from Missouri and Arkansas. July–Aug.

3/5

8. Hypericum cistifòlium Lam. Round-podded St. John's-wort. Fig. 2888.

Hypericum cistifolium Lam. Encycl. 4: 158. 1797.

H. sphaerocarpum Michx. Fl. Bor. Am. 2: 78. 1803.

Simple or branching, erect or ascending from a somewhat woody perennial base, 1°–2½° high; stems 4-angled. Leaves oblong or linear-oblong, obtuse, 1½′–3′ long, 3″–6″ wide, often with smaller ones in the axils; cymes terminal, several or many-flowered, naked; flowers sessile or nearly so, 5″–8″ broad; sepals linear, lanceolate or ovate, much shorter than or equalling the petals; stamens numerous, distinct; styles 3, united below; capsule strictly 1-celled, globose or ovoid-conic, 2″–2½″ long; seeds larger than in related species, rough-pitted.

On rocky banks, southwestern Ohio to Iowa, Kansas, Alabama and Arkansas. July–Sept.

Hypericum Bisséllii Robinson, known only from Southington, Connecticut, has smaller leaves, the cyme leafy-bracted, the sepals very unequal.

9. Hypericum dolabrifórme Vent. Straggling St. John's-wort. Fig. 2889.

Hypericum dolabriforme Vent. Hort. Cels. *pl. 45.* 1800.

Straggling and branching, decumbent, 6′–20′ high; branchlets slightly angled. Leaves linear or linear-lanceolate, 8″–20″ long, 1″–2″ wide, acute or obtusish, spreading or ascending, with smaller ones clustered in the axils; cymes terminal, leafy, few–several-flowered; pedicels about ½″ long; flowers nearly 1′ broad; sepals foliaceous, lanceolate or ovate, acute or acuminate, nearly or quite as long as the oblique pointed petals; stamens numerous, distinct; styles 3, united below; capsule ovoid-conical, coriaceous, 3″–4″ long, 1-celled; seeds rugose.

On dry hills, barrens of Kentucky and Tennessee to Georgia. July–Aug.

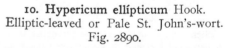

½

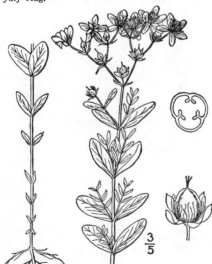

3/5

10. Hypericum ellípticum Hook. Elliptic-leaved or Pale St. John's-wort. Fig. 2890.

H. ellipticum Hook. Fl. Bor. Am. 1: 110. 1830.

Herbaceous, perennial; stem somewhat 4-angled, simple or with few branches, erect, 8′–20′ high. Leaves thin, spreading, elliptic or oval, obtuse, sessile, narrowed at the base or partly clasping, 8″–15″ long, 3″–5″ wide; cymes terminal, few-flowered, leafless but bracted; flowers pale yellow, nearly sessile, 5″–7″ broad; sepals spreading, oblong or oblanceolate, slightly shorter than the petals; styles 3, united below; stamens numerous; capsule ovoid-globose, 1-celled, about 2″ long; seeds striate; sepals and petals sometimes 4.

In swamps and along streams, Nova Scotia to Manitoba, Connecticut, northern New Jersey, Maryland, Michigan and Minnesota. July–Aug.

11. Hypericum virgàtum Lam. Virgate or Copper-colored St. John's-wort.
Fig. 2891.

Hypericum virgatum Lam. Encycl. **4**: 158. 1797.
H. angulosum Michx. Fl. Bor. Am. **2**: 78. 1803.
Hypericum virgatum ovalifolium Britton, Trans. N. Y. Acad. Sci. **9**: 10. 1889.

Slender, herbaceous, erect or ascending, simple, or branched above, 1°–2½° high, the stem and branches 4-angled. Leaves ascending or erect, oblong-lanceolate to elliptic, acute or obtuse, 15″ long or less, 2″–7″ wide, sessile; cyme terminal, ample, compound, bracted; pedicels ½″–2″ long; flowers numerous, copper-yellow, alternate, 4″–6″ broad; sepals foliaceous, ovate or lanceolate, keeled, more or less shorter than the petals; styles 3, distinct; stigmas capitate; capsule 1-celled, 2″ long, enclosed by the sepals.

In low grounds, New Jersey and Pennsylvania to Illinois, south to Florida and Tennessee. July–Sept.

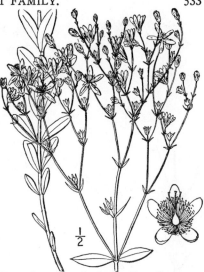

12. Hypericum perforàtum L.   Common St. John's-wort. Fig. 2892.

Hypericum perforatum L. Sp. Pl. 785. 1753.

Perennial, herbaceous from a woody base, 1°–2° high, much branched. Stems erect, with numerous barren shoots at base; leaves sessile, oblong or linear, 5″–10″ long, 1″–4″ wide, obtuse, more or less black-dotted; cymes terminal, several–many-flowered; flowers bright yellow, 8″–12″ broad; sepals lanceolate, acute, shorter than the copiously black-dotted petals; stamens united at their bases into 3 sets; styles 3; capsule ovoid, 2″–3″ long, 3-celled, glandular.

In fields and waste places, common throughout our area except the extreme north, and in the Southern States. Naturalized from Europe. Often a troublesome weed. Native also of northern Asia. June–Sept.   English names, amber, penny-john, rosin-rose, herb-john. Johnswort. Cammock. Touch-and-heal. Crushed herbage odorous.

13. Hypericum punctàtum Lam. Spotted or Corymbed St. John's-wort. Fig. 2893.

H. maculatum Walt. Fl. Car. 189. 1788. No Crantz.
H. punctatum Lam. Encycl. **4**: 164. 1797.
H. corymbosum Muhl.; Willd. Sp. Pl. **3**: 1457. 1803.
H. subpetiolatum Bicknell; Small, Fl. SE. U. S. 790. 1903.

Herbaceous, perennial from a woody base, erect, 1½°–3° high. Leaves sessile, short-petioled, or partly clasping, oblong or ovate-lanceolate, obtuse, 1′–3′ long, 4″–8″ wide, copiously black-dotted; cymes terminal, many-flowered; pedicels about 1″ long; flowers much crowded, 4″–7″ broad; sepals ovate-oblong, acute, about half as long as the conspicuously black-dotted petals; stamens numerous, united in 3 or 5 sets; styles 3, variable in length; capsule ovoid, 2″–3″ long, completely 3-celled.

In moist soil, Quebec and Ontario to Minnesota, Florida and Kansas. June–Sept.

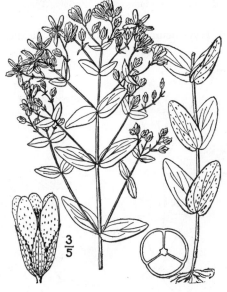

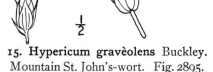

$\frac{1}{2}$

14. Hypericum pseudomaculàtum Bush. Large Spotted St. John's-wort. Fig. 2894.

Hypericum pseudomaculatum Bush; Britton, Man. 627. 1901.

Similar to the preceding species, but the leaves, at least the upper ones, acute, ovate to oblong-lanceolate; flowers larger; sepals lanceolate to ovate-lanceolate, acuminate; petals pale yellow, three to five times as long as the sepals, sometimes 10″ long; capsule completely 3-celled, narrowly ovoid, 3″–4″ long.

Woodlands and lawns, Illinois and Missouri to Texas, east to South Carolina and Florida. May–June.

15. Hypericum gravèolens Buckley. Mountain St. John's-wort. Fig. 2895.

Hypericum graveolens Buckley, Am. Journ. Sci. **45**: 174. 1843.

Herbaceous, perennial, similar to the preceding species. Stem erect, 1°–3° high, branched above; leaves oval, ovate or elliptic-oblong, sessile or clasping, obtuse, 1′–3′ long, ½′–1′ wide, sparingly black-dotted; cymes terminal, few–several-flowered; pedicels 1″–4″ long; flowers usually crowded, 1′ in breadth or more; sepals lanceolate, acute, much shorter than the sparingly dotted or dotless petals; stamens united in sets; styles 3; capsule ovoid, somewhat 3-lobed, 3-celled, 4″–6″ long.

Mountains of southwestern Virginia, Tennessee and North Carolina. June–Sept.

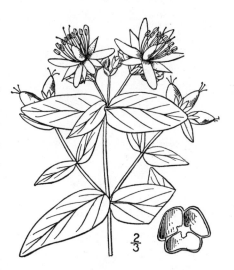

$\frac{2}{3}$

16. Hypericum boreàle (Britton) Bicknell. Northern St. John's-wort. Fig. 2896.

Hypericum canadense var. *boreale* Britton, Bull. Torr. Club **18**: 365. 1891.
H. boreale Bicknell, Bull. Torr. Club **22**: 213. 1894.

$\frac{2}{3}$

Perennial, sometimes stoloniferous; stem terete or slightly 4-angled, upright from a usually assurgent base, simple or branched, 1′–18′ high. Leaves elliptic, oval, oblong, or linear-oblong, 3″–16″ long, 1″–4″ wide, sessile or slightly clasping, obtuse, mostly 3-nerved, those of the lower part of the stem commonly much smaller than the upper and closer together; cymes few–several-flowered, leafy-bracted; flowers about 2½″ broad; sepals narrow, obtuse; capsules oblong, obtuse or obtusish, apiculate, 2″–2½″ long, purple, cross-wrinkled, longer than the sepals; seeds 3–5 times as long as wide, pale, longitudinally furrowed and finely cross-lined.

In wet soil, Newfoundland to Ontario, Vermont, New Jersey, Pennsylvania and Indiana. July–Sept.

17. Hypericum mùtilum L. Dwarf, Small-flowered or Slender St. John's-wort. Fig. 2897.

Hypericum mutilum L. Sp. Pl. 787. 1753.
Ascyrum Crux-Andreae L. Sp. Pl. 787. 1753.

Usually annual, slender, erect or ascending, generally tufted, abundantly branched, 6'-2½° high. Branchlets 4-angled; leaves oblong or ovate, sessile, clasping, obtuse, 4"-14" long, 2"-7" wide, 5-nerved at the base; cymes many-flowered, terminal, subulate-bracted; pedicels slender, 1"-6" long; flowers ½"-2" broad, light orange yellow; sepals foliaceous, linear, lanceolate or oblanceolate, much shorter than or slightly longer than the petals; stamens 5-12; styles 3; capsule ovoid, pointed, 1-celled, 1"-2" long, somewhat longer than the sepals.

In low grounds, Nova Scotia to Manitoba, Kansas, Florida and Texas. Ascends 3000 ft. in Virginia. July–Sept.

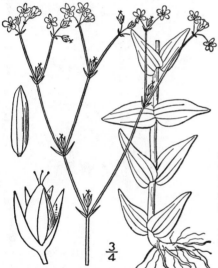

18. Hypericum gymnánthum Engelm. & Gray. Clasping-leaved St. John's-wort. Fig. 2898.

Hypericum gymnanthum Engelm. & Gray, Bost. Journ. Nat. Hist. **5**: 212. 1847.

Annual, erect, simple or sparingly branched, 10'-3° high. Leaves ovate, or the lower oval, cordate-clasping, often distant, 4"-10" long, 2"-4" wide, acute, or the lower obtuse, 3-7-nerved at the base; cymes terminal, loose, subulate-bracted; flowers numerous, 1"-2" broad; sepals lanceolate, acuminate, equalling or shorter than the petals and generally somewhat shorter than the 1-celled ovoid capsule; styles 3; stamens 10-12; capsule about 2" long.

In low grounds, southwestern New Jersey and Delaware to Ohio, Minnesota, Arkansas, Louisiana and Texas. July–Sept.

19. Hypericum màjus (A. Gray) Britton. Larger Canadian St. John's-wort. Fig. 2899.

Hypericum canadense var. *majus* A. Gray, Man. Ed. 5, 86. 1867.
Hypericum majus Britton, Mem. Torr. Club **5**: 225. 1894.

Annual or perennial, stouter than *H. canadense*, stem erect, 1°-3° high, usually branched above, the branches nearly erect. Leaves lanceolate or oblong-lanceolate, sessile or somewhat clasping, 10"-2½' long, 3"-6" wide, acute or obtuse at the apex, 5-7-nerved; cymes several–many-flowered; bracts subulate; flowers 3"-5" broad; sepals lanceolate, acuminate, about as long as the petals or shorter; styles 3; capsule narrowly conic, acute, 4"-5" long, longer than the narrowly lanceolate sepals; seeds minute, cross-lined and faintly longitudinally striate.

In moist soil, Quebec to Manitoba, British Columbia, New Jersey, Illinois and Colorado. June–Sept.

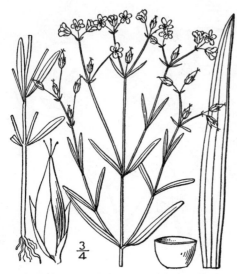

$\frac{3}{4}$

21. Hypericum Drummóndii (Grev. & Hook.) T. & G. Drummond's St. John's-wort. Fig. 2901.

Sarothra Drummondii Grev. & Hook. Bot. Misc. **3**: 236. 1833.
H. Drummondii T. & G. Fl. N. A. **1**: 165. 1838.

Annual, bushy-branched, 10′–30′ high, rigid. Leaves linear-subulate, 4″–12″ long, erect or narrowly ascending, ½″ wide, 1-nerved; flowers scattered along the upper part of leafy branches, numerous, peduncled, 2″ broad; sepals lance-linear, longer than the petals; stamens 10–20; styles 3; capsule 1-celled, ovoid, 2″ long, equalling or shorter than the sepals; seeds large, rugose.

In dry soil, Virginia to Georgia, Ohio, Illinois, Iowa, Kansas and Texas. July–Sept.

3. SARÒTHRA L. Sp. Pl. 272. 1753.

20. Hypericum canadénse L. Canadian St. John's-wort. Fig. 2900.

Hypericum canadense L. Sp. Pl. 785. 1753.

Annual or perennial, erect, 6′–20′ high, freely branching. Branches angular, erect or ascending; leaves linear, 6″–2′ long, 1″–2″ wide, obtuse, tapering to the base, 3-nerved; cymes terminal, several–many-flowered, subulate-bracted; flowers 2″–3″ broad; sepals lanceolate, acute, equalling or shorter than the petals; stamens 5–10; styles 3; capsule 1-celled, narrowly conic, acute, 2″–4″ long, much longer than the sepals; seeds striate.

In wet soil, Newfoundland to Manitoba, Georgia, Kentucky and Wisconsin. Ascends to 5000 ft. in North Carolina. July–Sept.

$\frac{1}{2}$

A low annual herb, the opposite leaves reduced to subulate scales, the mostly opposite branches erect-ascending, the very small yellow flowers alternate, very short-pedicelled or sessile along them in the axils of still smaller scales. Sepals 5, equal. Petals 5. Stamens 5–10. Styles 3, separate. Capsule elongated-conic, 1-celled, much longer than the sepals; seeds striate and pitted. [Greek, a broom.]

A monotypic genus of eastern North America.

1. Sarothra gentianoìdes L. Orange-grass. Pineweed. False John's-wort. Fig. 2902.

Sarothra gentianoides L. Sp. Pl. 272. 1753.
Hypericum Sarothra Michx. Fl. Bor. Am. **2**: 79. 1803.
Hypericum gentianoides B.S.P. Prel. Cat. N. Y. 9. 1888.

Erect, fastigiately branched, 4′–20′ high. Branches mainly opposite, filiform, erect, wiry; leaves minute, subulate, about 1″ long, appressed; flowers nearly sessile, 1″–1½″ wide, open in sunlight; sepals linear, about equalling the petals and very much shorter than the conic-cylindric acute purple pod; seeds very small.

$\frac{2}{3}$

In sandy soil, Maine to Florida, west to Ontario, Minnesota, Missouri and Texas. June–Oct. Ground-pine. Nit-weed.

4. TRIADÈNUM Raf. Med. Rep. (II.) 5: 352. 1808.

[ELODEA Pursh, Fl. Am. Sept. 360. 1814. Not Michx. 1803, nor *Elodes* Adans. 1763.]

Perennial marsh herbs, with opposite entire oblong-oval or ovate leaves, and pink or greenish purple flowers in terminal cymes, or also axillary. Calyx of 5 equal persistent sepals. Petals 5, not contorted, imbricated in the bud. Stamens 9, or sometimes more, in 3 sets, the sets alternating with 3 large hypogynous glands. Ovary 3-celled; styles 3. Capsule oblong-conic, much longer than the sepals. [Greek, three glands.]

Three species, natives of eastern North America. Type species: *Hypericum virginicum* L.

Leaves sessile; flower-clusters peduncled.   1. *T. virginicum.*
Leaves short-petioled; flower-clusters nearly sessile.   2. *T. petiolatum.*

1. Triadenum virgínicum (L.) Raf. Marsh St. John's-wort. Fig. 2903.

Hypericum virginicum L. Sp. Pl. Ed. 2, 1104. 1763.
Hypericum campanulatum Walt. Fl. Car. 191. 1788.
Elodea campanulata Pursh, Fl. Am. Sept. 379. 1814.
Elodea virginica Nutt. Gen. 2: 17. 1818.
Triadenum virginicum Raf. Fl. Tell. 3: 79. 1836.

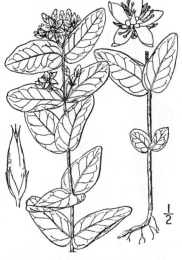

Glabrous, erect or ascending, nearly simple, often reddish, 1°–1½° high. Leaves sessile or cordate-clasping, ovate or oblong, 1'–3' long, 9"–12" wide, very obtuse, sometimes emarginate, glaucous beneath, black-dotted; flowers 6"–8" broad, in axillary and terminal peduncled leafy clusters; sepals ovate or lanceolate, acute, shorter than the straight petals; stamens 9 or more, united in 3 sets; styles 3, distinct; capsule oblong, 4'–5' long, acute, red-purple.

In swamps, Newfoundland to Florida, west to Manitoba, Nebraska and Louisiana. Also in northeastern Asia. Ascends to 2600 ft. in the Catskills. July–Sept.

Triadenum longifòlium Small, differing by longer leaves, narrowed at the base, inhabits the Southern States and ranges north into western Kentucky.

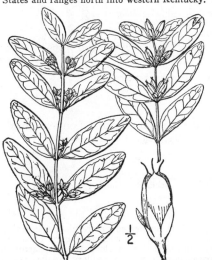

2. Triadenum petiolàtum (Walt.) Britton. Larger Marsh St. John's-wort. Fig. 2904.

Hypericum petiolatum Walt. Fl. Car. 191. 1788.

Elodea petiolata Pursh, Fl. Am. Sept. 379. 1814.

Triadenum petiolatum Britton; Britt. & Brown, Ill. Fl. 2: 437. 1897.

Similar to the preceding species, but often more branched and taller; leaves generally longer (2'–5'), petioled, or the upper sessile, not clasping, often narrowed at the base with petioles up to ½' long, pale beneath; flower-clusters axillary and terminal, sessile or very short-peduncled.

In swamps, New Jersey and Maryland to Florida, Indiana, Missouri, Arkansas and Louisiana. July–Aug.

Family 88. ELATINÀCEAE Lindl. Nat. Syst. Ed. 2, 88. 1836.

WATER-WORT FAMILY.

Low herbs, sometimes woody in tropical regions, with opposite or verticillate stipulate entire or serrate leaves, and small axillary solitary or fascicled flowers. Flowers regular, perfect. Sepals 2–5, imbricated. Petals the same number, hypogynous. Stamens the same number or twice as many. Ovary 2–5-celled; styles 2–5, stigmatic at the apex; ovules ∞, anatropous. Capsule with septicidal dehiscence. Placentae central. Seed-coat crustaceous, rugose or ribbed.

About 30 species, of wide geographic distribution.

Flowers 2–4-merous; glabrous aquatic or creeping herbs.   1. *Elatine.*
Flowers mainly 5-merous; pubescent ascending or diffuse herbs.   2. *Bergia.*

1. ELATINE L. Sp. Pl. 367. 1753.

Small glabrous or glabrate aquatic or creeping herbs, with opposite or verticillate leaves, and minute axillary mainly solitary flowers. Sepals 2–4, persistent, membranous, not ribbed. Petals of the same number, hypogynous. Stamens of the same number or twice as many. Styles or stigmas 2–4. Pod membranous, globose, 2–4-valved. Seeds ∞, straight, or slightly curved, striate longitudinally and transversely. [Greek, fir-like, with reference to the leaves.]

About 10 species, natives of temperate and warm regions. In addition to the following, another occurs in California and one in Montana. Type species: *Elatine Hydrópiper* L.

Petals and stamens 2; seeds distinctly sculptured.
     Leaves obovate; seeds with 9–10 longitudinal and 20–30 transverse striae.   1. *E. americana.*
     Leaves oblong or oval; seeds with 6–7 longitudinal and 10–12 transverse striae.
                                                   2. *E. brachysperma.*
Petals and stamens mostly 3; seeds little sculptured.   3. *E. triandra.*

1. Elatine americàna (Pursh) Arn. Water-wort. Mud-purslane. Fig. 2905.

Peplis americana Pursh, Fl. Am. Sept. 238. 1814.
Elatine americana Arn. Edinb. Journ. Sci. 1: 430. 1830.

Erect or spreading, tufted, aquatic or terrestrial, $\frac{1}{2}$–$1\frac{1}{2}'$ long, often submerged. Leaves obovate, obtuse, 1″–3″ long, 1″ wide or less; flowers sessile, axillary, minute, rarely opening in the submerged forms; sepals, petals, stamens and stigmas 2 (rarely 3 in the terrestrial forms); capsule globose, nearly $\frac{1}{2}$″ in diameter; seeds $\frac{1}{4}$″ to nearly $\frac{1}{2}$″ long, slightly curved, marked by 9–10 longitudinal striae and 20–30 cross-bars.

Margins of ponds and slow streams, Quebec to British Columbia, Virginia, Missouri, Texas and Mexico. Summer.

2. Elatine brachyspérma A. Gray. Short-seeded Water-wort. Fig. 2906.

Elatine brachysperma A. Gray, Proc. Am. Acad. 13: 361. 1878.

Terrestrial or sometimes submerged, spreading, tufted, 1′–2′ long. Leaves oblong, oval or lanceolate, narrowed at the base, 2″–3″ long, about 1″ wide, obtuse; flowers sessile, axillary, minute; sepals, petals, stamens and stigmas mainly 2; capsule nearly as in the preceding species; seeds short-oblong, nearly straight, about ·$\frac{1}{4}$″ long, marked by 6–7 longitudinal striae and 10–12 cross-bars.

Margins of ponds, Illinois and California, doubtless occurring between these limits. Summer.

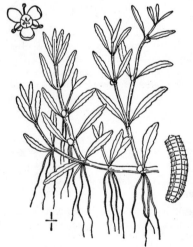

3. Elatine triándra Schk. Long-stemmed Water-wort. Fig. 2907.

Elatine triandra Schk. Bot. Hand. 1: 345. 1791.

Flaccid, tufted, immersed or creeping, stems 2′–4′ long, much branched. Leaves oblong or oblanceolate, very thin, obtuse, 2″–4″ long, 1″ wide, narrowed at the base; flowers minute, axillary, sessile; sepals commonly 2; petals, stamens and stigmas 3; seeds slightly curved, about the size of those of *E. americana*, slightly marked longitudinally and transversely.

Ponds, Illinois, South Dakota and Nebraska to Washington. Also in Europe. Summer.

2. BÉRGIA L. Mant. 1: 152, 241. 1771.

Herbs, or somewhat shrubby plants, branching, erect, ascending or prostrate, more or less pubescent, with opposite serrate or entire leaves, and small axillary solitary or clustered flowers. Parts of the flowers in 5's (very rarely in 4's or 3's). Sepals acute. Pod crustaceous, ovoid, 5-valved. Seeds numerous, striate longitudinally and transversely. [In honor of Dr. P. J. Bergius, 1723–1790, professor of Natural History in Stockholm.]

About 15 species, natives of warm and temperate regions. Type species : *Bergia capensis* L.

1. Bergia texàna (Hook.) Seub. Texas Bergia.
Fig. 2908.

Merimea texana Hook. Icon. Pl. *pl. 278.* 1840.

Bergia texana Seub.; Walp. Rep. 1 : 285. 1842.

Prostrate or ascending, diffusely branched, pubescent, stems 6'–10' long. Leaves spatulate or obovate, 1'–1½' long, 6"–8" wide, acutish or obtuse, serrate, narrowed into a short petiole ; stipules scarious, about 1" long, ciliate-serrulate ; flowers very short-peduncled, about 1½" broad, solitary or 2–3 together in the axils ; sepals ovate, acuminate, denticulate, slightly longer than the oblong obtuse petals ; capsule globose, 1" in diameter, its dehiscence septifragal ; seeds oblong, striate longitudinally and cross-barred.

Southern Illinois to Texas, west to Nevada and California. Summer.

$\frac{2}{3}$

Family 89. CISTÀCEAE Lindl. Nat. Syst. Ed. 2, 91. 1836.
ROCK-ROSE FAMILY.

Shrubs or low woody herbs, with alternate or opposite simple leaves, and solitary racemose clustered or paniculate flowers. Flowers regular, generally perfect. Sepals 3 or 5, persistent, when 5 the 2 exterior ones smaller and bract-like, the 3 inner convolute. Petals 5 or 3, or sometimes wanting, fugacious. Stamens ∞, hypogynous. Ovary 1, sessile, 1–several-celled ; ovules orthotropous, stalked ; style simple ; stigma entire or 3-lobed. Capsule dehiscent by valves. Seeds several or numerous ; embryo slender, straight or curved ; endosperm starchy or fleshy.

Eight genera and about 160 species, mostly natives of the northern hemisphere.

Petals 5, yellow, fugacious, or wanting.
  Leaves broad, lanceolate or oblong ; style short.   1. *Crocanthemum.*
  Leaves subulate or scale-like, imbricated ; style long.   2. *Hudsonia.*
Petals 3, not yellow, persistent ; flowers minute ; style none.   3. *Lechea.*

1. CROCÁNTHEMUM Spach, Ann. Sci. Nat. II. 6: 370. 1836.

Woody herbs or low shrubs, more or less branching, with showy yellow flowers, and with other much smaller apetalous cleistogamous ones. Petals in the larger flowers large, fugacious, the stamens numerous. Placentae or false septa 3. Ovules 2 on each placenta ; style short ; stigma capitate or 3-lobed ; capsule 1-celled ; seeds with long funicles ; embryo curved. [Greek, golden flower.]

About 20 species, natives of North and Central America, a few in South America. Besides the following, about 8 others occur in the Southern States. Type species : *Crocanthemum carolinianum* (L.) Spach. Some of the species are known as Rock-rose or Sun-rose. The genus has been included by authors in the Old World genera *Helianthemum* L., and *Halimium* Spach.

Petaliferous flowers solitary, few or several ; apetalous flowers in axillary sessile clusters.
  Petaliferous flowers 5–12, in a short terminal cymose raceme, their capsules 1½"–2" long, little, if at all, overtopped by the short later axillary branches ; capsules of the apetalous flowers about 1" in diameter.   1. *C. majus.*
  Petaliferous flowers solitary, rarely 2, their capsules 3"–4" long, much overtopped by the later elongated axillary branches ; capsules of the apetalous flowers nearly 2" in diameter.
                                               2. *C. canadense.*
Flowers all cymose at the summit of the stem, the petaliferous ones slender-pedicelled.
                                               3. *C. corymbosum.*

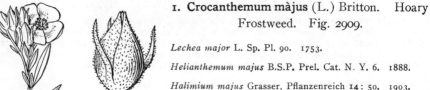

1. Crocanthemum màjus (L.) Britton. Hoary Frostweed. Fig. 2909.

Lechea major L. Sp. Pl. 90. 1753.

Helianthemum majus B.S.P. Prel. Cat. N. Y. 6. 1888.

Halimium majus Grasser, Pflanzenreich 14: 50. 1903.

Hoary-canescent, stems erect, 1°–2° high, at first simple, later with numerous short ascending branches. Leaves oblong-lanceolate or oblanceolate, acute or obtuse, 8″–18″ long, stellate-canescent beneath, darker above, short-petioled; petaliferous flowers 5–12 in a terminal cymose raceme, their corollas 7″–12″ broad, light yellow, their sepals densely canescent, the outer nearly as long as the inner, their capsules ovoid, 1½″–2″ long, little if at all overtopped by the later axillary branches; apetalous flowers appearing later, minute, clustered in the axils, nearly sessile, their capsules 1″–1½″ in diameter; seeds evenly reticulated.

In dry soil, Nova Scotia to Ontario, South Dakota, Nebraska, Colorado, South Carolina and Texas. Rock-rose. Petaliferous flowers June–July.

Helianthemum georgiànum Chapm. (*H. propinquum* Bicknell) differs in being lower, usually with more numerous stems, the longer-pedicelled petaliferous flowers short-racemose or subcorymbose, and ranges north from the Southern States into southern New Jersey and Long Island.

2. Crocanthemum canadénse (L.) Britton. Long-branched Frostweed. Scrofulaplant. Rock-rose. Frost-wort. Fig. 2910.

Cistus canadensis L. Sp. Pl. 526. 1753.
Helianthemum canadense Michx. Fl. Bor. Am.. 1: 308. 1803.
Halimium canadense Grasser, Pflanzenreich 14: 51. 1903.

Puberulent-canescent, erect, ascending, or sometimes diffuse, 3′–2° high, stem at first simple, later with slender elongated branches. Leaves oblong, linear-oblong or oblanceolate, nearly sessile, 6″–15″ long, 2″–4″ wide, rough and dark green above, paler and canescent beneath, the margins commonly revolute in drying; petaliferous flowers solitary, or rarely 2, bright yellow, 9″–20″ broad, their sepals pilose, the outer shorter than the inner, their capsules ovoid or obovoid, rounded above, 3″–4″ long, much overtopped by the later elongating axillary branches; apetalous flowers appearing later, axillary, nearly sessile, their capsules about 2″ in diameter; seeds papillose.

In dry rocky or sandy soil, Maine to Ontario, Indiana and Wisconsin, south to North Carolina and Mississippi. Petaliferous flowers May–July. In late autumn crystals of ice sometimes shoot from the base of the stem in this and the preceding species, whence the popular name frost-weed. Canadian rock-rose.

3. Crocanthemum corymbòsum (Michx.) Britton. Pine-barren Frostweed. Fig. 2911.

Helianthemum corymbosum Michx. Fl. Bor. Am. 1: 307. 1803.

Erect, branching from the base, 6'–12' high, finely and densely canescent. Leaves oblong, or the lowest obovate, 10"–16" long, obtuse or acutish, 3"–5" wide, entire, slightly revolute in drying, pale beneath, dark green above, short-petioled; flowers in nearly naked, fastigiate cymes at the summits of the stem and branches; the petaliferous 6"–10" broad, on slender pedicels 6"–8" long; apetalous flowers clustered, nearly sessile; calyx of both kinds woolly-pubescent; outer sepals about equalling the inner; capsules of the larger flowers 2"–3" broad, many-seeded; those of the apetalous ones smaller and few-seeded.

In sandy soil, New Jersey (?), North Carolina to Florida and Louisiana.

2. HUDSÒNIA L. Mant. 11, 74. 1767.

Low tufted diffusely branched shrubs, with small subulate or scale-like, imbricated leaves, and numerous yellow flowers terminating short branches. Petals 5, obovate-oblong. Stamens ∞. Style filiform, continuous with the ovary; placentae 3; stigma minute. Capsule 1-celled, 3-valved, included in the calyx. Seeds few; embryo slender, spirally curved. [Named for Wm. Hudson, 1730–1793, an English botanist.]

A genus of 3 species, natives of eastern North America, one inhabiting mountain tops in North Carolina. Plants of heath-like aspect, very showy when in bloom. Type species: *Hudsonia ericoides* L.

Flowers slender-pedicelled; leaves subulate.   1. *H. ericoides.*
Flowers nearly sessile or short-pedicelled; leaves scale-like.   2. *H. tomentosa.*

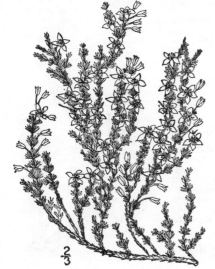

1. Hudsonia ericoìdes L. Heath-like Hudsonia. Fig. 2912.

Hudsonia ericoides L. Mant. 1: 74. 1767.

Bushy-branched from the base, greenish, softly-pubescent throughout, 4'–7' high, the principal branches slender, ascending. Leaves subulate, 3"–4" long, somewhat spreading, densely imbricated on the younger branches, more scattered on the older ones; pedicels very slender, 5"–8" long; flowers numerous, about 4" broad; sepals 2"–3" long, acutish; stamens 12–18; capsule oblong, slightly pubescent; seeds about 3.

In dry sandy soil, especially in pine-barrens, mainly near the coast, Newfoundland to New York and Virginia. Field-pine. Poverty-grass. American heath. May–June.

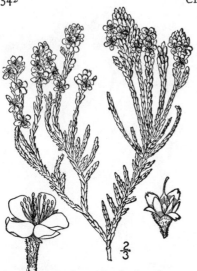

2. Hudsonia tomentòsa Nutt. Woolly Hudsonia. False Heather. Fig. 2913.

Hudsonia tomentosa Nutt. Gen. **2** : 5. 1818.

H. tomentosa intermedia Peck, Rep. N. Y. State Mus. **45** : 86. 1893.

Densely tufted and intricately branched, matted, hoary-pubescent, pale, 4′–8″ high; branches stout, ascending. Leaves about 1″ long, oval or oblong, densely imbricated and appressed; flowers sessile, or on rather stout pedicels less than 3″ long, numerous, slightly smaller than those of the preceding species; sepals obtuse; stamens 9–18; capsules ovoid, glabrous, usually 1-seeded.

In sands of the seashore and in pine-barrens, New Brunswick to Virginia, and on sand hills and lake and river shores west to Mackenzie, Manitoba, North Dakota and Wisconsin. May–July. Poverty- or beargrass. Dog's-dinner. Poverty-plant. Heath. Groundmoss or -cedar. Beach-heather.

3. LÉCHEA Kalm; L. Sp. Pl. 90. 1753.

Perennial branching herbs, often woody at the base, with small entire leaves and minute panicled greenish or purplish flowers. Sepals 5, the 2 outer smaller and narrower. Petals 3, ovate to linear, inconspicuous, persistent. Stamens 3–12. Stigmas 3, nearly sessile, laciniate, prominent when the plant is in flower. Capsule 3-valved, 3-celled, or by obliteration of the dissepiments 1-celled, about 6-seeded. Embryo curved or spiral. [Named for Johan Leche, a Swedish botanist, died 1764.]

A genus of about 14 species, 11 of them natives of eastern North America, 1 Texan, 1 Cuban and 1 Mexisan. Type species: *Lechea minor* L. Species indiscriminately known as Pin-weeds. The characteristic basal shoots appear late in the season.

Leaves of the basal shoots oblong or ovate, not more than 3 times as long as broad.
　Outer sepals longer than the inner; panicle very leafy.   1. *L. minor.*
　Outer sepals equalling or shorter than the inner.
　　Pod oblong; pedicels slender, 1″–2″ long.   2. *L. racemulosa.*
　　Pod globose; pedicels about ½″ long.
　　　Erect, villous-pubescent.   3. *L. villosa.*
　　　Ascending, bushy-branched, tomentose-canescent.   4. *L. maritima.*
Leaves of the basal shoots lanceolate or linear, usually more than 3 times as long as broad.
　Stem-leaves narrowly linear; inner sepals 1-nerved.   5. *L. tenuifolia.*
　Stem-leaves oblong-linear; inner sepals 3-nerved.
　　Plants green, more or less pubescent.
　　　Pod obovoid, ½″ in diameter; panicle-branches ascending or spreading. 6. *L. Leggettii.*
　　　Pod globose, about 1″ in diameter; panicle-branches nearly erect, loosely flowered;
　　　　flowers slender-pedicelled.   7. *L. intermedia.*
　　　Pod oval, about ½″ in diameter; panicle-branches erect-ascending, densely flowered;
　　　　flowers short-pedicelled.   8. *L. juniperina.*
　　Plant pale, canescent; pod globose, ½″ in diameter.   9. *L. stricta.*

1. Lechea mìnor L. Thyme-leaved Pin-weed.
Fig. 2914.

Lechea minor L. Sp. Pl. 90. 1753.

Lechea thymifolia Michx. Fl. Bor. Am. **1** : 77. 1803.

Lechea novae-caesareae Aust.; A. Gray, Man. Ed. 5, 81. 1867.

Erect, 6′–2° high, freely branching above, more or less pilose-pubescent with appressed hairs throughout. Branches slender, erect or ascending; stem-leaves oval or oblong, 4″–7″ long, 2″–3″ wide, acutish or obtuse, ciliate, the upper smaller and often narrower than the lower; petioles 1″ long; leaves of the basal shoots oval or oblong, obtusish, 3″–5″ long, 2½″–3″ wide; panicle very leafy; flowers close together, somewhat secund; outer sepals longer than the inner and longer than the obovoid or globose pod.

In dry open grounds, eastern Massachusetts to Ontario, Michigan, Florida and Louisiana. Petals red-purple. Aug.–Sept.

2. Lechea racemulòsa Lam. Oblong-fruited Pin-weed. Fig. 2915.

Lechea racemulosa Lam. Tabl. Encycl. 2: 432. pl. 281. f. 3. 1791.

Erect, 6'–18' high, freely branching above, slightly pubescent throughout with appressed hairs or at length nearly glabrous. Branches slender, divergent or ascending; leaves of the stem oblong or linear-oblong, obtuse or acutish, narrowed at the base, 4"–9" long, 1½"–2" wide; leaves of the basal shoots oval or oblong, 2"–4" long, 1½"–3" wide, obtuse; petioles about 1" long; panicle sparsely leafy, its branches spreading or ascending; flowers on slender divergent pedicels 1"–2" long; outer sepals equalling or shorter than the inner; pod oblong or ellipsoid.

In dry sandy and rocky soil, southeastern New York to Indiana, Florida and Tennessee. Ascends to 4200 ft. in North Carolina. July–Aug.

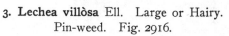

3. Lechea villòsa Ell. Large or Hairy. Pin-weed. Fig. 2916.

Lechea major Michx. Fl. Bor. Am. 1: 76. 1803. Not L. 1753.
Lechea villosa Ell. Bot. S. C. & Ga. 1: 184. 1817.

Erect, villous-pubescent with spreading hairs, 1°–2½° high, branching above, leafy. Branches rather stout, ascending; leaves of the stem oblong-elliptic, obtuse, but pointed, 8"–12" long, 3"–5" wide; petioles ½" long; leaves of the basal shoots oval or oblong, obtuse, 3"–4" long, 2"–3" wide; branches of the panicle ascending, the ultimate branchlets often recurved; pedicels ¼" long; flowers more or less secund-scorpioid, close together; outer sepals about equalling the inner; pod depressed-globose, ½" in diameter.

In dry soil, Vermont and Massachusetts to southern Ontario and Nebraska, south to Florida, Texas and northern Mexico. Petals greenish purple. July–Aug.

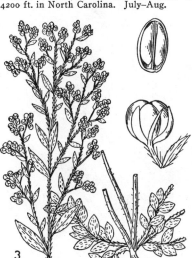

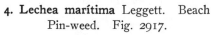

4. Lechea marítima Leggett. Beach Pin-weed. Fig. 2917.

L. maritima Leggett in Britt. Prel. Cat. N. Y. 13. 1881.
L. minor var. *maritima* A. Gray, Man. Ed. 6, 77. 1890.
L. maritima interior Robinson, Rhodora 10: 34. 1908.

Densely tufted, branching from the base, stout, rigid, 6'–15' high, tomentose-canescent with whitish hairs. Primary branches spreading or ascending, numerous; flowering branches slender, stiff, divergent, elongated; leaves of the stem linear or linear-oblong, blunt or acute, 4"–10" long, 1"–2" wide; leaves of the basal shoots oblong or ovate-oblong, mainly acute, 3"–4" long, 1½"–2" wide, densely canescent; pedicels ½"–1" long; flowers numerous, clustered; petals reddish; outer sepals shorter than the inner; pod globose, ½" in diameter.

Sands of the seashore and in sandy soil inland, Maine to Virginia and Georgia.

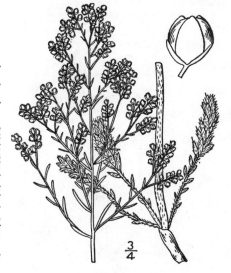

$\frac{3}{4}$

6. Lechea Leggéttii Britt. & Holl. Leg-gett's Pin-weed. Fig. 2919.

L. Leggettii Britt. & Holl. Prel. Cat. N. Y. 6. 1888.

Erect, rather slender, freely branching, more or less strigose-pubescent, 10'–2° high. Branches slender, spreading or ascending; leaves of the stem linear or linear-oblong, acute or obtuse, 5"–12" long, $\frac{1}{2}$"–1" wide, sessile or nearly so; leaves of the basal shoots oblong-linear, 2"–3" long, $\frac{1}{2}$" wide, acute; panicle open, its branches slender and divergent; inflorescence somewhat secund; pedicels $\frac{1}{2}$"–1" long; outer sepals nearly equalling the inner; capsule obovoid, $\frac{1}{2}$" in diameter.

In dry open places, Massachusetts to Indiana, south to North Carolina. Leaves of the basal shoots full-grown in November. Petals brownish purple. July–Aug.

Lechea monilifórmis Bicknell, from Nantucket Island, Mass., differs in a denser and more leafy panicle with flowers more secund, and oblong-obovoid capsules.

Lechea Tórreyi Leggett, a related pilose species of the Southeastern States, is erroneously recorded from southern Virginia.

5. Lechea tenuifòlia Michx. Narrow-leaved Pin-weed. Fig. 2918.

L. tenuifolia Michx. Fl. Bor. Am. 1 : 77. 1803.

Densely tufted, stems erect, slender, 4'–10' high, divaricately branched above, minutely strigose-pubescent. Branches slender, elongated; leaves of the stem narrowly linear, or sometimes nearly filiform, 2"–7" long, $\frac{1}{4}$" wide or less, acute, sessile, or very nearly so; leaves of the basal shoots linear, sessile, 3"–4" long, about $\frac{1}{2}$" wide; pedicels 1" long; flowers more or less secund, conspicuously bracted by the upper leaves; outer sepals equalling or exceeding the inner; pod globose-oval, $\frac{1}{2}$" in diameter, or more.

In dry open places, New Hampshire to Wisconsin, Nebraska, Florida and Texas. Petals red-purple. July–Aug.

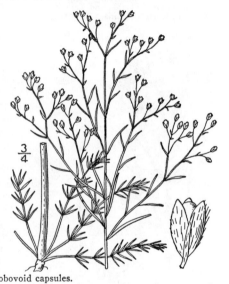

$\frac{3}{4}$

7. Lechea intermèdia Leggett. Large-podded Pin-weed. Fig. 2920.

Lechea intermedia Leggett; Britton, Bull. Torr. Club **21** : 252. 1894.

Erect, 8'–24' high, branching above, sparingly strigose-pubescent. Branches erect or ascending, short, slender; leaves of the stem oblong-linear, 6"–14" long, 1"–2$\frac{1}{2}$" wide, acute, nearly sessile, leaves of the basal shoots oblong-linear, shorter than those of the stem, 4"–5" long, $\frac{1}{2}$" wide, somewhat larger than those of *L. Leggettii;* pedicels 1"–2" long, slender; outer sepals about equalling the inner; capsule subglobose or depressed-globose, about 1" in diameter.

In dry open places, especially in hilly or mountainous regions, Pennsylvania and New Jersey to Nova Scotia, northern New York, Ontario, Wisconsin and Michigan. Leaves of the basal shoots full-grown in October or November. Petals brownish purple. July–Aug.

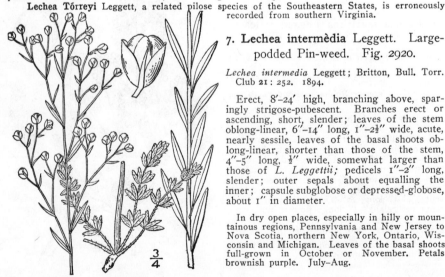

$\frac{3}{4}$

8. Lechea junipérina Bicknell. Maine Pin-weed. Fig. 2921

Lechea juniperina Bicknell, Bull. Torr. Club **24**: 88. 1897.

Tufted, 4′–20′ high, finely hoary to canescent. Branches short, ascending or erect, leafy, appressed, forming a dense narrow panicle; stemleaves numerous, ascending or appressed, glabrous, except the midrib and margins, linear-oblong to oblanceolate, 5″–10″ long, 1″–2″ wide; flowers numerous, crowded; pedicels ½″–1½″ long; fruiting calyx ovoid-ellipsoid, ¾″ long; inner sepals elliptic, nerveless or faintly 3-nerved, often deep purple, the outer shorter, bright green; leaves of basal shoots oblong or elliptic, 2″–3″ long, ½″–1″ wide.

Coast of Nova Scotia to New Hampshire. Aug. Petals brownish red. The basal shoots do not appear until September.

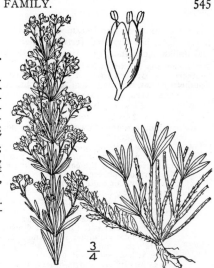

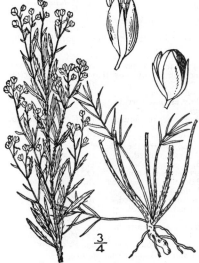

$\frac{3}{4}$

$\frac{3}{4}$

9. Lechea strícta Leggett. Bushy or Prairie Pin-weed. Fig. 2922.

Lechea stricta Leggett; Britton, Bull. Torr. Club **21**: 251. 1894.

Erect, 12′–16′ high, densely and fastigiately branched, densely strigose-canescent, pale, very bushy. Branches slender, ascending or nearly erect; leaves of the stem linear-oblong, 6″–12″ long, ½″–1″ wide, acute or bluntish; leaves of the basal shoots linear-oblong, much smaller than those of the stem, 2″–3″ long, ½″ wide or less, acute; pedicels slender, 1″–1½″ long; outer sepals shorter than or equalling the inner; capsule subglobose to oval, ½″–1″ in diameter.

In open dry places, western New York to Minnesota, Wisconsin and Nebraska. July–Aug.

Family 90. VIOLÀCEAE DC. Fl. Franc. 4: 801. 1805.

VIOLET FAMILY.

Herbs or shrubs, with alternate or basal (rarely opposite) simple entire lobed or laciniate stipulate leaves, and solitary or clustered flowers. Sepals 5, equal or unequal. Flowers perfect, mostly irregular. Petals 5, hypogynous, imbricated in the bud, the lower one generally larger or spurred. Perfect stamens 5, hypogynous; anthers erect, connivent in a ring, or syngenesious, sessile or on short filaments. Ovary 1, 1-celled; placentae 3, parietal; style simple; stigma generally oblique. Capsule dehiscent by valves (except in some tropical genera with berry-like fruit). Seeds anatropous, with a crustaceous testa; embryo mainly straight, in copious endosperm.

About 15 genera and 300 species, of wide distribution.

Sepals more or less prolonged posteriorly.	1. *Viola.*
Sepals not prolonged posteriorly.	
Petals nearly equal; stamens syngenesious.	2. *Cubelium.*
Petals very unequal; anthers only connivent.	3. *Calceolaria.*

1. VÌOLA [Tourn.] L. Sp. Pl. 933. 1753.*

Herbs, either leafy stemmed or stemless; petaliferous flowers mostly in early spring, succeeded, except in *V. pedata,* by cleistogamous flowers, that are usually without petals and never expand, but bear abundant seed; stamens five in the petaliferous flower, the two lowest with appendages that project into the spur or nectar sac of the odd petal, these two stamens alone developed in the cleistogamous flower. [The Latin name.]

Allied species freely hybridize when growing together; the hybrids commonly display

---

* Written by Dr. Ezra Brainerd.

characters more or less intermediate to those o_ the parent species, and show marked vegetative vigor, but impaired fertility; their offspring are often much unlike the mother plant and unlike each other, reverting variously to the characters of the two original species.

Some 200 species, widely distributed. Besides the following, about 35 others occur in the southern and western parts of North America. *Viola villosa* Walt. (*V. carolina* Greene), of the Southern States, may be looked for in southeastern Virginia. Type species: *Viola odorata* L.

* STEMLESS, THE LEAVES AND SCAPES DIRECTLY FROM A ROOTSTOCK OR FROM RUNNERS.

    † Flowers without marked fragrance; indigenous.

       ‡ PETALS VIOLET OR WHITE.

Cleistogamous flowers wanting; petals all beardless.   1. *V. pedata.*
Cleistogamous flowers present.

  A. *Rootstock thick, often stout, without stolons; lateral petals bearded.*

1. Cleistogamous flowers ovoid on short prostrate peduncles; their capsules mostly purplish.
    Leaves (except rarely the earliest) palmately 5–11-lobed or -parted.
      Plants villous-pubescent; seeds brown.   2. *V. palmata.*
      Plants nearly or quite glabrous; seeds buff.   3. *V. Stoneana.*
    Early and late leaves uncut; others 3–7-lobed or -parted, villous-pubescent.   4. *V. triloba.*
    Leaves all uncut; blades ovate to reniform, cordate, crenate-serrate.
      Plants nearly or quite glabrous.
        Petals violet-purple; seeds brown.
          Petioles smooth; plants of moist soil.   5. *V. papilionacea.*
          Petioles glandular roughened; plants of dry soil.   6. *V. latiuscula.*
        Petals pale violet, or nearly white; seeds buff.   7. *V. missouriensis.*
      Leaves villous, especially beneath and on petioles; seeds dark-brown.   8. *V. sororia.*
      Leaves hirsutulous above, otherwise glabrous; seeds buff.   9. *V. hirsutula.*

2. Cleistogamous flowers ovoid, on ascending peduncles soon elongate, their capsules purplish;
                            leaves cordate, none cut.
    Leaves pubescent beneath and on petioles.
      Sepals and their auricles ciliolate; blades broadly ovate, cordate.   10. *V. septentrionalis.*
      Sepals and auricles not ciliate; blades at flowering time narrowly ovate. 11. *V. novae-angliae.*
    Leaves glabrous beneath and on petioles.   12. *V. affinis.*

3. Cleistogamous flowers on erect peduncles, their capsules green.
    Leaves ovate to reniform, cordate, glabrous, uniformly crenate-serrate.
      Cleistogamous flowers ovoid; spurred petal villous.
        Mature leaves rounded at apex or bluntly pointed; sepals obtuse. 13. *V. nephrophylla.*
        Mature leaves abruptly acuminate; sepals acute.   14. *V. retusa.*
      Cleistogamous flowers long and slender, spurred petal glabrous.   15. *V. cucullata.*
    Leaves lobed, or the margins sharply incised or toothed toward the subcordate or truncate base.
      Spurred petal glabrous, lateral with clavate beard; leaves lobed.   16. *V. viarum.*
      Spurred petal villous, lateral with capillary beard.
        Blades of mature leaves ovate-oblong, ciliate, finely pubescent. 17. *V. fimbriatula.*
        Blades of mature leaves lanceolate, usually glabrous; petioles long. 18. *V. sagittata.*
        Blades of mature leaves broadly ovate or deltoid.
          Margin coarsely toothed near base; blades sometimes lobed. 19. *V. emarginata.*
          Margin sharply toothed toward base or pectinately incised. 20. *V. pectinata.*
        Blades of mature leaves primarily 3-lobed or 3-parted, segments variously cleft.
          Segments 2–3-cleft into linear or oblanceolate lobes; eastern. 21. *V. Brittoniana.*
          Segments 3-cleft, the subdivisions often 2–4-lobed; western. 22. *V. pedatifida.*
          Middle segment uncut, the outer usually 2–4-cleft; southern. 23. *V. septemloba.*

  B. *Rootstocks slender (thicker and scaly with age); plants usually from stolons.*
    Petals lilac or pale violet.
      Leaves minutely hairy on the upper surface; spur large, 3″ long. 24. *V. Selkirkii.*
      Leaves glabrous throughout; spur short, 1″ long. 25. *V. palustris.*
    Petals white, with dark purple lines on the three lower.
      Cleistogamous capsules ovoid, usually purplish; woodland plants.
        Leaves reniform, lateral petals beardless; stolons short. 26. *V. renifolia.*
        Leaves broadly ovate, acute, lateral petals bearded; seeds obtuse at base.
                             27. *V. incognita.*
      Leaves ovate, acute or acuminate; lateral petals beardless, seeds acute at base.
                             28. *V. blanda.*
      Cleistogamous capsules ellipsoid, always green, peduncles erect; bogs and wet meadows.
        Leaves broadly ovate or orbicular, cordate, obtuse. 29. *V. pallens.*
        Leaves oblong to ovate; base slightly cordate to tapering. 30. *V. primulifolia.*
        Leaves lanceolate or elliptical. 31. *V. lanceolata.*

       ‡‡ PETALS BRIGHT YELLOW. 32. *V. rotundifolia.*
       †† Flowers very fragrant; introduced. 33. *V. odorata.*

   ** LEAFY STEMMED; THE FLOWERS AXILLARY.

    † Style capitate, beakless, bearded near the summit; spur short; stipules nearly entire, soon scarious.

Stems at first short, flowers and leaves from near the base; later elongating. 34. *V. Nuttallii.*
Stems not leafly below; peduncles from axils of upper leaves.
    ‡*Petals yellow.*
    Rootstock short, woody, brown, bearing coarse fibrous roots. 35. *V. hastata.*
    Rootstock long, brittle, whitish, bearing crisp capillary roots.
      Sparingly pubescent; root-leaves usually 1–3 36. *V. eriocarpa.*
      Markedly pubescent; root-leaves usually wanting. 37. *V. pubescens.*

        ‡‡*Inner face of petals white with yellow base, outer face usually violet.*
Root-leaves and lower stem-leaves reniform, densely hirsutulous beneath. 38. *V. rugulosa.*
Root-leaves and lower stem-leaves broadly ovate, acuminate, subglabrous. 39. *V. canadensis.*

†† **Style not capitate; spur long; stipules bristly toothed, herbaceous.**

Spur 2″–4″ long; lateral petals bearded; style bent at tip, with short beard.
         Petals white or cream-colored.   40. *V. striata.*
         Petals violet-blue.
    Herbage glabrous or nearly so.
       Leaves orbicular or suborbicular.
         Stipules ovate-lanceolate, bristly serrate; leaves often 1¾′ wide. 41. *V. conspersa.*
         Stipules linear, entire except at base; leaves not over ¾′ wide. 42. *V. labradorica.*
       Leaves ovate; Canada and far west.   43. *V. adunca.*
    Herbage puberulent.
       Stems ascending; blades mostly ovate; Canada and bordering states. 44. *V. subvestita.*
       Stems prostrate; blades orbicular; Kentucky and southward.   45. *V. Walteri.*
Spur 4″–6″ long, lateral petals beardless; style straight and smooth. 46. *V. rostrata.*

††† **Style much enlarged upward into a globose, hollow summit; stipules large, leaf-like, pectinate at base.**

Upper leaves and middle lobe of stipules entire or nearly so; indigenous. 47. *V. Rafinesquii.*
Upper leaves and middle lobe of stipules plainly crenate; introduced from Europe.
    Petals large, 2–3 times as long as the sepals.   48. *V. tricolor.*
    Petals usually shorter than the sepals.   49. *V. arvensis.*

1. Viola pedàta L. Bird's-foot or Crowfoot Violet. Fig. 2923.

Viola pedata L. Sp. Pl. 933. 1753.
Viola pedata var. *bicolor* Pursh; Raf. in DC. Prodr. 1: 291. 1824.

Nearly glabrous; rootstock short, erect; leaves 3-divided, the lateral divisions pedately 3–5-parted or -cleft, the segments linear to spatulate, often 2–4-cleft or -toothed near the apex; the leaves of early spring and of late autumn often smaller and less deeply dissected; corolla ¾′–1¾′ broad, the upper petals dark violet, the three lower lilac-purple, all beardless; the orange tips of the stamens large and conspicuous at the center of the flower; capsules green, glabrous; seeds copper-colored; apetalous flowers wanting, but petaliferous frequent in late summer and autumn.

In dry fields and open woods, Massachusetts to Minnesota, south to Florida and Louisiana.

Var. **lineariloba** DC. with all the petals of the same lilac-purple color is the more common form. Sand-, snake-, wood-, horse or horseshoe violet. Pansy. Velvets. April–June.

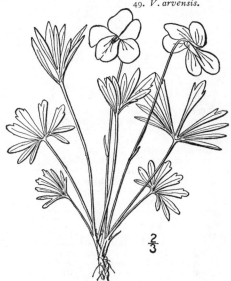

2. Viola palmàta L. Early Blue Violet. Fig. 2924.

Viola palmata L. Sp. Pl. 933. 1753.

Rootstock thick, usually oblique, sometimes branched; leaves palmately 5–11-lobed or -parted, the segments variously toothed or cleft, the middle segment usually the widest; petioles and veins of the lower surface villous, the upper surface often glabrous; corolla violet-purple, ¾′–1¼′ broad, sepals ovate-lanceolate, rather blunt; petaliferous flowers on erect peduncles, cleistogamous on prostrate peduncles, their capsules ovoid, 4″–6″ long; seeds brown, 1″ long.

Wooded hills in dry rich soil, western Massachusetts to Minnesota, south along the Alleghanies to Florida. A form with the lateral leaf-lobes linear occurs in the region of the Great Lakes. Hand- or hood-leaf violet. Chicken-fighters. Roosters. Johnny-jump-up. April–May.

Viola Egglestònii Brainerd, a glabrous species, the leaf-segments oblanceolate, first known from Tennessee, has recently been found in Kentucky.

3. Viola Stoneàna House. Witmer Stone's Violet. Fig. 2925.

Viola septemloba Stone, Proc. Acad. Phila. **1903**: 678
Not Le Conte 1826.
V. Stoneana House, Bull. Torr. Club **32**: 253. 1905.

Glabrous, except for very minute hairs along the margin of the leaves and on the veins; blades, except sometimes the earliest, 3-divided or -parted, the segments 2–3-cleft, the divisions cuneate or oblanceolate, acuminate, remotely toothed on the upper half, the middle division the widest, the two lower often lunate and coarsely toothed on the lower margin; mature leaves often 10'–14' high, the blades 3'–4' wide; flowers on peduncles 3'–4' high, large, violet, darker toward the throat, lateral petals bearded, spurred petal glabrous; cleistogamous flowers on short horizontal peduncles, their capsules ovoid, blotched with purple; seeds buff.

Moist woodlands, New Jersey, eastern Pennsylvania and Maryland. May.

4. Viola tríloba Schwein. Three-lobed Violet. Fig. 2926.

V. triloba Schwein. Am. Journ. Sci. **5**: 57. 1822.
V. congener Le Conte, Ann. Lyc. N. Y. **2**: 140. 1826.

Earliest leaves and those put forth in late summer usually with uncut blades, reniform, cordate, sparingly pubescent or glabrate; those unfolding at petaliferous flowering densely villous beneath and on the petioles, the blades 4'–6' wide when mature, 3-lobed or rarely 3-parted, the middle segment broad, the lateral lunate, divaricate, often coarsely toothed or cleft; peduncles mostly glabrous, shorter than the leaves; petals deep violet; outer sepals ovate-lanceolate, somewhat obtuse, slightly ciliate, cleistogamous capsules ovoid, purplish; seeds buff or brown.

Dry woodlands, southern New England and New York, south to Georgia and Alabama. Var. **dilatàta** (Ell.) Brainerd (*V. falcata* Greene), in which the pedately cut leaves have more numerous and deeper incisions, occurs from Missouri eastward to the coast and southward to Louisiana and Florida. April–May.

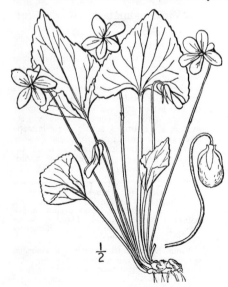

5. Viola papilionàcea Pursh. Meadow or Hooded Blue Violet. Fig. 2927.

Viola papilionacea Pursh, Fl. Am. Sept. **1**: 173. 1814.

Viola domestica Bicknell, Ill. Fl. **3**: 519. 1898.

Viola pratincola Greene, Pittonia **4**: 64. 1899.

Plants usually glabrous, robust from a stout branching rootstock; petioles sometimes sparingly pubescent, becoming much longer than the blades; these often 5' broad, reniform or ovate, cordate, acute or sometimes abruptly pointed; scapes shorter than the leaves; corolla deep violet, white or greenish yellow at the center, sometimes wholly white; the odd petal often narrow and boat-shaped, usually beardless; outer sepals ovate-lanceolate; capsules ellipsoid, green or dark purple, 5"–7" long; seeds 1" long, dark brown.

Moist fields and groves, frequently about dwellings, Massachusetts to Minnesota, south to Georgia and Oklahoma. Ascends to 6000 ft. in Virginia. Long-stemmed purple violet. Fighting cocks. Common blue violet. April–May.
Figured as *V. obliqua* in our first edition.

6. Viola latiúscula Greene. Broad-leaved Wood Violet. Fig. 2928.

Viola latiuscula Greene, Pittonia **5**: 93. 1902.

Glabrous except for more or less puberulence or granular roughness on the edges of the petiole near the blade; when in petaliferous flower 2½′–5′ high, the blades broadly ovate-deltoid, cordate, about 1′ wide, the earliest obtuse and tinged beneath with purple; mature leaves often 8′–12′ high, the blades 1½′–4′ wide, sometimes much dilated and abruptly pointed; flowers large, deep violet, the spurred petal villous at base; outer sepals lanceolate, glabrous, with short rounded auricles; cleistogamous flowers on short, horizontal peduncles, their capsules ellipsoid, flecked with purple, 4″–6″ long, the persistent sepals one-third as long; seeds brown.

Dry open woods in sand or gravel, western Vermont to New Jersey and northwestern Pennsylvania. May–June.

½

7. Viola missouriénsis Greene. Missouri Violet. Fig. 2929.

Viola missouriensis Greene, Pittonia **4**: 141. 1900.

Glabrous, cespitose, the stout ascending rootstock often branching; leaves at vernal flowering 3′–6′ high, the blades ovate-deltoid, cordate at base, often with concave upper margins; mature leaves 6′–12′ high, the blades 2½′–4′ wide, as long as broad, acuminate, rather coarsely crenate-serrate; corolla pale violet with a darker band above the white center, spurred petal glabrous; sepals lanceolate or ovate-oblong and obtuse, narrowly white-margined, slightly ciliolate; capsules from apetalous flowers broadly ellipsoid, finely dotted with brown, 5″–6″ long; seeds bright buff, nearly 1″ long.

River bottoms and low woods, Missouri and Oklahoma, south to Louisiana and Texas. April–May.

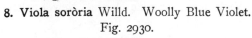

⅗

8. Viola soròria Willd. Woolly Blue Violet. Fig. 2930.

Viola sororia Willd. Enum. 263. 1809.
Viola cuspidata Greene, Pittonia **3**: 314. 1898.

Rootstock stout, often branching; petioles and under surface of young leaves, and often the scapes, villous-pubescent; the blades ovate to orbicular or even reniform, with an obtuse short point, cordate, crenate-serrate, sometimes 4′ wide when mature; corolla violet to lavender, and occasionally white; outer sepals ovate-oblong, commonly obtuse, all finely ciliate below the middle and on the short rounded auricles; cleistogamous flowers ovoid on short horizontal peduncles, usually underground, but lengthened and erect when the capsules ripen; capsules usually mottled with brown; seeds dark brown, 1″ long.

⅔

Moist meadows, shady ledges and dooryards, western Quebec and New England to Minnesota, south to North Carolina and Oklahoma. April–May.

9. Viola hirsùtula Brainerd. Southern Wood Violet. Fig. 2931.

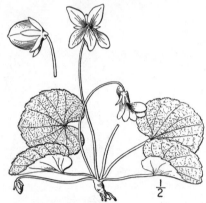

Viola villosa Nutt. and recent authors. Not Walt.
Viola hirsutula Brainerd, Rhodora **9**: 98. 1907.

Plants of small size; rootstock short, thick; leaves frequently appressed to the ground, the blades orbicular to reniform, cordate, obtuse, ¾′–2′ wide, purplish and glabrous beneath, silvery pubescent above; often purple-veined and mottled with different shades of green; flowers reddish purple on peduncles exceeding the leaves, lateral petals bearded, spur about 2″ long, very blunt; apetalous flowers small, ovoid, on short prostrate peduncles, their capsules ovoid, 3″–4″ long, purplish, bearing each 20–30 light brown seeds.

Copses in dry rich soil, southern New York to central Alabama and Georgia. Hairy violet. April–May.

10. Viola septentrionàlis Greene. Northern Blue Violet. Fig. 2932.

Viola septentrionalis Greene, Pittonia **3**: 334. 1898.

Rootstock at length stout and branching; scapes and leaves at vernal flowering 3′–5′ high, more or less hirsutulous except the earliest leaves; blades ovate to reniform, cordate, ciliate, somewhat pointed but the apex blunt, becoming 2′–3′ wide when mature; petioles slender, wiry, often purplish at base; petals variable, 4″–6″ wide, deep violet to pale lilac, rarely pure white or white suffused with violet, the three lowest villous at the base, all occasionally bearing scattered hairs; sepals ovate, usually obtuse, closely ciliolate nearly to the tip; cleistogamous flowers sagittate, on ascending peduncles; their mature capsules purple or sometimes green, subglobose, 2½″–4″ long, subtended by the spreading ciliolate auricles of the sepals; seeds dark brown.

Moist open woodlands, Prince Edward Island to Ontario, south to Connecticut and northern Pennsylvania. May.

11. Viola novae-ángliae House. New England Blue Violet. Fig. 2933.

Viola novae-angliae House, Rhodora **6**: 226. 1904.

In spring densely villous at the base except on petioles of earliest leaves; blades at petaliferous flowering narrowly ovate-triangular, cordate, about 1¾′ long, and ¾′ wide, glabrous above, more or less pubescent beneath, crenate-serrate at the base, distantly so toward the apex; the blades in summer becoming about 2′ wide, the breadth equalling the length; flowers large, violet-purple, on scapes 3′–4′ high, mostly above the leaves; the three lower petals densely villous, upper pair often with scattered hairs; sepals oblong, obtuse, glabrous; cleistogamous flowers sagittate, on ascending peduncles, their capsules nearly globose, mottled with purple, 3″–4″ long, subtended by spreading naked auricles; seeds nearly 1″ long.

Gravelly and sandy shores, or in crevices of rocks, along lakes or rivers, northern and central Maine, western Ontario and northern Wisconsin. May–June.

12. Viola affìnis Le Conte.　Le Conte's Violet.
Fig. 2934.

V. affinis Le Conte, Ann. Lyc. N. Y. **2**: 138. 1826.

Viola venustula Greene, Pittonia **3**: 335. 1898.

Nearly glabrous; leaves that unfold at vernal flowering narrowly cordate-ovate, and commonly attenuate toward the apex, becoming about 2′ wide in summer, the margins noticeably crenate-serrate; petioles slender; corolla violet with the white base conspicuous, spurred petal more or less villous; cleistogamous flowers small, ovoid, on ascending peduncles that lengthen as the capsules ripen; these ellipsoid, 2½″–4″ long, usually reddish brown, sometimes green, either glabrous or clothed with minute dense pubescence; sepals half the length of the capsule, with small appressed auricles; seeds normally buff, not quite 1″ long.

Moist meadows, low woods, and shady borders of streams, western New England to Wisconsin, south to Georgia and Alabama. April–May.

13. Viola nephrophýlla Greene.　Northern Bog Violet.　Fig. 2935.

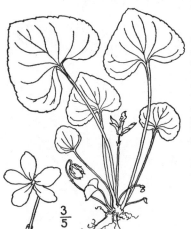

Viola nephrophylla Greene, Pittonia **3**: 144. 1896.
Viola vagula Greene, Pittonia **4**: 67. 1899.

Nearly or quite glabrous; earliest leaves orbicular or slightly reniform, later leaves broadly ovate, cordate, obtuse or bluntly pointed, crenate-serrate, 1¼′–2½′ wide; flowers large, violet, on peduncles exceeding the leaves; spurred petal villous, the lateral densely bearded, and the two upper often with scattered hairs; sepals ovate to lanceolate, obtuse and often rounded; cleistogamous flowers ovoid, on erect peduncles at length 1¾–4′ high; capsules green, glabrous, short-ellipsoid; seeds olive-brown, nearly 1″ long.

Cold mossy bogs and borders of streams and lakes, eastern Quebec to British Columbia, south to northwestern Connecticut, Wisconsin, New Mexico and Washington. May–June.

14. Viola retùsa Greene.　Western Blue Violet.　Fig. 2936.

Viola retusa Greene, Pittonia **4**: 6. 1899.

Glabrous; rootstock vertical, often stout and much branching; leaves at petaliferous flowering about 3′ high, the blades about 1′ wide, broadly ovate, cordate, slightly acuminate with obtuse apex; aestival leaves 2′–3′ wide, reniform, abruptly acuminate, the base cordate to truncate-decurrent, crenate-serrate; scapes somewhat exceeding the leaves; petals violet, the upper obovate, the lateral spatulate with clavate beard, the spur petal slightly hairy; sepals lanceolate, white margined; cleistogamous flowers ovoid, on erect peduncles becoming 4′–5′ long in fruit; capsules ellipsoid, green, 6″ long; seeds brown, 1″ long.

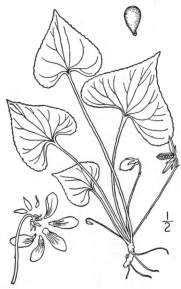

Low shady groves, central Kansas, and along streams in the foothills of eastern Colorado. May–June.

15. Viola cucullàta Ait. Marsh Blue Violet. Fig. 2937.

Viola cucullata Ait. Hort. Kew. 3: 228. 1789.

Glabrous; leaves except the earliest broadly ovate to reniform, cordate, acute or subacuminate, finely crenate-serrate, often 3½' wide when mature; peduncles usually much exceeding the leaves; corolla violet-blue, darker colored at the throat, sometimes white; lateral petals with strongly clavate beard, spurred petal glabrous, generally somewhat shorter than the lateral; sepals narrowly lanceolate; cleistogamous flowers long and slender, on erect, often elongate peduncles; capsules ovoid-cylindric, green, 5''-7½'' long, but little exceeding the long-auricled sepals; seeds nearly black, ¾'' long.

Wet places, Quebec and Ontario, south to the mountains of northern Georgia. *Viola dentata* Greene, not Pursh, is a not infrequent hybrid between this species and *V. fimbriatula*. April–June.

16. Viola viàrum Pollard. Plains Violet. Fig. 2938.

Viola viarum Pollard in Britton, Man. 635. 1901.

Glabrous; leaves broadly deltoid with the basal angles rounded; some undivided, merely crenate-serrate, or with a few slight incisions; others pedately 3–7-lobed or -parted, the middle segment broad acute serrate, the lower segments commonly lunate with outer margin sinuately serrate; corolla deep violet, the spurred petal glabrous narrow emarginate, the lateral pair narrow, bearing a sparse short clavate beard, the upper pair broader divergent emarginate; sepals narrowly lanceolate, with rather short auricles; cleistogamous fruit on peduncles somewhat shorter than the petioles; ripe capsules pale green, ovoid-cylindric; seeds olive-brown, nearly 1'' long.

Dry open ground, waysides, and rocky river-banks Missouri to Kansas. April–May.

17. Viola fimbriátula J. E. Smith. Ovate-leaved Violet. Fig. 2939.

Viola fimbriatula J. E. Smith in Rees' Cyclop. 37: no. 16. 1817.
Viola ovata Nutt. Gen. 1: 148. 1818.
V. sagittata var. *ovata* T. & G. Fl. N. A. 1: 133. 1838.

Rootstock becoming long and stout, usually erect; the blades of the earliest leaves ovate, obtuse, those of the later oblong-ovate, acute or somewhat obtuse, finely pubescent especially beneath, obscurely crenulate toward the apex, the lobes of the subcordate or truncate base often sharply toothed, incised, or auriculate; scapes usually much exceeding the leaves; sepals lanceolate, acuminate, with auricles somewhat spreading and ciliate; corolla violet-purple; capsules green, ovoid, 3''-5'' long; seeds brown; cleistogamous flowers on erect peduncles.

Dry fields and hillsides, Nova Scotia to Wisconsin, south to the mountains of northern Georgia. *Viola conjugens* Greene is apparently a hybrid between this species and *V. sagittata*. April–May. Fringed or rattle-snake violet.

18. Viola sagittàta Ait. Arrow-leaved Violet.
Fig. 2940.

Viola sagittata Ait. Hort. Kew. **3**: 287. 1789.

Usually glabrous, but the leaves often ciliate or finely pubescent throughout; petioles commonly longer than the blades; these lanceolate or oblong-lanceolate, becoming 1½′–4′ long, cordate to truncate, obtuse or acute, distantly and obscurely toothed above the middle, hastately or sagittately toothed or cleft at the base; the earliest leaves and those produced in late summer often deltoid-ovate, obtuse, merely crenate at the base; flowers on peduncles as long as the leaves, or somewhat longer; corolla violet-purple; sepals narrowly lanceolate, acute, glabrous; capsules 4″–7″ long, containing 50–70 brown seeds.

Moist banks and wet meadows, Massachusetts to Minnesota, south to Georgia and Louisiana. The pubescent form, frequently found in the East, is the prevalent form in the region of the Great Lakes. Early blue, spade-leaf or sand-violet. April–May.

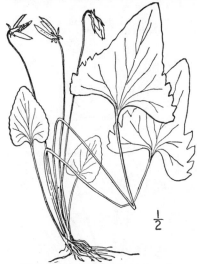

19. Viola emarginàta (Nutt.) Le Conte.
Triangle-leaved Violet. Fig. 2941.

V. sagittata var. *emarginata* Nutt. Gen. **1** : 147. 1818.
V. emarginata Le Conte, Ann. Lyc. N. Y. **2** : 142. 1826.

Glabrous, succulent, frequently cespitose; rootstock stout; petioles generally much longer than the blades; blades at petaliferous flowering narrowly ovate or triangular, subcordate, ¾′–1½′ long; those of later leaves broadly ovate or deltoid, 1½′–3¾′ wide when mature, often no longer than broad, the base subcordate or truncate, often decurrent, obscurely crenate-serrate above the middle, coarsely toothed or incised below; corolla violet-blue, the petals sometimes emarginate; cleistogamous capsules ellipsoid, 4″–7″ long, on erect peduncles somewhat shorter than the leaves; seeds brown.

Dry woods and hillsides, southern New York, south to northern Georgia and west to Oklahoma. Var. **acutíloba** Brainerd has the blades of mature leaves 5-cleft or 5-parted, the middle lobe long lanceolate, the lateral much shorter and narrower, the basal lunate with the outer margin coarsely sinuate-toothed. Staten Island, N. Y., and District of Columbia. April–May.

20. Viola pectinàta Bicknell. Cut-leaved
Violet. Fig. 2942.

Viola pectinata Bicknell, Torreya **4** : 129. 1904.

Plant from short erect rootstock, glabrous except sparsely hirtellous on the margins and veins of leaves; blades at petaliferous flowering narrowly ovate-deltoid, about 1¼′ long and ¾′ wide, subcordate, sharply dentate; blades of mature leaves in summer widely ovate-deltoid, commonly 2′ long and 2½′–3¼′ wide, the base truncate or nearly so, often decurrent, the apex acuminate, the margin closely and deeply dentate below the middle, or often pectinate with linear acute entire lobes; flowers on peduncles about the length of the leaves; petals deep violet, white at the base, the three lower villous-bearded, all often with scattered hairs; sepals narrowly lanceolate, with rather long auricles; capsules ovoid-cylindric, often 7″ long; seeds buff, about ¾″ long.

Low meadows, along the coast, eastern Massachusetts to Maryland. In all known stations growing with *Viola Brittoniana,* which it closely resembles except in leaf-outline. May–June.

$\frac{1}{2}$

21. Viola Brittoniàna Pollard. Coast Violet. Fig. 2943.

Viola Atlantica Britton, Bull. Torr. Club 24: 92. 1897. Not Pomel. 1874.
Viola Brittoniana Pollard, Bot. Gaz. 26: 332. 1898.

Rootstock thick, erect; scapes slender, 4'–8' high, mostly longer than the leaves; blades reniform to ovate in outline; 1¼'–2¾' wide when mature, 3-parted and the segments 2–4-cleft into linear or oblanceolate acute lobes, distantly serrulate, the middle lobe somewhat the widest; glabrous except for minute pubescence on the upper surface and margin; flowers large, rich violet with the white throat conspicuous; sepals linear-lanceolate, acuminate; capsules ovoid-cylindric, 5''–8'' long; seeds buff, ¼'' long.

In peaty or moist sandy soil along the coast, from southern Maine to Virginia. May–June.

22. Viola pedatífida Don. Prairie or Larkspur Violet. Fig. 2944.

Viola pedatifida Don, Gard. Dict. 1: 320. 1831.
Viola delphinifolia Nutt; T. & G. Fl. N. A. 1: 136. 1838.

Rootstock short, vertical; leaves palmately multifid, primarily 3-parted or -divided, each segment again 3-cleft or -parted into linear subdivisions, these often further cut into 2–4 lobes; leaves of late summer less deeply dissected, sometimes 3'–4' wide, usually cuneate at the base with prominent flabelliform veins, the lobes hirsutulous on the margin; scapes exceeding the leaves, bearing showy, violet flowers; cleistogamous capsules yellowish when ripe, 5''–7½'' long, on erect peduncles commonly shorter than the petioles; seeds 1'' long.

Prairies, Ohio to Saskatchewan, southwest to New Mexico and Arizona. April–June.

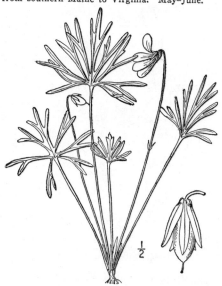

$\frac{1}{2}$

$\frac{2}{3}$

23. Viola septémloba Le Conte. Southern Coast Violet. Fig. 2945.

Viola septemloba Le Conte, Ann. Lyc. N. Y. 2: 141. 1826.

Glabrous; rootstock vertical; leaf-outline generally cordate-ovate; first leaves often and sometimes all the leaves uncut, others primarily 3-lobed, -cleft or -parted with widely open sinus; the middle segment uncut, relatively long and broad, usually narrowed at the base, the lateral segments sometimes uncut, but generally pedately cleft into 2–4 narrow divergent parts, that become smaller toward the base of the leaf; flowers violet, usually raised above the foliage, the three lower petals villous at the base; sepals narrowly lanceolate, with entire rounded auricles; cleistogamous flowers erect; capsules green, ovoid-cylindric, about 7'' long; seeds dark brown, 1'' long.

Open pine barrens in light soil, southeastern Virginia, south to Florida and southern Mississippi. March–April.

24. Viola Selkírkii Pursh.   Selkirk's or Great-spurred Violet.   Fig. 2946.

Viola Selkirkii Pursh; Goldie, Edinb. Phil. Journ. 6: 324. 1822.

Glabrous except for minute spreading hairs on the upper surface of the leaves; leaves and scapes 2'-4' high, usually from a slender rootstock or stolon; blades thin, crenate, ovate to suborbicular, deeply cordate, the basal lobes converging or overlapping, at vernal flowering about ¾' wide, when mature 1¼'-1¾' wide; sepals lanceolate or ovate-lanceolate, mostly acute; petals pale violet, all beardless, spur 2½''-3½'' long, much enlarged toward the rounded end; peduncles of cleistogamous flowers erect or ascending, the capsules short-ellipsoid, dotted with purple, 2''-3'' long; seeds small, pale buff.

Shaded ravines and cold mountain forests, New Brunswick to Pennsylvania and Minnesota, north to Greenland. April–May.

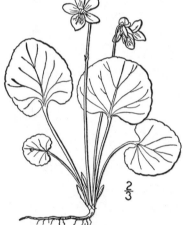

25. Viola palústris L.   Marsh Violet. Fig. 2947.

Viola palustris L. Sp. Pl. 934. 1753.

Glabrous, acaulescent; petioles and scapes arising from a very slender creeping or horizontal rootstock, the flowering scapes mostly exceeding the leaves; blades thin, cordate, broadly ovate, orbicular or reniform, 1'-2½' wide, crenulate; stipules ovate, acuminate; sepals ovate, obtuse or obtusish; petals pale lilac streaked with darker veins, or nearly white, 4''-6'' long, the lateral slightly bearded; spur about 1'' long, obtuse; stigma not bearded, somewhat beaked; capsule 3''-4'' long.

In wet or moist soil, Labrador to Alaska, south to the mountains of New England, in the Rocky Mountains to Colorado, and to Washington. Also in Europe and Asia. May–July.

26. Viola renifòlia A. Gray.   Kidney-leaved Violet.   Fig. 2948.

V. renifolia A. Gray, Proc. Am. Acad. 8: 288. 1870.
Viola blanda var. *renifolia* A. Gray, Bot. Gaz. 11: 255. 1886.

Pubescent throughout, or often nearly glabrous, especially the upper leaf-surface; rootstock slender in young plants, arising from short stolons, in old plants often stout and scaly; mature leaves with reniform blades narrowly cordate, distantly crenate-serrate, rounded at the apex, or occasional later leaves ending in a short blunt tip; sepals narrowly lanceolate; petals white, all beardless, the three lower with brownish veins, or often tinged with brown; capsules ellipsoid, those from cleistogamous flowers purple, on horizontal peduncles till ripe; stolons infrequent, short, often raceme-like, bearing cleistogamous flowers.

Arbor-vitae swamps and cold woods, Newfoundland to Mackenzie River, south to Pennsylvania, Michigan and Minnesota, and in the Rocky Mountains to Colorado. April–May.

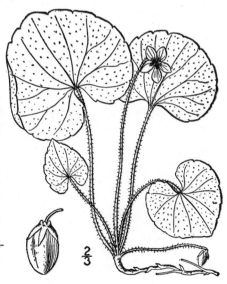

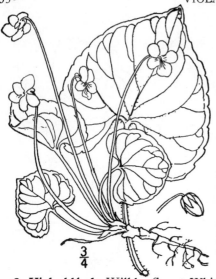

$\frac{3}{4}$

27. **Viola incógnita** Brainerd. Large-leaved White Violet. Fig. 2949.

Viola incognita Brainerd, Rhodora 7 : 84. 1905.

Rootstock slender, in older plants enlarging upward; peduncles, petioles and lower surface of leaves pubescent with soft white hairs, especially when young, the upper leaf-surface glabrous; blades at petaliferous flowering orbicular or reniform, $\frac{3}{4}'-1\frac{1}{2}'$ wide, the apex abruptly short-pointed; aestival leaves with large, rugose blades, broadly ovate, cordate usually with open sinus, mostly acute, $2\frac{1}{2}'-3'$ wide; scapes hardly taller than the leaves; petals white, the lateral bearded, the upper pair obovate, flowering early; seeds narrowly obovoid, obtuse at base, smooth, brown, $1''$ long; plant in summer producing numerous filiform runners.

Mountains and low moist woodlands, Newfoundland to Dakota, south to the mountains of eastern Tennessee. Var. **Forbesii** Brainerd is nearly or quite glabrous, except often for minute scattered hairs on the upper leaf-surface. April–May.

28. **Viola blánda** Willd. Sweet White Violet. Fig. 2950.

Viola blanda Willd. Hort. Berol. *pl. 24.* 1806.
V. amoena Le Conte, Ann. Lyc. N. Y. **2** : 144. 1826.
Viola blanda var. *palustriformis* A. Gray, Bot. Gaz. **11** : 255. 1886.

Petioles and scapes glabrous, usually tinged with red, the scapes much exceeding the leaves; blades ovate, cordate with narrow sinus, commonly acute, often somewhat acuminate, rarely over $2\frac{1}{2}'$ wide when mature, glabrous except for minute scattered hairs on the upper surface; lateral petals beardless, the upper pair often long, narrow, and strongly reflexed, sometimes twisted; cleistogamous capsules ovoid, dark purple; seeds dark brown, minutely rugose, acute at base, $\frac{3}{4}''$ long; plant freely producing in summer slender leafy runners.

Cool ravines and moist shady slopes in humus, western Quebec and western New England to Minnesota, south in the mountains to northern Georgia. In petaliferous flower 10–14 days later than either of the two preceding species. April–May.

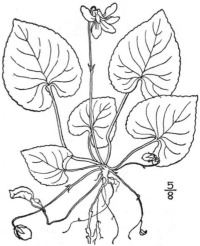

$\frac{5}{8}$

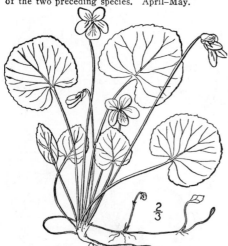

$\frac{2}{3}$

29. **Viola pállens** (Banks) Brainerd. Northern White Violet. Fig. 2951.

V. rotundifolia var. *pallens* Banks ; DC. Prodr.
  1 : 295. 1824.
Viola blanda recent authors. Not Willd.
Viola pallens Brainerd, Rhodora 7 : 247. 1905.

Petioles and scapes in summer often dotted with red and more or less hirsutulous; blades glabrous on both sides, broadly ovate or orbicular, cordate, $\frac{1}{2}'-2\frac{1}{2}'$ wide, crenate-serrate, obtuse or rounded at apex; flowers faintly fragrant, lateral petals usually bearing a small tuft of hairs, upper petals broadly obovate; capsules green, ellipsoid-cylindric; seeds $\frac{1}{2}''$ long, almost black; stolons slender, often bearing small leaves and cleistogamous flowers.

Springy land and along cold brooks, Labrador to Alberta, south to the mountains of South Carolina and Tennessee, and in the Rocky Mountains to Colorado. American sweet violet. Long mistaken for *V. blanda* Willd., and figured for that species in the first edition of this work. April–May.

30. Viola primulifòlia L.   Primrose-leaved
Violet. Fig. 2952.

Viola primulifolia L. Sp. Pl. 934. 1753.

Often quite glabrous, but usually somewhat
pubescent, especially toward the base of the petioles; blades oblong to ovate, obscurely crenate-
serrate, base slightly cordate, rounded or tapering, petioles often broadly winged above; scapes
2′–10′ high, often longer than the leaves; flowers
similar to those of *V. lanceolata;* sepals lanceolate, acuminate; the three lower petals purple-
veined, the lateral ones slightly bearded or beardless; capsules green, ellipsoid, 3″–5″ long, those
from the numerous late cleistogamous flowers on
rather short, erect peduncles; seeds reddish
brown, ¾″ long.

In moist open ground, New Brunswick to Florida
and Louisiana. Numerous leafy stolons appear from
vigorous plants in late summer.

31. Viola lanceolàta L.   Lance-leaved or
Water Violet. Fig. 2953.

Viola lanceolata L. Sp. Pl. 934. 1753.

Glabrous, usually profusely stoloniferous in late
summer, the stolons rooting at the nodes and bearing apetalous flowers; rootstock slender; scapes 2′–4′
high; mature leaves lanceolate or elliptical, the
blade 2½′–6′ long, 5″–10″ wide, gradually tapering
into the margined, often reddish petiole, obscurely
crenulate; sepals lanceolate, acuminate, 2″–3″ long;
petals 3″–4″ long, usually all beardless, the three
lower striped with purplish veins; capsules green,
ellipsoid, 3″–6″ long, those of the cleistogamous
flowers on erect peduncles, usually shorter than the
leaves; seeds dark brown.

Open bogs and moist meadows, Nova Scotia to Minnesota, south to the coastal plain, where it gives place to
the taller and narrower-leaved *Viola vittata* Greene.

32. Viola rotundifòlia Michx.   Round-
leaved or Yellow Violet. Fig. 2954.

V. rotundifolia Michx. Fl. Bor. Am. **2**: 150.
1803.

Rootstock long and stout, jagged with the
persistent bases of former leaves; stolons
short, usually without roots or leaves, bearing 1–4 cleistogamous flowers; leaves oval
or orbicular, obtuse, cordate with short and
narrow sinus, repand-crenulate, at vernal
flowering sparsely hirtellous, about 1′ wide;
in midsummer mostly glabrate, 2′–4′ wide,
prostrate; scapes 2′–4′ high; flowers bright
yellow, the three lower petals with brown
lines, the lateral bearded; style club-shaped,
abruptly capitate, beakless; capsule ovoid,
3″–4″ long, those from the cleistogamous
flowers on deflexed peduncles and closely
dotted with purple; seeds nearly white.

Cold woods, Maine to western Ontario, south
along the Alleghanies to northern Georgia. Ascends to 4500 ft. in Virginia. April–May.

$\frac{2}{3}$

34. Viola Nuttàllii Pursh. Nuttall's Violet. Fig. 2956.

V. Nuttallii Pursh, Fl. Am. Sept. 174. 1814.

Somewhat pubescent, or nearly glabrous; rootstock stout, deep-seated; leaves and petaliferous flowers in spring borne from near the base of short stems; these in summer much lengthened, erect or ascending, bearing cleistogamous flowers on axillary peduncles; blades of the leaves lanceolate or ovate-lanceolate, thickish, 1'–3' long, obscurely crenate-dentate or entire, tapering into margined petioles, 2'–6' long; sepals lanceolate or linear, attenuate, 3''–4'' long; petals yellow, 4''–7½'' long, slightly bearded or beardless; capsule subglobose or ellipsoid, about 3'' long.

On prairies and plains, Manitoba to Montana, south to Kansas and Arizona. Yellow prairie-violet. May.

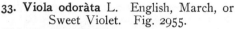

33. Viola odoràta L. English, March, or Sweet Violet. Fig. 2955.

Viola odorata L. Sp. Pl. 934. 1753.

Producing above ground leafy stolons rooting freely at the nodes and bearing numerous cleistogamous flowers in summer; petioles 2'–5' long; blades broadly ovate or orbicular, rounded or obtuse at the apex, cordate, crenate, 1'–2' wide, finely pubescent; flowers on scapes as long as the leaves or shorter; very fragrant, violet or white, lateral petals usually bearded; style hook-shaped; sepals oblong, mostly obtuse; cleistogamous flowers on slender recurving peduncles, broadly ovoid, angled, pubescent, purple; seeds large, cream-colored.

Native of Europe, often cultivated and occasionally adventive, as are some of its hybrids with allied European species. March–May. *Viola chinensis* L. (*Viola lancifolia* Pollard, not Thore), an Asiatic species, is spontaneous in botanical gardens at Washington, D. C., and elsewhere.

$\frac{1}{2}$

35. Viola hastàta Michx. Halberd- or Spear-leaved Yellow Violet. Fig. 2957.

Viola hastata Michx. Fl. Bor. Am. 2: 149. 1803.

Slightly puberulent; stem slender, 4'–10' high, from a long white brittle horizontal rootstock; stem-leaves 2–4, near the summit, halberd-shaped with rounded basal lobes, narrowly lanceolate above; or sometimes ovate-lanceolate and subcordate; radical leaves occasional, oblong-lanceolate, usually wider and more deeply cordate; all distantly serrulate; corolla yellow, the upper petals often tinged outside with violet; sepals linear-lanceolate, acute; capsules ovoid, glabrous, 4''–5'' long; stipules ovate, small, often with a few bristly teeth.

In mountain forests or hilly districts, Pennsylvania to Ohio, south to Liberty County, Florida. April–May.

36. Viola eriocàrpa Schwein. Smoothish Yellow Violet. Fig. 2958.

V. eriocarpa Schwein. Am. Journ. Sci. **5**: 75. 1822.
V. pubescens var. *scabriuscula* T. & G. Fl. N. A. **1**: 142. 1838.
V. scabriuscula Schwein.; Britt. & Brown, Ill. Fl. **2**: 453. 1897.

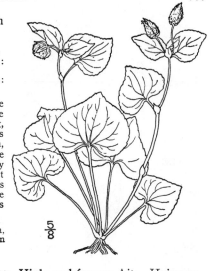

Glabrous except for minute pubescence on the upper part of the stem and on the lower surface of the leaves along the veins; stems ascending, commonly 2–4 from one rootstock; radical leaves 1–5, long-petioled, the blades ovate to reniform, cordate or truncate, mostly pointed; cauline leaves only on the upper half of the stem, broadly ovate, subcordate, acuminate, the uppermost smaller, truncate, nearly sessile; lateral petals bearded; sepals narrowly lanceolate; capsule ovoid, woolly or sometimes glabrous; seeds brown, a little more than 1″ long.

In low open woods, Nova Scotia to Manitoba, south to Georgia and Texas. Ascends to 4000 ft. in Virginia. April–May.

37. Viola pubéscens Ait. Hairy or Downy Yellow Violet. Fig. 2959.

Viola pubescens Ait. Hort. Kew. **3**: 290. 1789.

Softly pubescent; stems mostly stout, 8′–12′ high, often solitary; leaves either cauline, 2–4, near the summit, short-petioled, or occasionally a long-petioled root-leaf; blades broadly ovate or reniform, with cordate or truncate-decurrent base, crenate-dentate, somewhat pointed; stipules large, ovate-lanceolate; sepals narrowly lanceolate; petals bright yellow, the lateral bearded, the lower with short spur; capsules ovoid, 5″–6″ long, ovoid-conic, glabrous or sometimes woolly; seeds brown, 1¼″ long.

Dry rich woods, Nova Scotia to Dakota, south, especially in the mountains, to Virginia and Missouri. Often intergrading with *Viola eriocarpa*. April–May.

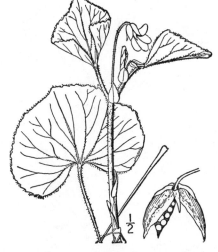

38. Viola rugulòsa Greene. Rydberg's Violet. Fig. 2960.

Viola rugulosa Greene, Pittonia **5**: 26. 1902.
Viola Rydbergii Greene, Pittonia **5**: 27. 1902.

Often widely spreading from long, thick, branching stolons; stems stout, 1°–2° high; radical leaves usually 3–5, long-petioled, the blades cordate-reniform, abruptly short-acuminate, often 4′ wide, densely hirsutulous beneath, sparsely so along the veins above; lower stem-leaves similar, the upper successively smaller and shorter-petioled, the blades becoming ovate-acuminate, the puberulence of the lower surface extending along the petioles and upper part of the stem; stipules lanceolate, nearly entire; flowers and fruit as in *V. canadensis;* petaliferous flowers often appearing in summer and autumn.

Rich woodlands, Iowa and Minnesota, west to the Rocky Mountains. May–Oct.

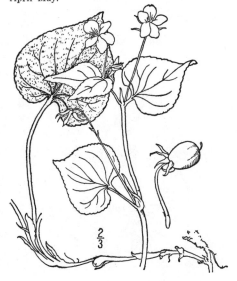

39. Viola canadénsis L.　Canada Violet.
Fig. 2961.

Viola canadensis L. Sp. Pl. 936. 1753.

Usually 8′–16′ high, glabrous or but sparsely and minutely pubescent; leaves broadly ovate, cordate, acuminate or acute, serrate; stipules sharply lanceolate; flowers single from the axils of cauline leaves, often appearing throughout the season; sepals subulate, spreading; inner surface of petals white above, bright yellow at the base, the outside more or less tinged with violet, the three lower striped with fine dark lines, the lateral pair bearded; capsules ovoid to subglobose, 3″–5″ long, often downy or puberulent; seeds brown, 1″ long.

In mountain forests or wooded uplands, New Brunswick to Saskatchewan, south to South Carolina, Alabama, Nebraska, and in the Rocky Mountains to Arizona and New Mexico. Ascends to 4000 ft. in Virginia. American sweet violet. Hens. June-flower. May–July.

40. Viola striàta Ait.　Pale or Striped Violet.
Fig. 2962.

Viola striata Ait. Hort. Kew. 3: 290. 1789.

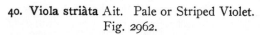

Stems several, angular, leafy, ascending, 6′–12′ long when in flower, in late summer often 2° long, decumbent; leaves glabrous or nearly so, orbicular to ovate, cordate, 1′–1½′ wide, usually acuminate, finely crenate-serrate; stipules large, oblong-lanceolate, fimbriate; flowers long-peduncled; sepals ciliolate, linear-lanceolate, attenuate; corolla white or cream-colored; spur thick, blunt, about 2″ long; style somewhat bearded below the beak; capsules ovoid, glabrous, 2″–3″ long; seeds light brown.

Low and shady ground, New York to Minnesota, south to Georgia and Missouri. Ascends to 3000 ft. in Virginia. April–May.

41. Viola conspérsa Reichenb.　American Dog Violet.　Fig. 2963.

V. conspersa Reichenb. Ic. Crit. 1: 44. 1823.

Viola Muhlenbergii Torr. Fl. U. S. 1: 256. 1824.

Glabrous; rootstock oblique, often much branched; stems 3½′–6′ high at time of vernal flowering; lower leaves orbicular, cordate, crenate-serrate, obtuse, becoming ¾′–1½′ wide; the upper somewhat smaller, subacuminate; stipules ovate-lanceolate, serrately ciliate especially toward the base; flowers numerous, usually pale violet, sometimes white, raised above the leaves on axillary peduncles 2′–3′ long; cleistogamous flowers in summer on short peduncles from the same axils that bore vernal flowers, or from axils of later leaves of the lengthened stems; style bent downward at the tip and slightly hairy; seeds light brown.

Low or shaded ground, Quebec to Minnesota, south to the mountains of northern Georgia. Regarded as not distinct from the following species in the first edition of this work. April–May. Early blue violet.

42. Viola labradórica Schrank. Alpine Violet. Fig. 2964.

4/5

V. labradorica Schrank, Denksch. Bot. Gesell.
Regensb. **2** : 12. 1818.
Viola punctata Schwein. Am. Journ. Sci. **5** : 67.
1822.
V. Muhlenbergiana var. *minor* Hook. Fl. Bor. Am.
1 : 78. 1830.

Rootstock long, tapering, scaly above, sometimes branching; stems few, slender, 1–3-
leaved, erect or ascending, usually about 2½′
high, bearing 1 or 2 petaliferous flowers on
long peduncles; lower leaves long-petioled,
blades orbicular, subcordate, glabrous, ½–¾′
wide; upper leaves on shorter petioles with
smaller blades, more or less ovate, obtuse,
sparsely hirtellous on the upper surface; stipules linear, attenuate, entire or with one or
two filiform appendages at the base; petals
deep violet; sepals lanceolate with round auricles; capsules subglobose, 2½″ long.

Alpine and subarctic; Greenland and Labrador, south to the high mountains of Maine, New
Hampshire and New York. July–Aug.

43. Viola adúnca J. E. Smith. Hooked Violet. Fig. 2965.

Viola adunca J. E. Smith in Rees' Cycl. **37** : No.
63. 1817.
Viola longipes Nutt.; T. & G. Fl. N. A. **1** : 140.
1838.
Viola canina L. var. *adunca* A. Gray, Proc. Am.
Acad. **8**. 377. 1872.

Glabrous or nearly so; rootstock woody,
jagged and chaffy from the remains of former
leaves; stems slender, several or many and
spreading, 1½–12′ high, bearing 1–3 axillary
flowers; basal and lower stem-leaves long-
petioled, the blades ovate, obtuse, finely crenate,
subcordate or more or less decurrent at the
base, 5″–10″ wide; upper leaves short-petioled,
narrower, less rounded at the apex; stipules
linear, attenuate, sparsely spinulose-serrulate;
flowers usually raised above the leaves on
peduncles 1½′–4′ long; petals violet to purple,
5″–7½″ long, the lateral bearded; spur rather
long, often curved upward or hooked; capsules
ellipsoid, 3½″ long.

Eastern Quebec, northern New Brunswick,
northern Ontario and in the mountains of Colorado and California, north to Alaska. May–July.

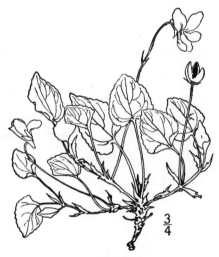

3/4

3/4

44. Viola subvestìta Greene. Sand Violet. Fig. 2966.

Viola canina var. *puberula* S. Wats. in A. Gray, Man.
Ed. 6, 81. 1890.
Viola subvestita Greene, Erythea **5** : 39. 1897.

Finely puberulent, stems several or many, spreading, 2′–6′ long. Petioles longer than the blades;
stipules linear-lanceolate with incised bristly teeth;
blades commonly ovate, ¾′–1′ long, crenulate, obtuse,
subcordate; peduncles slender, longer than the leaves;
sepals narrowly lanceolate; petals violet, spur about
3″ long, usually straight and blunt, but often with a
sharp point abruptly bent inward; cleistogamous flowers and capsules often abundant in late summer; capsule 2½″–4″ long; seeds dark brown, nearly 1″ long.

Sandy and sterile soil, Quebec and Maine, west to
Michigan, South Dakota, and the Rocky Mountains.
Referred in the first edition of this work to the Euro-
pean *V. arenaria* DC. May–July.

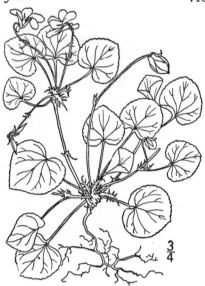

$\frac{3}{4}$

45. Viola Wálteri House. Prostrate Blue Violet. Fig. 2967.

Viola canina Walt. Fl. Car. 219. 1788. Not L.
V. Muhlenbergii var. *multicaulis* T. & G. Fl. 1: 140. 1838.
Viola multicaulis Britton, Mem. Torr. Club 5: 227. 1894. Not Jordan 1852.
Viola Wálteri House, Torreya 6: 172. 1906.

Finely puberulent; stems several, leafy, bearing in early spring small violet-blue flowers in the axils of basal leaves, at first ascending, later elongating, becoming prostrate, and bearing through the season apetalous flowers on long slender axillary peduncles; stems often surviving the winter and sending up in spring from their tips rosettes of leaves and petaliferous flowers, afterwards rooting and forming new plants; blades mostly orbicular, cordate, rounded or obtuse at the apex, crenulate, $\frac{3}{4}'-1\frac{1}{2}'$ wide, often mottled with darker green bordering the veins; stipules bristly fimbriate, $3''-5''$ long; capsules purplish, ovoid-globose, $3''$ long; seeds brown.

Dry woodlands, Kentucky to South Carolina, Florida and Texas. Feb.–July.

46. Viola rostràta Pursn. Long-spurred Violet. Fig. 2968.

Viola rostrata Pursh, Fl. Am. Sept. 174. 1814.

Stems often numerous, commonly $4'-8'$ high; leaves orbicular to broadly ovate, cordate, nearly or quite glabrous, serrate, the upper acute or pointed; petaliferous flowers raised on long peduncles above the leaves; petals spotted with darker violet, all beardless; spur slender, $5''-7''$ long; cleistogamous flowers, with minute or aborted petals, appearing later on short peduncles from the axils of the upper leaves; style straight, beakless, glabrous; capsules ovoid, $1\frac{1}{2}''-3''$ long, glabrous; seeds light brown.

Shady hillsides in leaf-mould, Quebec to Michigan, south in the mountains to Georgia. Beaked or canker-violet. June–July.

$\frac{1}{2}$

$\frac{2}{3}$

47. Viola Rafinésquii Greene. Field Pansy. Fig. 2969.

Viola tenella Muhl. Cat. 26. 1813. Not Poiret. 1810.
Viola Rafinesquii Greene, Pittonia 4: 9. 1899.

Glabrous, annual, with slender stem, $3'-8'$ high, often branched from the base; leaves small, the lowest $3''-5''$ wide, suborbicular, on slender petioles, the upper obovate to linear-oblanceolate, sparsely crenulate, attenuate at the base; stipules pectinately cut, the upper segment elongate, narrowly spatulate, mostly entire; internodes usually exceeding the leaves; flowers small, but the obovate bluish-white to cream-colored petals nearly twice the length of the lanceolate sepals; seeds light brown, a little more than $\frac{1}{2}''$ long.

In fields and open woods, New York to Michigan, south to Georgia and Texas. April–May. Field-violet.

48. Viola trícolor L. Pansy. Lady's-delight. Heartsease. Fig. 2970.

Viola tricolor L. Sp. Pl. 935. 1753.

Glabrous or pubescent, 4'–12' high; stem angled and often branched; upper leaves oval or lanceolate, ½'–1' long, the lower ovate, often cordate, all crenate-serrate; stipules foliaceous, laciniate or lyrate-pinnatifid; flowers 8''–1' broad, variously colored with yellow, purple or white.

In waste places, sparingly escaped from gardens. May–July. Introduced from Europe. English names from 40 to 50, among which are johnny jump-up or johnny jumper, monkey's face, love-in-idleness, fancy, biddy's eyes, herb trinity, cats' faces, flamy, garden gate. Garden- or trinity-violet. Kisses. Kiss-me. Hearts'-pansy. Battle-field flower. Stepmother. Cupid's-delight. None-so-pretty. Usually more or less impure, the garden pansy being the product of frequent crosses of *Viola tricolor* with allied species of the Old World.

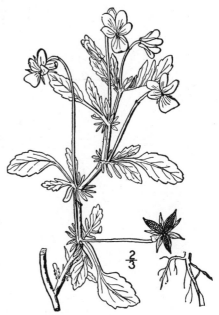

49. Viola arvénsis Murray. European Field Pansy. Fig. 2971.

Viola arvensis Murray, Prodr. Stirp. Goett. 73. 1770.

Similar to *V. Rafinesquii* but stouter, often 10'–13' high, erect, or branching and decumbent; leaf-blades ovate to lanceolate, noticeably crenate; stipules more coarsely pectinate, the upper lobe usually much enlarged, oblanceolate and sparsely crenate; petals usually shorter than the lanceolate acute sepals, pale yellow, sometimes the upper with violet tips, and the spurred petal deep yellow at the base; capsule globose; seeds brown, narrowly obovoid, about ¾'' long.

Cultivated fields, naturalized from Europe, Newfoundland and Ontario, south, occasionally, to North Carolina. April–Oct.

2. CUBÈLIUM Raf. Cat. Bot. Gard. Trans. 13. 1824.

[SOLEA Spreng. Pl. Min. Cog. Pug. 1 : 22. 1813. Not Spreng. 1800.]

Erect perennial leafy herbs, with entire sparingly toothed or undulate leaves, and small greenish white axillary flowers. Sepals 5, linear, equal, not prolonged at the base. Petals nearly equal, erect, imbricate, the lower one cordate, broader than the others, which are nearly alike in shape. Stamens 5, syngenesious, the sheath with a 2-lobed gland at the base; anthers almost sessile. Ovules 3 or 4 on each placenta; style hooked at the apex. Capsules slightly lobed, 3-valved, the valves infolded after dehiscence. Seeds obovoid-globose; embryo nearly the length of the endosperm. [Greek, from Cybele.]

A monotypic genus of eastern North America.

1. Cubelium cóncolor (Forst.) Raf. Green Violet. Fig. 2972.

Viola concolor Forst. Trans. Linn Soc. 6: 309. 1802.

Solea concolor Ging. in DC. Prodr. 1: 306. 1824.

Cubelium concolor Raf. Cat. Bot. Gard. Trans. 13. 1824.

Simple, 1°–2° high, more or less pubescent. Leaves alternate, ascending, oblong-lanceolate, 3′–4½′ long, 1′–1½′ wide, acuminate, attenuate at the base into a short petiole, entire, or with a few lateral teeth near the apex; stipules linear, acute, 3″–6″ long; flowers axillary, 1–3 together, about 4″ long, on recurved pedicels; sepals linear, about equalling the corolla; lower petal twice as broad as the others, gibbous at the base; capsule oblong, 8″–12″ long, dehiscent by 3 valves; seeds large.

In moist woods and copses, northern New York and southern Ontario to Michigan, south to North Carolina and Kansas. Ascends to 2500 ft. in Virginia. May–June.

3. CALCEOLÀRIA Loefl. Reise 244. 1766.

[SOLEA Spreng. in Schrad. Journ. Bot. 4: 192. 1800.]

[IONIDIUM Vent. Hort. Malm. *pl. 27.* 1803.]

Herbs, rarely shrubs, with mostly opposite leaves, and axillary or racemose flowers. Sepals somewhat unequal, not prolonged posteriorly. Petals unequal, the lower one longest, gibbous or saccate at the base, the two upper shorter than the lateral ones. Filaments distinct, the lower spurred or glandular; anthers connivent, not united. Capsule elastically 3-valved. Seeds ovoid-globose, with hard seed-coats. [Latin, slipper-like.]

A genus of about 60 species, mainly natives of tropical America, a few in Asia and Australia. Type species: *Viola Calceolaria* L.

1. Calceolaria verticillàta (Ort.) Kuntze. Nodding Violet. Whorl-leaf. Fig. 2973.

Viola verticillata Ort. Dec. Pl. 4: 50. 1797.

Ionidium polygalaefolium Vent. Jard. Malm. *pl. 27.* 1803.

Ionidium lineare Torr. Ann. Lyc. N. Y. 2: 168. 1827.

Calceolaria verticillata Kuntze, Rev. Gen. Pl. 41. 1891.

Somewhat pubescent or nearly glabrous, tufted from a woody base; stems erect or ascending, 4′–15′ high, simple or branched. Leaves alternate, or the lower sometimes opposite, linear, oblong or oblanceolate, entire, obtuse, 9″–20″ long, 1″–4″ wide, often with smaller ones fascicled in their axils, and thus appearing verticillate; stipules subulate or foliaceous; flowers white, axillary, solitary, nodding, 2″–3″ long; pedicels slender or filiform, 3″–7″ long; capsule obovoid, 2″ long; seeds nearly 1″ long.

In dry soil, Kansas to Texas, Mexico, Colorado and New Mexico. April–July.

Family 91. PASSIFLORACEAE Dumort. Anal. Fam. 37. 1829.

PASSION-FLOWER FAMILY.

Vines, climbing by tendrils, or erect herbs, with alternate petioled usually palmately-lobed leaves, and solitary or clustered perfect regular flowers. Calyx-tube short or elongated, persistent. Petals usually 5, inserted on the throat of the calyx, distinct, or in some species united. Stamens 5. Throat of the calyx crowned with a double or triple fringe. Filaments subulate or filiform, monadelphous, or separate. Ovary free from the calyx,·1-celled; placentae 3–5, parietal; styles 1–5. Fruit a berry or capsule, usually many-seeded.

About 18 genera and 350 species, of warm and tropical regions, most abundant in South America.

1. PASSIFLÒRA L. Sp. Pl. 955. 1753.

Climbing tendril-bearing herbaceous or woody vines, with lobed parted or entire alternate or rarely opposite leaves, and large showy axillary flowers, on jointed, often bracted
peduncles. Calyx-tube cup-shaped or campanulate, deeply 4–5-lobed, the lobes narrow, imbricated in the bud, its throat crowned with a double or triple fringe called the corona. Petals
4 or 5 (rarely none), inserted on the throat of the calyx. Ovary oblong, stalked. Filaments
monadelphous in a tube around the stalk of the ovary, separate above; anthers narrow, versatile. Fruit a many-seeded berry. Seeds pulpy-arilled, flat, ovate; endosperm fleshy. [Flower
of the Cross, or Passion, as emblematic of the crucifixion.]

About 300 species, mostly natives of tropical America, a few in Asia and Australia. Besides
the following, about 7 others occur in the southern and southwestern States. Type species: *Passiflora incarnata* L.

Leaves deeply 3–5-lobed; the lobes serrate; petals whitish; corona purple.   1. *P. incarnata.*
Leaves obtusely 3-lobed above the middle, the lobes entire; flowers yellowish.   2. *P. lutea.*

1. Passiflora incarnàta L. Passion-flower. Passion-vine. Fig. 2974.

Passiflora incarnata L. Sp. Pl. 959. 1753.

Stem glabrous, or slightly pubescent above,
striate when dry, climbing to a height of
10°–30°. Petioles ½–2′ long, with 2 glands
near the summit; leaves nearly orbicular in
outline, glabrous, or often somewhat pubescent, 3–5′ broad, somewhat cordate at the base,
deeply 3-lobed (rarely 5-lobed), the lobes ovate
or oval, acute or acutish, finely serrate; flowers
solitary, axillary, white with a purple or pink
corona, 1½–2′ broad; peduncles longer than the
petioles, usually 3-bracted just below the flowers; calyx-lobes linear, cuspidate on the back;
berry ovoid, nearly 2′ long, glabrous, yellow.

In dry soil, Virginia to Missouri, south to Florida and Texas. Fruit edible, called maypops.
May–July.

2. Passiflora lùtea L. Yellow Passion-flower. Fig. 2975.

Passiflora lutea L. Sp. Pl. 958. 1753.

Glabrous or very nearly so throughout,
herbaceous, climbing or trailing, 3°–10° long.
Petioles ½–1½′ long; leaves much broader than
long, more or less cordate at base, with 3 wide
obtuse rounded lobes, the lobes entire, often
mucronulate; stipules 1″–1½″ long; peduncles
slender, exceeding the petioles, usually in pairs
from the upper axils; flowers greenish yellow,
6″–10″ broad; calyx-lobes linear; berry globose-ovoid, 5″–6″ in diameter, glabrous, deep
purple.

In thickets, Pennsylvania to Illinois, Missouri,
Kansas, Florida and Texas. May–July.

Family 92. LOASÀCEAE Reichenb. Consp. 160. 1828.

LOASA FAMILY.

Erect or climbing branching herbs, often armed with hooked stinging or viscid
hairs, with alternate or opposite exstipulate leaves, and solitary racemose or
cymose, regular and perfect, white yellow or reddish flowers. Calyx-tube adnate
to the ovary, its limb 4–5-lobed, persistent. Petals 4 or 5, inserted on the throat
of the calyx. Stamens ∞, inserted with the petals; filaments filiform, commonly
arranged in clusters opposite the petals, the outer sometimes without anthers and
petaloid (staminodes); anthers introrse, longitudinally dehiscent. Ovary 1-celled

(rarely 2–3-celled), with 2 or 3 parietal placentae; style filiform, entire or 2–3-lobed; ovules anatropous Capsule usually 1-celled, crowned with the calyx-limb. Seeds mostly numerous; endosperm scanty.

About 20 genera and 250 species, all but 1 natives of America.

Seeds angled or prismatic, not separated by lamellae; mostly annuals.	1. *Mentzelia.*
Seeds flat, winged, separated by horizontal lamellae; perennials.	2. *Nuttallia.*

1. MENTZÈLIA L. Sp. Pl. 516. 1753.

Erect herbs, mostly annuals, with alternate entire lobed or pinnatifid leaves, and terminal solitary or cymose flowers. Calyx-tube cylindric, linear or club-shaped, its limb generally 5-lobed. Petals 5, spreading, convolute in the bud, deciduous Stamens 20–100. Ovary 1-celled; styles 3, more or less united; stigmas small, obtuse. Capsule dehiscent at the summit, few–many-seeded. Seeds mostly prismatic, not separated by horizontal lamellae, roughened or striate. [Named in honor of C Mentzel, a German botanist, died 1701.]

About 35 species, natives of America. Besides the following, some 20 others occur in the western parts of North America. Type species: *Mentzelia aspera* L.

Leaves sessile; stem little rough; calyx-lobes 2″ long.	1. *M. oligosperma.*
Leaves, at least the lower, petioled; stem very rough; calyx-lobes 3″ long.	2. *M. albicaulis.*

1. Mentzelia oligospérma Nutt. Few-seeded Mentzelia. Fig. 2976.

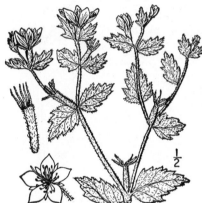

Mentzelia oligosperma Nutt. in Bot. Mag. *pl. 1760.* 1815.
Mentzelia aurea Nutt. Gen. 1: 300. 1818.

Rough and viscid-pubescent, 1°–3° high. Leaves ovate or oval, coarsely dentate or sinuate, acute or obtusish at the apex, 1′–3′ long, the upper rounded or truncate at the base and sessile, the lower narrowed at the base and usually petioled; flowers yellow, 5″–10″ broad, axillary or somewhat cymose, opening in sunshine; petals 5, oblong-cuneate, acute, about twice as long as the linear-lanceolate calyx-lobes; filaments 20–30, all filiform; capsule linear, 6″–8″ long, few-seeded; calyx-lobes about 3″ long; seeds oblong, wingless.

Prairies and plains, Illinois to South Dakota, Kansas, Colorado, Louisiana, Texas and Mexico. May–July.

2. Mentzelia albicaùlis Dougl. White-stemmed Mentzelia. Fig. 2977.

Mentzelia albicaulis Dougl.; T. & G Fl. N. A. 1: 534. 1840.
Bartonia albicaulis Dougl.; Hook. Fl. Bor. Am. 1: 222. 1833.

Stem nearly white, erect or ascending, slender, branched, shining, nearly smooth, or roughish above, 6′–2° high. Leaves sessile, mostly lanceolate in outline, sinuate-pinnatifid, sinuate-lobed, or the upper and lower sometimes entire, rough with short stiff hairs, 1′–3′ long; flowers yellow, few together at the ends of the branches, or also axillary, 6″–10″ broad, short-pedicelled or sessile; calyx-lobes linear-lanceolate, about 2″ long; filaments separate; capsule linear, 1′ long or less, many-seeded; seeds angled, tuberculate, wingless.

Western Nebraska to British Columbia, California and New Mexico. May–July.

2. NUTTÀLLIA Raf. Am. Month. Mag. 2: 175. 1817.

[BARTONIA Pursh; Sims. Bot. Mag. *pl. 1487.* 1812. Not. Muhl. 1801.]

Perennial herbs, with alternate lobed or pinnatifid leaves and terminal, cymose or solitary, large and showy flowers. Calyx-tube mostly obconic, the limb 5-lobed. Petals 5, in some species apparently 10, where the outer staminodes are petaloid. Stamens very numerous. Ovary 1-celled; styles 3. Capsule dehiscent at the summit, the placentae with horizontal lamellae between the 2-rowed seeds which are flat and more or less winged. [In honor of Thomas Nuttall, 1786–1859, American botanist.]

About 20 species, natives of western North America and Mexico. Type species: *Bartonia decapetala* Pursh.

Flowers about 2′ broad; calyx-tube bractless.
   Bracts at base of calyx linear, entire.   1. *N. nuda.*
   Bracts at base of calyx lanceolate, pinnatifid.   2. *N. stricta.*
Flowers about 4′ broad; calyx-tube bearing bracts.   3. *N. decapetala.*

1. Nuttallia nùda (Pursh) Greene.
Branched Nuttallia. Fig. 2978.

Bartonia nuda Pursh, Fl. Am. Sept. 328. 1814.

Mentzelia nuda T. & G. Fl. N. A. 1: 535. 1840.

Nuttallia nuda Greene, Leaflets 1: 210. 1906.

Rough with minute pubescence, slender, 1°–5° high, often widely branched, the stems light-colored. Leaves all sessile, lanceolate or oblong-lanceolate, acute at the apex, usually sharply and deeply dentate, or the upper pin-natifid, 1′–4′ long; flowers yellowish white, 1½′–2′ broad, opening in the evening; petals 10, about twice as long as the lanceolate calyx-lobes; calyx-tube not bracteolate, but 1 or 2 linear, mostly entire bracts at its base; stamens 100 or more, the outer ones somewhat petaloid; capsule oblong, 9″–12″ long, about 3″ thick; seeds numerous, wing-margined.

Plains, western Nebraska to Colorado and Wyoming. July–Aug.

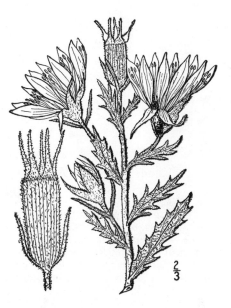

2. Nuttallia stricta (Osterhout) Greene.
Stiff Nuttallia. Fig. 2979.

Hesperaster strictus Osterhout, Bull. Torr. Club 29: 174. 1902.

Touterea stricta Osterhout; Rydb. Bull. Torr. Club 30: 276. 1903.

Nuttallia stricta Greene, Leaflets 1: 210. 1906.

Similar to the preceding species, but strict and less branched, 3° high or less, the stem white and rough-pubescent. Leaves lanceolate to oblong-lanceolate, obtuse or acute, sinuate-dentate, 3½′ long or less, not so deeply toothed as those of *N. nuda;* flowers several, corymbose, yellowish white, about 2′ broad; stamens numerous, many of the outer filaments petaloid; calyx-tube not bracteolate, but subtended by lanceolate deeply pinnatifid bracts; capsule 1′–1½′ long; seeds numerous, about 2″ long, wing-margined.

Plains and hills, South Dakota to Wyoming, Nebraska, Colorado and Texas. June–Aug.

$\frac{2}{5}$

3. Nuttallia decapétala (Pursh) Greene.
Prairie-lily. Showy Mentzelia. Fig. 2980.

Bartonia decapetala Pursh, in Bot. Mag. *pl. 1487.* 1812.
Bartonia ornata Pursh, Fl. Am. Sept. 327. 1814.
Mentzelia ornata T. & G. Fl. N. A. 1: 534. 1840.
Mentzelia decapetala Urban & Gilg, in Engl. & Prantl,
    Nat. Pfl. Fam. **3**: Abt. 6a, 111. 1894.
N. decapetala Greene, Leaflets 1: 210. 1906.

Roughish-pubescent, stout, seldom over 2° high.
Leaves oval, lanceolate or oblong, acute or acuminate at the apex, sinuate-pinnatifid, 2′–6′ long, the
upper sessile, the lower petioled; flowers mostly solitary and terminal, yellowish white, 3′–5′ broad, opening in the evening; petals about twice as long as
the lanceolate calyx-lobes; calyx-tube usually bracted;
filaments all filiform, very numerous (200–300); capsule oblong, 1½′–2′ long, 5″–6″ thick; seeds numerous,
margined, not winged.

Plains, Iowa to North Dakota, Saskatchewan, Montana, Nebraska and Texas. Gunebo-lily. June–Sept.

Nuttallia laevicaùlis (Dougl.) Greene [*Mentzelia
laevicaulis* (Dougl.) T. & G.] reported from Nebraska,
and admitted into our first edition, is not definitely
known within our area.

Family 93. CACTÀCEAE Lindl. Nat. Syst. Ed. 2, 53. 1836.

Cactus Family.

Fleshy plants, with flattened terete ridged or tubercled, continuous or jointed
stems, leafless, or with small leaves (only the tropical genera, *Pereskia* and *Peres-
kiopsis*, with large flat leaves), generally abundantly spiny, the spines developed
from cushions of hairs or bristles (areolae). Flowers mostly solitary, sessile, terminal or lateral, perfect, regular, showy. Calyx-tube adnate to the ovary, its
limb many-lobed or with distinct sepals. Petals numerous, imbricated in several
rows, mostly distinct. Stamens numerous, inserted on the throat of the calyx.
Filaments filiform; anthers small. Ovary 1-celled; ovules numerous, anatropous,
borne on several parietal placentae. Style terminal, elongated; stigmas numerous.
Fruit a berry, mostly fleshy, sometimes nearly dry. Seeds smooth, or tubercled,
arillate, the testa usually crustaceous or bony; endosperm little, or copious.

About 40 genera and 1000 species, all natives of America, except some species of the epiphytic
genus *Rhipsalis* in tropical Asia and Africa.

Stems subglobose, oval, ovoid or cylindric, tubercled, ribbed or angled; no proper leaves.
  Flowers borne on the tubercles or ribs, at or near the areolae.
    Flowers borne close to fully developed clusters of spines.   1. *Echinocereus.*
    Flowers borne close to areolae, from which the spines subsequently develope 2. *Pediocactus.*
  Flowers borne between the tubercles, distant from the areolae.   3. *Coryphantha.*
Plants jointed, the joints flattened, or cylindric; leaves present, terete and mostly early deciduous.
                                                                                             4. *Opuntia.*

---

1. ECHINOCÈREUS Engelm. Wisliz. Tour North. Mex. 91. 1848.

Stems ovoid, cylindric or oval, ribbed, or tubercled, the ribs or rows of tubercles usually
straight, mostly vertical; leaves none. Spine-bearing areolae on the ribs or tubercles. Flowers
borne on the ribs or tubercles, at or near the areolae, close to fully developed clusters of
spines. Calyx-tube with spine-bearing areolae, or scaly, prolonged beyond the ovary. Fruit
spiny. [Greek, hedgehog-*Cereus.*]

About 65 species, natives of America. Besides the following, some 30 others occur in the
southwestern United States. Type species: *Echinocereus viridiflòrus* Engelm.

Flowers greenish, about 1′ broad; fruit 5″–6″ long.   1. *E. viridiflorus.*
Flowers rose-purple, 2′–3′ broad; fruit 9″–10″ long.   2. *E. caespitosus.*

1. Echinocereus viridiflòrus Engelm.
Green-flowered Hedgehog Cereus.
Fig. 2981.

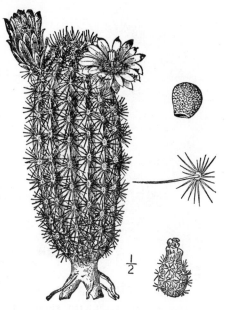

Echinocereus viridiflorus Engelm. Wisliz. Tour North. Mex. 91. 1848.

Cereus viridiflorus Engelm. Mem. Am. Acad. (II.) 4 : 50. 1849.

Stem subglobose to oval-cylindric, 1'–8' high, simple, or sparingly branched, 1'–2' in diameter. Ribs about 13; longer radial spines 12–18, with 2–6 setaceous upper ones, the lateral ones reddish brown, the others white or rarely purple; central spine stout, straight or curved, purple and white, or wanting; flowers about 1' broad, greenish brown without, yellowish green within; petals obtuse or acute; fruit ellipsoid, greenish, 5"–6" long; seeds tubercled.

South Dakota to Wyoming, Texas and New Mexico. Our figure is copied from plate 36, Cactaceae of the Mexican Boundary Survey, representing the *Cereus viridiflorus tubulosus* Coult. Contr. Nat. Herb. 3 : 383. 1896.

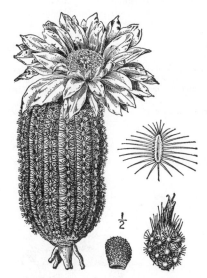

2. Echinocereus caespitòsus Engelm. &
Gray. Tufted Hedgehog Cereus.
Fig. 2982.

Cereus caespitosus Engelm. & Gray, Bost. Journ. Nat. Hist. 5 : 247. 1845.

Echinocereus caespitosus Engelm. Wisliz. Tour North. Mexico, 110. 1848.

Stems ovoid-globose to ovoid-cylindric, usually tufted, sometimes as many as 12 together, sometimes single, 1'–6' high, 1'–4' in diameter; ribs 12 or 13; radial spines 20–30, pectinate, white, the lateral ones the longer, 2"–4" long; central spines wanting, or sometimes 1 or 2 short ones; flowers rose-purple, 2'–3' broad, fruit ovoid, green, 9"–10" long; seeds tubercled, black, about ½" long.

Western Kansas (according to B. B. Smyth); Texas and Mexico.

2. PEDIOCÁCTUS Britton & Rose.

Stems globose, leafless, tubercled, the tubercles arranged in spiral rows bearing clusters of spines arising from areolae. Flowers borne on the tubercles, at or near areolae from which spines are developed. Calyx-tube prolonged beyond the ovary, its tube funnelform, bearing a few scales. Petals numerous, similar to the inner sepals, but larger, pinkish. Stamens numerous, borne on the tube of the calyx. Ovary green, globose; style columnar. Berry irregularly bursting, with a terminal scar, nearly or quite scaleless. Seeds tubercled, with a large subbasal hilum. [Greek, Plains-cactus.]

Three species, natives of central and western North America, the following typical.

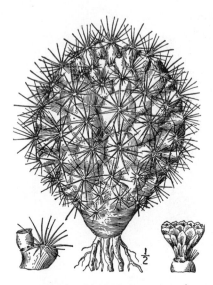

1. Pediocactus Símpsoni (Engelm.) Britton & Rose.   Simpson's Cactus.   Hedgehog-thistle.   Fig. 2983.

Echinocactus Simpsoni Engelm. Trans. St. Louis Acad. **2**: 197. 1863.

Stems single, globose or with a narrowed base, 3'–6' high, 3'–4' in diameter. Tubercles ovoid, somewhat 4-sided at base, 6"–8" long, arranged in spirals; central spines yellowish below, nearly black above, 5"–7" long, the exterior ones slightly shorter, whitish; flowers greenish pink, 8"–10" long and about as broad, borne to one side at the ends of the tubercles; petals oblong, crenulate and cuspidate at the apex; berry dry, 3"–3½" in diameter, bearing near its summit 2–3 scales which sometimes have short spines in their axils.

Kansas (according to B. B. Smyth); Colorado to Wyoming, Utah, New Mexico and Nevada. April–May.

3. CORYPHÁNTHA [Engelm.] Lemaire, Cact. 32. 1868.

Stems solitary or clustered, globose or ovoid, tubercled. Tubercles conic or cylindric, grooved, at least in many species, woolly and with clusters of spines at the apex. Leaves none. Flowers borne from areolae at the bases of the tubercles. Calyx-tube campanulate or funnel-form, produced beyond the ovary, which is often hidden between the tubercles. Petals in several rows. Ovary smooth, ovoid; style filiform. Berry ovoid or club-shaped, emersed, sometimes crowned by the withering corolla. [Greek, summit-flowering, the flowers being produced near the top.]

Perhaps 100 species, natives of warm and tropical America. Besides the following, many others occur in the southwestern States. The generic name *Cactus* used for these plants in our first edition belongs to the Turk's-head Cacti of tropical America. Type species: *Mamillaria sulcata* Engelm.

Flowers yellow or reddish ; central spine 1 ; berry scarlet, globose.   1. *C. missouriensis.*
Flowers purple ; central spines several ; berry green, ovoid.   2. *C. vivipara.*

1. Coryphantha missouriénsis (Sweet) Britton & Rose.   Missouri or Nipple Cactus.   Fig. 2984.

Cactus mamillaris Nutt. Gen. **1**: 295. 1818. Not L. 1753.

Mamillaria missouriensis Sweet, Hort. Brit. 171. 1827.

M. Nuttallii Engelm. Mem. Am. Acad. **4**: 49. 1849.

Cactus missouriensis Kuntze, Rev. Gen. Pl. 259. 1891.

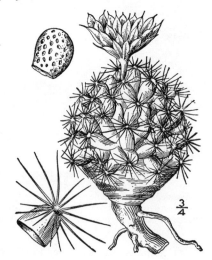

Stems mostly single, globose, 1'–2' high. Tubercles 6"–8" long, arranged in about 8 spiral rows, slightly grooved; spines gray, 10–20 together, the stouter central one 5"–6" long, or wanting; flowers yellow, or reddish, about 1' long and about the same breadth when expanded; petals 2"–3" wide, acute, abruptly mucronate; stigmas 2–5, very short, erect; berry globose, scarlet, 3"–4" in diameter, ripening the following spring; seeds black, globose, pitted, about ½" in diameter.

Plains and dry soil, North Dakota to Kansas and Texas, west to Colorado. Pelots. May.

Coryphantha sìmilis (Engelm.) Britton & Rose (*Mamillaria similis* Engelm.) has stems tufted; flowers 1′–2′ long; seeds about 1″ long, and ranges from Kansas and Colorado to Texas.

2. Coryphantha vivípara (Nutt.) Britton & Rose.　Purple Cactus.　Fig. 2985.

Cactus viviparus Nutt. Fraser's Cat. 1813.
Mamillaria vivipara Haw. Syn. Pl. Succ. Suppl. 72. 1819.

Stems single or tufted, 1′–5′ high, 1½′–2′ in diameter. Tubercles terete or nearly so, slightly grooved, bearing 3–8 slender reddish-brown spines 6″–10″ long, surrounded by 12–25 somewhat shorter, whitish or greenish ones in a single row; flowers purple, nearly 2′ long; petals lanceolate, narrow; sepals fringed; berry ovoid, 6″–9″ long, green; seeds light brown, obovoid, curved, pitted, about ¾″ long.

Plains and rocky soil, Minnesota to Manitoba, Alberta, Kansas, and Colorado.

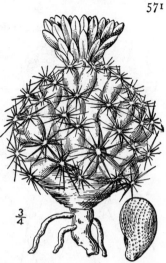

$\frac{3}{4}$

4. OPÚNTIA [Tourn.] Mill. Gard. Dict. Abr. Ed. 4. 1754.

Succulent plants, with jointed branching stems, the joints flat, or cylindric, and small mostly subulate deciduous spirally arranged leaves, the areolae axillary, often spine-bearing and almost always with barbed bristles (glochides). Flowers usually lateral. Calyx-tube not prolonged beyond the ovary, its lobes numerous, spreading. Petals numerous, slightly united at the base. Stamens very numerous, arranged in several rows; filaments distinct or slightly united. Ovary cylindric, exserted; style cylindric, longer than the stamens; stigma 2–7-rayed. Berry pear-shaped, often spiny. [Named from a town in Greece.]

About 200 species, natives of America. Besides the following, some 90 or more others occur in the western and southwestern States. Type species: *Cactus Opuntia* L.

Joints flattened, oval, oblong, obovate or orbicular; stems prostrate or ascending.
　Fruit fleshy, juicy, spineless or sparingly spiny.
　　Joints spineless, or with solitary stout spines.　　　　　　　　　1. *O. Opuntia.*
　　Joints spiny (no. 2 sometimes unarmed), the spines 1–15 at each areola.
　　　Spines white, gray or yellowish.
　　　　Joints 3′–5′ long; longer spines ½′–1½′ long.　　　　　　　2. *O. humifusa.*
　　　　Joints 6′–8′ long; longer spines 1′–2½′ long.　　　　　　　3. *O. tortispina.*
　　　Spines reddish brown to black; joints 6′–8′ long.　　　　　　4. *O. camanchica.*
　Fruit dry, with spine-bearing areoles.
　　Joints orbicular or broadly obovate, flat.　　　　　　　　　　5. *O. polyacantha.*
　　Joints little flattened, ovoid, or subglobose.　　　　　　　　6. *O. fragilis.*
Joints cylindric, or nearly so; stem erect.　　　　　　　　　　　7. *O. arborescens.*

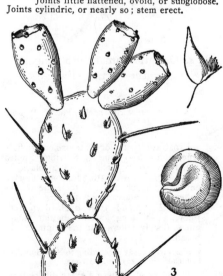

1. Opuntia Opúntia (L.) Coult. Eastern Prickly Pear.　Indian Fig. Fig. 2986.

Cactus Opuntia L. Sp. Pl. 468. 1753.

O. vulgaris Mill. Gard. Dict. Ed. 8, no. 1. 1768.

O. Opuntia Coult. Contr. Nat. Herb. **3**: 432. 1896.

Prostrate, or ascending, joints obovate, oval or orbicular, 2′–5′ long. Leaves subulate, appressed or somewhat spreading, 2″–4″ long, usually early deciduous; bristles greenish or yellowish brown; spines, when present, solitary, grayish or variegated, stout, not deflexed, 3″–1½′ long, often wanting; flowers yellow, sometimes with a reddish center, 2′–3′ broad; petals 8–10; fruit obovoid, fleshy, edible, 1′–1½′ long, red.

In dry sandy soil, or on rocks, eastern Massachusetts to eastern Pennsylvania, Kentucky and northern Florida. June–Aug. Prickly-pear cactus. Devil's-tongue. Barberry.

$\frac{3}{5}$

2. Opuntia humifùsa Raf.　Western Prickly Pear.　Devil's Tongue.
Fig. 2987.

Cactus humifusus Raf. Ann. Nat. 15.　1820.
Opuntia humifusa Raf. Med. Bot. 2 : 247.　1830.
O. mesacantha Raf. ; Ser. Bull. Bot. Gen. 216.　1830.
O. Rafinesquii Engelm. Pac. R. R. Rep. 4 : 41　1856.

Prostrate, similar to the preceding species; joints obovate to suborbicular, or oval, usually deep green, 2′–5′ long; leaves subulate, spreading, 3″–5″ long; bristles reddish brown; spines few, mostly near the margins of the joints, 1–4 together, whitish, or reddish at base and apex, deflexed, or the longer one spreading and ½′–1′ long; flowers yellow, often with a reddish centre, 2½′–3½′ broad; petals 10–12; fruit club-shaped, not spiny, fleshy, edible, 1½′–2′ long.

In dry sandy or rocky soil, Ohio to Minnesota, Kentucky, Missouri, Nebraska and Texas.　Summer.

Opuntia macrorhìza Engelm., a related species with a deep woody root, abundant in Texas, is reported to range northward into Missouri and Kansas.

3. Opuntia tortispìna Engelm.
Twisted-spined Cactus.
Fig. 2988.

Opuntia tortispina Engelm. Pac. R. R. Rep. 4 : 21.　1856.

Stems prostrate, the orbicular-obovate flattened joints 6′–8′ long.　Spines 3–5, yellowish, becoming whitish, angled and channeled, sometimes twisted, the longer ones 1½′–2½′ long, with 2–4 more slender and shorter ones; flowers sulphur-yellow, 2½′–3′ broad; fruit ovoid, fleshy, unarmed, about 2′ long and 1′ in diameter; seeds orbicular, slightly notched at the hilum, 2″–3″ wide.

Plains of Missouri and Nebraska to Texas. Summer.

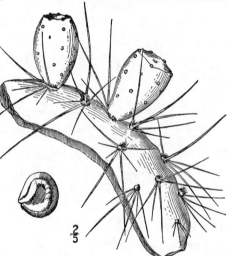

4. Opuntia camánchica Engelm.
Comanche Cactus.　Fig. 2989.

Opuntia camanchica Engelm. Pac. R. R. Rep. 4 : 40.　1856.

Prostrate, with obovate-orbicular flattened joints 6′–8′ long, 5′–8′ wide.　Spines 1–3, flattened, reddish brown to blackish, 1½′–3′ long, or with 3–6 additional shorter ones, the upper one suberect, the others deflexed or spreading; flowers yellow, about 2½′ broad; fruit oval, deep red, juicy, 1½′–2′ long; seeds angular, margined, deeply notched at the hilum, 2″–3″ broad.

Western Kansas (according to B. B. Smyth) ; Colorado to Texas and Arizona.

The plant of western Kansas differs from the typical Texan one by having more slender spines, lighter in color.　It hybridizes with *O. fragilis.*

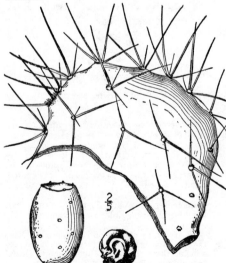

4. Opuntia polyacántha Haw. Many-spined Opuntia. Tuna. Fig. 2990.

Cactus ferox Nutt. Gen. 1: 296. 1818. Not Willd. 1813.

Opuntia polyacantha Haw. Syn. Pl. Succ. Suppl. 82. 1819.

Opuntia missouriensis DC. Prodr. 3: 472. 1828.

Prostrate, joints broadly obovate to orbicular, tubercled, pale green, 2'–6' long, about 6" thick, the tubercles 2" high, densely spiny and with cushions of fine bristles; spines 5–12, slender, 6"–2' long, whitish; leaves minute; flowers light yellow, 2'–3' broad; fruit dry, very prickly, 1'–1¼' long.

Plains and dry soil, Wisconsin to South Dakota, Athabasca, British Columbia, Nebraska, Missouri, Utah and New Mexico. May–June.

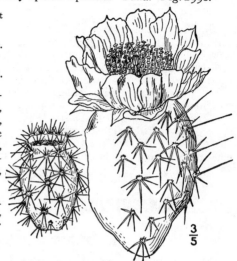

3/5

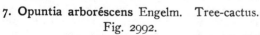

6. Opuntia frágilis (Nutt.) Haw. Brittle Opuntia. Tuna. Fig. 2991.

Cactus fragilis Nutt. Gen. 1: 296. 1818.

Opuntia fragilis Haw. Syn. Pl. Succ. Suppl. 82. 1819.

Decumbent or prostrate; joints ovoid, 1'–2' long, somewhat flattened or nearly terete. Leaves very small, reddish; cushions composed of few bristles; central spines 1–4, ½'–1½' long, gray, darker at the apex, surrounded by 4–6 smaller ones; flowers yellow, smaller than those of the preceding species; fruit nearly 1' long, becoming dry at maturity, provided with cushions of bristles usually bearing a few short spines.

Prairies and dry soil, Iowa, Wisconsin and Minnesota to South Dakota, British Columbia, Kansas and Utah. July–Sept.

3/5

7. Opuntia arboréscens Engelm. Tree-cactus. Fig. 2992.

Opuntia arborescens Engelm. Wisliz. Rep. 6. 1848.

Erect, tree-like, 4°–25° high, 4'–8' in diameter at the base, verticillately branched, the spiny branches spreading or drooping. Joints verticillate, mostly in 3's or 4's, cylindric, 2'–6' long, less than 1' in diameter, the prominent tubercles 7"–10" long; leaves terete, spreading, 6"–10" long; spines 8–30, terete, in yellowish sheaths, diverging, the interior ones the longer, often 1' long or more; flowers purple, 2½'–3' broad; fruit subglobose, crested-tuberculate, dry, or nearly so, yellow, unarmed, about 1' in diameter; seeds smooth, 1½"–2" wide.

Western Kansas, probably only in cultivation; Colorado to Texas, New Mexico, Arizona and Mexico.

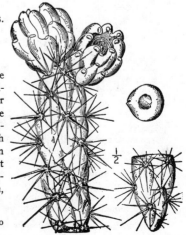

½

Family 94. **THYMELEÁCEAE** Reichenb. Consp. 82.   1828.

MEZEREUM FAMILY.

Shrubs or trees (rarely herbaceous), with tough fibrous or reticulated inner bark, and simple entire exstipulate leaves.   Flowers fascicled, capitate, racemose, or rarely solitary, regular, mostly perfect.   Calyx inferior, its tube cylindric or urn-shaped, 4–5-lobed or entire.   Petals none in our genera, present in many exotic ones.   Stamens borne on the calyx, twice as many as its lobes, or rarely fewer, often in two series; filaments long or short; anthers erect, 2-celled, the sacs longitudinally dehiscent.   Ovary 1-celled, 1-ovuled (2-celled and 2-ovuled in some Asiatic and Australasian genera); ovule anatropous, pendulous; style short or elongated; stigma terminal, mostly capitate.   Fruit a berry-like drupe in our plants.   Seed-coat mostly crustaceous; embryo straight; cotyledons fleshy; endosperm little or none, or copious in some exotic genera.

About 37 genera and 425 species, widely distributed, most abundant in Australia and South Africa.

Calyx-lobes 4, large; stamens included; style very short.   1. *Daphne.*
Calyx-limb almost wanting; stamens and style long, exserted.   2. *Dirca.*

1. DÁPHNE L. Sp. Pl. 356.   1753.

Erect or spreading shrubs, with alternate deciduous or evergreen leaves, and small purple pink or white flowers in fascicles, heads or racemes, borne in the following species at the leafless nodes of twigs of the preceding season.   Perianth tubular, its 4 lobes spreading. Stamens 8, in 2 series on the perianth-tube, included, or the upper 4 slightly exserted; filaments very short.   Disk none.   Ovary sessile or nearly so, 1-celled; style very short; stigma large, capitate.   Drupe ovoid, or oblong, the calyx deciduous or persistent.   [Mythological name.]

About 40 species, natives of Europe and Asia.   Type species : *Daphne Gnidium* L.

1. Daphne Mezèreum L.   Spurge Laurel.   Lady Laurel.   Mezereon.   Fig. 2993.

Daphne Mezereum L. Sp. Pl. 356.   1753.

A shrub 1°–4° high, the young twigs somewhat pubescent.   Leaves thin, deciduous, oblong-lanceolate or oblanceolate, acute or obtusish at the apex, 3′–5′ long, 4″–10″ wide, narrowed into short petioles; flowers in sessile fascicles of 2–5 at the nodes of twigs of the preceding season, very fragrant, expanding before the leaves or with them; perianth-tube appressed-pubescent, rose-purple or white, 6″ long or less, the ovate acute lobes nearly as long; drupe red, oval-ovoid, 3″–4″ long.

Escaped from cultivation, Quebec to Massachusetts, New York and Ontario.   Native of Europe and Asia.   Spurge-flax or -olive.   Dwarf bay.   Paradise- or mysterious plant. Wild pepper.   April–May.

2. DÍRCA L. Sp. Pl. 358.   1753.

Branching shrubs, with tough fibrous bark, alternate thin short-petioled deciduous leaves, and yellowish flowers in peduncled fascicles of 2–4 from scaly buds at the nodes of twigs of the preceding season, branches subsequently developing from the same nodes.   Perianth campanulate or funnelform, its limb undulately obscurely 4-toothed.   Stamens 8, borne on the perianth, exserted, the alternate ones longer; filaments very slender.   Disk obsolete.   Ovary nearly sessile, 1-celled; style filiform, exserted; stigma small, capitate.   Drupe red, oval-oblong.   [Named from a fountain in Thebes.]

Two known species, the following typical; *D. occidentàlis* A. Gray, in California.

1. Dirca palústris L. Leather- or Leaver-wood. Moose-wood. Wicopy. Fig. 2994.

Dirca palustris L. Sp. Pl. 358. 1753.

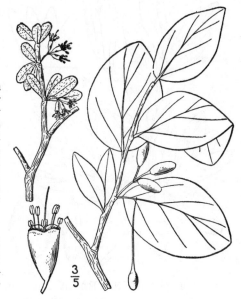

A shrub, 2°–6° high, the twigs yellowish green, glabrous, jointed. Leaves oval, or obovate, obtuse at the apex, rounded or narrowed at the base, pubescent when young, glabrous, or very nearly so, and 2′–3′ long when mature; bud-scales 3 or 4, oval, or oblong, very pubèscent with brown hairs, deciduous; peduncle about 2½″ long; flowers nearly sessile, expanding before the leaves; perianth 2″–3″ long; style longer than the stamens; drupe about 6″ long.

In woods and thickets, mostly in wet soil, New Brunswick to Ontario, Minnesota, Virginia, Tennessee, Florida and Missouri. Swamp-wood. Leather-bush. Wickup. American mezereon. Rope-bark. The bark produces violent vomiting; applied externally, it is an irritant to the skin. April–May.

Family 95. ELAEAGNÀCEAE Lindl. Nat. Syst. Ed. 2, 194. 1836.

OLEASTER FAMILY.

Shrubs or trees, mostly silvery-scaly, or stellate-pubescent, with entire alternate or opposite leaves, and perfect polygamous or dioecious flowers clustered in the axils or at the nodes of twigs of the preceding season, rarely solitary. Lower part of the perianth of perfect or pistillate flowers tubular or urn-shaped, enclosing the ovary and persistent, the upper part 4-lobed or 4-cleft, deciduous (obscurely 2-lobed in the Old World *Hippophaë*); perianth of staminate flowers 4-parted (2-parted in *Hippophaë*). Corolla none Stamens 4 or 8, those of perfect flowers borne on the throat of the perianth; filaments mostly short; anthers 2-celled, the sacs longitudinally dehiscent. Disk annular, or lobed. Ovary sessile, 1-celled; ovule 1, erect, anatropous; style slender. Fruit drupe-like, the perianth-base becoming thickened and enclosing the achene or nut. Seed erect; embryo straight; endosperm little or wanting.

Three known genera and about 20 species, widely distributed.

Stamens as many as the perianth-parts; flowers perfect or polygamous; leaves alternate.
                                                      1. *Elaeagnus.*
Stamens twice as many as the perianth-parts; flowers dioecious; leaves opposite. 2. *Lepargyraea.*

1. ELAEÁGNUS [Tourn.] L. Sp. Pl. 121. 1753.

Silvery-scaly shrubs, some exotic species trees, with alternate petioled leaves. Flowers solitary or 2–4 together in the axils, pedicelled, not bracted, perfect or polygamous. Perianth tubular below, constricted over the top of the ovary, the upper part campanulate or urn-shaped, 4-lobed, deciduous, the lobes valvate. Stamens 4, borne on the throat of the perianth. Style linear, long. Fruit drupe-like, the ripened perianth-base fleshy or mealy, enclosing the striate or grooved nut. [Greek, sacred olive.]

About 20 species, natives of Europe, Asia, Australia and North America. Only the following is known in North America. Type species: *Elaeagnus angustifolia* L.

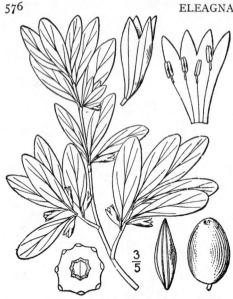

1. Elaeagnus argéntea Pursh. Silver-berry. Fig. 2995.

Elaeagnus argentea Pursh, Fl. Am. Sept. 114. 1814.

Stoloniferous, much branched, thornless, sometimes 12° high, the young twigs covered with brown scurf, becoming silvery. Leaves oblong, ovate or oval-lanceolate, densely silvery-scurfy on both sides, acute or obtuse, short-petioled, 1′–4′ long; flowers usually numerous, 1 to 3 in the axils, fragrant, silvery, 6″–8″ long; perianth silvery without, yellowish within, its lobes ovate, about 1″ long; fruit oval, silvery, 4″–6″ long, the stone 8-striate.

Quebec to Hudson Bay, Yukon, British Columbia, Minnesota, South Dakota and Utah. May–July. Fruit edible, ripe July–Aug.

2. LEPARGYRAÈA Raf. Am. Month. Mag. 2: 176. 1817.

[SHEPHERDIA Nutt. Gen. 2: 240. 1818.]

Shrubs, brown- or silvery-scurfy or stellate-pubescent, with opposite petioled leaves. Flowers small, dioecious, or sometimes polygamous, subspicate or fascicled at the nodes of the preceding season, or axillary, the pistillate few or sometimes solitary. Pistillate flowers with an urn-shaped or ovoid 4-lobed perianth, bearing an 8-lobed disk at its mouth which nearly closes it; style somewhat exserted. Staminate flowers with a 4-parted perianth and 8 stamens alternating with as many lobes of the disk; filaments short. Fruit drupe-like, the fleshy perianth-base enclosing a nut, or achene. [Greek, silvery-scaly.]

Three known species, the following and *L. rotundifolia* of Utah. Type species: *Hippophaë argéntea* Pursh.

Leaves ovate or oval, green above, silvery beneath; shrub thornless.   1. *L. canadensis.*
Leaves oblong, silvery on both sides; shrub mostly thorny.   2. *L. argentea.*

1. Lepargyraea canadénsis (L.) Greene. Canadian Buffalo-berry. Fig. 2996.

Elaeagnus canadensis L. Sp. Pl. 1024. 1753.

Shepherdia canadensis Nutt. Gen. 2: 240. 1818.

L. canadensis Greene, Pittonia 2: 122. 1890.

A thornless shrub, 4°–8° high, the young shoots brown-scurfy. Leaves ovate or oval, obtuse at the apex, rounded, or some of them narrowed at the base, 1′–1½′ long, green and sparingly stellate-scurfy above, densely silvery stellate-scurfy beneath, some of the scurf usually brown; petioles 2″–3″ long; flowers in short spikes at the nodes of the twigs, yellowish; buds globose, less than 1″ in diameter, forming in summer, expanding with or before the leaves early in the following spring; perianth about 2″ broad when expanded; fruit oval, red or yellowish, 2″–3″ long, the flesh insipid, the nut smooth.

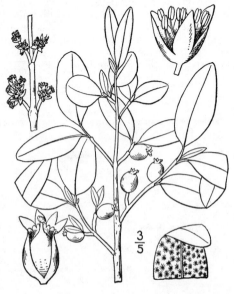

On banks, especially along streams, Newfoundland to Alaska, British Columbia, Maine, New York, Wisconsin and New Mexico. Wild oleaster- or olive-tree. Soopoo-lalia (Indian). April–June. Fruit ripe July–Aug.

2. Lepargyraea argéntea (Nutt.) Greene.   Buffalo-berry.   Rabbit-berry.
Fig. 2997.

Elaeagnus argentea Nutt. Fraser's Cat. 1813.

Hippophaë argentea Pursh, Fl. Am. Sept. 115. 1814.

Shepherdia argentea Nutt. Gen. **2**: 241. 1818.

L. argentea Greene, Pittonia **2**: 122. 1890.

A shrub, 4°–18° high, the twigs often terminating in thorns. Leaves oblong, or sometimes oblong-lanceolate, 1′–2′ long, rarely more than ½′ wide, obtuse at the apex, usually cuneate-narrowed at the base, densely silvery-scurfy on both sides; petioles 2″–6″ long; flowers fascicled at the nodes, the globose buds very silvery; fruit oval, or ovoid, scarlet, sour, 2″–3″ long, edible.

Minnesota to Manitoba, Saskatchewan, Kansas and Nevada. April–May. Called also beef-suet tree, silver leaf. Wild oleaster- or olive-tree. Bull-berry. Fruit ripe July–Aug.

Family 96. LYTHRÀCEAE Lindl. Nat. Syst. Ed. 2, 100. 1836.
LOOSESTRIFE FAMILY.

Herbs, shrubs, or often trees in tropical regions, mostly with opposite leaves and solitary or clustered mostly axillary perfect flowers. Stipules usually none. Calyx persistent, free from the ovary, but generally enclosing it, the limb toothed and often with accessory teeth in the sinuses. Petals as many as the primary calyx-teeth or none, inserted on the calyx. Disk annular or none. Stamens various, inserted on the calyx. Anthers versatile, longitudinally dehiscent. Ovary sessile or stipitate, 2–6-celled or sometimes 1-celled; style 1; stigma capitate or 2-lobed; ovules ∞, rarely few, anatropous. Capsule 1–several-celled, variously dehiscent or sometimes indehiscent. Seeds without endosperm; cotyledons flat, often auricled at the base.

About 21 genera and 400 species, of wide geographic distribution, most abundant in tropical America.

Calyx-tube campanulate or hemispheric; flowers regular.
  Flowers small, axillary, solitary or few; low herbs.
    Petals 4 in our species; capsule bursting irregularly.   1. *Ammannia.*
    Petals none; capsule indehiscent.   2. *Didiplis.*
    Petals 4; capsule septicidally dehiscent.   3. *Rotala.*
  Flowers large, in axillary cymes; large aquatic shrub.   4. *Decodon.*
Calyx-tube cylindric; flowers regular.   5. *Lythrum.*
Calyx-tube tubular, oblique; flowers irregular.   6. *Parsonsia.*

1. AMMÁNNIA [Houst.] L. Sp. Pl. 119. 1753.

Annual glabrous or glabrate herbs, mostly with 4-angled stems, opposite sessile narrow leaves, and small axillary solitary or cymose flowers. Calyx campanulate, globose or ovoid, 4-angled, 4-toothed, often with small appendages in the sinuses. Petals 4 in our species, deciduous. Stamens 4–8, inserted on the calyx-tube, filaments slender or short. Ovary enclosed in the calyx-tube, nearly globular, 2–4-celled, bursting irregularly. [Named for Johann Ammann, 1699–1741, a German botanist.]

About 20 species, of wide geographic distribution, most abundant in warm regions. Besides the following, another occurs in the Southern States. Type species: *Ammannia latifòlia* L.

Flowers sessile or very nearly so, solitary, or 2–3 together.
  Leaves linear-lanceolate, acuminate; style elongated.   1. *A. coccinea.*
  Leaves obovate or oblanceolate, obtuse; style very short.   2. *A. Koehnei.*
Flowers pedicelled, in axillary cymes.   3. *A. auriculata.*

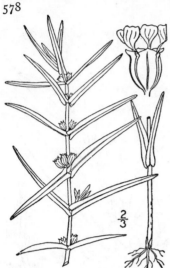

1. Ammannia coccínea Rottb. Long-leaved Ammannia. Fig. 2998.

Ammannia coccinea Rottb. Pl. Hort. Havn. Descr. 7. 1773.

Ammannia latifolia T. & G. Fl. N. A. 1 : 480. 1840. Not L. 1753.

Erect, glabrous, branching below, 6′–20′ high. Leaves linear-lanceolate, all obtusely cordate-auriculate and dilated at the somewhat clasping base, acuminate or acute at the apex, entire, 1′–3′ long, 1″–3″ wide; flowers 1–5 in each axil, sessile or very nearly so; petals purple, fugacious; style elongated, very slender, usually more than one-half the length of the capsule.

In swamps, New Jersey to Ohio, Indiana, Iowa, South Dakota, Florida, Louisiana, Texas, Mexico and Brazil. July–Sept.

2. Ammannia Koèhnei Britton. Koehne's Ammannia. Fig. 2999.

Ammannia Koehnei Britton, Bull. Torr. Club 18 : 271. 1891.

Ammannia humilis β T. & G. Fl. N. A. 1 : 480. 1840.

Erect, glabrous, 6′–20′ high, at length freely branching. Leaves obovate, oblance-olate, or somewhat spatulate, obtuse or obtusish at the apex, the upper ones clasping and more or less auriculate at the base, the lower narrowed and sessile or tapering into a short petiole; flowers 1–3 together in the axils, sessile; petals pink, fugacious; stamens very short, not exserted; style very short; capsule enclosed by the calyx.

In swamps, Hackensack marshes, N. J., to Florida. Tooth-cup. July–Sept.

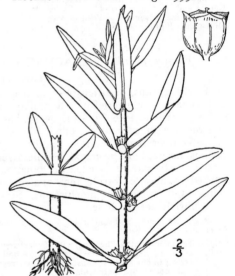

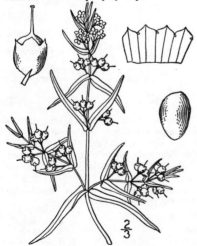

3. Ammannia auriculàta Willd. Wright's Ammannia. Fig. 3000.

A. auriculata Willd. Hort. Berol. 7. *pl.* 7. 1806.
Ammannia Wrightii A. Gray, Pl. Wright. 2 : 55. 1853.
A. latifolia pedicellata Carruth, Trans. Kans. Acad. Sci. 5 : 48. 1877.

Erect, 2′–10′ high, at length widely branching. Leaves sessile, linear-lanceolate or oblong, acute or acutish at the apex, auriculate at the base, ½′–1½′ long, about 2″ wide; flowers in axillary peduncled cymes; pedicels ½″–1½″ long; petals purple; style slender; stamens exserted; capsule partly enclosed by the calyx.

Missouri, Nebraska and Kansas to Texas, Ecuador and Brazil. Cuba. Also in Asia and Africa. May–June.

2. DÍDIPLIS Raf. Atl. Journ. 177. 1833.

An aquatic or marsh plant, rooting in the mud, with 4-angled stems, opposite linear entire leaves, and very small axillary solitary green flowers. Calyx hemispheric or campanulate, 4-lobed, with no appendages. Petals none. Stamens 2-4, usually 4, inserted on the calyx-tube; filaments very short. Ovary globose, enclosed by the calyx, 2-celled; style scarcely any; stigma obscurely 2-lobed; ovules ∞. Capsule globose, indehiscent, 2-celled. [Greek, twice double.]

A monotypic genus of east-central North America, closely related to the Old World genus *Peplis L.*

1. Didiplis diándra (Nutt.) Wood. Water Purslane. Fig. 3001.

Callitriche autumnalis(?) Michx. Fl. Bor. Am. 1: 2. 1803. Not L. 1753.
Peplis(?) diandra Nutt.; DC. Prodr. 3: 77. 1828.
Didiplis linearis Raf. Atl. Journ. 177. 1833.
Didiplis diandra Wood. Bot. & Fl. 124. 1870.

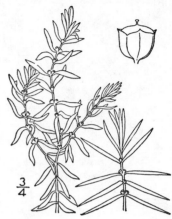

Submersed or rooting in the mud on shores, glabrous, 3'-12' long. Submersed leaves thin, elongated-linear or lanceolate, acute or acuminate at the apex, broader at the base, 6"-10" long; emersed leaves linear-oblong, narrowed at the base; flowers inconspicuous, about ½" long; capsule about ¼" in diameter.

Minnesota and Wisconsin to Texas and Mexico, east to North Carolina and Florida. Resembling *Callitriche* in habit. June-Aug.

3. ROTÀLA L. Mant. 2: 175. 1771.

Low annual mainly glabrous herbs, usually with opposite sessile or sometimes petioled leaves, 4-angled stems, and axillary mainly solitary small flowers. Calyx campanulate or globose, 4-lobed, the sinuses appendaged. Petals 4 in our species. Stamens 4, short. Ovary free from the calyx, globose, 4-celled. Capsule globose, enclosed by the membranous calyx, 4-celled, septicidally dehiscent, the valves very minutely and densely striate transversely. [Latin, wheel, from the whorled leaves of some species.]

About 30 species, of wide geographic distribution in warm and tropical regions. Type species: *Rotala verticillàris L.*

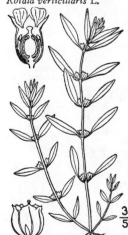

1. Rotala ramòsior (L.) Koehne. Tooth-cup. Fig. 3002.

Ammannia ramosior L. Sp. Pl. 120. 1753.

Ammannia humilis Michx. Fl. Bor. Am. 1: 99. 1803.

Boykinia humilis Raf. Aut. Bot. 9. 1840.

Rotala ramosior Koehne, in Mart. Fl. Bras. 13: Part 2, 194. 1875.

Glabrous, branched from the base or simple, ascending or erect, 2'-13' high. Leaves oblong or linear-oblong, 6"-15" long, 1"-3" wide, blunt at the apex, narrowed and sessile at the base or tapering into a short petiole, not auricled; flowers solitary or rarely 3 in the axils, very small; petals minute; style almost none.

In swamps, Massachusetts to Florida, Minnesota, Nebraska, Arkansas, Texas and Mexico. Also in California, Oregon, South America and the West Indies. July-Sept.

4. DÉCODON J. F. Gmel. Syst. Veg. 2: 677. 1791.

Herbaceous shrubs, with verticillate or opposite, short-petioled entire leaves, and showy purple pedicelled trimorphous flowers, in nearly sessile axillary cymes. Calyx broadly campanulate, or hemispheric, nerved, 5-7-toothed, with as many slender elongated accessory teeth in the sinuses. Stamens 10, rarely 8, alternately longer and shorter, inserted on the calyx-tube, the longer exserted. Style filiform; stigma small. Capsule globose, 3–5-celled, included in the calyx, loculicidally dehiscent. [Greek, ten-toothed, referring to the calyx.] A monotypic genus of eastern North America.

1. Decodon verticillàtus (L.) Ell. Swamp Loosestrife or Willow-herb. Fig. 3003.

Lythrum verticillatum L. Sp. Pl. 446. 1753.
Decodon aquaticus J. F. Gmel. Syst. 2: 677. 1791.
Decodon verticillatus Ell. Bot. S. C. & Ga. 1: 544. 1821.
Nesaea verticvillata H.B.K. Nov. Gen. 6: 191. 1823.

Aquatic, perennial, somewhat woody, with angular recurved glabrous or slightly pubescent stems 3°–10° long, which root from the tip when they reach the water or mud. Leaves lanceolate, 2′–5′ long, 4″–12″ wide, glabrous above, somewhat pubescent beneath, acute at both ends; petioles 2″–4″ long; cymes several-flowered; flowers nearly 1′ broad; petals cuneate at the base, pink-purple; filaments of the longer stamens very slender; capsule about 2½″ in diameter.

In swamps, Maine to Florida, west to southern Ontario, Minnesota, Tennessee and Louisiana. Stems clothed with parenchyma at the base. Flowers rarely double. Ascends to 2000 ft. in Pennsylvania. July–Sept. Peat- or slink-weed. Wild oleander. Grass-poly. Milk willow-herb.

Lagerstroemia índica L., crape myrtle, a large shrub with terminal panicles of showy white to purple irregular flowers, native of the East Indies is sparingly escaped from cultivation from Maryland southward.

5. LÝTHRUM L. Sp. Pl. 446. 1753.

Herbs or shrubs, with 4-angled stems, opposite alternate or rarely verticillate entire leaves, and solitary cymose-paniculate or spicate and terminal often dimorphous or trimorphous flowers. Calyx-tube cylindric, 8–12-ribbed, straight, not gibbous at the base, with 4–6 primary teeth and an equal number of appendages in the sinuses. Petals 4–6, usually obovate, rarely wanting. Stamens 4–12, inserted on the calyx-tube, included or exserted. Ovary oblong, sessile, 2-celled; style filiform; stigma mostly capitate; ovules numerous. Capsules enclosed by the calyx, membranous, 2-celled, 2-valved, or bursting irregularly. Seeds flat or angular. [Greek, gore, from the purple color of the flowers.]

About 30 species, of wide geographic distribution. Besides the following, about 5 others occur in the southern and western United States. Type species: *Lythrum Salicària* L.

Flowers axillary, solitary; stamens not more numerous than petals.
  Leaves mostly alternate.
    Leaves obtuse; stamens all included; annual.   1. *L. Hyssopifolia.*
    Leaves acute; stamens of short-styled flowers exserted; perennial.   2. *L. alatum.*
  Leaves mostly opposite, narrowly linear, narrowed at the base.   3. *L. lineare.*
Flowers in spicate panicles, terminal; stamens twice as many as petals.   4. *L. Salicaria.*

1. Lythrum Hyssopifòlia L. Hyssop Loosestrife. Grass Poly. Fig. 3004.

Lythrum Hyssopifolia L. Sp. Pl. 447. 1753.

Annual, glabrous, pale green, erect or assurgent, at length widely branched, 6′–24′ high. Leaves sessile, mainly alternate, the lowest sometimes opposite, oblong or linear-oblong, obtuse at the apex, rounded at the base, 4″–10″ long, 1″–4″ wide, those of the main stem larger than those of the branches; flowers solitary and sessile in the axils, not dimorphous, pink-purple, about ½″ broad; petals nearly erect; stamens all included; calyx 2½″–3″ long in fruit.

Borders of marshes, Maine to New Jersey and Pennsylvania. Also in California and along the coast of South America. Widely distributed in the Old World. June–Sept.

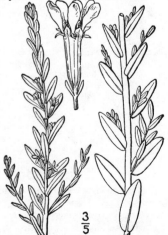

3/5

2. Lythrum alàtum Pursh. Wing-angled Loosestrife. Fig. 3005.

Lythrum alatum Pursh, Fl. Am. Sept. 334. 1814.

Perennial, erect, glabrous, usually much branched, dark green, 1°–4° high, the stem angled and often slightly winged. Leaves sessile, alternate or the lowest opposite, lanceolate or oblong, acute or acutish at the apex, rounded or cordate at the base, 6″–15″ long, 2″–5″ wide; flowers solitary in the upper axils, short-pedicelled, deep purple, 3″–5″ broad, dimorphous; petals erect-spreading; stamens of the short-styled flowers exserted; hypogynous ring fleshy; ovary nearly sessile; calyx 2½″–3″ long in fruit.

In low grounds, southern Ontario to Massachusetts, Kentucky, South Dakota, Utah, Kansas and Arkansas. The closely related *L. lanceolatum* Ell. of the southern states has the leaves narrowed or cuneate at the base. Milk willow-herb. June–Aug.

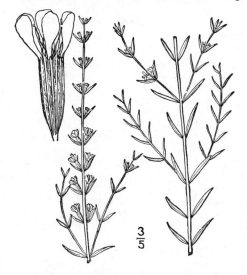

3. Lythrum lineàre L. Linear-leaved Loosestrife. Fig. 3006.

Lythrum lineare L. Sp. Pl. 447. 1753.

Perennial, slender, glabrous, rather pale green, much branched, 2°–4° high. Leaves narrowly linear, sessile, 6″–12″ long, 1″–2″ wide, nearly all opposite, acutish at the apex or the lowest obtuse, narrowed at the base; flowers solitary in the upper axils, light purple or nearly white, dimorphous, about 1½″ broad; stamens of the short-styled flowers exserted; no hypogynous ring; ovary short-stalked; fruiting calyx 1½″–2″ long.

Borders of salt marshes, New Jersey to Florida, west to Texas. Cuba. July–Sept.

Lythrum Vulnerària Ait., of Mexico, admitted into our first edition as recorded as found at St. Louis, Mo., is not definitely known within our area.

4. Lythrum Salicària L. Spiked or Purple Loosestrife Fig. 3007.

Lythrum Salicaria L. Sp. Pl. 446. 1753.

Perennial, erect, 2°–3° high, glabrous or pubescent, sometimes tomentose above, at length much branched. Leaves opposite or sometimes verticillate in 3's, sessile, lanceolate, cordate or clasping at the base, 2′–3′ long, 3″–5″ wide; flowers purple, trimorphous, 6″–8″ broad, in dense compound terminal interrupted bracted spikes; stamens 8–10, alternately longer and shorter, even the longer ones little exserted; ovary short-stalked; fruiting calyx about 3″ long; calyx-lobes shorter than the narrow appendages.

In swamps and wet meadows, Cape Breton Island to Ontario, south to southern New York, Delaware and the District of Columbia. Naturalized from Europe. June–Aug Widely distributed in the Old World. Spiked willowherb, long purples, soldiers. Purple-grass. Willow- or killweed. Sage-willow. Milk or purple willow-herb. Red sally. Rainbow-weed.

Lythrum virgàtum L., differing by leaves narrowed at the base, is recorded as established in eastern Massachusetts.

6. PARSÓNSIA P. Br.; Adans. Fam. Pl. 2: 234. 1763.

[CUPHEA P Br.; Adans. loc. cit. Hyponym. 1763.]

Herbs (some shrubs in tropical regions), with opposite or verticillate leaves. Flowers solitary or racemose, axillary, irregular and unsymmetrical. Calyx-tube elongated, tubular, 12-ribbed, gibbous or spurred at the base, oblique at the mouth with 6 primary teeth and usually as many appendanges. Petals 6, unequal. Stamens mostly 11 (sometimes 12 in our species), inserted on the throat of the calyx, unequal; filaments short. Ovary sessile or obliquely stipitate, with a curved gland at its base, unequally 2-celled; ovules several or numerous; style slender; stigma 2-lobed. Capsule included in the calyx, oblong, 1-celled, laterally dehiscent. Seeds flattened. [In honor of James Parsons, M. D., a Scotch botanist.]

About 200 species, natives of America. Besides the following, 2 others occur in the Southern States. Type species: *Lythrum Parsonsia* L.

1. Parsonsia petiolàta (L.) Rusby. Blue Wax-weed. Clammy Cuphea. Tar-weed. Wax-bush. Fig. 3008.

Lythrum petiolatum L. Sp. Pl. 446. 1753.
Cuphea viscosissima Jacq. Hort. Vind. 2: 83 *pl. 177.* 1772.
Cuphea petiolata Koehne, Engler's Bot. Jahrb. 2: 173. 1882. Not Pohl.
Parsonsia petiolata Rusby, Mem. Torr. Club 5: 231. 1894.

Annual, erect, very viscid-pubescent, branched, 6'–20' high. Leaves slender-petioled, ovate-lanceolate, scabrous, mostly rounded at the base and blunt-pointed at the apex, 1'–1½' long; flowers axillary, short-peduncled, purple, 3"–4" broad; petals ovate, clawed; stamens sometimes 12; fruiting calyx swollen, about 4" long; capsule dehiscent before the seeds are ripe, the placenta projecting through the lateral orifice.

In dry soil, New Hampshire to northern Illinois and Kansas, south to Georgia and Louisiana. Introduced into southern Ontario. Ascends to 3300 ft. in West Virginia. July–Oct.

½

Family 97. MELASTOMÀCEAE R Br. Exp. Congo, App. 5. 1818.

MEADOW-BEAUTY FAMILY.

Herbs (shrubs or trees in tropical regions), with opposite 3–9-nerved simple leaves, and regular perfect, often showy, but rarely odorous, generally clustered flowers. Stipules none. Calyx-tube adnate to or free from the ovary, usually 4–5-lobed, the lobes imbricated. Petals as many as the lobes of the calyx, and inserted on its throat, more or less oblique, imbricated. Stamens twice as many, or equal in number to the petals, often inclined or declined, the alternate ones sometimes shorter; anthers opening by a pore in our species. Ovary 2–several-celled (often 4-celled); style terminal, simple; stigma simple or lobed; ovules ∞, anatropous. Capsule included in the calyx-tube, irregularly or loculicidally dehiscent. Seeds mainly small, with no endosperm.

About 175 genera and 3000 species, widely distributed in tropical regions, most abundant in South America.

1. RHÉXIA L. Sp. Pl. 346. 1753.

Perennial herbs, often somewhat woody at the base, sometimes tuber-bearing, with mostly sessile opposite 3–5-nerved leaves, and terminal showy cymose or rarely solitary flowers. Calyx-tube urn-shaped or campanulate, constricted at the neck, its limb 4-lobed, the lobes triangular or subulate, shorter than the tube. Petals 4, obovate, oblique, rounded retuse, or aristate at the apex. Stamens 8, equal; anthers linear or oblong, incurved or inverted in the bud. Ovary free from the calyx, glabrous, 4-celled; style slender; stigma truncate. Capsule 4-celled, 4-valved. Placentae 4, central. Seeds numerous, coiled or bent, rough. [Greek, breaking, applied originally by Pliny to a different plant.]

About 14 species, natives of the eastern United States and Cuba. Type species: *Rhexia virginica* L.

Stem cylindric, very pubescent.	1. *R. mariana.*
Stem square or angled, pubescent or glabrous.	
Stem more or less pubescent; leaves ovate.	2. *R. virginica.*
Stem glabrous.	
Leaves oblong or lance-oblong; calyx with a few hairs above.	3. *R. aristosa.*
Leaves ovate, bristly-ciliate; calyx glabrous.	4. *R. ciliosa.*

1. Rhexia mariàna L. Maryland Meadow-Beauty. Fig. 3009.

Rhexia mariana L. Sp. Pl. 346. 1753.

Stem rather slender, cylindric, simple, or branched above, very hirsute-pubescent, 1°–2° high. Leaves spreading, short-petioled, oblong, or linear-oblong, mostly acute at the apex, narrowed at the base, 1′–1½′ long, 2″–5″ wide, pubescent with scattered bristly hairs on both surfaces, 3-nerved, the margins ciliate-serrulate; flowers loosely cymose, pedicelled, pale purple, about 1′ broad; pedicels and calyx-tube glandular-pubescent; petals rounded, or sometimes aristulate; anthers linear, curved, minutely spurred on the back.

In swamps, pine-barrens of Long Island to Florida, west to Kentucky, Missouri and Texas. June–Sept.

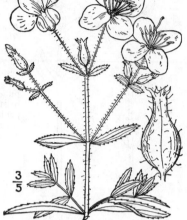

2. Rhexia virgínica L. Meadow-Beauty. Deer-grass. Fig. 3010.

Rhexia virginica L. Sp. Pl. 346. 1753.
Rhexia latifolia Bush, Rhodora 13 : 167. 1911.

Stem rather stout, simple or branched above, square, the angles often slightly winged, more or less pubescent, 1°–1½° high. Leaves ascending, sessile or short-petioled, ovate or ovate-oval, acute or acutish at the apex, rounded or rarely narrowed at the base, 1′–2′ long, 6″–12″ wide, usually with a few scattered hairs on both surfaces, mostly 5-nerved, the margins ciliate-serrulate; flowers bright purple, cymose, short-pedicelled, 1′–1½′ broad; calyx-tube and pedicels glandular-pubescent; petals rounded or slightly retuse; anthers linear, curved, minutely spurred on the back.

In sandy swamps, Maine to Florida, Ontario, northern New York, Iowa, Missouri and Louisiana. Ascends to 2000 ft. in Pennsylvania. Handsome Harry. July–Sept.

3. Rhexia aristòsa Britton. Awn-petaled Meadow-Beauty. Fig. 3011.

Rhexia aristosa Britton, Bull. Torr. Club 17 : 14.
pl. 99. 1890.

Stem square, slender, glabrous, branched or simple 1½°–2° high. Leaves sessile, erect, oblong or linear-oblong, obtusish at each end, 9″–15″ long, 1½″–3″ wide, 3-nerved, serrate toward the apex with appressed subulate teeth, glabrous or very nearly so beneath, but with a few scattered hairs above; flowers 1–4 together, short-pedicelled, magenta-red, 1′–1½′ broad; summit of the calyx-tube and its linear lobes with scattered subulate hairs; petals rounded, but obtusely pointed and aristate at the apex; anthers linear, minutely spurred on the back.

In sandy swamps, pine-barrens of New Jersey and Delaware to South Carolina and Georgia. Base of the stem with a coating of spongy tissue when growing in water. July–Aug.

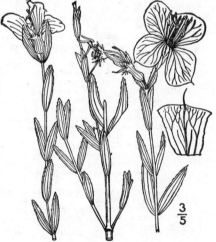

$\frac{3}{5}$

4. Rhexia ciliòsa Michx. Ciliate Meadow-Beauty.
Fig. 3012.

Rhexia petiolata Walt. Fl. Car. 130. 1788. (?)
Rhexia ciliosa Michx. Fl. Bor. Am. 1: 221. 1803.

Stem square, glabrous, simple or nearly so, 1°–2° high. Leaves ascending, ovate, very short-petioled, or sessile, acutish at the apex, mostly rounded at the base, 6″–10″ long, 4″–6″ wide, 3-nerved, glabrous or nearly so beneath, pubescent with a few scattered hairs above, the margins bristly-ciliate; cyme few-flowered; flowers very short-pedicelled, violet-purple, 1′–1½′ broad; calyx glabrous, or with a few hairs on its lobes; petals rounded, sometimes apiculate; anthers oblong, straight, back not spurred.

In swamps, Maryland to Florida and Louisiana. June–Aug.

Family 98. ONAGRÀCEAE Dumort. Anal.
Fam. 36. 1829.*
EVENING-PRIMROSE FAMILY.

Annual or perennial herbs, rarely shrubs, with alternate or opposite leaves, no stipules or mere glands in their places, and axillary spicate or racemose generally perfect regular or sometimes irregular flowers. Calyx-tube adnate to the ovary, often prolonged beyond it, the limb 2–6-lobed (usually 4-lobed). Petals 2–9 (usually 4), convolute in the bud, rarely none. Stamens usually as many or twice as many as the petals, inserted with them on the summit of the calyx-tube, or on the epigynous or perigynous disk. Ovary 1–6-celled (usually 4-celled); styles united; stigma capitate, discoid or 4-lobed; ovules ∞ in each cavity, generally anatropous. Fruit a capsule or small nut. Seeds mostly small; endosperm very little or none; embryo straight.

About forty genera and 400 species of wide geographic distribution, most abundant in America.

1. Floral whorls of 4 parts or more.
A. Fruit a many-seeded capsule, opening by valves or by a pore.
* Calyx-tube not prolonged beyond the ovary.
Seeds naked; calyx persistent on the fruit.
  Stamens 4, in 1 row.
    Leaves opposite; stems creeping or floating.
      Flowers sessile; petals none, or very small; leaves petioled; capsules short, the top flat.   1. *Isnardia.*
      Flowers long-stalked; petals conspicuous; leaves sessile; capsules elongated, curved, with a prominent 4-lobed stylopodium.   2. *Ludwigiantha.*
    Leaves alternate; stems erect or ascending.   3. *Ludwigia.*
  Stamens 8–12, in 2 rows.   4. *Jussiaea.*
Seeds furnished with a tuft of silky hairs; calyx deciduous.   5. *Chamaenerion.*
      ** Calyx-tube prolonged beyond the ovary; calyx deciduous.
Seeds furnished with a tuft of silky hairs.   6. *Epilobium.*
Seeds naked or sometimes tuberculate.
  Stamens equal in length.
    Stigma deeply 4-cleft, its segments linear.
      Ovules and seeds horizontal, in 2 or rarely more rows, prismatic-angled.   7. *Oenothera.*
      Ovules and seeds ascending, not angled.
        Buds erect; petals yellow; ovules and seeds in 2 rows.   8. *Raimannia.*
        Buds drooping; petals white or pink; ovules and seeds in 1 row.   9. *Anogra.*
    Stigmas entire or slightly 4-toothed.
      Calyx-tube longer than the ovary; stigma disk-like, entire.   16. *Galpinsia.*
      Calyx-tube shorter than the ovary; stigma disk-like, slightly 4-toothed.   17. *Meriolix.*
  Stamens unequal in length, the alternate longer.
    Ovules and seeds many, on slender funiculi; capsules club-shaped.
      Flowers yellow.   10. *Kneiffia.*
      Flowers white, pink or reddish.   11. *Hartmannia.*
    Ovules or seeds few, sessile, in 1 or 2 rows.
      Plants normally acaulescent.
        Capsules obtusely or retusely 4-angled; seeds furrowed along the raphe.
              12. *Pachylophus.*
        Capsules sharply 4-angled or winged; seeds with a tubercle at one end. 13. *Lavauxia.*
      Plants caulescent.
        Stems wiry, diffuse; capsules sharply 4-angled.   14. *Gaurella.*
        Stems stout, not diffuse; capsules 4-winged.   15. *Megapterium.*

* Text revised with the assistance of Dr. JOHN K. SMALL.

B. Fruit indehiscent, nut-like.
Calyx-tube obconic; filaments with scales at the base; ovary 4-celled.   18. *Gaura.*
Calyx-tube filiform; filaments unappendaged; ovary 1-celled.   19. *Stenosiphon.*
2. **Floral whorls of 2 parts.**   20. *Circaea.*

1. ISNÀRDIA L. Sp. Pl. 120. 1753.

Annual or perennial succulent herbs. Stems prostrate or decumbent, creeping or float-ing; leaves opposite, fleshy, narrowed into petioles which are slightly shorter than the blades. Flowers perefect, axillary, sessile, commonly apetalous. Calyx turbinate, its segments 4, shorter than the tube or slightly longer, persistent. Petals none, or 4, inconspicuous. Stamens 4; filaments very short; anthers ovoid or oblong. Ovary 4-celled, very short; styles often almost wanting; stigma 4-lobed; ovules numerous, in several rows. Capsule 4-angled, obovoid or turbinate, straight, flat at the apex, septicidal. Seeds numerous, often transversely wrinkled. [In honor of Antoine Dante Isnard, a French botanist, died 1724.]

About 4 species in Europe, North America, the West Indies and Mexico, the following typical.

1. Isnardia palústris L. Marsh Purslane. Fig. 3013.

Isnardia palustris L. Sp. Pl. 120. 1753.
Ludwigia palustris Ell. Bot. S. C. 1: 211. 1817.

Procumbent or floating, glabrous, rooting at the nodes, succulent. Stems branching, 4'-15' long; leaves opposite, oval, ovate or spatulate, acute or obtuse at the apex, 6"-12" long, narrowed into slender peti-oles; flowers axillary, solitary, sessile, about 1" broad; bractlets at base of the calyx usu-ally none; calyx-lobes triangular, acute; petals small, reddish or often wanting; cap-sule slightly longer than wide, about 1½" high, somewhat exceeding the calyx lobes.

In muddy ditches and swamps, Nova Scotia to Manitoba and Oregon, Florida, Louisiana, California and Mexico and the West Indies. Widely distributed in the Old World. Also called false or bastard loose-strife. Water-purslane. Phthisic-weed. June–Nov.

2. LUDWIGIÁNTHA Small, Bull. Torr. Club, 24: 178. 1897.

Annual or perennial fleshy herbs. Stems prostrate, creeping, usually little branched; leaves opposite, sessile, numerous. Flowers axillary, solitary, perfect, yellow, on slender bracted peduncles. Calyx narrowly obconic, its 4 segments narrow. Petals conspicuous, surpassing the calyx-segments. Stamens 4; filaments elongated, very slender; anthers ovoid. Ovary 4-celled; united styles filiform, elongated; stigma 4-lobed; ovules numerous. Capsules club-shaped, curved at the base at a right angle to the peduncle, about as long as the per-sistent calyx, crowned by a 4-lobed stylopodium. [Derivation as in Ludwigia.]

Two species of the southeastern United States, the first typical.

Peduncles much longer than the leaves; calyx-lobes linear-lanceolate.   1. *L. arcuata.*
Peduncles shorter than the leaves; calyx-lobes lanceolate.   2. *L. brevipes.*

1. Ludwigiantha arcuàta (Walt.) Small. Long-stalked Ludwigiantha. Fig. 3014.

Ludwigia arcuata Walt. Fl. Car. 89. 1788.
L. arcuata Small, Bull. Torr. Club 24: 178. 1897.

Creeping or floating, rooting at the nodes, glabrous or somewhat appressed-pubescent, little branched, 3'-12' long. Leaves opposite, oblanceolate, sessile, leathery, smooth, obtusish or acute at the apex, nar-rowed at the base, 6"-12" long; flowers 6"-10" broad on filiform, 2-bracted peduncles much longer than the leaves; calyx-lobes linear-lanceolate, acuminate, shorter than the obovate petals; filaments and fili-form style about 2" long; capsule club-shaped, some-what curved, glabrous, 4"-5" long, about equalling the calyx-lobes.

In swamps, Virginia to Florida. May–July.

2. Ludwigiantha brévipes Long, n. sp. Short-stalked Ludwigiantha. Fig. 3015.

Similar to the preceding species, creeping, glabrous. Leaves oblong-oblanceolate, acutish at the apex, narrowed to the sessile or nearly sessile base; flowers about ½' broad, on slender peduncles shorter than the leaves; calyx-lobes lanceolate to ovate-lanceolate; filaments about 1" long; filaments and stout style about 1" long; capsule a little longer than the calyx-lobes.

Moist sand, Long Beach Island, Ocean County, New Jersey. July–Aug.

3. LUDWÍGIA L. Sp. Pl. 118. 1753.

Perennial or annual herbs, with alternate usually entire leaves, and axillary or terminal, yellow or greenish flowers. Stems erect as ascending, sometimes angled, or winged. Calyx-tube cylindric, obpyramidal or top-shaped, not prolonged beyond the ovary, 3–5-lobed (usually 4-lobed), the lobes generally persistent. Petals usually 4, sometimes none, inserted under the margin of the disk. Stamens usually 4, inserted with the petals; filaments short. Ovary 4–5-celled; stigma capitate or 4-lobed. Capsule terete, ribbed or winged, crowned with the calyx-lobes, many-seeded, septicidally or irregularly dehiscent, or opening by an apical pore. [Named in honor of C. G. Ludwig, 1709–1773, Professor of Botany at Leipsic.]

About 25 species, natives of warm and temperate regions, most abundant in North America. Besides the following about 12 others occur in the southern and southwestern states. Type species: *Ludwigia alternifolia* L.

Flowers inconspicuous; petals none, or small, yellowish or greenish; valves of the capsule separating from the terminal disk.
Capsules subglobose or top-shaped.
  Bractlets at the base of the calyx minute, or none; capsule subglobose, finely pubescent.
  1. *L. sphaerocarpa.*
  Bractlets at the base of the calyx linear, about equalling the capsule; capsule top-shaped, glabrous.
  2. *L. polycarpa.*
Capsules cylindric or obpyramidal.
  Capsules cylindric.
  3. *L. glandulosa.*
  Capsules obpyramidal.
    Capsules as long as broad, or broader, the angles winged.
    4. *L. alata.*
    Capsules several times longer than broad, the angles obtuse.
    5. *L. linearis.*
Flowers showy, peduncled; petals large, bright yellow; capsules opening by an apical pore.
  Plants hirsute; capsules bristly pubescent.
  6. *L. hirtella.*
  Plants glabrous; capsules glabrous.
  7. *L. alternifolia.*

1. Ludwigia sphaerocàrpa Ell. Globe-fruited Ludwigia. Fig. 3016.

Ludwigia rudis Walt. Fl. Car. 89. 1788. ?

Ludwigia sphaerocarpa Ell. Bot. S. C. 1: 213. 1817.

Erect, branching, generally finely pubescent, stoloniferous, 2°–3° high, the lower part of the stem clothed with aerenchyma when growing in water. Leaves alternate, sessile, those of the stem and branches lanceolate, acute at both ends, 2'–4' long, scabrous and minutely denticulate, those of the stolons obovate; flowers solitary, sessile, greenish, about 1½''· broad; bractlets at base of calyx minute or none; calyx-lobes triangular-ovate, acute; petals commonly none; capsule subglobose, about 2'' high, scarcely longer than the calyx-lobes, finely pubescent.

In swamps, eastern Massachusetts to southern New York and Florida, west to Louisiana. July–Sept.

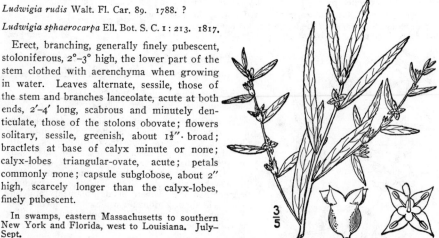

2. Ludwigia polycàrpa Short & Peter. Many-fruited Ludwigia. Fig. 3017.

Ludwigia polycarpa Short. & Peter, Translv. Journ. Med. **8**: 581. 1835.

Erect, glabrous, branching, 1°–3° high, producing stolons from the base. Leaves alternate, sessile, narrowly lanceolate, acute at each end, 2′–4′ long, rough-margined, those of the stolons broader and spatulate; bractlets at base of the calyx linear, 1½″–2″ long, usually persistent; flowers sessile, about 1½″ broad, greenish; calyxlobes triangular-lanceolate, acute, sometimes finely serrulate; petals minute, greenish; capsule glabrous, somewhat top-shaped but slightly 4-sided, about 2½″ high, often twice the length of the calyx-lobes, glabrous, at lenght dehiscent.

In swamps, Connecticut to Ontario, Minnesota, Tennessee, Nebraska and Kansas. July–Oct. False loosestrife.

3. Ludwigia glandulòsa Walt. Cylindric-fruited Ludwigia. Fig. 3018.

Ludwigia glandulosa Walt. Fl. Car. 88. 1788.

Jussiaea brachycarpa Lam. Encycl. **3**: 331. 1789.

L. cylindrica Ell. Bot. S. C. & Ga. **1**: 213. 1817.

Erect, glabrous, much branched, 1°–3° high. Leaves alternate, sessile or narrowed into a short petiole, oblong-lanceolate, acute at each end, 2′–4′ long; flowers axillary, solitary, or rarely 2 together, greenish, about 1″ broad; bractlets at base of calyx minute or none; calyx-lobes triangular-ovate, acute; petals none; capsule cylindric, 4-grooved, 3″–4″ long, glabrous, 4–5 times as long as the calyx-lobes, at length dehiscent.

In swamps, Virginia to southern Illinois, Missouri, Arkansas, Florida and Texas. July–Sept.

4. Ludwigia alàta Ell. Wing-stemmed Ludwigia. Fig. 3019.

Ludwigia alata Ell. Bot. S. C. & Ga. **1**: 212. 1817.

Perennial, slender, glabrous. Stems erect, 1°–3° tall, simple or branched, winged, often stoloniferous; leaves linear-oblanceolate to linear-lanceolate, or sometimes nearly linear, 1′–4′ long, acute or acutish, sessile or short-petioled, those of the stolons suborbicular or spatulate; flowers inconspicuous, about 2″ broad, white or greenish; spikes 2′–12′ long; calyx glabrous, its tube turbinate, its segments triangular-ovate, acute or acuminate; petals none; capsules broadly obpyramidal, 1½″–2″ high, sessile, the angles winged; seeds oval in outline, about ¼″ long, faintly pitted.

In marshes, North Carolina to Florida. Recorded from Missouri and Louisiana. June–Sept.

5. Ludwigia lineàris Walt. Linear-leaved Ludwigia. Fig. 3020.

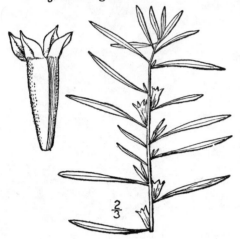

Ludwigia linearis Walt. Fl. Car. 89. 1788.

Erect, branching, glabrous, 1°–2½° high, often stoloniferous at the base and the lower part of the stem clothed with aerenchyma. Leaves alternate, those of the stem and branches narrowly linear, sessile, acute at each end, 1'–2' long, about 1'' wide, the margins roughish, those of the stolons obovate; flowers axillary, solitary, sessile, about 2'' broad; bractlets at the base of the calyx minute or none; calyx-lobes triangular-ovate, acute, slightly shorter than the yellowish petals; capsule narrowly obpyramidal, 4-sided, narrowed at the base, 3''–4'' long, glabrous, 3–5 times as long as the calyx-lobes, several times longer than broad, at length dehiscent.

In swamps, pine-barrens of New Jersey to Florida, west to Texas. July–Sept.

6. Ludwigia hirtélla Raf. Hairy Ludwigia. Fig. 3021.

Ludwigia hirtella Raf. Med. Rep. (II.) 5: 358. 1808.

Erect, branching, hirsute-pubescent, 1°–2° high, the clustered roots spindle-shaped. Leaves alternate, oblong-lanceolate or ovate-lanceolate, sessile, obtuse or acutish at the apex, rounded at the base, 1'–1½' long; pedicels 2-bracteolate; flowers axillary, solitary, peduncled, 6''–10'' broad; calyx-lobes ovate-lanceolate, acute, somewhat shorter than the yellow petals; capsules cubic with a rounded base, hirsute, about 2½'' high, shorter than the calyx-lobes, opening by an apical pore.

In swamps, pine-barrens of New Jersey to Florida, Arkansas and Texas. June–Sept.

7. Ludwigia alternifòlia L. Seed-box. Rattle-box. Fig. 3022.

Ludwigia alternifolia L. Sp. Pl. 118. 1753.

Ludwigia alternifolia linearifolia Britton, Bull. Torr. Club 17: 315. 1890.

Erect, branching, glabrous or finely pubescent, 2°–3½° high. Leaves alternate, short-petioled, lanceolate to linear-lanceolate, acute or acuminate at the apex, narrowed at the base, 2'–4½' long; flowers axillary, short peduncled, solitary, 6''–8'' broad; peduncles 2-bracted above the middle; calyx-lobes ovate to ovate-lanceolate, acuminate, about equalling the yellow petals which fall away when the plant is shocked; capsules glabrous, cubic with a rounded base, slightly wing-angled, about 2½'' high, opening by a pore at the base of the style and finally loculicidally dehiscent.

In swamps, New Hampshire to northern New York, Ontario, Michigan, Kansas, Florida and Texas. Roots often tuberous. June–Sept.

4. JUSSIAÈA L. Sp. Pl. 388. 1753.

Perennial herbs, with alternate, usually entire leaves, and white or yellow, axillary, solitary flowers. Peduncles mostly 2-bracted at the summit. Calyx-tube elongated, cylindric or prismatic, adnate to the ovary but not prolonged beyond it, the limb 4–6-lobed, the lobes acute, persistent. Petals 4–6 (rarely more), inserted under the margin of the disk. Stamens 8–12, in 2 rows, inserted with the petals; filaments short. Ovary 4–6-celled; stigma 4–6-lobed; ovules ∞. Capsule linear, oblong or club-shaped, angular or ribbed, septicidally dehiscent, crowned with the calyx-lobes. Seeds numerous. [In honor of Bernard de Jussieu, 1699–1777, founder of the Natural System of Botany.]

About 35 species, natives of warm and temperate regions most abundant in America. Besides the following about 7 others occur in the Southern States. Type species: *Jussiaea repens* L.

Creeping or floating; petals 5; pod cylindric.   1. *J. diffusa.*
Erect; petals 4; pod club-shaped, 4-sided.   2. *J. decurrens.*

1. Jussiaea diffùsa Forskal. Floating or Creeping Primrose-Willow. Fig. 3023.

J. diffusa Forskal, Fl. AEgypt. Arab. 210. 1775.
Jussiaea repens Sw. Obs. 172. 1791. Not L.

Stem creeping or floating, freely rooting from the nodes, glabrous, 1°–3° long. Leaves oval, oval-lanceolate or obovate, slender-petioled, glabrous, veiny, obtuse or acute at the apex, narrowed at the base, entire, 1′–4′ long; peduncles slender; flowers yellow, 6″–12″ broad; calyx-lobes 5, lanceolate, acute, shorter than the 5 obovate usually emarginate petals; stamens 10; capsule cylindric, tapering at the base, ridged, glabrous, 1′–1½′ long, 1½″–2″ thick; seeds in 1 row in each cell.

In ponds, Kentucky and Illinois to Kansas, Florida and Texas. Also in tropical America and Asia. Clove-strip. June–Aug.

½

2. Jussiaea decúrrens (Walt.) DC. Upright Primrose-Willow. Fig. 3024.

Ludwigia decurrens Walt. Fl. Car. 89. 1788.
Jussiaea decurrens DC. Prodr. 3: 56. 1828.

Erect, stem angled, branching, glabrous, 1°–2° high. Leaves lanceolate, acute or acuminate at the apex, narrowed at the base and decurrent on the stem, entire, 1′–4′ long; flowers very short-peduncled, yellow, 4″–6″ broad; calyx-lobes 4, ovate-lanceolate, acute, about equalling the 4 obovate petals; stamens 8; capsule club-shaped, 2–3 times as long as the peduncle, 4-sided, the angles somewhat winged; seeds in several rows in each cell.

In swamps, Maryland to Georgia and Florida, Illinois, Arkansas and Texas. July–Sept.

½

5. CHAMAENÈRION [Tourn.] Adans. Fam. Pl. 2: 85. 1763.

Showy perennial herbs, with tufted stems which are often woody at the base. Leaves alternate, leathery, entire; flowers perfect, irregular, showy, white or purple, in terminal racemes; calyx-tube not prolonged beyond the ovary, narrow, the 4 calyx-segments deciduous; petals 4, entire, broadest above the middle, spreading; stamens 8, declined; filaments dilated at the base; anthers oblong; ovary 4-celled; united styles filiform; stigmas 4-cleft; ovules numerous, in 2 rows, ascending. Capsule 4-celled, obtusely 4-angled, elongated, opening loculicidally. Seeds numerous, with a tuft of hairs. [Greek, ground rose-bay.]

About 4 species, chiefly in the north temperate zone. Type species: *Epilobium angustifolium* L.

Bracts small; lateral nerves of the leaves confluent in marginal loops; style pubescent at the base.   1. *C. angustifolium.*
Bracts leaf-like; lateral nerves of the leaves obsolete; style glabrous.   2. *C. latifolium.*

1. Chamaenerion angustifòlium (L.) Scop. Great or Spiked Willow-herb. Fire-weed. Fig. 3025.

Epilobium angustifolium L. Sp. Pl. 347. 1753.
C. angustifolium Scop. Fl. Carn. Ed. 2, 1 : 271. 1772.
Epilobium spicatum Lam. Fl. Fr. 3 : 482. 1778.

Erect, rather stout, simple or branched, glabrous or often finely pubescent above, 2°–8° high. Leaves alternate, very short-petioled, lanceolate, entire or denticulate, 2′–6′ long, 4″–12″ wide, pale beneath, acute at the apex, narrowed at the base, thin, the lateral veins confluent in marginal loops; flowers 8″–15″ broad, purple, or sometimes white, in elongated terminal spike-like racemes; bracts mostly shorter than the pedicels; petals entire; style pubescent at the base; stigma 4-lobed; capsules 2′–3′ long, about 1½″ thick, finely canescent, at least when young; seeds about ½″ long, smooth, or nearly so, the coma long, whitish.

In dry soil, Greenland to Alaska, North Carolina, Indiana, Kansas; the Rocky Mountains to Arizona; Pacific Coast to California. Europe and Asia. Often abundant after forest fires. French-, bay- or Persian-willow. Rose-bay. Fire-top. Burnt weed. Purple rocket. French or bay willow-herb. Indian wickup. Herb-wickopy. Flowering or blooming willow. Pigweed. Blooming sally (i. e., Salix). Sally-bloom. June–Sept.

2. Chamaenerion latifòlium (L.) Sweet. Broad-leaved Willow-herb. Fig. 3026.

Epilobium latifolium L. Sp Pl. 347. 1753.
C. latifolium Sweet, Hort. Brit. Ed. 2, 198. 1830.

Erect, usually branching, glabrate below, often quite canescent above, 6′–18′ high. Leaves mostly sessile, 1′–2′ long, 2″–6″ wide, denticulate or entire, lanceolate or ovate-lanceolate, acutish at both ends, thick, those of the branches opposite, the veins inconspicuous; flowers purple, 1′–2′ broad, in mainly short leafy-bracted racemes; petals entire; styles glabrous; stigma 4-lobed; capsules ½′–1½′ long, about 1½″ thick, canescent; seeds about 1″ long, nearly smooth; coma elongated, whitish.

Moist ground, Newfoundland to Alaska, south to Quebec, Colorado and Oregon. Also in Europe and Asia. June–Aug.

6. EPILÒBIUM L. Sp. Pl. 347. 1753.

Herbs, or sometimes shrubby plants, with alternate or opposite leaves, and axillary or terminal, solitary, spicate or racemose flowers. Calyx-tube linear, produced beyond the ovary, the limb 4-parted, deciduous. Petals 4, mostly obovate or obcordate. Stamens 8; anthers oblong or linear, short. Ovary 4-celled; united styles slender or filiform; stigma club-shaped or 4-lobed; ovules numerous. Capsule narrow, elongated, 4-sided, 4-celled, loculicidally dehiscent by 4 valves. Seeds small, numerous, with a tuft of hairs (coma) at the summit. [Greek, upon a pod, flower and pod appearing together.]

About 75 species, of wide geographic distribution, most abundant in temperate regions. Besides the following, about 35 others occur in the western and northwestern parts of North America. Type species: *Epilobium hirsutum* L.

Stigma deeply 4-lobed; flowers large.	1. *E. hirsutum.*
Stigma entire, or merely notched.	
Seeds smooth or nearly so; arctic or alpine species.	
Flowers white; leaves usually denticulate.	2. *E. alpinum.*
Flowers violet; leaves mostly entire.	3. *E. anagallidifolium.*
Seeds papillose.	
Leaves linear or lanceolate, entire or nearly so.	
Plants crisp-pubescent or canescent.	
Leaves sessile, not revolute-margined.	4. *E. palustre.*
Leaves petioled, very narrow, acute, revolute-margined.	5. *E. lineare.*
Plants glandular-pubescent, at least above.	

Densely pubescent throughout; leaves sessile.   6. *E. strictum.*
Glandular-pubescent above; leaves petioled.   7. *E. paniculatum.*
Leaves lanceolate or ovate, serrate.
  Leaves lanceolate, acute or acuminate; stems solitary.
    Seeds obconic, beakless; coma reddish; leaves narrowly lanceolate.
                                        8. *E. coloratum.*
    Seeds ellipsoid, short-beaked; coma white; leaves oblong-lanceolate to ovate-lanceolate.
                                      9. *E. adenocaulon.*
  Leaves ovate, thin, obtuse, or the upper acutish; stems tufted.   10. *E. Hornemanni.*

1. Epilobium hirsùtum L.   Great Hairy Willow-herb. Fig. 3027.

Epilobium hirsutum L. Sp. Pl. 347. 1753.

Stout, branched, 2°–4° high, softly hirsute-pubescent, spreading by subterranean shoots. Leaves lanceolate or oblong-lanceolate, usually opposite, sessile and often clasping at the base, acute at the apex, sharply serrulate, 1′–3′ long, 4″–6″ wide, thin, pubescent on both sides; flowers axillary, erect, rose-purple, about 1′ broad; petals notched, pubescent at the base within; stigma deeply 4-lobed; capsules stalked, 2′–3′ long, about 1″ thick, pubescent; seeds about ½″ long, smooth; coma whitish.

In waste places, Maine to central New York, Ontario, and in ballast about the sea-ports. Adventive or naturalized from Europe. English names, codlins-and-cream, fiddle-grass. Apple-, gooseberry- or cherry-pie [smell]. June–Sept.

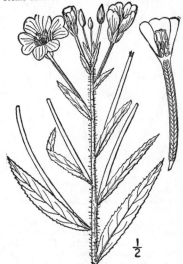

$\frac{1}{2}$

$\frac{1}{2}$

2. Epilobium alpìnum L.   Alpine Willow-herb. Fig. 3028

Epilobium alpinum L. Sp. Pl. 348. 1753.
E. lactiflorum Haussk. Oest. Bot. Zeit. 29: 89. 1879.

Slender, weak, tufted, glabrous or nearly so, 3′–12′ high. Leaves thin, pale, petioled, opposite, or the upper alternate, denticulate or entire, obtuse or obtusish at the apex, narrowed at the base, 6″–20″ long, 2″–8″ wide; flowers few, axillary, nearly erect, white or pink, 2″–3″ broad, petals notched; stigma nearly entire; capsules slender-stalked, 1′–2′ long, about ½″ thick, glabrous; seeds smooth, narrowed into a beak; coma whitish.

Labrador to Alaska, south to the White Mountains of New Hampshire, Colorado, Utah and Oregon. Also in Europe and Asia. Summer.

3. Epilobium anagallidifòlium Lam.   Pimpernel Willow-herb. Fig. 3029.

Epilobium anagallidifolium Lam. Encycl. 2: 376. 1786.

Low, usually tufted, 2′–8′ high, resembling the preceding species but generally smaller. Stems commonly pubescent in lines and nodding at the apex; leaves oblong or narrowly ovate, entire or nearly so, obtuse at the apex, narrowed at the base into a short petiole, 5″–10″ long, 1½″–2½″ wide; flowers few, axillary, clustered at the apex, pink or violet-purple, nodding, about 2½″ broad; stigma entire; capsule slender-peduncled, glabrous, purplish, about 1′ long, ½″ wide; seeds smooth, short-beaked, about ½″ long; coma dingy-white.

Labrador, Quebec, and through arctic America to Alaska, south in the Rocky Mountains to Nevada. Recorded from the mountains of New York and New England. Also in Europe and Asia. Summer.

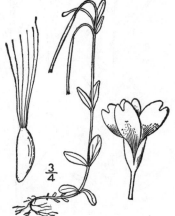

$\frac{3}{4}$

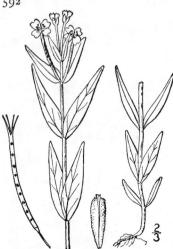

4. Epilobium palústre L.   Marsh or Swamp Willow-herb. Fig. 3030.

Epilobium palustre L. Sp. Pl. 348. 1753.
Epilobium oliganthum Michx. Fl. Bor. Am. 1: 223. 1803.

Erect or decumbent, slender, usually simple, 6'–18' high, perennial by subterranean shoots or stoloniferous, canescent above with incurved hairs, the stem terete. Leaves mostly opposite, sessile, oblong, or lanceolate-oblong, the lower often obtuse or subtruncate at the apex, 1'–2½' long, 1''–2½'' wide, erect or ascending, distinctly veined; flowers few in the upper axils, pink or whitish, usually nodding at first, 2''–3'' broad; stigma entire or nearly so; fruiting peduncles slender; capsules 1'–2' long, slightly more than ½'' thick, canescent; seeds about ½'' long, a little papillose, translucent, the apex scarcely narrowed; coma pale.

In bogs, Newfoundland to Alaska, south to Massachusetts, Ontario, Colorado and Washington. Also in Europe and Asia. Consists of several races differing in size and texture of leaves. Wickup. Summer.

5. Epilobium lineàre Muhl.   Linear-leaved Willow-herb. Fig. 3031.

Epilobium lineare Muhl. Cat. 39. 1813.
E. densum Raf. in Desv. Journ. Bot. 2: 271. 1814.
Epilobium palustre var. *lineare* A Gray, Man. Ed. 2, 130. 1856.

Slender, erect, canescent throughout with incurved hairs, 1°–2° high, at length much branched, perennial by subterranean shoots. Leaves linear or linear-lanceolate, mostly short-petioled, opposite or alternate, erect or ascending, acute at both ends, entire or very nearly so, 1'–2' long, ½''–2'' wide, the veins obscure, the margins revolute; flowers few or numerous in the upper axils, erect, pink or whitish, 2''–4'' broad; stigma entire or slightly notched; pedicels mostly slender; capsules about 2' long, finely canescent; seeds less than 1'' long, slightly papillose, the coma dingy.

In swamps, New Brunswick to Delaware, west to British Columbia, West Virginia, Kansas and Colorado. July–Sept. Sometimes produces bulblets near the base of the stem.

6. Epilobium stríctum Muhl.   Downy or Soft Willow-herb. Fig. 3032.

Epilobium strictum Muhl. Cat. 39. 1813

Epilobium molle Torr. Fl. U. S. 1: 393. 1824. Not Lam. 1805.

Erect, usually much branched, 1°–3° high, densely pubescent with whitish somewhat spreading hairs, perennial by subterranean shoots. Leaves sessile, ascending, broader than those of the preceding species, short-lanceolate, obtuse or obtusish, 9''–20'' long, 2''–4'' wide, alternate or opposite, mostly entire, evidently veined; flowers in the upper axils, pink or whitish, about 2'' broad; stigma entire or nearly so; capsules 2''–3'' long, nearly 1'' thick, short-peduncled, canescent; seeds obconic, papillose; coma dingy.

Bogs, Quebec to Athabasca, Virginia, Illinois and Minnesota. July–Sept.

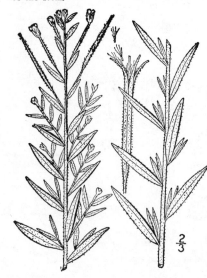

7. Epilobium paniculàtum Nutt.   Panicled Willow-herb.   Fig. 3033.

E. paniculatum Nutt.; T. & G. Fl. N. A. 1: 490. 1840.

Annual, slender, 1°–2° tall, loosely branched, glabrous below, glandular-pubescent above, the stem terete. Leaves alternate, varying from linear to linear-lanceolate, 1′–3′ long, acute, denticulate or nearly entire, attenuate into slender winged petioles, often involutely folded; pedicels subtended by narrow bracts or bearing these some distance from their bases; calyx often purple, its tube funnelform, 1″– 1½″ long, shorter than the lanceolate segments; petals cuneate, notched, 3″–4″ long, violet; capsules ascending, linear-fusiform, 10″–15″ long, curved; seeds obovoid, 1″ long, black, slightly papillose.

Lake Huron (according to Macoun); South Dakota to Alberta, to British Columbia, Colorado, Arizona and California. Summer.

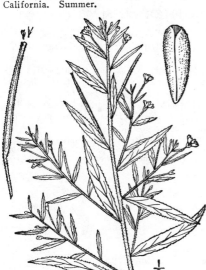

8. Epilobium coloràtum Muhl.   Purple-leaved or -veined Willow-herb.   Fig. 3034.

Epilobium coloratum Muhl.; Willd. Enum. 1: 411. 1809.

Erect, much branched, bushy, 1°–3° high, more or less canescent above, with incurved hairs often arranged in lines, glabrate below. Stem and leaves often purplish; leaves generally slender-petioled but sometimes sessile, narrowly lanceolate, acute or acuminate at the apex, narrowed at the base, sharply serrulate or denticulate, 2′–6′ long, 3″–8″ wide; flowers numerous in the axils, pink or white, 2″–3″ broad, generally nodding; stigma entire or merely notched; capsules short-peduncled, finely pubescent, 1′–2′ long, about 1″ thick; seeds obconic-fusiform, beakless, papillose, less than 1″ long; coma reddish-brown.

In low grounds, Maine to Ontario, Wisconsin, Nebraska, South Carolina, Tennessee and Kansas. Ascends to 2000 ft. in Virginia. Autumn basal shoots forming rosettes of leaves, as in the following species. July–Sept.

9. Epilobium adenocàulon Haussk.   Northern Willow-herb.   Fig. 3035.

Epilobium glandulosum Lehm. in Hook. Fl. Bor Am. 1: 206. 1833?

Epilobium adenocaulon Haussk. Oest. Bot. Zeit. 29: 119. 1879.

Closely resembling the preceding species, but the inflorescence and capsules glandular-pubescent. Leaves lanceolate or ovate-lanceolate, obtusish or sometimes acute, sparingly serrulate or denticulate, seldom over 2½′ long; flowers usually nodding at first; seeds obovoid, abruptly short-beaked, about ½″ long, papillose; coma white.

In moist grounds, Newfoundland to British Columbia, Massachusetts, Delaware, North Carolina, Iowa, New Mexico and California. Ascends to 4000 ft. in the Adirondacks. July–Sept.

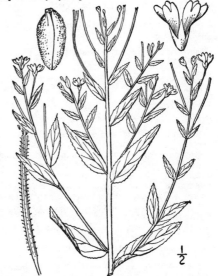

$\frac{2}{3}$

10. Epilobium Hornemánni Reichenb. Hornemann's Willow-herb. Fig. 3036.

E. Hornemanni Reichenb. Icon. Crit. **2** : 73. 1824.

E. alpinum var. *majus* A. Gray, Man. Ed. 5, 177. 1867.

Erect, 6'–12' high, simple or nearly so, slightly pubescent above, otherwise glabrous. Leaves short-petioled, ovate or elliptic, acutish or obtuse at the apex, narrowed or rounded at the base, entire or rather remotely denticulate, thin, 6"–20" long, 4"–10" wide; flowers few in the upper axils, purple or violet, 3"–3½" broad; stigma entire; capsules 1'–2½' long, nearly glabrous, slender-pedicelled; seeds about ½" long, papillose, nearly beakless; coma dingy-white.

Moist places, Labrador to Maine, New Hampshire, British Columbia, south in the Rocky Mountains to Colorado and to California. Also in Europe and Asia. Summer.

7. OENOTHÈRA L. Sp. Pl. 346. 1753.

[Onagra Adans. Fam. Pl. **2** : 85. 1763.]

Annual or biennial caulescent herbs, with mostly erect stems. Leaves alternate, undulate or toothed, sessile or short-petioled; buds erect. Flowers yellow, nocturnal, in terminal bracted spikes. Calyx-tube elongated, terete, gradually enlarged at the throat; calyx-segments narrow, the tips free in the bud. Petals 4, spreading. Stamens 8, equal in length; filaments filiform; anthers linear. Ovary 4-celled; united styles filiform; stigma 4-cleft; ovules numerous, in 2 or more rows, horizontal. Capsule 4-celled, 4-angled, more or less tapering, opening loculicidally. Seeds prismatic-angled, in 2 or more rows, horizontal. [Greek, wine-scenting, the roots being once used for that purpose.]

About 15 species, composed of many races, chiefly North American. The later flowers are often much smaller than the earlier ones on the same plant. The generic name *Onagra* was used for these species in our first edition, but it is properly a synonym of *Oenothera*. Type species: *Oenothèra biennis* L.

Flowers small; petals linear, 1"–2" broad.   1. *O. cruciata.*
Flowers large; petals ½'–2' broad.
    Plants and their capsules pubescent.
        Upper bracts shorter than the pods, deciduous.   2. *O. biennis.*
        Upper bracts as long as or longer than the pods, persistent.
            Puberulent and with long thick-based hairs.   3. *O. muricata.*
            Densely velvety-pubescent.   4. *O. Oakesiana.*
    Plants and their capsules wholly glabrous.   5. *O. argillicola.*

1. Oenothera cruciàta Nutt. Small-flowered Evening-Primrose. Fig. 3037.

Oenothera cruciata Nutt.; G. Don, Gen. Hist. **2** : 686. 1832.

Oenothera biennis var. *cruciata* T. & G. Fl. N. A. **1** : 492. 1840.

Onagra biennis cruciata Britton, Mem. Torr. Club **5** : 233. 1894.

Onagra cruciata Small, Bull. Torr. Club **23** : 169. 1896.

Annual, glabrate or sparingly villous. Stem erect, 2°–4° tall, usually simple, reddish or purple; leaves narrowly oblong or oblanceolate (the upper ones often lanceolate), 1½'–4' long, acute, serrate-denticulate, the lower ones slender-petioled, the uppermost nearly sessile; flowers small, yellow; spikes 4'–12' long, leafy-bracted. calyx-tube slender, ¾'–1' long, sparingly villous; calyx-segments linear-lanceolate, shorter than the tube; petals linear, 3"–6" long, ½"–2" broad, acutish; capsules 1'–1¼' long, gradually narrowed from the base, villous; seeds prismatic-angled, 1" long.

Sandy soil, Maine to New York and Massachusetts. Ascends to 2000 ft. in the Adirondacks. Aug.–Oct.

$\frac{3}{5}$

2. Oenothera biénnis L. Common Evening-Primrose. Night Willow-herb.
Fig. 3038.

Oenothera biennis L. Sp. Pl. 346. 1753.

Erect, generally stout, biennial, simple and wand-like or branched, 1°–6° high, more or less hirsute-pubescent, rarely glabrate. Leaves lanceolate to ovate-lanceolate, acute or acuminate, narrowed and sessile at the base or the lowest petioled, repand-denticulate, 1'–6' long; flowers opening in the evening, 1'–2½' broad; calyx-tube slender, much longer than the ovary, the lobes linear, contiguous at the base, reflexed; capsules oblong, narrowed above, erect, pubescent, ¾'–1½' long, 2½''–3'' thick, nearly terete, longer than the deciduous upper bracts.

Usually in dry soil, Labrador to Florida, Minnesota, Arkansas and Texas. Large rampion. Tree-primrose. Four-o-clock. Coffee- or fever-plant. King's-cure-all. Scurvish or scabish. June–Oct.

Oenothera grandiflòra Ait., of the Gulf States, is taller and has much larger flowers, up to 4' broad. Large-flowered races of the preceding species have been mistaken for it.

Oenothera Lamarckiàna Ser., a large-flowered plant, in some features intermediate between *O. biennis* and *O. grandiflora*, not definitely known in the wild state, but frequently cultivated, apparently originated in Old World gardens over one hundred years ago.

3. Oenothera muricàta L. Northern Evening-Primrose. Fig. 3039.

Oenothera muricata L. Syst. Ed. 12, 263. 1767.

Similar to the preceding species, usually simple, 3° high or less, the stem puberulent and with longer hairs enlarged at the base. Leaves lanceolate, mostly narrower than those of *O. biennis*, entire, or slightly repand-denticulate; flowers 1'–2' broad; capsules hirsute, narrowly oblong-cylindric, about 1' long, shorter than the persistent bracts.

Sandy and gravelly soil, Newfoundland to southeastern New York and New Jersey. July–Sept.

4. Oenothera Oakesiàna Robbins.   Oakes' Evening-Primrose.   Fig. 3040.

Oenothera biennis var. *Oakesiana* A. Gray, Man. Ed. 5, 178. 1867.
Oenothera Oakesiana Robbins; S. Wats. Bibl. Index I: 383. 1878.
Onagra Oakesiana Britton, Mem. Torr. Club 5: 233. 1894.

Resembling the two preceding species, usually annual, dull green, pubescent with appressed velvety hairs. Stem 1°–4° tall, mostly simple; leaves narrow, the basal narrowly oblanceolate, 3′–10′ long, the cauline lanceolate or linear-lanceolate, all acute, distantly dentate, sessile or short-petioled; flowers yellow, nocturnal, 1′–1½′ broad; spikes 4′–20′ long; calyx villous, its tube about 1′ long, its segments linear-lanceolate, one-half as long as the tube, rather prominently appendaged below the tip; petals obovate, ½′–¾′ long; capsule linear-pyramidal, gradually narrowed to the summit, 1¼′–1½′ long, 4-sided, curved; seeds prismatic. about 1″ long, the faces reticulated.

Sandy soil, Massachusetts to Long Island.   Summer.

Oenothera strigòsa Rydb. (*O. canovirens* Steele), of the Central States, ranging eastward to Illinois; resembles *O. Oakesiana* but has some long hairs and unappendaged calyx-segments. It may not be distinct from *O. biennis.*

5. Oenothera argillícola Mackenzie.   Narrow-leaved Evening-Primrose.   Fig. 3041.

Oe. argillicola Mackenzie, Torreya 4: 56. 1904.

Onagra argillicola Mackenzie, Torreya 4: 57. 1904.

Stems several from the same root, finely puberulent, 3°–4½° high. Rosette-leaves oblanceolate, 2½′–6′ long, 8″ wide or less, acute, sinuate, tapering into long petioles; stem-leaves linear-lanceolate, 2½′–3½′ long, glabrous, or slightly puberulent; calyx-tube very slender, glabrous, 1¼′–1¾′ long; petals obcordate, crenulate, 1¼′–1¾′ long; capsules glabrous, gradually tapering upward from the base, about 1′ long.

In rocky soil, Virginia and West Virginia.   July–Sept.

8. RAIMÁNNIA Rose, Contr. Nat. Herb. 8: 330.   1905.

Usually low annual biennial or perennial caulescent herbs, with prostrate or erect stems. Leaves alternate, sinuate or pinnatifid. Flowers perfect, yellow, axillary, or sometimes in terminal spikes, nocturnal; buds erect. Calyx-tube elongated, sometimes filiform, terete; calyx-segments 4, finally reflexed, deciduous. Petals 4, spreading. Stamens 8, equal in length; filaments filiform; anthers linear. Ovary 4-celled, elongated; united styles filiform; stigma deeply 4-cleft; ovules numerous, in 2 rows, ascending. Capsules usually narrowly cylindric, sometimes slightly tapering, spreading or ascending, obtusely 4-angled, loculicidal. Seeds numerous, in 2 rows, terete, crowned by a tubercle. [Name in honor of Rud. Raimann, a monographer of this family.]

About 20 species, in North and South America.   Type species: *Raimannia laciniata* (Hill) Rose.

Flowers axillary.
   Silvery-pubescent with appressed or ascending hairs; seeds striate.   **1.** *R. humifusa.*
   Glabrous or sparingly hirsute-pubescent; seeds pitted.   **2.** *R. laciniata.*
Flowers in terminal bracted spikes.   **3.** *R. rhombipetala.*

1. Raimannia humifùsa (Nutt.) Rose.   Seaside Evening-Primrose.   Fig. 3042.

Oenothera humifusa Nutt. Gen. 1 : 245. 1818.

Oenothera sinuata var. *humifusa* T. & G. Fl. N. A. 1 : 494. 1840.

Raimannia humifusa Rose, Contr. Nat. Herb. 8 : 331. 1905.

Spreading and decumbent or ascending, branched from the base and usually also above, silvery-pubescent with white appressed or ascending hairs; stems 8′–18′ long. Leaves lanceolate to oblanceolate, sessile or narrowed into a petiole, acutish or sometimes obtuse at the apex, ½′–2′ long, repand-denticulate, the lower pinnatifid; flowers axillary, yellow, nocturnal, 6″–15″ broad; calyx-lobes linear, obtusish, shorter than the tube, somewhat spreading; capsule linear, 6″–12″ long, about 1½″ thick, very pubescent; seeds striate longitudinally.

On sea-beaches, New Jersey to Florida. Bermuda. June–Sept.

2. Raimannia laciniàta (Hill) Rose.   Cut-leaved Evening-Primrose.   Fig. 3043.

Oenothera lacıniata Hill. Veg. Syst. 12 : 64. 1767.
Oenothera sinuata L. Mant. 2 : 228. 1771.
Oe. minima Pursh, Fl. Am. Sept. 262. *pl. 15.* 1814.
R. laciniata Rose, Contr. Nat. Herb. 8 : 330. 1905.

Decumbent or ascending, simple or sometimes branched, 4′–2½° high, glabrous or sparingly hirsute-pubescent. Leaves sessile or the lower petioled, oval-lanceolate or oblanceolate, acute or obtusish at the apex, sinuate-dentate or often pinnatifid, 1′–2′ long; flowers axillary (or on small plants sometimes solitary and terminal), 6″–2′ broad; calyx-lobes linear-lanceolate, reflexed, much shorter than the slender tube; capsule linear, 1′–1½′ long, about 1″ thick, more or less pubescent, straight or curved upward; seeds strongly pitted.

In sandy dry soil, southern New Jersey to Pennsylvania, Illinois and South Dakota, Florida, Texas and Mexico, extending into South America. Bermuda. May–June. Naturalized in Vermont.

Raimannia grándis (Britton) Rose, with large flowers, found from Missouri and Kansas to Texas, is probably a race of this species.

3. Raimannia rhombipétala (Nutt.) Rose.   Rhombic Evening-Primrose.   Fig. 3044.

Oenothera rhombipetala Nutt.; T. & G. Fl. N. A. 1 : 493. 1840.

R. rhombipetala Rose, Contr. Nat. Herb. 8 : 330. 1905.

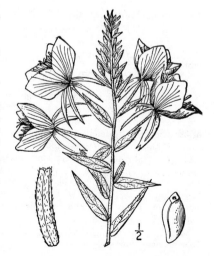

Erect, simple or rarely branched, finely and densely appressed pubescent, 2°–4° high. Leaves linear-lanceolate, sessile and rounded at the base or the lower narrowed into petioles, acuminate at the apex, remotely denticulate, 2′–4′ long; flowers in terminal, leafy-bracted spikes, yellow, nocturnal, 1′–2′ broad. calyx-lobes linear, reflexed, canescent, shorter than the very slender tube; petals rhombic-obovate; capsule columnar, curved upward, pubescent, 6″–8″ long, about 1″ thick; seeds obovoid, tuberculate at the top.

On prairies, Minnesota to Indiana, Nebraska and Texas. June–July.

9. ÁNOGRA Spach, Ann. Sci. Nat. (II.) 4: 164. 1835.

Low caulescent herbs. Stems often clothed with a papery bark. Leaves alternate, entire or usually pinnatifid. Buds drooping; flowers perfect, white or pink, usually axillary, diurnal. Calyx-tube elongated, gradually enlarged upward, calyx-segments narrow, finally reflexed, the acute tips free or united in the bud. Stamens 8, equal in length; filaments filiform; anthers linear. Ovary elongated, 4-celled; united styles filiform; stigma deeply 4-cleft; ovules numerous, in 1 row, ascending. Capsules elongated, spreading or ascending, 4-angled, loculicidal. Seeds ascending, in 1 row, terete. [Anagram of *Onagra*.]

About 10 species, chiefly in southern North America. Type species: *Anogra Douglasiana* Spach.

Tips of the calyx-segments not free in the bud.   1. *A. albicaulis.*
Tips of the calyx-segments free in the bud.
     Throat of the calyx-tube villous within.   2. *A. coronopifolia.*
     Throat of the calyx-tube glabrous within.
        Capsules narrowly ascending; leaves linear, entire or nearly so.   3. *A. Nuttallii.*
        Capsules widely spreading; leaves lanceolate, dentate.   4. *A. latifolia.*

1. Anogra albicaùlis (Pursh) Britton. Prairie Evening-Primrose. Fig. 3045.

Oenothera albicaulis Pursh, Fl. Am. Sept. 733. 1814.

Oenothera pinnatifida Nutt. Gen. 1: 245. 1818.

Anogra albicaulis Britton, Mem. Torr. Club 5: 234. 1894.

Annual or biennial, diffusely branched at the base; branches decumbent or ascending, more or less hirsutely pubescent or puberulent, whitish and often shreddy, 4'-12' long. Basal and lower leaves petioled, the upper sessile, oblanceolate or lanceolate in outline, deeply pinnatifid or the lowest repand-dentate (rarely entire), 1'-4' long; flowers axillary, diurnal, 1½'-3' broad, white, becoming rose-color; petals obcordate or emarginate; calyx-segments lanceolate, not free in the bud, acuminate, hirsute, finally reflexed, the throat naked; capsules linear, 1'-1½' long, about 1" thick, hirsute or puberulent; seeds finely pitted.

Prairies, North Dakota to Nebraska, New Mexico and Sonora. April–June.

2. Anogra coronopifòlia (T. & G.) Britton. Cut-leaved Evening-Primrose. Fig. 3046.

Oenothera coronopifolia T. & G. Fl. N. A. 1: 495. 1840.
Anogra coronopifolia Britton, Mem. Torr. Club 5: 234. 1894.
Raimannia coronopifolia Rose, Contr. Nat. Herb. 8: 330. 1905.

Perennial, erect, branched, 6'-2° high, more or less hispid, pubescent or canescent. Leaves lanceolate or oblanceolate in outline, sessile or the lowest petioled, 6"-2' long, usually finely and deeply pinnatifid into linear-oblong lobes; flowers axillary, white, turning pink, 9"-15" broad; calyx-segments linear, the tips free in the bud, reflexed, the throat villous within; petals broadly obovate; capsules oblong, abruptly constricted at the top, straight, pubescent and sometimes tuberculate, 4"-10" long, about 2" thick; seeds tuberculate.

Prairies, South Dakota to Colorado, Utah, Kansas and New Mexico. June–Sept.

3. Anogra Nuttàllii (Sweet) Spach. Nuttall's Evening-Primrose. Fig. 3047.

Oe. albicaulis Nutt. Fras. Cat. Name only. 1813.
Oe. Nuttallii Sweet, Hort. Brit. Ed. 2, 199. 1830.
A. Nuttalliana Spach, Ann. Sci. Nat. II. **4**: 164. 1835.

Perennial, erect, simple or branched, 6'-3° high, stems white or pale, glabrous, rarely with a few scattered long hairs, the bark often shreddy. Leaves linear, sessile or the lowest petioled, finely appressed-pubescent beneath, glabrous above, entire or sparingly denticulate, 1'-3½' long; flowers axillary, white, turning pink, 1'-1½' broad; segments of the calyx linear, the tips free in the bud, its throat glabrous within; petals nearly orbicular, entire or emarginate; capsules linear, erect-ascending, 1'-1½' long, about 1½" thick; seeds smooth.

Prairies, Minnesota to Saskatchewan, British Columbia, Nebraska and Colorado. White shrubby evening primrose. June–Aug. Included in the western *A. pallida* in our first edition.

4. Anogra latifòlia Rydb. Gray-leaved Evening-Primrose. Fig. 3048.

Oenothera pallida latifolia Rydb. Contr. U. S. Nat. Herb. **3**: 159. 1895.
Anogra latifolia Rydb. Bull. Torr. Club **31**: 570. 1904.

Perennial, often much branched, 2° high or less, the stout branches canescent, ascending. Leaves lanceolate to oblong, firm in texture, 2'-4' long, ¼'-1¼' wide, acute, sinuate-dentate, or sometimes nearly entire, ashy-canescent on both sides; flowers axillary, white, turning pink, 1¼'-2' wide; calyx strigose without; tips of the calyx-segments free in the bud; calyx-throat glabrous within; capsules linear, 1'-2' long, widely spreading or somewhat upcurved.

Dry soil, Nebraska and Kansas to Utah and New Mexico. June–Aug.

10. KNEÌFFIA Spach, Hist. Veg. **4**: 373. 1835.

Usually slender annual or perennial caulescent shrubby herbs. Leaves thinnish, mostly narrow, entire or shallowly toothed; buds mostly erect. Flowers yellow, diurnal, in terminal spikes or racemes. Calyx-tube slender, dilated at the throat; calyx-segments finally reflexed, the tips united in the bud or nearly so. Petals 4, spreading. Stamens 8, the alternate ones longer; filaments filiform; anthers linear. Ovary usually club-shaped, 4-angled; united styles filiform; stigma 4-cleft; ovules numerous, on slender stalks, in many rows. Capsules more or less club-shaped, nearly sessile or long-stalked, 4-winged or rarely sharply 4-angled. Seeds numerous, not angled, without a tubercle. [In honor of Prof. C. Kneiff, of Strassburg, who wrote on cryptogamic botany.]

About 12 species, mostly in temperate North America. **Type:** *Kneiffia glauca* (Michx.) Spach.

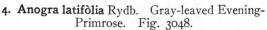

Stem-leaves filiform-linear; capsules 4-angled or very slightly 4-winged.   1. *K. linifolia.*
Stem-leaves never approaching filiform; capsules prominently winged.
  Capsules club-shaped.
    Pedicels and capsules pubescent.
      Stems decumbent, spreading.   2. *K. Alleni.*
      Stems erect or nearly so; body of the capsule more or less elongated.
        Capsule stalked.
          Pedicel longer than the body of the capsule, the wings thick and pubescent.
                3. *K. longipedicellata.*
          Pedicels shorter than the body of the capsule, the wings thin and glabrous.
                4. *K. linearis.*
        Capsule sessile.
          Hirsute; flowers 1½'-2½' wide.   5. *K. pratensis.*
          Merely puberulent; flowers 1' wide or less.   6. *K. pumila.*
    Pedicels and capsules glabrous or glabrate.
    Capsules oblong or nearly so.
      Plants not glaucous, usually pubescent; capsules less than 4" long.   7. *K. fruticosa.*
      Plants somewhat glaucous, glabrous; capsules more than 5" long.   8. *K. glauca.*

3/4

1. Kneiffia linifòlia (Nutt.) Spach. Thread-leaved Sundrops. Fig. 3049.

Oenothera linifolia Nutt. Journ. Acad. Phila. **2**: 120. 1821.
Kneiffia linifolia Spach, Nouv. Ann. Mus. Par. **4**: 368. 1835.

Erect, very slender, simple or branched, 6′–18′ high, glabrous or nearly so below, finely pubescent above. Stem-leaves filiform-linear, entire, crowded, 6″–15″ long; basal leaves tufted, oblanceolate or spatulate, petioled, about 1′ long; flowers in loose spike-like racemes, yellow, diurnal, 3″–4″ broad; calyx-lobes short, reflexed, the tube about 1″ long, rather shorter than the ovary; stigma-lobes very short; capsule obovoid, sessile or very nearly so, puberulent, sharply 4-sided but not winged, 2″–3″ long.

In dry soil, Illinois to Kansas, south to Georgia, Louisiana and Texas. May–July.

2. Kneiffia Álleni (Britton) Small. Allen's Sundrops. Fig. 3050.

Oenothera fruticosa var. humifusa Allen, Bull. Torr. Club **1**: 3. 1870. Not Oe. humifusa Nutt. 1818.
Kneiffia linearis Alleni Britton, Mem. Torr. Club **5**: 235. 1894.
Kneiffia Alleni Small, Bull. Torr. Club **23**: 177. 1896.

Low, perennial, finely appressed-pubescent, stems decumbent, at length diffusely branched, 3′–2° long, wiry and zigzag. Leaves oblanceolate to lanceolate, ½–1¼′ long, usually obtuse, undulate, sessile or short-petioled; flowers yellow, about ¾–1′ broad; racemes 1–2′ long, usually interrupted; calyx villous, its tube 2″–3″ long, striate, its segments linear-oblong, as long as the tube; petals orbicular-obovate, notched at the apex; capsules club-shaped, 3″–4″ long, winged, shorter than the pedicels; seeds obovoid, to oblong, ¼″ long, minutely pitted in rows.

In sand, eastern Long Island. Probably a decumbent race of K. linearis. June–Aug.

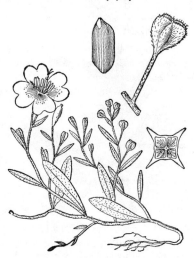

3. Kneiffia longipedicellàta Small. Long-stemmed Sundrops. Fig. 3051.

Kneiffia longipedicellata Small, Bull. Torr. Club **23**: 178. 1896.
Oenothera longipedicellata Robinson, Rhodora **10**: 34. 1908.

Perennial, slender, more or less puberulent; stems erect or assurgent, 1°–2½° tall, red, simple or sparingly branched above. Basal leaves spatulate or obovate-spatulate, 1½′–3′ long; stem-leaves few, linear-lanceolate 1′–2½′ long, obtuse or acutish, entire, sometimes undulate, short-petioled; flowers yellow, 1′–2′ broad; racemes 1′–4′ long; calyx hirsute, its tube slender, 5″–7″ long, its segments nearly linear, longer than the tube, the tips free in the bud; petals obovate, emarginate; capsules narrowly obovoid, the bodies about 5″ long, their angles with stout pubescent wings, their faces ridged, the pubescent pedicel longer than the body; seeds irregular, less than ½″ long, minutely papillose.

Moist soil, Connecticut to West Virginia and Florida. May–Aug.

½

4. Kneiffia lineàris (Michx.) Spach.   Narrow-leaved Sundrops.   Fig. 3052.

Oenothera linearis Michx. Fl. Bor. Am **1**: 225. 1803.
Kneiffia linearis Spach, Hist. Veg. **4**: 376. 1835.

Biennial or perennial, slender, puberulent, loosely pilose, or nearly glabrous. Stems erect or ascending, 6'–20' tall, simple or much-branched above, finally angled; basal leaves spatulate or broadly oblanceolate, 2'–3' long, entire or nearly so; cauline leaves linear, or linear-lanceolate, 1'–3' long, slightly toothed, acute or obtuse, short-petioled; flowers yellow, ¾'–1¾' broad; racemes 1'–4' long; calyx slightly pubescent, its tube 4''–6'' long, its segments linear-lanceolate, longer than the tube; petals obovate, shallowly notched at the apex and eroded; capsule oblong club-shaped, 4''–7'' long, the angles with papery glabrous wings, its faces ridged, narrowed into pedicels which are much shorter than the bodies; seeds irregular, ½'' long, angled.

In dry soil, Connecticut to Tennessee and Georgia. June–Sept.

Kneiffia ripària (Nutt.) Small is pubescent, has larger flowers, the fruit very much like that of *K. linearis;* it ranges from eastern Long Island to Georgia, near the coast.

5. Kneiffia praténsis Small.   Meadow Sundrops.
Fig. 3053.

K. pratensis Small, Fl. SE. U S. 842. 1903.

Oenothera pratensis Robinson, Rhodora **10**: 34. 1908.

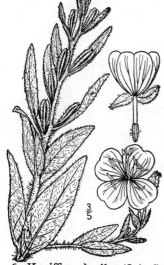

Erect or nearly so, perennial, 1½°–3½° high, often branched above, hirsute with spreading hairs. Leaves oblong-lanceolate or elliptic-lanceolate, 4½' long or less, 5''–10'' wide, the margins sinuate or entire, the apex acute, or that of the lower leaves obtuse; flowers leafy-bracted, 1½'–2½' broad; tube of the calyx somewhat hirsute, the lobes with narrow hirsute tips; capsule clavate, sessile, about 10'' long, hispid.

Low grounds, Ohio to Iowa, Missouri and Arkansas. Recorded from eastern New England. June–Aug.

6. Kneiffia pùmila (L.) Spach.   Small Sundrops.   Fig. 3054.

Oenothera pumila L. Sp. Pl. Ed. 2, 493. 1762.
Oenothera chrysantha Michx. Fl Bor. Am. **1**: 225. 1803
Kneiffia pumila Spach, Hist. Veg. **4**: 377. 1835.

Erect, branched or simple, finely puberulent, 8'–2° high. Leaves oblanceolate or oblong, obtuse or obtusish at the apex, narrowed at the base and often petioled, entire or very nearly so, 1'–2' long, 2''–4'' wide, usually glabrous; the basal ones broader and shorter; flowers in terminal, leafy-bracted spikes, yellow, diurnal, 4''–12'' broad; calyx-tube shorter than the ovary, the lobes linear-lanceolate, reflexed; petals obcordate; capsule sessile or short-stalked, glabrous, club-shaped, 3''–6'' long, the body obovoid, somewhat wing-angled.

In dry soil, Newfoundland to Manitoba, south to New Jersey, Georgia and Wisconsin; apparently erroneously recorded from Kansas. Ascends to 2200 ft. in Virginia. June–Aug.

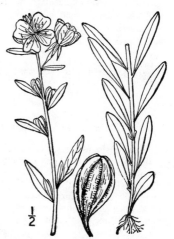

7. Kneiffia fruticòsa (L.) Raimann. Common Sundrops. Fig. 3055.

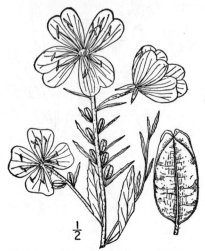

Oenothera fruticosa L. Sp. Pl. 346. 1753.
Kneiffia fruticosa Raimann, in Engl. & Prantl, Nat. Pfl. Fam. 3: Abt. 7, 214. 1893.
Kneiffia fruticosa pilosella Britton, Mem. Torr. Club 5: 234. 1894.
Oenothera pilosella Raf. Ann. Nat. 15. 1820.

Erect, usually branched, 1°–3° high, pubescent with short or long hairs, or nearly glabrous. Leaves lanceolate, ovate-lanceolate or oval-lanceolate, acute or obtusish at the apex, narrowed and sessile at the base or the lowest petioled, repand-denticulate, or rarely nearly entire, 1'–4' long; flowers yellow, diurnal, 1'–2' broad, in terminal leafy-bracted spikes; calyx-segments lanceolate, spreading, the tube mostly longer than the ovary; petals obcordate; capsule sessile or short-stalked, oblong, prominently winged, glabrous or pubescent, 3''–4'' long.

½

In dry soil, New Hampshire to Georgia, west to Minnesota and Louisiana. Recorded from Nova Scotia. Wild beet. Scabish. June–Aug.

Kneiffia Sumstìnei Jennings, of western Pennsylvania, seems to be a race of this species with abundant long hairs, probably not distinct from Oenothera pilosella Raf.

8. Kneiffia glàuca (Michx.) Spach. Glaucous Sundrops. Fig. 3056.

Oenothera glauca Michx. Fl. Bor. Am. 1: 224. 1803.

Kneiffia glauca Spach, Hist. Veg. 4: 374. 1835.

Erect, glabrous and glaucous, 1½°–3° high. Leaves sessile or the lower petioled, ovate or oval, repand-denticulate, 2'–5' long, 5''–15'' wide, acute or acutish at the apex, narrowed or rounded at the base; flowers bright yellow, diurnal, 1½'–3' broad, very showy in short, leafy corymbs; petals broadly obovate, emarginate; calyx-lobes ovate-lanceolate, acuminate, spreading, its tube very slender and 5–8 times as long as the ovary; capsule oblong, broadly 4-winged, glabrous, 5''–6'' long, borne on a short stalk.

½

In dry woods, mountains of Virginia and Kentucky to Georgia and Alabama. Scabish. May–Sept.

11. HARTMÁNNIA Spach, Hist. Veg. 4: 370. 1835.

Annual or perennial caulescent herbs with branched stems. Leaves alternate, commonly pinnatifid or lyrate; buds drooping. Flowers perfect, white, red or purple, diurnal, in terminal spikes or racemes. Calyx-tube funnelform; calyx-segments narrow, deciduous, their tips mostly free in the bud. Petals 4, spreading. Stamens 8, the alternate ones longer; filaments filiform; anthers linear. Ovary elongated, 4-celled; stigma 4-cleft; ovules numerous on slender stalks, in many rows. Capsules club-shaped, 4-winged, sessile or stalked. Seeds numerous, not tuberculate. [In honor of Emanuel Hartmann, a resident of Louisiana.]

About 10 species, in North and South America. Type species: Hartmannia faux-gaura Spach.

1. Hartmannia speciòsa (Nutt.) Small. Showy Primrose. Fig. 3057.

Oe. speciosa Nutt. Journ. Acad. Phil. **2**: 119. 1821.
Hartmannia speciosa Small, Bull. Torr. Club **23**: 181. 1896.

Erect, perennial, ascending or decumbent, more or less branched, 6′–3° high, puberulent or finely pubescent. Stem-leaves lanceolate or linear-lanceolate, sessile, or short-petioled, acutish, sinuate or pinnatifid, 2′–3′ long; basal leaves slender-petioled, oval or oval-lanceolate, repand or pinnatifid at the base; flowers white or pink, 1½′–3½′ broad, generally few, loosely spicate; petals broadly obovate, emarginate; calyx-lobes ovate-lanceolate, acuminate, spreading, the tube rather longer than the ovary; capsule club-shaped, strongly 4-ribbed, 4-winged, pubescent, 6″–9″ long, on a short stout pedicel.

Prairies, Missouri and Kansas to Louisiana, Texas, Arizona and Mexico. May–July. Extensively naturalized in Illinois, South Carolina and Georgia.

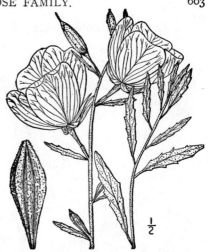

½

12. PACHÝLOPHUS Spach, Hist. Veg. 4: 365. 1835.

Perennial acaulescent or nearly acaulescent herbs. Leaves basal, leathery, pinnatifid or pinnately-toothed, petioled. Flowers basal, more or less tufted. Calyx pubescent, its tube linear-funnelform, its segments narrow, 2–3 times shorter than the tube. Petals white or pink, spreading. Stamens 8; filaments filiform, the alternate ones longer; anthers linear. United styles filiform; stigma 4-cleft. Capsules basal, woody, pyramidal, their angles retuse or obtuse, transversely wrinkled. Seeds sessile, in 1 or 2 rows, deeply furrowed along the raphe. [Greek, referring to the tuberculate edges of the valves of the capsule.]

Five or six species, of western North America, the following typical.

½

1. Pachylophus caespitòsa (Nutt.) Raimann. Scapose Primrose. Fig. 3058.

Oenothera caespitosa Nutt. Fras. Cat. 1813.
Oenothera scapigera Pursh, Fl. Am. Sept. 263. 1814.
P. Nuttallii Spach, Hist. Veg. **4**: 365. 1835.
Pachylophus caespitosa Raimann in Engl. & Prantl, Nat. Pfl. Fam. **3**: Abt. 7, 215. 1893.

Acaulescent or nearly so, perennial or biennial from a thick woody root. Leaves clustered at the base, narrowed into a slender petiole, lanceolate, oblanceolate or oval, acutish at the apex, densely pubescent, sinuate-dentate, often densely ciliate with white hairs, repand or pinnatifid, 3′–8′ long, usually less than 1′ wide; flowers few, white or rose, 1½′–3′ broad; petals obcordate; lobes of the calyx pubescent, narrowly lanceolate, reflexed-spreading, its tube 2′–7′ long, dilated at the mouth, many times longer than the ovary; capsule sessile, ovoid, strongly tuberculate on each side, the angles ribbed; seeds densely and minutely tuberculate.

Plains, South Dakota to Nebraska, Colorado and Utah. June–July.

13. LAVAÙXIA Spach, Hist. Veg. 4: 366. 1835.

Low usually acaulescent herbs, rarely producing short stems. Leaves mostly basal, pinnatifid, numerous. Flowers perfect, white, pink or pale yellow. Calyx-tube slender, dilated at the throat; calyx-segments finally reflexed, the tips free in the bud or united. Petals 4, spreading. Stamens 8, the alternate ones longer; filaments filiform; anthers linear. Ovary short, 4-angled; stigma 4-cleft; ovules few. Capsules stout, their angles sometimes winged above. Seeds few. [In honor of Francois Delavaux, founder of the botanical garden at Nismes.]

About 6 species, chiefly in southern North America. Type species: *Lavauxia tríloba* (Nutt.) Spach.

Leaves membranous; capsules beaked, glabrate.　　　　　　　　1. *L. triloba.*
Leaves leathery; capsules hardly beaked, pubescent.　　　　　2. *L. brachycarpa.*

1. Lavauxia tríloba (Nutt.) Spach.   Three-lobed Primrose.   Fig. 3059.

Oenothera triloba Nutt. Journ. Acad. Phil. **2**: 118. 1821.

Lavauxia triloba Spach, Hist. Veg. **4**: 367. 1835.

Perennial, nearly glabrous throughout. Leaves petioled, runcinate-pinnatifid, sometimes ciliate, oblong-lanceolate in outline, 3′–12′ long, sometimes 2′ wide, the apex acute or acutish; flowers white or pink, 1′–2½′ broad; calyx-lobes lanceolate, spreading, the tube slender, somewhat dilated at the summit, many times longer than the ovary, 2′–4′ long; petals often 3-lobed; capsule ovoid, 4-wing-angled, reticulate veined, 6″–12″ long; seeds finely and densely tuberculate.

In dry, often rocky soil, Kentucky and Tennessee to Kansas, Utah and California, south to Mississippi, Texas and northern Mexico. May–July.

Lavauxia Wàtsoni (Britton) Small, of Kansas and Nebraska, is described as differing from this species in being annual with smaller flowers and more abundant fruit. (*Oenothera triloba* var. *parviflora* S. Wats.)

2. Lavauxia brachycàrpa (A. Gray) Britton.   Short-podded Primrose. Fig. 3060.

Oenothera brachycarpa A. Gray, Pl. Wright. **1**: 70. 1852.

Lavauxia brachycarpa Britton, Mem. Torr. Club **5**: 235. 1894.

Low, perennial by a stout root, acaulescent or nearly so, softly canescent. Leaves basal, leathery, ovate to narrowly oblong, 3′–9′ long, acute or obtuse, lyrate-pinnatifid or sometimes nearly entire; petioles sometimes as long as the blade; flowers yellow, basal; calyx canescent, its tube 2′–4′ long, gradually dilated upward, its segments linear-lanceolate, about one-half as long as the tube, the tips free in the bud; petals 1′–1½′ long, undulate; capsules elliptic, 8″–9″ long, leathery or corky, the angles very thin, the faces somewhat wrinkled.

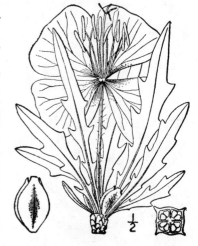

Montana to Kansas, Texas and New Mexico. April–July.

14. GAURÉLLA Small, Bull. Torr. Club **23**: 183. 1896.

Low perennial canescent or strigillose herbs with wiry diffusely branched stems. Leaves small, narrow, nearly entire or distantly toothed, narrowed into very short petioles. Flowers axillary, sessile. Calyx purplish, its tube cylindric, slightly dilated at the throat, its segments narrow, slightly longer than the tube, their tips united in the bud. Petals obovate, white or pink, spotted or striped with red. Stamens 8, the alternate ones longer; filaments filiform-subulate; anthers linear. Ovary 4-angled, short; united styles stout, enlarged above; stigmas filiform. Capsules ovoid-pyramidal, sessile, attenuate into a curved beak, sharply 4-angled, the faces swollen. Seeds obovoid, angled, delicately striate. [Diminutive of *Gaura*.]

A monotypic genus of the west-central United States.

1. Gaurella canescens (Torr.) Small. Spotted Primrose. Fig. 3061.

Oenothera canescens Torr. Frem. Rep. 315. 1845.
Oenothera guttulata Geyer; Hook. Lond. Journ.
  Bot. 6: 222. 1847.
Gaurella guttulata Small, Bull. Torr. Club **23**: 183.
  1896.

Diffusely branched from near or at the base,
4′–8′ high, canescent with appressed hairs, the
branches decumbent or ascending. Leaves
lanceolate or linear-lanceolate, nearly sessile
and narrowed at the base, obtusish at the apex,
4″–8″ long, 1½″–2″ wide, repand-denticulate or
entire; flowers axillary, white or pink, 9″–12″
wide; calyx-lobes lanceolate, canescent, the
tube longer than the ovary; petals obovate,
entire; capsule ovate, canescent, 4″–5″ long,
angled, not winged, sessile; seeds angled,
slipper-shaped.

Prairies, Nebraska to Texas, Colorado and New
Mexico. June–Sept.

15. MEGAPTÈRIUM Spach, Hist. Veg. 4: 363. 1835.

Low perennial herbs with stout sparingly branched stems. Leaves numerous, alternate,
narrow, entire or slightly toothed. Flowers perfect, few, but large and showy, axillary,
yellow. Calyx-tube much elongated, dilated toward the throat; calyx-segments narrow, the
tips free in the bud. Petals 4, spreading. Stamens 8, the alternate ones longer; filaments
filiform; anthers linear. Ovary 4-celled, 4-angled or 4-winged; united styles filiform; stigma
4-cleft; ovules few, sessile in rows. Capsules broadly 4-winged. Seeds few, crested. [Greek,
broad-winged.]

About 4 species, in North America and Mexico. Type species: *Megapterium Nuttallianum*
Spach.

Flowers 3′–6′ broad; capsules suborbicular, 2′–2¼′ long.   1. *M. missouriense.*
Flowers 1′–2′ broad; capsules oblong, 9″–14″ long.
  Densely finely canescent.   2. *M. Fremontii.*
  Glabrous.   3. *M. oklahomense.*

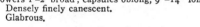

1. Megapterium missouriénse (Sims) Spach. Missouri Primrose. Fig. 3062.

Oenothera missouriensis Sims. Bot. Mag. *pl. 1592.*
  1814.
Oenothera macrocarpa Pursh, Fl. Amer. Sept.
  734. 1814.
Megapterium missouriense Spach, Hist. Veg. **4**:
  364. 1835.

Tufted, stems decumbent or ascending,
finely and densely canescent, 6′–12′ long.
Leaves thick, linear-lanceolate or oblong-
lanceolate, acuminate or acute at the apex,
narrowed at the base into a slender petiole
or the uppermost nearly sessile, entire or remotely denticulate, 2′–6′ long, 2″–8″ wide;
flowers 3′–6′ broad; calyx-lobes broadly lanceolate, spreading, the tube 2′–6′ long, 6–12
times the length of the ovary; capsule short-
stalked, nearly orbicular, very broadly winged,
finely canescent, or glabrate when mature,
1′–3′ long.

In dry soil, Missouri to Nebraska, Colorado
and Texas. May–July.

2. Megapterium Fremóntii (S. Wats.) Britton. Fremont's Primrose.
Fig. 3063.

$\frac{3}{5}$

Oenothera Fremontii S. Wats. Proc. Am. Acad.
8 : 587. 1873.
Megapterium Fremontii Britton, Mem. Torr.
Club 5 : 236. 1894.

Tufted, stems mostly simple, ascending, 2′–6′ high, densely appressed-pubescent or canescent. Leaves linear-lanceolate to somewhat oblanceolate, acuminate at the apex, narrowed at the base into a slender petiole, entire or very nearly so, silvery canescent, 1½′–3′ long, 2″–4″ wide; flowers 1′–2′ broad; calyx-lobes broadly lanceolate, acuminate, spreading, the tube canescent, very slender, 4–5 times the length of the ovary; capsule ovate, canescent, broadly winged, rounded at the summit, about 8″ long and 6″ wide, short-stalked.

Plains, Kansas to Texas. Summer.

3. Megapterium oklahoménse Norton. Oklahoma Primrose.
Fig. 3064.

Megapterium oklahomense Norton, Ann. Rep.
Mo. Bot. Gard. 9 : 153. 1898.

Glabrous throughout, even when young; stems decumbent or ascending, 1° long or less; leaves firm in texture, lanceolate, acuminate at the apex, narrowed at the base, remotely toothed or entire-margined, 2½′–4′ long; flowers 1½′–2′ broad; calyx-lobes linear-lanceolate, purple-spotted; capsules oblong, short-stalked, about 1′ long, its wings 3″–4″ wide.

Kansas and Oklahoma. Summer.

$\frac{1}{2}$

16. GALPÍNSIA Britton, Mem. Torr. Club 5 : 236. 1894.

[SALPINGIA Raimann, in Engler & Prantl, Nat. Pfl. Fam. 3 : Abt. 7, 217. 1893. Not *Salpinga* DC.]

Perennial caulescent herbs or shrubby plants with much branched or tufted stems. Leaves alternate, entire or toothed. Flowers perfect, yellow, axillary. Calyx-tube slender, narrowly funnelform, longer than the ovary; calyx-segments narrow, the tips free in the bud. Petals 4, spreading. Stamens 8, equal in length; filaments filiform; anthers linear. Ovary 4-celled, elongated; united styles filiform; stigma disk-like, entire. Capsules elongated, narrowed at the base, more or less curved. Seeds sometimes tuberculate. [Anagram of *Salpingia*.]

About 4 species, in the southern United States and Mexico. Type species : *Galpinsia Hartwegi* (Benth.) Britton.

Canescent or appressed-pubescent, low ; leaves narrow.   1. G. lavendulaefolia.
Hirsute-pubescent or tomentose ; leaves broad.   2. G. interior.

1. Galpinsia lavendulaefòlia (T. & G.) Small. Lavender-leaved Primrose. Fig. 3065.

Oenothera lavendulaefolia T. & G. Fl. N. A. 1: 501. 1840.

Galpinsia lavendulaefolia Small, Fl. SE. U. S. 845. 1903.

Somewhat woody, canescent, much branched, the branches decumbent or ascending, slender, 6′–15′ long. Leaves linear-oblong or lanceolate, acutish at the apex, sessile, 6″–2′ long, 1½″–2″ wide, entire or slightly repand-denticulate; flowers axillary, yellow, 1′–2′ broad; calyx-lobes lanceolate to linear-lanceolate, acuminate, reflexed-spreading, the tube dilated above, many times longer than the ovary; petals rhombic-obovate; stigma discoid; capsule nearly sessile, narrowly cylindric, canescent, 6″–12″ long, 1″–2″ thick.

Prairies and plains, Nebraska and Wyoming to Texas and Arizona. May–Sept. Included in our first edition in *G. Hartwegi* (Benth.) Britton, of the southwestern states and Mexico.

$\frac{3}{5}$

$\frac{3}{4}$

2. Galpinsia intèrior Small. Oblong-leaved Primrose.
Fig. 3066.

Galpinsia interior Small, Fl. SE. U. S. 845. 1903.

Somewhat woody, hirsute-pubescent, or tomentose, branched, 1° high or less, erect or ascending. Leaves oblong to oblong-lanceolate, entire, or nearly so, acute or obtuse at the apex, sessile by a somewhat clasping base, about 1′ long; calyx more or less hirsute, its lobes lanceolate, acuminate, 5″–8″ long; petals ½′–1′ long; capsules hirsute, 7″–10″ long.

On plains and stony hills, Nebraska and Kansas to Texas. June–Aug.

17. MERÌOLIX Raf. Am. Month. Mag. **4**: 192. 1818.

Biennial or perennial herbs with branched stems which sometimes become shrubby. Leaves alternate, narrow, entire or sharply serrate. Flowers perfect, regular, axillary, yellow. Calyx-tube funnelform, shorter than the ovary; calyx-segments narrow, keeled on the back, the tips free in the bud. Petals 4, often blotched at the base. Stamens 8, equal in length; filaments filiform; anthers narrow. Ovary 4-celled, 4-angled; stigma disk-like, 4-toothed; ovules numerous. Capsules linear, 4-angled, 4-celled, sessile. Seeds longitudinally grooved. [Name unexplained.]

Three or four species of temperate North America, the following typical.

1. Meriolix serrulàta (Nutt.) Walp. Tooth-leaved Primrose. Fig. 3067.

Oenothera serrulata Nutt. Gen. 1 : 246. 1818.

Meriolix serrulata Walp. Repert. 2 : 79. 1843.

M. intermedia Rydb.; Small, Fl. SE. U. S. 846. 1903.

Erect, simple or branched, canescent or glabrate, 4′–18′ high. Leaves linear-oblong, lanceolate or oblanceolate, acute or acutish at the apex, narrowed at the base and usually sessile, sharply dentate or denticulate, 1′–3′ long, 2″–3″ wide; flowers yellow, axillary, 6″–2′ broad; calyx-lobes ovate, acuminate, somewhat reflexed, the tube funnelform, silvery canescent, shorter than or equalling the ovary; petals obovate, crenulate; stigma discoid; capsule sessile, linear-cylindric, silvery canescent, 8″–15″ long, about 1″ thick, slightly grooved longitudinally.

In dry soil, Manitoba and Minnesota to Wisconsin, Texas and New Mexico. Consists of several races, differing in size, shape of leaves and size of flowers. May–July.

18. GAÙRA L. Sp. Pl. 347. 1753.

Annual biennial or perennial herbs, somewhat woody at the base, with alternate narrow sessile leaves, and white, pink or red flowers in terminal spikes or racemes. Calyx usually pubescent, its tube narrow, prolonged beyond the ovary, deciduous, 4-lobed (rarely 3-lobed), the lobes reflexed. Petals 4 (rarely 3), clawed, unequal. Stamens usually 8, declined; filaments filiform, each with a small scale at the base. Ovary 1-celled; united styles filiform, declined; stigma 4-lobed, surrounded by a cup-like border; ovules usually 4, pendulous. Fruit nut-like, ribbed or angled, indehiscent or nearly so, 1–4-seeded. Seeds unappendaged. [Greek, proud, some species being showy.]

About 18 species, natives of North America and Mexico. Type species: *Gaura biennis* L.

Fruit sessile or very nearly so; flowers spicate.
    Flowers 1½″–2″ broad; stigma little exserted beyond its cup.   1. *G. parviflora.*
    Flowers 4″–5″ broad; stigma exserted beyond its cup.
        Flowers red, turning scarlet; fruit canescent.   2. *G. coccinea.*
        Flowers white, turning pink; fruit villous.   3. *G. biennis.*
Fruit pedicelled; flowers racemose.
    Leaves mostly glabrous; fruit 7″ long, glabrous, its stout pedicel club-shaped.   4. *G. sinuata.*
    Leaves densely villous; fruit 5″ long, pubescent, its slender pedicel nearly filiform.
                                               5. *G. villosa.*

1. Gaura parviflòra Dougl. Small-flowered Gaura. Fig. 3068.

Gaura parviflora Dougl.; Hook. Fl. Bor. Am. 1 : 208. 1832.

Erect, branched, villous-pubescent with whitish hairs, 2°–5° high. Leaves ovate-lanceolate, acute or acuminate at the apex, repand-denticulate, narrowed at the base, softly pubescent, 1½′–4′ long, 4″–18″ wide; spikes elongated, usually densely flowered; flowers sessile, pink, 1½″–2″ broad, the ovary and calyx-tube slender; fruit sessile, narrowed at the base, 4-nerved, obtusely 4-angled, glabrous or nearly so, 3″–4″ long.

In dry soil, South Dakota to Iowa, Missouri, Louisiana, Texas, Mexico, Oregon, Utah and New Mexico. May–Aug.

2. Gaura coccínea Pursh.   Scarlet Gaura.
Fig. 3069.

Gaura coccinea Pursh, Fl. Am. Sept. 733. 1814.
G. marginata Lehm.; Hook. Fl. Bor. Am. 1: 208. 1833.

Erect or ascending, much branched, canescent, pubescent or glabrate, 6′–2° high. Leaves oblong, lanceolate, or linear-oblong, denticulate, repand or entire, acute or obtuse at the apex, narrowed at the base, 6″–18″ long, 2″–4″ wide; flowers sessile, red, turning scarlet, 4″–5″ broad; fruit sessile, terete below, 4-sided and narrowed above, canescent, 3″–4″ long.

Prairies and dry soil, Manitoba to Minnesota, Missouri, Nebraska and Texas, west to Montana, Utah, Arizona, and in Mexico. Adventive farther east. Wild honeysuckle (Texas). May–Aug.

Gaura glàbra Lehm. differs in having a glabrous shining stem, the foliage also glabrous or nearly so, the flowers often paler in color. It ranges from South Dakota to Nebraska, Montana and New Mexico, and is probably a race of *G. coccinea.*

3. Gaura biénnis L.   Biennial Gaura.
Fig. 3070.

Gaura biennis L. Sp. Pl. 347. 1753.

Erect, much branched, villous or downy-pubescent, 2°–5° high. Leaves lanceolate or oblong-lanceolate, acute or acuminate at each end, pubescent or finally glabrate above, remotely denticulate, 2′–4′ long, 2″–5″ wide; spikes slender; flowers sessile, white, turning pink, 4″–5″ broad; fruit sessile, narrowed at each end, 4-ribbed, villous-pubescent, 3″–4″ long.

In dry soil, Quebec and Ontario to Minnesota, Connecticut, Georgia, Nebraska and Arkansas. Ascends to 2200 ft. in Virginia. July–Sept.

Western races are shorter-pubescent and thicker-leaved than eastern, and have been separated as a species, *Gaura Pitcheri* (T. & G.) Small.

Gaura Michaūxii Spach (*G. filipes* Spach), admitted into our first edition as recorded from Virginia to

Illinois and Kansas, is not definitely known to grow north of South Carolina and Tennessee.

4. Gaura sinuàta Nutt.   Wavy-leaved
Gaura.   Fig. 3071.

Gaura sinuata Nutt.; Ser. in DC. Prodr. **3**: 44. 1828.

Perennial, erect or decumbent, glabrous, or rarely sparingly villous. Stem branched at the base or throughout, 1°–3° tall, usually naked above; leaves oblanceolate to lanceolate, or nearly linear, sinuate-toothed, 1′–3′ long, acute, on winged petioles or nearly sessile; calyx slightly pubescent, its tube above the ovary funnelform, 1″–2″ long, several times shorter than the linear segments; petals oblong-obovate, 4″–5″ long; stamens shorter than the petals; fruit about 7″ long, glabrous, 4-ridged and 4-grooved above the stout club-shaped pedicel.

In dry soil, Kansas to Arkansas and Texas. Wild honeysuckle. May–July.

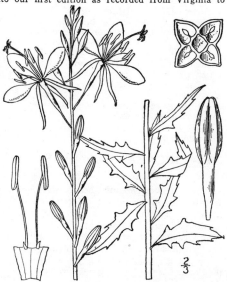

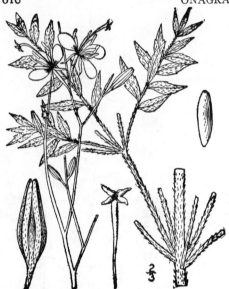

5. Gaura villòsa Torr. Woolly Gaura. Fig. 3072.

Gaura vilosa Torr. Ann. Lyc. N. Y. **2**: 200. 1827

Perennial, erect or nearly so, canescent or villous. Stems 1°–3° tall, simple or much branched, often naked above; leaves varying from lanceolate to oblanceolate or sometimes nearly linear, 1′–3′ long, sinuate-toothed or pinnatifid, acute or acuminate, sessile; calyx canescent, its tube above the ovary funnelform, 1″–2″ long, several times shorter than the linear acute segments; petals oblong-obovate, 5″–7″ long; stamens shorter than the petals; fruit about 5″ long, sparingly pubescent, the body sharply 4-angled, abruptly narrowed into a slender filiform pedicel.

In dry soil, Kansas to Arkansas and Texas. Wild honeysuckle. June–Sept.

19. STENOSÌPHON Spach, Nouv. Ann. Mus. Par **4**: 326. 1835.

Erect perennia. herbs, with slender upright branches, alternate sessile narrow leaves, and white sessile flowers in narrow terminal spikes. Calyx-tube filiform, much prolonged beyond the ovary, 4-lobed. Petals 4, clawed, unequal. Stamens 8, declined, not appendaged by scales at the base; filaments filiform. Ovary 1-celled; united styles slender; stigma 4-lobed, subtended by a cup-like border as in *Gaura;* ovules commonly 4. Fruit 8-ribbed, indehiscent, 1-celled, 1-seeded. Seed pendulous. [Greek, referring to the slender calyx-tube.]

A monotypic genus of the south-central United States.

1. Stenosiphon linifòlium (Nutt.) Britton. Flax-leaved Stenosiphon. Fig. 3073.

Gaura linifolia Nutt. in Long's Exp. **2**: 100. 1823.
Stenosiphon virgatus Spach, Nouv. Ann. Mus. Par. **4**: 326. 1835.
Stenosiphon linifolium Britton, Mem. Torr. Club **5**: 236. 1894.

Erect, slender, glabrous, 2°–5° high. Leaves sessile, lanceolate, linear-lanceolate or linear, acuminate or acute at the apex, narrowed or rounded at the base, entire, 1′–2′ long, the upper ones much smaller; spikes dense, narrow, sometimes 1°· long in fruit; flowers white, 4″–6″ broad; calyx-tube very slender, 4″–5″ long; fruit ovoid, pubescent, 1″–1½″ long, very much shorter than the linear-subulate bracts.

Prairies, hills and plains, Nebraska and Colorado to Texas. June–July.

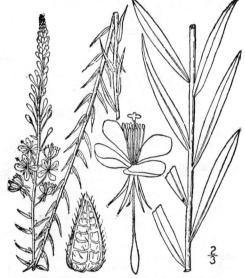

20. CIRCAÈA [Tourn.] L. Sp. Pl. 9. 1753.

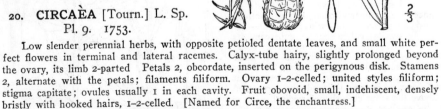

Low slender perennial herbs, with opposite petioled dentate leaves, and small white perfect flowers in terminal and lateral racemes. Calyx-tube hairy, slightly prolonged beyond the ovary, its limb 2-parted Petals 2, obcordate, inserted on the perigynous disk. Stamens 2, alternate with the petals; filaments filiform. Ovary 1–2-celled; united styles filiform; stigma capitate; ovules usually 1 in each cavity. Fruit obovoid, small, indehiscent, densely bristly with hooked hairs, 1–2-celled. [Named for Circe, the enchantress.]

Abous 8 species, natives of the northern hemisphere. Besides the following another occurs on the Pacific Coast. Type species: *Circaea lutetiana* L.

Plant 1°–2° high; leaves ovate; hairs of the 2-celled fruit stiff.　　　1. *C. lutetiana.*
Plant 3'–8' high; leaves cordate; hairs of the 1-celled fruit weak.　　　2. *C. alpina.*

1. Circaea lutetiàna L.　Enchanter's Nightshade.　Fig. 3074.

Circaea lutetiana L. Sp. Pl. 9. 1753.

Erect, branching, finely pubescent, at least above; stem swollen at the nodes, 1°–2° high. Leaves slender-petioled, ovate, acuminate at the apex, rounded or rarely slightly cordate at the base, remotely denticulate, 2'–4' long; pedicels 2"–4" long, slender, spreading in flower, reflexed in fruit; bracts deciduous or none; flowers about 1½" broad; fruit broadly obovoid, nearly 2" long, 2-celled, densely covered with stiff hooked hairs, or rarely glabrous.

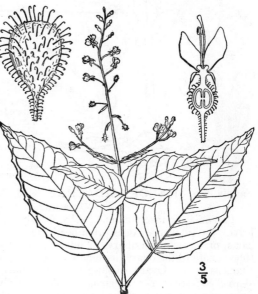

In woods, Nova Scotia to western Ontario, North Dakota, Georgia, Nebraska and Kansas. Also in Europe and Asia. Ascends to 2000 ft. in Virginia. Bindweed-nightshade. Mandrake. June-Aug. The specific name is from *Lutetia,* the ancient name of the City of Paris, France.

Circaea intermèdia Ehrh. has thinner, strongly toothed leaves, some of them cordate, and ranges from Quebec to Michigan, New Hampshire and Ohio, and is recorded from Tennessee.

$\frac{3}{5}$

2. Circaea alpìna L.　Smaller Enchanter's Nightshade.　Fig. 3075.

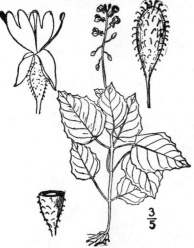

Circaea alpina L. Sp. Pl. 9. 1753.

Smaller, 3'–8' high, simple or branched, weak, glabrate, or pubescent above. Leaves ovate, slender-petioled, acute or acuminate at the apex, more or less cordate at the base, coarsely dentate, 1'–2' long; flowers about 1" broad; pedicels 1½"–2" long, reflexed in fruit; fruit narrowly obovoid, 1-celled, about 1" long, covered with weak soft hooked hairs.

$\frac{3}{5}$

In cold moist woods, Labrador to Alaska, south to Georgia, Indiana, Iowa, Michigan and South Dakota. Also in Europe and Asia. Leaves thin, somewhat shining. Ascends to 6300 ft. in North Carolina. July-Sept.

Family 99.　TRAPÀCEAE Dumort, Fl. Belg. 90. 1827.

WATER-NUT FAMILY.

Aquatic herbs, with opposite or verticillate pinnatifid submerged leaves, and clustered rhombic-ovate dentate floating ones with inflated petioles. Flowers perfect, axillary, solitary, short-peduncled. Calyx-tube short, the limb 4-parted, the lobes persistent. Petals 4, sessile, inserted on the perigynous disk. Stamens 4, inserted with the petals; filaments subulate-filiform. Ovary 2-celled, conic above; style subulate; ovule 1 in each cavity. Fruit coriaceous or bony, large, 2–4-spinose or swollen at the middle, 1-celled, 1-seeded, indehiscent. Seed inverted.

A single genus of 3 species, natives of Europe, tropical Asia and Africa.

1. TRÀPA L. Sp. Pl. 120. 1753.

Characters of the family. [Latin, calcitrapa, the caltrop.] Type species: *Trapa natans* L.

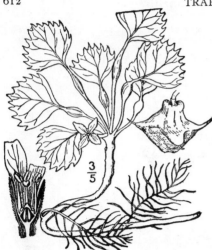

$\frac{3}{5}$

1. Trapa nàtans L   Swimming Water-
nut.   Water-Caltrop.   Fig. 3076.

Trapa natans L. Sp. Pl. 120.   1753.

Rooting in the mud at the bottom of lakes
or slow streams; stem often several feet long.
Submerged leaves approximate, pectinately
dissected, 1'–4' long; floating leaves in a
rosette sometimes 1° broad, their blades
rhombic-ovate, sharply dentate above, broadly
cuneate and entire below, about 1' wide, glabrous and shining above, the conspicuous veins
of the lower surface beset with short stiff
hairs; petioles of the floating leaves 2'–6' long,
inflated and spongy; flowers white, about 3"
broad; fruit 1'–2' long, armed with 4 somewhat recurved spines.

Naturalized in ponds and streams, eastern Massachusetts, and near Schenectady, N. Y.   Native
of Europe.   Called also sanghara-nut, Jesuit's
water-nut.   Seed mealy, edible.   June–July.

Family 100.   **HALORAGIDÀCEAE** Kl. & Garcke, Bot. Erg. Wald. 151.   1852.

WATER-MILFOIL FAMILY.

Perennial or rarely annual herbs, mainly aquatic, with alternate or verticillate
leaves, the submerged ones often pectinate-pinnatifid   Flowers perfect, or monoecious, or dioecious, axillary, in interrupted spikes, solitary or clustered.   Calyx-
tube adnate to the ovary, its limb entire or 2–4-lobed.   Petals small, 2–4, or none.
Stamens 1–8   Ovary ovoid-oblong, or short-cylindric, 2–8-ribbed or winged,
1–4-celled; styles 1–4; stigmas papillose or plumose.   Fruit a nutlet, or drupe,
compressed, angular, ribbed or winged, indehiscent, of 2–4 1-seeded carpels.
Endosperm fleshy; cotyledons minute.

Eight genera and about 100 species, of wide geographic distribution.

Stamen 1; ovary 1-celled.	1. *Hippuris.*
Stamens 2–8; ovary 3–4-celled.	
Fruit 3-angled or 4-angled.	2. *Proserpinaca.*
Fruit of 4 carpels.	3. *Myriophyllum.*

1. HIPPÙRIS L. Sp. Pl. 4.   1753.

Aquatic herbs, with simple erect stems, and verticillate simple entire leaves.   Flowers
small, axillary, perfect, or sometimes neutral or pistillate only.   Limb of the calyx minute,
entire.   Petals none.   Stamen 1, inserted on the margin of the calyx.   Style filiform, stigmatic its whole length, lying in a groove of the anther.
Fruit a small 1-celled 1-seeded drupe.   [Greek, mare's-tail.]

Three known species, natives of the north temperate and
arctic zone and of southern South America.   Besides the 2
following, the third occurs in northwestern arctic America.
Type species: *Hippuris vulgaris* L.

Leaves linear or lanceolate, in verticils of 5–12.   1. *H. vulgaris.*
Leaves obovate, oblong, or oblanceolate, in verticils of 4–6.
                             2. *H. tetraphylla.*

1. Hippuris vulgàris L.   Bottle Brush.   Mare's-
tail.   Joint-weed.   Fig. 3077.

Hippuris vulgaris L. Sp. Pl. 4.   1753.

Stem slender, glabrous, 8'–20' high.   Leaves linear or
lanceolate, acute, sessile, ¼"–12" long, 1"–2" wide, in
crowded verticils of 6–12, more or less sphacelate at the
apex; stamens with a short thick filament, and comparatively large 2-celled anther, dehiscent by lateral slits; seeds
ovoid, hollow; stigma persistent.

Swamps and bogs, Labrador and Greenland to Alaska, south
to Maine, New York, Illinois, Nebraska, in the Rocky Mountains to New Mexico, and on the Pacific Coast to California.
Also in Patagonia, and in Europe and Asia.   Summer.   Cat's-
tail.   Witches'-milk.   Paddock-pipes.   Knotgrass.

$\frac{2}{3}$

2. Hippuris tetraphýlla L. f.   Four-leaved Mare's-tail.
Fig. 3078.

Hippuris tetraphylla L. f. Suppl. 81. 1781.

Hippuris maritima Hell. Dissert. Hippur. *pl. 1.* 1786.

Smaller than the preceding species. Stem 4'-15' high; leaves obovate or oblanceolate, entire, in verticils of 4-6, not sphacelate at the apex or but slightly so, 4"-7" long.

Labrador and Quebec to Hudson Bay and Alaska. Also in northern Europe and Asia. Summer.

2. PROSERPINÀCA L. Sp. Pl. 88. 1753.

Aquatic herbs, with simple stems decumbent at the base. Leaves alternate, very various, dentate or pectinate-pinnatifid. Flowers perfect. Tube of the calyx adnate to the triquetrous ovary, the limb 3-4-parted. Petals none. Stamens 3-4. Styles 3-4, cylindric or conic-subulate stigmatic above the middle. Fruit bony, 3-4-angled, 3-4-celled, with 1 seed in each cavity. [Middle Latin, forward-creeping.]

Three or four species, natives of eastern North America, extending to the West Indies and Guatemala. Type species: *Proserpinaca palustris* L.

Emersed leaves linear-lanceolate to oblong, serrate ; fruit sharply angled.   1. *P palustris.*
Leaves all pectinate-pinnatifid ; fruit obtusely angled.   2. *P pectinata.*

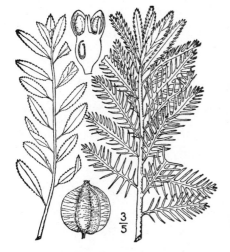

1. Proserpinaca palústris L.   Mermaid-weed. Fig. 3079.

Proserpinaca palustris L. Sp. Pl. 88   1753.

Glabrous, simple or sometimes branched, 8'-20' high. Emersed leaves oblong or linear-lanceolate, 10"-2' long, 1"-6" wide, sharply serrate, the submerged ones pectinate or pectinate-pinnatifid into stiff linear acute segments which are often serrulate, bearing a minute black spine in their axils; flowers solitary or several together, sessile in the axils of the emersed leaves; fruit about 2" long and 2" thick, sharply 3-angled, the faces concave, smooth or rugose.

In swamps, New Brunswick to Minnesota, Florida, Iowa, Texas and Central America. Also in Bermuda. July.

2. Proserpinaca pectinàta Lam.   Cut-leaved Mermaid-weed. Fig. 3080.

Proserpinaca pectinata Lam. Tabl. Encycl. *pl. 50. f. 1. 1*: 214. *1791.*

Proserpinaca pectinacea T. & G. Fl. N A. 1: 528. 1840.

Resembling the preceding species, but usually smaller. Leaves all pectinate or pinnatifid, the segments shorter and rarely serrulate, more subulate, or capillary; calyx-lobes broader; fruit smaller, about 1½" long by 1" thick, the faces flat or slightly convex, often wrinkled or somewhat tuberculate, the angles obtuse.

In sandy swamps near the coast, Maine to Florida, west to Louisiana. Summer.

Proserpinaca intermèdia Mackenzie, from swamps in southern New Jersey and Georgia, is quite intermediate between the two above species and may be a hybrid between them.

3. MYRIOPHÝLLUM [Vaill.] L. Sp. Pl. 992. 1753.

Aquatic herbs, with verticillate or alternate leaves, the emersed ones entire, dentate or pectinate, the submerged ones pinnatifid into capillary segments, the axillary commonly monoecious 2-bracted flowers often interruptedly spicate. Upper flowers generally staminate with a very short calyx-tube, its limb 2-4-lobed, or none; petals 2-4; stamens 4-8 Intermediate flowers often perfect. Lower flowers pistillate, the calyx more or less deeply 4-grooved and with 4 minute lobes, or none; ovary 2-4-celled; ovule 1 in each cavity, pendulous; styles 4, short, often plumose. Fruit splitting at maturity into 4 bony 1-seeded indehiscent carpels which are smooth, angled or tuberculate on the back. [Greek, myriad-leaved.]

About 20 species, of wide geographic distribution. In addition to the following, 2 others occur in the western United States. The plants flower in summer. Type species: *Myriophyllum spicatum* L.

Carpels smooth or minutely papillose.
　Stamens 8; petals fugacious.
　　Floral bracts verticillate.
　　　Floral bracts entire or toothed, shorter than the flowers.　　　1. *M. spicatum.*
　　　Floral bracts pectinate, shorter or longer than the flowers.　　2. *M. verticillatum.*
　　Floral bracts alternate.　　　　　　　　　　　　　　　　　　　　3. *M. alterniflorum.*
　Stamens 4; petals not fugacious.
　　Stem scape-like, erect, nearly leafless.　　　　　　　　　　　　　4. *M. tenellum.*
　　Stem creeping or floating, leafy.　　　　　　　　　　　　　　　　5. *M. humile.*
Carpels rough, tuberculate or ridged.
　Flowers on emersed spikes.
　　Floral leaves ovate or lanceolate, serrate.　　　　　　　　　　　6. *M. heterophyllum.*
　　Floral leaves linear, pectinate.　　　　　　　　　　　　　　　　7. *M. pinnatum.*
　Flowers on submersed stems.　　　　　　　　　　　　　　　　　　8. *M. Farwellii.*

1. Myriophyllum spicàtum L.　Spiked Water-Milfoil.　Fig. 3081.

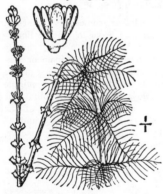

Myriophyllum spicatum L. Sp. Pl. 992. 1753.

Submerged leaves in whorls of 4's and 5's, dissected into capillary divisions. Floral leaves (bracts) ovate, entire or serrate, usually shorter than the flowers; spike 1'-3' long; petals 4, deciduous; stamens 8; stigmas short; fruit about 1" long and 1½" thick; carpels rounded on the back, with a deep wide groove between them, smooth, or very rarely slightly rugose.

In deep water, Newfoundland to Manitoba, Alaska, Maryland, Michigan, Kansas, New Mexico and California. Also in Europe and Asia. Both this species and the next have been erroneously recorded from Florida. Meakin. Water-navelwort.

2. Myriophyllum verticillàtum L.　Whorled Water-Milfoil.　Fig. 3082.

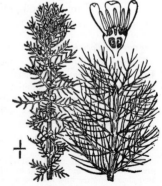

Myriophyllum verticillatum L. Sp. Pl. 992. 1753.

Submerged leaves in crowded whorls of 3's and 4's, the capillary divisions very slender, sometimes finer than those of *M. spicatum,* about 10 pairs, 1'-1½' long, often minutely scabrate. Floral leaves pectinate or pectinate-pinnatifid, longer or shorter than the flowers; spike 2'-6' long; petals of the staminate flowers 4, purplish; stamens 8; fruit 1"-1½" long, and about 1" thick, somewhat gibbous at the base.

In both deep and shallow water, Quebec and Ontario to New York, west to Minnesota and British Columbia. Also in Europe and Asia. Myriad-leaf.

3. Myriophyllum alterniflòrum DC. Loose-flowered Water-Milfoil. Fig. 3083.

Myriophyllum alterniflorum DC. Fl. Franc. Suppl. 529. 1815.

Submerged leaves usually in whorls of 3–5, occasionally scattered, the pinnate divisions capillary, 3″–5″ long. Spikes short, 1′–2′ long, numerous or several on the branching stems; uppermost floral leaves ovate or linear, entire or minutely toothed, smaller than the flowers, early deciduous; flowers mostly in pairs or solitary; petals of the staminate flowers 4, longer than the stamens, pale rose-color, deciduous; stamens 8; fruit nearly 1″ long, slightly less than 1″ thick; carpels rounded on the back, with a deep groove between them.

In deep water, Newfoundland to eastern Massachusetts and Ontario. Greenland. Common in Europe.

4. Myriophyllum tenéllum Bigel. Slender Water-Milfoil. Fig. 3084.

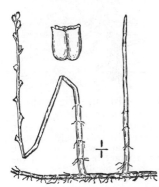

Myriophyllum tenellum Bigel. Fl. Bost. Ed. 2, 346. 1824.

Stems slender, scape-like, nearly leafless, simple, erect, 1½′–6′ or rarely 12′ high. Rhizome creeping, sending up many sterile stems; flowers alternate, solitary; uppermost bracts obovate, often longer than the monoecious flowers, the lower oblong, often shorter, the lowest minute or wanting; petals 4, purplish, longer than the 4 stamens; fruit ½″ long and about as thick at the top, sometimes enlarged at the base; carpels rounded or obtusely angled on the back, separated by a shallow groove.

Sandy bottoms of ponds and streams, Newfoundland to New Jersey, Pennsylvania, Ontario and Michigan.

5. Myriophyllum hùmile (Raf.) Morong. Low Water-Milfoil. Fig. 3085.

Burshia humilis Raf. Med. Rep. (II.) **5**: 361. 1808.

Myriophyllum ambiguum Nutt. Gen. **2**: 212. 1818.

Myriophyllum humile Morong, Bull. Torr. Club **18**: 242. 1891.

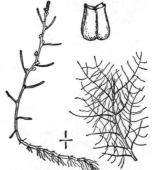

Typical form terrestrial, 1′–1½′ high, rooting in mud on shores. Leaves linear, entire or pectinate. Floating forms with stems often 12′ long, branched, with all or most of the leaves pectinate into capillary segments; these produce the typical form if they take root; petals 4, purplish; stamens 4; fruit usually less than 1″ long and about as thick at base, its carpels smooth, or rarely slightly roughened, separated by a shallow groove.

In ponds, Maine to Rhode Island, Maryland and recorded west to Illinois and Tennessee. Variable in appearance, but the variations are manifestly only conditions of the plant dependent upon its environment.

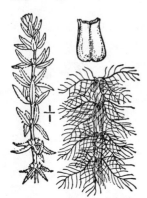

6. Myriophyllum heterophýllum Michx. Various-leaved Water-Milfoil. Fig. 3086.

Myriophyllum heterophyllum Michx. Fl. Bor. Am. **2**: 191. 1803.

Floral leaves in whorls of 3's to 5's, linear, ovate or lanceolate, serrate or rarely entire, much longer than the flowers. Submerged leaves subverticillate or scattered, crowded, pectinate-pinnatifid, about 10″ long, the divisions 6–10 pairs, capillary; flowering spike elongated (sometimes 18′ long); petals 4; stamens 4, rarely 6; fruit 1″ long, and slightly longer than thick; carpels 2-keeled on the back, their sides convex, usually slightly scabrous.

In ponds, Ontario and New York to Florida, west to Minnesota, Texas and Mexico.

Myriophyllum hippuroìdes Nutt., with narrower floral leaves and fruit slightly longer, a species of the Pacific United States, is recorded from southern Ontario.

7. Myriophyllum pinnàtum (Walt.) B.S.P. Pinnate Water-Milfoil. Fig. 3087.

Potamogeton pinnatum Walt. Fl. Car. 90. 1788.
Myriophyllum scabratum Michx. Fl. Bor. Am. **2**: 190. 1803.
Myriophyllum pinnatum B.S.P. Prel. Cat. N. Y. 16. 1888.

Leaves in whorls of 3's–5's, or sometimes scattered, the floral ones linear, serrate or pectinate, 2½″–6″ long, gradually passing into the submerged ones which are crowded, pinnately dissected, the divisions few and capillary; spikes 4′–8′ long; petals purplish; stamens 4, very rarely 6; carpels strongly 2-keeled and scabrous on the back, separated by deep grooves, their sides flat; mature fruit about 1″ long and somewhat more than ½″ thick.

In ponds, Massachusetts to Florida, Iowa, Missouri, Nebraska, Louisiana and Texas.

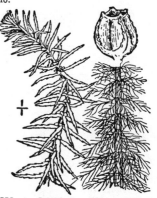

8. Myriophyllum Farwéllii Morong. Farwell's Water-Milfoil. Fig. 3088

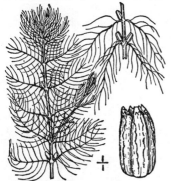

M. Farwellii Morong, Bull. Torr. Club **18**: 146. 1891.

Submerged; leaves in whorls of 3's–6's, or scattered, narrow, pinnately parted, the divisions finely capillary in 5–7 opposite or subopposite pairs, with minute black spines in the axils; flowers solitary in the axils of the leaves; petals 4, purplish, oblong; pistillate flowers only seen; styles 4, short; stamens 4, minute, abortive; fruit about 1″ long and ½″ thick; carpels crossed longitudinally by 3 or 4 rough tuberculate or slightly toothed ridges, 2 on the back and commonly 1 on each margin; groove between the carpels shallow.

In still water, Quebec to Michigan, Maine and New York.

Myriophyllum proserpinacoìdes Gill., the Chilian water-milfoil, or water-feather, with flowers on submersed stems, introduced into aquatic tanks in a nursery at Bordentown, New Jersey, and some years ago observed in a pond at Haddonfield, New Jersey, does not appear to have become established.

Family 101.   ARALIÀCEAE Vent. Tabl. 3: 2.   1799.

Ginseng Family.

Herbs, shrubs or trees, with alternate or verticillate (rarely opposite) leaves, and perfect or polygamous flowers in umbels, heads, racemes or panicles. Calyx-tube adnate to the ovary, its limb truncate or toothed. Petals usually 5, valvate or slightly imbricate, sometimes cohering together, inserted on the margin of the calyx. Stamens as many as the petals and alternate with them (rarely more), inserted on the epigynous disk; filaments filiform or short; anthers ovoid or oblong, introrse. Ovary inferior, 1–several-celled; styles as many as the cavities of the ovary; ovules 1 in each cavity, pendulous, anatropous. Fruit a berry or drupe. Seeds flattened, or somewhat 3-angled, the testa thin; endosperm copious, fleshy; embryo small, near the hilum; cotyledons ovate or oblong.

About 52 genera and 475 species, widely distributed in temperate and tropical regions.
Leaves compound.
    Herbs, shrubs or trees; leaves alternate, decompound; styles 5.
    Herbs; leaves verticillate, digitately compound; styles 2–3.   1. *Aralia.*
Leaves palmately lobed; styles 2.   2. *Panax.*
                                                                                   3. *Echinopanax.*

1. ARÀLIA [Tourn.] L. Sp. Pl. 273. 1753.

Perennial herbs, shrubs or trees, with alternate pinnately or ternately decompound leaves, and small polygamous or perfect flowers, in racemose, corymbose or paniculate umbels. Flowers white or greenish. Petioles sheathing at the base. Stipules none or inconspicuous. Pedicels jointed below the flowers. Calyx truncate or 5-toothed. Petals 5, spreading, obtuse, or with short inflexed points, valvate or slightly imbricate. Stamens 5. Disk depressed. Ovary 5-celled; style 5. Fruit a small berry enclosing about 5 seeds. [Name not explained.]

About 30 species, natives of North America and Asia. Besides the following, 2 others occur in the western and southwestern United States. Type species: *Aralia racemosa* L.

Umbels numerous, panicled or racemose.
    Spiny shrub or tree; leaflets thick, ovate.   1. *A. spinosa.*
    Branching unarmed herb; leaflets thin, large, cordate.   2. *A. racemosa.*
Umbels 2–7, or more, terminal or corymbose.
    Plant glabrate; leaf and peduncle arising from the rootstock.   3. *A. nudicaulis.*
    Plant bristly or hispid; stem leafy, erect.   4. *A. hispida.*

1. Aralia spinòsa L. Hercules' Club. Angelica or Spikenard Tree. Fig. 3089.

Aralia spinosa L. Sp. Pl. 273. 1753.

A shrub or tree, reaching a maximum height of about 40° and trunk diameter of 12′ but usually much smaller. Stem, branches and petioles spiny; leaves long-petioled, bipinnate, usuallly with a leaflet at the base of each pinna; leaflets ovate, thick, acute or acuminate, stalked, serrate, dark green above, glaucous and sometimes slightly pubescent beneath, 1′–4′ long; umbels very numerous, in terminal compound panicles; involucels of several short bractlets; peduncles and pedicels pubescent; flowers white, 2″ broad; pedicels 3″–4″ long in fruit; fruit ovoid, black, 5-lobed, about 3″ long; styles distinct.

In low grounds and along streams, southern New York to Florida, west to Indiana, Missouri and Texas. Freely planted for ornament, and sometimes escaping from cultivation further north. June–Aug. Wild orange. Pick or pigeon-tree. Prickly elder. Prickly ash. Toothache-tree.

2. Aralia racemòsa L. American Spikenard. Indian-root. Fig. 3090.

Aralia racemosa L. Sp. Pl. 273. 1753.

Herbaceous, divergently much branched, unarmed, 3°–6° high, glabrous or slightly pubescent. Roots large and thick, aromatic; leaves ternately or rarely quinately compound, the divisions pinnate; leaflets broadly ovate or orbicular, thin, acuminate at the apex, cordate at the base, 2′–6′ long, sharply and doubly serrate, sometimes pubescent on' the veins beneath; umbels numerous, racemose-paniculate; peduncles and pedicels puberulent; involucels of a few subulate bractlets; flowers greenish, about 1″ broad; fruit nearly globular, dark purple or reddish-brown, about 3″ in diameter; styles united below.

In rich woods, New Brunswick to Georgia, Minnesota, South Dakota and Missouri. July–Aug. Spignet. Spicebush. Petty morel. Life-of-man. Old maid's-root.

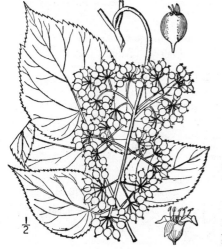

3. Aralia nudicaùlis L.   Wild or Virginian Sarsaparilla.   Fig. 3091.

Aralia nudicaulis L. Sp. Pl. 274. 1753.
Aralia nudicaulis prolifera A. C. Apgar, Bull. Torr. Club **14**: 166. 1887.
A. nudicaulis elongata Nash, loc. cit. **20**: 374. 1893.

Acaulescent or nearly so. Rootstock long; leaf arising with the peduncle from the very short stem, both sheathed at the base by dry thin scales; petioles erect, 6′–12′ long; primary divisions of the leaf ternate, slender-stalked, pinnately 3–5-foliolate; leaflets oval, ovate or ovate-lanceolate, acuminate, finely serrate, 2′–5′ long; umbels commonly 3, simple, rarely compound; involucre none; pedicels slender, glabrous; flowers greenish, 1½″ broad; fruit globose, purplish-black, about 3″ long, 5-lobed when dry.

In woods, Newfoundland to Manitoba, Idaho, Georgia, Missouri and Colorado. Small spikenard. Rabbit-root. False sarsaparilla. Wild liquorice. Shot-bush. May–June.

4. Aralia híspida Vent.   Bristly Sarsaparilla.   Wild Elder.   Fig. 3092.

Aralia hispida Vent. Hort. Cels, *pl. 41.* 1800.

Erect, leafy, 1°–3° high, the stem and petioles hispid with slender bristles. Leaves bipinnate; leaflets ovate or oval, acute, glabrous or pubescent on the veins beneath, sharply serrate, 1′–2′ long; umbels several, slender-peduncled, simple; pedicels glabrous; flowers white, 1″ broad; fruit dark purple, 3″–4″ in diameter, strongly 5-lobed when dry.

In rocky or sandy woods, and clearings, Newfoundland to North Carolina, Hudson Bay, Minnesota, Indiana and Michigan. June–July. Rough sarsaparilla. Dwarf elder. Hyeble. Pigeon-berry.

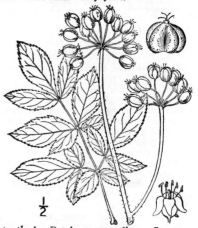

2. PÀNAX L. Sp. Pl. 1058. 1753.

Erect perennial herbs, from globose or elongated aromatic roots, with a verticil of digitately compound leaves at the summit of the stem. Umbels solitary, terminal, simple. Flowers greenish or white, polygamous. Calyx-limb obscurely 5-toothed. Petals 5, spreading. Stamens 5, alternate with the petals. Styles 2 or 3. Fruit a small drupe-like somewhat flattened berry, enclosing 2 or 3 seeds. [Greek, all-healing.]

About 7 species, of eastern North America and Asia.   Type species: *Panax quinquefolium* L.

Leaflets 5, ovate or obovate, stalked, acuminate.   1. *P. quinquefolium.*
Leaflets 3–5, oval, to oblanceolate, sessile, obtuse.   2. *P. trifolium.*

1. Panax quinquefòlium L.   Ginseng.   Red-berry.   Sang.   Fig. 3093.

Panax quinquefolium L. Sp. Pl. 1058. 1753.
Ginseng quinquefolium Wood, Bot. & Flor. 142. 1873.

Glabrous, 8′–15′ high. Root fusiform, deep. Petioles 1½′–4′ long; leaflets 5 (rarely 6–7), stalked, thin, ovate or obovate, acuminate, 2′–5′ long, 1′–2′ wide, irregularly dentate; peduncle slender, 1′–2′ long; umbel 6–20-flowered; pedicels 3″–6″ long in fruit; flowers about 1″ broad; styles usually 2; fruit somewhat didymous, bright crimson, 5″ broad.

In rich woods, Quebec to Alabama, Ontario, Minnesota, Nebraska and Missouri. July–Aug. The plant has become rare in most parts of its range by the gathering of its roots for export to China, but is now extensively cultivated in artificial shade.

2. Panax trifòlium L. Dwarf Ginseng or Ground-nut. Fig. 3094.

Panax trifolium L. Sp. Pl. 1059. 1753.
Ginseng trifolium Wood, Bot. & Flor. 142. 1873.

Glabrous, 3′–8′ high. Root globose, deep, about ½′ in diameter, pungent to the taste; petioles ½′–2′ long; leaflets 3–5, oval to oblanceolate, sessile, obtuse, usually narrowed at the base, 1′–1½′ long, 3″–8″ wide, dentate or serrate; peduncles 1′–2½′ long; pedicels 1″–1½″ long in fruit; flowers white, often monoecious, about 1″ broad; styles usually 3; fruit mostly 3-angled (or when with 2 styles, didymous), yellow, about 2″ broad.

In moist woods and thickets, Nova Scotia to Georgia, west to Ontario, Wisconsin and Iowa. April–June.

3. ECHINOPÀNAX Decne. & Pl. Rev. Hort. IV. 3: 105. 1854.

[RICINOPHYLLUM Pall.; Ledeb. Fl. Ross. 2: 375. Hyponym. 1844.]

A densely prickly shrub, with palmately lobed leaves and racemed or panicled umbels of small greenish-white flowers. Calyx-teeth obsolete; petals 5, valvate; stamens 5; filaments filiform; anthers oblong or ovate; ovary 2–3-celled; styles 2; stigma terminal. Fruit laterally compressed, of 2 carpels. [Greek, prickly *Panax*.]

A monotypic genus of northwestern North America and northeastern Asia.

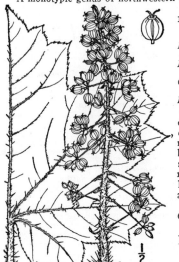

1. Echinopanax hórridum (J. E. Smith) Decne. & Planch. Devil's Club. Fig. 3095.

Panax horridum J. E. Smith, in Rees' Cyclop. 26: no. 10. 1819.
E. horridum Decne. & Planch.; Cooper, Pac. R. R. Rep. 12: 31. 1860.
Oplopanax horridum Miq. Ann. Mus. Bot. Lugd. Bat. 1: 116. 1863.
Fatsia horrida B. & H.; S. Wats. Bot. Cal. 1: 273. 1876.

Stems erect from a decumbent base, up to 13° high, densely prickly, leafy above; leaves nearly orbicular in outline, 6′–2° broad, cordate at the base with a rather narrow sinus, 3–11-lobed, with scattered prickles on both sides and puberulent beneath, the lobes acute, sharply irregularly serrate; inflorescence wooly, terminal, 4′–12′ long; peduncles subtended by a narrow laciniate bract; pedicels filiform; stamens about twice as long as the ovate petals; fruit 2″–2½″ long, scarlet.

In rocky places, Isle Royale, Lake Superior; Montana to Oregon and Alaska; also in Japan. June.

Family 102. AMMIÀCEAE Presl, Delic. Prag. 1. 1822.*

CARROT FAMILY.

Herbs, with alternate decompound, compound or sometimes simple leaves, the petioles often dilated at the base, the stems often hollow. Stipules none, or rarely present and minute. Flowers small, white, yellow, greenish, blue or purple, generally in compound or simple umbels, rarely in heads or capitate clusters, often polygamous. Umbels and umbellets commonly involucrate or involucellate. Calyx-tube wholly adnate to the ovary, its margin truncate or 5-toothed, the teeth seldom conspicuous. Petals 5, inserted on the margin of the calyx, usually with an inflexed tip, often emarginate or 2-lobed, those of the outer flowers sometimes larger than those of the inner. Stamens 5, inserted on the epigynous disk; filaments filiform; anthers versatile. Ovary inferior, 2-celled; styles 2, filiform, distinct, straight or recurved after flowering, persistent, often borne on a conic or depressed stylopodium; ovules 1 in each cavity, pendulous, anatropous. Fruit dry, composed of 2 carpels (mericarps), which generally separate from each other

_____
* Text prepared with the assistance of Dr. J. N. ROSE.

at maturity along the plane of their contiguous faces (the commissure). Fruit either flattened laterally (at right angles to the commissure), or dorsally (parallel to the commissure), or nearly terete (not flattened). Carpels after parting from each other supported on the summit of a slender axis (the carpophore), each with 5 primary ribs in their pericarps (rarely ribless), and in some genera with 4 additional secondary ones, the ribs or some of them often winged. Pericarp membranous or corky-thickened, usually containing oil-tubes between the ribs, or under the ribs and on the commissural sides, sometimes irregularly scattered, sometimes none. Seeds 1 in each carpel, usually adnate to the pericarp, their inner faces flat or concave; seed-coat thin; endosperm cartilaginous; embryo small, placed near the hilum; cotyledons ovate, oblong or linear.

About 250 genera and probably 2000 species, of wide geographic distribution, not abundant in tropical regions. The mature fruit is necessary for the certain determination of most of the genera and many of the species, the flowers being very much alike in all, and the leaves exhibiting great diversity in the same genus. The family is also known as UMBELLIFERAE, a misleading designation, many other plants bearing their flowers in umbels, and several of its genera bear them otherwise.

    1. Fruit ribless, scaly; flowers densely capitate (ERYNGIEAE).   1. *Eryngium.*
    2. Fruit ribbed or rarely ribless, not scaly; flowers umbelled, the umbels sometimes compact.
        A. Fruit ribless, covered with hooked prickles (SANICULAE).   2. *Sanicula.*
        B. FRUIT RIBBED, AT LEAST ITS BEAK, THE RIBS RARELY OBSOLETE.
a. *Fruit with both primary and secondary ribs, the latter the more prominent, armed with hooked prickles, primary ribs bristly* (CAUCALIEAE).
    Calyx-teeth obsolete; fruit dorsally flattened.   3. *Daucus.*
    Calyx-teeth prominent; fruit laterally flattened.   4. *Torilis.*
b. *Fruit with primary ribs only* (AMMINEAE).
* Fruit linear or linear-oblong, several times longer than **wide.**
    Fruit bristly.
        Fruit with a beak much longer than the body.   5. *Scandix.*
        Fruit beakless, narrowed to the base.   6. *Washingtonia.*
    Fruit not bristly.
        Fruit beaked, the beak shorter than the body; oil-tubes none.   7. *Cerefolium.*
        Fruit beakless, or short-beaked; with oil-tubes.
            Annual herbs, with decompound leaves.   8. *Chaerophyllum.*
            Perennial herb, with 3-foliolate leaves.   9. *Deringa.*
** Fruit oblong to ovoid or globose, not more than about twice as long as wide.
    † **Fruit much flattened dorsally, parallel with the commissure.**
    Leaf-segments entire.   10. *Pseudotaenidia.*
    Leaf-segments toothed or incised, or leaves dissected.
        Acaulescent or nearly so.
            Calyx-teeth obsolete; stylopodium none.   11. *Cogswellia.*
            Calyx-teeth distinct; stylopodium flat, evident.   12. *Cynomarathrum.*
        Leafy-stemmed; stylopodium conic or depressed.
            Flowers yellow or greenish-yellow; stylopodium depressed.
                Fruit with thickened corky margins, the ribs obscure; perennial, native.
                        13. *Pleiotaenia.*
                Fruit thin-margined, the ribs distinct; introduced plants.
                    Annual; leaves finely dissected.   14. *Anethum.*
                    Biennial or perennial; leaves pinnately compound with broad leaflets.
                        Umbels not involucrate.   15. *Pastinaca.*
                        Umbels involucrate, the bracts deflexed.   16. *Hipposelinum.*
        Flowers white or greenish-white; stylopodium mostly conic; involucre none, or of **a** few small bracts, or deciduous; perennials.
            Oil-tubes large, not extending to the base of the fruit.   17. *Heracleum.*
            Oil-tubes slender, extending to the base of the fruit or very nearly to the base.
                Lateral wings of the fruit distinct, forming a double border.
                    Leaves 2–3-pinnately decompound, with narrow segments; stylopodium depressed-conic.   18. *Conioselinum.*
                    Leaves ternately or pinnately compound, with broad segments; stylopodium depressed.   19. *Angelica.*
               Lateral wings of the fruit contiguous.
                  Native marsh herbs; leaves pinnate, or reduced to hollow phyllodes.
                        20. *Oxypolis.*
                  Introduced field herb; leaves ternate.   21. *Imperatoria.*
  †† **Fruit not flattened, or flattened laterally (at right angles to the commissure).**
    ‡ *Petals yellow or greenish-yellow (sometimes deep purple in Thaspium).*
    Leaves entire, perfoliate in our species; fruit without oil-tubes.   22. *Bupleurum.*
    Leaves compound; fruit with oil-tubes.
        Fruit not flattened, all its ribs winged; stylopodium none.   23. *Thaspium.*
        Fruit laterally flattened, its ribs not winged.
            Leaf-segments entire; stylopodium none; oil-tubes many.   24. *Taenidia.*
            Leaf-segments crenate, lobed or incised.
                Stylopodium none.   25. *Zizia.*
                Stylopodium present, conic or depressed.

Involucre of 2–4 linear bracts; stylopodium depressed. 26. *Apium.*
Involucre none.
　　Stylopodium large, conic; tall introduced plant with filiform leaf-segments.
　　　　　　　　　　　　　　　　　　　　　　　　　27. *Foeniculum.*
　　Stylopodium depressed; low native perennials with decompound leaves.
　　　　　　　　　　　　　　　　　　　　　　　　　28. *Musineon.*

‡‡ *Petals white, greenish-white or rarely pinkish.*

§ **Fruit nearly terete, not flattened either laterally or dorsally, or very slightly flattened.**
Umbels compound; leaves compound or simple.
　Ribs of the carpels all winged.
　　Involucre none.　　　　　　　　　　　　　　　　　29. *Cymopterus.*
　　Involucre of broad membranous bracts.　　　　　　30. *Phellopterus.*
　Ribs of the carpels distinct but not winged.
　Ribs all corky-thickened.
　　Annual; leaves finely dissected.　　　　　　　　　31. *Aethusa.*
　　Perennial; leaf-segments broad.　　　　　　　　　32. *Coelopleurum.*
　Dorsal ribs slender, the lateral sometimes corky.
　　Lateral ribs corky-thickened; leaves simple or simply pinnate.
　　　　　　　　　　　　　　　　　　　　　　　　　33. *Cynosciadium.*
　　None of the ribs corky-thickened; leaves compound.
　　　Annual; leaves dissected into filiform segments; fruit subglobose.
　　　　　　　　　　　　　　　　　　　　　　　　　34. *Coriandrum.*
　　　Perennial; leaf-segments broad; fruit oblong.　35. *Ligusticum.*
Umbels simple; leaves reduced to hollow jointed phyllodes.　36. *Lilaeopsis.*

§§ **Fruit laterally flattened.**
Umbels and leaves simple; no oil-tubes in the fruit.
Ribs of the fruit not anastomosing.　　　　　　　　　37. *Hydrocotyle.*
Ribs of the fruit anastomosing.　　　　　　　　　　　38. *Centella.*
Umbels compound.
Fruit tubercled or bristly.
　Seed-face concave.　　　　　　　　　　　　　　　39. *Spermolepis.*
　Seed face flat.　　　　　　　　　　　　　　　　　40. *Ammoselinum.*
Fruit smooth, neither tubercled nor bristly.
　Carpels strongly flattened laterally; fruit nearly orbicular; plants acaulescent.
　　　　　　　　　　　　　　　　　　　　　　　　　41. *Erigenia.*
　Carpels nearly terete, or only slightly flattened.
　　No oil-tubes in the fruit.
　　　Seed-face concave; involucre present.　　　　　42. *Conium.*
　　　Seed-face flat; involucre none.　　　　　　　　43. *Aegopodium.*
　　Fruit with oil-tubes.
　　　Seed-face concave; oil-tubes numerous; roots tuberous. 44. *Eulophus.*
　　　Seed-face flat.
　　　　Oil-tubes numerous; ribs filiform or inconspicuous.
　　　　　Pericarp thin.　　　　　　　　　　　　　45. *Pimpinella.*
　　　　　Pericarp corky-thickened.　　　　　　　　46. *Berula.*
　　　　Oil-tubes 1–3 in the intervals; fruit distinctly ribbed.
　　　　　Umbels terminal or axillary.
　　　　　　Stylopodium depressed; leaves once pinnate; oil-tubes 1–3 in
　　　　　　　the intervals.　　　　　　　　　　　47. *Sium.*
　　　　　　Stylopodium conic; oil-tubes solitary in the intervals.
　　　　　　　Ribs, at least the lateral ones, corky-thickened.
　　　　　　　　Annuals; leaves finely dissected. 48. *Ptilimnium.*
　　　　　　　　Perennials; leaves decompound. 49. *Cicuta.*
　　　　　　　Ribs not corky-thickened.
　　　　　　　　Leaves decompound.　　　　50. *Carum.*
　　　　　　　　Leaves reduced to hollow jointed phyllodes.
　　　　　　　　　　　　　　　　　　　　51. *Harperella.*
　　　　　Umbels, at least the lower, opposite the leaves.　52. *Celeri.*

1. ERÝNGIUM [Tourn.] L. Sp. Pl. 232. 1753.

Mostly perennial herbs, with spiny-toothed lobed dentate or sometimes dissected, rarely entire leaves, and dense bracted heads or spikes of small white or blue sessile flowers, subtended by bractlets. Calyx-teeth rigid, pungent, or acute. Petals erect, the apex emarginate with a long inflexed tip. Disk expanded. Styles slender. Fruit obovoid or ovoid, scaly or tuberculate, ribless, somewhat flattened laterally. Carpels nearly terete, the oil-tubes usually 5. [Greek, a kind of thistle.]

About 175 species, of wide geographic distribution in tropical and temperate regions. Besides the following, about 25 others occur in the southern and western parts of North America. Type species: *Eryngium maritimum* L.

Plants erect, tall; stem-leaves spiny or bristly-margined.
　Leaves elongated-linear, parallel-veined.　　　　　1. *E. aquaticum.*
　Leaves elongated-linear, reticulate-veined.　　　　2. *E. virginianum.*
　Stem-leaves palmately incised-pinnatifid.　　　　　3. *E. Leavenworthii.*
Plants prostrate, slender; leaves unarmed.　　　　　　4. *E. prostratum.*

$\frac{1}{2}$

2. Eryngium virginiànum Lam. Virginian Eryngo. Fig. 3097.

E. virginianum Lam. Encycl. 4: 759. 1797.

Stem slender, erect, glabrous, branched above, striate, 1°–3° high. Upper stem-leaves linear, acuminate, sessile and clasping at the base, 2′–8′ long, spiny-toothed or rarely laciniate, reticulate-veined; basal and lower leaves long-petioled, the blade linear-oblong, often obtuse, entire, or remotely denticulate; heads subglobose, 4″–7″ long, equalling or shorter than the lanceolate spiny-toothed or entire reflexed bracts; bractlets usually 3-cuspidate with the middle cusp longest; calyx-lobes lanceolate, cuspidate; fruit scaly.

In marshes near the coast, New Jersey to Florida, west to Texas. July–Sept.

1. Eryngium aquáticum L. Rattlesnakemaster. Button Snakeroot. Fig. 3096.

Eryngium aquaticum L. Sp. Pl. 232. 1753.

E. yuccaefolium Michx. Fl. Bor. Am. 1: 164. 1803.

Stout, 2°–6° high, glabrous; stem sriate, simple, or branched above. Leaves elongated-linear, acuminate at the apex, mostly clasping at the base, finely parellel-veined, the lower sometimes 3° long and 1½′ wide, the upper smaller, all with bristly margins, the bristles rather distant; heads stout-peduncled, globose-ovoid, 6″–10″ long, longer than the ovate or lanceolate cuspidate bracts; bractlets similar to the bracts but smaller; calyx-lobes ovate, acute; fruit scaly, about 1″ long.

In wet soil or upland, Connecticut to New Jersey, Illinois, South Dakota, Florida, Kansas and Texas. The name *aquaticum* is properly applied to this species, ascertained by a study of the Linnaean type specimen. June–Sept. Water-eryngo. Corn-snakeroot. Rattlesnake-flag or -weed.

$\frac{1}{2}$

3. Eryngıum Leavenwórthii T. & G. Leavenworth's Ervngo. Fig. 3098.

E. Leavenworthii T. & G. Fl. N. A. 1: 604. 1840.

Stout, glabrous, 1°–3° high, branched above. Stem-leaves sessile, or somewhat clasping at the base, palmately pinnatifid into narrow spiny-toothed segments; basal and lowest leaves oblanceolate, mostly obtuse, spinose-denticulate; heads peduncled, ovoid-oblong, 1′–2′ long, nearly 1′ thick, equalling or longer than the spinose bracts; bractlets 3–7-cuspidate, those of the upper part of the heads large and resembling the bracts; calyx-lobes pinnatifid, longer than the fruit.

In dry soil, Kansas and Arkansas to Texas. July–Oct. Briery thistle.

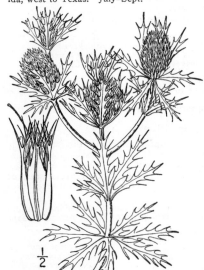

$\frac{1}{2}$

4. Eryngium prostràtum Nutt. Prostrate Eryngo. Fig. 3099.

Eryngium integrifolium Walt. Fl. Car. 112. 1788?

E. prostratum Nutt.; DC. Prodr. 4: 92. 1830.

Prostrate, diffusely branched, rooting from the nodes, the branches very slender, sometimes 18′ long. Lower and basal leaves slender-petioled, oval or oblong, mostly obtuse, entire, or crenate-dentate; stem-leaves smaller, often clustered at the nodes, ovate, few-toothed, or entire or some of them 3-parted; heads ovoid-oblong, dense, about 3″ long, mostly shorter than the lanceolate reflexed bracts.; bractlets very small; fruit about ½″ long, tuberculate.

In low grounds, Kentucky to Missouri, south to Florida and Texas. Summer.

2. SANÍCULA L. Sp. Pl. 235. 1753.

Perennial or biennial mostly glabrous herbs, with alternate palmately 3–7-foliolate or pinnatifid leaves and small yellowish, white or purplish, perfect and staminate flowers in compound generally few-rayed umbels. Umbellets globose. Involucre few-leaved, foliaceous; involucels small. Calyx-lobes membranous, mostly persistent. Petals obovate, or narrower, incurved at the apex, emarginate. Disk flat. Fruit somewhat flattened laterally, subglobose, covered with hooked bristles in our species. Carpels not ribbed; oil-tubes usually 5. [From the Latin, to heal.]

About 25 species, natives of the north temperate zone, South America and South Africa. Besides the following, about 14 others occur in the southern and western parts of the United States. Type species: *Sanicula europaea* L.

* **Perennial; some staminate flowers in separate heads; styles longer than the bristles.**
Petals and anthers greenish white; calyx-segments lanceolate, cuspidate; fruit 3″ long.
                                                             1. *S. marylandica.*
Petals and anthers yellow; calyx-lobes ovate, obtuse; fruit 1½″ long, or less.   2. *S. gregaria.*
** **Biennial or perennial; staminate flowers never in separate heads; styles shorter than the bristles.**
Leaves 3–5-divided; pedicels of staminate flowers 1″ long; fruit less than 2″ long.   3. *S. canadensis.*
Leaves 3-foliolate; pedicels of staminate flowers 2″ long; fruit 3″ long, or more. 4. *S. trifoliata.*

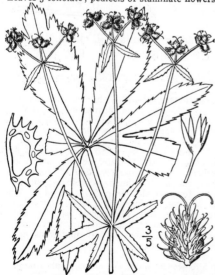

1. Sanicula marylándica L. Black Snake-root or Sanicle. Fig. 3100.

Sanicula marylandica L. Sp. Pl. 235. 1753.

Rather stout, 1½°–4° high, usually simple, topped by a 2–4-rayed umbel. Leaves firm, bluish green, the basal long-petioled, the upper sessile, 5–7-parted; segments 1½′–6′ long, obovate to oblanceolate, irregularly serrate or dentate, often incised; involucral leaves much smaller, 3-cleft; involucel-bracts small, rarely 1″ long; pedicels of staminate flowers 2″ long; calyx 1″ long, parted into subulate segments; petals greenish white, little exceeding the calyx; anthers greenish white; fruit sessile, ovoid, 3″ long, the slender recurved styles longer than the stout bristles; oil-tubes 5, large; seed furrowed dorsally.

In rich woods, Newfoundland to Alberta, Georgia and Colorado. May–July.

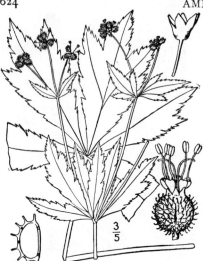

$\frac{3}{5}$

2. Sanicula gregària Bicknell. Clustered Snake-root. Fig. 3101.

S. gregaria Bicknell, Bull. Torr. Club **22**: 354. 1895.

Stems erect, weak, usually clustered, 1°–3° high, umbellate-branched, the branches slender. Leaves thin, bright green, 5-divided; segments stalked, obovate-cuneate to lanceolate, acute or acuminate, doubly serrate with bristle-tipped teeth, sharply incised, mostly less than 3′ long; basal leaves numerous, those of the stem only 1–2, petioled; involucral leaves large, 3-parted, those of the involucre foliaceous; pedicels of staminate flowers 1″–1½″ long, 3 or 4 times the length of the minute campanulate calyx; calyx-lobes ovate, obtuse; petals yellowish, much surpassing the calyx; anthers bright yellow; fruit stipitate, broadly obovoid, 1½″–2″ long, the slender styles recurved; bristles weak, very small; oil-tubes 5, small; seed not furrowed.

In moist woods and thickets, New Brunswick and Ontario to Minnesota, Georgia, Nebraska and Arkansas. May–June.

3. Sanicula canadénsis L. Short-styled Snake-root. Fig. 3102.

Sanicula canadensis L. Sp. Pl. 235. 1753.
S. marylandica var. *canadensis* Torr. Fl. U. S. 302. 1824.

Rather dull green, 1°–4° high, widely branched, the branches forked, the umbellate fruit-bearing rays only 1″–5″ long. Stem leafy; leaves petioled, 3–5-divided; segments cuneate-obovate to narrowly oblong, acute, mucronate-serrate, or incised, often small, but sometimes 3½′ long; involucral leaves small, those of the involucels bract-like; staminate flowers few, on pedicels 1″ long or less; calyx ½″ long, parted into linear-lanceolate acute lobes which exceed the minute white petals; fruit short-stipitate, subglobose, 1″–2½″ long; the bristles slender; styles short, included; oil-tubes 5; seed dorsally furrowed.

In dry woodlands, New Hampshire to Florida, South Dakota and Texas. June–Aug.

Sanicula Smàllii Bicknell, with yellowish or greenish petals, the styles about as long as the calyx-segments, is a related southern plant, ranging north to Missouri and North Carolina.

$\frac{1}{2}$

$\frac{1}{2}$

4. Sanicula trifoliàta Bicknell. Large-fruited Snake-root. Fig. 3103.

S. trifoliata Bicknell, Bull. Torr. Club **22**: 359. 1895.

Stem slender, 1°–2½° high, the branches alternate, the lower often nearly erect, simple or forked into numerous branchlets; umbels of 3–5 often irregular rays 4″–12″ long, leaves rather bright green, thin, slender-petioled, 3-divided, the lateral segments often cleft; segments stalked, broadly ovate, or obovate, or the lateral ones rhomboid, acute, coarsely doubly serrate, or incised, the teeth spinulose-cuspidate; staminate flowers few, on slender pedicels about 2″ long; calyx ½″ long, its linear rigid lobes incurved, subulate; petals white, about half as long as the calyx; styles short, included; fruit 3″ long, or more; larger oil-tubes 2, with numerous minute ones; seed not sulcate.

In hilly woods, Maine to Ontario, southeastern New York, West Virginia and Indiana. June–July.

3. DAÙCUS [Tourn.] L. Sp. Pl 242. 1753.

Biennial or annual, mostly hispid-pubescent herbs, with pinnately decompound finely divided leaves, and compound umbels of white or reddish flowers. Involucre of several foliaceous pinnately parted bracts in our species. Involucels of numerous entire or toothed bracts. Calyx-teeth obsolete. Petals obovate, the apex inflexed, those of the outer flowers often dilated and 2-lobed. Stylopodium depressed or none. Umbels very concave in fruit. Fruit oblong, somewhat flattened dorsally. Primary ribs 5, slender, bristly. Secondary ribs 4, winged, each bearing a row of barbed prickles. Oil-tubes solitary under the secondary ribs, and 2 on the commissural side of each carpel. [The ancient Greek name.]

About 25 species, of wide geographic distribution. Type species: *Daucus Carota* L

1. Daucus Caròta L.   Wild Carrot.   Fig. 3104.

Daucus Carota L. Sp. Pl. 242. 1753.

Bristly-hispid, usually biennial, erect, 1°–3° high, the root fleshy, deep, conic. Lower and basal leaves 2–3-pinnate, the segments lanceolate, dentate, lobed or pinnatifid; upper leaves smaller, less divided; bracts of the involucre parted into linear or filiform lobes; umbels 2′–4′ broad; rays numerous, crowded, ½′–2′ long, the inner ones shorter than the outer; pedicels very slender, 1″– 2″ long in fruit; flowers white, the central one of each umbel often purple, that of each umbellet occasionally so, all rarely pinkish; fruit 1½″–2″ long, bristly on the winged ribs.

In fields and waste places, very common nearly throughout our area, often a pernicious weed. Naturalized from Europe, and native also of Asia. The original of the cultivated carrot. Bird's- or crow's-nest. Queen Anne's-lace. Bird's-nest-plant. Lace-flower. Parsnip. Devil's-plague. Rantipole. June–Sept.

Daucus pusillus Michx., American carrot, of the Southern and Western States, has the stem retrorsely hispid, and linear leaf-segments; it enters our area in Kansas and Missouri.

4. TÓRILIS Adans. Fam. Pl. 2: 99, 612. 1763.

Annual, hispid or pubescent herbs, with pinnately decompound leaves, and compound umbels of white flowers. Calyx-teeth triangular, acute. Bracts of the involucre few and small or none. Involucels of several or numerous narrow bracts. Petals cuneate or obovate with an inflexed point, mostly 2-lobed. Stylopodium thick, conic. Fruit ovoid or oblong, laterally flattened. Primary ribs 5, filiform. Secondary ribs 4, winged, each bearing a row of barbed or hooked bristles or tubercles. Oil-tubes solitary under the secondary ribs, 2 on the commissural side. [Significance of the name unknown.]

About 20 species, natives of the northern hemisphere. Besides the following introduced ones, a native species occurs in western North America. Type species: *Tordylium Anthriscus* L. The generic name *Caucalis* L., used for these plants in our first edition, is now restricted to different Old World species. *C. latifolia* L. has been found on ballast grounds at Philadelphia.

Umbels sessile or short-stalked, capitate, opposite the leaves.	1. *C. nodosa.*
Umbels compound, long-peduncled; rays slender.	2. *C. Anthriscus.*

$\frac{3}{4}$

1. Torilis nodòsa (L.) Gaertn. Knotted Hedge-Parsley. Fig. 3105.

Tordylium nodosum L. Sp. Pl. 240. 1753.

Caucalis nodosa Huds. Fl. Angl. Ed. 2, 114. 1778.

Torilis nodosa Gaertn. Fruct. & Sem. 1: 82. *pl. 20. f. 6.* 1788.

Decumbent and spreading, branched at the base, the branches 6'–12' long. Leaves bipinnate, the segments linear-oblong, acute, entire or dentate; umbels sessile, or short-stalked, forming small capitate clusters opposite the leaves at the nodes; rays 1–3, very short; fruit sessile, ovoid, about 1½" long, the outer with barbed prickles on the secondary ribs, the inner with tubercles.

In waste places and on ballast, Philadelphia, Maryland and Iowa. Also in the Southern States, California, the West Indies, and South America. Adventive from Europe. May–Aug.

2. Torilis Anthríscus (L.) Gmel. Erect Hedge-Parsley. Fig. 3106.

Tordylium Anthriscus L. Sp. Pl. 240. 1753.

Caucalis Anthriscus Huds. Fl. Angl. Ed. 2, 114. 1778.

Torilis Anthriscus Gmel. Fl. Bad. 1: 615. 1806.

Erect, rather slender, 2°–3° high. Leaves bipinnate, or the uppermost simply pinnate, the segments lanceolate, obtuse, dentate or pinnatifid; umbels slender-peduncled, 1'–2' long; pedicels 1"–2" long in fruit; rays 3–8, slender, about ½' long; fruit ovoid-oblong, densely bristly on the secondary ribs, 1½"–2" long.

In waste places, New Jersey to the District of Columbia, western New York, Ohio, Missouri and Oklahoma. Adventive from Europe. Rough- or hemlock-chervil. Scabby head. Rough cicely. July–Sept.

$\frac{2}{3}$

5. SCÁNDIX [Tourn.] L. Sp. Pl. 256. 1753.

Annual herbs, with pinnately dissected leaves, the lobes very narrow. Flowers white, in compound several-rayed (rarely 1-rayed) umbels. Involucre none, or rarely of 1 bract. Involucels of several entire lobed or dissected bracts. Calyx-teeth minute or obsolete. Petals mostly unequal, the outer larger. Fruit linear, or linear-oblong, flattened laterally, prolonged into a beak mostly much longer than the body; primary ribs prominent; secondary ribs none; oil-tubes solitary, or wanting. Seed-face sulcate. Stylopodium short. [Greek name of the plant.]

About 10 species, natives of the Old World, the following typical.

1. Scandix Pécten-Véneris L.   Venus'- or Lady's-comb.   Shepherd's-needle.
Fig. 3107.

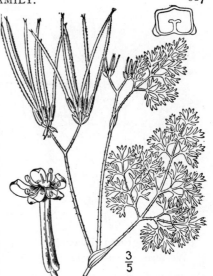

Scandix Pecten-Veneris L. Sp. Pl. 256. 1753.

Pubescent, stem 6'–18' high, branched, the branches ascending. Leaves 2–3-pinnately dissected, the lobes acute, less than ½" wide; lower leaves long-petioled; involucre none; involucels of several lanceolate bracts sometimes 2–3-lobed at the apex; flowers very nearly sessile; fruiting carpels 4"–6" long, strongly ribbed, terminated by a straight flat beak 1½'–2½' long, about 1" wide, its edges with stiff ascending hairs.

In waste places, northern New Jersey to the District of Columbia and in ballast about the sea-ports. Fugitive from Europe or Asia. May–July. Old English names, pink or Adam's-needle, beggar's-, crake- or crow-needles, devil's-darning-needles, hedge-hog, needle-chervil, poukenel.

6. WASHINGTÒNIA Raf. Am. Month. Mag. **2**: 176.   1818.

[OSMORRHIZA Raf. loc. cit. 1818.]

Perennial herbs with fleshy clustered thickish aromatic roots, decompound leaves, and loose few-rayed umbels of white flowers. Involucre and involucels of few narrow bracts, or none. Calyx-teeth obsolete. Petals incurved at the apex. Stylopodium small, conic. Fruit narrow, linear or oblong-linear, short-beaked, compressed, more or less bristly along the ribs, attenuated at the base. Carpels 5-angular, slightly flattened dorsally, the ribs acute and nearly equal; oil-tubes obsolete or none. [In honor of George Washington.]

About 15 species, natives of North America, eastern Asia and western South America. Besides the following about 8 others occur on the west coast and in the Rocky Mountains. Type species: *Myrrhis Claytoni* Michx.

Involucels of several persistent bracts.
    Style and stylopodium ½" long or less.   1. *W. Claytoni.*
    Style and stylopodium 1"–2" long.   2. *W. longistylis.*
Involucels none.
    Fruit beaked; stylopodium conic.   3. *W. divaricata.*
    Fruit blunt; stylopodium depressed.   4. *W. obtusa.*

1. Washingtonia Clàytoni (Michx.) Britton.   Woolly or Hairy Sweet-Cicely.
Sweet Javril.   Fig. 3108.

Myrrhis Claytoni Michx. Fl. Bor. Am. **1**: 170. 1803.
Osmorrhiza brevistylis DC. Prodr. **4**: 232. 1830.
O. Claytoni Clarke in Hook. f. Fl. Brit. Ind. **2**: 690. 1879.
W. Claytoni Britton in Britt. & Brown, Ill. Fl. **2**: 530. 1897.

Erect, at length widely branched above, 1½°–3° high, villous-pubescent throughout, especially when young. Lower leaves long-petioled, large, sometimes 1° wide, ternately decompound, the segments ovate or oval, incised-dentate; upper leaves nearly sessile, less compound; umbels long-peduncled, 2–6-rayed; rays divaricate, 1'–2' long in fruit; involucels of several subulate bracts; pedicels 3"–8" long; fruit about 6" long, about 1" wide; style and stylopodium ½" long, the stylopodium slender-conic.

In woods, Nova Scotia to South Dakota, North Carolina, Alabama, Illinois, Nebraska and Kansas. Ascends to 4000 ft. in Virginia. May–June.

2. Washingtonia longístylis (Torr.) Britton.
Smoother Sweet-Cicely. Anise-root.
Fig. 3109.

Myrrhis longistylis Torr. Fl U. S 310. 1824.
Osmorrhiza longistylis DC. Prodr 4: 232. 1830.
W longistylis Britton in Britt. & Brown, Ill. Fl. 2: 530.
1897.

Similar to the preceding species but the leaflets usually less deeply cleft, the stem either glabrous or densely villous; styles in fruit about 1″ long; bracts of the involucels lanceolate, 3″–4″ long, persistent.

In woods, Nova Scotia to Ontario, Assiniboia, Alabama, Tennessee, Kansas and Colorado. Ascends to 4200 ft. in North Carolina. Roots with a more spicy taste and stronger odor of anise than those of *W. Claytoni*. Plants with stems either glabrous or densely white villous are sometimes found growing together. May–June. Sweet-anise, -chervil or -javril. Cicely-root.

3. Washingtonia divaricàta Britton.
Western Sweet-Cicely. Fig. 3110.

Osmorrhiza divaricata Nutt.; T. & G. Fl N. A. 1: 639. Name only. 1840
W. divaricata Britton in Britt. & Brown, Ill. Fl. 2: 531. 1897.

Foliage pubescent; stem slender, somewhat pubescent or glabrous, 1½°–3° high, widely branched above; leaf-segments thin, ovate, acute, or acuminate, coarsely toothed and usually incised, ½′–2½′ long; umbels long-peduncled, 3–6-rayed, the very slender rays 2′–4′ long in fruit; involucels commonly none; pedicels very slender, 2″–1′ long; fruit about 6″ long, 1″ wide or rather more, beaked; style and stylopodium ¼″–1½″ long, the stylopodium slender-conic.

Woodlands, Quebec to New Hampshire; Manitoba to South Dakota, British Columbia, Utah and California. May–June.

4. Washingtonia obtùsa Coult. & Rose.
Blunt-fruited Sweet-Cicely. Fig. 3111.

Washingtonia obtusa Coult. & Rose, Contr. U. S. Nat. Herb. 7: 64. 1900.

Osmorrhiza obtusa Fernald, Rhodora 4: 154. 1902.

Glabrous or pubescent, 2½° high or less. Leaf-segments ovate to lanceolate, acute or acuminate, ½′–2½′ long; involucre none; umbels 3–5-rayed, the slender rays very widely spreading, or one or two of them deflexed; pedicels widely divergent, ½′–1′ long in fruit; fruit 6″–8″ long, rounded or short-tipped at the apex, the low stylopodium less than ¼″ high.

Woodlands, Newfoundland and Labrador to New Brunswick and Quebec; British Columbia and Assiniboia to California and Arizona. May–June.

7. CEREFÒLIUM (Rivin.) Haller, Stirp. Helv. 1: 327. 1768.

Annuals or biennials, with ternately or pinnately decompound leaves, and compound umbels of white flowers. Involucre none; involucels of few bracts Calyx-teeth obsolete or minute. Apex of the petals inflexed. Stylopodium depressed. Fruit linear, beaked, laterally compressed, smooth. Carpels nearly terete, ribless except at the beak; oil-tubes none. Seed-face channeled. [Latin; derivation as in the following genus.]

A few species, natives of warm and temperate regions of the Old World. Type species: *Scandix Cerefolium* L.

1. Cerefolium Cerefòlium (L.) Britton.
Garden Chervil or Beaked-Parsley.
Fig. 3112.

Scandix Cerefolium L. Sp. Pl. 368. 1753.
Chaerophyllum sativum Lam. Encycl. 1: 684. 1783.
Anthriscus Cerefolium Hoffm. Gen. Umb. 41. 1814.

Annual, glabrous, or finely pubescent above, much branched, 1½°–2° high. Basal and lower leaves slender-petioled, the upper smaller, nearly sessile, all ternately decompound into small segments; umbels numerous, rather short-peduncled, 3–6-rayed, the rays divergent, ¾′–1½′ long in fruit; pedicels stout, 2″–3″ long; bractlets of the involucels linear-lanceolate, acuminate, about 1″ long; fruit linear, 3″ long, glabrous and ribless, tipped with· a ribbed beak of one-third its own length

Roadsides and woodlands, Quebec and Pennsylvania. Naturalized from Europe. May–June.

Anthriscus Anthríscus (L.) Karst. (*A. vulgaris* Pers.) bur-chervil, readily recognized by its short-beaked muricate fruit, has been found as a waif in Nova Scotia.

8. CHAEROPHÝLLUM [Tourn.] L. Sp. Pl. 258. 1753.

Herbs, our species annuals, with ternately or pinnately decompound leaves and small compound umbels of white flowers. Involucre none or rarely of 1–2 bracts. Involucels of numerous small bracts. Calyx-teeth obsolete. Petals inflexed at the apex. Stylopodium small, conic. Fruit oblong or linear-oblong, glabrous or pubescent, flattened laterally. Carpels 5-angled, slightly flattened dorsally, the ribs slender, equal, obtuse or wanting; oil-tubes mostly solitary in the intervals. Seed-face channeled. [Greek, pleasant leaf, from the fragrance.]

About 40 species, natives of the warmer parts of the north temperate zone and northern Africa. Type species: *Chaerophyllum sylvestre* L.

Fruit not beaked, its ribs slender, narrower than the intervals between them.   1. *C. procumbens.*
Fruit beaked, its prominent ribs mostly as broad as the intervals.   2. *C. Teinturieri.*

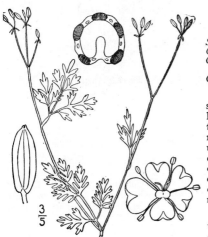

1. Chaerophyllum procúmbens (L.)
Crantz. Spreading Chervil. Fig. 3113.

Scandix procumbens L. Sp. Pl. 257. 1753.
C. procumbens Crantz, Class. Umb. 77. 1767.
Chaerophyllum procumbens Shortii T. & G. Fl. N. A.
   1: 637. 1840.
C. Shortii Bush, Trans. Acad. St. Louis 12: 59. 1902.

Much branched, more or less pubescent, slender, spreading, ascending or erect, 6′–20′ high. Lower leaves slender-petioled, ternately decompound, the divisions ovate, pinnatifid, the ultimate segments obtuse; upper leaves smaller, nearly sessile; umbels 2–6-rayed; rays 1′–½′ long in fruit; flowers few in the umbellets; bracts of the involucels ovate; fruit glabrous or minutely pubescent, oblong or linear-oblong, 2″–2½″ long, narrowed or blunt but not beaked at the summit, the ribs narrower than the intervals between them.

In moist ground, New York and southern Ontario to Michigan, south to North Carolina, Louisiana and Arkansas. April–June.

2. Chaerophyllum Teinturièri Hook. Teinturier's Chervil. Fig. 3114.

C. Teinturieri Hook. Comp. Bot. Mag. 1: 47. 1835.

Chaerophyllum procumbens var. *Teinturieri* C. & R. Bot. Gaz. 12: 160. 1887.

C. reflexum Bush. Trans. Acad. St. Louis 12: 62. 1902.

Similar to the preceding species, more or less pubescent, much branched, often taller. Ultimate leaf-segments acute or obtuse; rays of the umbels 1'–3' long; fruit 3''–4'' long, less than 1'' wide, glabrous or pubescent, narrowed above into a distinct beak, its prominent ribs as broad as the intervals between them, or broader.

In dry soil, southern Virginia to Tennessee, Kansas, Florida and Texas. March–May.

C. texànum Coult. & Rose differs by the fruit being less beaked, and ranges from Texas, northward into Missouri.

C. sylvéstre L. [*Anthriscus sylvestris* (L.) Hoffm.], wild chervil, dog-parsley or wild beaked-parsley, a tall annual with decompound leaves and smooth beakless fruit, has been found as a waif on Staten Island and in ballast about the seaports.

9. DÉRINGA Adans. Fam. Pl. 2: 498. 1763.

[CRYPTOTAENIA DC. Mem. Omb. 42. 1829.]

Perennial glabrous herbs, with 3-divided leaves, and compound irregular umbels of white flowers. Involucre and involucels none. Calyx-teeth obsolete Petals inflexed at the apex. Stylopodium conic; fruit narrowly oblong, laterally compressed, glabrous. Carpels nearly terete, the ribs equal, obtuse; oil-tubes solitary in the intervals and also beneath each rib. Seed-face flat or nearly so. [Said to be named for Deering or Dering.]

A monotypic genus of eastern North America and Japan.

1. Deringa canadénsis (L.) Kuntze. Honewort. Fig. 3115.

Sison canadense L. Sp. Pl. 252. 1753.
C. canadensis DC. Mem. Omb. 42. 1829.
D. canadensis Kuntze, Rev. Gen. Pl. 266. 1891.

Erect, rather slender, freely branching, 1°–3° high. Lower and basal leaves long-petioled, 3-divided, the segments thin, ovate, acute or acuminate at the apex, sharply and irregularly serrate, incised, or sometimes lobed, 1'–4' long, the lateral ones nearly sessile and oblique at the base, the terminal one abruptly narrowed into a margined incised stalk; upper leaves nearly sessile; umbels 4–10-rayed; pedicels unequal; fruit narrowed at both ends, 2''–3'' long, often curved.

In woods, New Brunswick to South Dakota, Missouri, Georgia and Texas. Ascends to 4200 ft. in North Carolina. June–July.

10. PSEUDOTAENÍDIA Mackenzie, Torreya 3: 158. 1903.

An erect glabrous and glaucous perennial, with stout rootstocks. Leaves ternately decompound, with entire segments. Umbels compound. Involucre and involucels wanting, or rarely of 1 or 2 bracts. Calyx-teeth short. Fruit oval or obovate, glabrous, strongly flattened dorsally, the dorsal and intermediate ribs filiform, much narrower than the intervals between them, the lateral ribs broadly winged; oil-tubes 1 or 2 in the intervals; stylopodium very short. [Greek, false Taenidia.]

A monotypic genus.

1. **Pseudotaenidia montàna** Mackenzie.
Virginia Mountain Pimpernel.
Fig. 3116.

Pseudotaenidia montàna Mackenzie, Torreya **3**: 159. 1903.

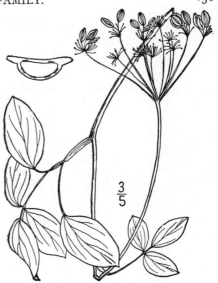

Stems striate, 2½° tall, or less. Leaves 2–3-ternate, the segments ovate to oblong-lanceo late or oblanceolate, ½′–1¼′ long, strongly veined beneath; petioles dilated and sheathing; peduncles 2½′–8′ long; umbel-rays 8–12, the longer up to 1¼′ long; rays of the umbellets 1½″–3½″ long; fruit 2½″–3″ long, 2″ wide.

Mountains of Virginia and West Virginia. Leaves almost the same as those of *Taenidia integerrima*. Flowers have not yet been collected.

---

11. **COGSWÉLLIA** Spreng.; Roem. & Schultes, Syst. Veg. **6**: XLVIII. 1820.

[Lomatium Raf. Journ. Phys. **89**: 101. 1819. Not *Lomatia* R. Br. 1810.]

Perennial herbs, acaulescent or nearly so, from thick fusiform or tuberous roots, with ternate, pinnate, or in our species bipinnate or finely dissected leaves, and compound umbels of white or yellow flowers. Involucre none. Involucels of several or numerous bracts. Calyx-teeth mostly obsolete. Stylopodium depressed or none. Fruit oval, oblong or orbicular, glabrous or pubescent, dorsally compressed. Carpels with filiform dorsal and intermediate ribs, the lateral ones broadly winged; oil-tubes 1–4 (rarely more) in the intervals, 2–10 on the commissural side. Seed-face flat or slightly concave. [Name in honor of Cogswell.]

About 60 species, of western North America. Type species: *Cogswellia villosa* (Raf.) Spreng. The species of this genus were previously referred to the Old World *Peucedanum* and their specific names wrongly applied.

Flowers white or pinkish.   1. *C. orientalis.*
Flowers yellow.
   Fruit glabrous; involucel-bracts united.   2. *C. daucifolia.*
   Fruit finely pubescent; involucel-bracts linear, distinct.   3. *C. foeniculacea.*

1. **Cogswellia orientàlis** (Coult. & Rose) M. E. Jones.   White-flowered Parsley.
Fig. 3117.

Lomatium orientale Coult. & Rose, Contr. U. S. Nat. Herb. **7**: 220. 1900.
Cogswellia orientalis M. E. Jones, Contr. West. Bot. **12**: 33. 1908.

Finely pubescent, the leaves and peduncles 3′–8′ high. Root elongated, often swollen in places. Leaves bipinnate, the segments oblong or ovate, generally pinnatifid into linear or linear-oblong obtusish lobes; bracts of the involucels lanceolate, scarious-margined; umbel 4–8-rayed, the rays unequal, ½′–1½′ long in fruit; pedicels 1″–3″ long; flowers white or pinkish; fruit broadly oval or orbicular, glabrous, 2″–3″ long, the lateral wings narrower than the carpel, the dorsal and intermediate ones inconspicuous; oil-tubes generally solitary in the intervals, about 4 on the commissural side.

In dry soil, Iowa and Minnesota to North Dakota, Washington, Kansas, Iowa and New Mexico. Confused in previous writings with *C. nudicaulis* of the Northwest. March–May.

2. Cogswellia daucifòlia (Nutt.) M. E. Jones.   Carrot-leaved Parsley.   Fig. 3118.

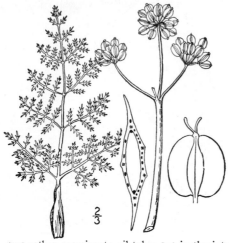

Peucedanum daucifolium Nutt.; T, & G. Fl. N.
    A. 1 : 627.   1840.
Peucedanum foeniculaceum daucifolium T. &
    G Fl. N. A. 1 : 627.   1840.
Cogswellia daucifolia M. E. Jones, Contr.
    West. Bot. 12 : 34.   1908.

Tomentose-pubescent, or becoming nearly
glabrous; peduncles 4'–10' high, usually
exceeding the leaves. Roots stout and
deep; leaves very finely dissected into short,
linear or filiform acute lobes and segments,
the primary divisions ternate or pinnate;
petioles strongly sheathing at the base;
umbels unequally 3–12-rayed, the rays ½'–
1½' long; bractlets of the involucels tomentose, united for more than half their length,
withering; flowers yellow; pedicels 2"–4"
long in fruit; fruit broadly oval, glabrous,
about 3" long, the lateral wings narrower
than the carpel, dorsal and intermediate
ones rather prominent; oil-tubes 1–3 in the intervals.

Prairies and plains, Missouri and Nebraska to Texas.   March–April.

3. Cogswellia foeniculàcea (Nutt.) Coult. & Rose.   Hairy Parsley.   Fig. 3119.

Ferula foeniculacea Nutt. Gen. 1 : 183. 1818.

Lomatium villosum Raf. Journ. Phys. 89. 101. 1819.

Cogswellia villosa Spreng.; Roem. & Schultes, Syst. 6 : 588.
    1820.

Cogswellia foeniculacea Coult. & Rose, Contr. U. S. Nat.
    Herb. 12 : 449. 1909.

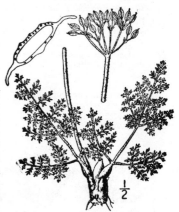

Tomentose-pubescent; peduncles 3'–8' long, exceeding
the leaves. Roots long and deep; leaves very finely dissected into narrowly oblong obtuse lobes and segments,
the primary divisions mostly ternate; umbel 4–10-rayed,
the rays 4"–10" long in fruit; bracts of the involucels
lanceolate, tomentose, or finely pubescent, separate or
nearly so; flowers yellow; fruit oval, finely pubescent,
3"–3½" long, about 2½" broad, the lateral wings narrower than the carpel, the dorsal and intermediate ribs
prominent; oil-tubes 3–4 in the intervals.

Plains and dry soil, North Dakota to Assiniboia, Wyoming, Nebraska and Texas.   April–May.

12. CYNOMÁRATHRUM Nutt.; Coult. & Rose, Contr. Nat. Herb. 7 : 244. 1900.

Perennial, acaulescent herbs, with stout rootstocks, pinnately compound leaves and
yellow flowers in compound cymes. Involucre mostly wanting. Involucels of a few narrow
bracts. Calyx-teeth evident. Fruit oblong, strongly flattened dorsally, the carpels with
sharp prominent dorsal and intermediate ribs, the lateral ribs broader and winged; oil-tubes
usually 3–5 in the intervals and several on the commissural side. Stylopodium flat, evident.
Seed-face flat. [Greek, dog-parsley.]

Six known species of the western United States, the following typical.

1. **Cynomarathrum Nuttàllii** (A. Gray)
Coult. & Rose. Nuttall's Dog-Parsley.
King's Parsley. Fig. 3120.

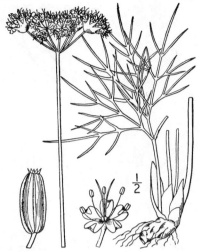

Seseli Nuttallii A. Gray, Proc. Am. Acad. **8**: 287.
1876.
Peucedanum graveolens S. Wats. Bot. King's Exp.
128. 1871.
Peucedanum Kingii S. Wats. Proc. Am. Acad. **22**:
474. 1887.
Cynomarathrum Nuttallii Coult. & Rose, Contr. Nat.
Herb. **7**: 245. 1900.

Glabrous, scape striate, 6′–20′ high, as long as
the leaves or somewhat longer. Leaves all basal,
long-petioled, pinnately or 2-pinnately divided
into narrowly linear segments ½″ wide or less;
umbel unequally 4–20-rayed; rays ½′–1½′ long;
involucels of several lanceolate at first partly
united bracts; calyx-teeth short; fruit oblong,
glabrous, 4″–6″ long, nearly 2″ wide, the carpels
with narrow lateral wings, the dorsal and intermediate ribs also somewhat winged; oil-tubes 3–6
in the intervals, and 6–10 on the commissural side.

In dry, often rocky soil, western Nebraska, Wyoming and Utah. June–Aug.

13. **PLEIOTAÉNIA** Coult. & Rose, Contr. Nat. Herb. **12**: 447. 1909.

[Polytaenia DC. Mem. Omb. 53. *pl. 13.* 1829. Not *Polytaenium* Desv. 1827.]

[Pachiloma Raf. New Fl. N. A. 33. 1836. Not *Pachyloma* DC. 1828.]

[?Phaiosperma Raf. loc. cit. 32. 1836.]

Perennial, nearly glabrous herbs, with pinnately decompound leaves, and compound
umbels of yellow flowers. Involucre none, or rarely of 1–2 linear bracts. Involucels of a
few subulate pubescent deciduous bracts. Calyx-teeth prominent, triangular. Petals obovate-
cuneate, with a long incurved tip. Stylopodium none. Fruit oval or obovate, much flattened
dorsally, thick and corky; dorsal and intermediate ribs obscure, the lateral ones with thick
wings which form a broad margin to the fruit, and are nerved toward the outer margin; oil-
tubes 12–18, contiguous, with numerous smaller ones irregularly disposed in the thick pericarp. Seed flat. [Greek, many-fillets, or oil-tubes.]

A monotypic genus of central North America.

1. **Pleiotaenia Nuttàllii** (DC.) Coult. & Rose.
Nuttall's Prairie Parsley. Fig. 3121.

Polytaenia Nuttallii DC. Mem. Omb. 53. *pl. 13.* 1829.

Pleiotaenia Nuttallii Coult. & Rose, loc. cit. 448. 1909.

Stem slightly scabrous, leafy, 1°–3° high; roots
fusiform. Leaves petioled, or the uppermost smaller
and sessile, pinnate, the segments deeply pinnatifid
or parted, 1′–3′ long, the lobes ovate, oblong or obovate, dentate or entire; umbels 6–12-rayed, 1′–2½′
broad; rays scabrous, ½′–2½′ long; pedicels finely
pubescent, 1″–2″ long; fruit glabrous, 3″–5″ long,
2½″–3½″ broad, ½″ thick, the margins obtuse, the
central part of both carpels depressed when dry.

Dry soil, Michigan and Wisconsin to Tennessee, Alabama, Kansas, Louisiana and Texas. April–May.

14. **ANÈTHUM** [Tourn.] L. Sp Pl. 263. 1753.

Annual glabrous erect herbs, with finely dissected leaves, and large compound umbels of
yellow flowers. Involucre and involucels wanting. Fruit oblong to elliptic, dorsally much
flattened, the lateral ribs winged, the dorsal ones slender, sharp. Oil-tubes solitary in the
intervals. [The ancient name.]

Two Asiatic species, the following typical.

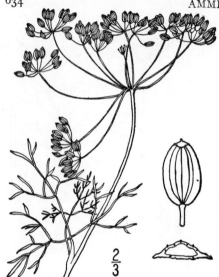

1. Anethum gravèolens L. Dill.
Fig. 3122.

Anethum graveolens L. Sp. Pl. *263*. 1753.

Stem usually branched above, striate, 1°–3° high. Leaves very finely dissected into almost filiform segments, similar to those of *Foeniculum,* the sheathing petioles strongly nerved and scarious-margined; umbels up to 6' broad, several–many-rayed, the rays 3' long or less; fruiting pedicels 5"–8" long; fruit about 3" long, 1½" wide.

Waste grounds, Connecticut to Virginia. Also in the West Indies. July–Sept.

$\frac{2}{3}$

15. PASTINÀCA L. Sp. Pl. 262. 1753.

Tall erect mostly biennial branching herbs, with thick roots, pinnate leaves, and compound umbels of yellow flowers. Involucre and involucels commonly none. Calyx-teeth obsolete. Stylopodium depressed. Fruit oval, glabrous, much flattened dorsally; dorsal and intermediate ribs filiform, the lateral winged, those of the two carpels contiguous and forming a broad margin to the fruit; oil-tubes solitary in the intervals and 2–4 on the commissural side. Seed very flat. [Latin *pastus,* food.]

About 7 species, natives of Europe and Asia, the following typica

1. Pastinaca satìva L. Wild Parsnip. Madnep. Tank. Fig. 2123.

Pastinaca sativa L. Sp. Pl. *262.* 1753.
Peucedanum sativum S. Wats. Bot. King's Exp. 128. 1871.

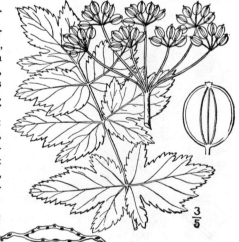

Biennial or rarely annual, glabrous, or somewhat downy-pubescent, 2°–5° high, the root long, conic, fleshy, the stem grooved. Lower and basal leaves petioled, pinnate, often 1½° long, the segments rather thin, ovate or oval, obtuse, sessile, lobed or incised and sharply dentate, 1'–3' long; upper leaves generally much reduced; umbels several or numerous, 2'–6' broad, 7–15-rayed, the rays slender, ½'–2' long; pedicels very slender, 3"–6" long in fruit; fruit broadly oval, 2½"–3½" long, 2"–3" broad, the dorsal and intermediate ribs not prominent but the oil-tubes conspicuous.

$\frac{3}{5}$

Roadsides and waste places, a very common weed in nearly all parts of our area. Naturalized from Europe. June–Sept. Queen-weed. Bird's-nest. Hart's-eye.

16. HIPPOSELÌNUM (Dalerech.) Britton & Rose.

A perennial herb, with decompound leaves, their segments broad, cuneate, and large umbels of whitish-yellow flowers. Involucre and involucels of many narrow bracts. Calyx-teeth very small. Fruit ovate-oblong, somewhat flattened dorsally; primary ribs winged; oil-tubes solitary in the intervals, 2 on the commissural side. [Greek, horse-parsley.]

A monotypic genus of the Old World.

1. Hipposelinum Levîsticum (L.) Britton & Rose. Lovage. Fig. 3124.

Ligusticum Levisticum L. Sp. Pl. 250. 1753.
Levisticum officinale Koch, Nov. Act Nat. Cur.
12¹: 101. 1824.
Levisticum Levisticum Karst. Deutsch. Fl. 844.
1882.

Stout, branched, 6° high or less, glabrous,
except the puberulent pedicels, the rootstock
stout, yellowish. Leaf-segments broadly ovate
or oblong, 2′–3′ long, often 2′ wide, entire and
cuneate at the base, sharply and coarsely lobed
or toothed above the middle; umbels 2′–3′
broad, the rays stout; pedicels short, about 2″
long, about as long as the fruits.

Roadsides and waste grounds, escaped from cultivation, Vermont to Pennsylvania. Native of
southern Europe. June–Aug.

17. HERACLÈUM L. Sp. Pl. 249. 1753.

Erect, mostly pubescent perennial herbs, with
ternately compound leaves, and compound
umbels of white or pinkish flowers. Bracts of the involucre few and deciduous, or none.
Involucels of numerous linear bracts. Calyx-teeth obsolete or small. Petals cuneate, or
clawed, those of the outer flowers dilated and obcordate or 2-lobed. Stylopodium thick,
conic. Fruit much flattened dorsally, broadly oval, obovate, or orbicular; dorsal and intermediate ribs filiform, the lateral ones broadly winged and the wings nerved near the outer
margin; oil-tubes extending only to about the middle of the carpels, conspicuous, 1 in each
interval, 2–4 on the commissural side. [Greek, to Hercules.]

About 60 species, natives of the northern
hemisphere, only the following in North America.
Type species: *Heracleum Sphondylium* L.

1. Heracleum lanàtum Michx. Cow-Parsnip. Fig. 3125.

H. lanatum Michx. Fl. Bor. Am. 1: 166. 1803.

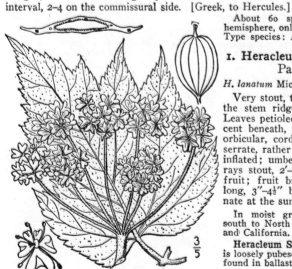

Very stout, tomentose-pubescent, 4°–8° high,
the stem ridged, often 2′ thick at the base.
Leaves petioled, ternately divided, very pubescent beneath, the segments broadly ovate, or
orbicular, cordate, stalked, lobed and sharply
serrate, rather thin, 3′–6′ broad; petioles much
inflated; umbels 6′–12′ broad, 8–30-rayed, the
rays stout, 2′–4′ long; pedicels 3″–9″ long in
fruit; fruit broadly oval, or obovate, 4″–6″
long, 3″–4½″ broad, finely pubescent, emarginate at the summit.

In moist ground, Newfoundland to Alaska,
south to North Carolina, Missouri, Kansas, Utah
and California. Master-wort. June–July.

Heracleum Sphondýlium L., of Europe, which
is loosely pubescent, with pinnate leaves, has been
found in ballast and waste grounds about the seaports.

18. CONIOSELÌNUM Hoffm. Umb. Ed. 2, 185. 1816.

Erect perennial glabrous branching herbs, with pinnately decompound leaves, and compound umbels of white flowers. Involucre none, or of a few short bracts. Involucels of
several narrowly linear bracts. Calyx-teeth obsolete. Petals with an infolded tip. Stylopodium depressed-conic. Fruit oval or oblong, dorsally flattened. Carpels with prominent
approximate dorsal and intermediate ribs, the lateral ones broadly winged and conspicuous.
Oil-tubes mostly 2–3 in the intervals, and 4–8 on the commissural side. Seed-face slightly
concave, its back strongly convex. [Greek, hemlock-parsley.]

About 10 species of the north temperate zone. Besides the following, some 3 others occur in
western North America. Type species: *Conioselinum tataricum* Hoffm.

1. Conioselinum chinénse (L.) B.S.P.   Hemlock-Parsley.   Fig. 3126.

Athamanta chinensis L. Sp. Pl. 245. 1753.

Selinum canadense Michx. Fl. Bor. Am. 1: 165. 1803.

C. (?) *canadense* T. & G. Fl. N. A. 1: 619. 1840.

Conioselinum chinense B.S.P. Prel. Cat. N. Y. 22. 1888.

Stem terete, striate, 2°–5° high. Lower leaves long-petioled, the upper nearly sessile, all decompound into linear-oblong acutish segments; petioles sheathing; umbels terminal and axillary, 2′–3′ broad, 9–16-rayed; rays rather slender, 1½′–2½′ long; pedicels very slender, 2″–3″ long; fruit prominently ribbed, broadly oval, about 2″ long.

In cold swamps, Newfoundland to southern New York, south in the mountains to North Carolina, west to Ontario, Indiana and Minnesota. Ascends to 5000 ft. in North Carolina. Aug.–Sept.

Conioselinum púmilum Rose, of Labrador, is a smaller plant, with umbel-rays only 6″–9″ long.

19. ANGÉLICA L. Sp. Pl. 250. 1753.

[ARCHANGELICA Hoffm. Gen. Umb. 166. 1814.]

Tall erect perennial branching herbs, with compound leaves and large terminal umbels of white flowers (in our species). Involucre none, or of a few small bracts. Involucels of several small bracts, or sometimes wanting. Calyx-teeth obsolete or small. Petals with an inflexed tip. Stylopodium depressed. Fruit ovate or oval, dorsally compressed, pubescent or glabrous. Dorsal and intermediate ribs prominent, approximate, the lateral ones broadly winged. Oil-tubes solitary, several or numerous in the intervals, 2–10 on the commissural side. Seed-face flat or somewhat concave. [Named for its supposed healing virtues.]

About 40 species, natives of the northern hemisphere and New Zealand. Besides the following, some 18 others occur in the southern and western parts of North America. Type species: *Angelica Archangelica* L.

Umbels glabrous, or nearly so; leaf-segments acute or acutish.
    Oil-tubes 1 (rarely 2–3) in the intervals; wings broader than the carpels.   1. *A. Curtisii.*
    Oil-tubes numerous and contiguous; wings narrower than the carpels.   2. *A. atropurpurea.*
Umbels densely tomentose; leaf-segments obtuse.   3. *A. villosa.*

1. Angelica Curtísii Buckl.   Curtis' Angelica.   Fig. 3127.

A. Curtisii Buckl. Am. Journ. Sci. 45: 173. 1843.

Glabrous, or the umbels and upper part of the stem slightly pubescent, 2°–3½° high. Leaves biternate, the divisions quinate or pinnate, the lower long-stalked, the upper mostly reduced to inflated petioles; segments rather thin, sometimes slightly pubescent on the veins beneath, ovate, acute or acuminate, sharply and irregularly dentate or incised, 2′–4′ long; umbels 3′–6′ broad, 9–25-rayed; rays rather stout, 1½′–3′ long; pedicels slender, 4″–6″ long, fruit oval, glabrous, 2″–3″ long, emarginate at the base, the lateral wings broader than the carpel; oil-tubes solitary or sometimes 2 or 3 in the intervals; seed adherent to the pericarp.

In woods, central Pennsylvania, south along the Alleghanies to North Carolina, where it ascends to 6400 ft., and to Georgia. Aug.–Sept.

2. Angelica atropurpùrea L.   Great High or Purple-stemmed Angelica. Fig. 3128.

Angelica atropurpurea L. Sp. Pl. 251. 1753.

Angelica triquinata Michx. Fl. Bor. Am. **1** : 167. 1803.

Archangelica atropurpurea Hoffm. Umbel. 161. 1814.

Stout, 4°-6° high, glabrous throughout, or the umbel slightly rough-hairy. Lower leaves often 2° wide, biternate and the divisions pinnate, the upper ones smaller, all with very broad dilated petioles; segments oval or ovate, acute or acutish, rather thin, sharply serrate and often incised, 1¼'-2' long; umbels sometimes 10' broad, 9-15-rayed, the rays 2'-4' long; pedicels very slender, 4"-8" long; fruit broadly oval, 3"-4" long, slightly emarginate at the base, the lateral wings narrower than the carpels; oil-tubes numerous and contiguous; seed becoming loose from the pericarp.

In swamps and moist ground, Newfoundland to Ontario, Minnesota, south to Delaware, Illinois and Iowa. June–July. Aunt Jerichos. Archangel. Masterwort.

3. Angelica villòsa (Walt.) B.S.P.   Pubescent or Hairy Angelica. Fig. 3129.

Ferula villosa Walt. Fl. Car. 115. 1788.
Angelica hirsuta Muhl. Cat. Ed. 2, 30. 1818.
Angelica villosa B.S.P. Prel. Cat. N. Y. **22**. 1888.

Rather slender, 2°-6° high, the umbels and upper part of the stem densely tomentose-canescent. Lower leaves ternate or biternate, often 1° long, the divisions pinnate, the segments thick, oval to lanceolate, equally and rather finely dentate, obtuse or obtusish, 1'-2' long, upper leaves mostly reduced to sheathing petioles; umbels 2'-4' broad, 7-30-rayed; rays slender, 1'-1½' long; pedicels about 2" long; fruit broadly oval, emarginate at the base, 3" long, finely pubescent; lateral wings about as broad as the carpels; oil-tubes generally 3-6 in the intervals; seed adhering to the pericarp.

In dry soil, Connecticut to Florida, Minnesota, Tennessee and Missouri. Ascends to 3200 ft. in Virginia. Aunt Jerichos. July–Aug.

Angelica sylvestris L., of Europe, which resembles this species, but is less pubescent, with ovate to lanceolate acute leaflets, glabrous fruit, and oil-tubes mostly only one in each interval, has been found on Cape Breton Island.

20.　OXÝPOLIS Raf. Neogen. 2. 1825.

[Tiedemannia DC. Mem. Omb. 51. 1829.]

[Archemora DC. Mem. Omb. 52. 1829.]

Erect perennial glabrous marsh herbs, with clustered tuberous roots, pinnate or ternate leaves, or in one species the leaves reduced to hollow jointed phyllodia, and compound umbels of white flowers. Involucre of a few linear bracts or wanting. Involucels of several small bracts, or none. Calyx-teeth acute. Stylopodium thick, conic. Fruit glabrous, dorsally compressed, oval or obovate; dorsal and intermediate ribs slender, the lateral ones winged, strongly nerved along the inner margin of the wing, the carpels appearing as if equally 5-ribbed. Oil-tubes solitary in the intervals, 2-6 on the commissural side. Seed-face nearly flat.

Five known species, natives of North America.   Type species: *Sium rigidius* L.

Leaves all reduced to hollow usually jointed phyllodia.　　　　　　　　　　　1. *O. filiformis.*
Leaves pinnate ; leaflets linear or lanceolate.　　　　　　　　　　　　　　2. *O. rigidius.*

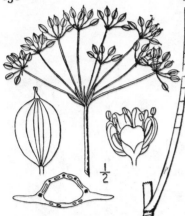

1. Oxypolis filifórmis (Walt.) Britton. Oxypolis. Fig. 3130.

Oenanthe filiformis Walt. Fl. Car. 113. 1788.
Oenanthe teretifolia Muhl. Cat. 31. 1813.
Tiedemannia teretifolia DC Mem. Omb. 51. *pl. 12.* 1829.
Oxypolis filiformis Britton, Mem. Torr. Club 5: 239. 1894.

Stem hollow, 2°–6° high. Leaves reduced to linear hollow usually jointed acute phyllodia 1′–18′ long; involucre of several linear-subulate bracts; umbels 2′–4′ broad, 6–15-rayed; rays slender, ½′–2′ long; pedicels 2″–4″ long; fruit oval, or slightly obovate, 2″–3″ long; oil-tubes large.

In ponds and swamps, southern Virginia to Florida, west to Louisiana. Aug.–Sept. Plants collected in Delaware, referred to this species, differ in having broadly oval corky-winged fruit, an inconspicuous disk, slender conic stylopodium and smaller oil-tubes. Water-dropwort.

2. Oxypolis rigídius (L.) Raf. Cowbane. Hemlock or Water Dropwort. Fig. 3131.

Sium rigidius L. Sp. Pl. 251. 1753.
O. rigida Raf.; Ser. Bull. Bot. 218. 1830.
O. longifolius Britton, Mem. Torr. Club 5: 239 1894.
Sium longifolium Pursh, Fl. Am. Sept. 194. 1814.

Rather slender, 2°–6° high. Leaves simply pinnate, the lower often 1° long or more; leaflets thick, ovate-lanceolate, lanceolate-linear, or oblong, entire, or remotely dentate, 1½′–3′ long, 3″–12″ wide; umbels 2′–4′ broad, 7–25-rayed; rays slender, 1′–4′ long; pedicels 2″–9″ long; fruit oval, 2½″–3″ long, 1½″–2″ broad; oil-tubes small.

In swamps, New York to Florida, Minnesota, Missouri and Louisiana. Aug.–Sept. Pig-potato.

21. IMPERATÒRIA [Tourn.] L. Sp. Pl. 259. 1753.

Tall perennial herbs, with large ternately divided or 2-pinnate leaves, sheathing petioles, and compound umbels of white flowers. Calyx-teeth obsolete. Petals ovate, mostly emarginate. Fruit much flattened dorsally, broadly oval, to nearly orbicular, cordate at both ends, the lateral ribs broadly winged all around, the intermediate and dorsal ribs slender, wingless; oil-tubes solitary in the intervals and 2 on the commissural side. Styles and conic stylopodium short. Seed-face flat. [Named for its supposed forceful medicinal properties.]

About 10 species, natives of the Old World, the following typical.

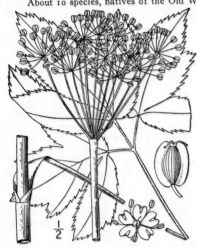

1. Imperatoria Ostrùthium L. Masterwort. Pellitory of Spain. Fig. 3132.

Imperatoria Ostruthium L. Sp. Pl. 259. 1753.

Glabrous, or sparingly pubescent; stem stout, hollow, erect, 2°–5° tall. Leaves ternately divided into very broad stalked ovate to obovate segments, which are often 3-parted nearly or quite to the base, sharply and unequally serrate and often incised, the segments of the long-petioled lower leaves often 5′ broad; rays of the umbels and pedicels very numerous, slender; involucre none, or of 1 or 2 lanceolate bracts; involucel-bracts few, narrow, deciduous; fruit broadly oval, about 2″ long.

In fields, Pocono plateau of Pennsylvania, and Michigan. Reported from Newfoundland. Naturalized or adventive from Europe. Broad-leaved hog's-fennel. Felon-grass. Imperial masterwort. Felonwort. May–July.

22. BUPLEÙRUM [Tourn.] L. Sp. Pl. 236. 1753.

Annual or perennial herbs, with simple entire clasping or perfoliate leaves, and compound umbels of yellow or greenish-yellow flowers. Involucre none in our species. Involucels of 5 ovate mucronate bracts. Calyx-teeth obsolete. Petals broad, the apex inflexed or infolded. Stylopodium conic. Styles short. Fruit oblong or oval, somewhat compressed laterally. Carpels angled, with slender equal ribs; oil-tubes none in our species. Seed-face concave. [Greek, ox-ribbed, referring to the leaves.]

About 65 species of wide geographic distribution. Besides the following another occurs in the Rocky Mountains and northwestern America. Type species: *Bupleurum rigidum* L.

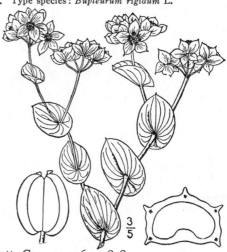

1. Bupleurum rotundifòlium L. Hare's Ear. Thorough-wax or -wort. Modesty. Fig. 3133.

Bupleurum rotundifolium L. Sp. Pl. 236. 1753.

Annual, erect, rather stiff, branching, glabrous, pale, 1°–2° high. Leaves broadly ovate, or oval, mostly obtuse, mucronate, 1′–1½′ long, perfoliate, or the lowest narrowed into a petiole; umbels terminal, 3–6-rayed, the rays seldom over 4″ long; bracts of the involucels about as long as the rays, yellowish; fruit glabrous, about 1½″ long.

In cultivated fields, New Hampshire to North Carolina, west to South Dakota, Tennessee, Kansas and Arizona. Naturalized from Europe. July–Aug.

Bupleurum Odontìtes L., also European, with narrowly linear leaves, is recorded as found in Massachusetts.

23. THÁSPIUM Nutt. Gen. 1: 196. 1818.

Perennial herbs, with ternate or ternately compound leaves, or the basal ones sometimes undivided, and compound umbels of yellow or purple flowers. Involucre none, or of 1–3 bracts. Involucels of several small bracts. Calyx-teeth prominent, acute. Stylopodium none. Style slender. Fruit ovoid or oblong, glabrous or nearly so, scarcely flattened. Carpels somewhat dorsally flattened, the ribs or at least some of them strongly winged; oil-tubes solitary in the intervals, 2 on the commissural side. Seed-face flat. [Name indirectly from the island Thapsus.]

Only the following species, natives of eastern North America. Type species: *Thaspium aureum* Nutt.

Leaves mostly ternate; segments crenate, thickish.   1. *T. trifoliatum.*
Leaves mostly biternate; segments incised or lobed, rather thin.
    Segments ovate, incised.   2. *T. barbinode.*
    Segments pinnatifid into oblong lobes.   3. *T. pinnatifidum.*

1. Thaspium trifoliàtum (L.) Britton. Purple Meadow-Parsnip. Fig. 3134.

Thapsia trifoliata L. Sp. Pl. 262. 1753.
Smyrnium atropurpureum Desr. in Lam. Encycl. 3: 667. 1789.
Thaspium aureum Nutt. Gen. 1: 196. 1818.
Thaspium atropurpureum Nutt. Gen. 1: 196. 1818.
T. trifoliatum Britton, Mem. Torr. Club 5: 240. 1894.
Thaspium trifoliatum aureum Britton, Mem. Torr. Club 5: 240. 1894.

Glabrous throughout; stems erect, more or less branched, 1°–2° high. Upper stem-leaves short-petioled, ternate, or rarely biternate, the segments ovate or ovate-lanceolate, 1′–2′ long, crenate-dentate all around; basal leaves long-petioled, sometimes undivided; umbels 1′–2′ broad; petals dark purple or yellow; fruit 2″ long, all the ribs usually winged.

In woods, Rhode Island to Georgia, Tennessee, Illinois, Missouri, Arkansas and Wyoming. Purple alexanders. Round-heart. The purple-flowered and yellow-flowered races are, apparently, otherwise indistinguishable. June–July.

2. Thaspium barbinòde (Michx.) Nutt.   Hairy-jointed Meadow Parsnip.
Fig. 3135.

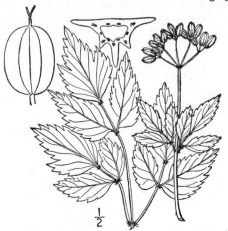

$\frac{1}{2}$

Smyrnium barbinode Michx. Fl. Bor. Am. 1: 167. 1803.
Thaspium barbinode Nutt. Gen. 1: 196. 1818.
T. barbinode angustifolium Coult. & Rose, Bot. Gaz. 12: 137. 1887.

Erect, divergently branched, 2°–4° high, pubescent at the joints and sometimes also on the young shoots and rays of the umbels. Leaves more or less petioled, mostly bipinnate (the upper often simply pinnate and the basal 3-pinnate); segments ovate to lanceolate, acute at both ends, or rounded at the base, rather thin, incised-serrate or cleft, 1′–2′ long; umbels 1′–2′ broad; flowers light yellow; fruit nearly 3″ long, 7 of the ribs commonly broadly winged.

Along streams, Ontario to Minnesota, Kansas, Florida, Kentucky and Arkansas. May–June.

3. Thaspium pinnatífidum (Buckl.) A. Gray.
Cut-leaved Meadow-Parsnip. Fig. 3136.

Zizia pinnatifida Buckl. Am. Journ. Sci. 45: 175. 1843.
Thaspium pinnatifidum A. Gray, Man. Ed. 2, 155. 1856.

Divergently branched, 2°–4° high, more pubescent than the preceding species. Leaves distant, ternately pinnatifid into numerous oblong or linear-oblong lobes, the basal ones long-petioled and very large; flowers light yellow; fruit 1½″–2¾″ long, puberulent, all the ribs winged, but 7 of the wings broader than the other 3.

In woods and copses, Kentucky to North Carolina and Tennessee. June.

$\frac{1}{2}$

24. TAENÍDIA Drude in E. & P. Nat. Pflf. 3[8]: 195. 1908.

A glabrous perennial herb, with 2–3-ternate leaves and compound umbels of yellow flowers. Involucre and involucels none. Calyx-teeth obsolete. Stylopodium broadly conic. Fruit oval, more or less compressed. Carpels obscurely 5-angled with slender equal distant ribs; oil-tubes numerous, 2–6 in the intervals. Seed-face flat or slightly convex. [Greek, with reference to the slender ribs.]

A monotypic genus.

$\frac{3}{5}$

1. Taenidia integérrima (L.) Drude. Yellow Pimpernel.
Fig. 3137.

Smyrnium integerrimum L. Sp. Pl. 263. 1753.
Zizia integerrima DC. Rap. Pl. Jard Genève 3: 7. 1830.
Pimpinella integerrima A. Gray, Proc. Am. Acad. 7: 345. 1868.
Taenidia integerrima Drude, loc. cit. 1908.

Erect, branched, glabrous, somewhat glaucous, 1°–3° high, slender. Leaves 2–3-ternate, the upper with short dilated petioles, the lower long-petioled; segments ovate, oval, or lanceolate, obtuse, or acutish and often mucronulate at the apex, entire, 6″–12″ long; umbels slender-peduncled; rays 10–20, 2′–4′ long in fruit; flowers yellow; pedicels slender; fruit oval, glabrous, about 2″ long.

In rocky or sandy soil, Quebec to North Carolina, Ontario, Minnesota, Arkansas and Mississippi. Ascends 4000 ft. in North Carolina. May–June. Golden alexanders.

25. ZÍZIA Koch, Nov. Act. Caes. Leop. Acad. 12 : 129. 1825.

Perennial mostly glabrous herbs, with ternate or ternately compound leaves, or the basal ones undivided as in *Thaspium,* and compound umbels of yellow flowers, the central fruit of each umbellet sessile. Involucre none; involucels of several small bracts. Calyx-teeth prominent. Stylopodium none. Styles elongated. Fruit ovoid, or oblong, glabrous, or nearly so, somewhat flattened at right angles to the commissure, the ribs filiform, not winged; oil-tubes solitary in the intervals, with a small one under each rib. Seed-face flat. [In honor of I. B. Ziz, a Rhenish botanist.]

Three species, mainly distinguished from the *Thaspia* by their wingless fruit. Type species: *Zizia aurea* (L.) Koch.

Basal leaves 2–3-ternately compound.
    Rays of the umbel numerous, stout; fruit 2″ long.   1. *Z. aurea.*
    Rays of the umbel 2–12, slender; fruit about 1″ long.   2. *Z. Bebbii.*
Basal leaves cordate, undivided; fruit about 1½″ long.   3. *Z. cordata.*

1. Zizia aùrea (L.) Koch. Early or Golden Meadow-Parsnip. Fig. 3138.

Smyrnium aureum L. Sp. Pl. 262. 1753.

Z. aurea Koch, Nov. Act. Caes. Leop. 12 : 129. 1825.

Thaspium aureum var. *apterum* A. Gray, Man. Ed. 2, 156. 1856.

Zizia aurea obtusifolia Bissell, Rhodora 2 : 225. 1900.

Erect, glabrous, branched, 1°–2½° high. Basal and lower leaves long-petioled, 2–3-ternately compound, the segments ovate, or ovate-lanceolate, acute, acuminate or obtusish at the apex, 1′–2′ long, sharply serrate; upper leaves shorter-petioled, ternate; rays of the umbels 9–25, stout, ascending, 1′–2′ long; fruit oblong, nearly 2″ long, about 1½″ wide.

In fields, meadows, and swamps, New Brunswick to Ontario, Saskatchewan, South Dakota, Florida and Texas. April–June. Golden alexanders. Wild parsley.

2. Zizia Bébbii (Coult. & Rose) Britton. Bebb's Zizia. Fig. 3139.

Zizia aurea var. *Bebbii* Coult. & Rose, Bot. Gaz. 12 : 138. 1887.

Zizia Bebbii Britton, Mem. Torr. Club 2 : 35. 1890.

Slender, ascending, simple or branched, 1°–2° high. Basal and lower leaves slender-petioled, 2–3-ternate, the segments ovate, oblong, or oval, mostly obtuse, ½′–1′ long, sharply serrate; stem-leaves ternate or biternate, short-petioled, or sessile, their segments lanceolate, generally narrower than those of the preceding species; rays of the umbel 2–12, slender, divergent, 1′–3′ long; fruit oval, or broader than long, about 1″ long, often 1¼″ wide.

In mountain woods, Virginia and West Virginia to North Carolina, Tennessee and Georgia. May. Golden alexanders.

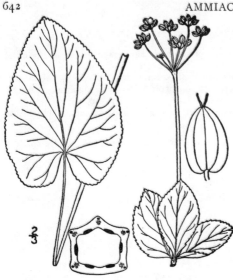

3. Zizia cordàta (Walt.) DC. Heart-leaved Alexanders. Fig. 3140.

Smyrnium cordatum Walt. Fl. Car. 114. 1788.

Zizia cordata DC. Prodr. 4: 100. 1830.

Thaspium trifoliatum var. *apterum* A. Gray, Man. Ed. 2, 156. 1856.

Stout, erect, branched, glabrous, or somewhat pubescent, 2°–3° high. Basal and lower leaves long-petioled, broadly ovate, or orbicular, undivided, deeply cordate at the base, sometimes 6' long, crenate all around; stem-leaves shorter-petioled, ternate, or rarely quinate, the segments ovate, or oval, crenate, or lobed; rays of the umbel 7–16, ascending, 1'–2' long; fruit ovate, or oval, about 1½" long and 1" wide.

In woods, Rhode Island to Minnesota, Alberta, Georgia, Missouri, Colorado and Oregon. Ascends to 3500 ft. in Virginia. **May–June.**

26. ÀPIUM [Tourn.] L. Sp. Pl. 264. 1753.

[PETROSELINUM Hoffm. Gen. Umb. 78, 177. 1814.]

Annual or biennial herbs, with 1–3-pinnate leaves, and yellow or yellowish flowers in compound umbels. Calyx-teeth obsolete. Stylopodium short-conic. Fruit ovate; carpels with 5 filiform ribs; oil-tubes solitary in the intervals, 2 on the commissural side. [Latin, parsley.]

A genus of 5 European species, the following typical.

1. Apium Petroselìnum L. Common or Garden Parsley. Ache. Fig. 3141.

Apium Petroselinum L. Sp. Pl. 264. 1753.
Petroselinum hortense Hoffm. Gen. Umb. 163. 1814.
Petroselinum sativum Hoffm. Gen. Umb. 177. 1814.
Petroselinum Petroselinum Karst. Deutsch. Fl. 831. 1882.

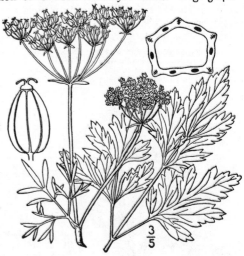

Erect, usually biennial, 1°–3° high, much branched, glabrous. Leaves bipinnate, triangular in outline, the segments ovate, dentate, or incised, or those of the upper leaves linear-oblong and entire; umbels peduncled, 1'–2½' broad, axillary and terminal, 15–20-rayed; rays 5"–12" long; pedicels about 1½" long; involucre of 2–4 linear bracts; bractlets of the involucels subulate; flowers greenish yellow; fruit ovate, glabrous, about 2" long, the ribs rather prominent when dry.

Maryland to Ontario, escaped from cultivation. Introduced from Europe. Native of the Mediterranean region. Leaves of some cultivated races crisped. Summer.

27. FOENÍCULUM Mill. Gard. Dict. Abr. Ed. 4. 1754.

Erect biennial or perennial glabrous herbs, with pinnately decompound leaves, the segments linear or capillary, and compound umbels of yellow flowers. Involucre and involucels none. Calyx-teeth obsolete. Petals obtuse or slightly retuse at the apex. Stylopodium large, conic. Fruit linear-oblong, glabrous, terete or nearly so. Carpels half-terete, dorsally flattened, prominently ribbed; oil-tubes solitary in the intervals. Seed-face flat, or slightly concave. [Latin, diminutive of foenum, hay, from its odor.]

About 4 species, natives of the Old World, the following typical.

1. Foeniculum Foeniculum (L.) Karst. Fennel. Fig. 3142.

Anethum Foeniculum L. Sp. Pl. 263. 1753.

Foeniculum vulgare Hill, Brit. Herb. 413. 1756.

Foeniculum Foeniculum Karst. Deutsch. Fl. 837. 1880–83.

Perennial, branched, 2°–4° high. Leaves very finely dissected into capillary segments; petioles broad, clasping; umbels large, 9–25-rayed, the rays rather stout, somewhat glaucous, 1'–3' long in fruit; pedicels 1"–4" long, slender; fruit about 3" long.

In waste places, Connecticut to Pennsylvania, Virginia, Missouri and Louisiana, escaped from gardens. Bermuda. Adventive or naturalized from Europe. Dill. Finkel. Spingel. July–Sept.

28. MUSÍNEON Raf. Journ. Phys. 91: 71. 1820.

[ADORIUM Raf. Neog. 3. 1825.]

[MUSENIUM Nutt.; T. & G. Fl. N. A. 1: 642. 1840.]

Low perennial resiniferous herbs, branching or acaulescent, with pinnately decompound leaves, and compound umbels of yellow or white flowers. Involucre none. Bracts of the involucels few, narrow. Calyx-teeth ovate. Petals clawed, the apex long and infolded. Stylopodium small, depressed. Fruit ovate or ovate-oblong, slightly compressed laterally, smooth or nearly so in our species (roughened in *M. Hookeri*). Carpels somewhat 5-angled, the ribs filiform, equal; oil-tubes usually 3 in the intervals, the middle one usually largest. Seed-face cancave. [A name of fennel.]

Four known species, natives of northwestern and central North America. Type species: *Seseli divaricatum* Pursh.

Stem leafy, branching; fruit about 2" long.   1. *M. divaricatum.*
Plant acaulescent, tufted; fruit about 1" long.   2. *M. tenuifolium.*

1. Musineon divaricàtum (Pursh) Nutt. Leafy Musineon. Fig. 3143.

Seseli divaricatum Pursh, Fl. Amer. Sept. 732. 1814.

Musenium divaricatum Nutt.; T. & G. Fl. N. A. 1: 642. 1840.

Adorium divaricatum Rydberg, Bot. Surv. Neb. 3: 37. 1894.

Decumbent or ascending, branched, glabrous, 6'–12' high. Leaves bipinnatifid, petioled, 2'–6' long, the rachis narrowly winged, the segments oblong or ovate, acutish, 3–5-dentate; umbels mostly long-peduncled, 1'–2½' broad, 8–25-rayed; rays rather stout, 3"–12" long; pedicels about 1½" long in fruit; flowers yellow; fruit smooth, or very nearly so, about 2" long.

Prairies, South Dakota to Manitoba and Oregon. May–June.

Musineon Hóokeri (Nutt.) T. & G. differs in being scabrous. It inhabits the Rocky Mountain region, ranging eastward into South Dakota and western Nebraska.

2. Musineon tenuifòlium Nutt. Scapose Musineon.
Fig. 3144.

Musenium tenuifolium Nutt.; T. & G. Fl. N. A. 1: 642. 1840.

Adorium tenuifolium Kuntze, Rev. Gen. Pl. 264. 1891.

Acaulescent from a woody root, tufted, glabrous, 2′–6′ high, pale and somewhat glaucous. Leaves petioled, decompound into linear acute incised segments; scape equalling or slightly exceeding the leaves; umbel ½′–1′ broad, 5–18-rayed; rays 2″–5″ long; flowers greenish white (?); pedicels ½″–2″ long in fruit; fruit oblong, nearly smooth, about 1″ long and ½″ thick, its ribs rather prominent when dry.

In dry rocky places, South Dakota, Nebraska, and in the Rocky Mountains. June–July.

29. CYMÓPTERUS Raf. Journ. Phys. 89: 100. 1819.

Perennial subscapose glabrous herbs, with thick roots, pinnately decompound leaves, and white flowers (in our species) in peduncled umbels. Involucre of several bracts or none. Involucels of 1 to numerous bracts. Calyx-teeth rather prominent. Petals inflexed at the apex. Stylopodium depressed. Fruit globose, ovoid or ellipsoid, flattened laterally or not at all. Carpels dorsally flattened, with 3–5 flat equal wings; oil-tubes several or solitary in the intervals, few or several on the commissural side. [Greek, wave-winged, referring to the fruit.]

About 13 species, natives of western and central North America, the following typical.

1. Cymopterus acaùlis (Pursh) Rydberg. Plains Cymopterus. Fig. 3145.

Selinum acaule Pursh, Fl. Am. Sept. 732. 1814.

Cymopterus glomeratus Raf. Journ. Phys. 89: 100. 1819.

Cymopterus acaulis Rydberg, Bot. Surv. Neb. 3: 38. 1894.

Low, the stem seldom over 1′ high. Leaves erect or ascending, bright green, 3′–8′ long, slender-petioled, pinnate or bipinnate into linear-oblong obtuse entire or lobed segments; umbels slender-peduncled, compact, 1′ or less broad, several-rayed; rays only 1″–2½″ long; pedicels very short; involucre none; involucel of a single palmately-lobed bractlet; fruit broadly oval, about 3″ in diameter when mature; oil-tubes 4–5 in the intervals; seed-face nearly flat.

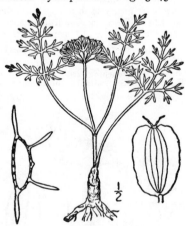

In dry soil, Minnesota, Wisconsin and Iowa to Arkansas, Assiniboia, British Columbia and Colorado. April–May.

30. PHELLÓPTERUS Nutt.; Coult. & Rose, Contr. U. S. Nat. Herb. 7: 166.
1900.

Perennial, nearly or quite acaulescent herbs, with 1–3-pinnate leaves, their segments small, short and broad, the flowers white or purple. Calyx-teeth distinct. Fruit glabrous, ovate to orbicular, each carpel with 3–5 broad thin wings. Stylopodium none. Oil-tubes 2 or 3 in each interval, 4–8 on the commissural side. [Greek, referring to the broad wings of the fruit.]

About 5 species, natives of the central and western United States, the following typical.

1. Phellopterus montànus Nutt. Mountain Cymopterus. Fig. 3146.

Cymopterus montanus T. & G. Fl. N. A. 1: 624. 1840.

Phellopterus montanus Nutt.; Coult. & Rose, Contr. U. S Nat. Herb. 7: 167. 1900.

Somewhat glaucous, or very slightly pubescent. Leaves 1'-6' high, stout-petioled, pinnate, or bipinnate, the segments oblong, obtuse, entire, toothed, or lobed; peduncles stout, 1'-6' high; involucre and involucels of broad membranous somewhat united veined bracts; umbels 1'-2' broad in fruit; rays several, 3"-9" long; pedicels 1"-2" long; fruit ellipsoid, 3"-6" long, the carpels broadly 3-5 winged; oil-tubes 1-3 in the intervals.

Dry soil, South Dakota to western Nebraska, Wyoming, Colorado and Texas. March–April.

31. AETHÙSA L. Sp. Pl. 256. 1753.

An annual glabrous herb, with pinnately dissected somewhat shining leaves, and compound umbels, both terminal and opposite the leaves. Involucre none, or of a single bract. Bracts of the involucels 1-5, setaceous, turned to one side. Calyx-teeth obsolete. Petals inflexed at the apex. Stylopodium broad, thick. Fruit globose-ovoid, glabrous. Carpels dorsally compressed, the 5 ribs prominent, corky, acute, nearly equal; oil-tubes solitary in the intervals, 2 on the commissural side. Seed-face flat. [Greek, burning, from the shining foliage.]

A monotypic genus of Europe and Asia.

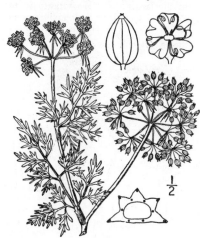

1. Aethusa Cynàpium L. Fool's Parsley or Cicely. Fig. 3147.

Aethusa Cynapium L. Sp. Pl. 256. 1753.

Erect, leafy, dichotomously branched, rather slender, 1°-2½° high. Leaves 2-3-pinnate, the lower slender-petioled, the upper nearly sessile; petiole-bases dilated; ultimate segments linear, acutish; umbels long-peduncled, 2'-3' broad in fruit, 8-12-rayed; rays ½'-1½' long; pedicels 1"-4" long; bractlets of the involucels 2-4, linear, turned downward; fruit about 1½" long, somewhat longer than broad; flowers white.

In waste places, Nova Scotia to Pennsylvania, Ontario and Minnesota. Poisonous. Adventive from Europe. False or dog's-parsley. Dog-poison. Small or lesser hemlock. June–Sept.

32. COELOPLEÙRUM Ledeb. Fl. Ross. 2: 361. 1844.

Stout and tall maritime perennials, with large 2-3-ternate leaves, inflated petioles, and compound umbels of greenish white flowers. Involucre of a few linear deciduous bracts, or none. Involucels of numerous linear bracts. Calyx-teeth obsolete. Petals with an inflexed apex. Stylopodium depressed. Fruit oblong to subglobose, scarcely flattened; dorsal and intermediate ribs prominent, corky-thickened, the lateral ones slightly broader, acute but not winged; oil-tubes solitary in the intervals, 1-2 under each rib and 2-4 on the commissural side. Seed loose in the pericarp, its face flat or slightly concave. [Greek, hollow-ribbed.]

Four or five species of North America and Asia. Type species: *Coelopleurum Gmélini* (DC.) Ledeb.

1. Coelopleurum actaeifolium (Michx.)
Coult. & Rose.   Sea-coast Angelica.
Fig. 3148.

Angelica Archangelica Schrank, Denks. Regens. Bot.
Gesell. 1: Abth. 2, 13. 1818. Not. L. 1753.
Archangelica peregrina Nutt.; T. & G. Fl. N. A. 1:
622. 1840.
Ligusticum actaeifolium Michx. Fl. Bor. Am. 1: 166.
1803.
Coelopleurum actaeifolium Coult. & Rose, Contr. U.
S. Nat. Herb. 7: 142. 1900.

Stout, branching, 2°–3° high, glabrous below,
the umbels and upper part of the stem puberulent.
Lower leaves large, 2–3-ternate, the segments thin,
ovate, acute or acuminate, sharply and irregularly
dentate and incised, 1½′–2¼′ long; umbels 3′–5′
broad, 10–25-rayed; rays 1′–2′ long; pedicels
slender, 3″–6″ long; fruit 2½″–3½″ long, the lateral
ribs scarcely stronger than the others.

Sea-coast, Greenland to Massachusetts, and on the
lower St. Lawrence river. Summer. Referred in
our first edition to *C. Gmelini* (DC.) Ledeb. of eastern Asia and Alaska, the type of the genus.

33. CYNOSCIÀDIUM DC. Mem. Omb. 44. *pl. 11.* 1829.

Glabrous slender branching annuals, the lower and basal leaves mostly linear and entire,
those of the stem mainly divided into few linear segments. Involucres and involucels of
several subulate or narrowly linear bracts, sometimes deciduous. Flowers small, white, in
terminal and lateral compound umbels. Calyx-teeth short, persistent. Fruit ovoid, or oblong,
nearly terete, glabrous, strongly ribbed, the lateral ribs the larger; oil-tubes solitary in the
intervals and 2 on the commissural side of each carpel. Seed-face flat. Stylopodium conic.
[Greek, dog-celery.]

Two known species, natives of the southern United States, the following typical.

1. Cynosciadium pinnàtum DC.   Pinnate
Cynosciadium. Fig. 3149.

C. pinnatum DC. Mem. Omb. 45 *pl. 11. f. B.* 1829.

Stem erect, or assurgent, 1°–2° high. Lower and
basal leaves petioled, the blades elongated-linear,
entire, acuminate or acute at each end, 1′–3′ long,
1½′–3′ wide; stem-leaves pinnately divided nearly to
the midvein into 3–9 narrowly linear entire segments,
the terminal segment much larger than the lateral
ones, or some of them entire; bracts of the involucres
2″–3″ long; umbels 4–10-rayed; rays very slender,
½′–1½′ long; fruit about 2″ long, less than 1″ wide,
tipped by the conic stylopodium and crowned by the
ovate calyx-teeth.

In wet soil, Missouri to Kansas, Oklahoma and Texas.
May–Aug.

34. CORIÁNDRUM [Tourn.] L. Sp. Pl. 256. 1753.

Annual glabrous herbs, with thin, pinnately divided or pinnately decompound leaves, and
compound umbels of white flowers. Involucre none. Involucels of a few narrow bracts.
Fruit subglobose, hard, scarcely flattened, not constricted at the commissure, its ribs slender.
Stylopodium conic, the styles slender. Calyx-teeth ovate, acute. Oil-tubes solitary in the
intervals, a few on the commissural side. [Ancient Latin name.]

Two species, of the warmer parts of the Old World, the following typical.

1. Coriandrum satìvum. L.   Coriander.   Fig. 3150.

Coriandrum sativum L. Sp. Pl 256. 1753.

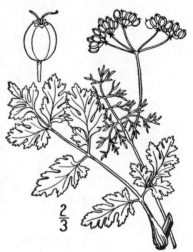

Erect, 2° high or less. Lower leaves pinnately divided, their segments broad, ovate to obovate, variously toothed and cleft; upper leaves pinnately decompound, with narrowly linear segments; flowering umbels 1′–2′ broad, the rays slender; pedicels 1″–2″ long; involucel-bracts deciduous; fruit about 2″ long and thick, its acutish ribs narrower than the intervals between them.

Waste grounds, eastern Massachusetts to Pennsylvania and North Carolina; South Dakota, and in the Western States. Adventive from the Old World. May–July.

Bifora americàna (DC.) S. Wats., of the southwest, an annual with finely dissected leaves, the characteristic fruit composed of two nearly separated subglobose carpels, has been recorded from Missouri, but is not definitely known to grow north of Arkansas.

Bifora ràdians Bieb., of southern Europe, with larger wrinkled fruit, has been collected on ballast and waste grounds in Rhode Island and Pennsylvania.

35. LIGÚSTICUM L. Sp. Pl. 250. 1753.

[LEVISTICUM Hill, Brit. Herb. 410. 1756.]

Perennial glabrous usually branching herbs, with aromatic roots, ternately compound leaves, and large compound umbels of white flowers. Involucre of several narrow mostly deciduous bracts or wanting. Involucels of numerous linear bracts. Calyx-teeth obsolete. Stylopodium conic. Fruit oblong or ovoid, scarcely flattened. Carpels dorsally compressed, the ribs prominent, acute, separated by broad intervals; oil-tubes 2–6 in the intervals, several on the commissural side. Seed-face flat or slightly concave. [Named from Liguria, where Lovage abounds.]

About 20 species, natives of the northern hemisphere. Besides the following, some 7 others occur in western North America. Type species: *Ligusticum scoticum* L.

Leaves thin; fruit ovoid; southern species.   1. *L. canadense.*
Leaves fleshy; fruit oblong; northern sea-coast species.   2. *L. scoticum.*

1. Ligusticum canadénse (L.) Britton. Nondo. Angelico. Fig. 3151.

Ferula canadensis L. Sp. Pl. 247. 1753.

Ligusticum canadense Britton, Mem. Torr. Club 5: 240. 1894.

Stout, erect, much branched above, 2°–6° high. Leaves thin, those of the stem sessile or nearly so, the lower and basal petioled, often 1° wide, their primary divisions ternate, the secondary ternate or pinnate; segments ovate, or oval, 1½′–5′ long, acute at the apex, rounded at the base, coarsely and sharply serrate, or those of the uppermost leaves linear-lanceolate and entire; umbels mostly twice compound, sometimes 10′ broad; bracts of the involucre 2–6, linear; bracts of the involucels several; pedicels 1″–2″ long in fruit; fruit ovoid, 2″–3″ long with prominent slightly winged ribs; oil-tubes 3–4 in the intervals; seed angled on the back.

In rich woods, southern Pennsylvania to Georgia, Missouri and Kentucky. Ascends to 4000 ft. in North Carolina. June–Aug.

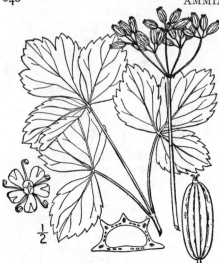

½

2. Ligusticum scóticum L. Scotch or Sea Lovage. Sea Parsley. Fig. 3152.

Ligusticum scoticum L. Sp. Pl. 250. 1753.

Stem simple, or rarely slightly branched, 10′–3° high. Leaves mostly biternate, the segments thick and fleshy, broadly obovate-ovate or oval, 1′–4′ long, shining, obtuse or acute at the apex, narrowed or the terminal one rounded at the base, dentate with blunt or sharp teeth; umbels 2′–4′ broad in fruit, the rays 1′–3′ long; pedicels 2″–5″ long; fruit oblong, 3″–5″ long, the ribs prominent and somewhat winged; seeds rounded on the back.

Along salt marshes, New York to Labrador and the lower St. Lawrence river. Also on the Pacific coast and the shores of northern Europe and Asia. The plant of the New England coast has more acute leaf-segments than the typical form. Shunis. July–Aug.

36. LILAEÓPSIS Greene, Pittonia 2: 192. 1891.

[Crantzia Nutt. Gen. 1: 177. 1818. Not Scop. 1777.]

Small creeping glabrous perennial marsh herbs, the leaves reduced to linear terete septate hollow petioles, with simple umbels of white flowers. Bracts of the involucre several, small. Calyx-teeth acute. Petals concave, acute, incurved at the apex. Stylopodium conic. Fruit glabrous, globose, somewhat flattened laterallly. Carpels nearly terete, the dorsal and intermediate ribs filiform, the lateral ones much larger and corky-thickened, the commissural faces each with a corky longitudinal projection; oil-tubes solitary in the intervals, 2 on the commissural side. Seed terete. [Greek, resembling the genus *Lilaea*.]

A genus of wide geographic distribution, usually regarded as monotypic.

1. Lilaeopsis lineàta (Michx.) Greene. Lilaeopsis. Fig. 3153.

Hydrocotyle chinensis L. Sp. Pl. 339. 1753?
Hydrocotyle lineata Michx. Fl. Bor. Am. 1: 162. 1803.
Crantzia lineata Nutt. Gen. 1: 178. 1818.
Lilaeopsis lineata Greene, Pittonia 2: 192. 1891.

Creeping, rooting in the mud, 2′–5′ long. Petioles linear-spatulate, very obtuse, generally 1′–3′ long but sometimes much longer, about 1½″ thick, hollow, distinctly jointed by transverse partitions; peduncles somewhat exceeding the leaves; umbels 5–10-rayed, the rays 1½″–3″ long; fruit about 1″ long.

In salt and brackish marshes, and on muddy river-shores, New Hampshire to eastern New York and Florida, west to Mississippi. June–Aug.

37. HYDROCÓTYLE L. Sp. Pl. 234. 1753.

Perennial herbs, prostrate and commonly rooting at the joints, with palmately lobed or veined, often peltate leaves, the bases of the petioles with 2 scale-like stipules, and small white flowers in peduncled or sessile simple or proliferous umbels or heads. Bracts of the involucre few and small, or none. Calyx-teeth minute. Petals entire. Disk flat. Fruit laterally compressed, orbicular or broader than high. Carpels with 5 primary ribs, the lateral ones usually curved; no large oil-tubes, but an oil-bearing layer of tissue beneath the epidermis. [Greek, water-cup.]

About 75 species of wide distribution. Besides the following another occurs in the Southwest and on the Pacific Coast. Type species: *Hydrocotyle vulgaris* L. The species are known as Marsh-, or Water-pennywort, or Water-cup.

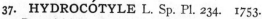

Leaves nearly orbicular, peltate.
 Umbels simple, rarely slightly proliferous; pedicels slender.   1. *H. umbellata*.
 Umbels, at least some of them, proliferous; pedicels, or some of them, short.
  Fruit notched at each end.   2. *H. Canbyi*.
  Fruit not notched at either end.   3. *H. verticillata*.

Leaves nearly orbicular, cordate, or reniform, not peltate.
　Flowers umbellate.
　　Leaves 5–9-lobed; umbels nearly sessile.
　　Leaves 3–7-cleft; umbels long-peduncled.
　Umbels capitate, the heads peduncled.

4. <i>H. americana.</i>
5. <i>H. ranunculoides.</i>
6. <i>H. rotundifolia..</i>

1. Hydrocotyle umbellàta L. Umbellate or Many-flowered Marsh-Pennywort. Fig. 3154.

Hydrocotyle umbellata L. Sp. Pl. 234. 1753.

Glabrous, stem creeping, several inches long, the subterranean branches tuberiferous. Petioles slender, erect, or ascending, 1′–6′ long; leaves peltate, orbicular, or broader than long, sometimes cordate at the base, ½′–2′ wide, crenately 7–11-lobed, the lobes broad, not deep, mostly crenulate; peduncles elongated; umbels simple or rarely with a proliferous extension; pedicels slender, 2″–6″ long; mature fruit notched at both ends, 1″–1½ broad, not quite as long; intermediate ribs corky-thickened; dorsal rib obtuse.

In swamps and low grounds, eastern Massachusetts to Florida and the West Indies, Minnesota, Texas and Mexico. Also in South America and South Africa. June–Sept. Water-navelwort. Water-grass.

$\frac{3}{5}$

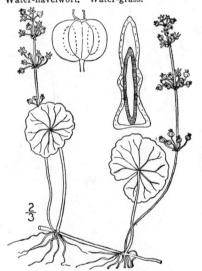

$\frac{2}{3}$

2. Hydrocotyle Cánbyi C. & R. Canby's Marsh-Pennywort. Fig. 3155.

Hydrocotyle umbellata var. ambigua A. Gray, Man. Ed. 5, 190. 1867. Not H. ambigua Pursh, 1814.
H. Canbyi Coult. & Rose, Bot. Gaz. 12: 103. 1887.

Stem creeping, sometimes 12′ long, the subterranean branches tuberiferous. Petioles short, or elongated; leaves peltate, orbicular or nearly so, ½′–1½′ wide, with 7–11 shallow broad mostly crenulate lobes; peduncles elongated; inflorescence mostly proliferous, rarely simply umbellate; verticils 3–10-flowered; pedicels 1″–2″ long, or some of them rarely 4″ long; fruit about 1″ long and 2″ broad, slightly notched at both ends when mature, much flattened, the intermediate ribs corky-thickened, the dorsal one very obtuse.

In moist ground, New Jersey to Maryland. The record of this species from Florida in our first edition should apply to <i>H. australis.</i> June–Sept.

3. Hydrocotyle verticillàta Thunb. Whorled Marsh-Pennywort. Fig. 3156.

H. verticillata Thunb. Diss. 2: 415. pl. 3. 1798.
Hydrocotyle interrupta Muhl. Cat. 30. 1813.

Similar to the two preceding species. Inflorescence always proliferous, 1′–2′ long; verticils 2–6-flowered; pedicels very short, usually less than ½″ long; fruit about 1″ long, 1½″–2″ broad, rounded or truncate at each end, not notched; intermediate ribs of the carpels filiform, not corky-thickened, the dorsal one acute.

In moist soil, Massachusetts to Florida, mainly near the coast, west to Texas, Arkansas and southern California, and in the West Indies, Central and South America. June–Sept.

Hydrocotyle austràlis Coult. & Rose has fruiting pedicels 1″–2″ long, but is otherwise similar to this species. It ranges from southeastern Virginia to Florida. Cuba.

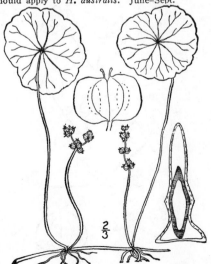

$\frac{2}{5}$

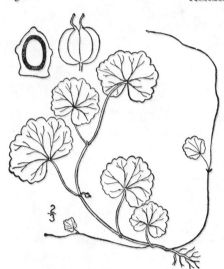

4. Hydrocotyle americàna L. American Marsh-Pennywort. Penny-Post. Fig. 3157.

Hydrocotyle americana L. Sp. Pl. 234. 1753.

Stems filiform, creeping, often bearing small tubers; petioles rather short, seldom over 2' long; leaves membranous, reniform, not peltate, deeply cordate, 1'-2' wide, with 9-13 shallow crenulate lobes; umbels sessile or very nearly so at the nodes, 1-5-flowered; pedicels less than 1'' long; fruit slightly more than $\frac{1}{2}''$ broad and nearly as high, the ribs all filiform.

In wet places, Nova Scotia to Ontario and Minnesota, south to southern New York, Pennsylvania, and in the mountains to North Carolina. Ascends to 3000 ft. in Virginia. June–Sept.

5. Hydrocotyle ranunculoìdes L. f. Floating Marsh-Pennywort. Fig. 3158.

Hydrocotyle ranunculoides L. f. Suppl. 177. 1781.
Hydrocotyle natans T. & G. Fl. N. A. 1 : 599. 1840.

Stem usually floating, sometimes creeping on shores, rather stout, abundantly rooting from the nodes, branched, 6'-24' long. Petioles elongated, weak; leaves reniform, 1'-2' wide, not peltate, 3-7-cleft, deeply cordate at the base, the lobes crenate; peduncles 1'-3' long, much shorter than the petioles, recurved in mature fruit; umbels simple, 5-10-flowered; fruit nearly orbicular, about $1\frac{1}{2}''$ broad, the ribs obscure and filiform.

In ponds and swamps, eastern Pennsylvania to Florida, near the coast, west to Texas, Arkansas, and on the Pacific Coast from Oregon to Lower California. Also in Cuba, Central and South America, Abyssinia and Italy. June–Sept.

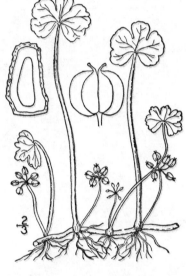

6. Hydrocotyle rotundifòlia Roxb. Asiatic Pennywort. Fig. 3159.

H. rotundifolia Roxb. Hort. Beng. 21. 1814.

Tufted and creeping, the stems very slender. Leaves reniform-orbicular with a narrow or broad sinus, glabrous on both sides or hispidulous beneath, 5''-10'' broad, their petioles slender or filiform; peduncles as long as the petioles, or shorter; capitate umbels several-flowered; fruit slightly notched at the base and apex; its ribs filiform.

Escaped into lawns from cultivation in greenhouses, Pennsylvania, Kentucky and District of Columbia. Native of tropical Asia. Summer.

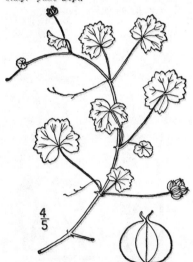

38. **CENTÉLLA** L. Sp. Pl. Ed. 2, 1393. 1763.

Perennial herbs (some African species shrubby), ours with prostrate stems rooting and sending up tufts of long-petioled leaves at the nodes, together with 1–3 long-rayed umbellets of small white flowers, the true umbel sessile. Petiole-bases sheathing. Bracts of the involucels 2–4, mostly prominent. Calyx-teeth none. Disk flat, or slightly concave. Styles filiform. Fruit somewhat flattened laterally, orbicular, reniform, or obcordate, rather prominently ribbed, the ribs mostly anastomosing; oil-tubes none. [Latin, diminutive of *centrum*, a prickle.]

About 20 species, of wide distribution, most abundant in South Africa. The following is the only one occurring in North America. Type species: *Centella villosa* L.

1. **Centella asiática** (L.) Urban. Ovate-leaved Marsh-Pennywort. Fig. 3160.

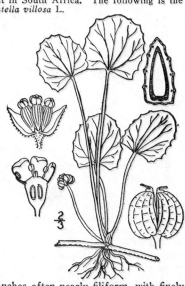

Hydrocotyle asiatica L. Sp. Pl. 234. 1753.
Hydrocotyle repanda Pers. Syn. 1: 302. 1805.
C. asiatica Urban in Mart. Fl. Bras. 11: 287. 1879.
Centella repanda Small, Fl. SE. U. S. 859. 1903.

Stem creeping, glabrous or somewhat pubescent, 1'–6' long. Petioles 3'–12' long, sometimes pubescent; blades ovate, rather thick, very obtuse and rounded at the apex, broadly cordate at the base, not peltate, 1'–1½' long, 9"–15" wide, repand-dentate; pedicels much shorter than the leaves, ½'–2' long; umbels capitate, 2–4-flowered, subtended by 2 ovate bracts; flowers nearly sessile; fruit 2"–2½" broad, about 1½" high, prominently ribbed and reticulated when mature.

In wet grounds, Maryland to Florida, west to Texas. Also in Bermuda, insular and continental tropical America, and Old World tropics. June–Sept.

39. **SPERMÓLEPIS** Raf. Neog. 2. 1825.

[LEPTOCAULIS Nutt.; DC. Mem. Omb. 39. 1829.]

Glabrous slender erect branching annuals, the branches often nearly filiform, with finely dissected petioled leaves, the leaf-segments very narrowly linear. Flowers very small, white, in compound unequal-rayed umbels. Involucre none; involucels of a few small narrow bracts, or none. Calyx-teeth obsolete. Fruit ovate, laterally flattened, tuberculate or bristly; ribs prominent, or obsolete; pericarp thick; oil-tubes solitary in the intervals or also under the ribs, 2 on the commissural side. Stylopodium short, conic. [Greek, scaly-seed, referring to the rough fruit.]

Four species, natives of the United States. Type species: *Daucus divaricatus* Walt.

Fruit tubercled.
  Umbel-rays divaricate.   1. *S. divaricatus.*
  Umbel-rays ascending.   2. *S. patens.*
Fruit covered with hooked bristles.   3. *S. echinatus.*

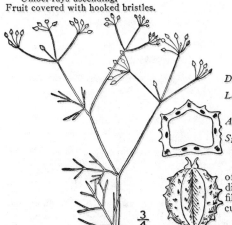

1. **Spermolepis divaricàtus** (Walt.) Britton. Rough-fruited Spermolepis. Fig. 3161.

Daucus divaricatus Walt. Fl. Car. 114. 1788.

Leptocaulis divaricatus DC. Mem. Omb. 39. *pl. 10.* 1829.

Apium divaricatum Wood, Bot. & Fl. 140. 1870.

Spermolepis divaricatus Britton, Mem. Torr. Club 5: 244. 1894.

Very slender and widely branching. Rays of the umbels almost filiform, ½'–1½' long, divaricate; flowers about ½" broad; pedicels filiform, 3"–6" long; fruit ovate, densely tuberculate, ½' long, the ribs rather prominent.

Nebraska to Texas, North Carolina and Florida. Also in ballast at Philadelphia. April–May.

2. Spermolepis pàtens (Nutt.) Robinson. Spreading Spermolepis. Fig. 3162.

Leptocaulis patens Nutt.; DC. Prodr. 4 : 107. 1830.
Apiastrum patens Coult. & Rose, Rev. 110. 1888
Spermolepis patens Robinson, Rhodora 10 : 34. 1908.

Erect, slender, 1°–2° high, divergently branched above. Stem-leaves short-petioled, biternately dissected into narrowly linear or filiform segments; umbels terminal, or axillary, ½'–1½' broad; rays 3''–6'' long; pedicels 1½''–2'' long in fruit; fruit ovate, slightly more than ½'' long, more or less tuberculate, usually densely so.

Sandy soil, Indiana to Missouri, Nebraska, Texas and New Mexico. June.

3. Spermolepis echinàtus (Nutt.) Heller. Bristly-fruited Spermolepis. Fig. 3163.

Leptocaulis echinatus Nutt.; DC. Prodr. 4 : 107. 1830.
S. echinatus Heller, Contr. Herb. F. & M. Coll. 1 : 73. 1895.

Resembling the preceding species, but lower, seldom over 1° high, the branches ascending or sometimes spreading. Rays of the umbel very slender, 1½' long, or less; fruit about ½'' long, covered with spreading hooked bristles, the ribs obsolete, the commissure narrow.

Alabama to Missouri, Texas and California. April–May.

40. AMMOSELÌNUM T. & G. Pac. R. R. Rep. 2 : 165. 1855.

Low branching annuals, with ternately divided finely dissected leaves, the ultimate leaf-segments linear, spatulate, or oblong, and small white flowers in terminal sessile or peduncled slender-rayed umbels. Involucels of a few linear or dissected bracts. Calyx-teeth obsolete. Fruit ovate to oval, laterally flattened, strongly ribbed, the ribs tuberculate or spinulose-tuberculate; pericarp very thick and dense; oil-tubes solitary in the intervals, and 2 on the commissural side. Styles and conic stylopodium short. [Greek, sand-parsley.]

Two known species, of the southwestern United States and Mexico, the following typical.

1. Ammoselinum Pòpei T. & G. Pope's Sand-parsley. Fig. 3164.

A. Popei T. & G. Pac. R. R. Rep. 2 : 165. 1855.
Apium Popei A. Gray, Proc. Am. Acad. 7 : 343. 1868.

A diffusely branched herb, 6'–15' high, the angled branches, rays of the umbels, and pedicels, rough. Lower leaves slender-petioled, the upper sessile, or nearly so, all dissected into linear obtuse or acutish segments about ½'' wide; involucre usually of 1 dissected leaf or more; involucel-bracts few, entire, or dissected; longer rays of the umbels 1' long in fruit, or less, the shorter ones often 1-flowered; fruit ovate, 2''–2½'' long, narrowed above, 1'' wide, or a little more, the ribs rather strongly tubercled, or even spinulose.

In sandy soil, Kansas to Texas. April–May.

Ammoselinum Bútleri (Engelm.) Coult. & Rose, of wet grounds from Arkansas to Texas, and recorded from Missouri, differs in being nearly smooth, with fruit only 1″ long.

41. ERIGENÌA Nutt. Gen. 1: 187. 1818.

A low glabrous nearly acaulescent perennial herb, arising from a deep tuber, with ternately decompound leaves, usually a single-leaved involucre, and small umbels of white flowers. Calyx-teeth obsolete. Petals flat, obovate or spatulate, entire. Fruit nearly orbicular, broader than long, notched at both ends, glabrous. Carpels incurved at top and bottom, with 5 slender ribs and 1–3 small oil-tubes in the intervals. [Greek, spring-born.]

A monotypic genus of central North America.

1. Erigenia bulbòsa (Michx.) Nutt. Harbinger of Spring. Fig. 3165.

Sison bulbosum Michx. Fl. Bor. Am. 1: 169. 1803.
Erigenia bulbosa Nutt. Gen. 1: 188. 1818.

Stem scapose, 3′–9′ high, bearing a leaf involucrate to the umbel. Basal leaves 2–4, petioled, ternately divided into thin oblong obtuse segments, the involucral one similar, smaller, short-petioled; petioles much dilated and sheathing at the base; umbels mostly compound, of 1–4 slender rays; involucels spatulate or sometimes foliaceous; pedicels very short in flower, 1″–2½″ long in fruit; fruit about 1″ long and 1½″ broad.

Ontario to the District of Columbia and Alabama, west to Minnesota and Kansas. Feb.–April. Turkey-pea. Pepper-and-salt.

42. CONÌUM L. Sp. Pl. 243. 1753.

Tall biennial glabrous poisonous herbs, with spotted stems, pinnately decompound leaves, and small white flowers in compound many-rayed umbels. Involucre and involucels of ovate-acuminate bracts. Calyx-teeth obsolete; petals obcordate, or entire with a short inflexed point; fruit broadly ovate, glabrous, somewhat flattened laterally. Carpels strongly wavy-ribbed; oil-tubes none, but a layer of oil-secreting tissue next the deeply concave seed. [Greek, hemlock.]

One, or perhaps two species, the following typical one native of Europe and Asia, the other of South Africa.

1. Conium maculàtum L. Poison Hemlock or Snakeweed. Fig. 3166.

Conium maculatum L. Sp. Pl. 243. 1753.

Erect, much-branched, 2°–5° high. Lower and basal leaves petioled, the upper sessile or nearly so, all pinnately dissected, the leaflets ovate in outline, thin, the ultimate segments dentate, or incised; petioles dilated and sheathing at the base; umbels 1′–3′ broad, the rays slender, 1′–1½′ long; pedicels filiform, 2″–3″ long in fruit; flowers about 1″ broad; fruit 1½″ long, about 1″ wide, its ribs very prominent when dry.

In waste places, Nova Scotia to Ontario, Delaware, Indiana and Michigan. Also in California and Mexico, Santo Domingo and South America. Naturalized from Europe. St. Bennet's-herb. Cashes. Wode-whistle. Poison or spotted parsley. Bunk. June–July.

43. AEGOPÒDIUM L. Sp. Pl. 265. 1753.

Perennial herbs, with 1–2-ternate leaves, and compound umbels of white flowers. Bracts of the involucre and involucels none, or rarely few and early deciduous. Calyx-teeth obsolete. Petals inflexed at the apex. Stylopodium thick, conic. Fruit ovate-oblong, glabrous, somewhat compressed. Carpels obscurely 5-angled, the ribs slender, equal, distant; oil-tubes none. Seed-face flat. [Greek, goat-foot.]

One or perhaps two species, natives of temperate Europe and Asia, the following typical.

1. Aegopodium Podagrària L. Goutweed. Goutwort. Herb-Gerard.
Fig. 3167.

3/5

A. Podagraria L. Sp. Pl. 265. 1753.

Erect, branched, glabrous, $1\frac{1}{2}°$–$2\frac{1}{2}°$ high. Basal and lower leaves long-petioled, biternate, the primary divisions stalked, the segments ovate, acute, or acuminate at the apex, rounded, or cordate and often oblique at the base, sharply serrulate, $1\frac{1}{2}'$–$3'$ long; upper leaves similar but smaller and usually simply ternate; umbels long-peduncled, $1\frac{1}{2}'$–$2\frac{1}{2}'$ broad, 9–25-rayed; rays $1'$ long in fruit or more; pedicels $2''$–$4''$ long; fruit about $2''$ long, scarcely $1''$ wide, the styles deflected.

In waste places, Massachusetts to New Jersey, Pennsylvania and Delaware. Adventive from Europe. Wild or English masterwort, Ax-ashe- or aise-weed. Dwarf or Bishop's-elder. Bishop's-weed. White-ash-herb. Garden-plague. Dog-elder. June-Aug.

44. EÙLOPHUS Nutt.; DC. Mon. Omb. 69. *pl. 2.* 1829.

Perennial slender glabrous branching herbs, from deep tuberous roots, with ternately or pinnately compound leaves, and long-peduncled compound umbels of white or pink flowers. Involucre generally of 1 bract, sometimes none. Involucels of several narrow bracts. Calyx-teeth usually prominent. Petals obovate, the tip inflexed. Stylopodium conic. Styles recurved. Fruit glabrous, linear to oblong in our species; ribs filiform, with 1–5 oil-tubes in the intervals. Seed-face concave. [Greek, well-plumed; application not apparent.]

About 8 species, natives of North America, extending into Mexico. Besides the following typical one, 5 others occur in the western United States.

1. Eulophus americànus Nutt. Eastern
Eulophus. Fig. 3168.

Eulophus americanus Nutt.; DC. Mem. Omb. 69. *pl. 2.* 1829.

3/5

Erect, $3°$–$5°$ high. Basal and lower leaves large, long-petioled, ternately compound into linear acute or obtusish segments; upper leaves similar, smaller and shorter-petioled; petioles sheathing at the base; umbels terminal, $3'$–$4'$ broad, the rays 6–12, very slender, $2'$–$4'$ long; involucre of 1–2 bracts, or none; involucels of several narrowly lanceolate acuminate bracts; pedicels almost filiform, $4''$–$8''$ long in fruit; flowers whitish; fruit oblong, $2''$–$3''$ long.

In dry soil, Ohio and Illinois to Kansas, Tennessee and Arkansas. July.

45. PIMPINÉLLA L. Sp. Pl. 263. 1753.

Glabrous, perennial herbs, with pinnate leaves and compound umbels of white flowers. Involucre and involucels none in our species. Calyx-teeth obsolete. Petals inflexed at the apex. Stylopodium thick, low, broadly conic. Fruit ovate, or oblong, more or less compressed. Carpels obscurely 5-angled with slender equal distant ribs; oil-tubes numerous, 2–6 in the intervals. Seed-face flat or slightly convex. [Latin; perhaps from bipinnula, *i. e.,* bipinnate.]

About 75 species, natives of the Old World, the following typical.

1. **Pimpinella Saxífraga** L. Bennet.
Pimpernel. Burnet Saxifrage.
Fig. 3169.

Pimpinella Saxifraga L. Sp. Pl. 263. 1753.

Erect, glabrous, 1°–2° high, somewhat branched. Leaves pinnate; segments of the lower 9–19, sharply serrate, or incised, ovate, or nearly orbicular, 8″–12″ long; upper leaves shorter-petioled and of fewer segments cut into narrower lobes; flowers white; umbels slender-peduncled, 7–20-rayed; rays slender, 1′–1½′ long in fruit; fruit oval, about 1″ long.

In waste places, New Brunswick to Pennsylvania, New Jersey, Delaware and Ohio. Adventive from Europe. June–Oct.

Pimpinella mágna L., a similar European species, taller and with larger leaves, has been found in waste grounds in Pennsylvania.

46. BÉRULA Hoffm.; Bess. Enum. Pl. Volh. 44. 1821.

A glabrous aquatic or marsh perennial, with pinnate leaves, serrate or sometimes incised leaf-segments, and terminal compound umbels of white flowers. Involucre and involucels of several narrow bracts. Calyx-teeth very small. Stylopodium conic; styles short. Fruit subglobose, emarginate at the base, slightly flattened laterally, glabrous, the ribs very slender, the pericarp thick and corky; oil-tubes numerous and close together along the inner side of the pericarp. Seed-face flat. [Latin name of the water cress.]

A monotypic genus of the north temperate zone.

1. **Berula erécta** (Huds.) Coville. Cut-leaved Water Parsnip. Fig. 3170.

Sium erectum Huds. Fl. Angl. 103. 1762.

Sium angustifolium L. Sp. Pl. Ed. 2, 1872. 1763.

Berula angustifolia Mert. & Koch, Deutsch. Flora 2: 433. 1826.

B. erecta Coville, Contr. Nat. Herb. 4: 115. 1893.

Erect, rather stout, much branched, 6′–3° high. Leaflets 7–19, ovate, oval, or linear-oblong, deeply serrate, crenate, laciniate, or lobed, 6″–18″ long, 2″–5″ wide, those of the upper leaves commonly more laciniate than those of the lower; umbels numerous, short-peduncled, 10–20-rayed; rays ½′–2½′ long in fruit; pedicels 1½″–3″ long; fruit less than 1″ long, nearly orbicular, somewhat cordate at the base, the ribs inconspicuous.

In swamps and streams, southern Ontario to British Columbia, south to Illinois, Nebraska; in the Rocky Mountains to New Mexico and to California. Also in Europe and Asia. Lesser, narrow-leaved, creeping or water-parsnip. July–Sept.

47. SÌUM [Tourn.] L. Sp. Pl. 251. 1753.

Perennial marsh herbs, with simply pinnate stem-leaves, the lower and basal ones often pinnatisected, and compound large umbels of white flowers. Involucre and involucels of numerous narrow bracts. Calyx-teeth minute. Petals inflexed at the apex. Stylopodium depressed. Styles short. Fruit ovate or oval, somewhat compressed. Carpels with prominent ribs; oil-tubes 1–3 in the intervals. Seed-face flat. [Greek name of a marsh plant.]

About 8 species, natives of the north temperate zone and South Africa. The following are the only ones known to occur in the United States. Type species: *Sium latifolium* L.

Plant stout, 2°–6° high; leaf-segments 7–17.   1. *S. cicutaefolium.*
Plant weak, 1°–3° high; leaf-segments 3–7.   2. *S. Carsoni.*

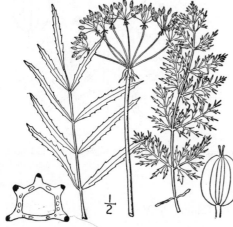

1. Sium cicutaefòlium Schrank.
Hemlock Water-Parsnip.
Fig. 3171.

Sium cicutaefolium Schrank, Bair. Fl. 1 : 558. 1789.
S. lineare Michx. Fl. Bor. Am. 1 : 167. 1803.
Sium latifolium of American authors, not of Linn.

Erect, stout, branched, 2°–6° high. Lower leaves long-petioled, the uppermost nearly sessile; petioles sheathing at the base; leaf-segments 7–17, linear, or lanceolate, 1½′–5′ long, 1½″–12″ wide, acuminate at the apex, sharply serrate, or the lowermost pectinately dissected; umbels 2′–3′ broad, 8–20-rayed; rays ½′–1½′ long; fruit ovate, compressed, about 1½″ long, the ribs prominent.

In swamps, Nova Scotia to British Columbia, south to Florida, Louisiana and California. Very variable in leaf-form. July–Oct.

2. Sium Càrsoni Durand. Carson's Water-Parsnip. Fig. 3172.

Sium Carsoni Durand; A. Gray, Man. Ed. 5, 196. 1867.

Stem slender, weak, 1°–2° long. Leaf-segments 3–7, those of the upper leaves linear, or lanceolate, acute, or acuminate, 1′–2′ long, 1½″–3″ wide, sharply serrate; lower leaves often floating and very thin, the segments broader and laciniate, or dissected; umbels 1′–2′ broad, 7–15-rayed; rays 6″–12″ long in fruit; fruit somewhat smaller than that of the preceding species.

In streams, Maine, Massachusetts and Rhode Island to Pennsylvania. Perhaps an aquatic race of *Sium cicutaefolium,* but appearing distinct in Pennsylvania. July–Aug.

48. PTILÍMNIUM Raf. Neog. 2. 1825.
[DISCOPLEURA DC. Mem. Omb. 38. 1829]

Annual erect glabrous branching herbs, with pinnately or ternately dissected leaves, and compound umbels of white flowers. Bracts of the involucre several, filiform or dissected in our species. Involucels present. Calyx-teeth obsolete. Petals obovate, the apex inflexed. Stylopodium conic; fruit ovate, slightly compressed, glabrous. Carpels dorsally compressed, the dorsal and intermediate ribs prominent, slender, the lateral ones very thick and corky; oil-tubes solitary in the intervals. Seed-face flat. [Greek, referring to the finely divided leaves.]

About 4 species. Besides the following, another occurs in Texas and one in the East Indies. Type species: *Ammi capillaceum* Michx.

Involucral bracts mostly pinnate; fruit 1″–1½″ long.   1. *P. capillaceum.*
Involucral bracts short, entire; fruit ½″–¾″ long.   2. *P. Nuttallii.*

1. Ptilimnium capillàceum (Michx.) Raf. Mock Bishop-weed. Fig. 3173.

Ammi majus Walt. Fl. Car. 113. 1788. Not L.
A. capillaceum Michx. Fl. Bor. Am. 1 : 164. 1803.
D. capillacea DC. Mem. Omb. 38. 1829.
Ptilimnium capillaceum Raf.; Seringe, Bull. Bot.
    217. 1830.
P. missouriense Coult. & Rose, Contr. Nat. Herb.
    12 : 444. 1909.

Slender, 1°–2° high or more, the branches
ascending or sometimes divaricate. Leaves
finely dissected into filiform segments, the
upper sessile, the lower more or less petioled;
involucral bracts, or some of them, pinnately
parted; involucels of several linear bracts;
umbels 2′–4′ broad, 5–20-rayed, the rays 1′–2′
long; pedicels 2″–8″ long; fruit ovate, acute,
1″–1½″ long.

In wet soil, especially brackish meadows, along
the coast, Massachusetts to Florida, west to Texas,
north to Kansas and Missouri. June–Oct. Called
also herb-william, wood-nep, bole- or bull-wort.

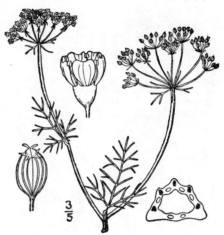

2. Ptilimnium Nuttàllii (DC.) Britton. Nuttall's Mock Bishop-weed. Fig. 3174.

Peucedanum verticillatum Raf. Fl. Ludov. 81. 1817?

Discopleura Nuttallii DC. Mem. Omb. 38. 1829.

Discopleura capillacea var. *Nuttallii* Coult. & Rose,
    Bot. Gaz. 12 : 292. 1887.

Ptilimnium Nuttallii Britton, Mem. Torr. Club 5 : 244.
    1894.

Similar to the preceding species, but generally
stouter, 2°–3° high, the branches nearly erect.
Umbels 7–25-rayed; bracts of the involucre linear,
entire, short, those of the involucels minute; fruit
nearly orbicular, obtusish, about ½″ long.

In swamps, Illinois to Kansas, Louisiana and Texas.
May–Sept.

49. CICÙTA L. Sp. Pl. 255. 1753.

Erect tall perennial glabrous herbs, with pinnate or pinnately compound leaves, and
compound terminal umbels of white flowers. Involucre of few bracts, or none; involucels
many-bracted. Calyx-teeth acute. Petals broad, the apex inflexed. Stylopodium short-
conic; fruit ovoid, or oblong, glabrous, slightly flattened laterally. Ribs corky, the lateral
ones rather the strongest; oil-tubes solitary in the intervals, 2 on the commissural side. Seed
nearly terete. [The ancient Latin name.]

About 8 species, natives of the north temperate zone and Mexico. Besides the following about
4 others occur in western North America. Type species: *Cicuta virosa* L.

Leaf-segments lanceolate.   1. *C. maculata.*
Leaf-segments narrowly linear.   2. *C. bulbifera.*

1. Cicuta maculàta L.   Water or Spotted Hemlock.   Musquash Root.   Fig. 3175.

Cicuta maculata L. Sp. Pl. 256. 1753.

Cicuta virosa var. *maculata* Coult. & Rose, Rev. Umb. 130. 1888.

Cicuta occidentalis Greene, Pittonia 2 : 7. 1889.

Stout, erect, branching, 3°–6° high, the stem marked with purple lines.   Roots several, fleshy, tuberiform, ovoid, or oblong; leaves petioled, bipinnate, or tripinnate, the lower often 1° long, and on long petioles, the upper smaller; leaf-segments lanceolate, or lance-oblong, coarsely and sharply serrate, 1′–5′ long, their veins apparently ending in the notches; umbellets many-flowered; pedicels unequal, 2″–4″ long in fruit; fruit oval to suborbicular, 1″–1½″ long.

In swamps and low grounds, New Brunswick to Manitoba, south to Florida and New Mexico. Poisonous.   Spotted cowbane.   Beaver-poison.   Children's-bane.   Musquash-poison.   Wild parsnip. Snakeweed.   Consists of several races, differing in width, thickness and serration of the leaf-segments, shape of fruit and thickness of its lateral ribs.   June–Aug.

Cicuta Curtissii Coult. & Rose differs in having nearly orbicular fruit, and often broader leaf-segments.   It inhabits the Southern States and is recorded as ranging northward into southern Virginia.

2. Cicuta bulbífera L.   Bulb-bearing Water Hemlock.   Fig. 3176.

Cicuta bulbifera L. Sp. Pl. 255. 1753.

Erect, slender, much branched, 1°–3½° high. Roots few, fleshy, tuberiform.   Leaves petioled, 2–3 pinnate, the upper ones less divided, smaller, and bearing numerous clustered bulblets in their axils; leaf-segments linear, sparingly serrate with distant teeth, ½′–1½′ long; fruit broadly ovate, slightly more than 1″ long, seldom formed along the southern range of the species.

In swamps, Nova Scotia to Maryland, British Columbia, Indiana, Nebraska and Oregon.   Ascends to 2600 ft. in the Catskills.   July–Sept.

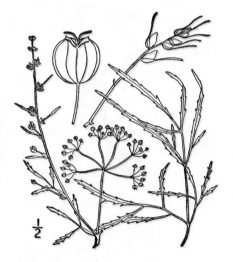

50.   CÀRUM L. Sp. Pl. 263.   1753.

Glabrous herbs, with thick roots, pinnate or ternately pinnatifid leaves, and small white or yellowish flowers in terminal compound umbels.   Calyx-teeth minute.   Petals inflexed at the apex.   Stylopodium conic; fruit ovate, or oblong, somewhat compressed, glabrous. Carpels somewhat 5-angled, the ribs filiform; oil-tubes solitary in the intervals and 2 on the commissural side.   Seed dorsally flattened, its face flat or slightly concave.   [Greek, caraway.]

About 50 species, natives of temperate and warm regions, the following typical.   Besides the following, about 4 others occur in western North America.

1. Carum Càrui L.   Caraway.   Car-
vies.   Fig. 3177.

Carum Carui L. Sp. Pl. 263. 1753.

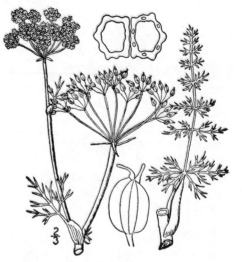

Biennial or sometimes perennial, erect,
branching, 1°–2° high. Lower and basal
leaves long-petioled, the uppermost nearly
sessile, all pinnatisected into linear or filiform segments; bases of the petioles widely
dilated; involucre of 1–3 linear bracts, or
none; involucels commonly none; umbels
1′–2½′ broad, 7–10-rayed; rays ½′–2′ long in
fruit; fruit oblong, usually slightly curved,
about 2″ long, the ribs conspicuous when
mature; flowers white.

Occasional in waste places, Newfoundland to
South Dakota, Pennsylvania and Colorado.
Adventive from Europe. May–July.

51. HARPERÉLLA Rose, Proc. Biol. Soc. Wash. **19**: 96. 1906.

Glabrous aquatic perennials. Leaves reduced to slender, terete, jointed phyllodes. Involucre and involucels inconspicuous. Flowers white. Calyx-teeth small, persistent. Fruit
flattened laterally, rounded at both ends, glabrous; carpels hardly flattened, terete, or somewhat angled in section; ribs rather prominent for the size of fruit, equal; stylopodium conic;
styles slender. Oil-tubes solitary in the intervals, two on the commissural side. Seeds
nearly terete in section. [Named for Roland M. Harper, a diligent student and collector.]

Three known species, natives of the southeastern United States. Type species: *Harperella
nodòsa* Rose.

1. Harperella vivípara Rose.   Viviparous
Harperella.   Fig. 3178.

Harperella vivipara Rose, Contr. U. S. Nat. Herb. **12**: 290.
1911.

Annual (?), stem slender, weak, at first erect, afterwards somewhat spreading, 4′–8′ long, usually simple,
sometimes with one or two branches, in age bearing
bulblets at the axils of all the leaves. Basal leaves 2
or 3, 2″–4″ long, terete, jointed, bright green, glabrous,
hollow, with a scarious stipular sheath at base; stem-
leaves similar but shorter, alternate, shorter than the
internodes; inflorescence a terminal umbel, with or
without other axillary ones; peduncle ½′–1½′ long; rays
1½″–5″ long; involucre, if present, consisting of one
small bract; bractlets of the involucels 4, minute; fruit
about 1″ long, broader than long.

Banks of the Potomac River, Maryland. July–Oct.

52. CÉLERI Adans. Fam. Pl. **2**: 498. 1753.

Perennial glabrous herbs, with pinnate or pinnately compound leaves, and white or greenish flowers in compound umbels. Involucre and involucels small or none. Calyx-teeth
obsolete. Petals ovate, mostly inflexed at the apex. Stylopodium depressed, or short-conic.
Fruit ovate, or broader than long, smooth. Carpels mostly with prominent ribs, somewhat
5-angled; oil-tubes mostly solitary in the intervals, 2 on the commissural side. Seed terete,
or nearly so. [The common name.]

Four or five species, natives of the Old World, southern South America and Australasia, the
following typical.

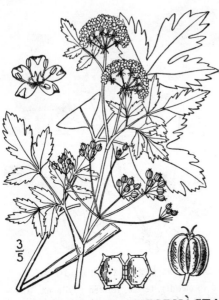

$\frac{3}{5}$

1. Celeri gravèolens (L.) Britton.
Celery. Smallage. Fig. 3179.

Apium graveolens L. Sp. Pl. 264. 1753.

Glabrous, stem erect, 1°–3° high, several-leaved. Leaves pinnate, the basal and lower ones long-petioled, the upper short-petioled, or nearly sessile; leaf-segments 3 or 5, stalked, or sessile, thin, broadly ovate to oval, coarsely toothed and often incised; ½'–1½' long; umbels opposite the leaves, and terminal, 3–7-rayed; involucre and involucels small, or none; flowers very small, white, very short-pedicelled; fruit oval, scarcely ½" long, the ribs somewhat winged.

In waste places, escaped from cultivation in Virginia, and naturalized on the coast of California. Also in ballast about the seaports. Native of Europe. Old English names, march, ache, marsh parsley, mile. May–July.

Apium Ammi (L.) Urban [*A. leptophyllum* (DC.) F. Muell.], a slender annual weed of the Southern States and tropical regions, with finely divided leaves and small umbels of white flowers opposite the petioles, found in ballast, and recorded from Missouri, is not definitely known to be established within our area.

Family 103. **CORNACEAE** Link, Handb. **2: 2.** 1831.
DOGWOOD FAMILY.

Shrubs, undershrubs or trees, with simple opposite, verticillate or alternate, usually entire leaves, and regular perfect polygamous or dioecious flowers in cymes, heads or rarely solitary. Calyx-tube adnate to the ovary, its limb 4–5-dentate, or none. Petals generally 4 or 5, sometimes wanting, valvate or imbricate, spreading, inserted at the base of the epigynous disc. Stamens as many as the petals or more numerous, inserted with them; filaments subulate or flat. Ovary inferior, 1–2-celled in our species; style 1, short or elongated; ovules 1 in each cavity, pendulous, anatropous. Fruit a drupe, the stone 1–2-celled, 1–2-seeded. Seeds oblong; embryo nearly as long as the endosperm; cotyledons foliaceous.

About 16 genera and 85 species, most abundant in the northern hemisphere.

Flowers perfect, 4-parted; ovary 2-celled.
　Flowers cymose, not involucrate.　　　　　　　　　　　　　　　　　　　1. *Cornus.*
　Flowers capitate, involucrate by 4 large white bracts.
　　Trees or shrubs.　　　　　　　　　　　　　　　　　　　　　　　2. *Cynoxylon.*
　　Undershrubs with creeping rootstocks.　　　　　　　　　　　　　3. *Chamaepericlymenum.*
Flowers polygamous or dioecious; petals minute or none; ovary 1-celled. 4. *Nyssa.*

1. CÓRNUS [Tourn.] L. Sp. Pl. 117. 1753.

Shrubs or trees, with simple mostly entire opposite verticillate or rarely alternate leaves, and small white greenish or purple flowers, in cymes. Calyx-tube top-shaped or campanulate, its limb minutely 4-toothed. Petals 4, valvate. Stamens 4. Ovary 2-celled; stigma truncate or capitate; ovules 1 in each cavity. Drupe ovoid or globular, the stone 2-celled and 2-seeded. [Greek, horn, from the toughness of the wood.]

About 20 species, natives of the north temperate zone, Mexico and Peru. Besides the following, 3 or 4 others occur in western North America. Type species: *Cornus Mas* L.

Leaves opposite.
　Leaves downy-pubescent beneath, at least when young (sometimes glabrate in No. 2).
　　Leaves broadly ovate or orbicular; fruit blue.　　　　　　　　1. *C. rugosa.*
　　Leaves ovate or ovate-lanceolate.
　　　Fruit blue; stone pointed at the base.　　　　　　　　　　2. *C. Amomum.*
　　　Fruit white.
　　　　Fruit 1½" in diameter, the stone longer than broad.　　3. *C. Priceae.*
　　　　Fruit 3" in diameter, the stone broader than long or as broad.
　　　　　Leaves scabrous above.　　　　　　　　　　　　　　4. *C. asperifolia.*
　　　　　Leaves not scabrous.　　　　　　　　　　　　　　　5. *C. Baileyi.*
　Leaves glabrate, or minutely appressed-pubescent beneath.
　　Leaves ovate, short-pointed; twigs purple.　　　　　　　　6. *C. stolonifera.*
　　Leaves ovate-lanceolate, acuminate.
　　　Fruit white; twigs grey.　　　　　　　　　　　　　　　7. *C. femina.*
　　　Fruit pale blue; twigs reddish.　　　　　　　　　　　　8. *C. stricta.*
Leaves alternate, clustered at the ends of the flowering branches; fruit blue.　9. *C. alternifolia.*

1. Cornus rugòsa Lam. Round-leaved Cornel or Dogwood. Fig. 3180.

Cornus rugosa Lam. Encycl. **2**: 115. 1786.

C. circinata L'Her. Cornus, *7. pl. 3.* 1788.

A shrub, 3°–10° high, the twigs warty, green and glabrous. Leaves petioled, entire, broadly ovate, orbicular, or even wider than long, acute, or short-acuminate at the apex, mostly rounded or truncate at the base, pale and densely soft-pubescent beneath, slightly pubescent above, 2′–6′ long; petioles 3″–9″ long; flowers white in rather dense cymes 1½′–2½′ broad, the pedicels usually somewhat pubescent; petals ovate; fruit globose, light blue, about 2½″ in diameter; stone subglobose, somewhat ridged.

In shady, often rocky situations, Nova Scotia to Manitoba, south to Virginia, Illinois, Iowa and North Dakota. Alder-leaved dogwood. Green osier. May–July.

$\frac{1}{2}$

2. Cornus Amòmum Mill. Silky Cornel. Kinnikinnik. Fig. 3181.

C. Amomum Mill. Gard. Dict. Ed. 8, no. 5. 1768.
Cornus sericea L. Mant. **2**: 199. 1771.
C. obliqua Raf. Ann. Nat. 13. 1820.
C. Purpusi Koehne, Gartenflora 1899: 388.

A shrub, 3°–10° high, with purplish twigs, the youngest commonly pubescent. Leaves petioled, ovate, oval, or ovate-lanceolate, acuminate at the apex, narrowed or rounded at the base, usually finely pubescent with brownish hairs beneath, glabrous or minutely appressed-pubescent above, 1′–5′ long; flowers white, in rather compact flat cymes 1½′–2½′ broad; petals narrowly oblong; fruit globose, light blue, 3″–3½″ in diameter, stone oblique, ridged, narrowed or pointed at base.

In low woods and along streams, Newfoundland to Ontario, Florida, North Dakota, Nebraska and Texas. Swamp dogwood. Blueberry-cornell. Red-osier; red-brush or -willow. Rose-willow. Squawbush. May–July.

$\frac{1}{2}$

3. Cornus Prìceae Small. Miss Price's Cornel. Fig. 3182.

Cornus Priceae Small, Torreya **1**: 54. 1901.

Svida Priceae Small, Fl. SE. U. S. 854. 1903.

A branching shrub, 3°–6° high, the twigs red, finely pubescent. Leaves numerous, elliptic to ovate-elliptic or ovate, usually acuminate at the apex, deep green and roughish pubescent above, pale and more copiously, but more softly pubescent, and prominently nerved beneath, 2′–4¾′ long; petioles ⅓–¾′ long, pubescent like the twigs; cymes closely flowered, 4–6 cm. broad at maturity; petals white, oblong-lanceolate to linear-lanceolate; fruit about 1½″ in diameter, subglobose, white; stone about 1″ long, slightly longer than broad, faintly ribbed.

On river banks, southern Kentucky and northern Tennessee. June.

$\frac{1}{2}$

$\frac{1}{2}$

5. Cornus Bàileyi Coult. & Evans. Bailey's Cornel or Dogwood. Fig. 3184.

C. Baileyi Coult. & Evans, Bot. Gaz. **15**: 37. 1890.

A shrub with reddish-brown twigs, much resembling the preceding species. Leaves slender-petioled, ovate or ovate-lanceolate, acute or acuminate at the apex, narrowed or rounded at the base, glabrate, or with finely appressed soft pubescence above, rather densely woolly-pubescent beneath, 1'–5' long; flower-buds ovoid; petals white, ovate-oblong; cymes compact, 1'–2' broad, the rays pubescent; fruit white, about 3'' in diameter; stone flattened, slightly oblique, channeled on the edge, much broader than high.

Lake shores and in moist ground, southern Ontario and Pennsylvania to Minnesota and Manitoba. May–June.

Svida intèrior Rydb., of central Nebraska, Colorado and Wyoming, with similar pubescence, but the stone of the fruit rather longer than thick, formerly included in this species, may be distinct.

4. Cornus asperifòlia Michx. Rough-leaved Cornel or Dogwood. Fig. 3183.

C. asperifolia Michx. Fl. Bor. Am. **1**: 93. 1803.
Cornus Drummondii C. A. Meyer, Mem. Acad. Petersb. (VI.) **5**: 210. 1845.

A shrub, 3°–15° high, the twigs reddish brown, the youngest very rough-pubescent. Leaves very slender-petioled, ovate-oval, or elliptic, acuminate at the apex, mostly obtuse at the base, pale and woolly-pubescent beneath, densely rough-pubescent above, 1½'–5' long; petioles and rays of the cyme rough-pubescent; cymes rather loosely-flowered, 2'–3' broad; flower-buds subcylindric; petals white, oblong-lanceolate; fruit globose, white, about 3'' in diameter; stone slightly furrowed, little compressed, often oblique, more or less broader than high.

In wet ground, or near streams, southern Ontario to Tennessee, Florida, Minnesota, Kansas and Texas. May–June.

$\frac{1}{2}$

6. Cornus stolonífera Michx. Red-osier Cornel or Dogwood. Fig. 3185.

C. alba Lam. Encycl. **2**: 115. 1786. Not L. 1767.
C. stolonifera Michx. Fl. Bor. Am. **1**: 92. 1803.

A shrub, 3°–10° high, usually stoloniferous, the twigs glabrous and bright reddish purple, or the youngest finely appressed-pubescent. Leaves slender-petioled, ovate, ovate-lanceolate or oval, acute or short-acuminate at the apex, rounded or narrowed at the base, finely appressed-pubescent above, white or whitish and sparingly pubescent beneath, or sometimes glabrous on both sides, 1'–5' long; cymes 1'–2' broad, flat-topped, usually minutely appressed-pubescent; petals white, ovate-oblong; fruit white to bluish, globose, 3''–4'' in diameter, the stone very variable in shape, either higher than broad or broader than high.

In moist soil, Newfoundland to the Yukon Territory, Virginia, Kentucky, Nebraska, Arizona and California. Ascends to 2400 ft. in the Adirondacks. Dogberry-tree. Waxberry-cornell. Kinnikinnik. Red brush. Squaw-bush. Gutter-tree. June–July.

$\frac{1}{2}$

7. Cornus fémina Mill. Panicled Cornel or Dogwood. Fig. 3186.

Cornus femina Mill. Gard. Dict. Ed. 8, No. 4. 1768.
Cornus candissima Marsh, Arb. Am. 35. 1785. Not Mill. 1768.
Cornus paniculata L'Her. Cornus 9. *pl. 15.* 1788.

A shrub, 6°–15° high, with gray smooth twigs, even the youngest glabrous or nearly so. Leaves petioled, lanceolate or ovate-lanceolate, long-acuminate at the apex, acute at the base, minutely appressed-pubescent on both sides, pale beneath, $1\frac{1}{2}'–4'$ long; cymes loosely flowered, somewhat paniculate, the rays mostly glabrous; petals white, lanceolate; fruit globose, or slightly depressed, white, about $3''$ in diameter; fruiting pedicels red; stone subglobose, slightly furrowed, or somewhat broader than high.

In rich soil, Maine and Ontario to North Carolina, Minnesota, Tennessee and Nebraska. White-fruited dogwood. White cornel. May–June.

8. Cornus strícta Lam. Stiff Cornel or Dogwood. Fig. 3187.

Cornus stricta Lam. Encycl. **2**: 116. 1786.
C. fastigiata Michx. Fl. Bor. Am. **1** : 92. 1803.

A shrub, 8°–15° high, resembling the preceding species, the twigs purplish or reddish brown. Leaves petioled, ovate or ovate-lanceolate, acute or acuminate at the apex, narrowed or sometimes rounded at the base, sparingly and finely appressed-pubescent on both sides, $1\frac{1}{2}'–3'$ long, the margins often minutely denticulate, green above and beneath; cymes rather loosely flowered, $1\frac{1}{2}'–2\frac{1}{2}'$ broad, their rays nearly or quite glabrous; petals white, ovate-lanceolate, or oblong; fruit pale blue, about $3''$ in diameter; stone globose, nearly smooth.

In swamps and along streams, Virginia to Georgia, Florida and Missouri. April–May. Panicled cornel.

9. Cornus alternifòlia L. f. Alternate-leaved Cornel or Dogwood. Fig. 3188.

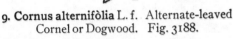

Cornus alternifolia L. f. Suppl. 125. 1781.

A shrub, or small tree, with smooth greenish bark, reaching a maximum height of about 30° and trunk diameter of 8'. Leaves slender-petioled, alternate, clustered near the ends of the branches, oval or ovate, acuminate at the apex, narrowed or sometimes rounded at the base, $2'–4'$ long, pale and appressed-pubescent beneath, glabrate above, the margins minutely denticulate; petioles $\frac{1}{2}'–1\frac{1}{2}'$ long; cymes $2'–4'$ broad, pubescent; petals white, or cream-color, lanceolate; fruit globular, or slightly depressed, blue, rarely yellow, about $4''$ in diameter; stone somewhat obovoid, channeled, scarcely flattened.

In woods, Miquelon Island and Nova Scotia to Georgia, Ontario, Minnesota, West Virginia, Alabama and Missouri. Ascends to 2500 ft. in Virginia. Wood hard, reddish brown; weight per cubic foot 42 lbs. Blue or purple dogwood. Umbrella-tree. Green osier. Pigeon-berry. May–July.

2. CYNÓXYLON Raf. Alsog. Amer. 59. 1838.

[BENTHAMIDIA Spach, Hist. Veg. **8**: 109. 1839.]

Trees, with opposite petioled pinnately veined leaves and small perfect yellowish or greenish flowers in heads subtended by a conspicuous involucre of 4 to 6 large white or pink bracts. Calyx 4-lobed; corolla of 4 valvate petals; stamens 4, with slender filaments and elliptic anthers; ovary sessile, 2-celled; style terminated by the depressed stigma; ovules 1 in each cavity of the ovary, pendulous. Fruit with thin acrid flesh, surmounted by the calyx, the stone 2-seeded; seeds oblong; endosperm fleshy; embryo straight.   [Greek, dogwood.]

Two species, the following typical one, and *C. Nuttallii*, of northwestern America.

1. Cynoxylon flóridum (L.) Raf.   Flowering Dogwood. Fig. 3189.

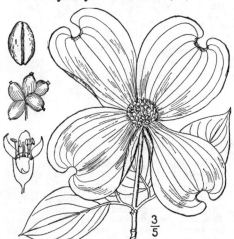

Cornus florida L. Sp. Pl. 117. 1753.
Cynoxylon floridum Raf.; Britton & Shafer, N. A. Trees 744. 1908.

A small tree, or large shrub, with very rough bark and spreading branches, reaching the maximum height of about 40° and trunk diameter of 1½°. Leaves petioled, ovate, or oval, rarely obovate, entire, pale and slightly pubescent on the veins beneath, dark green and glabrous, or minutely pubescent above, 3′–6′ long, acute at the apex, usually narrowed at the base; petioles 3″–10″ long; bracts of the involucre white or pinkish (rarely rose-red), very conspicuous, obovate, obcordate, or emarginate, strongly parallel-veined, 1′–2½′ long; flowers greenish-yellow, capitate; fruit ovoid, scarlet, 5″–6″ long, crowned with the persistent calyx; stone smooth, channeled, ovoid, 3″–4″ long.

In woods, Maine and Ontario to Florida, Minnesota, Kentucky, Kansas and Texas. Ascends to 4400 ft. in Virginia. Wood hard, brown; weight per cubic foot 50 lbs. Leaves bright red in autumn. Fruit often persistent over winter. Arrow-wood. Box-wood. Cornelian tree. False box or box-wood. Nature's-mistake. Florida dogwood. White cornel. Indian arrow-wood. April–June.

3. CHAMAEPERICLÝMENUM Graebn.; Asch. & Graebn. Fl. Nord. Flachl. 225, 539. 1898.

[CORNÉLLA Rydb. Bull. Torr Club **33**: 147. 1906.]

Low, almost herbaceous plants, woody only at the base, with nearly horizontal rootstocks, and erect stems bearing a solitary head of small greenish-purple or violet flowers subtended by an involucre of 4 large white bracts, the leaves opposite or whorled. Calyx-limb minutely 4-toothed, the teeth with a deciduous spinule on the back near the apex. Petals 4, valvate. Stamens 4. Ovary 2-celled. Drupe globose, red. [Greek, low *Periclymenum*.]

Two species, of the northern hemisphere. Type species: *Chamaepericlymenum suecicum* (L.) Asch. & Graebn.

1. Chamaepericlymenum canadénse (L.) Asch. & Graebn. Low or Dwarf Cornel. Bunch-berry or -plum. Fig. 3190.

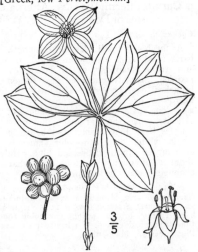

Cornus canadensis L. Sp. Pl. 117. 1753.
C. unalaschensis Ledeb. Fl. Ross. **2**: 378. 1844–46.
C. canadensis Rydb. Bull. Torr. Club **33**: 147. 1906.

Herbaceous, woody only at the base; flowering stems erect, scaly, 3′–9′ high. Rootstock nearly horizontal; leaves verticillate at the summit of the stem, or sometimes 1 or 2 pairs of opposite ones below, sessile, oval, ovate, or obovate, pinnately veined, glabrous or minutely appressed-pubescent, acute at each end, entire, 1′–3′ long; peduncle slender, ½′–1½′ long; involucral bracts 4–6, white, petaloid, ovate, 4″–9″ long; flowers greenish, capitate; petals ovate, one of them with a subulate appendage; fruit globose, bright red, about 3″ in diameter; stone smooth, globose, slightly longer than broad.

In low woods, Newfoundland to Alaska, New Jersey, West
Virginia, Indiana, Minnesota, Colorado and California; also in
eastern Asia. Rarely the upper leaves are opposite. May–July.
Cracker-berry.

2. Chamaepericlymenum suècicum (L.) Asch. & Graebn. Northern Dwarf Cornel. Lapland Cornel. Fig. 3191.

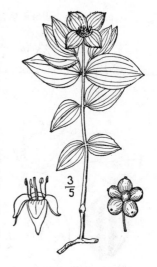

Cornus suecica L. Sp. Pl. 118. 1753.
Cornella suecica Rydb. Bull. Torr. Club 33 : 147. 1908.
Chamaepericlymenum suecicum Asch. & Graebn. Fl. Nord. Flachl.
539. 1898.

Flowering stems 2′–10′ high, sometimes branched above.
Rootstock horizontal. Leaves 3–6 pairs, all opposite, sessile,
ovate, or oval, acute or obtusish at the apex, mostly rounded
at the base, entire, minutely appressed-pubescent above, the
upper ½–1½′ long, the lower smaller, the veins all arising
from near the base; involucral bracts usually 4, ovate, 3″–6″
long, obtusish; flowers dark violet, capitate; fruit globose, red,
3″–4″ in diameter; stone flattened, slightly channeled on each
side, about as broad as long.

In cold, wet woods and wet cliffs, Newfoundland, Labrador and
Quebec through Arctic America to Alaska. Also in Greenland,
northern Europe and Asia. July–Aug.

4. NÝSSA L. Sp. Pl. 1058. 1753.

Trees or shrubs, with alternate petioled entire or dentate leaves. Flowers small, greenish, polygamo-dioecious, in capitate clusters, short racemes, or the fertile ones sometimes
solitary, borne at the summit of slender axillary peduncles, appearing with the leaves.
Staminate flowers numerous, the calyx small, 5-parted, the petals minute and fleshy, or
none; stamens 5–15; filaments slender; disk entire or lobed; pistil none or rudimentary.
Pistillate flowers 2–14, or solitary, bracted; calyx-limb 5-toothed, or truncate; petals minute
and fleshy, or none; stamens several, or commonly abortive; ovary 1-celled, with 1 pendulous ovule; style slender, recurved, stigmatic along one side near the apex. Drupe ovoid or
oval, the stone bony, compressed, ridged or terete, 1-seeded. [Name of a water nymph.]

About 7 species, natives of eastern North America, eastern and central Asia. Besides the following, another occurs in the Southern States. Type species : *Nyssa aquática* L.

Leaves usually entire ; pistillate flowers 2–14 ; fruit 3″–7″ long.	
Leaves mostly acute or acuminate ; stone little flattened.	1. *N. sylvatica.*
Leaves mostly obtuse ; stone much flattened.	2. *N. biflora.*
Leaves usually dentate ; pistillate flower solitary ; fruit 8″–15″ long.	3. *N. aquatica.*

1. Nyssa sylvática Marsh. Pepperidge. Sour Gum. Tupelo. Fig. 3192.

Nyssa sylvatica Marsh. Arb. Am. 97. 1785.
Nyssa multiflora Wang. Holz. 46. pl. 16. 1787.

A large tree, with rough bark, reaching a
maximum height of 110° and trunk diameter
of 5°; branches horizontal, especially when
the tree is young. Leaves obovate or oval,
acute, acuminate, or obtuse at the apex, usually
narrowed at the base, entire, glabrous and
shining above, more or less pubescent beneath,
2′–4′ long; petioles 4″–7″ long; staminate flowers in compound capitate clusters; pistillate
flowers larger, 2–14 together; fruit ovoid,
nearly black, 4″–7″ long, acid; stone ovoid,
more or less flattened and ridged.

In rich soil, most abundant in swamps, Maine
and Ontario to Florida, Michigan, Missouri and
Texas. Leaves crimson in autumn, rarely angu-
late-toothed on young trees. Wood soft, tough,
light yellow; weight per cubic foot 40 lbs. Black gum. Swamp-hornbeam. Yellow gum-tree.
Snag-tree. Beetle-bung. Hornbeam. Hornpipe. Hornbine. Hornpine. April–June.

2. Nyssa biflòra Walt. Southern Tupelo. Water Tupelo. Fig. 3193.

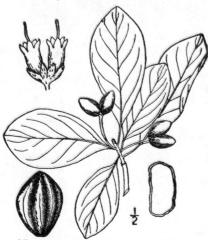

Nyssa biflora Walt. Fl. Car. 253. 1788.
Nyssa sylvatica var. *biflora* Sargent. Sylva **5**: 76.
pl. 218. 1893.

Similar to the preceding species, the base of the trunk much swollen. Leaves mostly smaller and narrower, thicker, oval, oblong or obovate, entire, obtuse, or sometimes acute at the apex, narrowed or rounded at the base, 1'–5' long, rarely more than 1½' wide, glabrous when mature, sometimes loosely pubescent when young; staminate flowers in compound or simple cymes; pistillate flowers only 1–3 together; fruit oval, or subglobose, 3"–6" long, acid; stone oval or oblong, distinctly flattened and furrowed.

In swamps and along ponds, New Jersey (according to Coulter and Evans); Maryland to Florida and Louisiana. Swamp-hornbeam. Water-gum. April–May.

3. Nyssa aquática L. Large Tupelo. Cotton or Tupelo Gum. Fig. 3194.

Nyssa aquatica L. Sp. Pl. 1058. 1753.
Nyssa uniflora Wang. Am. 83. *pl. 27. f. 57.* 1787.

A large tree, reaching a maximum height of about 100° and trunk diameter of 4°. Leaves slender-petioled, ovate or oval, angular-dentate, or entire, acute, or acuminate at the apex, rounded, often cordate, or sometimes narrowed at the base, downy-pubescent beneath, especially when young, becoming glabrate on both sides, 3'–10' long; staminate flowers in compound capitate clusters; pistillate flower larger, solitary; fruit oval, dark blue when ripe, 8"–15" long; stone narrowly obovate, flattened, spongy, with several sharp longitudinal ridges.

In swamps, southern Virginia to Florida, west to Illinois, Missouri and Texas. Wood soft, tough, light brown, or nearly white; weight per cubic foot 29 lbs. Black or sour gum. Swamp-tupelo or -hornbeam. March–May.

Series 2. *Gamopétalae.*

Petals partly or wholly united, rarely separate or wanting.

This series is also known as Sympetalae and has been called Monopetalae. The coherence of the petals is sometimes very slight or they are quite separate, as in Clethraceae, Pyrolaceae, some Ericaceae, Primulaceae, Styracaceae, Asclepiadaceae, Oleaceae, Curcurbitaceae and *Galax* in Diapensiaceae. From this condition the coherence varies through all stages to the tubular or funnelform corollas of some Convolvulaceae, Caprifoliaceae and Compositae. In most American species of *Fraxinus* (Oleaceae) and in *Glaux* (Primulaceae), there is no corolla.

Family 1. CLETHRÀCEAE Klotsch, Linnaea **24**: 12. 1851.

WHITE-ALDER FAMILY.

Shrubs or trees, more or less stellate-canescent, with alternate deciduous serrate or serrulate petioled leaves, in our species, and rather small white fragrant flowers in terminal, solitary or clustered, narrow usually elongated racemes. Calyx 5-cleft or 5-parted, persistent, the segments imbricated. Petals 5, slightly united at the base, obovate, oblong, or obcordate, imbricated, deciduous. Stamens 10; filaments slender; anthers sagittate, inverted in anthesis, the sacs opening by large apical pores; pollen-grains simple. Disk obsolete. Ovary 3-angled or

3-lobed, 3-celled, pubescent; ovules numerous; style slender; stigmas 3 in our species. Capsule subglobose, or 3-lobed, 3-celled, loculicidally 3-valved, the valves at length 2-cleft. Seeds very small, with a loose cellular coat.

1. CLÈTHRA L. Sp. Pl. 396. 1753.

Characters of the family. [Greek, alder, from the resemblance of the foliage.]

The family consists only of the following genus, comprising about 30 species, natives of eastern North America, Japan, Mexico, the West Indies and South America. Besides the following, another occurs in the Southern States. Several inhabit the mountains of the West Indies. Type species: *Clethra alnifolia* L.

Leaves obovate, acute or obtusish; filaments glabrous.   1. *C. alnifolia.*
Leaves oval or ovate, acuminate; filaments hirsute.   2. *C. acuminata.*

1. Clethra alnifòlia L. Sweet Pepper-bush. White or Spiked Alder. Fig. 3195.

Clethra alnifolia L. Sp. Pl. 396. 1753.

A shrub, 3°–10° high, the twigs minutely canescent. Leaves obovate, obtuse or acute at the apex, narrowed or cuneate at the base, sharply serrate, at least beyond the middle, glabrous or very nearly so and green on both sides, 1′–3′ long; petioles 1″–6″ long; racemes erect; bracts short, deciduous; pedicels, calyx and capsule canescent; calyx-lobes oblong, obtuse, nerved; flowers about 4″ broad, of spicy fragrance; filaments glabrous; style longer than the stamens; capsule subglobose, about 1½″ in diameter, about the length of the calyx.

In swamps and wet woods, or sometimes in dry soil, Maine to northern New Jersey, Florida and Mississippi, mostly near the coast. White bush. July–Aug.

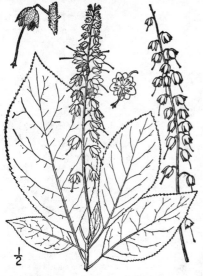

2. Clethra acuminàta Michx. Mountain Sweet Pepperbush. Fig. 3196.

C. acuminata Michx. Fl. Bor. Am. 1: 260. 1803.

A tall shrub or small tree, similar to the preceding species. Leaves oval, oblong, or ovate, acuminate at the apex, narrowed or rounded at the base, green above, pale and sometimes pubescent beneath, closely serrulate with very sharp-pointed teeth, 2′–7′ long, sometimes 3½′ wide; petioles 4″–12″ long; racemes spreading or recurved, solitary, or 2–3 together, 2′–8′ long, the rachis, pedicels and calyx densely pubescent or canescent; bracts longer than the flowers, caducous; filaments and bases of the petals hirsute; capsules pubescent.

In mountain woods, Virginia and West Virginia to Georgia. Ascends to 4500 ft. in North Carolina. July–Aug.

Family 2. PYROLÀCEAE Agardh, Cl. Pl. 18. 1825.

WINTERGREEN FAMILY.

Low mostly evergreen perennials, with branched rootstocks. Leaves petioled. Flowers perfect, nearly regular, racemose, solitary or corymbose, white to red. Calyx 4–5-lobed. Corolla very deeply 4–5-parted, or of 5 petals. Stamens twice as many as the divisions of the corolla, the anthers introrse in the bud, inverted at anthesis, opening by pores or short slits; pollen-grains in 4's. Ovary superior, 4–5-celled; style short or slender, often declined; stigma 5-lobed, or 5-crenate; ovules very numerous, anatropous. Fruit a loculicidally dehiscent capsule. Seeds very numerous, minute, the loose cellular coat much larger than the almost undifferentiated embryo.

Three genera and about 20 species, natives of the northern hemisphere.

Flowers racemose; leaves basal.	1. *Pyrola.*
Flowers solitary, corymbose or umbellate; leaves opposite or whorled.	
Stem leafy at base; flower solitary; style long.	2. *Moneses.*
Stem horizontal; branches erect, leafy; style very short.	3. *Chimaphila.*

1. PÝROLA [Tourn.] L. Sp. Pl. 396. 1753.

Low glabrous herbs, acaulescent or nearly so, stoloniferous, perennial. Leaves basal, persistent (one northwestern species leafless). Flowers nodding, or in one species ascending, white, yellowish, pink, or purple, racemose, on erect bracted scapes. Calyx 5-parted, persistent. Petals 5, concave, sessile, deciduous. Stamens 10, declined, or straight and connivent; filaments subulate, glabrous; anthers erect in the bud, emarginate or 2-beaked at the base, mostly reversed at flowering, each sac opening by a basal but apparently apical pore. Ovary 5-celled; style straight or declined, filiform, or thickened at the summit; stigma 5-lobed. Disk usually obsolete, rarely present and 10-lobed. Capsule subglobose, 5-lobed, 5-celled, loculicidally 5-valved from the base, the valves cobwebby on the margins when opening, the apex and base intruded. [Latin, diminutive of *Pyrus,* pear, from the similar leaves.]

About 15 species, natives of the northern hemisphere. Besides the following, 3 others occur in western North America. Type species: *Pyrola rotundifolia* L.

Style and stamens declined (slightly so in no. 6).	
Petals very obtuse; leaves rounded at the apex.	
Leaves rounded, truncate or narrowed at the base.	
Flowers white or greenish white; plants of dry woods.	
Calyx-lobes oblong or lanceolate; leaves shining.	1. *P. rotundifolia.*
Calyx-lobes ovate or triangular, short; leaves dull.	
Blades orbicular, coriaceous, mostly shorter than petioles.	2. *P. chlorantha.*
Blades oval, membranous, longer than their petioles.	3. *P. elliptica.*
Flowers pink or purple; bog plant.	4. *P. uliginosa.*
Leaves reniform or cordate, shining; flowers pink.	5. *P. asarifolia.*
Petals and leaves acute, the latter small.	6. *P. oxypetala.*
Style straight; stamens connivent.	
Style short; disk none; raceme regular.	7. *P. minor.*
Style elongated; disk 10-lobed; flowers in a 1-sided raceme.	8. *P. secunda.*

1. Pyrola americàna Sweet. Round-leaved American Wintergreen. Fig. 3197.

Pyrola americana Sweet, Hort. Brit. Ed. 2, 341. 1830.

Scape 6′–20′ high, 6–20-flowered, several-bracted. Leaf-blades orbicular or oval, spreading, obtuse, coriaceous, shining above, crenulate, narrowed, rounded, truncate or rarely subcordate at the base, 1′–3′ long; flowers white, nodding, very fragrant, 7″–9″ broad; pedicels 2″–3″ long, mostly longer than their bracts; calyx-lobes oblong or lanceolate, about one-third the length of the obtuse, converging, thick petals; stamens and style declined-ascending; style exserted, annular under the stigma; anther-sacs mucronate at base; capsule 2″–3″ in diameter.

In dry woods, Nova Scotia to South Dakota, Georgia and Ohio. False, larger, or pear-leaved wintergreen. Indian or canker lettuce. Wild or liverwort lettuce. Copper- or dollar-leaf. Consumption-weed. June–July. Included in *P. rotundifolia* L. in our first edition, which proves to be a distinct Old World species.

Pyrola grandiflòra Radius (*P. rotundifolia pumila* Hornem.), a high boreal species, extending south to mountain cliffs in Quebec, is smaller-leaved, lower, the flower white to crimson.

2. Pyrola chlorántha Sw. Greenish-flowered Wintergreen. Fig. 3198.

P. chlorantha Sw. Act. Holm. **1810**: 190. *pl. 5.* 1810.

Scape 4′–12′ high, 3–10-flowered. Blades orbicular, or broadly oval, mostly obtuse at both ends, but sometimes narrowed at the base, coriaceous, dull, obscurely crenulate, or entire, ½′–1½′ long, shorter than or equalling their petioles; flowers nodding, slightly odorous, greenish-white, 5″–7″ broad; pedicels 2″–3″ long, mostly longer than their bracts; calyx-lobes ovate, or triangular-ovate, acute or obtuse, about one-fourth the length of the obtuse converging petals; stamens and style declined-ascending; anther-sacs short-beaked; style exserted; capsule about 3″ in diameter.

In dry woods, Labrador to British Columbia, south to the District of Columbia, Illinois, Nebraska and in the Rocky Mountains to Arizona. Also in Europe. Shin-leaf. June–July.

3. Pyrola ellíptica Nutt. Shin-leaf. Fig. 3199.

Pyrola elliptica Nutt. Gen. 1: 273. 1818.

Scape 5′–10′ high, 7–15-flowered. Leaf-blades broadly oval, or elliptic, thin or membranous, dark green, obtuse, but usually mucronulate at the apex, narrowed or rounded at the base, plicate-crenulate with very low teeth, 1½′–3′ long, almost always longer than their petioles; flowers greenish-white, nodding, 6″–8″ broad, very fragrant; pedicels longer than or equalling their bracts; calyx-lobes ovate-triangular, acute or acuminate, about one-fourth as long as the obtuse, flat petals; stamens and style declined-ascending; anther-sacs scarcely beaked; style somewhat exserted; capsule about 3″ in diameter.

In rich, mostly dry woods, Nova Scotia to British Columbia, south to the District of Columbia, Illinois, Michigan, Iowa, South Dakota and in the Rocky Mountains to New Mexico. Wild lily-of-the-valley. June–Aug.

4. Pyrola uliginòsa Torr. Bog Wintergreen. Fig. 3200.

Pyrola uliginosa Torr. Fl. N. Y. 1: 453. *pl. 60.* 1843.
Pyrola rotundifolia var. *uliginosa* A. Gray, Man. Ed. 2, 259. 1856.

Scape 6′–15′ high, 7–15-flowered. Leaf-blades broadly oval, or orbicular, dull, rather thick, obscurely crenulate, obtuse at both ends, sometimes truncate at the base, equalling or shorter than their petioles; bracts shorter than or equalling the pedicels; flowers purple, 5″–8″ broad; calyx-lobes ovate-oblong or ovate-lanceolate, acute or obtuse, one-fourth to one-third the length of the obtuse petals; stamens and style declined-ascending; anther-sacs beaked; style slightly exserted; capsule about 2½″ in diameter.

In swamps and bogs, Newfoundland to Alaska, Vermont, central New York, Michigan, in the Rocky Mountains to Colorado, and to California. Similar to the Asiatic *P. incarnata* Fisch., and perhaps not specifically distinct from it. June–July.

5. Pyrola asarifòlia Michx.　Liver-leaf Wintergreen.　Fig. 3201.

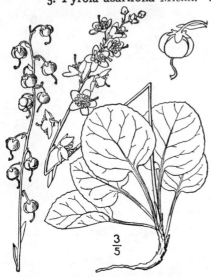

3/5

Pyrola asarifolia Michx. Fl. Bor. Am. 1 : 251. 1803.

Pyrola rotundifolia var. asarifolia Hook. Fl. Bor Am. 2 : 46. 1834.

Similar to the preceding species. Leaf-blades reniform, usually wider than long, coriaceous, shining above, obtuse at the apex, cordate at the base, crenulate, 1′–1½′ long, usually shorter than their narrowly margined petioles; flowers racemose, nodding, purple, or rose, 6″–8″ broad; calyx-lobes triangular-lanceolate or ovate-lanceolate, acute or acuminate, about one-third the length of the obtuse petals; stamens and style decurved-ascending; anther-sacs slightly beaked; style exserted; capsule about 3″ in diameter.

In wet woods and swamps, New Brunswick to Yukon Territory, south to Massachusetts, northern New York, Michigan, South Dakota, and in the Rocky Mountains to New Mexico. June–July.

6. Pyrola oxypétala Austin.　Sharp-petaled Wintergreen.　Fig. 3202.

Pyrola oxypetala Austin; A. Gray, Man. Ed. 5, 302. 1867.

Scape slender, 7′–9′ high, about 9-flowered. Blades ovate, coriaceous, dull, acute or acutish at the apex, narrowed at the base, obscurely crenulate, 7″–10″ long, shorter than their petioles; flowers racemose, ascending, greenish, 4″–5″ broad; bracts shorter than their pedicels; calyx-lobes tri-angular-ovate, acute, about one-third the length of the elliptic-lanceolate acuminate connivent petals; stamens and styles slightly declined; anther-sacs slightly horned.

Hills, Deposit, Delaware Co., N. Y. (C. F. Austin, 1860). The only station known, and the plant not subsequently collected. Perhaps a sharp-petaled race of P. chlorantha. June.

3/5

7. Pyrola mìnor L.　Lesser Wintergreen. Fig. 3203.

3/4

Pyrola minor L. Sp. Pl. 396. 1753.

Scapes slender, 8′ high or less, several-flowered. Leaf-blades rather thin, broadly oval, or nearly orbicular, dark green, crenulate, obtuse but sometimes mucronate at the apex, rounded, slightly narrowed, or subcordate at the base, 9″–18″ long; flowers racemose, nodding, white or pinkish, 3″–4″ broad; pedicels 1″–2½″ long, equalling or longer than the bracts; calyx-lobes mostly triangular-ovate and acute, much shorter than the connivent petals; style straight, included; stamens not declined, connivent around the pistil; petals oval or orbicular, obtuse; capsule about 2½″ in diameter.

In woods, Greenland and Labrador to Alaska, south to northern New England, Ontario, Michigan and Oregon, south in the Rocky Mountains to New Mexico. Also in Europe and Asia. Wood-lily. Shin-leaf. June–Aug.

8. Pyrola secúnda L.　Serrated or One-sided Wintergreen.　Fig. 3204.

Pyrola secunda L. Sp. Pl. 396. 1753.

Pyrola secunda pumila Paine, Cat. Plants Oneida Co., N. Y. 135.

Scapes usually several together from the much-branched rootstock, slender, 2′-10′ high. Leaf-blades ovate, or oval, or nearly orbicular, mostly thin, acute, or rarely obtuse at the apex, rounded or narrowed at the base, crenulate-serrulate, 6″-2′ long, longer than their petioles; flowers many, in a dense one-sided raceme, at first erect, soon drooping, white or green-ish-white, 3″-4″ broad; pedicels short; calyx-lobes ovate, obtuse, or obtusish, very short; petals oval, obtuse, with a pair of tubercles at the base, cam-panulate-connivent; style straight, exserted; stamens not declined, connivent around the pistil; capsule about 2″ in diameter.

In woods and thickets, Labrador to Alaska, south to the District of Columbia, Pennsylvania, Michigan, Ne-braska, along the Rocky Mountains to Mexico and to California. Ascends to 3000 ft. in the Adirondacks. Also in Europe and Asia. Shin-leaf. June–July.

2. MONÈSES Salisb.; S. F. Gray, Arr. Brit. Plants 2: 403. 1821.

A low perennial glabrous herb, with a decumbent leafy base, petioled evergreen crenu-late leaves, opposite, or verticillate in 3's, and a solitary drooping white or pink flower at the summit of a slender scape. Calyx 4–5 parted, persistent. Petals 4 or 5, spreading, broadly ovate or orbicular, sessile. Stamens 8 or 10, similar to those of Pyrola. Disk obsolete. Ovary globose, 4–5-celled; style straight, club-shaped at the summit; stigma 4–5-lobed; ovules very numerous in each cavity. Capsule subglobose, 4–5-lobed, 4–5-celled, loculicidally 4–5-valved from the summit, the valves glabrous on the margins. Seeds numerous, minute, the testa reticulated, produced at each end. [Greek, single-delight, from the single flower.]

A monotypic genus of the cooler parts of the northern hemisphere.

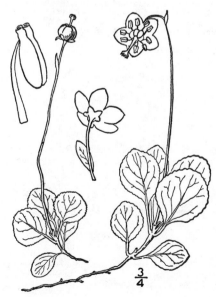

1. Moneses uniflòra (L.) A. Gray.　One-flowered Wintergreen.　Fig. 3205.

Pyrola uniflora L. Sp. Pl. 397. 1753.

Moneses grandiflora S. F. Gray, Arr. Brit. Pl. 2: 403. 1821.

Moneses uniflora A. Gray, Man. 273. 1848.

Stem bearing 1–3 pairs or whorls of leaves at the base, continued above into a bracted or naked scape 2′-6′ high. Blades orbicular or ovate, obtuse at the apex, narrowed, rounded or sometimes subcordate at the base, rather thin, 4″-12″ long, longer than or equalling their petioles; flower fragrant, 6″-10″ broad; calyx-lobes ovate, obtuse, about one-fifth the length of the petals; capsule erect, 3″-4″ in diameter, about as long as the persistent style and con-spicuously lobed stigma.

In woods, Labrador to Alaska, south to Connecti-cut, Pennsylvania, Michigan, in the Rocky Moun-tains to Colorado and to Oregon. Ascends to 4000 ft. in the Adirondacks. Also in Europe and Asia. June–Aug.

3. CHIMÁPHILA Pursh, Fl. Am. Sept. 279, 300. 1814.

Perennial herbs, with decumbent stems, ascending leafy branches, the leaves opposite, or verticillate, coriaceous, evergreen, short-petioled and serrate, and spreading or nodding white or purplish flowers in corymbs or umbels. Pedicels mostly bracteolate. Calyx 5-cleft, or 5-parted, persistent. Petals 5, concave, nearly orbicular, sessile, spreading or recurved. Stamens 10, similar to those of *Pyrola*, the filaments usually somewhat pubescent. Ovary globose, 5-lobed, 5-celled; ovules numerous in the cavities; style very short, obconic; stigma large, orbicular, 5-crenate. Capsule erect, globose, 5-lobed, 5-celled, loculicidally 5-valved from the top, the valves not woolly on the margins. Seeds numerous, minute, the testa reticulated, produced at each end. [Greek, winter-loving, from its evergreen leaves.]

About 6 species, natives of North America, Mexico, Santo Domingo and northeastern Asia. Besides the following another occurs on our Pacific Coast. Type species: *Chimaphila maculata* (L.) Pursh.

Leaves lanceolate, mottled with white.   1. *C. maculata.*
Leaves spatulate or cuneate-oblanceolate, bright green.   2. *C. umbellata.*

1. Chimaphila maculàta (L.) Pursh. Spotted Wintergreen. Fig. 3206.

Pyrola maculata L. Sp. Pl. 396. 1753.

C. maculata Pursh, Fl. Am. Sept. 300. 1814.

Stem extensively trailing, creeping or horizontally subterranean, sending up both sterile and flowering branches 3'–10' high. Leaves lanceolate, ovate-lanceolate, or the lower much shorter and ovate, acute or acuminate at the apex, rounded or narrowed at the base, sharply serrate with rather distant teeth, dark green and mottled with white along the veins, 1'–3' long, 3''–12'' wide below the middle; flowers few, corymbose or umbellate, white or pinkish, 6''–10'' broad; peduncle and pedicels puberulent; filaments villous at the middle; capsules erect, depressed-globose, about 4'' in diameter.

In dry woods, Maine and Ontario to Minnesota, south to Georgia and Mississippi. Ascends to 4200 ft. in North Carolina. June–Aug. Spotted pipsissiwa. Rheumatism-root. Dragon's-tongue. Wild arsenic. Ratsbane.

2. Chimaphila umbellàta (L.) Nutt. Pipsissewa. Prince's Pine. Fig. 3207.

Pyrola umbellata L. Sp. Pl. 396. 1753.
Chimaphila corymbosa Pursh, Fl. Am. Sept. 300. 1814.
Chimaphila umbellata Nutt. Gen. 1: 274. 1818.

Similar to the preceding species, the branches commonly stouter, sometimes 1° high and usually more leafy. Leaves spatulate or cuneate-oblanceolate, obtuse or acutish at the apex, sharply serrate, bright green and shining, not mottled, 1'–2½' long, 3''–12'' wide above the middle; flowers several, umbellate or subcorymbose, white or pinkish, commonly smaller than those of the preceding species, usually marked by a deep pink ring; filaments ciliate; capsule 3''–4'' in diameter.

In dry woods, Nova Scotia to British Columbia, south to Georgia, Mexico and California. Mountains of Santo Domingo. Also in Europe and Asia. Bitter wintergreen. Pine-tulip. Ground-holly. Bitter-sweet. Noble pine. Love-in-winter. King's-cure. June–Aug.

3/5

Family 3. **MONOTROPÀCEAE** Lindl. Nat. Syst. Ed. 2, 219. 1836.

INDIAN-PIPE FAMILY.

Humus-plants or saprophytes, with mostly simple, leafless bracted scapes, and solitary or clustered perfect regular flowers. Calyx 2–6-parted, free from the ovary; sepals erect, connate at the base, imbricated, deciduous. Corolla gamopetalous or polypetalous (wanting in the California *Allotropa*); lobes or petals 3–6. Stamens 6–12, hypogynous; filaments distinct, or united at base; anthers 2-celled or confluently 1-celled, attached to the filaments by their backs or bases; pollen-grains simple. Disk obsolete or 8–12-lobed. Ovary superior, 4–6-lobed, 1–6-celled; style short or elongated; stigma capitate or peltate; ovules numerous, anatropous. Capsule 4–6-lobed, or terete, 1–6-celled, loculicidally 4–6-valved, many seeded. Seeds minute, the testa reticulated.

About 9 genera and 12 species, mostly of the northern hemisphere, most abundant in North America.

Corolla gamopetalous, persistent.
　Corolla globose-ovoid; anthers 2-awned.　　　　　　　　　　　1. *Pterospora*.
　Corolla campanulate; anthers awnless.　　　　　　　　　　　2. *Monotropsis*.
Corolla polypetalous, deciduous.
　Flower solitary.　　　　　　　　　　　　　　　　　　　　3. *Monotropa*.
　Flowers racemose.　　　　　　　　　　　　　　　　　　　4. *Hypopitys*.

1. PTERÓSPORA Nutt. Gen. 1: 269. 1818.

Scape slender, glandular-pubescent, from a thick base of matted fibrous roots. Flowers and capsules racemose, pendulous. Calyx deeply 5-parted. Corolla gamopetalous, globose-ovoid, with 5 reflexed lobes. Stamens 10, included; filaments subulate, glabrous; anthers introrse, horizontal in the bud, the sacs longitudinally dehiscent, each with a deflexed awn near the base. Disk none. Ovary subglobose, 5-lobed, 5-celled; style short, columnar; stigma capitate, 5-lobed. Capsule depressed globose, 5-lobed, 5-celled, 5-valved, the apex and base intruded. Seeds horizontal, globose-ovoid, with a terminal reticulated wing. [Greek, wing-seeded.]

A monotypic genus of temperate North America.

1. Pterospora andromedèa Nutt. Giant Bird's-nest.
Pine Drops. Fig. 3208.

Plerospora andromedea Nutt. Gen. 1: 269. 1818.
Monotropa procera Torr.; Eaton, Man. Ed. 2, 324. 1818.

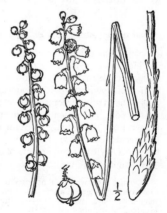

Roots very astringent, forming a rounded mass sometimes 2′ in diameter. Scape purplish or brown, 6′–4½° high, bracted, grooved, densely covered with viscid hairs. Bracts lanceolate, or linear, very numerous and crowded at the base; flowers numerous, racemose, white, 2″–4″ broad; pedicels at first spreading, soon recurved, 3″–10″ long, viscid; sepals oblong, about one-half the length of the corolla; capsule 4″–6″ in diameter.

In rich woods, Nova Scotia to New Hampshire, Pennsylvania, Michigan, British Columbia and California, south in the Rocky Mountains to Arizona and Mexico. Albany beech-drops. June–Aug.

As regards the two names given to this plant in 1818, Nuttall's "Genera," appeared before the second edition of Eaton's "Manual."

2. MONOTRÓPSIS Schwein.; Ell. Bot. S. C. & Ga. 1: 478. 1817.

[SCHWEINITZIA Nutt. Gen. 2: Add. 3. 1818.]

Scape slender, bracted; plants glabrous throughout. Sepals 5, oblong to linear. Corolla gamopetalous, oblong-campanulate, persistent, 5-saccate at the base, 5-lobed, the lobes not reflexed. Stamens 10, included; filaments subulate, glabrous; anthers horizontal in the bud, introrse, the sacs confluent, opening by large terminal pores, awnless. Disk 10-crenate. Ovary globose, 5-celled; style short, thick; stigma discoid, 5-angled. Capsule ovoid, 5-celled. Seeds very numerous. [Greek, resembling *Monotropa*.]

Three species, natives of southeastern North America, the following typical.

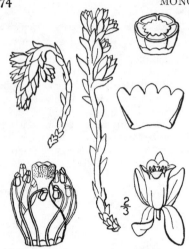

1. **Monotropsis odoràta** Ell. Sweet Pine-Sap. Carolina Beech-drops. Fig. 3209.

Monotropsis odorata Ell. Bot. S. C. & Ga. **1**: 479. 1817.

Schweinitzia caroliniana Don, Gen. Syst. **3**: 867. 1834.

Schweinitzia odorata DC. Prodr. **7**: 780. 1839.

Plant light purplish brown; scapes usually several in a cluster, 2'–4' high. Bracts numerous, ovate-oblong, obtuse, appressed, 2"–4" long; flowers few (usually 6–8), pink or white, spicate fragrant, 2-bracteolate at the base, spreading or erect, the spike at first recurved, becoming erect, 1'–2' long; sepals mostly oblong-lanceolate, acute, about as long as the corolla and the bractlets.

In woods, Maryland to North Carolina. Very rare. Feb.–May.

3. **MONÓTROPA** L. Sp. Pl. 387. 1753.

Scapose succulent white yellowish or red bracted herbs, with a solitary nodding flower, the capsule becoming erect. Sepals 2–4, deciduous. Petals 5 or 6, oblong, somewhat dilated at apex, erect, not saccate at the base, tardily deciduous. Stamens 10–12; filaments subulate-filiform; anthers short, peltate, horizontal, opening at first by 2 transverse chinks, becoming transversely 2-valved. Disk 10–12-toothed, confluent with the base of the ovary. Ovary 5-celled; style short, thick; stigma funnelform, its margin obscurely crenate, not ciliate. Capsule 5-celled, 5-valved, many-seeded. Seeds minute, the testa produced at each end. [Greek, once-turned.]

Two species, natives of North America, Mexico, Colombia, Japan and the Himalayas. The following typical one is the only one known in North America.

1. **Monotropa uniflòra** L. Indian Pipe. Fig. 3210.

Monotropa uniflora L. Sp. Pl. 387. 1753.

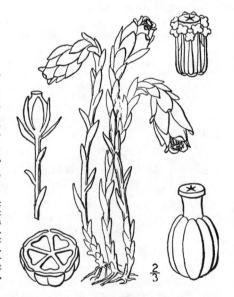

Scapes white, glabrous, usually clustered, 4'–10' high from a mass of matted brittle roots, turning dark in drying. Flower terminal, inodorous, nodding, oblong-campanulate, ½'–1' long, the fruit becoming erect; petals 4–5 (rarely 6), puberulent within, white, rather longer than the usually 10 stamens; filaments pubescent; ovary ovoid, acute, narrowed into the short style; capsule erect, obtusely angled, 5"–8" high, 4"–5" in diameter.

In moist rich woods, Anticosti to Florida, west to Washington and California, almost throughout temperate and warm North America and in Mexico. Ascends to 4200 ft. in North Carolina. Also in Japan and the Himalayas. Whole plant occasionally pink or red. American ice-plant. Ghost-flower, Corpse-plant. Eyebright. Convulsion-weed or -root. Dutchman's-pipe. Fit-root plant. Bird's-nest or pipe-plant. Fairy-smoke. June–Aug.

4. **HYPÓPITYS** Adans. Fam. Pl. **2**: 443. 1763.

Stems slender, pubescent at least above, bearing numerous white, pink, yellow or red flowers in a nodding one-sided raceme which soon becomes erect. Roots a dense mass of fleshy fibres. Terminal flower usually 5-parted, the lateral ones 3-4-parted. Sepals commonly as many as the petals. Petals saccate at the base. Stamens 6–10; filaments subulate-filiform; anthers horizontal, the 2 sacs becoming confluent, opening by 2 unequal valves, the larger valve spreading or reflexed, the smaller erect. Disk confluent with the base of the ovary, 8–10-toothed. Ovary 3–5-celled; style slender; stigma funnelform, sometimes glandular-ciliate. Capsule 3–5-celled, 3–5-valved, erect. [Greek, referring to its growth under firs.]

A genus of about 6 species of the north temperate zone. Type species: *Monotropa Hypopitys* L.

Stigma not retrorsely bearded; sepals and petals short-ciliate.   1. *H. americana.*
Stigma retrorsely bearded; sepals and petals long-ciliate.   2. *H. lanuginosa.*

1. Hypopitys americàna (DC.) Small. Pine-sap. False Beech-Drops. Fig. 3211.

Hypopitys multiflora americana DC. Prodr. 7²: 780. 1839.

Hypopitys americana Small, Fl. SE. U. S. 880. 1903.

Plants lemon-yellow, or sometimes pink, finely pubescent. Stems 4′–12′ tall; scales crowded at base of the stem, 2″–6″ long, the upper ones sometimes irregularly toothed; flowers several; sepals spatulate to oblanceolate, 3½″–5″ long, often irregularly toothed, ciliate with very short hairs; petals mainly cuneate, 9″–13″ long, sparingly pubescent, and ciliate like the sepals; style sparingly pubescent; stigma not retrorsely bearded; capsule oval or oblong-oval, 3½″–5″ long.

In woods, Ontario and New York, and southward in or near the Alleghenies to North Carolina. Yellow-bird's-nest. Fir-rope. July–Aug.

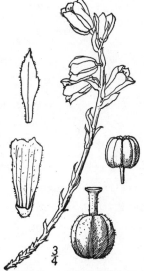

2. Hypopitys lanuginòsa (Michx.) Nutt. Hairy Pine-sap. Fig. 3212.

Monotropa lanuginosa Michx. Fl. Bor. Am. 2: 266. 1803.
Hypopitys lanuginosa Nutt. Gen. 1: 271. 1818.

Plants tawny and crimson, or sometimes pale, markedly or copiously pubescent. Stems 2′–14′ tall; scales 2½″–3½″ long; flowers few; sepals cuneate, oblanceolate or narrowly elliptic-spatulate, 3″–4½″ long, acute or acuminate, ciliate with relatively long hairs; petals cuneate to almost oblong, 5″–5½″ long, markedly pubescent without, ciliate like the sepals; style copiously pubescent; stigma retrorsely bearded; capsule globular, 2″–2½″ long.

In woods, Newfoundland and Quebec to Nova Scotia, Ontario and Indiana, and southward, especially in and near the mountains, to South Carolina and Tennessee, and to Florida. June–Aug. This species and the preceding one were included in *H. Hypopitys*, an Old World species, in our first edition.

Family 4. ERICÀCEAE DC. Fl. Franc. 3: 675. 1805.

HEATH FAMILY.

Shrubs, perennial herbs, or trees, with simple exstipulate leaves, and mostly perfect, gamopetalous or polypetalous flowers. Calyx inferior, free from the ovary, 4–5-parted or 4–5-cleft, mostly persistent. Corolla regular, or rarely somewhat 2-lipped and irregular, usually 4–5-toothed, -lobed or -parted. Stamens hypogynous, usually as many or twice as many as the corolla-lobes, teeth or petals; filaments mostly separate; anthers 2-celled, attached to the filaments by the back or base, the sacs often prolonged upwardly into tubes, dehiscent by terminal pores or chinks, or longitudinally, often awned. Disk crenate, lobed, or none. Ovary 2–5-celled; style elongated or short; stigma peltate or capitate; ovules usually numerous, anatropous. Fruit a capsule, berry or drupe. Seeds usually numerous and minute, or sometimes only 1 in each cavity; endosperm fleshy; embryo central; cotyledons short; radicle terete.

About 60 genera and 1100 species, of very wide geographic distribution.

* Fruit a septicidal capsule; corolla deciduous; anthers unappendaged. (RHODO-DENDREAE.)

Corolla of separate petals; capsule dehiscent from the base.   1. *Ledum.*

Corolla gamopetalous (polypetalous in no. 6); capsule dehiscent from the apex.

Corolla somewhat irregular (except in no. 5); seeds flat, winged.

Corolla funnelform to campanulate; stamens exserted.

Corolla funnelform, slightly 2-lipped; leaves deciduous.   2. *Azalea.*

Corolla 2-lipped, lower lip divided to the base; leaves deciduous.   3. *Rhodora.*

Corolla campanulate; leaves evergreen.   4. *Rhododendron.*

Corolla urn-shaped; stamens not exserted.   5. *Menziesia.*

Corolla regular; seeds angled, or rounded.

Corolla polypetalous.   6. *Dendrium.*

Corolla gamopetalous.

Stamens 5; capsule 2–3-celled.   7. *Chamaecistus.*

Stamens 10; capsule 5-celled.

Corolla saucer-shaped, 10-saccate.

Calyx-segments persistent; corolla-lobes rounded.   8. *Kalmia.*

Calyx-segments deciduous; corolla-lobes acute.   9. *Kalmiella.*

Corolla ovoid.   10. *Phyllodoce.*

**Fruit a loculicidal capsule (marginally septicidal in No. 21), berry or drupe; corolla deciduous; anthers often awned.

† *Fruit a dry capsule (fleshy in no. 21); calyx not accrescent, mostly small.* (ANDRO-MEDEAE.)

‡ Corolla campanulate, cylindric, urceolate or subglobose; anthers opening by terminal pores or chinks.

Low heath-like shrubs with small subulate leaves; corolla campanulate.

Peduncles lateral; corolla 5-lobed.   11. *Cassiope.*

Peduncles terminal; corolla 5-cleft.   12. *Harrimanella.*

Shrubs or trees, with linear to broadly oval leaves; corolla urceolate to cylindric or subglobose.

Anther-sacs opening only at the top; shrubs; capsule oblong, ovoid, obovoid, or depressed-globose.

Capsule dehiscent into 2 layers, the outer 5-valved, the inner 10-valved; anthers awnless.   13. *Chamaedaphne.*

Capsule simply 5-valved.

Sepals or calyx-lobes imbricated, at least in the bud.

Leaves evergreen; bracts persistent; anthers awnless.   14. *Leucothoë.*

Leaves and bracts deciduous; anther-sacs 1- or 2-awned.   15. *Eubotrys.*

Sepals or calyx-lobes valvate.

Anther-sacs awned; sutures of the capsule not thickened.

Seeds smooth and shining; awns of the anther-sacs ascending; narrow-leaved bog shrubs.   16. *Andromeda.*

Seeds with a loose cellular coat; awns of the anther-sacs deflexed; broad-leaved shrubs.   17. *Pieris.*

Anther-sacs awnless; sutures of the capsule thickened.

Filaments appendaged; glabrous shrubs.   18. *Neopieris.*

Filaments not appendaged; pubescent or lepidote shrubs   19. *Xolisma.*

Anther-sacs opening by long chinks; tree; capsule ovoid-pyramidal; calyx-lobes valvate.   20. *Oxydendrum*

‡‡ Corolla salverform; anthers longitudinally dehiscent; prostrate shrub. (EPIGAEAE).

      21. *Epigaea.*

†† *Fruit a drupe, or a capsule enclosed by the fleshy accrescent calyx.*

Fruit consisting of the fleshy calyx surrounding the capsule. (GAULTHERIEAE.) 22. *Gaultheria.*

Fruit a drupe with 4 or 5 nutlets. (ARBUTEAE.)

Nutlets coalescent; leaves persistent.   23. *Uva-Ursi.*

Nutlets separate; leaves deciduous.   24. *Mairania.*

*** Fruit a septicidal capsule; corolla withering-persistent; anthers appendaged. (ERI-CEAE.)

      25. *Calluna.*

1. LÈDUM L. Sp. Pl. 391. 1753.

Erect branching evergreen resinous shrubs, with scaly buds, the foliage fragrant when crushed. Leaves alternate, thick, short-petioled, oblong or linear, revolute-margined. Flowers white, numerous in terminal umbels or corymbs. Pedicels bracted at the base, the bracts scarious, deciduous. Calyx small or minute, 5-toothed, persistent. Petals 5, obovate or oval, obtuse, spreading, imbricated. Stamens 5 or 10 (rarely 5 to 7), exserted; filaments filiform; anthers small, attached by their backs to the filaments, globose-didymous, awnless, the sacs opening by terminal pores. Disk annular, 8–10-lobed. Ovary ovoid, scaly, 5-celled; ovules numerous; style filiform; stigma 5-lobed. Capsule oblong, 5-celled, septicidally 5-valved from the base. Seeds elongated. [Greek, ledon, the plant now called *Cistus Ledon.*]

About 5 species, natives of the north temperate and sub-arctic zones. Besides the following, 2 others occur on the Pacific Coast. Types species: *Ledum palustre* L.

Leaves linear, 1″–3″ wide; stamens about 10.

Leaves oblong, 3″–8″ wide; stamens 5–7.

1. *L. decumbens.*
2. *L. groenlandicum.*

1. Ledum decùmbens (Ait.) Lodd. Narrow leaved Labrador Tea. Fig. 3213.

L. palustre decumbens Ait. Hort. Kew. **2**: 65. 1789.
L. decumbens Lodd.; Steud. Nomencl. Ed. 2, 20. 1841.

A shrub, about 1° high, the twigs rusty-tomentose. Leaves linear, obtuse, dark green and somewhat rugose above, densely tomentose with brown wool beneath, strongly revolute-margined, ⅓′–¾′ long, 1″–2″ wide; flowers 3″–5″ broad; pedicels very pubescent, 4″–8″ long in fruit; stamens 10; capsule obovoid or oval, scurfy, about 2″ high and 1½″ in diameter, nodding; calyx-teeth less than ½″ long, broadly ovate to half-orbicular, obtuse.

In bogs, Newfoundland to Maine and Quebec, west to Alaska. Also in northern Asia. In our first edition included in *L. palustre* L., of Europe and Asia. Summer.

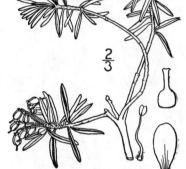

2. Ledum groenlándicum Oeder. Labrador Tea. Fig. 3214.

Ledum groenlandicum Oeder, Fl. Dan. *pl. 567.* 1771.

Ledum latifolium Ait. Hort. Kew. **2**: 65. 1789.

A shrub, 1°–4° high, similar to the preceding species, the twigs densely tomentose. Leaves oblong, obtuse, 1′–2′ long, 3″–8″ wide, green and slightly rugose above, densely brown-tomentose beneath, strongly revolute-margined; flowers 4″–5″ broad, umbellate or short-corymbose; pedicels brown-canescent or tomentose, 10″–12″ long and recurved in fruit; stamens 5–7; capsule oblong, canescent, nodding, 3″–3½″ long, 1″–1½″ in diameter.

In bogs and swamps, Greenland; Labrador to British Columbia, Massachusetts, eastern Pennsylvania, Wisconsin, Saskatchewan and Washington. May–Aug.

2. AZÀLEA L. Sp. Pl. 150. 1753.

Erect mostly tall branching shrubs, with alternate thin deciduous leaves. Flowers large, white, purple, yellow, pink, or orange, in terminal umbels developed from cone-like scaly buds. Calyx small or minute, 5-parted. Corolla funnelform, the tube mostly narrow, the limb nearly regularly 5-lobed or somewhat 2-lipped. Stamens 5 (rarely 10), exserted, usually declined; anthers awnless, attached to the filaments by their backs, the cells opening by terminal pores; styles slender, declined, exserted. Ovary 5-celled; ovules numerous in the cavities. Capsule oblong or linear-oblong, 5-celled, septicidally 5-valved from the summit, many-seeded. [Greek, dry, from the habitat of one of the original species.]

About 40 species, natives of North America and Asia. Besides the following, another occurs on the Pacific Coast and 2 or 3 in the Southern States. Type species: *Azalea índica* L. The genus is included in *Rhododendron* by some authors.

Flowers expanding before or with the leaves.
  Flowers pink or white.
    Leaves strigose on the midrib beneath; corolla-tube hirsute.
    Leaves canescent beneath; corolla-tube glandular.
  Flowers orange, yellow or red; leaves canescent beneath.
Flowers expanding later than the leaves.
  Leaves shining, glabrous beneath.
  Leaves strigose on the midrib beneath.

1. *A. nudiflora.*
2. *A. canescens.*
3. *A. lutea.*

4. *A. arborescens.*
5. *A. viscosa.*

1. **Azalea nudiflòra** L. Wild Honeysuckle. Pinkster-flower. Purple or Pink Azalea. Fig. 3215.

$\frac{1}{2}$

Azalea nudiflora L. Sp. Pl. Ed. 2, 214. 1762.
R. nudiflorum Torr. Fl. N. & Mid. U. S. 424. 1824.

A shrub, 2°–6° high, branched above, often simple below, the twigs glabrous, or with stiff hairs. Leaves oblong or obovate, acute at both ends, short-petioled, hairy on the midrib and sometimes on the lateral veins beneath, glabrous or with a few scattered hairs above when old, sometimes canescent on the lower surface when unfolding, 2′–4′ long, the margins ciliolate; pedicels strigose, 4″–7″ long; flowers pink to nearly white, expanding before or with the leaves, faintly odorous, the limb somewhat 2-lipped, 1½′–2′ broad, shorter than the narrow tube, which is pilose-pubescent and little or not at all glandular; stamens much exserted; capsule linear-oblong, strigose, 8″–9″ long, erect.

In dry sandy or rocky woods and thickets Massachusetts to Illinois, south to Florida and Texas. Ascends to 3000 ft. in Virginia. Reported from Canada and from Maine. Swamp or election-pink. Mayflower. Early, purple or swamp-honeysuckle. River-pink. April–May.

2. **Azalea canéscens** Michx. Mountain or Hoary Azalea. Fig. 3216.

Azalea canescens Michx. Fl. Bor. Am. 1: 150. 1803.
Rhodod. canesc. Porter, Bull. Torr. Club 16: 220. 1889.

A branching shrub, 4°–15° high, the twigs glabrous or sparingly pubescent. Leaves oval, elliptic or sometimes obovate, wider and shorter than those of the preceding species, permanently more or less soft-canescent and pale beneath and stiff-hairy or pubescent on the veins, varying to nearly glabrous, the margins ciliolate-serrulate; pedicels glandular; flowers rose-color to white, very fragrant, expanding with or before the leaves; corolla limb often 2′ broad, about equalling the rather stout, densely glandular but scarcely viscid tube; stamens slightly exserted; capsule linear-oblong, glandular, 6″–8″ long.

In woods, New Hampshire, New York and Pennsylvania, south, especially along the Alleghanies, to Florida and to Louisiana. April–May.

$\frac{3}{5}$

$\frac{1}{2}$

3. **Azalea lùtea** L. Flame Azalea. Fig. 3217.

Azalea lutea L. Sp. Pl. 150. 1753.
A. calendulacea Michx. Fl. Bor. Am. 1: 151. 1803.
Rhododendron calendulaceum Torr. Fl. N. & Mid. U. S. 425. 1824.

A shrub, 4°–15° high, similar to the preceding species, the twigs mostly glabrous. Leaves obovate or oval, permanently more or less canescent or tomentose beneath, glabrous, or with some scattered hairs above, the margins ciliolate-serrulate; pedicels short, pilose or glandular; flowers orange-yellow or red, very showy, slightly fragrant, expanding before or with the leaves; corolla-tube about the length of the nearly regular limb, glandular-pilose, the limb often 2′ broad; stamens long-exserted; capsule linear-oblong, about 8″ high, erect, more or less pubescent.

In dry woods, southern New York, and the mountains of Pennsylvania to Georgia and Tennessee, nearer the coast in North Carolina. Fine in cultivation. Yellow honeysuckle. May–June.

4. Azalea arboréscens Pursh. Smooth or Tree Azalea. Fig. 3218.

Azalea arborescens Pursh. Fl. Am. Sept. 152. 1814.

Rhododendron arborescens Torr. Fl. N. & Mid. U. S. 425. 1824.

A shrub, 8°–20° high, glabrous or nearly so throughout. Leaves obovate, oblanceolate or oval, acute at both ends or sometimes abruptly acuminate at the apex, manifestly petioled, firm, bright green and shining above, light green beneath, 2'–4' long, fragrant in drying, the margins ciliate; flowers white, or tinged with pink, very fragrant, the limb nearly regular, 1½'–2' broad, about as long as the slender glandular tube; pedicels short, glandular; stamens and style red, long-exserted; capsule oblong, densely glandular, 6"–8" long.

In woods, southern Pennsylvania to Georgia and eastern Tennessee. Ascends to 2500 ft. in North Carolina. Smooth honeysuckle. June–July.

5. Azalea viscòsa L. Swamp Pink or Honeysuckle. White Azalea. Fig. 3219.

Azalea viscosa L. Sp. Pl. 151. 1753.

Rhododendron viscosum Torr. Fl. N. & Mid. U. S. 424. 1824.

A shrub, 1°–8° high, usually much branched, the twigs hairy. Leaves obovate-oblong to oblanceolate, 1'–4' long, very short-petioled, obtuse and mucronulate or acute at the apex, narrowed at the base, glabrous or with a few scattered hairs above, more or less bristly hairy on the veins beneath, ciliolate, green on both sides, or glaucous beneath; flowers white, or sometimes pink, fragrant, later than the leaves; pedicels glandular, or bristly-hispid; corolla 1½'–2' long, the limb 1'–2' broad, more or less 2-lipped, much shorter than the slender, very viscid, densely glandular tube; capsule 5"–7" high, glandular-bristly.

In swamps, Maine to Ohio, Arkansas, Florida and Texas. Consists of several races differing in pubescence, size and shape of leaves and color of flowers. Clammy azalea. Meadow-pink. White or clammy honeysuckle. June–July.

3. RHODÒRA L. Sp. Pl. Ed. 2, 561. 1762.

A branching shrub, with deciduous oval or oblong short-petioled alternate leaves. Flowers umbellate or short-corymbose, short-pedicelled, rose-colored, purple, or nearly white, from terminal scaly buds. Calyx minute. Corolla 2-lipped, the upper lip unequally 2–3-lobed, the lower divided to the base, the segments recurved. Stamens 10, about equalling the corolla; anthers awnless, attached by their backs to the filaments, opening by terminal pores. Ovary 5-celled; ovules numerous in the cavities; style slender, slightly exserted; stigma capitate. Capsule linear-oblong, 5-celled, septicidally 5-valved from the summit, many-seeded. [From the Greek, *rhodon*, a rose.]

1. Rhodora canadénsis L.   Rhodora.   Fig. 3220.

Rhodora canadensis L. Sp. Pl. Ed. 2, 561. 1762.

Rhododendron Rhodora Gmel. Syst. 694. 1791.

Rhododendron canadense B.S.P. Prel. Cat. N. Y. 33. 1888.

A shrub, 1°–3° high, the branches slender, ascending or erect, the twigs sparingly strigose. Leaves oval or oblong, obtuse and mucronulate at the apex, narrowed at the base, entire, dark green and glabrous, or nearly so, above, light green or pale and glaucous and slightly pubescent, at least on the veins beneath, 1′–2′ long, 3″–7″ wide; flowers expanding with or before the leaves; pedicels very short, stiff, hairy; corolla about 1′ broad; lower lip divided into two linear-oblong obtuse segments; capsule oblong, puberulent, glaucous, 5″–7″ high.

In bogs and on wet hillsides, Newfoundland to New Jersey, west to Quebec, central New York and Pennsylvania. Lamb-kill. May.

4. RHODODÉNDRON L. Sp. Pl. 392. 1753.

Branching shrubs, with alternate persistent coriaceous leaves. Flowers large, or middle-sized, purple, rose-colored or white, corymbose or umbellate, from scaly cone-like buds. Calyx small, or minute, 5-lobed or 5-parted. Corolla campanulate, 5-lobed, nearly regular. Stamens 5–10 (usually 10), little exserted, declined or equally spreading. Anthers awnless, attached by their backs to the filaments, the sacs opening by terminal pores. Style slender; stigma capitate or 5–20-lobed; ovules numerous. Capsule short or elongated, mostly woody, septicidally dehiscent, 5–20-valved from the summit. Seeds numerous. [Greek, rose-tree.]

About 100 species, natives of the northern hemisphere, most abundant in Asia. Besides the following some 5 others occur in southern and western North America. Type species: *Rhododendron ferrugineum* L.

Arctic-alpine shrub, 4′–12′ high; leaves small, lepidote.   1. *R. lapponicum.*
Tall shrubs or low trees; leaves large, glabrous.
     Leaves usually acute at both ends; calyx-lobes oblong, obtuse.   2. *R. maximum.*
     Leaves mostly obtuse at both ends; calyx-lobes short, acute.   3. *R. catawbiense.*

1. Rhododendron lappónicum (L.) Wahl.   Lapland Rose Bay.   Fig. 3221.

Azalea lapponica L. Sp. Pl. 151. 1753.

Rhododendron lapponicum Wahl. Fl. Suec. 249. 1824.

Low, depressed or prostrate, branched, 2′–12′ high. Leaves oval, elliptic or oblong, obtuse and mucronulate at the apex, narrowed or rounded at the base, 4″–9″ long, 2″–4″ wide, densely covered with brownish scales on both sides, short-petioled; flowers few in the umbels, on short pedicels with scurfy scales; calyx-lobes oblong, obtuse, pubescent; corolla purple, 5-lobed, 7″–9″ broad, the lobes oblong, obtuse; stamens 5 or 10; capsule ovoid-oblong, 2″–3″ high.

Summits of the higher mountains of New England and the Adirondacks of New York; Quebec and Labrador to Greenland, west through arctic America to Alaska. Also in northern Europe and Asia. Laurel. Summer.

2. Rhododendron máximum L. Great Laurel. Rose Bay. Fig. 3222.

Rhododendron maximum L Sp. Pl. 392. 1753.

A tall shrub, or sometimes a tree, with maximum height of about 40° and trunk diameter of 1°. Leaves oblong, lanceolate-oblong or broadly oblanceolate, dark green on both sides, acute or abruptly short-acuminate at the apex, narrowed to a mostly acute base, 4'–7' long, 1'–2½' wide, glabrous, drooping in winter; petioles stout, ½'–1' long; pedicels glandular, viscid-pubescent, 1'–2' long; corolla 1½'–2' broad, about 1' long, rather deeply 5-cleft into oval obtuse lobes, rose-color, varying to white, sprinkled with yellowish or orange spots within; calyx-lobes oblong, obtuse; capsule oblong, puberulent, 5''–7'' high.

In low woods and along streams, Nova Scotia, Quebec, Ontario and Ohio to Georgia and Alabama, chiefly along the mountains, often forming almost impenetrable thickets. Wood hard, strong, light brown; weight per cubic foot 39 lbs. Deer-laurel. Big-leaf laurel. Wild or dwarf rose-bay. Cow-plant. Spoon-hutch. Mountain, horse- or bee-laurel. June–July.

3. Rhododendron catawbiénse Michx. Mountain Rose Bay. Catawba or Carolina Rhododendron. Fig. 3223.

Rhododendron catawbiense Michx. Fl. Bor. Am. **1**: 258. 1803.

A shrub, 3°–20° high. Leaves oval or broadly oblong, mostly rounded or obtuse at both ends, sometimes narrowed at the base, mucronate, 3'–5' long, 1½'–2' wide, dark green above, paler beneath; petioles stout, ½'–1½' long, pubescent when young; pedicels rather stout, pubescent, becoming glabrous; corolla lilac-purple, 1½'–2' long, 2'–2½' broad, 5-lobed, the lobes broad and rounded; calyx-lobes triangular-ovate, acute or acuminate, short; capsule linear-oblong, puberulent, 8''–10'' high.

Mountain summits, Virginia and West Virginia to Georgia and Tennessee. Laurel. May–June.

5. MENZIÈSIA J. E. Smith, Icon. Ined. 3. *pl. 56.* 1791.

Erect branching shrubs, with alternate membranous entire deciduous leaves, and small nodding greenish purple slender-pedicelled flowers, in terminal corymbs or umbels, developed from scaly buds. Calyx 4-toothed or 4-parted, persistent. Corolla urceolate-cylindric, or nearly globose, 4-toothed or 4-lobed. Stamens 8, included; filaments subulate, flattish, slightly dilated below; anthers linear-oblong, awnless, attached by their backs to the filaments, the sacs opening by terminal pores or chinks. Disk obscurely 8-crenate. Ovary mostly 4-celled; ovules numerous; style filiform; stigma 4-lobed or 4-toothed. Capsule subglobose or ovoid, 4-celled, septicidally 4-valved, many-seeded. Seeds slender, the testa membranous, prolonged at both ends. Parts of the flower rarely in 5's. [Named in honor of Archibald Menzies, surgeon and naturalist, died 1842.]

About 7 species, natives of North America and Japan. Besides the following, 2 others occur in the northwestern parts of North America. Type species: *Menziesia ferruginea* J. E. Smith.

Filaments glabrous; seeds pointed at each end.   1. *M. pilosa.*
Filaments pubescent below; seeds long-appendaged at each end.   2. *M. glabella.*

1. Menziesia pilòsa (Michx.) Pers. Alleghany Menziesia. Minnie-bush. Fig. 3224.

Azalea pilosa Michx. in Lam. Journ. Nat. Hist. 1 : 410. 1792.
Menziesia pilosa Pers. Syn. 1 : 420. 1805.
Menziesia globularis Salisb. Parad. Lond. 44. 1806.

A shrub, 2°–6° high, the twigs more or less chaffy and with stiff hairs. Leaves oval, oblong or obovate, thin, obtuse or acutish and glandular-mucronulate at the apex, narrowed at the base, rough-hairy above, pale glaucescent and sometimes chaffy on the veins beneath, 1′–2′ long, the margins ciliate; petioles 2″–5″ long, pubescent; flowers few in the umbels, drooping; pedicels filiform, glandular, ½′–1′ long; calyx-lobes short and broad, hirsute-ciliate; corolla urn-shaped or globose-ovoid, 2″–3″ long; filaments glabrous; capsule ovoid, about 2″ high, erect, glandular-bristly; seeds pointed at each end.

In mountain woods, Pennsylvania to Georgia. May–June.

2. Menziesia glabélla A. Gray. Smooth Menziesia. Fig. 3225.

Menziesia glabella A. Gray, Syn. Fl. N. A. 2 : Part 1, 39. 1878.

Similar to the preceding species, the twigs less chaffy. Leaves obovate, obtuse and glandular-mucronulate at the apex, pale, glaucous and glabrous or very nearly so beneath, sparingly pubescent above, 9″–18″ long, the margins ciliolate; flowers 1–5 in the umbels, spreading, becoming erect; pedicels ½′–1′ long, glandular; calyx-lobes short and broad, ciliate and pubescent; corolla urn-shaped, about 2″ long; filaments pubescent below; capsule oblong or obovoid, erect, about 2″ high, glabrous; seeds long-appendaged at each end

Minnesota Point, Lake Superior, west to Montana, Oregon and British Columbia. May–June.

6. DÉNDRIUM Desv. Journ. Bot. (II.) 1 : 36. 1813.

[LEIOPHYLLUM Pers. Syn. 1 : 477. 1805. Not Ehrh. 1780.]

A glabrous evergreen shrub, with coriaceous entire small mostly opposite leaves, and numerous small white or pinkish flowers, in terminal corymbs. Bud-scales coriaceous, persistent. Calyx 5-parted, the segments rigid, oblong-lanceolate, acute, persistent. Petals 5, sessile, ovate to obovate, spreading. Stamens 10, exserted; filaments filiform, glabrous; anthers small, globose-didymous, attached by their backs to the filaments, awnless, the sacs opening longitudinally. Disk 10-lobed. Ovary 2–5-celled; ovules numerous; style slender, straight; stigma simple, truncate. Capsule ovoid, 2–5-valved from the top. [Greek, a tree.]

Three species, of eastern North America, the following typical.

1. Dendrium buxifòlium (Berg.) Desv. Sand Myrtle. Sleek-leaf. Fig. 3226.

Ledum buxifolium Berg. Act. Upsal. **1777** : *pl. 3. f. 1*   1777.
Dendrium buxifolium Desv. Journ. Bot. (II) 1 : 36. 1813.
Leiophyllum buxifolium Ell. Bot. S. C. & Ga. 1 : 483. 1819–20.

A low shrub with box-like foliage, widely branching, 4′–18′ high. Leaves crowded, oblong or oval, thick, obtuse, dark green and shining above, lighter and black-dotted beneath, short-petioled, somewhat revolute-margined, 3″–7″ long, the midrib prominent, the lateral veins obscure; flowers about 2″ broad, several or numerous in short corymbs; anthers purple; pedicels filiform, 3″–5″ long in fruit; capsule acute, slightly over 1″ high, glabrous, puberulent, or roughened with short processes.

In sandy pine-barrens, New Jersey to Florida. April–June.

7. CHAMAECÍSTUS Oeder, Fl. Dan. 1: 4, *pl. 9.* 1761.

[LOISELEURIA Desv. Journ. Bot. (II.) 1: 35. 1813.]

A low glabrous depressed straggling branched shrub, with small linear-oblong petioled obtuse entire coriaceous and evergreen leaves, and small solitary or few flowers on terminal erect pedicels, the bud-scales few, persistent. Calyx 5-parted, the segments ovate-lanceolate, persistent. Corolla broadly campanulate, with 5 obtuse imbricated lobes. Stamens 5, included; filaments slender, adnate to the corolla; anthers globose-didymous, dorsally attached to the filaments, longitudinally dehiscent. Disk obscurely 5-lobed. Ovary globose, 2–3-celled; style short, straight; stigma capitate; ovules numerous. Capsule subglobose, 2–3-celled, septicidally 2–3-valved, the valves 2-cleft. Seeds ovoid, the testa granular. [Greek, ground cistus.]

A monotypic genus of the colder parts of the northern hemisphere.

1. Chamaecistus procúmbens (L.) Kuntze. Alpine or Trailing Azalea. Fig. 3227.

Azalea procumbens L. Sp. Pl. 151. 1753.
Loiseleuria procumbens Desv. Journ. Bot. (II) 1: 35. 1813.
C. serpyllifolia S. F. Gray, Bot. Arr. Brit. Pl. 2: 401. 1821.
Chamaecistus procumbens Kuntze, Rev. Gen. Pl. 388. 1891.

Tufted, much branched, diffuse, branches 2′–4′ long. Leaves mostly opposite, rather crowded, dark green above, paler beneath, 2″–4″ long, the midrib very prominent, on the lower side, the margins strongly revolute; petioles ½″ long or less; flowers 1–5 from terminal coriaceous buds; pedicels 3″–4″ long; corolla pink or white, about 2″ high, longer than the purplish sepals; capsule about 1″ thick.

Summits of the higher mountains of New England, Mt. Albert, Quebec; Nova Scotia; Newfoundland and Labrador to arctic America and Alaska. Also in Greenland, northern Europe and Asia. July–Aug.

8. KÁLMIA L. Sp. Pl. 391. 1753.

Erect branching shrubs, with entire evergreen coriaceous leaves, alternate, opposite, or verticillate in 3's. Flowers in naked umbels or corymbs. Calyx 5-parted or 5-divided, the segments imbricated in the bud, persistent. Corolla saucer-shaped, the limbs strongly 10-keeled in the bud, 5-lobed, with 10 pouches below the limb, the keels extending from the pouches to the lobes and sinuses. Stamens 10, shorter than the corolla; anthers oblong, awnless, the sacs opening by large terminal pores; filaments erect in the bud, soon curving outward, placing the anthers in the pouches of the corolla, straightening elastically when the flower is fully expanded. Disk 10-crenate. Ovary 5-celled; ovules numerous; style slender; stigma depressed-capitellate. Capsule subglobose, obscurely 5-lobed, 5-celled, septicidally 5-valved from the summit. Seeds small, subglobose. [Dedicated by Linnaeus to his pupil, Peter Kalm, 1715–1779, who travelled in America.]

Six known species, of North America. Type species: *Kalmia latifolia* L.

Flowers in mostly compound umbels or corymbs; twigs terete.
  Leaves oblong, mostly obtuse; flowers 3″–5″ broad.
    Leaves glabrous beneath or nearly so.   1. *K. angustifolia.*
    Leaves densely puberulent beneath.   2. *K. carolina.*
  Leaves elliptic or oval, acute at both ends; flowers 8″–12″ broad.   3. *K. latifolia.*
Flowers in simple terminal umbels; twigs 2-edged.   4. *K. polifolia.*

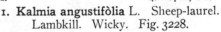

1. Kalmia angustifòlia L. Sheep-laurel. Lambkill. Wicky. Fig. 3228.

Kalmia angustifolia L. Sp. Pl. 391. 1753.

A shrub, 6′–3° high, with few nearly erect branches, and terete twigs. Leaves oblong or oblong-lanceolate, mostly opposite, or verticillate in 3's, obtuse or sometimes acute at the apex, narrowed at the base, petioled, glabrous, dark green above, light green beneath, 1′–2½′ long, 3″–10″ wide; young twigs and petioles often slightly glandular; flowers 3″–5″ broad, purple or crimson, numerous in lateral compound or simple corymbs; pedicels filiform, slightly glandular-canescent, 6″–12″ long, recurved in fruit; calyx-segments ovate, acute, glandular-canescent, persistent; capsule depressed-globose, 5-lobed, canescent, 1½″–2″ in diameter, the apex impressed; style long-persistent.

In moist soil, in swamps or on hillsides, Newfoundland to Hudson Bay, south to Georgia and Michigan. Spoon-wood-ivy. Kill-kid. Calf-kill. Sheep-poison. Dwarf laurel. June-July.

2. Kalmia carolìna Small. Southern Sheep-laurel. Fig. 3229.

Kalmia carolina Small, Fl. SE. U. S. 886. 1903.

Similar to *K. angustifolia* in habit, but with the foliage, especially the younger parts, copiously fine-pubescent. Leaves oval to oblong, $\frac{2}{3}'$–$1\frac{3}{4}'$ long, $4''$–$8''$ wide, obtuse, permanently canescent-tomentulose, at least beneath and paler beneath than above; flowers purplish, $3''$–$4\frac{1}{2}''$ broad, numerous in small corymbs; pedicels very slender, canescent, $3''$–$6''$ long; calyx-segments oblong-lanceolate; style finely pubescent; capsules spheroidal, pale-pubescent and glandular, about $2''$ in diameter.

In open woods, Virginia and North Carolina. June–July.

3. Kalmia latifòlia L. American or Mountain Laurel. Calico-bush. Fig. 3230.

Kalmia latifolia L. Sp. Pl. 391. 1753.
Kalmia latifolia myrtifolia Rand, Rhodod. 125. 1876.

A shrub with very stiff branches and terete twigs, often forming dense thickets, $3°$–$20°$ high, rarely becoming a tree with a maximum height of about $40°$ and trunk diameter of $18'$. Leaves alternate, or some of them opposite, or rarely verticillate in 3's, petioled, glabrous, oval, ovate-lanceolate, or elliptic, usually acute at both ends, rarely narrowly oblong-lanceolate, flat, green on both sides, persistent, $1'$–$5'$ long, $\frac{1}{4}'$–$1\frac{1}{2}'$ wide; flowers $9''$–$12''$ broad, pink to white, numerous and showy in compound terminal corymbs; pedicels bracted and 2-bracteolate at the base, slender, $\frac{1}{2}'$–$1\frac{1}{2}'$ long, densely glandular, erect, even in fruit; calyx and corolla glandular; capsule depressed-globose, 5-lobed, glandular, $2''$–$3''$ in diameter; calyx and filiform style long-persistent, the latter falling when the capsule begins to open.

In woods, preferring sandy or rocky soil, New Brunswick to Ontario, Indiana, western Kentucky, Florida and Louisiana. Wood very hard, brown; weight per cubic foot 44 lbs. Clamoun. Spoonwood. Broad-leaved kalmia. Ivy-bush. Wood- or small laurel. Big-leaved ivy. Spoonhunt. May–June.

4. Kalmia polifòlia Wang. Pale or Swamp Laurel. Fig. 3231.

K. polifolia Wang. Beob. Ges. Naturf. Freunde Berlin **2**: Part 2. 130. 1788.
Kalmia glauca Ait. Hort. Kew. **2**: 64. *pl 8.* 1811.

A glabrous shrub, $6'$–$2°$ high, with erect or ascending branches, the twigs 2-edged. Leaves opposite or sometimes in 3's, very nearly sessile, oblong or linear-oblong, mostly obtuse at the apex, narrowed at the base, green above, white-glaucous beneath, $\frac{1}{2}'$–$2'$ long, $2''$–$6''$ wide, the margins revolute, often strongly so; flowers in simple umbels terminating the branches, few (1–13), purple, $5''$–$9''$ broad; pedicels filiform, $\frac{1}{2}'$–$1\frac{1}{2}'$ long, erect, even in fruit; calyx-segments ovate, scarious-margined, acutish or obtuse, persistent; capsule depressed-globose, glabrous, about $2\frac{1}{2}''$ in diameter.

In bogs, Newfoundland to Hudson Bay and Alaska, south to Connecticut, northern New Jersey, Pennsylvania, Michigan, in the Rocky Mountains to Montana, and in the Sierra Nevada to California. Summer.

9. KALMIÉLLA Small, Fl. SE. U. S. 886. 1903.

Low shrubs, the foliage hirsute, the leaves small, alternate. Flowers mostly solitary in the axils of leaf-like bracts, slender-pedicelled pink or purple. Calyx-segments 5, foliaceous, hirsute or ciliate, deciduous. Corolla saucer-shaped, acutely 5-lobed, with 10 pouches below the limb. Stamens 10. [Diminutive of *Kalmia*.]

Three species, the following typical, the others Cuban.

1. Kalmiella hirsùta (Walt.) Small. Hairy Laurel. Fig. 3232.

Kalmia hirsuta Walt. Fl. Car. 138. 1788.
Kalmiella hirsuta Small, Fl. SE. U. S. 886. 1903.

A branching shrub, 1°–2° high, the branches ascending, hirsute. Leaves oblong or oblong-lanceolate, very nearly sessile, flat, or the margins slightly revolute, villous-hirsute, acute or obtusish, becoming glabrate in age, dark green above, lighter beneath, 3″–6″ long; flowers solitary, or rarely 2–3 together in the axils, rose-purple, 5″–9″ broad; pedicels very slender, nearly or quite glabrous; calyx-segments ovate-lanceolate, acute, or lanceolate, longer than the capsule; capsule depressed, about 1½″ in diameter, glabrous.

In moist pine-barrens, eastern Virginia to Florida. May–Aug.

10. PHYLLÓDOCE Salisb. Parad. Lond. *pl. 36.* 1806.

Low branching more or less glandular shrubs, with small crowded linear obtuse coriaceous evergreen leaves. Flowers long-pedicelled, nodding, mostly pink, blue or purple, in terminal umbels. Pedicels bracted at the base. Calyx 5-parted, persistent. Corolla ovoid or urceolate, contracted at the throat, 5-toothed. Stamens 10, included; filaments filiform; anthers attached to the filaments by their backs, oblong, obtuse, awnless, the sacs dehiscent by terminal oblique chinks. Disk obscurely lobed. Ovary 5-celled; ovules numerous; style filiform, included; stigma obscurely 5-lobed, or capitate. Capsule subglobose or globose-oblong, septicidally 5-valved to about the middle. Seeds minute, the testa coriaceous. [Greek, a sea nymph.]

About 8 species, natives of arctic and alpine regions of the northern hemisphere, the following typical. Besides the following, 5 or 6 others occur in northwest America.

1. Phyllodoce coerùlea (L.) Babingt. Mountain Heath. Fig. 3233.

Andromeda coerulea L. Sp. Pl. 393. **1753.**
A. taxifolia Pall. Fl. Ross. 1: 54. *pl. 72, f. 2.* 1784.
Phyllodoce coerulea Babingt. Man. Brit. Bot. 194. 1843.
Menziesia taxifolia Wood, First Lessons 185. 1856.
Bryanthus taxifolius A. Gray, Proc. Am. Acad. 7: 368. 1868.

A shrub 4′–6′ high, the branches ascending. Leaves yew-like, 3″–5″ long, less than 1″ wide, articulated with the branches, crowded above, their margins acutish, scabrous or serrulate-ciliolate; pedicels erect, very glandular, 5″–8″ long in flower, elongating in fruit, solitary or 2–6 at the ends of the branches; corolla 4″–5″ long, about 2″ in diameter, pink or purple, heath-like; calyx-segments lanceolate, acuminate, glandular; capsule erect, about 2″ high.

Summits of the higher mountains of Maine and New Hampshire; Mt. Albert, Quebec; Labrador and through arctic America to Alaska. Also in Greenland and in northern and alpine Europe and Asia. July–Aug.

11. CASSÍOPE D. Don, Edinb. Phil. Journ. 17: 157. 1834.

Low tufted branching heath-like evergreen shrubs, with small sessile opposite, crowded, entire apparently veinless leaves, appressed, so that the branches appear 4-sided, and axillary solitary peduncled white or pink nodding flowers, on pedicels bracted at the base. Sepals 4 or 5, imbricated at least in the bud, not bracted at the base, persistent, or at length deciduous. Corolla campanulate, 4–5-lobed, the lobes recurved. Stamens 8–10, included; filaments subulate, glabrous, anthers in one plane, attached to the filaments near the apex, the sacs opening by large terminal pores and tipped with a recurved awn. Ovary 4–5-celled; ovules numerous; style slender, elongated; stigma simple. Capsule globose or ovoid, 4–5-valved, each valve 2-cleft at the apex. Seeds minute, not winged, numerous. [Name from Cassiope, mother of Andromeda.]

About 8 species, natives of the colder parts of the northern hemisphere, the following typical. Besides the following, 2 others occur in the northwestern parts of North America.

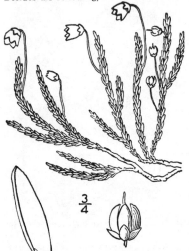

3/4

1. Cassiope tetragòna (L.) D. Don. Four-angled Cassiope. Fig. 3234.

Andromeda tetragona L. Sp. Pl. 393. 1753.
Cassiope tetragona D. Don, Edinb. New Phil. Journ. **17**: 158. 1834.

Tufted, much-branched, 4′–12′ high, the branches ascending or erect. Leaves thick, ovate or ovate-oblong, closely appressed, channeled on the back, concave or nearly flat on the inner (upper) surface, acute or the lower obtuse, usually puberulent when young, 1″–1½″ long; peduncles several or numerous, lateral, ascending or erect, slender, 5″–12″ long; flowers 3″–4″ broad; corolla 5-lobed; style slightly thickened below; capsule nearly globular, 1″–1½″ in diameter.

Labrador, Greenland and Hudson Bay to Alaska and Oregon. Also in arctic Europe and Asia. Summer.

12. HARRIMANÉLLA Coville, Proc. Wash. Acad. Sci. 3: 570. 1901.

Low heath-like evergreen shrubs, similar to *Cassiope*, the leaves imbricated in many ranks, the nodding flowers solitary at the ends of the branches. Sepals 5, imbricated in the bud, not bracted, persistent; corolla campanulate, vertically plaited at the base, deeply 5-cleft, its lobes overlapping. Stamens 10, included; anthers in 2 planes, their sacs awned just below the apex, opening by terminal pores. Ovary 5-celled; style short, stout; ovules numerous. Capsule globose, many-seeded, the numerous seeds oblong. [In honor of Edward H. Harriman, American financier and patron of science.]

Two species, of arctic and subarctic regions. Type species: *Harrimanella Stelleriana* (Pall.) Coville.

1. Harrimanella hypnoìdes (L.) Coville. Moss-plant. Fig. 3235.

Andromeda hypnoides L. Sp. Pl. 393. 1753.
Cassiope hypnoides D. Don, Edinb. New Phil. Journ. **17**: 157. 1834.
Harrimanella hypnoides Coville, Proc. Wash. Acad. Sci. **3**: 575. 1901.

Densely tufted, glabrous, usually much branched, 1′–4½′ high. Leaves linear-subulate, densely crowded and imbricated, somewhat spreading or appressed, acute, flat above, convex beneath, 1″–2″ long; flowers 3″–4″ broad; peduncles very slender, erect, 4″–12″ long; corolla nearly white; style conic; capsule about 1½″ in diameter, 2–3 times as long as the ovate calyx-lobes.

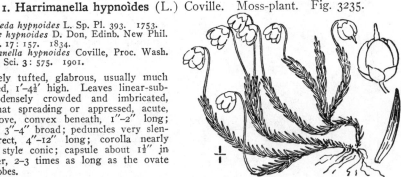

Summits of the higher mountains of New England and the Adirondacks of New York; Lake Superior; Quebec and Labrador to arctic America. Also in arctic Europe and Asia. Plant with the aspect of a moss. Moss-bush. Summer.

13. CHAMAEDÁPHNE Moench, Meth. 457. 1794.

[CASSANDRA D. Don, Edinb. New Phil. Journ. **17**: 158. 1834.]

An erect shrub, with stiff slender terete branches, alternate coriaceous evergreen short-petioled narrow leaves, and white short-pedicelled secund flowers, solitary in the axils of the small upper leaves, forming terminal leafy racemes. Calyx of 5 distinct imbricated persistent sepals, bracted at the base. Corolla oblong-cylindric, narrowed at the throat, 5-toothed, the teeth recurved. Stamens 10, included; filaments subulate, glabrous; anther-sacs tapering upward into tubular beaks, not awned, opening by terminal pores. Disk 10-toothed. Ovary 5-celled, 5-grooved; stigma simple. Capsule depressed-globose, the epicarp 5-valved, separating at length from the 10-valved endocarp. Seeds not winged. [Greek, ground or low Daphne.]

A monotypic genus of the north temperate zone.

1. Chamaedaphne calyculàta (L.) Moench.
Leather-leaf. Dwarf Cassandra.
Fig. 3236.

Andromeda calyculata L. Sp. Pl. 394. 1753.
Chamaedaphne calyculata Moench, Meth. 457. 1794.
Cassandra calyculata D. Don, Edinb. New Phil. Journ.
17: 158. 1834.

A branching shrub, 2°–4° high. Leaves oblong or oblanceolate, thick, coriaceous, obtuse or acute, narrowed at the base, densely covered on both sides with minute round scurfy scales, at least when young, ½′–1½′ long, the margins obscurely denticulate; upper leaves gradually smaller, the uppermost reduced to floral bracts; pedicels 1″ long or less; corolla about 3″ long; capsule depressed-globose, 2″ in diameter, about twice as long as the ovate sepals.

In bogs and swamps, Newfoundland to Alaska, south to southern New Jersey, Georgia, Illinois, Michigan and British Columbia. Also in northern Europe and Asia. April–June.

14. LEUCÓTHOË D. Don, Edinb. New Phil. Journ. 17: 159. 1834.

Shrubs, mostly tall, with alternate petioled entire or serrulate, in our species persistent leaves, and small usually white bracted flowers in axillary racemes, the bracts persistent. Sepals 5, distinct, imbricated, at least in the bud. Corolla cylindric or ovoid-urceolate, 5-toothed. Stamens 10, included; filaments subulate; anthers attached to the filaments near their bases, oblong, the sacs opening by terminal pores, obtuse, 2-mucronate, awnless. Disk 10-lobed. Ovary 5-celled; style slender; stigma 5-lobed; ovules numerous. Capsule depressed-globose, often 5-lobed, loculicidally 5-valved, the valves membranous, entire. Seeds numerous, minute, pendulous or spreading. [Name of a daughter of a Babylonian king.]

About 30 species, natives of North and South America and eastern Asia. Besides the following, 2 others occur in the southeastern States and one in California. Type species: *Leucothoë axillaris* (Lam.) D. Don.

Shoots puberulent; petioles 2″–4″ long; sepals imbricated in flower. 　　1. *L. axillaris.*
Shoots glabrous; petioles 4″–8″ long; sepals not imbricated in flower. 　　2. *L. Catesbaei.*

1. Leucothoë axillàris (Lam.) D. Don.
Downy Leucothoë. Fig. 3237.

Andromeda axillaris Lam. Encycl. 1: 157. 1783.
Leucothoë axillaris D. Don, Edinb. New Phil.
Journ. 17: 159. 1834.

A shrub, 2°–5° high, the twigs puberulent, at least when young. Leaves coriaceous, evergreen, oval to oblong-lanceolate, glabrous and dark green above, paler and sparsely beset with minute hairs beneath, acute or acuminate at the apex, narrowed or rarely rounded at the base, serrulate, at least near the apex, 2′–6′ long, ½′–1½′ wide; petioles usually pubescent, 2″–4″ long; racemes many-flowered, dense, catkin-like when expanding, sessile in the axils of the persistent leaves; bracts ovate, concave, persistent, borne near the base of the short pedicels; sepals broadly ovate, obtuse, imbricated even when expanded; corolla nearly cylindric, about 3″ long; stigma depressed, 5-rayed.

In moist woods, Virginia to Florida and Alabama, near the coast. April.

2. Leucothoë Catesbaèi (Walt.) A. Gray. Catesby's Leucothoë. Fig. 3238.

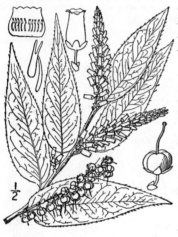

Andromeda Catesbaei Walt. Fl. Car. 137. 1788.

Andromeda spinulosa Pursh, Fl. Am. Sept. 293. 1814.

L. spinulosa G. Don, Gard. Dict. 3: 832. 1834.

Leucothoë Catesbaei A. Gray, Man. Ed. 2, 252. 1856.

A shrub, 3°–6° high, similar to the preceding species, the twigs glabrous. Leaves lanceolate or ovate-lanceolate, coriaceous and evergreen, acuminate at the apex, mostly rounded at the base, sharply serrulate with bristle-pointed teeth nearly all around, 3′–6′ long, 9″–18″ wide; petioles 4″–8″ long; racemes dense, axillary, many-flowered, catkin-like when expanding; bracts persistent, borne at the bases of the short petioles; sepals ovate or ovate-oblong, not at all or scarcely imbricated when the flower is expanded; corolla narrowly cylindric, about 2½″ long; capsule depressed, strongly 5-lobed, about 2″ in diameter.

Along streams, Virginia to Tennessee and Georgia. April. Dog-hobble. Dog-laurel.

15. EÙBOTRYS Nutt. Trans. Am. Phil. Soc. II. 8: 269. 1843.

Shrubs with broad deciduous serrulate leaves, and small white short-pedicelled bracted flowers in dense 1-sided racemes, lateral or terminating the twigs, the bracts deciduous, the calyx 2-bracteolate, the pedicels jointed with the rachis. Sepals 5, rigid, imbricated. Corolla nearly cylindric, 5-toothed, the teeth recurved. Stamens 10, included; filaments flat, narrowed above; anthers oblong, each sac 1-awned or 2-awned. Style slender, long; stigma capitate, truncate. Capsule depressed-globose, 5-celled, 5-valved. Seeds numerous, angular and flattened or winged. [Greek, referring to the racemose inflorescence.]

Only the following species, natives of eastern North America. Type species:*Eubotrys racemosa* (L.) Nutt.

Racemes recurved; capsule 5-lobed; anther-sacs 1-awned.   1. *E. recurva.*
Racemes erect or spreading; capsule not lobed; anther-sacs 2-awned.   2. *E. racemosa.*

1. Eubotrys recúrva (Buckl.) Britton. Mountain Eubotrys. Fig. 3239.

Andromeda recurva Buckl. Amer. Journ. Sci. 45: 172. 1843.

Leucothoë recurva A. Gray, Man. Ed. 2, 252. 1856.

A widely branched shrub, 2°–10° high, similar to the following species. Leaves thin, deciduous, ovate, ovate-lanceolate, or oval, often acuminate, pubescent on the veins beneath, 2′–4′ long; racemes terminating the branches, unfolding before the leaves, recurved, solitary or clustered; calyx 2-bracteolate, the bractlets persistent; sepals ovate; corolla about 3″ long; anther-sacs 1-awned; capsule strongly 5-lobed, about 2″ in diameter and 1″ high; seeds broadly winged.

In dry woods, mountains of Virginia to Tennessee, Georgia and Alabama. April–May.

2. Eubotrys racemòsa (L.) Nutt. Swamp Eubotrys. Fig. 3240.

Andromeda racemosa L. Sp. Pl. 394. 1753.
E. racemosa Nutt. Trans. Am. Phil. Soc. II. **8**: 269. 1843.
Leucothoë racemosa A. Gray, Man. Ed. 2, 252. 1856.

A shrub, 5°–12° high, with erect or divergent branches, terminal racemes, and glabrous or puberulent twigs. Leaves oblong to ovate, mostly acute at each end, thin, deciduous, short-petioled, glabrous, or with some short hairs above, pubescent, at least on the veins beneath, serrulate, 1′–3′ long, ½′–1′ wide; racemes solitary or clustered; flowers appearing with or before the leaves; calyx 2-bracteolate at the base, the bractlets firm, persistent; sepals much imbricated; pedicels about 1″ long, jointed with the rachis; corolla nearly cylindric, 3″–4″ long; anther-sacs 2-awned; style slender; stigma capitate; capsule slightly grooved, 1½″ in diameter, about equalling the sepals or a little longer; seeds smooth, wingless.

In swamps and moist thickets, Massachusetts to Pennsylvania, Tennessee, Florida and Louisiana, mostly near the coast. White ozier or pepper-bush. April–June.

Leucothoë elongàta Small, of the Southern States, is of this genus, differing from the preceding species in its relatively longer sepals; it is recorded as far north as Virginia.

16. ANDRÓMEDA L. Sp. Pl. 393. 1753.

A glabrous branching or rarely simple shrub. Leaves coriaceous, linear or oblong, entire, revolute-margined, evergreen, short-petioled, white-glaucous beneath. Flowers small, white, drooping, in terminal umbels. Calyx deeply 5-parted, persistent, the lobes not imbricated. Corolla globose-urceolate, 5-toothed, the teeth recurved. Stamens 10, included; filaments bearded; anthers attached to the filaments at about the middle, ovate, obtuse, the sacs opening by large terminal pores, each with an ascending awn. Disk 10-lobed. Ovary 5-celled; style columnar; stigma simple; ovules numerous. Capsule subglobose, 5-angled, loculicidally 5-valved, many-seeded, the top intruded. Seeds oval, spreading in all directions, the testa smooth, coriaceous, shining. [Named for Andromeda of mythology.]

A monotypic genus of the north temperate and subarctic zone.

1. Andromeda Polifòlia L. Wild Rosemary. Marsh Holy Rose. Moorwort. Fig. 3241.

Andromeda Polifolia L. Sp. Pl. 393. 1753.
A. glaucophylla Link, Enum. Hort. Berol. **1**: 394. 1821.

A shrub, 1°–3° high, usually little branched, the foliage acid. Leaves linear, linear-oblong or lanceolate-oblong, sometimes slightly spatulate, acute or obtusish, mucronulate, narrowed at the base, dark green above, prominently white-glaucous beneath, 1′–2½′ long, 2″–4″ wide, the margins strongly revolute; petioles about 1″ long; umbels few-flowered, terminal; bracts small, ovate, persistent; pedicels 4″–6″ long, straight or somewhat curved; calyx-lobes triangular-ovate, acute; corolla 2″–3″ in diameter; capsule about 2″ in diameter, about as long as the persistent style.

In bogs, Labrador and Newfoundland through arctic America to Alaska, south to northern New Jersey, Pennsylvania, Michigan and British Columbia. Also in northern Europe and Asia. Consists of several races, the southern (*A. glaucophylla*) with shorter and more curved pedicels. Marsh-rosemary. May–June.

17. PÌERIS D. Don, Edinb. New Phil. Journ. **17**: 159. 1834.

[PORTÙNA Nutt. Trans. Am. Phil. Soc. II. **8**: 268. 1843.]

Shrubs with evergreen serrulate leaves, and terminal or axillary, often panicled racemes of small white flowers, the pedicels subtended by small persistent bracts and 1–2-bracteolate. Calyx 5-cleft, the lobes or sepals valvate. Corolla ovoid-urceolate, 5-toothed, the teeth little spreading. Stamens 10; filaments smooth, not appendaged; anthers oblong, the sacs dehiscent by a terminal pore and bearing a deflexed awn on the back. Ovary 5-celled; style slender; stigma not lobed. Capsule globose to ovoid. Seeds several or numerous with a cellular-reticulated coat. [Named from one of the Muses.]

About 6 species, 2 of eastern North America, 1 of western Cuba, the others Asiatic. Type species: *Pieris formòsa* D. Don.

1. Pieris floribúnda (Pursh) Benth. & Hook. Mountain Fetter-bush. Fig. 3242.

Andromeda floribunda Pursh. Fl. Am. Sept. 293. 1814.
Portuna floribunda Nutt. Trans. Am. Phil. Soc. (II) **8**: 268. 1843.
Pieris floribunda Benth. & Hook. Gen. Pl. **2**: 588. 1876.

A shrub, 2°–6° high with nearly erect bristly or strigose-pubescent very leafy branches. Leaves oblong to ovate-lanceolate, coriaceous, persistent, evergreen, serrulate and bristly-ciliate, glabrous above, black-dotted beneath, acute or acuminate at the apex, usually rounded or obtuse at the base, $1\frac{1}{2}'$–3′ long, $\frac{1}{2}'$–1′ wide; petioles 2″–4″ long, very bristly, at least when young; flowers white, in terminal clustered slender dense racemes, drooping, about $3\frac{1}{2}''$ long; calyx-segments ovate-lanceolate, acute, valvate in the 5-angled bud; corolla slightly 5-angled, 5-saccate at the base; filaments unappendaged; anther-sacs each 1-awned; capsule globose-ovoid, about 2″ high, longer than the slender style; seeds linear-oblong, the testa loose and cellular.

Mountains of Virginia to Georgia. May.

18. NEOPÌERIS Britton, n. gen.

Shrubs or small trees. Leaves alternate, persistent or tardily deciduous, petioled, entire, firm in texture. Flowers mostly white, in axillary bracted umbels, the pedicels commonly 1–3-bracteolate. Calyx deeply 5-parted, the lobes ovate, acute, valvate in the bud, soon spreading, persistent. Corolla urceolate-cylindric, 5-toothed, the teeth recurved. Stamens 10, included; filaments narrow, glabrous, pubescent or ciliate, 2-toothed or 2-spurred at or below the apex; anthers oblong or ovoid, the sacs opening by large terminal oval pores, awnless. Disk 10-lobed. Ovary 5-celled; ovules numerous; style columnar; stigma truncate. Capsule globose or ovoid, 5-angled, 5-celled, the sutures thickened. Seeds numerous, linear-oblong, not winged, clavate or falcate, the testa smooth, membranous. [Name as in the preceding genus.]

Two species, natives of eastern North America. Type species: *Andromeda mariana* L.

Leaves coriaceous, evergreen, entire; flowers in axillary umbels.   1. *N. nitida.*
Leaves membranous, deciduous, entire; flowers in lateral umbels.   2. *N. mariana.*

1. Neopieris nítida (Bartr.) Britton. Fetter-bush. Fig. 3243.

Andromeda nitida Bartr.; Marsh. Arb. Amer. 8. 1788.
Pieris nitida Benth. & Hook. Gen. Pl. **2**: 588. 1876.

A glabrous shrub, 2°–6° high, the branches slender, ascending or erect, leafy, acutely angled, sparingly black-dotted. Leaves short-petioled, coriaceous, evergreen, shining, oblong, oval, oblong-lanceolate, or obovate, acuminate or acute at the apex, narrowed at the base, somewhat black-dotted beneath, the margins entire, revolute, bordered by an intra-marginal nerve; flowers in axillary umbels, nodding or spreading; pedicels 2″–4″ long; calyx-segments ovate-lanceolate, rigid, purplish, valvate in the bud, soon spreading; corolla white or red, ovoid-cylindric, narrowed at the throat, 3″–4″ long; filaments 2-spurred; style thickened above the middle; capsule globose, about as long as the calyx-segments; seeds club-shaped.

In wet woods, southeastern Virginia to Florida and Louisiana. Erroneously recorded from Cuba. Pipe-stem. April–May.

2. Neopieris mariàna (L.) Britton.
Stagger-bush. Fig. 3244.

Andromeda mariana L. Sp. Pl. 393. 1753.
Pieris mariana Benth. & Hook. Gen. Pl. 2: 588.
1876.

A shrub, 1°–4° high, the branches nearly erect, slender, glabrous or nearly so, black-dotted. Leaves rather thin, tardily deciduous, oval or oblong, glabrous above, sparingly pubescent on the veins and black-dotted beneath, acute or obtuse, narrowed or sometimes obtuse at the base, entire, 2′–3′ long, the margins slightly revolute; flowers nodding in lateral umbels on the nearly leafless branches of the preceding season, forming an elongated compound inflorescence; calyx-segments lanceolate, acuminate, almost foliaceous, deciduous; corolla ovoid-cylindric, white, or faintly pink, 5″–6″ long; filaments pubescent on the outer side, usually with 2 setose appendages below the summit; capsule ovoid-pyramidal, 1½″–2″ high, truncate, about as long as the sepals; seeds club-shaped.

In sandy soil, Rhode Island to Florida, mostly near the coast, extending west to Tennessee and Arkansas. Sorrel-tree. Wicks. May–July.

19. XOLÍSMA Raf. Am. Month. Mag. 4: 193. 1819.

[Lyonia Nutt. Gen. 1: 266. 1818. Not Raf. 1808, nor Ell. 1817.]

Tall shrubs, or small trees, with terete twigs, alternate short-petioled, lepidote or pubescent leaves, and small mostly white flowers in terminal or axillary, usually panicled racemes or clusters. Calyx 4–5-lobed or 4–5-cleft, the lobes not imbricated, valvate. Corolla globose, or urceolate, pubescent, 4–5-toothed, the teeth recurved. Stamens 8–10, included; filaments flat, incurved, pubescent, not appendaged; anthers attached to the filaments near their bases, truncate, not awned, the sacs opening by large terminal pores. Disk 8–10-lobed. Ovary 4–5-celled; style columnar; stigma truncate; ovules numerous, pendulous, attached to the upper part of the placentae. Capsule globose or ovoid, 4–5-angled, loculicidally 4–5-valved, its apex intruded, the sutures thickened. Seeds numerous, elongated, the testa membranous, loose, reticulated. [Name unexplained.]

About 20 species, natives of eastern North America, the West Indies and Mexico. Besides the following, 2 others occur in the southern United States. Type species: *Andromeda ferruginea* Walt.

1. Xolisma ligustrìna (L.) Britton. Privet
Andromeda. Fig. 3245.

Vaccinium ligustrinum L. Sp. Pl. 351. 1753.
Andromeda ligustrina Muhl. Cat. 43. 1813.
Lyonia ligustrina DC. Prodr. 7: 599. 1839.
X. ligustrina Britton, Mem. Torr. Club 4: 135. 1894.

A much branched shrub, 3°–12° high, the twigs puberulent or glabrous. Leaves obovate, oblong, oval or ovate, deciduous, minutely serrulate or entire, acute at each end or abruptly acuminate at the apex, usually quite glabrous above, more or less pubescent, at least on the veins, or glabrous when old, 1′–3½′ long; racemes numerous, mostly leafless, in terminal panicles or clusters, many-flowered; bracts small, caducous; pedicels single or clustered, 1″–3″ long, pubescent; calyx-lobes triangular-ovate, acute; corolla nearly globular, about 1½″ in diameter; capsule depressed-globose, obtusely 5-angled, about 1½″ in diameter.

In swamps and wet soil, Canada (according to Pursh), Maine to New York, Florida, Tennessee, Arkansas and Texas. White-wood. White-alder or pepper-bush. Seedy buckberry. Lyon's-andromeda. May–July.

Xolisma foliosiflòra (Michx.) Small, of the Southern States, differs in having the inflorescence leafy-bracted.

20. OXYDÉNDRUM DC. Prodr. 7: 601. 1839.

A tree, with alternate petioled deciduous sour leaves, and very numerous white flowers, in terminal panicled racemes. Pedicels 2-bracteolate at or above the middle. Sepals 5, slightly imbricated in the bud, early expanded, persistent. Corolla ovoid-cylindric, minutely canescent, narrowed at the throat, tardily expanding, 5-toothed. Stamens 10, about as long as the corolla; filaments wider than the linear anthers; anther-sacs opening by long chinks, not awned. Ovary ovoid, 5-celled; ovules numerous, near the base of the cavities; style columnar; stigma simple. Disk 10-toothed. Capsule ovoid-pyramidal, 5-angled, 5-valved. Seeds ascending or erect, elongated, the testa reticulated, loose and extended at each end beyond the linear nucleus. [Greek, sour-tree.]

A monotypic genus of southeastern North America.

1. Oxydendrum arbòreum (L.) DC. Sourwood. Sorrel-tree. Fig. 3246.

Andromeda arborea L. Sp. Pl. 394. 1753.
Oxydendrum arboreum DC. Prodr. 7: 601. 1839.

A smooth-barked tree, reaching a maximum height of about 60° and a trunk diameter of 15'. Leaves oblong, oval or oval-lanceolate, sharply serrulate, or entire, green and glabrous on both sides, finely reticulate-veined, acuminate at the apex, mostly narrowed at the base, 4'–6' long, 1'–3' wide; racemes numerous, long and slender, erect or curving, panicled at the ends of the branches, the rachis and short pedicels canescent; flowers $3\frac{1}{2}''$–3' long; capsule 2''–3'' long, canescent, tipped by the persistent style, the pedicels curving.

In woods, Pennsylvania and Maryland to Indiana, Alabama and Florida. Wood hard, reddish-brown; weight per cubic foot 46 lbs. Elk-tree. June–July.

21. EPIGAÈA L. Sp. Pl. 395. 1753.

Prostrate slightly woody more or less hirsute branching shrubs, with alternate petioled coriaceous evergreen entire leaves. Flowers rather large, perfect, heteromorphous or dioecious, bracted, sessile, white or pink, fragrant, clustered at the ends of the branches. Sepals 5, oblong, persistent, dry, much imbricated. Corolla salverform, the tube pubescent within, the limb 5-lobed (rarely 4- or 6-lobed). Stamens 10, about as long as the corolla-tube and attached to its base; filaments filiform; anthers linear-oblong, attached to the filaments below the middle. Disk 10-lobed. Ovary ovoid, hirsute, 5-lobed, 5-celled; ovules numerous; style columnar; stigma 5-lobed. Capsule depressed-globose, fleshy, hirsute, slightly 5-lobed, at length 5-valved. Seeds oval, the testa close and reticulated. [Greek, on the earth.]

Two species, the following of eastern North America, the other of Japan.

1. Epigaea rèpens L. Trailing Arbutus. Mayflower. Ground Laurel. Fig. 3247.

Epigaea repens L. Sp. Pl. 395. 1753.

Spreading on the ground, twigs hirsute, branches 6'–15' long. Leaves oval or nearly orbicular, thick, acute or obtuse and mucronulate at the apex, cordate or rounded at the base, mostly glabrous above, more or less hirsute beneath, green both sides, 1'–3' long, $\frac{3}{4}'$–$1\frac{1}{2}'$ wide; petioles hirsute, $\frac{1}{4}'$–2' long; flowers few or several in the clusters, 5''–8'' long, and nearly as broad when expanded; corolla-tube somewhat longer than the sepals; capsule splitting along the partitions into 5-valves, which spread backward into a 5-parted rosette, exposing the white succulent fleshy interior.

In sandy or rocky woods, especially under evergreen trees, Newfoundland to Saskatchewan, south to Florida, Kentucky and Wisconsin. Often forms large patches. Winter or mountain pink. Gravel-plant. Crocus. Shadflower. March–May.

22. GAULTHÈRIA Kalm.; L. Sp. Pl. 395. 1753.

Low or tall shrubs, with alternate coriaceous persistent evergreen leaves, and small axillary, solitary or racemose, white, red or pink flowers. Calyx 5-parted or 5-cleft, persistent. Corolla urn-shaped or campanulate, 5-toothed or 5-lobed, the lobes recurved or spreading. Stamens 10, included, inserted at the base of the corolla; filaments dilated above the base; anther-sacs opening by a terminal pore, commonly awned. Stigma obtuse, entire. Disk 10-toothed. Ovary 5-celled, 5-lobed. Calyx becoming fleshy and at length surrounding the capsule, forming a berry-like fruit. [Named after Dr. Gaultier, of Quebec.]

About 100 species, mostly of the Andes of South America, a few North American and Asiatic. Besides the following 3 others occur on the Pacific Coast, the following typical.

1. Gaultheria procúmbens L. Spring, Creeping or Spicy Wintergreen. Checkerberry. Fig. 3248.

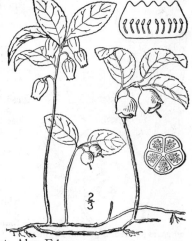

Gaultheria procumbens L. Sp. Pl. 395. 1753.

Nearly glabrous throughout, aromatic; stems slender, creeping or subterranean; branches erect, 2′-6′ high. Leaves mostly clustered at the ends of the branches, oval, oblong or obovate, obtuse or acute, narrowed at the base, short-petioled, the margins slightly revolute and serrate with low bristle-tipped teeth, dark green and shining above, pale beneath, 1′-2′ long; flowers usually solitary in the axils, on recurved peduncles 2″-4″ long, 2-bracteolate under the calyx; corolla ovoid-urceolate, white, 5-toothed, 2″-3″ long; fruit depressed-globose, slightly 5-lobed, bright red, 4″-6″ in diameter, mealy, very spicy in flavor.

In woods, especially under evergreen trees, Newfoundland to Manitoba, New Jersey, Georgia, West Virginia, Indiana and Michigan. June–Sept. Fruit ripe late in the autumn, remaining on the plant until spring. Chinks. One-berry. Drunkards. Chicken-berry. Red pollom. Box-, ground-, tea-, green- or partridge-berry. Deer-, hill-, ginger-, ivy-, grouse- or spice-berry. Ivory plum. Mountain- or Canada tea.

23. ÙVA-ÚRSI Mill. Gard. Dict. Abr. Ed. 4. 1754.
[ARCTOSTAPHYLOS Adans. Fam. Pl. 2: 165. 1763.]

Erect or spreading, low or tall shrubs (some western species small trees). Leaves alternate, petioled, firm or coriaceous, persistent, evergreen. Flowers small, nodding, bracted, pedicelled, white or pink, in terminal racemes, panicles or clusters. Calyx 4–5-parted, persistent. Corolla globose, ovoid, urceolate or oblong-campanulate, 4–5-lobed, the lobes recurved, imbricated in the bud. Stamens 10, rarely 8, included; filaments short, subulate; anthers short, erect, introrse, with 2 recurved awns on the back, the sacs opening by a terminal pore. Disk 8–10-lobed. Ovary 4–10-celled; ovules solitary in the cavities; style slender. Fruit a drupe, with 4–10 seed-like nutlets coherent into a solid stone. [Greek, bear-berry.]

About 40 species, the following typical one of the northern hemisphere, the others of western North America.

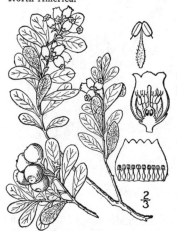

1. Uva-Ursi Ùva-Úrsi (L.) Britton. Red Bearberry. Kinnikinic. Fig. 3249.

Arbutus Uva-Ursi L. Sp. Pl. 395. 1753.
Arctostaphylos Uva-Ursi Spreng. Syst. 2: 287. 1825.

Trailing or spreading on the ground, branched; branches 6′-24′ long, the twigs puberulent. Leaves spatulate, coriaceous, obtuse, entire, evergreen, glabrous or minutely puberulent toward the base, ½′-1′ long, 2″-5″ wide, finely reticulate-veined; petioles about 1″ long, puberulent; flowers few in short racemes; pedicels 1″-2″ long; corolla ovoid, constricted at the throat, white, about 2″ long; drupe globose, red, glabrous, insipid, rather dry, 3″-5″ in diameter, usually containing 5 coalescent nutlets, each 1-nerved on the back.

In dry, sandy or rocky soil, Labrador and arctic America to Alaska, south to southern New Jersey, Pennsylvania, Illinois, Missouri, Nebraska, Colorado and California. Also in northern Europe and Asia. May–June. Mountainbox. Universe-vine. Rapper-dandies. Fox- or meal-plum or -berry. Bear's-grape-bilberry or -whortleberry. Rock- or crow-berry. Barren myrtle or bilberry. Mountain, upland, wild- or hog-crawberry. Barren myrtle.

24. MAIRÀNIA Neck.; Desv. Journ. Bot. II. 1: 36, 292. 1813.
[ARCTOUS Niedenzu, Engl. Bot. Jahrb. 11: 141. 1890.]

A low shrub, with shreddy bark, alternate thin deciduous leaves clustered toward the ends of the branches, and small white clustered pedicelled flowers. Calyx 4–5-parted.

Corolla 4–5-toothed, the short teeth spreading or recurved.　Stamens 8 or 10, included; anther with 2 recurved dorsal awns.　Ovary 4–5-celled; ovules 1 in each cavity.　Drupe globose, with 4 or 5 separate 1-seeded nutlets.　[Greek, referring to its shining leaves.]

A monotypic genus of the arctic zone and high mountain summits.

1. Mairania alpìna (L.) Desv.　Alpine or Black Bearberry.　Fig. 3250.

Arbutus alpina L. Sp. Pl. 395.　1753.
Mairania alpina Desv. Journ. Bot. (II) **1**: 37, 292.　1813.
Arctostaphylos alpina Spreng. Syst. **2**: 287.　1825.
Arctous alpina Niedenzu, Engl. Bot. Jahrb. **11**: 141.　1890.

Tufted or depressed-prostrate; branches 2′–5′ high, the twigs glabrous or very nearly so.　Leaves obovate, crenulate, conspicuously reticulate-veined, ciliate at least when young, $\frac{1}{2}$′–1′ long, 3″–7″ wide; flowers few, appearing from scaly buds before or with the leaves; corolla white, ovoid, constricted at the throat; drupe black (or bright red, according to Macoun), juicy, 3″–5″ in diameter.

Summits of the higher mountains of New England; Quebec to Newfoundland, Alaska and British Columbia.　Also in northern Europe and Asia.　Summer.

25. CALLÙNA Salisb. Trans. Linn. Soc. **6**: 317.　1802.

A low much branched evergreen shrub, with minute linear opposite crowded and imbricated leaves, and small white or pink flowers, in terminal one-sided dense, spike-like racemes.　Sepals 4, scarious, concave, obtuse, longer than and concealing the corolla.　Corolla campanulate when expanded, 4-parted, slightly twisted, persistent, becoming scarious.　Stamens 8, distinct; filaments short; anthers oblong, attached to the filaments by their backs, opening by a longitudinal slit, each sac with a dorsal reflexed appendage.　Disk 8-lobed.　Ovary depressed-globose, 8-angled; style slender; stigma capitellate.　Capsule somewhat 4-sided, 4-celled, septicidally 4-valved, few-seeded.　Seeds ovoid, pendulous, not winged.　[Greek to sweep, its twigs used for brooms.]

A monotypic genus of Europe and Asia.

1. Calluna vulgàris (L.) Salisb.　Ling.　Heather.　Moor.　Besom.　Fig. 3251.

Erica vulgaris L. Sp. Pl. 352.　1753.
C. vulgaris Salisb. Trans. Linn. Soc. **6**: 317.　1802.

A straggling shrub, the branches ascending, 3′–15′ high, the twigs puberulent or glabrous.　Leaves sessile, about $\frac{1}{4}$″ long, very numerous, imbricated in 4 rows, usually 2-auricled at the base, 3-angled, grooved on the back, glabrous, ciliate or canescent; calyx with 4 small bracts at the base; corolla about $1\frac{1}{2}$″ long, nearly concealed by the 4 scarious pink or white sepals.

Sandy or rocky soil, Newfoundland to New Jersey.　Naturalized or adventive from Europe.　Grig.　July–Sept.

Erìca cinèrea L., the Scotch heath, found at one spot on Nantucket Island, has an ovoid 4-toothed corolla, much longer than the calyx (about 3″ long) and linear leaves, mostly verticillate in 3's.

Erìca Tétralix L., the cross-leaved heath, also on Nantucket, has a similar corolla and linear leaves verticillate in 4's.　Both are waifs from Europe.

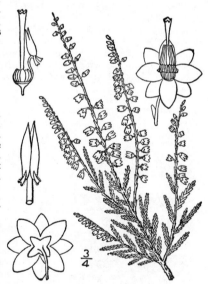

Family 5.　VACCINIÀCEAE Lindl. Veg. Kingd. 757.　1847.

HUCKLEBERRY FAMILY.

Erect or prostrate shrubs, or small trees, with alternate simple leaves, and small clustered or solitary perfect flowers, the pedicels commonly bracted.　Calyx-tube adnate to the ovary, the limb 4–5-lobed or 4–5-cleft.　Corolla gamopetalous, 4–5-lobed, or rarely divided into separate petals, deciduous, globose, campanulate, urceolate, or tubular.　Stamens twice as many as the corolla-lobes, epigynous, or inserted at the base of the corolla; filaments usually flattened, mostly short; anthers dorsally attached, 2-celled, the connective entire or 2-awned. Ovary inferior, 2–10-celled, crowned by the epigynous disk; style filiform; stigma simple, or minutely 4–5-dentate; ovules solitary, or several in each cavity, anatropous. Fruit a berry or drupe in our genera, globose; cells 1–several-seeded, or the drupe containing several nutlets. Seeds compressed; testa bony; endosperm fleshy; embryo central; radicle near the hilum.

About 20 genera and 300 species of wide geographic distribution.

Ovary 10-celled; fruit a berry-like drupe with 10 1-seeded nutlets.	1. *Gaylussacia.*
Ovary 4–5-celled; fruit a many-seeded berry.	
Corolla open-campanulate, 4–5-lobed.	
Flowers 4-parted; leaves small, coriaceous, persistent; low shrub.	2. *Vitis-Idaea.*
Flowers 5-parted; leaves large, thin, deciduous; tall shrubs.	
Flower not jointed with its pedicel; anthers exserted.	3. *Polycodium.*
Flower jointed with its pedicel; anthers included; berry black.	4. *Batodendron.*
Corolla cylindric, subglobose or urceolate.	
Erect shrubs; ovary entirely inferior; berries normally not white.	5. *Vaccinium.*
Low trailing shrub; ovary half inferior; berry snow-white.	6. *Chiogenes.*
Corolla deeply 4-cleft or 4-divided, the lobes reflexed.	7. *Oxycoccus.*

1. GAYLUSSÀCIA H.B.K. Nov. Gen. 3: 275. *pl. 257.* 1819.

[?ADNARIA Raf. Fl. Ludov. 56. 1817]

[DECAMERIUM Nutt. Trans. Am. Phil. Soc. II. **8**: 259. 1843.]

Branching shrubs, with alternate entire or serrate leaves, and small white or pink flowers in lateral bracted racemes. Pedicels mostly 2-bracteolate. Calyx-tube short, obconic, or turbinate, the limb 5-lobed or 5-toothed, persistent. Corolla urn-shaped, or tubular-campanulate, the tube terete or 5-angled, the limb 5-lobed, the lobes erect or recurved. Stamens 10, equal, usually included; filaments short and distinct; anther-sacs tapering upward into tubes, awnless, opening by terminal pores or chinks. Fruit a berry-like drupe with 10 seed-like nutlets, each containing a single seed. [Named for the celebrated chemist, Gay-Lussac.]

About 40 American species. Besides the following, another occurs in the southern Alleghenies. Type species: *Gaylussacia buxifolia* H.B.K.

Leaves pale and glaucous beneath, resinous; fruit blue with a bloom.	1. *G. frondosa.*
Leaves green both sides, resinous; fruit black, or sometimes blue.	
Bracts small, deciduous, mostly shorter than the pedicels.	2. *G. baccata.*
Bracts oval, large, persistent, longer than the pedicels.	3. *G. dumosa.*
Leaves thick, evergreen, serrate, not resinous; bracts scale-like.	4. *G. brachycera.*

1. Gaylussacia frondòsa (L.) T. & G. Blue Tangle. Tangleberry. Dangleberry. Huckleberry. Fig. 3252.

Vaccinium frondosum L. Sp. Pl. 351. 1753.
G. frondosa T. & G.; Torr. Fl. N. Y. 1: 449. 1843.

An erect shrub, 2°–4° high, with numerous spreading or ascending slender gray branches. Leaves oval to obovate, obtuse or retuse, entire, 1½′–2½′ long when mature, usually thin, the lower surface glabrous or pubescent, pale or glaucous, and sprinkled with resinous globules, the upper surface green, usually glabrous; petioles about 1″ long; flowers few, nodding, greenish pink in loose racemes; bracts linear-oblong, shorter than the filiform mostly 2-bracteolate pedicels, deciduous; corolla globose-campanulate, 1½″ long; filaments glabrous, shorter than the anthers; fruit globose, dark blue with a glaucous bloom, about 4″ in diameter, sweet.

In moist woods, New Hampshire to Virginia, Alabama, Ohio and Louisiana. Blue whortleberry. May–June. Fruit ripe July–Aug.

Gaylussacia ursìna (M. A. Curtis) T. & G., with acuminate leaves green on both sides and black fruit, native of the southern Alleghanies, is erroneously recorded from Kentucky.

3/5

2. Gaylussacia baccàta (Wang.) K. Koch. Black or High-bush Huckleberry. Fig. 3253.

Andromeda baccata Wang. Beitr. 111, *pl. 30. f. 69.* 1787.
Vaccinium resinosum Ait. Hort. Kew. 2: 12. 1789.
G. resinosa T. & G.; Torr. Fl. N. Y. 1: 449. 1843.
G. baccata K. Koch, Dendr. 2: 93. 1869-72.

A shrub, 1°-3° high, with ascending or erect stiff grayish branches, the young shoots commonly pubescent. Leaves oval or oblong, rarely obovate, obtuse or acutish, entire, very resinous when young, mucronulate, glabrous or very nearly so and green on both sides, firm, 1'-2' long; petioles about 1" long; flowers few, pink or red, in short one-sided racemes; bracts small, reddish, deciduous, shorter than or equalling the usually 2-bracteolate pedicels; corolla ovoid-conic, 5-angled, becoming campanulate-cylindric, 2"-2½" long; filaments ciliate; fruit black without bloom, or bluish and with a bloom, rarely white or pink, about 3" in diameter, sweet but seedy.

In woods and thickets, preferring sandy soil, New-foundland to Georgia, Manitoba, Wisconsin and Kentucky. Black-snap. Crackers. May-June. Fruit ripe July-Aug.

3. Gaylussacia dumòsa (Andr.) T. & G. Dwarf or Bush Huckleberry. Fig. 3254.

Vaccinium dumosum Andr. Bot. Rep. 2: *pl. 112.* 1800.
Vaccinium hirtellum Ait. f. Hort. Kew. Ed. 2, 2: 357. 1811.
G. dumosa T. & G.; A. Gray, Man. 259. 1848.
Gaylussacia dumosa hirtella A. Gray, Man. 259. 1848.

A branching shrub, 1°-2° high, from a horizontal or ascending base, the branches nearly erect, usually leafless below, the young twigs pubescent or hirsute, glandular. Leaves oblong-obovate or oblanceolate, obtuse, mucronate, entire, firm or coriaceous, green both sides, shining when old, sparingly pubescent or glabrous, resinous, or glandular, 1'-1½' long, sessile or nearly so; flowers white, pink or red, in rather long and loose racemes; bracts oval, foliaceous, persistent, pubescent or glandular, equalling or longer than the slender pubescent or hirsute 2-bracteolate pedicels; corolla campanulate, 2"-2½" long; filaments pubescent; calyx puberulent; fruit black, without bloom, 3"-4" in diameter, watery and rather insipid.

In sandy or rocky soil, often in swamps, Newfound-land to Florida and Louisiana. Gopher-berry. Races differ in pubescence and in shape of the leaves. May-June. Fruit July-Aug.

3/5

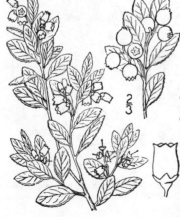

2/3

4. Gaylussacia brachýcera (Michx.) A. Gray. Box-Huckleberry. Fig. 3255.

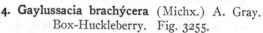

Vaccinium brachycerum Michx. Fl. Bor. Am. 1: 234. 1803.
Vaccinium buxifolium Salisb. Parad. Lond. *pl. 4.* 1806.
Gaylussacia brachycera A. Gray, Mem. Am. Acad. II. 3: 54. 1846.

A low branching shrub, 6'-15' high, from a horizontal or ascending base, the branches erect, angular, the twigs glabrous or very nearly so. Leaves thick, very coriaceous, glabrous, not resinous, persistent, evergreen, oval or oblong, obtuse or acutish, ½'-1' long, serrate with low teeth, the margins somewhat revolute; petioles 1" long or less; flowers few, white or pink in short racemes; bracts and bractlets scale-like, caducous; pedicels very short; corolla cylindric-ovoid, about 2" long; filaments ciliate; fruit (according to A. Wood) light blue.

In dry woods, Delaware and Pennsylvania to Virginia. May.

2. VÌTIS-IDAÈA (Tourn.) Hill, Brit. Herb. 516. 1756.

A low evergreen shrub, with creeping stems, alternate oval or obovate coriaceous leaves, and small white or pink nodding flowers, secund in small terminal clusters. Calyx 4-toothed. Corolla open-campanulate, 4-lobed. Stamens 8; anthers upwardly prolonged into tubes; filaments pubescent. Ovary 4-celled, inferior. Fruit a dark red acid many-seeded berry. [Ancient name.]

A monotypic genus of the north temperate and arctic zones.

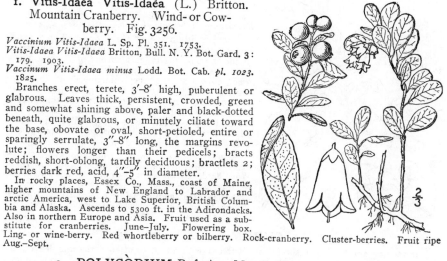

1. Vitis-Idaea Vìtis-Idaèa (L.) Britton. Mountain Cranberry. Wind- or Cowberry. Fig. 3256.

Vaccinium Vitis-Idaea L. Sp. Pl. 351. 1753.
Vitis-Idaea Vitis-Idaea Britton, Bull. N. Y. Bot. Gard. 3: 179. 1903.
Vaccinum Vitis-Idaea minus Lodd. Bot. Cab. pl. 1023. 1825.

Branches erect, terete, 3'-8' high, puberulent or glabrous. Leaves thick, persistent, crowded, green and somewhat shining above, paler and black-dotted beneath, quite glabrous, or minutely ciliate toward the base, obovate or oval, short-petioled, entire or sparingly serrulate, 3"-8" long, the margins revolute; flowers longer than their pedicels; bracts reddish, short-oblong, tardily deciduous; bractlets 2; berries dark red, acid, 4"-5" in diameter.

In rocky places, Essex Co., Mass., coast of Maine, higher mountains of New England to Labrador and arctic America, west to Lake Superior, British Columbia and Alaska. Ascends to 5300 ft. in the Adirondacks. Also in northern Europe and Asia. Fruit used as a substitute for cranberries. June–July. Flowering box. Ling- or wine-berry. Red whortleberry or bilberry. Rock-cranberry. Cluster-berries. Fruit ripe Aug.–Sept.

3. POLYCÒDIUM Raf. Am. Month. Mag. 2: 266. 1818.

Picrcoccus Nutt. Trans. Am. Phil. Soc. II. 8: 262. 1843.

Shrubs with alternate deciduous leaves, and purplish or yellowish green flowers in leafy-bracted racemes, jointed with their pedicels. Calyx 5-toothed. Corolla open-campanulate, 5-lobed. Stamens 10; anthers upwardly prolonged into tubes, exserted. Ovary 5-celled, inferior; style exserted. Berry green, nearly black, or yellow, globose to pyriform. [Greek, many bells.]

Three or four species of eastern North America. Type species: Vaccinium stamineum L.

1. Polycodium stamíneum (L.) Greene. Deerberry. Buckberry. Fig. 3257.

Vaccinium stamineum L. Sp. Pl. 350. 1753.

Polycodium stamineum Greene, Pittonia 3: 324. 1898.

A divergently branched shrub, 2°-5° high, with pubescent or glabrous twigs. Leaves oval, oblong or rarely obovate, acute or sometimes acuminate at the apex, petioled, entire, firm, green above, pale and glaucous or slightly pubescent beneath, 1'-4' long, ½'-1½' wide; flowers very numerous in graceful leafy-bracted racemes, jointed with their spreading or pendulous filiform pedicels; calyx glabrous or nearly so; corolla open-campanulate, purplish or yellowish green, deeply 5-cleft, 2"-3" long, 3"-5" broad; bracts usually persistent; berry globose or pear-shaped, green or yellow, 4"-5" in diameter, inedible.

In dry woods and thickets, Maine (?), Massachusetts to southern Ontario and Minnesota, south to Florida, Kentucky and Louisiana. Consists of several races, differing in amount of pubescence and in color of the fruit. Squawberry. Squaw-huckleberry or -whortleberry. Dangleberry. Gooseberry. April–June.

Polycodium melanocàrpum (C. Mohr) Small, is pubescent, with a pubescent calyx and deep purple palatable fruit. It inhabits the Southern States, and is recorded as far north as Missouri.

4. BATODÉNDRON Nutt. Trans. Am. Phil. Soc. II. **8**: 261. 1843.

Shrubs or small trees, with firm deciduous leaves, and white flowers in leafy-bracted racemes. Calyx 5-toothed. Corolla campanulate, 5-lobed. Stamens 10; anthers not exserted. Ovary inferior, 5-celled; style exserted. Berry black, globose, many-seeded. [Greek, black-berry tree.]

Two or three species of North America, or monotypic, with several races. Type species: *Batodendron arboreum* (Marsh.) Nutt.

2/3

1. Batodendron arbòreum (Marsh.) Nutt. Farkleberry. Tree-Huckleberry. Fig. 3258.

Vaccinium arboreum Marsh. Arb. Amer. 157. 1785.
Batodendron arboreum Nutt. loc. cit. 1843.

A divergently branched shrub or small tree, reaching a maximum height of about 30°, and trunk diameter of 9′, the twigs glabrous or slightly pubescent. Leaves obovate or oval, obtuse or acute and mucronulate at the apex, narrowed at the base, short-petioled, shining and bright green above, duller, and sometimes sparingly pubescent beneath, entire or glandular-denticulate, coriaceous, 1′–2′ long, ½′–1′ wide; flowers pendulous, slender-pedicelled; corolla white, campanulate, 5-lobed; bracts persistent; berry about 3″ in diameter, inedible.

In dry sandy soil, North Carolina to Kentucky, Indiana, Illinois, Missouri, Oklahoma, Florida and Texas. Wood hard, reddish brown, weight per cubic foot 47 lbs. Gooseberry. Sparkleberry. May–June.

Batodendron andrachnefórme Small, of Missouri, differs by its shorter-pedicelled smaller flowers, the corolla globular-campanulate.

5. VACCÍNIUM L. Sp. Pl. 349. 1753.

Branching shrubs (some species small trees) with alternate often coriaceous leaves, and small white, pink or red flowers, in terminal or lateral racemes or clusters, or rarely solitary in the axils. Calyx-tube globose, hemispheric or turbinate, not angled, adnate to the ovary, the limb 5-toothed or 5-lobed, persistent. Corolla urn-shaped or cylindric, rarely subglobose, its limb 5-toothed or 5-lobed. Stamens twice as many as the lobes of the corolla, distinct, the filaments short or elongated; anthers awned or awnless, upwardly prolonged into tubes, opening by terminal pores or chinks. Ovary 5-celled, or 10-celled by false partitions; ovules several or numerous in each cavity; style straight; stigma small. Fruit a many-seeded berry. [Latin name for these or related plants.]

About 150 species of wide geographic distribution. Besides the following some 11 others occur in southern and western North America. Type species: *Vaccinium Myrtillus* L.

Flowers solitary, or 2–4 together, on drooping pedicels; low shrubs; filaments glabrous; anthers 2-awned.
　Most or all the flowers 4-parted and stamens 8.　　　　　　　　　　　1. *V. uliginosum.*
　Flowers all or nearly all 5-parted, and stamens 10.
　　Shrub 3′–6′ high; leaves obovate or cuneate.　　　　　　　　　　2. *V. caespitosum.*
　　Shrubs 1°–12° high; leaves oval or oblong; northern species.
　　　Leaves serrulate, green both sides; berry purple-black.　　　　3. *V. membranaceum.*
　　　Leaves entire or nearly so, pale beneath; berry blue with bloom.　4. *V. ovalifolium.*
Flowers fascicled or racemose, short-pedicelled; filaments pubescent; anthers awnless.
　Fruit normally blue, with a bloom.
　　Corolla subcampanulate, greenish-pink.　　　　　　　　　　　　5. *V. pallidum..*
　　Corolla urceolate to subcylindric.
　　　Tall shrubs of marshes or wet soil; leaves large; corolla white.
　　　　Corolla subcylindric, 3″–6′ long.　　　　　　　　　　　　6. *V. corymbosum.*
　　　　Corolla urceolate, 2″–3″ long.　　　　　　　　　　　　　7. *V. caesariense.*
　　　Low upland or mountain shrubs, mostly less than 4° high, leaves small; corolla white to greenish pink.
　　　　Leaves oblong, lanceolate or narrowly elliptic, green on both sides.
　　　　　Leaves and twigs densely short-pubescent.　　　　　　　8. *V. canadense.*
　　　　　Leaves and twigs glabrous or nearly so.　　　　　　　　9. *V. angustifolium.*
　　　　　Leaves obovate to broadly oblong, pale beneath.　　　　10. *V. vacillans.*
　Fruit normally black, with no bloom or very little.
　　Corolla globose-ovoid to urceolate.
　　　Low shrub of rocky places; leaves glaucous beneath.　　　　11. *V. nigrum.*
　　　Tall shrubs; leaves green on both sides, somewhat paler beneath.
　　　　Leaves entire-margined, thin, densely pubescent beneath, 1½′–3′ long; marsh shrub.
　　　　　　　　　　　　　　　　　　　　　　　　　　　　　12. *V. atrococcum.*
　　　　Leaves serrulate, firm, glabrous or nearly so, 1′ long or less; pineland shrub.
　　　　　　　　　　　　　　　　　　　　　　　　　　　　　13. *V. Elliottii.*

Corolla nearly cylindric.
  Tall swamp shrub; corolla pink, 3″–4″ long.   14. *V. virgatum.*
  Low upland shrub; corolla white, 2″–3″ long.   15. *V. tenellum.*

1. Vaccinium uliginòsum L.   Great or Bog Bilberry. Bog Whortleberry.   Bleaberry.   Fig. 3259.

Vaccinium uliginosum L. Sp. Pl. 350. 1753.

A stiff much-branched shrub, 6′–24′ high. Leaves thick when mature, glabrous or nearly so on both sides, dull, pale or glaucous beneath, obovate, oblong, or oval, obtuse, or retuse, narrowed at the base, entire, nearly sessile, finely reticulate-veined, 5″–12″ long; flowers 2–4 together, or sometimes solitary near the ends of the branches, mostly shorter than the drooping pedicels; calyx 4-lobed (sometimes 5-lobed); corolla pink, ovoid or urn-shaped, 4–5-toothed; stamens 8–10; berry blue to black, with a bloom, about 3″ in diameter, sweet.

Summits of the mountains of New England and the Adirondacks, mainly above timber-line; Newfoundland and Labrador to Quebec, Maine, and shores of Lake Superior, to Alaska. Also in northern Europe and Asia. Bog-blueberry. June–July. Fruit ripe July–Aug.

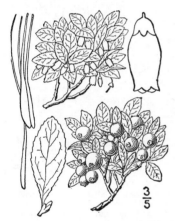

2. Vaccinium caespitòsum Michx.   Dwarf Bilberry.   Fig. 3260.

Vaccinium caespitosum Michx. Fl. Bor. Am. 1: 234. 1803.

A shrub, 3′–12′ high, much branched, nearly glabrous throughout, the twigs not angled. Leaves obovate or oblong-cuneate, obtuse or acute, 6″–12″ long, green and shining both sides, nearly sessile, serrulate with close bluntish teeth; flowers mostly solitary in the axils and longer than their drooping pedicels; calyx slightly 5-toothed (rarely 4-toothed); corolla obovoid or obovoid-oblong, pink or white, 5-toothed or rarely 4-toothed; stamens 10, rarely 8; berry blue with a bloom, sweet, about 3″ in diameter.

Rocky and gravelly soil, Labrador to Alaska, Maine, Vermont, northern New York, Wisconsin and south in the Rocky Mountains to Colorado, ascending to the highest mountain summits in New York and New England. June–July. Fruit ripe Aug.

3. Vaccinium membranàceum Dougl.   Thin-leaved Bilberry.   Fig. 3261.

Vaccinium myrtilloides Hook. Fl. Bor. Am. 2: 32. 1834. Not Michx. 1803.

Vaccinium membranaceum Dougl.; Torr. Bot. U. S. Expl. Exp. 377. 1874.

A branching shrub, 1°–5° high, nearly glabrous throughout, the twigs slightly angled. Leaves oval, oblong or ovate, thin or membranous, green both sides, not shining, acutish to acuminate, short-petioled, sharply and finely serrulate, 1′–2½′ long; flowers mostly solitary in the axils, their recurved pedicels becoming erect in fruit; calyx-limb entire or slightly toothed; corolla depressed-globose or globose-urceolate, greenish or purplish, mostly 5-toothed; stamens mostly 10; berry dark purple to black, rather acid.

In moist woods, northern Michigan; Oregon and British Columbia. June–July. Fruit ripe July–Aug.

3/5

2/3

4. Vaccinium ovalifòlium J. E. Smith.
Tall or Oval-leaved Bilberry.   Fig. 3262.

Vaccinium ovalifolium J. E. Smith in Rees' Cyclop. 36: No. 2.   1817.

A straggling branched shrub, 3°–12° high, the branches slender; twigs glabrous, jointed, sharply angled. Leaves oval, or elliptic, short-petioled, glabrous on both sides, green above, pale and glaucous beneath, rounded at both ends, or somewhat narrowed at the base, thin, sometimes mucronulate, entire or very nearly so, 1′–2′ long; flowers commonly solitary in the axils, on rather short recurved pedicels; calyx-limb slightly toothed; corolla ovoid; stamens 10; berry blue with a bloom, 4″–5″ in diameter.

Woods, Quebec to Michigan, Oregon and Alaska. Also in Japan.   June–July.   Fruit ripe July–Aug.

Vaccinium nubígenum Fernald, of mountain rocks in Quebec, has smaller serrulate elliptic leaves acute at both ends, the corolla urceolate, pink.

5. Vaccinium pállidum Ait.   Pale or
Mountain Blueberry.   Fig. 3263.

V. pallidum Ait. Hort. Kew. 2: 10.   1789.
Vaccinium corymbosum var. *pallidum* A. Gray, Man. Ed. 2, 250.   1856.
V. Constablei A. Gray, Am. Journ. Sci. 42: 42. 1842.

A branching shrub, 2°–8° high, with glabrous green warty twigs. Leaves oval, ovate or oblong, rather thin when mature, acute or acuminate, narrowed or rounded at the base, short-petioled, glabrous and light green above, pale and slightly glaucous beneath, serrulate, or nearly entire, 1′–3′ long; flowers several or numerous in the clusters, about equalling their slender pedicels; corolla oblong-cylindric to urceolate, slightly constricted at the throat, greenish-pink, 2″–2½″ long, 1½″–2″ thick; berry blue, 4″–6″ in diameter, delicious.

In woods, mountains of Virginia to South Carolina.   Fruit superior to all other blueberries. May–June.   Berries ripe July–Aug.

Vaccinium simulàtum Small, also of the southern mountains, and apparently extending north to New York, differs in having the leaves pubescent on the veins beneath.

6. Vaccinium corymbòsum L.   High-
bush or Tall Blueberry.   Fig. 3264.

Vaccinium corymbosum L. Sp. Pl. 350.   1753.
V. amoenum Ait. Hort. Kew. 2: 12.   1789.

A shrub, 6°–15° high, the twigs terete, minutely warty, greenish-brown, puberulent, or glabrous. Leaves oval or oblong, mostly acute at each end, entire or serrulate, sometimes ciliate, green and glabrous above, paler and often pubescent at least on the veins beneath, short-petioled, 1′–3′ long, ½′–1½′ wide; flowers in short racemes, appearing with the leaves, equalling or longer than their pedicels; bracts oblong or oval, deciduous; calyx 5-lobed; corolla cylindric, or slightly constricted at the throat, white or faintly pink, 3″–6″ long, 1½″–3″ thick, 5-toothed (rarely 5-lobed); stamens 10; berry blue with a bloom, 3″–4″ in diameter, pleasantly acid.

In swamps, thickets and woods, Maine to Virginia, Quebec, Minnesota and Louisiana, apparently erroneously recorded from farther north.   May–June.   Fruit ripe July–Aug.   Great whortleberry.   Seedy dewberry   Swamp-blueberry.   The late market blueberry.

7. Vaccinium caesariénse Mackenzie.   New Jersey Blueberry. Fig. 3265.

V. caesariense Mackenzie, Torreya **10**: 230. 1910.

A quite glabrous, much-branched shrub, 3°–10° high, the twigs green and warty. Leaves ovate to elliptic-lanceolate, very short-petioled, entire-margined, acute or acutish at the apex, narrowed or somewhat rounded at the base, dull green above, much paler beneath, 3′ long or less, about one-half grown at flowering time; racemes 6–12-flowered; pedicels about as long as the corolla; bracts ovate-oblong; calyx glaucous, its lobes broad, acute; corolla dull white, urceolate, 2″–3″ long, 1½″–2″ thick; style slightly exserted; berries dark blue, with a bloom, 3″–4″ in diameter.

Bogs, Long Island, N. Y., and in the pine-barrens of New Jersey. May.

8. Vaccinium canadénse Kalm.   Canada Blueberry. Fig. 3266.

V. canadense Kalm ; Richards. Frank. Journ. **736**.   1823.

A low pubescent branching shrub, 6′–2° high. Leaves oblong, oblong-lanceolate or narrowly elliptic, pubescent, at least beneath, entire, acute at the apex, narrowed at the base, 1′–1½′ long, 4″–8″ wide; flowers few in the clusters, which are sometimes numerous on naked branches, appearing with the leaves; pedicels usually shorter than the flowers; corolla oblong-campanulate, greenish-white, 2″–3″ long and 1½″ thick; berry blue or bluish-black, with a bloom (rarely white), sweet, 2½″–3″ in diameter.

In moist places, Labrador to Manitoba, south in the mountains to Virginia, and to Illinois and Michigan. May–June. Fruit ripe July–Aug.

9. Vaccinium angustifòlium Ait.   Dwarf, Sugar, Early or Low-bush Blueberry. Fig. 3267.

V. pennsylvanicum Lam. Encycl. **1**: 74.   1783. Not Mill. 1768.

Vaccinium pennsylvanicum angustifolium A. Gray, Man. **261**. 1848.

Vaccinium angustifolium Ait. Hort. Kew. **2**: 11. 1789.

V. Dobbini Burnham, Am. Bot. **12**: 8. 1907.

A low branching shrub, 6′–2° high, similar to the preceding species, but with green warty branches and usually nearly or quite glabrous throughout. Leaves oblong-elliptic or oblong-lanceolate, green and glabrous on both sides or slightly pubescent on the veins beneath, sharply serrulate, acute at both ends, 9″–18″ long, 1″–6″ wide; flowers few in the clusters, longer than the very short pedicels; corolla oblong-campanulate, slightly constricted at the throat, 2″–3½″ long, about 1½″ thick; white or pinkish; berry blue or nearly black, with a bloom, sometimes white, or reddish, very sweet, 3″–5″ in diameter.

In dry, rocky or sandy soil, Newfoundland to Saskatchewan, Virginia, Illinois and Wisconsin. Strawberry-huckleberry. May–June. Fruit ripe June–July. The early market blueberry.

10. Vaccinium vacíllans Kalm. Low Blueberry. Blue Huckleberry. Fig. 3268.

V. vacillans Kalm; Torr. Fl. N. Y. 1 : 444. 1843.

A stiff branching shrub, 6′–4° high, with glabrous or sometimes pubescent, yellowish-green warty branches and twigs. Leaves obovate, oval, or broadly oblong, acute or obtuse and usually mucronulate, narrowed or rounded at the base, firm, glabrous on both sides, or pubescent beneath, entire, or sparingly serrulate, pale, glaucous and finely reticulate-veined beneath, 1′–2½′ long, ½′–1¼′ wide; flowers several or few in the clusters which are sometimes racemose on naked branches, longer than or equalling their pedicels; corolla oblong-cylindric, somewhat constricted at the throat, greenish-pink, 2″–3″ long, 1½″–2″ thick; berry blue with a bloom, sweet, 2″–3½″ in diameter.

In dry soil, New Hampshire to Ontario and Michigan, south to Georgia, Tennessee and Kansas. May–June. Fruit ripe July–Aug.

11. Vaccinium nìgrum (Wood) Britton. Low Black Blueberry. Fig. 3269.

Vaccinium pennsylvanicum var. *nigrum* Wood, Bot. & Flor. 199. 1873.
V. nigrum Britton, Mem. Torr. Club 5 : 252. 1894.

Similar to *V. angustifolium* and often growing with it, 6′–12′ high, the twigs glabrous. Leaves oblong, oblanceolate or obovate, acute at the apex, narrowed or rounded at the base, finely serrulate, very nearly sessile, ½′–1′ long, 3″–6″ wide, glabrous on both sides, green above, pale and glaucous beneath; flowers few in the clusters, longer than their pedicels; corolla globose-ovoid, very little constricted at the throat, white or cream color, about 2″ long, 1½″ thick; berry black, without bloom, about 3″ in diameter.

In dry rocky soil, New Brunswick to New Jersey, Pennsylvania and Michigan. May. Fruit ripe in July.

$\frac{2}{3}$

12. Vaccinium atrocóccum (A. Gray) Heller. Black Blueberry. Fig. 3270.

$\frac{2}{3}$

Vaccinium disomorphum Bigel. Fl. Bost. Ed. 2, 151. 1824. Not Michx. 1803.
Vaccinium corymbosum var. *atrococcum* A. Gray, Man. Ed. 2, 250. 1856.
V. atrococcum Heller, Bull. Torr. Club 21 : 24. 1894.

A branching shrub with shreddy bark, 3°–10° high, closely resembling *Vaccinium corymbosum*, the branches green, minutely warty, the young twigs pubescent. Leaves oval or oblong, dark green above, light green and densely pubescent beneath even when old, entire, usually acute at both ends, mucronate, thick, 1½″–3′ long, ½′–1½′ wide; flowers in short racemes, appearing with the leaves, about the length of their slender pedicels; bracts and bractlets caducous; calyx 5-lobed; corolla short-cylindric or ovoid, pink or greenish-red, 2″–3″ long, about 1½″ thick, 5-toothed, constricted at throat; berry black, without bloom, sweet, 3″–5″ in diameter.

In swamps and wet woods, New Brunswick and Ontario to New Jersey, Pennsylvania and Alabama. May–June. Fruit ripe July–Aug.

13. Vaccinium Ellióttii Chapm. Elliott's Black Blueberry. Fig. 3271.

V. Elliottii Chapm. Fl. S. States 260. 1860.

A much-branched shrub, 3°–7° high, the young twigs greenish, pubescent, or glabrous, often rather densely leafy. Leaves nearly sessile, dark green, somewhat shining above, dull and glabrous, or sparingly pubescent on the veins beneath, ovate to elliptic, serrulate or nearly entire, acute at the apex, narrowed or rounded at the base, 4″–12″ long; racemes few-flowered; pedicels shorter than the corolla; calyx-lobes broad, acute; corolla reddish, conic-urceolate, 2½″–3″ long; berries black, 3″–4″ in diameter.

Pine lands, southeastern Virginia to Florida and Texas. March–May. Has been mistaken for *V. myrsinites* Lam., an evergreen shrub of the southeastern states, with blue berries, and obovate or oblanceolate leaves.

14. Vaccinium virgàtum Ait. Southern Black Huckleberry. Fig. 3272.

Vaccinium virgatum Ait. Hort. Kew. **2** : 12. 1789.

A shrub, 3°–12° high, the branches slender, green, the young twigs puberulent. Leaves narrowly oval-oblong, broadest at the middle, mucronate, short-petioled, entire, or finely serrulate, green and glabrous above, pale or glaucous beneath, veins pubescent, thick when old, 1′–2½′ long, ½′–1′ wide, the ends narrowed; flowers in short racemes or clusters, appearing before the leaves, equalling or longer than their pedicels; bracts and bractlets small, deciduous; calyx 5-lobed; corolla nearly cylindric, 3″–4″ long, 1″–1½″ thick, pink; stamens 10; berry black, with or without bloom, 2″–3″ in diameter.

In swamps, southern New York to Florida and Louisiana. April–May. Fruit ripe in July.

15. Vaccinium tenéllum Ait. Small Black Blueberry. Fig. 3273.

Vaccinium tenellum Ait. Hort. Kew. **2** : 12. 1789.

Vaccinium virgatum tenellum A. Gray. Syn. Fl. **2**¹ : 22. 1878.

A low shrub, with underground stems, the branches upright, 8′–16′ tall, finely pubescent. Leaves numerous, cuneate or narrowly elliptic-spatulate to elliptic, 5″–10″ long, acute or slightly acuminate at both ends, serrulate, pale green and rather conspicuously but delicately veined beneath, nearly sessile; flowers in often umbel-like racemes, appearing after the leaves; pedicels shorter than the corollas, slightly pubescent; corolla white, 2″–3″ long, nearly cylindric, slightly constricted at the throat, its lobes very short; berries subglobose, about 3″ long, black.

In dry woods, Virginia to Florida, Arkansas and Mississippi. April–May.

6. CHIÓGENES Salisb. Trans. Hort. Soc. Lond. **2** : 94. 1814.

Creeping prostrate evergreen branching shrubs, with alternate 2-ranked oval or ovate small leaves, and solitary axillary small white flowers, on short recurved peduncles. Calyx-tube adnate to the lower half of the ovary, 2-bracted at the base, its limb 4-cleft. Corolla short-campanulate, 4-cleft, its lobes rounded. Stamens 8, included; filaments short, nearly orbicular, roughish; anthers not awned nor prolonged into tubes, each sac 2-cuspidate at the apex and opening by a slit down to the middle. Ovary 4-celled, surrounded by the 8-lobed disk; style short. Berry globose to oval, snow-white, many-seeded, rather mealy. [Greek, snow-born, in allusion to the berries.]

A monotypic genus of North America and Japan.

1. Chiogenes híspídula (L.) T. & G. Creeping Snowberry. Ivory-plums. Fig. 3274.

Vaccinium hispidulum L. Sp. Pl. 352. 1753.
C. serpyllifolia Salisb. Trans. Hort. Soc. 2: 94. 1814.
Chiogenes hispidula T. & G.; Torr. Fl. N. Y. 1: 450. 1843.
Chiogenes japonica A. Gray, Syn. Fl. 2: Part 1, 26. 1878.

Branches strigose-pubescent, very slender, 3'-12' long. Leaves coriaceous, persistent, oval, ovate, or slightly obovate, short-petioled, acute at the apex, rounded or narrowed at the base, dark green, glabrous above, entire, sprinkled with appressed stiff brownish hairs beneath and on the revolute margins, 2''-5'' long; flowers few, solitary, axillary, nodding, about 2'' long, berry aromatic, usually minutely bristly, crowned by the 4 calyx-teeth, becoming almost wholly inferior, about 3'' in diameter.

In cold wet woods and bogs, Newfoundland to British Columbia, south to North Carolina and Michigan. Ascends to 5200 ft. in New Hampshire. May–June. Fruit ripe Aug.–Sept. Flavor of sweet birch. Mountain partridge-berry. Running birch. Moxie-berry. Maidenhair-berry.

7. OXYCÓCCUS [Tourn.] Hill, British Herbal, 324. 1756.

Glabrous, or slightly pubescent, trailing or erect shrubs, with alternate nearly sessile leaves, and axillary or terminal, solitary or several, pendulous or cernuous, slender-peduncled red or pink flowers. Calyx-tube nearly hemispheric, adnate to the ovary, the limb 4-5-cleft, persistent. Corolla long-conic in the bud, 4-5-parted or 4-5-divided into separate or nearly separate petals, these narrow and revolute. Stamens 8 or 10, the filaments distinct; anthers connivent into a cone, long-exserted when the flower is expanded, upwardly prolonged into hollow tubes dehiscent by a pore at the apex, not awned. Ovary 4-5-celled; style slender or filiform. Fruit an oblong or globose many-seeded juicy red acid berry. [Greek, sour berry.]

About 6 species, natives of the northern hemisphere. Type species: *Oxycoccus vulgaris* Hill.
Trailing bog shrubs; leaves evergreen, entire; flowers 1-6 from terminal buds.
     Leaves ovate, acute; berry globose.   1. *O. Oxycoccos.*
     Leaves oval or oblong, obtuse; berry ovoid or oblong.   2. *O. macrocarpus..*
Erect mountain shrub; leaves deciduous, serrulate; flowers solitary, axillary.   3. *O. erythrocarpus.*

1. Oxycoccus Oxycóccos (L.) MacM. Small or European Cranberry. Fig. 3275.

Vaccinium Oxycoccos L. Sp. Pl. 351. 1753.
V. Oxycoccus intermedium A. Gray. Syn. Fl. ed 2, 2¹: 396. 1886.
Oxycoccus palustris Pers. Syn. 1: 419. 1805.
O. Oxycoccus MacM. Bull. Torr. Club 19: 15. 1892.

Stems very slender, creeping, rooting at the nodes, 6'-18' long. Branches ascending or erect, 1'-6' high; leaves thick, evergreen, ovate, entire, acutish at the apex, rounded or cordate at the base, dark green above, white beneath, 2''-8'' long, 1''-3½'' wide, the margins more or less revolute; flowers 1-6, mostly umbellate, rarely racemose, from terminal scaly buds, nodding, on erect filiform pedicels, 2-bracteolate at or below the middle; corolla pink, about 4'' broad, divided nearly to the base; filaments puberulent, about half the length of the anthers; berry globose, 3''-5'' in diameter, often spotted when young.

In cold bogs, Newfoundland to Alaska, New Jersey, North Carolina, Michigan and British Columbia. Also in Europe and Asia. May–July. Fruit ripe Aug.–Sept. Bog- or marsh-wort. Moss-, bog-, fen- or moor-berry. Marsh-berry. Crone, cran-, cram- or crane-berry. Crow or craw-berry. Moss-millions [melons]. Sow- or sour-berry. Swamp red-berry.

2. Oxycoccus macrocàrpus (Ait.) Pursh. Large or American Cranberry. Fig. 3276.

Vaccinium macrocarpon Ait. Hort. Kew. **2**: 13. *pl. 7.* 1789.
O. palustris macrocarpus Pers. Syn. **1**: 419. 1805.
Oxycoccus macrocarpus Pursh, Fl. Am. Sept. 263. 1814.

Similar to the preceding species, but stouter and larger, the branches often 8' long. Leaves oval, oblong, or sometimes slightly obovate, obtuse at both ends, entire, 3"–9" long, 1"–4" wide, white or pale beneath, the margins slightly revolute; flowers several in mostly lateral somewhat racemose clusters, nodding on erect pedicels, 2-bracteolate above the middle; corolla light pink, 4"–5" broad, divided very nearly to the base; filaments puberulent, about one-third the length of the anthers; berry oblong or nearly globose, 4"–9" long.

In bogs, Newfoundland to western Ontario, Virginia, West Virginia, Michigan and Arkansas. Bear-berry. Marsh-cranberry. June–Aug. Fruit ripe Sept.–Oct.

3. Oxycoccus erythrocàrpus (Michx.) Pers. Southern Mountain Cranberry. Fig. 3277.

Vac. erythrocarpum Michx. Fl. Bor. Am. **1**: 227. 1803.
Oxycoccus erythrocarpus Pers. Syn. **1**: 419. 1805.

A divergently branched shrub, 1°–6° high, the twigs pubescent or glabrous. Leaves thin, green both sides, paler beneath than above, reticulate-veined, ovate, ovate-lanceolate, or ovate-oblong, acuminate at the apex, rounded, subcordate or the terminal ones narrowed at the base, finely serrulate with bristle-pointed teeth, flat, 1'–3' long, ½'–1' wide; flowers solitary in the axils; peduncles pendulous, filiform, usually minutely 2-bracteolate at the base and less than one-half as long as the leaves; corolla deeply 4-parted, red, about 5" broad; filaments villous, about one-fourth the length of the anthers; berry globose, dark red, 2"–3" in diameter.

In woods, mountains of Virginia to Georgia. June–July. Fruit ripe July–Sept.

Family 6. DIAPENSIÀCEAE Link. Handb. 1: 595. 1829.

DIAPENSIA FAMILY.

Low tufted shrubs, or perennial scapose herbs, with alternate or basal simple exstipulate leaves, and small white pink or purple gamopetalous or polypetalous perfect and regular flowers, solitary in the axils, or racemose at the summit of scapes. Calyx 5-parted, persistent; sepals imbricated in the bud. Corolla 5-lobed, 5-cleft, or 5-parted, deciduous. Stamens 5, inserted on the throat of the corolla and alternate with its lobes, or connate, sometimes with as many alternating staminodia; anther-sacs longitudinally or transversely dehiscent; pollen-grains simple. Disk none. Ovary free from the calyx, superior, 3-celled; style mostly stout, persistent; stigma 3-lobed; ovules few or numerous in the cavities, anatropous or amphitropous. Capsule 3-celled, loculicidally 3-valved. Seeds minute, the testa loose or close; endosperm fleshy; embryo terete; cotyledons short; radicle elongated.

Six genera and about 8 species, natives of the northern hemisphere.

Low tufted evergreen shrubs ; corolla gamopetalous.
  Tufted arctic-alpine shrub ; flowers terminal, peduncled.   1. *Diapensia.*
  Trailing shrub ; flowers solitary, sessile.   2. *Pyxidanthera.*
Tall scapose perennial herb ; flowers spicate-racemose ; petals separate.   3. *Galax.*

1. DIAPÉNSIA L. Sp. Pl. 141. 1753.

Densely tufted glabrous low evergreen shrubs, with thick rather fleshy imbricated narrow leaves, and solitary terminal erect peduncled white or pink flowers. Calyx 2–4-bracted at the base, the sepals oval, obtuse, somewhat rigid. Corolla campanulate, tardily deciduous, 5-lobed, the lobes obtuse. Stamens 5, inserted at the sinuses of the corolla; filaments short and broad; anther-cells pointed, divergent, obliquely 2-valved; staminodia none. Style slender; ovules numerous in the cells, anatropous. Seeds oblong-cubic, the testa close, reticulated. [Greek, by fives, alluding to the stamens and corolla-lobes.]

Two species, the following typical one of wide distribution in the colder parts of the northern hemisphere, the other Himalayan.

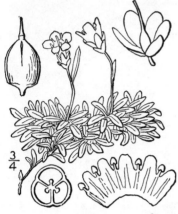

1. Diapensia lappónica L. Diapensia.
Fig. 3278.

Diapensia lapponica L. Sp. Pl. 141. 1753.

Glabrous, forming dense cushion-like tufts; stems simple or branched, erect or ascending, 1'–3' high. Leaves crowded below, thick, spatulate, sessile, obtuse or acutish, often curved, entire, 3"–6" long, about 1" wide, the margins usually revolute; peduncles rather stout, becoming 1'–2' long in fruit; sepals and bracts oval; corolla usually white, 3"–4" long, its tube about the length of the sepals and of its oval or oblong obtuse lobes; capsule ovoid, 2"–3" high.

Summits of the Adirondack Mountains, and of the mountains of New England; Mt. Albert, Quebec; Labrador and arctic America. Also in northern and alpine Europe and Asia. June–July.

2. PYXIDANTHÈRA Michx. Fl. Bor. Am. 1: 152. *pl. 17.* 1803.

A creeping tufted much-branched evergreen shrub, with small narrow alternate imbricated leaves, and numerous white or pinkish sessile flowers, solitary at the ends of the branches. Calyx bracted at the base, the sepals oblong, ciliate. Corolla short-campanulate, 5-lobed, tardily deciduous. Stamens inserted at the sinuses of the corolla; filaments broad and thick; anthers 2-celled, the sacs globose, transversely 2-valved, the lower valve cuspidate; staminodia none. Style columnar. Seeds globose-oblong, amphitropous, the testa black, cancellate. [Greek, box-anther.]

A monotypic genus of eastern North America.

1. Pyxidanthera barbulàta Michx. Pyxie.
Flowering Moss. Fig. 3279.

Pyxidanthera barbulata Michx. Fl. Bor. Am. 1: 152. *pl. 17.* 1803.
Diapensia barbulata Ell. Bot. S. C. & Ga. 1: 229. 1817.

Glabrous, or sparingly pubescent, very leafy, growing in mats or large patches on the ground, the main branches sometimes 1° long. Leaves sessile, linear, lanceolate or linear-oblong, acuminate or subulate-tipped, entire, pubescent at the base when young, 2"–4" long, about 1" wide, densely imbricated toward the ends of the branches, more scattered below; flowers usually very numerous, 2"–3" broad, mostly white; corolla-lobes cuneate-obovate, obtuse, retuse or eroded; capsule about 1" high, globose, sessile, surrounded by the upper leaves.

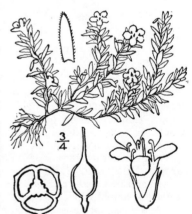

In dry sandy pine-barrens, southern New Jersey to North Carolina. Called also pine-barren beauty. Flowers sometimes pinkish. March–May.

3. GÀLAX L. Sp. Pl. 200. 1753.

An acaulescent perennial herb, with orbicular cordate crenate-dentate long-petioled basal leaves, and numerous small white flowers, spicate-racemose at the ends of tall mostly naked slender scapes. Calyx minutely 2-bracteolate at the base, 5-parted, the sepals nerveless. Corolla 5-divided, the petals oblong, entire, adnate to the bases of the monadelphous stamens. Stamen-tube 10-lobed at the summit, the lobes which are opposite the petals petaloid (staminodia), those alternate with the petals antheriferous; anthers nearly sessile, granular on the back, 1-celled, transversely 2-valved. Style very short. Seeds ovoid, the testa loose. [Greek, milk; name not characteristic of this genus.]

A monotypic genus of southeastern North America.

1. **Galax aphýlla** L. Galax. Galaxy. Beetle-weed. Fig. 3280.

Galax aphylla L. Sp. Pl. 200. 1753.

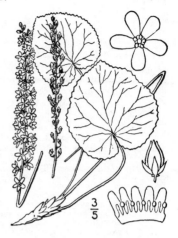

Scape 1½° high, terete, with red scaly bracts at the base and many red fibrous roots. Leaves orbicular, or broadly ovate, deeply cordate at the base with a rather narrow sinus, persistent, crenate-dentate or doubly denticulate with mucronulate or rounded teeth, shining, commonly shorter than their slender petioles, 1′–3′ in diameter; spike-like raceme dense, narrow, 2′–5′ long; flowers 1½″–2″ broad, spreading; bractlets deciduous; capsule ovoid, acute, erect, very short-pedicelled, 1″ long, slightly exceeding the lanceolate acutish sepals.

In dry woods, especially in the mountains, Virginia to Georgia. Ascends to 4500 ft. in North Carolina. Leaves bright green, shining. Colt- or colt's-foot. May–July.

Family 7. **PRIMULÀCEAE** Vent. Tabl. 2: 285. 1799.

PRIMROSE FAMILY.

Herbs, with alternate opposite verticillate or basal leaves, and perfect regular flowers, in terminal or axillary racemes, spikes, umbels or corymbs, or solitary in the axils or at the summit of a scape. Calyx free from the ovary (adnate to its lower part in *Samolus*), 4–9-parted or cleft (usually 5-parted), persistent or rarely deciduous. Corolla gamopetalous in our species (wanting in *Glaux*), 4–9-lobed or cleft (usually 5-cleft), rotate, funnelform, salverform or campanulate, deciduous. Stamens as many as the corolla-lobes and opposite them, hypogynous or rarely perigynous, inserted on the tube or base of the corolla; filaments distinct, or connate at the base; anthers introrse, attached by their backs to the filaments, 2-celled, the sacs longitudinally dehiscent. Disk obsolete, or none. Ovary superior (partly inferior in *Samolus*), 1-celled; placenta central, free; ovules anatropous, or mostly amphitropous; style 1; stigma simple, capitate, entire. Capsule 1-celled, 2–6-valved; rarely circumscissile or indehiscent, the valves erect or recurved, entire or 2-cleft. Seeds few or several, the testa adherent to the fleshy or horny copious endosperm; embryo small, straight; cotyledons obtuse.

About 28 genera and 400 species of wide distribution in the northern hemisphere, a few in southern South America and South Africa.

* **Lobes or segments of the corolla erect or spreading, not reflexed.**

† LOBES OF THE COROLLA IMBRICATED, AT LEAST IN THE BUD.

Ovary wholly superior.
    Terrestrial scapose plants; leaves not pinnatifid.

Corolla-tube longer than the calyx; style slender.	1. *Primula.*
Corolla-tube shorter than the calyx; style short.	2. *Androsace.*
Aquatic leafy-stemmed plant; leaves finely pinnatifid.	3. *Hottonia.*
Ovary adnate to the calyx.	4. *Samolus.*

†† LOBES OF THE COROLLA CONVOLUTE OR VALVATE, AT LEAST IN THE BUD (COROLLA WANTING IN NO. 9).

Capsule longitudinally dehiscent.
    Corolla rotate, or rarely short-funnelform.
        Stem leafy throughout; flowers yellow.

Staminodia none; corolla-lobes convolute; flowers axillary or racemed.	5. *Lysimachia.*
Staminodia 5; each corolla-lobe curved around its stamen.	6. *Steironema.*
Staminodia 5, tooth-like; flowers in axillary spike-like racemes.	7. *Naumburgia.*
Leaves whorled at the top of the stem; flowers white.	8. *Trientalis.*
Corolla none; flowers minute, solitary in the axils.	9. *Glaux.*

Capsule circumscissile; flowers axillary.

Corolla longer than the calyx; stamens borne on its base; leaves opposite.	10. *Anagallis.*
Corolla shorter than the calyx; stamens borne on its tube; leaves alternate.	11. *Centunculus.*

** **Segments of the corolla reflexed; plants scapose.**   12. *Dodecatheon.*

1. PRÍMULA L. Sp. Pl. 142. 1753.

Perennial scapose herbs, with basal leaves, and small or large white red purple or yellow dimorphous flowers, umbellate, or in involucrate or bracted racemose whorls at the summit of a scape. Calyx tubular, funnelform or campanulate, persistent, often angled, 5-lobed, the lobes imbricated, erect or spreading. Corolla funnelform or salverform, the tube longer than the calyx in our species, the limb 5-cleft, the lobes imbricated, entire, emarginate or 2-cleft. Stamens 5, inserted on the tube or at the throat of the corolla, included; filaments very short; anthers oblong, obtuse. Ovary superior, globose or ovoid; ovules numerous, amphitropous; style filiform; stigma capitate. Capsule oblong, ovoid or globose, 5-valved at the summit, many-seeded. Seeds peltate, the testa punctate. [Diminutive of the Latin primus, first, from the early blossoms.]

About 150 species, mostly of the northern hemisphere, a few in Java and at the Straits of Magellan. Besides the following, some 18 others occur in western and northwestern North America. Type species: *Primula veris* L.

Leaves almost always mealy beneath; scape 4'–18' high.	1. *P. farinosa.*
Leaves green both sides; scape 1'–6' high.	
Leaves spatulate or obovate, denticulate.	2. *P. mistassinica.*
Leaves oval or lance-ovate, entire.	3. *P. egaliksensis.*

1. Primula farinòsa L.   Bird's-eye or Mealy Primrose.   Fig. 3281.

Primula farinosa L. Sp. Pl. 143. 1753.

Leaves spatulate to obovate or oblong, obtuse at the apex, narrowed or somewhat cuneate at the base, tapering into petioles, or sessile, usually white- or yellow-mealy beneath at least when young, green above, 1'–4' long, 2"–6" wide, the margins crenulate-denticulate; scape 4'–18' high, 3–20-flowered; flowers umbellate; bracts of the involucre acute or acuminate; pedicels 2"–2' long; calyx-lobes acute, often mealy; corolla pink or lilac, usually with a yellowish eye, the tube slightly longer than the calyx, the lobes cuneate, retuse or obcordate, 2"–3" long; capsule narrowly oblong, erect, 2½"–6" long, longer than the calyx.

Cliffs and shores, Maine and Quebec to Greenland, west to Michigan and Minnesota. Consists of several races. Also in Europe and Asia. Summer.

2. Primula mistassínica Michx.   Mistassini or Dwarf Canadian Primrose.   Fig. 3282.

Primula mistassinica Michx. Fl. Bor. Am. 1: 124. 1803.

Similar to the preceding species, but smaller; scape very slender, 1'–6' high. Leaves spatulate to rhombic-ovate or obovate, green on both sides (rarely slightly mealy beneath), denticulate or repand, obtuse at the apex, narrowed or cuneate at the base, petioled or sessile, ½'–1½' long, 1½"–5" wide; flowers 2–8, umbellate; bracts of the involucre acute or acuminate; pedicels 2"–12" long; corolla pink, or pale purple, with or without a yellow eye, the tube distinctly longer than the calyx; corolla-lobes obcordate, 1½"–2½" long; capsule narrowly oblong, erect, 2½"–4" high.

On wet banks, Maine to Newfoundland, central New York, Michigan and Saskatchewan. Summer.

3. Primula egaliksénsis Hornem. Greenland Primrose. Fig. 3283.

Primula egaliksensis Hornem. Fl. Dan. *pl. 1511.* 1814.

Leaves green both sides, oval or lance-ovate, entire, or slightly undulate, obtuse or obtusish at the apex, ½′–1′ long, narrowed into petioles of about their own length; scape very slender, 2′–6′ high; umbels 2–6-flowered; bracts of the involucre lanceolate, acuminate; pedicels short, elongating in fruit; calyx-teeth short, acute; corolla-lobes 1″–2″ long, much shorter than the tube, obovate, sometimes cleft to the middle; capsule erect, about 3″ high, longer than the calyx.

Northern Labrador (Turner, according to A. Gray) and Greenland. Summer.

Several other boreal species have been described, but they are not definitely known within our range.

2. ANDRÓSACE [Tourn.] L. Sp. Pl. 141. 1753.

Low annual or perennial herbs, our species scapose, with tufted small basal leaves, and terminal umbellate or solitary involucrate small white or pink flowers. Calyx persistent, 5-lobed, -cleft or -parted, the lobes erect in flower, sometimes spreading in fruit. Corolla salverform or funnelform, the tube short, not longer than the calyx, the limb 5-lobed, the lobes imbricated. Stamens 5, included, inserted on the tube of the corolla; filaments very short; anthers short, oblong, obtuse. Ovary superior, turbinate or globose; ovules few, or numerous, amphitropous; style short; stigma capitellate. Capsule turbinate, ovoid or globose, 5-valved from the apex, few–many-seeded. [Greek, man's shield, from the shape of the leaf in some species.]

About 60 species, natives of the northern hemisphere. Besides the following, about 15 others occur in western and northwestern North America. Type species: *Androsace maxima* L.

1. Androsace occidentàlis Pursh. Androsace. Fig. 3284.

Androsace occidentalis Pursh, Fl. Am. Sept. 137. 1814.

Annual, minutely pubescent, or glabrate; scapes filiform, solitary or numerous from fibrous roots, erect or ascending, or diffuse, 1′–3′ long. Leaves oblong or spatulate, obtuse, entire, sessile, 3″–8″ long; bracts of the involucre similar to the leaves but much smaller, 1″–3″ long; pedicels several or numerous, filiform, 2″–6″ long in flower, often becoming 1′ long in fruit; calyx-tube obpyramidal in fruit, the lobes ovate or triangular-lanceolate, acute, as long as or longer than the tube, green, becoming foliaceous; corolla very small, white, shorter than the calyx; calyx longer than the several-seeded capsule.

In dry soil, Minnesota and Illinois to Kansas and Arkansas, west to Manitoba, Utah and New Mexico. April–June.

Androsace diffùsa Small, differing by narrower, lanceolate involucral bracts, enters our extreme northwestern limits in North Dakota.

3. HOTTÒNIA Boerh.; L. Sp. Pl. 145. 1753.

Aquatic glabrous herbs, rooting in the mud, or floating, with large pinnatifid submersed crowded leaves, and small white or purplish flowers, racemose-verticillate on bracted hollow erect emersed peduncles. Calyx deeply 5-parted, the lobes linear, imbricated, persistent. Corolla salverform, the tube short, the limb 5-parted, the lobes spreading, imbricated at least in the bud. Stamens 5, included, inserted on the tube of the corolla; filaments short; anthers oblong. Ovary ovoid; style filiform; stigma minute, capitate; ovules numerous, anatropous. Capsule subglobose, 5-valved. Seeds ellipsoid, numerous. [Dedicated to Peter Hotton, 1648–1709, professor at Leyden.]

Two species, the following of eastern North America, the other, the typical one, of Europe and eastern Asia.

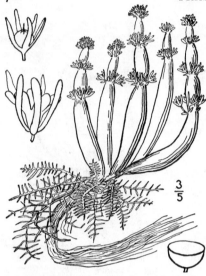

1. Hottonia inflàta Ell.   American
Featherfoil.   Fig. 3285.

Hottonia inflata Ell. Bot. S. C. & Ga. 1: *231.* 1817.

Stem entirely submerged, spongy, densely leafy, branched, sometimes 2° long. Leaves sessile, or nearly so, ovate or oblong in outline, divided very nearly to the rachis into narrowly linear entire segments ½'-2' long, ¼"-1" wide; peduncles several in a cluster at the ends of the stem and branches, partly emersed, hollow, jointed, constricted at the joints, 3'-8' high, the lower joint 2'-4' long, sometimes 1' thick, the others successively smaller; pedicels 2"-12" long; flowers 2"-3" long in verticils of 2-10 at the joints, subtended by linear bracts; corolla white, shorter than the calyx; capsule globose, about 1½" in diameter.

In shallow stagnant ponds, Maine and New Hampshire to central New York, Missouri, Arkansas, Florida and Louisiana. June-Aug. Called also water-feather, water-violet, water-yarrow.

4. SÁMOLUS [Tourn.] L. Sp. Pl. 171. 1753.

Perennial glabrous herbs, with alternate entire leaves, or the basal ones rosulate. Flowers small, white, in terminal racemes or panicles in our species. Calyx persistent, its tube adnate to the ovary below, its limb 5-cleft. Corolla perigynous, subcampanulate, 5-lobed or 5-parted, the lobes obtuse, imbricated, at least in the bud. Stamens 5, inserted on the tube of the corolla, opposite its lobes, alternating with as many staminodia (these wanting in *S. ebracteatus*), filaments short; anthers cordate. Ovary partly inferior; ovules numerous, amphitropous. Capsule globose or ovoid, 5-valved from the summit. Seeds minute. [Name Celtic.]

About 10 species, of wide distribution, most abundant in South Africa and Australasia. Besides the following 3 others occur in the southern United States. Type species: *Samolus Valerandi* L.

1. Samolus floribúndus H.B.K.   Water Pimpernel.   Brookweed.   Fig. 3286.

Samolus floribundus H.B.K. Nov. Gen. **2**: 224.   1817.
S. Valerandi var. *americanus* A. Gray, Man. Ed. 2, 274.   1856.

Erect or ascending, branched, at least at the base, 6'-18' high. Leaves membranous, 1'-3' long, ½'-1' wide, obovate, obtuse at the apex, narrowed at the base into petioles, the basal often in a rosulate tuft, the uppermost smaller and sometimes sessile; flowers commonly numerous, less than 1" broad, in loose elongated panicled racemes; pedicels filiform, spreading, 4"-12" long, bracteolate near the middle; calyx-lobes acute, shorter than the corolla; capsule 1"-1½" in diameter, the 5 apical valves spreading at maturity.

In swamps and brooks, often in brackish soil, New Brunswick to Florida, west to British Columbia, Texas and California. Also in Mexico, the West Indies and South America. May-Sept.

Samolus Valerándi L., of Europe and Asia, a smaller plant with mostly simple racemes and larger flowers and capsules, has been found in ballast about Philadelphia.

5. LYSIMÀCHIA [Tourn.] L. Sp. Pl. 146.   1753.

Herbs, mostly perennial, with leafy stems. Leaves entire, often glandular-punctate; flowers in our species yellow, solitary in the axils, or racemose, corymbose or paniculate. Calyx 5-7-parted or 5-7-divided, persistent, free from the ovary. Corolla rotate or campanulate, 5-7-parted, the tube very short, the lobes convolute at least in the bud. Stamens 5-7, inserted on the throat of the corolla; filaments separate, or connate at the base; anthers oblong or oval; staminodia none. Ovary globose or ovoid; ovules few or several; style filiform; stigma obtuse. Capsule ovoid or globose, 2-5-valved, few or several-seeded. [Greek, loose-strife.]

About 70 species, mostly natives of the northern hemisphere, a few in Africa and Australia. Besides the following, 3 others occur in the southern United States. Type species: *Lysimachia vulgaris* L.

Leaves verticillate in 3's-7's, or some of them rarely opposite.
    Corolla rotate-campanulate, pure yellow, 6"-12" broad.

Flowers in terminal panicles ; corolla-lobes glabrous.
Flowers axillary ; corolla-lobes glandular-ciliolate.
Corolla rotate, 4″–8″ broad, its lobes dark-streaked.
Leaves opposite, or some of them rarely alternate.
Flowers in a terminal virgate raceme ; stem erect.
Flowers axillary, solitary ; stem creeping.

1. *L. vulgaris.*
2. *L. punctata.*
3. *L. quadrifolia.*

4. *L. terrestris.*
5. *L. Nummularia.*

1. Lysimachia vulgàris L. Golden or Yellow Loosestrife or Willowherb. Fig. 3287.

Lysimachia vulgaris L. Sp. Pl. 146. 1753.

Densely downy-pubescent; stem erect, branched, 2°–
3½° high. Leaves verticillate in 3's or 4's, or some of
them opposite, short-petioled, ovate-lanceolate or ovate,
acute or acuminate at the apex, mostly narrowed at the
base, 2′–4′ long, ½′–1½′ wide; flowers 6″–10″ broad, in
terminal leafy panicles or compound corymbs; pedicels
2″–6″ long; sepals lanceolate or triangular-lanceolate,
acute or acuminate; corolla yellow, rotate-campanulate,
deeply parted, the segments glabrous; filaments monadelphous to about the middle, glandular; capsule about
1½″ in diameter, shorter than the sepals.

In fields and along roadsides, Maine to Ontario, southern
New York and Pennsylvania. Naturalized from Europe.
Native also of Asia. Willow-wort. Yellow rocket. June–Aug.

2. Lysimachia punctàta L. Spotted Loosestrife. Fig. 3288.

Lysimachia punctata L. Sp. Pl. 147. 1753.

Resembles the preceding species, usually
densely pubescent, sometimes glabrate; stem
simple or branched, 2°–3° high. Leaves verticillate in 3's or 4's or some of them opposite,
oval or ovate-lanceolate, acute or obtuse at the
apex, rounded or narrowed at the base, short-
petioled, 1′–3′ long, ½′–1½′ wide, usually proportionately shorter and broader than those of
L. vulgaris; flowers crowded in the upper axils
or racemose-verticillate, yellow, 8″–10″ broad;
pedicels 3″–10″ long; sepals lanceolate or
oblong-lanceolate, acute or obtusish; corolla-
segments glandular-ciliolate; filaments monadelphous at the base.

Waste places, Nova Scotia to New Jersey and
Pennsylvania. Adventive from Europe. June–July.

3. Lysimachia quadrifòlia L. Cross-wort. Whorled Loosestrife. Fig. 3289.

Lysimachia quadrifolia L. Sp. Pl. 147. 1753.

Pubescent, or glabrate, stem simple or rarely
branched, slender, erect, 1°–3° high. Leaves
verticillate in 3's–7's (commonly in 4's or 5's),
or some, or very rarely all of them opposite,
short-petioled or sessile, lanceolate, oblong or
ovate, acute or acuminate at the apex, 1′–4′ long,
3″–1½′ wide, usually black-punctate, the uppermost sometimes very small; flowers axillary,
3″–6″ broad, borne on filiform spreading peduncles
½′–1½′ long; sepals narrowly lanceolate, acute or
acuminate; corolla glabrous, dark-streaked, or
spotted; filaments monadelphous below; capsule
nearly as long as the sepals.

In thickets, New Brunswick to Ontario, Minnesota,
Tennessee, Georgia and Wisconsin. Five sisters. Yellow balm. Liberty-tea. June–Aug.

Lysimachia prodúcta (A. Gray) Fernald [*L. foliosa* Small] has characters intermediate between this species and the following, the flowers in leafy-bracted racemes, the leaves opposite or whorled, and may be a hybrid between them.

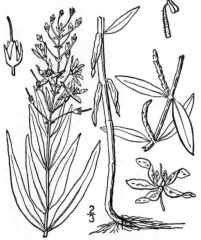

4. Lysimachia terréstris (L.) B.S.P. Bulb-bearing Loosestrife. Fig. 3290.

Viscum terrestre L. Sp. Pl. *1023.* 1753.
Lysimachia stricta Ait. Hort. Kew. 1: 199. 1789.
L. terrestris B.S.P. Prel. Cat. N. Y. 34. 1888.

Glabrous; stem erect, simple or branched, 8′–2° high, often bearing, after flowering, long bulblets (suppressed branches) in the axils. Leaves opposite or some of them rarely alternate, lanceolate or oblong-lanceolate, acute or acuminate at both ends, short-petioled, or sessile, usually black-punctate, 1′–3′ long, 2″–8″ wide; flowers 3″–5″ broad, in terminal bracted mostly elongated racemes; or some of them solitary or 2–3 together in the upper axils; pedicels slender or filiform, 5″–9″ long; sepals ovate or lanceolate, acute; corolla rotate, deeply parted, yellow with purple streaks or dots; filaments monadelphous below, glandular; capsule about 1½″ in diameter, nearly as long as sepals.

In swamps and moist thickets, Newfoundland and Manitoba, south to Georgia and Arkansas. The plant sometimes produces no flowers, but bears bulblets freely in the axils in the autumn, and in this condition was mistaken by Linnaeus for a terrestrial mistletoe. Swamp-candles. July–Sept.

5. Lysimachia Nummulària L. Money-wort. Creeping Loosestrife. Fig. 3291.

Lysimachia Nummularia L. Sp. Pl. 148. 1753

Glabrous; stems creeping, sometimes 2° long, often rooting at the nodes. Leaves opposite, orbicular or broadly oval, obtuse at both ends or truncate or cordate at the base, manifestly petioled, ½′–1′ long, sparingly black-punctate; flowers solitary in the axils, 8″–12″ broad; sepals cordate-ovate to lanceolate, acute, half as long as the rotate deeply 5-lobed yellow and dark-dotted corolla; filaments glandular, monadelphous at the base; capsule shorter than the sepals.

In moist places, Newfoundland to New Jersey, Virginia, Illinois and Michigan Naturalized from Europe. June–Aug. Lower leaves sometimes narrowed at the base. Creeping or wandering Jenny or Sally. Herb-twopence. Two-penny grass. Down-hill-of-life.

6. STEIRONÈMA Raf. Ann. Gen. Phys. 7: 192. 1820.

Perennial leafy herbs, with opposite or verticillate simple entire leaves, and axillary slender-peduncled nodding or spreading yellow flowers. Calyx 5-parted, persistent, the segments valvate in the bud. Corolla rotate, deeply 5-parted, with no proper tube, the lobes cuspidate or erose-denticulate, each separately involute or convolute around its stamen. Stamens 5; filaments distinct, or united into a ring at the very base, granulose-glandular; anthers linear, becoming curved; staminodia 5, subulate, alternate with the stamens. Ovary globose; ovules few or numerous. Capsule 5-valved, several–many-seeded. Seeds margined or angled. [Greek, sterile threads, from the abortive stamens.]

About five species, natives of North America. Type species: *Steironema ciliatum* (L.) Raf.
Leaves membranous, pinnately veined.
  Leaves ovate or ovate-lanceolate.
    Stem erect; flowers 6″–12″ broad.
      Petioles strongly ciliate; capsule longer than the calyx.   1. *S. ciliatum.*
      Petioles not ciliate, or slightly so at base; capsule not longer than calyx.
                                           2. *S. intermedium.*
    Stem reclined; flowers 3″–4″ broad; leaves not ciliate; petioles naked   3. *S. radicans.*
  Leaves lanceolate, oblong or linear; stem erect.   4. *S. lanceolatum.*
Leaves firm, linear, 1-nerved, the lateral veins obscure.   5. *S. quadriflorum.*

1. Steironema ciliàtum (L.) Raf. Fringed Loosestrife. Fig. 3292.

Lysimachia ciliata L. Sp. Pl. 147. 1753.
Steironema ciliatum Raf. Ann. Gen. Phys. **7**: 192. 1820.

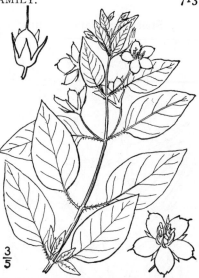

Stems erect, simple or branched, slender, mostly glabrous, 1°–4° high. Leaves membranous, ovate, ovate-oblong, or ovate-lanceolate, pinnately veined, acute or acuminate at the apex, obtuse, truncate or cordate at the base, 2′–6′ long, ½′–3′ wide, the margins ciliolate; petioles ciliate, ¼′–½′ long; peduncles filiform, ½′–2′ long; calyx-segments lanceolate, acuminate, shorter than the erose-denticulate commonly mucronate corolla-segments; flowers 6″–12″ broad; capsule longer than the calyx.

In moist thickets, Nova Scotia to British Columbia, south to Georgia, Alabama, Kansas, New Mexico and Arizona. Ascends to 6300 ft. in North Carolina. Naturalized in Europe. June–Aug.

2. Steironema intermèdium Kearney. Southern Loosestrife. Fig. 3293.

L. ciliata var. *tonsa* Wood, Class-book, 505. 1863.
Steironema intermedium Kearney, Bull. Torr. Club **21**: 263. 1894.
S. tonsum Bicknell; Britt. & Br. Ill. Fl. **2**: 590. 1897.

Stem erect, 1°–2° high, slender, obtusely 4-angled, glabrous below, minutely glandular-puberulent above. Leaves 2′–3′ long, 10″–20″ wide, ovate to ovate-lanceolate, acute at the apex, obtuse or subcordate at the base, minutely ciliolate, otherwise glabrous, the upper much smaller; petioles slender, glabrous, or ciliate only at the base; panicle open, leafy; pedicels slender, 2–6 times as long as the flowers; calyx-segments lanceolate, very acute; corolla 9″–10″ broad, its segments cuspidate; capsule shorter than calyx.

On dry rocks, Virginia to Kentucky, Tennessee and Alabama. June–July.

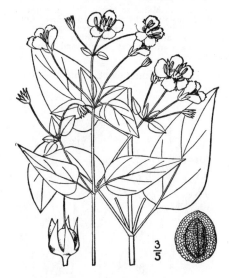

3. Steironema radìcans (Hook.) A. Gray. Trailing Loosestrife. Fig. 3294.

L. radicans Hook. Comp. Bot. Mag. **1**: 177. 1836.

S. radicans A. Gray, Proc. Am. Acad. **12**: 63. 1876.

Stem weak, at first erect, soon decumbent or reclined and often rooting at the joints, very slender, glabrous, much branched, 1°–3° long. Leaves membranous, pinnately veined, lanceolate to ovate-lanceolate, acute or acuminate at the apex, rounded or narrowed, but not cordate at the base, 1′–4′ long, ¼′–1′ wide; margins not ciliolate; petioles naked or very sparingly ciliolate, ¼′–1¼′ long; peduncles filiform, ½′–2′ long; calyx-segments ovate or lanceolate, acuminate, about equalling the erose-denticulate corolla-segments; flowers 3″–4″ broad; capsule about one-half as long as the calyx.

In swamps, Virginia and West Virginia to Arkansas and Texas. June–Aug.

4. Steironema lanceolàtum (Walt.) A. Gray. Lance-leaved Loosestrife. Fig. 3295.

Lysimachia lanceolata Walt. Fl. Car. 92. 1788.
L. hybrida Michx. Fl. Bor. Am. 1 : 126. 1803.
Steironema lanceolatum A. Gray, Proc. Am. Acad. 12 : 63. 1876.

Stem erect, slender, glabrous, simple or branched, 6'–3° high. Leaves lanceolate, linear or oblong-lanceolate, petioled or nearly sessile, membranous, pinnately veined, acute or acuminate at the apex, usually narrowed at the base, 1'–5' long, 2"–10" wide, the margins naked or ciliate; lower leaves shorter, often oblong or nearly orbicular; petioles 2"–8" long, naked or ciliate; peduncles slender or filiform, ½'–1½' long; calyx-segments lanceolate, acute or acuminate, nearly as long as or exceeding the erose and cuspidate-pointed corolla-segments; flowers 5"–9" broad; capsule nearly as long as the calyx-segments.

In moist soil, Maine to North Dakota, south to Florida, Louisiana and Arizona. June–Aug. Consists, apparently, of several races, regarded by some authors as species, which differ in width of leaves, length of petioles, length and shape of staminodes.

5. Steironema quadriflòrum (Sims) Hitchc. Prairie Moneywort. Linear-leaved Loosestrife. Fig. 3296.

L. quadriflora Sims, Bot. Mag. *pl. 660.* 1803.
L. longifolia Pursh, Fl. Am. Sept. 135. 1814.
Steironema longifolium A. Gray, Proc. Am. Acad. 12 : 63. 1876.
Steironema quadriflorum Hitchc. Trans. St. Louis Acad. 5 : 506. 1891.

Stem erect, strict, glabrous, simple or little branched, 4-sided, 6'–3° high. Stem-leaves all but the lowest sessile or very nearly so, firm, narrowly linear, 1-nerved, the lateral veins obscure, acute or acuminate at both ends, 1'–4' long, 1"–2½" wide, usually with smaller ones fascicled in the axils, glabrous, the margins slightly revolute; basal leaves oblong or linear-oblong, shorter, slender-petioled, acute or obtuse; peduncles filiform, ½'–1½' long; calyx-segments lanceolate, acute, shorter than the cuspidate and slightly erose corolla-segments; flowers 8"–12" broad, often somewhat clustered in 4's at the ends of the branches.

Along streams and lakes, Virginia to western New York, Ontario, Kentucky, Missouri, Iowa and Manitoba. June–July.

7. NAUMBÚRGIA Moench, Meth. Suppl. 23. 1802.

An erect perennial leafy herb, with slender rootstocks, opposite sessile lanceolate entire leaves, the lower much smaller or reduced to scales, and small yellow flowers in axillary peduncled spike-like racemes or heads. Calyx 5–7-divided, the sepals linear, slightly imbricated. Corolla deeply 5–7-parted, the tube exceedingly short, the segments narrow. Stamens 5–7, exserted; filaments slender, glabrous, slightly united at the base, alternating with as many small tooth-like staminodia at each sinus of the corolla. Ovary globose-ovoid; ovules few or several; style slender, equalling or exceeding the stamens; stigma capitate. Capsule 5–7-valved, few-seeded. Seeds not margined, somewhat angled. [In honor of Naumburg.]

A monotypic genus of the north temperate zone.

1. Naumburgia thyrsiflòra (L.) Duby. Tufted Loosestrife. Fig. 3297.

Lysimachia thyrsiflora L. Sp. Pl. 147. 1753.
Naumburgia guttata Moench, Meth. Suppl. 23. 1802.
Naumburgia thyrsiflora Duby, in DC. Prodr. 8 : 60. 1844.

Glabrous or somewhat pubescent; stems simple, erect, often tufted, 1°–2½° high. Leaves 2′–4′ long, 4″–10″ wide, the upper lanceolate or oblong-lanceolate, acute or acuminate at the apex, narrowed at the base, the lower smaller, the lowest reduced to ovate scales or these deciduous; peduncles solitary in the axils, rather stout, ½′–1½′ long; racemes dense, oblong or ovoid, ½′–1′ long, spike-like; pedicels very short; flowers 2″–3″ broad; sepals usually spotted; corolla-segments yellow with black spots; style very slender; anthers oblong; capsule globose, black-spotted, when mature slightly longer than the sepals, shorter than the style.]

In swamps, Nova Scotia to Alaska, south to southern New York, Pennsylvania, Missouri, Nebraska, Montana and California. Also in Europe and Asia. May–July.

$\frac{1}{2}$

8. TRIENTÀLIS L. Sp. Pl. 344. 1753.

Glabrous low perennial herbs, with simple slender erect stems, and lanceolate ovate or oblong leaves mostly clustered in a verticil at the summit. Flowers few or solitary, terminal, slender-peduncled, small, white or pink, deeply 5–9- (mostly 7-) parted. Sepals narrow, persistent, spreading. Corolla rotate, its tube almost none, its segments convolute in the bud, acute or acuminate, entire; filaments united into a narrow ring at the base; anthers linear-oblong, recurved after anthesis. Staminodia none. Ovary globose; ovules numerous; style filiform. Capsule globose, 5-valved, many-seeded. Seeds trigonous or spherical. [Latin, one-third of a foot, referring to the height of the plant.]

Four species, of the northern hemisphere. Two others occur in northwestern America, the typical *T. europeaea* L. in Europe and Asia.

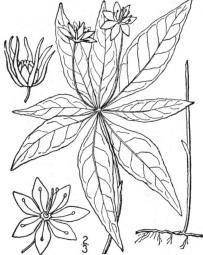

1. Trientalis americàna Pursh. Star-flower. Chickweed Wintergreen. Fig. 3298.

Trientalis americana Pursh, Fl. Am. Sept. 256. 1814.

Rootstock horizontal or creeping, sending up simple stem-like branches 3′–9′ high, which are naked or scaly below, the leaves all in a verticil of 5–10 at the summit, long stolons sometimes developed in their axils. Leaves membranous, lanceolate or oblong-lanceolate, acuminate at both ends, sessile or short-petioled, minutely crenulate, 1½′–4′ long, 4″–15″ wide; pedicels filiform, erect, 1′–2′ long; sepals narrowly lanceolate or subulate, cuspidate, about one-half as long as the oblong or somewhat obovate corolla-segments; flowers 4″–6″ broad; capsule shorter than the sepals.

In damp woods and thickets, Labrador to Manitoba, southern New Jersey, Virginia, Illinois and Michigan. May–June.

$\frac{2}{3}$

9. GLAÙX [Tourn.] L. Sp. Pl. 207. 1753.

A small succulent perennial leafy herb, with opposite entire obtuse small fleshy leaves, and minute dimorphous nearly sessile axillary pink or white flowers. Calyx 5-parted, the lobes petaloid, imbricated in the bud, about equalling the campanulate tube. Corolla none. Stamens 5, inserted at the base of the calyx and alternate with its lobes; filaments subulate-filiform; anthers cordate, attached by their backs to the filaments. Ovary superior, ovoid, glandular; ovules few; style filiform; stigma capitellate. Capsule globose-ovoid, beaked, 5-valved at the top, few-seeded. Seeds ellipsoid. [Greek, sea-green.]

A monotypic genus of salt marshes, sea-beaches and other saline situations in the northern hemisphere.

1. Glaux marítima L. Sea Milkwort. Black Saltwort. Fig. 3299.

Glaux maritima L. Sp. Pl. 207. 1753.

G. maritima obtusifolia Fernald, Rhodora 4: 215. 1902.

Perennial by slender rootstocks, glabrous, pale or glaucous, simple or branched, erect or diffuse, 2′–12′ high. Leaves oval, oblong or linear-oblong, rarely somewhat spatulate, sessile, 2″–7½″ long, 1″–4″ wide, the lower usually smaller than the upper; flowers about 1½″ broad, solitary and very nearly sessile in the axils, usually numerous; calyx-lobes oval, pink, purplish or white; stamens either shorter than the style or exceeding it; capsule nearly enclosed by the calyx, but free from and about equalling it.

In salt marshes and on sea-beaches, New Jersey to Newfoundland; in saline or subsaline soil from Minnesota to Manitoba, Alberta, Nebraska and Nevada; on the Pacific Coast from California to Alaska. Also in Europe and Asia. Called also sea-trifoly. June–Aug.

10. ANAGÁLLIS [Tourn.] L. Sp. Pl. 148. 1753.

Annual or perennial, diffuse or erect, branching mostly glabrous herbs, with opposite or verticillate (rarely alternate) sessile or short-petioled leaves, entire or nearly so, and small axillary peduncled red blue white or pink flowers. Calyx 5-parted, the lobes lanceolate or subulate, spreading, persistent. Corolla deeply 5-parted, rotate, the segments entire or erose, convolute in the bud, longer than the calyx. Stamens 5, inserted at the base of the corolla, filaments subulate, or filiform, puberulent, or pubescent, distinct, or united into a narrow ring at the base; anthers oblong, obtuse. Ovary globose, ovules numerous; stigma obtuse. Capsule globose, circumscissile, many-seeded. Seeds minute, flat on the back. [Greek, delightful.]

About 15 species, mostly of the Old World, 1 native in southern South America. The following European and Asiatic typical species is widely distributed as a weed.

1. Anagallis arvénsis L. Red or Scarlet Pimpernel. Poor Man's or Shepherd's Weather-glass. Fig. 3300.

Anagallis arvensis L. Sp. Pl. 148. 1753.
Anagallis coerulea Lam. Fl. Fr. 2: 285. 1778.
Anagallis arvensis coerulea Ledeb. Fl. Ross. 3: 30. 1846.

Annual, diffuse, usually much branched; branches 4″–12′ long, 4-sided. Leaves ovate or oval, membranous, opposite or rarely in 3's, sessile or somewhat clasping, obtuse or acutish, 3″–10″ long, black-dotted beneath; peduncles filiform, ½′–1½′ long, recurved in fruit; calyx-lobes keeled, rather rigid, slightly shorter than the crenate glandular-ciliate or glabrous corolla-segments; flowers scarlet or blue, sometimes white, usually with a darker center, 2″–3″ broad, opening only in bright weather; capsule glabrous, about 2″ in diameter.

In waste places, Newfoundland to Florida, west to Minnesota, Texas and Mexico, and on the Pacific Coast. Naturalized from Europe. Red chickweed. Burnet-rose. Shepherd's-clock. Bird's-eye or-tongue. Sunflower. Eyebright. Wink-a-peep. Shepherd's-delight. May–Aug.

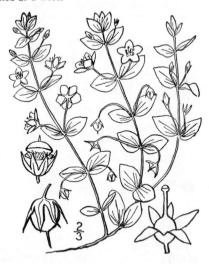

11. CENTÚNCULUS [Dill.] L. Sp. Pl. 116. 1753.

Low annual glabrous erect simple or branched herbs, with alternate small entire sessile or short-petioled leaves, or the lower opposite, and minute solitary axillary flowers. Calyx 4–5-parted, persistent, the lobes longer than the corolla. Corolla 4–5-cleft, marcescent, the tube subglobose, the lobes entire, acute, spreading. Stamens 4–5, inserted on the throat of the corolla; filaments short, glabrous, distinct; anthers ovate or cordate, obtuse; stigma capitate. Ovules numerous, amphitropous. Capsule globose, circumscissile, many-seeded. Seeds minute, flat on the back. [Latin, diminutive of *cento*, a patch.]

Three species, of wide geographic distribution. In addition to the following typical one, another occurs in Florida.

1. Centunculus mínimus L.   Chaffweed.   False Pimpernel.   Fig. 3301.

Centunculus minimus L. Sp. Pl. 116. 1753.

Simple or branched, very slender, 1'-6' high. Leaves spatulate, obovate or oblong, short-petioled, obtuse or acutish, 2''-4'' long, 1''-2'' wide; flowers sessile or very nearly so in the axils, shorter than the leaves, mostly 4-parted, 1''-2'' broad; calyx-lobes linear or linear-lanceolate, acuminate; corolla pink; capsule shorter than the calyx.

In moist soil, Illinois and Minnesota to British Columbia, south to Florida, Texas and Mexico. Also in Europe and South America. Bastard pimpernel. April–Sept.

12. DODECÀTHEON L. Sp. Pl. 144. 1753.

Glabrous scapose perennial herbs, with entire or repand basal leaves. Flowers large or middle-sized in involucrate umbels terminating scapes. Calyx deeply 5-lobed, persistent, the lobes at first reflexed. Corolla 5-parted, the lobes reflexed, slightly unequal, imbricated, the tube very short, thickened at the throat. Stamens 5, inserted on the throat of the corolla; filaments short, flat, monadelphous, connivent into a cone, exserted; anthers linear or lanceolate, connivent, attached by their bases to the filaments. Ovary ovoid or subglobose, superior; ovules numerous, amphitropous; style filiform, exserted; stigma simple. Capsule oblong or cylindric, erect, 5–6-valved at the apex or splitting to the base. Seeds numerous, minute; the testa punctate. [Greek, twelve gods; name used by Theophrastus for some different plant.]

About 30 species, natives of North America and northeastern Asia. Besides the following typical one, some 20 others occur in western and northwestern North America.

1. Dodecatheon Mèadia L.   Shooting Star.   American Cowslip.   Fig. 3302.

Dodecatheon Meadia L. Sp. Pl. 144. 1753.
Dodecatheon Meadia Frenchii Vasey; Wats. & Coult. in A. Gray, Man. Ed. 6, 735 b. 1891.

Perennial by a stout rootstock; roots fibrous; scape erect, 8'-2° high. Leaves oblong to ovate or oblanceolate, obtuse or obtusish at the apex, narrowed into margined petioles or subcordate, entire or toothed, 3'-12' long, ½'-4' wide; flowers few, several or numerous in the umbels, 9''-15'' long; bracts of the involucre lanceolate or linear, acute; pedicels recurved in flower, erect in fruit, unequal, the outer ones sometimes 4' long; calyx-lobes triangular-lanceolate, acute; corolla purple, pink or white; anthers 3''-4'' long; capsule narrowly ovoid, erect, 5-valved above, 6''-8'' high, much longer than the calyx.

On moist cliffs and prairies, Pennsylvania to Manitoba, south to Georgia and Texas. Indian-chief. Roosterheads. Johnny-jump. Pride-of-Ohio. April–May.

Dodecatheon brachycàrpa Small, with an ovoid capsule 5'' long, scarcely longer than the calyx, inhabits the Southern States and is erroneously recorded north to Maryland and Missouri.

Dodecatheon Hùgeri Small, with anthers prominently auricled at base, ranges north into Maryland.

Family 8. PLUMBAGINÀCEAE Lindl. Nat. Syst. Ed. 2, 269. 1836.

PLUMBAGO FAMILY.

Perennial mostly acaulescent erect herbs, with basal tufted leaves (stem often climbing and leafy in *Plumbago*), and small perfect regular clustered flowers. Calyx inferior, gamosepalous, tubular or funnelform, 5-toothed, plaited at the sinuses, the tube 5–15-ribbed. Corolla of 5 hypogynous clawed segments, connate at the base or united into a tube, convolute or imbricated in the bud. Stamens 5, opposite the corolla-segments, hypogynous; filaments separate, or united at the base; anthers 2-celled, attached by their backs to the filaments, the sacs longitudinally dehiscent. Disk none. Ovary superior, 1-celled; ovule solitary, anatropous, pendulous, the long funiculus arising from the base of the cavity; styles mostly 5, separate or united. Fruit a utricle or achene, enclosed by the calyx, rarely a dehiscent capsule. Seed solitary; testa membranous; endosperm mealy, or none; embryo straight; cotyledons entire.

About 10 genera and 350 species, of wide geographic distribution, mostly in saline situations. Inflorescence cymose-paniculate; flowers in one-sided spikes.   1. *Limonium.*
Flowers in a dense terminal head.   2. *Statice.*

1. LIMÒNIUM [Tourn.] Mill. Gard. Dict. Abr. Ed. 4. 1754.

[Statice Willd. Sp. Pl. 1: 1552. 1798.]

Herbs, mostly with flat basal leaves, and numerous very small flowers cymose-paniculate on the branches of bracted scapes, in 1–3-flowered bracteolate clusters, forming one-sided spikes. Calyx campanulate or tubular, the limb scarious, 5-toothed, the tube usually 10-ribbed. Petals 5, clawed. Stamens adnate to the bases of the petals. Styles mostly 5, separate in our species, stigmatic along the inner side. Fruit a utricle. [Ancient name of the wild beet.]

About 120 species. Besides the following, 5 others occur in the southern and western parts of the United States. Type species: *Statice Limonium* L.

1. Limonium carolinìànum (Walt.) Britton. Sea or Sea-side Lavender. Marsh Rosemary. Canker-root. Fig. 3303.

Statice caroliniana Walt. Fl. Car. 118. 1788.
S. Limonium var. *carolinianum* A. Gray, Man. Ed. 2, 270. 1856.
L. carolinianum Britton, Mem. Torr. Club 5: 255. 1894.

Glabrous, fleshy, root thick, fusiform or branched, astringent; scape terete, striate, slender, paniculately branched above, 6′–2° high. Leaves oblanceolate, obtuse or acutish and subulate-tipped at the apex, narrowed into margined petioles, entire, or slightly undulate, 3′–10′ long, ½′–1½′ wide, shorter than the scapes, the midvein prominent, the lateral veins very obscure; flowers erect, solitary or 2 or 3 together in the sessile secund bracteolate clusters, about 2″ high; calyx 5-toothed, sometimes with as many minute intermediate teeth in the sinuses; corolla pale purple; petals spatulate; ovary oblong or ovoid; styles filiform.

On salt meadows, Labrador to Florida and Texas. Bermuda. Lavender-thrift. Ink-root. Marsh-root. American thrift. July–Oct.

2. STÁTICE [Tourn.] L. Sp. Pl. 274. 1753.

[Armeria Willd. Enum. 333. 1809.]

Tufted acaulescent fleshy herbs, with slender mostly naked scapes, basal persistent rosulate narrow leaves with no differentiation into blade and petiole, and rather small short-pedicelled or sessile flowers, in dense terminal glomerate heads, subtended by scarious bracts and bractlets, the lower bracts forming a kind of involucre to the head, the two lowest reflexed and more or less united into a sheath. Calyx funnelform, 10-ribbed, 5-toothed, oblique at the base or decurrent on the pedicel, scarious. Petals 5, distinct, or more or less coherent. Filaments adnate to the bases of the petals. Styles united at the base, pubescent below the middle, longitudinally stigmatic above. Utricle 5-pointed at the summit, rarely dehiscent. [Greek, standing.]

About 20 species, natives of Europe, north Africa, western Asia, northern North America and southern South America. The following typical species is the only one known in North America.

1. Statice Armèria L. Thrift. Sea Pink. Ladies' Cushion. Fig. 3304.

Static Armeria L. Sp. Pl. 274. 1753.

Armeria vulgaris Willd. Enum. 333. 1809.

Scape glabrous or somewhat pubescent, 4′–18′ high. Leaves narrowly linear, acute or obtuse, flattish, obscurely 1-nerved, entire, numerous in a basal tuft, 1′–3′ long, ½″–1½″ wide; bracts scarious and obtuse, the 2 lower ones forming a sheath 3″–10″ long; head of flowers ½′–1′ in diameter; calyx-base decurrent on the very short pedicel, pubescent at least on the stronger nerves; corolla pink, purple or white, 2″–3″ broad; petals obtuse or cuspidate.

Along the sea-coast and on mountains, Quebec and Labrador to Alaska, south on the Pacific Coast to California. Also in Europe, northern Asia, and apparently the same species at the Strait of Magellan. Summer. Sea- or European-thrift. Sea-gilliflower. Sea-grass. Red-root.

Family 9. **SAPOTÀCEAE** Reichenb. Consp. 135. 1828.

SAPODILLA FAMILY.

Shrubs or trees, mostly with a milky juice. Leaves alternate, simple, entire, pinnately-veined, mostly coriaceous and exstipulate. Flowers small, regular and perfect, in axillary clusters. Calyx inferior, polysepalous; segments usually 4–7, persistent, much imbricated. Corolla gamopetalous, the tube campanulate or urceolate, 4–7-lobed, the lobes imbricated in the bud, sometimes with as many or twice as many lobe-like appendages borne on the throat. Stamens as many as the proper lobes of the corolla and inserted on its tube; staminodia usually present, alternate with the corolla-lobes; filaments mostly short, subulate; anthers attached by their bases to the filaments, or versatile, 2-celled, the sacs longitudinally dehiscent. Ovary superior, 2–5-celled, or rarely many-celled; ovules solitary in each cavity, anatropous or amphitropous; style conic or subulate; stigma simple. Fruit a fleshy berry, commonly 1-celled and 1-seeded, sometimes several-seeded. Seed large, the testa bony or crustaceous; embryo straight; endosperm fleshy, or none; cotyledons thick.

About 35 genera and 425 species, mostly of tropical regions in both the Old World and the New. Besides the following, 4 other genera occur in south Florida.

1. BUMÈLIA Sw. Prodr. 49. 1788.

Shrubs or trees, often spiny, with very hard wood, alternate coriaceous or membranous leaves, sometimes clustered on short spurs or at the nodes, and small pedicelled white or greenish flowers, fascicled in the axils. Calyx very deeply 5-parted, the segments much imbricated, unequal. Corolla 5-lobed, with a pair of lobe-like appendages at each sinus, its tube short. Stamens 5, inserted near the base of the corolla-tube; filaments filiform; anthers sagittate. Staminodia 5, petaloid, alternate with the stamens. Ovary 5-celled; style filiform. Berry globose or ellipsoid, small, the pericarp fleshy; enclosing a single erect seed. Seed shining, the hilum at the base. [Greek, ox [large] ash.]

About 35 species, natives of America. Besides the following, some 10 others occur in the southern and southwestern United States. Type species: *Bumelia retùsa* Sw.

Foliage, pedicels and calyx glabrous or very nearly so.　　　　　1. *B. lycioides.*
Foliage, pedicels and calyx tomentose-pubescent.　　　　　　　2. *B. lanuginosa.*

1. Bumelia lycioìdes (L.) Pers. Southern or Carolina Buckthorn. Fig. 3305.

Sideroxylon lycioides L. Sp. Pl. Ed. 2, 279. 1762.

Bumelia lycioides Pers. Syn. 1 : 237. 1805.

A shrub or small tree with maximum height of about 40° and trunk diameter of about 6', the bark gray, the twigs commonly spiny. Leaves rather firm, tardily deciduous, glabrous on both sides; finely reticulate-veined, oblong, elliptic, or oblanceolate, acute or acuminate at both ends, rarely obtuse at the apex, 2'–5' long, ¼'–1½' wide; petioles 2''–6'' long; flowers about 1½'' broad, numerous in the dense axillary clusters; pedicels about the length of the petioles, glabrous; calyx-segments obtuse, glabrous; staminodia ovate, boat-shaped, entire; berry subglobose, black, 4''–5'' long.

In moist thickets, Virginia to Illinois and Missouri, south to Florida and Texas. Wood hard, yellowish-brown; weight about 46 lbs. per cubic foot. Bumelia. Iron- or chittim-wood. Mock orange. Coma. June–Aug.

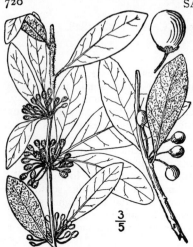

2. Bumelia lanuginòsa (Michx.) Pers.
Woolly Buckthorn. Fig. 3306.

Sideroxylon lanuginosum Michx. Fl. Bor. Am. 1: 122. 1803.
Bumelia lanuginosa Pers. Syn. 1: 237. 1805.

A shrub or tree, sometimes reaching a height of 60° and a trunk diameter of 3°, the twigs usually spiny. Leaves persistent, rather coriaceous, glabrous above, densely tomentose-pubescent beneath, oblanceolate, obovate or oblong, usually obtuse at the apex, narrowed or cuneate at the base, 1½′–3′ long, ¼′–1′ wide; petioles 2″–6″ long; flowers 3–18 in the fascicles, about 1½″ broad; pedicels tomentose, longer than the petioles; calyx-segments ovate, tomentose, obtusish; staminodia ovate, obscurely toothed; berry oval or globose, black, 4″–5″ long.

In woods and thickets, Illinois to Kansas, Georgia, Florida and Texas. Wood soft, weak, yellowish-brown; weight per cubic foot 41 lbs. Shittim-wood. Black haw. Gum-elastic. June–July.

Family 10. EBENÀCEAE Vent. Tabl. 2: 443. 1779.
EBONY FAMILY.

Trees or shrubs with very hard wood, alternate entire exstipulate leaves, and dioecious polygamous or rarely perfect regular flowers, solitary or cymose in the axils. Calyx inferior, 3–7-lobed, commonly accrescent and persistent. Corolla gamopetalous, deciduous, 3–7-lobed, the lobes usually convolute in the bud. Stamens 2–4 times as many as the lobes of the corolla in the sterile flowers, and inserted on its tube, usually some imperfect ones in the pistillate flowers; filaments short; anthers introrse, narrow, erect. Disk none. Ovary superior, several-celled, in the staminate flowers rudimentary or none; ovules 1–3 in each cavity, suspended; styles 2–8, distinct, or united below; stigmas terminal, sometimes 2-parted. Fruit a berry, containing several seeds, or but one. Seeds oblong, compressed or globose, the testa bony; endosperm copious, cartilaginous; embryo small, usually straight; cotyledons large, foliaceous.

About 6 genera and 275 species, mostly of tropical distribution.

1. DIOSPỲROS L. Sp. Pl. 1057. 1753.

Trees or shrubs, with broad leaves and lateral cymose racemose or solitary flowers, the pistillate commonly solitary, the staminate usually clustered. Calyx 4-6-cleft, enlarging in fruit. Corolla urceolate in our species, 4-6-lobed. Stamens 8–20 in the sterile flowers, few or several and mostly imperfect or none in the pistillate ones. Styles 2–6 in the pistillate flowers; ovary globose or ovoid, its cavities twice as many as the styles. Ovary rudimentary in the sterile flowers. Berry large, pulpy. Seeds 4–12, flat, oblong. [Greek, Zeus' wheat.]

About 160 species, abundant in Asia. Type species: *Diospyros Lotus* L.

1. Diospyros virginiàna L. Persimmon.
Date-plum. Lotus-tree. Fig. 3307.

Diospyros virginiana L. Sp. Pl. 1057. 1753.

A tree with maximum height of about 100° and trunk diameter of 2°, usually much smaller; bark hard, dark, furrowed. Leaves ovate or oval deciduous, pubescent when young, becoming glabrous, acute or acuminate, narrowed, rounded or subcordate at the base, dark green above, pale beneath, 2′–5′ long; petioles 3″–10″ long, loosely jointed with the twigs, the leaves falling away in drying; flowers mostly 4-parted; corolla greenish yellow, that of fertile flowers 5″–7″ long, about twice as large as that of the sterile; stamens of sterile flowers about 16, those of pistillate 8 or fewer; fruit globose, about 1′ long, reddish yellow and sweet when ripe, astringent when green, ripening after frost in the northern states.

In fields and woods, Connecticut to Iowa, Kansas, Florida and Texas. Wood hard, brown; weight per cubic foot 49 lbs. Jove's-fruit. Winter- or seeded-plum. Possum-wood. May–June. Fruit Sept.–Nov.

Family 11. **SYMPLOCÀCEAE** Miers; Lindl. Veg. Kingd. Ed. 3, 593. 1853.

SWEET-LEAF FAMILY.

Trees or shrubs, with entire or dentate broad leaves, and small or middle-sized regular mostly yellow and perfect flowers, in lateral or axillary clusters. Calyx-tube completely or partly adnate to the ovary, its limb 5-lobed, the lobes imbricated in the bud. Corolla 5-parted, sometimes very nearly to the base, the segments imbricated. Disk none. Stamens numerous in several series, inserted on the base or tube of the corolla; filaments filiform, usually slightly united in clusters at the base of each corolla-segment; anthers innate, laterally dehiscent. Ovary 2–5-celled, inferior or partly superior; ovules commonly 2 in each cavity, pendulous; style one; stigma one. Fruit a small mostly nearly dry drupe, usually with 1 oblong seed; embryo straight; endosperm fleshy.

Only the following genus, comprising about 200 species, natives of America, Asia and Australasia, most abundant in South America. The following is the only known North American species.

1. **SÝMPLOCOS** Jacq. Enum. Pl. Carib. 5, 24. 1760.

Characters of the family. Type species: *Symplocos martinicensis* Jacq. [Greek, connected, referring to the stamens.]

1. **Symplocos tinctòria** (L.) L'Her. Sweet-leaf. Horse-sugar. Fig. 3308.

Hopea tinctoria L. Mant. 105. 1767.

S. tinctoria L'Her. Trans. Linn. Soc. 1 : 176. 1791.

$\frac{2}{3}$

A shrub or small tree, sometimes attaining a height of 35° and a trunk diameter of 9′. Leaves rather coriaceous, oblong or slightly obovate, acute or acuminate at both ends, crenate-serrate with low teeth or repand, short-petioled, puberulent or pubescent on both sides when young, glabrous or nearly so above and dark green when old, pale and persistently pubescent beneath, 3′–6′ long, 1′–3′ wide, deciduous at the northern range of the species, persistent at the south, turning yellowish-green in drying; flowers bright yellow, fragrant, 4″–6″ broad, in sessile scaly-bracted clusters, appearing at the north before the leaves; corolla almost polypetalous, its segments oblong, obtuse, each bearing a cluster of stamens; drupe dry, nut-like, oblong, 3″–6″ long, pubescent, crowned with the small calyx lobes.

Woods and thickets, Delaware to Florida, Arkansas and Louisiana. Wood soft, weak, pale red or white; weight per cubic foot 33 lbs. Yellow wood. Florida laurel. Dye-leaves. March–April.

Family 12. **STYRACÀCEAE** A. DC. Prodr. 8: 244. 1844.

STORAX FAMILY.

Trees or shrubs, with alternate exstipulate leaves. Flowers regular, perfect, or rarely polygamo-dioecious, clustered, sometimes appearing before the leaves. Pubescence mostly stellate. Calyx more or less adnate to the ovary, 4–8-toothed, or entire. Corolla gamopetalous or polypetalous, the lobes or petals 4–8. Stamens twice as many as the lobes of the corolla or petals, or more, inserted on its tube or base, arranged in 1 series, the filaments monadelphous or 4–5-adelphous; anthers mostly introrse. Disk none. Ovary partly superior, 2–5-celled; ovules solitary or few in each cavity, anatropous; style slender; stigma simple or 2–5-lobed. Fruit a berry or drupe, or often nearly dry, winged in some genera, 1-seeded, or 2–5-celled with a seed in each cavity. Endosperm copious, fleshy; embryo usually straight; cotyledons flat.

About 7 genera and 75 species, mostly tropical, most abundant in South America.

Calyx superior, its tube obconic; fruit 2–4-winged.   1. *Halesia.*
Calyx nearly inferior, its tube campanulate; fruit globose or oblong.   2. *Styrax.*

1. HALESIA Ellis; L. Syst. Ed. 10, 2: 1044. 1759.

[MOHRODENDRON Britton, Gard. & For. **6**: 463. 1893.]

Small trees or shrubs, more or less stellate-pubescent, with membranous deciduous denticulate or dentate petioled leaves, and large white slender-pedicelled drooping bell-shaped flowers, in lateral fascicles or short racemes, appearing with or before the leaves. Calyx-tube obconic or obpyramidal, 4–5-ribbed, adnate to the ovary, the limb short, 4-toothed. Corolla campanulate, 4–5-cleft or 4–5-parted nearly to the base. Stamens 8–16; filaments flat, more or less monadelphous, slightly adnate to the corolla; anthers oblong. Ovary 2–4-celled; ovules about 4 in each cavity, the lower ascending, the upper pendulous. Fruit dry, oblong, 2–4-winged longitudinally, 1–4-celled, tipped with the style and the minute calyx-teeth, the seed cylindric. [In honor of Stephen Hales, 1677–1761, a distinguished English scientist.]

Three species, natives of southeastern North America, the following typical.

1. Halesia carolina L.   Silver-bell or Snow-drop Tree.   Fig. 3309.

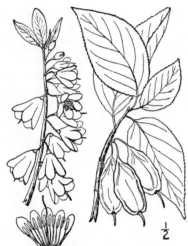

Halesia carolina L. Syst. Ed. 10, 1044. 1759.
Halesia tetraptera L. Sp. Pl. Ed. 2, 636. 1762.
Mohrodendron carolinum Britton, Gard. & For. **6**: 463. 1893.

A small tree with maximum height of about 45° and trunk diameter of about 20'. Leaves oval, ovate or ovate-oblong, denticulate, acuminate at the apex, mostly narrowed at the base, dark green and glabrous above when old, pale green and stellate-pubescent beneath, 2'–6' long, 1'–3' wide; flowers in lateral fascicles of 1–5 appearing with the leaves; pedicels filiform, ½'–1½' long; calyx at flowering time about 2″ long; corolla 6″–9″ long; ovary 4-celled; fruit oblong-ellipsoid, 4-winged, 1'–1½' long, usually longer than its pedicel, several times longer than the persistent style.

In woods and along streams, Virginia to Illinois, south to Florida and Alabama. Wood soft, light brown; weight per cubic foot 35 lbs. Calico-wood. Shittim- or Tiss-wood. Bell- or wild olive-tree. March–April.

2. STYRAX [Tourn.] L. Sp. Pl. 444. 1753.

Shrubs or small trees, with alternate leaves, deciduous in our species, and rather large mostly with drooping flowers, in lateral or terminal fascicles or leafy racemes, appearing before or with the leaves. Calyx persistent, nearly inferior, its tube campanulate, adnate to the lower part of the ovary, its limb minutely 5-toothed. Corolla 5-parted or 5-divided, the segments or petals imbricate, convolute or valvate in the bud. Stamens twice as many as the corolla lobes or petals (rarely fewer); filaments flat, monadelphous below or rarely separate, inserted on the base of the corolla; anthers linear. Ovary nearly superior, mostly 3-celled at the base; ovules several in each cavity, ascending; stigma 3-toothed, 3-lobed or capitate. Fruit globose or oblong, nearly dry, coriaceous or crustaceous, commonly only 1-seeded, 3-valved at the summit. [Greek name of Storax.]

About 75 species, natives of America, Asia and southern Europe. Besides the following, 2 others occur in the southern and western United States. Type species: *Styrax officinalis* L.

Foliage and inflorescence glabrous; calyx glandular-scurfy.   1. *S. americana.*
Lower surfaces of the leaves and inflorescence canescent or tomentose.
    Leaves oblong or oval, 1'–2½' long.   2. *S. pulverulenta.*
    Leaves obovate or oval, 2'–6' long.   3. *S. grandifolia.*

1. Styrax americàna Lam. Smooth Storax. Fig. 3310.

Styrax americana Lam. Encycl. 1 : 82. 1783.

A shrub 4°-10° high, the foliage glabrous or very nearly so throughout. Leaves green on both sides, oblong, oval or obovate, acute or obtuse at the apex, narrowed at the base, entire, or toothed, 1'-3' long, $\frac{1}{2}$'-1$\frac{1}{2}$' wide; petioles 2''-4'' long, often scurfy when young; flowers few in the mostly short racemes or sometimes solitary, 4''-7'' long, about the length of their pedicels; calyx and pedicels glandular-dotted; petals oblong-lanceolate, acute, puberulent on the outer surface or glabrous, valvate or but slightly overlapping in the bud; fruit sub-globose, puberulent, about 3'' in diameter.

In moist thickets and along streams, Virginia to Florida, Illinois, Missouri, Arkansas and Louisiana. Spring-orange. March–April.

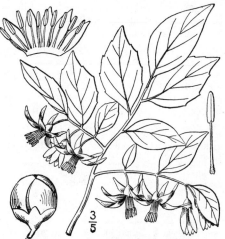

2. Styrax pulverulénta Michx. Downy Storax. Fig. 3311.

Styrax pulverulenta Michx. Fl. Bor. Am. **2** : 41. 1803.

Similar to the preceding species, but the lower surfaces of the leaves, the calyx and pedicels are densely stellate-pubescent or scurfy. Leaves oval or oblong, usually acute at each end and denticulate, short-petioled, 1'-2$\frac{1}{2}$' long, pale beneath; flowers in short terminal racemes and often in pairs in the axils, 4''-7'' long, usually longer than their pedicels; petals oblong-lanceolate, acute, puberulent on both sides or only on the exterior, convolute or imbricated in the bud; fruit globose, puberulent, about 3'' in diameter.

In moist woods and thickets, Virginia to Florida, Arkansas and Texas March–April.

3. Styrax grandifòlia Ait. Large-leaved Storax. Fig. 3312.

Styrax grandifolia Ait. Hort. Kew. **2** : 75. 1789.

A shrub, 5°-12° high. Leaves obovate or oval, dentate, denticulate or entire, short-petioled, tomentose or canescent and pale beneath, green and glabrous above, 2'-6' long, or on young shoots much larger; flowers 5''-8'' long, longer than their pedicels, mostly several in loose sometimes elongated racemes; rachis, pedicels and calyx stellate-tomentose; petals oblong, acutish, imbricated or convolute in the bud, puberulent without and often also within; fruit obovoid, puberulent, about 4'' long.

In woods, Virginia to Florida and Alabama. Mock-orange. March–May.

Family 13. OLEÀCEAE Lindl. Nat. Syst. 1830.

OLIVE FAMILY.

Trees or shrubs (a few genera almost herbaceous) with opposite or rarely alternate simple or pinnate exstipulate entire or dentate leaves and regular perfect polygamous or dioecious, 2–4-parted flowers in terminal or axillary panicles, cymes or fascicles. Calyx inferior, free from the ovary, usually small, sometimes none. Corolla gamopetalous, polypetalous, or none. Stamens 2–4, usually 2, inserted on the corolla; filaments usually short, separate; anthers mostly large, ovate, oblong or linear, 2-celled, the sacs longitudinally dehiscent. Ovary superior, 2-celled; ovules few in each cavity, anatropous or amphitropous; style usually short or none, rarely elongated. Fruit a capsule, samara, berry or drupe. Seeds erect or pendulous; endosperm fleshy, horny or wanting; embryo straight, rather large; cotyledons flat, or plano-convex; radicle usually short.

About 21 genera and 525 species, of wide distribution in temperate and tropical regions.

Fruit a loculicidal capsule; leaves simple; flowers complete. 1. *Syringa.*
Fruit a samara; leaves pinnate; flowers dioecious or polygamous. 2. *Fraxinus.*
Fruit a drupe or berry; leaves simple.
  Flowers dioecious, apetalous, from catkin-like scaly buds. 3. *Forestiera.*
  Flowers complete, polypetalous, paniculate; petals linear. 4. *Chionanthus.*
  Flowers complete, gamopetalous, paniculate. 5. *Ligustrum.*

1. SYRÍNGA L. Sp. Pl. 9. 1753.

Shrubs with opposite entire (rarely pinnatifid) leaves, and completely gamopetalous flowers, in dense terminal panicles or thyrses. Calyx campanulate, mostly 4-toothed, persistent. Corolla salverform, the tube cylindric, the limb 4-lobed, the lobes induplicate-valvate. Stamens 2, inserted near the summit of the corolla-tube; filaments short or slender; anthers ovate or oblong. Ovary 2-celled; ovules 2 in each cavity, pendulous; style elongated; stigma 2-cleft. Capsule narrowly oblong, somewhat compressed, coriaceous, loculicidally 2-valved from above, the valves concave. Seeds pendulous, compressed, obliquely winged. [Greek, a pipe, or tube.]

About 12 species, natives of Asia and eastern Europe, the following typical.

1. Syringa vulgàris L. Lilac. Fig. 3313.

Syringa vulgaris L. Sp. Pl. 9. 1753.

A glabrous shrub, 10°–25° high with terete branches. Leaves ovate, entire, deciduous, green on both sides, acuminate at the apex, truncate or subcordate at the base, 2′–5′ long, 1′–3′ wide; petioles ½′–1′ long; flowers lilac or white, very numerous, 5″–7″ long, 4″–5″ broad, in large terminal thyrses; calyx about 1″ long; corolla-tube about 1″ in diameter; ultimate pedicels short; capsule 8″–12″ long, 2″ thick.

Escaped from gardens to roadsides, Maine and New Hampshire to eastern New York and Pennsylvania. Native of eastern Europe. Pipe-tree. Pipe-privets. Blue-pipe. Blue-ash. Roman-willow. Flowers fragrant. April–May.

2. FRÁXINUS [Tourn.] L. Sp. Pl. 1057. 1753.

Trees, with opposite and in all our species odd-pinnate leaves, and small dioecious or polygamous (rarely perfect) greenish fasciculate or racemose-fasciculate flowers, appearing before or with the leaves from the axils of those of the previous season. Calyx small, 4-cleft, irregularly toothed, entire or none. Petals none or 2–4, separate, or united in pairs at the base, induplicate-valvate. Stamens 2 (rarely 3 or 4), inserted on the base of the petals or hypogynous; filaments short or elongated; anthers ovate, oblong or linear. Ovules 2 in each cavity of the ovary, pendulous; stigma 2-cleft. Fruit a flat samara, winged at the apex only or all around, usually 1-seeded. Seed oblong, pendulous. [The ancient Latin name.]

About 50 species, mostly of the north temperate zone. Besides the following, about 12 others occur in the Southern and Western States. Type species: *Fraxinus excelsior* L.

Lateral leaflets stalked; calyx mostly present, at least in the fertile flowers.
Body of the samara terete or nearly so, the wing chiefly terminal.
  Wing almost entirely terminal; leaves pale beneath.
    Twigs and leaves glabrous, or leaves pubescent beneath. 1. *F. americana.*
    Twigs and leaves densely pubescent. 2. *F. biltmoreana.*
  Wing manifestly extending down on the sides of the body.
    Wing of the samara long-linear, about 2″ wide. 3. *F. Darlingtonii.*
    Wing of the samara spatulate or oblong-spatulate, mostly 3″–5″ wide.
      Samara-body terete, slender.
      Samaras broadly spatulate; leaves firm, entire. *F. Michauxii.*

Samaras narrowly spatulate ; leaves thin, serrate or entire.   5. *F. pennsylvanica.*
Samara-body compressed ; leaflets entire.   6. *F. profunda.*
Body of the samara flat, the wing extending all around it.
Twigs terete ; leaflets 5–7 ; samara elliptic or spatulate.   7. *F. caroliniana.*
Twigs 4-sided ; leaflets 7–11 ; samara oblong or cuneate.   8. *F. quadrangulata.*
Lateral leaflets sessile ; calyx none ; samara winged all around.   9. *F. nigra.*

1. Fraxinus americàna L.   White Ash. Cane Ash.   Fig. 3314.

Fraxinus americana L. Sp. Pl. 1057. 1753.

A large forest tree, reaching a maximum height of about 130° and a trunk diameter of 6°. Twigs, petioles and rachis of the leaves glabrous; leaflets 5–9 (commonly 7), ovate, ovate-lanceolate, oblong or rarely slightly obovate, stalked, entire or denticulate, dark green above, pale or light green and often pubescent beneath, 3′–5′ long, 1′–2′ wide, acuminate or acute at the apex, mostly rounded at the base; flowers dioecious (rarely monoecious), the calyx of the pistillate present and persistent; anthers linear-oblong; samara 1′–2′ long, its body terete, not margined, winged only from near the summit, one-fourth to one-half the length of the linear-oblong or lanceolate wing.

In rich woods, Nova Scotia to Ontario, Minnesota, Florida, Kansas and Texas. Wood heavy, hard, strong, brown ; weight per cubic foot 41 lbs. April–June.

⅖

2. Fraxinus biltmoreàna Beadle.   Biltmore Ash.   Fig. 3315.

F. biltmoreana Beadle, Bot. Gaz. **25** : 358. 1898.

Similar to *Fraxinus americana,* becoming at least 60° high, but the young twigs, petioles and leaf-rachis densely pubescent or tomentose. Leaflets 7–9, stalked, ovate to oblong-lanceolate, entire-margined, or obscurely dentate, dark green and somewhat shining above, pale and more or less pubescent beneath; samara 1½′–2′ long, the narrow terminal wing 2–4 times as long as the oblong nearly terete plump body and but little decurrent upon it.

Woodlands and river-banks, Pennsylvania to Georgia. April–May.

½

3. Fraxinus Darlingtònii Britton.   Darlington's Ash.   Fig. 3316.

F. Darlingtonii Britton, Man. 725. 1901.

A tree, attaining a height of 70° or more, the twigs smooth or velvety, the twigs sometimes remaining velvety until the close of the growing season. Leaflets 5–7, ovate to oblong-ovate, usually denticulate, glabrous, or pubescent beneath, stalked, acute or acuminate, 3′ long or less; samara narrowly linear, not spatulate, 2′–3′ long, about 2″ wide, the narrow wing decurrent on the slender, terete, seed-bearing part only to about its middle.

Hillsides, river-banks and wet woods, Massachusetts to New York, Alabama and Louisiana. Wood hard, brown, strong. April–June.

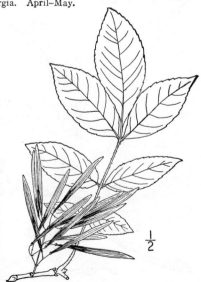

½

½

5. Fraxinus pennsylvánica Marsh. Green, Red, Blue or Black Ash. Fig. 3318.

Fraxinus pennsylvanica Marsh. Arb. Am. 51. 1785.
Fraxinus pubescens Lam. Encycl. 2: 548. 1786.
Fraxinus lanceolata Borck. Handb. Forst. Bot. 1: 826. 1800.
Fraxinus viridis Michx. f. Hist. Arb. Am. 3: 115. pl. 10. 1813.

A tree with maximum height of about 65° and trunk diameter of 3°, glabrous or nearly so throughout, or the twigs and leaves more or less pubescent, sometimes densely so. Leaflets 5-9, stalked, entire or denticulate, ovate or oblong-lanceolate, acuminate or acute at the apex, mostly narrowed at the base, green on both sides, 2′-6′ long, 1′-2′ wide; flowers dioecious, the calyx of the pistillate persistent; anthers linear-oblong; samara 1′-2′ long, the usually spatulate wing decurrent on the sides of the body sometimes to below the middle.

4. Fraxinus Michaùxii Britton. Michaux's Ash. Fig. 3317.

Fraxinus Michauxii Britton, Man. Ed. 2, 1075. 1905.

A tree, attaining a height of 40° or more, the bark rough and fissured, the young twigs glabrous or velvety. Leaflets 5-9, stalked, firm in texture, oblong-lanceolate, entire-margined, or slightly undulate, 4′-5′ long, 1′-2½′ wide, acute, dark green above, pale green, and more or less pubescent, at least on the veins beneath; flowers dioecious; samara broadly spatulate, 1½′-2′ long, 4″-5″ wide, the thick blunt or notched wing as long as or longer than the linear, nearly round body and decurrent upon it to or about the middle.

Wet grounds, southern New York to Indiana and North Carolina. April-May.

⅖

Moist soil, New Brunswick to Minnesota, Florida and Texas. Wood hard, strong, brown; weight per cubic foot 44 lbs. Water-, swamp- or river-ash. April-May.

Fraxinus campéstris Britton, with the lateral leaflets sessile, is a similar tree of the western plains, ranging eastward into Kansas.

6. Fraxinus profùnda Bush. Pumpkin Ash. Fig. 3319.

Fraxinus americana profunda Bush, Ann. Rep. Mo. Bot. Gard. 5: 147. 1894.
Fraxinus profunda Bush; Britton, Man. 725. 1901.

A tree up to 120° high, the thick bark gray and fissured, the young twigs velvety or smooth. Leaves large; leaflets 7-9, ovate-lanceolate to oblong-lanceolate, stalked, acuminate at the apex, bright green above, paler and pubescent or velvety beneath, 10′ long or less, the margins entire or nearly so; samara linear-oblong or slightly spatulate, 2′-3′ long, 4″-6″ broad, the rather thick, often notched wing longer than the linear, flattened seed-bearing part, and decurrent upon it to or below the middle.

In swamps, Virginia to western New York. Illinois, Missouri, Florida and Arkansas. April-May.

½

7. Fraxinus caroliniàna Mill.   Water or Carolina Ash. Fig. 3320.

F. caroliniana Mill. Dict. Ed. 8, no. 6. 1768.
F. platycarpa Michx. Fl. Bor. Am. **2**: 256. 1803.

A small tree, rarely over 40° high, the trunk reaching about 1° in diameter, with terete twigs and glabrous or slightly pubescent foliage. Leaflets 5–7 (rarely 9), ovate, ovate-lanceolate or oblong, acuminate or acute at the apex, narrowed, or the lower ones rounded at the base, long-stalked (4″–8″), sharply serrate, serrulate or sometimes entire, 2′–5′ long, $\frac{1}{2}$–$1\frac{1}{2}$′ wide; flowers dioecious, the calyx of the pistillate persistent; anthers linear-oblong; samara 1′–2′ long, 4″–9″ wide, elliptic or spatulate, the body linear, flat, broadly winged all around, extending more than half way to the apex of the fruit, the wing pinnately veined; samaras sometimes 3-winged.

In swamps and wet soil, southeastern Virginia to Florida, Missouri, Arkansas and Texas. Also in Cuba. Wood light, soft, weak, yellowish white; weight per cubic foot 22 lbs. Pop- or poppy-ash. March–April.

8. Fraxinus quadrangulàta Michx. Blue Ash. Fig. 3321.

Fraxinus quadrangulata Michx. Fl. Bor. Am. **2**: 255. 1803.

A large forest tree, sometimes becoming 110° high, the trunk reaching 3° in diameter, the twigs 4-sided, the foliage glabrous, or sparingly pubescent when young. Leaflets 7–11, ovate, oblong or lanceolate, acuminate at the apex, rounded or narrowed at the base, short-stalked (2″–3″), green on both sides, sharply serrate or serrulate, 3′–5′ long, 1′–2′ wide; flowers dioecious, the calyx of the pistillate ones obsolete; anthers linear-oblong; samara linear-oblong or cuneate, 1′–2′ long, 3″–7″ wide, winged all around, parallel-nerved, the body extending more than half-way to the apex.

In woods, Ontario, Minnesota and Michigan to Alabama, Iowa and Arkansas. Wood heavy, hard, not strong, yellowish brown; weight per cubic foot 47 lbs. March–April.

9. Fraxinus nìgra Marsh. Black or Brown Ash. Hoop Ash. Fig. 3322.

Fraxinus nigra Marsh. Arb. Am. **51**. 1785.
Fraxinus sambucifolia Lam. Encycl. **2**: 549. 1786.

A swamp tree, reaching a maximum height of about 100° and trunk diameter of 3°, the twigs terete, the foliage glabrous, except the midrib of the lower surfaces of the leaflets. Leaflets 7–11, sessile, green on both sides, oblong-lanceolate, long-acuminate at the apex, narrowed or rounded at the base, sharply serrate or serrulate, 3′–6′ long, 9″–18″ wide; flowers dioecious; calyx none; anthers short-oblong; samara oblong or linear-oblong, parallel-nerved, 1′–1$\frac{1}{2}$′ long, 3″–4″ wide, the body flat, winged all around, extending to or beyond the middle.

In swamps and wet woods, Newfoundland to Manitoba, south to Virginia, Illinois and Arkansas. Wood heavy, soft, not strong, dark brown; weight per cubic foot 39 lbs. April–May. Swamp-, basket- or water-ash.

3. FORESTIÈRA Poir. in Lam. Encycl. Suppl. 2: 664. 1811.

[ADELIA P. Br. Civ. & Nat. Hist. Jam. 361, hyponym. 1756.]

Shrubs with opposite simple serrulate or entire deciduous or persistent leaves (punctate in some southern species), and small yellow or greenish dioecious or polygamous flowers, fascicled, short-racemose or paniculate from scaly buds produced at the axils of the preceding season, appearing before or with the leaves. Calyx wanting, obsolete, or minute and 4-toothed or 4-parted. Corolla wanting, or of 1 or 2 small deciduous petals. Stamens 2–4; anthers ovate or oblong. Ovary ovoid, 2-celled; ovules 2 in each cell, pendulous; style slender; stigma 2-lobed. Fruit an oblong or subglobose drupe with 1 or rarely 2 seeds. [In honor of Charles Le Forestier, a French physician.]

About 15 species, natives of America. Besides the following, which is the type species, about 7 others occur in the southern and southwestern United States.

½

1. Forestiera acuminàta (Michx.) Poir. Adelia. Fig. 3323.

Adelia acuminata Michx. Fl. Bor. Am. **2**: 225. *pl. 48.* 1803.
Forestiera acuminata Poir. in Lam. Encycl. Suppl. **2**: 664. 1811.

A shrub or small tree, sometimes reaching a height of 30° and a trunk diameter of 8′, the branches somewhat spiny, the foliage glabrous. Leaves ovate, lanceolate or oblong, acuminate or acute at both ends, finely denticulate, 1′–4′ long, ½′–2′ wide; petioles slender, 4″–12″ long; staminate flowers fascicled; pistillate flowers short-paniculate; calyx obsolete; drupe narrowly oblong when mature, about ½′ long, when young fusiform and often curved.

River-banks, Indiana to Georgia, west to Missouri, Arkansas and Texas. Wood heavy, soft, not strong, yellowish brown; weight per cubic foot 40 lbs. March–April.

4. CHIONÁNTHUS L. Sp. Pl. 8. 1753.

Shrubs or small trees, with opposite simple entire leaves, and complete conspicuous white flowers, in large loose panicles from the axils of the upper leaves of the preceding season. Calyx small, 4-cleft or 4-parted, inferior, persistent. Corolla of 4 linear petals, slightly united at the very base, their margins slightly induplicate in the bud. Stamens 2 (rarely 3), inserted on the base of the corolla; filaments very short. Ovules 2 in each cavity of the ovary, pendulous; style short; stigma thick, emarginate or slightly 2-lobed. Fruit an oblong or ovoid usually 1-seeded drupe. [Greek, snow-blossom.]

About 3 species, the following typical one of southeastern North America, the others Chinese.

1. Chionanthus virgínica L. Fringe-tree. Fig. 3324.

Chionanthus virginica L. Sp. Pl. 8. 1753.

A shrub, or small tree, reaching a maximum height of about 35° and trunk diameter of about 8′, the young twigs, petioles and lower surfaces of the leaves pubescent, or sometimes glabrate. Leaves oval, oblong or some of them obovate, rather thick, acute, short-acuminate to obtuse at the apex, narrowed at the base, 3′–6′ long, 1′–3′ wide; the blade more or less decurrent on the petiole; panicles drooping, sometimes 10′ long, usually with some sessile oblong leaf-like bracts, its branches and the pedicels very slender; petals 1′ long or more, 1″ wide or less; drupe oblong or globose-oblong, nearly black, 5″–8″ long, the pulp thin.

In moist thickets, New Jersey and southern Pennsylvania to Florida, Missouri and Texas. Ascends to 2500 ft. in North Carolina. Wood heavy, hard, light brown; weight per cubic foot 40 lbs. Poison-, white- or flowering-ash. White- or American-fringe. Snow-flower-tree. Shavings. Old-man's beard. Gray-beard-tree. May–June.

½

5. LIGÚSTRUM [Tourn.] L. Sp. Pl. 7. 1753.

Shrubs or small trees, with opposite entire simple leaves, and small white complete flowers in terminal thyrses or panicles. Calyx small, truncate or 4-toothed, inferior. Corolla gamopetalous, funnelform, its tube mostly short, the limb 4-lobed, the lobes induplicate-valvate in the bud. Stamens 2, inserted on the tube of the corolla; filaments short. Ovary 2-celled; ovules 2 in each cavity, pendulous; style short or slender; stigma thickened. Fruit a 1–3-seeded mostly globose berry. [The classical Latin name.]

About 35 species, natives of the Old World, the following typical.

1. Ligustrum vulgàre L. Privet. Prim. Fig. 3325.

Ligustrum vulgare L. Sp. Pl. 7. 1753.

A shrub, 6°–10° high, the branches long and slender. Leaves firm, tardily deciduous, glabrous, lanceolate or oblong, acute or obtuse at the apex, narrowed at the base, short-petioled, 9″–2′ long, 3″–7″ wide, obscurely veined; panicles dense, short, minutely pubescent; flowers white, about 3″ broad; pedicels very short; stamens included; berries globose, black, 2″–3″ in diameter.

In thickets and along roadsides, escaped from cultivation, Maine and Massachusetts to Ontario, western New York, Pennsylvania and North Carolina. Native of Europe and Asia. Used for hedges. June–July. Old English names, primwort, print, skedge, skedgwith.

$\frac{3}{5}$

Family 14. LOGANIÀCEAE Dumort. Anal. Fam. 21. 1829.

LOGANIA FAMILY.

Herbs, shrubs, vines or some tropical genera trees, with opposite or verticillate simple stipulate leaves, or the leaf-bases connected by a stipular line or membrane, and regular perfect 4–5-parted mostly cymose or spicate flowers. Calyx inferior, the tube campanulate, sometimes short or none, the segments imbricated, at least in the bud. Corolla gamopetalous, funnelform, campanulate, or rarely rotate. Stamens as many as the lobes of the corolla, alternate with them, inserted on the tube or throat; anthers 2-celled, the sacs longitudinally dehiscent; pollen-grains simple. Disk usually none. Ovary superior, 2-celled (rarely 3–5-celled); style simple, 2–5-cleft or 2-divided, rarely 4-cleft; ovules numerous or few in each cavity, anatropous or amphitropous. Fruit a 2-valved capsule in our species. Seeds winged or wingless; embryo small, usually straight; endosperm copious; cotyledons narrow or foliaceous; radicle terete or conic.

About 30 genera and 400 species, widely distributed in warm and tropical regions.

Style 4-cleft; woody vine; flowers large, yellow.   1. *Gelsemium.*
Style simple, 2-lobed or 2-divided with a common stigma; herbs.
  Corolla-lobes valvate; capsule didymous or 2-lobed; leaves broad.
    Style simple, jointed; spike simple.   2. *Spigelia.*
    Style 2-divided below; spikes cymose.   3. *Cynoctonum.*
  Corolla-lobes imbricate; capsule subglobose; leaves linear.   4. *Polypremum.*

1. GELSÈMIUM Juss. Gen. 150. 1789.

Glabrous twining woody vines; leaves opposite, or rarely ternate, their bases connected by a stipular line, the very small stipules deciduous; flowers large, yellow, in axillary and terminal nearly sessile cymes, the pedicels scaly-bracteolate. Calyx deeply 5-parted, the segments dry, imbricated. Corolla funnelform, with 5 broad lobes imbricated in the bud. Stamens 5, inserted on the tube of the corolla; anthers linear-oblong. Ovary oblong, 2-celled; style slender or filiform, 4-cleft, the lobes stigmatic along the inner side; ovules numerous in each cavity, on linear placentae. Capsule elliptic, flattened contrary to the partition, septicidally dehiscent, the valves boat-shaped, 2-cleft at the summit; seeds several in each cell, flattened, winged. [From the Italian Gelsomino, the Jessamine.]

Two known species, the following typical one of the southeastern United States, the other of eastern Asia.

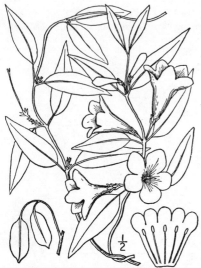

1. Gelsemium sempérvirens (L.) Ait. f. Yellow Jessamine. Carolina Jasmine. Fig. 3326.

Bignonia sempervirens L. Sp. Pl. 623. 1753.
G. nitidum Michx. Fl. Bor. Am. 1: 120. 1803.
G. sempervirens Ait. f. Hort. Kew. 2: 64. 1811.

Stem slender, climbing or trailing, sometimes 20° long. Leaves lanceolate, oblong-lanceolate or ovate-lanceolate, entire, short-petioled, persistent, evergreen, 1½′–3′ long, 5″–12″ wide; cymes 1–6-flowered; pedicels short; bractlets several, dry, oblong or lanceolate, 1″–2″ long; flowers dimorphous; sepals oblong, obtuse; corolla bright yellow, 1′–1½′ long; stigmas in one form short and anthers exserted, in the other form longer and anthers included; capsule flat, channeled on both sides, 4″–7″ long, cuspidate; seeds very flat, broadly winged at the summit.

In woods and thickets, eastern Virginia to Florida, Texas, Mexico and Guatemala, mostly near the coast. March–Oct. Called also Carolina wild woodbine, and evening trumpet-flower.

2. SPIGÈLIA L. Sp. Pl. 149. 1753.

Herbs, with opposite membranous entire pinnately veined leaves, small stipules, or the leaf-bases connected by a stipular line, and red yellow or purple flowers in scorpioid cymes or unilateral spikes, or terminal and in the forks of the branches. Calyx deeply 5-parted. Corolla narrowly funnelform, 5-lobed, the lobes valvate, the tube finely 15-nerved. Stamens 5, inserted on the corolla-tube; anthers 2-lobed at the base. Ovules numerous, on peltate placentae; style filiform, jointed near the middle, papillose above; stigma obtuse. Capsule didymous, 2-celled, somewhat flattened contrary to the dissepiment, circumscissile above the persistent base, the 2 carpels becoming 2-valved. Seeds peltate, not winged. [Named for Adrian von der Spigel, 1558–1625, physician.]

About 35 species, all American. Besides the following, 4 others occur in the Southern States. Type species: *Spigelia Anthelmia* L.

1. Spigelia marylándica L. Indian or Carolina Pink. Fig. 3327.

Lonicera marylandica L. Sp. Pl. 175. 1753.
Spigelia marylandica L. Syst. Ed. 12, 734. 1767.

Perennial, stem 4-angled, glabrous or very nearly so, simple, or branched at the base, erect, 1°–2° high. Leaves sessile, ovate, or ovate-lanceolate, acute or acuminate at the apex, rounded or narrowed at the base, 2′–4′ long, ½′–2′ wide, sparingly pubescent on the veins beneath; flowers in a solitary (rarely 2 or 3) terminal 1-sided peduncled spike; corolla scarlet outside, yellow within, 1′–2′ long, narrowed below, its lobes lanceolate, about 3″ long; calyx-segments subulate, as long as the corolla-lobes or shorter; style jointed below the middle, exserted or included.

In woods, North Carolina to Kentucky, Ohio, Wisconsin (?), Missouri, Florida and Texas. Erroneously recorded from New Jersey. May–July. Pink-root. Worm-grass. Star-bloom.

3. CYNÓCTONUM J. G. Gmel. Syst. 2: 443. 1791.

[MITRÈOLA R. Br. Prodr. Fl. Nov. Holl. 1: 450. 1810.]

Herbs, our species annual, with opposite entire membranous leaves, and minute stipules, or the leaf-bases connected by a stipular line. Flowers small, whitish, in one-sided spikes forming terminal or axillary cymes. Calyx 5-parted. Corolla urn-shaped, 5-lobed, the lobes valvate in the bud. Stamens 5, included; filaments short; anthers cordate. Ovules numerous, on peltate placentae; style short, 2-divided below, united above by the common stigma, the divisions becoming separate. Capsule 2-lobed at the summit; carpels divaricate, dehiscent along the inner side. Seeds numerous, small, tuberculate. [Greek, dog-killing.]

About 5 species, natives of warm and tropical regions. Type species: *Cynoctonum sessilifolium* J. G. Gmel.

1. Cynoctonum Mitrèola (L.) Britton.
Mitrewort. Fig. 3328.

Ophiorhiza Mitreola L. Sp. Pl. 150. 1753.
Anonymos petiolata Walt. Fl. Car. 108. 1788.
Cynoctonum petiolatum Gmel. Syst. **2**: 443. 1791.
Mitreola petiolata T. & G. Fl. N. A. **2**: 45. 1841.
Cynoctonum Mitreola Britton, Mem. Torr. Club **5**: 258. 1894.

Stem simple, or branched near the base, or sometimes also above, glabrous, slender, erect, terete, 1°–2° high. Leaves lanceolate or ovate, petioled, 1′–3′ long, 3″–1′ wide, acute at both ends, glabrous; cymes terminal and often also in the upper axils, slender-peduncled, the divisions slender, simple or forked; flowers about 1″ broad, numerous, sessile or very nearly so; capsule deeply 2-lobed, compressed, the lobes at length widely diverging, acute, dehiscent by a slit in the ventral suture near the summit.

In wet or moist soil, Virginia to Florida, Texas and Mexico. Also in the West Indies. June–Sept.

4. POLYPRÈMUM L. Sp. Pl. 111. 1753.

A glabrous diffusely branchel annual herb, with opposite linear-subulate leaves, their bases connected by a stipular membrane, and small white flowers in terminal bracted cymes. Calyx deeply 4-parted (rarely 5-parted), the segments subulate, scarious-margined below. Corolla rotate-campanulate, bearded in the throat, shorter than the calyx, 4-lobed (rarely 5-lobed), the lobes imbricated in the bud. Stamens 4 (rarely 5), inserted on the corolla, included; filaments short; anthers ovoid-globose. Ovules numerous in each cavity of the ovary, on oblong placentae; style short; stigma capitate or obscurely 2-lobed. Capsule globose-ovoid, slightly compressed, didymous, loculicidally 2-valved, the carpels at length septicidal. Seeds minute, smooth. [Greek, many-stemmed.]

A monotype, abundant in the warmer parts of America.

1. Polypremum procúmbens L. Polypremum.
Fig. 3329.

Polypremum procumbens L. Sp. Pl. 111. 1753.

Stems tufted, somewhat rigid, 4-angled, spreading on the ground, ascending or erect, usually much branched, 2′–12′ long. Leaves narrowly linear, ½′–1½′ long, ¼″–1″ wide, acute, sessile, minutely rough-toothed on the margins, often with smaller ones fascicled in their axils; flowers solitary, sessile in the forks of the cymes and along their branches, leafy-bracted, the bracts similar to the upper leaves; corolla 1″ or less long; capsule crustaceous, about 1″ in diameter, slightly 2-lobed, the lobes obtuse.

In dry sandy soil, New Jersey and Pennsylvania to Florida, Kentucky, Missouri, Texas and Mexico. Also in the West Indies. Occurs in cultivated fields as a weed. Probably adventive in its northern range. May–Sept.

INDEX OF LATIN GENERA IN VOLUME II.

[Classes and Families in SMALL CAPITALS; genera in Roman; synonyms in *Italics*.]

A CATALOGUE OF SELECTED DOVER BOOKS
IN ALL FIELDS OF INTEREST

A CATALOGUE OF SELECTED DOVER BOOKS
IN ALL FIELDS OF INTEREST

THE NOTEBOOKS OF LEONARDO DA VINCI, edited by J.P. Richter. Extracts from manuscripts reveal great genius; on painting, sculpture, anatomy, sciences, geography, etc. Both Italian and English. 186 ms. pages reproduced, plus 500 additional drawings, including studies for Last Supper, Sforza monument, etc. 860pp. 7⅞ x 10¾. USO 22572-0, 22573-9 Pa., Two vol. set $12.00

ART NOUVEAU DESIGNS IN COLOR, Alphonse Mucha, Maurice Verneuil, Georges Auriol. Full-color reproduction of Combinaisons ornamentales (c. 1900) by Art Nouveau masters. Floral, animal, geometric, interlacings, swashes — borders, frames, spots — all incredibly beautiful. 60 plates, hundreds of designs. 9⅜ x 8¹/₁₆ . 22885-1 Pa. $4.00

GRAPHIC WORKS OF ODILON REDON. All great fantastic lithographs, etchings, engravings, drawings, 209 in all. Monsters, Huysmans, still life work, etc. Introduction by Alfred Werner. 209pp. 9⅛ x 12¼. 21996-8 Pa. $6.00

EXOTIC FLORAL PATTERNS IN COLOR, E.-A. Seguy. Incredibly beautiful full-color pochoir work by great French designer of 20's. Complete Bouquets et frondaisons, Suggestions pour étoffes. Richness must be seen to be believed. 40 plates containing 120 patterns. 80pp. 9⅜ x 12¼. 23041-4 Pa. $6.00

SELECTED ETCHINGS OF JAMES A. McN. WHISTLER, James A. McN. Whistler. 149 outstanding etchings by the great American artist, including selections from the Thames set and two Venice sets, the complete French set, and many individual prints. Introduction and explanatory note on each print by Maria Naylor. 157pp. 9⅜ x 12¼. 23194-1 Pa. $5.00

VISUAL ILLUSIONS: THEIR CAUSES, CHARACTERISTICS, AND APPLICATIONS, Matthew Luckiesh. Thorough description, discussion; shape and size, color, motion; natural illusion. Uses in art and industry. 100 illustrations. 252pp. 21530-X Pa. $2.50

TEN BOOKS ON ARCHITECTURE, Vitruvius. The most important book ever written on architecture. Early Roman aesthetics, technology, classical orders, site selection, all other aspects. Stands behind everything since. Morgan translation. 331pp. 20645-9 Pa. $3.50

THE CODEX NUTTALL. A PICTURE MANUSCRIPT FROM ANCIENT MEXICO, as first edited by Zelia Nuttall. Only inexpensive edition, in full color, of a pre-Columbian Mexican (Mixtec) book. 88 color plates show kings, gods, heroes, temples, sacrifices. New explanatory, historical introduction by Arthur G. Miller. 96pp. 11⅜ x 8½. 23168-2 Pa. $7.50

MOTHER GOOSE'S MELODIES. Facsimile of fabulously rare Munroe and Francis "copyright 1833" Boston edition. Familiar and unusual rhymes, wonderful old woodcut illustrations. Edited by E.F. Bleiler. 128pp. 4½ x 6⅜. 22577-1 Pa. $1.00

MOTHER GOOSE IN HIEROGLYPHICS. Favorite nursery rhymes presented in rebus form for children. Fascinating 1849 edition reproduced in toto, with key. Introduction by E.F. Bleiler. About 400 woodcuts. 64pp. 6⅞ x 5¼. 20745-5 Pa. $1.00

PETER PIPER'S PRACTICAL PRINCIPLES OF PLAIN & PERFECT PRONUNCIATION. Alliterative jingles and tongue-twisters. Reproduction in full of 1830 first American edition. 25 spirited woodcuts. 32pp. 4½ x 6⅜. 22560-7 Pa. $1.00

MARMADUKE MULTIPLY'S MERRY METHOD OF MAKING MINOR MATHEMATICIANS. Fellow to Peter Piper, it teaches multiplication table by catchy rhymes and woodcuts. 1841 Munroe & Francis edition. Edited by E.F. Bleiler. 103pp. 4⅝ x 6.
22773-1 Pa. $1.25
20171-6 Clothbd. $3.00

THE NIGHT BEFORE CHRISTMAS, Clement Moore. Full text, and woodcuts from original 1848 book. Also critical, historical material. 19 illustrations. 40pp. 4⅝ x 6. 22797-9 Pa. $1.00

THE KING OF THE GOLDEN RIVER, John Ruskin. Victorian children's classic of three brothers, their attempts to reach the Golden River, what becomes of them. Facsimile of original 1889 edition. 22 illustrations. 56pp. 4⅝ x 6⅜.
20066-3 Pa. $1.25

DREAMS OF THE RAREBIT FIEND, Winsor McCay. Pioneer cartoon strip, unexcelled for beauty, imagination, in 60 full sequences. Incredible technical virtuosity, wonderful visual wit. Historical introduction. 62pp. 8⅜ x 11¼. 21347-1 Pa. $2.00

THE KATZENJAMMER KIDS, Rudolf Dirks. In full color, 14 strips from 1906-7; full of imagination, characteristic humor. Classic of great historical importance. Introduction by August Derleth. 32pp. 9¼ x 12¼. 23005-8 Pa. $2.00

LITTLE ORPHAN ANNIE AND LITTLE ORPHAN ANNIE IN COSMIC CITY, Harold Gray. Two great sequences from the early strips: our curly-haired heroine defends the Warbucks' financial empire and, then, takes on meanie Phineas P. Pinchpenny. Leapin' lizards! 178pp. 6⅛ x 8⅜. 23107-0 Pa. $2.00

WHEN A FELLER NEEDS A FRIEND, Clare Briggs. 122 cartoons by one of the greatest newspaper cartoonists of the early 20th century — about growing up, making a living, family life, daily frustrations and occasional triumphs. 121pp. 8½ x 9½.
23148-8 Pa. $2.50

THE BEST OF GLUYAS WILLIAMS. 100 drawings by one of America's finest cartoonists: The Day a Cake of Ivory Soap Sank at Proctor & Gamble's, At the Life Insurance Agents' Banquet, and many other gems from the 20's and 30's. 118pp. 8⅜ x 11¼. 22737-5 Pa. $2.50

HOUDINI ON MAGIC, Harold Houdini. Edited by Walter Gibson, Morris N. Young. How he escaped; exposés of fake spiritualists; instructions for eye-catching tricks; other fascinating material by and about greatest magician. 155 illustrations. 280pp. 20384-0 Pa. $2.50

HANDBOOK OF THE NUTRITIONAL CONTENTS OF FOOD, U.S. Dept. of Agriculture. Largest, most detailed source of food nutrition information ever prepared. Two mammoth tables: one measuring nutrients in 100 grams of edible portion; the other, in edible portion of 1 pound as purchased. Originally titled Composition of Foods. 190pp. 9 x 12. 21342-0 Pa. $4.00

COMPLETE GUIDE TO HOME CANNING, PRESERVING AND FREEZING, U.S. Dept. of Agriculture. Seven basic manuals with full instructions for jams and jellies; pickles and relishes; canning fruits, vegetables, meat; freezing anything. Really good recipes, exact instructions for optimal results. Save a fortune in food. 156 illustrations. 214pp. 6⅛ x 9¼. 22911-4 Pa. $2.50

THE BREAD TRAY, Louis P. De Gouy. Nearly every bread the cook could buy or make: bread sticks of Italy, fruit breads of Greece, glazed rolls of Vienna, everything from corn pone to croissants. Over 500 recipes altogether. including buns, rolls, muffins, scones, and more. 463pp. 23000-7 Pa. $3.50

CREATIVE HAMBURGER COOKERY, Louis P. De Gouy. 182 unusual recipes for casseroles, meat loaves and hamburgers that turn inexpensive ground meat into memorable main dishes: Arizona chili burgers, burger tamale pie, burger stew, burger corn loaf, burger wine loaf, and more. 120pp. 23001-5 Pa. $1.75

LONG ISLAND SEAFOOD COOKBOOK, J. George Frederick and Jean Joyce. Probably the best American seafood cookbook. Hundreds of recipes. 40 gourmet sauces, 123 recipes using oysters alone! All varieties of fish and seafood amply represented. 324pp. 22677-8 Pa. $3.00

THE EPICUREAN: A COMPLETE TREATISE OF ANALYTICAL AND PRACTICAL STUDIES IN THE CULINARY ART, Charles Ranhofer. Great modern classic. 3,500 recipes from master chef of Delmonico's, turn-of-the-century America's best restaurant. Also explained, many techniques known only to professional chefs. 775 illustrations. 1183pp. 6⅝ x 10. 22680-8 Clothbd. $17.50

THE AMERICAN WINE COOK BOOK, Ted Hatch. Over 700 recipes: old favorites livened up with wine plus many more: Czech fish soup, quince soup, sauce Perigueux, shrimp shortcake, filets Stroganoff, cordon bleu goulash, jambonneau, wine fruit cake, more. 314pp. 22796-0 Pa. $2.50

DELICIOUS VEGETARIAN COOKING, Ivan Baker. Close to 500 delicious and varied recipes: soups, main course dishes (pea, bean, lentil, cheese, vegetable, pasta, and egg dishes), savories, stews, whole-wheat breads and cakes, more. 168pp. USO 22834-7 Pa. $1.75

CONSTRUCTION OF AMERICAN FURNITURE TREASURES, Lester Margon. 344 detail drawings, complete text on constructing exact reproductions of 38 early American masterpieces: Hepplewhite sideboard, Duncan Phyfe drop-leaf table, mantel clock, gate-leg dining table, Pa. German cupboard, more. 38 plates. 54 photographs. 168pp. 8⅜ x 11¼. 23056-2 Pa. $4.00

JEWELRY MAKING AND DESIGN, Augustus F. Rose, Antonio Cirino. Professional secrets revealed in thorough, practical guide: tools, materials, processes; rings, brooches, chains, cast pieces, enamelling, setting stones, etc. Do not confuse with skimpy introductions: beginner can use, professional can learn from it. Over 200 illustrations. 306pp. 21750-7 Pa. $3.00

METALWORK AND ENAMELLING, Herbert Maryon. Generally conceded best all-around book. Countless trade secrets: materials, tools, soldering, filigree, setting, inlay, niello, repoussé, casting, polishing, etc. For beginner or expert. Author was foremost British expert. 330 illustrations. 335pp. 22702-2 Pa. $3.50

WEAVING WITH FOOT-POWER LOOMS, Edward F. Worst. Setting up a loom, beginning to weave, constructing equipment, using dyes, more, plus over 285 drafts of traditional patterns including Colonial and Swedish weaves. More than 200 other figures. For beginning and advanced. 275pp. 8¾ x 6⅜. 23064-3 Pa. $4.00

WEAVING A NAVAJO BLANKET, Gladys A. Reichard. Foremost anthropologist studied under Navajo women, reveals every step in process from wool, dyeing, spinning, setting up loom, designing, weaving. Much history, symbolism. With this book you could make one yourself. 97 illustrations. 222pp. 22992-0 Pa. $3.00

NATURAL DYES AND HOME DYEING, Rita J. Adrosko. Use natural ingredients: bark, flowers, leaves, lichens, insects etc. Over 135 specific recipes from historical sources for cotton, wool, other fabrics. Genuine premodern handicrafts. 12 illustrations. 160pp. 22688-3 Pa. $2.00

THE HAND DECORATION OF FABRICS, Francis J. Kafka. Outstanding, profusely illustrated guide to stenciling, batik, block printing, tie dyeing, freehand painting, silk screen printing, and novelty decoration. 356 illustrations. 198pp. 6 x 9. 21401-X Pa. $3.00

THOMAS NAST: CARTOONS AND ILLUSTRATIONS, with text by Thomas Nast St. Hill. Father of American political cartooning. Cartoons that destroyed Tweed Ring; inflation, free love, church and state; original Republican elephant and Democratic donkey; Santa Claus; more. 117 illustrations. 146pp. 9 x 12. 22983-1 Pa. $4.00
23067-8 Clothbd. $8.50

FREDERIC REMINGTON: 173 DRAWINGS AND ILLUSTRATIONS. Most famous of the Western artists, most responsible for our myths about the American West in its untamed days. Complete reprinting of *Drawings of Frederic Remington* (1897), plus other selections. 4 additional drawings in color on covers. 140pp. 9 x 12. 20714-5 Pa. $3.95

THE MAGIC MOVING PICTURE BOOK, Bliss, Sands & Co. The pictures in this book move! Volcanoes erupt, a house burns, a serpentine dancer wiggles her way through a number. By using a specially ruled acetate screen provided, you can obtain these and 15 other startling effects. Originally "The Motograph Moving Picture Book." 32pp. 8¼ x 11.   23224-7 Pa. $1.75

STRING FIGURES AND HOW TO MAKE THEM, Caroline F. Jayne. Fullest, clearest instructions on string figures from around world: Eskimo, Navajo, Lapp, Europe, more. Cats cradle, moving spear, lightning, stars. Introduction by A.C. Haddon. 950 illustrations. 407pp.   20152-X Pa. $3.50

PAPER FOLDING FOR BEGINNERS, William D. Murray and Francis J. Rigney. Clearest book on market for making origami sail boats, roosters, frogs that move legs, cups, bonbon boxes. 40 projects. More than 275 illustrations. Photographs. 94pp.
                     20713-7 Pa. $1.25

INDIAN SIGN LANGUAGE, William Tomkins. Over 525 signs developed by Sioux, Blackfoot, Cheyenne, Arapahoe and other tribes. Written instructions and diagrams: how to make words, construct sentences. Also 290 pictographs of Sioux and Ojibway tribes. 111pp. 6⅛ x 9¼.   22029-X Pa. $1.50

BOOMERANGS: HOW TO MAKE AND THROW THEM, Bernard S. Mason. Easy to make and throw, dozens of designs: cross-stick, pinwheel, boomabird, tumblestick, Australian curved stick boomerang. Complete throwing instructions. All safe. 99pp.   23028-7 Pa. $1.75

25 KITES THAT FLY, Leslie Hunt. Full, easy to follow instructions for kites made from inexpensive materials. Many novelties. Reeling, raising, designing your own. 70 illustrations. 110pp.   22550-X Pa. $1.25

TRICKS AND GAMES ON THE POOL TABLE, Fred Herrmann. 79 tricks and games, some solitaires, some for 2 or more players, some competitive; mystifying shots and throws, unusual carom, tricks involving cork, coins, a hat, more. 77 figures. 95pp.   21814-7 Pa. $1.25

WOODCRAFT AND CAMPING, Bernard S. Mason. How to make a quick emergency shelter, select woods that will burn immediately, make do with limited supplies, etc. Also making many things out of wood, rawhide, bark, at camp. Formerly titled Woodcraft. 295 illustrations. 580pp.   21951-8 Pa. $4.00

AN INTRODUCTION TO CHESS MOVES AND TACTICS SIMPLY EXPLAINED, Leonard Barden. Informal intermediate introduction: reasons for moves, tactics, openings, traps, positional play, endgame. Isolates patterns. 102pp. USO 21210-6 Pa. $1.35

LASKER'S MANUAL OF CHESS, Dr. Emanuel Lasker. Great world champion offers very thorough coverage of all aspects of chess. Combinations, position play, openings, endgame, aesthetics of chess, philosophy of struggle, much more. Filled with analyzed games. 390pp.   20640-8 Pa. $4.00

CATALOGUE OF DOVER BOOKS

INCIDENTS OF TRAVEL IN YUCATAN, John L. Stephens. Classic (1843) exploration of jungles of Yucatan, looking for evidences of Maya civilization. Travel adventures, Mexican and Indian culture, etc. Total of 669pp.
20926-1, 20927-X Pa., Two vol. set $5.50

LIVING MY LIFE, Emma Goldman. Candid, no holds barred account by foremost American anarchist: her own life, anarchist movement, famous contemporaries, ideas and their impact. Struggles and confrontations in America, plus deportation to U.S.S.R. Shocking inside account of persecution of anarchists under Lenin. 13 plates. Total of 944pp.
22543-7, 22544-5 Pa., Two vol. set $9.00

AMERICAN INDIANS, George Catlin. Classic account of life among Plains Indians: ceremonies, hunt, warfare, etc. Dover edition reproduces for first time all original paintings. 312 plates. 572pp. of text. 6⅛ x 9¼.
22118-0, 22119-9 Pa., Two vol. set $8.00
22140-7, 22144-X Clothbd., Two vol. set $16.00

THE INDIANS' BOOK, Natalie Curtis. Lore, music, narratives, drawings by Indians, collected from cultures of U.S.A. 149 songs in full notation. 45 illustrations. 583pp. 6⅝ x 9⅜.
21939-9 Pa. $5.00

INDIAN BLANKETS AND THEIR MAKERS, George Wharton James. History, old style wool blankets, changes brought about by traders, symbolism of design and color, a Navajo weaver at work, outline blanket, Kachina blankets, more. Emphasis on Navajo. 130 illustrations, 32 in color. 230pp. 6⅛ x 9¼.
22996-3 Pa. $5.00
23068-6 Clothbd. $10.00

AN INTRODUCTION TO THE STUDY OF THE MAYA HIEROGLYPHS, Sylvanus Griswold Morley. Classic study by one of the truly great figures in hieroglyph research. Still the best introduction for the student for reading Maya hieroglyphs. New introduction by J. Eric S. Thompson. 117 illustrations. 284pp.
23108-9 Pa. $4.00

THE ANALECTS OF CONFUCIUS, THE GREAT LEARNING, DOCTRINE OF THE MEAN, Confucius. Edited by James Legge. Full Chinese text, standard English translation on same page, Chinese commentators, editor's annotations; dictionary of characters at rear, plus grammatical comment. Finest edition anywhere of one of world's greatest thinkers. 503pp.
22746-4 Pa. $4.50

THE I CHING (THE BOOK OF CHANGES), translated by James Legge. Complete translation of basic text plus appendices by Confucius, and Chinese commentary of most penetrating divination manual ever prepared. Indispensable to study of early Oriental civilizations, to modern inquiring reader. 448pp.
21062-6 Pa. $3.50

THE EGYPTIAN BOOK OF THE DEAD, E.A. Wallis Budge. Complete reproduction of Ani's papyrus, finest ever found. Full hieroglyphic text, interlinear transliteration, word for word translation, smooth translation. Basic work, for Egyptology, for modern study of psychic matters. Total of 533pp. 6½ x 9¼.
EBE 21866-X Pa. $4.95

MODERN CHESS STRATEGY, Ludek Pachman. The use of the queen, the active king, exchanges, pawn play, the center, weak squares, etc. Section on rook alone worth price of the book. Stress on the moderns. Often considered the most important book on strategy. 314pp. 20290-9 Pa. $3.00

CHESS STRATEGY, Edward Lasker. One of half-dozen great theoretical works in chess, shows principles of action above and beyond moves. Acclaimed by Capablanca, Keres, etc. 282pp. USO 20528-2 Pa. $2.50

CHESS PRAXIS, THE PRAXIS OF MY SYSTEM, Aron Nimzovich. Founder of hyper-modern chess explains his profound, influential theories that have dominated much of 20th century chess. 109 illustrative games. 369pp. 20296-8 Pa. $3.50

HOW TO PLAY THE CHESS OPENINGS, Eugene Znosko-Borovsky. Clear, profound ex-aminations of just what each opening is intended to do and how opponent can counter. Many sample games, questions and answers. 147pp. 22795-2 Pa. $2.00

THE ART OF CHESS COMBINATION, Eugene Znosko-Borovsky. Modern explanation of principles, varieties, techniques and ideas behind them, illustrated with many examples from great players. 212pp. 20583-5 Pa. $2.00

COMBINATIONS: THE HEART OF CHESS, Irving Chernev. Step-by-step explanation of intricacies of combinative play. 356 combinations by Tarrasch, Botvinnik, Keres, Steinitz, Anderssen, Morphy, Marshall, Capablanca, others, all annotated. 245 pp. 21744-2 Pa. $2.50

HOW TO PLAY CHESS ENDINGS, Eugene Znosko-Borovsky. Thorough instruction manual by fine teacher analyzes each piece individually; many common endgame situations. Examines games by Steinitz, Alekhine, Lasker, others. Emphasis on understanding. 288pp. 21170-3 Pa. $2.75

MORPHY'S GAMES OF CHESS, Philip W. Sergeant. Romantic history, 54 games of greatest player of all time against Anderssen, Bird, Paulsen, Harrwitz; 52 games at odds; 52 blindfold; 100 consultation, informal, other games. Analyses by An-derssen, Steinitz, Morphy himself. 352pp. 20386-7 Pa. $2.75

500 MASTER GAMES OF CHESS, S. Tartakower, J. du Mont. Vast collection of great chess games from 1798-1938, with much material nowhere else readily available. Fully annotated, arranged by opening for easier study. 665pp. 23208-5 Pa. $6.00

THE SOVIET SCHOOL OF CHESS, Alexander Kotov and M. Yudovich. Authoritative work on modern Russian chess. History, conceptual background. 128 fully anno-tated games (most unavailable elsewhere) by Botvinnik, Keres, Smyslov, Tal, Petrosian, Spassky, more. 390pp. 20026-4 Pa. $3.95

WONDERS AND CURIOSITIES OF CHESS, Irving Chernev. A lifetime's accumulation of such wonders and curiosities as the longest won game, shortest game, chess problem with mate in 1220 moves, and much more unusual material — 356 items in all, over 160 complete games. 146 diagrams. 203pp. 23007-4 Pa. $3.50

THE ART DECO STYLE, ed. by Theodore Menten. Furniture, jewelry, metalwork, ceramics, fabrics, lighting fixtures, interior decors, exteriors, graphics from pure French sources. Best sampling around. Over 400 photographs. 183pp. 8⅜ x 11¼.
22824-X Pa. $4.00

THE GENTLEMAN AND CABINET MAKER'S DIRECTOR, Thomas Chippendale. Full reprint, 1762 style book, most influential of all time; chairs, tables, sofas, mirrors, cabinets, etc. 200 plates, plus 24 photographs of surviving pieces. 249pp. 9⅞ x 12¾.
21601-2 Pa. $5.00

PINE FURNITURE OF EARLY NEW ENGLAND, Russell H. Kettell. Basic book. Thorough historical text, plus 200 illustrations of boxes, highboys, candlesticks, desks, etc. 477pp. 7⅞ x 10¾.
20145-7 Clothbd. $12.50

ORIENTAL RUGS, ANTIQUE AND MODERN, Walter A. Hawley. Persia, Turkey, Caucasus, Central Asia, China, other traditions. Best general survey of all aspects: styles and periods, manufacture, uses, symbols and their interpretation, and identification. 96 illustrations, 11 in color. 320pp. 6⅛ x 9¼.
22366-3 Pa. $5.00

DECORATIVE ANTIQUE IRONWORK, Henry R. d'Allemagne. Photographs of 4500 iron artifacts from world's finest collection, Rouen. Hinges, locks, candelabra, weapons, lighting devices, clocks, tools, from Roman times to mid-19th century. Nothing else comparable to it. 420pp. 9 x 12.
22082-6 Pa. $8.50

THE COMPLETE BOOK OF DOLL MAKING AND COLLECTING, Catherine Christopher. Instructions, patterns for dozens of dolls, from rag doll on up to elaborate, historically accurate figures. Mould faces, sew clothing, make doll houses, etc. Also collecting information. Many illustrations. 288pp. 6 x 9. 22066-4 Pa. $3.00

ANTIQUE PAPER DOLLS: 1915-1920, edited by Arnold Arnold. 7 antique cut-out dolls and 24 costumes from 1915-1920, selected by Arnold Arnold from his collection of rare children's books and entertainments, all in full color. 32pp. 9¼ x 12¼.
23176-3 Pa. $2.00

ANTIQUE PAPER DOLLS: THE EDWARDIAN ERA, Epinal. Full-color reproductions of two historic series of paper dolls that show clothing styles in 1908 and at the beginning of the First World War. 8 two-sided, stand-up dolls and 32 complete, two-sided costumes. Full instructions for assembling included. 32pp. 9¼ x 12¼.
23175-5 Pa. $2.00

A HISTORY OF COSTUME, Carl Köhler, Emma von Sichardt. Egypt, Babylon, Greece up through 19th century Europe; based on surviving pieces, art works, etc. Full text and 595 illustrations, including many clear, measured patterns for reproducing historic costume. Practical. 464pp.
21030-8 Pa. $4.00

EARLY AMERICAN LOCOMOTIVES, John H. White, Jr. Finest locomotive engravings from late 19th century: historical (1804-1874), main-line (after 1870), special, foreign, etc. 147 plates. 200pp. 11⅜ x 8¼.
22772-3 Pa. $3.50

AUSTRIAN COOKING AND BAKING, Gretel Beer. Authentic thick soups, wiener schnitzel, veal goulash, more, plus dumplings, puff pastries, nut cakes, sacher tortes, other great Austrian desserts. 224pp. USO 23220-4 Pa. $2.50

CHEESES OF THE WORLD, U.S.D.A. Dictionary of cheeses containing descriptions of over 400 varieties of cheese from common Cheddar to exotic Surati. Up to two pages are given to important cheeses like Camembert, Cottage, Edam, etc. 151pp. 22831-2 Pa. $1.50

TRITTON'S GUIDE TO BETTER WINE AND BEER MAKING FOR BEGINNERS, S.M. Tritton. All you need to know to make family-sized quantities of over 100 types of grape, fruit, herb, vegetable wines; plus beers, mead, cider, more. 11 illustrations. 157pp. USO 22528-3 Pa. $2.00

DECORATIVE LABELS FOR HOME CANNING, PRESERVING, AND OTHER HOUSEHOLD AND GIFT USES, Theodore Menten. 128 gummed, perforated labels, beautifully printed in 2 colors. 12 versions in traditional, Art Nouveau, Art Deco styles. Adhere to metal, glass, wood, most plastics. 24pp. 8¼ x 11. 23219-0 Pa. $2.00

FIVE ACRES AND INDEPENDENCE, Maurice G. Kains. Great back-to-the-land classic explains basics of self-sufficient farming: economics, plants, crops, animals, orchards, soils, land selection, host of other necessary things. Do not confuse with skimpy faddist literature; Kains was one of America's greatest agriculturalists. 95 illustrations. 397pp. 20974-1 Pa. $2.95

GROWING VEGETABLES IN THE HOME GARDEN, U.S. Dept. of Agriculture. Basic information on site, soil conditions, selection of vegetables, planting, cultivation, gathering. Up-to-date, concise, authoritative. Covers 60 vegetables. 30 illustrations. 123pp. 23167-4 Pa. $1.35

FRUITS FOR THE HOME GARDEN, Dr. U.P. Hedrick. A chapter covering each type of garden fruit, advice on plant care, soils, grafting, pruning, sprays, transplanting, and much more! Very full. 53 illustrations. 175pp. 22944-0 Pa. $2.50

GARDENING ON SANDY SOIL IN NORTH TEMPERATE AREAS, Christine Kelway. Is your soil too light, too sandy? Improve your soil, select plants that survive under such conditions. Both vegetables and flowers. 42 photos. 148pp.
USO 23199-2 Pa. $2.50

THE FRAGRANT GARDEN: A BOOK ABOUT SWEET SCENTED FLOWERS AND LEAVES, Louise Beebe Wilder. Fullest, best book on growing plants for their fragrances. Descriptions of hundreds of plants, both well-known and overlooked. 407pp.
23071-6 Pa. $3.50

EASY GARDENING WITH DROUGHT-RESISTANT PLANTS, Arno and Irene Nehrling. Authoritative guide to gardening with plants that require a minimum of water: seashore, desert, and rock gardens; house plants; annuals and perennials; much more. 190 illustrations. 320pp. 23230-1 Pa. $3.50

SLEEPING BEAUTY, illustrated by Arthur Rackham. Perhaps the fullest, most delightful version ever, told by C.S. Evans. Rackham's best work. 49 illustrations. 110pp. 7⅞ x 10¾.   22756-1 Pa. $2.00

THE WONDERFUL WIZARD OF OZ, L. Frank Baum. Facsimile in full color of America's finest children's classic. Introduction by Martin Gardner. 143 illustrations by W.W. Denslow. 267pp.   20691-2 Pa. **$3.00**

GOOPS AND HOW TO BE THEM, Gelett Burgess. Classic tongue-in-cheek masquerading as etiquette book. 87 verses, 170 cartoons as Goops demonstrate virtues of table manners, neatness, courtesy, more. 88pp. 6½ x 9¼.
22233-0 Pa. **$2.00**

THE BROWNIES, THEIR BOOK, Palmer Cox. Small as mice, cunning as foxes, exuberant, mischievous, Brownies go to zoo, toy shop, seashore, circus, more. 24 verse adventures. 266 illustrations. 144pp. 6⅝ x 9¼.   21265-3 Pa. **$2.50**

BILLY WHISKERS: THE AUTOBIOGRAPHY OF A GOAT, Frances Trego Montgomery. Escapades of that rambunctious goat. Favorite from turn of the century America. 24 illustrations. 259pp.   22345-0 Pa. $2.75

THE ROCKET BOOK, Peter Newell. Fritz, janitor's kid, sets off rocket in basement of apartment house; an ingenious hole punched through every page traces course of rocket. 22 duotone drawings, verses. 48pp. 6⅞ x 8⅜ .   22044-3 Pa. $1.50

PECK'S BAD BOY AND HIS PA, George W. Peck. Complete double-volume of great American childhood classic. Hennery's ingenious pranks against outraged pomposity of pa and the grocery man. 97 illustrations. Introduction by E.F. Bleiler. 347pp.   20497-9 Pa. $2.50

THE TALE OF PETER RABBIT, Beatrix Potter. The inimitable Peter's terrifying adventure in Mr. McGregor's garden, with all 27 wonderful, full-color Potter illustrations. 55pp. 4¼ x 5½.   USO 22827-4 Pa. $1.00

THE TALE OF MRS. TIGGY-WINKLE, Beatrix Potter. Your child will love this story about a very special hedgehog and all 27 wonderful, full-color Potter illustrations. 57pp. 4¼ x 5½.   USO 20546-0 Pa. $1.00

THE TALE OF BENJAMIN BUNNY, Beatrix Potter. Peter Rabbit's cousin coaxes him back into Mr. McGregor's garden for a whole new set of adventures. A favorite with children. All 27 full-color illustrations. 59pp. 4¼ x 5½.
USO 21102-9 Pa. $1.00

THE MERRY ADVENTURES OF ROBIN HOOD, Howard Pyle. Facsimile of original (1883) edition, finest modern version of English outlaw's adventures. 23 illustrations by Pyle. 296pp. 6½ x 9¼.   22043-5 Pa. **$4.00**

TWO LITTLE SAVAGES, Ernest Thompson Seton. Adventures of two boys who lived as Indians; explaining Indian ways, woodlore, pioneer methods. 293 illustrations. 286pp.   20985-7 Pa. $3.00

CATALOGUE OF DOVER BOOKS

THE JOURNAL OF HENRY D. THOREAU, edited by Bradford Torrey, F.H. Allen. Complete reprinting of 14 volumes, 1837-1861, over two million words; the source-books for Walden, etc. Definitive. All original sketches, plus 75 photographs. Introduction by Walter Harding. Total of 1804pp. 8½ x 12¼.
20312-3, 20313-1 Clothbd., Two vol. set $50.00

MASTERS OF THE DRAMA, John Gassner. Most comprehensive history of the drama, every tradition from Greeks to modern Europe and America, including Orient. Covers 800 dramatists, 2000 plays; biography, plot summaries, criticism, theatre history, etc. 77 illustrations. 890pp. 20100-7 Clothbd. $10.00

GHOST AND HORROR STORIES OF AMBROSE BIERCE, Ambrose Bierce. 23 modern horror stories: The Eyes of the Panther, The Damned Thing, etc., plus the dream-essay Visions of the Night. Edited by E.F. Bleiler. 199pp. 20767-6 Pa. $2.00

BEST GHOST STORIES, Algernon Blackwood. 13 great stories by foremost British 20th century supernaturalist. The Willows, The Wendigo, Ancient Sorceries, others. Edited by E.F. Bleiler. 366pp. USO 22977-7 Pa. $3.00

THE BEST TALES OF HOFFMANN, E.T.A. Hoffmann. 10 of Hoffmann's most important stories, in modern re-editings of standard translations: Nutcracker and the King of Mice, The Golden Flowerpot, etc. 7 illustrations by Hoffmann. Edited by E.F. Bleiler. 458pp. 21793-0 Pa. $3.95

BEST GHOST STORIES OF J.S. LEFANU, J. Sheridan LeFanu. 16 stories by greatest Victorian master: Green Tea, Carmilla, Haunted Baronet, The Familiar, etc. Mostly unavailable elsewhere. Edited by E.F. Bleiler. 8 illustrations. 467pp. 20415-4 Pa. $4.00

SUPERNATURAL HORROR IN LITERATURE, H.P. Lovecraft. Great modern American supernaturalist brilliantly surveys history of genre to 1930's, summarizing, evaluating scores of books. Necessary for every student, lover of form. Introduction by E.F. Bleiler. 111pp. 20105-8 Pa. $1.50

THREE GOTHIC NOVELS, ed. by E.F. Bleiler. Full texts Castle of Otranto, Walpole; Vathek, Beckford; The Vampyre, Polidori; Fragment of a Novel, Lord Byron. 331pp. 21232-7 Pa. $3.00

SEVEN SCIENCE FICTION NOVELS, H.G. Wells. Full novels. First Men in the Moon, Island of Dr. Moreau, War of the Worlds, Food of the Gods, Invisible Man, Time Machine, In the Days of the Comet. A basic science-fiction library. 1015pp. USO 20264-X Clothbd. $6.00

LADY AUDLEY'S SECRET, Mary E. Braddon. Great Victorian mystery classic, beautifully plotted, suspenseful; praised by Thackeray, Boucher, Starrett, others. What happened to beautiful, vicious Lady Audley's husband? Introduction by Norman Donaldson. 286pp. 23011-2 Pa. $3.00

THE STYLE OF PALESTRINA AND THE DISSONANCE, Knud Jeppesen. Standard analysis of rhythm, line, harmony, accented and unaccented dissonances. Also pre-Palestrina dissonances. 306pp. 22386-8 Pa. $3.00

DOVER OPERA GUIDE AND LIBRETTO SERIES prepared by Ellen H. Bleiler. Each volume contains everything needed for background, complete enjoyment: complete libretto, new English translation with all repeats, biography of composer and librettist, early performance history, musical lore, much else. All volumes lavishly illustrated with performance photos, portraits, similar material. Do not confuse with skimpy performance booklets.

CARMEN, Georges Bizet. 66 illustrations. 222pp. 22111-3 Pa. $2.00
DON GIOVANNI, Wolfgang A. Mozart. 92 illustrations. 209pp. 21134-7 Pa. $2.50
LA BOHÈME, Giacomo Puccini. 73 illustrations. 124pp. USO 20404-9 Pa. $1.75
ÄIDA, Giuseppe Verdi. 76 illustrations. 181pp. 20405-7 Pa. $2.00
LUCIA DI LAMMERMOOR, Gaetano Donizetti. 44 illustrations. 186pp.
22110-5 Pa. $2.00

ANTONIO STRADIVARI: HIS LIFE AND WORK, W.H. Hill, et al. Great work of musicology. Construction methods, woods, varnishes, known instruments, types of instruments, life, special features. Introduction by Sydney Beck. 98 illustrations, plus 4 color plates. 315pp. 20425-1 Pa. $3.00

MUSIC FOR THE PIANO, James Friskin, Irwin Freundlich. Both famous, little-known compositions; 1500 to 1950's. Listing, description, classification, technical aspects for student, teacher, performer. Indispensable for enlarging repertory. 448pp.
22918-1 Pa. $4.00

PIANOS AND THEIR MAKERS, Alfred Dolge. Leading inventor offers full history of piano technology, earliest models to 1910. Types, makers, components, mechanisms, musical aspects. Very strong on offtrail models, inventions; also player pianos. 300 illustrations. 581pp. 22856-8 Pa. $5.00

KEYBOARD MUSIC, J.S. Bach. Bach-Gesellschaft edition. For harpsichord, piano, other keyboard instruments. English Suites, French Suites, Six Partitas, Goldberg Variations, Two-Part Inventions, Three-Part Sinfonias. 312pp. 8⅛ x 11.
22360-4 Pa. $5.00

COMPLETE STRING QUARTETS, Ludwig van Beethoven. Breitkopf and Härtel edition. 6 quartets of Opus 18; 3 quartets of Opus 59; Opera 74, 95, 127, 130, 131, 132, 135 and Grosse Fuge. Study score. 434pp. 9⅜ x 12¼. 22361-2 Pa. $7.95

COMPLETE PIANO SONATAS AND VARIATIONS FOR SOLO PIANO, Johannes Brahms. All sonatas, five variations on themes from Schumann, Paganini, Handel, etc. Vienna Gesellschaft der Musikfreunde edition. 178pp. 9 x 12. 22650-6 Pa. $4.00

PIANO MUSIC 1888-1905, Claude Debussy. Deux Arabesques, Suite Bergamesque, Masques, 1st series of Images, etc. 9 others, in corrected editions. 175pp. 9⅜ x 12¼. 22771-5 Pa. $4.00

DECORATIVE ALPHABETS AND INITIALS, edited by Alexander Nesbitt. 91 complete alphabets (medieval to modern), 3924 decorative initials, including Victorian novelty and Art Nouveau. 192pp. 7¾ x 10¾.   20544-4 Pa. $4.00

CALLIGRAPHY, Arthur Baker. Over 100 original alphabets from the hand of our greatest living calligrapher: simple, bold, fine-line, richly ornamented, etc. —all strikingly original and different, a fusion of many influences and styles. 155pp. 11⅜ x 8¼.   22895-9 Pa. $4.50

MONOGRAMS AND ALPHABETIC DEVICES, edited by Hayward and Blanche Cirker. Over 2500 combinations, names, crests in very varied styles: script engraving, ornate Victorian, simple Roman, and many others. 226pp. 8⅛ x 11.
22330-2 Pa. $5.00

THE BOOK OF SIGNS, Rudolf Koch. Famed German type designer renders 493 symbols: religious, alchemical, imperial, runes, property marks, etc. Timeless. 104pp. 6⅛ x 9¼.   20162-7 Pa. $1.75

200 DECORATIVE TITLE PAGES, edited by Alexander Nesbitt. 1478 to late 1920's. Baskerville, Dürer, Beardsley, W. Morris, Pyle, many others in most varied techniques. For posters, programs, other uses. 222pp. 8⅜ x 11¼.   21264-5 Pa. **$5.00**

DICTIONARY OF AMERICAN PORTRAITS, edited by Hayward and Blanche Cirker. 4000 important Americans, earliest times to 1905, mostly in clear line. Politicians, writers, soldiers, scientists, inventors, industrialists, Indians, Blacks, women, outlaws, etc. Identificatory information. 756pp. 9¼ x 12¾. 21823-6 Clothbd. $30.00

ART FORMS IN NATURE, Ernst Haeckel. Multitude of strangely beautiful natural forms: Radiolaria, Foraminifera, jellyfishes, fungi, turtles, bats, etc. All 100 plates of the 19th century evolutionist's Kunstformen der Natur (1904). 100pp. 9⅜ x 12¼.   22987-4 Pa. $4.00

DECOUPAGE: THE BIG PICTURE SOURCEBOOK, Eleanor Rawlings. Make hundreds of beautiful objects, over 550 florals, animals, letters, shells, period costumes, frames, etc. selected by foremost practitioner. Printed on one side of page. 8 color plates. Instructions. 176pp. 9³⁄₁₆ x 12¼.   23182-8 Pa. $5.00

AMERICAN FOLK DECORATION, Jean Lipman, Eve Meulendyke. Thorough coverage of all aspects of wood, tin, leather, paper, cloth decoration — scapes, humans, trees, flowers, geometrics — and how to make them. Full instructions. 233 illustrations, 5 in color. 163pp. 8⅜ x 11¼.   22217-9 Pa. $3.95

WHITTLING AND WOODCARVING, E.J. Tangerman. Best book on market; clear, full. If you can cut a potato, you can carve toys, puzzles, chains, caricatures, masks, patterns, frames, decorate surfaces, etc. Also covers serious wood sculpture. Over 200 photos. 293pp.   20965-2 Pa. $3.00

CATALOGUE OF DOVER BOOKS

EGYPTIAN MAGIC, E.A. Wallis Budge. Foremost Egyptologist, curator at British Museum, on charms, curses, amulets, doll magic, transformations, control of demons, deific appearances, feats of great magicians. Many texts cited. 19 illustrations. 234pp. USO 22681-6 Pa. $2.50

THE LEYDEN PAPYRUS: AN EGYPTIAN MAGICAL BOOK, edited by F. Ll. Griffith, Herbert Thompson. Egyptian sorcerer's manual contains scores of spells: sex magic of various sorts, occult information, evoking visions, removing evil magic, etc. Transliteration faces translation. 207pp. 22994-7 Pa. $2.50

THE MALLEUS MALEFICARUM OF KRAMER AND SPRENGER, translated, edited by Montague Summers. Full text of most important witchhunter's "Bible," used by both Catholics and Protestants. Theory of witches, manifestations, remedies, etc. Indispensable to serious student. 278pp. 6⅝ x 10. USO 22802-9 Pa. $3.95

LOST CONTINENTS, L. Sprague de Camp. Great science-fiction author, finest, fullest study: Atlantis, Lemuria, Mu, Hyperborea, etc. Lost Tribes, Irish in pre-Columbian America, root races; in history, literature, art, occultism. Necessary to everyone concerned with theme. 17 illustrations. 348pp. 22668-9 Pa. $3.50

THE COMPLETE BOOKS OF CHARLES FORT, Charles Fort. Book of the Damned, Lo!, Wild Talents, New Lands. Greatest compilation of data: celestial appearances, flying saucers, falls of frogs, strange disappearances, inexplicable data not recognized by science. Inexhaustible, painstakingly documented. Do not confuse with modern charlatanry. Introduction by Damon Knight. Total of 1126pp. 23094-5 Clothbd. $15.00

FADS AND FALLACIES IN THE NAME OF SCIENCE, Martin Gardner. Fair, witty appraisal of cranks and quacks of science: Atlantis, Lemuria, flat earth, Velikovsky, orgone energy, Bridey Murphy, medical fads, etc. 373pp. 20394-8 Pa. $3.00

HOAXES, Curtis D. MacDougall. Unbelievably rich account of great hoaxes: Locke's moon hoax, Shakespearean forgeries, Loch Ness monster, Disumbrationist school of art, dozens more; also psychology of hoaxing. 54 illustrations. 338pp. 20465-0 Pa. $3.50

THE GENTLE ART OF MAKING ENEMIES, James A.M. Whistler. Greatest wit of his day deflates Wilde, Ruskin, Swinburne; strikes back at inane critics, exhibitions. Highly readable classic of impressionist revolution by great painter. Introduction by Alfred Werner. 334pp. 21875-9 Pa. $4.00

THE BOOK OF TEA, Kakuzo Okakura. Minor classic of the Orient: entertaining, charming explanation, interpretation of traditional Japanese culture in terms of tea ceremony. Edited by E.F. Bleiler. Total of 94pp. 20070-1 Pa. $1.25